1996 Edition

Questionable Doctors

Disciplined by states or the federal government

Sidney Wolfe, M.D.
Mary Gabay
Phyllis McCarthy
Alana Bame
Benita Marcus Adler

A Public Citizen Health Research Group Report
March 1996

Public Citizen is a nonprofit membership organization in Washington, D.C., dedicated to advancing consumer rights through lobbying, litigation, research, publications, and information services.

Since its founding by Ralph Nader in 1971, Public Citizen has fought for consumer rights in the marketplace, for safe and secure health care, for fair trade, for clean and safe energy sources, and for corporate and government accountability.

First Printing

ISBN 0-937188-05-0

Table of Contents

Introduction		1
How To Use This Report		2
The U.S. "System" of Medical Quality Control		6
Findings		8
Table 1:	Public Citizen Ranking of Serious Doctor Disciplinary Actions By State Medical Licensing Boards--1994	11
Description of Tables 2 Through 11		17
Table 2:	Disciplinary Actions Each State or Federal Agency Reported to Public Citizen	21
Table 3:	Disciplinary Actions Reported to Public Citizen: A Breakdown of the Types of Disciplinary Actions Contained in this Report	22
Table 4:	Offenses for Which Doctors Were Disciplined	23
Table 5:	Disciplinary Actions Taken Against Doctors Cited for Sexual Abuse of or Sexual Misconduct with a Patient	24
Table 6:	Disciplinary Actions Taken Against Doctors Cited for Substandard Care, Incompetence or Negligence	24
Table 7:	Disciplinary Actions Taken Against Doctors Cited for Criminal Convictions	25
Table 8:	Disciplinary Actions Taken Against Doctors Cited for Misprescribing or Overprescribing Drugs	25

Table 9: Disciplinary Actions Taken Against Doctors Cited for Drug or Alcohol Abuse 26

Recommendations For the Federal Government 27

Recommendations For States 28

Recommendations To Consumers 31

Appendix 1: Glossary 33

Appendix 2: How We Compiled This Report 37

Appendix 3: Addresses of Federal Agencies 47

References 49

State Listings of Doctors

Acknowledgements

The authors would like to acknowledge the important efforts by many people and institutions which made this study possible.

First, we are grateful to those state licensing or disciplinary boards which cooperated with our requests for doctor-specific information by sending us lists which, in many cases, required them to reorganize data in a form which would be more useful to us. Similarly, the Inspector General's Office of the Department of Health and Human Services (HHS) has been extremely cooperative with our requests for information on those physicians who were sanctioned by the Peer Review Organizations and those who were the subject of other HHS sanctions. The Drug Enforcement Administration (DEA), belatedly, incompletely and only in the face of a lawsuit from Public Citizen, has begun to give us the data on doctors with uncontested restrictions or revocations of their narcotics licenses. Several consumer groups, including the New York Public Interest Research Group (NYPIRG) and the National Center for Patients' Rights, have also provided us with valuable information.

Special thanks to Elizabeth Schramm who assisted in production stages and Lauren Marshall who designed the cover and assisted in all stages of production.

But the lion's share of time spent on this report was in the time-consuming process of data entry, checking, rechecking and *rechecking* for accuracy and editing of information. A group of Public Citizen employees and former Public Citizen employees assisted in this enormous task including Laurie Mendelson and Lauren Dame.

Toufic Rahman, Public Citizen's computer consultant, spent many long hours refining our programs and providing computer assistance. Dr. Lynn Soffer provided us with critical advice on the computer formatting of these data and with a detailed system for ensuring that the data in the report accurately reflect those which we obtained from states and the Federal government. David Vladeck, an attorney with and Director of the Public Citizen Litigation Group, spent many long hours going over our summaries of the legal actions taken by state boards to ensure that they correctly interpreted the lengthier statements we received from the states.

Previous employees who worked on the first three editions include Dana Hull, Joan Stieber, Joanne Mott, Stephen Moore, Beverly Wellman, Kate Moore, Lauren Kanee, and Kathy Cashel.

Executive Summary

A license to practice medicine is a hard-won privilege. It is a privilege to hear our innermost thoughts, to see us naked, to cut us open, and to provide us with potentially dangerous drugs. Yet for too long the state and Federal government agencies chartered to protect us from those no longer fit to hold that privilege have fallen down on the job. Many state medical boards and other regulatory agencies have either entirely failed to catch doctors guilty of incompetence, drunkenness, or patient abuse, or have let them get away with slaps on the wrist such as fines or reprimands.

For just as long, doctors and their ostensible gate-keepers have failed to realize that consumers need to protect themselves. They have either refused to provide information on those shoddy doctors they have spotted, or they have made it awfully hard to get.

Information in the one Federal repository of disciplinary actions by State medical boards and Federal agencies--the National Practitioner Data Bank--is kept secret from both patients and from almost all physicians. It is partially in protest to this congressionally-mandated secrecy that Public Citizen's Health Research Group has established our own publicly-available data bank of doctors who have been disciplined. What follows are just a few of the main findings from our study of the data as reported in the national version of *13,012 Questionable Doctors* and in the state versions:

* *13,012 doctors disciplined by either state medical boards or Federal agencies are listed in the national books.* This represents an increase of 3,415 new physicians since the last time we analyzed the data in late 1993.

* These doctors had a total of *25,069 disciplinary actions* taken against them, the most common of which were probation (5,211 times), license revocation (2,321 times), license suspension (2,425 times) and license surrender (1,876 times). (See other types of disciplinary actions in Table 3, page 22.)

* For those doctors with disciplinary actions for which the states or Federal agencies supplied information on the offenses they had committed (about 2/3 of the doctors in the book), the following numbers of doctors committed the five most serious offenses (see Table 4, page 23 and the explanation of Table 4, page 18 for the more complete list of offenses):

Sexual abuse of or sexual misconduct with a patient: 264 doctors

Substandard care, incompetence or negligence: 1,622 doctors

Misprescribing or overprescribing of drugs: 1,378 doctors

Criminal Conviction (includes plea of guilty or no contest): 1,913 doctors

Drug or alcohol abuse: 1,059 doctors

* An analysis of the 1,208 doctors who were the subject of DEA disciplinary actions revealed that 376 or 31% were not the subject of any state disciplinary action even though their Federal narcotics license had been revoked or restricted.

* Similarly, of the 1,715 Medicare doctors who were the subjects of the 1,752 Medicare disciplinary actions, 520 or 30% were not disciplined by their state boards even though most (98.6% of actions) had involved exclusion from Medicare.

Thus, many states are not acting promptly, if at all, against physicians about whom a Federal agency has already compiled sufficient information to discipline them for very serious offenses.

Even for those states which do discipline doctors, for most of the serious offenses, some states frequently do little more than slap physicians on the wrist, leaving the majority free to practice with few if any restrictions.

* The only offense for which more than one-half of the disciplined physicians were at least temporarily taken out of practice was sexual abuse of or sexual misconduct with a patient, including some cases of rape. In this category, 70% of the 264 physicians listed in the book had licenses revoked, suspended or they surrendered their licenses but 30% (79 doctors) did not have to stop practicing at all. Many more of the 185 other doctors, especially those whose licenses were just temporarily suspended, are probably back in practice again. (See Table 5, page 24 and the explanation of Table 5, page 19 for details.)

* For the other four most serious offenses, the majority of physicians against whom disciplinary actions were taken escaped even a temporary cessation of their practices.

Substandard care, incompetence or negligence: 1,622 doctors. Only 33% of these physicians had to stop practicing, even temporarily. 67% or 1,087 were not required to stop. (See Table 6, page 24 and the explanation of Table 6, page 19 for details.)

Criminal conviction (includes plea of guilty or no contest): 1,913 doctors. Only 42% of these doctors had to stop practicing, even temporarily. 58% or 1,109 were not required to stop. (See Table 7, page 25 and the explanation of Table 7, page 19 for details.)

Misprescribing or overprescribing of drugs: 1,378 doctors. Only 32% of these physicians had to stop practicing, even temporarily. 68% or 937 were not required to stop. (See Table 8, page 25 and the explanation of Table 8, page 19 for details.)

Drug or alcohol abuse: 1,059 doctors.
Only 39% of these doctors had to stop practicing, even temporarily. 61% or 646 were not required to stop. (See Table 9, page 26 and the explanation of Table 9, page 19 for details.)

Thus, it is likely that most of the doctors in these above four categories of very serious offenses are currently practicing medicine, with few if any of their patients aware of these offenses.

Precisely because regulators provide so many protections for these health care practitioners, the Congressional Office of Technology Assessment recently concluded that a formal disciplinary action against a doctor provides a good reason to question his or her care.

Our study of the nation's medical quality control system led us to conclude that:

* *Too little discipline is still being done.* Less than one-half of 1% of the nation's doctors face any serious state sanctions each year.

* *Far too few state medical board disciplinary actions are for medical negligence or incompetence.* Of the 10,211 instances in which we knew the basis (the offense) for which a disciplinary action was taken and for which the basis of the action was not an action by another state, only 1,677 of those cases (16.4%) were for substandard care, incompetence or negligence.

This country's system for ensuring medical quality needs to be made much stronger. Below we suggest several avenues towards improvement:

* *Most states need to strengthen their medical practice statutes, restructure their medical boards, and dramatically increase both funding and staffing.* Most states should also establish programs to audit and weed out bad doctors so that patient injuries can be prevented rather than simply reacted to. The few states we are aware of that already have some kind of proactive program in place include Georgia, Mississippi, Missouri, Oregon, Utah, Virginia, and West Virginia.

The total number of serious state disciplinary actions against physicians increased 22% from 2,190 reported for 1993 to 2,675 in 1994 for a nationwide rate of 4.3 serious actions per 1,000 physicians. A difference greater than 25-fold exists between Wyoming, the state with the highest rate (12.41 per 1,000), and the District of Columbia, with the lowest rate, (0.48).

It is clear that state-by-state performance is spotty. None of the nation's dozen largest states is represented among those 15 states with the highest disciplinary rates. In fact, as seen in Table 1, page 11, all of the top 10 states had rates at least twice as high (7.94 or higher) as those of large states such as Pennsylvania (2.04 per 1,000), Illinois (2.92), Massachusetts (3.03), Michigan (3.28), California (3.28) and New York (3.97).

It is not unreasonable to estimate that at least 1 percent of doctors in this country deserve some serious disciplinary action each year. This would amount to 6,233 disciplined doctors a year, far in excess of the 2,675 doctors with serious disciplinary actions in 1994. If this had occurred, 3,558 more doctors would have had serious disciplinary actions that year.

Recommendations

* *Congress* should require cooperation and routine data-sharing between state medical boards, Medicare Peer Review Organizations, state Medicaid agencies, and the Drug Enforcement Administration in catching and sanctioning malfeasant physicians.

* *The National Practitioner Data Bank*, which began collecting information on questionable doctors in September 1990, should be opened to the public. This change will require legislation.

* *The Drug Enforcement Administration* should routinely tell the public and pharmacists which doctors' controlled substances prescription licenses it has pulled or restricted.

* *State medical boards* should be required to promptly make public all their disciplinary actions and the offenses for which their actions were taken, and to regularly distribute lists of actions to consumers, the press, and other health care consumer organizations.

Introduction

For more than 24 years, Public Citizen's Health Research Group has been striving to provide consumers with information they can use to make educated choices about their doctors. It has not been an easy road. Doctors generally don't like comparative information on quality to be released.

In the nation's first consumer's directory of local physicians, which we published in 1974 for Prince Georges County, Maryland, we wrote, "Most people can find out more about a car they plan to buy than they can about a doctor who may hold their life in his or her hands."[1] Unfortunately, that statement is still largely true today. In the process of collecting information from doctors for that directory, the Maryland State Medical Association threatened doctors who cooperated with loss of their license, arguing that "information that would point out differences between doctors" is illegal.

We have come a long way in the past 20 years and, for instance, several states now release computer tapes containing information on all hospital discharges for a given year. From these tapes we can discover which physicians have particularly high or low death rates from a certain procedure. The only problem is, the doctors are identified solely by code. Their names are withheld to preserve confidentiality.

Another example of the barriers to public access to information on specific doctors: the Federal Government began collecting information on state disciplinary actions, malpractice payments, and revocations and restrictions of hospital privileges for its National Practitioner Data Bank (NPDB) in September 1990. The problem is, consumers (and even doctors) are forbidden by law to have access to the data. This information is available primarily to hospitals, Health Maintenance Organizations, and government agencies that regulate the quality of medical care.[2,3,4]

In the wake of recent efforts to pass legislation to open up the NPDB, the American Medical Association, whose earlier efforts had succeeded in a prohibition against public disclosure when the law creating the NPDB was passed in 1986, passed a resolution at its 1993 annual convention stating: **"Resolved, that the American Medical Association...call for the dissolution of the National Practitioner Data Bank."** Now, as then, the AMA seems to want to protect the minority of American physicians about whom there is data in the NPDB from the scrutiny of their own patients and other physicians.

However, there has been some progress in the area of informing the public about poorly practicing physicians. Much information on state and federal government discipline of physicians is now public, although often difficult to obtain, and we have used that data to compile this report.

The United States has approximately 623,000 medical doctors, most of them competent and dedicated. *13,012 Questionable Doctors* includes only that **2.1%** of physicians whose care or conduct was substandard enough to be cited by a state medical disciplinary board, Medicare, or the federal Drug Enforcement Administration, or whose eligibility to participate in Food and Drug Administration (FDA) experiments was rescinded.

In a 1988 study on medical care quality assessment, the Congressional Office of Technology Assessment concluded that a sanction imposed on a physician by a state or a Medicare Peer Review Organization is good reason to question the quality of his or her care.[5] *"The rigorous due process followed by state medical boards lends credibility to the validity of their formal disciplinary actions against physicians,"* stated the report. *"State boards are reluctant to censure physicians and accord accused physicians extensive opportunities for appeal."*

How To Use This Report

1. If you are selecting a doctor...

-Call the medical board in the state where the doctor practices or used to practice. The board can frequently provide information on the physician's educational and specialty background, and whether the doctor has been disciplined or formally charged with misconduct. (Contact information for each state board is listed at the end of each state's section in this book.)

-Check to see if your local consumer group has published a guide to local doctors.

-Look your doctor up in the American Medical Association's *American Medical Directory* or the *Directory of Medical Specialists*, which can be found in all medical libraries and many large public libraries. These directories list the physician's educational background and whether or not he or she is board-certified in a specialty. You should not select a self-designated specialist who has not been trained in the specialty field.

-Ask the doctor for the names of hospitals where he or she has admitting privileges. Your local university teaching hospital will probably be the most selective about the physicians it admits to its staff. Also, should you need to be hospitalized, you will want a doctor who can admit you to the best hospital. *Washingtonian* magazine (most recently in the November 1995 issue),[6] and the *Washington Post*[7] have both published good articles on choosing a physician. There is also a book on the subject, *How to Choose a Good Doctor*, by G.D. LeMaitre, Andover Publishing Group, Andover MA, 1979.

2. If your current doctor is on this list...

-Check which state(s) or federal agency has disciplined him or her.

-Request a copy of the doctor's disciplinary file from the state or federal agency. State agency addresses are listed in the "Addresses" section of each state section. Federal addresses are on pages 47-48.

-Read the file before making a decision about whether to switch doctors. The information contained in our report is necessarily sketchy and may not include a full explanation of the reason for the disciplinary action because states may not have sent these details to us.

-Ask your doctor why he or she was disciplined. If your doctor can convince you that any problem that resulted in the disciplinary action has been resolved or is irrelevant to your future care, fine. Otherwise, you should consider switching.

3. If you have a complaint about a doctor...

-Find out what degree your doctor has, whether a medical doctor (M.D.), osteopathic physician (D.O.), chiropractor (D.C.), podiatrist (D.P.M.), or dentist (D.D.S. or D.M.D.). Different state agencies often regulate these different professionals.

-File your complaint with the state medical disciplinary agency. This agency is the only one that can remove dangerous or incompetent doctors from practice, impose limitations on a physician's license to practice, and truly protect other patients from being harmed. Your complaint could lead to the suspension or revocation of a doctor's license directly, or it could aid the medical board in detecting a pattern of poor medical care.

-File the complaint in the state where the doctor is licensed--i.e., where his or her office is located. Turn to that state's section under our "State by State Listings." Find the "Address" heading. Look for the address of the agency that regulates that type of doctor.

-If your care was within a hospital, you should also file a complaint with the hospital's peer review committee, which has the power to revoke or limit a doctor's privileges to practice there.

-You may also to file a complaint with Medicare (addresses, pages 47-48).

-Call the agency you have found to inquire about how to file a formal complaint. Some agencies have toll-free hotlines for complaints. Others require complaints to be filed on a specific form.

-Ask whether your complaint will remain confidential. State laws vary.

-File a written complaint containing as much information as possible. Make sure to include the doctor's full name, correctly spelled, office address, and the exact date when the conduct you are complaining of occurred. The state may also ask you to release your medical records for review.

-Ask the agency to notify you of the outcome of your complaint.

4. If you want to improve medical quality assurance in the state or the nation...

-Write your state representatives, your congressional representative, and your senators. Ask them to pass the legislation we recommend on page 27.

And Please Note...

* *Names sound alike. Just because a doctor whose name resembles your doctor's is listed in this report doesn't mean your doctor has been sanctioned. Many states failed to give us much identifying information on each doctor, and of the half a million doctors in this country, at least two are bound to have the same name.*

* *Many things change with time. While your doctor's license may be listed as having been revoked, suspended or restricted*

in this edition of the report, this doesn't necessarily mean those restrictions are still in effect. The information contained in this edition is information we received from the state medical boards by January 31, 1995. We also included information received through December 3, 1995 regarding previous actions which were either overturned or terminated, leaving the physician with an unrestricted license. However, the state may have fully reinstated a doctor's license or lifted their probation or other restrictions in materials received after our deadlines.

* *Boards don't always have the final say. Your doctor may have appealed his or her disciplinary action and had it overturned by a court. We do not have information on many appeals.*

The U.S. "System" of Medical Quality Control

The United States has a patchwork system for protecting the public from poor quality health care that is still largely uncoordinated and ineffective.

The first lines of defense are the state medical boards, the state government agencies charged with licensing physicians who meet certain standards. These boards are also responsible for catching already-licensed doctors who fall below standards of conduct or competence in any of a number of areas. They are legally empowered to discipline these doctors: to reprimand them, require them to take coursework, impose fines, place them on probation, and, in the worst cases, to suspend them from practice or revoke their licenses altogether.

These licensing and disciplinary systems vary from state to state. In some states the medical board is an independent state agency. In others, it is contained within the state department of licensing, of health, or of consumer affairs. In some states there is one board or agency for medical licensing and another for medical discipline. In a few states, one board or agency regulates all the health care professions--doctors, nurses, dentists, and so forth. In others, there are separate licensing and disciplinary boards for medical (allopathic) physicians, for osteopathic physicians, for dentists, and so on.[8]

In all states, the licensing boards are required to provide consumers with some disciplinary information about a specific doctor. The state agencies' addresses and phone numbers are listed in the "Addresses" section of each state's listing in this report.

The state agencies that run the Medicaid program, the joint state/federal program which funds health care for the poor, also sanctions doctors by excluding them from participation in Medicaid. Medicaid concentrates particularly on doctors guilty of insurance fraud. We did not receive any disciplinary information from such state Medicaid programs.

The U.S. Department of Health and Human Services, through its Medicare and Medicaid programs, also disciplines health practitioners. It excludes doctors from participation in Medicare or Medicaid for specified periods of time, and may fine them for violations as well.

The Department's Inspector General must exclude a doctor for at least five years for a criminal conviction related to the Medicare or Medicaid programs and for patient abuse or neglect.[9] It may also impose sanctions based on other types of convictions, on license revocation or suspension by a state agency, or on a sanction by any state Medicaid program.The Inspector General may also sanction a doctor for fraud, for accepting kickbacks, for failing to cooperate with investigators, and, based on a recommendation by the Medicare Peer Review Organizations for each state, for providing substandard or unnecessary care. The Inspector General's office accepts consumer complaints at the phone numbers and addresses listed on pages 47-48.

The Drug Enforcement Administration (DEA), which is part of the U.S. Department of Justice, tracks down doctors who overprescribe or abuse the so-called "scheduled drugs"--drugs such as narcotics, tranquilizers, and amphetamines that may be addictive or otherwise abused. The DEA issues licenses to doctors and dentists that allow them to prescribe these "controlled dangerous substances." No doctor may legally prescribe drugs listed as controlled substances without a valid DEA license. Some states require a separate state controlled substance license as well.

The DEA may deny a license to prescribe these drugs, restrict a doctor's prescription privileges, or revoke his or her privileges to prescribe controlled substances. It publishes notices of such disciplinary actions in the *Federal Register* when the actions have been contested. The address to direct complaints to the Drug Enforcement Administration is listed on page 47. After more than a year of trying to get information from the DEA on uncontested disciplinary cases, we finally received this data from the agency. This data on uncontested DEA actions covered only 1989. We requested such information for 1990-1991, but our request was denied. We appealed this decision, sued the DEA and they finally gave us additional data. These data include just some of the doctors with uncontested narcotics license actions for the years 1990-1992. Our most recent FOIA (Freedom of Information Act) request to the DEA, provided us with information on noncontested cases for the period from July 1993 through March 1994.

We also received information from the **Food and Drug Administration (FDA)** on physicians who were sanctioned because they had violated FDA laws, regulations, or policies regarding clinical research on patients.

State medical societies and specialty societies, both of which are unofficial trade associations for doctors, not government agencies, have peer review committees and have a role to play in medical discipline. However, they cannot prevent a doctor from continuing to practice, and their vested interest, in most cases, is in protecting their members, not the public.

Hospitals are required to have peer review committees to review the quality of medical care in their institutions. Consumers who have complaints about the quality of care in a hospital should file them with these committees. The committees may throw doctors off their staffs or restrict doctors' privileges to practice there. Unfortunately, most hospitals regard their peer review activities and disciplinary actions as confidential and will not inform patients about them. The National Practitioner Data Bank, as of April 30 1995, contained information on 4,306 clinical privilege actions against doctors[10] but, as mentioned above, these data are kept secret. There is also serious concern that hospitals are not reporting all of the hospital disciplinary actions against doctors as required by law. *During the first three years and four months of operation of the NPDB, 75 percent of U.S. hospitals had not reported even one physician to the NPDB.*[11]

Malpractice insurers can also play a role in quality control: they can cancel the policy of a physician who presents a bad risk, raise his or her rates, or offer coverage only if his or her practice is restricted.[12] Unfortunately, many states guarantee every doctor access to malpractice insurance, no matter how poor his or her record. Without an insurance policy, few doctors could afford to continue practicing and, in many states, would not be legally allowed to. Some state medical boards are informed when a doctor has had malpractice insurance canceled and will tell consumers.

Findings

Though it has been vastly improved during the past 15 years, the nation's system for protecting the public from medical incompetence and malfeasance is still far from adequate.

Gaps and breakdowns in communication still exist, although the National Practitioner Data Bank is helping to prevent doctors from being able to indiscriminately cross state lines to evade disciplinary boards. Those dangerous doctors who do fall through the cracks continue to kill, maim, defraud, and otherwise injure their unknowing patients.

Too many state medical boards, despite a clear duty to protect the public,[13] still believe their first responsibility is to rehabilitate "impaired physicians" and to protect *them* from the public's prying eyes. And the definition of "impaired" has expanded: it now covers doctors who may be drunk on the job, strung out on drugs, mentally ill, or habitual sex offenders.

While it is important for doctors who suffer from emotional problems or drug or alcohol addiction to receive appropriate treatment, this must be balanced with the state's responsibility to protect the public from doctors who are not able to deliver good medical care. Some states show a dangerous pattern of letting chemically dependent doctors return to practice after numerous failed attempts at rehabilitation. And while behavior that is sexually abusive may result from a mental illness, it is also a crime and is never acceptable in the context of patient care.

Although medical boards are now able to talk to each other, at least indirectly, to convey information about doctors they have disciplined, the boards are often far too slow to act on what they have learned. And many state medical boards seldom even communicate with the other agencies that guard against medical incompetence, fraud, and abuse--the federal Department of Health and Human Services, the Medicare Peer Review Organizations, the federal Drug Enforcement Administration, and the agencies that run state Medicaid programs.[14] Many of our recommendations to the states and federal government call for improved and regular communication between these groups.

Only a few of the country's better medical boards, for example those in Utah, West Virginia, Georgia, Oregon, and a few others attempt to act as sleuths, to seek out bad physicians before receiving complaints, in order to prevent misconduct and poor care.

The College of Physicians and Surgeons in the Canadian province of Ontario, by contrast, visits physicians' offices and performs random audits of their care in order to "be assured that licensed physicians meet minimal requirements for safe practice."[15,16] Physicians who fail to meet those standards, as many as 12% of family doctors and 2% of specialists, must undergo intensive educational retraining and in rare cases face disciplinary action. No American state has yet attempted such a far-reaching quality control program (to our knowledge).

Most importantly, most state medical boards have not refined the art of speaking to their primary constituency: the public.

Because of a commendable increase in requirements to report malpractice information to them, states are now repositories of masses of information on the quality of individual doctors, but they have few effective ways of disseminating it. For the first time, we received state doctor discipline data from Arkansas, leaving South Dakota as the only state which regulators and lawmakers apparently believe the general public has no need to know which doctors they have found substandard in conduct or in care unless consumers have a question about a specific physician. South Dakota continues to refuse to send us any information on specific doctors they have disciplined.

Many people trying to find a doctor still feel like they are floundering in the dark. They do not know what a medical board is. They do not know they can ask a board for disciplinary information, or that they can go there with complaints. Unwarned, too many of them see doctors guilty of previous acts of malpractice. And unwarned, too many of them are harmed.

Specifics

Too little discipline is still being done. Fewer than one-half of 1% of the nation's doctors face any serious state sanctions each year. 2,675 total serious disciplinary actions a year, the number state medical boards took in 1994,[17] is a pittance compared to the volume of injury and death of patients caused by negligence of doctors. It has been estimated that between 150,000 and 300,000 Americans are injured or killed each year in hospitals alone as a result of doctors' negligence based on the results of three studies.

1) Harvard researchers found that 1% of a representative sample of patients treated in New York state hospitals in 1984 were injured, and one-quarter of those died, because of medical negligence.[18] Nationwide, that translates into 234,000 injuries and 80,000 deaths in 1988 from negligence in American hospitals. Most of this involves physicians.

2) A similar study conducted in California in 1974 found that 0.8% of hospital patients had either been injured by negligence in the hospital or had been hospitalized because of negligent care.[19] Extrapolation of those findings yields an estimate of 249,000 injuries and deaths from malpractice in 1988.

3) In 1976 the HEW Malpractice Commission estimated similarly that one-half of 1% of all patients entering hospitals are injured there due to negligence. That estimate would indicate 156,000 injuries and deaths resulted from doctor negligence in 1988.[20]

Table 1 Public Citizen Ranking of Serious Doctor Disciplinary Actions By State Medical Licensing Boards -- 1994					
Rank 1994	**Rank 1993**	**State**	**Number of Serious Actions 1994**	**Number of Nonfederal MDs 1992**	**Serious Actions Per 1000 MDs 1994**
1	21	Wyoming	9	725	12.41
2	8	Alaska	9	797	11.29
3	14	Montana	15	1,546	9.70
4	4	Kentucky	69	7,175	9.62
5	2	Oklahoma	47	5,274	8.91
6	1	West Virginia	31	3,517	8.81
7	5	Iowa	41	4,890	8.38
8	10	Georgia	105	12,849	8.17
9	9	Mississippi	31	3,846	8.06
10	3	North Dakota	10	1,260	7.94
11	13	South Dakota	9	1,184	7.60
12	6	Colorado	57	8,189	6.96
13	12	Missouri	75	11,460	6.54
14	15	South Carolina	43	6,689	6.43
15	50	Nebraska	19	3,199	5.94
16	7	Indiana	60	10,149	5.91
17	16	Arizona	50	8,687	5.76
18	11	Louisiana	51	9,093	5.61
19	18	New Jersey	122	21,975	5.55
20	22/23	Oregon	39	7,094	5.50
21	19	Maryland	97	17,977	5.40
22	37/38	Kansas	26	5,057	5.14
23	28	Texas	170	33,846	5.02
24	22/23	Ohio	123	24,708	4.98

Table 1 Public Citizen Ranking of Serious Doctor Disciplinary Actions By State Medical Licensing Boards -- 1994					
Rank 1994	**Rank 1993**	**State**	**Number of Serious Actions 1994**	**Number of Nonfederal MDs 1992**	**Serious Actions Per 1000 MDs 1994**
25	25	Florida	163	33,802	4.82
26	42	Rhode Island	14	2,926	4.78
28	26	Arkansas	17	4,232	4.02
29	34	New York	258	64,927	3.97
30	37/38	Idaho	6	1,556	3.86
31	20	Nevada	8	2,117	3.78
32	30	Virginia	55	14,638	3.76
33	41	Maine	10	2,678	3.73
34/35	32	California	270	82,254	3.28
34/35	35	Michigan	65	19,810	3.28
36	40	North Carolina	45	14,665	3.07
37	45	Massachusetts	69	22,746	3.03
38	44	Tennessee	33	11,209	2.94
39	17	Vermont	5	1,707	2.93
40	31	Illinois	83	28,467	2.92
41	27	Wisconsin	30	10,701	2.80
42	36	Connecticut	31	11,335	2.73
43/44	49	New Mexico	9	3,340	2.69
43/44	29	Alabama	20	7,435	2.69
45	33	Minnesota	30	11,299	2.66
46	39	Utah	9	3,678	2.45
47	48	Pennsylvania	67	32,828	2.04
48	43	Delaware	3	1,549	1.94
49	47	New Hampshire	4	2,625	1.52
50	46	Hawaii	3	3,051	0.98
51	51	District of Columbia	2	4,168	0.48
		Totals	**2,675**	**623,378**	**4.29**

In *Table 1* on pages 11-12, based on data from the Federation of State Medical Boards, states are ranked in order from highest rate of serious disciplinary actions to lowest. The rate of serious actions per 1,000 physicians for the country or for each state is calculated by taking the number of "serious actions" as reported by the Federation and dividing by the number of non-federal physicians in that state as reported by the AMA. The result, in all cases a decimal fraction far smaller than 1, is then multiplied by 1,000 to get the rate per 1,000 physicians.

The total number of serious state disciplinary actions against physicians increased 22% from 2,190 reported for 1993 to 2,675 in 1994 for a nationwide rate of 4.3 serious actions per 1,000 physicians. A difference greater than 25-fold exists between Wyoming, the state with the highest rate (12.41 per thousand physicians), and the District of Columbia, with the lowest rate, (0.48).

It is clear that state-by-state performance is spotty. None of the nation's dozen biggest states is represented among those 15 states with the highest disciplinary rates. In fact, as seen in Table 1, all of the top 10 states had rates at least twice as high (7.94 or higher) as those of large states such as Pennsylvania (2.04 per thousand), Illinois (2.92), Massachusetts (3.03), Michigan (3.28), California (3.28) and New York (3.97).

It is not unreasonable to estimate that at least 1 percent of doctors in this country deserve some serious disciplinary action each year. This would amount to 6,233 disciplinary actions against doctors per year, far in excess of the 2,675 serious disciplinary actions in 1994. If this had occurred, 3,558 additional serious disciplinary actions would have had occurred that year.

State medical boards should be able to discipline at least as many doctors as malpractice carriers, since many boards now have the same information on claims and payments. A 1989 Tufts University study found that physician-owned malpractice insurers sanctioned 13.6 of every 1,000 doctors they covered. The insurers terminated policies of 6.6 of every 1,000 policyholders in 1985 because of negligence-prone behavior, and they restricted the practice or imposed other sanctions on another 7 of every 1,000 doctors whose care was found to be substandard.[21]

If this combined rate of malpractice insurance terminations by physician-owned insurance companies, 6.6 actions per 1,000 physicians, were applied to all physicians in the U.S., this rate would be more than one and one-half times as high as the actual 1994 average rate of serious disciplinary actions by state medical boards of 4.3 per 1,000 physicians.

This rate (6.6) is higher than the serious disciplinary action rates of all but 12 medical boards.

More doctors may not be getting caught. Much of the increased disciplinary activity has involved insuring that doctors, once caught by one state, are disciplined when they move to another.

Discipline is still too slow, though case backlogs in some states have been greatly reduced.

- Many state licensing departments have no mechanism for assigning priorities to investigations. Complaints based on murder convictions can get shoved to the bottom of the pile, beneath minor fee disputes.

- California actions can take 3 to 4 years or more to process, and they are automatically stayed pending appeal, which means a doctor can continue to practice while his or her case wends its way through the courts.

- In March of 1992 the case of Dr. Ivan C. Namihas, a Tustin gynecologist, made headlines in several California papers for nearly a week. The Medical Board eventually received over 140 complaints against Namihas, including many allegations of sexual abuse and inappropriate or improper medical treatment.[22] But the Board may have known about Namihas 20 years ago. A former part-time investigator for the Board told supervisors in 1970 that Namihas molested her that year. And in 1975 the Orange County Medical Association took the highly unusual step of sending a letter to the Board, stating that three local doctors had received several complaints about Namihas.[23] The Medical Board received another complaint against Namihas in 1982, and another in 1987, but it did not investigate these complaints due to what it termed insufficient evidence.[24] A senior investigator with the Board said the 1982 and 1987 complaints were never connected, but when she received the third complaint in 1990, she connected them.[25] Two more complaints were filed not long after, and when the story hit the newspapers, more than 100 additional complaints poured in. Namihas' license was eventually revoked on July 3, 1992.

- Medicare tries to exclude doctors whose state licenses have been revoked from receiving federal dollars. But it can take up to 18 months for the federal government to get the disciplinary documents from the states and act, said sanction program analyst Ron Ritchie.[26]

Questionable doctors can still cross state borders, though with less impunity than before. Data sharing between states has improved, but some states are either unwilling or unable to act on their information.

- A Brookings, Oregon family practitioner who surrendered his Oregon license during a disciplinary investigation simply moved over the state line to Smith River, California, to open a clinic.[27] During a 1990 hearing, Oregon Board of Medical Examiners executive director John Ulwelling said he knew of five similar cases in which doctors disciplined by Oregon were practicing in neighboring states; one such doctor's license had been revoked for incompetence. In that case, he said, even several phone calls to the other state's medical board had failed to prod them into action.[28]

- Oregon is one of the few states, Ulwelling testified, that bar an already-licensed physician from returning to practice there if a formal complaint is pending against him or her in another state. Most states, he said, have no means of discovering whether a doctor is under investigation elsewhere until they see notice of a formal disciplinary action against him or her on a Federation of State Medical Boards' report.[29]

The vast majority of states now require reporting of hospital disciplinary actions and malpractice claims or payments to the medical board, but few check whether the required reports have actually been filed. And some fail to act on the information they receive.

- An Oklahoma ob/gyn had his hospital privileges suspended and his malpractice insurance canceled in 1988. The hospital action, at least, should have been reported to the Oklahoma State Board of Medical Licensing and Supervision. But the Board did not act until the spring of 1990, more than six months after the doctor's wife died on his operating table from massive blood loss during liposuction.[30]

- A 1987 report by the New Jersey Commission of Investigation[31] detailed how hospitals in that state had utterly failed to comply with the state's 1983 law requiring disciplinary reporting, and how only half of the 1,000 malpractice awards submitted to the Board of Medical Examiners had even received superficial review. The state

Division of Consumer Affairs has recently created a special investigation division to review these claims.

- Michigan's lawmakers passed a law strengthening reporting requirements in 1987, but they didn't provide the funding to handle additional complaints. As a result, the 33% increase in complaints has gummed up the Bureau of Health Services' works. Furthermore, in February 1991 Governor John Engler disbanded the office that examines the thousands of malpractice lawsuits in search of those that are truly dangerous.[32] According to Dr. Donald Kuiper, a former member of the Board and Board chairman in the early 1980s, "This could jeopardize the public health and safety."[33]

Medical boards are much too forgiving. Many still see their priority as "rehabilitation," and their disciplinary actions are too light.

- The most common single disciplinary action states take is to place a doctor on probation (see Table 3, page 22). That's true for doctors found guilty of sexual abuse, substandard care, criminal offenses, prescription violations, and drug or alcohol abuse (Tables 5-9, pages 24-26).

- Revocations, license surrenders, and suspensions, those actions which actually remove a doctor from practice, made up less than one-third of the actions reported to us.

- Because they fail to remove chronic offenders from practice, many medical boards see the same doctors come back over and over and over again.

- Medical boards and other regulatory authorities generally don't have the resources to adequately monitor all the doctors they place on probation. When a doctor agrees to sign a probationary order, boards generally ask the doctor to designate a supervising physician to monitor his or her practice, and rely on that physician's reports. Few state boards have staff members (Oregon and Texas are two exceptions) actually visit the doctor's office to see if care is improving. (We note, however, that there may be as many as 340 doctors on probation with the Texas Board of Medical Examiners at any one time, but there previously have been two people whose job it is to ensure that physicians are complying with the conditions of their probation[34]). Many do use random urine tests to check for drug or alcohol use.

Far too few board actions, only 16.4% of the 10,211 actions for which we knew the exact offense, were for medical negligence or incompetence (see Table 4 page 23).

- Boards say proving incompetence is difficult, and investigations of substandard care soak up resources like a sponge.
- Instead, they use prescription violations and fraud convictions, offenses that are easy to document because they leave a paper trail, as potential indicators of substandard care. Inappropriate prescribing is often "the incipient sign of incompetence," says Oregon's John Ulwelling.[35]

Says former Department of Health and Human Services Inspector General Richard Kusserow, "If a surgeon was standing over my mother with a scalpel, and I had a choice between a crook that was competent and a very honest physician that was impaired by drugs, alcohol or age, I would choose the crook. And yet we seem to be very much better at finding the crooks."[36] (Most patients and Kusserow, we suspect, would prefer an honest *and* competent physician.)

Description of Tables 2 Through 9

The following tables provide a statistical national look at the disciplinary actions in this report. Please note that the period of years covered in our database varies from state to state--e.g. we may have received disciplinary materials covering six years for one state but only three years for another state. Therefore, our statistics should not be viewed as nationally representative for any specific time period.

Table 2, Disciplinary Actions Each State or Federal Agency Reported to Public Citizen, page 21 shows that of the 25,069 different disciplinary actions (representing actions against 13,012 different doctors) detailed in the state by state listings of our report, 1,267 or 5.1%, were DEA sanctions in contested and uncontested cases, 1,752 or 7.0% were fines and exclusions from the Medicare program, 19 were restrictions placed on a physician's eligibility to participate as investigators in FDA experiments, and the remaining 22,031 or 87.9% were disciplinary actions provided us by 49 states and the District of Columbia. South Dakota failed to provide us with any disciplinary actions for our listings. A description and statistical breakdown of the actions provided us by each state can be found in our State by State Listings. It should be noted that the counts presented in Table 2 include the two most serious disciplinary actions for each sanction reported. Some sanctions included more than two actions against the doctors. These less serious actions are not included in these counts.

It is interesting and worrisome that a computer analysis of the 1,208 doctors who were the subject of the 1,267 DEA actions, showed 376 or 31% were not the subject of any state disciplinary action even though their Federal narcotics license had been revoked or restricted, often several years ago.

Similarly, of the 1,715 Medicare doctors who were the subject of the 1,752 Medicare actions, 520 or 30% were not disciplined by their state boards even though most (98.6% of actions) had been serious enough to result in exclusions from Medicare.

Thus, many states are not acting promptly, if at all, against physicians about whom a Federal agency has compiled sufficient information to discipline them.

Table 3, Types of Disciplinary Actions Reported to Public Citizen, page 22, shows that the most common type of state disciplinary action of those submitted to us was probation. States imposed probation 20.8% of the time (5,211 times) when they disciplined practitioners. They revoked licenses 9.3% of the time (2,321 times), suspended licenses 9.7% of the time (2,425 times), and accepted a doctor's surrender of his or her license 7.5% of the time (1,876 times). Cumulatively, as shown in table 3, only 7,397 or 29.5% of the actions against doctors listed in this report resulted in at least a temporary loss of ability to practice medicine (revocation, suspension and surrender). Thus, most of the doctors who are listed in this book never had to stop practicing medicine and many more who had suspensions may once again be practicing. It is not likely that many of their patients are aware of these actions. **A total of 13,012 different physicians were the subject of the 25,069 disciplinary actions taken by state and Federal agencies.**

Table 4, Offenses for Which Doctors Were Disciplined, page 23. The reason an action was taken the offense was provided by state and Federal authorities for 13,696 of the records in our database. For a number of offenses, more than one action was taken. The most common single reason for which states disciplined doctors (among those 10,211 actions for which specific reasons other than discipline by another state or agency were reported) were the 1,989 instances (19.5% of all 10,211 actions for which a specific offense was stated) in which there was a *criminal conviction* (plea of guilty or nolo contendere--no contest).

A total of 1,913 different doctors were involved in these 1,989 criminal offenses.

Substandard care, incompetence or negligence, the second largest category, accounted for 1,677 or 16.4% of known offenses other than those listed as disciplinary action by another state. **A total of 1,622 different doctors were involved in these 1,677 offenses involving incompetence or negligence.**

Disciplinary actions taken because of *misprescribing or overprescribing drugs* accounted for an additional 1,436 or 14.1% of known offenses. **A total of 1,378 different doctors were involved in these 1,436 offenses.**

Drug or alcohol abuse formed the basis for an additional 1,200 or 11.8% of known offenses for which doctors were disciplined. **A total of 1,059 different doctors were involved in these 1,200 offenses.**

Sexual abuse of or sexual misconduct with a patient accounted for 282 offenses or 2.8% of the total. **A total of 264 different doctors were involved in these 282 offenses.**

The five offenses listed above, all extremely serious, accounted for 65% or almost two-thirds of all of those disciplinary actions in which a specific offense other than discipline by another state or agency was listed.

Table 5, Disciplinary Actions Taken Against Doctors Cited for Sexual Abuse of or Sexual Misconduct With a Patient, page 24, shows that of the 264 doctors who were disciplined for sexual abuse of or sexual misconduct with a patient, there were 184 actions (64 revocations, 23 surrenders, 60 suspensions plus 37 emergency suspensions) which took the doctors, at least temporarily, out of the practice of medicine. Thus, although 70% of the actions against these doctors (184/264) involved at least some cessation of their practice, 30% or almost a third were allowed to continue practicing, their behavior probably unknown to most of their patients. It is likely that others, especially those whose licenses were temporarily suspended, are once again practicing medicine.

Tables 6 through 9, the similar analyses for Substandard Care, Criminal Conviction, Misprescribing or Overprescribing of Drugs, and Drug or Alcohol Abuse (pages 24-26) show that only a minority of physicians (33%, 42%, 32% and 39% for these four categories, respectively) were given disciplinary actions (revocation, suspension or surrender of licenses) which stopped them, even temporarily, from practicing and about which most of their patients are probably unaware. Since suspension and emergency suspension were, collectively, the largest category of action among these and most suspended doctors return to practice, it is likely that most of the doctors in these four categories of very serious offenses are currently practicing medicine.

Table 2 Disciplinary Actions Each State or Federal Agency Reported to Public Citizen

Federal Agency	Number	Federal Agency	Number
DEA	1,267	FDA	19
Medicare	1,752		
Total Federal Actions	**3,038**		
States	**Number**	**States**	**Number**
Alabama	104	Missouri	491
Alaska	83	Montana	56
Arizona	462	Nebraska	77
Arkansas	34	Nevada	88
California	1,350	New Hampshire	39
Colorado	368	New Jersey	1,360
Connecticut	205	New Mexico	71
Delaware	31	New York	1,721
District	126	North Carolina	354
Florida	1,800	North Dakota	97
Georgia	865	Ohio	973
Hawaii	80	Oklahoma	223
Idaho	6	Oregon	291
Illinois	1,030	Pennsylvania	678
Indiana	438	Rhode Island	98
Iowa	425	South Carolina	375
Kansas	191	Tennessee	475
Kentucky	552	Texas	1,339
Louisiana	321	Utah	230
Maine	43	Vermont	92
Maryland	480	Virginia	542
Massachusetts	618	Washington	325
Michigan	669	West Virginia	395
Minnesota	686	Wisconsin	470
Mississippi	170	Wyoming	34
Total State Actions	**22,031**	**Total State/Federal Actions**	**25,069**

Table 3
Disciplinary Actions Reported to Public Citizen: A Breakdown of the Types of Disciplinary Actions Contained In This Report

Disciplinary Action	Number	Percent
Probation	5,211	20.8%
Suspension	2,425	9.7%
Revocation	2,321	9.3%
Fine	1,983	7.9%
Surrender	1,876	7.5%
Reprimand	1,774	7.1%
Exclusion from the Medicare Program	1,712	6.8%
Practice Restriction	1,340	5.3%
Revocation, Surrender, Suspension of Controlled Substance License	1,232	4.9%
Restriction of Controlled Substance License	891	3.6%
Emergency Suspension	775	3.1%
Education	638	2.5%
Physician Monitoring	611	2.4%
License Denial	394	1.6%
Required to Enter an Impaired Physicians Program or Drug or Alcohol Treatment	359	1.4%
Other Actions	1,527	6.1%
Total Actions	**25,069**	

Table 4
Offenses for Which Doctors Were Disciplined*

Offense	Number	Percent
Disciplinary Action Taken By Another State or Agency	3,485	25.4%
Criminal Conviction	1,989	14.5%
Substandard Care, Incompetence, or Negligence	1,677	12.2%
Misprescribing or Overprescribing Drugs	1,436	10.5%
Drug or Alcohol Abuse	1,200	8.8%
Professional Misconduct	998	7.3%
Noncompliance With a Board Order	774	5.7%
Noncompliance With a Professional Rule	633	4.6%
Practicing Without A License	408	3.0%
Providing False Information to Medical Board	319	2.3%
Sexual Abuse of or Sexual Misconduct With a Patient	282	2.1%
Mental or Physical Impairment	266	1.9%
Hospital Privilege Loss or Restriction	120	0.9%
Insurance or Medicare/Medicaid Fraud	52	0.4%
Falsifying/Altering Medical Records or Reports	31	0.2%
Overcharging	22	0.2%
Exceeding Professional Limitations	4	0.0%
Total Records With Offense Cited	**13,696**	

* Frequencies and types of violations cited by states or Federal Government for disciplinary actions. Includes only those actions for which an offense was reported and for which we had a corresponding term in our database.

Table 5
Disciplinary Actions Taken Against Doctors Cited for Sexual Abuse of or Sexual Misconduct With A Patient

Action	Number	Percent
Revocation	64	16.7%
Surrender	23	6.0%
Suspension	60	15.7%
Emergency Suspension	37	9.7%
Probation	87	22.7%
Fine	31	8.1%
Other Actions	81	21.1%
Total Actions	**383**	

Table 6
Disciplinary Actions Taken Against Doctors Cited For Substandard Care, Incompetence or Negligence

Action	Number	Percent
Revocation	164	7.0%
Surrender	116	4.9%
Suspension	201	8.6%
Emergency Suspension	55	2.3%
Probation	607	25.9%
Practice Restriction	191	8.1%
Fine	327	13.9%
Reprimand	226	9.6%
Other Actions	458	19.5%
Total Actions	**2,345**	

Table 7
Disciplinary Actions Taken Against Doctors Cited for Criminal Convictions

Action	Number	Percent
Revocation	348	14.8%
Surrender	84	3.6%
Suspension	325	13.8%
Emergency Suspension	52	2.2%
Probation	405	17.2%
Fine	106	4.5%
Other Actions	1,037	44.0%
Total Actions	**2,357**	

Table 8
Disciplinary Actions Taken Against Doctors Cited for Misprescribing or Overprescribing Drugs

Action	Number	Percent
Revocation	95	4.6%
Surrender	101	4.9%
Revocation, Surrender, or Suspension of Controlled Substance License	254	12.3%
Suspension	186	9.0%
Emergency Suspension	55	2.7%
Probation	508	24.6%
Restriction of Controlled Substance License	253	12.3%
Fine	226	10.9%
Education	109	5.3%
Other Actions	278	13.5%
Total Actions	**2,065**	

Table 9
Disciplinary Actions Taken Against Doctors Cited for Drug or Alcohol Abuse

Action	Number	Percent
Revocation	63	3.7%
Surrender	60	3.5%
Revocation, Surrender, or Suspension of Controlled Substance License	82	4.8%
Suspension	181	10.5%
Emergency Suspension	114	6.6%
Probation	532	30.9%
Restriction of Controlled Substance License	93	5.4%
Fine	36	2.1%
Required to Enter an Impaired Physician Program or Drug or Alcohol Treatment	170	9.9%
Other Actions	392	22.8%
Total Actions	**1,723**	

Recommendations For the Federal Government

1. **Create grants and standards.** Congress should create a small program of grants-in-aid to state medical boards. The grants should be tied to the boards' agreements to meet certain performance standards, which should be developed by the Public Health Service, as the Department of Health and Human Services Office of Inspector General recommended in 1990.[37]

In developing these standards the Public Health Service should work with the Federation of State Medical Boards' Assessment Task Force. In September 1990 the FSMB received a federal contract for $200,000 to undertake the development of a self-assessment instrument for state medical boards. The goal of the task force was to produce a sound and objective means by which boards could assess their performance over time and in comparison with other boards.[38] In April 1992 the Federation released its "Self-Assessment Instrument for State Medical Boards" and the accompanying handbook. The Instrument is a survey that each board can fill out regarding its own activities, enabling boards to eventually share information with each other and compare resources and performance.

The standards should include (but not be limited to) the following: processing complaints within a certain limited period of time; maintaining a certain level of staffing and having staff meet certain qualifications; disseminating disciplinary information to the public; having at least 30% of board members be consumer members; regularly publishing a newsletter that includes names of disciplined physicians and descriptions of the disciplinary actions taken against them; issuing an annual report that includes meaningful disciplinary statistics; and other standards.

2. **The Medicare Peer Review Organizations (PRO)**, which have been practically moribund in disciplining physicians for substandard care, should become more aggressive. The PROs should hire investigators and advisers trained in law enforcement so that fewer of their sanctions will be overturned.

As a 1990 Institute of Medicine report noted, the PROs are not evaluated on their ability to detect and correct poor quality care.[39] The Department of Health and Human Services should change its evaluation procedures to place more emphasis on quality.

3. **Open the National Practitioner Data Bank**. In 1986 Congress passed the Health Care Quality Improvement Act. This act mandated the establishment of a data bank containing information on adverse professional review actions taken against doctors, and on doctors who had been sued for malpractice and on whose behalf settlement or adjudicated payments had been made. Unfortunately, the law establishing the data bank also required that it be closed to the general public. Congress should pass legislation opening the data bank to consumers and loudly rebuke the American Medical Association's resolution to destroy the data bank.

4. **The Drug Enforcement Administration** should release a monthly list of all practitioners whose controlled substance prescription licenses have been revoked, restricted, or denied. The list should be widely distributed to pharmacies, state pharmacy and medical boards, and the general public.

Far too many doctors continue to prescribe controlled substances after their DEA licenses have expired or have been revoked. The DEA should consider requiring pharmacies to subscribe to an on-line service with which they could check the validity of these DEA license numbers.

5. **Require doctor recertification**. Congress should consider legislation proposed by Rep. Pete Stark, D-Calif., to require physicians who accept Medicare patients to be periodically recertified for competency.

Recommendations For States

1. **Strengthen the statutes.** States that have not already done so should adopt a version of the Model Medical Practice Act developed by the Federation of State Medical Boards,[40] or, preferably, stronger laws.

2. **Restructure the boards**. States should sever any remaining formal links between state licensing boards and state medical societies. Members of medical boards (and separate disciplinary boards, where present) should be appointed by the governor, and the governor's choice of appointees should not be limited to a medical society's nominees.

At least 50% of the members of each state medical board and disciplinary board should be well-informed and well trained public members who have no ties to health care providers.

The governor should appoint members to the Medical Board whose top priority is protecting the public's health, not providing assistance to physicians who are trying to evade disciplinary actions.

3. **Inform the public.** Each state's Open Records Law and its Medical Practice Act should state that all formal disciplinary actions against licensed professionals are fully public records.

Each legislature should require widespread dissemination of final disciplinary orders. Lists of those disciplined and full disciplinary orders should be promptly available by mail to all requesting them.

Notices of disciplinary actions should be sent to the local news media and to all hospitals, health maintenance organizations (HMOs), and other health care providers in the state, as well as to other state agencies, the federal Department of Health and Human Services, and the federal Drug Enforcement Administration. Federal law already requires that such information be reported to the National Practitioner Data Bank, which began operating on September 1, 1990.

4. **Strengthen board authority.** Every medical board should have the authority to impose emergency suspensions pending formal hearing in cases where a doctor poses a potential danger to the public health. Boards should aggressively use this authority when they learn of a potentially dangerous doctor.

Medical boards should have the authority to rapidly, after confirmation, accept the findings of other state boards and of the federal Department of Health and Human Services and the Drug Enforcement Administration. If a physician has been disciplined by another state, the second state's medical board should be required to impose sanctions at least as stringent as those imposed by the first state.

Each state should require physicians who have been licensed in other states and who seek licensure in a new state to submit affidavits that they are not under investigation elsewhere before being granted a new license. Physicians who are under investigation should not be permitted to practice until the board has heard the details of their case and can evaluate their competency.

Each legislature should grant its state medical licensing board the authority to examine physicians for physical, mental and professional competence and to test them for alcohol and drug use upon reason to believe that a problem exists in one of these areas.

5. **Encourage complaints.** Each legislature should provide for the protection of confidentiality and immunity to those who report violations of the Medical Practice Act to a board. Such protections should also be extended to board members, their staff, and consultants.

Each legislature should require all licensed health care practitioners to report Medical Practice Act violations by other practitioners to the medical board, with large civil penalties for failure to do so. Boards should aggressively use their authority to enforce the requirement that all health care providers report such violations. Each legislature should also require hospitals to report all revocations, restrictions, or voluntary surrenders of privileges.

Courts should be required to report all indictments and convictions of physicians to the medical disciplinary board. In addition, each legislature should require liability insurers to report all claims, payments, and policy cancellations to state medical disciplinary boards. It should request reports from other state agencies, Medicare, the DEA and other federal agencies. It should also require impaired physicians' programs to report the names of doctors who fail to successfully complete their programs.

Medical boards should conduct random audits of institutions to check compliance with these reporting requirements, and should fine those who fail to comply. After a doctor is disciplined, a board should fine any other practitioners who knew of that doctor's offense, but failed to report it.

6. **Keep the courts in check.** Each legislature should pass laws that make clear their intent that the judgements of the medical board be given extreme deference, and that, barring extraordinary circumstances, disciplinary actions should take immediate effect pending appeal.

Each legislature should adopt the 'Preponderance of the Evidence' standard of proof in medical disciplinary cases, replacing the tougher-to-meet 'Clear and Convincing Evidence' standard now in effect in most states. According to the August 1990 report on state medical boards issued by the Office of the Inspector General, "The 'clear and convincing evidence' standard of proof is more rigorous than the 'preponderance of evidence' standard that is typically required to justify tort damages for negligence in civil cases. The more rigorous standard provides greater protection for physicians, but adds complexity to the investigative process and appears to make it less likely that a board will persevere on a case through a full evidentiary hearing."[41]

Furthermore, the Project Work Panel of the Federation of State Medical Boards, in its August 1989 report *Elements of a Modern State Medical Board: A Proposal*, recommended that each state medical board "use preponderance of evidence as the standard of proof" and that they each have the power "to issue final decisions when acting as trier of fact in the performance of [their] adjudicatory duties".[42]

7. **Beef up funding and staffing.** Each legislature should permit the medical board to spend all the revenue from medical licensing fees, rather than being forced to give part to the state Treasury. The medical boards should raise their fees to $500 a year.

All boards could benefit from hiring new investigators and legal staff. Boards should employ adequate staff to process and investigate all complaints within 30 days, to review all malpractice claims filed with the board, to monitor and regularly visit doctors who have been disciplined to ensure their compliance with the sanctions imposed, and to ensure compliance with reporting requirements.

They should hire investigators to seek out errant doctors, through review of pharmacy records, consultation with medical examiners, and targeted office audits of those doctors practicing alone and suspected of poor care.

8. **Require risk prevention.** States should adopt a law, similar to one in Massachusetts, that requires all hospitals and other health care providers to have a meaningful, functioning risk prevention program designed to prevent injury to patients. Massachusetts also requires all adverse incidents occurring in hospitals or in doctors' offices to be reported to the medical board.

9. **Require periodic recertification of doctors** based on a written exam and audit of their patients' medical care records.

Recommendations To Consumers

1. **Complain.** File your complaints about poor medical care or medical misconduct with your state medical board and with the federal Department of Health and Human Services. If the offense occurred in a hospital, also file a complaint with the hospital peer review committee.

Your complaints are needed to protect others!

2. **Organize.** Form citizens' action or victims' rights groups to improve medical quality assurance in your area. The American Association of Retired Persons publishes a guide that can help you mobilize a group for reform.[43] Try to get a representative of your group appointed to the state medical board or the Medicare Peer Review Organization for your state.

3. **Write to your Congressperson** and voice your support for the opening of the National Practitioner Data Bank to the general public. This is especially important since the American Medical Association not only is against public disclosure, but has, in the face of "threats" of public disclosure, voted the "dissolution" of the data bank.

Appendix 1: Glossary

Controlled substances, controlled dangerous substances: drugs which are regulated under the federal Controlled Substances Act because of their potential for addiction or abuse.

D.O.: the academic degree awarded to osteopathic physicians.

DEA: the federal Drug Enforcement Administration, an agency of the U.S. Justice Department. Its mission is to enforce controlled substances laws.

DEA license, DEA registration, or DEA certificate: every person who handles or prescribes controlled substances, including physicians and dentists, must legally have a registration number issued by the Drug Enforcement Administration.

Disciplinary action: any of a number of ways a regulatory agency can limit or forbid a doctor's practice or formally indicate its displeasure. Includes license revocations, suspensions, and probations, consent agreements placing conditions on a doctor's continuing practice, monetary fines, and letters of reprimand.

Disciplinary action rate: total state disciplinary actions per 1,000 MDs practicing in a state.

Emergency suspension: a disciplinary action in which a medical board may remove a doctor from practice temporarily, without a formal disciplinary hearing, if it finds the doctor's continued practice could endanger the public health. Generally, boards are required to then hold a formal hearing on the case within a specified time period.

Impaired physicians program: a program to rehabilitate physicians suffering from an illness. Impaired physicians programs generally serve alcohol and drug abusers, but they have also been used to aid the mentally or physically ill, as well as habitual sex offenders.

Liability insurer: a company that insures doctors against malpractice lawsuits.

M.D.: the academic degree awarded to U.S. medical doctors, or allopathic physicians.

Medical board: used generically, any state regulatory agency that licenses and/or disciplines MDs. Medical boards may also license other practitioners and health care paraprofessionals.

Osteopath: a physician who graduated from a school of osteopathic medicine. Osteopaths have training in skeletal manipulation in addition to their medical training.

Peer review committee: a hospital committee that reviews the quality of care in the institution. The committee may admit physicians to the hospital staff or revoke or limit their privileges.

Peer Review Organization: a state-based group under contract to the federal Medicare program to audit the necessity and quality of Medicare patients' care.

Probation: a disciplinary action or agreement wherein a doctor must abide by certain conditions for a definite or indefinite period of time, or face a more severe penalty. Probationary conditions are generally tailored to the individual.

Reinstatement: issuance of a new medical license to a doctor who previously surrendered his or her license or had it revoked.

Reprimand: a formal letter to a doctor criticizing a particular episode of misconduct or poor care. Sometimes called an admonition or letter of censure.

Restriction: a disciplinary action which limits the type of medicine a doctor may practice. For instance, a doctor's license may be restricted to prevent him or her from practicing surgery, or to limit practice to a certain clinic.

Revocation: the cancellation of a doctor's state or DEA license. State laws regarding revocations vary: in some states, revocations are permanent; in others, doctors may reapply for a new license immediately; in others, doctors must wait for a certain time period before reapplying.

Sanction: a formal disciplinary action.

Schedule I: controlled substances such as marijuana and heroin, which are usually held to have no approved medical purpose.

Schedule II: controlled substances with approved medical uses, but with high potential for addiction or abuse. This category includes raw opium, codeine, amphetamines, and some barbiturates.

Schedule III: controlled substances whose use may lead to low-moderate physical dependence or high psychological dependence and are therefore considered to have some potential for abuse. This category includes many barbiturates and other depressant drugs, and narcotics which include moderate amounts of codeine.

Schedule IV: controlled substances whose use may lead to limited physical and psychological dependence. Includes Valium, Xanax, and other benzodiazepine tranquilizers, sleeping pills such as Halcion and anorectic stimulants, which are frequently used for weight loss.

Schedule V: controlled substances whose abuse potential is low; includes many non-prescription narcotic antidiarrheal drugs and cough suppressants.

Scheduled drugs: see Controlled Substances.

Serious disciplinary actions: Public Citizen's term for revocations, suspensions, surrenders, and probations, as they are reported by the Federation of State Medical Boards.

Serious disciplinary action rate: the number of revocations, suspensions, surrenders and probations per 1,000 MDs practicing in a state.

Summary suspension: see emergency suspension.

Surrender: a voluntary agreement by a doctor to give up his or her license to practice. Some surrender agreements permit a doctor to reapply for a new license; others are permanent.

State medical society: a local trade association of physicians. It serves no governmental function.

Stay: a stayed disciplinary action is like a suspended sentence: it does not take effect unless the doctor who has been disciplined disobeys the board or commits some further offense.

Suspension: the temporary removal of a doctor from practice. Some suspensions run for a definite period of time; others are indefinite, and a doctor must apply for the suspension to be lifted.

Triplicate prescription program: a program, now in effect in nine states, that requires copies of prescriptions for certain scheduled drugs to be sent to the state regulatory authority. Intended to prevent drug dealing and overprescribing of drugs that can easily be abused.

Appendix 2: How We Compiled This Report

1. Sources of Information:

A) Using a list published by the Federation of State Medical Boards, Public Citizen contacted all the medical boards from the 50 states and the District of Columbia in the fall of 1989 and requested a list of all the physicians they had disciplined since the beginning of 1985. We also asked to be put on their mailing lists to receive notification of future disciplinary orders. Since that initial request, we have periodically contacted the States to obtain new information on disciplinary actions. Most recently, we sent a letter to each state in November of 1994 requesting updated information for this edition of *Questionable Doctors*.

Not all states have been able to provide all the information we have requested. However, for this edition we have received information on disciplinary actions taken against one or more doctors from 49 states, the District of Columbia, the U.S. Department of Health and Human Services, the Drug Enforcement Administration and the Food and Drug Administration. This is the first edition of *Questionable Doctors* to include actions taken by the Arkansas Medical Board. South Dakota remains the only state board that has failed to provide us with the requested information. A description of the information we received from each state is included in the State by State Listing section of this report.

The time period covered by the disciplinary actions included in this edition of *Questionable Doctors* differs from state to state. If a state provided disciplinary actions from years prior to 1986, we included only actions from 1986 forward with one exception. Actions that occurred prior to 1986 are in the database if the physician they refer to was also disciplined in the 1986 to 1992 period (the time period covered by the 1993 edition of this report). Our cutoff date for inclusion of disciplinary materials in this report was January 31, 1995. Earlier editions of *Questionable Doctors* included disciplinary actions against dentists, chiropractors, and podiatrists if the State Board provided that information. Because we did not consistently receive information on such health care providers from all medical boards, we decided to eliminate entries on such professionals from our database.

B) Public Citizen obtained from the Inspector General's office of the U.S. Department of Health and Human Services a list of all health care providers excluded from the Medicare/Medicaid program for disciplinary purposes through December 1994. The list is called the *Medicare/Medicaid Sanction--Reinstatement Report*. It includes the doctor's name, degree and/or specialty, address, date of the sanction notice, period of exclusion from the program, and section of the Social Security Act violated. We included all physicians (both MDs and DOs) listed in these reports in our database. Previously, from May 1986 through October 1990, the Inspector General's office has also provided Public Citizen with copies of the notices of all sanctions, both fines and exclusions, imposed by the Department of Health and Human Services as a result of recommendations from Medicare Peer Review Organizations (PROs), which may sanction doctors for substandard or unnecessary care. The sanction notices include the physician's name, address, the PRO that recommended disciplinary action, the number of cases of substandard or unnecessary care for which the doctor was cited, sometimes the Department's findings about that care, the type of disciplinary action being taken, the length of an exclusion or the amount of a fine, and any information on appeals then available.

C) Public Citizen obtained from the *Federal Register* notices about doctors whose Drug Enforcement Administration registrations to prescribe controlled substances were revoked, restricted or denied following contested cases dated from 1988 through November 1994. Our list also includes some of the physicians who did not contest the DEA's decision and agreed to surrender or restrict their prescribing privileges. Although we asked DEA for all such uncontested actions, they have only partially fulfilled our request. *The Federal Register* notices included the doctor's name, address, and DEA certificate number, a description of the conduct that led to the agency's action, the type of action, and the effective date.

E) From the *Food and Drug Administration* Public Citizen obtained information on physicians who were sanctioned because they had violated FDA laws, regulations, or policies regarding clinical research on patients. These physicians are ineligible to receive investigational products for research purposes. Our database includes actions taken through March of 1994.

2. Generating the Database:

A) From the information we received from the states, the Drug Enforcement Administration, the Food and Drug Administration, and the Department of Health and Human Services, we created database entries on individual practitioners. In each entry we included (when available) the full name, degree, license number, date of birth, and location (street address, city and state) of each doctor, the state or agency that disciplined him or her, and the date of the disciplinary action. When we were not told whether a physician was an MD or DO, we listed the physician's degree as "DR".

We included up to two types of disciplinary actions taken on the given action date, and one violation or offense that served as the basis for that action (see below). Details and information on appeals, when available, are included under the "Notes" heading of our items on individual doctors. As we have previously stated, information regarding appeals was not generally available, and hence it is possible that some doctors have had their sanctions stayed or overturned on appeal. For this edition of *Questionable Doctors* we made a special effort to obtain information on court actions/decisions that overrule or change previous disciplinary actions taken by state boards. In September of 1995, we sent a letter to all boards requesting this information. Not all boards were able to fulfill our request, but given the information we did receive, we deleted from our database those actions that were overturned by the courts on appeal and for which litigation in the matter had ended in the physician's favor.

B) We classified each disciplinary action into one of 26 categories. For each disciplinary order, we chose what we viewed as the two most "severe" actions. We included those under the heading "Disciplinary action:" in our items on individual doctors. The heading "other actions" in both the national and state tables may include actions on this list which are not specified in the tables.

Following is a listing of our categories of disciplinary actions, in order of "severity":

- license revocation
- surrender of license
- nonrenewal of license
- revocation of license to prescribe controlled substances
- surrender of license to prescribe controlled substances
- nonrenewal of license to prescribe controlled substances
- denial of new license
- denial of license reinstatement (following surrender or revocation)
- license reinstatement (following surrender or revocation)
- license suspension
- suspension of authority to prescribe controlled substances
- emergency suspension (pending a formal disciplinary hearing)
- probation
- controlled substance license placed on probation
- fine
- restriction placed on license to practice

- restriction placed on license to prescribe controlled substances
- reprimand
- required to take additional medical education
- required to enter an impaired physician program or drug or alcohol treatment
- cease and desist order
- monitoring of physician performance
- private reprimand
- community service

Medicare/Medicaid program sanctions and actions taken against physicians by the Food and Drug Administration were classified in the following two categories respectively:

- exclusion from the Medicare and/or Medicaid programs
- investigator ineligible to receive investigational new drugs for experimental purposes

We placed any further details about disciplinary actions under the heading "Notes." Any disciplinary actions that do not fall into the above categories are detailed in the notes sections and classified as "Other actions" in our charts and statistical summaries.

C) When a state provided information on the legal violation or offense that led them to discipline a doctor, we classified that violation into one of 17 categories. If several violations were listed by the Board, we chose the one that appeared to contribute the most to the disciplinary decision. If that choice was unclear, we selected the offense that ranked highest on our hierarchy of offenses as listed below. We included the violation under the heading "Offense" in our items on individual doctors. The heading "other offenses" in both the national and state tables may include actions on this list which are not specified in the tables.

Following are the lists of our categories of offenses, and definitions as needed, in order of presumed importance:

- disciplinary action by another state or agency
- criminal conviction or plea of guilty, nolo contendere, or no contest to a crime
- practicing without a valid license or prescribing without a valid controlled substance license
- loss or restriction of hospital privileges
- failure to comply with a previous board order
- providing false information to the medical board

- substandard care, incompetence or negligence
- sexual abuse of or sexual misconduct with a patient
- drug or alcohol abuse
- overprescribing or misprescribing drugs
- physical or mental illness inhibiting the ability to practice with skill and safety
- insurance, Medicare or Medicaid fraud
- falsifying or altering patient records or medical reports
- overcharging
- exceeding professional limitations
- professional misconduct (see below)
- failure to comply with a professional rule (see below)

The category "professional misconduct" includes a variety of offenses that are more serious than the violation of a professional rule but don't fit into any of the other categories listed above. Some examples of offenses classified as professional misconduct are:

- "unprofessional conduct"
- a criminal offense of which the physician hasn't actually been convicted
- ordering or performing unnecessary or inappropriate procedures for a patient deliberately, rather than because of incompetence
- failing to supervise a physician's assistant, or other non-medical personnel
- permitting an unlicensed person to practice medicine
- tax violations
- intimidating a patient in an attempt to convince them not to seek a second opinion
- terminating a patient's medical care without transferring the patient to another's care
- abandonment of a patient
- making fraudulent representations in medical practice
- assuring a cure for an incurable disease
- offering to treat by a "secret method"
- accepting payments from laboratories for sending them patients' tests
- procuring a criminal abortion
- performing medical services that the board has declared to be of no value (frequently chelation therapy)
- soliciting patients in a deceitful manner
- disruption of residency program

- improperly transferring a patient from a treatment center to a hospital
- engaging in lewd conduct
- clearly excessive use of diagnostic procedures
- unlawful possession of a controlled substance outside the practice of medicine
- fraud in medical research
- operating an illegal drug lab
- unspecified perjury
- diversion of drugs (not specifically prescription drugs) or drug use
- presigning blank prescription pads so that an unlicensed person may practice medicine
- breaching physician-patient confidentiality
- charging for services as supervising physician even though not present during the course of treatment
- selling drugs and devices for financial gain
- sending out letters to request payment using an attorney's name without the attorney's knowledge or consent
- use of disposable syringes on multiple patients
- rendering a psychiatric evaluation without properly examining and treating the subject of said evaluation
- sexual abuse of a person other than a patient, or of an unspecified person
- not getting a consent form signed

Examples of the types of violations included in the category "Failure to comply with a professional rule" are:

- violation of restrictions on advertising
- failure to respond to the board
- failure to maintain sanitary practice conditions
- violation of medical records laws (except for falsifying records) including failure to provide copies of records when requested or excessive charges for providing records
- requiring patients to purchase drugs or devices from physician
- failure to keep required documents on file
- employing an agent to solicit patients
- making excessive claims of expertise
- violating AMA ethics standards
- failure to report a disciplinary action in another state
- failure to report child abuse
- failure to pay fees
- failure to display a valid license
- endorsing a product

- keeping outdated or misbranded drugs
- failure to keep proper controlled substance records
- failure to report other medical personnel who are violating the Medical Practice Act to the medical board
- fee-splitting
- failure to report a suspicious death to the police
- failure to meet continuing medical education requirements
- allowing someone not in the doctor's employ and not under direct supervision to demonstrate a TENS unit to patients
- two-tiered billing
- failure to have liability insurance
- practicing under a name other than the one on his or her physician's license
- nonpayment of student loan

3. Counting physicians and actions:

A) Counting physicians: It is impossible for us to know exactly how many physicians are in our database. There are two main reasons for this:

- Many states are not consistent in how they list the names of physicians who have been disciplined, i.e. they may have reported only a first and last name in one newsletter, but included a middle initial and suffix (such as Jr. or Sr.) in another. We made numerous phone calls to try and resolve questions about multiple actions taken against what appeared to be a single physician by a single state and in some cases made calls regarding multiple actions taken against what appeared to be the same person by different states.

- Many states do not include license numbers or dates of birth in their listings of disciplined doctors, which can quickly clarify situations in which names appear similar but are not exactly alike.

After we entered corrected information obtained through phone calls, we counted all the physicians in the database. We did this using a computer program that compared physician identifying information. The program used six database fields to "match" entries: last name, first name, middle name, the suffix (Jr., Sr., etc.), license number, and birth date. It compared two entries with the same first and last name and "matched" them if one or more of the following was true:

- they had the same birth date;
- they were sanctioned by the same state and had the same license number;
- a middle name in one matched the middle name in the other;

- a middle name in one matched the middle initial in the other; or,
- the first and last names matched and no other information was given to indicate a non-match.

Entries with the same first and last name were not matched if they had differing birth dates or license numbers (within the same state). When one record included a middle name and the other did not, the records were not considered a match unless the birth dates or license numbers matched. The same is true if one record had a suffix (Jr., Sr., etc.) and another did not.

B) Counting actions: Although each sanction may consist of several disciplinary actions, we entered only the two most serious disciplinary actions in each case. Both of these disciplinary actions were included when generating counts of actions taken by the state boards or federal agencies. Because we entered only the two most serious actions, our counts of the less serious actions (such as fines, restrictions, education, and monitoring) will not tell us how often these less serious actions were imposed. Rather, they will only tell us how often these actions were among the two most serious actions imposed.

4. Generation of the state-by-state lists:

A) In the "Disciplinary actions" sections of each state listing, we attempted to include doctors who had any connection with the state. Taking New York as an example, the New York "Disciplinary actions" section includes:

(i) All disciplinary actions taken by the New York State Board of Regents;

(ii) All disciplinary actions by other states, the Drug Enforcement Administration, the Food and Drug Administration or Medicare/Medicaid against doctors for whom a New York state address is given;

(iii) All other disciplinary actions against doctors with names like those included in (i) and (ii), i.e., actions taken by another state or agency that the computer program described above "matched" to doctors disciplined by New York or located in New York.

Any time a doctor's license number is listed in an action it is the license number of the state that is sanctioning the doctor. The only exception is that sometimes Drug Enforcement Administration actions list state license numbers.

Some state listings may include doctors with similar names who are not, in fact, the same doctor.

When state medical boards or other sources informed us that a physician listed in the book had died, we deleted all records for the deceased doctor from our database. We used the matching program to ensure that all records that matched to the physician's identifying information were deleted.

Although we have made every effort to match physician's names correctly, some materials we received did not include complete information on middle names, license numbers, or birth dates. Therefore, readers should remember that non-disciplined physicians and physicians with different disciplinary actions may have similar names to those physicians listed in the state listing of disciplinary actions. Readers should also remember that if they want the most current information on the status of a physician's license, they should contact the medical board of the state in which the physician practices or has practiced in the past.

5. Appeals, Reinstatements:

While we attempted to acquire as much up-to-date information as possible on doctors whose disciplinary actions have been appealed to and/or overturned by the courts, we do not have information on all appellate actions. Therefore, we cannot guarantee that a doctor listed here as being disciplined has not had that action overturned or stayed by a court. We entered into our database all disciplinary actions we received by January 31, 1995 and all reinstatements to an unrestricted license and court appeals we received by December 3, 1995. Again, the medical board should be contacted for more detailed and up-to-date information.

Some states did not supply us with information on license reinstatements or the lifting of license restrictions. We cannot guarantee that a physician listed as being suspended or restricted has not had that suspension or restriction lifted, or that a physician whose license was revoked has not obtained a new license.

6. Charts, Tables, Statistics:

This report uses data on disciplinary actions from two general sources: (1) Public Citizen's analysis of information on disciplinary actions provided by each state; and, (2) the 1994 statistical summaries of state serious disciplinary actions released by the Federation of State Medical Boards. This latter source is only used to generate Table 1 in both the national and state listings.

These two data sources are not always comparable. States may not have published or sent Public Citizen all the disciplinary actions they counted in their statistical summaries or reported to the Federation of State Medical Boards. Furthermore, our categorization of disciplinary actions may differ from the Federation's.

In our rankings of the numbers of serious state disciplinary actions, we use the Federation statistics because they are the only statistics that are relatively uniform from state to state. However, the Federation is dependent on the states to supply it with disciplinary information, and the types of actions reported may be different from state to state. This may lead to inconsistencies in the rankings. In this report we have ranked states based on the total number of serious disciplinary actions reported to the Federation (see Table 1, page 11).

For the tables summarizing the disciplinary actions taken by a state over a period of several years, we used our own method of counting *only those actions in our database*. Therefore, the numbers in these tables may look different from the numbers the Federation has released.

Appendix 3: Addresses of Federal Agencies

U.S. DEPARTMENT OF HEALTH AND HUMAN SERVICES
OFFICE OF INSPECTOR GENERAL

Use these addresses and phone numbers for information on the Medicare/Medicaid sanctions program:

June Gibbs Brown
Inspector General
Department of Health and Human Services
330 Independence Ave. SW
Room 5250 Cohen Bldg.
Washington, DC 20201
(202) 619-3148

Public Affairs Office
Office of Inspector General
Department of Health and Human Services
330 Independence Ave. SW
Room 5551 Cohen Building
Washington DC 20201
(202) 619-1343

To get a current list of those sanctioned, contact:

William M. Libercci, Deputy Director
Health Care Administrative Sanctions
Office of Investigations
Office of Inspector General
Department of Health and Human Services
Room 1-D-13 Oak Meadows Building
6325 Security Boulevard
Baltimore MD 21207
(410) 786-9603

DRUG ENFORCEMENT ADMINISTRATION
U.S. DEPARTMENT OF JUSTICE
1405 I Street, NW
Washington, D.C. 20005

Use these numbers and addresses to file complaints about health care providers with the Medicare sanctions program:

<u>Nationwide, 24-hour complaints hotline</u>
Toll free 1-800-447-8477

Region I - Boston
Regional Inspector General
Room 1409, JFK Federal Bldg.
Boston, MA 02203
(617) 565-2689
[Connecticut, Maine, Vermont, Massachusetts, New Hampshire, Rhode Island]

Region II - New York
Regional Inspector General
Room 3900B, Federal Bldg.
26 Federal Plaza
New York, NY 10278
(212) 264-1691
[New York, New Jersey, Puerto Rico, Virgin Isl.]

Region III - Philadelphia Regional Inspector General
P.O. Box 13716
Philadelphia, PA 19101
(215) 596-6743
[Pennsylvania, Delaware, Maryland, Virginia, West Virginia, District of Columbia]

Region IV - Atlanta
Regional Inspector General
101 Marietta Tower St. 1401
Atlanta, GA 30323
(404) 331-2131
[Alabama, Florida, Georgia, Kentucky, Mississippi, North Carolina, South Carolina, Tennessee]

References

1. Public Citizen Health Research Group, *A Consumer's Directory of Prince George's County Doctors*, 1974.

2. Public Health Service, Department of Health and Human Services, "National Practitioner Data Bank for Adverse Information on Physicians and other Health Care Providers," 45 CFR Part 60, *Federal Register*, October 17, 1989.

3. "The Health Care Quality Improvement Act of 1986," *New Jersey Medicine*, June 1987, 84 (6) 401-403.

4. Iglehart, John K., "Congress Moves to Bolster Peer Review: The Health Care Quality Improvement Act of 1986," *New England Journal of Medicine*, 1987, 316 (15) 960-964.

5. Office of Technology Assessment, *The Quality of Medical Care: Information for Consumers*, OTA-H-386. Washington, DC: U.S. Government Printing Office, June 1988.

6. Stevens, Carol, "Good Medicine: Finding the Right Care," *The Washingtonian*, November 1995, pp. 90-97.

7. Cohn, Victor, "How to Find a Doctor Who Delivers," *The Washington Post*, Health Section, October 14, 1984; "The Doctor Dilemma: Sorting Out Specialties," *The Washington Post*, Health Section, November 7, 1984; "The Doctor Checkup," *The Washington Post*, Health Section, November 21, 1984; Glazer, Sarah, "How Much Do You Know?", *The Washington Post*, Health Section, March 5, 1991.

8. Federation of State Medical Boards, Exchange. Section 3: *Physician Licensing Boards and Physician Discipline*, 1989/1990 edition; Federation of State Medical Boards, Exchange. Section 3: *Physician Licensing Boards and Physician Discipline*, 1988 edition.

9. Title II of the Social Security Act in Compilation of Social Security Laws including Social Security Act as amended and related enactments through January 1, 1989, Vol. 1, U.S. Government Printing Office 1989.

10. Health Resources and Services Administration, National Practitioner Data Bank Statistical Summary, As of Month Ending April 30, 1995.

11. Hospital reporting to the National Practitioner Data Bank. (OEI-01-94-00050). Office of the Inspector General, Department of Health and Human Services, February, 1995.

12. "Quality-of-Care Data Bank for Patients Coming Soon," *Internal Medicine News*, April 15-30, 1989, 22 (8) 9.

13. *Dent v. West Virginia*, 127 U.S. 114 (1889); see also *Klafter v. State Board of Examiners of Architects*, 259 Ill. 15, 102 N.E. 193 (1913); *In re Polk License Revocation*, 90 N.J. 550, 449 A.2nd 7 (1982).

14. "State Medical Boards and Medical Discipline," Office of Evaluation and Inspections, Office of the Inspector General, U.S. Department of Health and Human Services, draft report, April 1990.

15. McAuley, R.G., Letter to the Editor, *New England Journal of Medicine*, August 8, 1985.

16. Kusserow, Richard, Inspector General, U.S. Department of Health and Human Services, Testimony before the U.S. House of Representatives Committee on Small Business, Subcommittee on Regulation, Business Opportunities and Energy, June 8, 1990.

17. Federation of State Medical Boards, "1994 Summary of Board Actions Reported by State Licensing and Disciplinary Boards," April, 1994.

18. Harvard Medical Practice Study Group, "Patients, Doctors and Lawyers: Medical Injury, Malpractice Litigation and Patient Compensation in New York," 1990.

19. Mills, D.H. ed, *California Medical Association and California Hospital Association Report on the Medical Insurance Feasibility Study*, San Francisco: Sutter Publications, 1977.

20. *Journal of Legal Medicine*, February 1976.

21. Schwartz, William B., and Mendelson, Daniel N., "The Role of Physician-Owned Insurance Companies in the Detection and Deterrence of Negligence," *Journal of the American Medical Association* 1988, 260, (10):1342-1346.

22. Gewertz, Catherine, "O.C. Doctor's Practice is Shut Down by Court; Hearing: Gynecologist Accused of Sexual Misconduct Involving at Least 140 Patients is Called Danger to Public," *The Los Angeles Times*, Orange County Edition, March 14, 1992, part A, p. 1.

23. Weber, Tracy and Susan Peterson, "Doctor-Review System Sparks Fierce Criticism." *The Orange County Register*, March 15, 1992, Morning Edition, p. A1.

24. Gewertz, Catherine, "Court Order Sought to Shut Down Doctor; Tustin Gynecologist Accused of Molesting Scores of Patients Also Faces Possible Criminal Prosecution," *The Los Angeles Times*, Orange County Edition, March 13, 1992, part B, p. 1.

25. Gewertz, Catherine, "State Speeds Up Bid to Shut Down Doctor's Practice; Investigation: Dozens of Women Have Filed Complaints Alleging That a Tustin Gynecologist Sexually Molested Them," *The Los Angeles Times*, Orange County Edition, March 11, 1992, part B, p. 1.

26. Interview by Nicole Simmons with Ron Ritchie, 1990.

27. Griffith, John, "Doctor Who Gave up License May Build New Clinic," *The Oregonian*, March 1990.

28. Ulwelling, John, executive director, Oregon Board of Medical Examiners, testimony before the U.S. House of Representatives Committee on Small Business, Subcommittee on Regulation, Business Opportunities and Energy, June 8, 1990.

29. Ibid.

30. Fried, Jane, "Scar Removal Was Reason Sharon J. Reynolds Submitted to Cosmetic Surgery, Daughter Says," *The Public Medical News*, November 16, 1989, page 1; Fried, Jane, "Preliminary Hearing for Reynolds Set for May 30, Judge Decides. Physician Faces Second-degree Murder Charge," *The Public Medical News*, May 17, 1990.

31. Report and Recommendations of the State of New Jersey Commission of Investigation on Impaired and Incompetent Physicians, October 1987.

32. Goldstein, Avram, *The Detroit News*, "State's Doctor Investigation Unit Dropped," March 8, 1992.

33. Ibid.

34. SoRelle, Ruth, "Understaffing Mars Monitoring of Doctors on Probation", *The Houston Chronicle*, August 31, 1992, p. A 1.

35. Ulwelling, Testimony, op. cit.

36. Kusserow, Testimony, op. cit.

37. Lohr, Kathleen N., and Schroeder, Steven A., Institute of Medicine. "A Strategy for Quality Assurance in Medicare," *New England Journal of Medicine*, 1990, 322 (10).

38. "Federation Receives Federal Contract to Develop Self-Assessment Instrument for State Medical Boards," *FSMB Newsletter*, no. 36, September 1990.

39. Lohr, op. cit.

40. Federation of State Medical Boards, *Elements of a Modern State Medical Board: A Proposal*, August 1989.

41. "State Medical Boards and Medical Discipline," Office of Evaluation and Inspections, Office of the Inspector General, U.S. Department of Health and Human Services, August 1990, p. 9.

42. Federation of State Medical Boards, August 1989, op. cit.

43. American Association of Retired Persons, "Effective Physician Oversight: Prescription for Medical Licensing Board Reform," 1987.

TEXAS

1994 serious action rate: 5.02/1000
1994 ranking: 23rd

The Texas State Board of Medical Examiners sent us newsletters dated from the spring of 1985 to the winter of 1990. The disciplinary actions were not dated, but they cover roughly the period from late 1984 through October 1992. We entered the date of the newsletter as the action date for these records. Until the fall-winter 1988 newsletter, the newsletters only listed the most severe disciplinary actions taken: revocations, surrenders, suspensions, and some probations. Even the fall-winter 1988 newsletter did not fully describe the lesser disciplinary actions. Subsequent newsletters listed the physician's name, title, license number, city and state of residence, the date and type of action taken, and usually the reason for the action. The Board started sending us copies of disciplinary orders that accompany those listed in its newsletter from January 1992 through January 1995.

The information provided covers disciplinary actions taken against both allopathic physicians (MDs) and osteopathic physicians (DOs).

Besides disciplinary actions taken by the State Medical Board, this listing also includes actions taken by the Medicare/Medicaid programs, the FDA, and the DEA against physicians located in this state. Actions taken by other states against physicians located in this state or that match to a physician disciplined by this state (see pg. 43 for an explanation of our matching protocol) are also listed.

Although we have made every effort to match physician's names correctly, some materials we received did not include complete information on middle names, license numbers, birth dates or addresses. Therefore, readers should remember that non-disciplined physicians and physicians with different disciplinary actions may have similar names to those disciplined physicians listed in this state. Readers should also remember that if they want the most current information on the status on a physician's license, they should contact the medical board of the state in which the physician practices or had practiced.

According to the Federation of State Medical Boards, Texas took 170 serious disciplinary actions against MDs and DOs in 1994. Compared to the 33,846 MDs in the state, Texas had a serious disciplinary action rate of 5.02

serious actions per 1,000 MDs and a ranking of 23rd on that list (see Table 1, Findings, pg. 11).

The tables below summarize the data we received from Texas.

Table 1. Disciplinary Actions Against MDs and DOs January 1986 through January 1995*

Action	Number	Percent**
Revocation	86	6.4%
Surrender	118	8.8%
Suspension	80	6.0%
Probation	327	24.4%
Practice Restriction	127	9.5%
Action Taken Against Controlled Substance License	115	8.6%
Other Actions	486	36.3%
Total Actions	1,339	

* This table lists only the two most serious disciplinary actions taken against a physician, not additional, less serious actions.

** Percentages may not total 100% due to rounding.

Table 2. Offenses for which MDs and DOs Were Disciplined January 1986 through January 1995*

Offense	Number	Percent
Criminal Conviction	57	8.4%
Sexual Abuse of or Sexual Misconduct With a Patient	8	1.2%
Substandard Care, Incompetence or Negligence	86	12.7%
Misprescribing or Overprescribing Drugs	60	8.9%
Drug or Alcohol Abuse	132	19.6%
Disciplinary Action Taken Against License by Another State or Agency	130	19.3%
Other Offenses	202	29.9%
Total Records With Offense Listed	675	

* Includes only those actions for which an offense was listed and for which we had a corresponding term in our database.

- TEXAS -

Table 3. Disciplinary Actions Taken for Substandard Care, Incompetence or Negligence

Action	Number	Percent
Revocation	10	8.4%
Surrender	2	1.7%
Suspension	3	2.5%
Emergency Suspension	2	1.7%
Probation	38	31.9%
Practice Restriction	22	18.5%
Fine	3	2.5%
Reprimand	16	13.4%
Other Actions	23	19.3%
Total Actions	119	

Table 4. Disciplinary Actions Taken for Criminal Conviction

Action	Number	Percent
Revocation	23	35.4%
Surrender	3	4.6%
Suspension	13	20.0%
Emergency Suspension	2	3.1%
Probation	11	16.9%
Other Actions	13	20.0%
Total Actions	65	

- TEXAS -

Table 5. Disciplinary Actions Taken for Misprescribing or Overprescribing Drugs

Action	Number	Percent
Revocation	4	4.3%
Surrender	3	3.3%
Revocation, Surrender, or Suspension of Controlled Substance License	6	6.5%
Suspension	5	5.4%
Emergency Suspension	1	1.1%
Probation	25	27.2%
Restriction of Controlled Substance License	9	9.8%
Fine	1	1.1%
Education	12	13.0%
Other Actions	26	28.3%
Total Actions	92	

Table 6. Disciplinary Actions Taken for Drug or Alcohol Abuse

Action	Number	Percent
Revocation	3	1.4%
Surrender	1	0.5%
Revocation, Surrender, or Suspension of Controlled Substance License	19	9.0%
Suspension	25	11.9%
Emergency Suspension	14	6.7%
Probation	68	32.4%
Restriction of Controlled Substance License	10	4.8%
Required to Enter an Impaired Physician Program or Drug or Alcohol Treatment	21	10.0%
Other Actions	49	23.3%
Total Actions	210	

- TEXAS -

> If you feel that your doctor has not given you proper medical care or has mistreated you in any way--whether or not he or she is listed in this report--it is important that you let your state medical board know. Even if they do not immediately act on your complaint, it is important that the information be recorded in their files because it is possible that other people may have filed or will file complaints about the same doctor. Send a brief written description of what occurred to the addresses below or call the phone numbers listed for more information on how to file a complaint.

Address

Texas State Board of Medical Examiners
Bruce Levy, MD, JD, Executive Director
PO Box 149134
Austin, TX 78701
(512) 305-7010

- TEXAS -

Listing of Doctors Sanctioned by Offense

Criminal Conviction or Plea of Guilty, Nolo Contendere, or No Contest To A Crime

ABUD-SANCHEZ, DANILO
AGUIRRE-MORAN, RAFAEL
AVERY, BERT MILLS
BACHYNSKY, NICHOLAS
BOWLER, DONALD L
BRANCH, THOMAS COE
BROECKEL, PHILIP G
CALKINS, GREGORY PAUL
CHRIST, JOHN ERNEST
EARGLE, CANTRAL L JR
EMERSON, TIMOTHY JOE
FLEMING, JAMES MICHAEL
GARAS, GAMAL K
GARCIA, JOHN A
GINTHER, CLARK E
GOLD, JACOB CHARLES
GRIFFIN, STEVEN WAYNE
GROSS, GEORGE E
GUO, GEORGE S
HALEY, RICHARD K
HASSMANN, GARY C
HAWKINS, LARRY R
INGRAM, CHESTER WILLIAM JR
KAUFMAN, IRA S
KIEPFER, RICHARD FRANCIS
LAMURE, DAVID S SR
LEGGETT, JOSEPH EDWARD
LEVIN, IRA MARK
LEWIS, GEORGE E JR
LIGHTFOOT, STANLEY A
LINSTRUM, TOM ELTON
LOFTIS, M DEAN
MCKELLAR, DUNCAN L
MCLAUGHLIN, RICHARD A
MEDINA, AMANTE D
MILLER, MILTON M
MURPHY, JACK P JR
OBRIEN, RICHARD F
PATTEN, EDWARD LEE
PEARSON, LYNN LANIER
PETRUS, EDWARD J JR
RAMOS, BALTAZAR JR
REECE, DOUGLAS L
REYES, LUCIO ARTURO
SANDS, LARRY REX
SCHULTZE, JORGE
SHAUGHNESSY, DENNIS M
SINCLARE, ROSS
SOLANKI, KIRIT V
STANTON, ELBERT
TOMASEVIC, MIRA
WHITE, JAMES HARRISON

Drug or Alcohol Abuse

ALDERMAN, JOHN A
ANDERSON, BERNICE
ANDERSON, VICKI SPARKS
ANDRUCZK, ROBERT CORWIN
ARCHER, JIM PAUL
BAILEY, SHARON ANNE
BAKER, JOHN SCOTT
BALLARD, CHARLES DONALD
BALLI, EDWARD A
BARBA, PEDRO
BARTLEY, MICHAEL ALAN
BECK, KEITH DEXTER
BEDNER, TOM DAVID
BERRY, G L
BERRY, RICHARD WILLIAM
BIRDWELL, LARRY RAY
BOLIN, DANIEL HUFFMAN
BOWERS, STEVEN PAUL
BREITENSTEIN, LARRY JACK
BRITTAIN, ROBERT D III
BROUGH, ROYCE DONALD JR
BROWNE, DUNCAN JAMES
BRUNKEN, ROBERT B
BURCH, JOHN E JR
CAYLOR, ARTHUR BERNARD JR
CHESTER, JEREMY DAVID
CONRAD, EDGAR DONALD
CROPPER, KENNETH R
DARBY, CASTILLA ADOLPHUS JR
DELL, ROBERT VANCE
DOTSON, BEVERLY ANN
DOWD, DONNA CATHERINE
DUNCAN, JOHN DAVID
DYKE, MARSHALL JAMES
EARL, GENE MARKLEY JR
EIBAND, JOHN M
EPPS, DEBRA KENNAMER
ERICKSON, CARL F
FINLEY, OLIVIA I
GALLMAN, DOYLE F JR
GARNER, JAMES FRANCIS
GLIDDEN, WELDON EDWARD
GREEN, DEMETRIS A
GREEN, KENNETH WAYNE JR
HEWELL, GEORGE M
HOLLABAUGH, ERNEST R
HOLLEN, JAKE THOMAS
HOUSE, FLOYD LEON
HOWELL, WYATT ALLEN
HUBBARD, GREGORY GERARD
HUMMER, MICHAEL GORMAN
HUNTER, RICHARD BROOKSHIRE
JACKSON, NICHOLAS M

Caution: This list is designed to be used only in conjunction with the rest of this book which includes additional information on each physician such as license number, date of action and more complete descriptions of the offenses.

JONES, ROLAND WARD III
KENNEDY, JERETTA IRENE
KING, CLARENCE GORDON JR
KING, DENNIS MAURICE
KRAUS, VERNON J
KUO, LIMEI
KURTZ, IRWIN
LECONEY, THOMAS RATCLIFF
LEDLIE, WILLIAM BOYER
LEHMILLER, JOHN ERICH
LETT, CHARLES REGINALD
LEVIN, IRA MARK
LEWIS, ELBERT HAMPTON
LOCKWOOD, RICHARD L
LOVELACE, CHARLES RAY JR
MANION, ROBERT A
MARKSTROM, CARL ERIC
MARTIN, RAYMOND A
MASSEY, CHARLES R JR
MCCALLUM, MICHAEL H
MCCORKLE, BRANDT HALBERT
MCLEAN, PAUL EUGENE II
MOORE, M J
MORRISON, RICHARD FRANK
MURPHY, FRANK STUART
NEWMAN, NICK JAY
O'NEILL, PHILIP
OFFUTT, DONALD NIXON
PENNINGTON, KAREN
PRATER, WILLIAM WARREN
PUGH, MARION C JR
PULLIAM, KATHY A
QUENNEVILLE, KENNETH BRUCE
RANELLE, JOHN BARRY
RANKIN, DOUGLAS HALL
RICE, KARL WOODS
RIEDWEG, EDWARD ALBERT
RIVERA, RAUL
ROBINETT, KELLY E
ROBINSON, LUKE E
SABATES, FELIX NABOR JR
SAUCEDA, FRANCISCO BASIL
SCHEFFEY, ERIC H
SEGGER, FRANZJOSEF
SHARP, DOUGLAS ROBERT
SHAUGHNESSY, DENNIS M
SHERP, GARY ALLAN
SHIELDS, FREDERICK S
SORIANO, SALVADOR L
STANTON, JAMES MICHAEL
STEELE, JOHN GILBERT
STILL, ROBERT L JR
TAMEZ, RICHARD JOSEPH
TICAS, ROBERTO
ULDRICH, DENNIS ALAN
VICKERS, FRANK ALLEN
VILLEGAS, LEOPOLD III
WAKEFIELD, CORNELIUS III
WEST, PATRICIA BEATY
WESTBROOK, MARK DENTON
WHITMAN, PAUL F JR
WILLIAMSON, MARK A
WOMACK, JAMES CHANSLOR

Overprescribing or Misprescribing Drugs

ADELMAN, JACK ARNOLD
ALFORD, JACK ALLEN
ANDERSON, BERNICE
ANDREWS, RAWLE
AXELROD, WILLIAM
BENZAQUEN, MATHEWS
BILSING, WILLIAM ALBERT
BOONE, GEORGE DANIEL
BORCHERDING, HARLAN JAMES
BURLESON, JAMES D
CHAPPELL, TIMOTHY RAE
CHEN, RAY HUANG TSANG
CLARK, GEORGE B
COGBURN, CLARENCE G
COX, JOHNSTON STEWART
DEMETRIOU, CHRIS
DUBIN, JOSEPH
DUNN, FRANK LANIER
DWYER, PATRICK DAVID
FABIAN, HAROLD FRANK
FINCH, ALBERT B
FONTANIER, CHARLES EUGENE
GIPSON, EDDIE MACK
GIRTANNER, ROBERT EDWARD
GUSTAFSON, WESLEY C JR
HARDMAN, ROY E
HOLSTON, ROBERT G
HUDDLESTON, WILLIAM E
HUNT, JOHN D
JOHNSON, WILLIAM R
JONES, JAMES HOLLIS
KATERNDAHL, DAVID A
KILIAN, ROBERT JACK
LADLEY, DAVID MARK
LANE, RICHARD A
LEWIS, ALVIN M
LIPSEY, BILLY CLINT
LONG, JOSEPH MERL
MAZIQUE, EMORY E
MELENYZER, CHARLES L
MERWORTH, ROY W
PARKER, WAYLON M
PRANGLE, ROBERT E
REES, SEARLE BEAUFORT
REISCHMANN, EDDY
RHOADES, JOE WALKER
RICHTER, JAMES K
RUBINSTEIN, BARNEY
SCHULZE, JOHN P

Caution: This list is designed to be used only in conjunction with the rest of this book which includes additional information on each physician such as license number, date of action and more complete descriptions of the offenses.

- TEXAS -

SCHWARTZ, HAROLD ROBERT
SIMON, JEAN-CHARLES
STARR, THOMAS PIERCE SR
STAYER, DAVID SHELLENBERGER
STEGMAN, RONALD REGIS
STERN, STEVEN EMERY
STRINGER, DRENNON DURWOOD
THOMPSON, FRANK WILLIAM
VANBUSKIRK, RONALD
WOLF, GARY DUKE

Sexual Abuse of or Sexual Misconduct With A Patient

FILARDI, HECTOR HIRAM
HICKS, RAYMOND D
JOHNSTON, JAMES CHRISTOPHER
MCCLELLAN, DAVID MARK
MIRON, MORTON ARTHUR
SMITH, ART GLENN
WARREN, BRUCE HUNTINGTON

Substandard Care, Incompetence, Or Negligence

ALMOND, THOMAS HENRY
ATKINSON, WILLIAM H
BAGWELL, JERRY GLYN
BECK, KEITH DEXTER
BELUE, JOE BILL
BITTLE, CHARLES CARROLL JR
BORDELON, JERRY PHILLIP
BOUDREAU, DANIEL ALEXANDER
BROXTON, KYREL DARICE
BURKES, WALTER JOE
CHAMBERLIN, DAN STEVEN
CHONG, JUAN A
CHRISTIANSON, PAUL BARR
COLE, GEORGE MARTIN
CONTE, MAURICE S
DE LOS SANTOS, RAMIRO
DECARVALHO, GUARACY F
DENNIS, MICHAEL H
DESHEFY, ALAN
DIXON, JOSEPH ANDREW
DOTSON, DANIEL A
DRISCOLL, STEPHEN EDWARD
EDGEWORTH, LEWIS ANSON DAVID
ELAFIFI, BAYOUMI ABD
ERDMANN, RALPH R
EWING, CAROL T
FISCHER, ROY LEE
GAGLIANO, ANGELO VINCENT
GARCIA, EDUARDO I
GROSSMAN, MAURICE SIDNEY
GUERRERORAMIREZ, LUIS
GUIMBARDA, LUIS A
HAMAMCY, THARWAT M
HARDEY, CARLTON E
HARRISON, JACK WINFRED
HAYS, HARVEY JR
HEAD, WILLIAM JUSTUS III
HEALING, ROBERT DYSON
HERNANDEZ, ARTHUR
HOLT, CECIL ZENO
HOUSE, CHARLES HAROLD
JACKSON, JOSEPH JORDAN
JAMES, JOCELYN LEAH
JAVIER, RICARDO R
JOHNSON, NEAL D
JONES, JAMES WENDELL
KASNETZ, HERBERT ROY
KASTNER, AARON
KENNADY, DONALD SCOTT
KOROMPAI, FERENC L
LAWRENCE, RICHARD BURNETT III
LEE, HOWARD MONROE JR
LESHNOWER, ALAN C
LIU, KUO TAI
LOCKHART, ALBERT B
LONG, WALTER KEIRN JR
LUTHERER, BERTA DEL CARMEN
MALABANAN, BEN C
MARES, ALBERTO
MARTINEZ, MANUEL A JR
MCCASKILL, BERNIE L
MEHARRY, ROGER ALVIN
MIMS, ROBERT LEWIS
MURRAY, ROBERT VINCENT JR
PARIKH, KIRAN RAJEN
POEHLMANN, KURT S
RAMIREZ, HUGO A
RAMPOLDI, JAMES MOSES
READING, WILLIAM H
REYES, LUCIO ARTURO
ROBY, RUSSELL R
SANDERS, MARK S
SMILEY, EVELYN J K
SOTOODEH, BAGHER
SPEAK, KENNETH EDWIN
STRICKLAND, ALAN D
SWATE, TOMMY ERNEST
TAYLOR, ROOSEVELT JR
THOMPSON, WALTER FRED
VAN BOLDEN, VERNON II
VAUSE, DAVID DWIGHT
VEGGEBERG, KERMIT ROGER
VIOLA, CARLOS A
WINSLOW, DAVID EVERETT
WITHERSPOON, ROBERT GLYNN JR

Caution: This list is designed to be used only in conjunction with the rest of this book which includes additional information on each physician such as license number, date of action and more complete descriptions of the offenses.

DISCIPLINARY ACTIONS

ABADIER, ABDALLA MD, LICENSE NUMBER 00G8662, OF E GREENWICK, RI, WAS DISCIPLINED BY TEXAS ON JANUARY 6, 1995.
DISCIPLINARY ACTION: LICENSE REVOCATION
OFFENSE: PROFESSIONAL MISCONDUCT
NOTES: ORDER WILL BECOME FINAL WHEN ADMINISTRATIVE APPEALS HAVE BEEN EXHAUSTED; HAS 20 DAYS TO FILE A MOTION FOR REHEARING.

ABLE, ANTOINNE MD, DATE OF BIRTH FEBRUARY 28, 1958, OF 4041 MEDICAL DRIVE, SAN ANTONIO, TX, WAS DISCIPLINED BY MEDICARE ON MAY 23, 1993.
DISCIPLINARY ACTION: EXCLUSION FROM THE MEDICARE AND/OR MEDICAID PROGRAMS
OFFENSE: FAILURE TO COMPLY WITH A PROFESSIONAL RULE
NOTES: DEFAULTED ON HEALTH EDUCATION ASSISTANCE LOAN. REINSTATED ON 7/5/95.

ABRAHAM, MALOUF JR MD, DATE OF BIRTH MARCH 29, 1939, LICENSE NUMBER 00D1528, OF 720 ASH, CANADIAN, TX, WAS DISCIPLINED BY TEXAS ON APRIL 30, 1993.
DISCIPLINARY ACTION: REPRIMAND
OFFENSE: FAILURE TO COMPLY WITH A PROFESSIONAL RULE
NOTES: FAILED TO DOCUMENT THE HISTORY AND PHYSICAL OF SEVERAL PATIENTS INCLUDING REASON FOR ADMINISTERING MEDICATIONS.

ABUD-SANCHEZ, DANILO MD WAS DISCIPLINED BY NEW MEXICO ON JUNE 12, 1992.
DISCIPLINARY ACTION: SURRENDER OF LICENSE
NOTES: IN LIEU OF DISCIPLINARY HEARING.

ABUD-SANCHEZ, DANILO MD, LICENSE NUMBER 00H1545, OF EL PASO, TX, WAS DISCIPLINED BY TEXAS ON OCTOBER 9, 1992.
DISCIPLINARY ACTION: 60-MONTH PROBATION
OFFENSE: CRIMINAL CONVICTION OR PLEA OF GUILTY, NOLO CONTENDERE, OR NO CONTEST TO A CRIME
NOTES: CONVICTION OF FELONY FOR FILING FALSE, FICTITIOUS OR FRAUDULENT CLAIMS. SUSPENSION, STAYED. PROBATION UNDER TERMS AND CONDITIONS.

ABUD-SANCHEZ, DANILO MD, LICENSE NUMBER 00H1545, OF EL PASO, TX, WAS DISCIPLINED BY TEXAS ON JANUARY 6, 1995.
DISCIPLINARY ACTION: SURRENDER OF LICENSE
NOTES: ALLEGATIONS OF POSSIBLE VIOLATIONS OF MEDICAL PRACTICE ACT; HE DOES NOT ADMIT VIOLATIONS; SURRENDER IN LIEU OF FURTHER INVESTIGATION AND TO EFFECTUATE HIS RETIREMENT. SHALL NOT PETITION FOR REINSTATEMENT.

ADAMS, BARTON J DO, LICENSE NUMBER 0000516, WAS DISCIPLINED BY HAWAII ON FEBRUARY 24, 1992.
DISCIPLINARY ACTION: EMERGENCY SUSPENSION
OFFENSE: CRIMINAL CONVICTION OR PLEA OF GUILTY, NOLO CONTENDERE, OR NO CONTEST TO A CRIME
NOTES: CRIMINAL CONVICTION OF THREE COUNTS OF SEXUAL ASSAULT IN THE THIRD DEGREE. SUMMARY SUSPENSION EXTENDED 3/13/92.

ADAMS, BARTON J DO, LICENSE NUMBER 0000516, OF MAUI CORRECTIONAL CTR,600 WAIALE, WAILIKU, MAUI, HI, WAS DISCIPLINED BY HAWAII ON JUNE 1, 1992.
DISCIPLINARY ACTION: 24-MONTH LICENSE REVOCATION
OFFENSE: CRIMINAL CONVICTION OR PLEA OF GUILTY, NOLO CONTENDERE, OR NO CONTEST TO A CRIME
NOTES: SEXUALLY ASSAULTED A FEMALE EMPLOYEE WHILE EXAMINING AND TREATING HER. FOUND GUILTY OF THREE COUNTS OF SEXUAL ASSAULT AND SENTENCED TO TEN YEARS CONFINEMENT.

ADAMS, BARTON J DO, LICENSE NUMBER 00G7150, OF KAHULUI, HI, WAS DISCIPLINED BY TEXAS ON OCTOBER 9, 1992.
DISCIPLINARY ACTION: SURRENDER OF LICENSE
OFFENSE: DISCIPLINARY ACTION BY ANOTHER STATE OR AGENCY
NOTES: UNPROFESSIONAL OR DISHONORABLE CONDUCT LIKELY TO DECEIVE, DEFRAUD OR INJURE THE PUBLIC; CONVICTION OF A FELONY OR A CRIME OF A LESSER DEGREE THAT INVOLVES MORAL TURPITUDE; SUSPENSION, REVOCATION OR RESTRICTION BY ANOTHER STATE. LICENSE PERMANENTLY RETIRED.

ADAMS, BARTON J DO OF 261 LALO STREET, KAHULUI, HI, WAS DISCIPLINED BY DEA ON JANUARY 28, 1994.
DISCIPLINARY ACTION: REVOCATION OF CONTROLLED SUBSTANCE LICENSE
OFFENSE: DISCIPLINARY ACTION BY ANOTHER STATE OR AGENCY
NOTES: ON 3/29/90 HE SEXUALLY ASSAULTED A PATIENT AND WAS FOUND GUILTY OF SEXUAL ASSAULT IN HAWAII. ON 5/7/92 HE WAS SENTENCED TO TEN YEARS INCARCERATION AND A PSYCHOLOGICAL EVALUATION. ON 6/30/92 HIS STATE CONTROLLED SUBSTANCE REGISTRATION EXPIRED. AS A RESULT OF THIS CONVICTION, ON 7/10/92 HIS MEDICAL LICENSE WAS REVOKED IN HAWAII; ON 2/23/93 HE WAS EXCLUDED FROM PARTICIPATION IN THE MEDICARE PROGRAM FOR TEN YEARS.

ADAMS, BARTON JOSEPH DO, DATE OF BIRTH NOVEMBER 17, 1951, OF MAUI COMMUNITY CORRECTION CENTER, WAILUKU, HI, WAS DISCIPLINED BY MEDICARE ON MARCH 15, 1993.
DISCIPLINARY ACTION: 120-MONTH EXCLUSION FROM THE MEDICARE AND/OR MEDICAID PROGRAMS
OFFENSE: CRIMINAL CONVICTION OR PLEA OF GUILTY, NOLO CONTENDERE, OR NO CONTEST TO A CRIME
NOTES: CONVICTED OF THREE COUNTS OF SEXUAL ASSAULT OF PATIENTS.

ADAMS, BARTON JOSEPH DO, DATE OF BIRTH NOVEMBER 17, 1951, LICENSE NUMBER 0027020, OF 99902 MOANAHIA HIGHWAY, AIEA, HI, WAS DISCIPLINED BY GEORGIA ON NOVEMBER 9, 1993.
DISCIPLINARY ACTION: LICENSE REVOCATION
OFFENSE: DISCIPLINARY ACTION BY ANOTHER STATE OR AGENCY
NOTES: BASED ON ACTION BY HAWAII BOARD. SEXUAL ASSAULT OF FEMALE PATIENTS.

ADAMS, GEORGE L MD, LICENSE NUMBER 00E4982, OF CENTRE HARBOR, NH, WAS DISCIPLINED BY TEXAS ON APRIL 10, 1992.
NOTES: FINAL ACTION DEFERRED FOR ONE YEAR PENDING RESOLUTION OF CRIMINAL CASE. AGREED NOT TO PRACTICE MEDICINE IN TEXAS IN THE INTERIM.

ADDY, ERVIN E JR MD OF P.O. BOX 1309, CISCO, TX, WAS DISCIPLINED BY MEDICARE ON NOVEMBER 18, 1986.
DISCIPLINARY ACTION: 12-MONTH EXCLUSION FROM THE MEDICARE AND/OR MEDICAID PROGRAMS
OFFENSE: SUBSTANDARD CARE, INCOMPETENCE, OR NEGLIGENCE
NOTES: GROSSLY SUBSTANDARD CARE OF ONE PATIENT

ADELMAN, JACK ARNOLD MD, LICENSE NUMBER 00B6953, WAS

DISCIPLINED BY TEXAS ON AUGUST 20, 1993.
DISCIPLINARY ACTION: 36-MONTH PROBATION; REQUIRED TO TAKE ADDITIONAL MEDICAL EDUCATION
OFFENSE: OVERPRESCRIBING OR MISPRESCRIBING DRUGS
NOTES: ON VARIOUS OCCASIONS OVER SEVERAL YEARS, PRESCRIBED THE CONTROLLED SUBSTANCES TEMAZEPAM AND MORPHINE TO ONE PATIENT WITHOUT PROPERLY DOCUMENTING INTRACTABLE PAIN SO AS TO PROVIDE SUFFICIENT MEDICAL JUSTIFICATION; DID NOT DOCUMENT ADEQUATE FOLLOW-UP EXAMS AND MONITORING. SUSPENSION STAYED. CONDITIONS OF PROBATION: SHALL ATTEND AT LEAST 50 HOURS PER YEAR OF CONTINUING MEDICAL EDUCATION; IN ADDITION SHALL, WITHIN ONE YEAR, ENROLL IN AND SUBSEQUENTLY COMPLETE A PHARMACOLOGY COURSE FOR 10 HOURS OF CREDITS; SEPARATE FROM PATIENT RECORDS SHALL MAINTAIN A FILE OF EVERY PRESCRIPTION WRITTEN FOR CONTROLLED SUBSTANCES OR DANGEROUS DRUGS WHICH SHALL BE AVAILABLE FOR INSPECTION; SHALL NOT TELEPHONE ANY PRESCRIPTIONS FOR THESE DRUGS; SHALL APPEAR BEFORE THE BOARD ONCE A YEAR; SHALL COOPERATE WITH THE BOARD IN VERIFYING COMPLIANCE; SHALL INFORM BOARD OF CHANGE OF ADDRESS WITHIN 10 DAYS OR IF HE LEAVES THE STATE; TIME SPENT OUT OF TEXAS DOES NOT COUNT TOWARD PROBATION NOR WILL ANY PERIODS OF TIME AFTER WHICH HE RETIRES FROM THE PRACTICE OF MEDICINE. SHALL NOT SEEK MODIFICATION FOR ONE YEAR.

ADEN, GARY C MD, DATE OF BIRTH NOVEMBER 18, 1935, OF 2403 CORONA CT, LA JOLLA, CA, WAS DISCIPLINED BY MEDICARE ON MAY 23, 1990.
DISCIPLINARY ACTION: EXCLUSION FROM THE MEDICARE AND/OR MEDICAID PROGRAMS
OFFENSE: DISCIPLINARY ACTION BY ANOTHER STATE OR AGENCY
NOTES: LICENSE REVOCATION OR SUSPENSION.

ADEN, GARY C MD, DATE OF BIRTH NOVEMBER 18, 1935, LICENSE NUMBER 0014167, OF LA JOLLA, CA, WAS DISCIPLINED BY COLORADO ON JUNE 7, 1991.
DISCIPLINARY ACTION: SURRENDER OF LICENSE
OFFENSE: DISCIPLINARY ACTION BY ANOTHER STATE OR AGENCY
NOTES: GROSSLY NEGLIGENT MEDICAL PRACTICE, ENGAGING IN A SEXUAL ACT WITH A PATIENT DURING THE COURSE OF PATIENT CARE, AND REVOCATION OF HIS CALIFORNIA LICENSE. AGREEMENT NEVER TO REQUEST REINSTATEMENT OR APPLY FOR A NEW LICENSE.

ADEN, GARY CARL MD, LICENSE NUMBER C026644, OF SAN DIEGO, CA, WAS DISCIPLINED BY CALIFORNIA ON OCTOBER 9, 1989.
DISCIPLINARY ACTION: LICENSE REVOCATION
OFFENSE: SEXUAL ABUSE OF OR SEXUAL MISCONDUCT WITH A PATIENT
NOTES: BIZARRE SEXUAL MISCONDUCT WITH PATIENTS; FAILED TO COMPLY WITH BOARD ORDER COMPELLING PSYCHIATRIC EXAM; DEFAULT DECISION.

ADEN, GARY CARL MD, LICENSE NUMBER 00D2974, OF LA JOLLA, CA, WAS DISCIPLINED BY TEXAS ON OCTOBER 5, 1991.
DISCIPLINARY ACTION: LICENSE REVOCATION
OFFENSE: DISCIPLINARY ACTION BY ANOTHER STATE OR AGENCY
NOTES: CALIFORNIA LICENSE WAS REVOKED BECAUSE OF SEXUALLY ABUSIVE AND VIOLENT TREATMENT OF SEVEN PATIENTS UNDER HIS PSYCHIATRIC CARE; ALSO FAILED TO COMPLY WITH CALIFORNIA BOARD ORDER OF 10/9/89 TO UNDERGO A PSYCHIATRIC EVALUATION.

ADKINS, MARGO M MD, DATE OF BIRTH JANUARY 13, 1960, OF 2500 E 22ND STREET #213, AUSTIN, TX, WAS DISCIPLINED BY MEDICARE ON APRIL 16, 1994.
DISCIPLINARY ACTION: EXCLUSION FROM THE MEDICARE AND/OR MEDICAID PROGRAMS
OFFENSE: FAILURE TO COMPLY WITH A PROFESSIONAL RULE
NOTES: DEFAULTED ON PUBLIC HEALTH SERVICE EDUCATION LOAN.

ADLOF, CAROLYN MD, LICENSE NUMBER 00C7426, OF THREE RIVERS, TX, WAS DISCIPLINED BY TEXAS ON JANUARY 28, 1989.
DISCIPLINARY ACTION: SURRENDER OF CONTROLLED SUBSTANCE LICENSE
NOTES: SHALL SURRENDER FEDERAL AND STATE CONTROLLED SUBSTANCE REGISTRATIONS AND NOT REREGISTER WITHOUT PRIOR BOARD AUTHORITY; SHALL MAINTAIN ADEQUATE MEDICAL RECORDS ON ALL PATIENT OFFICE VISITS; SHALL NOT USE NUBAIN OR STADOL IN PATIENT TREATMENT; SHALL OBTAIN PHYSICAL EXAMINATION BY NEUROLOGIST.

AGUIRRE-MORAN, RAFAEL MD, LICENSE NUMBER 00D6922, OF WINNIE, TX, WAS DISCIPLINED BY TEXAS ON SEPTEMBER 20, 1994.
DISCIPLINARY ACTION: EMERGENCY SUSPENSION
OFFENSE: CRIMINAL CONVICTION OR PLEA OF GUILTY, NOLO CONTENDERE, OR NO CONTEST TO A CRIME
NOTES: THE FOLLOWING ALLEGATIONS WERE MADE: ON 6/17/94 A COMPLAINT WAS FILED WITH SHERIFF'S DEPARTMENT BY A PATIENT WHO ALLEGED INAPPROPRIATE AND UNSOLICITED TOUCHING BY HIM DURING AN EXAM; ON 6/22/94 AN ASSAULT CLASS C MISDEMEANOR WAS FILED AGAINST HIM TO WHICH HE PLED GUILTY; ON 8/30/94 HE WAS ARRESTED AND CHARGED WITH ONE COUNT OF INDECENCY WITH A MINOR WHOM HE MOLESTED DURING AN EXAM; FROM 1992 TO 1994 HE PRESCRIBED LARGE QUANTITIES OF CONTROLLED SUBSTANCES TO FOUR PATIENTS WITHOUT ADEQUATE DOCUMENTED EVALUATION AND NO APPARENT MEDICAL INDICATION OR ADEQUATE LEGITIMATE MEDICAL BASIS; HAD SOME FORM OF SEXUAL ENCOUNTER WITH THREE PATIENTS IN EXCHANGE FOR CONTROLLED SUBSTANCES AND PRESCRIPTION PADS.

ALDERMAN, JOHN A DO, LICENSE NUMBER 00E3639, OF ODESSA, TX, WAS DISCIPLINED BY TEXAS ON OCTOBER 1, 1987.
DISCIPLINARY ACTION: PROBATION
OFFENSE: DRUG OR ALCOHOL ABUSE
NOTES: SUSPENSION PROBATED AS LONG AS HE CONFORMS TO PROBATION TERMS.

ALEXANDER, JAMES ALAN MD, LICENSE NUMBER 00C9263, OF HOUSTON, TX, WAS DISCIPLINED BY TEXAS ON OCTOBER 27, 1993.
DISCIPLINARY ACTION: 60-MONTH PROBATION; REQUIRED TO TAKE ADDITIONAL MEDICAL EDUCATION
OFFENSE: PROFESSIONAL MISCONDUCT
NOTES: IN SEVERAL CASES DURING LATE 1989 AND EARLY 1990 PERSISTENTLY AND FLAGRANTLY OVERCHARGED AND OVERTREATED PATIENTS INCLUDING PERFORMING UNNECESSARY PROCEDURES; IN SOME OF THESE CASES THERE WAS INADEQUATE DOCUMENTATION. SUSPENSION STAYED. CONDITIONS OF PROBATION:

SHALL PERFORM 10 HOURS PER MONTH OF COMMUNITY SERVICE FOR FIVE YEARS; SHALL ATTEND AT LEAST 50 HOURS PER YEAR OF CONTINUING MEDICAL EDUCATION AND DURING THE FIRST YEAR OF PROBATION SHALL COMPLETE A BOARD-APPROVED ETHICS COURSE OR PROGRAM; SHALL UTILIZE A SYSTEM OF PATIENT RECORD KEEPING THAT ACCURATELY REFLECTS INFORMATION AND SHALL BE MONITORED BY A PHYSICIAN WHO SHALL CONDUCT RANDOM REVIEWS OF THESE RECORDS AND PROVIDE REPORTS EVERY FOUR MONTHS; SHALL GIVE A COPY OF THIS ORDER TO ANY HEALTH CARE ENTITY WHERE HE HAS PRIVILEGES; SHALL COOPERATE WITH THE BOARD IN VERIFYING COMPLIANCE; SHALL INFORM BOARD OF CHANGE OF ADDRESS WITHIN 10 DAYS OR IF HE LEAVES THE STATE; TIME SPENT OUT OF TEXAS DOES NOT COUNT TOWARD PROBATION. HAS 20 DAYS TO FILE A MOTION FOR REHEARING. ORDER WILL BECOME FINAL WHEN ALL APPEALS HAVE BEEN EXHAUSTED.

ALFORD, JACK ALLEN MD, DATE OF BIRTH APRIL 2, 1930, LICENSE NUMBER 00C4971, OF 6550 MAPLERIDGE, SUITE 101C, HOUSTON, TX, WAS DISCIPLINED BY TEXAS ON JUNE 17, 1992.
DISCIPLINARY ACTION: 60-MONTH PROBATION
OFFENSE: OVERPRESCRIBING OR MISPRESCRIBING DRUGS
NOTES: NONTHERAPEUTIC PRESCRIBING. SUSPENSION, STAYED. PROBATION UNDER TERMS AND CONDITIONS. ON 8/20/93 ORDER TERMINATED; LICENSE FREE AND CLEAR OF ANY PREVIOUS RESTRICTIONS.

ALLEN, BRADY L MD OF DALLAS, TX, WAS DISCIPLINED BY FDA ON DECEMBER 11, 1990.
DISCIPLINARY ACTION: INELIGIBLE TO RECEIVE INVESTIGATIONAL NEW DRUGS FOR EXPERIMENTAL PURPOSES

ALLEN, EDMUND L MD, LICENSE NUMBER 00E3838, OF ABILENE, TX, WAS DISCIPLINED BY TEXAS ON DECEMBER 1, 1988.
NOTES: SETTLEMENT AGREEMENT AND UNSPECIFIED DISCIPLINARY ACTION

ALLEN, GWENDOLYN JOYCE MD, LICENSE NUMBER 00G4784, OF SAN SABA, TX, WAS DISCIPLINED BY TEXAS ON JUNE 10, 1991.
DISCIPLINARY ACTION: 36-MONTH PROBATION; RESTRICTION PLACED ON LICENSE
OFFENSE: PROFESSIONAL MISCONDUCT
NOTES: AIDING OR ABETTING, DIRECTLY OR INDIRECTLY, THE PRACTICE OF MEDICINE BY ANY PERSON, PARTNERSHIP, ASSOCIATION, OR CORPORATION NOT DULY LICENSED TO PRACTICE MEDICINE BY THE BOARD. CONDITIONS OF PROBATION INCLUDE: SHALL NOT ACCEPT EMPLOYMENT OR ENTER INTO CONTRACTUAL RELATIONSHIPS WHEREIN LICENSEE WOULD BE COMPENSATED TO DIAGNOSE AND/OR TREAT PATIENTS BY A LAYPERSON, CORPORATION, OR OTHER ENTITY NOT COMPRISED EXCLUSIVELY OF TEXAS LICENSED PHYSICIANS; SHALL NOT ALLOW SIGNATURE TO BE DUPLICATED AND USED AS A RUBBER STAMP OR ANY DOCUMENT UTILIZED IN HER PRACTICE OF MEDICINE FOR EITHER TREATMENT OF PATIENTS OR BILLING PURPOSES.

ALLGOOD, HOMER JR MD, DATE OF BIRTH DECEMBER 5, 1924, LICENSE NUMBER 00D7517, OF 708 S FIRST STREET, MULESHOE, TX, WAS DISCIPLINED BY TEXAS ON JUNE 12, 1990.
DISCIPLINARY ACTION: 60-MONTH PROBATION; RESTRICTION PLACED ON CONTROLLED SUBSTANCE LICENSE
NOTES: STIPULATED ORDER. MUST COMPLETE PRECEPTORSHIP ON PREVENTION AND TREATMENT OF DRUG ABUSE, SURRENDER ALL UNUSED TRIPLICATE PRESCRIPTION FORMS, NOT TREAT ANY PATIENT FOR WEIGHT CONTROL OR OBESITY WITH ANY CONTROLLED SUBSTANCE OR OVER THE COUNTER DRUGS BUT MAY TREAT WITH COUNSELLING, DIET, AND EXERCISE REGIMEN, NOT PRESCRIBE, ADMINISTER OR POSSESS SCHEDULE II CONTROLLED DRUG EXCEPT FOR ORDERING FOR HOSPITALIZED PATIENTS, ATTEND CONTINUING MEDICAL EDUCATION COURSES, MAINTAIN SEPARATE FILE OF COPY OF EVERY PRESCRIPTION WRITTEN FOR CONTROLLED SUBSTANCES, AND APPEAR BEFORE BOARD SEMI-ANNUALLY. ON 1/29/93, HIS REQUEST FOR TERMINATION OF PROBATION IS DENIED, HOWEVER, HE IS GRANTED PERMISSION TO REAPPLY TO THE DRUG ENFORCEMENT ADMINISTRATION AND THE TEXAS DEPARTMENT OF PUBLIC SAFETY FOR SCHEDULE II CONTROLLED SUBSTANCE REGISTRATION AND FOR TRIPLICATE PRESCRIPTION FORMS. RESTRICTIONS ON PRESCRIBING, ADMINISTERING OR POSSESSING ANY DRUGS CLASSIFIED AS SCHEDULE II CONTROLLED SUBSTANCES EXCEPT FOR ORDERING SUCH DRUGS FOR HOSPITALIZED PATIENTS ARE LIFTED. ON 8/20/93, ORDER MODIFIED SO HE SHALL ATTEND 50 HOURS PER YEAR OF CONTINUING MEDICAL EDUCATION. ALL OTHER TERMS AND CONDITIONS REMAIN IN EFFECT. ON 6/22/94 BOARD DENIED HIS REQUEST FOR TERMINATION OF THIS ORDER.

ALLISON, STANLEY C MD, LICENSE NUMBER 0C29575, OF TACOMA, WA, WAS DISCIPLINED BY CALIFORNIA ON MARCH 30, 1988.
DISCIPLINARY ACTION: LICENSE REVOCATION
OFFENSE: DISCIPLINARY ACTION BY ANOTHER STATE OR AGENCY
NOTES: DISCIPLINED BY WASHINGTON STATE MEDICAL BOARD. DEFAULT DECISION.

ALLISON, STANLEY C MD, LICENSE NUMBER 00D2339, OF OLYMPIA, WA, WAS DISCIPLINED BY TEXAS ON OCTOBER 24, 1988.
DISCIPLINARY ACTION: SURRENDER OF LICENSE
OFFENSE: DISCIPLINARY ACTION BY ANOTHER STATE OR AGENCY
NOTES: DISCIPLINED IN WASHINGTON AND CALIFORNIA

ALMARASHI, ABDUL-HUSEIN S H MD, LICENSE NUMBER 00E5664, OF GLADEWATER, TX, WAS DISCIPLINED BY TEXAS ON MARCH 31, 1990.
OFFENSE: OVERCHARGING
NOTES: MUST ADJUST CHARGES AND CEASE CHARGING FOR CERTAIN EXTRANEOUS MATTERS. ON 6/22/94 PROBATION TERMINATED DUE TO SUCCESSFUL COMPLETION AND COMPLIANCE WITH TERMS OF HIS ORDER.

ALMOND, THOMAS HENRY MD, LICENSE NUMBER 00D4908, OF WIMBERLEY, TX, WAS DISCIPLINED BY TEXAS ON DECEMBER 4, 1991.
DISCIPLINARY ACTION: RESTRICTION PLACED ON CONTROLLED SUBSTANCE LICENSE
OFFENSE: SUBSTANDARD CARE, INCOMPETENCE, OR NEGLIGENCE
NOTES: WAS RESPONSIBLE FOR AVAILABILITY OF EQUIPMENT NECESSARY TO ADMINISTER ANESTHESIA AND FOR DEVELOPMENT OF SAFETY REGULATIONS AT BRAZOSPORT MEMORIAL HOSPITAL IN 3/88; ADEQUATE RULES AND PROCEDURES TO ENSURE SAFETY OF

ANESTHESIA WERE NOT ESTABLISHED; ON 3/31/88 A PATIENT AND HER FETUS DIED APPARENTLY AS A RESULT OF IMPROPER INTUBATION BY A CRNA. INDEFINITELY EXCLUDED FROM ADMINISTERING ANY ANESTHETIC DRUGS; SHALL COOPERATE WITH BOARD IN VERIFYING COMPLIANCE; SHALL ADVISE THE BOARD OF CHANGE OF ADDRESS WITHIN 10 DAYS.

ALVORD, REX JR MD OF 407A IRONDALE DRIVE, EL PASO, TX, WAS DISCIPLINED BY NEW MEXICO ON OCTOBER 6, 1994.
OFFENSE: DRUG OR ALCOHOL ABUSE
NOTES: LICENSE PLACED UNDER UNSPECIFIED CONDITIONS.

AMARO, MICHAEL ANTHONY MD, DATE OF BIRTH JULY 6, 1956, LICENSE NUMBER 00G6431, OF 3807 FM 1092 SUITE 310, MISSOURI CITY, TX, WAS DISCIPLINED BY TEXAS ON JUNE 15, 1993.
DISCIPLINARY ACTION: 60-MONTH PROBATION; RESTRICTION PLACED ON CONTROLLED SUBSTANCE LICENSE
OFFENSE: LOSS OR RESTRICTION OF HOSPITAL PRIVILEGES
NOTES: IN 10/91 WHILE HOLDING TEMPORARY PRIVILEGES AT A HOSPITAL HE WAS REQUIRED TO PARTICIPATE IN A MONITORING PROGRAM REQUIRING RANDOM DRUG SCREENS; SCREEN ON 9/14/92 WAS POSITIVE FOR COCAINE METABOLITES AND HIS HOSPITAL PRIVILEGES WERE SUSPENDED AT TWO HOSPITALS; COMPLETED INPATIENT TREATMENT AND CONTINUES TO PARTICIPATE IN OUTPATIENT TREATMENT AND AA, AND SEE A PSYCHIATRIST; HOSPITAL PRIVILEGES HAVE BEEN REINSTATED UNDER CONDITIONS. SUSPENSION STAYED. CONDITIONS OF PROBATION: SHALL ATTEND AT LEAST 50 HOURS PER YEAR OF CONTINUING MEDICAL EDUCATION; SHALL CONTINUE TO RECEIVE PSYCHIATRIC TREATMENT WITH QUARTERLY REPORTS TO THE BOARD; SHALL ABSTAIN FROM THE CONSUMPTION OF ALCOHOL/DRUGS IN ANY FORM UNLESS PRESCRIBED BY ANOTHER PHYSICIAN FOR A LEGITIMATE AND THERAPEUTIC PURPOSE; SHALL SURRENDER ALL UNUSED TRIPLICATE PRESCRIPTION FORMS AND SHALL NOT ATTEMPT TO ORDER MORE; SHALL NOT PRESCRIBE, ADMINISTER OR DISPENSE SCHEDULE II CONTROLLED SUBSTANCES EXCEPT TO HOSPITAL PATIENTS AND SHALL KEEP A LOG OF THESE PRESCRIPTIONS SUBJECT TO REVIEW; SHALL KEEP A SEPARATE LOG OF ALL PRESCRIPTIONS FOR OTHER CONTROLLED SUBSTANCES SUBJECT TO REVIEW; SHALL PARTICIPATE IN ACTIVITIES OF AN IMPAIRED PHYSICIAN'S GROUP AND ATTEND WEEKLY MEETINGS WITH QUARTERLY REPORTS; SHALL SUBMIT HIMSELF FOR APPROPRIATE EXAMS INCLUDING DRUG OR ALCOHOL SCREENS; SHALL PARTICIPATE IN AA'S PROGRAM NOT LESS THAN ONCE A WEEK WITH QUARTERLY REPORTS TO THE BOARD; SHALL COMPLY WITH CONDITIONS REQUIRED FOR HOSPITAL PRIVILEGES REINSTATEMENT; SHALL APPEAR BEFORE THE BOARD ONCE A YEAR; SHALL GIVE A COPY OF THIS ORDER TO ANY HEALTH CARE ENTITY WHERE HE HAS PRIVILEGES; SHALL COOPERATE WITH THE BOARD IN VERIFYING COMPLIANCE; SHALL INFORM BOARD OF CHANGE OF ADDRESS WITHIN 10 DAYS OR IF HE LEAVES THE STATE; TIME SPENT OUT OF TEXAS DOES NOT COUNT TOWARD PROBATION. SHALL NOT SEEK MODIFICATION FOR ONE YEAR. REQUEST FOR TERMINATION WAS DENIED ON 8/19/94.

AMARO, MICHAEL ANTHONY MD, DATE OF BIRTH JULY 6, 1956, LICENSE NUMBER 0029835, OF 15700 LEXINGTON SUITE 1108, SUGAR LAND, TX, WAS DISCIPLINED BY GEORGIA ON DECEMBER 1, 1993.
DISCIPLINARY ACTION: PROBATION
OFFENSE: DISCIPLINARY ACTION BY ANOTHER STATE OR AGENCY
NOTES: ACTION BASED ON ACTION TAKEN BY TEXAS BOARD. IMPAIRMENT.

AMAYO, EMMANUEL P K MD, DATE OF BIRTH JULY 13, 1943, LICENSE NUMBER 0039094, OF 30840 NORTHWESTERN HWY, FARMINGTON HILLS, MI, WAS DISCIPLINED BY MICHIGAN ON NOVEMBER 20, 1991.
DISCIPLINARY ACTION: 24-MONTH LICENSE SUSPENSION; FINE
OFFENSE: SUBSTANDARD CARE, INCOMPETENCE, OR NEGLIGENCE
NOTES: $20,945 FINE.

AMAYO, EMMANUEL P K MD, LICENSE NUMBER 00F4737, OF FARMINGTON HILLS, MI, WAS DISCIPLINED BY TEXAS ON JUNE 17, 1992.
DISCIPLINARY ACTION: 24-MONTH LICENSE SUSPENSION
OFFENSE: DISCIPLINARY ACTION BY ANOTHER STATE OR AGENCY
NOTES: ACTION TAKEN BY ANOTHER STATE BOARD FOR UNPROFESSIONAL OR DISHONORABLE CONDUCT LIKELY TO DECEIVE, DEFRAUD OR INJURE THE PUBLIC; AND PROFESSIONAL FAILURE TO PRACTICE MEDICINE IN AN ACCEPTABLE MANNER CONSISTENT WITH PUBLIC HEALTH AND WELFARE. SUBJECT TO TERMS AND CONDITIONS OF MICHIGAN BOARD ORDER.

AMAYO, EMMANUEL P MD, LICENSE NUMBER 0004462, OF PONTIAC, MI, WAS DISCIPLINED BY VIRGINIA ON FEBRUARY 1, 1993.
DISCIPLINARY ACTION: REPRIMAND
OFFENSE: PROVIDING FALSE INFORMATION TO THE BOARD
NOTES: MISREPRESENTATION ON APPLICATION FOR INTERN/RESIDENT'S LICENSE; LICENSE EXPIRED 06/30/92.

AMICK, ROGER MD, LICENSE NUMBER 00F4739, OF LITTLE ROCK, AR, WAS DISCIPLINED BY TEXAS ON AUGUST 24, 1991.
DISCIPLINARY ACTION: LICENSE REVOCATION; SURRENDER OF CONTROLLED SUBSTANCE LICENSE
OFFENSE: FAILURE TO COMPLY WITH A PREVIOUS BOARD ORDER
NOTES: VIOLATION OF TERMS AND CONDITIONS OF PREVIOUS BOARD ORDER. SHALL NOT ATTEMPT TO REREGISTER OR OTHERWISE OBTAIN CONTROLLED SUBSTANCES REGISTRATION WITHOUT APPROVAL FROM THE BOARD; SHALL SURRENDER ALL UNUSED TRIPLICATE PRESCRIPTION FORMS AND NOT ATTEMPT TO ORDER MORE WITHOUT BOARD APPROVAL.

AMORUSO, ANTHONY V JR MD, LICENSE NUMBER 00E9093, OF CERRITOS, CA, WAS DISCIPLINED BY TEXAS ON AUGUST 25, 1989.
DISCIPLINARY ACTION: RESTRICTION PLACED ON LICENSE
NOTES: SHALL NOT TREAT OR SERVE AS PHYSICIAN, PRESCRIBE, DISPENSE, ADMINISTER OR WRITE PRESCRIPTIONS FOR CONTROLLED SUBSTANCES OR OTHER DRUGS SUBJECT TO ABUSE FOR SELF OR FAMILY MEMBERS; ADMINISTER TO SELF AND FAMILY ONLY THOSE DRUGS PRESCRIBED BY OTHER PHYSICIANS. SHALL RECEIVE PRIOR APPROVAL FROM BOARD IF RETURNING TO TEXAS TO PRACTICE.

ANDERS, STEPHEN ODELL DO, DATE OF BIRTH SEPTEMBER 24, 1952, LICENSE NUMBER 00F5452, OF 4101 AIRPORT FREEWAY #101, BEDFORD, TX, WAS DISCIPLINED BY TEXAS ON JUNE 15, 1993.
DISCIPLINARY ACTION: RESTRICTION PLACED ON LICENSE

OFFENSE: PHYSICAL OR MENTAL ILLNESS INHIBITING THE ABILITY TO PRACTICE WITH SKILL AND SAFETY
NOTES: CURRENTLY SUFFERS FROM AN ILLNESS AND HAS NOT PRACTICED SINCE 10/91 DUE TO THAT ILLNESS; AGREES TO REFRAIN FROM PRACTICE UNTIL BOARD DETERMINES HIS HEALTH ALLOWS HIM TO PRACTICE WITH REASONABLE SAFETY AND SKILL. SHALL PROVIDE ADEQUATE DOCUMENTATION TO THE BOARD ESTABLISHING THIS; SHALL GIVE A COPY OF THIS ORDER TO ANY HEALTH CARE ENTITY WHERE HE HAS PRIVILEGES.

ANDERS, STEPHEN ODELL DO, DATE OF BIRTH SEPTEMBER 24, 1952, LICENSE NUMBER 00F5452, OF BEDFORD, TX, WAS DISCIPLINED BY TEXAS ON JANUARY 6, 1995.
DISCIPLINARY ACTION: SURRENDER OF LICENSE
OFFENSE: PHYSICAL OR MENTAL ILLNESS INHIBITING THE ABILITY TO PRACTICE WITH SKILL AND SAFETY
NOTES: HAS UNDERGONE THERAPY SINCE ENTRY OF 6/15/93 ORDER; CONTINUES TO SUFFER FROM A DISABLING ILLNESS WHICH PREVENTS HIM FROM RETURNING TO THE PRACTICE OF MEDICINE. MAY SEEK REINSTATEMENT.

ANDERSON, BERNICE DO, DATE OF BIRTH MAY 23, 1955, LICENSE NUMBER 00H9489, WAS DISCIPLINED BY TEXAS ON OCTOBER 16, 1991.
DISCIPLINARY ACTION: EMERGENCY SUSPENSION
OFFENSE: DRUG OR ALCOHOL ABUSE
NOTES: ALLEGED INTEMPERATE USE OF DRUGS AND DIVERSION OF CONTROLLED SUBSTANCES THROUGH FALSE PRESCRIPTIONS AND OTHER MISREPRESENTATIONS. MUST HAVE A PSYCHIATRIC EXAMINATION, INCLUDING NEUROPSYCHOLOGIC EVALUATION WITH COGNITIVE EVALUATIONS, FROM A BOARD-APPROVED PSYCHIATRIST.

ANDERSON, BERNICE DO, DATE OF BIRTH MAY 23, 1955, LICENSE NUMBER 00H9489, OF PO BOX 1050, PALACIOS, TX, WAS DISCIPLINED BY TEXAS ON JANUARY 24, 1992.
DISCIPLINARY ACTION: LICENSE SUSPENSION; 60-MONTH PROBATION
OFFENSE: OVERPRESCRIBING OR MISPRESCRIBING DRUGS
NOTES: WROTE FALSE OR FICTITIOUS PRESCRIPTIONS FOR DANGEROUS DRUGS; AND UNPROFESSIONAL OR DISHONORABLE CONDUCT LIKELY TO DECEIVE, DEFRAUD OR INJURE THE PUBLIC. SUSPENDED UNTIL SUCH TIME AS SHE IS EVALUATED BY A PSYCHIATRIST SPECIALIZING IN ADDICTIONOLOGY SATISFACTORY TO THE EXECUTIVE DIRECTOR OF THE BOARD AND FURNISHES REPORTS TO THE BOARD FROM THE PSYCHIATRIST INDICATING THAT SHE IS BOTH MENTALLY AND PHYSICALLY ABLE TO SAFELY PRACTICE MEDICINE. UPON RECEIPT AND VERIFICATION OF SUCH REPORTS, THE SUSPENSION SHALL BE STAYED AND PLACED ON PROBATION UNDER TERMS AND CONDITIONS. PROBATION MODIFIED 12/10/92: DUE TO WORK LOCATION AND PLACE OF RESIDENCE HAD DIFFICULTY COMPLYING WITH REQUIREMENT TO PARTICIPATE IN COUNTY MEDICAL SOCIETY COMMITTEE ON PHYSICIAN HEALTH AND REHABILITATION; THEREFORE, PERMISSION GRANTED TO MEET THE REQUIREMENT BY PARTICIPATION IN EITHER COUNTY MEDICAL SOCIETY OR A REHABILITATION GROUP OF THE TEXAS OSTEOPATHIC MEDICAL ASSOCIATION UNDER THE SAME TERMS AND CONDITIONS.

ANDERSON, BERNICE DO, DATE OF BIRTH MAY 23, 1955, LICENSE NUMBER 00H9489, OF PO BOX 1050, PALACIOS, TX, WAS DISCIPLINED BY TEXAS ON MAY 10, 1993.
DISCIPLINARY ACTION: LICENSE SUSPENSION
OFFENSE: FAILURE TO COMPLY WITH A PREVIOUS BOARD ORDER
NOTES: ON 1/24/92 SHE ENTERED INTO AN AGREEMENT WITH THE BOARD TO ADDRESS HER DIVERSION OF CONTROLLED SUBSTANCES; ONE OF THE CONDITIONS OF PROBATION WAS THAT SHE ABSTAIN FROM THE CONSUMPTION OF CONTROLLED SUBSTANCES IN ANY FORM AND THAT SHE SHALL NOT POSSESS, ADMINISTER DISPENSE OR PRESCRIBE THEM; DURING THE FIRST QUARTER OF 1993 SHE INGESTED CONTROLLED SUBSTANCES; THERE IS NO INDICATION THAT SHE HARMED ANY PATIENTS DUE TO THIS FAILURE TO COMPLY.

ANDERSON, BERNICE DO, DATE OF BIRTH MAY 23, 1955, LICENSE NUMBER 00H9489, OF SAN ANTONIO, TX, WAS DISCIPLINED BY TEXAS ON APRIL 22, 1994.
DISCIPLINARY ACTION: SURRENDER OF CONTROLLED SUBSTANCE LICENSE; 120-MONTH PROBATION
NOTES: AS REQUIRED BY THE PREVIOUS ORDER HAS APPEARED BEFORE BOARD AND PROVIDED SUFFICIENT EVIDENCE TO SHOW SHE IS PHYSICALLY, MENTALLY AND OTHERWISE COMPETENT TO PRACTICE. CONDITIONS OF PROBATION: SHALL NOT PRACTICE AS A SOLO PRACTITIONER OR IN ANY SETTING NOT PREAPPROVED BY THE BOARD; SHALL BE SUPERVISED BY BOARD-APPROVED PHYSICIAN WITH REPORTS THREE TIMES A YEAR; SHALL ABSTAIN FROM THE CONSUMPTION OF ALCOHOL/CHEMICAL SUBSTANCES IN ANY FORM UNLESS PRESCRIBED BY ANOTHER PHYSICIAN FOR A LEGITIMATE AND THERAPEUTIC PURPOSE; SHALL SUBMIT HERSELF FOR APPROPRIATE EXAMS INCLUDING DRUG OR ALCOHOL SCREENS; SHALL NOT TREAT OR OTHERWISE SERVE AS PHYSICIAN, PRESCRIBE, DISPENSE OR ADMINISTER DRUGS THAT MAY BE SUBJECT TO ABUSE TO HERSELF OR ANY MEMBER OF HER FAMILY; SHALL SURRENDER DEA AND TEXAS CONTROLLED SUBSTANCES CERTIFICATES, ALL UNUSED TRIPLICATE PRESCRIPTION FORMS AND ALL UNUSED CONTROLLED SUBSTANCES INCLUDING SAMPLES IN HER POSSESSION; SHALL NOT REREGISTER FOR THESE CERTIFICATES WITHOUT PERMISSION; SEPARATE FROM PATIENT RECORDS SHALL MAINTAIN A FILE OF EVERY PRESCRIPTION WRITTEN FOR DANGEROUS DRUGS WITH POTENTIAL FOR ABUSE WHICH SHALL BE AVAILABLE FOR INSPECTION; SHALL PARTICIPATE IN ACTIVITIES OF A PHYSICIAN HEALTH AND REHABILITATION COMMITTEE AND ATTEND WEEKLY MEETINGS WITH QUARTERLY REPORTS; SHALL PARTICIPATE IN AA'S PROGRAM NOT LESS THAN THREE TIMES A WEEK WITH QUARTERLY REPORTS TO THE BOARD; SHALL SUBMIT HERSELF FOR EXAMINATION AND TREATMENT TO A BOARD-APPROVED PSYCHIATRIST; SHALL ATTEND AT LEAST 50 HOURS PER YEAR OF CONTINUING MEDICAL EDUCATION; SHALL APPEAR BEFORE THE BOARD TWICE A YEAR; SHALL GIVE A COPY OF THIS ORDER TO ANY HEALTH CARE ENTITY WHERE SHE HAS PRIVILEGES; SHALL COOPERATE WITH THE BOARD IN VERIFYING COMPLIANCE; SHALL INFORM BOARD OF CHANGE OF ADDRESS WITHIN 10 DAYS OR IF SHE LEAVES THE STATE; TIME SPENT OUT OF TEXAS DOES NOT COUNT TOWARD PROBATION. SHALL NOT SEEK MODIFICATION

FOR ONE YEAR.

ANDERSON, BERNICE L DO, LICENSE NUMBER 0075475, OF 410 COMMERCE STREET, PALACIOS, TX, WAS DISCIPLINED BY DEA ON JULY 21, 1993.
DISCIPLINARY ACTION: SURRENDER OF CONTROLLED SUBSTANCE LICENSE
OFFENSE: DISCIPLINARY ACTION BY ANOTHER STATE OR AGENCY
NOTES: TEXAS LICENSE SUSPENDED PENDING PSYCHIATRIC EXAM AND REHEARING AND PUBLIC INTEREST REVOCATION PROCEEDINGS TO BE INITIATED UNLESS BOARD SURRENDERED

ANDERSON, ELI T MD, DATE OF BIRTH JUNE 29, 1944, OF 221 NORFOLK SUITE 505, HOUSTON, TX, WAS DISCIPLINED BY MEDICARE ON MAY 26, 1988.
DISCIPLINARY ACTION: 60-MONTH EXCLUSION FROM THE MEDICARE AND/OR MEDICAID PROGRAMS
OFFENSE: CRIMINAL CONVICTION OR PLEA OF GUILTY, NOLO CONTENDERE, OR NO CONTEST TO A CRIME
NOTES: PROGRAM-RELATED CONVICTION.

ANDERSON, KENNETH CARL MD, LICENSE NUMBER 00F0855, OF HUMBLE, TX, WAS DISCIPLINED BY TEXAS ON MARCH 5, 1994.
DISCIPLINARY ACTION: REPRIMAND
OFFENSE: PROFESSIONAL MISCONDUCT
NOTES: IN 7/92 AFTER ESTABLISHING A PHYSICIAN-PATIENT RELATIONSHIP WITH ONE PATIENT WITH AN ECTOPIC PREGNANCY FAILED TO TREAT HER OR PROPERLY REFER HER TO ANOTHER PHYSICIAN. HAD HIS OFFICE STAFF DISMISS THIS PATIENT, RESULTING IN ABANDONMENT OF THE PATIENT. SHALL GIVE A COPY OF THIS ORDER TO ANY HEALTH CARE ENTITY WHERE HE HAS PRIVILEGES; SHALL COOPERATE WITH THE BOARD IN VERIFYING COMPLIANCE; SHALL INFORM BOARD OF CHANGE OF ADDRESS WITHIN 10 DAYS. SHALL NOT SEEK MODIFICATION FOR ONE YEAR.

ANDERSON, VICKI SPARKS MD, LICENSE NUMBER 00E6215, OF PFLUGERVILLE, TX, WAS DISCIPLINED BY TEXAS ON MARCH 5, 1994.
DISCIPLINARY ACTION: LICENSE SUSPENSION
OFFENSE: DRUG OR ALCOHOL ABUSE
NOTES: SHE HAS ADMITTED TO A DECLINE IN HER COGNITIVE ABILITES AND DEXTERITY DUE TO A CONTUSION OF THE RIGHT FRONTAL LOBE OF THE BRAIN WHICH SHE SUFFERED AS A RESULT OF AN AUTO ACCIDENT IN 1983; HOSPITALIZED DURING 1/93 PURSUANT TO AN INVOLUNTARY COMMITMENT DUE TO SUICIDAL IDEATION AND DISCHARGED IN 2/93 WITH A DIAGNOSIS OF BIPOLAR DISORDER; HAS ADMITTED A LONG HISTORY OF ALCOHOL ABUSE; CLAIMS A SOBRIETY DATE OF 3/90 BUT ADMITS A RELAPSE FROM SPRING TO JULY OF 1993. SUSPENSION UNTIL SHE CAN APPEAR BEFORE THE BOARD AND DEMONSTRATE SHE IS ABLE TO PRACTICE WITH REASONABLE SKILL AND SAFETY. IF SHE IS ALLOWED TO PRACTICE IT WILL BE UNDER SPECIFIED CONDITIONS; SHALL COOPERATE WITH THE BOARD IN VERIFYING COMPLIANCE; SHALL INFORM BOARD OF CHANGE OF ADDRESS WITHIN 10 DAYS AND IF SHE LEAVES THE STATE; TIME SPENT OUT OF TEXAS DOES NOT COUNT TOWARD SUSPENSION. SHALL NOT SEEK MODIFICATION FOR ONE YEAR.

ANDERSON, VICKI SPARKS MD, LICENSE NUMBER 00E6215, OF AUSTIN, TX, WAS DISCIPLINED BY TEXAS ON AUGUST 19, 1994.
DISCIPLINARY ACTION: 120-MONTH PROBATION; RESTRICTION PLACED ON CONTROLLED SUBSTANCE LICENSE
NOTES: HAS SATISFIED THE MINIMUM REQUIREMENTS OF AGREED ORDER OF 3/5/94 AND SUSPENSION IS NOW STAYED. CONDITIONS OF PROBATION: SHALL TREAT NO PATIENTS UNTIL SHE PASSESS THE EXAMS NECESSARY FOR OBTAINING ACLS AND ATLS CERTIFICATION; SHALL ATTEND AT LEAST 50 HOURS PER YEAR OF CONTINUING MEDICAL EDUCATION IN EMERGENCY OR FAMILY MEDICINE; SHALL SUBMIT HERSELF FOR EVALUATION AND TREATMENT BY A BOARD-APPROVED PSYCHIATRIST WITH REPORTS TO THE BOARD; SHALL ABSTAIN FROM THE CONSUMPTION OF ALCOHOL/CHEMICAL SUBSTANCES IN ANY FORM UNLESS PRESCRIBED BY ANOTHER PHYSICIAN FOR A LEGITIMATE AND THERAPEUTIC PURPOSE; SHALL SUBMIT HERSELF FOR APPROPRIATE EXAMS INCLUDING ALCOHOL OR DRUG SCREENS; SHALL NOT TREAT OR OTHERWISE SERVE AS PHYSICIAN, PRESCRIBE, DISPENSE OR ADMINISTER DRUGS THAT MAY BE SUBJECT TO ABUSE TO HERSELF OR ANY MEMBER OF HER FAMILY; SEPARATE FROM PATIENT RECORDS, SHALL MAINTAIN A FILE OF EVERY PRESCRIPTION WRITTEN FOR CONTROLLED SUBSTANCES OR DANGEROUS DRUGS WHICH SHALL BE AVAILABLE FOR INSPECTION; SHALL NOT TELEPHONE PRESCRIPTIONS TO A PHARMACY FOR CONTROLLED SUBSTANCES OR DANGEROUS DRUGS OR PERMIT ANYONE NOT LICENSED BY THIS BOARD TO DO SO ON HER BEHALF; SHALL PARTICIPATE IN AA'S PROGRAM NOT LESS THAN THREE TIMES A WEEK WITH QUARTERLY REPORTS TO BOARD; SHALL PARTICIPATE IN THE ACTIVITIES OF A PHYSICIAN HEALTH AND REHABILITATION COMMITTEE AND ATTEND WEEKLY MEETINGS WITH QUARTERLY REPORTS; SHALL PASS THE SPEX EXAM WITHIN ONE YEAR; SHALL APPEAR BEFORE THE BOARD TWICE A YEAR; SHALL COOPERATE WITH THE BOARD IN VERIFYING COMPLIANCE; SHALL INFORM BOARD OF CHANGE OF ADDRESS WITHIN 10 DAYS OR IF SHE LEAVES THE STATE; TIME SPENT OUT OF TEXAS DOES NOT COUNT TOWARD PROBATION. SHALL NOT SEEK MODIFICATION FOR ONE YEAR.

ANDREWS, RAWLE MD, LICENSE NUMBER 00D1963, OF HOUSTON, TX, WAS DISCIPLINED BY TEXAS ON APRIL 15, 1994.
DISCIPLINARY ACTION: REQUIRED TO TAKE ADDITIONAL MEDICAL EDUCATION
OFFENSE: OVERPRESCRIBING OR MISPRESCRIBING DRUGS
NOTES: PRESCRIBED CONTROLLED SUBSTANCES AND SUBSTANCES WITH ADDICTIVE POTENTIAL TO TWO PATIENTS FOR EXTENDED PERIODS OF TIME WITHOUT ADEQUATE INDICATION. LICENSE RESTRICTED FOR FIVE YEARS WITH THE FOLLOWING CONDITIONS: WITHIN ONE YEAR WILL ENROLL IN, AND SUBSEQUENTLY COMPLETE, A TWO WEEK PRECEPTORSHIP ON THE PREVENTION AND TREATMENT OF DRUG ABUSE AND ONE ON PAIN MANAGEMENT; SHALL MAINTAIN ADEQUATE, LEGIBLE MEDICAL RECORDS ON ALL PATIENT OFFICE VISITS AND MAKE THESE AVAILABLE FOR INSPECTION; SHALL REFRAIN FROM THE PRESCRIPTION OR ADMINISTRATION OF ANY DRUG THAT IS NOT MEDICALLY INDICATED; SEPARATE FROM PATIENT RECORDS SHALL MAINTAIN A FILE OF EVERY PRESCRIPTION WRITTEN FOR ANY DANGEROUS DRUG WHICH MAY BE HABIT-FORMING WHICH SHALL BE AVAILABLE FOR INSPECTION; SHALL APPEAR BEFORE

THE BOARD ONCE A YEAR; SHALL GIVE A COPY OF THIS ORDER TO ANY HEALTH CARE ENTITY WHERE HE HAS PRIVILEGES; SHALL COOPERATE WITH THE BOARD IN VERIFYING COMPLIANCE; SHAL INFORM BOARD OF CHANGE OF ADDRESS WITHIN 10 DAYS OR IF HE LEAVES THE STATE; TIME SPENT OUT OF TEXAS DOES NOT COUNT TOWARD PROBATION. SHALL NOT SEEK MODIFICATION FOR ONE YEAR.

ANDRUCZK, ROBERT CORWIN MD, LICENSE NUMBER 00G7390, OF DALLAS, TX, WAS DISCIPLINED BY TEXAS ON OCTOBER 29, 1988.
DISCIPLINARY ACTION: SURRENDER OF CONTROLLED SUBSTANCE LICENSE; MONITORING OF PHYSICIAN
OFFENSE: DRUG OR ALCOHOL ABUSE
NOTES: SURRENDER FEDERAL AND STATE CONTROLLED SUBSTANCE REGISTRATIONS INCLUDING ALL SCHEDULES AND TO NOT REREGISTER WITHOUT BOARD AUTHORIZATION; SHALL PARTICIPATE IN AA AND WEDNESDAY NIGHT PHYSICIANS GROUP ACTIVITIES; SHALL REQUEST AND AUTHORIZE SPECIFIC PHYSICIAN TO REPORT HIS PROGRESS AND PROGNOSIS; SHALL SUBMIT HIMSELF FOR APPROPRIATE EXAMINATIONS TO DETERMINE FREEDOM FROM ALCOHOL OR DRUGS. THIS BOARD ORDER MODIFIED EFFECTIVE 12/4/91 SUCH THAT HE IS GRANTED PERMISSION TO REAPPLY TO THE DRUG ENFORCEMENT ADMINISTRATION AND THE TEXAS DEPARTMENT OF PUBLIC SAFETY FOR SCHEDULES II, IIN, III, IIIN, IV OR V; SHALL REFRAIN FROM THE PRESCRIPTION OR ADMINISTRATION OF ANY DRUG UNLESS THE DRUG IS MEDICALLY INDICATED AND PRESCRIBED IN THERAPEUTIC DOSES; SHALL CONDUCT ADEQUATE FOLLOW-UP EXAMINATIONS ON ALL PATIENTS TO DETERMINE WHETHER THE COURSE OF TREATMENT, INCLUDING THE PRESCRIBING OF DRUGS, IS APPROPRIATE; SHALL NOT TREAT OR OTHERWISE SERVE AS PHYSICIAN, TO PRESCRIBE, DISPENSE, OR ADMINISTER CONTROLLED SUBSTANCES OR ANY OTHER DRUGS THAT MAY BE SUBJECT TO ABUSE FOR HIMSELF OR ANY FAMILY MEMBER; SHALL PARTICIPATE IN AA AND ATTEND AT LEAST SIX TIMES PER WEEK, WITH QUARTERLY REPORTS TO BOARD; TREATING PHYSICIAN SHALL REPORT QUARTERLY TO THE BOARD; SHALL SUBMIT TO RANDOM TESTS OF BODILY FLUIDS; SHALL COOPERATE WITH THE BOARD IN VERIFYING COMPLIANCE. UNLESS MODIFIED, ORDER SHALL REMAIN IN EFFECT UNTIL 8/4/93; MAY PETITION FOR MODIFICATION NO SOONER THAN 8/4/89.

ANKLESARIA, MANEK E MD, LICENSE NUMBER 0013574, OF 2325 S. HARVARD SUITE 104, TULSA, OK, WAS DISCIPLINED BY OKLAHOMA ON NOVEMBER 23, 1992.
DISCIPLINARY ACTION: LICENSE SUSPENSION
OFFENSE: SEXUAL ABUSE OF OR SEXUAL MISCONDUCT WITH A PATIENT
NOTES: EXHIBITED INAPPROPRIATE SEXUAL BEHAVIOR WITH TWO OPHTHALMOLOGIC PATIENTS, ONE IN THE FALL OF 1990 AND THE OTHER MAY 6, 1991 INCLUDING SEXUAL COMMENTS, PLACING PATIENTS HAND ON HIS PENIS, AND FONDLING AND KISSING PATIENT. SUSPENSION IN EFFECT UNTIL PRESENTS EVIDENCE OF MEDICAL IN-PATIENT EVALUATION AND SUCCESSFUL COMPLETION OF TREATMENT. ON 5/20/93 SUSPENSION CONTINUED. HE WILL IMMEDIATELY UNDERGO FULL IN-PATIENT EVALUATION AND COMPLETE ANY NECESSARY TREATMENT; WILL NOT REAPPEAR BEFORE THE BOARD AND REQUEST TERMINATION OR MODIFICATION UNLESS HE CAN PROVIDE EVIDENCE OF SUCCESSFUL COMPLETION OF EVALUATION AND ANY NECESSARY TREATMENT AND ASSURANCE TO THE BOARD BY THE TREATMENT PROVIDER THAT HE MAY RETURN SAFELY TO PRACTICE MEDICINE.

ANKLESARIA, MANEK E MD, LICENSE NUMBER 0013574, OF 2325 S HARVARD AVE #104, TULSA, OK, WAS DISCIPLINED BY OKLAHOMA ON OCTOBER 11, 1993.
DISCIPLINARY ACTION: 60-MONTH PROBATION; RESTRICTION PLACED ON LICENSE
NOTES: LICENSE REINSTATED FROM 11/21/92 SUSPENSION. CONDITIONS OF PROBATION BEGINNING 10/1/93: SHALL SUBMIT BIOLOGICAL FLUID SPECIMENS; SHALL FULFILL CONDITIONS RECOMMENDED BY SPECIFIED MD AND/OR THE STAFF OF SPECIFIED CENTER; SHALL ALLOW STAFF TO SPEAK WITH BOARD TO VERIFY COMPLIANCE; WHEN EXAMINING ANY FEMALE PATIENT SHALL HAVE A FEMALE MEDIAL PROFESSIONAL PRESENT; SHALL CONTINUE UNDER PSYCHIATRIC CARE WITH BOARD-APPROVED PHYSICIAN; SHALL NOTIFY ANY HEALTH CARE ENTITY WHERE HE HOLDS OR APPLIES FOR STAFF PRIVILEGES OF THE CONDITIONS OF THE ORDER; SHALL FURNISH BOARD WITH ADDRESS AND/OR CHANGE OF ADDRESS; SHALL APPEAR BEFORE THE BOARD UPON REQUEST AND SUBMIT REQUIRED REPORTS; SHALL PAY COSTS. ON 3/31/94 ORDER MODIFIED SUCH THAT BIOLOGICAL FLUID SPECIMENS WERE NO LONGER REQUIRED.

ANKLESARIA, MANEK EDALJI MD, DATE OF BIRTH APRIL 15, 1949, LICENSE NUMBER 00F2155, OF 2325 SO HARVARD SUITE 104, TULSA, OK, WAS DISCIPLINED BY TEXAS ON APRIL 30, 1993.
DISCIPLINARY ACTION: SURRENDER OF LICENSE
NOTES: LICENSE PERMANENTLY CANCELLED.

ANKLESARIA, MANEK EDALJI MD, DATE OF BIRTH APRIL 15, 1949, LICENSE NUMBER 0020520, OF TULSA, OK, WAS DISCIPLINED BY NORTH CAROLINA ON DECEMBER 3, 1993.
DISCIPLINARY ACTION: SURRENDER OF LICENSE

ANKLESARIA, MANEK EDALJI MD, DATE OF BIRTH APRIL 15, 1949, LICENSE NUMBER 0033882, OF 2325 S. HARVARD AVE., TULSA, OK, WAS DISCIPLINED BY NEW JERSEY ON DECEMBER 28, 1993.
DISCIPLINARY ACTION: CEASE AND DESIST ORDER
OFFENSE: DISCIPLINARY ACTION BY ANOTHER STATE OR AGENCY
NOTES: DISCIPLINARY ACTION TAKEN IN OKLAHOMA. SHALL HAVE LEAVE TO SURRENDER HIS LICENSE TO PRACTICE MEDICINE AND SURGERY IN NEW JERSEY WITH PREJUDICE TO SEEKING REINSTATEMENT AT ANY FUTURE DATE.

APPLEBY, HOMER Q MD, LICENSE NUMBER 00C1745, OF SLAUGHTER, LA, WAS DISCIPLINED BY TEXAS ON OCTOBER 1, 1987.
DISCIPLINARY ACTION: LICENSE REVOCATION
OFFENSE: DISCIPLINARY ACTION BY ANOTHER STATE OR AGENCY
NOTES: DISCIPLINARY ACTION BY LOUISIANA.

ARCHER, JIM PAUL DO, LICENSE NUMBER 0062644, OF 4242 MEDICAL DR #7150, SAN ANTONIO, TX, WAS DISCIPLINED BY DEA ON OCTOBER 26, 1990.
DISCIPLINARY ACTION: SURRENDER OF CONTROLLED SUBSTANCE LICENSE
OFFENSE: PROFESSIONAL MISCONDUCT
NOTES: VIOLATIONS OF OBTAINING CONTROLLED SUBSTANCES BY FRAUD.

ARCHER, JIM PAUL DO, LICENSE NUMBER 00D2978, OF 8434 FREDERICKSBURG RD., SAN ANTONIO, TX, WAS DISCIPLINED BY TEXAS ON DECEMBER 4, 1991.
DISCIPLINARY ACTION: PROBATION; REQUIRED TO ENTER AN IMPAIRED PHYSICIAN PROGRAM OR DRUG OR ALCOHOL TREATMENT
OFFENSE: DRUG OR ALCOHOL ABUSE
NOTES: ADDICTION TO DEMEROL, MORPHINE, DILAUDID, VICODIN, AND TALWIN, WHICH RENDERS HIM UNABLE TO PRACTICE MEDICINE WITH REASONABLE SKILL AND SAFETY TO PATIENTS; ISSUED FALSE OR FICTITIOUS TRIPLICATE PRESCRIPTIONS; FAILED TO KEEP ADEQUATE INVENTORY OR DISPENSATION RECORDS; FAILED TO KEEP ADEQUATE PATIENT RECORDS REGARDING PRESCRIBING PRACTICES. REVOCATION STAYED; PLACED ON INDEFINITE PROBATION UNDER THE FOLLOWING TERMS AND CONDITIONS: SHALL ABSTAIN FROM THE CONSUMPTION OF ALCOHOL/CHEMICAL SUBSTANCES IN ANY FORM, EXCEPT AS PRESCRIBED BY ANOTHER PHYSICIAN; SHALL PARTICIPATE IN THE ACTIVITIES OF AN IMPAIRED PHYSICIANS PROGRAM, INCLUDING WEEKLY MEETINGS, WITH QUARTERLY REPORTS TO THE BOARD; SHALL PARTICIPATE IN AA NOT LESS THAN THREE TIMES A WEEK FOR THE FIRST YEAR OF PROBATION, AND TWO TIMES THEREAFTER, WITH QUARTERLY REPORTS TO THE BOARD; SHALL SUBMIT TO RANDOM TESTS OF BODILY FLUIDS; SHALL ABIDE BY RECOMMENDATIONS OF A BOARD-APPROVED PSYCHIATRIST; SHALL REFRAIN FROM THE USE OF AND SHALL NOT POSSESS, ADMINISTER, OR PRESCRIBE ANY CONTROLLED SUBSTANCE OR ANY OTHER DRUG REQUIRING A PRESCRIPTION; SHALL APPEAR BEFORE THE BOARD TWICE A YEAR; SHALL NOT ATTEMPT TO REREGISTER CONTROLLED SUBSTANCES LICENSES WITHOUT BOARD PERMISSION; SHALL GIVE A COPY OF THIS ORDER TO ANY HOSPITAL WHERE HE HAS PRIVILEGES; SHALL COOPERATE WITH THE BOARD IN VERIFYING COMPLIANCE; SHALL ADVISE THE BOARD OF A CHANGE IN ADDRESS WITHIN 10 DAYS; TIME SPENT OUT OF TEXAS DOES NOT COUNT TOWARDS PROBATION. ON 8/19/94 HIS REQUEST FOR TERMINATION OF THIS ORDER DENIED.

ARNDT-HAGAN, MARY L MD, DATE OF BIRTH AUGUST 26, 1956, OF 13510 TOM FIELD ROAD, DALLAS, TX, WAS DISCIPLINED BY MEDICARE ON AUGUST 13, 1993.
DISCIPLINARY ACTION: EXCLUSION FROM THE MEDICARE AND/OR MEDICAID PROGRAMS
OFFENSE: FAILURE TO COMPLY WITH A PROFESSIONAL RULE
NOTES: DEFAULTED ON HEALTH EDUCATION ASSISTANCE LOAN. REINSTATED ON 9/28/93.

ATHARI, MOHAMMAD MD, LICENSE NUMBER 00E6718, OF BAYTOWN, TX, WAS DISCIPLINED BY TEXAS ON APRIL 14, 1989.
DISCIPLINARY ACTION: 12-MONTH RESTRICTION PLACED ON LICENSE; 42-MONTH MONITORING OF PHYSICIAN
NOTES: MUST FAMILIARIZE HIMSELF WITH STATUTE AND RULES OF BOARD REGARDING PROPER DELEGATION TO NON-PHYSICIANS; HAVE ALL HIS MEDICAL ASSISTANTS WEAR NAME TAGS WHILE ON DUTY; FURNISH BOARD COPIES OF EXECUTED STANDING DELEGATION ORDERS; AGREEMENT AND ORDER EFFECTIVE UNTIL OCTOBER 16, 1992. FOR ONE YEAR, MUST OBTAIN SECOND OPINIONS ON CERTAIN WORKER'S COMPENSATION CASES.

ATKINSON, WILLIAM H MD, LICENSE NUMBER 00E2448, OF WAXAHACHIE, TX, WAS DISCIPLINED BY TEXAS ON APRIL 10, 1992.
DISCIPLINARY ACTION: 60-MONTH PROBATION
OFFENSE: SUBSTANDARD CARE, INCOMPETENCE, OR NEGLIGENCE
NOTES: PROFESSIONAL FAILURE TO PRACTICE MEDICINE IN AN ACCEPTABLE MANNER CONSISTENT WITH PUBLIC HEALTH AND WELFARE. LICENSE SUSPENDED, SUSPENSION STAYED; PROBATION UNDER TERMS AND CONDITIONS.

ATLAS, RUTH M MD, LICENSE NUMBER 00G7616, OF HOUSTON, TX, WAS DISCIPLINED BY TEXAS ON AUGUST 24, 1991.
DISCIPLINARY ACTION: REPRIMAND
OFFENSE: PROFESSIONAL MISCONDUCT
NOTES: UNPROFESSIONAL OR DISHONORABLE CONDUCT LIKELY TO DECEIVE, DEFRAUD, OR INJURE THE PUBLIC.

AVERY, BERT MILLS MD, LICENSE NUMBER 00F2529, OF LAWTON, OK, WAS DISCIPLINED BY TEXAS ON NOVEMBER 19, 1993.
OFFENSE: CRIMINAL CONVICTION OR PLEA OF GUILTY, NOLO CONTENDERE, OR NO CONTEST TO A CRIME
NOTES: ON 5/27/93 WAS CONVICTED OF ONE COUNT OF FELONY CONSPIRACY TO COMMIT MAIL FRAUD AND EIGHT COUNTS OF FELONY MAIL FRAUD IN U.S. DISTRICT COURT, WESTERN DISTRICT OF OKLAHOMA; CONVICTIONS REFERRED TO BILLING CHAMPUS FOR TUBAL REVERSAL SURGERY WHICH WAS NOT A COVERED PROCEDURE; WAS SENTENCED TO 21 MONTHS OF COMMUNITY SERVICE AT 40 HOURS PER WEEK; HAS APPEALED THE CONVICTION AND WAS AWAITING DISPOSITION OF THIS MATTER BY THE OKLAHOMA STATE BOARD OF MEDICAL EXAMINERS AT THE TIME OF THE ORDER; DOES NOT NOW WISH TO PRACTICE IN TEXAS. PRIOR TO PRACTICING MEDICINE IN TEXAS SHALL OBTAIN THE APPROVAL OF THE BOARD; RESERVES THE RIGHT TO A CONTESTED HEARING REGARDING THE ALLEGATIONS ADDRESSED; SHALL GIVE A COPY OF THIS ORDER TO ANY HEALTH CARE ENTITY IN TEXAS WHERE HE HAS PRIVILEGES; SHALL INFORM BOARD OF CHANGE OF ADDRESS WITHIN 10 DAYS. ON 3/4/95 BOARD GRANTED HIS PETITION FOR TERMINATION OF ORDER RETROACTIVE TO 11/19/93 BASED ON COURT OF APPEALS REVERSAL OF FELONY CONVICTION.

AXELROD, WILLIAM MD, DATE OF BIRTH JANUARY 9, 1918, LICENSE NUMBER 00B6608, OF 1109 MEDICAL TOWERS 1700 DRYDEN, HOUSTON, TX, WAS DISCIPLINED BY TEXAS ON APRIL 30, 1993.
DISCIPLINARY ACTION: 60-MONTH PROBATION; RESTRICTION PLACED ON CONTROLLED SUBSTANCE LICENSE
OFFENSE: OVERPRESCRIBING OR MISPRESCRIBING DRUGS
NOTES: FROM 2/3/89 THROUGH 7/20/92 HE COMMITTED SEVERAL PRESCRIPTION VIOLATIONS INCLUDING FAILING TO JUSTIFY IN HIS MEDICAL RECORDS THE USE OF INJECTABLE DEMEROL FOR TWO PATIENTS FOR WHOM HE WAS NOT THEIR TREATING PHYSICIAN; PRESCRIBED DEMEROL FOR ONE OF THESE PATIENTS WHICH WAS ADMINISTERED TO THE OTHER; FAILED TO KEEP COMPLETE AND ACCURATE RECORDS OF PURCHASES AND DISPOSALS OF DANGEROUS DRUGS AND/OR CONTROLLED SUBSTANCES; FAILED TO MAINTAIN ACQUISITION AND DISPENSING RECORDS FOR TALWIN; ON 8/17/92 HE SURRENDERED DEA AND

DPS REGISTRATIONS WHICH WERE THEN REVOKED. FIVE YEAR SUSPENSION STAYED. CONDITIONS OF PROBATION: MAY APPLY FOR REINSTATEMENT OF CONTROLLED SUBSTANCE REGISTRATIONS FOR SCHEDULES III, IV AND V BUT NOT SCHEDULE II; SHALL APPEAR BEFORE THE BOARD ONCE A YEAR; SHALL GIVE A COPY OF THIS ORDER TO ANY HEALTH CARE ENTITY WHERE HE HAS PRIVILEGES; SHALL COOPERATE WITH THE BOARD IN VERIFYING COMPLIANCE; SHALL INFORM THE BOARD OF CHANGE OF ADDRESS WITHIN 10 DAYS OR IF HE LEAVES THE STATE; TIME SPENT OUT OF TEXAS DOES NOT COUNT TOWARD PROBATION. SHALL NOT SEEK MODIFICATION FOR ONE YEAR.

AXELROD, WILLIAM MD, DATE OF BIRTH JANUARY 9, 1918, LICENSE NUMBER 00B6608, OF 1109 MEDICAL TOWERS, HOUSTON, TX, WAS DISCIPLINED BY DEA ON SEPTEMBER 20, 1993.
DISCIPLINARY ACTION: RESTRICTION PLACED ON CONTROLLED SUBSTANCE LICENSE
OFFENSE: FAILURE TO COMPLY WITH A PROFESSIONAL RULE
NOTES: EXCESSIVE PURCHASE REPORT. ORDERED EXCESSIVE AMOUNTS OF DEMEROL WITHOUT MAINTAINING RECORDS. VOLUNTARY SURRENDER OF REGISTRATION ON 08/17/92. SEIZED 9 MLS DEMEROL AND 10 MLS TALWIN. SUBMITTED APPLICATION FOR REGISTRATION ON 07/01/93. APPROVAL OF APPLICATION.

AZEVEDO, FERNANDO W MD, LICENSE NUMBER 00D8138, OF MISSOURI CITY, TX, WAS DISCIPLINED BY TEXAS ON JANUARY 24, 1992.
DISCIPLINARY ACTION: SURRENDER OF LICENSE
NOTES: LICENSE PLACED ON RETIREMENT STATUS IN LIEU OF FURTHER INVESTIGATION AND DISCIPLINARY ACTION.

BACHYNSKY, NICHOLAS MD, LICENSE NUMBER 00E1495, OF HOUSTON, TX, WAS DISCIPLINED BY TEXAS ON JANUARY 26, 1990.
DISCIPLINARY ACTION: LICENSE REVOCATION
OFFENSE: CRIMINAL CONVICTION OR PLEA OF GUILTY, NOLO CONTENDERE, OR NO CONTEST TO A CRIME
NOTES: PLEADED GUILTY 7/13/89 TO FRAUD IN U.S. DISTRICT COURT FOR THE SOUTHERN DISTRICT OF TEXAS

BACHYNSKY, NICHOLAS MD, LICENSE NUMBER 0168030, OF HOUSTON, TX, WAS DISCIPLINED BY NEW YORK ON MAY 13, 1991.
DISCIPLINARY ACTION: LICENSE REVOCATION

BACHYNSKY, NICHOLAS MD, LICENSE NUMBER 0047143, OF FT WORTH, TX, WAS DISCIPLINED BY FLORIDA ON DECEMBER 30, 1991.
DISCIPLINARY ACTION: LICENSE REVOCATION; FINE
OFFENSE: DISCIPLINARY ACTION BY ANOTHER STATE OR AGENCY
NOTES: LICENSE REVOKED IN ANOTHER STATE; CONVICTED OR FOUND GUILTY OF, OR ENTERED PLEA OF NOLO CONTENDERE TO, REGARDLESS OF ADJUDICATION, A CRIME IN ANY JURISDICTION WHICH DIRECTLY RELATES TO THE PRACTICE OF MEDICINE OR THE ABILITY TO PRACTICE MEDICINE. $10,000 FINE.

BAGWELL, JERRY GLYN MD, LICENSE NUMBER 00D1130, OF GATESVILLE, TX, WAS DISCIPLINED BY TEXAS ON NOVEMBER 3, 1994.
DISCIPLINARY ACTION: 120-MONTH PROBATION; REQUIRED TO TAKE ADDITIONAL MEDICAL EDUCATION
OFFENSE: SUBSTANDARD CARE, INCOMPETENCE, OR NEGLIGENCE
NOTES: TREATED A 28 YEAR OLD FEMALE ON MARCH 15 AND 16, 1993; HER MEDICAL RECORDS SHOW A HISTORY OF SEIZURES, PEPTIC ULCER DISEASE, CERVICAL DYSPLASIA AND LOWER EXTREMITY DEEP VEIN THROMBOSIS; ALSO NOTED IN HER RECORDS WAS ONGOING COUMADIN THERAPY; ON 3/16/93 HE NOTED BLEEDING INTO HER SKIN AND ORDERED LAB TESTING; HER PROTHROMBIN TIME WAS GREATER THAN 50; HE FAILED TO ALTER THE DOSAGE OF, OR TO DISCONTINUE, HER COUMADIN; WAS PLACED ON PROBATION BECAUSE OF THIS BY THE TEXAS DEPARTMENT OF CRIMINAL JUSTICE PEER REVIEW COMMITTEE FOR TWO MONTHS WHICH ENDED 12/26/93. SUSPENSION STAYED. CONDITIONS OF PROBATION: SHALL MAINTAIN ADEQUATE MEDICAL RECORDS ON ALL PATIENT VISITS WHICH SHALL BE AVAILABLE FOR INSPECTION; SHALL NOT SIGN ANY PATIENT RECORD UNLESS HE HAS PERSONALLY EXAMINED THE PATIENT OR CLEARLY NOTES IN THE RECORD THAT HE DID NOT; SHALL ATTEND AT LEAST 50 HOURS PER YEAR OF CONTINUING MEDICAL EDUCATION, 10 HOURS OF WHICH SHALL BE IN RISK MANAGEMENT AND 40 HOURS OF WHICH SHALL BE IN FAMILY PRACTICE; WITHIN SIX MONTHS SHALL PASS THE SPEX EXAM AND THE MEDICAL JURISPRUDENCE EXAM; SHALL APPEAR BEFORE THE BOARD TWICE A YEAR; SHALL GIVE A COPY OF THIS ORDER TO ANY HEALTH CARE ENTITY WHERE HE HAS PRIVILEGES; SHALL COOPERATE WITH THE BOARD IN VERIFYING COMPLIANCE; SHALL INFORM BOARD OF CHANGE OF ADDRESS WITHIN 10 DAYS OR IF HE LEAVES THE STATE; TIME SPENT OUT OF TEXAS DOES NOT COUNT TOWARD PROBATION. SHALL NOT SEEK MODIFICATION FOR ONE YEAR.

BAILEY, DENNIS L MD, LICENSE NUMBER 0022299, OF 2183 SHANCEY LANE, COLLEGE PARK, GA, WAS DISCIPLINED BY GEORGIA ON JUNE 11, 1985.
DISCIPLINARY ACTION: LICENSE REVOCATION

BAILEY, DENNIS L MD OF EAST POINT, GA, WAS DISCIPLINED BY TEXAS ON DECEMBER 1, 1986.
DISCIPLINARY ACTION: LICENSE REVOCATION
OFFENSE: DISCIPLINARY ACTION BY ANOTHER STATE OR AGENCY

BAILEY, SHARON ANNE DO, LICENSE NUMBER 00G0654, OF DALLAS, TX, WAS DISCIPLINED BY TEXAS ON APRIL 20, 1991.
DISCIPLINARY ACTION: 120-MONTH PROBATION; REQUIRED TO ENTER AN IMPAIRED PHYSICIAN PROGRAM OR DRUG OR ALCOHOL TREATMENT
OFFENSE: DRUG OR ALCOHOL ABUSE
NOTES: SHALL COMPLY WITH TERMS OF IMPAIRED HEALTH PROFESSIONAL'S TREATMENT CONTRACT OF THE TEXAS OSTEOPATHIC MEDICAL ASSOCIATION; AFTER EXPIRATION OF THIS CONTRACT, SHALL PARTICIPATE IN AA ON A REGULAR BASIS; SHALL SUBMIT TO ALCOHOL OR DRUG SCREENS; SHALL CONTINUE TREATMENT WITH A BOARD-APPROVED PHYSICIAN, WITH TWICE YEARLY REPORTS TO THE BOARD; SHALL OBTAIN AND CONTINUE TO HAVE A RECOVERING ABUSE SPONSOR WHO IS A HEALTH CARE PROFESSIONAL.

BAKER, JOHN A MD OF ARGYLE, TX, WAS DISCIPLINED BY MISSOURI ON FEBRUARY 16, 1994.
DISCIPLINARY ACTION: NONRENEWAL OF LICENSE
OFFENSE: FAILURE TO COMPLY WITH A PROFESSIONAL RULE
NOTES: DURING 1992 HE FAILED TO OBTAIN THE REQUIRED 25

HOURS OF CONTINUING MEDICAL EDUCATION CREDITS AND FAILED TO REPORT OBTAINING SUCH HOURS BY 05/20/93 AS REQUIRED BY BOARD RULE.

BAKER, JOHN SCOTT MD, LICENSE NUMBER 00J1853, OF WINSTON-SALEM, NC, WAS DISCIPLINED BY TEXAS ON NOVEMBER 19, 1993.
OFFENSE: DRUG OR ALCOHOL ABUSE
NOTES: IN 11/92 WAS GRANTED LICENSURE; BOARD LATER RECEIVED INFORMATION THAT HE HAD PROVIDED FALSE INFORMATION ABOUT HIS ABUSE OF ALCOHOL; IN 1/93 REPORTED HIMSELF TO THE BOARD AND SUPERVISING PHYSICIANS IN NORTH CAROLINA; COMPLETED INPATIENT TREATMENT AND ENTERED THREE MONTHS OF EXTENDED CARE; HAS SIGNED A CONTRACT WITH NORTH CAROLINA IMPAIRED PHYSICIANS PROGRAM; FULL LICENSURE STATUS WITH NORTH CAROLINA IS PENDING AS OF THE DATE OF THE ORDER. PRIOR TO PRACTICING IN TEXAS SHALL APPEAR BEFORE THE BOARD TO RECEIVE APPROVAL; SHALL PROVIDE TO TEXAS BOARD ANY REQUESTED COPIES OF REPORTS SUBMITTED TO NORTH CAROLINA; SHALL FOLLOW THE TERMS OF THE NORTH CAROLINA CONTRACT AND ALL CONDITIONS IMPOSED BY THE NORTH CAROLINA BOARD; SHALL GIVE A COPY OF THIS ORDER TO ANY HEALTH CARE ENTITY WHERE HE HAS PRIVILEGES; SHALL COOPERATE WITH THE BOARD IN VERIFYING COMPLIANCE; SHALL INFORM THE BOARD OF CHANGE OF ADDRESS WITHIN 10 DAYS. SHALL NOT SEEK MODIFICATION FOR ONE YEAR.

BALDWIN, RICHARD E DO, DATE OF BIRTH JULY 19, 1938, OF 313 EAST MAIN STREET, DAVIS, OK, WAS DISCIPLINED BY MEDICARE ON DECEMBER 13, 1989.
DISCIPLINARY ACTION: 60-MONTH EXCLUSION FROM THE MEDICARE AND/OR MEDICAID PROGRAMS
OFFENSE: CRIMINAL CONVICTION OR PLEA OF GUILTY, NOLO CONTENDERE, OR NO CONTEST TO A CRIME
NOTES: PROGRAM-RELATED CONVICTION.

BALDWIN, RICHARD E DO OF DAVIS, OK, WAS DISCIPLINED BY MISSOURI ON JULY 27, 1990.
DISCIPLINARY ACTION: 2-MONTH LICENSE SUSPENSION; 22-MONTH PROBATION
OFFENSE: DISCIPLINARY ACTION BY ANOTHER STATE OR AGENCY
NOTES: TWO MONTH SUSPENSION RETROACTIVE TO 6/15/89, TWENTY-TWO MONTH PROBATION RETROACTIVE TO 8/16/89.

BALDWIN, RICHARD E DO, LICENSE NUMBER 00E3192, OF DAVIS, OK, WAS DISCIPLINED BY TEXAS ON AUGUST 18, 1990.
OFFENSE: DISCIPLINARY ACTION BY ANOTHER STATE OR AGENCY
NOTES: STIPULATED ORDER. MUST COMPLY WITH OKLAHOMA BOARD ORDER, RECEIVE PERMISSION OF TEXAS BOARD BEFORE RETURNING TO PRACTICE MEDICINE IN TEXAS, AND BE SUBJECT TO ANY TERMS IMPOSED.

BALDWIN, RICHARD E DO, DATE OF BIRTH JULY 19, 1938, LICENSE NUMBER 0018743, OF DAVIS, OK, WAS DISCIPLINED BY COLORADO ON FEBRUARY 21, 1992.
DISCIPLINARY ACTION: SURRENDER OF LICENSE
OFFENSE: CRIMINAL CONVICTION OR PLEA OF GUILTY, NOLO CONTENDERE, OR NO CONTEST TO A CRIME
NOTES: FELONY CONVICTION FOR MEDICAID FRAUD.

BALLARD, CHARLES DONALD MD, DATE OF BIRTH JULY 19, 1952, LICENSE NUMBER 00F9165, OF 15187 HILLVIEW ROAD, TYLER, TX, WAS DISCIPLINED BY TEXAS ON JUNE 17, 1992.
DISCIPLINARY ACTION: 60-MONTH PROBATION
OFFENSE: DRUG OR ALCOHOL ABUSE
NOTES: INTEMPERATE USE OF DRUGS. SUSPENSION, STAYED. PROBATION UNDER TERMS AND CONDITIONS. ON 6/15/93 BOARD MODIFIED THIS ORDER AS FOLLOWS: HE MAY SEEK TO OBTAIN HIS DRUG ENFORCEMENT ADMINISTRATION AND TEXAS DEPARTMENT OF PUBLIC SAFETY CONTROLLED SUBSTANCES REGISTRATION CERTIFICATE; UPON OBTAINING THESE CERTIFICATES, HE MAY POSSESS, ADMINISTER, AND PRESCRIBE DRUGS ONLY IN HOSPITALS FOR INPATIENTS OR IN HOSPITAL EMERGENCY ROOMS FOR EMERGENCY ROOM PATIENTS. IN THE CASE OF ER PATIENTS, CAN ONLY PRESCRIBE IN QUANTITIES LIMITED TO ADDRESS THE IMMEDIATE NEEDS OF THE PATIENTS TO PROVIDE THERAPEUTIC CARE OF EMERGENCY CONDITIONS UNTIL SUCH TIME AS THE PATIENT CAN BE SEEN BY A TREATING OR ATTENDING PHYSICIAN FOR CONTINUED CARE.

BALLI, EDWARD A MD, LICENSE NUMBER 00H5691, OF SAN ANTONIO, TX, WAS DISCIPLINED BY TEXAS ON SEPTEMBER 9, 1991.
DISCIPLINARY ACTION: 60-MONTH PROBATION; REQUIRED TO ENTER AN IMPAIRED PHYSICIAN PROGRAM OR DRUG OR ALCOHOL TREATMENT
OFFENSE: DRUG OR ALCOHOL ABUSE
NOTES: FROM LATE 1989 TO 5/24/90 HE ABUSED RITALIN AND VICODIN FOR NON-MEDICAL PURPOSES WHILE ACTIVELY ENGAGED IN THE PRACTICE OF MEDICINE; ENTERED A TREATMENT PROGRAM 5/24/90 FOR TREATMENT OF CHEMICAL DEPENDENCY AND WAS DISCHARGED 7/4/90; EXECUTED A 2 YEAR AFTERCARE CONTRACT. SUSPENSION STAYED; CONDITIONS OF PROBATION INCLUDE: REFRAINING FROM USE OF ALCOHOL OR DRUGS EXCEPT MEDICATION PRESCRIBED BY HIS PRIMARY CARE PHYSICIAN; SHALL SUBMIT FOR ALCOHOL OR DRUG SCREENS; SHALL PARTICIPATE IN BEXAR COUNTY MEDICAL SOCIETY COMMITTEE ON PHYSICIAN HEALTH AND REHABILITATION, WITH WEEKLY REPORTS TO THE BOARD; SHALL PARTICIPATE IN AA NOT LESS THAN TWICE A WEEK; SHALL COMPLY WITH THE TERMS AND CONDITIONS OF THE AFTERCARE CONTRACT EXECUTED WITH LAUREL RIDGE PSYCHIATRIC HOSPITAL; SHALL APPEAR BEFORE THE BOARD TWICE YEARLY; SHALL ADVISE THE BOARD OF A CHANGE IN ADDRESS; TIME SPENT OUT OF TEXAS DOES NOT COUNT TOWARD PROBATION. SHALL NOT PETITION THE BOARD FOR MODIFICATION OF ORDER FOR AT LEAST ONE YEAR.

BALLI, EDWARD A MD, LICENSE NUMBER 00H5691, OF SEGUIN, TX, WAS DISCIPLINED BY TEXAS ON AUGUST 20, 1992.
DISCIPLINARY ACTION: 2-MONTH LICENSE SUSPENSION; 60-MONTH PROBATION
OFFENSE: DRUG OR ALCOHOL ABUSE
NOTES: ADDITIONAL FIVE-YEAR SUSPENSION, STAYED. PROBATION UNDER TERMS AND CONDITIONS. ON 11/3/94 ORDER MODIFIED AS FOLLOWS: SEPARATE FROM PATIENT RECORDS, HE SHALL MAINTAIN A LOG CONSISTING OF A COPY OF EVERY PRESCRIPTION WRITTEN FOR CONTROLLED SUBSTANCES OR DANGEROUS DRUGS BY DATE ISSUED WHICH SHALL BE AVAILABLE TO BOARD FOR INSPECTION; MAY TELEPHONE PRESCRIPTIONS OR REFILLS FOR

DANGEROUS DRUGS IN TO PHARMACIES BUT NOT FOR CONTROLLED SUBSTANCES; SHALL MAINTAIN A LOGBOOK FOR ALL PRESCRIPTIONS OR REFILLS TELEPHONED IN CHRONOLOGICAL ORDER BY DATE.

BALUCH, ABDUL MD, LICENSE NUMBER 00F7693, OF MIDLAND, TX, WAS DISCIPLINED BY TEXAS ON MAY 20, 1989.
DISCIPLINARY ACTION: MONITORING OF PHYSICIAN
NOTES: SHALL REPORT NAMES OF PATIENTS WHO UNDERGO CERTAIN PROCEDURES IN THE OFFICE; SHALL MODIFY CRITERIA FOR PRESCRIBING OR ADMINISTERING CERTAIN MEDICATIONS AND FOR DETERMINING OFFICE CHARGES; SHALL MAINTAIN ADEQUATE MEDICAL RECORDS AS DIRECTED AND FACILITATE REVIEW OF CHARTS AS DIRECTED; SHALL APPEAR SEMIANNUALLY BEFORE BOARD.

BARBA, PEDRO MD, LICENSE NUMBER 00F7695, OF PACUHCA, MEXICO, WAS DISCIPLINED BY TEXAS ON APRIL 15, 1994.
DISCIPLINARY ACTION: LICENSE SUSPENSION
OFFENSE: DRUG OR ALCOHOL ABUSE
NOTES: FAILED TO KEEP RECORDS OF PURCHASES AND DISPOSALS OF CONTROLLED DRUGS; STARTED SELF-PRESCRIBING DRUGS FOR BACK PAIN MANAGEMENT AFTER AN AUTO ACCIDENT IN 1989 LEADING TO HIS ADDICTION TO LORTAB AND DEMEROL; CLOSED HIS PRACTICE TO ADDRESS HIS DRUG PROBLEM IN 1/92 AND HAS BEEN TREATED; HAS BEEN LIVING IN MEXICO. SUSPENSION UNTIL HE OBTAINS AN IN-PATIENT PSYCHIATRIC EVALUATION AND APPEARS BEFORE THE BOARD PROVIDING SUFFICIENT INFORMATION THAT HE IS PHYSICALLY, MENTALLY AND OTHERWISE COMPETENT TO SAFELY PRACTICE.

BARBER, FOREST C MD, LICENSE NUMBER 00C2329, OF FORT WORTH, TX, WAS DISCIPLINED BY TEXAS ON JANUARY 28, 1989.
DISCIPLINARY ACTION: SURRENDER OF LICENSE

BARBER, FOREST C MD OF 2929 RACE, FT. WORTH, TX, WAS DISCIPLINED BY DEA ON APRIL 13, 1989.
DISCIPLINARY ACTION: SURRENDER OF CONTROLLED SUBSTANCE LICENSE
OFFENSE: PROFESSIONAL MISCONDUCT
NOTES: TEXAS STATE MEDICAL EXAMINERS CANCELLED LICENSES. VOLUNTARILY SURRENDERED LICENSE IN LIEU OF FORMAL HEARING BEFORE TEXAS STATE MEDICAL EXAMINERS BOARD FOR UNPROFESSIONAL CONDUCT LIKELY TO DECEIVE, DEFRAUD OR INJURE THE PUBLIC.

BARBER, FOREST C MD, DATE OF BIRTH DECEMBER 22, 1917, OF 3001 RACE STREET, FORT WORTH, TX, WAS DISCIPLINED BY MEDICARE ON JULY 28, 1989.
DISCIPLINARY ACTION: EXCLUSION FROM THE MEDICARE AND/OR MEDICAID PROGRAMS
OFFENSE: DISCIPLINARY ACTION BY ANOTHER STATE OR AGENCY
NOTES: LICENSE REVOCATION OR SUSPENSION.

BARON, JAY KENT MD, LICENSE NUMBER 00D5675, OF HOUSTON, TX, WAS DISCIPLINED BY TEXAS ON JUNE 13, 1989.
DISCIPLINARY ACTION: 60-MONTH REQUIRED TO TAKE ADDITIONAL MEDICAL EDUCATION; 60-MONTH MONITORING OF PHYSICIAN
NOTES: OBTAIN CONTINUING MEDICAL EDUCATION; RECEIVE PSYCHIATRIC EVALUATION AND FOLLOW RECOMMENDATIONS; APPEAR BEFORE BOARD IN 1989 AND 1990 AND THEREAFTER SUBMIT LETTER REGARDING PRACTICE; OBTAIN LETTERS OF RECOMMENDATION REFLECTING CALIBER AS PHYSICIAN; OBTAIN BOARD APPROVAL FOR ANY MEDICAL PRACTICE CHANGE.

BARON, JAY KENT DR OF PASADENA, TX, WAS DISCIPLINED BY ILLINOIS ON AUGUST 1, 1991.
DISCIPLINARY ACTION: 60-MONTH LICENSE SUSPENSION
OFFENSE: DISCIPLINARY ACTION BY ANOTHER STATE OR AGENCY
NOTES: DISCIPLINED BY TEXAS FOR FAILING TO PROVIDE ACCEPTABLE MEDICAL TREATMENT TO A PATIENT CONSISTENT WITH PUBLIC HEALTH AND WELFARE. INDEFINITE SUSPENSION FOR A MINIMUM OF FIVE YEARS.

BARON, JAY KENT MD, LICENSE NUMBER 00D5675, OF HOUSTON, TX, WAS DISCIPLINED BY TEXAS ON MARCH 6, 1992.
DISCIPLINARY ACTION: 84-MONTH PROBATION
OFFENSE: PROFESSIONAL MISCONDUCT
NOTES: AIDING OR ABETTING THE PRACTICE OF MEDICINE BY ANY PERSON, PARTNERSHIP, ASSOCIATION OR CORPORATION NOT DULY LICENSED TO PRACTICE MEDICINE BY THE BOARD. LICENSE REVOKED, REVOCATION STAYED; PROBATION UNDER TERMS AND CONDITIONS.

BARTLEY, MICHAEL ALAN MD, LICENSE NUMBER 00H6033, OF HOUSTON, TX, WAS DISCIPLINED BY TEXAS ON MAY 15, 1992.
DISCIPLINARY ACTION: EMERGENCY SUSPENSION

BARTLEY, MICHAEL ALAN MD, LICENSE NUMBER 00H6033, OF HOUSTON, TX, WAS DISCIPLINED BY TEXAS ON JUNE 17, 1992.
DISCIPLINARY ACTION: 12-MONTH LICENSE SUSPENSION
OFFENSE: DRUG OR ALCOHOL ABUSE

BARTLEY, MICHAEL ALAN MD, LICENSE NUMBER 00H6033, WAS DISCIPLINED BY TEXAS ON SEPTEMBER 10, 1993.
DISCIPLINARY ACTION: 120-MONTH PROBATION; RESTRICTION PLACED ON LICENSE
NOTES: PURSUANT TO THE TERMS OF THE 6/17/92 SUSPENSION ORDER HE PROVIDED EVIDENCE TO SHOW THAT HE IS MENTALLY, PHYSICALLY AND OTHERWISE COMPETENT TO PRACTICE MEDICINE INCLUDING PROOF OF A DOCUMENTED AFTERCARE PROGRAM SATISFACTORY TO THE BOARD. SUSPENSION LIFTED AND STAYED. CONDITIONS OF PROBATION: PRACTICE LIMITED TO THAT ASSOCIATED WITH A FELLOWSHIP PROGRAM WITH QUARTERLY REPORTS; SHALL NOT APPLY FOR OR POSSESS ANY DEA OR TEXAS CONTROLLED SUBSTANCES REGISTRATION CERTIFICATES; SHALL ABSTAIN FROM THE CONSUMPTION OF ALCOHOL OR DRUGS IN ANY FORM UNLESS PRESCRIBED BY ANOTHER PHYSICIAN FOR A LEGITIMATE AND THERAPEUTIC PURPOSE; SHALL PARTICIPATE IN AA NOT LESS THAN TWICE A WEEK WITH QUARTERLY REPORTS TO THE BOARD; SHALL PARTICIPATE IN ACTIVITIES OF A PHYSICIAN COUNSELING COMMITTEE WITH QUARTERLY REPORTS; SHALL SUBMIT HIMSELF FOR APPROPRIATE EXAMS INCLUDING DRUG OR ALCOHOL SCREENS; SHALL GIVE A COPY OF THIS ORDER TO ANY HEALTH CARE ENTITY WHERE HE HAS PRIVILEGES; SHALL COOPERATE WITH THE BOARD IN VERIFYING COMPLIANCE; SHALL INFORM BOARD OF CHANGE OF ADDRESS WITHIN 10 DAYS OR IF HE LEAVES THE STATE; TIME SPENT OUT OF TEXAS DOES NOT COUNT TOWARD PROBATION. ON 11/24/93 THIS ORDER MODIFIED BECAUSE OF A LACK OF

AVAILABILITY OF A FELLOWSHIP PROGRAM UNTIL 7/1/94; HIS MEDICAL PRACTICE WILL BE LIMITED TO THAT ASSOCIATED WITH TWO HOSPITALS WITH SUPERVISOR MAKING QUARTERLY REPORTS UNTIL FELLOWSHIP BECOMES AVAILABLE.

BASKIN, TONEY W MD OF FORT BRAGG, NC, WAS DISCIPLINED BY LOUISIANA ON OCTOBER 22, 1992.
DISCIPLINARY ACTION: 36-MONTH PROBATION
OFFENSE: DISCIPLINARY ACTION BY ANOTHER STATE OR AGENCY
NOTES: ADMINISTRATIVE ACTION TAKEN BY TEXAS; HABITUAL OR RECURRING ABUSE OF DRUGS, INCLUDING ALCOHOL. SUBJECT TO CONTINUING FULL COMPLIANCE WITH ORDER PREVIOUSLY ENTERED BY TEXAS; PRIOR NOTICE TO BOARD OF INTENT TO RELOCATE PRACTICE TO LOUISIANA; ABSTINENCE FROM THE USE OF ALCOHOL AND OTHER MOOD-ALTERING SUBSTANCES.

BASKIN, TONEY WILLIAM MD, LICENSE NUMBER 00D8502, OF FORT BRAGG, NC, WAS DISCIPLINED BY TEXAS ON MARCH 6, 1992.
DISCIPLINARY ACTION: 36-MONTH PROBATION
OFFENSE: DISCIPLINARY ACTION BY ANOTHER STATE OR AGENCY
NOTES: DISCIPLINARY ACTION TAKEN BY ANOTHER STATE OR UNIFORMED SERVICES OF THE UNITED STATES FOR INTEMPERATE USE OF ALCOHOL OR DRUGS. LICENSE SUSPENDED, SUSPENSION STAYED; PROBATION UNDER TERMS AND CONDITIONS. PROBATION TERMINATED ON 6/22/94.

BATTLE, CLINTON C MD, DATE OF BIRTH JANUARY 4, 1927, OF BOX 423, PORT GIBSON, MS, WAS DISCIPLINED BY MEDICARE ON NOVEMBER 18, 1988.
DISCIPLINARY ACTION: EXCLUSION FROM THE MEDICARE AND/OR MEDICAID PROGRAMS
OFFENSE: DISCIPLINARY ACTION BY ANOTHER STATE OR AGENCY
NOTES: LICENSE REVOCATION OR SUSPENSION.

BATTLE, CLINTON CHARLES MD, LICENSE NUMBER 00F1368, OF FORT WORTH, TX, WAS DISCIPLINED BY TEXAS ON DECEMBER 3, 1990.
DISCIPLINARY ACTION: RESTRICTION PLACED ON CONTROLLED SUBSTANCE LICENSE; REQUIRED TO TAKE ADDITIONAL MEDICAL EDUCATION
OFFENSE: FAILURE TO COMPLY WITH A PROFESSIONAL RULE
NOTES: FAILED TO KEEP INVENTORIES AND RECORDS OF CONTROLLED SUBSTANCES DISPENSED; FAILED TO CREATE RECORDS ADEQUATE TO SUPPORT PRESCRIPTION DECISIONS. SHALL NOT PRESCRIBE, ORDER, ADMINISTER, OR DISPENSE SCHEDULE II CONTROLLED SUBSTANCES TO ANY PERSON EXCEPT FOR PATIENTS WHO ARE ADMITTED TO A HOSPITAL OR A HOSPITAL EMERGENCY ROOM; SHALL NOT PRESCRIBE, ADMINISTER, OR DISPENSE SEDATIVES OR STIMULANT MEDICATIONS FOR ANY PATIENT FOR LONGER THAN 90 DAYS IN ANY ONE-YEAR PERIOD; SHALL NOT PRESCRIBE, ADMINISTER, OR DISPENSE ANY NARCOTIC DRUG TO A PATIENT FOR RELIEF OF CHRONIC OR ACUTE PAIN FOR LONGER THAN 60 DAYS IN ANY ONE-YEAR PERIOD; SHALL MAINTAIN ADEQUATE MEDICAL RECORDS ON ALL PATIENT OFFICE VISITS AND MAKE PATIENT MEDICAL RECORDS AVAILABLE FOR COPYING AND EVALUATION BY INVESTIGATORS, CONSULTANTS OR MEMBERS OF THE BOARD; SHALL ENROLL IN, AND SUBSEQUENTLY COMPLETE WITHIN 12 MONTHS FROM THE DATE OF THIS ORDER, A 2 WEEK PRECEPTORSHIP ON THE PREVENTION AND TREATMENT OF DRUG ABUSE; SHALL MAINTAIN IN A FILE SEPARATE FROM PATIENT RECORDS, A COPY OF EVERY PRESCRIPTION WRITTEN FOR CONTROLLED SUBSTANCES AND DANGEROUS DRUGS, BY DATE ISSUED, AND SUCH FILE OF PRESCRIPTION COPIES SHALL BE AVAILABLE FOR INSPECTION BY INVESTIGATORS OR AGENTS OF THE BOARD DURING REGULAR OFFICE HOURS WITHOUT NOTICE; SHALL APPEAR BEFORE THE BOARD OR A COMMITTEE OF THE BOARD SEMIANNUALLY, WHEN REQUESTED IN WRITING. RESTRICTIONS TERMINATED EFFECTIVE 2/6/92; LICENSE FREE OF ANY RESTRICTION OR LIMITATION.

BATTLE, ROBERT MCREE MD, LICENSE NUMBER 00D2355, OF HOUSTON, TX, WAS DISCIPLINED BY TEXAS ON OCTOBER 26, 1990.
DISCIPLINARY ACTION: 24-MONTH PROBATION; REPRIMAND
NOTES: MUST OBTAIN CONTINUING MEDICAL EDUCATION; PERFORM PHYSICAL EXAMINATIONS AND TAKE HISTORY BEFORE PERFORMING OTHER TESTS ON OR TREATING ANY PATIENT.

BAUM, SHELDON E DO, LICENSE NUMBER 0OS2499, OF BORGER, TX, WAS DISCIPLINED BY FLORIDA ON OCTOBER 22, 1987.
DISCIPLINARY ACTION: NONRENEWAL OF LICENSE
OFFENSE: DISCIPLINARY ACTION BY ANOTHER STATE OR AGENCY

BAUMAN, DALE V MD OF SHREVEPORT, LA, WAS DISCIPLINED BY LOUISIANA ON JANUARY 29, 1992.
DISCIPLINARY ACTION: 36-MONTH PROBATION; FINE
OFFENSE: PROVIDING FALSE INFORMATION TO THE BOARD
NOTES: FRAUD, DECEIT OR PERJURY IN OBTAINING A LICENSE; PROFESSIONAL OR MEDICAL INCOMPETENCY. PROBATION INCLUDES CONTINUING PROCTORING AND REVIEW OF ALL SURGICAL PROCEDURES WITH QUARTERLY REPORTS TO THE BOARD, SUCCESSFUL PASSAGE OF RECERTIFICATION EXAMINATION OF AMERICAN BOARD OF OBSTETRICS AND GYNECOLOGY, $3000 FINE.

BAUMAN, DALE VICTOR MD, LICENSE NUMBER 00E5348, OF SHREVEPORT, LA, WAS DISCIPLINED BY TEXAS ON AUGUST 20, 1992.
DISCIPLINARY ACTION: 36-MONTH PROBATION
OFFENSE: DISCIPLINARY ACTION BY ANOTHER STATE OR AGENCY
NOTES: SUSPENSION, STAYED. PROBATION UNDER TERMS AND CONDITIONS.

BAURER, MARTIN MD OF HEWITT, TX, WAS DISCIPLINED BY ILLINOIS ON OCTOBER 1, 1994.
DISCIPLINARY ACTION: PROBATION
OFFENSE: DISCIPLINARY ACTION BY ANOTHER STATE OR AGENCY
NOTES: DISCIPLINED IN TEXAS. INDEFINITE PROBATION.

BAURER, MARTIN E MD, LICENSE NUMBER 00F5829, OF GATESVILLE, TX, WAS DISCIPLINED BY TEXAS ON AUGUST 20, 1992.
DISCIPLINARY ACTION: 36-MONTH PROBATION
OFFENSE: FAILURE TO COMPLY WITH A PROFESSIONAL RULE
NOTES: FAILURE TO KEEP COMPLETE AND ACCURATE RECORDS OF PURCHASES AND DISPOSALS OF CONTROLLED SUBSTANCES. ORDERED TO UNDERGO A PSYCHIATRIC EXAM. SUSPENSION, STAYED. PROBATION UNDER TERMS AND CONDITIONS. ON 1/14/94 ORDER MODIFIED SO THAT THE REQUIREMENT THAT HE PARTICIPATE IN ACTIVITIES OF THE CORYELL OR MCCLENNAN COUNTY MEDICAL SOCIETY ON PHYSICIAN HEALTH AND REHABILITATION IS DELETED; REQUIRED

TO MAKE ANNUAL APPEARANCES BEFORE THE BOARD DURING EACH YEAR OF PROBATION.

BECK, KEITH DEXTER MD, LICENSE NUMBER 00G0607, OF SAN ANTONIO, TX, WAS DISCIPLINED BY TEXAS ON JUNE 10, 1991.
DISCIPLINARY ACTION: 60-MONTH PROBATION; RESTRICTION PLACED ON CONTROLLED SUBSTANCE LICENSE
OFFENSE: DRUG OR ALCOHOL ABUSE
NOTES: INTEMPERATE USE OF ALCOHOL OR DRUGS. CONDITIONS OF PROBATION: SHALL APPEAR BEFORE THE BOARD ONCE A YEAR; SHALL NOT PRESCRIBE TO OR TREAT IMMEDIATE FAMILY; MAY ADMINISTER TO SELF OR FAMILY ONLY DRUGS PRESCRIBED BY OTHER PHYSICIANS; DEA AND DPS REGISTRATIONS LIMITED TO SCHEDULES III, III-N, IV AND V; SHALL SURRENDER ALL UNUSED TRIPLICATE PRESCRIPTION FORMS; SHALL SUBMIT TO DRUG AND ALCOHOL SCREENS; SHALL PARTICIPATE IN IMPAIRED PHYSICIANS PROGRAM; SHALL PARTICIPATE IN AA NOT LESS THAN THREE TIMES PER WEEK.

BECK, KEITH DEXTER MD, LICENSE NUMBER 00G0607, OF SAN ANTONIO, TX, WAS DISCIPLINED BY TEXAS ON AUGUST 20, 1992.
DISCIPLINARY ACTION: 45-MONTH PROBATION
OFFENSE: SUBSTANDARD CARE, INCOMPETENCE, OR NEGLIGENCE
NOTES: PROFESSIONAL FAILURE TO PRACTICE MEDICINE IN AN ACCEPTABLE MANNER CONSISTENT WITH PUBLIC HEALTH AND WELFARE. SUSPENSION, STAYED. PLACED ON PROBATION UNDER TERMS AND CONDITIONS UNTIL 6/10/96. IF HE IS NOT BOARD CERTIFIED BY THIS DATE, THE PROBATION CONTINUES INDEFINITELY UNTIL HE GETS CERTIFICATION.

BECK, KEITH DEXTER MD, LICENSE NUMBER 00G0607, OF 11 DEVONWOOD, SAN ANTONIO, TX, WAS DISCIPLINED BY DEA ON OCTOBER 29, 1993.
DISCIPLINARY ACTION: RESTRICTION PLACED ON CONTROLLED SUBSTANCE LICENSE
OFFENSE: DISCIPLINARY ACTION BY ANOTHER STATE OR AGENCY
NOTES: LICENSE RESTRICTED FOR SELF PRESCRIBING RITALIN AND DEVELOPING AN ADDICTION TO THE DRUG. RESTRICTED BY TEXAS STATE BOARD TO SCHEDULES III, IIIN, IV AND V.

BECKSTROM, HARRIETT M P DO, LICENSE NUMBER 00E4970, WAS DISCIPLINED BY TEXAS ON OCTOBER 5, 1991.
DISCIPLINARY ACTION: 60-MONTH RESTRICTION PLACED ON LICENSE
OFFENSE: DISCIPLINARY ACTION BY ANOTHER STATE OR AGENCY
NOTES: A HOSPITAL REMOVED ANESTHESIA PRIVILEGES ON 2/4/87; SHE NEITHER ADMITS NOR DENIES VIOLATING MEDICAL PRACTICE ACT. TERMS AND CONDITIONS OF RESTRICTION ARE AS FOLLOWS: SHALL REFRAIN FROM PERFORMING GENERAL ANESTHESIA, AND SHALL NOT PETITION THE BOARD FOR MODIFICATION OF THIS ORDER FOR A PERIOD OF AT LEAST ONE YEAR; SHALL COOPERATE WITH THE BOARD IN VERIFYING COMPLIANCE; SHALL ADVISE THE BOARD OF A CHANGE OF ADDRESS WITHIN 10 DAYS; TIME SPENT OUT OF TEXAS DOES NOT COUNT TOWARD RESTRICTION.

BEDNER, TOM DAVID MD, LICENSE NUMBER 00D3149, OF HOUSTON, TX, WAS DISCIPLINED BY TEXAS ON JANUARY 6, 1995.
DISCIPLINARY ACTION: LICENSE SUSPENSION
OFFENSE: DRUG OR ALCOHOL ABUSE
NOTES: HAS NOT PRACTICED FOR APPROXIMATELY THE LAST TWO YEARS DUE TO A REPORTED DISABILITY FROM DEPRESSION, ANXIETY, PANIC DISORDER AND ALCOHOLISM; HAS A HISTORY OF CHRONIC AND ACUTE ALCOHOLISM FOR WHICH HE RECEIVED TREATMENT IN 1987 AND 1991; RELAPSES IN 4/94, 9/94 AND 11/94 LED TO HOSPITAL ADMISSIONS; PARTICIPATING IN TREATMENT AND ATTENDS AA ON A REGULAR BASIS; IN LIEU OF FURTHER INVESTIGATION HE AGREES TO THIS ORDER. SUSPENSION UNTIL HE PERSONALLY APPEARS BEFORE THE BOARD AND PROVIDES SUFFICIENT EVIDENCE WHICH INDICATES HE IS PHYSICALLY, MENTALLY AND OTHERWISE COMPETENT TO SAFELY PRACTICE INCLUDING BUT NOT LIMITED TO COPIES OF MEDICAL RECORDS AND REPORTS OF PSYCHOLOGICAL AND NEUROPSYCHIATRIC EVALUATIONS.

BELUE, JOE BILL MD, LICENSE NUMBER 00D2088, OF TYLER, TX, WAS DISCIPLINED BY TEXAS ON JUNE 22, 1994.
DISCIPLINARY ACTION: REPRIMAND; REQUIRED TO TAKE ADDITIONAL MEDICAL EDUCATION
OFFENSE: SUBSTANDARD CARE, INCOMPETENCE, OR NEGLIGENCE
NOTES: MISTAKENLY ARTIFICIALLY INSEMINATED A FEMALE PATIENT DUE TO RELYING TOO MUCH ON THE CHART PLACED ON THE DOOR OF THE EXAMINING ROOM; PATIENT WENT TO ROOM WHEN NURSE CALLED A NAME THAT WAS SIMILAR TO BUT NOT HERS; WAS SCHEDULED FOR A VAGINAL EXAM; HE FAILED TO PROMPTLY INFORM PATIENT OF MISTAKE UNTIL SHE TELEPHONED THAT AFTERNOON; APOLOGIZED IN WRITING TO PATIENT AND INSERTED THAT LETTER IN FILE; DID NOT SPECIFICALLY MARK THE ERROR DOWN ON PATIENT CHART AS HE FELT THE LETTER WAS SUFFICIENT. CONDITIONS OF THREE YEAR RESTRICTION: SHALL ATTEND AT LEAST 50 HOURS PER YEAR OF CONTINUING MEDICAL EDUCATION WITH AT LEAST ONE COURSE IN RISK MANAGEMENT AND OFFICE PROCEDURE; SHALL APPEAR BEFORE THE BOARD ONCE A YEAR; SHALL MAINTAIN ADEQUATE RECORDS ON ALL PATIENT OFFICE VISITS WHICH SHALL BE AVAILABLE FOR INSPECTION; SHALL NOT SIGN ANY PATIENT CHARTS UNLESS HE HAS PERSONALLY EXAMINED THE PATIENT UNLESS THE CHART CLEARLY REFLECTS THAT HE DID NOT; SHALL UTILIZE AN ADEQUATE SYSTEM OF PATIENT RECORD KEEPING; SHALL GIVE A COPY OF THIS ORDER TO ANY HEALTH CARE ENTITY WHERE HE HAS PRIVILEGES; SHALL COOPERATE WITH THE BOARD IN VERIFYING COMPLIANCE; SHALL INFORM BOARD OF CHANGE OF ADDRESS WITHIN 10 DAYS OR IF HE LEAVES THE STATE; TIME SPENT OUT OF TEXAS DOES NOT COUNT TOWARD RESTRICTION. SHALL NOT SEEK MODIFICATION FOR ONE YEAR. ON 10/13/95 ORDER TERMINATED BASED ON COMPLIANCE WITH TERMS AND CHANGES HE HAS EFFECTED IN HIS OFFICE PRACTICE.

BENDEL, WILLIAM JR MD OF MINNETONKA, MN, WAS DISCIPLINED BY LOUISIANA ON MARCH 24, 1988.
DISCIPLINARY ACTION: LICENSE REVOCATION
OFFENSE: DISCIPLINARY ACTION BY ANOTHER STATE OR AGENCY
NOTES: REVOCATION OF LICENSE BY ANOTHER STATE.

BENDEL, WILLIAM L JR MD, LICENSE NUMBER 0017501, WAS DISCIPLINED BY MINNESOTA ON NOVEMBER 21, 1987.
DISCIPLINARY ACTION: SURRENDER OF LICENSE
OFFENSE: DRUG OR ALCOHOL ABUSE
NOTES: MUST SURRENDER LICENSE IN MINNESOTA AND ALSO

IN INDIANA, LOUISIANA, MICHIGAN, TEXAS AND ANY OTHER STATE WHERE HE IS LICENSED

BENDEL, WILLIAM L JR MD, LICENSE NUMBER 0021039, OF 14501 ATRIUM WAY, MINNETONKA, MN, WAS DISCIPLINED BY INDIANA ON DECEMBER 16, 1987.
DISCIPLINARY ACTION: SURRENDER OF LICENSE

BENDEL, WILLIAM L JR MD, LICENSE NUMBER 0017861, WAS DISCIPLINED BY MICHIGAN ON SEPTEMBER 21, 1988.
DISCIPLINARY ACTION: SURRENDER OF LICENSE

BENDEL, WILLIAM L JR MD, LICENSE NUMBER 00D3457, OF MINNETONKA, MN, WAS DISCIPLINED BY TEXAS ON SEPTEMBER 24, 1988.
DISCIPLINARY ACTION: SURRENDER OF LICENSE
OFFENSE: DISCIPLINARY ACTION BY ANOTHER STATE OR AGENCY
NOTES: DUE TO STIPULATION AND ORDER WITH MINNESOTA BOARD; TEXAS BOARD FOUND HE HAD VIOLATED THE MEDICAL PRACTICE ACT AND REVOKED HIS LICENSE.

BENZAQUEN, MATHEWS MD, LICENSE NUMBER 00D3560, OF SAN ANTONIO, TX, WAS DISCIPLINED BY TEXAS ON NOVEMBER 11, 1994.
DISCIPLINARY ACTION: SURRENDER OF CONTROLLED SUBSTANCE LICENSE; LICENSE SUSPENSION
OFFENSE: OVERPRESCRIBING OR MISPRESCRIBING DRUGS
NOTES: IN 1991 DEA INVESTIGATED HIM FOR NON-THERAPEUTIC PRESCRIBING; TWO AGENTS OBTAINED PHENTERMINE FROM HIM FROM 3/7/91 THROUGH 11/13/91 BY REPRESENTING THEMSELVES AS TRUCK DRIVERS WHO WANTED TO STAY AWAKE FOR LONG PERIODS OF TIME; THE DRUGS WERE DISPENSED BY DR. BENZAQUEN DIRECTLY FROM HIS OFFICE; SUBSEQUENTLY SURRENDERED HIS OFFICE SUPPLY OF PHENTERMINE TO DEA DIVERSION; HE INFORMED BOARD HE HAD ORDERED PHENTERMINE TO BEGIN A DIET PROGRAM IN THE AREA OF HIS OFFICE PRACTICE; ON 7/23/93 AN AGREED JUDGMENT ASSESSING A FINE OF $5,000 WAS ENTERED AGAINST HIM IN SETTLEMENT TO RESOLVE THE ALLEGATIONS; BOARD FOUND HIS MEDICAL RECORDS FAILED TO SUPPORT OR OTHERWISE PROVIDE A LEGITIMATE MEDICAL BASIS FOR DISPENSING AND THAT PRESCRIBING OF PAIN MEDICATIONS TO ONE PATIENT WAS EXCESSIVE. SUSPENSION STAYED AFTER SEVEN DAYS. CONDITIONS OF FIVE-YEAR PROBATION: SHALL SURRENDER DEA AND TEXAS CONTROLLED SUBSTANCES CERTIFICATES, ALL UNUSED TRIPLICATE PRESCRIPTION FORMS, AND ALL CONTROLLED SUBSTANCES IN HIS POSSESSION INCLUDING SAMPLES; SHALL NOT SEEK REREGISTRATION WITHOUT PERMISSION; SHALL MAINTAIN ADEQUATE MEDICAL RECORDS ON ALL PATIENT OFFICE VISITS WHICH SHALL BE AVAILABLE FOR INSPECTION; SEPARATE FROM PATIENT RECORDS SHALL MAINTAIN A LOG OF EVERY PRESCRIPTION FOR DANGEROUS DRUGS WHICH SHALL BE AVAILABLE FOR INSPECTION; SHALL NOT TELEPHONE PRESCRIPTIONS TO A PHARMACY FOR DANGEROUS DRUGS OR PERMIT OTHER PEOPLE TO DO SO ON HIS BEHALF; SHALL ATTEND AT LEAST 50 HOURS PER YEAR OF CONTINUING MEDICAL EDUCATION WITH AT LEAST 20 HOURS IN PHARMACOLOGY OR ADDICTIONOLOGY DURING THE FIRST YEAR; WITHIN ONE YEAR SHALL PASS THE SPEX EXAM AND THE MEDICAL JURISPRUDENCE EXAM; SHALL APPEAR BEFORE THE BOARD ONCE A YEAR; SHALL GIVE A COPY OF THIS ORDER TO ANY HEALTH CARE ENTITY WHERE HE HAS PRIVILEGES; SHALL COOPERATE WITH THE BOARD IN VERIFYING COMPLIANCE; SHALL INFORM BOARD OF CHANGE OF ADDRESS WITHIN 10 DAYS OR IF HE LEAVES THE STATE; TIME SPENT OUT OF TEXAS DOES NOT COUNT TOWARD PROBATION. SHALL NOT SEEK MODIFICATION FOR ONE YEAR.

BEREZOSKI, ROBERT N MD, LICENSE NUMBER 0C37375, OF DAYTON, OH, WAS DISCIPLINED BY CALIFORNIA ON MAY 21, 1990.
DISCIPLINARY ACTION: SURRENDER OF LICENSE
NOTES: VOLUNTARY SURRENDER ACCEPTED WHILE CHARGES PENDING.

BEREZOSKI, ROBERT N MD, LICENSE NUMBER 00E0812, OF STAFFORD, TX, WAS DISCIPLINED BY TEXAS ON MAY 24, 1990.
OFFENSE: DISCIPLINARY ACTION BY ANOTHER STATE OR AGENCY
NOTES: STIPULATED ORDER. MUST SUBMIT TO PSYCHIATRIST FOR EVALUATION/TREATMENT, APPEAR FOR ANNUAL REPORT TO BOARD, INFORM TEXAS BOARD OF ANY CHANGES IN OHIO MEDICAL LICENSURE STATUS OR CONCERNING FELONY CONVICTION IN OHIO RESULTING FROM PENDING LEGAL ACTION. ORDER EFFECTIVE FOR FIVE YEARS.

BERGES, BENJAMIN MD, LICENSE NUMBER 0096099, OF 435 WEST MERRICK ROAD, FREEPORT, NY, WAS DISCIPLINED BY NEW YORK ON JANUARY 31, 1994.
DISCIPLINARY ACTION: LICENSE REVOCATION
OFFENSE: CRIMINAL CONVICTION OR PLEA OF GUILTY, NOLO CONTENDERE, OR NO CONTEST TO A CRIME
NOTES: CONVICTED OF SEXUAL ABUSE IN THE SECOND DEGREE.

BERGES, BENJAMIN MD, DATE OF BIRTH OCTOBER 19, 1935, OF 435 WEST MERRICK ROAD, FREEPORT, NY, WAS DISCIPLINED BY MEDICARE ON JULY 17, 1994.
DISCIPLINARY ACTION: EXCLUSION FROM THE MEDICARE AND/OR MEDICAID PROGRAMS
OFFENSE: DISCIPLINARY ACTION BY ANOTHER STATE OR AGENCY
NOTES: LICENSE REVOKED FOR REASONS BEARING ON PROFESSIONAL PERFORMANCE.

BERGES, BENJAMIN MD, LICENSE NUMBER 00G0356, OF 435 WEST MERRICK ROAD, FREEPORT, NY, WAS DISCIPLINED BY TEXAS ON SEPTEMBER 30, 1994.
DISCIPLINARY ACTION: SURRENDER OF LICENSE
OFFENSE: DISCIPLINARY ACTION BY ANOTHER STATE OR AGENCY
NOTES: ON 12/23/92 PLED GUILTY TO AND WAS CONVICTED OF SEXUAL ABUSE IN THE SECOND DEGREE; THE PERSON INVOLVED WAS A PATIENT; HE WAS SENTENCED TO THREE YEARS PROBATION; ON 10/20/93 NEW YORK LICENSE WAS REVOKED BASED ON THE CRIMINAL CONVICTION. SHALL NOT PETITION THE BOARD FOR REINSTATEMENT OF HIS TEXAS LICENSE.

BERKSON, BURTON MD OF EL PASO, TX, WAS DISCIPLINED BY KANSAS ON NOVEMBER 30, 1988.
NOTES: STIPULATION, UNSPECIFIED

BERNDT, JACK EDWARD MD, LICENSE NUMBER 00H0177, OF GALVESTON, TX, WAS DISCIPLINED BY TEXAS ON DECEMBER 1, 1988.
NOTES: SETTLEMENT AGREEMENT AND UNSPECIFIED DISCIPLINARY ACTION

BERRY, G L DO, DATE OF BIRTH FEBRUARY 8, 1939, LICENSE

NUMBER 00F3409, OF 130 DAFFODIL, LAKE JACKSON, TX, WAS DISCIPLINED BY TEXAS ON JUNE 15, 1993.
DISCIPLINARY ACTION: EMERGENCY SUSPENSION
OFFENSE: DRUG OR ALCOHOL ABUSE
NOTES: APPEARED ON 4/20/93 TO DISCUSS ALLEGATIONS OF INTEMPERATE USE OF DRUGS AND ALCOHOL; BOARD RECEIVED INFORMATION THAT HE OFTEN SMELLED OF ALCOHOL WHEN PERFORMING DUTIES AS PHYSICIAN; HAD RECEIVED TREATMENT IN 1992 IN CALIFORNIA FOR ALCOHOL ABUSE; BOARD CHOSE TO RECOMMEND CLOSING THAT INVESTIGATION DUE TO LACK OF EVIDENCE; ON 5/20/93 HE APPEARED FOR DUTY UNDER THE INFLUENCE OF ALCOHOL AND WAS DISCIPLINED BY EMPLOYER.

BERRY, G L DO, DATE OF BIRTH FEBRUARY 8, 1939, LICENSE NUMBER 00F3409, OF 130 DAFFODIL, LAKE JACKSON, TX, WAS DISCIPLINED BY TEXAS ON AUGUST 20, 1993.
DISCIPLINARY ACTION: LICENSE SUSPENSION
OFFENSE: DRUG OR ALCOHOL ABUSE
NOTES: UNABLE TO PRACTICE WITH REASONABLE SKILL AND SAFETY BECAUSE OF THE INTEMPERATE USE OF ALCOHOL. SUSPENSION UNTIL SUCH TIME AS HE PERSONALLY APPEARS BEFORE BOARD TO PROVIDE SUFFICIENT EVIDENCE TO SHOW HE IS COMPETENT TO PRACTICE INCLUDING A CURRENT PSYCHIATRIC EXAMINATION; SHALL GIVE A COPY OF THIS ORDER TO ANY HEALTH CARE ENTITY WHERE HE HAS PRIVILEGES; SHALL COOPERATE WITH THE BOARD IN VERIFYING COMPLIANCE; SHALL INFORM BOARD OF CHANGE OF ADDRESS WITHIN 10 DAYS.

BERRY, RICHARD WILLIAM MD, LICENSE NUMBER 00E0814, OF AUSTIN, TX, WAS DISCIPLINED BY TEXAS ON JUNE 22, 1994.
DISCIPLINARY ACTION: REQUIRED TO TAKE ADDITIONAL MEDICAL EDUCATION; MONITORING OF PHYSICIAN
OFFENSE: DRUG OR ALCOHOL ABUSE
NOTES: ADMITTED TO THE USE OF MARIJUANA ON A LIMITED BASIS PRIOR TO 3/91; IS CURRENTLY COUNSELED AND TREATED BY A PSYCHIATRIST; VOLUNTARILY ADMITTED HIMSELF FOR RECOVERY TREATMENT IN 2/91 AND SIGNED AN AFTERCARE AGREEMENT; REVIEW OF RECORDS REVEALED NO EVIDENCE OF IMPROPER PATIENT CARE; SELF-PRESCRIBED AND INGESTED FIORICET IN 9/92 DUE TO SEVERE HEADACHES; DENIES ANY VIOLATION OF THE RULE AGAINST INTEMPERATE USE OF ALCOHOL OR DRUGS THAT COULD ENDANGER THE LIVES OF PATIENTS BUT DESIRES TO RESOLVE THIS MATTER AND THUS SIGNED THE FOLLOWING AGREED ORDER. CONDITIONS OF FIVE YEAR RESTRICTION: SHALL CONTINUE COUNSELING WITH PRESENT PSYCHIATRIST WITH QUARTERLY REPORTS; SHALL OBTAIN SERVICES OF A PRIMARY CARE PHYSICIAN AND INFORM THE BOARD WHO THIS IS; SHALL ABSTAIN FROM THE CONSUMPTION OF ALCOHOL OR DRUGS WITH ADDICTIVE POTENTIAL IN ANY FORM UNLESS PRESCRIBED, DISPENSED OR AUTHORIZED BY ANOTHER PHYSICIAN FOR A LEGITIMATE OR THERAPEUTIC PURPOSE; SHALL SUBMIT HIMSELF FOR APPROPRIATE EXAMS INCLUDING DRUG OR ALCOHOL SCREENS; SHALL PARTICIPATE IN AA'S PROGRAM AT LEAST TWICE A WEEK WITH QUARTERLY REPORTS TO THE BOARD; SHALL NOT TREAT OR OTHERWISE SERVE AS PHYSICIAN, PRESCRIBE, DISPENSE OR ADMINISTER DRUGS THAT MAY BE SUBJECT TO ABUSE TO HIMSELF OR ANY MEMBER OF HIS FAMILY; SHALL ATTEND AT LEAST 50 HOURS PER YEAR OF CONTINUING MEDICAL EDUCATION; SHALL APPEAR BEFORE THE BOARD ONCE A YEAR; SHALL GIVE A COPY OF THIS ORDER TO ANY HEALTH CARE ENTITY WHERE HE HAS PRIVILEGES; SHALL COOPERATE WITH THE BOARD IN VERIFYING COMPLIANCE; SHALL INFORM BOARD OF CHANGE OF ADDRESS WITHIN 10 DAYS OR IF HE LEAVES THE STATE; TIME SPENT OUT OF TEXAS DOES NOT COUNT TOWARD RESTRICTION. SHALL NOT SEEK MODIFICATION FOR ONE YEAR.

BERRY, RONALD E MD, LICENSE NUMBER 0TXF217, OF 1318 W NOEL, RT.1, BOX 1A, MEMPHIS, TX, WAS DISCIPLINED BY DEA ON JULY 11, 1989.
DISCIPLINARY ACTION: RESTRICTION PLACED ON CONTROLLED SUBSTANCE LICENSE
OFFENSE: OVERPRESCRIBING OR MISPRESCRIBING DRUGS
NOTES: EXCESSIVE AND NONTHERAPEUTIC PRESCRIBING OF CONTROLLED SUBSTANCES

BETTY, CLAUDE W MD OF 3020 GARNETT DRIVE, PERRYTON, TX, WAS DISCIPLINED BY MEDICARE ON NOVEMBER 20, 1986.
DISCIPLINARY ACTION: 48-MONTH EXCLUSION FROM THE MEDICARE AND/OR MEDICAID PROGRAMS
OFFENSE: SUBSTANDARD CARE, INCOMPETENCE, OR NEGLIGENCE
NOTES: GROSSLY SUBSTANDARD CARE IN 10 CASES; LACK OF DIAGNOSTIC EVALUATION AND TREATMENT OF SEVERE MEDICAL CONDITIONS; LACK OF UNDERSTANDING OF THE BASIC MEDICAL TREATMENT CONCEPT IN FLUID BALANCE AND ELECTROLYTES, ANTIBIOTICS AND BACTERIOLOGY, TREATMENT OF CARDIAC AND PULMONARY DISEASE

BIANCHINE, JOSETTE W MD, LICENSE NUMBER 0082807, OF CEDAR GROVE, NJ, WAS DISCIPLINED BY NEW YORK ON JULY 16, 1986.
DISCIPLINARY ACTION: 12-MONTH PROBATION
NOTES: 1 YEAR SUSPENSION, STAYED

BIANCHINE, JOSETTE W MD OF CEDAR GROVE, NJ, WAS DISCIPLINED BY TEXAS ON DECEMBER 1, 1986.
DISCIPLINARY ACTION: SURRENDER OF LICENSE

BIANCHINE, JOSETTE W MD WAS DISCIPLINED BY OHIO ON JANUARY 14, 1988.
DISCIPLINARY ACTION: LICENSE REINSTATEMENT; RESTRICTION PLACED ON CONTROLLED SUBSTANCE LICENSE
NOTES: CONSENT AGREEMENT. MAY NOT PRESCRIBE OR DISPENSE ADDICTIVE DRUGS.IF SHE INTENDS TO PRACTICE IN OHIO, BOARD MAY REQUIRE PRIOR EVALUATION.

BIANCHINE, JOSETTE W MD, DATE OF BIRTH MARCH 20, 1929, LICENSE NUMBER 000D605, WAS DISCIPLINED BY MARYLAND ON JANUARY 28, 1991.
DISCIPLINARY ACTION: PROBATION; REPRIMAND
OFFENSE: DISCIPLINARY ACTION BY ANOTHER STATE OR AGENCY
NOTES: ON 1/11/82 SHE PLEADED GUILTY TO 7 COUNTS OF MAKING, UTTERING OR SELLING A FALSE OR FORGED PRESCRIPTION IN COURT OF COMMON PLEAS, FRANKLIN COUNTY, OHIO. OHIO SUSPENDED LICENSE ON 7/14/82, THEN STAYED THE SUSPENSION SUBJECT TO THE FOLLOWING CONDITIONS: MUST NOT PRESCRIBE ANY HABIT FORMING DRUGS; MUST APPEAR QUARTERLY BEFORE BOARD. WHEN SHE FAILED TO APPEAR, OHIO SUSPENDED HER LICENSE ON 12/4/83. IN APPLYING FOR MARYLAND RENEWAL ON

8/31/84 SHE LIED ABOUT LICENSE BEING SUSPENDED IN ANOTHER STATE AND ABOUT THE CONVICTION. NEW YORK SUSPENDED LICENSE 6/24/86 BASED ON OHIO ACTION. FAILED TO SUBMIT AN APPLICATION FOR RENEWAL OF MARYLAND LICENSE ON OR BEFORE 9/30/86. OHIO REINSTATED LICENSE SUBJECT TO CONDITIONS ON 12/4/87. LIED ON 12/29/88 APPLICATION FOR REINSTATEMENT OF MARYLAND LICENSE. LICENSE GRANTED ON FOLLOWING CONDITIONS OF PROBATION: SIGNED RELEASES AUTHORIZING BOARD TO OBTAIN INFORMATION FROM ANY RELEVANT INDIVIDUALS OR ORGANIZATIONS; MUST TAKE AND PASS SPEX WITH A SCORE OF 75; MAY NOT PRACTICE UNTIL A PRACTICE SETTING IS APPROVED; MUST ARRANGE FOR MONTHLY REPORTS FROM SUPERVISOR. MAY PETITION FOR PERMISSION TO PRACTICE WITHOUT SUPERVISION AFTER ONE YEAR.

BIANCHINE, JOSETTE W MD, DATE OF BIRTH MARCH 20, 1929, OF PO BOX 304, CEDAR GROVE, NJ, WAS DISCIPLINED BY NEW JERSEY ON FEBRUARY 8, 1991.
DISCIPLINARY ACTION: DENIAL OF NEW LICENSE
OFFENSE: PROVIDING FALSE INFORMATION TO THE BOARD
NOTES: SUBMITTED INACCURATE INFORMATION ON HER APPLICATION BY SAYING THAT SHE HAD NEVER BEEN CHARGED WITH OR CONVICTED OF A CRIME, AND FAILED TO NOTE ACTIONS BY TEXAS AND NEW YORK.

BIBEAU, GUY R MD, LICENSE NUMBER 000T580, OF SAN ANGELO, TX, WAS DISCIPLINED BY SOUTH CAROLINA ON FEBRUARY 15, 1990.
DISCIPLINARY ACTION: RESTRICTION PLACED ON LICENSE
NOTES: TEMPORARY LICENSE ISSUED WITH CONDITIONS

BICKERS, PETER W MD, LICENSE NUMBER 00G6267, OF AMARILLO, TX, WAS DISCIPLINED BY TEXAS ON APRIL 15, 1994.
DISCIPLINARY ACTION: SURRENDER OF LICENSE
NOTES: IN LIEU OF FURTHER INVESTIGATION OR A HEARING ON ALLEGATIONS. SHALL NOT PETITION FOR REINSTATEMENT.

BIDDIX, JERRY WAYNE MD, LICENSE NUMBER 00E3855, OF BUNA, TX, WAS DISCIPLINED BY TEXAS ON DECEMBER 1, 1988.
NOTES: SETTLEMENT AGREEMENT AND UNSPECIFIED DISCIPLINARY ACTION. ON 06/11/91 LICENSE FREE OF ANY RESTRICTION OF LIMITATION.

BIDDIX, JERRY WAYNE MD OF TX, WAS DISCIPLINED BY NORTH CAROLINA ON MARCH 15, 1989.
NOTES: CONSENT ORDER, UNSPECIFIED.

BIGGS, CHARLES R DO, DATE OF BIRTH DECEMBER 31, 1931, LICENSE NUMBER 00D9747, OF INGRAM HILLS ROAD, INGRAM, TX, WAS DISCIPLINED BY TEXAS ON FEBRUARY 4, 1988.
DISCIPLINARY ACTION: RESTRICTION PLACED ON LICENSE
NOTES: MUST REFRAIN FROM PERFORMING SURGICAL OR NON-SURGICAL INVASIVE PROCEDURES (NOT INCLUDING INJECTIONS, IMMUNIZATIONS, EMG STUDIES OR INJECTION OF TRIGGER POINTS FOR PATIENTS WITH MYOFACIAL PROBLEMS). ON 8/20/93 BOARD GRANTED TERMINATION OF THIS ORDER; LICENSE FREE AND CLEAR OF ANY PREVIOUS RESTRICTIONS.

BIGGS, CHARLES R DO OF FT WORTH, TX, WAS DISCIPLINED BY OHIO ON AUGUST 9, 1989.
DISCIPLINARY ACTION: LICENSE SUSPENSION
NOTES: INDEFINITE SUSPENSION

BIGGS, CHARLES R DO OF AUSTIN, TX, WAS DISCIPLINED BY MISSOURI ON FEBRUARY 28, 1990.
DISCIPLINARY ACTION: RESTRICTION PLACED ON LICENSE
OFFENSE: DISCIPLINARY ACTION BY ANOTHER STATE OR AGENCY
NOTES: AGREEMENT NOT TO PERFORM SURGERY OR NON-SURGICAL INVASIVE PROCEDURES.

BILDERBACK, ROBERT D MD, LICENSE NUMBER 00D3822, OF SAN ANTONIO, TX, WAS DISCIPLINED BY TEXAS ON NOVEMBER 5, 1988.
DISCIPLINARY ACTION: LICENSE REVOCATION
OFFENSE: PHYSICAL OR MENTAL ILLNESS INHIBITING THE ABILITY TO PRACTICE WITH SKILL AND SAFETY
NOTES: UNABLE TO PRACTICE WITH REASONABLE SKILL AND SAFETY BY REASON OF ILLNESS AND MENTAL CONDITION; FAILED TO PRACTICE IN ACCEPTABLE MANNER CONSISTENT WITH PUBLIC HEALTH AND WELFARE

BILDERBACK, ROBERT D MD OF ST. LOUIS, MO, WAS DISCIPLINED BY MISSOURI ON DECEMBER 7, 1988.
DISCIPLINARY ACTION: LICENSE REVOCATION
OFFENSE: DISCIPLINARY ACTION BY ANOTHER STATE OR AGENCY
NOTES: ALSO MENTAL ILLNESS AND INABILITY TO PRACTICE WITH REASONABLE SKILL AND CARE.

BILDERBACK, ROBERT DOUG MD, LICENSE NUMBER C032983, OF SAN ANTONIO, TX, WAS DISCIPLINED BY CALIFORNIA ON JANUARY 30, 1991.
DISCIPLINARY ACTION: LICENSE REVOCATION
OFFENSE: DISCIPLINARY ACTION BY ANOTHER STATE OR AGENCY
NOTES: DISCIPLINED BY TEXAS BOARD AND MISSOURI BOARD FOR MENTAL ILLNESS. DEFAULT DECISION.

BILLIG, DONAL M MD, LICENSE NUMBER 0080740, OF WASHINGTON, DC, WAS DISCIPLINED BY NEW YORK ON MAY 13, 1987.
DISCIPLINARY ACTION: LICENSE REVOCATION

BILLIG, DONAL M DR, LICENSE NUMBER 0030537, WAS DISCIPLINED BY MASSACHUSETTS ON JUNE 3, 1987.
DISCIPLINARY ACTION: LICENSE REVOCATION
OFFENSE: CRIMINAL CONVICTION OR PLEA OF GUILTY, NOLO CONTENDERE, OR NO CONTEST TO A CRIME
NOTES: GROSS MISCONDUCT. REINSTATEMENT ON 9/20/89.

BILLIG, DONAL M MD, LICENSE NUMBER 00D4388, OF KANSAS CITY, MO, WAS DISCIPLINED BY TEXAS ON OCTOBER 1, 1987.
DISCIPLINARY ACTION: EMERGENCY SUSPENSION
OFFENSE: DISCIPLINARY ACTION BY ANOTHER STATE OR AGENCY
NOTES: DISCIPLINARY ACTION TAKEN BY UNIFORMED SERVICES OF THE U.S.

BILSING, WILLIAM ALBERT MD, LICENSE NUMBER 00C2986, OF NORMANGEE, TX, WAS DISCIPLINED BY TEXAS ON JANUARY 14, 1994.
DISCIPLINARY ACTION: SURRENDER OF CONTROLLED SUBSTANCE LICENSE; 60-MONTH PROBATION
OFFENSE: OVERPRESCRIBING OR MISPRESCRIBING DRUGS
NOTES: ALLEGATIONS CONCERNING HIS NON-THERAPEUTIC PRESCRIBING OF CONTROLLED SUBSTANCES TO 11 PATIENTS, AT LEAST ONE OF WHICH WAS ALLEGED TO BE A SUBSTANCE ABUSER; FAILED TO KEEP ANY MEDICAL REPORTS ON ANY OF THESE PATIENTS. CONDITIONS OF PROBATION: SHALL MAINTAIN ADEQUATE MEDICAL RECORDS ON ALL PATIENT OFFICE VISITS AND SHALL MAKE THESE RECORDS AVAILABLE

FOR REVIEW; SHALL SURRENDER DEA AND TEXAS CONTROLLED SUBSTANCES CERTIFICATIONS AND SHALL NOT ATTEMPT TO REREGISTER THESE WITHOUT PERMISSION; PUBLIC REPRIMAND; SHALL GIVE A COPY OF THIS ORDER TO ANY HEALTH CARE ENTITY WHERE HE HAS PRIVILEGES; SHALL COOPERATE WITH THE BOARD IN VERIFYING COMPLIANCE; SHALL INFORM BOARD OF CHANGE OF ADDRESS WITHIN 10 DAYS OR IF HE LEAVES THE STATE; TIME SPENT OUT OF TEXAS OR IN OFFICIAL RETIRED STATUS WITH THE BOARD DOES NOT COUNT TOWARD PROBATION. SHALL NOT SEEK MODIFICATION FOR ONE YEAR.

BILSING, WILLIAM ALBERT MD, LICENSE NUMBER 00C2986, OF #1 WILSON NURSERY ROAD, NORMANGEE, TX, WAS DISCIPLINED BY DEA ON FEBRUARY 11, 1994.
DISCIPLINARY ACTION: SURRENDER OF CONTROLLED SUBSTANCE LICENSE

BIRDWELL, LARRY RAY DO, LICENSE NUMBER 00F6445, OF HONEY GROVE, TX, WAS DISCIPLINED BY TEXAS ON NOVEMBER 9, 1991.
DISCIPLINARY ACTION: LICENSE SUSPENSION
OFFENSE: DRUG OR ALCOHOL ABUSE
NOTES: SUSPENDED INDEFINITELY.

BIRDWELL, LARRY RAY DO, LICENSE NUMBER 00F6445, WAS DISCIPLINED BY TEXAS ON DECEMBER 2, 1991.
DISCIPLINARY ACTION: SURRENDER OF CONTROLLED SUBSTANCE LICENSE; LICENSE SUSPENSION
OFFENSE: DRUG OR ALCOHOL ABUSE
NOTES: ENGAGED IN THE INTEMPERATE USE OF ALCOHOL OR DRUGS THAT COULD ENDANGER THE LIVES OF HIS PATIENTS. AS A RESULT OF THIS, ON 11/8/91 HE SIGNED AN INITIAL IMPAIRED PHYSICIANS CONTRACT WITH THE TEXAS OSTEOPATHIC MEDICAL ASSOCIATION, IN WHICH HE AGREED TO ENTER INTO A TREATMENT PROGRAM. CONDITIONS OF HIS SUSPENSION ARE AS FOLLOWS: SHALL SURRENDER HIS DEA AND TEXAS CONTROLLED SUBSTANCE REGISTRATION CERTIFICATES; SHALL SURRENDER ALL UNUSED TRIPLICATE PRESCRIPTION FORMS IN HIS POSSESSION, AND SHALL NOT ATTEMPT TO ORDER ANY MORE TRIPLICATE PRESCRIPTION FORMS UNTIL HE HAS WRITTEN AUTHORITY; SHALL SURRENDER ALL CONTROLLED SUBSTANCES, INCLUDING SAMPLES, PRESENTLY IN HIS POSSESSION, AND MAY NOT POSSESS ANY CONTROLLED SUBSTANCES IN THE FUTURE; SHALL GIVE A COPY OF THIS ORDER TO ALL HOSPITALS WHERE HE HAS PRIVILEGES; SHALL COOPERATE WITH THE BOARD IN VERIFYING COMPLIANCE; SHALL ADVISE THE BOARD OF ANY CHANGE OF ADDRESS WITHIN 10 DAYS.

BIRDWELL, LARRY RAY DO, LICENSE NUMBER 00F6445, OF SAN MARCOS, TX, WAS DISCIPLINED BY TEXAS ON JUNE 26, 1992.
DISCIPLINARY ACTION: 60-MONTH PROBATION
NOTES: REQUEST FOR LIFTING OF SUSPENSION IMPOSED 11/9/91 GRANTED; LICENSE SUSPENDED, SUSPENSION STAYED. PROBATION UNDER TERMS AND CONDITIONS. ON 8/19/94 ORDER MODIFIED AS FOLLOWS: REQUIREMENT TO PARTICIPATE IN THE ACTIVITIES OF THE PHYSICIANS ASSISTANCE PROGRAM COMMITTEE AND TO ABIDE BY THE TERMS OF HIS 24 MONTH AFTERCARE PROGRAM CONTRACT IS DELETED.

BITTLE, CHARLES CARROLL JR MD, LICENSE NUMBER 00H0184, OF SANGER, TX, WAS DISCIPLINED BY TEXAS ON APRIL 15, 1994.
DISCIPLINARY ACTION: REQUIRED TO TAKE ADDITIONAL MEDICAL EDUCATION
OFFENSE: SUBSTANDARD CARE, INCOMPETENCE, OR NEGLIGENCE
NOTES: FAILED TO PERFORM SUFFICIENT FOLLOW-UP VISITS ON NINE GERIATRIC PATIENTS ADMITTED TO A HOSPITAL; ONE WAS DISCHARGED WITH A HIGH FEVER; DR. BITTLE IS PRESENTLY WORKING IN PRIMARILY AN ADMINISTRATIVE CAPACITY. FOR THREE YEARS LICENSE UNDER THE FOLLOWING RESTRICTIONS: SHALL ATTEND AT LEAST 50 HOURS PER YEAR OF CONTINUING MEDICAL EDUCATION INCLUDING AT LEAST 10 HOURS IN RISK MANAGEMENT OR RECORD-KEEPING COURSES; SHALL MAINTAIN ADEQUATE MEDICAL RECORDS ON ALL PATIENT OFFICE VISITS WHICH SHALL BE AVAILABLE FOR INSPECTION; SHALL NOT SIGN ANY PATIENT RECORD UNLESS HE HAS PERSONALLY EXAMINED THE PATIENT OR CLEARLY NOTES IN THE RECORD THAT HE DID NOT; SHALL APPEAR BEFORE THE BOARD ONCE A YEAR; SHALL GIVE A COPY OF THIS ORDER TO ANY HEALTH CARE ENTITY WHERE HE HAS PRIVILEGES; SHALL COOPERATE WITH THE BOARD IN VERIFYING COMPLIANCE; SHALL INFORM BOARD OF CHANGE OF ADDRESS WITHIN 10 DAYS OR IF HE LEAVES THE STATE; TIME SPENT OUT OF TEXAS DOES NOT COUNT TOWARD RESTRICTION. SHALL NOT SEEK MODIFICATION FOR ONE YEAR.

BLACK, JAMES WILLIAM JR MD, DATE OF BIRTH OCTOBER 2, 1936, LICENSE NUMBER 00D4036, OF 12854 SPURLING DRIVE, DALLAS, TX, WAS DISCIPLINED BY TEXAS ON APRIL 30, 1993.
DISCIPLINARY ACTION: SURRENDER OF LICENSE
OFFENSE: PROFESSIONAL MISCONDUCT
NOTES: BOARD HAS INVESTIGATED ALLEGATIONS OF UNPROFESSIONAL CONDUCT WHICH HE DENIES; RETIRED FROM PRACTICE 1/92. SURRENDER IS PERMANENT; SHALL GIVE A COPY OF THIS ORDER TO ANY HEALTH CARE ENTITY WHERE HE HAS PRIVILEGES.

BLAISDELL, GLENN D MD, LICENSE NUMBER 00C5606, OF COLLEGE STATION, TX, WAS DISCIPLINED BY TEXAS ON OCTOBER 9, 1992.
DISCIPLINARY ACTION: SURRENDER OF LICENSE
NOTES: IN LIEU OF FURTHER DISCIPLINARY ACTION.

BLAISDELL, GLENN D MD OF MOSCOW, ID, WAS DISCIPLINED BY MISSOURI ON MARCH 24, 1994.
DISCIPLINARY ACTION: LICENSE REVOCATION
OFFENSE: DISCIPLINARY ACTION BY ANOTHER STATE OR AGENCY
NOTES: TEXAS LICENSE WAS FINALLY AND UNCONDITIONALLY REVOKED FOR FELONY CONVICTION OF POSSESSION OF A FIREARM, TERMINAL MISCHIEF AND INTEMPERATE USE OF ALCOHOL OR DRUGS. NO REAPPLICATION FOR LICENSE FOR SEVEN YEARS.

BLANCHETT, LEO M III MD, LICENSE NUMBER 00E6240, OF EL PASO, TX, WAS DISCIPLINED BY TEXAS ON SEPTEMBER 28, 1990.
NOTES: MAY NOT PRACTICE MEDICINE UNTIL HE RECEIVES BOARD APPROVAL TO REENTER SUCH PRACTICE OF MEDICINE UNDER TERMS AS BOARD MAY DETERMINE APPROPRIATE, PASSES SPECIAL PURPOSE EXAMINATION, AND PROVIDES BOARD WITH PSYCHIATRIC REPORT; CORRESPOND WITH BOARD REGARDING CURRENT MEDICAL AND OCCUPATIONAL STATUS.

BLANTON, GEORGE E DO OF EL PASO, TX, WAS DISCIPLINED BY TEXAS ON SEPTEMBER 1, 1985.
DISCIPLINARY ACTION: SURRENDER OF LICENSE

BLANTON, GEORGE E DO, LICENSE NUMBER 00S3719, OF CORAL SPRINGS, FL, WAS DISCIPLINED BY FLORIDA ON APRIL 29, 1987.
DISCIPLINARY ACTION: 12-MONTH PROBATION
OFFENSE: DISCIPLINARY ACTION BY ANOTHER STATE OR AGENCY

BLESIUS, CORNELIUS K MD, LICENSE NUMBER 00D4714, OF EL PASO, TX, WAS DISCIPLINED BY TEXAS ON AUGUST 20, 1992.
DISCIPLINARY ACTION: REPRIMAND
OFFENSE: PROFESSIONAL MISCONDUCT
NOTES: CONDUCT LIKELY TO DECEIVE THE PUBLIC.

BLISSARD, PAUL KING MD, LICENSE NUMBER 00F6453, OF HUNTSVILLE, TX, WAS DISCIPLINED BY TEXAS ON DECEMBER 3, 1990.
DISCIPLINARY ACTION: 12-MONTH PROBATION; REQUIRED TO TAKE ADDITIONAL MEDICAL EDUCATION
NOTES: MUST MAINTAIN ADEQUATE MEDICAL RECORDS ON ALL PATIENT OFFICE VISITS; ATTEND AT LEAST 50 HOURS OF CONTINUING MEDICAL EDUCATION APPROVED FOR CATEGORY I CREDITS, AND PROVIDE PROOF OF ATTENDANCE.

BLOCK, ROBERT JEROME MD, LICENSE NUMBER 00C6174, OF LINCOLNWOOD, IL, WAS DISCIPLINED BY TEXAS ON MARCH 6, 1992.
DISCIPLINARY ACTION: SURRENDER OF LICENSE
OFFENSE: DISCIPLINARY ACTION BY ANOTHER STATE OR AGENCY
NOTES: ACTION TAKEN BY ANOTHER STATE BOARD. LICENSE VOLUNTARILY SURRENDERED IN LIEU OF FURTHER DISCIPLINARY ACTION.

BLOSSMAN, ROBERT CHARLES MD, LICENSE NUMBER 00D5591, OF HOUMA, LA, WAS DISCIPLINED BY TEXAS ON OCTOBER 26, 1990.
NOTES: IF DESIRING TO PRACTICE MEDICINE IN TEXAS, MUST DEMONSTRATE TO TEXAS BOARD HIS CAPACITY TO PRACTICE WITH REASONABLE SKILL AND SAFETY AND PROVIDE REPORT ON STATUS OF LOUISIANA LICENSE AND ANY OTHER MEDICAL LICENSE HELD AT THAT TIME; IF GRANTED PERMISSION TO PRACTICE, MAY HAVE IMPOSED PROBATIONARY TERMS AS BOARD MAY DETERMINE APPROPRIATE.

BLUM, JACK MD, LICENSE NUMBER 0C28144, OF FAIR OAKS, CA, WAS DISCIPLINED BY CALIFORNIA ON JUNE 22, 1990.
DISCIPLINARY ACTION: SURRENDER OF LICENSE
NOTES: VOLUNTARY SURRENDER ACCEPTED WHILE CHARGES PENDING.

BLUM, JACK MD, LICENSE NUMBER 0006978, OF CONROE, TX, WAS DISCIPLINED BY MISSISSIPPI ON NOVEMBER 21, 1991.
DISCIPLINARY ACTION: SURRENDER OF LICENSE
OFFENSE: DISCIPLINARY ACTION BY ANOTHER STATE OR AGENCY
NOTES: ACTION TAKEN IN CALIFORNIA.

BLUM, JACK MD, LICENSE NUMBER 0005293, WAS DISCIPLINED BY ARIZONA ON JANUARY 23, 1992.
DISCIPLINARY ACTION: PROBATION
OFFENSE: DISCIPLINARY ACTION BY ANOTHER STATE OR AGENCY
NOTES: CALIFORNIA LICENSE SURRENDERED EFFECTIVE 6/22/90 IN CONJUNCTION WITH DISCIPLINARY PROCEEDINGS PENDING AGAINST HIM IN CALIFORNIA. ADMITTED THAT HE USED OR ADMINISTERED TO HIMSELF CONTROLLED SUBSTANCES AND DANGEROUS DRUGS WHICH CAUSED URINE SAMPLES TO TEST POSITIVE ON SIX TESTS DURING THE PERIOD FROM 4/18/88 THROUGH 6/22/89. DR. BLUM IS GUILTY OF UNPROFESSIONAL CONDUCT FOR USE OF CONTROLLED SUBSTANCES EXCEPT IF PRESCRIBED BY ANOTHER PHYSICIAN FOR USE DURING A PRESCRIBED COURSE OF TREATMENT. SHALL MEET WITH THE ARIZONA BOARD PRIOR TO PRACTICING MEDICINE IN ARIZONA AND SHALL BE SUBJECT TO ANY PSYCHIATRIC, PSYCHOMETRIC AND PHYSICAL EVALUATION OR COMPETENCY TESTS THAT THE BOARD MAY DEEM NECESSARY PRIOR TO PERMITTING HIM TO PRACTICE MEDICINE.

BLUM, JACK MD, LICENSE NUMBER 0003057, OF DALLAS, TX, WAS DISCIPLINED BY VERMONT ON OCTOBER 15, 1992.
OFFENSE: DISCIPLINARY ACTION BY ANOTHER STATE OR AGENCY
NOTES: SURRENDERED LICENSE IN CALIFORNIA ON 3/29/90. DISCIPLINED FOR UNPROFESSIONAL CONDUCT, IN THAT HE ADMITTED HE USED OR ADMINISTERED TO HIMSELF CONTROLLED SUBSTANCES AND DANGEROUS DRUGS WHICH CAUSED URINE SAMPLES TO TEST POSITIVE BETWEEN 1/19/89 AND 6/22/89. IF HE SHOULD REAPPLY FOR LICENSURE IN CALIFORNIA, HIS APPLICATION SHALL BE TREATED AS AN ORIGINAL APPLICATION AND HE SHALL BE REQUIRED TO MEET ALL THE REQUIREMENTS OF A NEW APPLICANT. BEFORE PRACTICING IN VERMONT, WILL APPEAR BEFORE THE BOARD AND BE SUBJECT TO ANY COMPETENCY TESTS THEY DEEM NECESSARY.

BLUM, JACK MD, LICENSE NUMBER 0013563, OF DALLAS, TX, WAS DISCIPLINED BY WASHINGTON ON NOVEMBER 20, 1992.
DISCIPLINARY ACTION: PROBATION
OFFENSE: DISCIPLINARY ACTION BY ANOTHER STATE OR AGENCY
NOTES: CHARGES OF SUSPENSION, REVOCATION, OR RESTRICTION OF THE LICENSE TO PRACTICE IN ANOTHER JURISDICTION. UNABLE TO PRACTICE IN WASHINGTON UNTIL CERTAIN CONDITIONS ARE MET.

BLUM, JACK MD, DATE OF BIRTH JANUARY 9, 1934, LICENSE NUMBER 00D2660, OF 10044 INWOOD ROAD, DALLAS, TX, WAS DISCIPLINED BY TEXAS ON JANUARY 29, 1993.
DISCIPLINARY ACTION: 60-MONTH PROBATION; RESTRICTION PLACED ON CONTROLLED SUBSTANCE LICENSE
OFFENSE: DISCIPLINARY ACTION BY ANOTHER STATE OR AGENCY
NOTES: DISCIPLINED BY CALIFORNIA BOARD FOR SELF-ADMINISTRATION OF DANGEROUS OR CONTROLLED SUBSTANCES LEADING TO SURRENDER OF HIS LICENSE; MISSISSIPPI LICENSE ALSO SURRENDERED ALTHOUGH HE HAD NEVER PRACTICED THERE; DISCIPLINED BY ARIZONA BOARD ALTHOUGH HE NEVER PRACTICED THERE; SELF-ADMINISTERED DIAZEPAM, CODEINE, PHENERGAN, AND PROCARDIA; CURRENTLY PRACTICING IN GEORGIA. 5 YEAR SUSPENSION STAYED. CONDITIONS OF PROBATION: SHALL PARTICIPATE IN ACTIVITIES OF A PHYSICIAN HEALTH AND REHABILITATION COMMITTEE AND ATTEND WEEKLY MEETINGS WITH QUARTERLY REPORTS; SHALL PARTICIPATE IN AA'S 12 STEP PROGRAM NOT LESS THAN 2 TIMES A WEEK WITH QUARTERLY REPORTS; SHALL FURNISH THE BOARD WITH WRITTEN REPORTS ON HIS MEDICAL CONDITION AND COMPLIANCE WITH THIS ORDER WHEN REQUESTED; SHALL ABSTAIN FROM THE CONSUMPTION OF ALCOHOL/CONTROLLED SUBSTANCES IN ANY FORM; SHALL SUBMIT HIMSELF FOR APPROPRIATE EXAMS INCLUDING DRUG OR ALCOHOL SCREENS; SHALL NOT TREAT OR OTHERWISE

SERVE AS THE PHYSICIAN, PRESCRIBE, DISPENSE OR ADMINISTER DRUGS THAT MAY BE SUBJECT TO ABUSE TO HIMSELF OR ANY MEMBER OF HIS FAMILY; SHALL NOT POSSESS, ADMINISTER, DISPENSE OR PRESCRIBE SCHEDULE II OR IIN CONTROLLED SUBSTANCES OUTSIDE OF A HOSPITAL SETTING; SHALL MAINTAIN A SEPARATE LOG OF ALL PRESCRIPTIONS WRITTEN FOR CONTROLLED SUBSTANCES WHICH SHALL BE AVAILABLE FOR INSPECTION; SHALL OBTAIN THE SERVICES OF A PRIMARY CARE PHYSICIAN WHO SHALL RELEASE INFORMATION TO THE BOARD; BOARD WILL BE INFORMED IF ANY DRUG HAVING ADDICTION-FORMING OR ADDICTION-SUSTAINING LIABILITY IS PRESCRIBED; SHALL OBTAIN NO PRESCRIPTIONS FROM ANY OTHER PHYSICIAN UNLESS IT IS APPROVED IN WRITING WITHIN 24 HOURS; ANY PRESCRIPTIONS WRITTEN CAN BE FILLED ONLY AT BOARD-APPROVED PHARMACIES; SHALL BE EVALUATED BY A BOARD-APPROVED PSYCHIATRIST TO WHOM HE WILL PROVIDE A COPY OF THE ORDER; SHALL COOPERATE WITH THE BOARD IN VERIFYING COMPLIANCE; SHALL INFORM BOARD OF CHANGE OF ADDRESS WITHIN 10 DAYS; TIME SPENT OUT OF TEXAS OR GEORGIA DOES NOT COUNT TOWARD PROBATION; SHALL APPEAR BEFORE THE BOARD ONCE A YEAR; SHALL APPEAR BEFORE THE BOARD PRIOR TO PRACTICING IN TEXAS. SHALL NOT SEEK MODIFICATION UNTIL FEBRUARY 6, 1994.

BLUM, JACK MD, DATE OF BIRTH JANUARY 9, 1934, LICENSE NUMBER 0016004, OF 101 BOWENS MILL ROAD, DOUGLAS, GA, WAS DISCIPLINED BY GEORGIA ON JUNE 28, 1993.
DISCIPLINARY ACTION: EMERGENCY SUSPENSION
NOTES: IMPAIRMENT.

BLUM, JACK MD, DATE OF BIRTH JANUARY 9, 1934, LICENSE NUMBER 0016004, OF 10044 INWOOD ROAD, DALLAS, TX, WAS DISCIPLINED BY GEORGIA ON OCTOBER 7, 1993.
DISCIPLINARY ACTION: LICENSE SUSPENSION
NOTES: IMPAIRMENT; SHALL NOT ENGAGE IN OR RETURN TO PRACTICE OF MEDICINE IN GEORGIA UNTIL FURTHER ORDER OF THE BOARD.

BLUM, JACK MD, LICENSE NUMBER 00D2660, OF DALLAS, TX, WAS DISCIPLINED BY TEXAS ON OCTOBER 14, 1993.
DISCIPLINARY ACTION: EMERGENCY SUSPENSION
OFFENSE: FAILURE TO COMPLY WITH A PREVIOUS BOARD ORDER
NOTES: VIOLATED 1/29/93 ORDER IN THAT HE REFUSED TO SUPPLY A URINE SAMPLE IN 8/93 AND INGESTED CONTROLLED SUBSTANCES IN 9/93.

BLUM, JACK MD, LICENSE NUMBER 00D2660, OF 10044 INWOOD ROAD, DALLAS, TX, WAS DISCIPLINED BY DEA ON NOVEMBER 24, 1993.
DISCIPLINARY ACTION: SURRENDER OF CONTROLLED SUBSTANCE LICENSE
NOTES: CONTINUES TO ATTEMPT TO OBTAIN CONTROLLED SUBSTANCES BY CALL-IN PRESCRIPTIONS.

BLUM, JACK MD, LICENSE NUMBER 00D2660, OF DALLAS, TX, WAS DISCIPLINED BY TEXAS ON JUNE 22, 1994.
DISCIPLINARY ACTION: PROBATION
OFFENSE: FAILURE TO COMPLY WITH A PREVIOUS BOARD ORDER
NOTES: VIOLATED 1/29/93 TEXAS ORDER IN THAT HE REFUSED TO SUPPLY A URINE SAMPLE ON 8/26/93, INGESTED CONTROLLED SUBSTANCES THREE TIMES IN 9/93; SURRENDERED HIS DEA CONTROLLED SUBSTANCES REGISTRATION ON 11/22/93. SUSPENSION STAYED. CONDITIONS OF INDEFINITE PROBATION: SHALL NOT PRACTICE MEDICINE UNTIL HE HAS UNDERGONE A 72 HOUR INPATIENT EVALUATION FOR CHEMICAL DEPENDENCY, HAS OBTAINED A COMPLETE NEUROLOGIC EXAM FROM A BOARD-APPROVED PSYCHIATRIST, CAN DEMONSTRATE COMPLIANCE WITH THIS PSYCHIATRIST'S RECOMMENDATIONS AND APPEARS BEFORE THE BOARD TO REQUEST PERMISSION TO PRACTICE. UPON AN ADEQUATE SHOWING BEFORE THE BOARD THAT HE IS ABLE TO SAFELY PRACTICE MEDICINE, HE SHALL BE ALLOWED TO RESUME THE PRACTICE OF MEDICINE UNDER VARIOUS TERMS AND CONDITIONS.

BLUM, JACK MD, LICENSE NUMBER 00D2660, WAS DISCIPLINED BY TEXAS ON JANUARY 5, 1995.
DISCIPLINARY ACTION: 120-MONTH PROBATION; RESTRICTION PLACED ON CONTROLLED SUBSTANCE LICENSE
OFFENSE: FAILURE TO COMPLY WITH A PREVIOUS BOARD ORDER
NOTES: SUSPENSION STAYED. CONDITIONS OF PROBATION: SHALL ABSTAIN FROM THE CONSUMPTION OR ALCOHOL OR CONTROLLED SUBSTANCES IN ANY FORM UNLESS PRESCRIBED BY ANOTHER PHYSICIAN FOR A LEGITIMATE AND THERAPEUTIC PURPOSE; SHALL SUBMIT HIMSELF FOR APPROPRIATE EXAMS INCLUDING DRUG OR ALCOHOL SCREENS; SHALL NOT TREAT OR OTHERWISE SERVE AS PHYSICIAN FOR HIMSELF OR ANY MEMBER OF HIS FAMILY AND SHALL NOT PRESCRIBE, DISPENSE OR ADMINISTER ANY DRUGS THAT MAY BE SUBJECT TO ABUSE TO HIMSELF OR ANY MEMBER OF HIS FAMILY; SHALL ONLY ORDER AND ADMINISTER CONTROLLED SUBSTANCES FOR PERSONS UNDERGOING INPATIENT PROCEDURES AND/OR TREATMENTS AT A HOSPITAL FOR PURPOSES OF INPATIENT CARE; SHALL SURRENDER ALL UNUSED TRIPLICATE PRESCRIPTION FORMS AND CONTROLLED SUBSTANCES IN HIS POSSESSION INCLUDING SAMPLES; SHALL BE MONITORED BY A BOARD-APPROVED PHYSICIAN WITH QUARTERLY REPORTS TO THE BOARD; SEPARATE FROM PATIENT RECORDS SHALL MAINTAIN A FILE OF EVERY PRESCRIPTION WRITTEN FOR DANGEROUS DRUGS WHICH SHALL BE AVAILABLE FOR REVIEW; SHALL NOT TELEPHONE ANY PRESCRIPTION TO A PHARMACY FOR DANGEROUS DRUGS THAT MAY BE HABIT-FORMING; SHALL PARTICIPATE IN THE ACTIVITIES OF A PHYSICIANS' HEALTH AND REHABILITATION COMMITTEE AND ABIDE BY TERMS OF AN AFTERCARE PROGRAM CONTRACT WITH QUARTERLY REPORTS; SHALL PARTICIPATE IN AA'S PROGRAMS NOT LESS THAN THREE TIMES A WEEK WITH QUARTERLY REPORTS TO THE BOARD; SHALL SUBMIT HIMSELF FOR EVALUATION AND TREATMENT TO A BOARD-APPROVED PSYCHIATRIST WITH QUARTERLY REPORTS; SHALL ATTEND AT LEAST 40 HOURS OF CONTINUING MEDICAL EDUCATION PER YEAR; SHALL APPEAR BEFORE THE BOARD TWICE A YEAR; SHALL GIVE A COPY OF THIS ORDER TO ANY HEALTH CARE ENTITY WHERE HE HAS PRIVILEGES; SHALL COOPERATE WITH THE BOARD IN VERIFYING COMPLIANCE; SHALL INFORM BOARD OF CHANGE OF ADDRESS WITHIN 10 DAYS OR IF HE LEAVES THE STATE; TIME SPENT OUT OF TEXAS DOES NOT COUNT TOWARD PROBATION. SHALL NOT SEEK MODIFICATION FOR ONE YEAR.

BLUME, HORST G MD, DATE OF BIRTH MARCH 12, 1926, LICENSE

NUMBER 0017208, OF SIOUX CITY, IA, WAS DISCIPLINED BY IOWA ON FEBRUARY 22, 1990.
DISCIPLINARY ACTION: 60-MONTH PROBATION; 3-MONTH RESTRICTION PLACED ON CONTROLLED SUBSTANCE LICENSE
NOTES: MAY NOT PRESCRIBE ADMINISTER OR DISPENSE CONTROLLED SUBSTANCES EXCEPT IN HOSPITAL

BLUME, HORST G MD WAS DISCIPLINED BY ARIZONA ON JUNE 21, 1991.
OFFENSE: DISCIPLINARY ACTION BY ANOTHER STATE OR AGENCY
NOTES: PLACED ON PROBATION FOR 5 YEARS BY IOWA. BOARD ACCEPTED THE SIGNED STIPULATION AND ORDER SAYING THAT HE WILL NOT PRACTICE MEDICINE IN ARIZONA UNTIL HE HAS FIRST MET WITH THE BOARD.

BLUME, HORST G MD WAS DISCIPLINED BY NEBRASKA ON NOVEMBER 21, 1991.
DISCIPLINARY ACTION: PROBATION
OFFENSE: DISCIPLINARY ACTION BY ANOTHER STATE OR AGENCY

BLUME, HORST G MD OF SIOUX CITY, IA, WAS DISCIPLINED BY MISSOURI ON OCTOBER 1, 1992.
DISCIPLINARY ACTION: 60-MONTH PROBATION
OFFENSE: DISCIPLINARY ACTION BY ANOTHER STATE OR AGENCY
NOTES: ALSO PRESCRIPTION VIOLATIONS.

BLUME, HORST GUNTHER MD, LICENSE NUMBER 00D1551, OF SIOUX CITY, IA, WAS DISCIPLINED BY TEXAS ON OCTOBER 26, 1990.
NOTES: MUST COMPLY WITH IOWA RESTRICTIONS AND AUTHORIZE IOWA BOARD TO RELEASE INFORMATION AS TO STATUS AND PROBATIONARY COMPLIANCE; MUST RECEIVE APPROVAL FROM TEXAS BOARD PRIOR TO PRACTICING MEDICINE IN TEXAS.

BOLIN, DANIEL HUFFMAN MD, LICENSE NUMBER 00E6042, OF WICHITA FALLS, TX, WAS DISCIPLINED BY TEXAS ON OCTOBER 5, 1991.
DISCIPLINARY ACTION: 120-MONTH PROBATION; REQUIRED TO ENTER AN IMPAIRED PHYSICIAN PROGRAM OR DRUG OR ALCOHOL TREATMENT
OFFENSE: DRUG OR ALCOHOL ABUSE
NOTES: INTEMPERATE USE OF HISTUSSIN FROM 9/90 UNTIL 7/91, WHEN HE ENTERED INPATIENT TREATMENT FOR HIS DRUG USE. REVOCATION STAYED AND PUT ON PROBATION WITH FOLLOWING TERMS AND CONDITIONS: SHALL ABSTAIN FROM THE CONSUMPTION OF ALCOHOL/CHEMICAL SUBSTANCES IN ANY FORM; SHALL PARTICIPATE IN THE ACTIVITIES OF THE IMPARIED PHYSICIANS PROGRAM, INCLUDING WEEKLY MEETINGS, WITH QUARTERLY REPORTS TO THE BOARD; SHALL PARTICIPATE IN ALCOHOLICS ANONYMOUS ON A REGULAR BASIS, INCLUDING A 12-STEP PROGRAM, OF NOT LESS THAN FOUR TIMES A WEEK; SHALL SUBMIT HIMSELF FOR RANDOM SCREENS OF BIOLOGICAL FLUIDS; SHALL OBTAIN TREATMENT FROM A BOARD-APPROVED PSYCHIATRIST, WITH QUARTERLY REPORTS TO BOARD; SHALL NOT TREAT OR OTHERWISE SERVE AS THE PHYSICIAN, PRESCRIBE, DISPENSE, OR ADMINISTER CONTROLLED SUBSTANCES, OR ANY OTHER DRUGS THAT MAY BE SUBJECT TO ABUSE, FOR HIMSELF OR ANY MEMBER OF HIS IMMEDIATE FAMILY; SHALL MAINTAIN A LOG BOOK FOR THE RECEIPT AND DISPENSING OF ALL DRUG SAMPLES AND SHALL PROVIDE THEM TO BOARD UPON REQUEST; SHALL APPEAR BEFORE THE BOARD TWICE A YEAR; SHALL COOPERATE WITH BOARD IN VERIFYING COMPLIANCE; SHALL ADVISE THE BOARD OF CHANGE OF ADDRESS WITHIN 10 DAYS; TIME SPENT OUT OF TEXAS DOES NOT COUNT TOWARDS PROBATION.

BOLLING, DAVID RANDOLPH JR MD, LICENSE NUMBER 00D4039, OF SAN ANTONIO, TX, WAS DISCIPLINED BY TEXAS ON APRIL 15, 1994.
DISCIPLINARY ACTION: LICENSE SUSPENSION
OFFENSE: PHYSICAL OR MENTAL ILLNESS INHIBITING THE ABILITY TO PRACTICE WITH SKILL AND SAFETY
NOTES: ON 3/3/94 HE WAS ADJUDGED OF UNSOUND MIND BY A PROBATE COURT; CONSENTED TO THIS ORDER THROUGH HIS GUARDIAN. SUSPENSION UNTIL HE CAN APPEAR BEFORE THE BOARD AND PROVIDE INFORMATION TO PROVE HIS COMPETENCY.

BOMMAKANTI, SWAMISARAN MD, LICENSE NUMBER 0164833, OF OSHKOSH, WI, WAS DISCIPLINED BY NEW YORK ON NOVEMBER 5, 1990.
DISCIPLINARY ACTION: LICENSE SUSPENSION; 36-MONTH PROBATION
NOTES: PARTIAL SUSPENSION UNTIL THE SUCCESSFUL COMPLETION OF RETRAINING COURSES. APPLICATION FOR RECONSIDERATION GRANTED EFFECTIVE 1/28/92; ORDER MODIFIED AND MANDATES THE HEALTH DEPARTMENT TO SELECT, OBTAIN, AND NOTIFY THE PHYSICIAN OF AN ACCEPTABLE RETRAINING PROGRAM OR ACCEPT ONE AS ORDERED BY THE BOARD OF REGENTS.

BOMMAKANTI, SWAMISARAN MD, LICENSE NUMBER 00G8532, OF OSHKOSH, WI, WAS DISCIPLINED BY TEXAS ON JUNE 10, 1991.
DISCIPLINARY ACTION: 60-MONTH PROBATION; RESTRICTION PLACED ON LICENSE
OFFENSE: DISCIPLINARY ACTION BY ANOTHER STATE OR AGENCY
NOTES: DISCIPLINARY ACTION TAKEN BY ANOTHER STATE BOARD DUE TO PROFESSIONAL MISCONDUCT. LICENSE PARTIALLY SUSPENDED IN THE AREA OF SURGERY; UPON TERMINATION OF THE SUSPENSION OF NEW YORK LICENSE, TEXAS LICENSE SHALL BE PLACED ON PROBATION FOR FIVE YEARS; PRIOR TO PRACTICING MEDICINE IN TEXAS, SHALL APPEAR BEFORE AND RECEIVE APPROVAL FROM THE TEXAS BOARD.

BOONE, GEORGE DANIEL MD, LICENSE NUMBER 00F6460, OF KERRVILLE, TX, WAS DISCIPLINED BY TEXAS ON JANUARY 14, 1994.
DISCIPLINARY ACTION: REPRIMAND
OFFENSE: OVERPRESCRIBING OR MISPRESCRIBING DRUGS
NOTES: IN 1991 AFTER ADVISING THE PATIENTS OF THE RISKS OF STEROID USE AND DANGERS OF BLACK MARKET STEROIDS, HE PRESCRIBED ANABOLIC STEROIDS TO TWO PATIENTS FOR NON-MEDICAL PURPOSES RELATED TO WEIGHT GAIN AND BODY BUILDING, NO OTHER COMPLAINTS HAVE BEEN FILED AGAINST HIM WITH BOARD.

BORCHERDING, HARLAN JAMES DO, LICENSE NUMBER 00D7531, OF HOUSTON, TX, WAS DISCIPLINED BY TEXAS ON AUGUST 19, 1994.
DISCIPLINARY ACTION: 120-MONTH PROBATION; RESTRICTION PLACED ON CONTROLLED SUBSTANCE LICENSE
OFFENSE: OVERPRESCRIBING OR MISPRESCRIBING DRUGS
NOTES: ON 3/20/92 HE ENTERED A GUILTY PLEA TO FRAUD OF A CONTROLLED SUBSTANCE, A MISDEMEANOR, AND RECEIVED DEFERRED ADJUDICATION WITH TWO YEARS PROBATION; ON 5/25/94 HE GAVE TESTIMONY IN

REGARD TO A DEA AUDIT OF HIS OFFICE ON 2/19/93 WHICH IDENTIFIED VARIOUS VIOLATIONS PERTAINING TO HIS PRESCRIBING PRACTICES AND RECORD KEEPING; ENTERED INTO A SETTLEMENT AGREEMENT WITH DEA WITH NO ADMISSION OF GUILT; ADMITS TO PREVIOUSLY POOR RECORD KEEPING AND ASSERTS HE IS WORKING TO IMPROVE THIS; DENIES EVER SELLING A PRESCRIPTION. SUSPENSION STAYED. CONDITIONS OF PROBATION: SHALL MAINTAIN ADEQUATE MEDICAL RECORDS ON ALL PATIENT OFFICE VISITS WHICH SHALL BE AVAILABLE FOR INSPECTION; SHALL NOT SIGN ANY PATIENT RECORD UNLESS HE HAS PERSONALLY EXAMINED THE PATIENT OR CLEARLY NOTES IN THE RECORD THAT HE DID NOT; SHALL REQUEST MODIFICATION OF DEA AND TEXAS CONTROLLED SUBSTANCES CERTIFICATES TO BE LIMITED TO SCHEDULES III, IV AND V; SHALL NOT ATTEMPT TO REREGISTER WITHOUT PERMISSION; SHALL PASS THE JURISPRUDENCE EXAM WITHIN ONE YEAR; SHALL COMPLETE A BOARD-APPROVED PHARMACOLOGY COURSE AND AN ETHICS COURSE; SHALL ATTEND AT LEAST 50 HOURS PER YEAR OF CONTINUING MEDICAL EDUCATION; SHALL APPEAR BEFORE THE BOARD TWICE A YEAR; SHALL GIVE A COPY OF THIS ORDER TO ANY HEALTH CARE ENTITY WHERE HE HAS PRIVILEGES; SHALL COOPERATE WITH THE BOARD IN VERIFYING COMPLIANCE; SHALL INFORM BOARD OF CHANGE OF ADDRESS WITHIN 10 DAYS OR IF HE LEAVES THE STATE; TIME SPENT OUT OF TEXAS DOES NOT COUNT TOWARD PROBATION. SHALL NOT SEEK MODIFICATION FOR THREE YEARS.

BORDELON, JERRY PHILLIP MD, LICENSE NUMBER 00D8998, OF AUSTIN, TX, WAS DISCIPLINED BY TEXAS ON NOVEMBER 3, 1994.
DISCIPLINARY ACTION: REPRIMAND
OFFENSE: SUBSTANDARD CARE, INCOMPETENCE, OR NEGLIGENCE
NOTES: ON 11/1/93 HE PERFORMED LASER SURGERY ON A PATIENT TO REMOVE PAPILLOMAS FROM THE THROAT AREA; INDICATORS WERE THAT HELIOX WAS THE REQUIRED ANESTHESIA GAS, HOWEVER, THE ANESTHESIOLOGIST ADMINISTERED ESSENTIALLY PURE OXYGEN; DR. BORDELON WAS NOT AWARE OF THIS AND USED A LASER; AN ACCIDENT ENSUED AND THE PATIENT DIED NEARLY TWO MONTHS LATER FROM COMPLICATIONS; MAINTAINS THE ANESTHESIOLOGIST NEVER WARNED HIM THAT HE ADMINISTERED PURE OXYGEN; NEITHER ADMITS NOR DENIES ALLEGATIONS BUT CONSENTS TO THE ORDER TO REACH AN EXPEDITIOUS RESOLUTION. SHALL WITHIN SIX MONTHS OBTAIN A BOARD-APPROVED COURSE IN RISK MANAGEMENT; SHALL GIVE A COPY OF THIS ORDER TO ANY HEALTH CARE ENTITY WHERE HE HAS PRIVILEGES; SHALL COOPERATE WITH THE BOARD IN VERIFYING COMPLIANCE; SHALL INFORM CHANGE OF ADDRESS WITHIN 10 DAYS. SHALL NOT SEEK MODIFICATION FOR SIX MONTHS.

BORGE, ADOLF NORMAN MD, LICENSE NUMBER 00D1555, OF FORT WORTH, TX, WAS DISCIPLINED BY TEXAS ON MARCH 31, 1990.
DISCIPLINARY ACTION: 60-MONTH PROBATION; REQUIRED TO TAKE ADDITIONAL MEDICAL EDUCATION
NOTES: STIPULATED ORDER. REVOCATION STAYED. MUST ATTEND CONTINUING MEDICAL EDUCATION,OBTAIN WRITTEN CONSULTATIONS ON HOSPITALIZATIONS AND HOSPITAL QUALITY ASSURANCE COMMITTEE. MUST SUBMIT QUARTERLY REPORTS TO BOARD. PROBATION TERMINATED EFFECTIVE 4/30/93; LICENSE FREE OF ANY RESTRICTION OR LIMITATION.

BOUDREAU, DANIEL ALEXANDER DO, LICENSE NUMBER 00D5354, OF MESQUITE, TX, WAS DISCIPLINED BY TEXAS ON JANUARY 6, 1995.
DISCIPLINARY ACTION: 60-MONTH RESTRICTION PLACED ON LICENSE; REQUIRED TO TAKE ADDITIONAL MEDICAL EDUCATION
OFFENSE: SUBSTANDARD CARE, INCOMPETENCE, OR NEGLIGENCE
NOTES: DURING 3/91 PERFORMED A MICRODISKECTOMY AT THE WRONG LEVEL ON A PATIENT DUE TO A MISCALCULATION; THE PATIENT FILED A MALPRACTICE ACTION WHICH WAS SETTLED FOR $200,000; SINCE THEN HE REPORTS REVISING HIS PROCEDURES TO BETTER IDENTIFY THE CORRECT SURGICAL LEVEL; NO LONGER PERFORMING BACK SURGERIES; HE AGREES TO THE ENTRY OF THE ORDER IN LIEU OF FURTHER INVESTIGATION. CONDITIONS OF RESTRICTION: SHALL NOT PERFORM BACK SURGERIES OF ANY KIND BUT MAY ASSIST AT BACK SURGERIES PERFORMED BY ANOTHER SURGEON; SHALL MAINTAIN ADEQUATE MEDICAL RECORDS ON ALL PATIENT OFFICE VISITS WHICH SHALL BE AVAILABLE FOR INSPECTION; SHALL OBTAIN AT LEAST 50 HOURS PER YEAR OF CONTINUING MEDICAL EDUCATION; SHALL APPEAR BEFORE THE BOARD ONCE A YEAR OR UPON REQUEST; SHALL COOPERATE WITH THE BOARD IN VERIFYING COMPLIANCE; SHALL PROVIDE AS NEEDED ALL MEDICAL RELEASES AND RELEASES OF PEER REVIEW RECORDS; SHALL GIVE A COPY OF THIS ORDER TO ANY HEALTH CARE ENTITY WHERE HE HAS OR APPLIES FOR PRIVILEGES AND ANYONE ELSE WHO ASKS FOR IT; SHALL ENSURE ANY INQUIRIES REGARDING HIS TEXAS LICENSURE STATUS ARE ANSWERED BY REFERENCE TO THIS ORDER; SHALL INFORM BOARD OF CHANGE OF ADDRESS WITHIN 10 DAYS OR IF HE LEAVES THE STATE; TIME SPENT OUT OF TEXAS DOES NOT COUNT TOWARD RESTRICTION. SHALL NOT SEEK MODIFICATION FOR ONE YEAR.

BOWERS, STEVEN PAUL MD, LICENSE NUMBER 00E0828, OF DALLAS, TX, WAS DISCIPLINED BY TEXAS ON OCTOBER 27, 1989.
DISCIPLINARY ACTION: 60-MONTH MONITORING OF PHYSICIAN
OFFENSE: DRUG OR ALCOHOL ABUSE

BOWLER, DONALD L MD, LICENSE NUMBER 00D2928, OF HUNTSVILLE, TX, WAS DISCIPLINED BY TEXAS ON AUGUST 24, 1991.
DISCIPLINARY ACTION: LICENSE SUSPENSION
OFFENSE: CRIMINAL CONVICTION OR PLEA OF GUILTY, NOLO CONTENDERE, OR NO CONTEST TO A CRIME
NOTES: FELONY CONVICTION OF FRAUD IN THE PRESCRIPTION AND DELIVERY OF A CONTROLLED SUBSTANCE.

BOYCE, ALFRED EVERSLEY DO, DATE OF BIRTH NOVEMBER 8, 1929, LICENSE NUMBER 00F0898, OF 1007 15TH STREET, WELLINGTON, TX, WAS DISCIPLINED BY TEXAS ON JANUARY 29, 1993.
DISCIPLINARY ACTION: 60-MONTH PROBATION; RESTRICTION PLACED ON LICENSE
OFFENSE: LOSS OR RESTRICTION OF HOSPITAL PRIVILEGES
NOTES: ON 1/16/91 HOSPITAL PRIVILEGES WERE RESTRICTED DUE TO INSUFFICIENT DOCUMENTATION OF QUALIFICATIONS TO DO SURGERY BY THE CHILLICOTHE HOSPITAL; THEY TERMINATED HIS CONTRACT 8/91 DUE TO AN UNACCEPTABLE COMPLICATION RATE DURING

SURGERY. A BOARD REVIEW OF 20 PATIENT CHARTS REVEALED THE FOLLOWING DEFICIENCIES: FAILED TO ADEQUATELY DOCUMENT THE HISTORY AND TREATMENT OF PATIENTS; FAILED TO DEMONSTRATE AN ADEQUATE KNOWLEDGE OF PHARMACOLOGY OR AN ABILITY TO CARE FOR PATIENTS IN ACUTE AND CRITICAL CARE EMERGENCIES; DID NOT RECOGNIZE CONGESTIVE HEART FAILURE AND DIABETIC KETOACIDOSIS; FAILED TO TRANSFER PATIENTS IN A TIMELY MANNER. 5 YEAR SUSPENSION STAYED. CONDITIONS OF PROBATION: SHALL TAKE AND PASS THE SPEX EXAM; SHALL TAKE AT LEAST 50 CREDITS CONTINUING MEDICAL EDUCATION PER YEAR; SHALL BE MONITORED BY A BOARD-APPROVED PHYSICIAN WITH BI-MONTHLY REPORTS TO THE BOARD; WITHIN THREE MONTHS SHALL ENROLL IN A PHARMACOLOGY RETRAINING COURSE; SHALL COMPLETE AN INTENSIVE REVIEW COURSE OF AREAS RELEVANT TO FAMILY PRACTICE, INCLUDING HANDS-ON WORKSHOPS WITHIN 6 MONTHS; SHALL BE ACCEPTED IN A SPECIFIED PERSONALIZED CONTINUING MEDICAL EDUCATION ACUTE MINI-RESIDENCY WITHIN ONE MONTH WHICH SHALL BE APPROVED BY THE BOARD; SHALL MAINTAIN ADEQUATE MEDICAL RECORDS ON ALL PATIENT OFFICE VISITS; SHALL COMPLETE AN ADVANCED CARDIAC LIFE SUPPORT PROGRAM AND AN ADVANCED TRAUMA LIFE SUPPORT PROGRAM; IS RESTRICTED FROM PERFORMING ANY MAJOR SURGERY IN AN OUTPATIENT OR HOSPITAL SETTING; SHALL GIVE A COPY OF THIS ORDER TO ANY HEALTH CARE ENTITY WHERE HE HAS PRIVILEGES; SHALL COOPERATE WITH THE BOARD IN VERIFYING COMPLIANCE; SHALL INFORM BOARD OF CHANGE OF ADDRESS WITHIN 10 DAYS OR IF HE LEAVES THE STATE; TIME SPENT OUT OF TEXAS DOES NOT COUNT TOWARD PROBATION; SHALL NOT SEEK MODIFICATION OF THIS ORDER.

BOYCE, ALFRED EVERSLEY DO, DATE OF BIRTH NOVEMBER 8, 1929, LICENSE NUMBER 00F0898, OF 1007 15TH STREET, WELLINGTON, TX, WAS DISCIPLINED BY TEXAS ON MAY 21, 1993.
DISCIPLINARY ACTION: EMERGENCY SUSPENSION
OFFENSE: FAILURE TO COMPLY WITH A PREVIOUS BOARD ORDER
NOTES: AS A CONDITION OF 01/29/93 PROBATION HE WAS ORDERED TO TAKE AND PASS SPEX EXAM; HE DID NOT PASS EXAM 0N 3/18/93. LICENSE SUSPENDED UNTIL HE PASSES THE EXAM.

BOYCE, ALFRED EVERSLEY DO, DATE OF BIRTH NOVEMBER 8, 1929, LICENSE NUMBER 00F0898, OF WELLINGTON, TX, WAS DISCIPLINED BY TEXAS ON APRIL 15, 1994.
DISCIPLINARY ACTION: SURRENDER OF LICENSE
OFFENSE: FAILURE TO COMPLY WITH A PREVIOUS BOARD ORDER
NOTES: DID NOT TAKE THE SPEX EXAM IN 12/93 AS REQUIRED BY A PREVIOUS ORDER; BOARD ALSO RECEIVED ALLEGATIONS OF OTHER VIOLATIONS WHICH HE DENIED. SURRENDER IN LIEU OF FURTHER INVESTIGATION OR A HEARING ON THE ALLEGATIONS. SHALL NOT APPLY FOR REINSTATEMENT OF LICENSE.

BRAMANTI, HENRY R MD, DATE OF BIRTH JUNE 8, 1940, LICENSE NUMBER 00E3214, OF 2512 HORNE STREET SUITE A, FORT WORTH, TX, WAS DISCIPLINED BY TEXAS ON APRIL 30, 1993.
DISCIPLINARY ACTION: 24-MONTH PROBATION; REPRIMAND
OFFENSE: LOSS OR RESTRICTION OF HOSPITAL PRIVILEGES
NOTES: DURING THE COURSE OF A DELIVERY ON 9/23/91 HE INTERACTED WITH STAFF IN AN ABRASIVE AND ABUSIVE MANNER; MADE INSENSITIVE COMMENTS IN THE PRESENCE OF THE PATIENT AND HER HUSBAND; DUE TO COMPLICATIONS THE INFANT SUFFERED A PERIOD OF OXYGEN DEPRIVATION BUT APPARENTLY RECOVERED; AFTER THIS HE ENTERED INTO A CONTINUATION OF PRACTICE AGREEMENT WITH HOSPITAL REQUIRING HIM TO UNDERGO REGULAR COUNSELING WITH A PSYCHIATRIST. CONDITIONS OF PROBATION: SHALL COMPLY WITH ALL TERMS OF CONTINUATION OF PRACTICE AGREEMENT WITH HOSPITAL; SHALL CONTINUE TO RECEIVE COUNSELING WITH QUARTERLY REPORTS; SHALL ATTEND AT LEAST 50 HOURS PER YEAR OF CONTINUING MEDICAL EDUCATION; SHALL APPEAR BEFORE THE BOARD TWICE DURING THE FIRST YEAR OF PROBATION AND AT LEAST ONCE DURING THE SECOND; SHALL GIVE A COPY OF THIS ORDER TO ANY HEALTH CARE ENTITY WHERE HE HAS PRIVILEGES; SHALL COOPERATE WITH THE BOARD IN VERIFYING COMPLIANCE; SHALL INFORM BOARD OF ADDRESS CHANGE WITHIN 10 DAYS OR IF HE LEAVES THE STATE; TIME SPENT OUT OF TEXAS DOES NOT COUNT TOWARD PROBATION. SHALL NOT SEEK MODIFICATION FOR ONE YEAR.

BRANCH, THOMAS COE MD, LICENSE NUMBER 00C8909, OF PLAINVIEW, TX, WAS DISCIPLINED BY TEXAS ON JUNE 22, 1994.
DISCIPLINARY ACTION: 120-MONTH PROBATION; REQUIRED TO TAKE ADDITIONAL MEDICAL EDUCATION
OFFENSE: CRIMINAL CONVICTION OR PLEA OF GUILTY, NOLO CONTENDERE, OR NO CONTEST TO A CRIME
NOTES: ON 5/15/92 DURING REGULAR BUSINESS HOURS ENGAGED IN SEXUAL INTERCOURSE WITH AN EMPLOYEE OF METHODIST HOSPITAL AT HIS MEDICAL OFFICE; ON 5/20/92 CONSUMED AN EXCESSIVE AMOUNT OF ALCOHOL AND BENZODIAZEPINES; IN 1993 ENTERED A PLEA OF NOLO CONTENDERE TO DRIVING WHILE INTOXICATED RELATED TO THIS AND CONSEQUENTLY WAS FINED AND PLACED ON TWO YEARS PROBATION; PRIVILEGES AT METHODIST HOSPITAL WERE SUMMARILY SUSPENDED WHICH HE DID NOT CONTEST OR APPEAL; HAS BEGUN A MONITORING PROGRAM WITH PHYSICIANS HEALTH AND REHABILITATION COMMITTEE AND BEGAN ATTENDING AA ON A REGULAR BASIS. SUSPENSION STAYED. CONDITIONS OF PROBATION: SHALL ABSTAIN FROM THE CONSUMPTION OF ALCOHOL/CHEMICAL SUBSTANCES IN ANY FORM UNLESS PRESCRIBED BY ANOTHER PHYSICIAN FOR A LEGITIMATE AND THERAPEUTIC PURPOSE; SHALL SUBMIT HIMSELF FOR APPROPRIATE EXAMS INCLUDING DRUG OR ALCOHOL SCREENS; SHALL NOT TREAT OR OTHERWISE SERVE AS PHYSICIAN, PRESCRIBE, DISPENSE OR ADMINISTER DRUGS THAT MAY BE SUBJECT TO ABUSE TO HIMSELF OR ANY MEMBER OF HIS FAMILY; SHALL PARTICIPATE IN AA'S PROGRAM NOT LESS THAN THREE TIMES A WEEK WITH QUARTERLY REPORTS TO THE BOARD; SHALL SUBMIT HIMSELF FOR EVALUATION AND TREATMENT TO A BOARD-APPROVED PSYCHIATRIST WITH QUARTERLY REPORTS; SHALL COMPLETE 10 HOURS OF ETHICS COURSES OR AN ETHICS PROGRAM WITHIN ONE YEAR AND 50 HOURS OF CONTINUING MEDICAL EDUCATION PER YEAR; SHALL APPEAR BEFORE THE BOARD TWICE A YEAR; SHALL GIVE A COPY OF THIS ORDER TO ANY HEALTH CARE ENTITY WHERE HE HAS PRIVILEGES; SHALL COOPERATE WITH THE BOARD IN VERIFYING COMPLIANCE; SHALL INFORM BOARD OF CHANGE OF ADDRESS WITHIN 10 DAYS OR IF HE LEAVES THE STATE; TIME SPENT OUT OF TEXAS DOES NOT COUNT

TOWARD PROBATION. SHALL NOT SEEK MODIFICATION FOR ONE YEAR.

BRANSFORD, PARIS MD, LICENSE NUMBER 00D7920, OF HOUSTON, TX, WAS DISCIPLINED BY TEXAS ON DECEMBER 1, 1989.
DISCIPLINARY ACTION: 6-MONTH LICENSE SUSPENSION; 120-MONTH PROBATION
OFFENSE: PROFESSIONAL MISCONDUCT
NOTES: LICENSE REVOKED/STAYED; DURING SUSPENSION MUST RECEIVE PSYCHIATRIC EVALUATION, TREATMENT AND CONTINUING MEDICAL EDUCATION. PROBATION PERIOD INCLUDES RESTRICTIONS ON GYNECOLOGICAL PRACTICE AND REQUIREMENT TO APPEAR REGULARLY BEFORE THE BOARD. ON APPEAL TO TRAVIS COUNTY DISTRICT COURT. ON 12/04/91 REQUEST FOR TERMINATION OF PROBATION DENIED; REQUEST FOR MODIFICATION OF PROBATION IS GRANTED WITH FOLLOWING CONDITIONS: MAY PRACTICE IN THE OBSTETRICS/GYNECOLOGICAL FIELD; SHALL APPEAR AT THE BOARD ONCE A YEAR TO REPORT ON COMPLIANCE WITH HIS PROBATION AND THE MEDICAL PRACTICE ACT; ALL OTHER TERMS AND CONDITIONS OF ORIGINAL PROBATION REMAIN IN EFFECT.

BRASWELL, ROY B II MD, LICENSE NUMBER 00G2915, OF SULPHUR, LA, WAS DISCIPLINED BY TEXAS ON JANUARY 12, 1991.
NOTES: MUST SUBMIT TO PSYCHIATRIST FOR EVALUATION, IF APPLICABLE, UNDERGO RECOMMENDED TREATMENT

BRASWELL, ROY B II MD OF MONTEREY, LA, WAS DISCIPLINED BY LOUISIANA ON AUGUST 30, 1991.
DISCIPLINARY ACTION: 60-MONTH PROBATION; REQUIRED TO ENTER AN IMPAIRED PHYSICIAN PROGRAM OR DRUG OR ALCOHOL TREATMENT
OFFENSE: DISCIPLINARY ACTION BY ANOTHER STATE OR AGENCY
NOTES: ALSO CHARGED WITH EXCESSIVE USE OF ALCOHOL. PROBATION CONDITIONED ON CONTINUING PSYCHIATRIC TREATMENT AND MONITORING, EXECUTION OF TREATMENT CONTRACT WITH IMPAIRED PHYSICIANS PROGRAM, PERIODIC REPORTS TO BOARD BY SUPERVISING PHYSICIAN, AND OBTAIN SPECIFIED CONTINUING MEDICAL EDUCATION.

BREITENSTEIN, LARRY J DO, DATE OF BIRTH OCTOBER 17, 1942, LICENSE NUMBER 0041326, OF 1110 KINGWOOD DRIVE, SUITE 201, KINGWOOD, TX, WAS DISCIPLINED BY NEW JERSEY ON DECEMBER 16, 1994.
DISCIPLINARY ACTION: 120-MONTH PROBATION; RESTRICTION PLACED ON CONTROLLED SUBSTANCE LICENSE
OFFENSE: DISCIPLINARY ACTION BY ANOTHER STATE OR AGENCY
NOTES: BASED ON ACTION BY TEXAS. TEN YEAR SUSPENSION STAYED. CONDITIONS OF PROBATION: SHALL NOT WRITE ANY PRESCRIPTIONS FOR CONTROLLED SUBSTANCES; SHALL APPEAR BEFORE A COMMITTEE OF THE BOARD TO DISCUSS THE STATUS OF LICENSURE PRIVILEGES IN ALL OTHER JURISDICTIONS, HIS PARTICIPATION IN CONTINUING MEDICAL EDUCATION AND HIS PLANS FOR NEW JERSEY PRACTICE PRIOR TO PRACTICE IN NEW JERSEY.

BREITENSTEIN, LARRY JACK DO, LICENSE NUMBER 00D5923, OF 818 BURNING TREE, KINGWOOD, TX, WAS DISCIPLINED BY TEXAS ON OCTOBER 27, 1993.
DISCIPLINARY ACTION: EMERGENCY SUSPENSION
OFFENSE: DRUG OR ALCOHOL ABUSE
NOTES: BETWEEN 12/92 AND 8/93 ENGAGED IN THE INTEMPERATE USE OF DRUGS INCLUDING COCAINE, VICODIN AND XANAX WHICH COULD ENDANGER THE LIVES OF PATIENTS; ALSO DURING 1993 INJECTED OR OTHERWISE PROVIDED COCAINE TO AN ADULT FEMALE WHO SUBSEQUENTLY DIED OF ACUTE COCAINE TOXICITY ON 8/11/93.

BREITENSTEIN, LARRY JACK DO OF 1110 KINGWOOD DRIVE SUITE 201, KINGWOOD, TX, WAS DISCIPLINED BY DEA ON NOVEMBER 17, 1993.
DISCIPLINARY ACTION: SURRENDER OF CONTROLLED SUBSTANCE LICENSE
OFFENSE: PROFESSIONAL MISCONDUCT
NOTES: SEIZURE OF COCAINE FROM RESIDENCE 08/11/93 IN KINGWOOD TEXAS DURING CONSENT TO SEARCH.

BREITENSTEIN, LARRY JACK DO, LICENSE NUMBER 00D5923, OF KINGWOOD, TX, WAS DISCIPLINED BY TEXAS ON NOVEMBER 19, 1993.
DISCIPLINARY ACTION: LICENSE SUSPENSION; REQUIRED TO ENTER AN IMPAIRED PHYSICIAN PROGRAM OR DRUG OR ALCOHOL TREATMENT
OFFENSE: DRUG OR ALCOHOL ABUSE
NOTES: HAS ATTEMPTED TO GET INPATIENT TREATMENT SINCE EMERGENCY SUSPENSION; HOWEVER ECONOMIC PROBLEMS AND THE SCARCITY OF AVAILABLE BEDS HAS PREVENTED HIS ADMISSION INTO INPATIENT TREATMENT; MAINTAINS HE REMAINS DRUG-FREE SINCE 8/11/93. SUSPENSION UNTIL HE SUCCESSFULLY COMPLETES INPATIENT TREATMENT AND SHOWS THE BOARD HE IS PHYSICALLY, MENTALLY AND OTHERWISE COMPETENT TO SAFELY PRACTICE MEDICINE. SUSPENSION WILL THEN BE STAYED TO 10 YEAR PROBATION WITH CONDITIONS. SHALL NOT SEEK MODIFICATION FOR ONE YEAR.

BRIGGS, ROBERT B DO OF CLIFTON, NJ, WAS DISCIPLINED BY TEXAS ON DECEMBER 1, 1986.
DISCIPLINARY ACTION: SURRENDER OF LICENSE

BRIGGS, ROBERT B DO, LICENSE NUMBER 0OS4222, OF CLIFTON, NJ, WAS DISCIPLINED BY FLORIDA ON JULY 29, 1988.
DISCIPLINARY ACTION: FINE; REPRIMAND
OFFENSE: DISCIPLINARY ACTION BY ANOTHER STATE OR AGENCY
NOTES: FINE OF $1000; CRIMINAL CONVICTION

BRITTAIN, ROBERT D III MD, LICENSE NUMBER 00G4858, OF SAN ANTONIO, TX, WAS DISCIPLINED BY TEXAS ON AUGUST 24, 1991.
DISCIPLINARY ACTION: 60-MONTH PROBATION; MONITORING OF PHYSICIAN
OFFENSE: DRUG OR ALCOHOL ABUSE
NOTES: ALCOHOL ABUSE. LICENSE SUSPENDED, STAYED; SHALL PARTICIPATE IN AA; SHALL CONTINUE TREAMENT FROM DESIGNATED PHYSICIAN; SHALL SUBMIT TO DRUG OR ALCOHOL SCREENS; SHALL APPEAR BEFORE THE BOARD TWICE YEARLY DURING PROBATION.

BRODY, MICHAEL P MD, LICENSE NUMBER 00D5690, OF SANTA ANA, CA, WAS DISCIPLINED BY TEXAS ON APRIL 1, 1987.
DISCIPLINARY ACTION: LICENSE REVOCATION
OFFENSE: LOSS OR RESTRICTION OF HOSPITAL PRIVILEGES
NOTES: SUBMITTED FALSE OR MISLEADING STATEMENT, DOCUMENT OR CERTIFICATE TO BOARD FOR LICENSURE; INTEMPERATELY USED ALCOHOL OR DRUGS THAT COULD ENDANGER PATIENTS; EXHIBITED UNPROFESSIONAL OR DISHONORABLE CONDUCT

LIKELY TO INJURE PUBLIC; UNABLE TO PRACTICE MEDICINE WITH REASONABLE SKILL AND SAFETY TO PATIENTS; FAILED TO PRACTICE MEDICINE IN ACCEPTABLE MANNER; DISCIPLINED BY LICENSED HOSPITAL, SUCH ACTION BASED ON PROFESSIONAL INCOMPETENCE LIKELY TO HARM PUBLIC.

BROECKEL, PHILIP MD, LICENSE NUMBER G002717, OF SAN JUAN, TX, WAS DISCIPLINED BY CALIFORNIA ON DECEMBER 4, 1989.
DISCIPLINARY ACTION: LICENSE REVOCATION
OFFENSE: DISCIPLINARY ACTION BY ANOTHER STATE OR AGENCY
NOTES: DISCIPLINED BY TEXAS FOR CONVICTION OF FOUR SEPARATE FELONIES; DEFAULT DECISION.

BROECKEL, PHILIP G MD, LICENSE NUMBER 00G3950, OF SAN JUAN, TX, WAS DISCIPLINED BY TEXAS ON DECEMBER 1, 1988.
DISCIPLINARY ACTION: LICENSE REVOCATION
OFFENSE: CRIMINAL CONVICTION OR PLEA OF GUILTY, NOLO CONTENDERE, OR NO CONTEST TO A CRIME
NOTES: CONVICTED OF FELONIES INVOLVING SEXUAL INDECENCY WITH CHILD, SEXUAL ASSAULT, AND AGGRAVATED SEXUAL ASSAULT

BROECKEL, PHILLIP G MD, DATE OF BIRTH DECEMBER 8, 1927, OF ROUTE 1, BOX 540, SAN JUAN, TX, WAS DISCIPLINED BY MEDICARE ON APRIL 27, 1989.
DISCIPLINARY ACTION: EXCLUSION FROM THE MEDICARE AND/OR MEDICAID PROGRAMS
OFFENSE: DISCIPLINARY ACTION BY ANOTHER STATE OR AGENCY
NOTES: SUSPENSION OR EXCLUSION UNDER A FEDERAL OR STATE HEALTH CARE PROGRAM.

BROOKS, JESSE MILES MD, LICENSE NUMBER 00B5748, OF ATLANTA, TX, WAS DISCIPLINED BY TEXAS ON AUGUST 18, 1990.
DISCIPLINARY ACTION: REQUIRED TO TAKE ADDITIONAL MEDICAL EDUCATION
NOTES: STIPULATED ORDER. MUST OBTAIN CONTINUING MEDICAL EDUCATION, PARTICIPATE IN PRECEPTORSHIP PROGRAM TO INCLUDE SPECIFIC CURRICULUM, CONCLUDE AGREEMENT REGARDING ACCEPTANCE OF CERTAIN PATIENTS, AND OBTAIN PHYSICIAN TO JOIN HOSPITAL STAFF WHO WILL BE AVAILABLE FOR BACKUP COVERAGE.

BROOKS, JESSE MILES MD, LICENSE NUMBER 00B5748, OF ATLANTA, TX, WAS DISCIPLINED BY TEXAS ON APRIL 15, 1994.
DISCIPLINARY ACTION: MONITORING OF PHYSICIAN
OFFENSE: PROFESSIONAL MISCONDUCT
NOTES: DURING 1990 AND 1991 HE ORDERED EXCESSIVE LAB TESTS AND CHARGED FOR THEM IN THE CASE OF TWO PATIENTS; MADE DIAGNOSES FOR THESE PATIENTS THAT ARE NOT SUPPORTED BY MEDICAL RECORDS AND PRESCRIBED MEDICATIONS TO THEM THAT WERE NOT MEDICALLY INDICATED. CONDITIONS OF ORDER: HE SHALL SUBMIT ONE OUT OF EVERY FIVE PATIENT FILES HOSPITALIZED FOR A PERIOD OF 24 HOURS OR MORE TO A HOSPITAL REVIEW COMMITTEE EACH WEEK; COMMITTEE WILL SUBMIT REPORTS TO BOARD; THE NUMBER OF FILES CHOSEN FOR REVIEW WILL BE REDUCED IF NO PROBLEMS ARE SEEN FOR ONE YEAR; PROGRAM WILL DISCONTINUE IN TWO YEARS IF NO PROBLEMS ARE FOUND; SHALL MAINTAIN ADEQUATE MEDICAL RECORDS AND SHALL MAKE THESE RECORDS AVAILABLE FOR INSPECTION; SHALL REFRAIN FROM PRESCRIBING ANY DRUG THAT IS NOT MEDICALLY INDICATED; SHALL GIVE A COPY OF THIS ORDER TO ANY HEALTH CARE ENTITY WHERE HE HAS PRIVILEGES; SHALL COOPERATE WITH THE BOARD IN VERIFYING COMPLIANCE; SHALL INFORM BOARD OF CHANGE OF ADDRESS WITHIN 10 DAYS OR IF HE LEAVES THE STATE; TIME SPENT OUT OF TEXAS DOES NOT COUNT TOWARD RESTRICTIONS. SHALL NOT SEEK MODIFICATION FOR ONE YEAR.

BROOKS, MARSHALL J J MD, LICENSE NUMBER 00B5369, OF ATLANTA, TX, WAS DISCIPLINED BY TEXAS ON AUGUST 18, 1990.
DISCIPLINARY ACTION: REQUIRED TO TAKE ADDITIONAL MEDICAL EDUCATION
NOTES: STIPULATED ORDER. MUST OBTAIN CONTINUING MEDICAL EDUCATION, PARTICIPATE IN PRECEPTORSHIP PROGRAM TO INCLUDE SPECIFIC CURRICULUM, CONCLUDE AGREEMENT REGARDING ACCEPTANCE OF CERTAIN PATIENTS, AND OBTAIN PHYSICIAN TO JOIN HOSPITAL STAFF WHO WILL BE AVAILABLE FOR BACKUP COVERAGE.

BROOKS, THOMAS C MD, LICENSE NUMBER 00B8251, OF DAYTON, TX, WAS DISCIPLINED BY TEXAS ON DECEMBER 1, 1990.
DISCIPLINARY ACTION: LICENSE REVOCATION
OFFENSE: PROFESSIONAL MISCONDUCT
NOTES: IMPERSONATED A LICENSED PRACTITIONER OR PERMITTED OR ALLOWED ANOTHER TO USE LICENSE TO PRACTICE MEDICINE. AIDED OR ABETTED, DIRECTLY OR INDIRECTLY, THE PRACTICE OF MEDICINE BY ANY PERSON, PARTNERSHIP, ASSOCIATION, OR CORPORATION NOT LICENSED TO PRACTICE.

BROUGH, ROYCE DONALD JR MD, DATE OF BIRTH MAY 7, 1943, LICENSE NUMBER 00E4808, OF 2020 NAOMI, HOUSTON, TX, WAS DISCIPLINED BY TEXAS ON JANUARY 29, 1993.
DISCIPLINARY ACTION: 60-MONTH PROBATION; MONITORING OF PHYSICIAN
OFFENSE: DRUG OR ALCOHOL ABUSE
NOTES: ON 9/14/92 VOLUNTARILY BEGAN A TREATMENT PROGRAM AND WAS SUCCESSFULLY DISCHARGED; HAS ENTERED AN AFTERCARE PROGRAM CONTRACT. 5 YEAR SUSPENSION STAYED. CONDITIONS OF PROBATION: SHALL APPEAR BEFORE THE BOARD ONCE A YEAR; SHALL NOT SELF-TREAT OR OTHERWISE SERVE AS PHYSICIAN, PRESCRIBE, DISPENSE OR ADMINISTER DRUGS THAT MAY BE SUBJECT TO ABUSE FOR HIMSELF OR ANY MEMBER OF HIS FAMILY; SHALL ABSTAIN FROM THE CONSUMPTION OF ALCOHOL/CHEMICAL SUBSTANCES IN ANY FORM UNLESS PRESCRIBED BY ANOTHER PHYSICIAN FOR A LEGITIMATE AND THERAPEUTIC PURPOSE; SHALL PARTICIPATE IN ACTIVITIES OF A PHYSICIAN COUNSELING COMMITTEE WITH QUARTERLY REPORTS; SHALL PARTICIPATE IN AA NOT LESS THAN 3 TIMES A WEEK WITH QUARTERLY REPORTS TO THE BOARD; SHALL SUBMIT HIMSELF FOR APPROPRIATE EXAMS INCLUDING DRUG OR ALCOHOL SCREENS; SHALL CONTINUE TO RECEIVE TREATMENT FROM THE ADDICTIONOLOGIST AND PSYCHIATRIST HE IS NOW SEEING; SHALL FURNISH THE BOARD WITH WRITTEN REPORTS ON HIS MEDICAL CONDITION AND COMPLIANCE WITH THIS ORDER WHEN REQUESTED; SHALL COMPLY WITH THE TERMS OF HIS AFTERCARE CONTRACT; SHALL GIVE A COPY OF THIS ORDER TO ANY HEALTH CARE ENTITY WHERE HE HAS PRIVILEGES; SHALL COOPERATE WITH THE BOARD IN VERIFYING COMPLIANCE; SHALL INFORM THE BOARD OF CHANGE OF ADDRESS OR IF HE LEAVES THE STATE; TIME SPENT OUT OF TEXAS DOES NOT COUNT TOWARD

PROBATION. SHALL NOT SEEK MODIFICATION FOR 1 YEAR.

BROUGH, ROYCE DONALD JR MD, DATE OF BIRTH MAY 7, 1943, LICENSE NUMBER 0006701, OF 400 SECOND AVE NORTH, AMORY, MS, WAS DISCIPLINED BY MISSISSIPPI ON JULY 15, 1993.
DISCIPLINARY ACTION: PROBATION; MONITORING OF PHYSICIAN
OFFENSE: DISCIPLINARY ACTION BY ANOTHER STATE OR AGENCY
NOTES: BASED ON ACTIONS IN TEXAS. FIVE YEAR SUSPENSION STAYED; HE IS SUBJECT TO TERMS AND CONDITIONS INCLUDING RANDOM, UNANNOUNCED AND WITNESSED BLOOD AND URINE SCREENS.

BROWN, CYNTHIA A MD, LICENSE NUMBER 0D26655, OF 16816 5TH AVENUE SE, BUTHELL, WA, WAS DISCIPLINED BY MARYLAND ON MARCH 12, 1990.
DISCIPLINARY ACTION: SURRENDER OF LICENSE; SURRENDER OF CONTROLLED SUBSTANCE LICENSE
OFFENSE: SUBSTANDARD CARE, INCOMPETENCE, OR NEGLIGENCE
NOTES: HAS NOT PRACTICED IN MARYLAND SINCE 10/26/88; LICENSED IN TEXAS AND HAS APPLIED IN WASHINGTON STATE; MAY APPLY FOR REINSTATEMENT UPON COMPLETION OF A BOARD-APPROVED TRAINING PROGRAM

BROWN, CYNTHIA A MD, LICENSE NUMBER 00D8160, OF BOTHELL, WA, WAS DISCIPLINED BY TEXAS ON FEBRUARY 22, 1991.
NOTES: MAY NOT PRACTICE IN TEXAS UNTIL THE MARYLAND BOARD HAS ACTED ON ANY PETITION SHE HAS FILED OR MAY FILE FOR REINSTATEMENT OF HER LICENSE; RECEIVE PERMISSION OF TEXAS BOARD BEFORE RETURNING TO PRACTICE MEDICINE IN TEXAS AND BE SUBJECT TO ANY TERMS IMPOSED

BROWN, STEVEN M MD, LICENSE NUMBER 0A49127, OF DALLAS, TX, WAS DISCIPLINED BY CALIFORNIA ON JULY 14, 1994.
DISCIPLINARY ACTION: 60-MONTH PROBATION
OFFENSE: CRIMINAL CONVICTION OR PLEA OF GUILTY, NOLO CONTENDERE, OR NO CONTEST TO A CRIME
NOTES: THREE SUBSTANCE ABUSE CONVICTIONS IN TEXAS, 1985 TO 1988; FAILED TO DISCLOSE THEM IN HIS APPLICATION FOR CALIFORNIA LICENSE IN 1989. REVOCATION STAYED.

BROWN, STUART L MD OF 1258 PROSPECT STREET, LA JOLLA, CA, WAS DISCIPLINED BY DEA ON APRIL 12, 1990.
DISCIPLINARY ACTION: SURRENDER OF CONTROLLED SUBSTANCE LICENSE
OFFENSE: SUBSTANDARD CARE, INCOMPETENCE, OR NEGLIGENCE
NOTES: MEDICAL LICENSE REVOKED 09/21/89 FOR GROSS NEGLIGENCE, INCOMPETENCE AND SEXUAL MISCONDUCT.

BROWN, STUART L MD, DATE OF BIRTH JANUARY 10, 1933, OF 6687 LA JOLLA SCENIC DR, LA JOLLA, CA, WAS DISCIPLINED BY MEDICARE ON MAY 22, 1990.
DISCIPLINARY ACTION: EXCLUSION FROM THE MEDICARE AND/OR MEDICAID PROGRAMS
OFFENSE: DISCIPLINARY ACTION BY ANOTHER STATE OR AGENCY
NOTES: LICENSE REVOCATION OR SUSPENSION.

BROWN, STUART L MD, DATE OF BIRTH JANUARY 10, 1933, LICENSE NUMBER 0016045, OF 1258 PROSPECT, LA JOLLA, CA, WAS DISCIPLINED BY MINNESOTA ON NOVEMBER 14, 1992.
DISCIPLINARY ACTION: SURRENDER OF LICENSE
OFFENSE: DISCIPLINARY ACTION BY ANOTHER STATE OR AGENCY
NOTES: DISCIPLINARY ACTION BY ANOTHER STATE; ENGAGING IN CONDUCT WITH A PATIENT WHICH IS SEXUAL OR MAY REASONABLY BE INTERPRETED BY THE PATIENT AS SEXUAL.

BROWN, STUART LEO MD, LICENSE NUMBER 00C7341, OF LA JOLLA, CA, WAS DISCIPLINED BY TEXAS ON MAY 24, 1990.
DISCIPLINARY ACTION: SURRENDER OF LICENSE
NOTES: STIPULATED ORDER. MEDICAL LICENSE VOLUNTARILY SURRENDERED IN LIEU OF DISCIPLINARY HEARING

BROWN, THOMAS J MD, LICENSE NUMBER 0020063, OF TX, WAS DISCIPLINED BY ARIZONA ON OCTOBER 13, 1993.
DISCIPLINARY ACTION: MONITORING OF PHYSICIAN
NOTES: INFORMATION RECEIVED ALLEGING THAT HE REQUIRES CONTINUED MEDICAL CARE. SHALL OBTAIN A SOLE TREATING PSYCHIATRIST APPROVED BY THE BOARD AND TAKE ONLY THOSE MEDICATIONS PRESCRIBED BY HIM WITH QUARTERLY REPORTS TO THE BOARD, INDICATING DIAGNOSIS, PROGNOSIS, COMPLIANCE WITH MEDICATIONS, RESULTS OF LABORATORY TESTS AND DATE OF VISITS. THE BOARD WILL GET WRITTEN FEEDBACK AT LEAST QUARTERLY FROM EACH OF HIS EMPLOYERS FOR THE PAST QUARTER INDICATING HIS ABILITY TO COMPETENTLY PRACTICE MEDICINE AS WELL AS THE NUMBER OF HOURS WORKED IN THE PREVIOUS QUARTER AND THE TYPE OF WORK DONE; ORDER IS NOT DISCIPLINARY IN NATURE BUT IS DESIGNATED FOR PERSONAL REHABILITATIVE PURPOSES.

BROWNE, DUNCAN JAMES MD, LICENSE NUMBER 00H9193, OF HOUSTON, TX, WAS DISCIPLINED BY TEXAS ON JUNE 22, 1994.
DISCIPLINARY ACTION: 60-MONTH RESTRICTION PLACED ON LICENSE; REQUIRED TO TAKE ADDITIONAL MEDICAL EDUCATION
OFFENSE: DRUG OR ALCOHOL ABUSE
NOTES: HAS A HISTORY OF ABUSING THE DRUG NITROUS OXIDE SINCE 1991; DRUG USE SECONDARY TO DEPRESSION DUE TO FAMILY MATTERS; RECEIVED OUTPATIENT TREATMENT IN 1991 AND UNDERWENT PSYCHIATRIC CARE; SOBRIETY DATE IS 6/17/92; COMPLETED A ONE YEAR RECOVERY AND SUPERVISION PROGRAM WITH THE UNIVERSITY OF TEXAS; CURRENTLY MEETS WITH PSYCHIATRIST AND PSYCHOLOGIST ONCE A MONTH. LICENSE RESTRICTED FIVE YEARS WITH THE FOLLOWING CONDITIONS: SHALL ABSTAIN FROM THE CONSUMPTION OF ALCOHOL/CHEMICAL SUBSTANCES IN ANY FORM UNLESS PRESCRIBED BY ANOTHER PHYSICIAN FOR A LEGITIMATE AND THERAPEUTIC PURPOSE; SHALL NOT TREAT OR OTHERWISE SERVE AS PHYSICIAN, PRESCRIBE, DISPENSE, OR ADMINISTER DRUGS THAT MAY BE SUBJECT TO ABUSE TO HIMSELF OR ANY MEMBER OF HIS FAMILY; SHALL LIMIT MEDICAL PRACTICE SOLELY TO THE PRACTICE OF ANESTHESIOLOGY IN A HOSPITAL OR OUTPATIENT PAIN SETTING; SHALL NOT POSSESS, ADMINISTER, DISPENSE OR PRESCRIBE ANY CONTROLLED SUBSTANCES OR DANGEROUS DRUGS EXCEPT AS NECESSARY FOR TREATMENT OF INPATIENTS IN HOSPITAL OR OUTPATIENT PAIN SETTING; SHALL CONTINUE TO PARTICIPATE IN AA'S PROGRAM AT LEAST THREE TIMES A WEEK WITH QUARTERLY REPORTS TO THE BOARD; SHALL SUBMIT HIMSELF FOR APPROPRIATE EXAMS INCLUDING DRUG OR ALCOHOL SCREENS; SHALL CONTINUE TO MEET WITH PSYCHIATRIST AND

PSYCHOLOGIST MONTHLY WITH QUARTERLY REPORTS; SHALL ATTEND AT LEAST 50 HOURS PER YEAR OF CONTINUING MEDICAL EDUCATION; SHALL APPEAR BEFORE THE BOARD ONCE A YEAR; SHALL GIVE A COPY OF THIS ORDER TO ANY HEALTH CARE ENTITY WHERE HE HAS PRIVILEGES; SHALL COOPERATE WITH THE BOARD IN VERIFYING COMPLIANCE; SHALL INFORM BOARD OF CHANGE OF ADDRESS WITHIN 10 DAYS OR IF HE LEAVES THE STATE; TIME SPENT OUT OF TEXAS DOES NOT COUNT TOWARD PROBATION. SHALL NOT SEEK MODIFICATION FOR ONE YEAR.

BROXTON, KYREL DARICE MD, DATE OF BIRTH JUNE 18, 1952, LICENSE NUMBER 00G2333, OF 17070 RED OAK DRIVE SUITE 101, HOUSTON, TX, WAS DISCIPLINED BY TEXAS ON AUGUST 20, 1993.
DISCIPLINARY ACTION: REPRIMAND; REQUIRED TO TAKE ADDITIONAL MEDICAL EDUCATION
OFFENSE: SUBSTANDARD CARE, INCOMPETENCE, OR NEGLIGENCE
NOTES: INAPPROPRIATELY HANDLED THE FLUID AND ELECTROLYTE BALANCE OF A 20 MONTH OLD CHILD AND INAPPROPRIATELY TREATED HIS HYPERGLYCEMIA ON 12/19/88 WHEN THE PATIENT APPEARED IN AN EMERGENCY ROOM IN RESPIRATORY DISTRESS; SHE OBTAINED CONSULTATION WHEN SHE RECOGNIZED THE CHILD'S CARE WAS BEYOND HER CAPABILITIES. FOR THREE YEARS SHE SHALL ATTEND AT LEAST 50 HOURS PER YEAR OF CONTINUING MEDICAL EDUCATION INCLUDING COURSES RELATING TO FLUID AND ELECTROLYTE MANAGMENT AND METABOLIC AND ACUTE-CARE MANAGEMENT; SHALL GIVE A COPY OF THIS ORDER TO ANY HEALTH CARE ENTITY WHERE SHE HAS PRIVILEGES; SHALL COOPERATE WITH THE BOARD IN VERIFYING COMPLIANCE; SHALL INFORM BOARD OF CHANGE OF ADDRESS WITHIN 10 DAYS OR IF SHE LEAVES THE STATE; TIME SPENT OUT OF TEXAS DOES NOT COUNT TOWARDS ORDER. SHALL NOT SEEK MODIFICATION FOR ONE YEAR. ON 9/30/94 ORDER WAS TERMINATED.

BRUNKEN, ROBERT B MD, LICENSE NUMBER 00C3593, OF DALLAS, TX, WAS DISCIPLINED BY TEXAS ON AUGUST 19, 1994.
DISCIPLINARY ACTION: 60-MONTH PROBATION; MONITORING OF PHYSICIAN
OFFENSE: DRUG OR ALCOHOL ABUSE
NOTES: ENTERED TREATMENT AND PARTICIPATED WITH A PROFESSIONALS TREATMENT PROGRAM FOR LONG TERM TREATMENT OF ALCOHOL DEPENDENCE; SELF-REPORTED THIS TREATMENT TO THE BOARD; IS BEING TREATED BY A PSYCHIATRIST, ATTENDS AA AND HAS REGULAR URINE SCREENS. SUSPENSION STAYED. CONDITIONS OF PROBATION: SHALL ABSTAIN FROM THE CONSUMPTION OF ALCOHOL/CHEMICAL SUBSTANCES IN ANY FORM UNLESS PRESCRIBED BY ANOTHER PHYSICIAN FOR LEGITIMATE AND THERAPEUTIC PURPOSES; SHALL SUBMIT HIMSELF FOR APPROPRIATE EXAMS INCLUDING DRUG OR ALCOHOL SCREENS; SHALL PARTICIPATE IN AA'S PROGRAM NOT LESS THAN THREE TIMES A WEEK WITH QUARTERLY REPORTS TO THE BOARD; SHALL SUBMIT HIMSELF FOR EVALUATION AND TREATMENT TO A BOARD-APPROVED PSYCHIATRIST WITH REPORTS TO THE BOARD; SHALL NOT TREAT OR OTHERWISE SERVE AS PHYSICIAN, PRESCRIBE, DISPENSE OR ADMINISTER ANY DRUGS THAT MAY BE SUBJECT TO ABUSE TO HIMSELF OR ANY MEMBER OF HIS FAMILY; SHALL APPEAR BEFORE THE BOARD ONCE A YEAR; SHALL GIVE A COPY OF THIS ORDER TO ANY HEALTH CARE ENTITY WHERE HE HAS PRIVILEGES; SHALL COOPERATE WITH THE BOARD IN VERIFYING COMPLIANCE; SHALL INFORM BOARD OF CHANGE OF ADDRESS WITHIN 1O DAYS OR IF HE LEAVES THE STATE; TIME SPENT OUT OF TEXAS DOES NOT COUNT TOWARD PROBATION. SHALL NOT SEEK MODIFICATION FOR ONE YEAR.

BUI, RAU VAN MD, LICENSE NUMBER 0A35749, OF SAN JOSE, CA, WAS DISCIPLINED BY CALIFORNIA ON DECEMBER 8, 1986.
DISCIPLINARY ACTION: 3-MONTH LICENSE SUSPENSION; 57-MONTH PROBATION
OFFENSE: CRIMINAL CONVICTION OR PLEA OF GUILTY, NOLO CONTENDERE, OR NO CONTEST TO A CRIME
NOTES: CONVICTION FOR FILING FALSE MEDI-CAL CLAIMS. REVOCATION STAYED.

BUI, RAU VAN MD, LICENSE NUMBER 00F7412, OF SAN JOSE, CA, WAS DISCIPLINED BY TEXAS ON AUGUST 1, 1988.
DISCIPLINARY ACTION: 60-MONTH PROBATION
OFFENSE: DISCIPLINARY ACTION BY ANOTHER STATE OR AGENCY
NOTES: CALIFORNIA LICENSE PROBATED, RESTRICTED AND CONDITIONED; REVOCATION STAYED

BUKA, NORMAN JOHN MD, LICENSE NUMBER 0023337, OF 777 HEMLOCK STREET, MACON, GA, WAS DISCIPLINED BY GEORGIA ON APRIL 4, 1985.
DISCIPLINARY ACTION: 18-MONTH PROBATION
NOTES: REVIEW AND EVALUATION 8/4/86.

BUKA, NORMAN JOHN MD OF MACON, GA, WAS DISCIPLINED BY TEXAS ON DECEMBER 1, 1986.
DISCIPLINARY ACTION: PROBATION
OFFENSE: DISCIPLINARY ACTION BY ANOTHER STATE OR AGENCY
NOTES: 18-MONTH SUSPENSION STAYED AND BUKA PLACED ON STIPULATED PROBATION; PROBATION SUBSEQUENTLY LIFTED

BUNDRANT, BRADLY M MD, LICENSE NUMBER 00H7275, OF EL PASO, TX, WAS DISCIPLINED BY TEXAS ON MAY 22, 1992.
DISCIPLINARY ACTION: EMERGENCY SUSPENSION
NOTES: 6/22/92: TEMPORARY SUSPENSION LIFTED; REINSTATED UNDER TERMS AND CONDITIONS OF PREVIOUS BOARD ORDER DATED 5/24/90. 11/13/92: 5/24/90 ORDER AMENDED. SHALL CONTINUE TO PARTICIPATE IN PSYCHOTHERAPY, AND SUBMIT HIMSELF FOR APPROPRIATE EXAMINATIONS, INCLUDING SCREENING FOR ALCOHOL OR DRUGS.

BUNN, RUSSELL B DO, LICENSE NUMBER 00C5945, OF MT ENTERPRISE, TX, WAS DISCIPLINED BY TEXAS ON MARCH 1, 1990.
DISCIPLINARY ACTION: 120-MONTH CEASE AND DESIST ORDER
NOTES: STIPULATED ORDER. MUST CEASE PRESCRIBING, ADMINISTERING, SUPPLYING OR DISPENSING CONTROLLED SUBSTANCES AND DANGEROUS DRUGS. ORDER IN EFFECT FOR TEN YEARS BEGINNING 90 DAYS FROM 12/4/89.

BUNN, RUSSELL BURTON DO OF PO BOX 160, MOUNT ENTERPRISE, TX, WAS DISCIPLINED BY DEA ON MARCH 12, 1990.
DISCIPLINARY ACTION: SURRENDER OF CONTROLLED SUBSTANCE LICENSE
OFFENSE: OVERPRESCRIBING OR MISPRESCRIBING DRUGS
NOTES: PRESCRIBED CONTROLLED SUBSTANCES FOR NONTHERAPEUTIC REASON AND FAILED TO KEEP PROPER RECORDS AND MAINTAIN INVENTORIES OF CONTROLLED SUBSTANCES DISPENSED TO PATIENTS.

BURCH, JOHN E JR MD, LICENSE NUMBER 00G9267, OF FORT WORTH, TX, WAS DISCIPLINED BY TEXAS ON APRIL 14, 1989.
DISCIPLINARY ACTION: REQUIRED TO ENTER AN IMPAIRED PHYSICIAN PROGRAM OR DRUG OR ALCOHOL TREATMENT; MONITORING OF PHYSICIAN
OFFENSE: DRUG OR ALCOHOL ABUSE
NOTES: SHALL PARTICIPATE IN AA AND IMPAIRED PHYSICIAN GROUP ACTIVITIES; SHALL SUBMIT FOR APPROPRIATE EXAMINATIONS INCLUDING ALCOHOL OR DRUG SCREENINGS; SHALL OBTAIN RECOVERY ABUSE SPONSOR; SHALL ENCOURAGE FAMILY ATTENDANCE IN CERTAIN ALCOHOL EDUCATION PROGRAMS; SHALL ABSTAIN FROM ALCOHOL AND DRUGS; SHALL APPEAR BEFORE BOARD UPON REQUEST. ON 10/1/93 ORDER TERMINATED.

BURKES, WALTER JOE MD, LICENSE NUMBER 00G6909, OF MEMPHIS, TN, WAS DISCIPLINED BY TEXAS ON JULY 1, 1990.
DISCIPLINARY ACTION: LICENSE SUSPENSION
OFFENSE: SUBSTANDARD CARE, INCOMPETENCE, OR NEGLIGENCE
NOTES: FAILURE TO PRACTICE MEDICINE IN ACCEPTABLE MANNER CONSISTENT WITH PUBLIC HEALTH AND WELFARE. DISCIPLINED BY LICENSED HOSPITAL OR MEDICAL STAFF. LICENSE SUSPENDED INDEFINITELY UNTIL HE APPEARS BEFORE BOARD AND SHOWS GOOD CAUSE WHY LICENSE SHOULD BE REINSTATED.

BURKETT, DAVID GARY MD, LICENSE NUMBER 00E9555, OF MONROE, LA, WAS DISCIPLINED BY TEXAS ON OCTOBER 26, 1990.
NOTES: MUST COMPLY WITH LOUISIANA RESTRICTIONS AND AUTHORIZE LOUISIANA BOARD TO RELEASE INFORMATION AS TO STATUS AND PROBATIONARY COMPLIANCE; RECEIVE APPROVAL FROM TEXAS BOARD PRIOR TO PRACTICING MEDICINE IN TEXAS.

BURLESON, JAMES D MD, LICENSE NUMBER 00H1932, OF BIG SPRING, TX, WAS DISCIPLINED BY TEXAS ON AUGUST 19, 1994.
DISCIPLINARY ACTION: 60-MONTH PROBATION; RESTRICTION PLACED ON CONTROLLED SUBSTANCE LICENSE
OFFENSE: OVERPRESCRIBING OR MISPRESCRIBING DRUGS
NOTES: ADMITTED THAT HE WROTE PRESCRIPTIONS FOR CONTROLLED SUBSTANCES, SPECIFICALLY DEMEROL, IN THE NAME OF A PATIENT AND THEN DIVERTED THE SUBSTANCES TO A RELATIVE; HAS BEEN UNDER SIGNIFICANT STRESS DUE TO HIS DAUGHTER'S ILLNESS; HAS RECEIVED TREATMENT REGARDING CO-DEPENDENCY PROBLEMS; IS CURRENTLY SEEING A PSYCHOLOGIST. SUSPENSION STAYED. CONDITIONS OF PROBATION: SHALL ABSTAIN FROM THE CONSUMPTION OF ALCOHOL/CHEMICAL SUBSTANCES IN ANY FORM UNLESS PRESCRIBED BY ANOTHER PHYSICIAN FOR A LEGITIMATE AND THERAPEUTIC PURPOSE; SHALL SUBMIT HIMSELF FOR APPROPRIATE EXAMS INCLUDING DRUG OR ALCOHOL SCREENS; WITHIN ONE YEAR SHALL PASS THE MEDICAL JURISPRUDENCE EXAM; SHALL ATTEND AT LEAST 50 HOURS PER YEAR OF CONTINUING MEDICAL EDUCATION; SHALL SURRENDER ALL UNUSED TRIPLICATE PRESCRIPTION FORMS AND 222 FORMS IN HIS POSSESSION OTHER THAN THOSE ASSOCIATED WITH HIS EMS DIRECTORSHIP; SEPARATE FROM PATIENT RECORDS, SHALL MAINTAIN A FILE OF EVERY PRESCRIPTION WRITTEN FOR DANGEROUS DRUGS WHICH SHALL BE AVAILABLE FOR INSPECTION; SHALL NOT CALL IN ANY PRESCRIPTIONS FOR CONTROLLED SUBSTANCES OR DANGEROUS DRUGS; SHALL NOT POSSESS, ADMINISTER, DISPENSE OR PRESCRIBE ANY CONTROLLED SUBSTANCES BUT MAY ORDER THEM TO BE ADMINISTERED TO HOSPITAL OR NURSING HOME PATIENTS; SHALL NOT TREAT OR OTHERWISE SERVE AS PHYSICIAN, PRESCRIBE, DISPENSE OR ADMINISTER DRUGS THAT MAY BE SUBJECT TO ABUSE TO HIMSELF OR ANY MEMBER OF HIS FAMILY; SHALL CONTINUE TO RECEIVE PSYCHIATRIC TREATMENT WITH QUARTERLY REPORTS; SHALL COMPLY WITH TERMS OF HIS CONTRACT WITH SCENIC MOUNTAIN MEDICAL CENTER; SHALL APPEAR BEFORE THE BOARD ONCE A YEAR; SHALL GIVE A COPY OF THIS ORDER TO ANY HEALTH CARE ENTITY WHERE HE HAS PRIVILEGES; SHALL COOPERATE WITH THE BOARD IN VERIFYING COMPLIANCE; SHALL INFORM BOARD OF CHANGE OF ADDRESS WITHIN 10 DAYS OR IF HE LEAVES THE STATE; TIME SPENT OUT OF TEXAS DOES NOT COUNT TOWARD PROBATION. SHALL NOT SEEK MODIFICATION FOR ONE YEAR.

BURNETT, JOSEPH R DO, LICENSE NUMBER 00C0015, OF SALEM, MO, WAS DISCIPLINED BY TEXAS ON JUNE 13, 1989.
DISCIPLINARY ACTION: SURRENDER OF LICENSE

BUSCH, GERALD I MD OF HOUSTON, TX, WAS DISCIPLINED BY TEXAS ON JULY 1, 1986.
DISCIPLINARY ACTION: SURRENDER OF LICENSE

BUSCH, GERALD IRWIN MD, LICENSE NUMBER 00F9260, OF 1300 MOURSUND, HOUSTON, TX, WAS DISCIPLINED BY DEA ON JUNE 9, 1989.
DISCIPLINARY ACTION: RESTRICTION PLACED ON CONTROLLED SUBSTANCE LICENSE
OFFENSE: CRIMINAL CONVICTION OR PLEA OF GUILTY, NOLO CONTENDERE, OR NO CONTEST TO A CRIME
NOTES: ARRESTED 10/14/85 IN HOUSTON, TEXAS FOR OBTAINING DRUGS BY FRAUD; CONTROLLED SUBSTANCE PRIVILEGES SURRENDERED; MEDICAL LICENSE VOLUNTARILY SURRENDERED; PLED NOLO CONTENDERE 01/22/86 AND GIVEN 1 YEAR DEFERRED ADJUDICATION AND $1,000 FINE; REQUEST FOR ORDER TO SHOW CAUSE 05/12/88 IN HOUSTON, TX; RESTRICTION OF CONTROLLED SUBSTANCES REGISTRATION.

BUSHART, JAMES F MD OF DALLAS, TX, WAS DISCIPLINED BY LOUISIANA ON MAY 21, 1992.
DISCIPLINARY ACTION: PROBATION
OFFENSE: DISCIPLINARY ACTION BY ANOTHER STATE OR AGENCY
NOTES: ADMINISTRATIVE ACTION BY TEXAS; HABITUAL OR RECURRING ABUSE OF ALCOHOL. PROBATION FOR PERIOD CONCURRENT WITH PROBATION IMPOSED BY TEXAS STATE BOARD OF MEDICAL EXAMINERS, SUBJECT TO CONTINUING COMPLETE COMPLIANCE WITH TERMS OF ORDER PREVIOUSLY ENTERED BY TEXAS BOARD, PRIOR NOTICE TO BOARD OF INTENT TO RELOCATE PRACTICE TO LOUISIANA, MAINTENANCE OF COMPLETE ABSTINENCE FROM THE USE OF ALCOHOL AND OTHER MOOD-ALTERING SUBSTANCES.

BUSHART, JAMES FREDERICK MD, LICENSE NUMBER 00G5869, OF DALLAS, TX, WAS DISCIPLINED BY TEXAS ON AUGUST 24, 1991.
DISCIPLINARY ACTION: 36-MONTH PROBATION; MONITORING OF PHYSICIAN
OFFENSE: FAILURE TO COMPLY WITH A PREVIOUS BOARD ORDER
NOTES: VIOLATION OF PREVIOUS AGREED ORDER. SHALL PARTICIPATE IN AA; SHALL APPEAR BEFORE BOARD ONCE A YEAR; SHALL SUBMIT TO DRUG OR ALCOHOL

SCREENS.

BUSHART, JAMES FREDERICK MD, LICENSE NUMBER 00G5869, OF RIDGELAND, MS, WAS DISCIPLINED BY TEXAS ON JUNE 22, 1994.
DISCIPLINARY ACTION: LICENSE SUSPENSION
OFFENSE: LOSS OR RESTRICTION OF HOSPITAL PRIVILEGES
NOTES: LICENSE WAS PLACED ON PROBATION FOR FIVE YEARS ON 10/20/86; EXHIBITED A HISTORY OF ALCOHOL AND OPIATE ABUSE BETWEEN 1986 AND 1990 AND SUFFERED RELAPSES IN 8/88 AND 5/90; LICENSE AGAIN PLACED ON PROBATION ON 8/24/91; SUFFERED RELAPSES IN 9/92 AND 9/93 AFTER WHICH HE WAS ADMITTED FOR TREATMENT; IN OCTOBER 1993 AND DECEMBER 1993 HOSPITAL PRIVILEGES WERE TERMINATED AT TWO FACILITIES. BASED ON THE RELAPSE. SUSPENSION UNTIL SUCH TIME AS HE APPEARS BEFORE THE BOARD AND PROVIDES SUFFICIENT EVIDENCE THAT INDICATES HE IS PHYSICALLY, MENTALLY AND OTHERWISE COMPETENT TO SAFELY PRACTICE.

CADDELL, JAMES DONALD DO, LICENSE NUMBER 00F6497, OF DALLAS, TX, WAS DISCIPLINED BY TEXAS ON APRIL 21, 1990.
NOTES: STIPULATED ORDER. MUST MAINTAIN COMPLETE AND ACCURATE RECORDS OF PURCHASES AND DISPOSALS OF CONTROLLED SUBSTANCES. ORDER EFFECTIVE FOR THREE YEARS.

CADENHEAD, JAMES F MD OF P.O. BOX 938, HASKELL, TX, WAS DISCIPLINED BY MEDICARE ON JULY 29, 1987.
DISCIPLINARY ACTION: 24-MONTH EXCLUSION FROM THE MEDICARE AND/OR MEDICAID PROGRAMS
OFFENSE: SUBSTANDARD CARE, INCOMPETENCE, OR NEGLIGENCE
NOTES: GROSSLY SUBSTANDARD CARE OF 5 PATIENTS, INCLUDING POOR KNOWLEDGE OF CARDIOVASCULAR ILLNESS, LACK OF AGGRESSIVE DIAGNOSTIC UTILIZATION, POOR KNOWLEDGE OF LABORATORY EVALUATION, UNTIMELY AND INJUDICIOUS USE OF LABORATORY, X-RAY AND ELECTROCARDIOGRAPHIC DIAGNOSIS OF A PATIENT ADMITTED WITH UNCONSCIOUSNESS

CAIAZZA, STEPHEN S MD, LICENSE NUMBER 0128177, OF NEW YORK, NY, WAS DISCIPLINED BY NEW YORK ON FEBRUARY 18, 1987.
DISCIPLINARY ACTION: 36-MONTH PROBATION
NOTES: 3 YEAR SUSPENSION, STAYED

CAIAZZA, STEPHEN S MD, DATE OF BIRTH AUGUST 9, 1943, LICENSE NUMBER 0031909, OF 240 E. 27TH STREET, 8B, NEW YORK, NY, WAS DISCIPLINED BY NEW JERSEY ON APRIL 11, 1988.
DISCIPLINARY ACTION: 36-MONTH PROBATION
OFFENSE: OVERPRESCRIBING OR MISPRESCRIBING DRUGS
NOTES: 3 YEAR SUSPENSION STAYED; BASED ON CONTROLLED DANGEROUS SUBSTANCES IMPROPRIETIES IN NEW YORK

CAIAZZA, STEPHEN S MD, LICENSE NUMBER 00F8818, OF NEW YORK, NY, WAS DISCIPLINED BY TEXAS ON MAY 20, 1989.
DISCIPLINARY ACTION: MONITORING OF PHYSICIAN
OFFENSE: DISCIPLINARY ACTION BY ANOTHER STATE OR AGENCY
NOTES: ACCEPTED TEXAS ORDER SIMILAR TO NEW YORK BOARD ORDER; SHALL BE SUBJECT TO VISITS WITH SELECTED NEW YORK REPRESENTATIVE TO DETERMINE COMPLIANCE REGARDING CONTROLLED SUBSTANCE PRESCRIBING; PRACTICE SUBJECT TO MONITORING REGARDING FITNESS TO PRACTICE, INCLUDING DRUG TESTS; SHALL RECEIVE TEXAS BOARD APPROVAL PRIOR TO PRACTICING IN TEXAS.

CALKINS, GREGORY P MD, LICENSE NUMBER 0015302, OF IN, WAS DISCIPLINED BY WEST VIRGINIA ON JUNE 16, 1989.
OFFENSE: CRIMINAL CONVICTION OR PLEA OF GUILTY, NOLO CONTENDERE, OR NO CONTEST TO A CRIME
NOTES: CONVICTED IN HAMMOND INDIANA FOR INCOME TAX EVASION, A FELONY. TEXAS ATTACHED CONDITIONS ON HIS LICENSE ON 9/24/88. HE MUST NOTIFY BOARD IN WRITING OF ANY DISCIPLINARY ACTIONS TAKEN BY OTHER STATES WHERE HE IS LICENSED AS A RESULT OF INCOME TAX EVASION CONVICTION. MUST NOTIFY THE BOARD OF ANY CHANGE OF ADDRESS.

CALKINS, GREGORY P MD, DATE OF BIRTH NOVEMBER 23, 1950, LICENSE NUMBER 0025811, WAS DISCIPLINED BY KENTUCKY ON JANUARY 4, 1990.
DISCIPLINARY ACTION: 24-MONTH PROBATION; FINE
NOTES: FINE $500.00

CALKINS, GREGORY P MD OF CINCINNATI, OH, WAS DISCIPLINED BY OHIO ON MARCH 19, 1990.
DISCIPLINARY ACTION: 1-MONTH LICENSE SUSPENSION; 60-MONTH PROBATION
OFFENSE: CRIMINAL CONVICTION OR PLEA OF GUILTY, NOLO CONTENDERE, OR NO CONTEST TO A CRIME
NOTES: FELONY CONVICTION (INCOME TAX EVASION); REVOCATION STAYED

CALKINS, GREGORY P MD, DATE OF BIRTH NOVEMBER 23, 1950, LICENSE NUMBER 0026343, OF 817 GLENWOOD AVENUE, JOLIET, IL, WAS DISCIPLINED BY IOWA ON DECEMBER 23, 1991.
DISCIPLINARY ACTION: SURRENDER OF LICENSE
OFFENSE: DISCIPLINARY ACTION BY ANOTHER STATE OR AGENCY

CALKINS, GREGORY PAUL MD, LICENSE NUMBER 00G8583, OF JOLIET, IL, WAS DISCIPLINED BY TEXAS ON SEPTEMBER 24, 1988.
OFFENSE: CRIMINAL CONVICTION OR PLEA OF GUILTY, NOLO CONTENDERE, OR NO CONTEST TO A CRIME
NOTES: MUST NOTIFY BOARD WITHIN 10 DAYS FROM DATE ON WHICH HE IS NOTIFIED BY ANY STATE WHERE LICENSED OF ANY DISCIPLINARY ACTION ARISING OUT OF HIS INCOME TAX EVASION CONVICTION.

CALKINS, GREGORY PAUL MD, LICENSE NUMBER 040120E, WAS DISCIPLINED BY PENNSYLVANIA ON JANUARY 26, 1990.
DISCIPLINARY ACTION: REPRIMAND

CALKINS, GREGORY PAUL MD, LICENSE NUMBER 0017859, WAS DISCIPLINED BY ARIZONA ON JUNE 30, 1990.
DISCIPLINARY ACTION: EMERGENCY SUSPENSION
OFFENSE: CRIMINAL CONVICTION OR PLEA OF GUILTY, NOLO CONTENDERE, OR NO CONTEST TO A CRIME
NOTES: PLED GUILTY TO INCOME TAX EVASION IN INDIANA 10/28/87 AND PLACED ON CRIMINAL PROBATION FOR FIVE YEARS WITH A $1000 FINE AND 500 HOURS OF COMMUNITY SERVICE. TEXAS BOARD ALSO REQUIRED HIM TO INFORM THEM OF ANY ACTION TAKEN BASED ON THIS CONVICTION.

CALKINS, GREGORY PAUL MD WAS DISCIPLINED BY HAWAII ON JULY 18, 1990.
DISCIPLINARY ACTION: LICENSE REVOCATION

CANALE, SALVADOR L MD OF LAS VEGAS, NV, WAS DISCIPLINED

BY TEXAS ON DECEMBER 1, 1986.
DISCIPLINARY ACTION: LICENSE REVOCATION
OFFENSE: DISCIPLINARY ACTION BY ANOTHER STATE OR AGENCY

CANO, ABRAHAM MD, LICENSE NUMBER 00F0912, OF HARLINGEN, TX, WAS DISCIPLINED BY TEXAS ON DECEMBER 1, 1988.
NOTES: SETTLEMENT AGREEMENT AND UNSPECIFIED DISCIPLINARY ACTION

CANTU, JULIAN R JR MD, LICENSE NUMBER 00D8867, OF SAN ANTONIO, TX, WAS DISCIPLINED BY TEXAS ON DECEMBER 1, 1988.
NOTES: SETTLEMENT AGREEMENT AND UNSPECIFIED DISCIPLINARY ACTION

CARAWAY, BENJAMIN D MD OF LUBBOCK, TX, WAS DISCIPLINED BY OHIO ON NOVEMBER 2, 1988.
NOTES: CONSENT AGREEMENT, UNSPECIFIED. ON 1/10/91 PROBATION TERMINATED; LICENSE TO PRACTICE NOW UNRESTRICTED.

CARIN, SANTIAGO O MD, DATE OF BIRTH FEBRUARY 19, 1937, OF 141 YANKEE JIM COURT, VALLEJO, CA, WAS DISCIPLINED BY MEDICARE ON FEBRUARY 17, 1988.
DISCIPLINARY ACTION: 60-MONTH EXCLUSION FROM THE MEDICARE AND/OR MEDICAID PROGRAMS
OFFENSE: CRIMINAL CONVICTION OR PLEA OF GUILTY, NOLO CONTENDERE, OR NO CONTEST TO A CRIME
NOTES: PROGRAM-RELATED CONVICTION. REINSTATED ON 2/17/95.

CARIN, SANTIAGO O MD, LICENSE NUMBER 00E7574, OF VALLEJO, CA, WAS DISCIPLINED BY TEXAS ON SEPTEMBER 24, 1988.
DISCIPLINARY ACTION: SURRENDER OF LICENSE

CARIN, SANTIAGO O MD OF BENECIA, CA, WAS DISCIPLINED BY MISSOURI ON OCTOBER 28, 1988.
DISCIPLINARY ACTION: SURRENDER OF LICENSE
OFFENSE: CRIMINAL CONVICTION OR PLEA OF GUILTY, NOLO CONTENDERE, OR NO CONTEST TO A CRIME
NOTES: SUBSTANDARD CARE

CARIN, SANTIAGO O MD, LICENSE NUMBER 0106298, OF VENECIA, CA, WAS DISCIPLINED BY NEW YORK ON AUGUST 30, 1989.
DISCIPLINARY ACTION: 12-MONTH LICENSE SUSPENSION; 48-MONTH PROBATION
NOTES: SUSPENSION 5 YEARS, STAY LAST 4 YEARS

CARIN, SANTIAGO O MD, DATE OF BIRTH FEBRUARY 19, 1937, LICENSE NUMBER 0017051, OF 864 CAMDEN COURT, BENICIA, CA, WAS DISCIPLINED BY WISCONSIN ON NOVEMBER 15, 1990.
DISCIPLINARY ACTION: SURRENDER OF LICENSE
OFFENSE: DISCIPLINARY ACTION BY ANOTHER STATE OR AGENCY
NOTES: SURRENDERED LICENSE IN OKLAHOMA ON 9/11/87 FOLLOWING CONVICTION OF BLUE CROSS/SHIELD FRAUD AND BOARD CHARGES THAT HE OBTAINED LICENSE BY FRAUD OR MISREPRESENTATION. LICENSE SUBSEQUENTLY SURRENDERED IN MISSOURI ON 4/13/88.

CARIN, SANTIAGO O MD, LICENSE NUMBER C041005, OF BENICIA, CA, WAS DISCIPLINED BY CALIFORNIA ON APRIL 3, 1991.
DISCIPLINARY ACTION: 1-MONTH LICENSE SUSPENSION; 59-MONTH PROBATION
OFFENSE: DISCIPLINARY ACTION BY ANOTHER STATE OR AGENCY
NOTES: ACTION BASED ON DISCIPLINE BY OKLAHOMA BOARD, ALSO CRIMINAL CONVICTION, FOR RETENTION OF CHECK FROM BLUE CROSS THAT SHOULD HAVE BEEN DEPOSITED WITH THE U.S. GOVERNMENT. REVOCATION STAYED.

CARNINE, KENNETH S MD, LICENSE NUMBER 0010798, OF MT VERNON, WA, WAS DISCIPLINED BY WASHINGTON ON MARCH 11, 1993.
DISCIPLINARY ACTION: EMERGENCY SUSPENSION
OFFENSE: SEXUAL ABUSE OF OR SEXUAL MISCONDUCT WITH A PATIENT
NOTES: ALLEGATIONS OF MORAL TURPITUDE, ABUSE AND/OR SEXUAL CONTACT WITH A PATIENT.

CARNINE, KENNETH S MD, LICENSE NUMBER 00D4946, OF MT VERNON, WA, WAS DISCIPLINED BY TEXAS ON SEPTEMBER 30, 1994.
DISCIPLINARY ACTION: SURRENDER OF LICENSE
OFFENSE: DISCIPLINARY ACTION BY ANOTHER STATE OR AGENCY
NOTES: ALLEGATIONS OF DISCIPLINARY ACTION BY ANOTHER STATE OR BY THE UNIFORMED SERVICES OF THE U.S. SURRENDER IN LIEU OF FURTHER INVESTIGATION; SHALL NOT PETITION FOR REINSTATEMENT OF LICENSE.

CARPENTER, CHARLES ELFORD MD, LICENSE NUMBER 0018621, OF 2005 NICHOLSON ST, MISSION, TX, WAS DISCIPLINED BY GEORGIA ON JANUARY 8, 1987.
DISCIPLINARY ACTION: RESTRICTION PLACED ON LICENSE
OFFENSE: DISCIPLINARY ACTION BY ANOTHER STATE OR AGENCY
NOTES: DISCIPLINARY ACTION IN TEXAS. CANNOT PRACTICE IN GEORGIA UNTIL FURTHER ORDER.

CARPENTER, CHARLES ELFORD MD, LICENSE NUMBER 0018621, OF 2005 NICHOLSON ST, MISSION, TX, WAS DISCIPLINED BY GEORGIA ON AUGUST 9, 1989.
DISCIPLINARY ACTION: NONRENEWAL OF LICENSE
NOTES: DISCIPLINARY ACTION IN TEXAS; FAILED TO RENEW DURING PENDING DISCIPLINARY PROCEEDINGS.

CARSTENSEN, HAROLD G MD, LICENSE NUMBER 0C17546, OF HARLINGEN, TX, WAS DISCIPLINED BY CALIFORNIA ON MAY 25, 1990.
DISCIPLINARY ACTION: LICENSE REVOCATION
OFFENSE: DISCIPLINARY ACTION BY ANOTHER STATE OR AGENCY
NOTES: DISCIPLINED BY TEXAS BOARD FOR PROVOCATIVE TOUCHING OF FEMALE PATIENT. NO APPEARANCE BY DOCTOR.

CARTER, PETER JOSEPH MD, LICENSE NUMBER 00C4265, OF FORT WORTH, TX, WAS DISCIPLINED BY TEXAS ON JUNE 10, 1991.
DISCIPLINARY ACTION: SURRENDER OF LICENSE
NOTES: LICENSE PLACED ON IRREVOCABLE RETIREMENT STATUS IN LIEU OF DISCIPLINARY ACTION.

CASEY, JAMES GORDON MD, LICENSE NUMBER 00C6128, OF ABILENE, TX, WAS DISCIPLINED BY TEXAS ON OCTOBER 10, 1992.
DISCIPLINARY ACTION: LICENSE REVOCATION
OFFENSE: PROFESSIONAL MISCONDUCT
NOTES: UNPROFESSIONAL AND DISHONORABLE CONDUCT LIKELY TO DECEIVE, DEFRAUD OR INJURE THE PUBLIC.

CASSELLA, ROBERT R MD, LICENSE NUMBER 027634L, OF RUSK, TX, WAS DISCIPLINED BY PENNSYLVANIA ON APRIL 23, 1987.
DISCIPLINARY ACTION: 24-MONTH LICENSE SUSPENSION
OFFENSE: SUBSTANDARD CARE, INCOMPETENCE, OR NEGLIGENCE
NOTES: TWO YEAR SUSPENSION RETROACTIVE TO JANUARY 1,

1987. PETITION FOR RECONSIDERATION TO HEARING EXAMINER DENIED ON 05/29/87.

CASSELLA, ROBERT R MD, LICENSE NUMBER 027634L, OF RUSK, TX, WAS DISCIPLINED BY PENNSYLVANIA ON DECEMBER 9, 1987.
DISCIPLINARY ACTION: LICENSE REVOCATION
OFFENSE: SUBSTANDARD CARE, INCOMPETENCE, OR NEGLIGENCE
NOTES: DEPARTED FROM STANDARDS OF ACCEPTABLE AND PREVAILING MEDICAL PRACTICE IN THE TREATMENT OF THREE PATIENTS. ORDER OF HEARING EXAMINER VACATED BY BOARD. BOARD DECISION AFFIRMED IN COMMONWEALTH COURT.

CAVER, CLAUDE V JR MD, LICENSE NUMBER 00CO662, OF QUEZON CITY, PHILIPPINES, WAS DISCIPLINED BY TEXAS ON DECEMBER 1, 1988.
DISCIPLINARY ACTION: SURRENDER OF LICENSE
NOTES: LICENSE PLACED ON RETIREMENT STATUS

CAYLOR, ARTHUR BERNARD JR MD, LICENSE NUMBER 00F9287, OF 1600 UNIVERSITY DRIVE, COLLEGE STATION, TX, WAS DISCIPLINED BY DEA ON SEPTEMBER 27, 1993.
DISCIPLINARY ACTION: SURRENDER OF CONTROLLED SUBSTANCE LICENSE

CAYLOR, ARTHUR BERNARD JR MD, LICENSE NUMBER 00F9287, OF COLLEGE STATION, TX, WAS DISCIPLINED BY TEXAS ON JUNE 22, 1994.
DISCIPLINARY ACTION: SURRENDER OF CONTROLLED SUBSTANCE LICENSE; 60-MONTH PROBATION
OFFENSE: DRUG OR ALCOHOL ABUSE
NOTES: ADMITS TO CHEMICAL DEPENDENCY, SPECIFICALLY HYDROCODONE, AND RECEIVED INPATIENT TREATMENT ONCE IN 1987 AND ONCE IN 1993; FAILED TO KEEP ACCURATE AND COMPLETE RECORDS OF THE CONTROLLED SUBSTANCE, VICODIN WHICH HE ORDERED IN LARGE QUANTITIES FROM A PHARMACEUTICAL SUPPLY HOUSE; DENIES USE OF ALCOHOL; SURRENDERED HIS DEA REGISTRATION IN 9/93; IS IN TREATMENT WITH A PSYCHOTHERAPIST AND UNDER THE CARE OF A PRIMARY CARE PHYSICIAN FOR HIS PHYSICAL CONDITION WHICH IS DESCRIBED AS AN AUTOIMMUNE DISEASE MANIFESTED BY GASTRITIS, DUODENITIS, NEUROSENSORY HEARING LOSS, AXONAL MOTOR DEGENERATION WITH PROXIMAL MYOPATHY, MYELODYSPLASIA AND BASEL CELL CARCINOMA OF THE FOREHEAD; HIS CONDITION IS PRESENTLY STABILIZED; PARTICIPATES IN AA AND HAS COMPLETED THE 12 STEPS. SUSPENSION STAYED. CONDITIONS OF PROBATION: SHALL APPEAR BEFORE THE BOARD ONCE A YEAR; SHALL ABSTAIN FROM THE CONSUMPTION OF ALCOHOL/CHEMICAL SUBSTANCES IN ANY FORM UNLESS PRESCRIBED BY ANOTHER PHYSICIAN FOR A LEGITIMATE AND THERAPEUTIC PURPOSE; SHALL NOT TREAT OR OTHERWISE SERVE AS PHYSICIAN, PRESCRIBE, DISPENSE OR ADMINISTER DRUGS THAT MAY BE SUBJECT TO ABUSE TO HIMSELF OR ANY MEMBER OF HIS FAMILY; SHALL SUBMIT HIMSELF FOR APPROPRIATE EXAMS INCLUDING DRUG OR ALCOHOL SCREENS; SHALL SUBMIT HIMSELF TO A BOARD-APPROVED PSYCHIATRIST FOR EVALUATION AND TREATMENT WITH REPORTS TO THE BOARD; SHALL PARTICIPATE IN AA'S PROGRAM NOT LESS THAN THREE TIMES A WEEK WITH QUARTERLY REPORTS TO THE BOARD; SHALL PARTICIPATE IN ACTIVITIES OF A PHYSICIAN'S HEALTH AND REHABILITATION COMMITTEE AND ATTEND WEEKLY MEETINGS WITH QUARTERLY REPORTS; SHALL ATTEND AT LEAST 50 HOURS PER YEAR OF CONTINUING MEDICAL EDUCATION; SHALL SURRENDER DEA AND TEXAS CONTROL SUBSTANCES REGISTRATION CERTIFICATES; SHALL NOT REAPPLY FOR THESE WITHOUT APPROVAL; SEPARATE FROM PATIENT RECORDS, SHALL MAINTAIN A FILE OF EVERY PRESCRIPTION WRITTEN FOR DANGEROUS DRUGS WHICH SHALL BE AVAILABLE FOR INSPECTION; SHALL GIVE A COPY OF THIS ORDER TO ANY HEALTH CARE ENTITY WHERE HE HAS PRIVILEGES; SHALL COOPERATE WITH THE BOARD IN VERIFYING COMPLIANCE; SHALL INFORM BOARD OF CHANGE OF ADDRESS WITHIN 10 DAYS OR IF HE LEAVES THE STATE; TIME SPENT OUT OF TEXAS DOES NOT COUNT TOWARD PROBATION. SHALL NOT SEEK MODIFICATION FOR ONE YEAR.

CECIL, JOHN G MD WAS DISCIPLINED BY NEVADA ON MAY 25, 1988.
DISCIPLINARY ACTION: SURRENDER OF LICENSE
OFFENSE: OVERPRESCRIBING OR MISPRESCRIBING DRUGS
NOTES: IRREVOCABLE VOLUNTARY SURRENDER

CECIL, JOHN G MD OF PAHRUMP, NV, WAS DISCIPLINED BY DEA ON MAY 18, 1989.
DISCIPLINARY ACTION: REVOCATION OF CONTROLLED SUBSTANCE LICENSE
OFFENSE: DISCIPLINARY ACTION BY ANOTHER STATE OR AGENCY
NOTES: SURRENDERED NEVADA LICENSE ON MAY 16, 1988. INVENTORY SHOWED SIGNIFICANT SHORTAGES OF HIS OFFICE SUPPLIES OF CONTROLLED SUBSTANCES. ISSUED PRESCRIPTIONS IN FICTITIOUS NAMES. MAINTAINED AT LEAST ONE DRUG-DEPENDENT PATIENT ON DILAUDID.

CECIL, JOHN G MD, LICENSE NUMBER 0003410, OF PAHRUMP, NV, WAS DISCIPLINED BY SOUTH CAROLINA ON JULY 14, 1989.
DISCIPLINARY ACTION: SURRENDER OF LICENSE
NOTES: NOT ELIGIBLE FOR REINSTATEMENT

CECIL, JOHN G MD, LICENSE NUMBER 00B5151, OF SEDONA, AZ, WAS DISCIPLINED BY TEXAS ON AUGUST 25, 1989.
DISCIPLINARY ACTION: SURRENDER OF LICENSE

CECIL, JOHN G MD, DATE OF BIRTH NOVEMBER 19, 1905, OF 625 DEER PASS DRIVE, SEDONA, AZ, WAS DISCIPLINED BY MEDICARE ON JULY 22, 1991.
DISCIPLINARY ACTION: EXCLUSION FROM THE MEDICARE AND/OR MEDICAID PROGRAMS
OFFENSE: DISCIPLINARY ACTION BY ANOTHER STATE OR AGENCY
NOTES: LICENSE REVOCATION OR SUSPENSION.

CHALAIRE, FRANK M MD, LICENSE NUMBER 00D0375, OF SAN ANTONIO, TX, WAS DISCIPLINED BY TEXAS ON APRIL 21, 1990.
DISCIPLINARY ACTION: 60-MONTH PROBATION; RESTRICTION PLACED ON CONTROLLED SUBSTANCE LICENSE
NOTES: STIPULATED ORDER. MUST NOT DISPENSE CONTROLLED SUBSTANCES EXCEPT TO MEET IMMEDIATE NEEDS OF PATIENT FOR TREATMENT OF ANY MEDICAL CONDITION, MUST PROVIDE PRESCRIPTIONS WHEN AND TO DEGREE CALLED FOR BY CURRENT MEDICAL PRACTICE, MUST NOT PRESCRIBE CONTROLLED SUBSTANCE OR DANGEROUS DRUG FOR OBESITY PATIENT EXCEPT AFTER COMPLETION OF DIAGNOSTIC WORK-UP AS SPECIFIED.

CHALAIRE, FRANK M MD OF SAN ANTONIO, TX, WAS DISCIPLINED BY LOUISIANA ON APRIL 11, 1991.
DISCIPLINARY ACTION: PROBATION
OFFENSE: DISCIPLINARY ACTION BY ANOTHER STATE OR AGENCY
NOTES: CHARGED WITH ACTION TAKEN BY TEXAS STATE BOARD OF MEDICAL EXAMINERS. LICENSE ON PROBATION CONCURRENTLY WITH FIVE-YEAR PROBATION IMPOSED BY TEXAS, SUBJECT TO STRICT COMPLIANCE WITH PENDING ORDER OF TEXAS STATE BOARD OF MEDICAL EXAMINERS, PRIOR WRITTEN NOTICE TO BOARD OF INTENT TO RELOCATE TO LOUISIANA.

CHALAIRE, FRANK M MD, LICENSE NUMBER 0C24984, OF SAN ANTONIO, TX, WAS DISCIPLINED BY CALIFORNIA ON SEPTEMBER 5, 1992.
DISCIPLINARY ACTION: SURRENDER OF LICENSE
NOTES: VOLUNTARY SURRENDER WHILE CHARGES PENDING.

CHAMBERLIN, DAN STEVEN DO, LICENSE NUMBER 00H2295, OF PORT ARANSAS, TX, WAS DISCIPLINED BY TEXAS ON SEPTEMBER 9, 1992.
DISCIPLINARY ACTION: LICENSE REVOCATION
OFFENSE: SUBSTANDARD CARE, INCOMPETENCE, OR NEGLIGENCE
NOTES: UNPROFESSIONAL OR DISHONORABLE CONDUCT LIKELY TO DECEIVE, DEFRAUD OR INJURE THE PUBLIC; AND PROFESSIONAL FAILURE TO PRACTICE MEDICINE IN AN ACCEPTABLE MANNER CONSISTENT WITH PUBLIC HEALTH AND WELFARE.

CHAN, KWOK WEI MD, LICENSE NUMBER 0043820, OF 119 BELMONT STREET, WORCESTER, MA, WAS DISCIPLINED BY MASSACHUSETTS ON NOVEMBER 17, 1993.
DISCIPLINARY ACTION: FINE; MONITORING OF PHYSICIAN
OFFENSE: PROFESSIONAL MISCONDUCT
NOTES: VIOLATION OF A BOARD REGULATION. $10,000 FINE, ADMONISHMENT, PLAN FOR JOINT PSYCHOTHERAPY, REPORTS FROM DEPARTMENT HEAD.

CHAN, KWOK WEI MD, LICENSE NUMBER 0039381, OF 5 NORTHLAND ROAD, SHREWSBURY, MA, WAS DISCIPLINED BY VIRGINIA ON OCTOBER 13, 1994.
DISCIPLINARY ACTION: REPRIMAND
OFFENSE: DISCIPLINARY ACTION BY ANOTHER STATE OR AGENCY
NOTES: ON 11/17/93 LICENSE TO PRACTICE MEDICINE WAS RESTRICTED BY THE MASSACHUSETTS BOARD, WAS FINED $10,000 AND REQUIRED TO ENGAGE IN PSYCHOTHERAPY AND SUBJECTED TO MONITORING OF HIS CLINICAL PRACTICE FOR ENGAGING IN A PHYSICAL ALTERCATION WITH A COLLEAGUE IN THE PRESENCE OF AN ANESTHETIZED PATIENT; HE WAS SANCTIONED BY THE HOSPITAL AND FAILED TO REPORT THIS SANCTION TO THE BOARD WITHIN 30 DAYS AS REQUIRED.

CHAN, KWOK WEI MD OF SHREWSBURY, MA, WAS DISCIPLINED BY PENNSYLVANIA ON NOVEMBER 15, 1994.
DISCIPLINARY ACTION: FINE; REPRIMAND
OFFENSE: DISCIPLINARY ACTION BY ANOTHER STATE OR AGENCY
NOTES: RECIPROCAL ACTION TAKEN IN MASSACHUSETTS. $500 CIVIL PENALTY.

CHAN, KWOK WEI MD, DATE OF BIRTH OCTOBER 18, 1950, LICENSE NUMBER 00G7184, OF WORCESTER, MA, WAS DISCIPLINED BY TEXAS ON FEBRUARY 1, 1995.
DISCIPLINARY ACTION: SURRENDER OF LICENSE
OFFENSE: DISCIPLINARY ACTION BY ANOTHER STATE OR AGENCY
NOTES: LICENSE IN MASSACHUSETTS ADMONISHED AND FINED AFTER GETTING INTO A FIGHT WITH ANOTHER PHYSICIAN IN AN OPERATING ROOM; THE HOSPITAL PLACED HIM ON FIVE YEARS PROBATION WHICH HE DID NOT REPORT TO MASSACHUSETTS BOARD. SURRENDER IS PERMANENT.

CHANDLER, DONALD S MD, DATE OF BIRTH SEPTEMBER 30, 1941, LICENSE NUMBER 0030857, OF 1453 BAR HARBOR DRIVE, DALLAS, TX, WAS DISCIPLINED BY MICHIGAN ON MAY 19, 1993.
DISCIPLINARY ACTION: 35-MONTH PROBATION; REPRIMAND
OFFENSE: SUBSTANDARD CARE, INCOMPETENCE, OR NEGLIGENCE
NOTES: NEGLIGENCE AND INCOMPETENCE.

CHANDLER, DONALD S MD, DATE OF BIRTH AUGUST 3, 1941, LICENSE NUMBER 0013501, OF 900 N COKRELL HILL RD, DESOTO, TX, WAS DISCIPLINED BY GEORGIA ON SEPTEMBER 2, 1994.
DISCIPLINARY ACTION: 60-MONTH PROBATION
OFFENSE: DISCIPLINARY ACTION BY ANOTHER STATE OR AGENCY
NOTES: DISCIPLINARY ACTION IN TEXAS AND MICHIGAN.

CHANDLER, DONALD STANLEY MD, LICENSE NUMBER 00G0967, OF DALLAS, TX, WAS DISCIPLINED BY TEXAS ON APRIL 20, 1991.
DISCIPLINARY ACTION: 60-MONTH PROBATION; RESTRICTION PLACED ON LICENSE
NOTES: SUSPENSION STAYED. TERMS OF PROBATION: SHALL APPEAR BEFORE THE BOARD TWICE A YEAR; SHALL REFRAIN FROM ACCEPTING EMPLOYMENT OR ENTERING INTO CONTRACTUAL ARRANGEMENTS WHEREIN HE WOULD BE COMPENSATED TO DIAGNOSE AND/OR TREAT PATIENTS BY A LAY PERSON, CORPORATION, OR OTHER ENTITY NOT COMPRISED EXCLUSIVELY OF LICENSED PHYSICIANS; SHALL NOT PRACTICE BARIATRIC MEDICINE ON ANY PATIENT EXCEPT OVERWEIGHT PEDIATRIC PATIENTS WHO ARE APPROPRIATE CANDIDATES FOR WEIGHT CONTROL TREATMENT; SHALL ATTEND 50 HOURS CATEGORY I CONTINUING MEDICAL EDUCATION PER YEAR; MUST COMPLETE COURSE IN MEDICAL ETHICS. ON 4/15/94 HIS REQUEST FOR TERMINATION OF ORDER DENIED. HOWEVER, ORDER IS MODIFIED AS FOLLOWS: HE SHALL APPEAR BEFORE THE BOARD ONCE A YEAR DURING EACH YEAR OF PROBATION TO REPORT ON HIS COMPLIANCE. ALL OTHER PROVISIONS OF THIS ORDER REMAIN IN EFFECT. ON 10/13/95 ORDER TERMINATED.

CHANDLER, HAROLD M MD, LICENSE NUMBER 0007636, OF 11101 MAPLE GROVE, OKLAHOMA CITY, OK, WAS DISCIPLINED BY OKLAHOMA ON MAY 20, 1993.
DISCIPLINARY ACTION: 12-MONTH LICENSE SUSPENSION
OFFENSE: DRUG OR ALCOHOL ABUSE
NOTES: IN 1992 WAS USING ALCOHOL IN EXCESSIVE AMOUNTS AND IN 9/92 ADMITTED HIMSELF FOR ASSESSMENT AND TREATMENT; CONTINUED OUTPATIENT TREATMENT INCLUDING AA PARTICIPATION, PSYCHIATRIC TREATMENT AND ADDITIONAL HOSPITALIZATION; ALSO WAS DIAGNOSED WITH A BRAIN TUMOR AND UNDERWENT SURGERY FOR REMOVAL. WHEN HE APPLIES FOR REINSTATEMENT MUST PROVIDE COPIES OF ALL EVALUATIONS, REPORTS AND PROGNOSIS FROM RECOVERY CENTER AND EVALUATIONS OF RECOVERY FROM BRAIN SURGERY.

CHANDLER, HAROLD M MD, LICENSE NUMBER 0007636, WAS DISCIPLINED BY OKLAHOMA ON FEBRUARY 17, 1994.

DISCIPLINARY ACTION: 60-MONTH PROBATION; RESTRICTION PLACED ON LICENSE
NOTES: IN COMPLIANCE WITH 5/14/93 SUSPENSION ORDER HAS COMPLETED IN-PATIENT EVALUATION AND TREATMENT AND PROVIDED DISCHARGE SUMMARY AND LETTERS OF SUPPORT AND AN MRI DATED 2/2/94. LICENSE REINSTATED FROM SUSPENSION. PROBATION TO BEGIN 2/11/94. CONDITIONS OF PROBATION: SHALL MEET REGULARLY WITH PHYSICIAN RECOVERY COMMITTEE; SHALL NOT PRESCRIBE, ADMINISTER OR DISPENSE ANY MEDICATIONS FOR HIS PERSONAL USE AND TAKE NO MEDICATION UNLESS IT IS AUTHORIZED BY ANOTHER PHYSICIAN FOR A LEGITIMATE MEDICAL NEED; SHALL ABSTAIN FROM THE CONSUMPTION OF ALCOHOL OR ANY SUBSTANCE WHICH WOULD ADVERSELY AFFECT HIS ABILITY TO PRACTICE MEDICINE; SHALL NOT INGEST ANY SUBSTANCE THAT WOULD TEST POSITIVE FOR ALCOHOL OR ANY CONTROLLED SUBSTANCE; SHALL SUBMIT BIOLOGICAL FLUID SPECIMENS; SHALL HAVE HIS PHYSICIAN MONITOR LITHIUM LEVELS AND PROVIDE QUARTERLY REPORTS; SHALL PRACTICE UNDER A BOARD-APPROVED MONITOR; SHALL HAVE HIS PATIENTS SIGN A PATIENT'S RIGHTS STATEMENT; SHALL FURNISH BOARD WITH ADDRESS AND/OR CHANGE OF ADDRESS; SHALL APPEAR BEFORE THE BOARD UPON REQUEST AND PROVIDE REQUIRED REPORTS; SHALL PAY COSTS; SHALL SUPPLY A COPY OF THIS ORDER TO ANY HEALTH CARE ENTITY WHERE HE HAS PRIVILEGES; SHALL NOT SUPERVISE A PHYSICIAN'S ASSISTANT.

CHANDLER, HAROLD MULLINS MD, LICENSE NUMBER 00H5382, OF BEAUMONT, TX, WAS DISCIPLINED BY TEXAS ON APRIL 15, 1994.
DISCIPLINARY ACTION: 60-MONTH PROBATION; REQUIRED TO TAKE ADDITIONAL MEDICAL EDUCATION
OFFENSE: DISCIPLINARY ACTION BY ANOTHER STATE OR AGENCY
NOTES: ON 5/20/93 OKLAHOMA SUSPENDED HIS LICENSE FOR ONE YEAR BASED ON INTEMPERATE USE OF ALCOHOL; ADMITS HE IS AN ALCOHOLIC AND HAS SOUGHT IN-PATIENT TREATMENT ON HIS OWN INITIATIVE IN THE PAST; HAS BEEN SOBER SINCE 9/8/92; HE IS CURRENTLY PRACTICING PSYCHIATRY IN TEXAS AND BEING TREATED BY HIS PHYSICIAN IN OKLAHOMA; OKLAHOMA REINSTATED HIS LICENSE ON PROBATION ON 2/11/94. SUSPENSION STAYED. CONDITIONS OF PROBATION: SHALL ABSTAIN FROM THE CONSUMPTION OF ALCOHOL/CHEMICAL SUBSTANCES IN ANY FORM UNLESS PRESCRIBED BY ANOTHER PHYSICIAN FOR A LEGITIMATE AND THERAPEUTIC PURPOSE; SHALL NOT TREAT OR OTHERWISE SERVE AS PHYSICIAN, PRESCRIBE, DISPENSE OR ADMINISTER DRUGS THAT MAY BE SUBJECT TO ABUSE TO HIMSELF OR ANY MEMBER OF HIS FAMILY; SHALL SUBMIT HIMSELF FOR APPROPRIATE EXAMS INCLUDING DRUG AND ALCOHOL SCREENS; SHALL PARTICIPATE IN AA'S PROGRAM NOT LESS THAN TWO TIMES A WEEK WITH QUARTERLY REPORTS TO THE BOARD; SHALL CONTINUE TREATMENT WITH HIS PRESENT PHYSICIAN AND MONITORING WITH HIS PRESENT SUPERVISOR WITH QUARTERLY REPORTS; SHALL ATTEND AT LEAST 50 HOURS PER YEAR OF CONTINUING MEDICAL EDUCATION INCLUDING COURSES ADDRESSING ADDICTIONOLOGY, DRUG ABUSE, AND CO-DEPENDENCY; SHALL PERFORM TWO HOURS PER WEEK OF COMMUNITY SERVICE FOR FIVE YEARS; SHALL FOLLOW ALL TERMS OF OKLAHOMA ORDER AND PROVIDE TEXAS BOARD ALL DOCUMENTS SUBMITTED TO OKLAHOMA BOARD; SHALL APPEAR BEFORE THE BOARD TWICE A YEAR; SHALL GIVE A COPY OF THIS ORDER TO ANY HEALTH CARE ENTITY WHERE HE HAS PRIVILEGES; SHALL COOPERATE WITH THE BOARD IN VERIFYING COMPLIANCE; SHALL INFORM BOARD OF CHANGE OF ADDRESS WITHIN 10 DAYS OR IF HE LEAVES THE STATE; TIME SPENT OUT OF TEXAS DOES NOT COUNT TOWARD PROBATION. SHALL NOT SEEK MODIFICATION FOR ONE YEAR.

CHANEY, MARTIN H MD, LICENSE NUMBER 00C8220, OF HUNTSVILLE, TX, WAS DISCIPLINED BY TEXAS ON AUGUST 24, 1991.
NOTES: PROBATION TERMINATED; LICENSE FREE OF RESTRICTION.

CHAPPELL, TIMOTHY RAE MD, LICENSE NUMBER 00E7029, OF PLANO, TX, WAS DISCIPLINED BY TEXAS ON JUNE 22, 1994.
DISCIPLINARY ACTION: REPRIMAND; REQUIRED TO TAKE ADDITIONAL MEDICAL EDUCATION
OFFENSE: OVERPRESCRIBING OR MISPRESCRIBING DRUGS
NOTES: PRESCRIBED HYCODAN FOR ONE PATIENT FROM 11/89 TO 5/92 IN INCREASING QUANTITIES WHEN HE HAD REASON TO SUSPECT SHE WAS ADDICTED AS EARLY AS 8/90; TALKED WITH PATIENT ABOUT THIS CONCERN BUT DID NOT INSIST SHE SEEK TREATMENT. SHALL WITHIN SIX MONTHS COMPLETE A BOARD-APPROVED CLINICAL PHARMACOLOGY OR PAIN MANAGEMENT COURSE AND ETHICS COURSE OR PROGRAM; SHALL GIVE A COPY OF THIS ORDER TO ANY HEALTH CARE ENTITY WHERE HE HAS PRIVILEGES; SHALL COOPERATE WITH THE BOARD IN VERIFYING COMPLIANCE; SHALL INFORM BOARD OF CHANGE OF ADDRESS WITHIN 10 DAYS OR IF HE LEAVES THE STATE; TIME SPENT OUT OF TEXAS DOES NOT COUNT TOWARD ORDER. SHALL NOT SEEK MODIFICATION FOR ONE YEAR.

CHEN, RAY HUANG TSANG MD, DATE OF BIRTH JANUARY 2, 1942, LICENSE NUMBER 00E5356, OF 6305 NEWCASTLE, BELLAIRE, TX, WAS DISCIPLINED BY TEXAS ON JANUARY 29, 1993.
DISCIPLINARY ACTION: 60-MONTH PROBATION; RESTRICTION PLACED ON CONTROLLED SUBSTANCE LICENSE
OFFENSE: OVERPRESCRIBING OR MISPRESCRIBING DRUGS
NOTES: PRESCRIBED DEMEROL AND VALIUM TO HIS EX-WIFE IN EXCESSIVE AMOUNTS WHEN HE KNEW SHE WAS HABITUATED TO CONTROLLED SUBSTANCES. 5 YEAR SUSPENSION STAYED. CONDITIONS OF PROBATION: SHALL SURRENDER ALL UNUSED TRIPLICATE PRESCRIPTION FORMS AND NOT ORDER ANY MORE WITHOUT WRITTEN AUTHORITY; SHALL NOT POSSESS, ADMINISTER, DISPENSE OR PRESCRIBE ANY CONTROLLED SUBSTANCES OUTSIDE OF A HOSPITAL SETTING; SHALL NOT TREAT OR OTHERWISE SERVE AS PHYSICIAN, PRESCRIBE, DISPENSE OR ADMINISTER CONTROLLED SUBSTANCES THAT MAY BE SUBJECT TO ABUSE TO HIMSELF OR ANY MEMBER OF HIS FAMILY; SHALL MAINTAIN ADEQUATE MEDICAL RECORDS ON ALL OFFICE VISITS WHICH SHALL BE AVAILABLE FOR INSPECTION; SHALL APPEAR BEFORE THE BOARD ONCE A YEAR; SHALL GIVE A COPY OF THIS ORDER TO ANY HEALTH CARE ENTITY WHERE HE HAS PRIVILEGES; SHALL COOPERATE WITH THE BOARD IN VERIFYING COMPLIANCE; SHALL INFORM BOARD OF CHANGE OF ADDRESS WITHIN 10 DAYS OR IF HE LEAVES THE STATE; TIME SPENT OUT OF TEXAS DOES NOT COUNT

TOWARD PROBATION. SHALL NOT SEEK MODIFICATION UNLESS HE LOCATES PRACTICE OUTSIDE OF TEXAS AND AT LEAST ONE YEAR HAS ELAPSED.

CHERIAN, FRANCIS MD, LICENSE NUMBER 00F8052, OF BRYAN, TX, WAS DISCIPLINED BY TEXAS ON OCTOBER 27, 1989.
DISCIPLINARY ACTION: RESTRICTION PLACED ON CONTROLLED SUBSTANCE LICENSE
NOTES: STIPULATED ORDER. PROHIBITED FROM DISPENSING DRUGS FROM OFFICE.

CHERIAN, RANY MD, LICENSE NUMBER 00G6918, OF BRYAN, TX, WAS DISCIPLINED BY TEXAS ON OCTOBER 27, 1989.
DISCIPLINARY ACTION: RESTRICTION PLACED ON CONTROLLED SUBSTANCE LICENSE
NOTES: STIPULATED ORDER. PROHIBITED FROM DISPENSING DRUGS FROM OFFICE.

CHESNICK, JOHN JR DO, LICENSE NUMBER 00E7855, OF CORPUS CHRISTI, TX, WAS DISCIPLINED BY TEXAS ON DECEMBER 1, 1988.
NOTES: SETTLEMENT AGREEMENT AND UNSPECIFIED DISCIPLINARY ACTION

CHESNICK, JOHN JR DO, LICENSE NUMBER 0004376, WAS DISCIPLINED BY MICHIGAN ON JANUARY 5, 1989.
DISCIPLINARY ACTION: SURRENDER OF LICENSE

CHESNICK, JOHN J JR DO OF CORPUS CHRISTI, TX, WAS DISCIPLINED BY MISSOURI ON JANUARY 18, 1989.
DISCIPLINARY ACTION: SURRENDER OF LICENSE
OFFENSE: DISCIPLINARY ACTION BY ANOTHER STATE OR AGENCY

CHESTER, JEREMY DAVID MD, LICENSE NUMBER 00H4234, OF DUNCANVILLE, TX, WAS DISCIPLINED BY TEXAS ON SEPTEMBER 25, 1993.
DISCIPLINARY ACTION: 60-MONTH RESTRICTION PLACED ON CONTROLLED SUBSTANCE LICENSE; MONITORING OF PHYSICIAN
OFFENSE: DRUG OR ALCOHOL ABUSE
NOTES: HAS SUFFERED FROM DEPRESSION, POST-TRAUMATIC STRESS AND CHEMICAL DEPENDENCE INVOLVING ABUSE OF FENTANYL; UNDERWENT INPATIENT TREATMENT FOR CHEMICAL DEPENDENCE FROM 7/91 THROUGH 11/91 AND INPATIENT CARE FOR DEPRESSION AND POST-TRAUMATIC STRESS BEGINNING 12/92; PARTICIPATES IN AA AND IS IN THERAPY. CONDITIONS OF RESTRICTION: SHALL ABSTAIN FROM THE CONSUMPTION OF ALCOHOL/CHEMICAL SUBSTANCES IN ANY FORM UNLESS PRESCRIBED BY ANOTHER PHYSICIAN FOR A LEGITIMATE AND THERAPEUTIC PURPOSE; SHALL SUBMIT HIMSELF FOR APPROPRIATE EXAMS INCLUDING DRUG OR ALCOHOL SCREENS; SHALL CONTINUE TO RECEIVE TREATMENT FROM SPECIFIED PHYSICIANS WITH QUARTERLY REPORTS; SHALL PARTICIPATE IN AA'S PROGRAM NOT LESS THAN TWO TIMES A WEEK; SHALL PARTICIPATE IN ACTIVITIES OF A PHYSICIAN HEALTH AND REHABILITATION COMMITTEE AND ATTEND WEEKLY MEETINGS WITH QUARTERLY REPORTS; SHALL NOT POSSESS, ADMINISTER, OR PRESCRIBE CONTROLLED SUBSTANCES EXCEPT IN A HOSPITAL EMERGENCY ROOM; SEPARATE FROM PATIENT RECORDS, SHALL MAINTAIN A WRITTEN RECORD OF EVERY DANGEROUS DRUG ORDERED OR PRESCRIBED; SHALL NOT TELEPHONE IN ANY PRESCRIPTIONS; EMPLOYER SHALL SUBMIT REPORTS TO THE BOARD EVERY SIX MONTHS; SHALL GIVE A COPY OF THIS ORDER TO ANY HEALTH CARE ENTITY WHERE HE HAS PRIVILEGES; SHALL COOPERATE WITH THE BOARD IN VERIFYING COMPLIANCE; SHALL INFORM BOARD OF CHANGE OF ADDRESS WITHIN 10 DAYS OR IF HE LEAVES THE STATE; TIME SPENT OUT OF TEXAS DOES NOT COUNT TOWARD RESTRICTION. SHALL NOT SEEK MODIFICATION FOR ONE YEAR.

CHILDRESS, MARVIN A MD OF 1219 PARKER STREET, GOLDTHWAITE, TX, WAS DISCIPLINED BY MEDICARE ON DECEMBER 12, 1986.
DISCIPLINARY ACTION: 60-MONTH EXCLUSION FROM THE MEDICARE AND/OR MEDICAID PROGRAMS
OFFENSE: SUBSTANDARD CARE, INCOMPETENCE, OR NEGLIGENCE
NOTES: GROSSLY SUBSTANDARD CARE OF 10 PATIENTS INCLUDING FAILURE TO ACT PROMPTLY AND AGGRESSIVELY IN TREATING LIFE-THREATENING ILLNESSES AND TREATING PATIENTS WHOSE ILLNESSES WERE BEYOND CHILDRESS' CLINICAL SKILLS. CHILDRESS HAS TRIED TO IMPROVE HIS SKILLS BUT INSPECTOR GENERAL DETERMINED HE WAS UNABLE TO DO SO

CHILDRESS, MARVIN A MD, LICENSE NUMBER 00C0817, OF GOLDTHWAITE, TX, WAS DISCIPLINED BY TEXAS ON DECEMBER 1, 1988.
NOTES: SETTLEMENT AGREEMENT AND UNSPECIFIED DISCIPLINARY ACTION

CHIN, FRANK T W MD OF BOX 870, 3150 HORTON ROAD, FORT WORTH, TX, WAS DISCIPLINED BY MEDICARE ON MARCH 10, 1986.
DISCIPLINARY ACTION: 120-MONTH EXCLUSION FROM THE MEDICARE AND/OR MEDICAID PROGRAMS
OFFENSE: CRIMINAL CONVICTION OR PLEA OF GUILTY, NOLO CONTENDERE, OR NO CONTEST TO A CRIME
NOTES: PROGRAM-RELATED CONVICTION.

CHIN, FRANK T W DR WAS DISCIPLINED BY CALIFORNIA ON OCTOBER 1, 1987.
DISCIPLINARY ACTION: DENIAL OF NEW LICENSE
OFFENSE: CRIMINAL CONVICTION OR PLEA OF GUILTY, NOLO CONTENDERE, OR NO CONTEST TO A CRIME
NOTES: FEDERAL CONVICTION FOR PRESCRIBING CONTROLLED DRUGS WITHOUT MEDICAL CAUSE. CONVICTION IN LOUISIANA FOR MEDICAID FRAUD. DENIED SOMETIME BETWEEN JULY AND OCTOBER 1987

CHIN, FRANK T W MD OF WEST MONROE, LA, WAS DISCIPLINED BY KANSAS ON APRIL 26, 1989.
DISCIPLINARY ACTION: DENIAL OF NEW LICENSE

CHODOSH, THOMAS B DO, LICENSE NUMBER 00D6394, OF CORPUS CHRISTI, TX, WAS DISCIPLINED BY TEXAS ON JUNE 13, 1989.
DISCIPLINARY ACTION: 60-MONTH RESTRICTION PLACED ON LICENSE; 60-MONTH REQUIRED TO TAKE ADDITIONAL MEDICAL EDUCATION
NOTES: OBTAIN PRE-PARTUM CONSULTATIONS ON PATIENT HIGH RISK PREGNANCIES AND REFER OR OBTAIN DELIVERY ROOM ASSISTANCE; APPEAR SEMI-ANNUALLY BEFORE BOARD; REPORT ON OBSTETRICAL PATIENTS AND OBTAIN REVIEW OF SUCH REPORTS; OBTAIN CONTINUING MEDICAL EDUCATION.

CHODOSH, THOMAS B DO OF CORPUS CHRISTI, TX, WAS DISCIPLINED BY MISSOURI ON SEPTEMBER 7, 1990.
OFFENSE: DISCIPLINARY ACTION BY ANOTHER STATE OR AGENCY

NOTES: UNSUCCESSFULLY ATTEMPTED A NORMAL DELIVERY BY A 15-YEAR-OLD MOTHER USING FORCEPS IN A RECKLESS AND DANGEROUS MANNER; UNDUE DELAY IN OBTAINING A C-SECTION RESULTED IN BRAIN DAMAGE TO THE INFANT AND UNNECESSARY DAMAGE TO THE MOTHER AND CHILD IN GENERAL. AGREEMENT - MUST APPEAR BEFORE BOARD BEFORE RETURNING TO PRACTICE IN MISSOURI

CHOKSHI, SUSHIL B MD, LICENSE NUMBER 00F5865, OF JACKSBORO, TX, WAS DISCIPLINED BY TEXAS ON DECEMBER 4, 1989.
NOTES: STIPULATED ORDER. MUST MAINTAIN COMPLETE AND ACCURATE RECORDS OF PURCHASES AND DISPOSALS OF CONTROLLED SUBSTANCES AND ADEQUATELY SUPERVISE ACTIVITIES OF EMPLOYEES TO DETERMINE COMPLIANCE WITH LAWS INVOLVING PRACTICE OF MEDICINE.

CHONG, JUAN A MD, LICENSE NUMBER 00E0855, OF CLEVELAND, TX, WAS DISCIPLINED BY TEXAS ON OCTOBER 5, 1991.
DISCIPLINARY ACTION: 48-MONTH RESTRICTION PLACED ON LICENSE; REQUIRED TO TAKE ADDITIONAL MEDICAL EDUCATION
OFFENSE: SUBSTANDARD CARE, INCOMPETENCE, OR NEGLIGENCE
NOTES: INAPPROPRIATE OBSTETRICAL/ GYNECOLOGICAL TREATMENT OF NINE PATIENTS; VOLUNTARILY AGREED TO A HOSPITAL REVIEW OF RECORDS, TO GET SECOND OPINIONS ON ALL SURGERY CASES, AND TO OBTAIN FURTHER EDUCATION; VOLUNTARILY RELINQUISHED HIS GYNECOLOGICAL PRIVILEGES AT CHARTER REGIONAL MEDICAL CENTER UNTIL THEY HIRED A QUALIFIED PHYSICIAN WHO COULD REVIEW HIS RECORDS, WHICH WAS ACCEPTED BY THE HOSPITAL ON 2/22/91; HAS NOT PRACTICED OBSTETRICS FOR MORE THAN A YEAR. LICENSE IS RESTRICTED UNDER THE FOLLOWING TERMS AND CONDITIONS: SHALL ATTEND AT LEAST 50 HOURS PER YEAR OF CATEGORY I CONTINUING MEDICAL EDUCATION; SHALL NOT PRACTICE OBSTETRICS UNTIL SUCH TIME AS THE MEDICAL EXECUTIVE COMMITTEE OF AN ACCREDITED HOSPITAL IS PREPARED TO EXTEND HOSPITAL OBSTETRICS PRIVILEGES; SHALL REFRAIN FROM PERFORMING GYNECOLOGICAL SURGERY UNLESS PERFORMED IN A ACCREDITED HOSPITAL WHERE HE HAS PRIVILEGES TO PERFORM SUCH SURGERY; SHALL HAVE A BOARD-APPROVED SUPERVISOR WITH QUARTERLY REPORTS TO THE BOARD; SHALL COOPERATE WITH THE BOARD IN VERIFYING COMPLIANCE; SHALL ADVISE THE BOARD OF ANY ADDRESS CHANGE WITHIN 10 DAYS; TIME SPENT OUT OF TEXAS DOES NOT COUNT TOWARD PROBATION; SHALL NOT SEEK MODIFICATION OF ORDER FOR AT LEAST ONE YEAR. ON 3/5/94 ORDER TERMINATED.

CHOUTEAU, ROBERT M DO, LICENSE NUMBER 00E9578, OF DALLAS, TX, WAS DISCIPLINED BY TEXAS ON JANUARY 6, 1995.
DISCIPLINARY ACTION: REPRIMAND
OFFENSE: FAILURE TO COMPLY WITH A PROFESSIONAL RULE
NOTES: INADEQUATELY DOCUMENTED THE CARE AND TREATMENT OF A PATIENT. SHALL GIVE A COPY OF THIS ORDER TO ANY HEALTH CARE ENTITY WHERE HE HAS PRIVILEGES.

CHRIST, JOHN E MD, LICENSE NUMBER 0123047, OF BISHOP COUNTY JAIL, BASTROP, TX, WAS DISCIPLINED BY NEW YORK ON OCTOBER 24, 1994.
DISCIPLINARY ACTION: LICENSE REVOCATION
OFFENSE: DISCIPLINARY ACTION BY ANOTHER STATE OR AGENCY
NOTES: CONVICTED OF ATTEMPTED MURDER AND FOUND GUILTY OF MISCONDUCT BY THE TEXAS BOARD.

CHRIST, JOHN E MD, LICENSE NUMBER 0055213, OF 6560 FANNIN STREET, HOUSTON, TX, WAS DISCIPLINED BY MASSACHUSETTS ON NOVEMBER 9, 1994.
DISCIPLINARY ACTION: LICENSE REVOCATION
OFFENSE: DISCIPLINARY ACTION BY ANOTHER STATE OR AGENCY
NOTES: DISCIPLINE BY TEXAS; CRIMINAL CONVICTION

CHRIST, JOHN ERNEST MD, LICENSE NUMBER 00E0856, OF HOUSTON, TX, WAS DISCIPLINED BY TEXAS ON JANUARY 14, 1994.
DISCIPLINARY ACTION: LICENSE SUSPENSION
OFFENSE: CRIMINAL CONVICTION OR PLEA OF GUILTY, NOLO CONTENDERE, OR NO CONTEST TO A CRIME
NOTES: ON 9/16/93 JUDGMENT ENTERED WHICH FOUND HIM GUILTY OF ATTEMPTED MURDER; SENTENCED TO 20 YEARS IN PRISON AND A $10,000 FINE; IS PRESENTLY INCARCERATED; IS IN THE PROCESS OF APPEALING THIS CONVICTION. IF APPEAL OF CONVICTION IS SUCCESSFUL SUSPENSION SHALL BE LIFTED UNLESS LICENSE HAS BEEN SUSPENDED FOR MORE THAN 24 MONTHS; IN THAT CASE SUSPENSION SHALL REMAIN IN EFFECT UNTIL HE PASSES SPEX EXAM; IF CONVICTION IS UPHELD, LICENSE SHALL BE REVOKED.

CHRISTENSEN, DENNIS W MD, LICENSE NUMBER 0012595, OF CONWAY, SC, WAS DISCIPLINED BY SOUTH CAROLINA ON JULY 24, 1990.
DISCIPLINARY ACTION: PROBATION; FINE
OFFENSE: PROVIDING FALSE INFORMATION TO THE BOARD
NOTES: SUBSTANCE ABUSE AND FALSE ANSWER ON REREGISTRATION. SUSPENSION STAYED; $1,000 FINE AND INDEFINITE PROBATION.

CHRISTENSEN, DENNIS W MD, LICENSE NUMBER 0012595, OF CONWAY, SC, WAS DISCIPLINED BY SOUTH CAROLINA ON DECEMBER 5, 1990.
DISCIPLINARY ACTION: LICENSE REVOCATION
OFFENSE: FAILURE TO COMPLY WITH A PREVIOUS BOARD ORDER
NOTES: VIOLATED CONDITIONS OF PROBATION.

CHRISTENSEN, DENNIS W MD, LICENSE NUMBER 00C8923, OF CONWAY, SC, WAS DISCIPLINED BY TEXAS ON APRIL 20, 1991.
DISCIPLINARY ACTION: REQUIRED TO ENTER AN IMPAIRED PHYSICIAN PROGRAM OR DRUG OR ALCOHOL TREATMENT; MONITORING OF PHYSICIAN
OFFENSE: DISCIPLINARY ACTION BY ANOTHER STATE OR AGENCY
NOTES: PRIOR TO PRACTICING IN TEXAS MUST APPEAR BEFORE THE BOARD; CONTINUE TO PARTICIPATE IN A MAINTENANCE PROGRAM FOR RECOVERING ALCOHOLICS; MUST ABSTAIN FROM THE CONSUMPTION OF ALCOHOL/CHEMICAL SUBSTANCES; MUST SUBMIT TO ALCOHOL AND DRUG SCREENS.

CHRISTENSEN, DENNIS W MD OF CONWAY, SC, WAS DISCIPLINED BY NORTH CAROLINA ON SEPTEMBER 30, 1991.
DISCIPLINARY ACTION: SURRENDER OF LICENSE

CHRISTIANSON, PAUL BARR MD, LICENSE NUMBER 00G6487, OF GRIFFISS AFB, NY, WAS DISCIPLINED BY TEXAS ON JANUARY 24, 1992.
DISCIPLINARY ACTION: SURRENDER OF LICENSE
OFFENSE: SUBSTANDARD CARE, INCOMPETENCE, OR

NEGLIGENCE
NOTES: PROFESSIONAL FAILURE TO PRACTICE MEDICINE IN AN ACCEPTABLE MANNER CONSISTENT WITH PUBLIC HEALTH AND WELFARE. LICENSE VOLUNTARILY SURRENDERED IN LIEU OF FURTHER DISCIPLINARY ACTION.

CISNEROS, ALFREDO A MD, LICENSE NUMBER 00E4817, OF ROSEBUD, TX, WAS DISCIPLINED BY TEXAS ON DECEMBER 1, 1988.
NOTES: SETTLEMENT AGREEMENT AND UNSPECIFIED DISCIPLINARY ACTION

CLARK, CORDELL MD OF 7231 FLAMELEAF PLACE, DALLAS, TX, WAS DISCIPLINED BY MEDICARE ON JULY 10, 1986.
DISCIPLINARY ACTION: 36-MONTH EXCLUSION FROM THE MEDICARE AND/OR MEDICAID PROGRAMS; FINE

CLARK, GEORGE B DO, LICENSE NUMBER 00D1400, OF DALLAS, TX, WAS DISCIPLINED BY TEXAS ON JANUARY 6, 1995.
DISCIPLINARY ACTION: REPRIMAND
OFFENSE: OVERPRESCRIBING OR MISPRESCRIBING DRUGS
NOTES: FROM 1984 THROUGH 7/93 PRESCRIBED CONTROLLED SUBSTANCES TO AN ADULT FEMALE PATIENT WITHOUT ADEQUATE INDICATION OR APPROPRIATE DOCUMENTATION; KNEW OR SHOULD HAVE KNOWN SHE WAS AN ABUSER OF CONTROLLED SUBSTANCES; AGREES TO THE ENTRY OF THIS ORDER IN LIEU OF FURTHER INVESTIGATION.

CLARK, ROBERT ERNEST III MD, LICENSE NUMBER 00F6532, OF HEREFORD, TX, WAS DISCIPLINED BY TEXAS ON AUGUST 20, 1992.
DISCIPLINARY ACTION: 60-MONTH PROBATION
OFFENSE: DISCIPLINARY ACTION BY ANOTHER STATE OR AGENCY
NOTES: UNPROFESSIONAL OR DISHONORABLE CONDUCT LIKELY TO DECEIVE, DEFRAUD OR INJURE THE PUBLIC; AND DISCIPLINARY ACTION BY A PEER REVIEW ENTITY. SUSPENSION, STAYED. PROBATION UNDER TERMS AND CONDITIONS.

CLARK, WILLIAM M MD, LICENSE NUMBER 00G1357, OF PRAIRIE VIEW, TX, WAS DISCIPLINED BY TEXAS ON APRIL 1, 1987.
DISCIPLINARY ACTION: LICENSE REVOCATION
OFFENSE: PROFESSIONAL MISCONDUCT
NOTES: UNPROFESSIONAL OR DISHONORABLE CONDUCT LIKELY TO DECEIVE OR DEFRAUD PUBLIC.

CLARK, WILLIAM M MD OF PRAIRIE VIEW, TX, WAS DISCIPLINED BY LOUISIANA ON JULY 2, 1987.
DISCIPLINARY ACTION: LICENSE REVOCATION
OFFENSE: DISCIPLINARY ACTION BY ANOTHER STATE OR AGENCY
NOTES: REVOCATION OF A LICENSE ISSUED BY ANOTHER STATE.

COATS, ROBERT EUGENE JR DO, DATE OF BIRTH AUGUST 12, 1946, LICENSE NUMBER 00G7795, OF 103 E ADKINS, SEAGOVILLE, TX, WAS DISCIPLINED BY TEXAS ON MARCH 26, 1993.
DISCIPLINARY ACTION: RESTRICTION PLACED ON LICENSE; RESTRICTION PLACED ON CONTROLLED SUBSTANCE LICENSE
NOTES: ALLEGATIONS MADE WHICH QUESTION HIS ABILITY TO SAFELY PRACTICE DUE TO MEDICAL PROBLEMS ASSOCIATED WITH A DAMAGED HIP AND POSSIBLE INTEMPERATE USE OF DRUGS; HE DOES NOT ADMIT THESE ALLEGATIONS. AFTER 3/31/93 SHALL NOT PRACTICE MEDICINE UNTIL HE IS EVALUATED BY A BOARD-APPROVED PSYCHIATRIST AND ORTHOPEDIST. SHALL NOT REQUEST RENEWAL OF DEA AND DPS CONTROLLED SUBSTANCES REGISTRATIONS WHICH EXPIRE ON 3/31/93; SHALL KEEP A SEPARATE LOG OF ALL SUCH PRESCRIPTIONS WRITTEN BETWEEN 3/13/93 AND 3/31/94 WHICH IS TO BE AVAILABLE FOR INSPECTION.

COATS, ROBERT EUGENE JR DO, DATE OF BIRTH AUGUST 12, 1946, LICENSE NUMBER 00G7795, OF ARLINGTON, TX, WAS DISCIPLINED BY TEXAS ON MARCH 5, 1994.
DISCIPLINARY ACTION: 84-MONTH PROBATION; RESTRICTION PLACED ON CONTROLLED SUBSTANCE LICENSE
OFFENSE: PHYSICAL OR MENTAL ILLNESS INHIBITING THE ABILITY TO PRACTICE WITH SKILL AND SAFETY
NOTES: ADMITS THAT PHYSICAL AILMENTS INCLUDING TWO TOTAL HIP REPLACEMENTS AND MAJOR BACK SURGERY HAVE IMPAIRED HIS ABILITY TO PRACTICE; CONTENDS HE HAS NEVER ABUSED PAIN MEDICATIONS AND NEVER PRESCRIBED MEDICATIONS WITHOUT ADEQUATE INDICATION; HE BELIEVES HE NO LONGER HAS ANY IMPAIRMENT THAT WOULD AFFECT HIS ABILITY TO PRACTICE MEDICINE SAFELY; VOLUNTARILY SUBMITTED TO PSYCHIATRIC AND ORTHOPEDIC EVALUATIONS REQUIRED BY PREVIOUS ORDER; IN LIEU OF A CONTESTED HEARING, THE FOLLOWING ORDER WAS AGREED TO. SUSPENSION STAYED. CONDITIONS OF PROBATION: SHALL APPEAR BEFORE THE BOARD TWICE A YEAR; SHALL ATTEND AT LEAST 50 HOURS PER YEAR OF CONTINUING MEDICAL EDUCATION; SHALL MAINTAIN ADEQUATE MEDICAL RECORDS ON ALL PATIENT OFFICE VISITS AND SHALL MAKE SUCH RECORDS AVAILABLE FOR REVIEW; SHALL NOT SIGN ANYTHING ON A PATIENT RECORD UNLESS HE HAS PERSONALLY SEEN AND EXAMINED THE PATIENT UNLESS THE RECORD CLEARLY REFLECTS HE HAS NOT; SHALL ABSTAIN FROM THE CONSUMPTION OF ALCOHOL/CHEMICAL SUBSTANCES IN ANY FORM UNLESS PRESCRIBED BY ANOTHER PHYSICIAN FOR A LEGITIMATE AND THERAPEUTIC PURPOSE; SHALL NOT TREAT OR OTHERWISE SERVE AS PHYSICIAN, PRESCRIBE, DISPENSE OR ADMINISTER DRUGS THAT MAY BE SUBJECT TO ABUSE TO HIMSELF OR ANY MEMBER OF HIS FAMILY; SEPARATE FROM PATIENT RECORDS SHALL MAINTAIN A FILE OF EVERY PRESCRIPTION WRITTEN FOR DANGEROUS DRUGS WHICH SHALL BE AVAILABLE FOR INSPECTION; SHALL NOT PERMIT AN UNLICENSED PERSON TO PHONE IN A PRESCRIPTION ON HIS BEHALF UNLESS HE HAS FIRST PERFORMED AN EXAM AND MADE A DIAGNOSIS; SHALL SUBMIT HIMSELF FOR APPROPRIATE EXAMS INCLUDING DRUG OR ALCOHOL SCREENS; SHALL CONTINUE TO RECEIVE PSYCHIATRIC TREATMENT WITH QUARTERLY REPORTS; SHALL SUBMIT TO THE CARE AND TREATMENT OF A BOARD-APPROVED ORTHOPEDIC PHYSICIAN; SHALL PROVIDE WRITTEN REPORTS VERIFYING COMPLIANCE UPON REQUEST; MAY REAPPLY FOR DEA AND TEXAS CONTROLLED SUBSTANCES CERTIFICATES FOR SCHEDULES II AND III BUT SHALL LIMIT PRESCRIBING TO A HOSPITAL, EMERGENCY ROOM OR MINOR EMERGENCY CLINIC; SHALL GIVE A COPY OF THE ORDER TO ANY HEALTH CARE ENTITY WHERE HE HAS PRIVILEGES; SHALL COOPERATE WITH THE BOARD IN VERIFYING COMPLIANCE; SHALL INFORM BOARD OF ANY CHANGE OF ADDRESS WITHIN 10 DAYS OR IF HE LEAVES THE STATE; TIME PERIOD SPENT OUT OF TEXAS DOES NOT COUNT TOWARD PROBATION. SHALL NOT SEEK

MODIFICATION FOR ONE YEAR. ON 10/10/94 THIS ORDER CORRECTED SUCH THAT HE WAS GIVEN PERMISSION TO APPLY FOR SCHEDULE IV AND V CONTROLLED SUBSTANCES CERTIFICATES.

COE, RICHARD O JR MD OF PRAIRIE VILLAGE, KS, WAS DISCIPLINED BY KANSAS ON FEBRUARY 11, 1989.
DISCIPLINARY ACTION: EMERGENCY SUSPENSION

COE, RICHARD O JR MD OF OVERLAND PARK, KS, WAS DISCIPLINED BY MISSOURI ON MARCH 3, 1989.
DISCIPLINARY ACTION: SURRENDER OF LICENSE
OFFENSE: DISCIPLINARY ACTION BY ANOTHER STATE OR AGENCY
NOTES: DRUG OR ALCOHOL ABUSE.

COE, RICHARD O JR MD OF OVERLAND PARK, KS, WAS DISCIPLINED BY KANSAS ON AUGUST 12, 1989.
DISCIPLINARY ACTION: RESTRICTION PLACED ON LICENSE

COE, RICHARD OREN JR MD, LICENSE NUMBER 00C5634, OF OVERLAND PARK, KS, WAS DISCIPLINED BY TEXAS ON DECEMBER 1, 1988.
NOTES: SETTLEMENT AGREEMENT AND UNSPECIFIED DISCIPLINARY ACTION

COE, RICHARD OREN JR MD, LICENSE NUMBER 00C5634, OF OLATHE, KS, WAS DISCIPLINED BY TEXAS ON MARCH 31, 1990.
DISCIPLINARY ACTION: 60-MONTH PROBATION; REQUIRED TO ENTER AN IMPAIRED PHYSICIAN PROGRAM OR DRUG OR ALCOHOL TREATMENT
OFFENSE: DISCIPLINARY ACTION BY ANOTHER STATE OR AGENCY
NOTES: STIPULATED ORDER. MUST COMPLY WITH STIPULATION ENTERED INTO WITH KANSAS BOARD AND TERMS OF KANSAS IMPAIRED PHYSICIAN MONITORING CONTRACT, FURNISH TEXAS BOARD REPORTS AND RECEIVE APPROVAL FROM BOARD PRIOR TO PRACTICING MEDICINE IN TEXAS.

COE, RICHARD OREN JR MD, LICENSE NUMBER 00C5634, OF OVERLAND PARK, KS, WAS DISCIPLINED BY TEXAS ON JUNE 10, 1991.
DISCIPLINARY ACTION: LICENSE REVOCATION
OFFENSE: DISCIPLINARY ACTION BY ANOTHER STATE OR AGENCY
NOTES: ALCOHOL ABUSE LED TO DISCIPLINARY ACTION BY ANOTHER STATE.

COGBURN, CLARENCE G DO, LICENSE NUMBER 00C7270, OF HOUSTON, TX, WAS DISCIPLINED BY TEXAS ON JANUARY 28, 1989.
DISCIPLINARY ACTION: SURRENDER OF CONTROLLED SUBSTANCE LICENSE; REQUIRED TO TAKE ADDITIONAL MEDICAL EDUCATION

COGBURN, CLARENCE G DO, LICENSE NUMBER 00C7270, OF HOUSTON, TX, WAS DISCIPLINED BY TEXAS ON JUNE 22, 1994.
DISCIPLINARY ACTION: REPRIMAND; REQUIRED TO TAKE ADDITIONAL MEDICAL EDUCATION
OFFENSE: OVERPRESCRIBING OR MISPRESCRIBING DRUGS
NOTES: NON-THERAPEUTICALLY PRESCRIBED TO ONE PATIENT IN THAT ON 9/10/93 HE DISPENSED 200 SOMA TABLETS AND AT THE SAME TIME PRESCRIBED OR DISPENSED 60 ANEXSIA TABLETS; CLAIMED THE PATIENT REQUESTED THIS QUANTITY OF DRUGS DUE TO TRAVEL PLANS; WAS OPERATING AN UNLICENSED PHARMACY BY DISPENSING BEYOND THE PATIENT'S IMMEDIATE NEEDS. CONDITIONS OF LICENSE RESTRICTION: SHALL NOT ORDER OR MAINTAIN IN HIS POSSESSION ANY CONTROLLED SUBSTANCES OR DANGEROUS DRUGS, INCLUDING SAMPLES, UNLESS PRESCRIBED OR DISPENSED BY ANOTHER PHYSICIAN FOR A LEGITIMATE MEDICAL NEED; SEPARATE FROM PATIENT RECORDS, SHALL MAINTAIN A LOG OF ALL PRESCRIPTIONS HE WRITES FOR CONTROLLED SUBSTANCES OR DANGEROUS DRUGS WHICH SHALL BE AVAILABLE FOR INSPECTION; SHALL ATTEND AT LEAST 50 HOURS PER YEAR OF CONTINUING MEDICAL EDUCATION; SHALL APPEAR BEFORE THE BOARD ONCE A YEAR; SHALL GIVE A COPY OF THIS ORDER TO ANY HEALTH CARE ENTITY WHERE HE HAS PRIVILEGES; SHALL COOPERATE WITH THE BOARD IN VERIFYING COMPLIANCE; SHALL INFORM BOARD OF CHANGE OF ADDRESS WITHIN 10 DAYS OR IF HE LEAVES THE STATE; TIME SPENT OUT OF TEXAS SHALL NOT COUNT TOWARD RESTRICTION. SHALL NOT SEEK MODIFICATION FOR ONE YEAR.

COGBURN, CLARENCE GILBERT DO OF 5901 LAURA KOPPE, HOUSTON, TX, WAS DISCIPLINED BY DEA ON FEBRUARY 9, 1989.
DISCIPLINARY ACTION: SURRENDER OF CONTROLLED SUBSTANCE LICENSE
OFFENSE: PROFESSIONAL MISCONDUCT
NOTES: EXCESSIVE PURCHASE REPORT; SOLD 61 TABS OF POSSIBLE LORAZEPAM 04/08/88 IN HOUSTON, TEXAS; ACCOUNTABILITY INVESTIGATION; VOLUNTARY SURRENDER OF CONTROLLED SUBSTANCES PRIVILEGES 01/25/89.

COGHE, DAVID W MD, LICENSE NUMBER 00G9579, OF AUSTIN, TX, WAS DISCIPLINED BY TEXAS ON JULY 28, 1989.
NOTES: SUBMIT TO PSYCHIATRIC EVALUATION AND FOLLOW RECOMMENDATIONS. EFFECTIVE UNTIL ALL REQUIREMENTS HAVE BEEN COMPLIED WITH. AS OF 04/20/91 LICENSE FREE OF ANY RESTRICTION OR LIMITATION.

COHN, JACQUELINE ELLEN MD, LICENSE NUMBER TXE7862, OF 1521 S STAPLES #801, CORPUS CHRISTI, TX, WAS DISCIPLINED BY DEA ON SEPTEMBER 14, 1992.
DISCIPLINARY ACTION: RESTRICTION PLACED ON CONTROLLED SUBSTANCE LICENSE
NOTES: HAD SURRENDERED SCHEDULES II AND IIN IN 1983 ACCORDING TO ORDER BY THE TEXAS STATE BOARD OF MEDICAL EXAMINERS. IN 1985 SHE WAS GIVEN PERMISSION TO REAPPLY. SCHEDULES II AND IIN PRIVILEGES WERE REINSTATED 09/14/92. ALIAS: JACQUELINE COHN BUCK.

COLE, GEORGE MARTIN DO, LICENSE NUMBER 00F5175, OF AMARILLO, TX, WAS DISCIPLINED BY TEXAS ON NOVEMBER 13, 1992.
DISCIPLINARY ACTION: 36-MONTH RESTRICTION PLACED ON LICENSE
OFFENSE: SUBSTANDARD CARE, INCOMPETENCE, OR NEGLIGENCE
NOTES: PROFESSIONAL FAILURE TO PRACTICE MEDICINE IN AN ACCEPTABLE MANNER CONSISTENT WITH PUBLIC HEALTH AND WELFARE.

COLEMAN, MILBURN LEE DO, LICENSE NUMBER 00D7549, OF DALLAS, TX, WAS DISCIPLINED BY TEXAS ON SEPTEMBER 8, 1992.
DISCIPLINARY ACTION: RESTRICTION PLACED ON LICENSE
OFFENSE: PROFESSIONAL MISCONDUCT
NOTES: VIOLATION OF THE LAWS OF TEXAS CONNECTED WITH HIS PRACTICE OF MEDICINE.

CONNER, PATRICK T MD, LICENSE NUMBER 0C41076, OF SPRINGFIELD, MO, WAS DISCIPLINED BY CALIFORNIA ON MAY 19, 1993.
DISCIPLINARY ACTION: 60-MONTH PROBATION
NOTES: REVOCATION STAYED.

CONNER, PATRICK TRAVIS MD, LICENSE NUMBER 00G3243, OF SPRINGFIELD, MO, WAS DISCIPLINED BY TEXAS ON OCTOBER 26, 1990.
NOTES: MUST COMPLY WITH MISSOURI RESTRICTIONS AND AUTHORIZE MISSOURI BOARD TO RELEASE INFORMATION AS TO STATUS AND PROBATIONARY COMPLIANCE; RECEIVE APPROVAL FROM TEXAS BOARD PRIOR TO PRACTICING MEDICINE IN TEXAS. ON 11/3/94 ORDER TERMINATED.

CONRAD, EDGAR DONALD DO, LICENSE NUMBER 00C7271, OF WEATHERFORD, TX, WAS DISCIPLINED BY TEXAS ON DECEMBER 3, 1990.
DISCIPLINARY ACTION: LICENSE SUSPENSION; 120-MONTH PROBATION
OFFENSE: DRUG OR ALCOHOL ABUSE
NOTES: LICENSE SUSPENDED FOR ADMISSION INTO A SUBSTANCE ABUSE TREATMENT PROGRAM. ON 4/19/91 REINSTATED AND PLACED ON PROBATION UNDER CONDITIONS INCLUDING: MUST APPEAR BEFORE THE BOARD OR A COMMITTEE OF THE BOARD TWO TIMES A YEAR DURING EACH YEAR OF PROBATION; CONTINUING PARTICIPATION IN THE ACTIVITIES OF THE TARRANT COUNTY MEDICAL SOCIETY COMMITTEE ON PHYSICIAN HEALTH AND REHABILITATION, INCLUDING PARTICIPATION IN THE WEEKLY MEETINGS; CONTINUING PARTICIPATION IN THE ACTIVITIES AND PROGRAMS OF ALCOHOLICS ANONYMOUS ON A REGULAR BASIS; MAINTENANCE OF ADEQUATE MEDICAL RECORDS ON ALL PATIENT OFFICE VISITS; SUBMISSION FOR APPROPRIATE CHEMICAL EXAMINATIONS AT THE REQUEST OF THE BOARD OR ITS REPRESENTATIVE.

CONRAD, EDGAR DONALD DO, LICENSE NUMBER 00C7271, OF WEATHERFORD, TX, WAS DISCIPLINED BY TEXAS ON OCTOBER 4, 1991.
DISCIPLINARY ACTION: LICENSE REVOCATION
OFFENSE: FAILURE TO COMPLY WITH A PROFESSIONAL RULE
NOTES: LICENSE SUSPENDED ON 12/3/90 UNTIL HE COMPLETED AN INPATIENT SUBSTANCE ABUSE PROGRAM; ON 4/19/91 LICENSE WAS REINSTATED ON 10 YEARS PROBATION SUBJECT TO TERMS AND CONDITIONS, INCLUDING RANDOM DRUG SCREENS; ON 5/23/91 TESTED POSITIVE FOR ALCOHOL ON A DRUG SCREEN.

CONTE, MAURICE S MD, DATE OF BIRTH SEPTEMBER 4, 1937, LICENSE NUMBER 00E7036, OF HOUSTON, TX, WAS DISCIPLINED BY TEXAS ON MAY 24, 1990.
DISCIPLINARY ACTION: REQUIRED TO TAKE ADDITIONAL MEDICAL EDUCATION
NOTES: STIPULATED ORDER. SHALL ATTEND CONTINUING MEDICAL EDUCATION COURSES, UTILIZE PATIENT RECORD-KEEPING SYSTEM TO ACCURATELY REFLECT CERTAIN INFORMATION, AND MAKE ANNUAL APPEARANCES BEFORE BOARD OR BOARD COMMITTEE.

CONTE, MAURICE S MD, DATE OF BIRTH SEPTEMBER 4, 1937, LICENSE NUMBER 00E7036, OF HOUSTON, TX, WAS DISCIPLINED BY TEXAS ON MARCH 6, 1992.
DISCIPLINARY ACTION: RESTRICTION PLACED ON LICENSE
OFFENSE: SUBSTANDARD CARE, INCOMPETENCE, OR NEGLIGENCE
NOTES: PROFESSIONAL FAILURE TO PRACTICE MEDICINE IN AN ACCEPTABLE MANNER CONSISTENT WITH PUBLIC HEALTH AND WELFARE.

CONTE, MAURICE S MD, DATE OF BIRTH SEPTEMBER 4, 1937, LICENSE NUMBER 00E7036, OF HENDERSON, NV, WAS DISCIPLINED BY TEXAS ON FEBRUARY 8, 1993.
DISCIPLINARY ACTION: LICENSE SUSPENSION
OFFENSE: FAILURE TO COMPLY WITH A PREVIOUS BOARD ORDER
NOTES: HE WAS REQUIRED BY AN ORDER OF 3/6/92 TO TAKE AND PASS THE SPEX EXAM; HE HAS TAKEN THE EXAM TWICE IN 9/92 AND 12/92 AND FAILED BOTH TIMES. LICENSE SUSPENDED UNTIL HE PASSES THE SPEX EXAM. ON 3/3/95 SUSPENSION TERMINATED.

CONTE, MAURICE S MD, DATE OF BIRTH SEPTEMBER 4, 1937, LICENSE NUMBER 0021080, OF 1313 SPYGLASS, AUSTIN, TX, WAS DISCIPLINED BY NEW JERSEY ON JUNE 27, 1994.
DISCIPLINARY ACTION: LICENSE SUSPENSION
NOTES: MUST APPEAR BEFORE A COMMITTEE OF THIS BOARD FOR A STATUS CONFERENCE PRIOR TO RESUMING NEW JERSEY PRACTICE. LICENSE IS SUSPENDED UNTIL SUCH TIME THAT HE DEMONSTRATES TO THE BOARD THAT HIS LICENSE TO PRACTICE MEDICINE IN TEXAS IS REINSTATED.

CONTIN, JUAN U MD, LICENSE NUMBER 00D7815, OF EL PASO, TX, WAS DISCIPLINED BY TEXAS ON OCTOBER 5, 1991.
DISCIPLINARY ACTION: 36-MONTH PROBATION; REQUIRED TO TAKE ADDITIONAL MEDICAL EDUCATION
OFFENSE: PROFESSIONAL MISCONDUCT
NOTES: WHILE ACTING AS MEDICAL DIRECTOR OF THE SOUTHWEST PAIN MANAGEMENT/BIOFEEDBACK CLINIC, HE AFFIXED HIS SIGNATURE TO INSURANCE CLAIM FORMS WITHOUT ADEQUATE KNOWLEDGE OF THE UNDERLYING BASIS FOR THE CLAIMS AND WITHOUT CONSIDERING THE REPRESENTATIONS TO INSURANCE CARRIERS WHICH WERE BEING MADE BY VIRTUE OF HIS SIGNATURES ON THESE CLAIM FORMS. SUSPENSION STAYED AND PLACED ON PROBATION WITH FOLLOWING TERMS AND CONDITIONS: SHALL OBTAIN 25 HOURS OF ETHICS CREDITS THROUGH SUCCESSFUL COMPLETION OF ETHICS COURSES OR PROGRAMS WITHIN ONE YEAR; DURING THE FIRST YEAR OF PROBATION, SHALL TAKE AND PASS THE MEDICAL JURISPRUDENCE EXAMINATION GIVEN BY THE TEXAS BOARD; SHALL APPEAR BEFORE THE BOARD ONCE A YEAR; SHALL COOPERATE WITH BOARD IN VERIFYING COMPLIANCE; SHALL ADVISE THE BOARD OF CHANGE OF ADDRESS WITHIN 10 DAYS; TIME SPENT OUT OF TEXAS DOES NOT COUNT TOWARDS PROBATION; SHALL NOT SEEK MODIFICATION OF ORDER FOR AT LEAST ONE YEAR.

CONTIN, JUAN U MD, DATE OF BIRTH APRIL 25, 1936, LICENSE NUMBER 0026570, OF 5728 KINGSFIELD AVENUE, EL PASO, TX, WAS DISCIPLINED BY NEW JERSEY ON FEBRUARY 9, 1993.
DISCIPLINARY ACTION: 36-MONTH PROBATION
OFFENSE: DISCIPLINARY ACTION BY ANOTHER STATE OR AGENCY
NOTES: DISCIPLINED IN TEXAS FOR UNPROFESSIONAL CONDUCT. THREE YEAR SUSPENSION STAYED. PRIOR TO RESUMING PRACTICE IN NEW JERSEY, MUST DEMONSTRATE SATISFACTORY COMPLETION OF ALL REQUIREMENTS IN TEXAS AND APPEAR BEFORE A

COMMITTEE OF THE BOARD FOR A STATUS CONFERENCE.

CONTIN, JUAN U MD, LICENSE NUMBER 0017694, OF EL PASO, TX, WAS DISCIPLINED BY FLORIDA ON APRIL 16, 1993.
DISCIPLINARY ACTION: SURRENDER OF LICENSE
OFFENSE: DISCIPLINARY ACTION BY ANOTHER STATE OR AGENCY
NOTES: CHARGED WITH HAVING A LICENSE ACTED AGAINST, BY THE LICENSING AUTHORITY OF ANOTHER JURISDICTION AND FAILING TO REPORT TO THE BOARD, IN WRITING, WITHIN 30 DAYS OF THIS ACTION. IN LIEU OF FURTHER PROSECUTION, ACCEPTED A VOLUNTARY RELINQUISHMENT OF LICENSE WITH THE AGREEMENT NEVER AGAIN TO APPLY FOR LICENSURE AS A PHYSICIAN IN FLORIDA.

COOK, TED A MD, LICENSE NUMBER 00D1589, OF PORTLAND, OR, WAS DISCIPLINED BY TEXAS ON APRIL 20, 1991.
DISCIPLINARY ACTION: PROBATION
OFFENSE: DISCIPLINARY ACTION BY ANOTHER STATE OR AGENCY
NOTES: DISCIPLINARY ACTION TAKEN BY ANOTHER STATE FOR UNPROFESSIONAL CONDUCT. MUST COMPLY WITH ALL TERMS OF OREGON PROBATION; PRIOR TO PRACTICING IN TEXAS, MUST APPEAR BEFORE BOARD FOR APPROVAL.

COOK, TED ALLEN MD, LICENSE NUMBER 0013047, OF PORTLAND, OR, WAS DISCIPLINED BY OREGON ON AUGUST 10, 1990.
DISCIPLINARY ACTION: 3-MONTH PROBATION; FINE

COOKE, THOMAS R DO, LICENSE NUMBER 00E6056, OF CHEHALIS, WA, WAS DISCIPLINED BY TEXAS ON FEBRUARY 22, 1991.
NOTES: MUST COMPLY WITH WASHINGTON STATE BOARD ORDER; RECEIVE PERMISSION OF TEXAS BOARD BEFORE RETURNING TO PRACTICE OF OBSTETRICS IN TEXAS AND BE SUBJECT TO ANY TERMS IMPOSED.

COOMANSINGH, BELDEN J L MD, LICENSE NUMBER 00F8446, OF FORT WORTH, TX, WAS DISCIPLINED BY TEXAS ON JUNE 22, 1994.
DISCIPLINARY ACTION: 120-MONTH PROBATION; RESTRICTION PLACED ON LICENSE
OFFENSE: LOSS OR RESTRICTION OF HOSPITAL PRIVILEGES
NOTES: BOARD INVESTIGATED ALLEGATIONS HE HAD MADE INAPPROPRIATE COMMENTS TO THREE PATIENTS INCLUDING ASKING THEM OUT ON DATES; ALSO OFFERED PAIN MEDICATIONS TO ONE PATIENT IN EXCHANGE FOR SEXUAL FAVORS; ALSO INAPPROPRIATELY TOLD A PATIENT SHE HAD AN URGENT NEED FOR SEXUAL GRATIFICATION; HE DENIES THESE ALLEGATIONS; IN 3/93 RESTRICTIONS PUT ON HOSPITAL PRIVILEGES BECAUSE HIS CARE AND TREATMENT OF EIGHT PATIENTS DEMONSTRATED A DEFICIENCY IN DEALING WITH HIGH RISK PREGNANCIES, INCLUDING TREATING PREGNANCY INDUCED HYPERTENSION WITH ALDOMET AND PHENOBARB; HOSPITAL SUBSEQUENTLY TERMINATED HIS PRIVILEGES WHEN HE DID NOT MEET ONE OF THE REQUIREMENTS, OBTAINING A RISK MANAGEMENT COURSE; SOUGHT DISTRICT COURT ACTION REGARDING THE TERMINATION WHICH WAS STILL PENDING AS OF THE ORDER DATE; IN 1/91 HE WAS NOT REAPPOINTED TO STAFF OF ANOTHER HOSPITAL BASED UPON SEVEN QUALITY OF CARE CASES REGARDING HIS MANAGEMENT OF PREGNANCY INDUCED HYPERTENSION, PITOCIN AUGMENTATION THERAPY, SUSPECTED SEPSIS, CLASS III PAP SMEARS AND HIS LACK OF APPRECIATION OF INDICATIONS FOR C-SECTIONS; HOSPITAL RECOMMENDED A RESIDENCY TYPE TRAINING PROGRAM; HE DID NOT APPEAL THIS DECISION; RECENTLY SUFFERED A MYOCARDIAL INFARCTION AND WISHES TO LIMIT HIS PRACTICE. SUSPENSION STAYED. CONDITIONS OF PROBATION: SHALL APPEAR BEFORE THE BOARD ONCE A YEAR; SHALL ATTEND AT LEAST 50 HOURS PER YEAR OF CONTINUING MEDICAL EDUCATION; SHALL BE SUPERVISED BY A BOARD-APPROVED PHYSICIAN WITH QUARTERLY REPORTS; SHALL MAINTAIN ADEQUATE MEDICAL RECORDS ON ALL PATIENT OFFICE VISITS WHICH SHALL BE AVAILABLE FOR INSPECTION; SHALL COMPLETE A SIX MONTH MINI-RESIDENCY IN OBSTETRICS/GYNECOLOGY PRIOR TO PRACTICING OB/GYN OTHER THAN IN A FAMILY PRACTICE SETTING; SHALL NOT PERFORM ANY PHYSICAL EXAM ON A FEMALE PATIENT WITHOUT THE PRESENCE OF A CHAPERONEE AND THIS SHALL BE DOCUMENTED IN THE RECORD; SHALL GIVE A COPY OF THIS ORDER TO ANY HEALTH CARE ENTITY WHERE HE HAS PRIVILEGES; SHALL COOPERATE WITH THE BOARD IN VERIFYING COMPLIANCE; SHALL INFORM BOARD OF CHANGE OF ADDRESS WITHIN 10 DAYS OR IF HE LEAVES THE STATE; TIME SPENT OUT OF TEXAS DOES NOT COUNT TOWARD PROBATION. SHALL NOT SEEK MODIFICATION FOR ONE YEAR.

COOMBS, CLARENCE J MD OF 7410 VILLAGE ROAD #11, SYKESVILLE, MD, WAS DISCIPLINED BY MEDICARE ON FEBRUARY 28, 1986.
DISCIPLINARY ACTION: 60-MONTH EXCLUSION FROM THE MEDICARE AND/OR MEDICAID PROGRAMS
OFFENSE: CRIMINAL CONVICTION OR PLEA OF GUILTY, NOLO CONTENDERE, OR NO CONTEST TO A CRIME
NOTES: PROGRAM-RELATED CONVICTION. REINSTATED ON 2/2/93.

COOMBS, CLARENCE J MD OF AUSTIN, TX, WAS DISCIPLINED BY TEXAS ON DECEMBER 1, 1986.
DISCIPLINARY ACTION: LICENSE REVOCATION
OFFENSE: DISCIPLINARY ACTION BY ANOTHER STATE OR AGENCY
NOTES: COMMITTED A FELONY

CORNITIUS, TIMOTHY G MD OF ROUTE 1, BOX 321, CADOO MILLS, TX, WAS DISCIPLINED BY KANSAS ON JUNE 14, 1993.
DISCIPLINARY ACTION: MONITORING OF PHYSICIAN
OFFENSE: DRUG OR ALCOHOL ABUSE
NOTES: PRIOR TO APPLYING FOR LICENSURE ON 3/26/93, SUFFERED FROM IMPAIRMENT DUE TO CHEMICAL ABUSE; WAS SUCCESSFULLY DISCHARGED FROM INPATIENT TREATMENT ON 4/23/93. RESTRICTIONS INCLUDE: ENTERING INTO A MONITORING CONTRACT WITH KANSAS MEDICAL SOCIETY AND IMPAIRED PROVIDER PROGRAM WHICH MAY DISCUSS OR OTHERWISE COMMUNICATE TO THE BOARD DETAILS OF HIS CASE AS NECESSARY; HE AGREES TO RELEASE ALL MATERIAL IN HIS PROGRAM FILE IN THE EVENT THAT HE IS TERMINATED FROM PROGRAM FOR NONCOMPLIANCE; PROGRAM LENGTH SHALL BE AT LEAST FOUR YEARS WITH OPTION TO RENEW PROGRAM FOR ADDITIONAL TIME AT THE DISCRETION OF PROGRAM OR THE BOARD; CONDITIONS OF PROGRAM INCLUDE: URINALYSIS TESTING THREE TIMES A WEEK AT RANDOM TIMES FOR SIX MONTHS. AGREES NOT TO USE ANY MIND ALTERING DRUG OR SUBSTANCE INCLUDING ALCOHOL, WILL NOT DO ANY SELF PRESCRIBING, ANY CHANGE OF ADDRESS OR

NEED FOR MEDICATION WILL IMMEDIATELY BE COMMUNICATED TO PROGRAM.

CORNITIUS, TIMOTHY GAVIN MD, LICENSE NUMBER 00H0266, OF DODGE CITY, KS, WAS DISCIPLINED BY TEXAS ON JANUARY 6, 1995.
DISCIPLINARY ACTION: SURRENDER OF LICENSE
OFFENSE: DISCIPLINARY ACTION BY ANOTHER STATE OR AGENCY
NOTES: IN 1992 AND FOR APPROXIMATELY A YEAR AND A HALF ENGAGED IN THE INTEMPERATE USE OF THE CONTROLLED SUBSTANCES XANAX AND DARVOCET; VOLUNTARILY ADMITTED HIMSELF FOR TREATMENT IN 3/93 AND SUCCESSFULLY COMPLETED INPATIENT TREATMENT; ENTERED AN AGREEMENT AND ENFORCEMENT ORDER WITH KANSAS BOARD ON 6/14/93 AND HAS REPORTED FULL COMPLIANCE WITH THIS ORDER TO TEXAS; IN LIEU OF FURTHER INVESTIGATION AGREES TO THIS ORDER. SHALL NOT PETITION FOR REINSTATEMENT.

CORRAL, EDGAR MD OF HOUSTON, TX, WAS DISCIPLINED BY TEXAS ON DECEMBER 1, 1986.
DISCIPLINARY ACTION: SURRENDER OF LICENSE

CORRAL, EDGAR M DR OF 7603 BELLFORT BLVD, HOUSTON, TX, WAS DISCIPLINED BY ILLINOIS ON JULY 1, 1989.
DISCIPLINARY ACTION: LICENSE REVOCATION; REVOCATION OF CONTROLLED SUBSTANCE LICENSE
OFFENSE: DISCIPLINARY ACTION BY ANOTHER STATE OR AGENCY
NOTES: PLED GUILTY IN TEXAS DISTRICT COURT TO UNLAWFUL DELIVERY OF A CONTROLLED SUBSTANCE.

COWDEN, WILLIAM L MD, LICENSE NUMBER 00F1483, OF DALLAS, TX, WAS DISCIPLINED BY TEXAS ON JANUARY 6, 1995.
DISCIPLINARY ACTION: REPRIMAND; REQUIRED TO TAKE ADDITIONAL MEDICAL EDUCATION
OFFENSE: PROFESSIONAL MISCONDUCT
NOTES: ON FOUR OCCASIONS DURING 1992 HE ADMINISTERED AN INJECTION OF A SUBSTANCE UNDER DEVELOPMENT IN ENGLAND TO A PATIENT SUFFERING FROM HODGKIN'S DISEASE WITHOUT KNOWING THE VARIOUS COMPONENTS, SIDE EFFECTS, TOXICITY OR CONTRAINDICATIONS OF THE DRUG; DRUG WAS FOR PALLIATION OF SYMPTOMS NOT CURE; SUBSTANCE NOT FDA APPROVED; ALSO DURING 1991 AND 1992 PRESCRIBED CYTOMEL TO A PATIENT WITHOUT APPROPRIATE INDICATION OR DOCUMENTATION; NEITHER ADMITS NOR DENIES THE ALLEGATIONS. CONDITIONS OF TWO YEAR RESTRICTION ON LICENSE INCLUDE: SHALL OBTAIN AT LEAST 50 HOURS PER YEAR OF CONTINUING MEDICAL EDUCATION INCLUDING AT LEAST ONE COURSE PER YEAR IN PHARMACOLOGY AND ENDOCRINOLOGY; SHALL APPEAR BEFORE THE BOARD ONCE A YEAR OR UPON REQUEST; SHALL COOPERATE WITH THE BOARD IN VERIFYING COMPLIANCE; SHALL GIVE A COPY OF THIS ORDER TO ANY HEALTH CARE ENTITY WHERE HE HAS OR APPLIES FOR PRIVILEGES OR ANYONE ELSE THAT REQUESTS IT; SHALL ENSURE ANY INQUIRIES REGARDING HIS TEXAS LICENSURE STATUS ARE ANSWERED BY REFERENCE TO THIS ORDER; SHALL INFORM BOARD OF CHANGE OF ADDRESS WITHIN 10 DAYS OR IF HE LEAVES THE STATE; TIME SPENT OUT OF TEXAS DOES NOT COUNT TOWARD RESTRICTION. SHALL NOT SEEK MODIFICATION FOR ONE YEAR.

COX, JOHNSTON STEWART MD, LICENSE NUMBER 00F6546, OF VICTORIA, TX, WAS DISCIPLINED BY TEXAS ON AUGUST 19, 1994.
DISCIPLINARY ACTION: FINE; REQUIRED TO TAKE ADDITIONAL MEDICAL EDUCATION
OFFENSE: OVERPRESCRIBING OR MISPRESCRIBING DRUGS
NOTES: HE PRESCRIBED CONTROLLED SUBSTANCES TO A SINGLE PATIENT WHO EXHIBITED SIGNS OF HABITUATION WITHOUT ADEQUATE JUSTIFICATION AND DOCUMENTATION OF PHYSICAL EXAMS, REFERRALS OR CONSULTATIONS REGARDING POSSIBLE CHRONIC PAIN AND WITHOUT OBJECTIVE TESTING OR FINDINGS. CONDITIONS OF RESTRICTION: SHALL ATTEND AT LEAST 50 HOURS PER YEAR OF CONTINUING MEDICAL EDUCATION INCLUDING 10 HOURS IN RISK MANAGEMENT AND 25 HOURS IN PHARMACOLOGY/ADDICTIONOLOGY IN THE FIRST YEAR; SHALL NOT TREAT OR OTHERWISE SERVE AS PHYSICIAN, PRESCRIBE, DISPENSE OR ADMINISTER DRUGS THAT MAY BE SUBJECT TO ABUSE TO HIMSELF OR ANY MEMBER OF HIS FAMILY; SHALL MAINTAIN ADEQUATE MEDICAL RECORDS ON ALL PATIENT OFFICE VISITS WHICH SHALL BE AVAILABLE FOR INSPECTION; SHALL PERSONALLY EXAMINE PATIENTS WHENEVER ANY FORM CERTIFIES THAT A PERSONAL EXAM HAS BEEN PERFORMED BY A PHYSICIAN, WHERE STATE LAW REQUIRES THIS OR WHERE AN INITIAL DIAGNOSIS OF PROBABLE DISEASE OR INJURY HAS BEEN MADE; SHALL PERSONALLY EXAMINE THE PATIENT DURING THE FIRST VISIT; SHALL NOT SIGN ANY PATIENT RECORD UNLESS HE HAS PERSONALLY EXAMINED THE PATIENT OR CLEARLY NOTES IN THE RECORD THAT HE HAS NOT; $1,000 ADMINISTRATIVE PENALTY; SHALL APPEAR BEFORE THE BOARD ONCE A YEAR; SHALL GIVE A COPY OF THIS ORDER TO ANY HEALTH CARE ENTITY WHERE HE HAS PRIVILEGES; SHALL COOPERATE WITH THE BOARD IN VERIFYING COMPLIANCE; SHALL INFORM BOARD OF CHANGE OF ADDRESS WITHIN 10 DAYS OR IF HE LEAVES THE STATE; TIME SPENT OUT OF TEXAS DOES NOT COUNT TOWARD PROBATION. SHALL NOT SEEK MODIFICATION FOR ONE YEAR.

CRAWFORD, ROBERT R DO, LICENSE NUMBER 00D3580, OF BEDFORD, TX, WAS DISCIPLINED BY TEXAS ON DECEMBER 1, 1988.
NOTES: SETTLEMENT AGREEMENT AND UNSPECIFIED DISCIPLINARY ACTION

CRAWFORD, ROBERT R DO OF BEDFORD, TX, WAS DISCIPLINED BY MISSOURI ON JUNE 16, 1989.
DISCIPLINARY ACTION: 60-MONTH RESTRICTION PLACED ON LICENSE
OFFENSE: DISCIPLINARY ACTION BY ANOTHER STATE OR AGENCY
NOTES: RESTRICTION RETROACTIVE TO 1/4/88, DATE OF TEXAS ACTION.

CROPPER, KENNETH R MD, LICENSE NUMBER 00D5948, OF LAKE JACKSON, TX, WAS DISCIPLINED BY TEXAS ON NOVEMBER 3, 1994.
DISCIPLINARY ACTION: LICENSE SUSPENSION
OFFENSE: DRUG OR ALCOHOL ABUSE
NOTES: ON 4/16/94 WENT TO A HOSPITAL EMERGENCY ROOM CLAIMING TO HAVE KIDNEY STONES AND ASKING FOR DEMEROL WHICH HE RECEIVED; HE RETURNED THE NEXT DAY AND WAS ADMITTED FOR PAIN; SPECIALIST FOUND NO EVIDENCE OF KIDNEY STONES AND WHEN THE HOSPITAL REFUSED TO INCREASE DEMEROL HE CHECKED OUT AGAINST MEDICAL ADVICE; ACTED

INAPPROPRIATELY IN THE HOSPITAL INCLUDING CURSING AT THE STAFF; TOLD BOARD HE WAS UNDER THE CARE OF A PSYCHIATRIST DUE TO CHEMICAL DEPENDENCY AND THAT HE WAS HOSPITALIZED ON 5/20/94 FOR SUBSTANCE ABUSE AND DEPRESSION; REPORTEDLY RESPONDED WELL TO TREATMENT WITH MEDICATIONS AND PSYCHOTHERAPY; HE IS CURRENTLY SEEING A PSYCHIATRIST AND ATTENDS AA; REPORTED SOBRIETY DATE IS 4/19/94; IS CURRENTLY ON DISABILITY. SUSPENSION UNTIL HE PERSONALLY APPEARS BEFORE THE BOARD AND PROVIDES SUFFICIENT EVIDENCE AND INFORMATION WHICH ADEQUATELY INDICATES THAT HE IS PHYSICALLY, MENTALLY AND OTHERWISE COMPETENT TO SAFELY PRACTICE MEDICINE INCLUDING AT A MINIMUM COMPLETE LEGIBLE COPIES OF MEDICAL RECORDS AND REPORTS OF PSYCHOLOGICAL AND NEUROPSYCHIATRIC EVALUATIONS.

CROSS, CRISS C MD, LICENSE NUMBER 00H7286, OF SAN ANTONIO, TX, WAS DISCIPLINED BY TEXAS ON OCTOBER 9, 1992.
DISCIPLINARY ACTION: 120-MONTH PROBATION
OFFENSE: FAILURE TO COMPLY WITH A PREVIOUS BOARD ORDER
NOTES: NONCOMPLIANCE WITH 4/20/90 ORDER. REVOCATION, STAYED. PROBATION UNDER TERMS AND CONDITIONS.

CULLEN, AUBREY P MD, DATE OF BIRTH JANUARY 22, 1921, OF 10220 MEMORIAL #38, HOUSTON, TX, WAS DISCIPLINED BY MEDICARE ON JULY 25, 1989.
DISCIPLINARY ACTION: 60-MONTH EXCLUSION FROM THE MEDICARE AND/OR MEDICAID PROGRAMS
OFFENSE: CRIMINAL CONVICTION OR PLEA OF GUILTY, NOLO CONTENDERE, OR NO CONTEST TO A CRIME
NOTES: CONVICTION RELATED TO FRAUD.

DAIL, ROBERT WOOD MD, LICENSE NUMBER 00E3244, OF CHATTANOOGA, TN, WAS DISCIPLINED BY TEXAS ON APRIL 15, 1994.
DISCIPLINARY ACTION: SURRENDER OF LICENSE
OFFENSE: PROFESSIONAL MISCONDUCT
NOTES: ALLEGATIONS CONCERING ORDERING OF MULTIPLE MODALITIES FOR AUTO ACCIDENT PATIENTS; BOARD FINDS THAT VARIOUS PATIENTS RECEIVED UNNECESSARY TREATMENT; PRACTICES IN TENNESSEE AND DOES NOT PLAN ON PRACTICING IN TEXAS. SHALL NOT SEEK REINSTATEMENT OF LICENSE.

DANIEL, ROSS H MD, LICENSE NUMBER 00E3245, OF WHARTON, TX, WAS DISCIPLINED BY TEXAS ON DECEMBER 1, 1989.
DISCIPLINARY ACTION: LICENSE REVOCATION

DARBY, CASTILLA ADOLPHUS JR MD, LICENSE NUMBER 00F8840, OF GARLAND, TX, WAS DISCIPLINED BY TEXAS ON MARCH 4, 1994.
DISCIPLINARY ACTION: EMERGENCY SUSPENSION
OFFENSE: DRUG OR ALCOHOL ABUSE
NOTES: EVIDENCE AND INFORMATION INDICATE THAT BETWEEN 1/7/91 AND 12/30/93 HE WAS HOSPITALIZED FOR SEVERE PSYCHIATRIC DISORDERS AND POLYSUBSTANCE ABUSE RELATED TO HIS USE OF ALCOHOL, STREET DRUGS AND PRESCRIPTION MEDICATIONS AT LEAST SEVEN TIMES. EVIDENCE ALSO INDICATES HE HAS FAILED TO COMPLY WITH REQUIREMENTS FOR OUTPATIENT THERAPY, PARTICIPATION IN AA AND IMPAIRED PHYSICIANS GROUP ACTIVITIES; HAS A LONG HISTORY OF SUBSTANCE ABUSE AND PSYCHOTIC SYMPTOMS.

DARBY, CASTILLA ADOLPHUS JR MD, LICENSE NUMBER 00F8840, OF GARLAND, TX, WAS DISCIPLINED BY TEXAS ON APRIL 15, 1994.
DISCIPLINARY ACTION: LICENSE SUSPENSION
OFFENSE: DRUG OR ALCOHOL ABUSE
NOTES: ON 3/4/94 PLACED HIS LICENSE ON A TEMPORARY SUSPENSION DUE TO ADMITTED ALCOHOL ABUSE FOR APPROXIMATELY 20 YEARS AND PROBLEMS WITH BENZODIAZEPINES; HAS BEEN IN THERAPY SINCE 3/11/94; CLAIMS A SOBRIETY DATE FROM ALCOHOL OF 1/2/93 AND BENZODIAZEPINES FROM 11/26/93. SUSPENSION UNTIL HE APPEARS BEFORE THE BOARD AND PROVIDES SUFFICIENT EVIDENCE THAT HE IS PHYSICALLY, MENTALLY AND OTHERWISE COMPETENT TO SAFELY PRACTICE. SHALL NOT SEEK MODIFICATION FOR ONE YEAR.

DARBY, FRANK JOSEPH JR MD, LICENSE NUMBER 00D3195, OF PASADENA, TX, WAS DISCIPLINED BY TEXAS ON AUGUST 24, 1991.
DISCIPLINARY ACTION: LICENSE REVOCATION
OFFENSE: PROFESSIONAL MISCONDUCT
NOTES: UNPROFESSIONAL AND DISHONORABLE CONDUCT LIKELY TO INJURE THE PUBLIC.

DAROCHA, TADEUSZ MD OF 819 HILLSIDE STREET, CANADIAN, TX, WAS DISCIPLINED BY MEDICARE ON OCTOBER 6, 1987.
DISCIPLINARY ACTION: 24-MONTH EXCLUSION FROM THE MEDICARE AND/OR MEDICAID PROGRAMS
OFFENSE: SUBSTANDARD CARE, INCOMPETENCE, OR NEGLIGENCE
NOTES: EXCLUSION WAS OVERTURNED BY AN ADMINISTRATIVE LAW JUDGE ON JUNE 20, 1988. ORIGINAL SANCTION BASED ON IMPROPER USE OF ANTIBIOTICS WITHOUT CHECKING FOR SENSITIVITIES ON 5 PATIENTS. JUDGE FOUND THAT DAROCHA PROMISED TO CHANGE HIS PRACTICE AND THAT HIS CONTINUED PRACTICE WOULD NOT POSE A RISK TO MEDICARE PATIENTS

DAVENPORT, MARK R MD, LICENSE NUMBER 0039514, OF 1700 N MOORE ST, DALLAS, TX, WAS DISCIPLINED BY VIRGINIA ON JULY 5, 1989.
DISCIPLINARY ACTION: PROBATION; FINE
OFFENSE: OVERPRESCRIBING OR MISPRESCRIBING DRUGS
NOTES: ON PROBATION UNTIL FURTHER ORDER FOR INDISCRIMINATE AND EXCESSIVE PRESCRIBING. $7500 FINE IMPOSED ON DOCTOR, $2500 FINE IMPOSED ON MEDICAL PRACTICE. PROBATION TERMINATED ON 5/25/93; REINSTATED TO A FULL AND UNRESTRICTED LICENSE.

DAVIS, ANTHONY A MD, LICENSE NUMBER 00H2329, OF BAYTOWN, TX, WAS DISCIPLINED BY TEXAS ON SEPTEMBER 30, 1994.
DISCIPLINARY ACTION: REPRIMAND; MONITORING OF PHYSICIAN
OFFENSE: PROFESSIONAL MISCONDUCT
NOTES: ADMITTED THAT MISCOMMUNICATION BETWEEN HIMSELF AND OFFICE STAFF RESULTED IN A PATIENT RECEIVING DUPLICATE PRESCRIPTIONS WHICH THE PATIENT USED IN A SUICIDE ATTEMPT; REPORTS THAT HE HAS NOW INSTITUTED RECORD KEEPING PROCEDURES IN ORDER TO AVOID FUTURE MISCOMMUNICATIONS. CONDITIONS OF ORDER; SHALL MAINTAIN ADEQUATE MEDICAL RECORDS ON ALL PATIENT OFFICE VISITS WHICH SHALL BE AVAILABLE FOR INSPECTION; SHALL ADEQUATELY SUPERVISE THE ACTIVITIES OF ALL EMPLOYEES; SHALL GIVE A COPY OF THIS ORDER TO ANY HEALTH CARE ENTITY WHERE HE HAS PRIVILEGES; SHALL COOPERATE WITH THE

BOARD IN VERIFYING COMPLIANCE; SHALL INFORM BOARD OF CHANGE OF ADDRESS WITHIN 10 DAYS.

DAVIS, DONALD FLOYD MD, LICENSE NUMBER 00D0105, OF MCCAMEY, TX, WAS DISCIPLINED BY TEXAS ON OCTOBER 1, 1987.
DISCIPLINARY ACTION: 120-MONTH PROBATION
NOTES: PREVIOUS BOARD ORDER AMENDED. SUSPENSION STAYED.

DAVIS, HERBERT A MD, DATE OF BIRTH FEBRUARY 7, 1940, LICENSE NUMBER 0021196, OF TYLER, TX, WAS DISCIPLINED BY COLORADO ON SEPTEMBER 17, 1993.
DISCIPLINARY ACTION: SURRENDER OF LICENSE
OFFENSE: SUBSTANDARD CARE, INCOMPETENCE, OR NEGLIGENCE
NOTES: ALLEGATIONS OF SUBSTANDARD PATIENT CARE.

DAVIS, HERBERT A MD, LICENSE NUMBER 00D2408, OF TYLER, TX, WAS DISCIPLINED BY TEXAS ON AUGUST 19, 1994.
DISCIPLINARY ACTION: REPRIMAND
OFFENSE: DISCIPLINARY ACTION BY ANOTHER STATE OR AGENCY
NOTES: ON 8/4/93 HE VOLUNTARILY SURRENDERED COLORADO LICENSE IN LIEU OF FURTHER PROCEEDINGS. HE TREATED A PATIENT BETWEEN 1985 AND 1988 AND TOWARDS THE END OF TREATMENT A SOCIAL AND LATER SEXUAL RELATIONSHIP DEVELOPED; HE CLAIMED THE SEXUAL RELATIONSHIP OCCURRED AFTER TERMINATION OF TREATMENT; HE UNDERSTANDS THE RELATIONSHIP WAS NON-THERAPEUTIC AND DETRIMENTAL TO THE PATIENT. NO OTHER COMPLAINTS ABOUT HIS PRACTICE IN TEXAS HAVE BEEN RECEIVED. SHALL SUBMIT TO A FULL EXAMINATION FOR SEXUAL DISORDERS/ADDICTION WITHIN 30 DAYS; SHALL GIVE A COPY OF THIS ORDER TO ANY HEALTH CARE ENTITY WHERE HE HAS PRIVILEGES; SHALL COOPERATE WITH THE BOARD IN VERIFYING COMPLIANCE. SHALL NOT SEEK MODIFICATION FOR ONE YEAR. THE BOARD RESERVES THE RIGHT TO SEEK OR IMPOSE ADDITIONAL DISCIPLINARY ACTION SHOULD AN UNFAVORABLE REPORT BE RECEIVED FROM THE AFOREMENTIONED EXAMINATION.

DAVIS, ROBERT M MD OF BROOKHAVEN, MS, WAS DISCIPLINED BY TEXAS ON SEPTEMBER 1, 1985.
DISCIPLINARY ACTION: LICENSE SUSPENSION
NOTES: INDEFINITE SUSPENSION

DAVIS, ROBERT M MD, LICENSE NUMBER 00C4292, OF BOERNE, TX, WAS DISCIPLINED BY TEXAS ON DECEMBER 1, 1988.
DISCIPLINARY ACTION: PROBATION
OFFENSE: FAILURE TO COMPLY WITH A PREVIOUS BOARD ORDER
NOTES: VIOLATED PROBATIONARY TERMS; RETAINED ON PROBATION WITH ADDITIONAL STIPULATIONS

DE LOS SANTOS, RAMIRO MD, LICENSE NUMBER 00F5182, OF EAGLE PASS, TX, WAS DISCIPLINED BY TEXAS ON OCTOBER 1, 1993.
DISCIPLINARY ACTION: 60-MONTH PROBATION; REQUIRED TO TAKE ADDITIONAL MEDICAL EDUCATION
OFFENSE: SUBSTANDARD CARE, INCOMPETENCE, OR NEGLIGENCE
NOTES: FROM 3/10/89 THROUGH 6/30/89 PERFORMED REPEAT C-SECTIONS ON THREE PATIENTS WITHOUT MEDICAL INDICATIONS; EVEN THOUGH SONOGRAMS WERE NORMAL AND THERE WAS NO EVIDENCE OF FETAL DISTRESS, THE BABIES WERE DELIVERED AT 37 WEEKS GESTATION; ON 4/27/89 HE FAILED TO ADEQUATELY TREAT A PATIENT IN THE EMERGENCY ROOM AND PREMATURELY DISCHARGED HER PRIOR TO STABILIZING HER BLOOD PRESSURE; ON 8/5/89 HE PERFORMED AN ABORTION ON ONE PATIENT AND KNOWINGLY DISCHARGED HER WITH FETAL TISSUE REMAINING IN THE UTERUS; FROM 3/10/89 THROUGH 8/5/89 HE FAILED TO ACCURATELY DOCUMENT PATIENT MEDICAL RECORDS. SUSPENSION STAYED. CONDITIONS OF PROBATION: SHALL ATTEND AT LEAST 50 HOURS PER YEAR OF CONTINUING MEDICAL EDUCATION 60 PERCENT OF WHICH SHALL BE IN BOARD-APPROVED COURSES ON OBSTETRICS AND HIGH-RISK PREGNANCY; SHALL MAINTAIN ADEQUATE PATIENT MEDICAL RECORDS WHICH WILL BE MADE AVAILABLE FOR REVIEW; SHALL APPEAR BEFORE THE BOARD ONCE A YEAR; SHALL COOPERATE WITH THE BOARD IN VERIFYING COMPLIANCE; SHALL INFORM BOARD OF CHANGE OF ADDRESS WITHIN 10 DAYS OR IF HE LEAVES THE STATE; TIME SPENT OUT OF TEXAS DOES NOT COUNT TOWARD PROBATION. SHALL NOT SEEK MODIFICATION FOR ONE YEAR.

DE QUEVEDO, ANA J GARCIA MD, DATE OF BIRTH SEPTEMBER 13, 1945, OF 2151 S KIRKWOOD ROAD #256, HOUSTON, TX, WAS DISCIPLINED BY MEDICARE ON OCTOBER 10, 1994.
DISCIPLINARY ACTION: EXCLUSION FROM THE MEDICARE AND/OR MEDICAID PROGRAMS
OFFENSE: DISCIPLINARY ACTION BY ANOTHER STATE OR AGENCY
NOTES: LICENSE REVOKED FOR REASONS BEARING ON PROFESSIONAL COMPETENCE.

DECARVALHO, GUARACY F MD, LICENSE NUMBER 00E3677, OF GEORGE WEST, TX, WAS DISCIPLINED BY TEXAS ON DECEMBER 1, 1990.
DISCIPLINARY ACTION: 60-MONTH PROBATION
OFFENSE: SUBSTANDARD CARE, INCOMPETENCE, OR NEGLIGENCE
NOTES: UNPROFESSIONAL CONDUCT LIKELY TO DECEIVE, DEFRAUD, OR INJURE PUBLIC. DISCIPLINED BY HOSPITAL OR HOSPITAL MEDICAL STAFF INCLUDING REMOVAL, SUSPENSION OR LIMITATION OF HOSPITAL PRIVILEGES OR OTHER DISCIPLINARY ACTIONS. FAILURE TO PRACTICE MEDICINE IN ACCEPTABLE MANNER CONSISTENT WITH PUBLIC HEALTH AND WELFARE. SUSPENSION STAYED. PROBATIONARY CONDITIONS INCLUDE CHANGE IN OBSTETRICAL PRACTICE, COMPLETION OF CONTINUING MEDICAL EDUCATION, REQUIREMENT FOR FEMALE STAFF MEMBER OR CHAPERONEE DURING CERTAIN EXAMINATIONS AND/OR TREATMENTS.

DELAFLOR, RICARDO MD, LICENSE NUMBER 00D9778, OF EL PASO, TX, WAS DISCIPLINED BY TEXAS ON APRIL 14, 1989.
DISCIPLINARY ACTION: 60-MONTH RESTRICTION PLACED ON CONTROLLED SUBSTANCE LICENSE
NOTES: SHALL TENDER DEA AND DPS CONTROLLED SUBSTANCE REGISTRATIONS FOR REISSUANCE TO EXCLUDE SCHEDULES II-N, III AND III-N. SHALL COOPERATE WITH BOARD IN VERIFYING COMPLIANCE; SHALL ADVISE THE BOARD OF ANY CHANGE OF ADDRESS WITHIN 10 DAYS; TIME PERIOD DURING WHICH RESTRICTIONS SHALL REMAIN IN EFFECT SHALL NOT INCLUDE TIME SPENT OUT OF TEXAS.

DELAFLOR, RICARDO MD, LICENSE NUMBER 0TXD977, OF 423 SAN SABA, EL PASO, TX, WAS DISCIPLINED BY DEA ON JUNE 12, 1989.

DISCIPLINARY ACTION: RESTRICTION PLACED ON CONTROLLED SUBSTANCE LICENSE
OFFENSE: OVERPRESCRIBING OR MISPRESCRIBING DRUGS
NOTES: WROTE PRESCRIPTIONS FOR VICODIN IN EXCESSIVE AMOUNTS TO PATIENT FOR NONTHERAPEUTIC PURPOSES.

DELAFLOR, RICARDO MD, DATE OF BIRTH MARCH 30, 1908, LICENSE NUMBER 0021641, OF 423 SAN SABA, EL PASO, TX, WAS DISCIPLINED BY NEW JERSEY ON MAY 5, 1990.
DISCIPLINARY ACTION: SURRENDER OF LICENSE
OFFENSE: DISCIPLINARY ACTION BY ANOTHER STATE OR AGENCY
NOTES: DISCIPLINED IN TEXAS DUE TO QUESTIONABLE CONTROLLED SUBSTANCE PRESCRIBING.

DELGADO, VICTOR MANUEL MD, LICENSE NUMBER TX08250, OF 1602 LORRAINE, HOUSTON, TX, WAS DISCIPLINED BY DEA ON JULY 5, 1990.
DISCIPLINARY ACTION: RESTRICTION PLACED ON CONTROLLED SUBSTANCE LICENSE
OFFENSE: OVERPRESCRIBING OR MISPRESCRIBING DRUGS
NOTES: PURSUANT TO AN AGREEMENT WITH THE TEXAS MEDICAL BOARD, DR. DELGADO SURRENDERED SCHEDULES II AND IIN OF HIS DEA REGISTRATION, BASED ON AN APPEARANCE BEFORE THE BOARD ON 10/28/85 TO DISCUSS HIS ALLEGED NONTHERAPEUTIC PRESCRIBING OF CONTROLLED SUBSTANCES. THE AGREEMENT WITH THE BOARD INCLUDES THE FOLLOWING STIPULATIONS: MUST SURRENDER ALL UNUSED TRIPLICATE PRESCRIPTIONS; SHALL REFRAIN FROM TREATING ANY PATIENTS FOR WEIGHT CONTROL WITH CONTROLLED SUBSTANCES; SHALL NOT PETITION THE TEXAS STATE BOARD OF MEDICAL EXAMINERS FOR MODIFICATION OF THE AGREEMENT FOR ONE YEAR; THE AGREEMENT WILL BE IN EFFECT FOR FIVE YEARS.

DELL, ROBERT V MD, LICENSE NUMBER 0009654, OF SAN ANTONIO, TX, WAS DISCIPLINED BY SOUTH CAROLINA ON OCTOBER 31, 1990.
DISCIPLINARY ACTION: SURRENDER OF LICENSE
NOTES: VOLUNTARY SURRENDER; NOT ELIGIBLE FOR REINSTATEMENT

DELL, ROBERT V MD OF POPLAR BLUFF, MO, WAS DISCIPLINED BY MISSOURI ON NOVEMBER 6, 1990.
DISCIPLINARY ACTION: 24-MONTH LICENSE SUSPENSION; 60-MONTH PROBATION
OFFENSE: DISCIPLINARY ACTION BY ANOTHER STATE OR AGENCY
NOTES: DISCIPLINARY ACTION TAKEN IN KANSAS BASED ON PERSONAL IMPAIRMENT. TWO YEAR SUSPENSION RETROACTIVE TO 9/15/88.

DELL, ROBERT V MD OF HANNIBAL, MO, WAS DISCIPLINED BY MISSOURI ON JUNE 16, 1993.
DISCIPLINARY ACTION: 84-MONTH PROBATION
OFFENSE: FAILURE TO COMPLY WITH A PREVIOUS BOARD ORDER
NOTES: ALSO DRUG USE, SUBSTANDARD CARE, LIMITATION OF CONTROLLED SUBSTANCE AUTHORITY.

DELL, ROBERT VANCE MD OF HATTIESBURG, MS, WAS DISCIPLINED BY KANSAS ON APRIL 15, 1989.
NOTES: MUST ENTER THERAPY FOR EITHER DRUG OR ALCOHOL ABUSE OR MENTAL PROBLEMS

DELL, ROBERT VANCE MD, LICENSE NUMBER 00G1372, OF POPLAR BLUFF, MO, WAS DISCIPLINED BY TEXAS ON OCTOBER 27, 1989.
DISCIPLINARY ACTION: 60-MONTH PROBATION; REQUIRED TO ENTER AN IMPAIRED PHYSICIAN PROGRAM OR DRUG OR ALCOHOL TREATMENT
OFFENSE: DRUG OR ALCOHOL ABUSE
NOTES: STIPULATED ORDER. REVOCATION STAYED. MUST PARTICIPATE IN MISSOURI PHYSICIANS HEALTH PROGRAM AND AA, OBTAIN EXAMINATIONS TO DETERMINE FREEDOM FROM DRUGS AND ALCOHOL, REFRAIN FROM ALCOHOL CONSUMPTION, NOT TREAT, SERVE AS PHYSICIAN, PRESCRIBE, DISPENSE OR ADMINISTER CONTROLLED SUBSTANCES FOR SELF OR FAMILY, PROVIDE TEXAS BOARD WITH REPORTS AS SUBMITTED TO MISSOURI BOARD, AND RECEIVE APPROVAL FROM TEXAS BOARD PRIOR TO PRACTICING IN TEXAS.

DEMATTEIS, ALBERT A MD, LICENSE NUMBER 0016911, OF ST. PETERSBURG, FL, WAS DISCIPLINED BY FLORIDA ON NOVEMBER 12, 1986.
DISCIPLINARY ACTION: LICENSE SUSPENSION; FINE
OFFENSE: OVERPRESCRIBING OR MISPRESCRIBING DRUGS
NOTES: $1000 FINE; LICENSE PLACED ON INACTIVE STATUS AND NOT ACTIVATED EXCEPT UPON AGREEMENT OF THE BOARD. MISCONDUCT; FAILING TO KEEP ADEQUATE RECORDS JUSTIFYING TREATMENT

DEMATTEIS, ALBERT A MD, LICENSE NUMBER 00C6133, OF ST. PETERSBURG, FL, WAS DISCIPLINED BY TEXAS ON DECEMBER 1, 1988.
NOTES: SETTLEMENT AGREEMENT AND UNSPECIFIED DISCIPLINARY ACTION

DEMETRIOU, CHRIS DO, LICENSE NUMBER 00C6180, OF PASADENA, TX, WAS DISCIPLINED BY TEXAS ON OCTOBER 1, 1987.
DISCIPLINARY ACTION: LICENSE REVOCATION
OFFENSE: OVERPRESCRIBING OR MISPRESCRIBING DRUGS
NOTES: PRESCRIBED DRUGS NONTHERAPEUTICALLY; FAILED TO PRACTICE MEDICINE IN ACCEPTABLE MANNER; FAILED TO ADEQUATELY SUPERVISE ACTIVITIES OF THOSE ACTING UNDER HIS SUPERVISION.

DEMETRIOU, CHRIS DO OF PASADENA, TX, WAS DISCIPLINED BY MISSOURI ON MARCH 10, 1989.
DISCIPLINARY ACTION: LICENSE REVOCATION
OFFENSE: DISCIPLINARY ACTION BY ANOTHER STATE OR AGENCY
NOTES: PRESCRIPTION VIOLATIONS.

DENNIS, MICHAEL H MD, LICENSE NUMBER 00G0612, OF TAYLOR, TX, WAS DISCIPLINED BY TEXAS ON JUNE 10, 1991.
DISCIPLINARY ACTION: 60-MONTH PROBATION; MONITORING OF PHYSICIAN
OFFENSE: SUBSTANDARD CARE, INCOMPETENCE, OR NEGLIGENCE
NOTES: PROFESSIONAL FAILURE TO PRACTICE MEDICINE IN AN ACCEPTABLE MANNER CONSISTENT WITH PUBLIC HEALTH AND WELFARE. SHALL APPEAR BEFORE BOARD ONCE A YEAR; SHALL PARTICIPATE IN AA; SHALL HAVE A RECOVERING ABUSE SPONSOR; SHALL SUBMIT TO DRUG OR ALCOHOL SCREENS.

DENNIS, MICHAEL H MD, LICENSE NUMBER 00G0612, OF TAYLOR, TX, WAS DISCIPLINED BY TEXAS ON MARCH 6, 1992.
DISCIPLINARY ACTION: 60-MONTH PROBATION
OFFENSE: SUBSTANDARD CARE, INCOMPETENCE, OR NEGLIGENCE
NOTES: PROFESSIONAL FAILURE TO PRACTICE MEDICINE IN AN

ACCEPTABLE MANNER CONSISTENT WITH PUBLIC HEALTH AND WELFARE. LICENSE SUSPENDED, SUSPENSION STAYED; PROBATION UNDER TERMS AND CONDITIONS.

DENNIS, MICHAEL H MD, LICENSE NUMBER 00G0612, OF TAYLOR, TX, WAS DISCIPLINED BY TEXAS ON APRIL 29, 1992.
DISCIPLINARY ACTION: EMERGENCY SUSPENSION

DENNIS, MICHAEL H MD, LICENSE NUMBER 00G0612, OF TAYLOR, TX, WAS DISCIPLINED BY TEXAS ON JUNE 17, 1992.
DISCIPLINARY ACTION: SURRENDER OF LICENSE
OFFENSE: FAILURE TO COMPLY WITH A PREVIOUS BOARD ORDER
NOTES: IN LIEU OF FURTHER DISCIPLINARY ACTION DUE TO VIOLATION OF PREVIOUS BOARD ORDER.

DESHEFY, ALAN MD, LICENSE NUMBER 00G6163, OF FORT WORTH, TX, WAS DISCIPLINED BY TEXAS ON JULY 1, 1990.
DISCIPLINARY ACTION: EMERGENCY SUSPENSION
OFFENSE: SUBSTANDARD CARE, INCOMPETENCE, OR NEGLIGENCE
NOTES: DISCIPLINED BY HOSPITAL MEDICAL STAFFS FOR UNPROFESSIONAL CONDUCT OR PROFESSIONAL INCOMPETENCE LIKELY TO HARM PUBLIC. SHALL SUBMIT TO EXAMINATION TO DETERMINE IF HE IS UNABLE TO PRACTICE MEDICINE WITH REASONABLE SKILL AND SAFETY AND PENDING BOARD ACTION ON REPORT, LICENSE SHALL BE SUSPENDED.

DESHEFY, ALAN N MD, LICENSE NUMBER 0052572, OF 2823 NW 29TH ST, FORT WORTH, TX, WAS DISCIPLINED BY DEA ON AUGUST 16, 1990.
DISCIPLINARY ACTION: SURRENDER OF CONTROLLED SUBSTANCE LICENSE
NOTES: MEDICAL LICENSE SUSPENDED 03/31/90.

DESHEFY, ALAN N MD, DATE OF BIRTH JANUARY 4, 1954, OF 6006 NW 70 AVE, TAMARAC, FL, WAS DISCIPLINED BY MEDICARE ON APRIL 10, 1992.
DISCIPLINARY ACTION: EXCLUSION FROM THE MEDICARE AND/OR MEDICAID PROGRAMS
OFFENSE: DISCIPLINARY ACTION BY ANOTHER STATE OR AGENCY
NOTES: LICENSE REVOCATION OR SUSPENSION.

DHESI, TARSEM S MD, LICENSE NUMBER 00F6575, OF HOUSTON, TX, WAS DISCIPLINED BY TEXAS ON JANUARY 6, 1995.
DISCIPLINARY ACTION: FINE
OFFENSE: PROFESSIONAL MISCONDUCT
NOTES: DURING 1992 AND 1993 FAILED TO ADEQUATELY OVERSEE THE BILLING FOR PATIENT CARE RENDERED THROUGH PHYSICAL THERAPY CLINICS OWNED IN PART BY HIM AND FOR WHICH HE WAS A MEDICAL DIRECTOR WHICH RESULTED IN BILLING WHICH DID NOT ACCURATELY REFLECT THE HEALTH-CARE PROVIDER WHO RENDERED THE SERVICE; USED IN-HOUSE BILLING AND MANAGEMENT; REPORTS HE HAS SOLD THE CLINICS DUE TO THE DIFFICULTY INVOLVED WITH KEEPING UP WITH THE WORKLOAD; IN LIEU OF FURTHER INVESTIGATION AGREES TO THIS ORDER. $1,000 ADMINISTRATIVE PENALTY TO BE PAID WITHIN FOUR MONTHS.

DIAZ, GUSTAVO A MD, LICENSE NUMBER 0026064, OF GOLIAD, TX, WAS DISCIPLINED BY FLORIDA ON FEBRUARY 18, 1991.
DISCIPLINARY ACTION: REQUIRED TO TAKE ADDITIONAL MEDICAL EDUCATION
OFFENSE: PROVIDING FALSE INFORMATION TO THE BOARD
NOTES: CHARGED WITH RENEWING A LICENSE BY FRAUDULENT MISREPRESENTATIONS IN THAT HE FALSELY CERTIFIED THAT HE COMPLETED THE CONTINUING MEDICAL EDUCATION REQUIREMENTS FOR LICENSURE RENEWAL; VIOLATED A BOARD RULE IN THAT HE FAILED TO SUBMIT DOCUMENTATION VERIFYING CONTINUING MEDICAL EDUCATION IN RESPONSE TO THE BOARD'S RANDOM AUDIT. IN LIEU OF FURTHER PROSECUTION, HE MUST PAY $1000 ADMINISTRATIVE COST AND APPEAR BEFORE THE BOARD AND DEMONSTRATE COMPLETION OF ALL CONTINUING MEDICAL EDUCATION REQUIREMENTS; MUST ALSO COMPLETE FIVE HOURS OF CATEGORY I CONTINUING MEDICAL EDUCATION IN RISK MANAGEMENT WITHIN 180 DAYS OF 02/18/91; ATTACH TO SUBSEQUENT LICENSE RENEWAL APPLICATIONS DOCUMENTATION OF COMPLETION OF THE CONTINUING MEDICAL EDUCATION REQUIREMENTS.

DICKERSON, JOE WESLEY MD, LICENSE NUMBER 00B6104, OF JASPER, TX, WAS DISCIPLINED BY TEXAS ON DECEMBER 1, 1988.
NOTES: SETTLEMENT AGREEMENT AND UNSPECIFIED DISCIPLINARY ACTION

DITTEMORE, HAROLD E MD OF 3400 ANDREWS HIGHWAY, MIDLAND, TX, WAS DISCIPLINED BY NEW MEXICO ON DECEMBER 22, 1993.
DISCIPLINARY ACTION: SURRENDER OF LICENSE
NOTES: IN LIEU OF ACTION.

DIXON, JOSEPH ANDREW MD, DATE OF BIRTH JULY 31, 1959, LICENSE NUMBER 00H2342, OF 6300 HUMANA PLAZA SUITE 875, ABILENE, TX, WAS DISCIPLINED BY TEXAS ON JANUARY 29, 1993.
DISCIPLINARY ACTION: REPRIMAND
OFFENSE: SUBSTANDARD CARE, INCOMPETENCE, OR NEGLIGENCE
NOTES: WHILE ENROLLED IN A RESIDENCY PROGRAM IN 12/88 FAILED TO APPROPRIATELY READ A LUMBAR X-RAY OF A PATIENT WHILE HE WORKED UNSUPERVISED IN A HOSPITAL EMERGENCY ROOM AND TO MAKE AN APPROPRIATE DIAGNOSIS.

DOBBS, ROBERT MAYS MD, LICENSE NUMBER 00D7558, OF PHOENIX, AZ, WAS DISCIPLINED BY TEXAS ON JUNE 24, 1988.
DISCIPLINARY ACTION: 60-MONTH REQUIRED TO ENTER AN IMPAIRED PHYSICIAN PROGRAM OR DRUG OR ALCOHOL TREATMENT
OFFENSE: DISCIPLINARY ACTION BY ANOTHER STATE OR AGENCY
NOTES: CONTINUE IN ARIZONA IMPAIRED PHYSICIANS PROGRAMS WHILE SUBMITTING REPORTS TO TEXAS BOARD; ABSTAIN FROM ALCOHOL, DRUGS, MEDICATIONS UNLESS PRESCRIBED BY TREATING PHYSICIAN AND MAINTAIN LOG OF THESE MEDICATIONS; SUBMIT TO THERAPY; PARTICIPATE IN AFTERCARE; MUST PROVIDE REPORT ON ARIZONA LICENSE STATUS IF DESIRING TO PRACTICE IN TEXAS.

DOBSON, WALTER A DO, LICENSE NUMBER 00F2636, OF GRAND PRAIRIE, TX, WAS DISCIPLINED BY TEXAS ON OCTOBER 5, 1991.
DISCIPLINARY ACTION: 60-MONTH PROBATION; REQUIRED TO TAKE ADDITIONAL MEDICAL EDUCATION
OFFENSE: OVERCHARGING
NOTES: FOR SERVICE PROVIDED TO EIGHT PATIENTS, HE OR HIS OFFICE PERSONNEL MADE ONE OR MORE OF THE FOLLOWING ERRORS: UPCODING; UNBUNDLED FEES; INCORRECTLY IDENTIFYING SERVICES; AND PERFORMING IV SEDATION AND MONITORING IN CASES

NOT REQUIRING SAME, WHICH RESULTED IN THE UNNECESSARY USE OF AN OPERATING AND RECOVERY ROOM. ACTIONS CONSTITUTED PERSISTENT AND FLAGRANT OVERCHARGING AND OVERTREATNG OF PATIENTS. SUSPENSION STAYED, TERMS AND CONDITIONS OF PROBATION ARE AS FOLLOWS: SHALL COMPLETE AT LEAST 50 HOURS PER YEAR OF CATEGORY I CONTINUING MEDICAL EDUCATION, 25 HOURS OF WHICH SHALL BE IN GYNECOLOGY AND THE REMAINDER SHALL BE IN GENERAL MEDICAL COURSES AND IN ETHICS; SHALL UTILIZE THE BLUE CROSS/BLUE SHIELD, MCGRAW HILL, MEDICARE OR COMPARABLE GUIDELINES FOR ESTABLISHING HIS CHARGES FOR SERVICES RENDERED; SHALL ADEQUATELY SUPERVISE THE ACTIVITIES OF ALL OF HIS EMPLOYEES; SHALL HAVE COLPOSCOPY CASES REVIEWED BY BOARD-APPROVED GYNECOLOGIC SURGEON; SHALL PERFORM COLPOSCOPIES ONLY AFTER THE PATIENT HAS OBTAINED A SECOND AGREEING OPINION FROM A BOARD CERTIFIED GYNECOLOGICAL SURGEON; SHALL APPEAR BEFORE THE BOARD TWICE A YEAR; SHALL COOPERATE WITH THE BOARD IN VERIFYING COMPLIANCE; SHALL INFORM THE BOARD OF CHANGE OF ADDRESS WITHIN 10 DAYS; TIME SPENT OUT OF TEXAS DOES NOT COUNT TOWARDS PROBATION; SHALL NOT PETITION FOR MODIFICATION FOR ONE YEAR. ON 11/19/93, ORDER MODIFIED TO DELETE THE PROVISION REQUIRING A SECOND OPINION FROM A BOARD CERTIFIED GYNECOLOGICAL SURGEON PRIOR TO PERFORMING COLPOSCOPIES.

DOLENZ, BERNARD J MD, LICENSE NUMBER 00C7391, OF DALLAS, TX, WAS DISCIPLINED BY TEXAS ON NOVEMBER 12, 1990.
DISCIPLINARY ACTION: PROBATION
OFFENSE: FAILURE TO COMPLY WITH A PROFESSIONAL RULE
NOTES: FAILURE TO KEEP COMPLETE AND ACCURATE RECORDS OF PURCHASES AND DISPOSALS OF DRUGS LISTED IN THE TEXAS CONTROLLED SUBSTANCES ACT; FAILURE TO PRACTICE MEDICINE IN ACCEPTABLE MANNER CONSISTENT WITH PUBLIC HEALTH AND WELFARE. ONE YEAR SUSPENSION, SUSPENSION PROBATED WITH CONDITIONS. ON APPEAL TO TRAVIS COUNTY DISTRICT COURT.

DONOVAN, JOSEPH L JR MD, LICENSE NUMBER 00H7291, OF SAN DIEGO, CA, WAS DISCIPLINED BY TEXAS ON JUNE 28, 1991.
NOTES: PROBATION TERMINATED; LICENSE FREE OF ANY RESTRICTIONS.

DOOLITTLE, J B DO, LICENSE NUMBER 00C2451, OF MEXICO, MO, WAS DISCIPLINED BY TEXAS ON MAY 20, 1989.
DISCIPLINARY ACTION: SURRENDER OF CONTROLLED SUBSTANCE LICENSE
NOTES: SHALL RECEIVE BOARD APPROVAL PRIOR TO OPENING OFFICE OR PRACTICING IN TEXAS.

DOOLITTLE, J B DO, LICENSE NUMBER 00C2451, OF MEXICO, MO, WAS DISCIPLINED BY TEXAS ON DECEMBER 1, 1990.
DISCIPLINARY ACTION: LICENSE REVOCATION
OFFENSE: DISCIPLINARY ACTION BY ANOTHER STATE OR AGENCY
NOTES: DISCIPLINED BY MISSOURI, REQUESTED TEXAS ACCEPT SURRENDER. MAY SEEK REINSTATEMENT OF TEXAS LICENSE NO SOONER THAN ONE YEAR FROM ORDER DATE BY COMPLYING WITH CERTAIN PROVISIONS.

DOOLITTLE, J B DO OF MEXICO, MO, WAS DISCIPLINED BY MISSOURI ON MARCH 24, 1994.
DISCIPLINARY ACTION: LICENSE REVOCATION
OFFENSE: CRIMINAL CONVICTION OR PLEA OF GUILTY, NOLO CONTENDERE, OR NO CONTEST TO A CRIME
NOTES: PLED GUILTY IN THE CIRCUIT COURT OF AUDRAIN COUNTY, MISSOURI TO UNLAWFUL POSSESSION OF A CONTROLLED SUBSTANCE. NO REAPPLICATION FOR LICENSE FOR SEVEN YEARS.

DORSEY, EUGENE MD OF 2524 MARTIN LUTHER KING, DALLAS, TX, WAS DISCIPLINED BY MEDICARE ON DECEMBER 14, 1982.
DISCIPLINARY ACTION: 60-MONTH EXCLUSION FROM THE MEDICARE AND/OR MEDICAID PROGRAMS
OFFENSE: CRIMINAL CONVICTION OR PLEA OF GUILTY, NOLO CONTENDERE, OR NO CONTEST TO A CRIME
NOTES: PROGRAM-RELATED CONVICTION.

DORSEY, EUGENE MD, LICENSE NUMBER 0008752, OF 944 S CORNITH ST RD, DALLAS, TX, WAS DISCIPLINED BY GEORGIA ON APRIL 2, 1986.
DISCIPLINARY ACTION: 60-MONTH PROBATION; RESTRICTION PLACED ON CONTROLLED SUBSTANCE LICENSE
OFFENSE: DRUG OR ALCOHOL ABUSE
NOTES: PERSONAL USE OR ADDICTION. MAY NOT WRITE PRESCRIPTION FOR CONTROLLED SUBSTANCES WITHOUT FEDERAL AND STATE DEA REGISTRATION.

DOTSON, BEVERLY ANN MD, LICENSE NUMBER 00D3204, OF GRAHAM, TX, WAS DISCIPLINED BY TEXAS ON DECEMBER 1, 1990.
DISCIPLINARY ACTION: LICENSE REVOCATION
OFFENSE: DRUG OR ALCOHOL ABUSE
NOTES: INTEMPERATE USE OF ALCOHOL AND DRUGS, UNPROFESSIONAL OR DISHONORABLE CONDUCT LIKELY TO DECEIVE, DEFRAUD, OR INJURE PUBLIC, PROFESSIONAL FAILURE TO PRACTICE MEDICINE IN ACCEPTABLE MANNER CONSISTENT WITH PUBLIC HEALTH AND WELFARE. MOTION FOR REHEARING FILED.

DOTSON, DANIEL A MD, LICENSE NUMBER 00D4096, OF GRAHAM, TX, WAS DISCIPLINED BY TEXAS ON DECEMBER 1, 1990.
DISCIPLINARY ACTION: LICENSE REVOCATION
OFFENSE: SUBSTANDARD CARE, INCOMPETENCE, OR NEGLIGENCE
NOTES: UNPROFESSIONAL OR DISHONORABLE CONDUCT LIKELY TO DECEIVE, DEFRAUD OR INJURE PUBLIC, PROFESSIONAL FAILURE TO PRACTICE MEDICINE IN ACCEPTABLE MANNER CONSISTENT WITH PUBLIC HEALTH AND WELFARE. FILED MOTION FOR REHEARING.

DOTSON, DANIEL A MD, DATE OF BIRTH NOVEMBER 14, 1941, LICENSE NUMBER 0025062, OF PUEBLO, CO, WAS DISCIPLINED BY COLORADO ON SEPTEMBER 11, 1992.
DISCIPLINARY ACTION: SURRENDER OF CONTROLLED SUBSTANCE LICENSE
OFFENSE: SUBSTANDARD CARE, INCOMPETENCE, OR NEGLIGENCE
NOTES: TWO OR MORE ACTS OR OMISSIONS WHICH FAILED TO MEET GENERALLY ACCEPTED STANDARDS OF MEDICAL PRACTICE. PERMANENT SURRENDER OF DRUG ENFORCEMENT ADMINISTRATION CERTIFICATE (ALL SCHEDULES). NOT TO SEEK CERTIFICATE REINSTATEMENT IN FUTURE.

DOTSON, RODNEY N MD WAS DISCIPLINED BY ARIZONA ON APRIL 10, 1991.
DISCIPLINARY ACTION: DENIAL OF NEW LICENSE

OFFENSE: DISCIPLINARY ACTION BY ANOTHER STATE OR AGENCY
NOTES: ACTION BASED ON LICENSE RESTRICTION IN TEXAS.

DOTSON, RODNEY N MD WAS DISCIPLINED BY ARIZONA ON JUNE 21, 1991.
DISCIPLINARY ACTION: DENIAL OF NEW LICENSE
NOTES: FAILURE TO MEET STATUTORY REQUIREMENTS FOR LICENSURE.

DOTSON, RODNEY NORMAN MD, LICENSE NUMBER 00D9988, OF TEXARKANA, TX, WAS DISCIPLINED BY TEXAS ON JANUARY 12, 1991.
DISCIPLINARY ACTION: 60-MONTH PROBATION; RESTRICTION PLACED ON LICENSE
NOTES: IMMEDIATE CESSATION OF CERVICAL CAUTERY EXCEPT UNDER DIRECT SUPERVISION OF A PHYSICIAN AS PART OF AN APPROVED FAMILY PRACTICE RESIDENCY OR PRECEPTORSHIP, PRESCRIBING OR ADMINISTERING CERTAIN DRUGS, OR PROVIDING ONGOING PRENATAL CARE, EXCEPT WITH PRIOR ARRANGEMENTS FOR DELIVERY AND FOLLOW-UP; LIMITATION OF MANAGEMENT OF YEAST INFECTION PATIENTS; NO TREATMENT OF ATTENTION DEFICIT DISORDER OR HYPERACTIVE PATIENTS WITHOUT ONGOING CONSULTATION WITH A PEDIATRICIAN; PERFORMANCE OF CIRCUMCISIONS LIMITED TO NEONATAL PATIENTS UNLESS UNDER DIRECT SUPERVISION OF A PHYSICIAN AS PART OF A FAMILY PRACTICE RESIDENCY OR PRECEPTORSHIP; OBTAINING AN ARIZONA LICENSE TO PRACTICE MEDICINE IMMEDIATELY, OR SURRENDER OF TEXAS MEDICAL LICENSE EFFECTIVE 7/1/91 UNLESS ENTERED INTO A ONE-YEAR PRECEPTORSHIP OR FAMILY PRACTICE RESIDENCY WITH TIMELY AND SUCCESSFUL COMPLETION.

DOUGLAS, AUBRY C MD, LICENSE NUMBER 00E7895, OF 2000 CRAWFORD, SUITE 850, HOUSTON, TX, WAS DISCIPLINED BY DEA ON AUGUST 2, 1993.
DISCIPLINARY ACTION: SURRENDER OF CONTROLLED SUBSTANCE LICENSE

DOUGLAS, JAKE S MD, LICENSE NUMBER 00B5654, OF BEAUMONT, TX, WAS DISCIPLINED BY TEXAS ON JANUARY 24, 1992.
DISCIPLINARY ACTION: SURRENDER OF LICENSE
OFFENSE: PHYSICAL OR MENTAL ILLNESS INHIBITING THE ABILITY TO PRACTICE WITH SKILL AND SAFETY
NOTES: POSSIBLE INABILITY TO PRACTICE MEDICINE WITH REASONABLE SKILL AND SAFETY TO PATIENTS BY REASON OF ILLNESS. LICENSE VOLUNTARILY RETIRED IN LIEU OF DISCIPLINARY ACTION.

DOWD, DONNA CATHERINE MD, DATE OF BIRTH SEPTEMBER 4, 1952, LICENSE NUMBER 00F3913, OF 9147 POWHATAN, SAN ANTONIO, TX, WAS DISCIPLINED BY TEXAS ON JUNE 15, 1993.
DISCIPLINARY ACTION: 60-MONTH PROBATION; MONITORING OF PHYSICIAN
OFFENSE: DRUG OR ALCOHOL ABUSE
NOTES: HAS BEEN DIAGNOSED AS SUFFERING FROM AN ACUTE AND CHRONIC INFECTION BY THE EPSTEIN-BARR VIRUS SECONDARY TO A B CELL LYMPHOCYTIC DISORDER; DURING 1991 AND 1992 SELF-PRESCRIBED TYLENOL #3 FOR MUSCLE PAIN AND CONSUMED EXCESSIVE QUANTITIES WITHOUT A SUFFICIENT MEDICAL JUSTIFICATION; SHE VOLUNTARILY SOUGHT MEDICAL ASSISTANCE AND PSYCHIATRIC COUNSELING IN 10/92 AND TOOK A MEDICAL LEAVE OF ABSENCE; EVIDENCE DOES NOT INDICATE EXCESSIVE CONSUMPTION CAUSED PATIENT HARM. SUSPENSION STAYED. CONDITIONS OF PROBATION: SHALL NOT SELF-PRESCRIBE DANGEROUS DRUGS OR CONTROLLED SUBSTANCES; SHALL ABSTAIN FROM THE CONSUMPTION OF DANGEROUS DRUGS OR CONTROLLED SUBSTANCES IN ANY FORM UNLESS PRESCRIBED BY ANOTHER PHYSICIAN FOR A LEGITIMATE MEDICAL PURPOSE; SHALL SUBMIT HERSELF FOR APPROPRIATE EXAMS INCLUDING DRUG SCREENS; SHALL KEEP A SEPARATE RECORD OF EVERY PRESCRIPTION WRITTEN FOR CONTROLLED SUBSTANCES OR DANGEROUS DRUGS WHICH SHALL BE AVAILABLE FOR INSPECTION; SHALL CONTINUE TO RECEIVE TREATMENT WITH QUARTERLY REPORTS TO THE BOARD; SHALL APPEAR BEFORE THE BOARD ONCE A YEAR; SHALL GIVE A COPY OF THIS ORDER TO ANY HEALTH CARE ENTITY WHERE SHE HAS PRIVILEGES; SHALL COOPERATE WITH THE BOARD IN VERIFYING COMPLIANCE; SHALL INFORM BOARD OF CHANGE OF ADDRESS WITHIN 10 DAYS OR IF SHE LEAVES THE STATE; TIME SPENT OUT OF TEXAS DOES NOT COUNT TOWARD PROBATION. SHALL NOT SEEK MODIFICATION FOR ONE YEAR.

DOWD, DONNA CATHERINE MD, DATE OF BIRTH SEPTEMBER 4, 1952, LICENSE NUMBER 00F3913, OF SAN ANTONIO, TX, WAS DISCIPLINED BY TEXAS ON JANUARY 6, 1995.
DISCIPLINARY ACTION: 48-MONTH PROBATION; MONITORING OF PHYSICIAN
OFFENSE: FAILURE TO COMPLY WITH A PREVIOUS BOARD ORDER
NOTES: IN VIOLATION OF 06/15/93 ORDER BETWEEN 11/93 AND 3/94 SHE SELF-PRESCRIBED PRESCRIPTIONS FOR DIAZOXIDE, PYRIDIUM AND SEPTRA AND ON 6/20/94 INGESTED BARBITURATES AND BENZODIAZEPINES WHICH WERE PRESCRIBED BY TREATING PHYSICIAN BUT NOT REPORTED TO THE BOARD. SUSPENSION STAYED. CONDITIONS OF PROBATION: SHALL NOT SELF-PRESCRIBE DANGEROUS DRUGS; SHALL ABSTAIN FROM THE CONSUMPTION OF ALCOHOL/CHEMICAL SUBSTANCES IN ANY FORM UNLESS PRESCRIBED BY ANOTHER PHYSICIAN FOR A LEGITIMATE AND THERAPEUTIC PURPOSE; SHALL SUBMIT HERSELF FOR APPROPRIATE EXAMS INCLUDING DRUG OR ALCOHOL SCREENS; SEPARATE FROM PATIENT RECORDS, SHALL MAINTAIN A FILE OF EVERY PRESCRIPTION FOR CONTROLLED SUBSTANCES OR DANGEROUS DRUGS WHICH SHALL BE AVAILABLE FOR INSPECTION; SHALL NOT TELEPHONE ANY PRESCRIPTION TO A PHARMACY FOR THESE DRUGS; SHALL CONTINUE TO RECEIVE TREATMENT FROM SPECIFIED PHYSICIAN WITH QUARTERLY REPORTS; UPON VISIT TO ANY PHYSICIAN SHALL PROVIDE THEM WITH A REPORT OF MEDICATIONS SHE HAS BEEN PRESCRIBED OR IS CONSUMING WITH INITIALS OF THE PRESCRIBING PHYSICIAN; SHALL APPEAR BEFORE THE BOARD ONCE A YEAR; SHALL GIVE A COPY OF THIS ORDER TO ANY HEALTH CARE ENTITY WHERE SHE HAS PRIVILEGES; SHALL COOPERATE WITH THE BOARD IN VERIFYING COMPLIANCE; SHALL INFORM BOARD OF CHANGE OF ADDRESS WITHIN 10 DAYS OR IF SHE LEAVES THE STATE; TIME SPENT OUT OF TEXAS DOES NOT COUNT TOWARD PROBATION. SHALL NOT SEEK MODIFICATION FOR ONE YEAR. ALSO KNOWN AS DONNA C. CROMWELL.

DOWLING, GEORGE W MD, LICENSE NUMBER 0009159, OF

ANDREWS, TX, WAS DISCIPLINED BY FLORIDA ON SEPTEMBER 25, 1991.
DISCIPLINARY ACTION: SURRENDER OF LICENSE
OFFENSE: PROVIDING FALSE INFORMATION TO THE BOARD
NOTES: CHARGED WITH FRAUDULENT MISREPRESENTATION IN THAT HE FALSELY CERTIFIED THAT HE HAD COMPLETED CONTINUING MEDICAL EDUCATION REQUIREMENTS FOR LICENSE RENEWAL; FAILED TO SUBMIT DOCUMENTATION VERIFYING COMPLETION OF RISK MANAGEMENT AND HIV/AIDS CONTINUING MEDICAL EDUCATION IN RESPONSE TO THE BOARD'S RANDOM AUDIT. AGREES NEVER AGAIN TO APPLY FOR LICENSURE AS A PHYSICIAN IN FLORIDA.

DOWNING, LLOYD L MD, LICENSE NUMBER 00C0314, OF SAN ANGELO, TX, WAS DISCIPLINED BY TEXAS ON DECEMBER 1, 1988.
NOTES: SETTLEMENT AGREEMENT AND UNSPECIFIED DISCIPLINARY ACTION

DRAKE, GEORGE K MD, LICENSE NUMBER 00C6915, OF HOUSTON, TX, WAS DISCIPLINED BY TEXAS ON DECEMBER 1, 1988.
NOTES: SETTLEMENT AGREEMENT AND UNSPECIFIED DISCIPLINARY ACTION

DRISCOLL, EDWARD THOMAS MD, LICENSE NUMBER 00B6008, OF ODESSA, TX, WAS DISCIPLINED BY TEXAS ON NOVEMBER 13, 1992.
DISCIPLINARY ACTION: RESTRICTION PLACED ON LICENSE
NOTES: PRACTICE OF MEDICINE RESTRICTED TO NO MORE THAN EIGHT HOURS PER WEEK AND NO MORE THAN FOUR HOURS PER 24 HOUR PERIOD; PRACTICE LIMITED TO THE PHYSICAL CONFINES OF THE DRISCOLL CLINIC LOCATED IN ODESSA, TEXAS; SHALL NOT PERFORM SURGERY.

DRISCOLL, STEPHEN EDWARD MD, LICENSE NUMBER 00F1514, OF ODESSA, TX, WAS DISCIPLINED BY TEXAS ON APRIL 20, 1992.
DISCIPLINARY ACTION: 24-MONTH PROBATION; REPRIMAND
OFFENSE: SUBSTANDARD CARE, INCOMPETENCE, OR NEGLIGENCE
NOTES: SEVERAL VIOLATIONS OF THE MEDICAL PRACTICE ACT, INCLUDING PROFESSIONAL FAILURE TO PRACTICE MEDICINE IN AN ACCEPTABLE MANNER CONSISTENT WITH PUBLIC HEALTH AND WELFARE. LICENSE SUSPENDED, SUSPENSION STAYED; PROBATION UNDER TERMS AND CONDITIONS.

DUBIN, JOSEPH DO, LICENSE NUMBER 00C2154, OF DALLAS, TX, WAS DISCIPLINED BY TEXAS ON JUNE 22, 1994.
DISCIPLINARY ACTION: REPRIMAND
OFFENSE: OVERPRESCRIBING OR MISPRESCRIBING DRUGS
NOTES: ALLEGATIONS OF NON-THERAPEUTIC PRESCRIBING OF PHENMETRAZINE, PHENTERMINE HYDROCHLORIDE AND THYROID MEDICATIONS FOR WEIGHT LOSS; STAFF CONTENDS VIOLATION OF MEDICAL ACT; HE CONTENDS THAT THERE IS NO VIOLATION EXCEPT AS TO INADEQUATE RECORD-KEEPING; ALLEGATIONS RELATE TO EVENTS BETWEEN 1984 AND 1989; NO EVIDENCE THAT HE HAS TREATED PATIENTS FOR WEIGHT LOSS SINCE 1989; HE AGREED TO THIS ORDER IN LIEU OF A HEARING. SHALL GIVE A COPY OF THE ORDER TO ANY HEALTH CARE ENTITY WHERE HE HAS PRIVILEGES.

DUGGER, DAVID LEON MD OF MEDFORD, NY, WAS DISCIPLINED BY LOUISIANA ON APRIL 14, 1989.
DISCIPLINARY ACTION: CEASE AND DESIST ORDER
OFFENSE: PROFESSIONAL MISCONDUCT
NOTES: FRAUDULENT, FALSE, DECEPTIVE OR MISLEADING SOLICITATION OR SELF PROMOTION; PROHIBITED FROM ADVERTISING OR UNDERTAKING TREATMENT OF LEARNING DISABILITIES THROUGH "CRANIAL MANIPULATION."

DUGGER, DAVID LEON MD, DATE OF BIRTH DECEMBER 26, 1944, LICENSE NUMBER 0006909, OF 3626 NORTH MACARTHUR, IRVING, TX, WAS DISCIPLINED BY MISSISSIPPI ON JANUARY 18, 1990.
DISCIPLINARY ACTION: RESTRICTION PLACED ON LICENSE
NOTES: CONSENT ORDER RESTRICTED LICENSE.

DUNCAN, JOHN DAVID MD, LICENSE NUMBER 00D4980, OF DUMAS, TX, WAS DISCIPLINED BY TEXAS ON OCTOBER 1, 1993.
DISCIPLINARY ACTION: SURRENDER OF CONTROLLED SUBSTANCE LICENSE; 84-MONTH PROBATION
OFFENSE: DRUG OR ALCOHOL ABUSE
NOTES: HAS DEVELOPED AN ADMITTED ALCOHOL PROBLEM WHICH BECAME MORE ACUTE DURING 1992; HAS NOT CONSUMED ALCOHOL SINCE 10/92; HAS PERIODICALLY ATTENDED AA AND PARTICIPATED WITH PHYSICIANS HEALTH COMMITTEE; CHARGES WERE PENDING AS OF ORDER DATE FOR AN ALCOHOL-RELATED AUTOMOBILE-PEDESTRIAN ACCIDENT. SUSPENSION STAYED. CONDITIONS OF PROBATION: SHALL ABSTAIN FROM THE CONSUMPTION OF ALCOHOL/CHEMICAL SUBSTANCES UNLESS PRESCRIBED BY ANOTHER PHYSICIAN FOR A LEGITIMATE AND THERAPEUTIC PURPOSE; SHALL SUBMIT HIMSELF FOR APPROPRIATE EXAMS INCLUDING DRUG OR ALCOHOL SCREENS; SHALL SURRENDER HIS DEA AND TEXAS CONTROLLED SUBSTANCES CERTIFICATE AND ALL UNUSED TRIPLICATE PRESCRIPTION FORMS; SHALL NOT ATTEMPT TO REREGISTER THESE REGISTRATIONS WITHOUT PERMISSION; SHALL CONTINUE TO PARTICIPATE IN AA'S PROGRAM NOT LESS THAN ONCE A WEEK WITH QUARTERLY REPORTS; SHALL CONTINUE TO PARTICIPATE IN ACTIVITIES OF A PHYSICIAN HEALTH AND REHABILITATION COMMITTEE AND ATTEND WEEKLY MEETINGS WITH QUARTERLY REPORTS; SHALL SUBMIT HIMSELF FOR EVALUATION AND TREATMENT TO A BOARD-APPROVED PSYCHIATRIST; SHALL GIVE A COPY OF THIS ORDER TO ANY HEALTH CARE ENTITY WHERE HE HAS PRIVILEGES; SHALL COOPERATE WITH THE BOARD IN VERIFYING COMPLIANCE; SHALL INFORM THE BOARD OF CHANGE OF ADDRESS WITHIN 10 DAYS OR IF HE LEAVES THE STATE; TIME SPENT OUT OF TEXAS DOES NOT COUNT TOWARD PROBATION; SHALL APPEAR BEFORE THE BOARD ONCE A YEAR. SHALL NOT SEEK MODIFICATION FOR ONE YEAR.

DUNCAN, RICHARD PERRY DO, LICENSE NUMBER 00D0452, OF HOUSTON, TX, WAS DISCIPLINED BY TEXAS ON JANUARY 12, 1991.
DISCIPLINARY ACTION: SURRENDER OF CONTROLLED SUBSTANCE LICENSE; 120-MONTH CONTROLLED SUBSTANCE LICENSE PLACED ON PROBATION
NOTES: MUST SURRENDER ALL UNUSED TRIPLICATE PRESCRIPTION FORMS AND NOT ATTEMPT TO ORDER MORE UNTIL HE HAS BOARD PERMISSION; SURRENDER DEA AND TEXAS CONTROLLED SUBSTANCE REGISTRATION CERTIFICATES; NOT ATTEMPT TO REREGISTER OR OTHERWISE OBTAIN CONTROLLED SUBSTANCES REGISTRATIONS UNTIL HE HAS BOARD PERMISSION; SURRENDER ALL CONTROLLED SUBSTANCES, INCLUDING SAMPLES, IN HIS POSSESSION OR SUBJECT TO HIS CONTROL, NOR

POSSESS ANY SUCH CONTROLLED SUBSTANCES; ABSTAIN FROM CONSUMPTION OF ALCOHOL/CHEMICAL SUBSTANCES; PARTICIPATE OR CONTINUE TO PARTICIPATE IN HARRIS COUNTY MEDICAL SOCIETY COMMITTEE ON PHYSICIAN HEALTH AND REHABILITATION, ALCOHOLICS ANONYMOUS, AND TEXAS OSTEOPATHIC MEDICAL ASSOCIATION PHYSICIAN ASSISTANCE PROGRAM; REPORT IMMEDIATELY ANY INCIDENT IN WHICH HE CONSUMES ALCOHOL OR USES CONTROLLED SUBSTANCE NOT PRESCRIBED BY ANOTHER PHYSICIAN; SUBMIT TO APPROPRIATE EXAMINATIONS TO DETERMINE FREEDOM FROM DRUGS AND ALCOHOL; MAINTAIN ADEQUATE MEDICAL RECORDS ON PATIENT OFFICE VISITS TO INCLUDE SPECIFIC INFORMATION. ORDER TERMINATED ON 5/11/95.

DUNN, FRANK LANIER MD, LICENSE NUMBER 00B9641, OF KERRVILLE, TX, WAS DISCIPLINED BY TEXAS ON APRIL 26, 1991.
DISCIPLINARY ACTION: LICENSE SUSPENSION
OFFENSE: OVERPRESCRIBING OR MISPRESCRIBING DRUGS
NOTES: NONTHERAPEUTIC PRESCRIBING AND INADEQUATE MEDICAL PRACTICES.

DUNN, FRANK LANIER MD, LICENSE NUMBER 00B9641, OF KERRVILLE, TX, WAS DISCIPLINED BY TEXAS ON JUNE 16, 1992.
DISCIPLINARY ACTION: LICENSE REVOCATION
OFFENSE: DISCIPLINARY ACTION BY ANOTHER STATE OR AGENCY
NOTES: ALSO VIOLATIONS INVOLVING THE PRESCRIBING OF CONTROLLED SUBSTANCES. PROFESSIONAL FAILURE TO PRACTICE MEDICINE CONSISTENT WITH PUBLIC HEALTH AND WELFARE.

DWYER, EDWARD J MD, DATE OF BIRTH DECEMBER 18, 1942, LICENSE NUMBER 0032223, OF 2906 MEDICAL ARTS ST., AUSTIN, TX, WAS DISCIPLINED BY NEW JERSEY ON AUGUST 17, 1988.
DISCIPLINARY ACTION: REQUIRED TO ENTER AN IMPAIRED PHYSICIAN PROGRAM OR DRUG OR ALCOHOL TREATMENT
OFFENSE: DRUG OR ALCOHOL ABUSE
NOTES: REQUIRED TO PARTICIPATE WITH APPROPRIATE PHYSICIANS' SUPPORT AND REHAB GROUP IN TEXAS. PRIOR TO PRACTICING SHALL APPEAR FOR STATUS CONFERENCE; ACTION BASED ON SUBSTANCE ABUSE

DWYER, EDWARD J MD, LICENSE NUMBER 00D6582, OF AUSTIN, TX, WAS DISCIPLINED BY TEXAS ON DECEMBER 1, 1988.
NOTES: SETTLEMENT AGREEMENT AND UNSPECIFIED DISCIPLINARY ACTION

DWYER, EDWARD J MD, LICENSE NUMBER C037662, OF AUSTIN, TX, WAS DISCIPLINED BY CALIFORNIA ON JUNE 28, 1989.
DISCIPLINARY ACTION: SURRENDER OF LICENSE

DWYER, EDWARD J MD, LICENSE NUMBER 00D6582, OF AUSTIN, TX, WAS DISCIPLINED BY TEXAS ON AUGUST 24, 1991.
DISCIPLINARY ACTION: 60-MONTH PROBATION; RESTRICTION PLACED ON LICENSE
OFFENSE: FAILURE TO COMPLY WITH A PREVIOUS BOARD ORDER
NOTES: VIOLATED PREVIOUS BOARD ORDER. REVOCATION STAYED. TERMS OF PROBATION: SHALL ATTEND 10 HOURS PER YEAR OF AN ETHICS COURSE IN ADDITION TO 50 HOURS REQUIRED UNDER PREVIOUS ORDER; SHALL OBTAIN BLUE CROSS/BLUE SHIELD AND MEDICARE GUIDELINES FOR PHYSICIAN CHARGES; SHALL REFRAIN FROM PRESCRIBING OR ADMINISTERING TENS UNIT TREATMENT; SHALL MAKE REFUNDS TO PARTICULAR PATIENTS; SHALL APPEAR BEFORE BOARD TWICE A YEAR.

DWYER, EDWARD J MD, DATE OF BIRTH DECEMBER 18, 1943, LICENSE NUMBER 00D6582, OF 3410 FAR WEST BOULEVARD #145, AUSTIN, TX, WAS DISCIPLINED BY TEXAS ON AUGUST 20, 1993.
DISCIPLINARY ACTION: SURRENDER OF LICENSE
OFFENSE: PHYSICAL OR MENTAL ILLNESS INHIBITING THE ABILITY TO PRACTICE WITH SKILL AND SAFETY
NOTES: HAS VOLUNTARILY CEASED PRACTICING MEDICINE DUE TO AN ILLNESS. SHALL SURRENDER HIS DEA AND TEXAS CONTROLLED SUBSTANCES REGISTRATION AND ALL UNUSED PRESCRIPTION AND TRIPLICATE PRESCRIPTION FORMS. LICENSE WILL BE REINSTATED UNDER THE FOLLOWING CONDITIONS: SHALL SUBMIT HIMSELF FOR EVALUATION TO TWO BOARD-APPROVED PSYCHIATRISTS AND BOTH MUST CONCLUDE HIS HEALTH HAS BEEN RESTORED OR HIS ILLNESS IS CAPABLE OF BEING TREATED AND CONTROLLED ON A CONTINUING BASIS TO SUCH AN EXTENT THAT HE IS CAPABLE OF PRACTICING.

DWYER, EDWARD JOSEPH MD OF 3410 FAR WEST BLVD, AUSTIN, TX, WAS DISCIPLINED BY DEA ON SEPTEMBER 21, 1993.
DISCIPLINARY ACTION: SURRENDER OF CONTROLLED SUBSTANCE LICENSE
NOTES: SURRENDERED FOR CAUSE TO TEXAS STATE BOARD OF MEDICAL EXAMINERS.

DWYER, PATRICK DAVID MD, LICENSE NUMBER 00E7393, OF SUGAR LAND, TX, WAS DISCIPLINED BY TEXAS ON APRIL 15, 1994.
DISCIPLINARY ACTION: 60-MONTH PROBATION; REQUIRED TO TAKE ADDITIONAL MEDICAL EDUCATION
OFFENSE: OVERPRESCRIBING OR MISPRESCRIBING DRUGS
NOTES: PROVIDED MEDICATIONS TO HIS WIFE WITHOUT INDICATIONS OVER THE COURSE OF SEVERAL YEARS ENDING IN 1991; FAILED TO KEEP ADEQUATE RECORDS OF DRUGS AND THE QUANTITY OF THOSE DRUGS SUPPLIED TO HIS WIFE. SUSPENSION STAYED. CONDITIONS OF PROBATION: WITHIN ONE YEAR SHALL COMPLETE A TWO WEEK PRECEPTORSHIP ON THE PREVENTION AND TREATMENT OF DRUG ABUSE; SHALL REFRAIN FROM PRESCRIBING ANY DRUG THAT IS NOT MEDICALLY INDICATED; SHALL REFRAIN FROM THE USE OF AND SHALL NOT POSSESS, ADMINISTER OR PRESCRIBE ANY PRESCRIPTION DRUG UNLESS PRESCRIBED BY ANOTHER PHYSICIAN FOR A LEGITIMATE AND THERAPEUTIC PURPOSE; SHALL NOT TREAT OR OTHERWISE SERVE AS PHYSICIAN, PRESCRIBE, DISPENSE, OR ADMINISTER DRUGS THAT MAY BE SUBJECT TO ABUSE TO HIMSELF OR ANY MEMBER OF HIS FAMILY; HE SHALL MAINTAIN A FILE SEPARATE FROM PATIENT RECORDS OF EVERY PRESCRIPTION WRITTEN FOR CONTROLLED SUBSTANCES OR DANGEROUS DRUGS, A LOG OF ANY PRESCRIPTIONS CALLED INTO A PHARMACY. AND ADEQUATE MEDICAL RECORDS ON PATIENT OFFICE VISITS ALL OF WHICH SHALL BE AVAILABLE FOR INSPECTION; SHALL ATTEND AT LEAST 50 HOURS PER YEAR OF CONTINUING MEDICAL EDUCATION; SHALL APPEAR BEFORE THE BOARD ONCE A YEAR; SHALL GIVE A COPY OF THIS ORDER TO ANY HEALTH CARE ENTITY WHERE HE HAS PRIVILEGES; SHALL COOPERATE WITH THE BOARD IN VERIFYING COMPLIANCE; SHALL INFORM BOARD OF CHANGE OF ADDRESS WITHIN 10 DAYS OR IF HE LEAVES THE STATE; TIME SPENT OUT OF TEXAS DOES NOT COUNT TOWARD PROBATION. SHALL NOT SEEK MODIFICATION

FOR ONE YEAR.

DYKE, MARSHALL JAMES MD, LICENSE NUMBER 00D1619, OF CONROE, TX, WAS DISCIPLINED BY TEXAS ON DECEMBER 4, 1991.
DISCIPLINARY ACTION: 60-MONTH PROBATION; RESTRICTION PLACED ON LICENSE
OFFENSE: DRUG OR ALCOHOL ABUSE
NOTES: HAS ENGAGED IN THE INTEMPERATE USE OF COCAINE SINCE 4/91; VOLUNTARILY ADMITTED HIMSELF TO THE HOSPITAL ON 8/6/91. SUSPENSION STAYED; CONDITIONS OF PROBATION: SHALL SURRENDER SCHEDULE II AND IIN OF DEA AND TEXAS CONTROLLED SUBSTANCES REGISTRATIONS, AND SHALL NOT ATTEMPT TO REREGISTER OR OTHERWISE OBTAIN THESE LICENSES WITHOUT WRITTEN AUTHORITY OF THE BOARD; SHALL SURRENDER ALL UNUSED TRIPLICATE PRESCRIPTION FORMS; SHALLL APPEAR BEFORE THE BOARD TWICE A YEAR; SHALL NOT TREAT OR PRESCRIBE DRUGS TO HIMSELF OR ANY MEMBER OF HIS IMMEDIATE FAMILY; SHALL ABSTAIN FROM THE CONSUMPTION OF ALCOHOL/CHEMICAL SUBSTANCES, WITH EXPLANATION TO THE BOARD WITHIN 24 HOURS IF HE DOES SO; SHALL PARTICIPATE IN IMPAIRED PHYSICIANS PROGRAM, WITH QUARTERLY REPORTS TO THE BOARD; SHALL PARTICIPATE IN AA OR NARCOTICS ANONYMOUS, INCLUDING A 12-STEP PROGRAM, AT LEAST 3 TIMES PER WEEK; SHALL SUBMIT TO RANDOM SCREENING OF BODILY FLUIDS, AND SHALL ALWAYS BE SCREENED TWICE ON DAYS HE PERFORMS SURGERY; SHALL CONTINUE IN EITHER INPATIENT OR OUTPATIENT CARE AS DETERMINED BY HIS TREATING PHYSICIAN, WITH QUARTERLY REPORTS TO THE BOARD; SHALL IMMEDIATELY NOTIFY THE BOARD IF HE DISCONTINUES TREATMENT; SHALL SUBMIT TO PSYCHIATRIC EVALUATION BY A BOARD-APPROVED PSYCHIATRIST AND ABIDE BY RECOMMENDATIONS; SHALL NOT OPERATE ON ANY PATIENT UNLESS ANOTHER OTOLARYNGOLOGIST IS AVAILABLE IN THE BUILDING; SHALL GET BOARD PERMISSION TO CHANGE HIS SPECIALTY; SHALL COOPERATE WITH BOARD IN VERIFYING COMPLIANCE; SHALL ADVISE THE BOARD OF A CHANGE OF ADDRESS WITHIN 10 DAYS; TIME SPENT OUT OF TEXAS DOES NOT COUNT TOWARDS PROBATION; SHALL NOT SEEK MODIFICATION OF ORDER FOR AT LEAST ONE YEAR.

DYKE, MARSHALL JAMES MD, LICENSE NUMBER 00D1619, OF CONROE, TX, WAS DISCIPLINED BY TEXAS ON MARCH 4, 1994.
DISCIPLINARY ACTION: EMERGENCY SUSPENSION
OFFENSE: FAILURE TO COMPLY WITH A PREVIOUS BOARD ORDER
NOTES: ALLEGATIONS OF NONCOMPLIANCE WITH 12/4/91 ORDER INCLUDING INGESTING COCAINE AS INDICATED BY A POSITIVE REPORT OF A BLOOD SAMPLE TAKEN ON 2/17/94 NOT PURSUANT TO A PRESCRIPTION BY A PRIMARY CARE PHYSICIAN AND NOT REPORTED TO THE BOARD; HOSPITAL PRIVILEGES WERE TEMPORARILY SUSPENDED PENDING A HEARING ON HIS USE OF COCAINE.

EARGLE, CANTRAL L JR MD, LICENSE NUMBER 00G0694, OF DALLAS, TX, WAS DISCIPLINED BY TEXAS ON JUNE 22, 1994.
DISCIPLINARY ACTION: REPRIMAND
OFFENSE: CRIMINAL CONVICTION OR PLEA OF GUILTY, NOLO CONTENDERE, OR NO CONTEST TO A CRIME
NOTES: ON 4/23/90 WAS CONVICTED OF THREE COUNTS OF WILLFUL FAILURE TO FILE INCOME TAX RETURNS; ON 1/2/91 CONVICTION WAS AFFIRMED BY THE U.S. COURT OF APPEALS. SHALL GIVE A COPY OF THIS ORDER TO ANY HEALTH CARE ENTITY WHERE HE HAS PRIVILEGES.

EARGLE, CANTRAL LESTER JR MD, LICENSE NUMBER 0010915, OF 5329 N MACARTHUR #1094, IRVING, TX, WAS DISCIPLINED BY GEORGIA ON AUGUST 6, 1986.
DISCIPLINARY ACTION: SURRENDER OF LICENSE
OFFENSE: DISCIPLINARY ACTION BY ANOTHER STATE OR AGENCY
NOTES: ACTION IN CALIFORNIA. AGREES NOT TO PRACTICE UNTIL FURTHER ORDER OF THE BOARD.

EARL, GENE MARKLEY JR MD, LICENSE NUMBER 00D9991, OF TYLER, TX, WAS DISCIPLINED BY TEXAS ON APRIL 15, 1994.
DISCIPLINARY ACTION: SURRENDER OF CONTROLLED SUBSTANCE LICENSE; 60-MONTH PROBATION
OFFENSE: DRUG OR ALCOHOL ABUSE
NOTES: BEGINNING IN 1990 SELF-PRESCRIBED ADDICTIVE SCHEDULED CONTROLLED SUBSTANCES DUE TO PAIN ASSOCIATED WITH SURGERIES HE HAD UNDERGONE; SUBSEQUENTLY BECAME ADDICTED TO THESE SUBSTANCES; TO SUPPORT HIS ADDICTION HE WROTE AND CALLED IN PRESCRIPTIONS IN THE NAME OF FAMILY MEMBERS FROM 1/1/92 TO 6/1/93 WHEN HE ENTERED A TREATMENT PROGRAM; SOBRIETY DATE IS 6/10/93; PARTICIPATED IN AA MEETINGS; HOSPITAL PLACED CERTAIN RESTRICTIONS ON HIS PRACTICE; IS CURRENTLY UNDER THE CARE OF A PSYCHOTHERAPIST AND AN ADDICTIONOLOGIST. SUSPENSION STAYED. CONDITIONS OF PROBATION: SHALL COMPLY WITH RESTRICTIONS IMPOSED BY HOSPITAL WHICH INCLUDE SPECIFYING HIS PRIMARY PHYSICIAN AND HIS SUPERVISOR WITH THE IMPAIRED PHYSICIAN'S GROUP; PROVIDING COPIES OF AFTERCARE CONTRACT AND LETTERS DETAILING THE FINDINGS OF HIS PHYSICIAN REGARDING AFTERCARE; SHALL HAVE PRIMARY CARE PHYSICIAN PROVIDE REPORTS; SHALL SUBMIT TO RANDOM TESTS OF BODILY FLUIDS; REPORTS WILL BE OBTAINED FROM THE DIRECTOR OF NURSING; REVIEWS WILL BE MADE OF A RANDOM SELECTION OF HIS INPATIENT CHARTS; ADDITIONAL CONDITIONS IMPOSED BY THE BOARD: SHALL INFORM THE BOARD WITHIN 10 DAYS IF PRIVILEGES AT HOSPITAL ARE TERMINATED; SHALL COMPLY WITH THE AFOREMENTIONED REQUIREMENTS IMPOSED BY HOSPITAL AND FORWARD ALL REPORTS SUBMITTED TO THE HOSPITAL TO THE BOARD; SHALL BE SUPERVISED BY A BOARD-APPROVED PHYSICIAN WITH QUARTERLY REPORTS; SHALL ABSTAIN FROM THE CONSUMPTION OF ALCOHOL/CHEMICAL SUBSTANCES IN ANY FORM UNLESS PRESCRIBED BY ANOTHER PHYSICIAN FOR A LEGITIMATE AND THERAPEUTIC PURPOSE; SHALL NOT TREAT OR OTHERWISE SERVE AS PHYSICIAN, PRESCRIBE, DISPENSE OR ADMINISTER DRUGS THAT MAY BE SUBJECT TO ABUSE TO HIMSELF OR ANY MEMBER OF HIS FAMILY; SHALL SURRENDER HIS DEA AND TEXAS CONTROLLED SUBSTANCES CERTIFICATES, ALL UNUSED TRIPLICATE PRESCRIPTION FORMS, AND ALL CONTROLLED SUBSTANCES INCLUDING SAMPLES IN HIS POSSESSION; SHALL NOT ATTEMPT TO REREGISTER WITHOUT APPROVAL; SHALL CONTINUE TO PARTICIPATE IN AA'S PROGRAM NOT LESS THAN THREE TIMES A WEEK WITH QUARTERLY REPORTS TO THE BOARD; SHALL SUBMIT HIMSELF FOR APPROPRIATE EXAMS INCLUDING DRUG OR ALCOHOL SCREENS; SHALL CONTINUE TREATMENT WITH HIS

PSYCHOTHERAPIST WITH QUARTERLY REPORTS; SHALL APPEAR BEFORE THE BOARD TWICE A YEAR; SHALL GIVE A COPY OF THIS ORDER TO ANY HEALTH CARE ENTITY WHERE HE HAS PRIVILEGES; SHALL COOPERATE WITH THE BOARD IN VERIFYING COMPLIANCE; SHALL INFORM BOARD OF CHANGE OF ADDRESS WITHIN 10 DAYS OR IF HE LEAVES THE STATE; TIME SPENT OUT OF TEXAS DOES NOT COUNT TOWARD PROBATION. SHALL NOT SEEK MODIFICATION FOR ONE YEAR.

ECHOLS, BEN HARRIS MD, DATE OF BIRTH SEPTEMBER 20, 1949, LICENSE NUMBER 00F6227, OF 7400 FANNIN SUITE 1118, HOUSTON, TX, WAS DISCIPLINED BY TEXAS ON JANUARY 29, 1993.
DISCIPLINARY ACTION: REPRIMAND
OFFENSE: PROFESSIONAL MISCONDUCT
NOTES: AIDED AND ABETTED THE UNLICENSED PRACTICE OF MEDICINE BY BEST RECOVERY HEALTH CARE, INC. A CONTRACT WITH WHICH AWARDED HIM 10% OF REVENUE COLLECTED FROM THE METHADONE CLINIC; HE NEVER COLLECTED THIS REVENUE. SHALL GIVE A COPY OF THIS ORDER TO ANY HEALTH CARE ENTITY WHERE HE HAS PRIVILEGES; SHALL INFORM THE BOARD OF CHANGE OF ADDRESS WITHIN 10 DAYS.

EDGEWORTH, LEWIS ANSON DAVID MD, LICENSE NUMBER 00E5743, OF BRIDGEPORT, TX, WAS DISCIPLINED BY TEXAS ON JANUARY 24, 1992.
DISCIPLINARY ACTION: 24-MONTH PROBATION
OFFENSE: SUBSTANDARD CARE, INCOMPETENCE, OR NEGLIGENCE
NOTES: PROFESSIONAL FAILURE TO PRACTICE MEDICINE IN AN ACCEPTABLE MANNER CONSISTENT WITH PUBLIC HEALTH AND WELFARE. LICENSE SUSPENDED, SUSPENSION STAYED; PROBATION UNDER TERMS AND CONDITIONS.

EIBAND, JOHN M MD, LICENSE NUMBER 00C5037, OF HOUSTON, TX, WAS DISCIPLINED BY TEXAS ON DECEMBER 4, 1991.
DISCIPLINARY ACTION: 60-MONTH PROBATION; REQUIRED TO ENTER AN IMPAIRED PHYSICIAN PROGRAM OR DRUG OR ALCOHOL TREATMENT
OFFENSE: DRUG OR ALCOHOL ABUSE
NOTES: ABUSED DEMEROL AND ALCOHOL FROM 12/89 THROUGH 2/91; WAS SUSPENDED FROM HOSPITAL PRIVILEGES FROM 2/17/91 TO 4/91; HAS REACHED A MONITORING AGREEMENT WITH HOSPITAL; HAS NOT ABUSED DEMEROL OR ALCOHOL SINCE 2/91 AFTER COMPLETING INPATIENT HOSPITALIZATION. FIVE YEAR SUSPENSION STAYED; CONDITIONS OF PROBATION: SHALL ABSTAIN FROM THE CONSUMPTION OF ALCOHOL/CHEMICAL SUBSTANCES IN ANY FORM; SHALL CONTINUE TO MEET WITH IMPAIRED PHYSICIANS COMMITTEE, WITH QUARTERLY REPORTS TO THE BOARD; SHALL PARTICIPATE IN AA, INCLUDING A 12-STEP PROGRAM, ATTENDING NOT LESS THAN 3 TIMES A WEEK, WITH QUARTERLY REPORTS TO THE BOARD; SHALL INITIATE TREATMENT, MONITORING, AND SUPERVISION, WITH THE STARTING POINT PROGRAM WITH QUARTERLY REPORTS TO THE BOARD; SHALL PARTICIPATE IN SCREENING OF BIOLOGICAL FLUIDS; SHALL IMMEDIATELY NOTIFY THE BOARD UPON DISCONTINUATION OF TREATMENT; SHALL MAINTAIN A LOG OF EVERY PRESCRIPTION WRITTEN FOR CONTROLLED SUBSTANCES OR DANGEROUS DRUGS, WHICH SHALL BE AVAILABLE FOR INSPECTION ON DEMAND; SHALL NOT PRESCRIBE FOR OR TREAT HIMSELF OR HIS IMMEDIATE FAMILY; SHALL APPEAR BEFORE THE BOARD TWICE A YEAR; SHALL SUPPLY WRITTEN REPORTS OF HIS MEDICAL CONDITION WHEN REQUESTED; MUST ADVISE THE BOARD OF ADDRESS CHANGE OR IF HE LEAVES THE STATE; TIME SPENT OUT OF TEXAS DOES NOT COUNT TOWARDS PROBATION; SHALL NOT PETITION FOR MODIFICATION OF ORDER AT LEAST UNTIL AFTER 10/1/93. ON 3/5/94 HIS REQUEST FOR TERMINATION OF ORDER DENIED. HOWEVER, ORDER MODIFIED AS FOLLOWS: WRITTEN REPORTS OF HIS PARTICIPATION IN THE PHYSICIANS COUNSELING COMMITTEE WILL BE REQUIRED EVERY SIX MONTHS INSTEAD OF EVERY THREE MONTHS; REQUIREMENT OF PARTICIPATION IN AA AND REQUIREMENT TO INITIATE TREATMENT, MONITORING AND SUPERVISION FROM THE STARTING POINT PROGRAM ARE DELETED; ALLOWED TO REQUEST TERMINATION OR MODIFICATION ONCE EVERY SIX MONTHS. ON 8/19/94 PROBATION TERMINATED.

EITEL, JOHN BEN DO, LICENSE NUMBER 00B8453, OF PORT NECHES, TX, WAS DISCIPLINED BY TEXAS ON APRIL 15, 1994.
DISCIPLINARY ACTION: SURRENDER OF CONTROLLED SUBSTANCE LICENSE
OFFENSE: FAILURE TO COMPLY WITH A PROFESSIONAL RULE
NOTES: FAILED TO MAINTAIN ADEQUATE RECORDS RELATING TO CONTROLLED SUBSTANCES; PLED GUILTY TO A PORTION OF THE CHARGES AGAINST HIM, LEADING TO THE IMPOSITION OF A FINE AND SURRENDER OF DEA AND TEXAS CONTROLLED SUBSTANCES CERTIFICATES. SHALL NOT HOLD THESE CERTIFICATES AND SHALL NOT REAPPLY WITHOUT BOARD APPROVAL; SHALL GIVE A COPY OF THIS ORDER TO ANY HEALTH CARE ENTITY WHERE HE HAS PRIVILEGES; SHALL COOPERATE WITH THE BOARD IN VERIFYING COMPLIANCE; SHALL INFORM BOARD OF CHANGE OF ADDRESS WITHIN 10 DAYS. SHALL NOT SEEK MODIFICATION FOR ONE YEAR.

ELAFIFI, BAYOUMI ABD MD, LICENSE NUMBER 00E2552, OF HOUSTON, TX, WAS DISCIPLINED BY TEXAS ON DECEMBER 5, 1988.
DISCIPLINARY ACTION: LICENSE SUSPENSION
OFFENSE: SUBSTANDARD CARE, INCOMPETENCE, OR NEGLIGENCE
NOTES: FAILED TO PRACTICE IN ACCEPTABLE MANNER CONSISTENT WITH PUBLIC HEALTH AND WELFARE; DISCIPLINARY ACTION BY PROFESSIONAL ASSOCIATION OR HOSPITAL BASED ON UNPROFESSIONAL CONDUCT OR INCOMPETENCE. INDEFINITE SUSPENSION.

ELKIN, SCOTT RICHARD DO, DATE OF BIRTH APRIL 8, 1950, LICENSE NUMBER 00G1644, OF 5806 MESA DRIVE SUITE 375, AUSTIN, TX, WAS DISCIPLINED BY TEXAS ON DECEMBER 4, 1991.
DISCIPLINARY ACTION: 60-MONTH PROBATION; 60-MONTH REQUIRED TO TAKE ADDITIONAL MEDICAL EDUCATION
OFFENSE: PROFESSIONAL MISCONDUCT
NOTES: SEVERAL TIMES BETWEEN 11/6/89 AND 2/14/90 HE SIGNED INSURANCE FORMS FOR A PATIENT REPRESENTING HE HAD PROVIDED PSYCHOTHERAPY, WHEN IN FACT IT HAD BEEN PERFORMED BY AN UNLICENSED PSYCHOTHERAPIST. SUSPENSION STAYED. CONDITIONS OF PROBATION: SHALL COMPLETE FIVE HOURS PER YEAR OF AN ETHICS COURSE; SHALL REFRAIN FROM SIGNING INSURANCE FORMS AND/OR ATTENDING PHYSICIAN STATEMENTS FOR PATIENTS HE HAS NOT PERSONALLY TREATED;

SHALL APPEAR BEFORE THE BOARD ONCE A YEAR; SHALL COOPERATE WITH BOARD IN VERIFYING COMPLIANCE; SHALL ADVISE THE BOARD OF CHANGE OF ADDRESS WITHIN 10 DAYS; TIME SPENT OUT OF TEXAS DOES NOT COUNT TOWARD PROBATION; MAY NOT PETITION FOR MODIFICATION FOR AT LEAST ONE YEAR. ON 8/20/93, ORDER TERMINATED AND LICENSE FREE AND CLEAR OF ANY PREVIOUS RESTRICTIONS.

ELKIN, SCOTT RICHARD DO, DATE OF BIRTH APRIL 8, 1950, LICENSE NUMBER 0023916, WAS DISCIPLINED BY COLORADO ON FEBRUARY 11, 1994.
DISCIPLINARY ACTION: REPRIMAND
OFFENSE: DISCIPLINARY ACTION BY ANOTHER STATE OR AGENCY
NOTES: DISCIPLINARY ACTION TAKEN BY TEXAS.

ELTERMAN, ROY DANA MD OF 12801 N CENTRAL EXPRESSWAY #580, DALLAS, TX, WAS DISCIPLINED BY DEA ON MARCH 7, 1990.
DISCIPLINARY ACTION: SURRENDER OF CONTROLLED SUBSTANCE LICENSE
OFFENSE: DRUG OR ALCOHOL ABUSE
NOTES: WROTE PRESCRIPTION FOR PERSONAL USE. ADMITTED TO SUBSTANCE ABUSE PROBLEM WITH PRESCRIPTION MEDICATION.

ELTERMAN, ROY DANA MD, LICENSE NUMBER 00E9188, OF DALLAS, TX, WAS DISCIPLINED BY TEXAS ON SEPTEMBER 28, 1990.
DISCIPLINARY ACTION: 36-MONTH PROBATION; MONITORING OF PHYSICIAN
NOTES: MUST COMPLY WITH HIS AGREEMENT WITH HUMANA HOSPITAL-MEDICAL CITY DALLAS; CONTINUE PSYCHIATRIC TREATMENT; SUBMIT FOR APPROPRIATE EXAMINATIONS TO DETERMINE FREEDOM FROM DRUGS AND ALCOHOL; PARTICIPATE IN ALCOHOLICS ANONYMOUS; REPORT ANY INCIDENT IN WHICH HE PARTAKES OF ALCOHOL OR USES CONTROLLED SUBSTANCE NOT PRESCRIBED BY ANOTHER PHYSICIAN FOR LEGITIMATE AND THERAPEUTIC CONDITION; NOT TREAT OR SERVE AS PHYSICIAN, PRESCRIBE, DISPENSE, OR ADMINISTER CONTROLLED SUBSTANCES OR ANY OTHER DRUGS THAT MAY BE SUBJECT TO ABUSE, OR WRITE PRESCRIPTIONS FOR CONTROLLED SUBSTANCES OR ANY OTHER DRUGS THAT MAY BE SUBJECT TO ABUSE FOR SELF OR IMMEDIATE FAMILY; ADMINISTER TO SELF OR IMMEDIATE FAMILY ONLY DRUGS AS PRESCRIBED BY OTHER PHYSICIANS; NOT TREAT HIMSELF FOR RECURRING MEDICAL CONDITION NOR ADMINISTER OR PRESCRIBE MOOD ELEVATORS OR CONTROLLED SUBSTANCES FOR PERSONAL USE; ABSTAIN FROM ALCOHOL CONSUMPTION; REFRAIN FROM USE OF, AND NOT POSSESS, ADMINISTER, OR PRESCRIBE CONTROLLED SUBSTANCES OR ANY DRUG OR MEDICATION REQUIRING PRESCRIPTION UNLESS SUCH IS PRESCRIBED, ADMINISTERED, OR DISPENSED BY PHYSICIAN TREATING HIM FOR LEGITIMATE MEDICAL NEED, AND SUCH TREATING PHYSICIAN REPORTS TO BOARD CONDITION BEING TREATED AND DRUG PRESCRIBED; APPEAR BEFORE BOARD WHEN REQUESTED.

EMANUEL, RAPHAEL JOHN MD, LICENSE NUMBER 00E7592, OF DALLAS, TX, WAS DISCIPLINED BY TEXAS ON OCTOBER 5, 1991.
DISCIPLINARY ACTION: 24-MONTH PROBATION; REPRIMAND
OFFENSE: OVERCHARGING
NOTES: INADVERTENTLY USED THE WRONG BILLING CODES FOR PULMONARY AND VASCULAR TESTING ON TWO PATIENTS IN MARCH AND AUGUST 1988. CONDITIONS OF PROBATION: SHALL ATTEND AT LEAST 20 HOURS OF CATEGORY I CONTINUING MEDICAL EDUCATION IN RISK MANAGEMENT WITHIN ONE YEAR; SHALL APPEAR BEFORE THE BOARD ONCE A YEAR; SHALL COOPERATE WITH THE BOARD IN VERIFYING COMPLIANCE; SHALL ADVISE THE BOARD OF ANY CHANGE OF ADDRESS WITHIN 10 DAYS; TIME SPENT OUT OF STATE DOES NOT COUNT TOWARDS PROBATION.

EMERSON, TIMOTHY JOE MD, LICENSE NUMBER 00G8831, OF SAN ANGELO, TX, WAS DISCIPLINED BY TEXAS ON DECEMBER 4, 1991.
DISCIPLINARY ACTION: LICENSE SUSPENSION
OFFENSE: CRIMINAL CONVICTION OR PLEA OF GUILTY, NOLO CONTENDERE, OR NO CONTEST TO A CRIME
NOTES: SEVERAL TIMES DURING 1986 AND ON 3/25/87 HE ENGAGED IN SEXUAL CONTACT WITH A FEMALE CHILD YOUNGER THAN 17; PLED GUILTY TO SEXUAL ASSAULT OF A FEMALE CHILD YOUNGER THAN 17 ON 8/10/87; COURT PLACED HIM ON PROBATION FOR 10 YEARS WITH TERMS, INCLUDING THE REQUIREMENT THAT HE ATTEND PSYCHOLOGICAL COUNSELING SESSIONS. SUSPENSION UNTIL SUCH TIME AS HE SHOWS HE IS MENTALLY, PHYSICALLY AND OTHERWISE COMPETENT TO PRACTICE MEDICINE.

EMERSON, TIMOTHY JOE MD, LICENSE NUMBER 00G8831, WAS DISCIPLINED BY TEXAS ON AUGUST 31, 1993.
DISCIPLINARY ACTION: 84-MONTH PROBATION; RESTRICTION PLACED ON LICENSE
NOTES: PURSUANT TO TERMS OF 12/4/91 ORDER HE PROVIDED EVIDENCE TO SHOW HE IS MENTALLY, PHYSICALLY AND OTHERWISE COMPETENT TO PRACTICE MEDICINE. SUSPENSION LIFTED AND STAYED. CONDITIONS OF PROBATION: WITHIN ONE YEAR SHALL COMPLETE 50 HOURS OF CONTINUING MEDICAL EDUCATION IN FAMILY PRACTICE; WHEN PERFORMING PHYSICAL EXAMS ON CHILDREN AND FEMALE PATIENTS SHALL BE MONITORED AND CHAPERONEED BY A FEMALE MONITOR WHO SHALL DOCUMENT HER PRESENCE; SHALL SUBMIT HIMSELF FOR EVALUATION AND TREATMENT TO A BOARD-APPROVED PSYCHIATRIST; UNTIL HE HAS SUCCESSFULLY COMPLETED THE AFOREMENTIONED 50 HOURS OF CONTINUING MEDICAL EDUCATION, SHALL BE MONITORED OR SUPERVISED BY A BOARD-APPROVED PHYSICIAN WHO WILL REPORT TO THE BOARD EVERY FOUR MONTHS; SHALL GIVE A COPY OF THIS ORDER TO ALL HEALTH CARE ENTITIES WHERE HE HAS PRIVILEGES; SHALL COOPERATE WITH BOARD IN VERIFYING COMPLIANCE; SHALL INFORM BOARD OF CHANGE OF ADDRESS WITHIN 10 DAYS OR IF HE LEAVES THE STATE; TIME SPENT OUT OF TEXAS DOES NOT COUNT TOWARD PROBATION. SHALL NOT SEEK MODIFICATION FOR ONE YEAR.

EMERSON, TIMOTHY JOE MD OF SAN ANGELO, TX, WAS DISCIPLINED BY NORTH CAROLINA ON FEBRUARY 1, 1994.
DISCIPLINARY ACTION: LICENSE REVOCATION

EPPS, DEBRA KENNAMER MD, LICENSE NUMBER 00H2360, OF DALLAS, TX, WAS DISCIPLINED BY TEXAS ON DECEMBER 4, 1991.
DISCIPLINARY ACTION: SURRENDER OF CONTROLLED SUBSTANCE LICENSE; 120-MONTH PROBATION
OFFENSE: DRUG OR ALCOHOL ABUSE
NOTES: DURING THE PERIOD OF 7/86 TO 7/91 SHE ABUSED FIORICET, FIORINAL #3, LORCET PLUS, DARVOCET N-100, MORPHINE, AND INJECTABLE DEMEROL

OBTAINED THROUGH THE USE OF SAMPLES AND PRESCRIPTIONS SHE WROTE USING OTHER PEOPLE'S NAMES; WAS UNABLE TO ADEQUATELY CARE FOR PATIENTS DUE TO IMPAIRMENT; HAS BEEN ENROLLED IN A TREATMENT PROGRAM FOR CHEMICAL DEPENDENCY SINCE 7/13/91. SUSPENSION STAYED; CONDITIONS OF PROBATIONS: SHALL REFRAIN FROM CONSUMING ALL MOOD ALTERING DRUGS INCLUDING ALCOHOL; MUST SUBMIT TO APPROPRIATE EXAMINATIONS INCLUDING SCREENS OF BODILY FLUIDS: MUST PARTICIPATE WITH IMPAIRED PHYSICIANS GROUP, INCLUDING WEEKLY MEETINGS, WITH QUARTERLY WRITTEN REPORTS TO THE BOARD; MUST PARTICIPATE IN AA, INCLUDING A 12-STEP PROGRAM, NOT LESS THAN TWICE A WEEK, WITH WRITTEN QUARTERLY REPORTS TO THE BOARD; TREATING PHYSICIAN SHALL ALSO SUBMIT REPORTS TO BOARD QUARTERLY; SHALL SURRENDER DEA AND TEXAS CONTROLLED SUBSTANCES REGISTRATIONS: SHALL NOT REAPPLY FOR THESE WITHOUT WRITTEN CONSENT FROM THE BOARD; SHALL SURRENDER ALL UNUSED TRIPLICATE PRESCRIPTION FORMS AND ALL CONTROLLED SUBSTANCES, INCLUDING SAMPLES; SHALL ENROLL IN AND COMPLETE, WITHIN SIX MONTHS, A REMEDIAL PHARMACOLOGY COURSE WITH PROOF OF COMPLETION SUBMITTED; SHALL APPEAR BEFORE THE BOARD TWICE A YEAR; SHALL COOPERATE WITH BOARD IN VERIFYING COMPLIANCE; SHALL ADVISE THE BOARD OF ANY ADDRESS CHANGE WITHIN 10 DAYS; TIME SPENT OUT OF TEXAS DOES NOT COUNT TOWARDS PROBATION; SHALL NOT PETITION FOR MODIFICATION OF ORDER FOR AT LEAST ON YEAR.

EPPS, DEBRA KENNAMER MD, LICENSE NUMBER 00H2360, OF DALLAS, TX, WAS DISCIPLINED BY TEXAS ON AUGUST 20, 1992.
DISCIPLINARY ACTION: LICENSE SUSPENSION
OFFENSE: FAILURE TO COMPLY WITH A PREVIOUS BOARD ORDER
NOTES: VIOLATION OF PREVIOUS BOARD ORDER.

EPPS, DEBRA KENNAMER MD, LICENSE NUMBER 00H2360, WAS DISCIPLINED BY TEXAS ON SEPTEMBER 7, 1993.
DISCIPLINARY ACTION: 60-MONTH PROBATION; RESTRICTION PLACED ON CONTROLLED SUBSTANCE LICENSE
NOTES: BASED ON HER PROGRESS AND PSYCHIATRIC EVALUATION BOARD GRANTED REQUEST TO TERMINATE SUSPENSION ENTERED ON 8/20/92. CONDITIONS OF PROBATION: SHALL ABSTAIN FROM THE CONSUMPTION OF ALCOHOL/CHEMICAL SUBSTANCES; SHALL SUBMIT HERSELF FOR APPROPRIATE EXAMS INCLUDING DRUG OR ALCOHOL SCREENS; SHALL CONTINUE TO PARTICIPATE IN THE ACTIVITIES OF THE BEXAR COUNTY MEDICAL SOCIETY AND ATTEND WEEKLY MEETINGS WITH QUARTERLY REPORTS; SHALL CONTINUE TO PARTICIPATE IN AA'S 12 STEP PROGRAM NOT LESS THAN THREE TIMES A WEEK WITH QUARTERLY REPORTS TO THE BOARD; SHALL CONTINUE TO RECEIVE PSYCHIATRIC COUNSELING WITH QUARTERLY REPORTS TO THE BOARD; SHALL ATTEND AT LEAST 50 HOURS PER YEAR OF CONTINUING MEDICAL EDUCATION; SHALL BE MONITORED BY A BOARD-APPROVED PHYSICIAN WITH QUARTERLY REPORTS; SHALL APPEAR BEFORE THE BOARD TWICE A YEAR; SHALL COOPERATE WITH THE BOARD IN VERIFYING COMPLIANCE; SHALL INFORM BOARD OF CHANGE OF ADDRESS WITHIN 10 DAYS OR IF SHE LEAVES THE STATE; TIME SPENT OUT OF TEXAS DOES NOT COUNT TOWARD PROBATION. SHALL NOT SEEK MODIFICATION FOR ONE YEAR. ORDER MODIFIED ON 10/1/93 GRANTING HER PERMISSION TO REAPPLY TO THE DEA AND TEXAS DEPARTMENT OF PUBLIC SAFETY FOR SCHEDULES IV AND V CONTROLLED SUBSTANCE AUTHORITY; SHALL NOT POSSESS, ADMINISTER, DISPENSE OR PRESCRIBE ANY CONTROLLED SUBSTANCES BUT MAY ORDER THEM TO BE ADMINISTERED TO HOSPITALIZED PATIENTS IF THEY ARE COUNTERSIGNED. ORDER FURTHER MODIFIED ON 9/30/94 SUCH THAT SHE WOULD BE ABLE TO APPLY FOR SCHEDULE III SUBSTANCE AUTHORITY, THE REQUIREMENT THAT ALL PRESCRIPTIONS FOR CONTROLLED SUBSTANCES BE COUNTERSIGNED IS DROPPED AND THE CONDITION ADDED THAT SEPARATE FROM PATIENT RECORDS SHE SHALL MAINTAIN A FILE OF EVERY PRESCRIPTION WRITTEN FOR CONTROLLED SUBSTANCES OR DANGEROUS DRUGS WHICH SHALL BE AVAILABLE FOR INSPECTION.

ERDMANN, RALPH R MD, LICENSE NUMBER 00C7350, OF LUBBOCK, TX, WAS DISCIPLINED BY TEXAS ON AUGUST 20, 1992.
DISCIPLINARY ACTION: SURRENDER OF LICENSE
OFFENSE: SUBSTANDARD CARE, INCOMPETENCE, OR NEGLIGENCE
NOTES: UNPROFESSIONAL OR DISHONORABLE CONDUCT LIKELY TO DECEIVE, DEFRAUD OR INJURE THE PUBLIC; PROFESSIONAL FAILURE TO PRACTICE MEDICINE IN AN ACCEPTABLE MANNER CONSISTENT WITH PUBLIC HEALTH AND WELFARE; AND COMMITTING AN ACT THAT IS IN VIOLATION OF THE LAWS OF TEXAS. LICENSE RETIRED IN LIEU OF FURTHER DISCIPLINARY PROCEEDINGS.

ERICKSON, CARL F MD, LICENSE NUMBER 00H2361, OF SAN ANTONIO, TX, WAS DISCIPLINED BY TEXAS ON AUGUST 24, 1991.
DISCIPLINARY ACTION: 60-MONTH PROBATION; REQUIRED TO ENTER AN IMPAIRED PHYSICIAN PROGRAM OR DRUG OR ALCOHOL TREATMENT
OFFENSE: DRUG OR ALCOHOL ABUSE
NOTES: INTEMPERATE USE OF ALCOHOL OR DRUGS. SUSPENSION STAYED. CONDITIONS OF PROBATION: MUST REFRAIN FROM ALCOHOL OR DRUG CONSUMPTION; MUST SUBMIT TO ALCOHOL OR DRUG SCREENS; MUST PARTICIPATE IN IMPAIRED PHYSICIANS PROGRAM; MUST PARTICIPATE IN AA; MUST APPEAR TWICE YEARLY BEFORE THE BOARD. ON 9/30/94 PROBATION TERMINATED.

ESPIRITU, EDGARDO T MD, LICENSE NUMBER 00E4321, OF NEDERLAND, TX, WAS DISCIPLINED BY TEXAS ON DECEMBER 5, 1988.
DISCIPLINARY ACTION: 59-MONTH RESTRICTION PLACED ON LICENSE
NOTES: SHALL REFRAIN FROM GASTROPLASTY SURGERY WITHOUT BOARD APPROVAL; SHALL OBTAIN SPECIFIC CONSULTATION AND CONCURRING OPINION THAT SURGERY IS NECESSARY AND HAVE APPROPRIATE BOARD CERTIFIED SURGEON AS HIS ASSISTANT IN SURGERY ON ALL MAJOR ABDOMINAL SURGERIES

ESPIRITU, EDGARDO T MD, DATE OF BIRTH FEBRUARY 23, 1940, LICENSE NUMBER 0031366, OF 2100 HIGHWAY 365, NEDERLAND, TX, WAS DISCIPLINED BY MICHIGAN ON MARCH 20, 1991.
DISCIPLINARY ACTION: LICENSE REVOCATION; FINE
OFFENSE: SUBSTANDARD CARE, INCOMPETENCE, OR NEGLIGENCE
NOTES: $250 FINE.

ESPIRITU, EDGARDO T MD, LICENSE NUMBER 00E4321, WAS DISCIPLINED BY TEXAS ON SEPTEMBER 9, 1991.
NOTES: REQUEST FOR TERMINATION OF AGREED ORDER OF 12/5/88 WAS DENIED WHEN BOARD FOUND INSUFFICIENT BASIS FOR GRANTING THE REQUEST.

ESPIRITU, ERNESTO T MD, LICENSE NUMBER 00G0873, OF FANNETT, TX, WAS DISCIPLINED BY TEXAS ON MAY 24, 1990.
DISCIPLINARY ACTION: 120-MONTH RESTRICTION PLACED ON CONTROLLED SUBSTANCE LICENSE; REQUIRED TO TAKE ADDITIONAL MEDICAL EDUCATION
NOTES: STIPULATED ORDER. MUST IMMEDIATELY DISPOSE OF CONTROLLED SUBSTANCES IN HIS POSSESSION OR SUBJECT TO HIS CONTROL, REFRAIN FROM PRESCRIBING, DISPENSING, OR ADMINISTERING CONTROLLED SUBSTANCES IN ALL SCHEDULES AND UNDER ALL CIRCUMSTANCES EXCEPT IN HOSPITAL EMERGENCY ROOMS, AND ATTEND CONTINUING MEDICAL EDUCATION COURSES. ORDER EFFECTIVE FOR TEN YEARS.

EVANS, WILLIAM G MD, LICENSE NUMBER 00C1081, OF LUBBOCK, TX, WAS DISCIPLINED BY TEXAS ON OCTOBER 1, 1987.
DISCIPLINARY ACTION: SURRENDER OF LICENSE

EWING, CAROL T MD, LICENSE NUMBER 00E3260, OF PORT ARTHUR, TX, WAS DISCIPLINED BY TEXAS ON JANUARY 24, 1992.
DISCIPLINARY ACTION: 60-MONTH PROBATION
OFFENSE: SUBSTANDARD CARE, INCOMPETENCE, OR NEGLIGENCE
NOTES: PROFESSIONAL FAILURE TO PRACTICE MEDICINE IN AN ACCEPTABLE MANNER CONSISTENT WITH PUBLIC HEALTH AND WELFARE. PROBATION UNDER TERMS AND CONDITIONS. ON 8/19/94 HER REQUEST FOR TERMINATION OF THIS ORDER DENIED.

FABIAN, HAROLD FRANK MD, DATE OF BIRTH DECEMBER 12, 1924, LICENSE NUMBER 00C3651, OF P.O. BOX 500, MCLEAN, TX, WAS DISCIPLINED BY TEXAS ON AUGUST 24, 1991.
DISCIPLINARY ACTION: SURRENDER OF LICENSE
OFFENSE: OVERPRESCRIBING OR MISPRESCRIBING DRUGS
NOTES: NONTHERAPEUTIC PRESCRIBING. SHALL SURRENDER DEA AND DPS CONTROLLED SUBSTANCE REGISTRATION CERTIFICATE; SHALL NOT ATTEMPT TO REREGISTER OR OTHERWISE OBTAIN REGISTRATION WITHOUT PRIOR BOARD APPROVAL. ON 6/15/93 ORDER MODIFIED SO THAT HE MAY SEEK TO OBTAIN HIS DRUG ENFORCEMENT ADMINISTRATION AND TEXAS DEPARTMENT OF PUBLIC SAFETY CONTROLLED SUBSTANCES REGISTRATION CERTIFICATES; UPON OBTAINING THESE CERTIFICATES MAY ADMINISTER AND PRESCRIBE DRUGS WHICH ARE SUBJECT TO THESE REGISTRATIONS FOR LEGITIMATE THERAPEUTIC PURPOSES ONLY; SEPARATE FROM PATIENT RECORDS, HE SHALL MAINTAIN A FILE CONSISTING OF A COPY OF EVERY PRESCRIPTION WRITTEN BY HIM FOR CONTROLLED SUBSTANCES BY DATE ISSUED WHICH SHALL BE AVAILABLE FOR INSPECTION BY THE BOARD; HE SHALL NOT TELEPHONE ANY PRESCRIPTION TO A PHARMACY FOR CONTROLLED SUBSTANCES.

FARLEY, PATRICK C MD, LICENSE NUMBER 0030541, OF SEATTLE, WA, WAS DISCIPLINED BY WASHINGTON ON JULY 27, 1994.
DISCIPLINARY ACTION: EMERGENCY SUSPENSION
OFFENSE: PHYSICAL OR MENTAL ILLNESS INHIBITING THE ABILITY TO PRACTICE WITH SKILL AND SAFETY
NOTES: UNABLE TO PRACTICE WITH REASONABLE SKILL AND SAFETY DUE TO A MENTAL OR PHYSICAL CONDITION. HE HAS COMMITTED ACTS OF MORAL TURPITUDE AND HE MISREPRESENTED A FACT IN HIS APPLICATION FOR A LICENSE TO PRACTICE MEDICINE.

FARLEY, PATRICK C MD, LICENSE NUMBER 00G2696, OF SEATTLE, WA, WAS DISCIPLINED BY TEXAS ON OCTOBER 27, 1994.
DISCIPLINARY ACTION: EMERGENCY SUSPENSION
OFFENSE: DISCIPLINARY ACTION BY ANOTHER STATE OR AGENCY
NOTES: AVAILABLE EVIDENCE AND INFORMATION INDICATE THE FOLLOWING: HAS ENGAGED IN CONDUCT INDICATIVE OF A MENTAL CONDITION WHICH CAUSES HIM TO BE UNABLE TO PRACTICE WITH REASONABLE SKILL AND SAFETY; HAS UNDERGONE AN INDEPENDENT PSYCHIATRIC EXAM WHICH LED TO A DIAGNOSIS OF SUCH A MENTAL CONDITION; ON 7/27/94 WASHINGTON SUMMARILY SUSPENDED HIS LICENSE BASED ON THIS.

FAYMORE, LEONARD F DO WAS DISCIPLINED BY OHIO ON DECEMBER 2, 1981.
DISCIPLINARY ACTION: LICENSE REVOCATION

FAYMORE, LEONARD F DO OF ELYRIA, OH, WAS DISCIPLINED BY TEXAS ON SEPTEMBER 1, 1985.
DISCIPLINARY ACTION: SURRENDER OF LICENSE

FAYMORE, LEONARD F DO OF OXFORD, WI, WAS DISCIPLINED BY MISSOURI ON DECEMBER 29, 1987.
DISCIPLINARY ACTION: LICENSE REVOCATION

FERNANDEZ, CARLOS A MD, LICENSE NUMBER 00C2460, OF EL PASO, TX, WAS DISCIPLINED BY TEXAS ON FEBRUARY 22, 1991.
DISCIPLINARY ACTION: 60-MONTH PROBATION; RESTRICTION PLACED ON LICENSE
NOTES: MUST SUBMIT TO PSYCHIATRIC EVALUATION AND UNDERGO RECOMMENDED TREATMENT; APPEAR FOR ANNUAL REPORT TO BOARD; EXAMINE NO FEMALE PATIENTS UNLESS A CHAPERONEE IS PRESENT IN THE EXAMINATION ROOM.

FERNANDEZ-VILA, WILFREDO MD, LICENSE NUMBER 00D3864, OF SOUTH HOUSTON, TX, WAS DISCIPLINED BY TEXAS ON OCTOBER 29, 1988.
DISCIPLINARY ACTION: REVOCATION OF CONTROLLED SUBSTANCE LICENSE; 46-MONTH PROBATION
NOTES: MUST COMPLY WITH MEMO OF AGREEMENT WITH DEA, COMPLETE DRUG ABUSE PRECEPTORSHIP AND NOT REAPPLY FOR DEA AND TEXAS CONTROLLED SUBSTANCES REGISTRATIONS WITHOUT BOARD PERMISSION

FERNANDEZ-VILA, WILFREDO MD, LICENSE NUMBER 0TXD386, OF 1712 HOUSTON BLVD, SOUTH HOUSTON, TX, WAS DISCIPLINED BY DEA ON AUGUST 29, 1989.
DISCIPLINARY ACTION: RESTRICTION PLACED ON CONTROLLED SUBSTANCE LICENSE
OFFENSE: PROFESSIONAL MISCONDUCT
NOTES: ARRESTED 09/09/86 IN SOUTH HOUSTON, TEXAS FOR ILLEGAL DISTRIBUTION OF OXYCODONE; CHARGES DISMISSED 04/22/87 DUE TO LACK OF SPEEDY TRIAL. SURRENDERED LICENSE TO PRACTICE MEDICINE.

FERNANDEZ-VILA, WILFREDO MD, LICENSE NUMBER 0D03201, OF 1714 HOUSTON BOULEVARD, SOUTH HOUSTON, TX, WAS DISCIPLINED BY MARYLAND ON MAY 23, 1990.
DISCIPLINARY ACTION: SURRENDER OF LICENSE
OFFENSE: DISCIPLINARY ACTION BY ANOTHER STATE OR AGENCY

NOTES: ON 9/4/87 HE ENTERED INTO A MEMORANDUM OF AGREEMENT WITH THE DEA IN WHICH HE AGREED NOT TO PRESCRIBE, ORDER, OR HANDLE SCHEDULE II, IIN, III OR IIIN CONTROLLED SUBSTANCES, OR ANY SCHEDULE V NARCOTIC SUBSTANCES, FOR FIVE YEARS. ORIGINALLY PLACED ON PROBATIONARY STATUS BY TEXAS BOARD UNTIL SEPTEMBER 3, 1992. AS PART OF HIS AGREED BOARD ORDER, HE WAS ALSO REQUIRED TO ENROLL AND COMPLETE A TWO WEEK PRECEPTORSHIP ON THE PREVENTION AND TREATMENT OF DRUG ABUSE.

FERNANDEZ-VILA, WILFREDO MD, DATE OF BIRTH JULY 1, 1916, LICENSE NUMBER 0012162, OF 1714 HOUSTON BLVD, SOUTH HOUSTON, TX, WAS DISCIPLINED BY GEORGIA ON NOVEMBER 15, 1990.
DISCIPLINARY ACTION: LICENSE REVOCATION
OFFENSE: DISCIPLINARY ACTION BY ANOTHER STATE OR AGENCY

FERNANDEZ-VILA, WILFREDO MD, LICENSE NUMBER 0100494, OF 1714 HOUSTON BOULEVARD, SOUTH HOUSTON, TX, WAS DISCIPLINED BY NEW YORK ON AUGUST 2, 1993.
DISCIPLINARY ACTION: LICENSE REVOCATION
OFFENSE: DISCIPLINARY ACTION BY ANOTHER STATE OR AGENCY
NOTES: FOUND GUILTY BY THE DRUG ENFORCEMENT ADMINISTRATION OF VIOLATING FEDERAL LAWS AND REGULATIONS RELATING TO THE PRESCRIBING OF CONTROLLED SUBSTANCES.

FILARDI, HECTOR HIRAM MD, LICENSE NUMBER 00C5531, OF GRANBURY, TX, WAS DISCIPLINED BY TEXAS ON APRIL 15, 1994.
DISCIPLINARY ACTION: RESTRICTION PLACED ON LICENSE
OFFENSE: SEXUAL ABUSE OF OR SEXUAL MISCONDUCT WITH A PATIENT
NOTES: CRIMINAL COMPLAINT HAS BEEN FILED AGAINST HIM ALLEGING THAT HE HAS ENGAGED IN BEHAVIOR CONSTITUTING SEXUAL INDECENCY WITH VARIOUS MINORS WHO WERE HIS PATIENTS; DENIES ALL OF THE ALLEGATIONS AND WHILE MAKING NO ADMISSION REGARDING ANY PENDING ACCUSATIONS VOLUNTARILY AGREED TO THE ENTRY OF THIS ORDER. PRACTICE RESTRICTED IN THAT HE SHALL NOT EXAMINE OR TREAT ANY PEDIATRIC PATIENT UNDER 16 YEARS OF AGE; IN THE EVENT THE CRIMINAL CHARGES ARE DISPOSED OF THROUGH DISMISSAL OR ACQUITTAL THIS RESTRICTION SHALL TERMINATE; SHALL COOPERATE WITH THE BOARD IN VERIFYING COMPLIANCE; SHALL INFORM BOARD OF CHANGE OF ADDRESS WITHIN 10 DAYS.

FINCH, ALBERT B MD, LICENSE NUMBER 00C3297, OF ODESSA, TX, WAS DISCIPLINED BY TEXAS ON OCTOBER 1, 1987.
DISCIPLINARY ACTION: RESTRICTION PLACED ON CONTROLLED SUBSTANCE LICENSE; REPRIMAND
OFFENSE: OVERPRESCRIBING OR MISPRESCRIBING DRUGS
NOTES: EXHIBITED UNPROFESSIONAL OR DISHONORABLE CONDUCT LIKELY TO DECEIVE OR DEFRAUD PUBLIC; PRESCRIBED OR ADMINISTERED DRUGS NONTHERAPEUTICALLY. RESTRICTIONS INCLUDED BEING PREVENTED FROM PRESCRIBING AMPHETAMINE OR AMPHETAMINE-LIKE DRUGS FOR WEIGHT CONTROL.

FINCHER, MARK L MD OF 1512 BARWICK, NORMAN, OK, WAS DISCIPLINED BY DEA ON JUNE 22, 1992.
DISCIPLINARY ACTION: REVOCATION OF CONTROLLED SUBSTANCE LICENSE
OFFENSE: DISCIPLINARY ACTION BY ANOTHER STATE OR AGENCY
NOTES: EFFECTIVE 06/22/91 OKLAHOMA SUSPENDED HIS MEDICAL LICENSE FOR TWO YEARS BASED ON HIS FRAUDULENT MISREPRESENTATION OF HIS PREVIOUS CRIMINAL RECORD IN AN APPLICATION THAT HE SUBMITTED FOR REINSTATEMENT OF HIS MEDICAL LICENSE. ALSO, AS OF 01/28/92 HE CONTINUED TO BE UNREGISTERED WITH THE CONTROLLED SUBSTANCES LICENSING AUTHORITY IN OKLAHOMA.

FINCHER, MARK LYNN MD, LICENSE NUMBER 0014822, OF 1512 BARWICK, NORMAN, OK, WAS DISCIPLINED BY OKLAHOMA ON JUNE 22, 1991.
DISCIPLINARY ACTION: 24-MONTH LICENSE SUSPENSION
OFFENSE: PROVIDING FALSE INFORMATION TO THE BOARD
NOTES: ON 5/31/90, ARRESTED IN STEPHENS COUNTY, OKLAHOMA, AND CHARGED WITH TWO COUNTS OF LARCENY OF DOMESTIC ANIMALS. FORMALLY CHARGED ON 6/1/90. ON 10/2/90, SUBMITTED AN APPLICATION FOR REINSTATEMENT OF LICENSE, AND FALSELY ANSWERED TWO QUESTIONS; SPECIFICALLY, ANSWERED "NO" TO "HAVE YOU EVER BEEN CHARGED WITH OR CONVICTED OF A FELONY OR MISDEMEANOR?" BEFORE NEXT BOARD APPEARANCE, SHALL PRESENT EVIDENCE FROM PSYCHIATRIST THAT HE IS FREE OF ANY MENTAL CONDITION THAT WOULD PREVENT HIM FROM PRACTICING WITH REASONABLE SKILL AND SAFETY.

FINCHER, MARK LYNN MD, LICENSE NUMBER 00H7413, OF NORMAN, OK, WAS DISCIPLINED BY TEXAS ON JUNE 17, 1992.
DISCIPLINARY ACTION: SURRENDER OF LICENSE
OFFENSE: DISCIPLINARY ACTION BY ANOTHER STATE OR AGENCY

FINLEY, OLIVIA I MD, LICENSE NUMBER 00G6105, OF SAN ANTONIO, TX, WAS DISCIPLINED BY TEXAS ON DECEMBER 1, 1988.
NOTES: SETTLEMENT AGREEMENT AND UNSPECIFIED DISCIPLINARY ACTION

FINLEY, OLIVIA I MD, LICENSE NUMBER 00G6105, WAS DISCIPLINED BY TEXAS ON OCTOBER 5, 1991.
NOTES: ORDER OF 2/15/88 PLACING LICENSE ON 10 YEAR PROBATION IS VACATED AND LICENSE IS NOW FREE OF ANY RESTRICTION OR LIMITATION.

FINLEY, OLIVIA I MD, LICENSE NUMBER 00G6105, OF KERRVILLE, TX, WAS DISCIPLINED BY TEXAS ON MARCH 24, 1994.
DISCIPLINARY ACTION: EMERGENCY SUSPENSION
OFFENSE: DRUG OR ALCOHOL ABUSE
NOTES: ON TWO OCCASIONS IN 3/94 EVIDENCE AND INFORMATION INDICATE THAT SHE WAS UNDER THE INFLUENCE OF COCAINE WHILE TREATING PATIENTS AND THAT AS A RESULT OF THIS SUBSTANCE ABUSE SHE HAS FAILED TO SHOW UP AT WORK IN A TIMELY MANNER AND TO PROVIDE COVERAGE FOR HER PATIENTS DURING HER ABSENCE; THESE FAILURES CONSTITUTE ABANDONMENT OF PATIENTS.

FINLEY, OLIVIA I MD, LICENSE NUMBER 00G6105, OF KERRVILLE, TX, WAS DISCIPLINED BY TEXAS ON SEPTEMBER 30, 1994.
DISCIPLINARY ACTION: LICENSE SUSPENSION
OFFENSE: DRUG OR ALCOHOL ABUSE
NOTES: SHE HAS ADMITTED TO THE INTEMPERATE USE OF COCAINE ON VARIOUS OCCASIONS AFTER SUBSTANCE ABUSE TREATMENT INCLUDING USE AS RECENTLY AS 11/93. SUSPENSION UNTIL SHE PERSONALLY APPEARS

BEFORE THE BOARD AND PROVIDES SUFFICIENT EVIDENCE THAT SHE IS PHYSICALLY, MENTALLY AND OTHERWISE COMPETENT TO PRACTICE; EVIDENCE SHALL INCLUDE BUT NOT BE LIMITED TO COMPLETE MEDICAL RECORDS AND REPORTS OF PSYCHOLOGICAL, NEUROPSYCHIATRIC AND PHYSICAL EVALUATIONS.

FISCHER, ROY LEE DO, LICENSE NUMBER 00C4317, OF DALLAS, TX, WAS DISCIPLINED BY TEXAS ON JULY 1, 1990.
DISCIPLINARY ACTION: LICENSE REVOCATION
OFFENSE: SUBSTANDARD CARE, INCOMPETENCE, OR NEGLIGENCE
NOTES: ACTIONS CONSTITUTED PROFESSIONAL FAILURE TO PRACTICE MEDICINE IN ACCEPTABLE MANNER CONSISTENT WITH PUBLIC HEALTH AND WELFARE. RECURRING MERITORIOUS HEALTH CARE LIABILITY CLAIMS FILED AGAINST HIM EVIDENCE PROFESSIONAL INCOMPETENCE LIKELY TO INJURE PUBLIC.

FISHER, ALLEN M DO OF MIDLAND, TX, WAS DISCIPLINED BY TEXAS ON JULY 1, 1986.
DISCIPLINARY ACTION: LICENSE REVOCATION
OFFENSE: FAILURE TO COMPLY WITH A PREVIOUS BOARD ORDER
NOTES: PRESCRIBED CONTROLLED SUBSTANCES NONTHERAPEUTICALLY AND EXHIBITED UNPROFESSIONAL OR DISHONORABLE CONDUCT LIKELY TO INJURE PUBLIC; VIOLATED PRIOR AGREEMENT WITH THE BOARD; MOTION FOR REHEARING DENIED

FLEMING, JAMES M DO, LICENSE NUMBER 0004511, OF SEABROOK, TX, WAS DISCIPLINED BY OHIO ON APRIL 12, 1991.
DISCIPLINARY ACTION: LICENSE REVOCATION
OFFENSE: CRIMINAL CONVICTION OR PLEA OF GUILTY, NOLO CONTENDERE, OR NO CONTEST TO A CRIME
NOTES: CONVICTION OF SIX FELONY COUNTS OF MEDICAID FRAUD. PERMANENT REVOCATION.

FLEMING, JAMES M DO, DATE OF BIRTH DECEMBER 28, 1943, LICENSE NUMBER 0006308, OF 1087 DENNISON AVE, COLUMBUS, OH, WAS DISCIPLINED BY MICHIGAN ON JANUARY 21, 1992.
DISCIPLINARY ACTION: LICENSE REVOCATION
OFFENSE: CRIMINAL CONVICTION OR PLEA OF GUILTY, NOLO CONTENDERE, OR NO CONTEST TO A CRIME

FLEMING, JAMES M DO, DATE OF BIRTH DECEMBER 28, 1943, OF 2711 LITTLE YORK ROAD SUITE 200, HOUSTON, TX, WAS DISCIPLINED BY MEDICARE ON JUNE 2, 1993.
DISCIPLINARY ACTION: 60-MONTH EXCLUSION FROM THE MEDICARE AND/OR MEDICAID PROGRAMS
OFFENSE: CRIMINAL CONVICTION OR PLEA OF GUILTY, NOLO CONTENDERE, OR NO CONTEST TO A CRIME
NOTES: CONVICTED OF SUBMITTING FALSE STATEMENTS TO THE MEDICAID PROGRAM FOR PHYSICIAN SERVICES.

FLEMING, JAMES MICHAEL DO, LICENSE NUMBER 00E0006, OF SEABROOK, TX, WAS DISCIPLINED BY TEXAS ON AUGUST 24, 1991.
DISCIPLINARY ACTION: REPRIMAND
OFFENSE: CRIMINAL CONVICTION OR PLEA OF GUILTY, NOLO CONTENDERE, OR NO CONTEST TO A CRIME
NOTES: CONVICTED OF MEDICAID FRAUD.

FLORES, ALBERTO MD, DATE OF BIRTH FEBRUARY 7, 1955, OF 1611 ROCKDALE DRIVE, ARLINGTON, TX, WAS DISCIPLINED BY MEDICARE ON MARCH 6, 1994.
DISCIPLINARY ACTION: EXCLUSION FROM THE MEDICARE AND/OR MEDICAID PROGRAMS
OFFENSE: FAILURE TO COMPLY WITH A PROFESSIONAL RULE
NOTES: DEFAULTED ON PUBLIC HEALTH SERVICE EDUCATION LOAN. REINSTATED ON 6/8/94.

FLORY, WILLIAM D MD, LICENSE NUMBER 00D5527, OF ANDREWS, TX, WAS DISCIPLINED BY TEXAS ON JULY 28, 1989.
DISCIPLINARY ACTION: REQUIRED TO TAKE ADDITIONAL MEDICAL EDUCATION
NOTES: MUST SELECT COURSE IN OBSTETRICAL MEDICINE WITHIN CERTAIN TIME FRAME OR CEASE OBSTETRICAL PRACTICE UNTIL DONE.

FLYNN, PATRICK WILLIAM MD, LICENSE NUMBER 00C8283, OF CARSON CITY, NV, WAS DISCIPLINED BY TEXAS ON AUGUST 26, 1988.
NOTES: SETTLEMENT AGREEMENT AND UNSPECIFIED DISCIPLINARY ACTION. ON 3/5/94 ORDER IS TERMINATED BASED ON HIS RELEASE FROM AN ARIZONA ORDER WHICH HAD EXPIRED.

FLYNN, PATRICK WILLIAM MD, LICENSE NUMBER 0004384, WAS DISCIPLINED BY ARIZONA ON JANUARY 19, 1990.
DISCIPLINARY ACTION: 60-MONTH PROBATION; REQUIRED TO ENTER AN IMPAIRED PHYSICIAN PROGRAM OR DRUG OR ALCOHOL TREATMENT
OFFENSE: FAILURE TO COMPLY WITH A PREVIOUS BOARD ORDER
NOTES: ON 4/10/87 ENTERED INTO BOARD ORDER WITH TERMS INCLUDING ABSTAINING FROM ALCOHOL AND ALL OTHER DRUGS AND CONTINUING CARE AND TREATMENT FOR SUBSTANCE ABUSE. CEASED PRACTICING MEDICINE IN ARIZONA ON OR BEFORE 12/87. ON OR ABOUT 12/11/87 ENTERED INTO STIPULATION WITH NEVADA BOARD, WHICH WAS AMENDED ON OR ABOUT 11/21/88. ON 10/24/88 SUBMITTED URINE SAMPLE WHICH TESTED POSITIVE FOR ALCOHOL AND ON 6/19/89 SUBMITTED URINE SAMPLE WHICH TESTED POSITIVE FOR BARBITURATES. ENTERED SUBSTANCE ABUSE PROGRAM IN ATLANTA IN 10/89. CONDITIONS OF PROBATION: MUST HAVE NEVADA BOARD SUBMIT EVALUATIONS OF HIS PROGRESS EVERY SIX MONTHS AND IMMEDIATELY INFORM THE ARIZONA BOARD IN THE EVENT HE VIOLATES THE NEVADA STIPULATION; MUST NOT PRACTICE IN ARIZONA WITHOUT BOARD APPROVAL; MUST OBTAIN CARE FROM BOARD-APPROVED PRIMARY CARE PHYSICIAN WHO IS A CERTIFIED ADDICTIONOLOGIST AND WHO MUST SUBMIT QUARTERLY REPORTS TO THE BOARD; MUST ABSTAIN FROM USE OF ALCOHOL AND ANY OTHER DRUGS; MUST COMPLY WITH REQUESTS FOR RANDOM BIOLOGICAL FLUID TESTS; MUST SUBMIT TO ANY EXAMS AND THERAPY ORDERED BY BOARD; MUST PARTICIPATE IN 12-STEP RECOVERY PROGRAM FOR SUBSTANCE ABUSE AS DETERMINED BY THERAPIST AND ATTEND AT LEAST THREE WEEKLY MEETINGS; MUST IMMEDIATELY PARTICIPATE IN ARIZONA MEDICAL ASSOCIATION PHYSICIAN'S HEALTH COMMITTEE PROGRAM WITH QUARTERLY REPORTS TO BOARD; MUST APPEAR BEFORE BOARD FOR INTERVIEWS UPON REQUEST; MUST MAINTAIN A LOG OF ALL MEDICATIONS TAKEN; MUST ADVISE BOARD OF CHANGE IN OFFICE OR HOME ADDRESSES OR IF PLANS TO BE AWAY FOR MORE THAN FIVE DAYS. ON 4/17/93 ORDER TERMINATED.

FLYNN, STEPHEN EUGENE MD, LICENSE NUMBER 00C6937, OF PHOENIX, AZ, WAS DISCIPLINED BY TEXAS ON MARCH 6, 1992.
DISCIPLINARY ACTION: 60-MONTH PROBATION
OFFENSE: DISCIPLINARY ACTION BY ANOTHER STATE OR AGENCY
NOTES: DISCIPLINARY ACTION TAKEN BY ANOTHER STATE BOARD AND INTEMPERATE USE OF ALCOHOL OR DRUGS. LICENSE SUSPENDED, SUSPENSION STAYED; PROBATION UNDER TERMS AND CONDITIONS.

FLYNN, STEPHEN EUGENE MD, LICENSE NUMBER 00C6937, OF PHOENIX, AZ, WAS DISCIPLINED BY TEXAS ON OCTOBER 9, 1992.
DISCIPLINARY ACTION: SURRENDER OF LICENSE
NOTES: PERMANENTLY SURRENDERED.

FOLLETT, WILLIAM WALLACE III MD, LICENSE NUMBER 00D4118, OF EL PASO, TX, WAS DISCIPLINED BY TEXAS ON MARCH 5, 1994.
DISCIPLINARY ACTION: 84-MONTH PROBATION; REQUIRED TO TAKE ADDITIONAL MEDICAL EDUCATION
OFFENSE: PROFESSIONAL MISCONDUCT
NOTES: FROM 5/27/92 THROUGH 6/2/92 MAINTAINED AN INAPPROPRIATE SOCIAL RELATIONSHIP WITH A FEMALE PATIENT; FAILED TO RECOGNIZE THE OCCURRENCE OF TRANSFERENCE AND COUNTERTRANSFERENCE WHILE TREATING THE PATIENT AND THAT SHE WAS IN A VULNERABLE POSITION RELATING TO THE DEATH OF HER HUSBAND; PATIENT BELIEVES SHE WAS EXPLOITED BY DR. FOLLETT; HE DOES NOT HAVE A PAST DISCIPLINARY HISTORY. SUSPENSION STAYED. CONDITIONS OF PROBATION: SHALL ATTEND AT LEAST 50 HOURS OF CONTINUING MEDICAL EDUCATION AND AN ADDITIONAL SIX HOURS OF ETHICS COURSES PER YEAR; SHALL SUBMIT HIMSELF TO A BOARD-APPROVED PSYCHIATRIST FOR EVALUATION AND FOLLOW RECOMMENDATIONS FOR CARE AND TREATMENT IF ANY; SHALL GIVE THIS PSYCHIATRIST A COPY OF THE BOARD ORDER; SHALL APPEAR BEFORE THE BOARD ONCE A YEAR; SHALL NOT MAINTAIN A PERSONAL OR SOCIAL RELATIONSHIP WITH PATIENTS; WITHIN ONE YEAR SHALL SUBMIT A PUBLISHABLE PAPER REGARDING DOCTOR-PATIENT BOUNDARIES; SHALL COOPERATE WITH THE BOARD IN VERIFYING COMPLIANCE; SHALL INFORM BOARD OF CHANGE OF ADDRESS WITHIN 10 DAYS OR IF HE LEAVES THE STATE; TIME SPENT OUT OF TEXAS DOES NOT COUNT TOWARD PROBATION. SHALL NOT SEEK MODIFICATION FOR ONE YEAR.

FONTANIER, CHARLES EUGENE DO, LICENSE NUMBER 00F3960, OF HOUSTON, TX, WAS DISCIPLINED BY TEXAS ON APRIL 15, 1994.
DISCIPLINARY ACTION: 60-MONTH RESTRICTION PLACED ON LICENSE; REQUIRED TO TAKE ADDITIONAL MEDICAL EDUCATION
OFFENSE: OVERPRESCRIBING OR MISPRESCRIBING DRUGS
NOTES: AS RECENTLY AS 1991 HE HAS REGULARLY DISPENSED QUANTITIES OF FASTIN WHICH EXCEEDED AMOUNTS NECESSARY TO MEET PATIENTS' IMMEDIATE NEEDS; REGULARLY PRESCRIBED TO PATIENTS FOR WEIGHT CONTROL QUANTITIES OF FASTIN AND OTHER ANOREXICS FOR PERIODS OF TIME WHICH EXCEED THOSE RECOMMENDED BY THE MANUFACTURER. SHALL ATTEND AT LEAST 50 HOURS PER YEAR OF CONTINUING MEDICAL EDUCATION; SHALL MAINTAIN ADEQUATE MEDICAL RECORDS ON ALL PATIENT OFFICE VISITS AND SEPARATE FROM PATIENT RECORDS SHALL MAINTAIN A FILE OF EVERY PRESCRIPTION WRITTEN FOR CONTROLLED SUBSTANCES OR DANGEROUS DRUGS BOTH OF WHICH SHALL BE AVAILABLE FOR INSPECTION; SHALL REFRAIN FROM PRESCRIBING ANY DRUG UNLESS MEDICALLY INDICATED; SHALL NOT TREAT ANY PATIENT FOR WEIGHT CONTROL OR OBESITY WITH ANY DRUGS; MAY TREAT SUCH PATIENTS ONLY WITH COUNSELING, DIET AND EXERCISE; WITHIN TWO YEARS SHALL COMPLETE ADDITIONAL TRAINING IN PHARMACOLOGY AND FAMILY PRACTICE; SHALL APPEAR BEFORE THE BOARD ONCE A YEAR; SHALL GIVE A COPY OF THIS ORDER TO ANY HEALTH CARE ENTITY WHERE HE HAS PRIVILEGES; SHALL COOPERATE WITH THE BOARD IN VERIFYING COMPLIANCE; SHALL INFORM BOARD OF CHANGE OF ADDRESS WITHIN 10 DAYS OR IF HE LEAVES THE STATE; TIME SPENT OUT OF TEXAS DOES NOT COUNT TOWARD RESTRICTION. SHALL NOT SEEK MODIFICATION FOR ONE YEAR. ON 10/13/95 ORDER TERMINATED BASED ON COMPLIANCE WITH TERMS.

FORTNER, BENNIE R MD, LICENSE NUMBER 00D3224, OF AMARILLO, TX, WAS DISCIPLINED BY TEXAS ON DECEMBER 1, 1988.
NOTES: SETTLEMENT AGREEMENT AND UNSPECIFIED DISCIPLINARY ACTION

FOWLER, DONALD H MD OF 1301 N MAIN ST, MARION, SC, WAS DISCIPLINED BY DEA ON NOVEMBER 6, 1990.
DISCIPLINARY ACTION: SURRENDER OF CONTROLLED SUBSTANCE LICENSE
OFFENSE: OVERPRESCRIBING OR MISPRESCRIBING DRUGS
NOTES: OVERPRESCRIBING PERCODAN, DARVON, VALIUM AND TALWIN NX AND NOT KEEPING ADEQUATE RECORDS OF DRUGS. ON 06/12/90 LICENSE INDEFINITELY SUSPENDED WITH REINSTATEMENT STIPULATIONS TO PROBATIONARY STATUS AFTER SIX MONTHS, $10,000 FINE AND SURRENDER OF SOUTH CAROLINA REGISTRATION.

FOWLER, DONALD H MD, LICENSE NUMBER 00C6321, OF MARION, SC, WAS DISCIPLINED BY TEXAS ON APRIL 20, 1991.
DISCIPLINARY ACTION: PROBATION
OFFENSE: DISCIPLINARY ACTION BY ANOTHER STATE OR AGENCY
NOTES: ACTION TAKEN BY ANOTHER STATE BOARD FOR PRESCRIBING CONTROLLED SUBSTANCES AND DANGEROUS DRUGS IN QUANTITIES THAT WERE WITHOUT VALID DOCUMENTED MEDICAL JUSTIFICATION AND FOR OTHER THAN DOCUMENTED LEGITIMATE PURPOSES. MUST RECEIVE APPROVAL FROM THE TEXAS BOARD PRIOR TO PRACTICING MEDICINE IN TEXAS.

FREDMAN, RAPHA P MD, LICENSE NUMBER 00G1397, OF ATLANTA, GA, WAS DISCIPLINED BY TEXAS ON DECEMBER 3, 1990.
DISCIPLINARY ACTION: 60-MONTH PROBATION; REQUIRED TO ENTER AN IMPAIRED PHYSICIAN PROGRAM OR DRUG OR ALCOHOL TREATMENT
NOTES: CONTINUED PARTICIPATION IN ACTIVITIES AND PROGRAMS OF ALCOHOLICS ANONYMOUS OR COCAINE ANONYMOUS ON A REGULAR BASIS; SUBMISSION FOR APPROPRIATE CHEMICAL EXAMINATIONS AT THE REQUEST OF A REPRESENTATIVE OF THE BOARD; CONTINUATION OF COMPLIANCE WITH TERMS AND CONDITIONS OF AFTER CARE CONTRACT, AND CONTINUATION OF WORK WITH RECOVERING ABUSE SPONSOR.

FREDMAN, RAPHA P MD, LICENSE NUMBER 00G1397, WAS DISCIPLINED BY TEXAS ON JANUARY 14, 1994.

DISCIPLINARY ACTION: 36-MONTH PROBATION; MONITORING OF PHYSICIAN
OFFENSE: FAILURE TO COMPLY WITH A PREVIOUS BOARD ORDER
NOTES: DURING 1993 CONCERNS WERE RAISED ABOUT COMPLIANCE WITH 12/3/90 ORDER BECAUSE OF DIFFICULTIES OF MAINTAINING ADEQUATE COMMUNICATION BETWEEN DR. FREDMAN AND COMPLIANCE OFFICER; ALLEGATIONS OF UNTIMELY SUBMISSION OF AA REPORTS, FAILURE TO OBTAIN AN AA SPONSOR, AND A POSITIVE URINALYSIS FOR MARIJUANA METABOLITES; HE EXPLAINED COMMUNICATION PROBLEMS AS A PRODUCT OF HIS SURGICAL SCHEDULE; DENIES USING MARIJUANA AND SUBSEQUENT SCREENS DO NOT SHOW ANY EVIDENCE OF MARIJUANA USE. 1990 PROBATION EXTENDED WITH ADDITIONAL CONDITIONS: SHALL CONTACT THE BOARD COMPLIANCE OFFICER WITHIN EIGHT HOURS AFTER WHICH A MESSAGE IS LEFT; SHALL SUBMIT HIMSELF FOR APPROPRIATE EXAMS INCLUDING DRUG AND ALCOHOL SCREENS WITHIN 24 HOURS AFTER A REQUEST; ALL OTHER TERMS OF THE 1990 ORDER ARE STILL IN EFFECT; SHALL GIVE A COPY OF THIS ORDER TO ANY HEALTH CARE ENTITY WHERE HE HAS PRIVILEGES. SHALL NOT SEEK MODIFICATION FOR ONE YEAR.

FULLER, CHARLES III MD OF DALLAS, TX, WAS DISCIPLINED BY TEXAS ON JULY 1, 1986.
DISCIPLINARY ACTION: SURRENDER OF LICENSE

GAGLIANO, ANGELO VINCENT MD, LICENSE NUMBER 00H6820, OF SAN ANTONIO, TX, WAS DISCIPLINED BY TEXAS ON JANUARY 6, 1995.
DISCIPLINARY ACTION: REPRIMAND
OFFENSE: SUBSTANDARD CARE, INCOMPETENCE, OR NEGLIGENCE
NOTES: IN 8/92 HE ADMINISTERED ANESTHESIA ON A NON-EMERGENT CRITICALLY ILL SURGICAL PATIENT WITHOUT FIRST ESTABLISHING APPROPRIATE MONITORING; AGREED TO THIS ORDER IN LIEU OF FURTHER INVESTIGATION.

GALINDO, CONRADO G III MD, DATE OF BIRTH JANUARY 9, 1947, LICENSE NUMBER 00F0189, OF 1300 BEDELL, DEL RIO, TX, WAS DISCIPLINED BY TEXAS ON DECEMBER 3, 1990.
DISCIPLINARY ACTION: 60-MONTH PROBATION; RESTRICTION PLACED ON CONTROLLED SUBSTANCE LICENSE
NOTES: PARTICIPATION IN PRECEPTORSHIP PROGRAM TO INCLUDE SPECIFIC CURRICULUM; ATTENDANCE AT CONTINUING MEDICAL EDUCATION COURSES; NOT PRESCRIBING ANY SCHEDULE II CONTROLLED DRUG EXCEPT FOR HOSPITALIZED PATIENTS; CONTINUATION OF TREATMENT FROM A PSYCHIATRIST; APPEARANCE BEFORE BOARD TWICE ANNUALLY; SUBMIT HIMSELF FOR APPROPRIATE EXAMINATIONS AND SCREENINGS TO DETERMINE FREEDOM FROM DRUGS OR ALCOHOL; PARTICIPATION IN ACTIVITIES AND PROGRAMS OF ALCOHOLICS ANONYMOUS ON A REGULAR BASIS. ON 8/20/93 BOARD DENIED HIS REQUEST FOR TERMINATION AND MODIFIED THIS ORDER SO THAT HE IS REQUIRED TO MAKE ANNUAL RATHER THAN SEMI-ANNUAL APPEARANCES BEFORE THE BOARD. ALL OTHER PROVISIONS OF THIS ORDER REMAIN IN EFFECT. ON 8/19/94 HIS REQUEST FOR TERMINATION OF THIS ORDER DENIED.

GALLMAN, DOYLE F JR DO, LICENSE NUMBER 00H2391, OF MANSFIELD, TX, WAS DISCIPLINED BY TEXAS ON AUGUST 19, 1994.
DISCIPLINARY ACTION: 60-MONTH PROBATION; RESTRICTION PLACED ON CONTROLLED SUBSTANCE LICENSE
OFFENSE: DRUG OR ALCOHOL ABUSE
NOTES: AFTER UNDERGOING KNEE SURGERY IN 1989 HE BECAME ADDICTED TO THE VICODIN HE WAS TAKING FOR PAIN RELIEF; OCCASIONALLY USED IM INJECTABLE MEDICINE SUCH AS NUBAIN, TALWIN AND DEMEROL; INITIATED HIS OWN TREATMENT AND WAS HOSPITALIZED FROM 8/16/93 THROUGH 9/16/93; IS PRESENTLY IN OUTPATIENT THERAPY. SUSPENSION STAYED. CONDITIONS OF PROBATION: SHALL APPEAR BEFORE BOARD TWICE A YEAR; SHALL NOT TREAT OR OTHERWISE SERVE AS PHYSICIAN, PRESCRIBE, DISPENSE OR ADMINISTER DRUGS THAT MAY BE SUBJECT TO ABUSE TO HIMSELF OR ANY MEMBER OF HIS FAMILY; SHALL NOT POSSESS, ADMINISTER, DISPENSE OR PRESCRIBE ANY CONTROLLED SUBSTANCES BUT MAY ORDER THEM TO BE ADMINISTERED TO HOSPITAL OR NURSING HOME PATIENTS AND MAY WRITE PRESCRIPTIONS FOR CONTROLLED SUBSTANCES FOR PATIENTS SEEN IN OTHER PHYSICIAN'S OFFICES IN THE COURSE OF HIS LOCUM TENENS WORK; SHALL SUBMIT HIMSELF FOR APPROPRIATE EXAMS INCLUDING DRUG OR ALCOHOL SCREENS; SHALL CONTINUE TO PARTICIPATE IN AA'S PROGRAM NOT LESS THAN THREE TIMES A WEEK WITH MONTHLY REPORTS; SHALL ABSTAIN FROM THE CONSUMPTION OF ALCOHOL/CHEMICAL SUBSTANCES IN ANY FORM UNLESS PRESCRIBED BY ANOTHER PHYSICIAN FOR A LEGITIMATE AND THERAPEUTIC PURPOSE; SHALL CONTINUE TO PARTICIPATE IN ACTIVITIES OF THE TEXAS OSTEOPATHIC MEDICAL ASSOCIATION AND ATTEND WEEKLY MEETINGS WITH QUARTERLY REPORTS; SHALL CONTINUE TO RECEIVE TREATMENT FROM SPECIFIED PHYSICIAN WITH QUARTERLY REPORTS; WITHIN ONE YEAR SHALL TAKE A BOARD-APPROVED COURSE IN ADDICTIONOLOGY; SEPARATE FROM PATIENT RECORDS SHALL MAINTAIN A FILE OF EVERY PRESCRIPTION WRITTEN FOR DANGEROUS DRUGS WHICH SHALL BE AVAILABLE FOR INSPECTION; SHALL GIVE A COPY OF THIS ORDER TO ANY HEALTH CARE ENTITY WHERE HE HAS PRIVILEGES; SHALL COOPERATE WITH THE BOARD IN VERIFYING COMPLIANCE; SHALL INFORM BOARD OF CHANGE OF ADDRESS WITHIN 10 DAYS OR IF HE LEAVES THE STATE; TIME SPENT OUT OF TEXAS DOES NOT COUNT TOWARD PROBATION. SHALL NOT SEEK MODIFICATION FOR ONE YEAR.

GALLOWAY, ROBERT E MD, LICENSE NUMBER 00E9198, OF HOUSTON, TX, WAS DISCIPLINED BY TEXAS ON MARCH 5, 1994.
DISCIPLINARY ACTION: 60-MONTH PROBATION; REQUIRED TO TAKE ADDITIONAL MEDICAL EDUCATION
OFFENSE: PROVIDING FALSE INFORMATION TO THE BOARD
NOTES: SINCE 1978 HE HAS SUBMITTED OR ALLOWED OFFICE STAFF TO SUBMIT INFORMATION TO 10 HOSPITALS THAT HE IS AMERICAN BOARD OF INTERNAL MEDICINE CERTIFIED WHEN HE IS NOT; VOLUNTARILY AGREED TO A PSYCHIATRIC EXAM; HAS NOT BEEN THE SUBJECT OF HOSPITAL OR PATIENT COMPLAINTS. ONE YEAR SUSPENSION STAYED. CONDITIONS OF PROBATION: SHALL APPEAR BEFORE THE BOARD TWICE A YEAR; SHALL ATTEND AT LEAST 50 HOURS PER YEAR OF CONTINUING EDUCATION; SHALL ALSO ATTEND SIX HOURS OF AN ETHICS COURSE OR PROGRAM PER

YEAR FOR FIVE YEARS; WITHIN ONE YEAR SHALL PASS THE BOARD'S JURISPRUDENCE EXAM; SHALL PERFORM EIGHT HOURS PER MONTH OF COMMUNITY SERVICE FOR THREE YEARS; SHALL CONTINUE TO RECEIVE PSYCHIATRIC TREATMENT WITH QUARTERLY REPORTS; SHALL COOPERATE WITH THE BOARD IN VERIFYING COMPLIANCE; SHALL INFORM BOARD OF CHANGE OF ADDRESS WITHIN 10 DAYS OR IF HE LEAVES THE STATE; TIME SPENT OUT OF TEXAS DOES NOT COUNT TOWARD PROBATION. SHALL NOT SEEK MODIFICATION FOR ONE YEAR.

GALLOWAY, ROBERT E MD, LICENSE NUMBER 00E9198, OF HOUSTON, TX, WAS DISCIPLINED BY TEXAS ON JUNE 22, 1994.
DISCIPLINARY ACTION: 60-MONTH PROBATION; REQUIRED TO TAKE ADDITIONAL MEDICAL EDUCATION
OFFENSE: PROFESSIONAL MISCONDUCT
NOTES: FAILED TO ADEQUATELY SUPERVISE THE ACTIVITIES OF HIS ASSISTANT WHO WAS NOT REGISTERED AS A PHYSICIAN'S ASSISTANT; IN 4/90 FAILED TO FOLLOW UP ON LAB WORK OF ONE PATIENT WHO WAS LATER FOUND TO HAVE CANCER OF THE DUODENUM. ON 3/5/94 HE ENTERED INTO AN AGREED ORDER WHICH IS INCORPORATED WITH THIS ORDER. ONE YEAR SUSPENSION STAYED. CONDITIONS OF PROBATION: SHALL OBTAIN AT LEAST EIGHT HOURS OF CONTINUING MEDICAL EDUCATION IN RISK MANAGEMENT WITHIN ONE YEAR FROM THE DATE OF THIS ORDER; SHALL SUBMIT WRITTEN PROTOCOL OF SUPERVISION OF HIS PHYSICIAN ASSISTANT WITHIN 30 DAYS; SHALL NOT PRESIGN PRESCRIPTIONS FOR CONTROLLED SUBSTANCES OR DANGEROUS DRUGS; SHALL DOCUMENT ON EACH RECORD THAT HE HAS PERSONALLY SEEN OR REVIEWED EACH PATIENT CHART; SHALL KEEP A SEPARATE LIST OF PATIENTS SEEN BY THE PHYSICIAN'S ASSISTANT WHICH SHALL BE AVAILABLE FOR REVIEW; SHALL MAINTAIN A COMPLETE CREDENTIALS/PERSONNEL FILE ON EACH EMPLOYEE AND ENSURE THAT ALL NECESSARY DOCUMENTATION HAS BEEN OBTAINED; SHALL MAINTAIN RESPONSIBILITY FOR THE ACTS OR OMISSIONS OF HIS EMPLOYEES; SHALL GIVE A COPY OF THIS ORDER TO ANY HEALTH CARE ENTITY WHERE HE HAS PRIVILEGES; SHALL COOPERATE WITH THE BOARD IN VERIFYING COMPLIANCE; SHALL INFORM BOARD OF CHANGE OF ADDRESS WITHIN 10 DAYS OR IF HE LEAVES THE STATE. TIME SPENT OUT OF TEXAS DOES NOT COUNT TOWARD PROBATION. SHALL NOT SEEK MODIFICATION FOR ONE YEAR.

GANACIAS, ADELA RAMIREZ MD, OF 1619 KINGSPOINT DRIVE, CARROLLTON, TX, WAS DISCIPLINED BY OKLAHOMA ON JULY 1, 1993.
DISCIPLINARY ACTION: DENIAL OF NEW LICENSE
NOTES: HAS FAILED THE FLEX EXAM 10 TIMES, WHICH RAISES SERIOUS ISSUES AS TO CLINICAL COMPETENCY AND FITNESS TO PRACTICE. DENIAL REAFFIRMED ON 12/2/93.

GARAS, GAMAL K MD OF 16 MCCALL ROAD, WINCHESTER, MA, WAS DISCIPLINED BY MEDICARE ON DECEMBER 2, 1985.
DISCIPLINARY ACTION: 240-MONTH EXCLUSION FROM THE MEDICARE AND/OR MEDICAID PROGRAMS
OFFENSE: CRIMINAL CONVICTION OR PLEA OF GUILTY, NOLO CONTENDERE, OR NO CONTEST TO A CRIME
NOTES: PROGRAM-RELATED CONVICTION. REINSTATED ON 12/3/93.

GARAS, GAMAL K MD, LICENSE NUMBER 0024812, OF SYLVANIA, NEW SOUTH WALES, AUSTRALIA, WAS DISCIPLINED BY GEORGIA ON JULY 27, 1986.
DISCIPLINARY ACTION: LICENSE REVOCATION
OFFENSE: DISCIPLINARY ACTION BY ANOTHER STATE OR AGENCY
NOTES: BOARD ACTION IN MISSOURI; CONVICTION FOR MEDICAID FRAUD.

GARAS, GAMAL K MD OF SYLVANIA, AUSTRALIA, WAS DISCIPLINED BY TEXAS ON DECEMBER 1, 1986.
DISCIPLINARY ACTION: LICENSE REVOCATION
OFFENSE: CRIMINAL CONVICTION OR PLEA OF GUILTY, NOLO CONTENDERE, OR NO CONTEST TO A CRIME
NOTES: CONVICTION OF FELONY

GARAS, GAMAL K MD, LICENSE NUMBER 034679L, OF UNIVERSITY CITY, MO, WAS DISCIPLINED BY PENNSYLVANIA ON MAY 7, 1987.
DISCIPLINARY ACTION: 12-MONTH LICENSE SUSPENSION
OFFENSE: DISCIPLINARY ACTION BY ANOTHER STATE OR AGENCY
NOTES: SUSPENSION OF LICENSE TO PRACTICE MEDICINE IN INDIANA BASED UPON FELONY CONVICTION FOR MEDICARE FRAUD.

GARAS, GAMAL K MD, LICENSE NUMBER 0050310, WAS DISCIPLINED BY MASSACHUSETTS ON JULY 15, 1987.
DISCIPLINARY ACTION: LICENSE REVOCATION
OFFENSE: CRIMINAL CONVICTION OR PLEA OF GUILTY, NOLO CONTENDERE, OR NO CONTEST TO A CRIME
NOTES: OTHER OFFENSE LISTED WAS MEDICAID FRAUD. LICENSE WAS REINSTATED ON 5/3/89.

GARAS, GAMAL K MD, LICENSE NUMBER 1032284, OF 2548 MEDINAH, EVERGREEN, CO, WAS DISCIPLINED BY INDIANA ON MARCH 23, 1989.
DISCIPLINARY ACTION: EMERGENCY SUSPENSION
NOTES: EMERGENCY SUSPENSION CONTINUED 5/3/89

GARAS, GAMAL K MD, LICENSE NUMBER 1032284, OF 2548 MEDINAH, EVERGREEN, CO, WAS DISCIPLINED BY INDIANA ON JULY 28, 1989.
DISCIPLINARY ACTION: SURRENDER OF LICENSE

GARCIA, CLOTILDE P MD, LICENSE NUMBER 00C4322, OF HOSPITAL BLVD SUITE 118, CORPUS CHRISTI, TX, WAS DISCIPLINED BY DEA ON JANUARY 24, 1994.
DISCIPLINARY ACTION: SURRENDER OF CONTROLLED SUBSTANCE LICENSE

GARCIA, EDUARDO I MD, LICENSE NUMBER 00F3978, OF HOUSTON, TX, WAS DISCIPLINED BY TEXAS ON JANUARY 24, 1992.
DISCIPLINARY ACTION: 24-MONTH PROBATION
OFFENSE: SUBSTANDARD CARE, INCOMPETENCE, OR NEGLIGENCE
NOTES: PROFESSIONAL FAILURE TO PRACTICE MEDICINE IN AN ACCEPTABLE MANNER CONSISTENT WITH PUBLIC HEALTH AND WELFARE. LICENSE SUSPENDED, SUSPENSION STAYED; PROBATION UNDER TERMS AND CONDITIONS.

GARCIA, JOHN A MD OF AUSTIN, TX, WAS DISCIPLINED BY TEXAS ON DECEMBER 1, 1986.
DISCIPLINARY ACTION: LICENSE REVOCATION
OFFENSE: CRIMINAL CONVICTION OR PLEA OF GUILTY, NOLO CONTENDERE, OR NO CONTEST TO A CRIME
NOTES: CONVICTION OF FELONY

GARCIA, JOSE GERARDO MD, DATE OF BIRTH NOVEMBER 21, 1935, LICENSE NUMBER 00D1310, OF LAREDO, TX, WAS DISCIPLINED BY TEXAS ON AUGUST 24, 1991.
DISCIPLINARY ACTION: 36-MONTH PROBATION; REQUIRED TO TAKE ADDITIONAL MEDICAL EDUCATION
OFFENSE: PROFESSIONAL MISCONDUCT
NOTES: UNPROFESSIONAL AND/OR DISHONORABLE CONDUCT LIKELY TO DECEIVE, DEFRAUD, OR INJURE THE PUBLIC. LICENSE SUSPENDED, STAYED; CONDITIONS OF PROBATION INCLUDE: COMPLETION OF TEN HOURS OF AN ETHICS COURSE PER YEAR FOR THREE YEARS; SUBMITTING TO PSYCHIATRIC EVALUATION AND TREATMENT BY A PSYCHIATRIST APPROVED BY THE BOARD ONCE A YEAR; SHALL APPEAR BEFORE THE BOARD ONCE ANNUALLY DURING EACH YEAR OF PROBATION. ORDER TERMINATED ON 6/21/93; LICENSE FREE AND CLEAR OF RESTRICTIONS.

GARCIAARECHA, LUIS A MD, LICENSE NUMBER 00D9140, OF SAN ANTONIO, TX, WAS DISCIPLINED BY TEXAS ON JANUARY 12, 1991.
DISCIPLINARY ACTION: REPRIMAND

GARDINER, HENRY GEORGE MD, LICENSE NUMBER 00C4120, OF FORT WORTH, TX, WAS DISCIPLINED BY TEXAS ON AUGUST 24, 1991.
DISCIPLINARY ACTION: 60-MONTH PROBATION; RESTRICTION PLACED ON CONTROLLED SUBSTANCE LICENSE
OFFENSE: PROFESSIONAL MISCONDUCT
NOTES: UNPROFESSIONAL OR DISHONORABLE CONDUCT LIKELY TO DECIEVE, DEFRAUD, OR INJURE THE PUBLIC; PROFESSIONAL FAILURE TO PRACTICE MEDICINE IN AN ACCEPTABLE MANNER CONSISTENT WITH PUBLIC HEALTH AND WELFARE. REVOCATION STAYED. CONDITIONS OF PROBATION: SHALL SURRENDER SCHEDULE II AND II-N DEA AND DPS CONTROLLED SUBSTANCES REGISTRATIONS; SHALL NOT ATTEMPT TO REREGISTER WITHOUT PRIOR BOARD APPROVAL; SHALL SURRENDER ALL UNUSED TRIPLICATE PRESCRIPTION FORMS AND NOT ATTEMPT TO ORDER MORE WITHOUT PRIOR APPROVAL OF THE BOARD; SHALL NOT PRESCRIBE, ADMINISTER, OR POSSESS ANY SCHEDULE III, IV, OR V CONTROLLED SUBSTANCES EXCEPT FOR HOSPITALIZED PATIENTS; SHALL ATTEND AT LEAST 50 HOURS PER YEAR FOR THREE YEARS OF CATEGORY I CONTINUING MEDICAL EDUCATION, TO INCLUDE AT LEAST FIVE HOURS IN RISK MANAGEMENT.

GARDNER, ROBERT L MD, LICENSE NUMBER 00D7045, OF LANCASTER, TX, WAS DISCIPLINED BY TEXAS ON OCTOBER 26, 1990.
DISCIPLINARY ACTION: REPRIMAND; REQUIRED TO TAKE ADDITIONAL MEDICAL EDUCATION
NOTES: MUST OBTAIN MONITOR FOR CASES; UNDERGO PHYSICAL EXAMINATION AND FOLLOW ANY RECOMMENDED TREATMENT; SUBMIT FOR PSYCHIATRIC EVALUATION AND FOLLOW ANY RECOMMENDED TREATMENT; OBTAIN CONTINUING MEDICAL EDUCATION; VISIT BOARD ANNUALLY FOR NEXT FIVE YEARS

GARNER, JAMES FRANCIS MD, DATE OF BIRTH NOVEMBER 3, 1950, LICENSE NUMBER 00E6363, OF 1606 MORSE STREET, HOUSTON, TX, WAS DISCIPLINED BY TEXAS ON JANUARY 29, 1993.
DISCIPLINARY ACTION: 120-MONTH PROBATION; RESTRICTION PLACED ON LICENSE
OFFENSE: DRUG OR ALCOHOL ABUSE
NOTES: ON 2/3/91 HE FAILED TO DIAGNOSE A FOUR-YEAR-OLD'S PNEUMONIA AND PRESCRIBED CHLORDIAZEPOXIDE FOR WHICH THERE WAS NO VALID MEDICAL REASON; HAD PREVIOUSLY INGESTED CODEINE ON MULTIPLE OCCASIONS WITHOUT A LEGITIMATE MEDICAL PURPOSE; IN JULY 1991 ADMITTED HIMSELF FOR INPATIENT TREATMENT AND THEN ENTERED INTO A MONITORING CONTRACT WITH A PHYSICIAN'S COUNSELING COMMITTEE; NOW PRACTICES ONLY AT INDIGENT CLINICS. SUSPENSION STAYED. CONDITIONS OF PROBATION: SHALL NOT WORK IN AN EMERGENCY ROOM SETTING, URGENT CARE FACILITY OR SIMILAR CLINIC AND SHALL RESTRICT PRACTICE TO THE TWO INDIGENT CLINICS WHERE HE CURRENTLY PRACTICES; SHALL OBTAIN WRITTEN APPROVAL OF THE BOARD BEFORE CHANGING HIS PRACTICE; ANY CHANGE WILL BE LIMITED TO A GROUP OR CLINIC PRACTICE; SHALL SUBMIT HIMSELF FOR EVALUATION AND TREATMENT TO A BOARD-APPROVED PSYCHIATRIST WHO WILL HAVE A COPY OF THIS ORDER; SHALL PARTICIPATE IN ACTIVITIES OF A PHYSICIAN HEALTH AND REHABILITATION COMMITTEE AND SHALL ATTEND WEEKLY MEETINGS WITH QUARTERLY REPORTS; SHALL ABSTAIN FROM THE CONSUMPTION OF ALCOHOL/DRUGS IN ANY FORM UNLESS PRESCRIBED BY ANOTHER PHYSICIAN FOR A LEGITIMATE AND THERAPEUTIC PURPOSE; SHALL SUBMIT HIMSELF FOR APPROPRIATE EXAMS INCLUDING DRUG OR ALCOHOL SCREENS; SHALL NOT ADMINISTER, PRESCRIBE, DISPENSE ANY CONTROLLED SUBSTANCES EXCEPT AS IS MEDICALLY NECESSARY TO TREAT HIV/AIDS PATIENTS AT THE CLINICS WHERE HE WORKS AND LIMITED TO ENUMERATED SUBSTANCES; SHALL MAINTAIN A SEPARATE WRITTEN LOG OF THESE PRESCRIPTIONS WHICH SHALL BE AVAILABLE FOR INSPECTION; SHALL ATTEND AT LEAST 50 HOURS PER YEAR OF CONTINUING MEDICAL EDUCATION; SHALL APPEAR BEFORE THE BOARD TWICE A YEAR; SHALL GIVE A COPY OF THIS ORDER TO ANY HEALTH CARE ENTITY WHERE HE HAS PRIVILEGES; SHALL COOPERATE WITH THE BOARD IN VERIFYING COMPLIANCE; SHALL INFORM BOARD OF CHANGE OF ADDRESS WITHIN 10 DAYS AND IF HE LEAVES THE STATE; TIME SPENT OUT OF TEXAS DOES NOT COUNT TOWARD PROBATION; SHALL NOT SEEK MODIFICATION FOR ONE YEAR.

GEAGAN, EDWARD RICHARD DO, DATE OF BIRTH DECEMBER 23, 1917, OF 10910 PRESTON TRAILS DR, AUSTIN, TX, WAS DISCIPLINED BY MEDICARE ON OCTOBER 23, 1990.
DISCIPLINARY ACTION: 60-MONTH EXCLUSION FROM THE MEDICARE AND/OR MEDICAID PROGRAMS
OFFENSE: SUBSTANDARD CARE, INCOMPETENCE, OR NEGLIGENCE
NOTES: HE VIOLATED HIS OBLIGATION TO PROVIDE SERVICES THAT MEET PROFESSIONAL STANDARDS IN THREE CASES THROUGH PROVIDING GENERALIZED INADEQUATE CARE, DISCHARGING PATIENTS PRIOR TO ACHIEVING MEDICAL STABILITY, CONTINUING USE OF A MEDICATION INAPPROPRIATELY IN PRESENCE OF DEHYDRATION AND RENAL IMPAIRMENT, AND FAILING TO RECOGNIZE, DIAGNOSE AND TREAT HYPOKALEMIA, URINARY TRACT INFECTION, ANEMIA, CHEST PAIN, RENAL FAILURE, LIVER DYSFUNCTION AND PNEUMONIA. HE WAS ALSO DETERMINED TO HAVE A POOR UNDERSTANDING OF PHARMACOLOGY.

GEAGAN, EDWARD RICHARD DO, LICENSE NUMBER 00D5607, OF

AUSTIN, TX, WAS DISCIPLINED BY TEXAS ON APRIL 20, 1991.
NOTES: LICENSE PLACED ON IRREVOCABLE RETIREMENT STATUS IN LIEU OF FURTHER INVESTIGATION AND DISCIPLINARY ACTION.

GEMOETS, THOMAS H MD, LICENSE NUMBER 00C5678, OF HOUSTON, TX, WAS DISCIPLINED BY TEXAS ON OCTOBER 27, 1989.
DISCIPLINARY ACTION: 36-MONTH RESTRICTION PLACED ON LICENSE; REQUIRED TO TAKE ADDITIONAL MEDICAL EDUCATION
NOTES: STIPULATED ORDER. MUST REFRAIN FROM ACCEPTING EMPLOYMENT OR ENTERING INTO CERTAIN CONTRACTUAL RELATIONSHIPS, REDUCE ANY EMPLOYMENT OR INDEPENDENT CONTRACTOR ARRANGEMENT TO WRITING AND SUBMIT TO BOARD FOR APPROVAL, ATTEND RISK MANAGEMENT COURSE AND OBTAIN CONTINUING MEDICAL EDUCATION

GEORGE, PHILIP N MD, DATE OF BIRTH SEPTEMBER 5, 1955, LICENSE NUMBER 0026283, OF 13311 INNSHIRE, HOUSTON, TX, WAS DISCIPLINED BY IOWA ON AUGUST 20, 1993.
DISCIPLINARY ACTION: LICENSE REVOCATION
OFFENSE: SUBSTANDARD CARE, INCOMPETENCE, OR NEGLIGENCE
NOTES: CHARGES OF SUBSTANDARD MEDICAL CARE. ALSO CHARGES OF VIOLATING MISDEMEANOR STATUTE RELATED TO PRACTICE OF MEDICINE.

GETTINS, EDWIN T DO, LICENSE NUMBER 000S841, OF ORLANDO, FL, WAS DISCIPLINED BY FLORIDA ON APRIL 29, 1987.
DISCIPLINARY ACTION: PROBATION
OFFENSE: OVERPRESCRIBING OR MISPRESCRIBING DRUGS
NOTES: FAILED TO KEEP WRITTEN MEDICAL RECORDS, JUSTIFYING THE COURSE OF TREATMENT; MISPRESCRIBED SCHEDULE II DRUGS; ALSO MONITORING PHYSICIAN AND REPORTS TO THE BOARD

GETTINS, EDWIN T DO, LICENSE NUMBER 00B8462, OF ORLANDO, FL, WAS DISCIPLINED BY TEXAS ON DECEMBER 1, 1988.
NOTES: SETTLEMENT AGREEMENT AND UNSPECIFIED DISCIPLINARY ACTION

GIBSON, JOSEPH P MD OF 814 MEYER LANE, KERMIT, TX, WAS DISCIPLINED BY MEDICARE ON JULY 2, 1987.
DISCIPLINARY ACTION: 36-MONTH EXCLUSION FROM THE MEDICARE AND/OR MEDICAID PROGRAMS
OFFENSE: SUBSTANDARD CARE, INCOMPETENCE, OR NEGLIGENCE
NOTES: GROSSLY SUBSTANDARD CARE OF 2 PATIENTS

GIBSON, JOSEPH V JR MD, LICENSE NUMBER 00C3381, OF CORSICANA, TX, WAS DISCIPLINED BY TEXAS ON JANUARY 30, 1990.
DISCIPLINARY ACTION: SURRENDER OF LICENSE
NOTES: STIPULATED ORDER. LICENSE RETIRED

GIFFORD, LORING A MD, LICENSE NUMBER 0140544, OF ANTHONY, TX, WAS DISCIPLINED BY NEW YORK ON JANUARY 21, 1987.
DISCIPLINARY ACTION: LICENSE REVOCATION

GILBERT, LEON N JR MD, LICENSE NUMBER 00C1874, OF BETHANY, OK, WAS DISCIPLINED BY TEXAS ON JUNE 13, 1989.
NOTES: MUST APPEAR BEFORE TEXAS BOARD BEFORE COMMENCING TEXAS PRACTICE.

GILL, KATHERINE E MD, LICENSE NUMBER 00E8509, OF HOUSTON, TX, WAS DISCIPLINED BY TEXAS ON DECEMBER 1, 1988.
NOTES: SETTLEMENT AGREEMENT AND UNSPECIFIED DISCIPLINARY ACTION

GILMORE, ROBERT M MD, LICENSE NUMBER 00C5684, OF PORTLAND, TX, WAS DISCIPLINED BY TEXAS ON DECEMBER 1, 1988.
NOTES: SETTLEMENT AGREEMENT AND UNSPECIFIED DISCIPLINARY ACTION

GINTHER, CLARK E MD, LICENSE NUMBER 00C1099, OF BISHOP, TX, WAS DISCIPLINED BY TEXAS ON AUGUST 19, 1994.
OFFENSE: CRIMINAL CONVICTION OR PLEA OF GUILTY, NOLO CONTENDERE, OR NO CONTEST TO A CRIME
NOTES: ON 4/5/93 HE WAS CONVICTED OF AIDING AND ABETTING THE ATTEMPTED ILLEGAL POSSESSION OF PHENTERMINE AND DIAZEPAM TO TWO PATIENTS WHO WERE UNDERCOVER DEA AGENTS, A MISDEMEANOR OFFENSE; WAS PLACED ON PROBATION FOR ONE YEAR WITH A FINE OF $5,000 AND REQUIRED COMMUNITY SERVICE; SURRENDERED DEA REGISTRATION AS A RESULT OF CONVICTION. HE DENIES ANY MISCONDUCT IN PRESCRIBING TO THE TWO DEA AGENTS. SHALL RETIRE FROM PRACTICE EFFECTIVE 12/31/94 AND MEDICAL LICENSE SHALL BE CANCELLED; SHALL GIVE A COPY OF THIS ORDER TO ANY HEALTH CARE ENTITY WHERE HE HAS PRIVILEGES; SHALL COOPERATE WITH THE BOARD IN VERIFYING COMPLIANCE; SHALL INFORM BOARD OF CHANGE OF ADDRESS WITHIN 10 DAYS.

GIPSON, EDDIE MACK MD, LICENSE NUMBER 00C8982, OF DALLAS, TX, WAS DISCIPLINED BY TEXAS ON JANUARY 24, 1992.
DISCIPLINARY ACTION: 60-MONTH PROBATION
OFFENSE: OVERPRESCRIBING OR MISPRESCRIBING DRUGS
NOTES: SEVERAL VIOLATIONS OF THE MEDICAL PRACTICE ACT, INCLUDING NONTHERAPEUTIC PRESCRIBING AND INABILITY TO PRACTICE MEDICINE WITH REASONABLE SKILL AND SAFETY TO PATIENTS BY REASON OF ILLNESS, DRUNKENNESS, EXCESSIVE USE OF DRUGS, NARCOTICS, CHEMICALS, OR ANY OTHER TYPE OF MATERIAL OR AS A RESULT OF ANY MENTAL OR PHYSICAL CONDITION. LICENSE SUSPENDED, SUSPENSION STAYED; PROBATION UNDER TERMS AND CONDITIONS.

GIPSON, EDDIE MACK MD, LICENSE NUMBER 00C8982, OF WHITNEY, TX, WAS DISCIPLINED BY TEXAS ON AUGUST 28, 1992.
DISCIPLINARY ACTION: EMERGENCY SUSPENSION
OFFENSE: FAILURE TO COMPLY WITH A PREVIOUS BOARD ORDER
NOTES: FAILURE TO COMPLY WITH TERMS OF JANUARY 1992 ORDER.

GIPSON, EDDIE MACK MD, LICENSE NUMBER 00C8982, OF WHITNEY, TX, WAS DISCIPLINED BY TEXAS ON NOVEMBER 13, 1992.
DISCIPLINARY ACTION: LICENSE SUSPENSION
NOTES: SUSPENDED UNTIL SUCH TIME AS HE PERSONALLY APPEARS BEFORE THE BOARD AND PROVIDES EVIDENCE WHICH IN THE JUDGMENT OF THE BOARD IS SUFFICIENT TO SHOW THAT HE IS PHYSICALLY, MENTALLY, AND OTHERWISE COMPETENT TO SAFELY PRACTICE MEDICINE.

GIPSON, EDDIE MACK MD, LICENSE NUMBER 0030840, OF 2042 SOUTH BUCKNER BOULEVARD, DALLAS, TX, WAS DISCIPLINED BY MASSACHUSETTS ON MAY 11, 1994.
OFFENSE: DISCIPLINARY ACTION BY ANOTHER STATE OR AGENCY
NOTES: DISCIPLINE BY TEXAS; MENTAL IMPAIRMENT.

SUSPENSION OF INCHOATE RIGHT TO RENEW LICENSE.

GIRTANNER, ROBERT EDWARD MD, LICENSE NUMBER 00D7983, OF HOUSTON, TX, WAS DISCIPLINED BY TEXAS ON SEPTEMBER 30, 1994.
DISCIPLINARY ACTION: LICENSE SUSPENSION; 60-MONTH PROBATION
OFFENSE: OVERPRESCRIBING OR MISPRESCRIBING DRUGS
NOTES: FROM 4/88 THROUGH 4/92 ON MULTIPLE OCCASIONS ORDERED OR PRESCRIBED CONTROLLED SUBSTANCES TO THREE PATIENTS WITHOUT ADEQUATELY DOCUMENTING A SUFFICIENT MEDICAL BASIS FOR THIS ONE OF WHOM IS A FAMILY MEMBER WHO HAD A DRUG ADDICTION PROBLEM WHICH HE KNEW ABOUT; ON MULTIPLE OCCASIONS FROM 6/88 THROUGH 2/91 HE ORDERED OR PRESCRIBED CONTROLLED SUBSTANCES IN THE NAMES OF INDIVIDUALS WHO HE DID NOT INTEND TO RECEIVE THE MEDICATIONS AND WHICH HE SUBSEQUENTLY DIVERTED FOR THE USE OF THE FAMILY MEMBER REFERENCED ABOVE; DURING 1991 AND 1992 HE SELF-PRESCRIBED TYLENOL #4 WITHOUT MAINTAINING DOCUMENTATION OF THE BASIS FOR THE PRESCRIBING. SUSPENSION STAYED AFTER SEVEN DAYS. CONDITIONS OF PROBATION: SHALL NOT TREAT OR OTHERWISE SERVE AS PHYSICIAN, PRESCRIBE, DISPENSE OR ADMINISTER DRUGS THAT MAY BE SUBJECT TO ABUSE TO HIMSELF OR ANY MEMBER OF HIS IMMEDIATE FAMILY; SHALL ABSTAIN FROM THE CONSUMPTION OF CONTROLLED SUBSTANCES OR DANGEROUS DRUGS WITH POTENTIAL FOR ABUSE IN ANY FORM UNLESS PRESCRIBED BY ANOTHER PHYSICIAN FOR A LEGITIMATE AND THERAPEUTIC PURPOSE; SHALL ENSURE ANY PRESCRIPTION WRITTEN FOR SCHEDULE II OR III CONTROLLED SUBSTANCES SHALL BE COUNTERSIGNED BY ANOTHER LICENSED TEXAS PHYSICIAN WORKING WITHIN HIS PLACE OF EMPLOYMENT; PRESCRIBING, DISPENSING, ORDERING OR ADMINISTERING OF CONTROLLED SUBSTANCES AND DANGEROUS DRUGS LIMITED TO PATIENTS RECEIVING CARE WITHIN THE HEALTH CARE DELIVERY SYSTEM OF THE BAYLOR COLLEGE OF MEDICINE; SHALL SUBMIT HIMSELF FOR APPROPRIATE EXAMS INCLUDING DRUG OR ALCOHOL SCREENS; SHALL SUBMIT HIMSELF FOR EVALUATION AND TREATMENT TO A BOARD-APPROVED PSYCHIATRIST WITH REPORTS TO THE BOARD; SHALL BE SUPERVISED BY A BOARD-APPROVED PHYSICIAN WITH QUARTERLY REPORTS; SHALL ATTEND AT LEAST 50 HOURS PER YEAR OF CONTINUING MEDICAL EDUCATION; SHALL MAINTAIN ADEQUATE MEDICAL RECORDS ON ALL PATIENT OFFICE VISITS WHICH SHALL BE AVAILABLE FOR INSPECTION; SHALL APPEAR BEFORE THE BOARD ONCE A YEAR; SHALL GIVE A COPY OF THIS ORDER TO ANY HEALTH CARE ENTITY WHERE HE HAS PRIVILEGES; SHALL COOPERATE WITH THE BOARD IN VERIFYING COMPLIANCE; SHALL INFORM BOARD OF CHANGE OF ADDRESS WITHIN 10 DAYS OR IF HE LEAVES THE STATE; TIME SPENT OUT OF TEXAS DOES NOT COUNT TOWARD PROBATION. SHALL NOT SEEK MODIFICATION FOR ONE YEAR.

GLIDDEN, WELDON EDWARD DO, LICENSE NUMBER 00G3397, OF QUANAH, TX, WAS DISCIPLINED BY TEXAS ON NOVEMBER 3, 1994.
DISCIPLINARY ACTION: 60-MONTH PROBATION; RESTRICTION PLACED ON CONTROLLED SUBSTANCE LICENSE
OFFENSE: DRUG OR ALCOHOL ABUSE
NOTES: FROM 1/92 THROUGH 3/94 INGESTED LARGE NUMBERS OF TYLENOL #4 WITHOUT A LEGITIMATE MEDICAL PURPOSE; CALLED FICTITIOUS PRESCRIPTIONS TO SEVERAL PHARMACIES IN VARIOUS NAMES AND DIVERTED THESE FOR HIS OWN USE; HAD NO PATIENT RECORDS CORRESPONDING TO THE NAMES HE USED TO OBTAIN THE CONTROLLED SUBSTANCES; ON 3/10/94 HE CONTACTED IMPAIRED PHYSICIANS PROGRAM AND SIGNED A CONTRACT WITH THEM; ON 3/15/94 HE NOTIFIED THE BOARD THAT HE WAS RECEIVING INPATIENT TREATMENT; STATES SOBRIETY DATE AS 3/12/94; HAS ATTENDED AA MEETINGS REGULARLY AFTER DISCHARGE FROM INPATIENT TREATMENT. SUSPENSION STAYED. CONDITIONS OF PROBATION: SHALL ABSTAIN FROM THE CONSUMPTION OF ALCOHOL/CHEMICAL SUBSTANCES WITH ADDICTIVE POTENTIAL UNLESS PRESCRIBED, DISPENSED OR AUTHORIZED BY ANOTHER PHYSICIAN FOR A LEGITIMATE THERAPEUTIC PURPOSE; WITHIN 30 DAYS SHALL SUBMIT TO A PSYCHIATRIC EVALUATION TO INCLUDE A COMPLETE NEUROPSYCHIATRIC EVALUATION BY A BOARD-APPROVED PSYCHIATRIST; SHALL FOLLOW THE PSYCHIATRIST'S RECOMMENDATIONS REGARDING TREATMENT THAT AT A MINIMUM WILL INCLUDE FOLLOW-UP CARE AND COUNSELING AT LEAST ONCE PER MONTH; SHALL NOT TREAT OR OTHERWISE SERVE AS PHYSICIAN, PRESCRIBE, DISPENSE OR ADMINISTER DRUGS THAT MAY BE SUBJECT TO ABUSE TO HIMSELF OR ANY MEMBER OF HIS FAMILY; SHALL CONTINUE TO PARTICIPATE IN AA'S PROGRAM NOT LESS THAN THREE TIMES A WEEK WITH QUARTERLY REPORTS TO THE BOARD; SHALL ADHERE TO THE TERMS OF 24 MONTH AFTERCARE CONTRACT WITH IMPAIRED PHYSICIANS PROGRAM; SHALL SUBMIT HIMSELF FOR APPROPRIATE EXAMS INCLUDING DRUG OR ALCOHOL SCREENS; SHALL SURRENDER ALL CONTROLLED SUBSTANCES AND DANGEROUS DRUGS IN HIS POSSESSION INCLUDING SAMPLES; SHALL NOT TELEPHONE PRESCRIPTIONS FOR CONTROLLED SUBSTANCES OR DANGEROUS DRUGS TO A PHARMACY OR PERMIT ANYONE TO DO SO ON HIS BEHALF; SEPARATE FROM PATIENT RECORDS, SHALL MAINTAIN A FILE OF EVERY PRESCRIPTION WRITTEN FOR CONTROLLED SUBSTANCES OR DANGEROUS DRUGS WHICH SHALL BE AVAILABLE FOR INSPECTION; MAY ORDER ALL SCHEDULED DRUGS AND DANGEROUS DRUGS FOR INPATIENTS IN HOSPITAL AND NURSING HOME SETTINGS, BUT MAY NOT OTHERWISE PRESCRIBE, ADMINISTER, DISPENSE OR POSSESS SUCH DRUGS WITH THE FOLLOWING EXCEPTIONS -- MAY PRESCRIBE ALL SCHEDULED AND DANGEROUS DRUGS FOR OUTPATIENTS SUFFERING FROM ATTENTION DEFICIT DISORDER AND MAY PRESCRIBE SCHEDULE IV DRUGS AND THOSE DANGEROUS DRUGS WHICH ARE NOT GENERALLY CONSIDERED TO HAVE ADDICTIVE POTENTIAL TO ALL OTHER OUTPATIENTS. SHALL ATTEND AT LEAST 50 HOURS PER YEAR OF CONTINUING MEDICAL EDUCATION; SHALL APPEAR BEFORE THE BOARD ONCE A YEAR; SHALL GIVE A COPY OF THIS ORDER TO ANY HEALTH CARE ENTITY WHERE HE HAS PRIVILEGES; SHALL COOPERATE WITH THE BOARD IN VERIFYING COMPLIANCE; SHALL INFORM BOARD OF CHANGE OF ADDRESS WITHIN 10 DAYS OR IF HE LEAVES THE STATE; TIME SPENT OUT OF TEXAS DOES NOT COUNT TOWARD PROBATION. SHALL NOT SEEK MODIFICATION FOR ONE YEAR.

GLOVER, GEORGE E JR MD, LICENSE NUMBER 00B9108, OF VICTORIA, TX, WAS DISCIPLINED BY TEXAS ON AUGUST 25, 1989.
DISCIPLINARY ACTION: 60-MONTH PROBATION; REQUIRED TO TAKE ADDITIONAL MEDICAL EDUCATION
NOTES: LICENSE SUSPENDED, SUSPENSION STAYED. PROBATION CONDITIONS INCLUDE CONTINUING MEDICAL PSYCHIATRIC TREATMENT, AA PARTICIPATION, ALCOHOL/DRUG SCREENING, REFRAIN FROM INGESTING ALCOHOL AND SELF-PRESCRIBING OF CONTROLLED SUBSTANCES.

GOLD, JACOB CHARLES MD OF 5411 NORDLING, HOUSTON, TX, WAS DISCIPLINED BY DEA ON MARCH 12, 1990.
DISCIPLINARY ACTION: SURRENDER OF CONTROLLED SUBSTANCE LICENSE
OFFENSE: CRIMINAL CONVICTION OR PLEA OF GUILTY, NOLO CONTENDERE, OR NO CONTEST TO A CRIME
NOTES: CONVICTED 05/03/89 IN HOUSTON, TEXAS FOR DISTRIBUTING METHAMPHETAMINE, PHENTERMINE, ETHCHLORVYNOL, PHENDIMETRAZINE AND DEXTROAMPHETAMINE AND SENTENCED 08/21/89 TO SIX MONTHS PRISON, FIVE YEARS PROBATION AND $4950 SPECIAL ASSESSMENT FEE.

GOLD, JACOB CHARLES MD, LICENSE NUMBER 00C5685, OF HOUSTON, TX, WAS DISCIPLINED BY TEXAS ON JULY 1, 1990.
DISCIPLINARY ACTION: SURRENDER OF CONTROLLED SUBSTANCE LICENSE
OFFENSE: CRIMINAL CONVICTION OR PLEA OF GUILTY, NOLO CONTENDERE, OR NO CONTEST TO A CRIME
NOTES: CONVICTED OF FELONY. SUSPENSION STAYED PENDING OUTCOME OF APPEAL, MUST SURRENDER ALL NARCOTIC LICENSES, PERMITS, AND REGISTRATIONS. LICENSE TO BE AUTOMATICALLY RESTORED IF APPEAL UPHELD.

GOLD, JACOB CHARLES MD, DATE OF BIRTH FEBRUARY 26, 1925, OF 15922 MILLER RD #1, HOUSTON, TX, WAS DISCIPLINED BY MEDICARE ON MAY 24, 1991.
DISCIPLINARY ACTION: 120-MONTH EXCLUSION FROM THE MEDICARE AND/OR MEDICAID PROGRAMS
OFFENSE: CRIMINAL CONVICTION OR PLEA OF GUILTY, NOLO CONTENDERE, OR NO CONTEST TO A CRIME
NOTES: CONVICTION RELATING TO CONTROLLED SUBSTANCES.

GOLD, JACOB CHARLES MD, LICENSE NUMBER 00C5685, OF HOUSTON, TX, WAS DISCIPLINED BY TEXAS ON DECEMBER 4, 1991.
DISCIPLINARY ACTION: LICENSE REVOCATION
OFFENSE: CRIMINAL CONVICTION OR PLEA OF GUILTY, NOLO CONTENDERE, OR NO CONTEST TO A CRIME
NOTES: ON 5/3/89 HE WAS CONVICTED ON SIX COUNTS FOR KNOWINGLY AND UNLAWFULLY DISPENSING BY PRESCRIPTION TO ONE PATIENT DESOXYN, FASTIN, AND PLACIDYL NOT IN THE USUAL COURSE OF PROFESSIONAL PRACTICE AND NOT FOR A LEGITIMATE MEDICAL PURPOSE; WAS ALSO CONVICTED OF 93 COUNTS OF DISPENSING BY PRESCRIPTION TO ANOTHER PATIENT THESE SAME DRUGS AND ALSO PRELU-2 AND DEXEDRINE NOT FOR A LEGITIMATE MEDICAL PURPOSE. ON 8/21/89 HE WAS SENTENCED TO SIX MONTHS IMPRISONMENT, FOLLOWED BY A FIVE YEAR PROBATION; PRESENTLY INCARCERATED. VOLUNTARILY SURRENDERED HIS LICENSE. SHALL SURRENDER DEA AND TEXAS CONTROLLED SUBSTANCES REGISTRATION CERTIFICATES, ALL UNUSED TRIPLICATE PRESCRIPTION FORMS, AND ALL CONTROLLED SUBSTANCES PRESENTLY IN HIS OFFICE, INCLUDING SAMPLES.

GOOD, EDWARD F MD, LICENSE NUMBER 0014447, OF WEBSTER, TX, WAS DISCIPLINED BY FLORIDA ON APRIL 20, 1992.
DISCIPLINARY ACTION: FINE
OFFENSE: FAILURE TO COMPLY WITH A PROFESSIONAL RULE
NOTES: CHARGED WITH FAILING TO MAINTAIN AND SUBMIT DOCUMENTATION VERIFYING COMPLETION OF HIV/AIDS AND RISK MANAGEMENT CONTINUING MEDICAL EDUCATION IN RESPONSE TO THE BOARD'S RANDOM AUDIT. $1,000 FINE.

GORDON, GENE STEPHEN MD, DATE OF BIRTH JANUARY 15, 1947, LICENSE NUMBER 00F1033, OF 6 PEMBROKE HILL DEVONWOOD, FARMINGTON, CT, WAS DISCIPLINED BY TEXAS ON JANUARY 29, 1993.
DISCIPLINARY ACTION: 60-MONTH PROBATION; RESTRICTION PLACED ON LICENSE
OFFENSE: DISCIPLINARY ACTION BY ANOTHER STATE OR AGENCY
NOTES: CONNECTICUT LICENSE PUT ON PROBATION 6/18/91 BASED ON HIS MISHANDLING MEDICATION REGIMES FOR PATIENTS; FAILED TO ESTABLISH AND MAINTAIN APPROPRIATE BOUNDARIES FOR HIS PATIENTS; BREACHED PATIENT CONFIDENTIALITY ON NUMEROUS OCCASIONS; FAILED TO MAINTAIN ADEQUATE AND COMPLETE MEDICAL RECORDS; TESTIFIED FALSELY UNDER OATH AS TO AUTHORSHIP OF CERTAIN DOCUMENTS RELATING TO HIS ROLE AS AN EXPERT WITNESS. 5 YEAR SUSPENSION STAYED. CONDITIONS OF PROBATION: SAME AS THOSE OF CONNECTICUT ORDER INCLUDING CONSULTING A BOARD-APPROVED PSYCHIATRIST WEEKLY, HAVING A PSYCHIATRIST MONITOR HIS PRACTICE -- BOTH OF WHOM SHALL SUBMIT REPORTS, SHALL NOT CONDUCT GROUP THERAPY SESSIONS WITHOUT A CO-FACILITATOR, AND SHALL NOT SERVE AS AN EXPERT WITNESS; PRIOR TO PRACTICING IN TEXAS SHALL APPEAR BEFORE THE BOARD; SHALL INFORM THE BOARD IF HE LEAVES TEXAS OR CONNECTICUT; TIME SPENT OUT OF THESE TWO STATES DOES NOT COUNT TOWARD PROBATION. SHALL NOT SEEK MODIFICATION FOR ONE YEAR.

GOUGER, DONALD T MD, LICENSE NUMBER 0096763, OF HOUSTON, TX, WAS DISCIPLINED BY NEW YORK ON MAY 13, 1987.
NOTES: 2 YEAR SUSPENSION STAYED

GREEN, DEMETRIS A MD, LICENSE NUMBER 00J4168, OF HOUSTON, TX, WAS DISCIPLINED BY TEXAS ON NOVEMBER 3, 1994.
DISCIPLINARY ACTION: LICENSE SUSPENSION
OFFENSE: DRUG OR ALCOHOL ABUSE
NOTES: ON 10/7/94 WAS INVOLUNTARILY ADMITTED TO AN ADDICTION TREATMENT PROGRAM FOR SYMPTOMS RELATED TO COCAINE ADDICTION; DURING 1994 INGESTED COCAINE WITHOUT A LEGITIMATE MEDICAL PURPOSE. SUSPENSION UNTIL HE PERSONALLY APPEARS BEFORE THE BOARD AND PROVIDES SUFFICIENT EVIDENCE THAT HE IS PHYSICALLY, MENTALLY AND OTHERWISE COMPETENT TO PRACTICE SAFELY INCLUDING BUT NOT LIMITED TO COMPLETE LEGIBLE COPIES OF MEDICAL RECORDS AND REPORTS OF PSYCHOLOGICAL AND NEUROPSYCHIATRIC EVALUATIONS.

GREEN, KENNETH W JR MD, DATE OF BIRTH APRIL 27, 1957, OF

2728 OAKLAWN AVENUE, DALLAS, TX, WAS DISCIPLINED BY MEDICARE ON JUNE 30, 1994.
DISCIPLINARY ACTION: EXCLUSION FROM THE MEDICARE AND/OR MEDICAID PROGRAMS
OFFENSE: FAILURE TO COMPLY WITH A PROFESSIONAL RULE
NOTES: DEFAULTED ON PUBLIC HEALTH SERVICE EDUCATION LOAN.

GREEN, KENNETH WAYNE JR MD, LICENSE NUMBER 00H2414, OF DALLAS, TX, WAS DISCIPLINED BY TEXAS ON APRIL 10, 1992.
DISCIPLINARY ACTION: 120-MONTH PROBATION
OFFENSE: DRUG OR ALCOHOL ABUSE
NOTES: SEVERAL VIOLATIONS OF THE MEDICAL PRACTICE ACT, INCLUDING INTEMPERATE USE OF ALCOHOL OR DRUGS AND INABILITY TO PRACTICE MEDICINE WITH REASONABLE SKILL AND SAFETY TO PATIENTS. LICENSE SUSPENDED, SUSPENSION STAYED; PROBATION UNDER TERMS AND CONDITIONS.

GREEN, KENNETH WAYNE JR MD, LICENSE NUMBER 00H2414, OF DALLAS, TX, WAS DISCIPLINED BY TEXAS ON NOVEMBER 13, 1992.
DISCIPLINARY ACTION: EMERGENCY SUSPENSION
OFFENSE: FAILURE TO COMPLY WITH A PREVIOUS BOARD ORDER
NOTES: INTEMPERATE USE OF DRUGS AND VIOLATION OF PROBATION. TEMPORARILY SUSPENDED UNTIL A HEARING BEFORE THE STATE OFFICE OF ADMINISTRATIVE HEARINGS CAN BE CONDUCTED.

GREEN, KENNETH WAYNE JR MD, LICENSE NUMBER 00H2414, WAS DISCIPLINED BY TEXAS ON AUGUST 28, 1993.
DISCIPLINARY ACTION: PROBATION; MONITORING OF PHYSICIAN
OFFENSE: FAILURE TO COMPLY WITH A PREVIOUS BOARD ORDER
NOTES: IN SPITE OF DISCREPANCIES IN PROCEDURES TESTING A URINE SAMPLE HE GAVE ON 6/5/92 AND HIS CLAIM THAT A VITAMIN HE WAS TAKING TRIGGERED A POSITIVE RESULT ON THE DRUG SCREEN, THE BOARD DETERMINED THAT EMPIRICAL, SCIENTIFIC EVIDENCE SHOWED HE HAD INGESTED COCAINE ON OR ABOUT 6/5/92 IN VIOLATION OF THE 4/10/92 ORDER. TEN YEAR SUSPENSION STAYED. CONDITIONS OF 4/10/92 PROBATION MODIFIED: SHALL CONTINUE TREATMENT WITH COUNSELORS AND SHALL PARTICIPATE IN SCREENS AS DIRECTED BY THEM WITH REPORTS TO THE BOARD UPON REQUEST OR IMMEDIATELY IF ANY SCREEN IS POSITIVE; IF HE RECEIVED A DRUG FROM A PHYSICIAN FOR A LEGITIMATE AND THERAPEUTIC PURPOSE THE PHYSICIAN SHALL IMMEDIATELY REPORT THIS TO THE BOARD WITH DETAILS; TREATING PHYSICIAN SHALL BE GIVEN A COPY OF THIS ORDER; SHALL IN ADDITION TO DRUG SCREENS REQUESTED BY BOARD SUBMIT TO 12 PER YEAR TO BE ORDERED BY THE PHYSICIAN REHABILITATION COMMITTEE WITH RESULTS PROVIDED TO THE BOARD. SHALL NOT SEEK MODIFICATION FOR ONE YEAR.

GREEN, KENNETH WAYNE JR MD, LICENSE NUMBER 00H2414, OF DALLAS, TX, WAS DISCIPLINED BY TEXAS ON AUGUST 19, 1994.
DISCIPLINARY ACTION: LICENSE REVOCATION
OFFENSE: FAILURE TO COMPLY WITH A PREVIOUS BOARD ORDER
NOTES: IN VIOLATION OF 4/10/92 AND 8/20/93 ORDERS, ON 11/2/93 HE REFUSED TO PROVIDE A REQUESTED URINE SAMPLE; HE DID COMPLY THREE HOURS LATER; THIS SAMPLE TESTED POSITIVE FOR AMPHETAMINES AND METHAMPHETAMINES WHICH HAD NOT BEEN PRESCRIBED BY HIS ATTENDING PHYSICIAN; CONTINUED DRUG USAGE AND RELAPSES DO NOT PRESENT A FAVORABLE PICTURE IN TERMS OF POTENTIAL FOR REHABILITATION. ORDER WILL BECOME FINAL WHEN ADMINISTRATIVE APPEALS HAVE BEEN EXHAUSTED; HE HAS 20 DAYS TO FILE FOR A REHEARING.

GREEN, KENNETH WAYNE JR MD OF 729 GRAPEVINE HIGHWAY, HURST, TX, WAS DISCIPLINED BY DEA ON NOVEMBER 10, 1994.
DISCIPLINARY ACTION: REVOCATION OF CONTROLLED SUBSTANCE LICENSE
OFFENSE: DRUG OR ALCOHOL ABUSE
NOTES: TEXAS MEDICAL BOARD PLACED HIS LICENSE ON PROBATION IN 4/92 FOR TEN YEARS BASED UPON HIS ABUSE OF DEMEROL AND VICODIN WHICH RESULTED IN HIM LOSING HIS CLINICAL PRIVILEGES AT A MEDICAL CENTER IN 4/91. ON 6/5/92 URINE SAMPLE COLLECTED FROM HIM TESTED POSITIVE FOR COCAINE WHICH WAS AGAINST THE TERMS OF THE PREVIOUS ORDER AND HIS LICENSE WAS SUSPENDED FOR TEN YEARS WITH SUSPENSION STAYED. VIOLATED PROVISIONS OF BOTH BOARD ORDERS AND CONSEQUENTLY HAD HIS TEXAS LICENSE REVOKED ON 08/19/94.

GREGORIO, CESAR P JR MD, LICENSE NUMBER 00E7611, OF ROCKWALL, TX, WAS DISCIPLINED BY TEXAS ON JUNE 10, 1991.
DISCIPLINARY ACTION: 36-MONTH PROBATION; REQUIRED TO TAKE ADDITIONAL MEDICAL EDUCATION
OFFENSE: PROFESSIONAL MISCONDUCT
NOTES: PROFESSIONAL FAILURE TO PRACTICE IN AN ACCEPTABLE MANNER CONSISTENT WITH PUBLIC HEALTH AND WELFARE. CONDITIONS OF PROBATION INCLUDE: 50 HOURS PER YEAR OF CONTINUING MEDICAL EDUCATION CLASSES APPROVED BY THE EXECUTIVE DIRECTOR; MUST APPEAR BEFORE THE BOARD ONCE A YEAR; MUST MAINTAIN SEPARATE FILES OF THOSE RECORDS THAT INDICATE A NEED TO DO PLETHYSMOGRAPHIC TESTS.

GRIER, RAYMOND E MD, LICENSE NUMBER 0A32041, OF GREENSBORO, NC, WAS DISCIPLINED BY CALIFORNIA ON SEPTEMBER 7, 1987.
DISCIPLINARY ACTION: 36-MONTH PROBATION
OFFENSE: OVERPRESCRIBING OR MISPRESCRIBING DRUGS
NOTES: REVOCATION STAYED; PRESCRIBING DANGEROUS DRUGS WITHOUT GOOD FAITH PRIOR EXAM AND MEDICAL INDICATION; GROSS NEGLIGENCE IN PRACTICE; INADEQUATE SUPERVISION OF PHYSICIAN ASSISTANTS

GRIER, RAYMOND E MD OF GREENSBORO, NC, WAS DISCIPLINED BY OHIO ON NOVEMBER 9, 1988.
DISCIPLINARY ACTION: LICENSE SUSPENSION
NOTES: INDEFINITE SUSPENSION

GRIER, RAYMOND E MD, LICENSE NUMBER 00G4586, OF GREENSBORO, NC, WAS DISCIPLINED BY TEXAS ON DECEMBER 1, 1988.
NOTES: SETTLEMENT AGREEMENT AND UNSPECIFIED DISCIPLINARY ACTION

GRIER, RAYMOND EDWARD MD OF GREENSBORO, NC, WAS DISCIPLINED BY NORTH CAROLINA ON DECEMBER 1, 1988.
DISCIPLINARY ACTION: 36-MONTH PROBATION
NOTES: REVOCATION STAYED.

GRIFFIN, JOHN MD OF 11808 BROAD OAKS, AUSTIN, TX, WAS DISCIPLINED BY MEDICARE ON FEBRUARY 13, 1980.
DISCIPLINARY ACTION: 36-MONTH EXCLUSION FROM THE

MEDICARE AND/OR MEDICAID PROGRAMS
OFFENSE: CRIMINAL CONVICTION OR PLEA OF GUILTY, NOLO CONTENDERE, OR NO CONTEST TO A CRIME
NOTES: PROGRAM-RELATED CONVICTION.

GRIFFIN, JOHN MD, DATE OF BIRTH NOVEMBER 27, 1932, LICENSE NUMBER 0017641, WAS DISCIPLINED BY IOWA ON JULY 25, 1989.
DISCIPLINARY ACTION: FINE
OFFENSE: FAILURE TO COMPLY WITH A PROFESSIONAL RULE
NOTES: FAILURE TO REPORT SEXUAL CHILD ABUSE

GRIFFIN, STEVEN WAYNE MD OF DALLAS, TX, WAS DISCIPLINED BY TEXAS ON MAY 1, 1985.
DISCIPLINARY ACTION: SURRENDER OF LICENSE

GRIFFIN, STEVEN WAYNE MD, LICENSE NUMBER 00E2587, OF MINEOLA, TX, WAS DISCIPLINED BY TEXAS ON AUGUST 24, 1991.
DISCIPLINARY ACTION: SURRENDER OF LICENSE
OFFENSE: CRIMINAL CONVICTION OR PLEA OF GUILTY, NOLO CONTENDERE, OR NO CONTEST TO A CRIME
NOTES: LICENSE VOLUNTARILY SURRENDERED IN LIEU OF FURTHER DISCIPLINARY ACTION DUE TO FELONY CONVICTION OF CONSPIRACY TO OBTAIN A CONTROLLED SUBSTANCE.

GRIFFITH, KARL EDWARD MD, DATE OF BIRTH JULY 11, 1950, LICENSE NUMBER 00G5121, OF 6816 MCCALLUM, DALLAS, TX, WAS DISCIPLINED BY TEXAS ON AUGUST 20, 1993.
DISCIPLINARY ACTION: 120-MONTH PROBATION; RESTRICTION PLACED ON LICENSE
OFFENSE: LOSS OR RESTRICTION OF HOSPITAL PRIVILEGES
NOTES: IN 11/90 WAS ADMITTED FOR POLYSUBSTANCE ABUSE TREATMENT; THEN ENTERED RECOVERY RESIDENCE PROGRAM AT A HOSPITAL; EXPERIENCED DRUG-RELATED WORK DIFFICULTIES DUE TO A RELAPSE IN RECOVERY; HOSPITAL REQUIRED RANDOM DRUG SCREENS; TESTED POSITIVE FOR BENZODIAZEPINES IN 6/91; ALSO ABUSED SUFENTA, FENTANYL AND FORANE ANESTHETIC GAS; WAS REPLACED ON A SURGICAL CASE IN 12/91 WHEN HE WAS NOTED TO BE UNRESPONSIVE, SPONGES SOAKED IN FORANE WERE DISCOVERED IN THE SURGICAL MASK HE WAS WEARING; ANESTHESIA PRIVILEGES WERE SUSPENDED; WAS DISCHARGED FROM A TREATMENT PROGRAM ON 3/27/92 AND HAS CONTINUED AFTERCARE TREATMENT INCLUDING REGULAR AA ATTENDANCE AND THERAPY. REVOCATION STAYED. CONDITIONS OF PROBATION: SHALL ABSTAIN FROM THE CONSUMPTION OF ALCOHOL/DRUGS IN ANY FORM UNLESS PRESCRIBED BY ANOTHER PHYSICIAN FOR A LEGITIMATE AND THERAPEUTIC PURPOSE; SHALL SUBMIT HIMSELF FOR APPROPRIATE EXAMS INCLUDING DRUG OR ALCOHOL SCREENS; UPON BOARD REQUEST SHALL SUBMIT HIMSELF TO SARA CAPNOGRAPH TESTS; SHALL NOT POSSESS, ADMINISTER, DISPENSE OR PRESCRIBE ANY CONTROLLED SUBSTANCES EXCEPT FOR TREATMENT OF INPATIENTS AS A CLINICAL INSTRUCTOR IN ANESTHESIOLOGY; SHALL LIMIT PRACTICE SOLELY TO THE DUTIES OF CLINICAL INSTRUCTOR OF ANESTHESIOLOGY; SHALL BE UNDER THE OBSERVATION OF A PHYSICIAN OR CERTIFIED REGISTERED NURSE ANESTHESIOLOGIST WHILE ADMINISTERING OR SUPERVISING THE ADMINISTRATION OF ANESTHESIA; SHALL CONTINUE TREATMENT BY AN ADDICTIONOLOGIST WITH QUARTERLY REPORTS; SHALL SUBMIT HIMSELF FOR EVALUATION AND TREATMENT TO A BOARD-APPROVED PSYCHIATRIST; SHALL PARTICIPATE IN ACTIVITIES OF A PHYSICIAN HEALTH AND REHABILITATION COMMITTEE AND ATTEND WEEKLY MEETINGS WITH QUARTERLY REPORTS; SHALL PARTICIPATE IN AA'S PROGRAM NOT LESS THAN THREE TIMES A WEEK WITH QUARTERLY REPORTS TO THE BOARD; SHALL ATTEND AT LEAST 50 HOURS PER YEAR OF CONTINUING MEDICAL EDUCATION; SHALL PERFORM 12 HOURS PER MONTH OF COMMUNITY SERVICE WITH QUARTERLY REPORTS TO THE BOARD; SHALL GIVE A COPY OF THIS ORDER TO ANY HEALTH CARE ENTITY WHERE HE HAS PRIVILEGES; SHALL COOPERATE WITH THE BOARD IN VERIFYING COMPLIANCE; SHALL INFORM BOARD OF CHANGE OF ADDRESS WITHIN 10 DAYS OR IF HE LEAVES THE STATE; TIME SPENT OUT OF TEXAS DOES NOT COUNT TOWARD PROBATION. SHALL NOT SEEK MODIFICATION FOR ONE YEAR. ON 1/6/95 ORDER MODIFIED SUCH THAT HE MAY ALSO PRACTICE AS ASSISTANT OR ASSOCIATE PROFESSOR OF ANESTHESIOLOGY; SHALL BE UNDER THE SUPERVISION OF THE HOSPITAL RATHER THAN A SPECIFIED PERSON; COMMUNITY SERVICE REQUIREMENT IS DELETED.

GRISWOLD, NEIL L DO WAS DISCIPLINED BY MINNESOTA ON FEBRUARY 20, 1975.
DISCIPLINARY ACTION: DENIAL OF NEW LICENSE

GRISWOLD, NEIL L DO, LICENSE NUMBER 00D3484, OF SAUK RAPIDS, MN, WAS DISCIPLINED BY TEXAS ON DECEMBER 1, 1988.
NOTES: SETTLEMENT AGREEMENT AND UNSPECIFIED DISCIPLINARY ACTION

GROSS, GEORGE E DO OF GRAND PRAIRIE, TX, WAS DISCIPLINED BY TEXAS ON DECEMBER 1, 1986.
DISCIPLINARY ACTION: LICENSE REVOCATION
OFFENSE: CRIMINAL CONVICTION OR PLEA OF GUILTY, NOLO CONTENDERE, OR NO CONTEST TO A CRIME
NOTES: CONVICTED OF FELONY INVOLVING CONTROLLED SUBSTANCES.

GROSSMAN, GERALD MD, LICENSE NUMBER 0106920, OF BIG SPRING, TX, WAS DISCIPLINED BY NEW YORK ON MAY 13, 1987.
DISCIPLINARY ACTION: 24-MONTH LICENSE SUSPENSION

GROSSMAN, MAURICE SIDNEY MD, DATE OF BIRTH JUNE 1, 1927, LICENSE NUMBER 00C3062, OF 1001 LOUISIANA PARKWAY SUITE 307, CORPUS CHRISTI, TX, WAS DISCIPLINED BY TEXAS ON JANUARY 29, 1993.
DISCIPLINARY ACTION: REPRIMAND
OFFENSE: SUBSTANDARD CARE, INCOMPETENCE, OR NEGLIGENCE
NOTES: ON 4/22/87 A PATIENT CAME TO HIS OFFICE WITH ABDOMINAL PAINS; PRIOR TO AND DURING A PLANNED COLONSCOPY, A COMBINATION OF VALIUM, DEMEROL IV AND DEMEROL IM AND PHENERGAN WAS ADMINISTERED; THE PATIENT SUFFERED RESPIRATORY AND CARDIAC ARREST, BECAME NEUROLOGICALLY UNRESPONSIVE AND WAS TRANSPORTED TO A HOSPITAL WHERE RESUSCITATION WAS ATTEMPTED; SHE DIED ONE WEEK LATER. SHALL GIVE A COPY OF THIS ORDER TO ANY HEALTH CARE ENTITY WHERE HE HAS PRIVILEGES; SHALL INFORM THE BOARD OF CHANGE OF ADDRESS WITHIN 10 DAYS.

GUERRERORAMIREZ, LUIS MD, LICENSE NUMBER 00E0946, OF HOUSTON, TX, WAS DISCIPLINED BY TEXAS ON APRIL 9, 1992.
DISCIPLINARY ACTION: LICENSE REVOCATION
OFFENSE: SUBSTANDARD CARE, INCOMPETENCE, OR

NEGLIGENCE
NOTES: SEVERAL VIOLATIONS OF THE MEDICAL PRACTICE ACT, INCLUDING PROFESSIONAL FAILURE TO PRACTICE MEDICINE IN AN ACCEPTABLE MANNER CONSISTENT WITH PUBLIC HEALTH AND WELFARE. HE HAS FILED A MOTION FOR REHEARING WHICH HAD NOT BEEN RULED ON AS OF SUMMER 1992.

GUIMBARDA, LUIS A MD, LICENSE NUMBER 00D2945, OF SAN ANTONIO, TX, WAS DISCIPLINED BY TEXAS ON OCTOBER 5, 1991.
DISCIPLINARY ACTION: 24-MONTH PROBATION; REQUIRED TO TAKE ADDITIONAL MEDICAL EDUCATION
OFFENSE: SUBSTANDARD CARE, INCOMPETENCE, OR NEGLIGENCE
NOTES: INADEQUATE TREATMENT AND RECORD KEEPING REGARDING THREE PATIENTS SHOWED FAILURE TO PRACTICE MEDICINE IN AN ACCEPTABLE MANNER. CONDITIONS OF PROBATION: SHALL ATTEND AT LEAST 50 HOURS OF CATEGORY I CONTINUING MEDICAL EDUCATION WITH 10 HOURS OF DIABETES MANAGEMENT PER YEAR; SHALL OBTAIN CONSULTATION WITH ANOTHER PHYSICIAN WITHIN 48 HOURS OF ADMITTING ANY PATIENT; SHALL NOT PETITION FOR MODIFICATION FOR AT LEAST ONE YEAR; SHALL COOPERATE WITH BOARD IN VERIFYING COMPLIANCE; SHALL ADVISE THE BOARD OF ANY CHAGE OF ADDRESS; TIME SPENT OUT OF STATE DOESN'T COUNT TOWARDS PROBATION.

GULLION, JERRY C MD, LICENSE NUMBER 00C9001, OF MARSHALL, TX, WAS DISCIPLINED BY TEXAS ON JANUARY 26, 1990.
DISCIPLINARY ACTION: 36-MONTH REPRIMAND; REQUIRED TO TAKE ADDITIONAL MEDICAL EDUCATION
NOTES: STIPULATED ORDER.

GUO, GEORGE S MD, DATE OF BIRTH JUNE 19, 1961, LICENSE NUMBER 00H4368, OF 11123 ASHCOTT, HOUSTON, TX, WAS DISCIPLINED BY TEXAS ON JANUARY 29, 1993.
DISCIPLINARY ACTION: LICENSE REVOCATION
OFFENSE: CRIMINAL CONVICTION OR PLEA OF GUILTY, NOLO CONTENDERE, OR NO CONTEST TO A CRIME
NOTES: CONVICTED OF THE FELONY OFFENSE OF BURGLARY OF A HABITATION AND SENTENCED TO 10 YEARS CONFINEMENT WITH SHOCK PROBATION AFTER 90 DAYS AND A FINE; HAS PRACTICED NO MEDICINE SINCE HIS ARREST ON 11/23/90. ORDER WILL BECOME FINAL WHEN ALL APPEALS HAVE BEEN EXHAUSTED.

GURAV, RAMCHANDRA S MD, DATE OF BIRTH MARCH 27, 1935, LICENSE NUMBER 0030126, OF 520 HOSPITAL DRIVE #2, NEW BOSTON, TX, WAS DISCIPLINED BY NEW JERSEY ON MARCH 22, 1991.
DISCIPLINARY ACTION: SURRENDER OF LICENSE
NOTES: SHOULD DR. GURAV SEEK TO PRACTICE IN NEW JERSEY IN THE FUTURE, MUST APPEAR BEFORE THE BOARD FOR A STATUS CONFERENCE. THIS MATTER IS RESOLVED WITHOUT ANY FORMAL FINDING BEING MADE BY THE BOARD OF MEDICAL EXAMINERS. THIS DOES NOT CONSTITUTE A SUSPENSION OR REVOCATION.

GURAV, RAMCHANDRA S MD, LICENSE NUMBER 0025523, OF NEW BOSTON, TX, WAS DISCIPLINED BY VIRGINIA ON DECEMBER 16, 1993.
DISCIPLINARY ACTION: LICENSE SUSPENSION
OFFENSE: CRIMINAL CONVICTION OR PLEA OF GUILTY, NOLO CONTENDERE, OR NO CONTEST TO A CRIME
NOTES: CRIMINAL CONVICTION OF UNLAWFUL DISPENSING OF SCHEDULE IV CONTROLLED SUBSTANCES.

GURAV, RANCHANDRA S MD, LICENSE NUMBER 0025523, OF 520 HOSPITAL DRIVE, SUITE 2, NEW BOSTON, TX, WAS DISCIPLINED BY VIRGINIA ON JUNE 16, 1994.
DISCIPLINARY ACTION: PROBATION; RESTRICTION PLACED ON CONTROLLED SUBSTANCE LICENSE
OFFENSE: CRIMINAL CONVICTION OR PLEA OF GUILTY, NOLO CONTENDERE, OR NO CONTEST TO A CRIME
NOTES: ON 6/8/91 CONVICTED IN TEXAS FOR KNOWINGLY, INTENTIONALLY AND UNLAWFULLY DISPENSING AND CAUSING TO BE DISPENSED A SCHEDULE IV CONTROLLED SUBSTANCE NOT IN THE USUAL COURSE OF PROFESSIONAL PRACTICE FOR A LEGITIMATE MEDICAL PURPOSE. LICENSE REINSTATED FROM SUSPENSION. PROBATION WITH FOLLOWING TERMS AND CONDITIONS: SHALL BE PROHIBITED FROM PRESCRIBING SCHEDULE II CONTROLLED SUBSTANCES IN VIRGINIA EXCEPT IN A HOSPITAL SETTING.

GUSTAFSON, W C JR MD OF 7500 BEECHNUT, HOUSTON, TX, WAS DISCIPLINED BY DEA ON NOVEMBER 19, 1993.
DISCIPLINARY ACTION: SURRENDER OF CONTROLLED SUBSTANCE LICENSE
OFFENSE: FAILURE TO COMPLY WITH A PROFESSIONAL RULE
NOTES: VIOLATIONS OF THE CONTROLLED SUBSTANCE ACT.

GUSTAFSON, WESLEY C JR MD, LICENSE NUMBER 00C9002, OF HOUSTON, TX, WAS DISCIPLINED BY TEXAS ON JANUARY 28, 1989.
DISCIPLINARY ACTION: REQUIRED TO TAKE ADDITIONAL MEDICAL EDUCATION; MONITORING OF PHYSICIAN
NOTES: SHALL MODIFY CRITERIA FOR ADMINISTERING AND PRESCRIBING MEDICATIONS AS DIRECTED; SHALL COMPLETE PRECEPTORSHIP ON PREVENTION AND TREATMENT OF DRUG ABUSE; SHALL REEVALUATE HIS CRITERIA FOR REFERRAL OF CERTAIN CHRONIC PATIENTS; SHALL CREATE AND MAINTAIN PRESCRIPTION AND MEDICAL RECORDS FOR REVIEW;

GUSTAFSON, WESLEY C JR MD, LICENSE NUMBER 00C9002, OF SEMINOLE, TX, WAS DISCIPLINED BY TEXAS ON JUNE 22, 1994.
DISCIPLINARY ACTION: SURRENDER OF CONTROLLED SUBSTANCE LICENSE; 60-MONTH PROBATION
OFFENSE: OVERPRESCRIBING OR MISPRESCRIBING DRUGS
NOTES: BETWEEN 1/93 AND 12/93 PRESCRIBED LARGE QUANTITIES OF PROPOXYPHENE, HYDROCODONE, SOMA, RESTORIL, PHENERGAN WITH CODEINE, PENTAZOCINE, DIAZEPAM AND TEGRETOL TO TWO PATIENTS WITHOUT ANY LEGITIMATE MEDICAL REASON AND FOR A PERIOD AND IN QUANTITIES FAR IN EXCESS OF THAT INDICATED BY THE PATIENTS' MEDICAL CONDITIONS; THESE PERSONS WERE KNOWN TO HAVE A HISTORY OF SUBSTANCE ABUSE AND HE SHOULD HAVE KNOWN THEY WERE HABITUAL USERS OF DANGEROUS DRUGS; SURRENDERED HIS DEA AND TEXAS CONTROLLED SUBSTANCES CERTIFICATES ON 11/18/93. SUSPENSION STAYED. CONDITIONS OF PROBATION: SHALL APPEAR BEFORE THE BOARD ONCE A YEAR; SHALL ATTEND AT LEAST 50 HOURS PER YEAR OF CONTINUING MEDICAL EDUCATION AT LEAST FIVE HOURS OF WHICH SHALL BE IN THE AREA OF RECORD KEEPING AND/OR RISK MANAGEMENT AND 20 HOURS OF WHICH SHALL BE IN THE AREA OF ADDICTIONOLOGY AND/OR SUBSTANCE ABUSE; SHALL MAINTAIN ADEQUATE MEDICAL RECORDS ON ALL PATIENT OFFICE

VISITS WHICH SHALL BE AVAILABLE FOR INSPECTION; SHALL PERSONALLY EXAMINE PATIENTS WHENEVER ANY FORM CERTIFIES THAT A PERSONAL EXAMINATION HAS BEEN PERFORMED AND ALWAYS ON A FIRST VISIT; SHALL NOT TREAT OR OTHERWISE SERVE AS PHYSICIAN, PRESCRIBE, DISPENSE OR ADMINISTER DRUGS THAT MAY BE SUBJECT TO ABUSE TO HIMSELF OR ANY MEMBER OF HIS IMMEDIATE FAMILY; SHALL SURRENDER DEA AND TEXAS CONTROLLED SUBSTANCES CERTIFICATES IF HE HAS NOT ALREADY DONE SO AS WELL AS ALL UNUSED TRIPLICATE PRESCRIPTION FORMS AND ALL CONTROLLED SUBSTANCES IN HIS POSSESSION INCLUDING SAMPLES; SHALL NOT REAPPLY WITHOUT PERMISSION; SEPARATE FROM PATIENT RECORDS, SHALL MAINTAIN A FILE OF ALL PRESCRIPTIONS WRITTEN FOR DANGEROUS DRUGS WHICH SHALL BE AVAILABLE FOR INSPECTION; SHALL NOT TELEPHONE IN ANY PRESCRIPTIONS FOR DANGEROUS DRUGS OR PERMIT ANY PERSON WHO IS NOT LICENSED TO DO SO ON HIS BEHALF; SHALL NOT SERVE AS PHYSICIAN TO CHRONIC PAIN PATIENTS; SHALL GIVE A COPY OF THIS ORDER TO ANY HEALTH CARE ENTITY WHERE HE HAS PRIVILEGES; SHALL COOPERATE WITH THE BOARD IN VERIFYING COMPLIANCE; SHALL INFORM BOARD OF CHANGE OF ADDRESS OR IF HE LEAVES THE STATE; TIME SPENT OUT OF TEXAS DOES NOT COUNT TOWARD PROBATION. SHALL NOT SEEK MODIFICATION FOR ONE YEAR.

GUYETTE, WILLIAM A MD, DATE OF BIRTH MAY 17, 1949, LICENSE NUMBER 0022109, WAS DISCIPLINED BY KENTUCKY ON JULY 1, 1988.
DISCIPLINARY ACTION: SURRENDER OF CONTROLLED SUBSTANCE LICENSE; 24-MONTH PROBATION
NOTES: VOLUNTARILY RELINQUISHED PRESCRIBING PRIVILEGES. DISCHARGED FROM PROBATION ON 11/14/90.

GUYETTE, WILLIAM A MD, LICENSE NUMBER 00F9517, OF SALEM, KY, WAS DISCIPLINED BY TEXAS ON JULY 28, 1989.
OFFENSE: DISCIPLINARY ACTION BY ANOTHER STATE OR AGENCY
NOTES: MUST COMPLY WITH TERMS OF KENTUCKY ORDER. MUST DEMONSTRATE CAPACITY TO PRACTICE WITH REASONABLE SKILL AND SAFETY TO PATIENTS AND PROVIDE KENTUCKY LICENSE STATUS REPORT IF SEEKING PERMISSION TO PRACTICE IN TEXAS.

HADAD, ANIBAL R MD OF P.O. BOX 890526, HOUSTON, TX, WAS DISCIPLINED BY MEDICARE ON MARCH 9, 1987.
DISCIPLINARY ACTION: FINE
OFFENSE: SUBSTANDARD CARE, INCOMPETENCE, OR NEGLIGENCE
NOTES: FINED $5,046.11. PERFORMED UNNECESSARY FEMORAL TIBIAL GRAFTS IN A 75 YEAR OLD MAN FOR CLAUDICATION. NO LONGER LISTED AS EXCLUDED AS OF 9/30/92.

HAFFKE, OSCAR WILLIAM MD, LICENSE NUMBER 00B8894, OF FORT WORTH, TX, WAS DISCIPLINED BY TEXAS ON MARCH 31, 1994.
DISCIPLINARY ACTION: SURRENDER OF LICENSE
NOTES: HAS NOT ADMITTED VIOLATIONS OF MEDICAL PRACTICE ACT; SURRENDER IN LIEU OF FURTHER INVESTIGATION; SHALL NOT PETITION FOR REINSTATEMENT OF LICENSE.

HAGER, JEROME P MD, LICENSE NUMBER 0G39489, OF RIVERSIDE, CA, WAS DISCIPLINED BY CALIFORNIA ON DECEMBER 19, 1992.
DISCIPLINARY ACTION: SURRENDER OF LICENSE
NOTES: VOLUNTARY SURRENDER WHILE CHARGES PENDING.

HAGER, JEROME P MD, DATE OF BIRTH JULY 15, 1923, OF 7101 MAGNOLIA AVENUE SUITE A, RIVERSIDE, CA, WAS DISCIPLINED BY MEDICARE ON AUGUST 2, 1993.
DISCIPLINARY ACTION: 60-MONTH EXCLUSION FROM THE MEDICARE AND/OR MEDICAID PROGRAMS
OFFENSE: CRIMINAL CONVICTION OR PLEA OF GUILTY, NOLO CONTENDERE, OR NO CONTEST TO A CRIME
NOTES: CONVICTED OF A CRIME RELATED TO THE MEDI-CAL PROGRAM.

HAGER, JEROME PETER MD, LICENSE NUMBER 00D2233, OF RIVERSIDE, CA, WAS DISCIPLINED BY TEXAS ON APRIL 16, 1994.
DISCIPLINARY ACTION: LICENSE REVOCATION
OFFENSE: DISCIPLINARY ACTION BY ANOTHER STATE OR AGENCY
NOTES: ON 12/19/92 CALIFORNIA BOARD ACCEPTED SURRENDER OF HIS LICENSE BASED ON FINDINGS THAT HE WAS GUILTY OF SEXUAL MISCONDUCT AND SEXUAL RELATIONS WITH TWO CASES WHO WERE PSYCHIATRIC PATIENTS, GROSS NEGLIGENCE AND GENERAL UNPROFESSIONAL CONDUCT. ORDER WILL BECOME FINAL WHEN APPEALS HAVE BEEN EXHAUSTED. HE HAS 20 DAYS TO FILE A MOTION FOR REHEARING.

HAIDINYAK, JOHN G MD, DATE OF BIRTH APRIL 13, 1949, OF 311 FAIRWAY DRIVE, NACOGDOCHES, TX, WAS DISCIPLINED BY MEDICARE ON NOVEMBER 9, 1989.
DISCIPLINARY ACTION: 60-MONTH EXCLUSION FROM THE MEDICARE AND/OR MEDICAID PROGRAMS
OFFENSE: CRIMINAL CONVICTION OR PLEA OF GUILTY, NOLO CONTENDERE, OR NO CONTEST TO A CRIME
NOTES: PROGRAM-RELATED CONVICTION.

HALBERT, DAVID S MD, LICENSE NUMBER 00C7626, OF ABILENE, TX, WAS DISCIPLINED BY TEXAS ON JANUARY 28, 1989.
DISCIPLINARY ACTION: REPRIMAND; REQUIRED TO TAKE ADDITIONAL MEDICAL EDUCATION
NOTES: SHALL COMPLETE PRECEPTORSHIP ON PREVENTION AND TREATMENT OF DRUG ABUSE

HALBERT, HORACE B MD OF P.O. DRAWER 518, ROSEBUD, TX, WAS DISCIPLINED BY MEDICARE ON MARCH 25, 1987.
DISCIPLINARY ACTION: 24-MONTH EXCLUSION FROM THE MEDICARE AND/OR MEDICAID PROGRAMS
OFFENSE: SUBSTANDARD CARE, INCOMPETENCE, OR NEGLIGENCE
NOTES: GROSSLY SUBSTANDARD CARE OF 8 PATIENTS. LACK OF KNOWLEDGE OF CURRENT MEDICAL MANAGEMENT OF HOSPITALIZED DIABETIC PATIENTS

HALBERT, HORACE B JR MD, LICENSE NUMBER 00C6965, OF ROSEBUD, TX, WAS DISCIPLINED BY TEXAS ON OCTOBER 29, 1988.
DISCIPLINARY ACTION: RESTRICTION PLACED ON LICENSE; REQUIRED TO TAKE ADDITIONAL MEDICAL EDUCATION
NOTES: MUST MODIFY CRITERIA FOR PRESCRIBING OR ADMINISTERING CERTAIN MEDICATIONS; SHALL NOT SERVE AS PHYSICIAN FOR SELF OR FAMILY; SHALL COMPLY WITH PRESCRIBED REGIMENT FOR MAINTENANCE OF OWN HEALTH; SHALL OBTAIN 50 HOURS OF CONTINUING MEDICAL EDUCATION PER YEAR; SHALL NOT PERFORM CERTAIN SURGERIES

UNLESS ASSISTED AS DIRECTED;

HALBERT, HORACE BURNARD JR MD, LICENSE NUMBER 00C6965, OF FRANKSTON, TX, WAS DISCIPLINED BY TEXAS ON JANUARY 14, 1994.
DISCIPLINARY ACTION: 60-MONTH PROBATION; REQUIRED TO TAKE ADDITIONAL MEDICAL EDUCATION
OFFENSE: FAILURE TO COMPLY WITH A PROFESSIONAL RULE
NOTES: INVESTIGATED ALLEGATIONS RELATED TO ALLEGED ACTION TAKEN BY TEXAS MEDICAL FOUNDATION; FOUND THAT MANY, IF NOT ALL OF HIS PROBLEMS AROSE FROM HIS FAILURE TO ADEQUATELY DOCUMENT PATIENT RECORDS DUE TO HIS EXTREMELY HEAVY PATIENT LOAD; HE DENIES ANY WRONGDOING. IN LIEU OF A CONTESTED CASE HEARING THIS AGREEMENT WAS REACHED. FIVE YEAR SUSPENSION STAYED. CONDITIONS OF PROBATION: SHALL APPEAR BEFORE THE BOARD ONCE A YEAR; SHALL ATTEND AT LEAST 50 HOURS PER YEAR OF CONTINUING MEDICAL EDUCATION; SHALL BE SUPERVISED BY A BOARD-APPROVED PHYSICIAN WITH REPORTS TO THE BOARD THREE TIMES A YEAR; SHALL MAINTAIN ADEQUATE MEDICAL RECORDS ON ALL PATIENT OFFICE VISITS WHICH SHALL BE AVAILABLE FOR REVIEW; SHALL COOPERATE WITH THE BOARD IN VERIFYING COMPLIANCE; SHALL INFORM BOARD OF CHANGE OF ADDRESS WITHIN 10 DAYS OR IF HE LEAVES THE STATE; TIME SPENT OUT OF TEXAS DOES NOT COUNT TOWARD PROBATION. SHALL NOT SEEK MODIFICATION FOR ONE YEAR.

HALCOMB, WILLIAM W DO, LICENSE NUMBER 00E5774, OF MESA, AZ, WAS DISCIPLINED BY TEXAS ON SEPTEMBER 28, 1990.
DISCIPLINARY ACTION: SURRENDER OF LICENSE

HALEY, RICHARD K DO, LICENSE NUMBER 00C9286, OF WESTERVILLE, OH, WAS DISCIPLINED BY TEXAS ON JANUARY 24, 1992.
DISCIPLINARY ACTION: LICENSE REVOCATION
OFFENSE: CRIMINAL CONVICTION OR PLEA OF GUILTY, NOLO CONTENDERE, OR NO CONTEST TO A CRIME
NOTES: CONVICTION OF FELONY.

HALEY, RONALD ANTHONY MD, LICENSE NUMBER 00D4663, OF HOUSTON, TX, WAS DISCIPLINED BY TEXAS ON APRIL 14, 1989.
OFFENSE: PROFESSIONAL MISCONDUCT
NOTES: SHALL FAMILIARIZE HIMSELF WITH LAWS AND RULES REGARDING PROPER DELEGATION OF AUTHORITY TO NON-PHYSICIANS AND COMPLY WITH SAME; SHALL BECOME FAMILIAR WITH PHYSICIAN RESPONSIBILITIES REGARDING UTILIZATION OF MEDICAL TECHNICIANS AND MEDICAL PERSONNEL AND COMPLY WITH SAME. ORDER TERMINATED ON 5/11/95.

HALFON, VICTOR J MD, DATE OF BIRTH DECEMBER 5, 1916, LICENSE NUMBER 00D1664, OF 6521 HARRISBURG, HOUSTON, TX, WAS DISCIPLINED BY TEXAS ON JUNE 15, 1993.
DISCIPLINARY ACTION: 60-MONTH RESTRICTION PLACED ON CONTROLLED SUBSTANCE LICENSE; REQUIRED TO TAKE ADDITIONAL MEDICAL EDUCATION
OFFENSE: DISCIPLINARY ACTION BY ANOTHER STATE OR AGENCY
NOTES: ON 7/19/91 DEA ISSUED AN ORDER TO SHOW CAUSE PROPOSING TO REVOKE HIS DEA CERTIFICATE ALLEGING THAT FROM 8/89 TO 1/90 HE SOLD AND DISPENSED PHENTERMINE, A SCHEDULE IV CONTROLLED SUBSTANCE TO DEA UNDERCOVER OFFICERS WITHOUT A LEGITIMATE MEDICAL PURPOSE; IN LIEU OF A HEARING AND WITHOUT ADMITTING TO CHARGES HE ENTERED INTO A MEMO OF AGREEMENT WITH THE DEA WITH VARIOUS CONDITIONS. LICENSE RESTRICTED FOR FIVE YEARS WITH THE FOLLOWING CONDITIONS: SHALL NOT DISPENSE ANY CONTROLLED SUBSTANCES OR SHALL NOT ORDER, REQUEST, PURCHASE OR RECEIVE ANY FOR OFFICE USE; SHALL PRESCRIBE NO MORE THAN A 14 A DAY SUPPLY OF CONTROLLED SUBSTANCES PER PATIENT FOR WEIGHT REDUCTION; SHALL MAINTAIN A SEPARATE FILE CONSISTING OF A COPY OF EVERY PRESCRIPTION WRITTEN FOR CONTROLLED SUBSTANCES WHICH SHALL BE AVAILABLE FOR INSPECTION; SHALL COMPLY WITH ALL TERMS OF DEA MEMORANDUM OF AGREEMENT; SHALL COMPLETE WITHIN ONE YEAR A CONTINUING MEDICAL EDUCATION PHARMACOLOGY COURSE OR COURSES FOR A TOTAL OF 20 HOURS OF CATEGORY I CREDITS; IN ADDITION SHALL COMPLETE 50 HOURS PER YEAR OF CATEGORY I CREDITS; SHALL APPEAR BEFORE THE BOARD ONCE A YEAR UPON REQUEST; SHALL GIVE A COPY OF THIS ORDER TO ANY HEALTH CARE ENTITY WHERE HE HAS PRIVILEGES; SHALL COOPERATE WITH THE BOARD IN VERIFYING COMPLIANCE; SHALL INFORM BOARD OF CHANGE OF ADDRESS WITHIN 10 DAYS OR IF HE LEAVES THE STATE; TIME SPENT OUT OF TEXAS DOES NOT COUNT TOWARD RESTRICTION. SHALL NOT SEEK MODIFICATION FOR ONE YEAR. ON 1/6/95 BOARD DENIED REQUEST TO TERMINATE THE ORDER; HOWEVER IT WAS MODIFIED SUCH THAT THE TIME ALLOWED FOR COMPLETION OF 20 HOURS OF A PHARMACOLOGY COURSE WAS EXTENDED TO WITHIN ONE YEAR OF THE MODIFICATION ORDER.

HALFON, VICTOR J MD, LICENSE NUMBER 00D1664, OF 6521 HARRISBURG, HOUSTON, TX, WAS DISCIPLINED BY DEA ON NOVEMBER 16, 1993.
DISCIPLINARY ACTION: RESTRICTION PLACED ON CONTROLLED SUBSTANCE LICENSE
NOTES: MEMORANDUM OF AGREEMENT SIGNED ON 08/29/91.

HALL, JAMES A MD, LICENSE NUMBER 0007604, OF ORMOND BEACH, FL, WAS DISCIPLINED BY FLORIDA ON DECEMBER 19, 1990.
DISCIPLINARY ACTION: SURRENDER OF LICENSE
NOTES: IN LIEU OF FURTHER PROSECUTION, AGREED TO NEVER AGAIN APPLY FOR LICENSURE IN FLORIDA.

HALL, JAMES A MD, LICENSE NUMBER 00C9003, OF DALLAS, TX, WAS DISCIPLINED BY TEXAS ON FEBRUARY 22, 1991.
DISCIPLINARY ACTION: REPRIMAND
OFFENSE: PROFESSIONAL MISCONDUCT
NOTES: ENGAGED IN INAPPROPRIATE PHYSICAL CONTACT WITH A PATIENT.

HAMAMCY, THARWAT DR OF MILLSAP, TX, WAS DISCIPLINED BY ILLINOIS ON OCTOBER 1, 1994.
DISCIPLINARY ACTION: LICENSE REVOCATION
OFFENSE: DISCIPLINARY ACTION BY ANOTHER STATE OR AGENCY
NOTES: DISCIPLINED IN TEXAS.

HAMAMCY, THARWAT M MD, DATE OF BIRTH SEPTEMBER 20, 1943, LICENSE NUMBER 00G2715, OF 925 SANTA ISABEL, LAGUNA VISTA, TX, WAS DISCIPLINED BY TEXAS ON JUNE 25, 1993.
DISCIPLINARY ACTION: LICENSE REVOCATION
OFFENSE: SUBSTANDARD CARE, INCOMPETENCE, OR NEGLIGENCE

NOTES: PRACTICE INCONSISTENT WITH PUBLIC HEALTH AND WELFARE INCLUDING: CHARGING A PATIENT 3 TIMES FOR THE SAME TREATMENT; DID NOT USE, AT THE PATIENT'S REQUEST, AN IV DURING A HERNIA OPERATION PERFORMED IN HIS OFFICE WHICH WAS IMPORTANT FOR THE PATIENT'S SAFETY; WROTE HIS OPERATIVE REPORT FOR THIS SURGERY TWO YEARS LATER TO SUBMIT TO THE BOARD WITH REPORT FALSELY DATED WITH THE DATE OF SURGERY; IN SEVERAL INSTANCES FAILED TO DOCUMENT IN MEDICAL RECORDS SUFFICIENT INFORMATION OF PATIENTS TO WHOM HE HAD GIVEN PRENATAL CARE; TREATED A PATIENT WITH FLAGYL DURING HER FIRST TRIMESTER EVEN THOUGH FLAGYL IS CONTRAINDICATED UNLESS OTHER TREATMENTS HAVE BEEN TRIED; FAILED TO ORDER PRENATAL LAB TESTS FOR ONE PATIENT; FAILED TO ARRANGE MEDICAL COVERAGE WITH ANOTHER DOCTOR IN HIS ABSENCE FOR THIS PATIENT; DID NOT TRANSFER THIS PATIENT TO A MORE APPROPRIATELY EQUIPPED HOSPITAL; FAILED TO ADEQUATELY TREAT THE HIGH BLOOD PRESSURE OF ANOTHER PATIENT. ORDER WILL BECOME FINAL WHEN ALL APPEALS HAVE BEEN EXHAUSTED.

HAMMOND, AULDINE COLQUHOU DO OF PO DRAWER 5726, BEAUMONT, TX, WAS DISCIPLINED BY DEA ON MAY 5, 1989.
DISCIPLINARY ACTION: SURRENDER OF CONTROLLED SUBSTANCE LICENSE
OFFENSE: PROFESSIONAL MISCONDUCT
NOTES: SUPPLIED 56 UNITS PHENDIMETRAZINE 01/21/88 IN LUMBERTON, TEXAS. EXCESSIVE PURCHASES OF PHENDIMETRAZINE. SOLD 168 UNITS OF 35 MG PHENDIMETRAZINE, 77 UNITS ZINC GLUCONATE, AND 84 UNITS WESTHROID FOR NONMEDICAL PURPOSES 03/14/88 IN LUMBERTON, TX. SOLD 336 PHENDIMETRAZINE TABS FOR NON-LEGITIMATE MEDICAL PURPOSE 04/05/88 AND 07/06/88 IN LUMBERTON. SEIZURE ON 08/03/88 IN LUMBERTON OF 52,164 UNITS PHENDIMETRAZINE AND REAL ESTATE WORTH $94,220. VOLUNTARY SURRENDER OF CONTROLLED SUBSTANCES PRIVILEGES ON 03/07/89.

HANSEN, WILLIAM M MD OF WESTMINSTER, CA, WAS DISCIPLINED BY TEXAS ON DECEMBER 1, 1986.
DISCIPLINARY ACTION: SURRENDER OF LICENSE

HANSON, MICHAEL W MD, LICENSE NUMBER 00F9532, OF PUEBLO, CO, WAS DISCIPLINED BY TEXAS ON DECEMBER 1, 1988.
DISCIPLINARY ACTION: PROBATION
OFFENSE: DISCIPLINARY ACTION BY ANOTHER STATE OR AGENCY
NOTES: REQUIRED TO COMPLY WITH COLORADO STATE BOARD ORDER AND OTHER RELATED CONDITIONS

HARDEY, CARLTON E MD, LICENSE NUMBER 00C3071, OF ARLINGTON, TX, WAS DISCIPLINED BY TEXAS ON FEBRUARY 26, 1990.
DISCIPLINARY ACTION: RESTRICTION PLACED ON LICENSE; REPRIMAND
OFFENSE: SUBSTANDARD CARE, INCOMPETENCE, OR NEGLIGENCE
NOTES: PROFESSIONAL FAILURE TO PRACTICE MEDICINE IN ACCEPTABLE MANNER CONSISTENT WITH PUBLIC HEALTH AND WELFARE. REQUIRED TO ATTEND RISK MANAGEMENT COURSE. MUST HAVE ATTENDANT PRESENT WHEN PERFORMING CERTAIN EXAMINATIONS. ON 6/22/94 THIS ORDER WAS TERMINATED.

HARDMAN, ROY E MD, LICENSE NUMBER 00D9481, OF SAN ANTONIO, TX, WAS DISCIPLINED BY TEXAS ON OCTOBER 5, 1991.
DISCIPLINARY ACTION: SURRENDER OF LICENSE
OFFENSE: OVERPRESCRIBING OR MISPRESCRIBING DRUGS
NOTES: BOARD INVESTIGATED ALLEGATIONS THAT HE ENGAGED IN FOLLOWING ACTIVITIES: CORPORATE PRACTICE AT THE BROADWAY CLINIC; ALLOWED DEA REGISTRATION TO BE USED BY A NONPHYSICIAN TO ORDER CONTROLLED SUBSTANCES; INAPPROPRIATELY PRESCRIBED DANGEROUS DRUGS IN COMBINATION WITH ANORECTIC MEDICATIONS; MISTREATMENT OF ONE PATIENT; INAPPROPRIATELY PRESCRIBED CONTROLLED SUBSTANCES TO 10 DIFFERENT PATIENTS; MISTREATED ONE PATIENT; FAILED TO COMPLY WITH BOARD'S SUBPOENA FOR PATIENTS' MEDICAL RECORDS. SHALL NOT SEEK RELICENSURE FOR AT LEAST ONE YEAR.

HARDMAN, ROY EUGENE MD, DATE OF BIRTH JUNE 6, 1935, LICENSE NUMBER 0057092, OF 665 LAKEWOOD LANE, MARQUETTE, MI, WAS DISCIPLINED BY MICHIGAN ON NOVEMBER 21, 1991.
DISCIPLINARY ACTION: EMERGENCY SUSPENSION
OFFENSE: CRIMINAL CONVICTION OR PLEA OF GUILTY, NOLO CONTENDERE, OR NO CONTEST TO A CRIME
NOTES: CRIMINAL SEXUAL CONDUCT CONVICTION.

HARDMAN, ROY EUGENE MD, DATE OF BIRTH JUNE 6, 1935, OF CHIPPEWA TEMP CORRECTIONAL FACIL, KINCHELOE, MI, WAS DISCIPLINED BY DEA ON OCTOBER 30, 1992.
DISCIPLINARY ACTION: REVOCATION OF CONTROLLED SUBSTANCE LICENSE
OFFENSE: DISCIPLINARY ACTION BY ANOTHER STATE OR AGENCY
NOTES: ON 11/20/91, MICHIGAN SUMMARILY SUSPENDED HIS MEDICAL LICENSE RESULTING IN A NULLIFICATION OF HIS CONTROLLED SUBSTANCE LICENSE.

HARDMAN, ROY EUGENE MD, DATE OF BIRTH JUNE 6, 1935, LICENSE NUMBER 0057092, OF 665 LAKEWOOD LANE, MARQUETTE, MI, WAS DISCIPLINED BY MICHIGAN ON NOVEMBER 30, 1993.
DISCIPLINARY ACTION: 12-MONTH LICENSE SUSPENSION
OFFENSE: CRIMINAL CONVICTION OR PLEA OF GUILTY, NOLO CONTENDERE, OR NO CONTEST TO A CRIME
NOTES: CONVICTION/CRIMINAL SEXUAL CONDUCT.

HARDY, ROBERT HOWARD MD, LICENSE NUMBER 00E6401, OF COLLEYVILLE, TX, WAS DISCIPLINED BY TEXAS ON APRIL 20, 1991.
DISCIPLINARY ACTION: 60-MONTH PROBATION; MONITORING OF PHYSICIAN
NOTES: CONDITIONS OF PROBATION INCLUDE: MUST APPEAR ANNUALLY BEFORE THE BOARD; MUST PARTICIPATE IN AA; MUST SUBMIT TO ALCOHOL OR DRUG SCREENS; MUST CONTINUE TREATMENT WITH SPECIFIED PHYSICIAN WHO WILL SUBMIT QUARTERLY REPORTS TO THE BOARD. ON 4/15/94 ORDER MODIFIED AS FOLLOWS: PARTICIPATION IN AA REDUCED TO ONCE A WEEK; REQUIREMENT OF QUARTERLY REPORTS TO THE BOARD FROM HIS TREATING PHYSICIAN MODIFIED TO BIANNUAL REPORTS.

HARGIS, THOMAS C MD OF RODEO, NM, WAS DISCIPLINED BY TEXAS ON SEPTEMBER 1, 1985.
OFFENSE: DISCIPLINARY ACTION BY ANOTHER STATE OR AGENCY
NOTES: MUST OBTAIN PRIOR BOARD APPROVAL TO RETURN TO TEXAS TO PRACTICE

HARGIS, THOMAS C MD, LICENSE NUMBER 0008441, WAS DISCIPLINED BY ARIZONA ON JUNE 20, 1991.
DISCIPLINARY ACTION: REQUIRED TO ENTER AN IMPAIRED PHYSICIAN PROGRAM OR DRUG OR ALCOHOL TREATMENT; MONITORING OF PHYSICIAN
OFFENSE: DRUG OR ALCOHOL ABUSE
NOTES: MUST IMMEDIATELY PARTICIPATE IN THE ARIZONA MEDICAL ASSOCIATION'S MONITORED AFTERCARE TREATMENT PROGRAM WHOSE THERAPIST MUST SUBMIT QUARTERLY REPORTS; SHALL PARTICIPATE IN 90 12-STEP MEETINGS APPROPRIATE FOR SUBSTANCE ABUSE AND ACCEPTABLE TO THE BOARD WITHIN 90 DAYS OF THIS ORDER; AFTER COMPLETION OF THIS REQUIREMENT, MUST PARTICIPATE IN A 12-STEP RECOVERY PROGRAM FOR SUBSTANCE ABUSE AND ATTEND AT LEAST 3 WEEKLY MEETINGS; SHALL OBTAIN A SOLE BOARD-APPROVED TREATING PHYSICIAN; SHALL ABSTAIN COMPLETELY FROM THE CONSUMPTION OF ALCOHOLIC BEVERAGES AND SHALL TAKE NO DRUGS OR MEDICATIONS UNLESS PRESCRIBED BY HIS TREATING PHYSICIAN; SHALL COMPLY WITH REQUESTS FOR RANDOM BODILY FLUID TESTS; SHALL MAINTAIN A LOG OF ANY AND ALL MEDICATIONS TAKEN; SHALL SUBMIT TO MENTAL, PHYSICAL OR MEDICAL COMPETENCY EXAMINATIONS, OR ANY THERAPY ORDERED BY THE BOARD; SHALL COMPLY WITH REQUESTS FOR RANDOM BIOLOGICAL FLUID TESTS; SHALL APPEAR BEFORE THE BOARD FOR INTERVIEWS UPON REQUEST AND MUST INFORM BOARD OF ADDRESS CHANGE OR IF AWAY FOR MORE THAN FIVE DAYS.

HARGIS, THOMAS C MD, LICENSE NUMBER 0008441, WAS DISCIPLINED BY ARIZONA ON JULY 15, 1994.
DISCIPLINARY ACTION: 60-MONTH PROBATION; REQUIRED TO ENTER AN IMPAIRED PHYSICIAN PROGRAM OR DRUG OR ALCOHOL TREATMENT
OFFENSE: FAILURE TO COMPLY WITH A PREVIOUS BOARD ORDER
NOTES: ON 6/20/91, ENTERED INTO A REHABILITATION STIPULATION INCLUDING A REQUIREMENT THAT HE TAKE NO DRUGS; SEVEN TIMES BETWEEN 8/91 AND 11/93 HE TESTED POSITIVE FOR DRUGS NOT PRESCRIBED BY TREATING PHYSICIAN; AS A RESULT, BOARD ORDERED EVALUATION FOR SUBSTANCE ABUSE; ENTERED LONG TERM RESIDENTIAL TREATMENT ON 3/2/94. MUST IMMEDIATELY PARTICIPATE IN A BOARD-APPROVED MONITORED AFTERCARE TREATMENT PROGRAM WHOSE THERAPIST MUST SUBMIT QUARTERLY REPORTS; MUST PARTICIPATE IN A 12-STEP RECOVERY PROGRAM AS DETERMINED BY HIS TREATING THERAPIST AND ATTEND AT LEAST THREE WEEKLY MEETINGS; SHALL OBTAIN A BOARD-APPROVED TREATING PHYSICIAN; SHALL ABSTAIN COMPLETELY FROM THE CONSUMPTION OF ALCOHOLIC BEVERAGES AND DRUGS EXCEPT WHEN PRESCRIBED BY HIS TREATING PHYSICIAN; MUST SUBMIT TO WITNESSED RANDOM BIOLOGICAL FLUID COLLECTION; KEEP A LOG OF ANY AND ALL MEDICATIONS PRESCRIBED FOR HIM; SHALL SUBMIT TO ANY EXAMINATIONS OR THERAPY ORDERED BY BOARD; SHALL APPEAR BEFORE BOARD FOR INTERVIEWS UPON REQUEST; SHALL INFORM BOARD OF CHANGE OF ADDRESS OR IF AWAY FOR MORE THAN FIVE DAYS.

HARRISON, JACK WINFRED MD, DATE OF BIRTH SEPTEMBER 10, 1935, LICENSE NUMBER 00D4777, OF 217 AVALON, DE SOTO, TX, WAS DISCIPLINED BY TEXAS ON JUNE 10, 1991.
DISCIPLINARY ACTION: 60-MONTH PROBATION; RESTRICTION PLACED ON LICENSE
OFFENSE: SUBSTANDARD CARE, INCOMPETENCE, OR NEGLIGENCE
NOTES: PROFESSIONAL INCOMPETENCE LIKELY TO INJURE THE PUBLIC, INABILITY TO PRACTICE MEDICINE WITH REASONABLE SKILL AND SAFETY TO PATIENTS, AND INTEMPERATE USE OF ALCOHOL OR DRUGS. SHALL NOT PERFORM ANY SURGERY; MUST SUBMIT TO ALCOHOL OR DRUG SCREENS. ON 8/20/93 ORDER TERMINATED AND LICENSE FREE AND CLEAR OF ANY PREVIOUS RESTRICTIONS.

HART, WALTER F MD, LICENSE NUMBER 00B7075, OF GLADEWATER, TX, WAS DISCIPLINED BY TEXAS ON AUGUST 25, 1989.
DISCIPLINARY ACTION: SURRENDER OF LICENSE

HARTHCOCK, KERRY A MD WAS DISCIPLINED BY WASHINGTON ON APRIL 15, 1988.
DISCIPLINARY ACTION: PROBATION; REQUIRED TO ENTER AN IMPAIRED PHYSICIAN PROGRAM OR DRUG OR ALCOHOL TREATMENT
OFFENSE: DRUG OR ALCOHOL ABUSE
NOTES: LICENSE ISSUED ON INDEFINITE PROBATION; RANDOM URINE TESTS; SHALL PARTICIPATE IN NARCOTICS ANONYMOUS OR AA TWICE WEEKLY WITH QUARTERLY REPORTS TO THE BOARD; REGULAR INTERVIEWS WITH THE BOARD; SHALL SUBMIT QUARTERLY PROGRESS REPORTS TO THE BOARD. MONITORED TREATMENT PROGRAM HAD BEEN REQUIRED BY PREVIOUS BOARD ORDER.

HARTHCOCK, KERRY ALFRED MD, LICENSE NUMBER 00G1428, OF SEATTLE, WA, WAS DISCIPLINED BY TEXAS ON JANUARY 26, 1990.
OFFENSE: DISCIPLINARY ACTION BY ANOTHER STATE OR AGENCY
NOTES: STIPULATED ORDER. SHALL COMPLY WITH PROBATIONARY REQUIREMENTS OF WASHINGTON BOARD ORDER, TEXAS BOARD TO HAVE ACCESS TO WASHINGTON BOARD DOCUMENTS, MUST OBTAIN APPROVAL FROM TEXAS BOARD PRIOR TO PRACTICING IN TEXAS. AS OF 4/20/91 PROBATION TERMINATED; LICENSE FREE OF ANY RESTRICTION OR LIMITATION.

HARTIN, RICHARD B JR MD, DATE OF BIRTH NOVEMBER 29, 1952, LICENSE NUMBER 00G6524, OF 2506 GRANDRIDGE TRAIL, CEDAR PARK, TX, WAS DISCIPLINED BY TEXAS ON JUNE 10, 1991.
DISCIPLINARY ACTION: 60-MONTH PROBATION; MONITORING OF PHYSICIAN
OFFENSE: LOSS OR RESTRICTION OF HOSPITAL PRIVILEGES
NOTES: INABILITY TO PRACTICE MEDICINE WITH REASONABLE SKILL AND SAFETY, LOSS OF HOSPITAL PRIVILEGES, AND UNPROFESSIONAL CONDUCT OR PROFESSIONAL INCOMPETENCE LIKELY TO HARM THE PUBLIC. SHALL SUBMIT TO ALCOHOL OR DRUG SCREENS; SHALL CONTINUE TO PARTICIPATE IN ACTIVITIES OF IMPAIRED PHYSICIANS PROGRAM. ON 8/20/93 ORDER TERMINATED AND LICENSE FREE AND CLEAR OF ANY PREVIOUS RESTRICTIONS.

HARTLEY, LAWRENCE J MD OF 100 MEDICAL DR, LAKE JACKSON, TX, WAS DISCIPLINED BY DEA ON JULY 3, 1990.
DISCIPLINARY ACTION: SURRENDER OF CONTROLLED SUBSTANCE LICENSE
NOTES: PLACED ON FIVE YEARS PROBATION BY TEXAS STATE BOARD OF MEDICAL EXAMINERS.

HARTLEY, LAWRENCE JUSTICE MD, LICENSE NUMBER 00C8117, OF LAKE JACKSON, TX, WAS DISCIPLINED BY TEXAS ON MAY 24, 1990.
DISCIPLINARY ACTION: SURRENDER OF CONTROLLED SUBSTANCE LICENSE; 60-MONTH PROBATION
NOTES: STIPULATED ORDER. MUST APPEAR BEFORE BOARD TWICE YEARLY, SURRENDER CONTROLLED SUBSTANCES REGISTRATION CERTIFICATES AND ALL UNUSED TRIPLICATE PRESCRIPTION FORMS AND NOT ATTEMPT TO ORDER MORE, COMPLETE PRECEPTORSHIP ON PREVENTION AND TREATMENT OF DRUG ABUSE, NOT TREAT OR OFFER TO TREAT ANY DISEASE OR DISORDER OR ANY PHYSICAL DEFORMITY OR INJURY BY ANY SYSTEM OR METHOD OR TO EFFECT CURES THEREOF, AND NOT PRESCRIBE FOR OR TREAT ANY PATIENTS EXCEPT IN EMERGENCY SITUATIONS. ON 10/1/93, ORDER TERMINATED.

HASKELL, ROBERT MD, DATE OF BIRTH JANUARY 28, 1926, LICENSE NUMBER 0A29045, OF SAN RAFAEL, CA, WAS DISCIPLINED BY CALIFORNIA ON MARCH 1, 1992.
DISCIPLINARY ACTION: 60-MONTH PROBATION
OFFENSE: SUBSTANDARD CARE, INCOMPETENCE, OR NEGLIGENCE
NOTES: REPEATED NEGLIGENT ACTS IN WEIGHT REDUCTION PRACTICE; INCLUDING MULTIPLE REPEATED INJECTIONS OF VITAMIN B12, CHROMIUM AND PROCAINE; REPEATED USE OF THYROID EXTRACT FOR WEIGHT LOSS; FAILURE TO MONITOR FOR SIDE EFFECTS. REVOCATION, STAYED. PROBATION WITH TERMS AND CONDITIONS.

HASKELL, ROBERT DO, LICENSE NUMBER 00D2787, OF SAN RAFAEL, CA, WAS DISCIPLINED BY TEXAS ON MARCH 5, 1994.
DISCIPLINARY ACTION: SURRENDER OF LICENSE
OFFENSE: DISCIPLINARY ACTION BY ANOTHER STATE OR AGENCY
NOTES: ON 12/9/91 LICENSE WAS SANCTIONED BY CALIFORNIA BOARD FOR REPEATED NEGLIGENT ACTS IN THE CARE AND TREATMENT OF ONE PATIENT. HE DOES NOT WISH TO MAINTAIN A TEXAS LICENSE OR CONTEST THE CALIFORNIA PROCEEDINGS. LICENSE IS SURRENDERED IN LIEU OF FURTHER DISCIPLINARY ACTION.

HASSMANN, GARY C MD, LICENSE NUMBER 00E3302, OF TEMPLE, TX, WAS DISCIPLINED BY TEXAS ON SEPTEMBER 24, 1988.
DISCIPLINARY ACTION: LICENSE REVOCATION
OFFENSE: CRIMINAL CONVICTION OR PLEA OF GUILTY, NOLO CONTENDERE, OR NO CONTEST TO A CRIME
NOTES: CONVICTED OF FELONY; HAD HOSPITAL PRIVILEGES REMOVED ON BASIS OF UNPROFESSIONAL CONDUCT, ENGAGED IN UNPROFESSIONAL OR DISHONORABLE CONDUCT LIKELY TO DECEIVE, DEFRAUD OR INJURE PUBLIC; FAILED TO PRACTICE MEDICINE IN ACCEPTABLE MANNER CONSISTENT WITH PUBLIC HEALTH AND WELFARE

HASSMANN, GARY C MD, DATE OF BIRTH APRIL 6, 1941, OF POST OFFICE BOX 1000, EL RENO, OK, WAS DISCIPLINED BY MEDICARE ON APRIL 13, 1989.
DISCIPLINARY ACTION: EXCLUSION FROM THE MEDICARE AND/OR MEDICAID PROGRAMS
OFFENSE: DISCIPLINARY ACTION BY ANOTHER STATE OR AGENCY
NOTES: LICENSE REVOCATION OR SUSPENSION.

HASSMANN, GARY CHARLES MD, LICENSE NUMBER 0017579, OF 3207 RIVERSIDE DR, TULSA, OK, WAS DISCIPLINED BY OKLAHOMA ON FEBRUARY 1, 1991.
DISCIPLINARY ACTION: 60-MONTH PROBATION; RESTRICTION PLACED ON LICENSE
NOTES: LICENSED UNDER PROBATIONARY TERMS AND CONDITIONS: MUST NOT PRESCRIBE, ADMINISTER OR DISPENSE ANY MEDICATIONS, INCLUDING CONTROLLED DANGEROUS SUBSTANCES, FOR HIS PERSONAL USE; MUST NOT PRESCRIBE, ADMINISTER OR DISPENSE ANY SCHEDULE DRUGS, OR ANY LEGEND DRUGS PRIOR TO OBTAINING PERMISSION FROM BOARD; MUST ABSTAIN FROM ALCOHOL OR ANY SUBSTANCE WHICH WOULD ADVERSELY AFFECT HIS ABILITY TO PRACTICE OR ANY MEDICATION NOT PRESCRIBED BY HIS DOCTOR; MUST SUBMIT BIOLOGICAL FLUID SPECIMENS FOR ANALYSIS; MUST TAKE SPEX; SHALL COMPLETE 50 HOURS OF CLASS I CONTINUING MEDICAL EDUCATION EACH YEAR OF PROBATION; SHALL NOT PERFORM ANY SURGERY OR SURGICAL PROCEDURES UNTIL FURTHER ORDER; SHALL NOTIFY ANY HOSPITAL WHERE HE HOLDS STAFF PRIVILEGES, OR CLINIC OR GROUP OF THE TERMS AND CONDITIONS; SHALL FURNISH BOARD WITH ADDRESS AND/OR CHANGE OF ADDRESS; SHALL APPEAR BEFORE BOARD UPON REQUEST. ON 3/11/93 MOTION TO TERMINATE PROBATION DENIED. ON 2/18/94 ORDER MODIFIED ALLOWING HIM TO PRESCRIBE, ADMINISTER OR DISPENSE LEGEND DRUGS BUT ONLY ON SERIALLY NUMBERED DUPLICATE PRESCRIPTION PADS WITH COPIES AVAILABLE TO THE BOARD; PROVISIONS REQUIRING HIM TO SUBMIT BIOLOGICAL FLUID SPECIMENS FOR ANALYSIS WERE DROPPED.

HASSMANN, GARY CHARLES MD, LICENSE NUMBER 0017579, WAS DISCIPLINED BY OKLAHOMA ON NOVEMBER 18, 1994.
DISCIPLINARY ACTION: MONITORING OF PHYSICIAN
OFFENSE: DRUG OR ALCOHOL ABUSE
NOTES: ON 2/11/94 BOARD HAD MODIFIED TERMS OF PREVIOUS PROBATION DELETING REQUIREMENTS THAT HE ABSTAIN FROM THE CONSUMPTION OF ALCOHOL AND TO SUBMIT BIOLOGICAL FLUID SPECIMENS; WAS ARRESTED FOR DRIVING UNDER THE INFLUENCE OF ALCOHOL ON 3/25/94. THESE TWO REQUIREMENTS WERE REINSTATED AND ALL OTHER TERMS OF PROBATION STILL IN EFFECT.

HAUSER, BILL OLIVER MD, LICENSE NUMBER 00D0158, OF SAN ANTONIO, TX, WAS DISCIPLINED BY TEXAS ON JANUARY 24, 1992.
DISCIPLINARY ACTION: 36-MONTH PROBATION
OFFENSE: PROFESSIONAL MISCONDUCT
NOTES: AIDING OR ABETTING, DIRECTLY OR INDIRECTLY, THE PRACTICE OF MEDICINE BY ANY PERSON, PARTNERSHIP, ASSOCIATION, OR CORPORATION NOT DULY LICENSED TO PRACTICE MEDICINE BY THE BOARD. LICENSE SUSPENDED, SUSPENSION STAYED; PROBATION UNDER TERMS AND CONDITIONS.

HAVARD, THOMAS III DO, LICENSE NUMBER 00E5103, OF LUFKIN, TX, WAS DISCIPLINED BY TEXAS ON APRIL 1, 1987.
DISCIPLINARY ACTION: LICENSE SUSPENSION

HAVARD, THOMAS JEFFERSON III DO, LICENSE NUMBER 0016924, OF PO BOX 1, HUNT, TX, WAS DISCIPLINED BY GEORGIA ON JANUARY 13, 1988.
DISCIPLINARY ACTION: LICENSE SUSPENSION
OFFENSE: DISCIPLINARY ACTION BY ANOTHER STATE OR AGENCY

HAVARD, THOMAS JEFFERSON III DO, LICENSE NUMBER 0016924, OF PO BOX 1, HUNT, TX, WAS DISCIPLINED BY GEORGIA ON NOVEMBER 14, 1988.

DISCIPLINARY ACTION: PROBATION
OFFENSE: DISCIPLINARY ACTION BY ANOTHER STATE OR AGENCY
NOTES: ACTION IN TEXAS. SUSPENSION LIFTED BUT STILL ON PROBATION.

HAWKINS, ELMER JOHN MD, LICENSE NUMBER 00B8604, OF JAYTON, TX, WAS DISCIPLINED BY TEXAS ON APRIL 1, 1987.
DISCIPLINARY ACTION: SURRENDER OF LICENSE

HAWKINS, LARRY R MD, LICENSE NUMBER 00G3441, OF AUSTIN, TX, WAS DISCIPLINED BY TEXAS ON DECEMBER 1, 1988.
DISCIPLINARY ACTION: RESTRICTION PLACED ON LICENSE
OFFENSE: CRIMINAL CONVICTION OR PLEA OF GUILTY, NOLO CONTENDERE, OR NO CONTEST TO A CRIME
NOTES: REQUIRED TO COMPLY WITH COURT PROBATION TERMS AND LIMIT HIMSELF TO PRESENT PRACTICE FOR AT LEAST 18 MONTHS;CONVICTED OF FELONY FOR INDECENCY WITH A CHILD.

HAYS, HARVEY JR MD, LICENSE NUMBER 00C2491, OF BORGER, TX, WAS DISCIPLINED BY TEXAS ON APRIL 10, 1992.
DISCIPLINARY ACTION: 36-MONTH PROBATION
OFFENSE: SUBSTANDARD CARE, INCOMPETENCE, OR NEGLIGENCE
NOTES: PROFESSIONAL FAILURE TO PRACTICE MEDICINE IN AN ACCEPTABLE MANNER CONSISTENT WITH PUBLIC HEALTH AND WELFARE. LICENSE SUSPENDED, SUSPENSION STAYED; PROBATION UNDER TERMS AND CONDITIONS.

HAYS, HARVEY JR MD, LICENSE NUMBER 00C2491, OF BORGER, TX, WAS DISCIPLINED BY TEXAS ON JUNE 22, 1994.
DISCIPLINARY ACTION: RESTRICTION PLACED ON LICENSE; RESTRICTION PLACED ON CONTROLLED SUBSTANCE LICENSE
OFFENSE: FAILURE TO COMPLY WITH A PREVIOUS BOARD ORDER
NOTES: HE ENTERED AN AGREED ORDER ON 4/10/92 BASED ON FINDINGS THAT HE HAD PRESCRIBED METHADONE TO A PATIENT WITHOUT BEING REGISTERED AS A METHADONE CLINIC AND HAD PRESCRIBED CONTROLLED SUBSTANCES TO ADDICTED INDIVIDUALS; ONE OF THE CONDITIONS OF THE ORDER WAS THAT HE COMPLETE A PHARMACOLOGY RETRAINING COURSE WITHIN SIX MONTHS; HAS FAILED TO COMPLETE SUCH A COURSE; HIS FAILURE TO COMPLY HAS BEEN CONTRIBUTED TO BY TEMPORARY HEALTH PROBLEMS WHICH HE HAS EXPERIENCED; HAS SURRENDERED HIS DEA AND TEXAS CONTROLLED SUBSTANCES CERTIFICATES, ALL UNUSED TRIPLICATE PRESCRIPTION FORMS AND ALL CONTROLLED SUBSTANCES; HAS CEASED PRIVATE PRACTICE AND IS NOT INVOLVED IN DIRECT PATIENT SERVICES. SHALL NOT ATTEMPT TO REENTER PRIVATE PRACTICE OR BE INVOLVED IN DIRECT PATIENT SERVICES; SHALL NOT ATTEMPT TO REREGISTER CONTROLLED SUBSTANCES CERTIFICATES WITHOUT BOARD PERMISSION; SHALL GIVE A COPY OF THIS ORDER TO ANY HEALTH CARE ENTITY WHERE HE HAS PRIVILEGES; SHALL COOPERATE WITH THE BOARD IN VERIFYING COMPLIANCE; SHALL INFORM BOARD OF CHANGE OF ADDRESS WITHIN 10 DAYS. SHALL NOT SEEK MODIFICATION FOR ONE YEAR.

HEAD, WILLIAM J III MD, DATE OF BIRTH JANUARY 29, 1954, LICENSE NUMBER 0033365, OF 4126 SOUTHWEST FREEWAY, STE 500, HOUSTON, TX, WAS DISCIPLINED BY MINNESOTA ON SEPTEMBER 12, 1992.
OFFENSE: DISCIPLINARY ACTION BY ANOTHER STATE OR AGENCY
NOTES: SUSPENSION STAYED UPON COMPLIANCE WITH THE FOLLOWING: SHALL COMPLY WITH ALL TERMS AND CONDITIONS IMPOSED ON TEXAS LICENSE. SHALL CAUSE COMPLIANCE REPORT TO BE SENT FROM TEXAS BOARD. IF HE MOVES TO MINNESOTA TO PRACTICE, SHALL MEET WITH COMPLAINT REVIEW COMMITTEE WHICH MAY THEN CONDITION OR RESTRICT HIS LICENSE AS DEEMED NECESSARY.

HEAD, WILLIAM JUSTUS III MD, LICENSE NUMBER 00F6730, OF HOUSTON, TX, WAS DISCIPLINED BY TEXAS ON SEPTEMBER 5, 1991.
DISCIPLINARY ACTION: 60-MONTH PROBATION; RESTRICTION PLACED ON LICENSE
OFFENSE: SUBSTANDARD CARE, INCOMPETENCE, OR NEGLIGENCE
NOTES: PERFORMED A CATARACT EXTRACTION AND AN INTRAOCULAR LENS IMPLANT IN A PATIENT ON 1/26/88; THE SURGERY WAS UNNECESSARY. REVOCATION STAYED; TERMS OF PROBATION INCLUDE; ATTENDING AT LEAST 40 HOURS APPROVED CATEGORY I CONTINUING MEDICAL EDUCATION PER YEAR; MUST ATTEND 10 HOURS OF AN ETHICS COURSE OR PROGRAM PER YEAR FOR FIVE YEARS; SHALL PERFORM NO PROCEDURE INVOLVING SURGERY ON THE ADNEXA OF THE EYE UNLESS HE FIRST OBTAINS A SECOND OPINION FROM AN OPHTHALMOLOGIST WHO CONCURS WITH THE DECISION TO PERFORM THE SURGERY; MUST PERFORM 50 HOURS PER MONTH OF COMMUNITY SERVICE; MUST APPEAR BEFORE THE BOARD TWO TIMES A YEAR; TIME SPENT OUT OF TEXAS DOES NOT COUNT TOWARDS PROBATION. ON 11/19/93 PROBATION MODIFIED: HE MAY PERFORM MEDICALLY NECESSARY SURGERY ON THE ADNEXA OF THE EYE WITHOUT OBTAINING A CONCURRING SECOND OPINION FROM ANOTHER OPHTHALMOLOGIST; SHALL NOT, HOWEVER, PERFORM INTRAOCULAR PROCEDURES REQUIRING AN INCISION INTO THE EYE OF ANY KIND UNLESS HE FIRST OBTAINS A SECOND OPINION FROM AN OPHTHALMOLOGIST WHO CONCURS WITH HIS DECISION TO PERFORM THE PROCEDURE. PHYSICIANS WHO PROVIDE SUCH A SECOND OPINION SHALL HAVE NO BUSINESS RELATIONSHIP WITH HIM. ON 11/3/94 ORDER MODIFIED AS FOLLOWS: REQUIREMENT THAT HE NOT PERFORM INTRAOCULAR PROCEDURES REQUIRING AN INCISION INTO THE EYE UNLESS HE FIRST OBTAINS A SECOND OPINION FROM AN OPHTHALMOLOGIST IS DELETED AND HIS RECORDS OF ANY SURGERY PREFORMED SHALL BE SUBJECT TO RANDOM REVIEW.

HEADLEY, DAVID M MD OF PORT GIBSON, MS, WAS DISCIPLINED BY LOUISIANA ON OCTOBER 26, 1989.
OFFENSE: DISCIPLINARY ACTION BY ANOTHER STATE OR AGENCY
NOTES: INVESTIGATION RELATIVE TO SUSPECTED DISPENSING OF CONTROLLED SUBSTANCES IN OTHER THAN A LEGAL OR LEGITIMATE MANNER AND DISCIPLINARY ACTION AGAINST MEDICAL LICENSE BY MISSISSIPPI; MUST STRICTLY COMPLY WITH TERMS AND CONDITIONS MANDATED BY MISSISSIPPI, MUST INFORM BOARD OF INTENT TO RELOCATE TO LOUISIANA.

HEADLEY, DAVID M MD, LICENSE NUMBER 00G0724, OF PORT GIBSON, MS, WAS DISCIPLINED BY TEXAS ON AUGUST 18, 1990.
OFFENSE: DISCIPLINARY ACTION BY ANOTHER STATE OR AGENCY
NOTES: STIPULATED ORDER. MUST COMPLY WITH MISSISSIPPI BOARD ORDER AND OBTAIN PERMISSION OF BOARD

BEFORE PRACTICING IN TEXAS AND COMPLY WITH ANY PROBATIONARY TERMS WHICH MAY BE IMPOSED.

HEADLEY, DAVID M MD OF PORT GIBSON, MS, WAS DISCIPLINED BY DEA ON OCTOBER 29, 1993.
DISCIPLINARY ACTION: DENIAL OF LICENSE REINSTATEMENT
OFFENSE: DRUG OR ALCOHOL ABUSE
NOTES: IN 7/88 THE MISSISSIPPI BOARD RECEIVED COMPLAINTS REGARDING HIS ALLEGED POOR HANDLING OF OBSTETRICS AND GYNECOLOGICAL PATIENTS, HIS ALLEGED PERSONAL ABUSE OF NON-CONTROLLED SUBSTANCES, AS WELL AS PROBLEMS INVOLVING HIS ASSAULT AND BATTERY ON HIS WIFE. BOARD'S INVESTIGATION REVEALED THAT BETWEEN EARLY 1987 AND LATE 1988 HE PRESCRIBED LARGE QUANTITIES OF FIORINAL, HALCION, DARVON AND DARVOCET FOR HIS WIFE'S PERSONAL USE AND FAILED TO MAINTAIN AN INVENTORY OF THE NON-CONTROLLED SUBSTANCES THAT HE DISPENSED AND ADMINISTERED. HE ENTERED INTO A CONSENT AGREEMENT WITH THE MISSISSIPPI MEDICAL BOARD ON 9/28/88 IN WHICH HE WAS ORDERED NOT TO DISPENSE, ADMINISTER OR PRESCRIBE TO HIMSELF OR FAMILY MEMBERS ANY ADDICTIVE DRUGS, AND TO SUBMIT TO RANDOM URINE AND/OR BLOOD SCREENS. TESTED POSITIVE ON TWO OCCASIONS FOR CONTROLLED SUBSTANCES USE. AS A RESULT, THE BOARD ISSUED AN ORDER EFFECTIVE 8/11/89 PROHIBITING HIM FROM PRACTICING MEDICINE IN MISSISSIPPI UNTIL HE UNDERGOES AN EVALUATION FOR CHEMICAL DEPENDENCY AND IS DEEMED CAPABLE OF RETURNING TO PRACTICE. ON 10/24/89, HE ENTERED INTO A SECOND CONSENT AGREEMENT WHERE HE WAS ORDERED TO SUBMIT TO RANDOM, UNANNOUNCED URINE AND/OR BLOOD SCREENS FOR A PERIOD OF AT LEAST FIVE YEARS AND MUST SUCCESSFULLY COMPLETE ALL REQUIRED PHASES OF TREAMENT AT MISSISSIPPI IMPAIRED PROFESSIONALS PROGRAM; HE WAS ALSO ORDERED TO SURRENDER HIS DEA CERTIFICATE OF REGISTRATION.

HEALING, ROBERT DYSON MD, LICENSE NUMBER 00G2986, OF HAMLIN, TX, WAS DISCIPLINED BY TEXAS ON JUNE 17, 1992.
DISCIPLINARY ACTION: 36-MONTH RESTRICTION PLACED ON LICENSE
OFFENSE: SUBSTANDARD CARE, INCOMPETENCE, OR NEGLIGENCE
NOTES: NONTHERAPEUTIC PRESCRIBING AND PROFESSIONAL FAILURE TO PRACTICE MEDICINE IN AN ACCEPTABLE MANNER CONSISTENT WITH PUBLIC HEALTH AND WELFARE. ON 8/19/94 ORDER TERMINATED.

HEDGES, DON W DO, DATE OF BIRTH OCTOBER 2, 1940, OF 6463 FOURTH STREET NW, ALBUQUERQUE, NM, WAS DISCIPLINED BY MEDICARE ON JUNE 14, 1991.
DISCIPLINARY ACTION: 60-MONTH EXCLUSION FROM THE MEDICARE AND/OR MEDICAID PROGRAMS
OFFENSE: CRIMINAL CONVICTION OR PLEA OF GUILTY, NOLO CONTENDERE, OR NO CONTEST TO A CRIME
NOTES: PROGRAM-RELATED CONVICTION.

HEDGES, DON WALTER DO, LICENSE NUMBER 00E3303, OF ALBUQUERQUE, NM, WAS DISCIPLINED BY TEXAS ON MARCH 5, 1994.
DISCIPLINARY ACTION: REPRIMAND
OFFENSE: INSURANCE, MEDICARE, OR MEDICAID FRAUD
NOTES: WHILE PRACTICING IN NEW MEXICO HE INTENTIONALLY SUBMITTED INACCURATE DIAGNOSES TO MEDICARE FOR FIVE PATIENTS HE WAS TREATING WITH A DIET PLAN SO THAT HE WOULD RECEIVE REIMBURSEMENT SINCE THE DIET PLAN WAS NOT A COVERED BENEFIT.

HELFER, LEWIS M MD, LICENSE NUMBER 00B4517, OF NO 4 FLINTSTONE COURT, SAN ANTONIO, TX, WAS DISCIPLINED BY DEA ON NOVEMBER 16, 1993.
DISCIPLINARY ACTION: RESTRICTION PLACED ON CONTROLLED SUBSTANCE LICENSE

HENNARD, GEORGES MARCEL MD, LICENSE NUMBER 00F3494, OF HOUSTON, TX, WAS DISCIPLINED BY TEXAS ON OCTOBER 27, 1989.
DISCIPLINARY ACTION: 60-MONTH PROBATION; RESTRICTION PLACED ON LICENSE
NOTES: STIPULATED ORDER. REVOCATION STAYED. MUST REFRAIN FROM ACCEPTING EMPLOYMENT OR ENTERING INTO CERTAIN CONTRACTUAL RELATIONSHIPS, MUST NOT TREAT PATIENTS FOR WEIGHT CONTROL OR OBESITY WITH CONTROLLED SUBSTANCES, DANGEROUS DRUGS, OR OVER-THE-COUNTER DRUGS BUT MAY TREAT WITH COUNSELING, DIET, AND EXERCISE REGIMEN, MUST APPEAR ANNUALLY BEFORE BOARD, ORDER CONSTITUTES A PUBLIC REPRIMAND. PROBATION TERMINATED EFFECTIVE 12/4/91; LICENSE FREE OF ANY RESTRICTION OR LIMITATION.

HERMAN, WESLEY K MD, LICENSE NUMBER 00G0727, OF DALLAS, TX, WAS DISCIPLINED BY TEXAS ON DECEMBER 1, 1988.
NOTES: SETTLEMENT AGREEMENT AND UNSPECIFIED DISCIPLINARY ACTION

HERNANDEZ, ARTHUR MD, LICENSE NUMBER 00G1674, OF SAN ANTONIO, TX, WAS DISCIPLINED BY TEXAS ON OCTOBER 5, 1991.
DISCIPLINARY ACTION: REPRIMAND
OFFENSE: SUBSTANDARD CARE, INCOMPETENCE, OR NEGLIGENCE
NOTES: ON 8/14/87 HE INFUSED A PATIENT WITH APPROPRIATE ANESTHETIC MEDICATIONS FOR SURGERY; AFTER DRUGS WERE ADMINISTERED THE SURGERY WAS CANCELLED; HE REVERSED, TO THE EXTENT POSSIBLE, THE NARCOTIC PREVIOUSLY ADMINISTERED, AND CHOSE NOT TO REVERSE THE MUSCLE RELAXANT SINCE THE DOSE WAS SMALL; PATIENT SUFFERED A SEIZURE AND BRAIN DAMAGE DUE TO DEPRIVATION OF OXYGEN; FAILED TO TAKE ADEQUATE PRECAUTIONS TO SAFEGUARD PATIENT'S HEALTH DESPITE AVAILABLE INFORMATION WHICH MAY HAVE SUGGESTED POOR OXYGEN EXCHANGE; HOSPITAL REPRIMANDED HIM FOR ERRORS IN JUDGMENT; REVIEWED 100 PERCENT OF HIS CASES FOR SIX MONTHS; FOUND THAT HIS PROFESSIONAL CONDUCT USUALLY FOLLOWS ACCEPTABLE STANDARDS OF CARE AND THAT THIS INCIDENT DID NOT REPRESENT HIS TYPICAL CARE; HAS SUCCESSFULLY COMPLETED THE SIX MONTH REVIEW AND HAS HAD NO SUBSEQUENT PROBLEMS.

HEWELL, GEORGE M MD, LICENSE NUMBER 00D9493, OF PLANO, TX, WAS DISCIPLINED BY TEXAS ON DECEMBER 4, 1989.
DISCIPLINARY ACTION: 24-MONTH RESTRICTION PLACED ON CONTROLLED SUBSTANCE LICENSE; REQUIRED TO TAKE ADDITIONAL MEDICAL EDUCATION
OFFENSE: DRUG OR ALCOHOL ABUSE
NOTES: STIPULATED ORDER. MUST COMPLETE PRECEPTORSHIP ON PREVENTION AND TREATMENT OF DRUG ABUSE, MUST NOT PRESCRIBE FOR SELF OR

FAMILY, MUST SUBMIT FOR APPROPRIATE EXAMINATIONS TO DETERMINE FREEDOM FROM DRUGS AND ALCOHOL, MUST NOT ADMINISTER OR POSSESS SCHEDULE II CONTROLLED DRUGS EXCEPT FOR HOSPITALIZED PATIENTS, MUST MAINTAIN SEPARATE FILE OF PRESCRIPTIONS WRITTEN FOR SCHEDULED CONTROLLED SUBSTANCES, MUST NOT TELEPHONE TO PHARMACIES OF PRESCRIPTIONS FOR SCHEDULED CONTROLLED SUBSTANCES, MUST SURRENDER UNUSED TRIPLICATE PRESCRIPTIONS FORMS AND NOT ORDER MORE WITHOUT BOARD PERMISSION.

HICKS, RAYMOND D MD, LICENSE NUMBER 00D9495, OF DALLAS, TX, WAS DISCIPLINED BY TEXAS ON AUGUST 19, 1994.
DISCIPLINARY ACTION: LICENSE SUSPENSION; 120-MONTH PROBATION
OFFENSE: SEXUAL ABUSE OF OR SEXUAL MISCONDUCT WITH A PATIENT
NOTES: IN 10/93 STAFF AT A CLINIC REPORTED ALCOHOL ON HIS BREATH; ADMITTED TO IMPAIRED PHYSICIAN'S COMMITTEE THAT HE HAD BEEN DRINKING REGULARLY DURING OFFICE HOURS; PRIVILEGES WERE SUSPENDED AND HE ENTERED ALCOHOL TREATMENT; NOTIFIED THE BOARD OF THIS ON 11/17/93; TREATMENT RECORDS REVEALED A LENGTHY HISTORY OF DEPRESSIVE SYMPTOMS BECOMING MORE SEVERE FOLLOWING A MYOCARDIAL INFARCTION IN 1985; ADMITTED TO DRINKING REGULARLY THROUGHOUT THE DAY SINCE 1986; DURING TREATMENT REVEALED A HISTORY OF SEXUAL ACTIVITY WITH PATIENTS AND PROSTITUTES AS LATE AS 7/93; IN 11/92 HE PLED NO CONTEST TO CHARGES OF SOLICITATION OF PROSTITUTION; REQUESTED EVALUATION NOTED HE MET THE CRITERIA FOR PSYCHOSEXUAL DISORDER WITH ADDICTIVE FEATURES; COMPLETED TREATMENT AND IS UNDER THE CARE OF AN ADDICTIONOLOGIST; SOBRIETY DATE IS 9/29/93. SUSPENSION STAYED TO PROBATION AFTER 14 DAYS. CONDITIONS OF PROBATION: SHALL APPEAR BEFORE THE BOARD TWICE A YEAR; SHALL ABSTAIN FROM THE CONSUMPTION OF ALCOHOL/CHEMICAL SUBSTANCES IN ANY FORM UNLESS PRESCRIBED BY ANOTHER PHYSICIAN FOR A LEGITIMATE AND THERAPEUTIC PURPOSE; SHALL PARTICIPATE IN THE ACTIVITIES OF A PHYSICIAN HEALTH AND REHABILITATION COMMITTEE AND ATTEND WEEKLY MEETINGS WITH QUATERLY REPORTS; SHALL PARTICIPATE IN AA'S PROGRAM AND SEXUAL ADDICTION ANONYMOUS NOT LESS THAN THREE TIMES A WEEK FOR EACH PROGRAM WITH QUARTERLY REPORTS TO THE BOARD; SHALL SUBMIT HIMSELF FOR APPROPRIATE EXAMS INCLUDING DRUG OR ALCOHOL SCREENS; SHALL CONTINUE TREATMENT WITH PRESENT ADDICTIONOLOGIST AT LEAST ONCE A MONTH WITH QUARTERLY REPORTS; SHALL NOT TREAT OR OTHERWISE SERVE AS PHYSICIAN, PRESCRIBE, DISPENSE OR ADMINISTER DRUGS THAT MAY BE SUBJECT TO ABUSE TO HIMSELF OR TO ANY MEMBER OF HIS FAMILY; SHALL BE SUPERVISED BY A BOARD-APPROVED PHYSICIAN WITH QUARTERLY REPORTS; SHALL LIMIT PRACTICE TO A BOARD-APPROVED INSTITUTIONAL SETTING WITH SUFFICIENT PROTOCOLS TO ENSURE HIS PRACTICE IS SUFFICIENTLY MONITORED; SHALL HAVE A CHAPERONEE PRESENT FOR THE EXAMINATION OF ALL FEMALE PATIENTS WHICH SHALL BE DOCUMENTED IN THEIR RECORDS; SHALL FOLLOW TERMS OF ALL AFTERCARE CONTRACTS; SHALL EXECUTE RELEASES FOR TREATMENT RECORDS WITHIN 10 DAYS OF A REQUEST FROM THE BOARD; SHALL GIVE A COPY OF THIS ORDER TO ANY HEALTH CARE ENTITY WHERE HE HAS PRIVILEGES; SHALL COOPERATE WITH THE BOARD IN VERIFYING COMPLIANCE; SHALL INFORM BOARD OF CHANGE OF ADDRESS WITHIN 10 DAYS OR IF HE LEAVES THE STATE; TIME SPENT OUT OF TEXAS DOES NOT COUNT TOWARD PROBATION. SHALL NOT SEEK MODIFICATION FOR ONE YEAR.

HILDERBRAND, HAROLD MD OF P.O. BOX 467, MERIDIAN, TX, WAS DISCIPLINED BY MEDICARE ON OCTOBER 5, 1987.
DISCIPLINARY ACTION: 60-MONTH EXCLUSION FROM THE MEDICARE AND/OR MEDICAID PROGRAMS
OFFENSE: SUBSTANDARD CARE, INCOMPETENCE, OR NEGLIGENCE
NOTES: GROSSLY SUBSTANDARD CARE OF 4 PATIENTS

HILDERBRAND, HAROLD E MD, LICENSE NUMBER 00B9578, OF MERIDIAN, TX, WAS DISCIPLINED BY TEXAS ON DECEMBER 1, 1989.
DISCIPLINARY ACTION: SURRENDER OF LICENSE
NOTES: MUST RECEIVE WRITTEN AUTHORITY FROM BOARD IF DESIRING TO PRACTICE IN TEXAS.

HILL, JAMES LEE DO OF DUNCANVILLE, TX, WAS DISCIPLINED BY MISSOURI ON JANUARY 24, 1989.
DISCIPLINARY ACTION: 36-MONTH PROBATION
OFFENSE: CRIMINAL CONVICTION OR PLEA OF GUILTY, NOLO CONTENDERE, OR NO CONTEST TO A CRIME

HILL, ROBERT D MD, LICENSE NUMBER 00C6143, OF ODESSA, TX, WAS DISCIPLINED BY TEXAS ON JANUARY 6, 1995.
DISCIPLINARY ACTION: 60-MONTH PROBATION; REQUIRED TO TAKE ADDITIONAL MEDICAL EDUCATION
OFFENSE: LOSS OR RESTRICTION OF HOSPITAL PRIVILEGES
NOTES: ON 4/7/92 A HOSPITAL SUMMARILY SUSPENDED HIS PRIVILEGES DUE TO THE FOLLOWING: HE EXAMINED A NEWBORN INFANT WHO HIS NOTES REFLECTED WAS NORMAL, A POOR EATER, AND STATED "WATCH"; NURSES' NOTES REFLECT THE BABY WAS SPITTING UP EMESIS, REFUSING TO NURSE, WAS NOT STOOLING AND WAS NOT AROUSABLE; IN SPITE OF THIS DR. HILL DISCHARGED PATIENT AND ADVISED PARENTS TO CALL IF EATING DID NOT IMPROVE; THEY DID CALL LATER THAT DAY AND HE REFUSED TO SEE THE CHILD AS HE BELIEVED THE PROBLEM WOULD RESOLVE ITSELF; ANOTHER PHYSICIAN HOSPITALIZED THE INFANT THAT SAME DAY; THE INFANT WAS DIAGNOSED WITH CYSTIC FIBROSIS. HE RESIGNED FROM THE HOSPITAL AFTER BEING ADVISED THAT THE HOSPITAL'S EXECUTIVE COMMITTEE WOULD RECOMMEND A PERMANENT SUSPENSION. SUSPENSION STAYED. CONDITIONS OF PROBATION: SHALL HAVE A BOARD-APPROVED MONITORING PHYSICIAN WITH MONTHLY REPORTS; SHALL ATTEND AT LEAST 50 HOURS PER YEAR OF CONTINUING MEDICAL EDUCATION; SHALL APPEAR BEFORE THE BOARD ONCE A YEAR; SHALL COOPERATE WITH THE BOARD IN VERIFYING COMPLIANCE; SHALL INFORM BOARD OF CHANGE OF ADDRESS WITHIN 10 DAYS OR IF HE LEAVES THE STATE; TIME SPENT OUT OF TEXAS DOES NOT COUNT TOWARD PROBATION. SHALL NOT SEEK MODIFICATION FOR ONE YEAR.

HILL, WELTON E MD OF 235 W. PALM, BELLVILLE, TX, WAS DISCIPLINED BY MEDICARE ON MARCH 27, 1987.
DISCIPLINARY ACTION: 12-MONTH EXCLUSION FROM THE

MEDICARE AND/OR MEDICAID PROGRAMS
OFFENSE: SUBSTANDARD CARE, INCOMPETENCE, OR NEGLIGENCE
NOTES: GROSSLY SUBSTANDARD CARE OF 8 PATIENTS, INCLUDING LACK OF CAPABILITY TO EVALUATE AND TREAT MEDICAL PROBLEMS IN THE AREA OF CARDIOLOGY, PULMONOLOGY, INFECTIOUS DISEASE AND METABOLIC DISEASES, INAPPROPRIATE AND UNTIMELY USE OF AVAILABLE LABORATORY AND RADIOLOGIC SERVICES AND INATTENTION TO THE RESULTS OF LABORATORY TESTS AND RADIOLOGIC FINDINGS

HINKLEY, BRUCE S MD, LICENSE NUMBER 0009999, OF 2212 VALLEY VIEW, CEDAR HILL, TX, WAS DISCIPLINED BY OKLAHOMA ON MAY 23, 1991.
NOTES: 9/7/88 URINE SAMPLE TESTED POSITIVE FOR COCAINE; MCALESTER REGIONAL HEALTH CENTER PLACED HIM ON PROBATION. ON 11/25/88, FOUND WITH A GUN CRAWLING IN A PASTURE SAYING THE MAFIA OR NAZIS WERE AFTER HIM; URINE SAMPLES FROM THAT DAY ALSO TESTED POSITIVE FOR COCAINE. SINCE 12/88 OR 1/89 HAS NOT PRACTICED; HAS BEEN VOLUNTARY PATIENT AT A CENTER FOR ADDICTIVE DISEASES. PLACED ON 5 YEARS PROBATION 6/9/89. IS IN SUBSTANTIAL COMPLIANCE WITH THE TERMS AND CONDITIONS; PRESENTLY PRACTICING UNDER SUPERVISION AT ORTHOPEDIC PRACTICE IN ARLINGTON, TEXAS. PROBATION MODIFIED 5/23/91: CAN BE REDUCED TO LEVEL IV SUPERVISION; MAY PRESCRIBE OR WRITE ORDERS FOR SCHEDULE II, III, IV AND V FOR HOSPITAL IN-PATIENTS OR OUT-PATIENTS ON SERIALLY NUMBERED, DUPLICATE PRESCRIPTION PADS. OTHER TERMS OF 6/9/89 ORDER WHICH ARE STILL IN EFFECT INCLUDE: SHALL NOT PRESCRIBE, ADMINISTER OR DISPENSE ANY MEDICATION, INCLUDING CONTROLLED DANGEROUS SUBSTANCES, FOR HIS PERSONAL OR ANY FAMILY MEMBER'S USE; SHALL TAKE NO MEDICATIONS UNLESS AUTHORIZED BY TREATING PHYSICIAN; SHALL ABSTAIN FROM ALCOHOL OR ANY SUBSTANCE WICH WOULD ADVERSELY AFFECT HIS ABILITY TO PRACTICE; SHALL SUBMIT BIOLOGICAL FLUID SPECIMENS FOR ANALYSIS; SHALL CONTINUE TO PARTICIPATE IN RECOVERY COMMITTEE; SHALL FURNISH BOARD WITH ADDRESS AND/OR CHANGE OF ADDRESS; SHALL APPEAR BEFORE BOARD UPON REQUEST; SHALL NOTIFY ANY HOSPITAL WHERE HE HOLDS STAFF PRIVILEGES, OR CLINIC OR GROUP OF THE TERMS AND CONDITIONS. ON 3/12/92, APPLICATION FOR REINSTATEMENT OF LICENSE WAS DENIED. LICENSE HAD LAPSED DUE TO NON-RENEWAL.

HINKLEY, BRUCE STANTON MD, LICENSE NUMBER 00D9497, OF DALLAS, TX, WAS DISCIPLINED BY TEXAS ON AUGUST 25, 1989.
DISCIPLINARY ACTION: SURRENDER OF CONTROLLED SUBSTANCE LICENSE; 120-MONTH PROBATION
OFFENSE: DISCIPLINARY ACTION BY ANOTHER STATE OR AGENCY
NOTES: REVOCATION STAYED. PROBATION TERMS: COMPLY WITH AND PROVIDE OKLAHOMA BOARD ORDER AND REPORTS TO EACH BOARD; PARTICIPATE IN SUBSTANCE ABUSE PROGRAMS AND NARCOTICS ANONYMOUS, RECEIVE PSYCHIATRIC EVALUATION AND TREATMENT; SUBMIT TO ALCOHOL/DRUG SCREENING; REFRAIN FROM USE OR POSSESSION, OF ADMINISTRATION OR PRESCRIBING OF CONTROLLED SUBSTANCES OR ANY PRESCRIPTION DRUG OR MEDICATION UNLESS PRESCRIBED BY PHYSICIAN; SURRENDER CONTROLLED SUBSTANCE REGISTRATION CERTIFICATES; SURRENDER UNUSED TRIPLICATE PRESCRIPTION FORMS; APPEAR SEMI-ANNUALLY BEFORE BOARD.

HINKLEY, BRUCE STANTON MD, LICENSE NUMBER 00D9497, OF ARLINGTON, TX, WAS DISCIPLINED BY TEXAS ON AUGUST 24, 1991.
DISCIPLINARY ACTION: RESTRICTION PLACED ON CONTROLLED SUBSTANCE LICENSE
NOTES: PROBATION MODIFIED AS FOLLOWS: ALLOWED TO REAPPLY FOR DEA AND DPS CONTROLLED SUBSTANCES REGISTRATION CERTIFICATES IN SCHEDULES II, II-N, III, III-N, IV, AND V FOR USE FOR HOSPITAL PATIENTS ONLY; SHALL REQUEST ANOTHER PHYSICIAN TO PRESCRIBE FOR OFFICE PATIENTS IN NEED OF CONTROLLED SUBSTANCES OR DANGEROUS DRUGS. ON 11/19/93 ORDER MODIFIED SO HE MAY REAPPLY TO THE DRUG ENFORCEMENT ADMINISTRATION AND TEXAS DEPARTMENT OF PUBLIC SAFETY FOR CONTROLLED SUBSTANCES REGISTRATION CERTIFICATES IN ALL SCHEDULES AND FOR ALL PATIENTS. ALL OTHER PROVISIONS OF THIS ORDER REMAIN IN FULL FORCE.

HIRSCH, EDWARD MD, LICENSE NUMBER 00F3499, OF EL PASO, TX, WAS DISCIPLINED BY TEXAS ON OCTOBER 9, 1992.
DISCIPLINARY ACTION: RESTRICTION PLACED ON LICENSE
OFFENSE: PROFESSIONAL MISCONDUCT
NOTES: AIDING THE UNLICENSED PRACTICE OF MEDICINE BY AN ASSOCIATION OR CORPORATION. SHALL REFRAIN FROM PRACTICING MEDICINE UNTIL PASSAGE OF SPEX.

HIRSCH, EDWARD MD, LICENSE NUMBER 00F3499, OF EL PASO, TX, WAS DISCIPLINED BY TEXAS ON NOVEMBER 19, 1993.
DISCIPLINARY ACTION: SURRENDER OF LICENSE
NOTES: LICENSE IS PERMANENTLY CANCELED; SHALL NOT PETITION THE BOARD FOR REINSTATEMENT.

HOLBROOK, JAMES M MD, LICENSE NUMBER 00F5233, OF FORT WORTH, TX, WAS DISCIPLINED BY TEXAS ON SEPTEMBER 24, 1988.
OFFENSE: DISCIPLINARY ACTION BY ANOTHER STATE OR AGENCY
NOTES: SHALL CONTINUE TO COMPLY WITH HIS MEMO OF UNDERSTANDING WITH DEA; AND TO COOPERATE WITH TARRANT COUNTY METHADONE CLINICS AND LAW ENFORCEMENT COMMUNITY

HOLLABAUGH, ERNEST R MD, LICENSE NUMBER 00D0476, OF DALLAS, TX, WAS DISCIPLINED BY TEXAS ON MAY 20, 1989.
DISCIPLINARY ACTION: 60-MONTH REQUIRED TO ENTER AN IMPAIRED PHYSICIAN PROGRAM OR DRUG OR ALCOHOL TREATMENT; 60-MONTH MONITORING OF PHYSICIAN
OFFENSE: DRUG OR ALCOHOL ABUSE
NOTES: SHALL PARTICIPATE IN AA AND DALLAS COUNTY MEDICAL SOCIETY ON PHYSICIAN HEALTH AND REHABILITATION; SHALL CONTINUE COUNSELING AND TREATMENT; SHALL SUBMIT TO APPROPRIATE EXAMS INCLUDING ALCOHOL OR DRUG SCREENINGS; SHALL REFRAIN FROM CONTROLLED SUBSTANCE USE UNLESS SUCH PRESCRIBED OR ADMINISTERED BY ANOTHER PHYSICIAN FOR DIAGNOSED THERAPEUTIC PURPOSE; SHALL CAUSE REPORT TO BE MADE TO BOARD BY RECOVERING ABUSE SPONSOR

HOLLEN, JAKE THOMAS MD, DATE OF BIRTH AUGUST 8, 1951,

LICENSE NUMBER 00G5926, OF JENNINGS, LA, WAS DISCIPLINED BY TEXAS ON OCTOBER 29, 1988.
DISCIPLINARY ACTION: REQUIRED TO ENTER AN IMPAIRED PHYSICIAN PROGRAM OR DRUG OR ALCOHOL TREATMENT; MONITORING OF PHYSICIAN
OFFENSE: DRUG OR ALCOHOL ABUSE
NOTES: SHALL PARTICIPATE IN AA AND IMPAIRED PHYSICIAN GROUP; CHAIRMAN TO SUBMIT REPORTS TWICE A YEAR; SHALL SUBMIT SELF FOR APPROPRIATE EXAMS INCLUDING ALCOHOL AND DRUG SCREENINGS AT BOARD'S REQUEST

HOLLEN, JAKE THOMAS MD, DATE OF BIRTH AUGUST 8, 1951, LICENSE NUMBER 00G5926, OF LAKE CHARLES, LA, WAS DISCIPLINED BY TEXAS ON AUGUST 28, 1992.
DISCIPLINARY ACTION: EMERGENCY SUSPENSION
OFFENSE: FAILURE TO COMPLY WITH A PREVIOUS BOARD ORDER
NOTES: NONCOMPLIANCE WITH PREVIOUS BOARD ORDER.

HOLLEN, JAKE THOMAS MD, DATE OF BIRTH AUGUST 8, 1951, LICENSE NUMBER 00G5926, OF 701 CRICKETT ROAD, LAKE CHARLES, LA, WAS DISCIPLINED BY TEXAS ON JANUARY 30, 1993.
DISCIPLINARY ACTION: 120-MONTH PROBATION; RESTRICTION PLACED ON CONTROLLED SUBSTANCE LICENSE
OFFENSE: FAILURE TO COMPLY WITH A PREVIOUS BOARD ORDER
NOTES: FAILED TO COMPLY WITH 1988 BOARD ORDER IN THAT HE: FAILED TO SUBMIT SPECIMENS OF BODILY FLUIDS; FAILED TO SUBMIT PROOF OF ATTENDANCE OF AA MEETINGS OR ATTENDANCE AND PARTICIPATION WITH AN IMPAIRED PHYSICIANS GROUP AND FAILED TO COOPERATE WITH THE BOARD; TEN YEAR SUSPENSION STAYED, PROBATION ISSUED WITH FOLLOWING CONDITIONS: SHALL PARTICIPATE IN ACTIVITIES OF A PHYSICIAN HEALTH AND REHABILITATION COMMITTEE AND ATTEND WEEKLY MEETINGS WITH QUARTERLY REPORTS; SHALL PARTICIPATE IN AA'S 12 STEP PROGRAM NOT LESS THAN 3 TIMES A WEEK WITH QUARTERLY REPORTS TO THE BOARD; SHALL FURNISH THE BOARD WITH WRITTEN REPORTS ON HIS MEDICAL CONDITION AND COMPLIANCE WITH THIS ORDER WHEN REQUESTED; SHALL ABSTAIN FROM THE CONSUMPTION OF ALCOHOL/CHEMICAL SUBSTANCES IN ANY FORM; SHALL SUBMIT HIMSELF FOR APPROPRIATE EXAMS INCLUDING DRUG OR ALCOHOL SCREENS; SHALL NOT TREAT OR OTHERWISE SERVE AS THE PHYSICIAN, PRESCRIBE, DISPENSE OR ADMINISTER DRUGS THAT MAY BE SUBJECT TO ABUSE FOR HIMSELF OR ANY MEMBER OF HIS FAMILY; DEA AND CONTROLLED SUBSTANCES REGISTRATION LIMITED TO SCHEDULES III THROUGH V; SHALL NOT ATTEMPT TO REREGISTER WITHOUT BOARD AUTHORIZATION; SHALL MAINTAIN A COPY OF EVERY PRESCRIPTION WRITTEN FOR CONTROLLED SUBSTANCES OR DANGEROUS DRUGS WHICH SHALL BE AVAILABLE FOR INSPECTION; SHALL NOT TELEPHONE IN ANY PRESCRIPTION FOR SUCH DRUGS; SHALL OBTAIN THE SERVICES OF A PRIMARY CARE PHYSICIAN WHO SHALL RELEASE INFORMATION TO THE BOARD AND NOTIFY THEM IF ANY DRUG HAVING ADDICTION-FORMING OR ADDICTION-SUSTAINING LIABILITY IS PRESCRIBED; SHALL OBTAIN NO PRESCRIPTIONS FROM ANY OTHER PHYSICIAN UNLESS IT IS APPROVED IN WRITING WITHIN 24 HOURS; ANY PRESCRIPTIONS WRITTEN BY PRIMARY CARE PHYSICIAN CAN BE FILLED ONLY AT BOARD-APPROVED PHARMACIES; SHALL BE EVALUATED BY A BOARD-APPROVED PSYCHIATRIST TO WHOM HE WILL PROVIDE A COPY OF THE ORDER; SHALL COOPERATE WITH THE BOARD IN VERIFYING COMPLIANCE; SHALL INFORM BOARD OF CHANGE OF ADDRESS WITHIN 10 DAYS OR IF HE LEAVES THE STATE; TIME SPENT OUT OF TEXAS OR LOUISIANA DOES NOT COUNT TOWARD PROBATION; SHALL APPEAR BEFORE THE BOARD ONCE A YEAR; SHALL MEET WITH PROBATION OFFICER 3 TIMES PER YEAR; SHALL APPEAR BEFORE THE BOARD PRIOR TO PRACTICING IN TEXAS. SHALL NOT SEEK MODIFICATION UNTIL DECEMBER 1, 1996.

HOLLEN, JAKE THOMAS MD OF LAKE CHARLES, LA, WAS DISCIPLINED BY LOUISIANA ON JUNE 24, 1993.
DISCIPLINARY ACTION: 120-MONTH PROBATION; RESTRICTION PLACED ON CONTROLLED SUBSTANCE LICENSE
OFFENSE: DISCIPLINARY ACTION BY ANOTHER STATE OR AGENCY
NOTES: ACTION TAKEN BY TEXAS. SUBJECT TO FULL COMPLIANCE WITH TERMS OF CONSENT AGREEMENT WITH TEXAS BOARD, PROHIBITION ON PRESCRIPTION OF SCHEDULE II CONTROLLED SUBSTANCES, BOARD AUDITING OF RECORDS OF CONTROLLED SUBSTANCE PRESCRIPTIONS.

HOLLEN, JAKE THOMAS MD, LICENSE NUMBER 0013982, OF ELTON ROAD, JENNINGS, LA, WAS DISCIPLINED BY DEA ON AUGUST 25, 1993.
DISCIPLINARY ACTION: RESTRICTION PLACED ON CONTROLLED SUBSTANCE LICENSE
OFFENSE: DISCIPLINARY ACTION BY ANOTHER STATE OR AGENCY
NOTES: TEXAS MEDICAL LICENSE PUT ON PROBATION 08/28/92. LOUISIANA AND TEXAS MEDICAL BOARDS REVOKED SCHEDULE II.

HOLSTON, ROBERT G DO, LICENSE NUMBER 00E3308, OF FORT WORTH, TX, WAS DISCIPLINED BY TEXAS ON NOVEMBER 5, 1988.
DISCIPLINARY ACTION: LICENSE REVOCATION
OFFENSE: FAILURE TO COMPLY WITH A PREVIOUS BOARD ORDER
NOTES: VIOLATED PROBATIONARY TERMS

HOLSTON, ROBERT G DO, LICENSE NUMBER 00E3308, OF KENNEDALE, TX, WAS DISCIPLINED BY TEXAS ON DECEMBER 1, 1988.
DISCIPLINARY ACTION: PROBATION
OFFENSE: OVERPRESCRIBING OR MISPRESCRIBING DRUGS
NOTES: REVOCATION STAYED; EXHIBITED INTEMPERANCE IN USE OF DRUGS, WROTE FALSE OR FICTITIOUS PRESCRIPTIONS FOR CONTROLLED SUBSTANCES, AND PRESCRIBED OR ADMINISTERED DRUGS NONTHERAPEUTICALLY.

HOLSTON, ROBERT G DO OF KENNEDALE, TX, WAS DISCIPLINED BY TENNESSEE ON AUGUST 1, 1989.
DISCIPLINARY ACTION: 60-MONTH PROBATION; REQUIRED TO ENTER AN IMPAIRED PHYSICIAN PROGRAM OR DRUG OR ALCOHOL TREATMENT
OFFENSE: DISCIPLINARY ACTION BY ANOTHER STATE OR AGENCY
NOTES: PROBATION 5-8 YEARS; MUST HAVE PSYCHIATRIST FURNISH MONTHLY REPORTS INCLUDING DRUG SCREEN; MUST SUBMIT TO BOARDS COPIES OF EACH PRESCRIPTION WRITTEN FOR CONTROLLED SUBSTANCES AND MAY NOT PRESCRIBE ANY DRUGS FOR SELF USE; SHALL ABIDE BY CONTRACT WITH IMPAIRED PHYSICIANS COMMITTEE; MAY NOT REAPPLY FOR DEA NUMBER FOR TWO YEARS

HOLSTON, ROBERT GEORGE DO, LICENSE NUMBER 0TXE330, OF 619 N LITTLE ROAD, KENNEDALE, TX, WAS DISCIPLINED BY DEA

ON JANUARY 23, 1989.
DISCIPLINARY ACTION: SURRENDER OF CONTROLLED SUBSTANCE LICENSE
OFFENSE: PROFESSIONAL MISCONDUCT
NOTES: LICENSE REVOKED 11/05/88; VOLUNTARILY SURRENDERED REGISTRATION 01/23/89 IN ARLINGTON, TEXAS. CHARGED WITH OBTAINING CONTROLLED SUBSTANCES BY FRAUD 10/03/88 IN FT. WORTH, TX; CANNOT REAPPLY FOR REGISTRATION UNTIL 08/91.

HOLSTON, ROBERT GEORGE DO, DATE OF BIRTH JANUARY 29, 1947, OF PO BOX 1043, JAMESTOWN, TN, WAS DISCIPLINED BY MEDICARE ON JUNE 12, 1989.
DISCIPLINARY ACTION: EXCLUSION FROM THE MEDICARE AND/OR MEDICAID PROGRAMS
OFFENSE: DISCIPLINARY ACTION BY ANOTHER STATE OR AGENCY
NOTES: LICENSE REVOCATION OR SUSPENSION. MEDICARE PRIVILEGES REINSTATED ON 7/9/92.

HOLT, CECIL ZENO MD, LICENSE NUMBER 00B8784, OF WAXAHACHIE, TX, WAS DISCIPLINED BY TEXAS ON APRIL 10, 1992.
DISCIPLINARY ACTION: 60-MONTH PROBATION
OFFENSE: SUBSTANDARD CARE, INCOMPETENCE, OR NEGLIGENCE
NOTES: PROFESSIONAL FAILURE TO PRACTICE MEDICINE IN AN ACCEPTABLE MANNER CONSISTENT WITH PUBLIC HEALTH AND WELFARE. LICENSE SUSPENDED, SUSPENSION STAYED; PROBATION UNDER TERMS AND CONDITIONS.

HONG, SEUNG KOOK MD, LICENSE NUMBER 00F5950, OF RICHARDSON, TX, WAS DISCIPLINED BY TEXAS ON JANUARY 12, 1991.
DISCIPLINARY ACTION: 60-MONTH PROBATION; RESTRICTION PLACED ON LICENSE
NOTES: SHALL NOT PRACTICE OBSTETRICS OR SURGERY, EXCEPT FOR MINOR OFFICE PRACTICE SURGERY, WITHOUT MEETING ALL QUALIFICATIONS FOR BOARD CERTIFICATION IN GENERAL SURGERY, WHICH WOULD THEN BE PERMITTED; SHALL TREAT NO PATIENTS UNDER FOUR YEARS OF AGE EXCEPT TO PROVIDE IMMUNIZATIONS; OBTAIN CONTINUING MEDICAL EDUCATION; TAKE AND PASS THE SPECIAL PURPOSE EXAM (SPEX) WITHIN SIX MONTHS OF APPROVAL OF THIS ORDER.

HONG, SEUNG KOOK MD, LICENSE NUMBER 00F5950, OF RICHARDSON, TX, WAS DISCIPLINED BY TEXAS ON OCTOBER 17, 1994.
DISCIPLINARY ACTION: 9-MONTH PROBATION; REQUIRED TO TAKE ADDITIONAL MEDICAL EDUCATION
OFFENSE: FAILURE TO COMPLY WITH A PREVIOUS BOARD ORDER
NOTES: ON 1/12/91 HE ENTERED INTO AN AGREEMENT WITH BOARD DUE TO THE FINDING THAT HE HAD MERITORIOUS MEDICAL LIABILITY CLAIMS AGAINST HIM FOR TREATMENT RENDERED IN 1980. 1981, 1983 AND 1985 INVOLVING BOTH OBSTETRICS AND SURGERY; ONE OF THE TERMS OF THIS AGREEMENT WAS THAT HE WOULD PASS THE SPEX EXAM WITHIN 6 MONTHS; HE TOOK THE EXAM TWICE ONCE IN 9/91 AND ONCE IN 6/92 AND DID NOT PASS NOR DID HE COMPLETE THE EXAM ON BOTH OCCASIONS; CLAIMED HE HAD FAMILY PROBLEMS WHICH MADE IT DIFFICULT TO STUDY AND IT WAS DIFFICULT FOR HIM TO FINISH THE EXAM IN THE ALLOTTED TIME BECAUSE ENGLISH IS NOT HIS FIRST LANGUAGE. SUSPENSION STAYED. CONDITIONS OF PROBATION: SHALL PASS THE SPEX EXAM WITHIN TWO YEARS; SHALL BE GIVEN ONE AND A HALF NORMAL TIME ALLOTMENT TO TAKE THE EXAM; SHALL COMPLETE A 150 HOUR PRACTICAL REVIEW COURSE APPROVED BY THE BOARD WITHIN ONE YEAR; ALL OTHER TERMS OF 1/12/91 ORDER REMAIN IN EFFECT FOR TWO YEARS FROM THE DATE OF THIS ORDER. THE BOARD ORDER WILL BECOME FINAL WHEN ADMINISTRATIVE APPEALS HAVE BEEN EXHAUSTED; HE HAS 20 DAYS TO FILE A MOTION FOR REHEARING.

HOOPER, LAWRENCE H JR MD, LICENSE NUMBER 00G1293, OF EL PASO, TX, WAS DISCIPLINED BY TEXAS ON DECEMBER 3, 1990.
DISCIPLINARY ACTION: PROBATION
NOTES: PLACED ON TEMPORARY PROBATION PENDING THE OUTCOME OF CRIMINAL TRIAL. PROBATION TERMINATED EFFECTIVE 6/17/92; LICENSE FREE OF ANY RESTRICTION OR LIMITATION.

HOUSE, CHARLES HAROLD MD, LICENSE NUMBER 00D0390, OF KILLEEN, TX, WAS DISCIPLINED BY TEXAS ON SEPTEMBER 24, 1988.
DISCIPLINARY ACTION: 63-MONTH REQUIRED TO TAKE ADDITIONAL MEDICAL EDUCATION

HOUSE, CHARLES HAROLD MD, LICENSE NUMBER 00D0390, OF KILLEEN, TX, WAS DISCIPLINED BY TEXAS ON JUNE 22, 1994.
DISCIPLINARY ACTION: 60-MONTH PROBATION; RESTRICTION PLACED ON LICENSE
OFFENSE: SUBSTANDARD CARE, INCOMPETENCE, OR NEGLIGENCE
NOTES: BETWEEN 8/19/91 AND 11/93 IN REGARD TO MULTIPLE PATIENTS, FAILED TO ADEQUATELY FOLLOW-UP GYNECOLOGICAL PROBLEMS, FAILED TO APPROPRIATELY INSTITUTE TREATMENT IN RESPONSE TO ABNORMAL PAP SMEARS, FAILED TO PROPERLY UTILIZE COLPOSCOPY AND CAUTERY AND FAILED TO OBTAIN A DEFINITE DIAGNOSIS OR KNOW PATIENT PATHOLOGY FROM PAP SMEAR OR BIOPSY REPORT BEFORE INITIATING TREATMENT; FAILED TO USE A PROGESTATIONAL AGENT IN CONJUNCTION WITH ESTROGEN THEREBY PUTTING PATIENTS AT RISK FOR ENDOMETRIAL CANCER; PATIENT CHART REVIEW REVEALED NUMEROUS SUCH DEFICIENCIES; IS NOT AMERICAN BOARD CERTIFIED BUT ADVERTISES THAT HE IS A FAMILY PRACTICE SPECIALIST WITH A SUBSPECIALTY IN OBSTETRICS/GYNECOLOGY. SUSPENSION STAYED. CONDITIONS OF PROBATION: SHALL NOT PRACTICE GYNECOLOGY UNTIL HE HAS OBTAINED 25 HOURS OF OUT- PATIENT GYNECOLOGICAL TRAINING INCLUDING A BOARD-APPROVED COLPOSCOPY COURSE; UPON COMPLETION OF THIS TRAINING SHALL BE SUPERVISED BY A BOARD-APPROVED PHYSICIAN FOR ALL GYNECOLOGIC CASES WITH REPORTS THREE TIMES A YEAR; SHALL REFER ALL ABNORMAL PAP SMEARS BEYOND CLASS II FOR A SECOND OPINION TO A BOARD-APPROVED PHYSICIAN; SHALL ATTEND AT LEAST 50 HOURS PER YEAR OF CONTINUING MEDICAL EDUCATION 25 HOURS OF WHICH SHALL BE IN OUT-PATIENT GYNECOLOGY; SHALL GIVE A COPY OF THIS ORDER TO ANY HEALTH CARE ENTITY WHERE HE HAS PRIVILEGES; SHALL COOPERATE WITH THE BOARD IN VERIFYING COMPLIANCE; SHALL INFORM BOARD OF ADDRESS CHANGE WITHIN 10 DAYS OR IF HE LEAVES THE STATE; TIME SPENT OUT OF TEXAS DOES NOT COUNT TOWARD PROBATION. SHALL NOT SEEK

MODIFICATION FOR ONE YEAR.

HOUSE, FLOYD LEON MD, LICENSE NUMBER 00D9501, OF VICTORIA, TX, WAS DISCIPLINED BY TEXAS ON JULY 1, 1990.
DISCIPLINARY ACTION: LICENSE REVOCATION
OFFENSE: DRUG OR ALCOHOL ABUSE
NOTES: INTEMPERATE USE OF ALCOHOL WHICH IN BOARD'S OPINION COULD ENDANGER LIVES OF PATIENTS, UNPROFESSIONAL CONDUCT LIKELY TO DECEIVE, DEFRAUD, OR INJURE PUBLIC; REVOCATION STAYED PENDING JUDICIAL REVIEW. JUDGE UPHELD BOARD'S DECISION.

HOUSE, FLOYD LEON MD, DATE OF BIRTH FEBRUARY 22, 1944, LICENSE NUMBER 00D9501, OF 5603 EL CAMINO REAL, HARLINGEN, TX, WAS DISCIPLINED BY TEXAS ON MAY 14, 1993.
DISCIPLINARY ACTION: LICENSE REINSTATEMENT; 120-MONTH PROBATION
NOTES: REINSTATEMENT FROM REVOCATION OF 10/12/90. TEN YEAR SUSPENSION STAYED. CONDITIONS OF PROBATION: RESTRICTED TO THE PRACTICE OF PSYCHIATRY AT ONE OF TWO FACILITIES; SHALL SUBMIT HIMSELF TO EVALUATION AND TREATMENT BY A BOARD-APPROVED PSYCHIATRIST TO WHOM HE SHALL PROVIDE A COPY OF THIS ORDER AND WHO SHALL MAKE MONTHLY REPORTS TO THE BOARD; SHALL BE SUPERVISED BY A BOARD-APPROVED PHYSICIAN WHO SHALL SUBMIT QUARTERLY REPORTS TO THE BOARD; SHALL ATTEND AT LEAST 50 HOURS OF CONTINUING MEDICAL EDUCATION AND SIX HOURS OF AN ETHICS COURSE PER YEAR; SHALL ABSTAIN FROM THE CONSUMPTION OF ALCOHOL/CHEMICAL SUBSTANCES IN ANY FORM; SHALL PARTICIPATE IN ACTIVITIES OF A PHYSICIAN HEALTH AND REHABILITATION COMMITTEE AND ATTEND WEEKLY MEETINGS WITH QUARTERLY REPORTS; THIS CONDITION MODIFIED ON 8/20/93 SUCH THAT HE SHALL PARTICIPATE IN AND BE SUBJECT TO REVIEW BY ANY PEER REVIEW COMMITTEE OF ANY STATE OF TEXAS MENTAL HEALTH AND MENTAL RETARDATION FACILITY WHERE HE PRACTICES WITH QUARTERLY REPORTS; SHALL PARTICIPATE IN AA'S PROGRAM NOT LESS THAN THREE TIMES A WEEK WITH QUARTERLY REPORTS TO THE BOARD; SHALL SUBMIT HIMSELF FOR APPROPRIATE EXAMS INCLUDING DRUG AND ALCOHOL SCREENS; SHALL FURNISH WRITTEN REPORTS TO THE BOARD UPON REQUEST TO VERIFY COMPLIANCE; ANY CHANGE IN EMPLOYMENT SHALL BE REPORTED TO THE BOARD; SHALL NOT HAVE ANY PERSONAL RELATIONSHIP WITH ANY PATIENT; SHALL NOT TREAT OR OTHERWISE SERVE AS PHYSICIAN, PRESCRIBE, DISPENSE OR ADMINISTER DRUGS THAT MAY BE SUBJECT TO ABUSE FOR HIMSELF OR ANY MEMBER OF HIS FAMILY; SHALL APPEAR BEFORE THE BOARD TWICE A YEAR; SHALL ARRANGE A PAYMENT PLAN TO PAY COURT COSTS ASSOCIATED WITH THE ORIGINAL REVOCATION ACTION TAKEN AGAINST HIS LICENSE; SHALL GIVE A COPY OF THIS ORDER TO ANY HEALTH CARE ENTITY WHERE HE HAS PRIVILEGES; SHALL COOPERATE WITH THE BOARD IN VERIFYING COMPLIANCE; SHALL INFORM THE BOARD OF CHANGE OF ADDRESS WITHIN 10 DAYS OR IF HE LEAVES THE STATE; TIME SPENT OUT OF TEXAS DOES NOT COUNT TOWARD PROBATION. ON 6/22/94 A REQUEST TO ALLOW HIM TO ENGAGE IN PART-TIME PRIVATE PRACTICE WAS DENIED.

HOUSE, FLOYD LEON MD, LICENSE NUMBER 00D9501, OF 1901 S 24TH STREET, EDINBURG, TX, WAS DISCIPLINED BY DEA ON JULY 28, 1993.
DISCIPLINARY ACTION: RESTRICTION PLACED ON CONTROLLED SUBSTANCE LICENSE
OFFENSE: DISCIPLINARY ACTION BY ANOTHER STATE OR AGENCY
NOTES: REGISTRATION REVOKED 10/12/90 IN TEXAS FOR INTEMPERATE USE OF ALCOHOL OR DRUGS AND UNPROFESSIONAL CONDUCT.

HOWARD, ANNETTE M MD, DATE OF BIRTH AUGUST 24, 1958, OF 3221 MILBURN STREET, HOUSTON, TX, WAS DISCIPLINED BY MEDICARE ON MARCH 6, 1994.
DISCIPLINARY ACTION: EXCLUSION FROM THE MEDICARE AND/OR MEDICAID PROGRAMS
OFFENSE: FAILURE TO COMPLY WITH A PROFESSIONAL RULE
NOTES: DEFAULTED ON PUBLIC HEALTH SERVICE EDUCATION LOAN. REINSTATED ON 3/2/95.

HOWELL, SHELLEY M DO, LICENSE NUMBER 00E3310, OF TEMPLE, TX, WAS DISCIPLINED BY TEXAS ON JUNE 13, 1989.
NOTES: PRESCRIBE WEIGHT LOSS MEDICATION IN ACCORDANCE WITH PHYSICIAN'S DESK REFERENCE. ORDER EFFECTIVE FOR 3 YEARS.

HOWELL, WYATT ALLEN MD, LICENSE NUMBER 00D8276, OF SEMINOLE, TX, WAS DISCIPLINED BY TEXAS ON AUGUST 20, 1992.
DISCIPLINARY ACTION: 60-MONTH PROBATION
OFFENSE: DRUG OR ALCOHOL ABUSE
NOTES: INTEMPERATE USE OF ALCOHOL OR DRUGS AND DISCIPLINARY ACTION TAKEN BY HIS PEERS. SUSPENSION, STAYED. PROBATION UNDER TERMS AND CONDITIONS.

HUBBARD, GREGORY GERARD DO, LICENSE NUMBER 00G3480, OF ARLINGTON, TX, WAS DISCIPLINED BY TEXAS ON MARCH 6, 1992.
DISCIPLINARY ACTION: 120-MONTH PROBATION
OFFENSE: DRUG OR ALCOHOL ABUSE
NOTES: ALSO WRITING FALSE OR FICTITIOUS PRESCRIPTIONS FOR DANGEROUS DRUGS. LICENSE REVOKED, REVOCATION STAYED; PROBATION UNDER TERMS AND CONDITIONS.

HUBBARD, GREGORY GERARD DO, LICENSE NUMBER 00G3480, OF BEDFORD, TX, WAS DISCIPLINED BY TEXAS ON JANUARY 14, 1994.
DISCIPLINARY ACTION: 120-MONTH PROBATION; RESTRICTION PLACED ON CONTROLLED SUBSTANCE LICENSE
OFFENSE: FAILURE TO COMPLY WITH A PREVIOUS BOARD ORDER
NOTES: IN VIOLATION OF THE 3/92 BOARD ORDER HE ABUSED STADOL NASAL SPRAY FROM 8/93 THROUGH 10/93 BY INGESTING IT WITHOUT A LEGITIMATE MEDICAL REASON; SELF-REPORTED THIS TO THE BOARD, HIS MONITORING PHYSICIAN AND THE PHYSICIAN HEALTH AND REHABILITATION COMMITTEE; ENTERED A SIX WEEK OUTPATIENT TREATMENT PROGRAM; IS UNDER THE CONTINUING CARE OF A PSYCHIATRIST. REVOCATION STAYED. CONDITIONS OF PROBATION: SHALL CONTINUE PSYCHIATRIC TREATMENT WITH QUARTERLY REPORTS; SHALL FURNISH WRITTEN REPORTS UPON REQUEST VERIFYING COMPLIANCE; SHALL ABSTAIN FROM THE CONSUMPTION OF ALCOHOL/CHEMICAL SUBSTANCES IN ANY FORM UNLESS PRESCRIBED BY ANOTHER PHYSICIAN FOR A LEGITIMATE AND THERAPEUTIC PURPOSE; SHALL SUBMIT HIMSELF FOR APPROPRIATE EXAMS INCLUDING DRUG AND ALCOHOL SCREENS; SHALL SURRENDER DEA AND TEXAS CONTROLLED SUBSTANCES

CERTIFICATES AND UNUSED TRIPLICATE PRESCRIPTION FORMS; SHALL NOT REREGISTER WITHOUT PERMISSION; SHALL NOT PRESCRIBE, DISPENSE, ADMINISTER OR POSSESS ANY CONTROLLED SUBSTANCE UNLESS PRESCRIBED TO HIM BY A TREATING PHYSICIAN; SHALL NOT TREAT OR OTHERWISE SERVE AS PHYSICIAN, PRESCRIBE, DISPENSE OR ADMINISTER DRUGS THAT MAY BE SUBJECT TO ABUSE TO HIMSELF OR ANY MEMBER OF HIS FAMILY; SHALL PARTICIPATE IN ACTIVITIES OF A PHYSICIAN HEALTH AND REHABILITATION COMMITEE AND ATTEND WEEKLY MEETINGS WITH QUARTERLY REPORTS; SHALL BE SUPERVISED BY A BOARD-APPROVED PHYSICIAN WITH REPORTS THREE TIMES A YEAR; SHALL APPEAR BEFORE THE BOARD TWICE A YEAR; SHALL GIVE A COPY OF THIS ORDER TO ANY HEALTH CARE ENTITY WHERE HE HAS PRIVILEGES; SHALL COOPERATE WITH THE BOARD IN VERIFYING COMPLIANCE; SHALL INFORM BOARD OF CHANGE OF ADDRESS WITHIN 10 DAYS OR IF HE LEAVES THE STATE; TIME SPENT OUT OF TEXAS DOES NOT COUNT TOWARD PROBATION. SHALL NOT SEEK MODIFICATION FOR ONE YEAR.

HUBBARD, GREGORY GERARD DO, LICENSE NUMBER 00G3480, OF BEDFORD, TX, WAS DISCIPLINED BY TEXAS ON OCTOBER 27, 1994.
DISCIPLINARY ACTION: EMERGENCY SUSPENSION
OFFENSE: FAILURE TO COMPLY WITH A PREVIOUS BOARD ORDER
NOTES: AVAILABLE EVIDENCE AND INFORMATION INDICATE THE FOLLOWING: THAT ON 3/17/94 HE INGESTED AN UNSPECIFIED BARBITURATE AND ON 3/17/94 AND 9/13/94 HE INGESTED STADOL NOT PURSUANT TO A PRESCRIPTION FROM ANOTHER PHYSICIAN FOR A LEGITIMATE MEDICAL REASON AND IN VIOLATION OF A 1/14/94 AGREED ORDER; DID NOT SELF-REPORT THE SECOND INCIDENT; THIS WAS DETECTED BY A URINE SCREEN IN BOTH CASES; BETWEEN 9/23/94 AND 10/18/94 HE OBTAINED FOUR PRESCRIPTIONS FOR STADOL BY FRAUDULENT MEANS IN THAT PRESCRIPTIONS WERE WRITTEN FOR AN INDIVIDUAL WHO WAS NOT A PATIENT ON PREPRINTED FORMS WHICH HE SIGNED; HE PERSONALLY PRESENTED THE LAST PRESCRIPTION ON 10/18/94, ATTEMPTED TO LEAVE THE STORE WITHOUT PAYING AND WAS ARRESTED.

HUCKABY, HENRY L MD, DATE OF BIRTH JULY 26, 1934, OF 2000 CRAWFORD SUITE 124, HOUSTON, TX, WAS DISCIPLINED BY MEDICARE ON APRIL 21, 1988.
DISCIPLINARY ACTION: 120-MONTH EXCLUSION FROM THE MEDICARE AND/OR MEDICAID PROGRAMS
OFFENSE: CRIMINAL CONVICTION OR PLEA OF GUILTY, NOLO CONTENDERE, OR NO CONTEST TO A CRIME
NOTES: PROGRAM-RELATED CONVICTION.

HUCKABY, HENRY L MD, LICENSE NUMBER 00E0334, OF HOUSTON, TX, WAS DISCIPLINED BY TEXAS ON OCTOBER 29, 1988.
DISCIPLINARY ACTION: 120-MONTH PROBATION; 60-MONTH REQUIRED TO TAKE ADDITIONAL MEDICAL EDUCATION
NOTES: SUSPENSION STAYED; SHALL APPEAR FOR SEMI-ANNUAL REPORTS; SHALL ATTEND 50 HOURS CONTINUING MEDICAL EDUCATION PER YEAR

HUCKABY, HENRY L MD, LICENSE NUMBER 0010966, OF PO BOX 130687, HOUSTON, TX, WAS DISCIPLINED BY GEORGIA ON AUGUST 10, 1990.
DISCIPLINARY ACTION: LICENSE REVOCATION
OFFENSE: DISCIPLINARY ACTION BY ANOTHER STATE OR AGENCY
NOTES: ON 10/29/88 THE TEXAS BOARD SUSPENDED HIS LICENSE, STAYED THE SUSPENSION, AND PLACED HIM ON PROBATION FOR 10 YEARS AFTER HE PLED GUILTY TO MAKING FALSE CLAIMS IN MEDICARE STATEMENTS. ON 12/13/89 ON GEORGIA LICENSE RENEWAL FORM HE SAID NO STATE BOARD HAD TAKEN DISCIPLINARY ACTION AGAINST HIM AND THAT HE HAD NOT BEEN CONVICTED OF ANY FEDERAL, STATE, OR LOCAL STATUTES.

HUDDLESTON, WILLIAM E MD, LICENSE NUMBER 00C5501, OF BRIDGEPORT, TX, WAS DISCIPLINED BY TEXAS ON AUGUST 19, 1994.
DISCIPLINARY ACTION: MONITORING OF PHYSICIAN
OFFENSE: OVERPRESCRIBING OR MISPRESCRIBING DRUGS
NOTES: PRESCRIBED CONTROLLED SUBSTANCES FOR WHICH THERE WAS LITTLE DOCUMENTATION SUPPORTING THE NECESSITY OF THE PRESCRIPTION; DID NOT ADEQUATELY DOCUMENT TREATMENTS OR WHETHER CONSULTANTS WERE OBTAINED; DOES NOT ADMIT TO THE SPECIFIC ALLEGATIONS BUT AGREES TO THE ORDER. SEPARATE FROM PATIENT RECORDS SHALL MAINTAIN A FILE OF EVERY PRESCRIPTION WRITTEN FOR CONTROLLED SUBSTANCES OR DANGEROUS DRUGS WHICH SHALL BE AVAILABLE FOR INSPECTION; SHALL MAINTAIN ADEQUATE MEDICAL RECORDS ON ALL PATIENT OFFICE VISITS WHICH SHALL BE AVAILABLE FOR INSPECTION; SHALL COOPERATE WITH THE BOARD IN VERIFYING COMPLIANCE; SHALL INFORM BOARD OF CHANGE OF ADDRESS WITHIN 10 DAYS OR IF HE LEAVES THE STATE; TIME SPENT OUT OF TEXAS DOES NOT COUNT TOWARD ORDER. SHALL NOT SEEK MODIFICATION FOR ONE YEAR.

HUDSON, RICHARD C DO, DATE OF BIRTH OCTOBER 22, 1946, LICENSE NUMBER 00E9485, OF BRIDGEPORT, TX, WAS DISCIPLINED BY TEXAS ON AUGUST 24, 1991.
DISCIPLINARY ACTION: 60-MONTH PROBATION; RESTRICTION PLACED ON LICENSE
OFFENSE: DISCIPLINARY ACTION BY ANOTHER STATE OR AGENCY
NOTES: DISCIPLINARY ACTION TAKEN BY THE U.S. AIR FORCE. CONDITIONS OF PROBATION: SHALL APPEAR BEFORE THE BOARD ONCE A YEAR; SUBMIT FOR EVALUATION AND TREATMENT OF A PSYCHIATRIST APPROVED BY THE BOARD; MUST NOT CONDUCT ANY EXAMINATION UPON ANY FEMALE PATIENT UNLESS A THIRD PARTY IS PRESENT DURING EXAMINATION.

HUDSON, RICHARD C DO, DATE OF BIRTH OCTOBER 22, 1946, LICENSE NUMBER 00E9485, OF 4001 NW OZMUN, LAWTON, OK, WAS DISCIPLINED BY TEXAS ON JUNE 15, 1993.
DISCIPLINARY ACTION: SURRENDER OF LICENSE
NOTES: BOARD HAS RECEIVED ALLEGATIONS CONCERNING POSSIBLE VIOLATIONS OF THE MEDICAL PRACTICE ACT; WHILE NOT ADMITTING THESE HE VOLUNTARILY SURRENDERS HIS LICENSE IN LIEU OF FURTHER INVESTIGATION OR A HEARING. SHALL NOT PETITION THE BOARD FOR REINSTATEMENT.

HUMMER, MICHAEL GORMAN MD, LICENSE NUMBER 00G7827, OF AUSTIN, TX, WAS DISCIPLINED BY TEXAS ON JUNE 22, 1994.
DISCIPLINARY ACTION: 120-MONTH PROBATION; MONITORING OF PHYSICIAN
OFFENSE: DRUG OR ALCOHOL ABUSE
NOTES: HE SELF-REPORTED THE INTEMPERATE USE OF

VICODIN DURING THE TIME PERIOD OF 1989 TO 1993; HAS A HISTORY OF ONE PRIOR SUBSTANCE ABUSE TREATMENT; DEVELOPED CHRONIC SHOULDER PAIN IN 1989 TO 1990; DURING 1993 WAS TAKING 10 TO 16 VICODIN TABLETS PER DAY; ENTERED RECOVERY PROGRAM IN 10/93; SOBRIETY DATE IS 10/13/93; IS ATTENDING AA DAILY AND RECEIVING TREATMENT FROM A PSYCHIATRIST AND A PRIMARY CARE PHYSICIAN. SUSPENSION STAYED. CONDITIONS OF PROBATION: SHALL ABSTAIN FROM THE CONSUMPTION OF ALCOHOL/CHEMICAL SUBSTANCES IN ANY FORM UNLESS PRESCRIBED BY ANOTHER PHYSICIAN FOR A LEGITIMATE AND THERAPEUTIC PURPOSE; SHALL NOT TREAT OR OTHERWISE SERVE AS PHYSICIAN, PRESCRIBE, DISPENSE OR ADMINISTER DRUGS THAT MAY BE SUBJECT TO ABUSE TO HIMSELF OR ANY MEMBER OF HIS FAMILY; SHALL CONTINUE TO PARTICIPATE IN THE ACTIVITIES OF A PHYSICIAN HEALTH AND REHABILITATION COMMITTEE AND ATTEND WEEKLY MEETINGS WITH QUARTERLY REPORTS. SHALL FOLLOW THE TERMS OF HIS AFTERCARE CONTRACT; SHALL CONTINUE TREATMENT WITH HIS PRIMARY CARE PHYSICIAN; SHALL SUBMIT HIMSELF FOR APPROPRIATE EXAMS INCLUDING DRUG OR ALCOHOL SCREENS; SHALL PARTICIPATE IN AA'S PROGRAM NOT LESS THAN THREE TIMES A WEEK WITH QUARTERLY REPORTS TO THE BOARD; SHALL SUBMIT HIMSELF FOR EVALUATION AND TREATMENT BY A BOARD-APPROVED PSYCHIATRIST; UPON DEMAND HE SHALL SUBMIT TO AN EXAMINATION BY A PHYSICIAN SPECIALIST; SHALL APPEAR BEFORE THE BOARD TWICE A YEAR; SHALL GIVE A COPY OF THIS ORDER TO ANY HEALTH CARE ENTITY WHERE HE HAS PRIVILEGES; SHALL COOPERATE WITH THE BOARD IN VERIFYING COMPLIANCE; SHALL INFORM BOARD OF CHANGE OF ADDRESS WITHIN 10 DAYS OR IF HE LEAVES THE STATE; TIME SPENT OUT OF TEXAS DOES NOT COUNT TOWARD PROBATION. SHALL NOT SEEK MODIFICATION FOR ONE YEAR.

HUNT, JACKIE HANSEN MD, LICENSE NUMBER 00C1908, OF MASON, TX, WAS DISCIPLINED BY TEXAS ON JUNE 17, 1992.
DISCIPLINARY ACTION: SURRENDER OF LICENSE
NOTES: HEALTH REASONS. PERMANENT RETIREMENT.

HUNT, JOHN D MD, LICENSE NUMBER 00G4476, OF SAN ANGELO, TX, WAS DISCIPLINED BY TEXAS ON OCTOBER 9, 1992.
DISCIPLINARY ACTION: 36-MONTH PROBATION
OFFENSE: OVERPRESCRIBING OR MISPRESCRIBING DRUGS
NOTES: NONTHERAPEUTIC PRESCRIBING. SUSPENSION, STAYED. PROBATION UNDER TERMS AND CONDITIONS. ON 1/6/95 PROBATION TERMINATED.

HUNTER, RICHARD BROOKSHIRE MD, LICENSE NUMBER 00C2062, OF DALLAS, TX, WAS DISCIPLINED BY TEXAS ON OCTOBER 1, 1987.
DISCIPLINARY ACTION: PROBATION
OFFENSE: FAILURE TO COMPLY WITH A PREVIOUS BOARD ORDER
NOTES: VIOLATED PROBATIONARY TERMS. PLACED UNDER EXTENDED PROBATION WITH ADDITIONAL STIPULATIONS.

HUNTER, RICHARD BROOKSHIRE MD, LICENSE NUMBER 00C2062, OF DALLAS, TX, WAS DISCIPLINED BY TEXAS ON MARCH 6, 1992.
DISCIPLINARY ACTION: EMERGENCY SUSPENSION
OFFENSE: FAILURE TO COMPLY WITH A PREVIOUS BOARD ORDER
NOTES: VIOLATION OF PREVIOUS BOARD ORDER DUE TO INTEMPERATE USE OF ALCOHOL OR DRUGS. LICENSE TEMPORARILY SUSPENDED.

HUNTER, RICHARD BROOKSHIRE MD, DATE OF BIRTH AUGUST 22, 1925, LICENSE NUMBER 00C2062, OF DALLAS, TX, WAS DISCIPLINED BY TEXAS ON AUGUST 22, 1992.
DISCIPLINARY ACTION: 120-MONTH PROBATION
OFFENSE: DRUG OR ALCOHOL ABUSE
NOTES: UNPROFESSIONAL OR DISHONORABLE CONDUCT LIKELY TO DECEIVE, DEFRAUD OR INJURE THE PUBLIC. SUSPENSION, STAYED. PROBATION UNDER TERMS AND CONDITIONS.

HUNTER, RICHARD BROOKSHIRE MD, DATE OF BIRTH AUGUST 22, 1925, LICENSE NUMBER 00C2062, OF 3600 GASTON 1006 BARNETT TOWER, DALLAS, TX, WAS DISCIPLINED BY TEXAS ON MARCH 26, 1993.
DISCIPLINARY ACTION: SURRENDER OF LICENSE
OFFENSE: FAILURE TO COMPLY WITH A PREVIOUS BOARD ORDER
NOTES: AN 8/22/92 ORDER PLACED TERMS AND CONDITIONS ON HIS CONTINUED PRACTICE; IN LIGHT OF HIS LONG CAREER AND PRACTICAL DIFFICULTIES IN COMPLYING WITH THESE TERMS, THE BOARD ALLOWED HIM TO PERMANENTLY RETIRE.

HURDIS-GRANT, HELEN LINDA MD, DATE OF BIRTH APRIL 2, 1947, OF PO BOX 1708, DENVER CITY, TX, WAS DISCIPLINED BY MEDICARE ON APRIL 16, 1994.
DISCIPLINARY ACTION: EXCLUSION FROM THE MEDICARE AND/OR MEDICAID PROGRAMS
OFFENSE: FAILURE TO COMPLY WITH A PROFESSIONAL RULE
NOTES: DEFAULTED ON PUBLIC HEALTH SERVICE EDUCATION LOAN. REINSTATED ON 8/5/94.

HURDISS, LAWRENCE MD, LICENSE NUMBER G029320, OF CORPUS CHRISTI, TX, WAS DISCIPLINED BY CALIFORNIA ON MAY 7, 1987.
DISCIPLINARY ACTION: LICENSE REVOCATION
OFFENSE: DISCIPLINARY ACTION BY ANOTHER STATE OR AGENCY
NOTES: DISCIPLINE BY TEXAS BOARD

HUTCHENS, JEROME E MD, LICENSE NUMBER 0017829, OF 7827 PRESTWOOD DR, HOUSTON, TX, WAS DISCIPLINED BY GEORGIA ON DECEMBER 3, 1986.
DISCIPLINARY ACTION: PROBATION
OFFENSE: DISCIPLINARY ACTION BY ANOTHER STATE OR AGENCY
NOTES: REVOCATION STAYED; PROBATION CONSISTENT WITH TEXAS BOARD.

HUTCHENS, JEROME ENOS MD, LICENSE NUMBER TXC5733, OF BIG SPRING STATE HOSP BOX 231, BIG SPRING, TX, WAS DISCIPLINED BY DEA ON SEPTEMBER 23, 1992.
DISCIPLINARY ACTION: RESTRICTION PLACED ON CONTROLLED SUBSTANCE LICENSE
OFFENSE: CRIMINAL CONVICTION OR PLEA OF GUILTY, NOLO CONTENDERE, OR NO CONTEST TO A CRIME
NOTES: STATE MEDICAL LICENSE REVOKED 06/16/81; SURRENDERED DEA REGISTRATION CERTIFICATE 10/26/81. WROTE PRESCRIPTIONS FOR DILAUDID TABS. CONVICTED 04/12/82 OF KNOWINGLY AND INTENTIONALLY DISPENSING HYDROMORPHONE WITHOUT VALID MEDICAL PURPOSE AND NOT IN THE COURSE OF PROFESSIONAL PRACTICE. SENTENCED TO FIVE YEARS IN PRISON. ALIAS: JEROME HUTCHINS.

HUTCHENS, JEROME ENOS MD, LICENSE NUMBER 1040961, OF 8510 KENPREDGE, HOUSTON, TX, WAS DISCIPLINED BY INDIANA ON DECEMBER 10, 1992.

DISCIPLINARY ACTION: PROBATION
NOTES: PROBATIONARY LICENSE ISSUED. PROBATION WITHDRAWN ON 12/13/93.

HUTCHENS, JEROME ENOS MD OF HOUSTON, TX, WAS DISCIPLINED BY OHIO ON AUGUST 11, 1993.
DISCIPLINARY ACTION: DENIAL OF NEW LICENSE
OFFENSE: DISCIPLINARY ACTION BY ANOTHER STATE OR AGENCY
NOTES: PRIOR REVOCATION OF HIS TEXAS MEDICAL LICENSE BY THE TEXAS BOARD; FELONY DRUG CONVICTION.

INGRAM, CHESTER WILLIAM JR MD, LICENSE NUMBER 00G1048, OF LIVINGSTON, TX, WAS DISCIPLINED BY TEXAS ON FEBRUARY 23, 1991.
DISCIPLINARY ACTION: RESTRICTION PLACED ON LICENSE
NOTES: HEARING CONTINUED BECAUSE OF PENDING CRIMINAL TRIAL, TO RESUME ON OR BEFORE 5/31/91 IF SAID TRIAL HAS NOT BEEN COMMENCED BY 5/20/91; LIMITATION OF GYNECOLOGICAL PRACTICE TO HAVING TWO ADULTS PRESENT THROUGHOUT THE TIME OF EXAMINATION, WITH THE WITNESSES WRITING THEIR NAMES IN PATIENTS' CHARTS.

INGRAM, CHESTER WILLIAM JR MD, LICENSE NUMBER 00G1048, WAS DISCIPLINED BY TEXAS ON SEPTEMBER 17, 1991.
DISCIPLINARY ACTION: LICENSE SUSPENSION
OFFENSE: CRIMINAL CONVICTION OR PLEA OF GUILTY, NOLO CONTENDERE, OR NO CONTEST TO A CRIME
NOTES: ON 9/12/91 HE WAS SENTENCED TO 40 YEARS IN PRISON FOR CONVICTION OF AGGRAVATED KIDNAPPING.

INGRAM, CHESTER WILLIAM JR MD, LICENSE NUMBER 0007526, OF TX, WAS DISCIPLINED BY ALABAMA ON MARCH 25, 1992.
DISCIPLINARY ACTION: LICENSE REVOCATION
OFFENSE: DISCIPLINARY ACTION BY ANOTHER STATE OR AGENCY
NOTES: CONVICTED IN THE STATE COURT OF TEXAS OF THE OFFENSE OF AGGRAVATED KIDNAPPING AND SENTENCED TO A TERM OF IMPRISONMENT OF 40 YEARS; LICENSE TO PRACTICE MEDICINE IN TEXAS SUSPENDED DUE TO FELONY CONVICTION.

INGRAM, CHESTER WILLIAM JR MD, DATE OF BIRTH DECEMBER 20, 1949, LICENSE NUMBER 0021525, OF 3114 3RD ST NE, BIRMINGHAM, AL, WAS DISCIPLINED BY GEORGIA ON NOVEMBER 5, 1992.
DISCIPLINARY ACTION: LICENSE SUSPENSION
OFFENSE: CRIMINAL CONVICTION OR PLEA OF GUILTY, NOLO CONTENDERE, OR NO CONTEST TO A CRIME
NOTES: CONVICTION OF A FELONY IN TEXAS. SUSPENSION INDEFINITE.

IVERSON, DALE ARTHUR MD OF THE WOODLANDS, TX, WAS DISCIPLINED BY NORTH DAKOTA ON DECEMBER 11, 1992.
DISCIPLINARY ACTION: RESTRICTION PLACED ON LICENSE
NOTES: QUALITY OF CARE ISSUES.

IVERSON, DALE ARTHUR MD, DATE OF BIRTH NOVEMBER 11, 1936, LICENSE NUMBER 00D0180, OF THE WOODLANDS, TX, WAS DISCIPLINED BY TEXAS ON MARCH 5, 1994.
DISCIPLINARY ACTION: 60-MONTH PROBATION
OFFENSE: DISCIPLINARY ACTION BY ANOTHER STATE OR AGENCY
NOTES: LICENSE DISCIPLINED IN NORTH DAKOTA 12/10/92 FOR A CONSISTENT FAILURE TO DOCUMENT AN ADEQUATE HISTORY OR PHYSICAL EXAM; PATIENT CARE WAS SUBSTANDARD. SUSPENSION STAYED. CONDITIONS OF PROBATION: SHALL FULLY COMPLY WITH TERMS OF NORTH DAKOTA STIPULATION; SHALL PROVIDE TO TEXAS COPIES OF ALL DOCUMENTS SENT TO NORTH DAKOTA BOARD INCLUDING CONTINUING MEDICAL EDUCATION VERIFICATION; SHALL GIVE A COPY OF THIS ORDER TO ANY HEALTH CARE ENTITY WHERE HE HAS PRIVILEGES; SHALL COOPERATE WITH THE BOARD IN VERIFYING COMPLIANCE; SHALL INFORM BOARD OF CHANGE OF ADDRESS WITHIN 10 DAYS OR IF HE LEAVES THE STATE; TIME SPENT OUT OF TEXAS DOES NOT COUNT TOWARD PROBATION. SHALL NOT SEEK MODIFICATION FOR ONE YEAR.

JACKSON, JOSEPH JORDAN MD, LICENSE NUMBER 00F9614, OF DALLAS, TX, WAS DISCIPLINED BY TEXAS ON SEPTEMBER 30, 1994.
DISCIPLINARY ACTION: LICENSE REVOCATION
OFFENSE: SUBSTANDARD CARE, INCOMPETENCE, OR NEGLIGENCE
NOTES: ON 5/22/93 WHILE HE WAS THE ONLY PHYSICIAN AT AN EMERGENCY ROOM HE BECAME ANGRY WITH THE NURSING STAFF AND TELEPHONED ANOTHER PHYSICIAN TO SAY HE WAS LEAVING; LEFT BEFORE THE OTHER DOCTOR COULD GET THERE TO RELIEVE HIM; IT IS STANDARD PRACTICE FOR DOCTORS LEAVING AN EMERGENCY ROOM TO BRIEF INCOMING DOCTORS ABOUT PATIENTS, PARTICULARLY CRITICAL CONDITION PATIENTS; HIS CONDUCT CONSTITUTES ABANDONING PATIENTS AND IS BELOW THE STANDARD OF CARE; ON THE SAME NIGHT ANOTHER PATIENT CAME TO EMERGENCY ROOM COMPLAINING OF CHEST PAIN, DIZZINESS, SHORTNESS OF BREATH AND BEING CLOSE TO PASSING OUT; DR. JACKSON BERATED THIS PATIENT FOR COMING TO THE HOSPITAL AND SAID HE WAS NOT HAVING A HEART ATTACK; HE THEN SENT THE PATIENT HOME WITHOUT CHECKING HIS CARDIAC ENZYMES, IV ACCESS, RECHECKING HIS BLOOD PRESSURE AND WATCHING HIM LONGER, CONDUCT WHICH WAS BELOW THE STANDARD OF CARE; THE PATIENT WAS ADMITTED TO THE HOSPITAL THE NEXT DAY FOR HYPERTENSION AND STAYED FIVE DAYS; ANOTHER PATIENT THAT NIGHT WAS IN CRITICAL CONDITION SUFFERING FROM HEAD TRAUMA AS A RESULT OF AN AUTO ACCIDENT AND HIS FAILURE TO RENDER RAPID AND IMMEDIATE ATTENTION WAS BELOW THE STANDARD OF CARE AS WAS HIS LEAVING THE HOSPITAL WITHOUT BRIEFING HIS REPLACEMENT ABOUT THIS PATIENT; FAILED TO DOCUMENT FINDINGS REGARDING FIVE PATIENTS HE SAW THAT NIGHT IN HOSPITAL RECORDS WHICH COULD CAUSE INJURY OR STRESS TO PATIENTS BECAUSE THE ONCOMING PHYSICIANS WOULD NOT BE INFORMED OF THE PATIENT'S HISTORY; LOUDLY AND RUDELY ACCUSED THE NURSING STAFF OF FRAUDULENT AND CRIMINAL ACTIVITIES RELATING TO MEDICARE AND ADMISSION POLICIES; HIS CONTINUED PRACTICE IS AN IMMINENT PERIL TO THE PUBLIC HEALTH.

JACKSON, NICHOLAS M MD, LICENSE NUMBER 00E2632, WAS DISCIPLINED BY TEXAS ON JUNE 22, 1994.
DISCIPLINARY ACTION: 84-MONTH PROBATION; RESTRICTION PLACED ON CONTROLLED SUBSTANCE LICENSE
OFFENSE: DRUG OR ALCOHOL ABUSE
NOTES: HE HAS ENGAGED IN THE INTEMPERATE USE OF DALGAN AND DEVELOPED AN ADDICTION TO THE DRUG; WAS TREATED IN 1991, SUFFERED A RELAPSED AND ENTERED TREATMENT IN 6/93; HAS ADMITTED TO EXPERIMENTING WITH LSD, METHAMPHETAMINES AND

MARIJUAN IN COLLEGE AND OCCASIONALLY USING MARIJUANA AND ALCOHOL DURING MEDICAL SCHOOL; ADMITS ALLOWING DALGAN ACCESS TO ONE PERSON WHO EVENTUALLY NEEDED TREATMENT FOR ADDICTION TO THE DRUG; HAS MAINTAINED SOBRIETY SINCE 6/29/93; CURRENTLY UNDER THE CARE OF A PSYCHIATRIST AND ENTERED A REHABILITATION CONTRACT WITH PHYSICIANS HEALTH AND REHABILITATION COMMITTEE. SUSPENSION STAYED. CONDITIONS OF PROBATION: SHALL APPEAR BEFORE THE BOARD TWICE A YEAR; SHALL ABSTAIN FROM THE CONSUMPTION OF ALCOHOL/CHEMICAL SUBSTANCES IN ANY FORM UNLESS PRESCRIBED BY ANOTHER PHYSICIAN FOR A LEGITIMATE AND THERAPEUTIC PURPOSE; SHALL PARTICIPATE IN AA'S PROGRAM NOT LESS THAN THREE TIMES A WEEK WITH QUARTERLY REPORTS TO THE BOARD; SHALL SUBMIT HIMSELF FOR APPROPRIATE EXAMS INCLUDING DRUG AND ALCOHOL SCREENS; SHALL SUBMIT HIMSELF FOR EVALUATION AND TREATMENT TO A BOARD-APPROVED PSYCHIATRIST; SHALL NOT TREAT OR OTHERWISE SERVE AS PHYSICIAN, PRESCRIBE DISPENSE OR DRUGS THAT MAY BE SUBJECT TO ABUSE TO HIMSELF OR ANY MEMBER OF HIS FAMILY; SHALL SURRENDER HIS DEA AND TEXAS CONTROLLED SUBSTANCES CERTIFICATES AND NOT REAPPLY WITH PERMISSION; SHALL ATTEND AT LEAST 50 HOURS PER YEAR OF CONTINUING MEDICAL EDUCATION; SHALL COMPLY WITH TERMS OF CONTRACT WITH THE PHYSICIANS HEALTH AND REHABILITATION COMMITTEE AND PROVIDE A COPY OF THIS CONTRACT; SHALL GIVE A COPY OF THIS ORDER TO ANY HEALTH CARE ENTITY WHERE HE HAS PRIVILEGES; SHALL COOPERATE WITH THE BOARD IN VERIFYING COMPLIANCE; SHALL INFORM BOARD OF CHANGE OF ADDRESS OR IF HE LEAVES THE STATE; TIME SPENT OUT OF TEXAS DOES NOT COUNT TOWARD PROBATION. SHALL NOT SEEK MODIFICATION FOR ONE YEAR.

JACOBI, RUDOLPH E MD, LICENSE NUMBER 00C2269, OF HOUSTON, TX, WAS DISCIPLINED BY TEXAS ON APRIL 10, 1992.
DISCIPLINARY ACTION: SURRENDER OF LICENSE
NOTES: LICENSE PERMANENTLY RETIRED IN LIEU OF FURTHER DISCIPLINARY ACTION.

JACOBSON, KAREN S MD, LICENSE NUMBER 00F9615, OF AUSTIN, TX, WAS DISCIPLINED BY TEXAS ON JUNE 22, 1994.
DISCIPLINARY ACTION: REPRIMAND
OFFENSE: PROFESSIONAL MISCONDUCT
NOTES: IN 1991 SHE ORDERED NUBAIN FOR A PATIENT WITH WHOM SHE BECAME PERSONALLY ACQUAINTED WHO HAD BEEN DIAGNOSED WITH CANCER; ALLEGES THAT SHE TOOK A HISTORY AND PHYSICAL OF THE PATIENT AND THAT THE PATIENT TOLD HER THAT OTHER PAIN MEDICATIONS WERE NOT BEING TAKEN; FAILED TO CONFER WITH PATIENT'S TREATING PHYSICIAN; ALLEGES THAT FOR TWO YEARS SHE KEPT THE APPROPRIATE RECORDS BUT DOES NOT KNOW WHERE THOSE RECORDS ARE; ALLEGES SHE DID NOT CHARGE THE PATIENT; THIS ORDER IS A SETTLEMENT IN LIEU OF A CONTESTED HEARING. SHALL GIVE A COPY OF THIS ORDER TO ANY HEALTH CARE ENTITY WHERE SHE HAS PRIVILEGES.

JAIKARAN, JACQUES S MD, LICENSE NUMBER 00F2731, OF HUMBLE, TX, WAS DISCIPLINED BY TEXAS ON OCTOBER 9, 1992.
DISCIPLINARY ACTION: REPRIMAND
OFFENSE: FAILURE TO COMPLY WITH A PROFESSIONAL RULE
NOTES: FALSE ADVERTISING.

JAIN, ROSHAN L MD, LICENSE NUMBER 0220079, OF 18339 CAPE BAHAMAS, HOUSTON, TX, WAS DISCIPLINED BY WISCONSIN ON MARCH 21, 1990.
DISCIPLINARY ACTION: LICENSE REVOCATION
OFFENSE: DISCIPLINARY ACTION BY ANOTHER STATE OR AGENCY
NOTES: LICENSE WAS REVOKED IN NEW YORK IN 1986 BECAUSE OF 7 COUNTS OF UNPROFESSIONAL CONDUCT.

JAIN, ROSHAN L MD, DATE OF BIRTH SEPTEMBER 21, 1936, OF 18339 CAPE BAHAMAS, HOUSTON, TX, WAS DISCIPLINED BY MEDICARE ON JULY 23, 1991.
DISCIPLINARY ACTION: EXCLUSION FROM THE MEDICARE AND/OR MEDICAID PROGRAMS
OFFENSE: DISCIPLINARY ACTION BY ANOTHER STATE OR AGENCY
NOTES: LICENSE REVOCATION OR SUSPENSION.

JAIN, ROSHAN LAL MD, LICENSE NUMBER 0138688, OF HOUSTON, TX, WAS DISCIPLINED BY NEW YORK ON JANUARY 21, 1987.
DISCIPLINARY ACTION: LICENSE REVOCATION

JAIN, ROSHAN LAL MD WAS DISCIPLINED BY NEW HAMPSHIRE ON NOVEMBER 7, 1987.
DISCIPLINARY ACTION: LICENSE REVOCATION
OFFENSE: DISCIPLINARY ACTION BY ANOTHER STATE OR AGENCY

JAMES, JOCELYN LEAH MD, LICENSE NUMBER 00G6668, OF SAN ANTONIO, TX, WAS DISCIPLINED BY TEXAS ON OCTOBER 9, 1992.
DISCIPLINARY ACTION: 60-MONTH PROBATION
OFFENSE: SUBSTANDARD CARE, INCOMPETENCE, OR NEGLIGENCE
NOTES: PROFESSIONAL FAILURE TO PRACTICE MEDICINE IN AN ACCEPTABLE MANNER CONSISTENT WITH PUBLIC HEALTH AND WELFARE. SUSPENSION STAYED. PROBATION UNDER TERMS AND CONDITIONS. ON 11/3/94 PROBATION TERMINATED.

JAREM, BOHDAN J MD WAS DISCIPLINED BY ARIZONA ON DECEMBER 2, 1993.
OFFENSE: DISCIPLINARY ACTION BY ANOTHER STATE OR AGENCY
NOTES: TEXAS ISSUED AN ORDER IN 01/93 SUSPENDING HIS LICENSE FOR FIVE YEARS. HE SIGNED AND ENTERED INTO A STIPULATION AND ORDER NOT TO PRACTICE MEDICINE IN ARIZONA.

JAREM, BOHDAN JOHN MD, DATE OF BIRTH JULY 22, 1941, LICENSE NUMBER 00D9829, OF 5400 PRESTON OAKS #2003, DALLAS, TX, WAS DISCIPLINED BY TEXAS ON JANUARY 30, 1993.
DISCIPLINARY ACTION: EMERGENCY SUSPENSION
OFFENSE: PHYSICAL OR MENTAL ILLNESS INHIBITING THE ABILITY TO PRACTICE WITH SKILL AND SAFETY
NOTES: SUFFERS FROM A BIPOLAR DISORDER IN THE MANIC PHASE AND IS IN NEED OF PSYCHIATRIC COUNSELING.

JAREM, BOHDAN JOHN MD, DATE OF BIRTH JULY 22, 1941, LICENSE NUMBER 00D9829, OF 4118 KEYSTONE, GARLAND, TX, WAS DISCIPLINED BY TEXAS ON JUNE 15, 1993.
DISCIPLINARY ACTION: 60-MONTH PROBATION; MONITORING OF PHYSICIAN
NOTES: FROM 1/7/93-2/22/93 HE RECEIVED INPATIENT PSYCHIATRIC TREATMENT FOR A BIPOLAR DISORDER IN THE MANIC PHASE; DISORDER IS CURRENTLY IN REMISSION AND HE IS RECEIVING PSYCHIATRIC COUNSELING. FIVE YEAR SUSPENSION STAYED.

CONDITIONS OF PROBATION: SHALL CONTINUE TO RECEIVE PSYCHIATRIC TREATMENT WITH QUARTERLY REPORTS TO THE BOARD; SHALL OBTAIN A BOARD-APPROVED PSYCHIATRIST AND CONTINUE TREATMENT IF HE RELOCATES; SHALL SUBMIT HIMSELF FOR RANDOM LAB TESTING OF HIS LITHIUM LEVEL; SHALL APPEAR BEFORE THE BOARD TWICE A YEAR; SHALL GIVE A COPY OF THIS ORDER TO ANY HEALTH CARE ENTITY WHERE HE HAS PRIVILEGES; SHALL COOPERATE WITH THE BOARD IN VERIFYING COMPLIANCE; SHALL INFORM BOARD OF CHANGE OF ADDRESS WITHIN 10 DAYS OR IF HE LEAVES TEXAS; TIME SPENT OUT OF TEXAS DOES NOT COUNT TOWARD PROBATION. SHALL NOT SEEK MODIFICATION FOR ONE YEAR.

JAREM, BOHDAN JOHN MD, LICENSE NUMBER 0029241, OF GARLAND, TX, WAS DISCIPLINED BY OHIO ON MARCH 16, 1994.
DISCIPLINARY ACTION: LICENSE SUSPENSION; PROBATION
OFFENSE: DISCIPLINARY ACTION BY ANOTHER STATE OR AGENCY
NOTES: PRIOR ACTION BY TEXAS BOARD DUE TO HIS BIPOLAR DISORDER. INDEFINITE SUSPENSION. CONDITIONS FOR REINSTATEMENT ESTABLISHED; PROBATION FOR AT LEAST TWO YEARS.

JAVIER, RICARDO R MD, LICENSE NUMBER 00D9186, OF HUBBARD, TX, WAS DISCIPLINED BY TEXAS ON MARCH 5, 1994.
DISCIPLINARY ACTION: 36-MONTH RESTRICTION PLACED ON LICENSE; REQUIRED TO TAKE ADDITIONAL MEDICAL EDUCATION
OFFENSE: SUBSTANDARD CARE, INCOMPETENCE, OR NEGLIGENCE
NOTES: IN 5/84 HE INITIATED A SURGICAL PROCEDURE AT A HOSPITAL INSUFFICIENTLY EQUIPPED TO HANDLE IT AND FAILED TO REFER THE PATIENT TO A SURGEON AND FACILITY BETTER ABLE TO CARE FOR THE PATIENT IN A TIMELY MANNER; IN 8/94 FAILED TO ADDRESS THE ACUTE ABDOMEN OF A PATIENT IN A TIMELY MANNER ALTHOUGH THERE WERE CLINICAL INDICATIONS FOR SURGERY; IN 1990 FAILED TO ADEQUATELY EVALUATE A NURSING HOME PATIENT ON A SUFFICIENTLY REGULAR BASIS OR TO ADEQUATELY DOCUMENT SUCH EVALUATIONS; HE NO LONGER PERFORMS SURGERY AND HAS NOT SEEN NURSING HOME PATIENTS FOR TWO YEARS. SHALL MAINTAIN A CURRENT ADVANCED CARDIAC LIFE SUPPORT AND ADVANCED TRAUMA LIFE SUPPORT CERTIFICATION; SHALL NOT ACT AS A PRIMARY SURGEON ON ANY SURGICAL CASE EXCEPT FOR OFFICE PROCEDURES REQUIRING ONLY LOCAL ANESTHESIA; SHALL ATTEND AT LEAST 50 HOURS CONTINUING MEDICAL EDUCATION PER YEAR; DURING THE FIRST YEAR SHALL PROVIDE AT LEAST ONE LETTER OF RECOMMENDATION FROM A PHYSICIAN AT EACH HOSPITAL WHERE HE WORKS; SHALL GIVE A COPY OF THIS ORDER TO ANY HEALTH CARE ENTITY WHERE HE HAS PRIVILEGES; SHALL COOPERATE WITH THE BOARD IN VERIFYING COMPLIANCE; SHALL INFORM BOARD OF CHANGE OF ADDRESS WITHIN 10 DAYS OR IF HE LEAVES THE STATE; TIME SPENT OUT OF TEXAS DOES NOT COUNT TOWARD RESTRICTION. SHALL NOT SEEK MODIFICATION FOR ONE YEAR.

JAYANTY, SATYA VIKRAM MD, LICENSE NUMBER 00G4609, OF HOUSTON, TX, WAS DISCIPLINED BY TEXAS ON AUGUST 25, 1989.
DISCIPLINARY ACTION: REPRIMAND

JOHNSON, GERALD WAYNE MD, DATE OF BIRTH MARCH 11, 1940, LICENSE NUMBER 00D6462, OF 17115 RED OAK DRIVE #211, HOUSTON, TX, WAS DISCIPLINED BY TEXAS ON AUGUST 24, 1991.
DISCIPLINARY ACTION: RESTRICTION PLACED ON LICENSE
NOTES: AGREES TO LIMIT HIMSELF TO REMOVING NO MORE THAN 2000 CCS. OF FAT DURING A LIPOSUCTION DAY SURGERY PROCEDURE; NO MORE THAN 4000 CCS. OF FAT IN A HOSPITAL SETTING; IF NECESSARY, MUST TRANSFUSE ONE UNIT OF BLOOD WHEN 2000 CCS. ARE REMOVED, WITH ANOTHER UNIT OF BLOOD WHEN 3000-4000 CCS. OF FAT ARE REMOVED. ALSO AGREES TO ENSURE THAT BEFORE BEGINNING ANY PLASTIC SURGERY PROCEDURE, TRANSPORTATION IS AVAILABLE TO A HOSPITAL FACILITY WITHIN A FIVE-MILE RADIUS FROM THE SURGICAL SITE FOR ANY PATIENT WHO EXPERIENCES COMPLICATIONS. ON 8/20/93 ORDER TERMINATED AND LICENSE FREE AND CLEAR OF ANY PREVIOUS RESTRICTIONS.

JOHNSON, HAROLD Z MD WAS DISCIPLINED BY WASHINGTON ON SEPTEMBER 8, 1989.
DISCIPLINARY ACTION: EMERGENCY SUSPENSION
OFFENSE: DRUG OR ALCOHOL ABUSE
NOTES: HAS BEEN OBSERVED EXHIBITING SIGNS OF SUBSTANCE ABUSE AND/OR A PHYSICAL OR MENTAL IMPAIRMENT WHICH RENDERS HIM INCAPABLE OF PRACTICING; ALLEGEDLY PROVIDED INCOMPETENT, NEGLIGENT OR SUBSTANDARD MEDICAL SERVICE TO 25 PATIENTS

JOHNSON, HAROLD Z MD, LICENSE NUMBER 00D0926, OF ADA, OK, WAS DISCIPLINED BY TEXAS ON JUNE 10, 1991.
OFFENSE: DISCIPLINARY ACTION BY ANOTHER STATE OR AGENCY
NOTES: SHOULD HE DESIRE TO PRACTICE MEDICINE IN TEXAS, MUST DEMONSTRATE TO BOARD HIS CAPACITY TO PRACTICE WITH REASONABLE SKILL AND SAFETY AND PROVIDE STATUS REPORT OF WASHINGTON LICENSE; IF TEXAS GRANTS HIM PERMISSION TO PRACTICE, TEXAS BOARD MAY IMPOSE ADDITIONAL PROBATIONARY TERMS.

JOHNSON, HAROLD ZAY MD, LICENSE NUMBER 0G18683, OF LONG BEACH, CA, WAS DISCIPLINED BY CALIFORNIA ON MAY 1, 1994.
DISCIPLINARY ACTION: LICENSE REVOCATION
OFFENSE: DISCIPLINARY ACTION BY ANOTHER STATE OR AGENCY
NOTES: DISCIPLINED BY WASHINGTON STATE BOARD BASED ON ALLEGED IMPAIRMENT DUE TO ALCOHOLISM. TEXAS DISCIPLINE BASED ON ABOVE ACTION. DEFAULT DECISION.

JOHNSON, LECTOY T MD, DATE OF BIRTH NOVEMBER 28, 1931, OF 1919 LABRANCH, HOUSTON, TX, WAS DISCIPLINED BY MEDICARE ON OCTOBER 14, 1988.
DISCIPLINARY ACTION: 60-MONTH EXCLUSION FROM THE MEDICARE AND/OR MEDICAID PROGRAMS
OFFENSE: CRIMINAL CONVICTION OR PLEA OF GUILTY, NOLO CONTENDERE, OR NO CONTEST TO A CRIME
NOTES: PROGRAM-RELATED CONVICTION.

JOHNSON, NEAL D MD, LICENSE NUMBER 00G3500, OF AUSTIN, TX, WAS DISCIPLINED BY TEXAS ON JUNE 22, 1994.
DISCIPLINARY ACTION: REQUIRED TO TAKE ADDITIONAL MEDICAL EDUCATION
OFFENSE: SUBSTANDARD CARE, INCOMPETENCE, OR NEGLIGENCE
NOTES: FAILED TO CONSIDER AND/OR DIAGNOSE APPENDICITIS IN ONE PATIENT EVEN AFTER SERIAL PRESENTATIONS. SHALL WITHIN ONE YEAR ATTEND AT LEAST 50 HOURS

OF CONTINUING MEDICAL EDUCATION WITH SIX HOURS IN RISK MANAGEMENT AND NINE HOURS IN AREAS DEALING WITH THE DIAGNOSIS OF ACUTE ABDOMINAL PAIN; SHALL GIVE A COPY OF THIS ORDER TO ANY HEALTH CARE ENTITY WHERE HE HAS PRIVILEGES; SHALL COOPERATE WITH THE BOARD IN VERIFYING COMPLIANCE; SHALL INFORM BOARD OF ADDRESS CHANGE WITHIN 10 DAYS. SHALL NOT SEEK MODIFICATION FOR SIX MONTHS. ON 6/28/95, BOARD GRANTED HIS PETITION FOR TERMINATION OF ORDER BASED ON HIS COMPLIANCE WITH ALL CONDITIONS.

JOHNSON, WILLIAM R MD, LICENSE NUMBER 00DO573, OF AUSTIN, TX, WAS DISCIPLINED BY TEXAS ON AUGUST 18, 1990.
DISCIPLINARY ACTION: LICENSE REVOCATION
OFFENSE: OVERPRESCRIBING OR MISPRESCRIBING DRUGS
NOTES: STIPULATED ORDER. LICENSE IMMEDIATELY AND PERMANENTLY RETIRED IN LIEU OF CONTINUING CONTESTED CASE HEARING CONCERNING ALLEGATIONS OF NONTHERAPEUTIC PRESCRIBING OF CONTROLLED SUBSTANCES.

JOHNSON, WILLIAM RICHARD MD OF BOX 1507 BUNA, BUNA, TX, WAS DISCIPLINED BY DEA ON OCTOBER 18, 1990.
DISCIPLINARY ACTION: SURRENDER OF CONTROLLED SUBSTANCE LICENSE
OFFENSE: OVERPRESCRIBING OR MISPRESCRIBING DRUGS
NOTES: NON-THERAPEUTIC PRESCRIBING.

JOHNSTON, JAMES CHRISTOPHER MD, LICENSE NUMBER 00G8880, OF NACOGDOCHES, TX, WAS DISCIPLINED BY TEXAS ON JUNE 22, 1994.
DISCIPLINARY ACTION: RESTRICTION PLACED ON LICENSE
OFFENSE: SEXUAL ABUSE OF OR SEXUAL MISCONDUCT WITH A PATIENT
NOTES: AS RECENTLY AS 6/8/94 CRIMINAL COMPLAINTS WERE FILED AGAINST HIM ALLEGING HE ENGAGED IN BEHAVIOR CONSTITUTING ATTEMPTED SEXUAL ASSAULT AGAINST INDIVIDUALS WHO WERE PATIENTS; DENIES ALLEGATIONS; BECAUSE HE DESIRES TO FOCUS RESOURCES AND TIME ON DEFENSE OF THE CRIMINAL CASE. AGREES TO THIS ORDER WITH THE BOARD. LICENSE IS RESTRICTED AS FOLLOWS: SHALL NOT EXAMINE OR TREAT PATIENTS AFTER THE ORDER DATE; WITHIN 30 DAYS SHALL SUBMIT HIMSELF FOR ASSESSMENT THROUGH THE BEHAVIOR CARE NETWORK PROGRAM OR OTHER BOARD-APPROVED PROGRAM WHICH WILL FOCUS ON THE DISPARITY BETWEEN THE COMPLAINTS AGAINST HIM AND HIS OWN VERSION OF EVENTS AND ATTEMPT TO DETERMINE THE DEGREE OF RISK TO THE PUBLIC INVOLVED IN HIS CONTINUED PRACTICE; SHOULD THIS EVALUATION INDICATE HIS PRACTICE CONSTITUTES NO THREAT TO THE PUBLIC HEALTH HE SHALL BE PERMITTED TO RESUME PRACTICE PENDING FURTHER ORDER OF THE BOARD PROVIDED HE SEES PATIENTS ONLY WHEN ACCOMPANIED BY A CHAPERONEE APPROVED IN ADVANCE WHO WILL SIGN ALL CHARTS TO INDICATE PRESENCE; SHALL COOPERATE WITH THE BOARD IN VERIFYING COMPLIANCE; SHALL INFORM BOARD OF CHANGE OF ADDRESS WITHIN 10 DAYS.

JONES, GARY ROY MD, LICENSE NUMBER 00D0928, OF AUSTIN, TX, WAS DISCIPLINED BY TEXAS ON OCTOBER 26, 1990.
DISCIPLINARY ACTION: 24-MONTH PROBATION; RESTRICTION PLACED ON LICENSE
NOTES: MUST SUBMIT FOR PSYCHIATRIC EVALUATION AND FOLLOW ANY RECOMMENDED TREATMENT; HAVE NURSE/ASSISTANT PRESENT DURING CERTAIN EXAMINATIONS.

JONES, JAMES HOLLIS MD, LICENSE NUMBER 00C2516, OF DENTON, TX, WAS DISCIPLINED BY TEXAS ON MARCH 5, 1994.
DISCIPLINARY ACTION: SURRENDER OF CONTROLLED SUBSTANCE LICENSE; 60-MONTH PROBATION
OFFENSE: OVERPRESCRIBING OR MISPRESCRIBING DRUGS
NOTES: BETWEEN JUNE 1989 AND APRIL 1993 HE COMMITTED NUMEROUS PRESCRIPTION VIOLATIONS INCLUDING PRESCRIBING CONTROLLED SUBSTANCES SUCH AS LORTAB AND HYDROCODONE TO PATIENTS HE KNEW OR SHOULD HAVE KNOWN WERE HABITUAL USERS OF NARCOTIC DRUGS; PRESCRIBED VARIOUS CONTROLLED SUBSTANCES SUCH AS HYDROCODONE, XANAX, ANEXSIA, DARVOCET, FIORINAL, VALIUM, MOTRIN, AND TUSSIONEX TO PATIENTS WHO HAD NO EXAMINATIONS OR REASON FOR THE PRESCRIPTION NOTED IN THEIR RECORDS. FIVE YEAR SUSPENSION STAYED. CONDITIONS OF PROBATION: SHALL APPEAR BEFORE THE BOARD TWICE A YEAR; SHALL SURRENDER DEA AND TEXAS CONTROLLED SUBSTANCES REGISTRATION CERTIFICATES AND SHALL NOT REREGISTER WITHOUT THE BOARDS APPROVAL; SHALL NOT SIGN OR INDICATE IN ANY MANNER IN PATIENT RECORDS THAT HE HAS SEEN PATIENTS UNLESS HE ACTUALLY HAS SEEN AND EXAMINED THE PATIENT UNLESS IT IS CLEARLY NOTED THAT HE DID NOT PERSONALLY EXAMINE THE PATIENT; SHALL PERSONALLY EXAMINE PATIENT ON THE FIRST VISIT; SHALL ATTEND 50 HOURS PER YEAR OF CONTINUING MEDICAL EDUCATION; SHALL WITHIN SIX MONTHS COMPLETE A BOARD-APPROVED ADDICTIONOLOGY COURSE; SHALL GIVE A COPY OF THIS ORDER TO ANY HEALTH CARE ENTITY WHERE HE HAS PRIVILEGES; SHALL COOPERATE WITH THE BOARD IN VERIFYING COMPLIANCE; SHALL INFORM BOARD OF CHANGE OF ADDRESS WITHIN 10 DAYS OR IF HE LEAVES THE STATE; TIME SPENT OUT OF TEXAS DOES NOT COUNT TOWARD PROBATION. SHALL NOT SEEK MODIFICATION FOR ONE YEAR.

JONES, JAMES W DO, LICENSE NUMBER 0120716, OF 10545 MAYLEE, DALLAS, TX, WAS DISCIPLINED BY NEW YORK ON SEPTEMBER 30, 1993.
DISCIPLINARY ACTION: 36-MONTH PROBATION
OFFENSE: DISCIPLINARY ACTION BY ANOTHER STATE OR AGENCY
NOTES: DISCIPLINED BY THE TEXAS BOARD. 3 YEAR SUSPENSION STAYED.

JONES, JAMES WENDELL DO, LICENSE NUMBER 00E2032, OF DALLAS, TX, WAS DISCIPLINED BY TEXAS ON APRIL 21, 1990.
DISCIPLINARY ACTION: REQUIRED TO TAKE ADDITIONAL MEDICAL EDUCATION; MONITORING OF PHYSICIAN
NOTES: STIPULATED ORDER. MUST MAINTAIN LIST OF ALL PATIENTS SEEN DURING EACH CALENDAR QUARTER AND AUTHORIZE PHYSICIAN TO REPORT TO BOARD CONCERNING QUALITY AND APPROPRIATENESS OF PHYSICIAN'S DIAGNOSTIC AND TREATMENT DECISIONS, OBTAIN CONTINUING MEDICAL EDUCATION, ATTEND RISK MANAGEMENT COURSE, COMPLETE FAMILY PRACTICE REVIEW OR REFRESHER COURSE, AND APPEAR ANNUALLY BEFORE BOARD.

JONES, JAMES WENDELL DO, LICENSE NUMBER 00E2032, OF DALLAS, TX, WAS DISCIPLINED BY TEXAS ON MARCH 6, 1992.

DISCIPLINARY ACTION: 36-MONTH PROBATION
OFFENSE: SUBSTANDARD CARE, INCOMPETENCE, OR NEGLIGENCE
NOTES: PROFESSIONAL FAILURE TO PRACTICE MEDICINE IN AN ACCEPTABLE MANNER CONSISTENT WITH PUBLIC HEALTH AND WELFARE. LICENSE SUSPENDED, SUSPENSION STAYED; PROBATION UNDER TERMS AND CONDITIONS. EFFECTIVE 4/30/93 LICENSE FREE OF ANY RESTRICTION OR LIMITATION.

JONES, ROLAND W III MD OF ORANGE, TX, WAS DISCIPLINED BY LOUISIANA ON DECEMBER 19, 1989.
DISCIPLINARY ACTION: LICENSE SUSPENSION
OFFENSE: DISCIPLINARY ACTION BY ANOTHER STATE OR AGENCY
NOTES: DISCIPLINED BY TEXAS; LICENSE SUSPENDED PENDING RESTORATION BY TEXAS LICENSING AUTHORITY AND PETITION TO THE BOARD FOR REINSTATEMENT.

JONES, ROLAND W III MD OF ORANGE, TX, WAS DISCIPLINED BY DEA ON AUGUST 24, 1994.
DISCIPLINARY ACTION: REVOCATION OF CONTROLLED SUBSTANCE LICENSE
OFFENSE: DISCIPLINARY ACTION BY ANOTHER STATE OR AGENCY
NOTES: ON 11/9/90 TEXAS BOARD PLACED HIS LICENSE ON PROBATION FOR TEN YEARS WITH SEVERAL TERMS AND CONDITIONS BECAUSE IT FOUND HE HAD ENGAGED IN THE INTEMPERATE USE OF ALCOHOL. HAD BEEN DISCIPLINED BY A HOSPITAL AND FAILED TO KEEP ACCURATE RECORDS OF PURCHASES AND DISPOSALS OF CONTROLLED SUBSTANCES. ON 6/26/92 HIS STATE REGISTRATION TO HANDLE CONTROLLED SUBSTANCES WAS CANCELLED. ON 8/20/92 BOARD SUSPENDED HIS LICENSE FOR FAILURE TO FOLLOW TERMS OF THIS PROBATION. THEREFORE HE LACKS STATE AUTHORIZATION TO PRESCRIBE CONTROLLED SUBSTANCES.

JONES, ROLAND WARD III MD, LICENSE NUMBER 00E9726, OF ORANGE, TX, WAS DISCIPLINED BY TEXAS ON OCTOBER 26, 1990.
DISCIPLINARY ACTION: 120-MONTH PROBATION; RESTRICTION PLACED ON LICENSE
OFFENSE: LOSS OR RESTRICTION OF HOSPITAL PRIVILEGES
NOTES: DISCIPLINED BY LICENSED HOSPITAL OR MEDICAL STAFF OF HOSPITAL, INCLUDING REMOVAL, SUSPENSION, LIMITATION OF HOSPITAL PRIVILEGES OR OTHER DISCIPLINARY ACTION; FAILURE TO KEEP COMPLETE AND ACCURATE RECORDS OF PURCHASES AND DISPOSALS OF DRUGS OR CONTROLLED SUBSTANCES; INTEMPERANCE IN USE OF ALCOHOL OR DRUGS THAT COULD ENDANGER LIVES OF PATIENTS; INABILITY TO PRACTICE MEDICINE WITH REASONABLE SKILL AND SAFETY TO PATIENTS BY REASON OF ILLNESS, DRUNKENNESS, EXCESSIVE USE OF DRUGS, NARCOTICS, CHEMICALS, OR OTHER TYPE OF MATERIAL OR AS RESULT OF MENTAL OR PHYSICAL CONDITION.

JONES, ROLAND WARD III MD, LICENSE NUMBER 00E9726, OF ORANGE, TX, WAS DISCIPLINED BY TEXAS ON MAY 21, 1992.
DISCIPLINARY ACTION: EMERGENCY SUSPENSION

JONES, ROLAND WARD III MD, LICENSE NUMBER 00E9726, OF ORANGE, TX, WAS DISCIPLINED BY TEXAS ON AUGUST 20, 1992.
DISCIPLINARY ACTION: 12-MONTH LICENSE SUSPENSION
OFFENSE: DRUG OR ALCOHOL ABUSE
NOTES: UNPROFESSIONAL OR DISHONORABLE CONDUCT LIKELY TO DECEIVE, DEFRAUD OR INJURE THE PUBLIC; AND INABILITY TO PRACTICE MEDICINE WITH REASONABLE SKILL AND SAFETY TO PATIENTS. SUSPENSION UNDER TERMS AND CONDITIONS. ON 4/16/94 HIS REQUEST FOR REINSTATEMENT OF HIS LICENSE WAS DENIED.

JONES, SEABORN E DO, LICENSE NUMBER 00C4382, OF MINEOLA, TX, WAS DISCIPLINED BY TEXAS ON JULY 28, 1989.
DISCIPLINARY ACTION: 12-MONTH RESTRICTION PLACED ON CONTROLLED SUBSTANCE LICENSE
NOTES: REFRAIN FROM PRESCRIBING, DISPENSING OR ADMINISTERING SCHEDULE II, II-N, III CONTROLLED SUBSTANCES; REFRAIN FROM PRESCRIPTION OR ADMINISTRATION OF DRUGS FOR PATIENTS UNLESS THERAPEUTIC; REFRAIN FROM PRESCRIBING, ADMINISTERING OR DISPENSING DRUGS WITH ABUSE POTENTIAL UNTIL SATISFIED OF LEGITIMATE NEED; UNDERSTAND ABUSE POTENTIAL OF CONTROLLED SUBSTANCES AND PRESCRIPTION DRUGS BY PATIENTS; CONDUCT PROPER FOLLOW-UP EXAMS, MAINTAIN MEDICAL RECORDS ACCORDING TO PROFESSIONAL STANDARDS.

JONES, SHELLIE JR MD OF LEESVILLE, LA, WAS DISCIPLINED BY LOUISIANA ON SEPTEMBER 25, 1989.
DISCIPLINARY ACTION: 6-MONTH LICENSE SUSPENSION; 54-MONTH PROBATION
OFFENSE: CRIMINAL CONVICTION OR PLEA OF GUILTY, NOLO CONTENDERE, OR NO CONTEST TO A CRIME
NOTES: ALSO MISPRESCRIBING CONTROLLED SUBSTANCES; REMAINDER OF 5 YEAR SUSPENSION STAYED, LIFETIME PROHIBITION ON PRESCRIBING SCHEDULE II CONTROLLED SUBSTANCES, PROHIBITION DURING PROBATION ON PRESCRIPTION OF SCHEDULE III-V CONTROLLED SUBSTANCES, CONTINUING MEDICAL EDUCATION; $2500 FINE

JONES, SHELLIE J JR MD, LICENSE NUMBER 00C4383, OF LEESVILLE, LA, WAS DISCIPLINED BY TEXAS ON AUGUST 18, 1990.
OFFENSE: DISCIPLINARY ACTION BY ANOTHER STATE OR AGENCY
NOTES: STIPULATED ORDER. MUST COMPLY WITH LOUISIANA ORDER, PROVIDE TEXAS BOARD WITH ANY REQUESTED REPORTS AND OBTAIN PERMISSION OF BOARD BEFORE PRACTICING IN TEXAS.

JOSEY, WILLIE L MD, DATE OF BIRTH NOVEMBER 18, 1946, LICENSE NUMBER 0023878, OF 815 MAIN STREET, SOUTH SHORE, KY, WAS DISCIPLINED BY KENTUCKY ON APRIL 11, 1985.
DISCIPLINARY ACTION: 24-MONTH PROBATION
OFFENSE: DRUG OR ALCOHOL ABUSE
NOTES: DEPENDENCY ON ORAL OXYCODONE. CONDITIONS OF PROBATION: SHALL DEVELOP AND MAINTAIN A RELATIONSHIP WITH THE COMMITTEE ON IMPAIRED PHYSICIANS; SHALL ACTIVELY PARTICIPATE IN AA AND NARCOTICS ANONYMOUS AND ATTEND AT LEAST ONE MEETING PER WEEK. ON 4/11/87 HE WAS DISCHARGED FROM PROBATION.

JOSEY, WILLIE L MD, LICENSE NUMBER 0055467, OF 18480 W 5TH STREET, BELOIT, OH, WAS DISCIPLINED BY DEA ON MARCH 20, 1990.
DISCIPLINARY ACTION: SURRENDER OF CONTROLLED SUBSTANCE LICENSE
OFFENSE: DISCIPLINARY ACTION BY ANOTHER STATE OR AGENCY
NOTES: OHIO STATE MEDICAL BOARD HAS PLACED RESTRICTIONS ON HIS MEDICAL LICENSE. ONE OF THE CONDITIONS IMPOSED WAS THAT HE COULD NO

LONGER POSSESS A DEA CERTIFICATE OF REGISTRATION.

JOSEY, WILLIE L MD, DATE OF BIRTH NOVEMBER 18, 1946, LICENSE NUMBER 0023878, OF 815 MAIN STREET, SOUTH SHORE, KY, WAS DISCIPLINED BY KENTUCKY ON JUNE 21, 1990.
DISCIPLINARY ACTION: 60-MONTH PROBATION; RESTRICTION PLACED ON CONTROLLED SUBSTANCE LICENSE
NOTES: IMPLEMENTATION OF ORDER STAYED UNTIL HE RELOCATES TO PRACTICE IN KENTUCKY. CONDITIONS OF PROBATION: SHALL SUBMIT QUARTERLY DECLARATIONS OF COMPLIANCE WITH ORDER; SHALL SURRENDER HIS DEA CERTIFICATE AND SHALL NOT APPLY FOR REGISTRATION WITH DEA WITHOUT PRIOR BOARD APPROVAL AND NOT FOR A MINIMUM OF SIX MONTHS; UPON REINSTATEMENT SHALL KEEP A LOG OF ALL CONTROLLED SUBSTANCES PRESCRIBED, DISPENSED OR ADMINISTERED; SHALL ABSTAIN COMPLETELY FROM THE POSSESSION OR PERSONAL USE OF DRUGS EXCEPT AS DISPENSED BY ANOTHER PERSON WITH SUCH AUTHORITY WHO KNOWS OF HIS HISTORY OF CHEMICAL DEPENDENCY; SHALL ABSTAIN FROM CONSUMING ALCOHOL; SHALL SUBMIT URINE OR BLOOD SPECIMENS UPON REQUEST; SHALL HAVE A BOARD-APPROVED MONITORING PHYSICIAN WITH QUARTERLY REPORTS TO THE BOARD; SHALL PROVIDE ALL HOSPITALS WHERE HE HAS PRIVILEGES WITH A COPY OF THE ORDER; SHALL COOPERATE WITH THE KENTUCKY IMPAIRED PHYSICIANS COMMITTEE WITH QUARTERLY REPORTS. ON 2/9/93 AN AMENDED ORDER PLACED HIS LICENSE ON PROBATION FOR FIVE YEARS WITH THE CONDITION THAT HE SHALL KEEP A LOG OF ALL CONTROLLED SUBSTANCES PRESCRIBED, DISPENSED OR ADMINISTERED; ALL OTHER TERMS OF THE ORIGINAL ORDER REMAIN IN FORCE.

JOSEY, WILLIE L MD, LICENSE NUMBER 00G6076, OF ALLIANCE, OH, WAS DISCIPLINED BY TEXAS ON AUGUST 18, 1990.
OFFENSE: DISCIPLINARY ACTION BY ANOTHER STATE OR AGENCY
NOTES: STIPULATED ORDER. MUST COMPLY WITH OHIO BOARD ORDER, OBTAIN PERMISSION OF BOARD BEFORE PRACTICING IN TEXAS AND COMPLY WITH ANY ADDITIONAL PROBATIONARY TERMS WHICH MAY BE IMPOSED.

JOSEY, WILLIE LEROY MD, LICENSE NUMBER 0055467, OF SOUTH SHORE, KY, WAS DISCIPLINED BY OHIO ON JULY 2, 1987.
DISCIPLINARY ACTION: PROBATION
NOTES: INDEFINITE PROBATION WITH CONDITIONS. PROBATION CONTINUED ON 11/8/89. PROBATION MODIFIED ON 10/10/91 AUTHORIZING HIM TO PRESCRIBE CONTROLLED SUBSTANCES WITH A LOG MAINTAINED OF ALL SUCH PRESCRIBING. REQUEST TO CHANGE FREQUENCY OF RANDOM URINE SCREENS COLLECTED FROM ONE PER WEEK TO ONE PER MONTH GRANTED ON 6/18/92. BOARD GRANTED HIS REQUEST TO REDUCE REQUIRED BOARD APPEARANCES TO ONCE EVERY SIX MONTHS ON 9/8/93.

KAIN, THOMAS R MD, LICENSE NUMBER 00E3966, WAS DISCIPLINED BY TEXAS ON OCTOBER 5, 1991.
DISCIPLINARY ACTION: EMERGENCY SUSPENSION
OFFENSE: LOSS OR RESTRICTION OF HOSPITAL PRIVILEGES
NOTES: HOSPITAL PRIVILEGES WERE SUSPENDED BY DEPARTMENT OF THE ARMY, UNITED STATES ARMY MEDICAL DEPARTMENT ACTIVITY, FORT HOOD, TEXAS, DUE TO INCOMPETENCY IN PERFORMING ANESTHETIC SERVICES.

KAN, DANIEL MD, LICENSE NUMBER 0041683, OF SAN ANTONIO, TX, WAS DISCIPLINED BY FLORIDA ON OCTOBER 11, 1991.
DISCIPLINARY ACTION: FINE
OFFENSE: PROFESSIONAL MISCONDUCT
NOTES: AIDING, ASSISTING, PROCURING, OR ADVISING AN UNLICENSED PERSON TO PRACTICE MEDICINE IN THAT HE ACTED AS A SUPERVISOR FOR AN UNLICENSED PHYSICIAN ASSISTANT; DELEGATING PROFESSIONAL RESPONSIBILITIES TO A PERSON HE KNEW OR HAD REASON TO KNOW WAS NOT QUALIFIED BY TRAINING, EXPERIENCE, OR LICENSURE TO PERFORM THEM, IN THAT AN UNLICENSED PERSON FUNCTIONED AS A PHYSICIAN ASSISTANT WHILE UNDER HIS SUPERVISION. $250 FINE, LETTER OF CONCERN.

KASNER, MARTIN MD, LICENSE NUMBER 0031141, OF FT LAUDERDALE, FL, WAS DISCIPLINED BY FLORIDA ON JUNE 19, 1990.
DISCIPLINARY ACTION: 24-MONTH LICENSE SUSPENSION; 36-MONTH PROBATION
OFFENSE: SUBSTANDARD CARE, INCOMPETENCE, OR NEGLIGENCE
NOTES: GROSS MALPRACTICE AND FAILING TO PRACTICE MEDICINE WITH AN ACCEPTABLE LEVEL OF CARE AND SKILL. ALSO FOUND GUILTY OF PRESCRIBING, DISPENSING, ADMINISTERING, MIXING, OR OTHERWISE PREPARING A LEGEND DRUG OTHER THAN IN THE COURSE OF PROFESSIONAL PRACTICE; FAILURE TO KEEP WRITTEN MEDICAL RECORDS JUSTIFYING THE COURSE OF TREATMENT OF A PATIENT; AND MAKING DECEPTIVE, UNTRUE OR FRAUDULENT REPRESENTATIONS OR EMPLOYING A TRICK OR SCHEME IN THE PRACTICE OF MEDICINE. MUST PAY $5000 FINE; PROBATION SUBJECT TO TERMS AND CONDITIONS TO BE SET AT THE TIME OF REINSTATEMENT FROM SUSPENSION WITH SPECIAL EMPHASIS ON USE OF SCHEDULED CONTROLLED SUBSTANCES.

KASNER, MARTIN MD, DATE OF BIRTH AUGUST 2, 1934, OF 3550 GALT OCEAN DR #1809, FT LAUDERDALE, FL, WAS DISCIPLINED BY MEDICARE ON SEPTEMBER 24, 1990.
DISCIPLINARY ACTION: 60-MONTH EXCLUSION FROM THE MEDICARE AND/OR MEDICAID PROGRAMS
OFFENSE: CRIMINAL CONVICTION OR PLEA OF GUILTY, NOLO CONTENDERE, OR NO CONTEST TO A CRIME
NOTES: CONVICTION RELATING TO CONTROLLED SUBSTANCES.

KASNER, MARTIN MD, LICENSE NUMBER 00F5251, OF FT LAUDERDALE, FL, WAS DISCIPLINED BY TEXAS ON AUGUST 24, 1991.
DISCIPLINARY ACTION: SURRENDER OF LICENSE
OFFENSE: DISCIPLINARY ACTION BY ANOTHER STATE OR AGENCY
NOTES: ACTION TAKEN BY ANOTHER STATE BOARD FOR NONTHERAPEUTIC PRESCRIBING. SURRENDER IN LIEU OF FURTHER DISCIPLINARY ACTION.

KASNER, MARTIN MD, LICENSE NUMBER 0005992, OF MONTREAL, QUEBEC, CANADA, WAS DISCIPLINED BY VERMONT ON OCTOBER 28, 1991.
DISCIPLINARY ACTION: LICENSE REVOCATION
OFFENSE: DISCIPLINARY ACTION BY ANOTHER STATE OR AGENCY
NOTES: DISCIPLINARY ACTION TAKEN IN FLORIDA CONCERNING HIS PRESCRIBING VALIUM AND PERCODAN TO HIS

PATIENT WITHOUT A VALID MEDICAL PURPOSE AND PRESCRIBING VALIUM IN EXCESSIVE AMOUNTS; FLORIDA LICENSE WAS RESTRICTED ON 8/23/88 AND SUSPENDED ON 6/12/90; IN HIS VERMONT RENEWAL APPLICATIONS IN 2/89 AND 10/90 HE STATED THERE HAD BEEN NO ACTION TAKEN AGAINST HIS LICENSE.

KASNER, MARTIN MD, LICENSE NUMBER 0005992, OF MONTREAL, QUEBEC, CANADA, WAS DISCIPLINED BY VERMONT ON JANUARY 8, 1992.
DISCIPLINARY ACTION: LICENSE REVOCATION
OFFENSE: CRIMINAL CONVICTION OR PLEA OF GUILTY, NOLO CONTENDERE, OR NO CONTEST TO A CRIME
NOTES: ON 12/5/89 CONVICTED IN BROWARD COUNTY CIRCUIT COURT ON TEN COUNTS OF UNLAWFUL DELIVERY OF DIAZEPAM AND OXYCODONE BY ISSUING PRESCRIPTIONS TO TWO INDIVIDUALS; LIED ABOUT THIS CONVICTION ON RENEWAL APPLICATION 10/22/90. WILL CONSIDER REINSTATEMENT IN NO SOONER THAN FIVE YEARS; THIS ORDER COMBINED WITH ONE ISSUED 10/28/91.

KASNER, MARTIN MD, LICENSE NUMBER 0031141, OF FT LAUDERDALE, FL, WAS DISCIPLINED BY FLORIDA ON APRIL 8, 1992.
DISCIPLINARY ACTION: FINE; REPRIMAND
OFFENSE: FAILURE TO COMPLY WITH A PREVIOUS BOARD ORDER
NOTES: CHARGED WITH VIOLATING AN ORDER OF THE BOARD IN THAT HE FAILED TO PAY A $5,000 ADMINISTRATIVE FINE IMPOSED BY FINAL ORDER OF 6/19/90. SHALL PAY $400/MONTH UNTIL SUCH TIME AS THE FINE IS PAID IN FULL. LICENSE SHALL NOT BE ELIGIBLE FOR REINSTATEMENT UNTIL AFTER THE $5,000 FINE HAS BEEN PAID.

KASNETZ, HERBERT ROY MD, DATE OF BIRTH JULY 22, 1935, LICENSE NUMBER 00D3908, OF 1420 N MACARTHUR BLVD, IRVING, TX, WAS DISCIPLINED BY TEXAS ON AUGUST 20, 1993.
DISCIPLINARY ACTION: REPRIMAND
OFFENSE: SUBSTANDARD CARE, INCOMPETENCE, OR NEGLIGENCE
NOTES: ADMINISTERED GAMMA GOBULIN SHOTS TO A PATIENT WITH A TOTAL SERUM IGG LEVEL OF 1210 WITHOUT SUFFICIENT OBJECTIVE AND CLINICAL INDICATIONS REFLECTED IN THE PATIENT'S CHART. SHALL GIVE A COPY OF THIS ORDER TO ANY HEALTH CARE ENTITY WHERE HE HAS PRIVILEGES.

KASTNER, AARON MD, LICENSE NUMBER 00E7133, OF GARLAND, TX, WAS DISCIPLINED BY TEXAS ON APRIL 10, 1992.
DISCIPLINARY ACTION: 48-MONTH PROBATION
OFFENSE: SUBSTANDARD CARE, INCOMPETENCE, OR NEGLIGENCE
NOTES: UNPROFESSIONAL OR DISHONORABLE CONDUCT LIKELY TO DECEIVE, DEFRAUD OR INJURE THE PUBLIC; AND PROFESSIONAL FAILURE TO PRACTICE MEDICINE IN AN ACCEPTABLE MANNER CONSISTENT WITH PUBLIC HEALTH AND WELFARE. LICENSE REVOKED, REVOCATION STAYED; PROBATION UNDER TERMS AND CONDITIONS.

KATERNDAHL, DAVID A MD WAS DISCIPLINED BY OHIO ON JULY 8, 1987.
DISCIPLINARY ACTION: REPRIMAND

KATERNDAHL, DAVID A MD, DATE OF BIRTH NOVEMBER 20, 1950, LICENSE NUMBER 00H2144, OF DEPT. FAMILY PRACTICE UTHSC, SAN ANTONIO, TX, WAS DISCIPLINED BY TEXAS ON DECEMBER 4, 1991.
DISCIPLINARY ACTION: 36-MONTH PROBATION; RESTRICTION PLACED ON CONTROLLED SUBSTANCE LICENSE
OFFENSE: OVERPRESCRIBING OR MISPRESCRIBING DRUGS
NOTES: PROVIDED CONTROLLED SUBSTANCES, IN A NONTHERAPEUTIC MANNER, TO A FAMILY MEMBER DURING 1988 AND 1989. ENTERED INTO IMPAIRED PHYSICIANS PROGRAM IN 9/89 AND HAS COMPLIED WITH REQUIREMENTS OF THAT CONTRACT. THREE YEAR SUSPENSION STAYED, PROBATION ISSUED WITH FOLLOWING CONDITIONS: SHALL APPEAR BEFORE BOARD TWICE A YEAR FOR COMPLIANCE REVIEW; SHALL WITHIN SIX MONTHS SUCCESSFULLY COMPLETE A MEDICAL PHARMACOLOGY COURSE; SHALL BE MONITORED BY A BOARD-APPROVED PHYSICIAN WITH QUARTERLY REPORTS; SHALL REFRAIN FROM THE PRESCRIPTION OR ADMINISTRATION OF ANY DRUG FOR ANY PATIENT UNLESS THE DRUG IS MEDICALLY INDICATED AND PRESCRIBED IN THERAPEUTIC DOSES; SHALL REFRAIN FROM THE USE OF AND POSSESSION, ADMINISTERING, OR PRESCRIBING OF ANY CONTROLLED SUBSTANCES OR ANY OTHER DRUG OR MEDICATION REQUIRING A PRESCRIPTION, OR PRESCRIBING SAME TO FAMILY; REGISTRATIONS ARE LIMITED TO SCHEDULES III, III-N, IV, AND V IF DEA APPROVES; SHALL SUBMIT HIMSELF FOR APPROPRIATE EXAMINATIONS, INCLUDING DRUG OR ALCOHOL SCREENINGS; SHALL CONTINUE TREATMENT WITH QUARTERLY REPORTS TO THE BOARD; SHALL PROVIDE A COPY OF THE ORDER TO EMPLOYER; SHALL COOPERATE WITH BOARD IN VERIFYING COMPLIANCE; SHALL INFORM BOARD OF CHANGE OF ADDRESS WITHIN 10 DAYS OR IF HE LEAVES TEXAS; TIME SPENT OUT OF TEXAS DOES NOT COUNT TOWARD PROBATION; MAY NOT SEEK MODIFICATION OF ORDER FOR ONE YEAR. ON 1/29/93 MODIFICATION OF ORDER GRANTING HIM PERMISSION TO APPLY FOR ISSUANCE OF TEXAS DEPARTMENT OF PUBLIC SAFETY AND DRUG ENFORCEMENT ADMINISTRATION CONTROLLED SUBSTANCE REGISTRATION CERTIFICATES. ALL OTHER TERMS OF THIS ORDER REMAIN IN EFFECT. ON 1/14/94 PROBATION TERMINATED.

KATERNDAHL, DAVID ARTHUR MD, LICENSE NUMBER 0042398, OF SAN ANTONIO, TX, WAS DISCIPLINED BY OHIO ON JANUARY 13, 1993.
DISCIPLINARY ACTION: 36-MONTH PROBATION
OFFENSE: DISCIPLINARY ACTION BY ANOTHER STATE OR AGENCY
NOTES: TEXAS SANCTION IMPOSED BECAUSE OF HIS PROVISION OF CONTROLLED SUBSTANCES IN A NON-THERAPEUTIC MANNER TO A FAMILY MEMBER. PROBATION CALCULATED FROM 12/4/91 AND TO RUN CONCURRENTLY WITH PROBATION IMPOSED BY TEXAS.

KAUFFMANN, ADOLPH FREDERICK III MD, LICENSE NUMBER 00B6910, OF FORT WORTH, TX, WAS DISCIPLINED BY TEXAS ON FEBRUARY 22, 1991.
DISCIPLINARY ACTION: 60-MONTH PROBATION; RESTRICTION PLACED ON LICENSE
NOTES: MUST MAINTAIN ADEQUATE MEDICAL RECORDS ON ALL PATIENTS; OBTAIN SECOND OPINION FROM A BOARD CERTIFIED GENERAL SURGEON FOR ANY POSSIBLE BREAST SURGERY OR BREAST BIOPSY; APPEAR FOR ANNUAL REPORT TO BOARD. ON 6/22/94 REQUEST FOR TERMINATION OF THIS ORDER DENIED.

KAUFMAN, IRA S MD, LICENSE NUMBER 00E9731, OF HOUSTON, TX, WAS DISCIPLINED BY TEXAS ON AUGUST 19, 1994.
DISCIPLINARY ACTION: SURRENDER OF CONTROLLED SUBSTANCE LICENSE; 120-MONTH PROBATION
OFFENSE: CRIMINAL CONVICTION OR PLEA OF GUILTY, NOLO CONTENDERE, OR NO CONTEST TO A CRIME
NOTES: ON 6/30/93 HE PLED NOLO CONTENDERE TO TWO SECOND DEGREE FELONY CHARGES OF OBTAINING DRUGS BY FRAUD; THE CASES INVOLVED TWO PRESCRIPTIONS HE ISSUED ONE ON 2/7/92 AND ONE ON 9/24/92 FOR MEPERIDINE IN THE NAMES OF TWO PEOPLE WHO WERE NOT HIS PATIENTS; THERE WAS NO MEDICAL PURPOSE FOR PRESCRIBING THE DRUG; HE PRESENTED THESE PRESCRIPTIONS TO PHARMACISTS HIMSELF; ALSO PLED NOLO CONTENDERE TO A MISDEMEANOR OFFENSE OF CARRYING A WEAPON; BEGINNING ON 2/7/92 CONSUMED DRUGS INCLUDING MEPERIDINE FOR NO VALID MEDICAL PRACTICE SOME OF WHICH HE OBTAINED PRESCRIPTIONS FOR IN THE MANNER PREVIOUSLY DESCRIBED; WAS IMPAIRED BY THE USE OF DRUGS AND ALCOHOL PRIOR TO RECEIVING INPATIENT TREATMENT FROM 1/18/93 THROUGH 2/12/93; PROBATION REQUIRES HIM TO RECEIVE PSYCHIATRIC COUNSELING. SUSPENSION STAYED. CONDITIONS OF PROBATION: SHALL ABSTAIN FROM THE CONSUMPTION OF ALCOHOL/CHEMICAL SUBSTANCES IN ANY FORM UNLESS PRESCRIBED BY ANOTHER PHYSICIAN FOR A LEGITIMATE AND THERAPEUTIC PURPOSE; SHALL SUBMIT HIMSELF FOR APPROPRIATE EXAMS INCLUDING DRUG OR ALCOHOL SCREENS; SHALL PARTICIPATE IN ACTIVITIES OF A PHYSICIAN HEALTH AND REHABILITATION COMMITTEE AND ATTEND WEEKLY MEETINGS WITH QUARTERLY REPORTS; SHALL PARTICIPATE IN AA'S PROGRAM NOT LESS THAN THREE TIMES A WEEK WITH QUARTERLY REPORTS TO THE BOARD; SHALL SURRENDER DEA AND TEXAS CONTROLLED SUBSTANCES CERTIFICATES, UNUSED TRIPLICATE PRESCRIPTION FORMS AND ALL CONTROLLED SUBSTANCES IN HIS POSSESSION INCLUDING SAMPLES; SHALL NOT ATTEMPT TO REREGISTER WITHOUT PERMISSION; SHALL NOT TELEPHONE A PRESCRIPTION TO ANY PHARMACY; SHALL SUBMIT HIMSELF TO A BOARD-APPROVED PSYCHIATRIST FOR EXAMINATION AND TREATMENT AND SEE THIS PSYCHIATRIST AT LEAST ONCE A MONTH; SHALL ATTEND AT LEAST 50 HOURS PER YEAR OF CONTINUING MEDICAL EDUCATION; WITHIN ONE YEAR SHALL PASS THE MEDICAL JURISPRUDENCE EXAM; SHALL GIVE A COPY OF THIS ORDER TO ANY HEALTH CARE ENTITY WHERE HE HAS PRIVILEGES; SHALL COOPERATE WITH THE BOARD IN VERIFYING COMPLIANCE; SHALL INFORM BOARD OF CHANGE OF ADDRESS WITHIN 10 DAYS OR IF HE LEAVES THE STATE; TIME SPENT OUT OF TEXAS DOES NOT COUNT TOWARD PROBATION. SHALL NOT SEEK MODIFICATION FOR ONE YEAR.

KAUFMANN, GARY E MD, LICENSE NUMBER 00D3624, OF ATLANTA, GA, WAS DISCIPLINED BY TEXAS ON DECEMBER 1, 1988.
NOTES: SETTLEMENT AGREEMENT AND UNSPECIFIED DISCIPLINARY ACTION

KAUFMANN, GARY EDMUND MD, LICENSE NUMBER 0010979, OF 415 SPALDING DRIVE, ATLANTA, GA, WAS DISCIPLINED BY GEORGIA ON JULY 21, 1986.
DISCIPLINARY ACTION: EMERGENCY SUSPENSION
OFFENSE: PHYSICAL OR MENTAL ILLNESS INHIBITING THE ABILITY TO PRACTICE WITH SKILL AND SAFETY
NOTES: MENTAL IMPAIRMENT; UNPROFESSIONAL CONDUCT.

KAUFMANN, GARY EDMUND MD, LICENSE NUMBER 0010979, OF 415 SPALDING DRIVE, ATLANTA, GA, WAS DISCIPLINED BY GEORGIA ON AUGUST 6, 1986.
DISCIPLINARY ACTION: SURRENDER OF LICENSE
OFFENSE: PROFESSIONAL MISCONDUCT
NOTES: NARCOTICS VIOLATIONS/USE. PENDING A HEARING/ORDERED INTO AN EVALUATION.

KAUFMANN, GARY EDMUND MD, LICENSE NUMBER 0010979, OF 415 SPALDING DRIVE, ATLANTA, GA, WAS DISCIPLINED BY GEORGIA ON NOVEMBER 6, 1986.
DISCIPLINARY ACTION: RESTRICTION PLACED ON LICENSE; REQUIRED TO ENTER AN IMPAIRED PHYSICIAN PROGRAM OR DRUG OR ALCOHOL TREATMENT
NOTES: SUSPENSION LIFTED; NO SURGERY, EMERGENCY ROOM OR HOSPITAL PRACTICE; REMAIN IN PSYCHOTHERAPY; QUARTERLY REPORTS.

KAY, BILLY F MD, DATE OF BIRTH FEBRUARY 12, 1934, LICENSE NUMBER 00E9260, OF 6960 BELLAIRE BLVD APT 2214, HOUSTON, TX, WAS DISCIPLINED BY TEXAS ON APRIL 30, 1993.
DISCIPLINARY ACTION: LICENSE SUSPENSION
OFFENSE: PHYSICAL OR MENTAL ILLNESS INHIBITING THE ABILITY TO PRACTICE WITH SKILL AND SAFETY
NOTES: UNABLE TO PRACTICE WITH REASONABLE SKILL AND SAFETY DUE TO INSUFFICIENT INTELLECTUAL FUNCTIONING. SUSPENSION A MINIMUM OF 1 YEAR; BEFORE MAKING AN APPLICATION FOR REINSTATEMENT HE SHALL SUBMIT HIMSELF FOR AN INDEPENDENT MENTAL AND PHYSICAL EXAM; SHALL PROVIDE PROOF OF A DOCUMENTED AFTERCARE PROGRAM; SHALL INFORM THE BOARD OF CHANGE OF ADDRESS WITHIN 10 DAYS OR IF HE LEAVES THE STATE; TIME SPENT OUT OF TEXAS DOES NOT COUNT TOWARD SUSPENSION.

KAY, BILLY F MD, LICENSE NUMBER 0013277, OF 6960 BELLAIRE BLVD, SUITE 2214, HOUSTON, TX, WAS DISCIPLINED BY KANSAS ON JUNE 20, 1994.
DISCIPLINARY ACTION: DENIAL OF LICENSE REINSTATEMENT
OFFENSE: DISCIPLINARY ACTION BY ANOTHER STATE OR AGENCY
NOTES: ON 04/09/92, TEXAS BOARD TEMPORARILY SUSPENDED HIS TEXAS MEDICAL LICENSE DUE TO LONG-TERM ALCOHOL ABUSE AND MENTAL ILLNESS. ON 04/30/93 LICENSE WAS INDEFINITELY SUSPENDED BY TEXAS. HE HAS THE INABILITY TO PRACTICE MEDICINE WITH REASONABLE SKILL AND SAFETY TO PATIENTS BY REASON OF BIPOLAR DISORDER, ALCOHOL DEPENDENCY AND DEMENTIA ASSOCIATED WITH ALCOHOLISM. HE IS UNWILLING TO ENTER INTO A MONITORING CONTRACT WITH THE KANSAS MEDICAL SOCIETY WHICH WOULD INCLUDE ATTENDANCE OF AA MEETINGS AND RANDOM URINE SCREENING. APPLICATION FOR STATUS CHANGE FROM INACTIVE TO ACTIVE IS THEREFORE DENIED.

KELLER, WAYNE F MD, LICENSE NUMBER 00D0190, OF 909 FROSTWOOD STE 362, HOUSTON, TX, WAS DISCIPLINED BY DEA ON DECEMBER 28, 1992.
DISCIPLINARY ACTION: RESTRICTION PLACED ON CONTROLLED SUBSTANCE LICENSE
OFFENSE: OVERPRESCRIBING OR MISPRESCRIBING DRUGS
NOTES: SHALL NOT PRESCRIBE, ADMINISTER, POSSESS OR

DISPENSE ANY DRUG IN SCHEDULES II, IIN, III OR IIIN CONTROLLED SUBSTANCES, WITH THE EXCEPTION THAT HE MAY ORDER SUCH MEDICATIONS FOR PATIENTS WHO ARE IN THE HOSPITAL. AGREED TO THE RESTRICTIONS DUE TO ALLEGATIONS THAT HE WAS PRESCRIBING EXCESSIVE AMOUNTS OF SCHEDULE II CONTROLLED SUBSTANCES TO PATIENTS. REGISTRATION MODIFIED ON 03/15/89.

KELLER, WAYNE FRANCIS MD, LICENSE NUMBER 00D0190, OF 909 FROSTWOOD STE 362, HOUSTON, TX, WAS DISCIPLINED BY TEXAS ON JANUARY 28, 1989.
DISCIPLINARY ACTION: RESTRICTION PLACED ON CONTROLLED SUBSTANCE LICENSE
NOTES: SHALL NOT PRESCRIBE, ADMINISTER, POSSESS OR DISPENSE SCHEDULE II, II-N OR III-N DRUGS EXCEPT TO HOSPITAL PATIENTS. ON 4/15/94 ORDER TERMINATED.

KELLY, PATRICK M DO, LICENSE NUMBER 00D6653, OF CEDAR PARK, TX, WAS DISCIPLINED BY TEXAS ON SEPTEMBER 1, 1992.
DISCIPLINARY ACTION: SURRENDER OF LICENSE
NOTES: PERMANENTLY SURRENDERED.

KENNADY, DONALD SCOTT MD, LICENSE NUMBER 00C4389, OF NEW BRAUNFELS, TX, WAS DISCIPLINED BY TEXAS ON JANUARY 6, 1995.
DISCIPLINARY ACTION: 60-MONTH RESTRICTION PLACED ON LICENSE; REQUIRED TO TAKE ADDITIONAL MEDICAL EDUCATION
OFFENSE: SUBSTANDARD CARE, INCOMPETENCE, OR NEGLIGENCE
NOTES: FROM 1987 THROUGH 1992 HE FAILED TO CONDUCT ADEQUATE EXAMS OF ONE PATIENT WHILE PRESCRIBING THYROID MEDICATION AND ESTINYL; PATIENT HAD BEEN SUBSEQUENTLY DIAGNOSED BY ANOTHER PHYSICIAN AS HAVING A TONSILLAR TUMOR; AGREED TO THIS ORDER IN LIEU OF FURTHER INVESTIGATION. CONDITIONS OF FIVE YEAR RESTRICTION: PRACTICE SHALL BE MONITORED BY A BOARD-APPROVED PHYSICIAN WITH QUARTERLY REPORTS; SHALL MAINTAIN ADEQUATE MEDICAL RECORDS ON ALL PATIENT OFFICE VISITS WHICH SHALL BE AVAILABLE FOR INSPECTION; SHALL OBTAIN AT LEAST 50 HOURS PER YEAR OF CONTINUING MEDICAL EDUCATION INCLUDING IN THE FIRST YEAR 15 HOURS IN DIAGNOSIS AND MANAGEMENT OF DISORDERS IN THE HEAD AND NECK AND FIVE HOURS IN RISK MANAGEMENT; WITHIN ONE YEAR SHALL PASS THE SPEX EXAM; SHALL APPEAR BEFORE THE BOARD ONCE A YEAR OR UPON REQUEST; SHALL COOPERATE WITH THE BOARD IN VERIFYING COMPLIANCE; SHALL EXECUTE ANY RELEASES NECESSARY FOR BOARD TO OBTAIN RECORDS PERTAINING TO HIS PRIVILEGES AT HOSPITALS OR HEALTH CARE FACILITIES; SHALL GIVE A COPY OF THIS ORDER TO ANY HEALTH CARE ENITY WHERE HE HAS OR APPLIES FOR PRIVILEGES OR ANYONE ELSE WHO REQUESTS THEM; SHALL ENSURE ANY INQUIRIES REGARDING HIS TEXAS LICENSURE STATUS ARE ANSWERED BY REFERENCE TO THIS ORDER; SHALL INFORM BOARD OF CHANGE OF ADDRESS WITHIN 1O DAYS OR IF HE LEAVES THE STATE; TIME SPENT OUT OF TEXAS DOES NOT COUNT TOWARD RESTRICTION. SHALL NOT SEEK MODIFICATION FOR ONE YEAR.

KENNEDY, JERETTA IRENE MD, LICENSE NUMBER 00C5745, OF HITCHCOCK, TX, WAS DISCIPLINED BY TEXAS ON APRIL 24, 1991.
DISCIPLINARY ACTION: LICENSE REVOCATION
OFFENSE: DRUG OR ALCOHOL ABUSE
NOTES: INTEMPERATE USE OF ALCOHOL OR DRUGS AND INABILITY TO PRACTICE WITH REASONABLE SKILL AND SAFETY TO PATIENTS. ON APPEAL.

KENNEDY, JERETTA IRENE MD OF 1172 SAILFISH DR, HITCHCOCK, TX, WAS DISCIPLINED BY DEA ON JUNE 6, 1991.
DISCIPLINARY ACTION: SURRENDER OF CONTROLLED SUBSTANCE LICENSE
OFFENSE: PROFESSIONAL MISCONDUCT
NOTES: VOLUNTARY SURRENDER 05/15/90 IN HITCHCOCK, TEXAS DUE TO DIVERSION OF DEMEROL.

KEPPLER, JOHN PAUL MD, DATE OF BIRTH NOVEMBER 14, 1950, LICENSE NUMBER 0029482, OF 1669 PHOENIX PKWY #102, ATLANTA, GA, WAS DISCIPLINED BY GEORGIA ON MARCH 23, 1990.
DISCIPLINARY ACTION: EMERGENCY SUSPENSION
OFFENSE: DRUG OR ALCOHOL ABUSE
NOTES: IN 1982 HE VOLUNTARILY ENTERED AND COMPLETED A TREATMENT PROGRAM FOR DEPENDENCY ON ALCOHOL AND DRUGS. AN APRIL 1987 CONSENT ORDER PUTTING KEPPLER ON PROBATION WAS TERMINATED 4/24/89. BOARD RECEIVED RELIABLE INFORMATION THAT HE HAD SUFFERED RELAPSE. HE IS ALSO REQUIRED TO SUBMIT TO A 72-HOUR INPATIENT MENTAL/PHYSICAL EVALUATION.

KEPPLER, JOHN PAUL MD OF 4015 SOUTH COBB DR STE 100, SMYRNA, GA, WAS DISCIPLINED BY DEA ON AUGUST 17, 1990.
DISCIPLINARY ACTION: SURRENDER OF CONTROLLED SUBSTANCE LICENSE
OFFENSE: DRUG OR ALCOHOL ABUSE
NOTES: SUSPENSION OF LICENSE TO PRACTICE MEDICINE 03/23/90 IN GEORGIA FOR ADDICTION TO LORACET AND HYDROCODONE.

KEPPLER, JOHN PAUL MD, LICENSE NUMBER 00F9100, OF ATLANTA, GA, WAS DISCIPLINED BY TEXAS ON DECEMBER 3, 1990.
DISCIPLINARY ACTION: SURRENDER OF LICENSE
NOTES: SURRENDERED LICENSE IN LIEU OF DISCIPLINARY HEARING.

KEPPLER, JOHN PAUL MD, DATE OF BIRTH NOVEMBER 14, 1950, LICENSE NUMBER 0029482, OF 1669 PHOENIX PKWY #102, ATLANTA, GA, WAS DISCIPLINED BY GEORGIA ON APRIL 3, 1991.
DISCIPLINARY ACTION: PROBATION
NOTES: SUSPENSION LIFTED. MAY RESUME PRACTICE UNDER TERMS AND CONDITIONS OF A CONSENT ORDER, INCLUDING SUPERVISED PROBATION. MAY PETITION FOR TERMINATION OF PROBATION AFTER DOCUMENTING SEVEN YEARS OF CONTINUOUS SOBRIETY OR UNTIL 3/10/87, WHICHEVER IS LATER. ON 10/7/92 ORDER MODIFYING THIS ORDER ISSUED. MAY UTILIZE DEA PERMIT FOR SCHEDULE IV TO BE FILLED IN CLINIC. SUPPLY TWO SPECIMENS MONTHLY AS OPPOSED TO THREE TIMES WEEKLY, AND QUARTERLY REPORTS AS OPPOSED TO MONTHLY REPORTS.

KEPPLER, JOHN PAUL MD, DATE OF BIRTH NOVEMBER 14, 1950, LICENSE NUMBER 0029482, OF 141 WEST SOLOMON STREET, GRIFFIN, GA, WAS DISCIPLINED BY GEORGIA ON JANUARY 12, 1994.
DISCIPLINARY ACTION: EMERGENCY SUSPENSION
NOTES: IMPAIRMENT.

KEPPLER, JOHN PAUL MD, DATE OF BIRTH NOVEMBER 14, 1950, LICENSE NUMBER 0029482, OF 141 W SOLOMON STREET, GRIFFIN, GA, WAS DISCIPLINED BY GEORGIA ON MAY 16, 1994.
DISCIPLINARY ACTION: PROBATION
NOTES: IMPAIRMENT. SUSPENSION LIFTED WITH INDEFINITE PROBATION.

KEPPLER, JOHN PAUL MD, DATE OF BIRTH NOVEMBER 14, 1950, LICENSE NUMBER 0029482, OF 141 W SOLOMON STREET, GRIFFIN, GA, WAS DISCIPLINED BY GEORGIA ON JUNE 9, 1994.
DISCIPLINARY ACTION: EMERGENCY SUSPENSION
NOTES: IMPAIRMENT; RELAPSE.

KEPPLER, JOHN PAUL MD, DATE OF BIRTH NOVEMBER 14, 1950, LICENSE NUMBER 0029482, OF 141 W SOLOMAN STREET, GRIFFIN, GA, WAS DISCIPLINED BY GEORGIA ON SEPTEMBER 23, 1994.
DISCIPLINARY ACTION: LICENSE REVOCATION
OFFENSE: DRUG OR ALCOHOL ABUSE
NOTES: DRUG ADDICTION.

KESLER, KEITH E DO, LICENSE NUMBER 00G9758, OF AUSTIN, TX, WAS DISCIPLINED BY TEXAS ON JANUARY 14, 1994.
DISCIPLINARY ACTION: SURRENDER OF CONTROLLED SUBSTANCE LICENSE; 60-MONTH PROBATION
OFFENSE: LOSS OR RESTRICTION OF HOSPITAL PRIVILEGES
NOTES: ON 7/27/93 DIVERTED DEMEROL FOR HIS OWN USE FROM THE EMERGENCY ROOM OF HOSPITAL WHERE HE WAS EMPLOYED; PRIVILEGES WERE THEN SUSPENDED AT THIS HOSPITAL BECAUSE OF SUSPECTED IMPAIRMENT; ON 7/28/93 ENTERED TREATMENT FOR CHEMICAL DEPENDENCY AND THEN AN AFTERCARE CONTRACT AND A CONTRACT WITH IMPAIRED PHYSICIANS COMMITTEE. SUSPENSION STAYED. CONDITIONS OF PROBATION: SHALL ABSTAIN FROM THE CONSUMPTION OF ALCOHOL/CHEMICAL SUBSTANCES IN ANY FORM UNLESS PRESCRIBED BY ANOTHER PHYSICIAN FOR A LEGITIMATE AND THERAPEUTIC PURPOSE; SHALL SUBMIT HIMSELF FOR APPROPRIATE EXAMS INCLUDING DRUG OR ALCOHOL SCREENS; SHALL CONTINUE TO PARTICIPATE IN AA'S PROGRAM NOT LESS THAN THREE TIMES A WEEK WITH QUARTERLY REPORTS TO THE BOARD; SHALL SURRENDER DEA AND TEXAS CONTROLLED SUBSTANCES REGISTRATION AND SHALL NOT REREGISTER WITHOUT PERMISSION; SHALL PARTICIPATE IN ACTIVITIES OF A PHYSICIAN HEALTH AND REHABILITATION COMMITTEE AND ATTEND WEEKLY MEETINGS WITH QUARTERLY REPORTS; SHALL PARTICIPATE IN ALL ACTIVITIES AS REQUIRED BY HIS AFTERCARE CONTRACT; SHALL ATTEND AT LEAST 50 HOURS PER YEAR OF CONTINUING MEDICAL EDUCATION; SHALL GIVE A COPY OF THIS ORDER TO ANY HEALTH CARE ENTITY WHERE HE HAS PRIVILEGES; SHALL COOPERATE WITH THE BOARD IN VERIFYING COMPLIANCE; SHALL INFORM BOARD OF CHANGE OF ADDRESS WITHIN 10 DAYS OR IF HE LEAVES THE STATE; TIME SPENT OUT OF TEXAS DOES NOT COUNT TOWARD PROBATION; SHALL APPEAR BEFORE THE BOARD ONCE A YEAR. SHALL NOT SEEK MODIFICATION FOR ONE YEAR UNLESS HE IS ADMITTED TO A RESIDENCY TRAINING PROGRAM IN WHICH CASE HE MAY REQUEST PERMISSION TO REAPPLY FOR CONTROLLED SUBSTANCES CERTIFICATES. HE WAS ACCEPTED INTO A PSYCHIATRIC RESIDENCY PROGRAM AND ON 6/22/94 HE WAS GRANTED PERMISSION TO REAPPLY FOR SCHEDULE IV AND V CONTROLLED SUBSTANCES REGISTRATION. IF THESE CERTIFICATES ARE REISSUED THE FOLLOWING CONDITIONS ALSO APPLY: SHALL NOT POSSESS, ADMINISTER, DISPENSE OR PRESCRIBE CONTROLLED SUBSTANCES EXCEPT FOR PURPOSES OF TREATMENT OF PATIENTS IN THE CONTEXT OF HIS PSYCHIATRIC RESIDENCY PROGRAM; SHALL NOT TREAT OR OTHERWISE SERVE AS PHYSICIAN, PRESCRIBE, DISPENSE OR ADMINISTER DRUGS THAT MAY BE SUBJECT TO ABUSE TO HIMSELF OR ANY MEMBER OF HIS FAMILY; SEPARATE FROM PATIENT RECORDS, SHALL MAINTAIN A FILE OF EVERY PRESCRIPTION WRITTEN FOR CONTROLLED SUBSTANCES OR DANGEROUS DRUGS WHICH SHALL BE AVAILABLE FOR REVIEW; SHALL BE SUPERVISED BY THE DIRECTOR OF HIS PROGRAM WITH QUARTERLY REPORTS. ALL OTHER PROVISIONS OF THE ORDER REMAIN IN EFFECT.

KESLER, KEITH E MD, LICENSE NUMBER 00C8220, OF 5105 QUAIL RUN, AUSTIN, TX, WAS DISCIPLINED BY ARKANSAS ON DECEMBER 1, 1994.
DISCIPLINARY ACTION: SURRENDER OF LICENSE

KESLER, KEITH ELDON DO, LICENSE NUMBER 00G9758, OF 2701 CLEARVIEW DRIVE, AUSTIN, TX, WAS DISCIPLINED BY DEA ON MARCH 14, 1994.
DISCIPLINARY ACTION: SURRENDER OF CONTROLLED SUBSTANCE LICENSE
OFFENSE: DISCIPLINARY ACTION BY ANOTHER STATE OR AGENCY
NOTES: INVOLVED IN DEMEROL DIVERSION FROM HOSPITAL. MEDICAL LICENSE SUSPENDED 01/14/94. SUSPENSION STAYED AND PLACED ON PROBATION.

KESZLER, BERNEY R MD OF 302 N. RAGUET, LUFKIN, TX, WAS DISCIPLINED BY MEDICARE ON JULY 13, 1987.
DISCIPLINARY ACTION: 60-MONTH EXCLUSION FROM THE MEDICARE AND/OR MEDICAID PROGRAMS
OFFENSE: CRIMINAL CONVICTION OR PLEA OF GUILTY, NOLO CONTENDERE, OR NO CONTEST TO A CRIME
NOTES: PROGRAM-RELATED CONVICTION.

KESZLER, BERNEY R MD, DATE OF BIRTH JULY 18, 1942, OF PO BOX 151706, LUFKIN, TX, WAS DISCIPLINED BY MEDICARE ON NOVEMBER 1, 1990.
DISCIPLINARY ACTION: 120-MONTH EXCLUSION FROM THE MEDICARE AND/OR MEDICAID PROGRAMS; FINE
NOTES: IMPOSITION OF A CIVIL MONEY PENALTY OR ASSESSMENT. NO LONGER LISTED AS EXCLUDED AS OF 9/30/92.

KHOLEIF, ALI A R MD, DATE OF BIRTH OCTOBER 20, 1938, LICENSE NUMBER 0021542, OF OTTUMWA, IA, WAS DISCIPLINED BY IOWA ON MAY 11, 1990.
DISCIPLINARY ACTION: EMERGENCY SUSPENSION
NOTES: ON 6/5/90 SUSPENSION WAS LIFTED.

KHOLEIF, ALI A R MD, DATE OF BIRTH OCTOBER 20, 1938, LICENSE NUMBER 0021542, OF OTTUMWA, IA, WAS DISCIPLINED BY IOWA ON DECEMBER 6, 1990.
DISCIPLINARY ACTION: LICENSE REVOCATION
OFFENSE: SUBSTANDARD CARE, INCOMPETENCE, OR NEGLIGENCE
NOTES: ALSO ETHICAL VIOLATIONS.

KHOLEIF, ALI A R MD, DATE OF BIRTH OCTOBER 20, 1938, OF RR 7 BOX 188A, OTTUMWA, IA, WAS DISCIPLINED BY MEDICARE ON MAY 10, 1991.
DISCIPLINARY ACTION: EXCLUSION FROM THE MEDICARE AND/OR

MEDICAID PROGRAMS
OFFENSE: DISCIPLINARY ACTION BY ANOTHER STATE OR AGENCY
NOTES: LICENSE REVOCATION OR SUSPENSION.

KHOLEIF, ALI ABDEL RAHIM MD OF WOODLAND, TX, WAS DISCIPLINED BY MISSOURI ON FEBRUARY 22, 1993.
DISCIPLINARY ACTION: LICENSE REVOCATION
OFFENSE: DISCIPLINARY ACTION BY ANOTHER STATE OR AGENCY
NOTES: SUBSTANDARD CARE AND MISCONDUCT. NO REINSTATEMENT OF LICENSE FOR SEVEN YEARS.

KIEPFER, RICHARD F MD OF 208 WOLLSCHLAGER DRIVE, BOERNE, TX, WAS DISCIPLINED BY DEA ON SEPTEMBER 29, 1993.
DISCIPLINARY ACTION: SURRENDER OF CONTROLLED SUBSTANCE LICENSE
OFFENSE: CRIMINAL CONVICTION OR PLEA OF GUILTY, NOLO CONTENDERE, OR NO CONTEST TO A CRIME
NOTES: CONVICTED OF FAILURE TO MAKE, KEEP AND FURNISH CONTROLLED SUBSTANCES RECORDS ON PHENTOBARBITAL. SENTENCED 6/25/93 TO PROBATION, FINE AND COMMUNITY SERVICE; LICENSE SUSPENDED 8/20/93.

KIEPFER, RICHARD FRANCIS MD, DATE OF BIRTH APRIL 12, 1937, LICENSE NUMBER 00F7503, OF 208 WOLLSCHLAEGER, BOERNE, TX, WAS DISCIPLINED BY TEXAS ON AUGUST 20, 1993.
DISCIPLINARY ACTION: LICENSE SUSPENSION
OFFENSE: CRIMINAL CONVICTION OR PLEA OF GUILTY, NOLO CONTENDERE, OR NO CONTEST TO A CRIME
NOTES: ON 6/25/93 HE WAS FOUND GUILTY IN KENDALL COUNTY TEXAS OF THE FELONY OFFENSE OF FAILURE TO MAKE, KEEP AND FURNISH CONTROLLED SUBSTANCE RECORDS OF THE SCHEDULE II CONTROLLED SUBSTANCE PENTOBARBITAL; PLACED ON PROBATION FOR SIX YEARS AND FINED $10,000; IS IN THE PROCESS OF APPEALING THE CONVICTION. IF CONVICTION IS OVERTURNED WITHIN TWO YEARS BOARD WILL LIFT SUSENSION; IF LONGER THAN TWO YEARS HE SHALL PASS SPEX EXAM BEFORE THE SUSPENSION IF LIFTED; IF CONVICTION IS UPHELD LICENSE WILL AUTOMATICALLY BE REVOKED.

KIEPFER, RICHARD FRANCIS MD, DATE OF BIRTH APRIL 12, 1937, LICENSE NUMBER 0021180, OF 1 ST. JOSEPH TERRACE, WOODBRIDGE, NJ, WAS DISCIPLINED BY NEW JERSEY ON JUNE 2, 1994.
DISCIPLINARY ACTION: LICENSE REVOCATION
OFFENSE: CRIMINAL CONVICTION OR PLEA OF GUILTY, NOLO CONTENDERE, OR NO CONTEST TO A CRIME
NOTES: FINDING OF GUILT IN TEXAS ON THE FELONY OFFENSE OF FAILURE TO MAKE, KEEP AND FURNISH CONTROLLED SUBSTANCE RECORDS FOR SCHEDULE II CONTROLLED DANGEROUS SUBSTANCES MEDICATION. SENTENCING OF A SIX-YEAR PRISON SENTENCE WAS STAYED AND HE WAS PLACED ON SIX YEARS PROBATION AND FINED $10,000.

KILIAN, ROBERT JACK MD, LICENSE NUMBER 00D9333, OF LAKE JACKSON, TX, WAS DISCIPLINED BY TEXAS ON NOVEMBER 19, 1993.
DISCIPLINARY ACTION: 60-MONTH PROBATION; REPRIMAND
OFFENSE: OVERPRESCRIBING OR MISPRESCRIBING DRUGS
NOTES: FROM 6/28/84 THROUGH 3/92 PRESCRIBED VARIOUS NARCOTIC DRUGS TO 15 PATIENTS FOR CHRONIC PAIN MANAGEMENT FOR WHICH HE FAILED TO TAKE ADEQUATE HISTORIES, TO ORDER FURTHER DIAGNOSTIC STUDIES AS INDICATED, MAINTAIN A COMPREHENSIVE PAIN AND DRUG ABUSE MANAGEMENT PLAN, APPROPRIATELY DOCUMENT MEDICAL RECORDS TO JUSTIFY TREATMENT AND PERFORM PERIODIC PHYSICAL EXAMS; WITHOUT HIS KNOWLEDGE SOME OF THE DRUGS WERE SOLD BY TWO PATIENTS WHICH RESULTED IN THEIR ARREST. CONDITIONS OF PROBATION: SHALL MAINTAIN ADEQUATE MEDICAL RECORDS ON ALL PATIENT OFFICE VISITS AND MAKE THESE RECORDS AVAILABLE FOR REVIEW; SHALL HAVE HIS PRACTICE MONITORED BY A BOARD-APPROVED PHYSICIAN WITH QUARTERLY REPORTS; SHALL CONSULT WITH HIS MONITORING PHYSICIAN REGARDING APPROPRIATE MANAGEMENT OF ALL PATIENTS HE MAINTAINS ON CONTROLLED SUBSTANCES FOR LONGER THAN SIX MONTHS; WITHIN SIX MONTHS WILL ENROLL IN A REMEDIAL PHARMACOLOGY COURSE AND SHALL ATTEND 50 HOURS PER YEAR OF CONTINUING MEDICAL EDUCATION WITH AT LEAST ONE COURSE PER YEAR ON THE POTENTIAL FOR ABUSE OF CONTROLLED SUBSTANCES AND OTHER PRESCRIPTION DRUGS; DUPLICATE COPIES OF ALL PRESCRIPTIONS FOR CONTROLLED SUBSTANCES SHALL BE MAINTAINED AND AVAILABLE FOR REVIEW; SHALL APPEAR BEFORE THE BOARD TWICE A YEAR; SHALL GIVE A COPY OF THIS ORDER TO ANY HEALTH CARE ENTITY WHERE HE HAS PRIVILEGES; SHALL COOPERATE WITH THE BOARD IN VERIFYING COMPLIANCE; SHALL INFORM BOARD OF CHANGE OF ADDRESS WITHIN 10 DAYS OR IF HE LEAVES THE STATE; TIME SPENT OUT OF TEXAS DOES NOT COUNT TOWARD PROBATION. SHALL NOT SEEK MODIFICATION FOR ONE YEAR.

KIM, YOUNGHOO MD, LICENSE NUMBER 00H7442, OF LOVELAND, CO, WAS DISCIPLINED BY TEXAS ON JUNE 17, 1992.
DISCIPLINARY ACTION: SURRENDER OF LICENSE

KIMBROUGH, RICHARD LEE MD, LICENSE NUMBER 00D8308, OF HOUSTON, TX, WAS DISCIPLINED BY TEXAS ON OCTOBER 27, 1989.
DISCIPLINARY ACTION: REPRIMAND
NOTES: STIPULATED ORDER. SHALL NOT ORDER INDUCTION OF GENERAL ANESTHESIA UNLESS APPROPRIATE DIAGNOSTIC STUDIES AND LAB TESTS HAVE BEEN PERFORMED TO PROPERLY ASSESS PATIENTS' FITNESS FOR SURGERY.

KINDRICK, JAMES W MD, LICENSE NUMBER 00H5181, OF ODESSA, TX, WAS DISCIPLINED BY TEXAS ON SEPTEMBER 28, 1990.
DISCIPLINARY ACTION: 36-MONTH PROBATION; MONITORING OF PHYSICIAN
NOTES: MUST CONTINUE PSYCHIATRIC TREATMENT; CONFER WITH BOARD-APPROVED LOCAL PHYSICIAN TO MONITOR OFFICE MEDICAL PRACTICE AND PROCEDURES; APPEAR BEFORE BOARD YEARLY.

KINDRICK, JAMES W MD OF FALLS CHURCH, VA, WAS DISCIPLINED BY VIRGINIA ON DECEMBER 4, 1990.
DISCIPLINARY ACTION: LICENSE REVOCATION
OFFENSE: PROVIDING FALSE INFORMATION TO THE BOARD
NOTES: INTERN/RESIDENT LICENSE REVOKED FOR SUBMITTING A FALSE APPLICATION TO BOARD.

KINDRICK, JAMES W MD, LICENSE NUMBER 0056108, OF ABILENE, TX, WAS DISCIPLINED BY OHIO ON FEBRUARY 13, 1991.
DISCIPLINARY ACTION: LICENSE REVOCATION
OFFENSE: DISCIPLINARY ACTION BY ANOTHER STATE OR AGENCY

NOTES: SUSPENSION OF CLINICAL PRIVILEGES BY AIR FORCE; PRIOR DISCIPLINARY ACTION AGAINST LICENSE IN NEW JERSEY. PERMANENT REVOCATION.

KINDRICK, JAMES W MD, DATE OF BIRTH JUNE 21, 1958, OF 6200 WILSON BLVD #306, FALLS CHURCH, VA, WAS DISCIPLINED BY MEDICARE ON DECEMBER 4, 1991.
DISCIPLINARY ACTION: EXCLUSION FROM THE MEDICARE AND/OR MEDICAID PROGRAMS
OFFENSE: DISCIPLINARY ACTION BY ANOTHER STATE OR AGENCY
NOTES: LICENSE REVOCATION OR SUSPENSION.

KINDRICK, JAMES W MD, LICENSE NUMBER 00H5181, OF ROCKVILLE, MD, WAS DISCIPLINED BY TEXAS ON JANUARY 24, 1992.
DISCIPLINARY ACTION: LICENSE REVOCATION
OFFENSE: DISCIPLINARY ACTION BY ANOTHER STATE OR AGENCY
NOTES: UNPROFESSIONAL OR DISHONORABLE CONDUCT LIKELY TO DECEIVE, DEFRAUD OR INJURE THE PUBLIC.

KINDRICK, JAMES W MD, DATE OF BIRTH JUNE 21, 1958, WAS DISCIPLINED BY MARYLAND ON SEPTEMBER 7, 1993.
DISCIPLINARY ACTION: DENIAL OF NEW LICENSE
OFFENSE: DISCIPLINARY ACTION BY ANOTHER STATE OR AGENCY
NOTES: ON 10/31/88 HE WAS DISCIPLINED BY THE AIR FORCE FOR INAPPROPRIATE PATIENT CARE; ON 6/15/90 WAS ASKED TO RESIGN FROM A FAMILY PRACTICE RESIDENCY IN TEXAS DUE TO MEDICAL REASONS AND SUBSEQUENTLY HAD HIS TEXAS LICENSE PLACED ON PROBATION; ON 12/4/90 HAD HIS LICENSE REVOKED IN VIRGINIA BASED ON THE TEXAS ACTION AND FALSE STATEMENTS ON HIS VIRGINIA LICENSE APPLICATION REGARDING PREVIOUS DISCIPLINE; ON 2/3/91 OHIO REVOKED HIS LICENSE BASED ON THE AIR FORCE AND TEXAS ACTIONS; IN HIS 7/91 APPLICATION IN MARYLAND DID NOT DISCLOSE THE OHIO AND TEXAS ACTIONS. ALSO KNOWN AS JAMEY LEE WEST.

KING, CLARENCE GORDON JR MD, LICENSE NUMBER 00E1883, OF SAN ANTONIO, TX, WAS DISCIPLINED BY TEXAS ON AUGUST 18, 1990.
DISCIPLINARY ACTION: 60-MONTH RESTRICTION PLACED ON CONTROLLED SUBSTANCE LICENSE; REQUIRED TO ENTER AN IMPAIRED PHYSICIAN PROGRAM OR DRUG OR ALCOHOL TREATMENT
OFFENSE: DRUG OR ALCOHOL ABUSE
NOTES: STIPULATED ORDER. SHALL NOT POSSESS, ADMINISTER OR DISPENSE ANY SCHEDULE II OR II-N CONTROLLED SUBSTANCES BUT MAY ORDER SUCH TO BE ADMINISTERED BY STAFF MEMBER TO PATIENT IN HOSPITAL, HOSPITAL EMERGENCY ROOM, OR NURSING HOME. SHALL NOT ORDER TRIPLICATE PRESCRIPTION FORMS. SHALL NOT TREAT OR SERVE AS PHYSICIAN, DISPENSE, OR ADMINISTER CONTROLLED SUBSTANCES OR OTHER DRUGS THAT MAY BE SUBJECT TO ABUSE FOR ANY MEMBER OF IMMEDIATE FAMILY OR SELF, AND ADMINISTER TO SELF OR IMMEDIATE FAMILY ONLY SUCH DRUGS AS PRESCRIBED BY OTHER PHYSICIANS. MUST PARTICIPATE IN AA AND BEXAR COUNTY MEDICAL SOCIETY COMMITTEE ON PHYSICIAN HEALTH AND REHABILITATION, SUBMIT TO PSYCHIATRIC EVALUATION AND FOLLOW RECOMMENDATIONS, PROVIDE URINE OR BLOOD SAMPLES ON NO-NOTICE BASIS, NOT TREAT ANY PATIENT WHILE UNDER INFLUENCE OF CONTROLLED SUBSTANCE OR ALCOHOL, DISPOSE OF CONTROLLED SUBSTANCE SAMPLES IN POSSESSION AND NOT ACCEPT OR RECEIVE SUCH SAMPLES, SUBMIT HIMSELF FOR APPROPRIATE EXAMINATIONS AND SCREENINGS TO DETERMINE FREEDOM FROM DRUGS AND ALCOHOL, AND APPEAR BEFORE BOARD TWICE ANNUALLY. ON 4/15/94 ORDER TERMINATED.

KING, DANIEL ALBERT MD, LICENSE NUMBER 00G3011, OF 2307 MILL CREEK, SUGAR LAND, TX, WAS DISCIPLINED BY DEA ON MARCH 14, 1989.
DISCIPLINARY ACTION: SURRENDER OF CONTROLLED SUBSTANCE LICENSE
OFFENSE: CRIMINAL CONVICTION OR PLEA OF GUILTY, NOLO CONTENDERE, OR NO CONTEST TO A CRIME
NOTES: RESTRICTED TO ADMINISTERING OR DISPENSING CONTROLLED SUBSTANCES TO HOSPITAL INPATIENTS ONLY. WROTE FALSE AND FICTITIOUS PRESCRIPTIONS FOR PERCODAN BETWEEN 09/87 AND 07/88. PLED NOLO CONTENDERE 02/24/89 IN TEXAS TO DELIVERY OF PRESCRIPTIONS; SENTENCED TO 5 YEARS PROBATION, A $500 FINE AND COURT COSTS OF $82.50.

KING, DANIEL ALBERT MD, LICENSE NUMBER 00G3011, OF PASADENA, TX, WAS DISCIPLINED BY TEXAS ON AUGUST 25, 1989.
DISCIPLINARY ACTION: 120-MONTH PROBATION; REQUIRED TO TAKE ADDITIONAL MEDICAL EDUCATION
NOTES: LICENSE SUSPENDED; STAYED 10 YEARS. RECEIVE PSYCHIATRIC TREATMENT, ALCOHOL ABUSE PROGRAMS, ABSTAIN FROM CONTROLLED SUBSTANCES, MOOD ALTERING DRUGS AND ALCOHOL, SUBMIT TO APPROPRIATE EXAMS TO DETERMINE FREEDOM FROM DRUGS AND ALCOHOL, APPEAR SEMI-ANNUALLY BEFORE THE BOARD. ON 8/19/94 PROBATION TERMINATED.

KING, DENNIS MAURICE MD, LICENSE NUMBER 00D7122, OF AUSTIN, TX, WAS DISCIPLINED BY TEXAS ON JANUARY 14, 1994.
DISCIPLINARY ACTION: 60-MONTH PROBATION; MONITORING OF PHYSICIAN
OFFENSE: DRUG OR ALCOHOL ABUSE
NOTES: HAS HAD ALCOHOL, MARIJUANA AND COCAINE PROBLEMS (INCLUDING IV COCAINE USAGE); TREATED IN GEORGIA; TREATING PHYSICIANS DO NOT RECOMMEND RE-ENTRY INTO MEDICAL PROFESSION. FIVE YEAR SUSPENSION STAYED. CONDITIONS OF PROBATION: PRIOR TO PRACTICING MEDICINE IN TEXAS SHALL APPEAR BEFORE BOARD AND DEMONSTRATE THAT HE IS PHYSICALLY, MENTALLY AND OTHERWISE COMPETENT TO PRACTICE AND OBTAIN APPROVAL AS TO ABILITY TO PRESCRIBE, DISPENSE OR ADMINISTER CONTROLLED SUBSTANCE DRUGS II-V; SHALL APPEAR BEFORE THE BOARD TWICE A YEAR; SHALL NOT TREAT OR OTHERWISE SERVE AS PHYSICIAN, PRESCRIBE, DISPENSE OR ADMINISTER DRUGS THAT MAY BE SUBJECT TO ABUSE TO HIMSELF OR ANY MEMBER OF HIS FAMILY; SHALL ABSTAIN FROM THE CONSUMPTION OF ALCOHOL/CHEMICAL SUBSTANCES IN ANY FORM UNLESS PRESCRIBED BY ANOTHER PHYSICIAN FOR A LEGITIMATE AND THERAPEUTIC PURPOSE; SHALL PARTICIPATE IN ACTIVITIES OF A PHYSICIAN HEALTH AND REHABILITATION COMMITTEE AND ATTEND WEEKLY MEETINGS WITH QUARTERLY REPORTS; SHALL PARTICIPATE IN AA'S PROGRAM NOT LESS THAN THREE TIMES A WEEK WITH QUARTERLY REPORTS TO THE BOARD; SHALL SUBMIT HIMSELF FOR APPROPRIATE EXAMS INCLUDING DRUG OR ALCOHOL SCREENS; SHALL CONTINUE TREATMENT WITH SPECIFIED

PHYSICIAN WITH QUARTERLY REPORTS; SHALL GIVE A COPY OF THIS ORDER TO ANY HEALTH CARE ENTITY WHERE HE HAS PRIVILEGES; SHALL COOPERATE WITH THE BOARD IN VERIFYING COMPLIANCE; SHALL INFORM BOARD OF CHANGE OF ADDRESS WITHIN 10 DAYS OR IF HE LEAVES THE STATE; TIME SPENT OUT OF TEXAS DOES NOT COUNT TOWARD PROBATION. SHALL NOT SEEK MODIFICATION FOR ONE YEAR.

KINZIE, DANIEL HARPINE IV MD, DATE OF BIRTH JULY 8, 1935, LICENSE NUMBER 00G8562, OF 6302 CYPRESS CREEK ROAD, SAN ANTONIO, TX, WAS DISCIPLINED BY TEXAS ON JANUARY 29, 1993.
DISCIPLINARY ACTION: RESTRICTION PLACED ON LICENSE; REPRIMAND
OFFENSE: PROFESSIONAL MISCONDUCT
NOTES: FAILED TO SUPERVISE THE ACTIVITIES OF ONE OF HIS EMPLOYEES WHO REPRESENTED HIMSELF AS A PHYSICIAN'S ASSISTANT WHEN HE WAS NOT REGISTERED AS ONE; THIS PERSON ENGAGED IN THE EXAMINATION AND TREATMENT OF PATIENTS; DR. KINZIE WAS UNAWARE OF THIS DECEPTION OR THAT HE WAS ENGAGING IN THE TREATMENT OF PATIENTS. SHALL APPEAR BEFORE THE BOARD TWICE A YEAR; SHALL NOT SIGN ANY PATIENT RECORDS UNLESS HE HAS PERSONALLY SEEN AND EXAMINED THE PATIENT UNLESS IT IS CLEARLY SPELLED OUT IN THE CHART THAT HE DID NOT SEE THE PATIENT; SHALL ADEQUATELY SUPERVISE THE ACTIVITIES OF ALL HIS EMPLOYEES; SHALL PROVIDE BOARD WITH ANNUAL REPORTS REGARDING EMPLOYMENT DETAILS ON HIS EMPLOYEES, ASSOCIATES OR ANY PHYSICIANS WHO COVER FOR HIM; SHALL GIVE A COPY OF THIS ORDER TO ANY HEALTH CARE ENTITY WHERE HE HAS PRIVILEGES; SHALL COOPERATE WITH THE BOARD IN VERIFYING COMPLIANCE; SHALL INFORM BOARD OF ANY ADDRESS CHANGE WITHIN 10 DAYS; SHALL NOT SEEK MODIFICATION FOR ONE YEAR. ON 8/19/94 BASED ON HIS SUCCESSFULLY MEETING AND COMPLYING WITH ALL TERMS OF THE ORDER, THE ORDER WAS TERMINATED.

KIRKPATRICK, JAMES L MD OF 5130 82ND STREET, LUBBOCK, TX, WAS DISCIPLINED BY MEDICARE ON JULY 17, 1987.
DISCIPLINARY ACTION: 12-MONTH EXCLUSION FROM THE MEDICARE AND/OR MEDICAID PROGRAMS
OFFENSE: SUBSTANDARD CARE, INCOMPETENCE, OR NEGLIGENCE
NOTES: GROSSLY SUBSTANDARD CARE OF TWO PATIENTS; GENERAL LACK OF KNOWLEDGE OF PHARMACOLOGY AND INADEQUATE UNDERSTANDING OF PHYSIOLOGY. REINSTATED ON 6/23/94.

KIRLIN, PATRICK JOSEPH DO, LICENSE NUMBER 00C9448, OF GRAND PRAIRIE, TX, WAS DISCIPLINED BY TEXAS ON NOVEMBER 19, 1993.
DISCIPLINARY ACTION: REPRIMAND
OFFENSE: FAILURE TO COMPLY WITH A PROFESSIONAL RULE
NOTES: FAILED TO ADEQUATELY DOCUMENT THE EXAMINATION OF A PATIENT WHO IS ALSO ONE OF HIS EMPLOYEES. SHALL GIVE A COPY OF THIS ORDER TO ALL HEALTH CARE ENTITIES WHERE HE HAS PRIVILEGES.

KITTEN, CLIFFORD M MD, LICENSE NUMBER 00E4456, OF HOUSTON, TX, WAS DISCIPLINED BY TEXAS ON DECEMBER 1, 1988.
NOTES: SETTLEMENT AGREEMENT AND UNSPECIFIED DISCIPLINARY ACTION

KLEBER, RONALD J MD OF MARIETTA, GA, WAS DISCIPLINED BY LOUISIANA ON SEPTEMBER 29, 1988.
DISCIPLINARY ACTION: 6-MONTH LICENSE SUSPENSION; PROBATION
OFFENSE: DISCIPLINARY ACTION BY ANOTHER STATE OR AGENCY
NOTES: SUBJECT TO STRICT COMPLIANCE WITH TERMS, CONDITIONS AND RESTRICTIONS IMPOSED BY PRIOR CONSENT ORDER OF GEORGIA BOARD. PLEADED GUILTY TO MAKING OR SUBMITTING FALSE OR DECEPTIVE CLAIMS TO A GOVERNMENTAL AUTHORITY FOR THE PURPOSE OF OBTAINING MONETARY COMPENSATION FOR SERVICES RENDERED.

KLEBER, RONALD JON MD, LICENSE NUMBER 0012335, OF PO BOX 1787, MARIETTA, GA, WAS DISCIPLINED BY GEORGIA ON MAY 12, 1988.
DISCIPLINARY ACTION: 6-MONTH LICENSE SUSPENSION
OFFENSE: CRIMINAL CONVICTION OR PLEA OF GUILTY, NOLO CONTENDERE, OR NO CONTEST TO A CRIME
NOTES: MEDICAID FRAUD.

KLEBER, RONALD JON MD, LICENSE NUMBER 00D0932, OF MARIETTA, GA, WAS DISCIPLINED BY TEXAS ON OCTOBER 27, 1989.
DISCIPLINARY ACTION: 60-MONTH RESTRICTION PLACED ON LICENSE
OFFENSE: DISCIPLINARY ACTION BY ANOTHER STATE OR AGENCY
NOTES: STIPULATED ORDER. LICENSE SUSPENDED, SUSPENSION STAYED UNDER FOLLOWING CONDITIONS: IF HE PETITIONS FOR TERMINATION OF GEORGIA SUSPENSION SHALL PROVIDE TEXAS WITH EVIDENCE THAT HE IS ABLE TO PRACTICE WITH SKILL AND SAFETY, THAT HE IS IN COMPLIANCE WITH PROBATION, THAT CONTINUING MEDICAL EDUCATION IS COMPLETED, THAT HE HAS MADE A RESTITUTION FOR WRONGFULLY BILLED PAYMENTS. DURING GEORGIA MEDICAL LICENSE PROBATION, SHALL ABIDE BY CONDITIONS OF CRIMINAL PROBATION. IF AUTHORIZED TO PRACTICE IN GEORGIA, SHALL COMPLY WITH REQUIREMENTS RELATING TO DIAGNOSIS, TREATMENT AND RECORD KEEPING, ALLOW INSPECTION OF RECORDS, HAVE REPORTS SUBMITTED ON HEALTH STATUS, SHALL NOT PARTICIPATE IN MEDICARE OR MEDICAID IN EITHER STATE FOR 15 YEARS COMMENCING 6/28/87 WITHOUT AUTHORIZATION FROM HHS. IF DESIRING TO PRACTICE MEDICINE IN TEXAS, MUST DEMONSTRATE CAPACITY TO PRACTICE WITH REASONABLE SKILL AND SAFETY TO PATIENTS AND FURNISH REPORT ON GEORGIA MEDICAL LICENSE STATUS. IF GRANTED PERMISSION TO PRACTICE IN TEXAS WHILE GEORGIA BOARD PROBATION IN EFFECT, TEXAS MAY IMPOSE APPROPRIATE PROBATIONARY TERMS.

KNIGHT, PATRICK L MD, LICENSE NUMBER 00E7638, OF PHOENIX, AZ, WAS DISCIPLINED BY TEXAS ON AUGUST 18, 1990.
OFFENSE: DISCIPLINARY ACTION BY ANOTHER STATE OR AGENCY
NOTES: STIPULATED ORDER. MUST COMPLY WITH ARIZONA BOARD ORDER, OBTAIN PERMISSION OF BOARD BEFORE PRACTICING IN TEXAS, AND FOLLOW SUCH TERM AS MAY BE IMPOSED.

KNIGHT, RALPH WALKER MD, LICENSE NUMBER 00C3112, OF WICHITA FALLS, TX, WAS DISCIPLINED BY TEXAS ON OCTOBER 1, 1987.
DISCIPLINARY ACTION: PROBATION
OFFENSE: LOSS OR RESTRICTION OF HOSPITAL PRIVILEGES

NOTES: PRESCRIBED DRUGS NONTHERAPEUTICALLY;DISCIPLINED BY LICENSED HOSPITAL, SUCH ACTION BASED ON PROFESSIONAL INCOMPETENCE LIKELY TO HARM PUBLIC; UNABLE TO PRACTICE MEDICINE WITH REASONABLE SKILL AND SAFETY TO PATIENTS BY REASON OF MENTAL CONDITION; PRESCRIBED FOR KNOWN HABITUAL DRUG USER; EXHIBITED UNPROFESSIONAL OR DISHONORABLE CONDUCT LIKELY TO DECEIVE OR DEFRAUD PUBLIC. LICENSE INDEFINITELY SUSPENDED AND PROBATED UNDER STIPULATED CONDITIONS.

KODSY, RAOUF ABDALLAH TWEFIK DR, DATE OF BIRTH DECEMBER 19, 1955, OF 12126 CARRIAGE HILL, HOUSTON, TX, WAS DISCIPLINED BY IOWA ON APRIL 29, 1993.
DISCIPLINARY ACTION: DENIAL OF NEW LICENSE
OFFENSE: PROVIDING FALSE INFORMATION TO THE BOARD
NOTES: BASED ON FALSIFIED MEDICAL APPLICATION. PERMANENT MEDICAL LICENSE DENIED.

KOKERNOT, ROBERT H MD, LICENSE NUMBER 00G2024, OF LOS FREANOS, TX, WAS DISCIPLINED BY CALIFORNIA ON JANUARY 6, 1988.
DISCIPLINARY ACTION: LICENSE REVOCATION
OFFENSE: DISCIPLINARY ACTION BY ANOTHER STATE OR AGENCY
NOTES: DEFAULT DECISION; DISCIPLINED BY ILLINOIS MEDICAL BOARD

KOMER, ROBERT A DO, LICENSE NUMBER 1005414, WAS DISCIPLINED BY MICHIGAN ON JUNE 7, 1990.
DISCIPLINARY ACTION: LICENSE REVOCATION

KOMER, ROBERT A DO, DATE OF BIRTH NOVEMBER 30, 1938, OF 12600 MELVILLE, APT 219, MONTGOMERY, TX, WAS DISCIPLINED BY MEDICARE ON OCTOBER 1, 1990.
DISCIPLINARY ACTION: EXCLUSION FROM THE MEDICARE AND/OR MEDICAID PROGRAMS
OFFENSE: DISCIPLINARY ACTION BY ANOTHER STATE OR AGENCY
NOTES: LICENSE REVOCATION OR SUSPENSION.

KOMER, ROBERT A DO, LICENSE NUMBER 0002512, OF MONTGOMERY, TX, WAS DISCIPLINED BY OHIO ON JANUARY 13, 1992.
DISCIPLINARY ACTION: LICENSE REVOCATION
OFFENSE: DISCIPLINARY ACTION BY ANOTHER STATE OR AGENCY
NOTES: MICHIGAN DISCIPLINARY ACTION FOR INAPPROPRIATE SEXUAL ACTIVITIES WITH PATIENTS AND IMPROPER PRESCRIBING PRACTICES; FRAUD, MISREPRESENTATION, OR DECEPTION IN RENEWING OHIO LICENSE. PERMANENT REVOCATION.

KOMER, ROBERT A DO OF MONTGOMERY, TX, WAS DISCIPLINED BY MISSOURI ON FEBRUARY 11, 1993.
DISCIPLINARY ACTION: LICENSE REVOCATION
OFFENSE: DISCIPLINARY ACTION BY ANOTHER STATE OR AGENCY
NOTES: SEX ABUSE AND PRESCRIPTION VIOLATION. NO REINSTATEMENT OF LICENSE FOR SEVEN YEARS.

KOMER, ROBERT ALLAN DO, LICENSE NUMBER 00E5553, OF HUNTSVILLE, TX, WAS DISCIPLINED BY TEXAS ON JANUARY 12, 1991.
DISCIPLINARY ACTION: 36-MONTH PROBATION
OFFENSE: DISCIPLINARY ACTION BY ANOTHER STATE OR AGENCY
NOTES: MICHIGAN MEDICAL LICENSE SUMMARILY SUSPENDED BY THE MICHIGAN BOARD. CONTINUED TREATMENT BY A SPECIFIC PSYCHIATRIST FOR NO LESS THAN THREE YEARS, WITH REGULAR REPORTS FROM THAT PSYCHIATRIST.

KOMER, ROBERT ALLAN DO, LICENSE NUMBER 00R2435, OF MONTGOMERY, TX, WAS DISCIPLINED BY ARKANSAS ON MAY 19, 1993.
DISCIPLINARY ACTION: LICENSE REVOCATION
OFFENSE: SEXUAL ABUSE OF OR SEXUAL MISCONDUCT WITH A PATIENT
NOTES: PRESCRIBED MEDICATION WITHOUT MEDICAL INDICATIONS; FOUND GUILTY OF SEXUAL MISCONDUCT WITH PATIENTS.

KOMOROV, JOSEPH DR OF HOUSTON, TX, WAS DISCIPLINED BY CALIFORNIA ON APRIL 10, 1986.
DISCIPLINARY ACTION: DENIAL OF NEW LICENSE
OFFENSE: PROVIDING FALSE INFORMATION TO THE BOARD
NOTES: EJECTED FROM FLEX EXAM FOR CHEATING

KONDEJEWSKI, RICHARD JOSEPH MD, LICENSE NUMBER 00F0548, OF LEAGUE CITY, TX, WAS DISCIPLINED BY TEXAS ON JANUARY 14, 1994.
DISCIPLINARY ACTION: 60-MONTH PROBATION; RESTRICTION PLACED ON LICENSE
OFFENSE: PROFESSIONAL MISCONDUCT
NOTES: IN 1981 WHILE TREATING A PATIENT FOR WEIGHT LOSS HE MAINTAINED A PERSONAL RELATIONSHIP WITH HER THAT WAS NOT TERMINATED UNTIL 1984 INCLUDING ALLOWING HER TO STAY AT HIS HOME WITH HIS FAMILY; FAILING TO OBTAIN PROFESSIONAL PSYCHIATRIC CARE WHEN SHE OBVIOUSLY NEEDED IT; TRIED TO TREAT HER PSYCHIATRIC PROBLEMS WHEN HE WAS NOT QUALIFIED TO DO SO; PURCHASING ONE OR MORE GIFTS FOR HER; PATIENT ALLEGES THAT SHE HAD SEX WITH HIM ON AT LEAST TWO OCCASIONS AND WAS GIVEN SEXUALLY EXPLICIT MATERIAL TO READ; HE ACKNOWLEDGES POOR JUDGMENT BUT DENIES HAVING SEX WITH HER OR EXHIBITING ANY ROMANTIC OVERTURES. SUSPENSION STAYED. CONDITIONS OF PROBATION: SHALL COMPLETE SIX HOURS OF ETHICS COURSES EACH YEAR; SHALL SUBMIT HIMSELF TO A BOARD-APPROVED PSYCHIATRIST FOR EVALUATION AND FOLLOW RECOMMENDATIONS REGARDING CARE AND TREATMENT; SHALL GIVE PSYCHIATRIST A COPY OF THIS ORDER AND HAVE HIM SUBMIT REPORTS THREE TIMES A YEAR IN THE EVENT TREATMENT IS NECESSARY; SHALL APPEAR BEFORE THE BOARD TWICE A YEAR; SHALL REFRAIN FROM TREATING ANY PATIENTS FOR PSYCHIATRIC PROBLEMS AND DEPRESSION; SHALL NOT EXAMINE ANY FEMALE PATIENT WITHOUT A CHAPERONEE IN EXAMINING ROOM AND SUCH PRESENCE WILL BE DOCUMENTED IN THE PATIENT'S RECORD; SHALL COOPERATE WITH THE BOARD IN VERIFYING COMPLIANCE; SHALL INFORM BOARD OF CHANGE OF ADDRESS WITHIN 10 DAYS OR IF HE LEAVES THE STATE; TIME SPENT OUT OF TEXAS DOES NOT COUNT TOWARD PROBATION. SHALL NOT SEEK MODIFICATION FOR ONE YEAR.

KONES, RICHARD J MD, DATE OF BIRTH APRIL 8, 1941, OF PO BOX 630547, HOUSTON, TX, WAS DISCIPLINED BY MEDICARE ON FEBRUARY 11, 1982.
DISCIPLINARY ACTION: 60-MONTH EXCLUSION FROM THE MEDICARE AND/OR MEDICAID PROGRAMS
OFFENSE: CRIMINAL CONVICTION OR PLEA OF GUILTY, NOLO CONTENDERE, OR NO CONTEST TO A CRIME
NOTES: PROGRAM-RELATED CONVICTION.

KONES, RICHARD J MD, LICENSE NUMBER 0031124, WAS DISCIPLINED BY MASSACHUSETTS ON FEBRUARY 3, 1988.
DISCIPLINARY ACTION: LICENSE REVOCATION
OFFENSE: DISCIPLINARY ACTION BY ANOTHER STATE OR AGENCY
NOTES: CRIMINAL CONVICTION FOR MEDICAID FRAUD

KOROMPAI, FERENC L MD, LICENSE NUMBER 00D0936, OF PECS, HU, WAS DISCIPLINED BY TEXAS ON JANUARY 6, 1995.
DISCIPLINARY ACTION: FINE; 60-MONTH RESTRICTION PLACED ON LICENSE
OFFENSE: SUBSTANDARD CARE, INCOMPETENCE, OR NEGLIGENCE
NOTES: ON 7/19/91 REMOVED WHAT HE THOUGHT WAS A PATIENT'S NON-FUNCTIONING KIDNEY ALTHOUGH HE DID NOT OBTAIN CONSENT TO REMOVE IT UNDER THE BELIEF THAT IT WAS A POTENTIAL SOURCE OF INCREASED BLOOD PRESSURE; REMOVED THE SOLE FUNCTIONING KIDNEY INSTEAD; AGREED TO THIS ORDER IN LIEU OF FURTHER INVESTIGATION. CONDITIONS OF FIVE YEAR RESTRICTION: SHALL ATTEND AT LEAST 50 HOURS PER YEAR OF CONTINUING MEDICAL EDUCATION INCLUDING AT LEAST 10 HOURS IN RISK MANAGEMENT AND 25 IN CARDIOVASCULAR SURGERY; SHALL MAINTAIN ADEQUATE MEDICAL RECORDS ON ALL PATIENT OFFICE VISITS WHICH SHALL BE AVAILABLE FOR INSPECTION; SHALL NOT SIGN ANY PATIENT RECORD UNLESS HE HAS PERSONALLY EXAMINED THE PATIENT OR CLEARLY NOTES IN THE RECORD THAT HE DID NOT; SHALL PAY $5,000 ADMINISTRATIVE PENALTY; SHALL PERFORM 75 HOURS PER YEAR OF COMMUNITY SERVICE; SHALL APPEAR BEFORE THE BOARD ONCE A YEAR OR UPON REQUEST; SHALL COOPERATE WITH THE BOARD IN VERIFYING COMPLIANCE; SHALL GIVE A COPY OF THIS ORDER TO ANY HEALTH CARE ENTITY WHERE HE HAS OR APPLIES FOR PRIVILEGES OR ANYONE WHO REQUESTS IT; SHALL ENSURE ANY INQUIRIES REGARDING HIS TEXAS LICENSURE STATUS ARE ANSWERED BY REFERENCING THIS ORDER; SHALL INFORM BOARD OF CHANGE OF ADDRESS WITHIN 10 DAYS OR IF HE LEAVES THE STATE; TIME SPENT OUT OF TEXAS DOES NOT COUNT TOWARD RESTRICTION. SHALL NOT SEEK MODIFICATION FOR ONE YEAR. PUBLIC REPRIMAND.

KRATZ, ARTHUR WILLIAM DO, LICENSE NUMBER 00C3950, OF DALLAS, TX, WAS DISCIPLINED BY TEXAS ON AUGUST 19, 1994.
DISCIPLINARY ACTION: 60-MONTH RESTRICTION PLACED ON CONTROLLED SUBSTANCE LICENSE; REQUIRED TO TAKE ADDITIONAL MEDICAL EDUCATION
OFFENSE: DISCIPLINARY ACTION BY ANOTHER STATE OR AGENCY
NOTES: IN 9/92 SURRENDERED HIS DEA CONTROLLED SUBSTANCE CERTIFICATE IN THE FACE OF ALLEGATIONS THAT HE FAILED TO COMPLETELY ACCOUNT FOR 7,000 TABLETS OF ACETAMINOPHEN WITH CODEINE; IN 4/93 ENTERED INTO A MEMO OF UNDERSTANDING WITH DEA WHICH GRANTED HIM AUTHORITY TO PRESCRIBE ONLY SCHEDULE IV AND V CONTROLLED SUBSTANCES; THESE ACTIONS WERE IN LARGE PART PROMPTED BY HIS FAILURE TO COMPLETELY ACCOUNT FOR CONTROLLED SUBSTANCES WHICH WERE ORDERED BY HIS WIFE AND DISPENSED BY HER TO FAMILY MEMBERS; HE MAINTAINS HE WAS UNAWARE THAT HIS WIFE HAD BEEN DOING THIS; ENTERED INTO THIS AGREEMENT WITH DEA TO AVOID THE PURSUIT OF CRIMINAL CHARGES CONTEMPLATED WITH REGARD TO HIS WIFE. CONDITIONS OF FIVE YEAR RESTRICTION: SHALL REQUEST MODIFICATION OF DEA AND TEXAS CONTROLLED SUBSTANCES CERTIFICATES SUCH THAT HE CANNOT PRESCRIBE SCHEDULES II AND III AND SHALL NOT SEEK REREGISTRATION WITHOUT PERMISSION; SHALL SURRENDER ALL UNUSED TRIPLICATE PRESCRIPTION FORMS; SEPARATE FROM PATIENT RECORDS SHALL MAINTAIN A FILE OF EVERY PRESCRIPTION WRITTEN FOR CONTROLLED SUBSTANCES OR DANGEROUS DRUGS WHICH SHALL BE AVAILABLE FOR INSPECTION; SHALL NOT TELEPHONE ANY PRESCRIPTION TO A PHARMACY FOR CONTROLLED SUBSTANCES OR DANGEROUS DRUGS; SHALL NOT EMPLOY HIS WIFE AS A MEMBER OF HIS MEDICAL STAFF; SHALL NOT PRESCRIBE, ADMINISTER OR DISPENSE DRUGS THAT MAY BE SUBJECT TO ABUSE TO HIMSELF OR ANY MEMBER OF HIS FAMILY; SHALL ATTEND AT LEAST 50 HOURS PER YEAR OF CONTINUING MEDICAL EDUCATION; SHALL GIVE A COPY OF THIS ORDER TO ANY HEALTH CARE ENTITY WHERE HE HAS PRIVILEGES; SHALL COOPERATE WITH THE BOARD IN VERIFYING COMPLIANCE; SHALL INFORM BOARD OF CHANGE OF ADDRESS WITHIN 10 DAYS OR IF HE LEAVES THE STATE; TIME SPENT OUT OF TEXAS DOES NOT COUNT TOWARD RESTRICTION. SHALL NOT SEEK MODIFICTAION FOR ONE YEAR.

KRAUS, VERNON J MD, DATE OF BIRTH SEPTEMBER 25, 1940, LICENSE NUMBER 00D8747, OF FORT WORTH, TX, WAS DISCIPLINED BY TEXAS ON APRIL 21, 1990.
DISCIPLINARY ACTION: REQUIRED TO ENTER AN IMPAIRED PHYSICIAN PROGRAM OR DRUG OR ALCOHOL TREATMENT; MONITORING OF PHYSICIAN
OFFENSE: DRUG OR ALCOHOL ABUSE
NOTES: STIPULATED ORDER. MUST SUBMIT TO TESTS TO DETERMINE PRESENCE OF DRUGS OR ALCOHOL (CONSISTENT WITH HIS AFTERCARE AGREEMENT REQUIREMENTS), CONTINUE ATTENDING IMPAIRED PHYSICIAN COMMITTEE MEETINGS AND AA OR NARCOTICS ANONYMOUS MEETINGS, HAVE CONTACT WITH TARRANT COUNTY MEDICAL SOCIETY'S PHYSICIAN HEALTH AND REHABILITATION COMMITTEE, MEET WITH SPECIFIC PHYSICIAN AS PART OF HIS CONTINUED REHABILITATION PROGRAM, AND APPEAR BEFORE BOARD ANNUALLY. RESTRICTIONS MODIFIED EFFECTIVE 6/17/92. RESTRICTIONS ON LICENSE TERMINATED EFFECTIVE 4/30/93.

KRAUS, VERNON J MD, LICENSE NUMBER 0C29717, OF FORT WORTH, TX, WAS DISCIPLINED BY CALIFORNIA ON SEPTEMBER 11, 1992.
DISCIPLINARY ACTION: 60-MONTH PROBATION
OFFENSE: DISCIPLINARY ACTION BY ANOTHER STATE OR AGENCY
NOTES: DISCIPLINED BY TEXAS BOARD FOR IMPAIRMENT DUE TO SUBSTANCE ABUSE. REVOCATION STAYED. PROBATION WITH TERMS AND CONDITIONS.

KROHN, DOUGLAS RUSSELL MD, LICENSE NUMBER 00H8713, OF SOMERSET, NJ, WAS DISCIPLINED BY TEXAS ON AUGUST 24, 1991.
DISCIPLINARY ACTION: REPRIMAND
OFFENSE: DISCIPLINARY ACTION BY ANOTHER STATE OR AGENCY
NOTES: ACTION TAKEN BY ANOTHER STATE BOARD FOR SEXUAL MISCONDUCT. PRIOR TO PRACTICING MEDICINE IN TEXAS, MUST APPEAR BEFORE AND RECEIVE APPROVAL FROM THE TEXAS BOARD.

KRUEGER, PHILIP MICHAEL MD, LICENSE NUMBER 00D4187, OF BOISE, ID, WAS DISCIPLINED BY TEXAS ON APRIL 20, 1991.
DISCIPLINARY ACTION: PROBATION
OFFENSE: DISCIPLINARY ACTION BY ANOTHER STATE OR AGENCY
NOTES: MUST INFORM BOARD IN WRITING OF INTENT TO RESUME PRACTICING MEDICINE IN TEXAS.

KRUK, KATHLEEN ADELE DR, LICENSE NUMBER 0017571, OF 10 HAPPY HILL, WICHITA FALLS, TX, WAS DISCIPLINED BY OKLAHOMA ON JANUARY 12, 1991.
DISCIPLINARY ACTION: 60-MONTH PROBATION; MONITORING OF PHYSICIAN
NOTES: HISTORY OF TREATMENT FOR DEPRESSION STARTING IN 1989. CURRENTLY UNDERGOING OUT-PATIENT TREATMENT. ISSUES RAISED AS TO HER PHYSICAL AND MENTAL FITNESS TO PRACTICE. LICENSE GRANTED UNDER PROBATIONARY TERMS AND CONDITIONS: SHALL CONTINUE PSYCHIATRIC/PSYCHOLOGICAL CARE AND MAKE RECORDS AVAILABLE TO BOARD; SHALL SUBMIT BIOLOGICAL FLUID SPECIMENS FOR ANALYSIS; SHALL NOTIFY ANY HOSPITAL WHERE SHE HOLDS STAFF PRIVILEGES, OR CLINIC OR GROUP OF THE TERMS AND CONDITIONS; SHALL FURNISH BOARD WITH ADDRESS AND/OR CHANGE OF ADDRESS; SHALL APPEAR BEFORE BOARD UPON REQUEST.

KUHL, IVAN WALTER MD, DATE OF BIRTH DECEMBER 2, 1920, LICENSE NUMBER 00C4396, OF 1111 N 10TH, MCALLEN, TX, WAS DISCIPLINED BY TEXAS ON APRIL 30, 1993.
OFFENSE: PROFESSIONAL MISCONDUCT
NOTES: THROUGH 1990 HE PRESCRIBED ASIATIC CAPSULES CONTAINING ARSENIC TRIOXIDE FOR THE TREATMENT OF PSORIASIS; NOT IN THE PURVIEW OF ACCEPTABLE CURRENT MEDICAL PRACTICE. SHALL NOT PRESCRIBE, ADMINISTER OR DISPENSE ARSENIC TRIOXIDE; SHALL GIVE A COPY OF THIS ORDER TO ANY HEALTH CARE ENTITY WHERE HE HAS PRIVILEGES; SHALL COOPERATE WITH THE BOARD IN VERIFYING COMPLIANCE; SHALL INFORM BOARD OF CHANGE OF ADDRESS WITHIN 10 DAYS.

KULA, GARY P MD, LICENSE NUMBER 00F4183, OF NORMAN, OK, WAS DISCIPLINED BY TEXAS ON DECEMBER 1, 1988.
NOTES: SETTLEMENT AGREEMENT AND UNSPECIFIED DISCIPLINARY ACTION

KUO, LIMEI MD, LICENSE NUMBER 00F5811, OF BELLAIRE, TX, WAS DISCIPLINED BY TEXAS ON JULY 23, 1992.
DISCIPLINARY ACTION: EMERGENCY SUSPENSION
OFFENSE: DRUG OR ALCOHOL ABUSE
NOTES: INTEMPERATE USE OF DRUGS.

KUO, LIMEI MD, LICENSE NUMBER 00F5811, OF BELLAIRE, TX, WAS DISCIPLINED BY TEXAS ON NOVEMBER 13, 1992.
DISCIPLINARY ACTION: 12-MONTH LICENSE SUSPENSION
NOTES: MAY MAKE APPLICATION FOR REINSTATEMENT AFTER ONE YEAR.

KURTZ, IRWIN MD, LICENSE NUMBER 00C7021, OF 4402 VANCE JACKSON, SAN ANTONIO, TX, WAS DISCIPLINED BY TEXAS ON JULY 14, 1994.
DISCIPLINARY ACTION: EMERGENCY SUSPENSION
OFFENSE: DRUG OR ALCOHOL ABUSE
NOTES:

KURTZ, IRWIN MD, LICENSE NUMBER 00C7021, OF SAN ANTONIO, TX, WAS DISCIPLINED BY TEXAS ON AUGUST 19, 1994.
DISCIPLINARY ACTION: LICENSE SUSPENSION
OFFENSE: DRUG OR ALCOHOL ABUSE
NOTES: LICENSE WAS TEMPORARILY SUSPENDED ON 7/14/94 AFTER HE WAS DIAGNOSED AS POLYSUBSTANCE DEPENDENT, HYPOMANIC, AND HAVING BIPOLAR DISEASE; HE TESTED POSITIVE FOR BENZODIAZEPINES AND METHADONE ON 7/1/94; HAS ENGAGED IN THE INTEMPERATE USE OF PRESCRIPTION DRUGS; HAS ADMITTED TO A HISTORY OF POLYSUBSTANCE DEPENDENCE AND INTEMPERATE USE OF DRUGS, AS RECENTLY AS JULY 1994. SUSPENDED UNTIL SUCH TIME AS HE APPEARS BEFORE THE BOARD AND PROVIDES SUFFICIENT EVIDENCE THAT HE IS PHYSICALLY, MENTALLY AND OTHERWISE COMPETENT TO SAFELY PRACTICE MEDICINE. UPON SHOWING HE IS ABLE TO SAFELY PRACTICE, THE SUSPENSION WILL BE STAYED AND HIS LICENSE WILL BE PLACED ON PROBATION WITH VARIOUS TERMS AND CONDITIONS.

LADLEY, DAVID M MD, DATE OF BIRTH JUNE 19, 1953, OF 202 FM 1960 EAST BYPASS, HUMBLE, TX, WAS DISCIPLINED BY MEDICARE ON FEBRUARY 28, 1994.
DISCIPLINARY ACTION: EXCLUSION FROM THE MEDICARE AND/OR MEDICAID PROGRAMS
OFFENSE: DISCIPLINARY ACTION BY ANOTHER STATE OR AGENCY
NOTES: LICENSE REVOKED FOR REASONS BEARING ON PROFESSIONAL PERFORMANCE AND COMPETENCE.

LADLEY, DAVID MARK MD, LICENSE NUMBER 0025455, OF 105 N HIGH ST, HENDERSON, TX, WAS DISCIPLINED BY GEORGIA ON AUGUST 28, 1991.
DISCIPLINARY ACTION: NONRENEWAL OF LICENSE
OFFENSE: DISCIPLINARY ACTION BY ANOTHER STATE OR AGENCY
NOTES: DISCIPLINARY ACTION IN TEXAS. ADMINISTRATIVE REVOCATION FOR FAILURE TO RENEW.

LADLEY, DAVID MARK MD, LICENSE NUMBER 00G7839, OF HUMBLE, TX, WAS DISCIPLINED BY TEXAS ON DECEMBER 7, 1992.
OFFENSE: OVERPRESCRIBING OR MISPRESCRIBING DRUGS
NOTES: SEVERAL VIOLATIONS OF THE MEDICAL PRACTICE ACT, INCLUDING NONTHERAPEUTIC PRESCRIBING, PRACTICE INCONSISTENT WITH PUBLIC HEALTH AND WELFARE, AND IMPAIRMENT DUE TO ILLNESS OR CHEMICAL ABUSE. ORDER OF REVOCATION. ON 12/30/92, HE FILED MOTION FOR REHEARING WHICH WAS DENIED ON 1/11/93. ON 1/28/93, HE FILED AN APPEAL IN TRAVIS COUNTY AND A DECISION IS CURRENTLY PENDING. ORDER WILL BECOME FINAL WHEN ALL APPEALS HAVE BEEN EXHAUSTED.

LAFLEUR, MELANIE KOHOUT MD, LICENSE NUMBER 00H3482, OF MESA, AZ, WAS DISCIPLINED BY TEXAS ON JANUARY 6, 1995.
OFFENSE: DISCIPLINARY ACTION BY ANOTHER STATE OR AGENCY
NOTES: ENTERED INTO A REHABILITATION STIPULATION AND ORDER WITH THE ARIZONA BOARD ON 5/25/93 WHICH PLACED HER UNDER TERMS AND CONDITIONS BUT DOES NOT CONSTITUTE A DISCIPLINARY ORDER. SHALL NOT PRACTICE IN TEXAS UNTIL SHE PERSONALLY APPEARS BEFORE THE BOARD AND PROVIDES SUFFICIENT EVIDENCE THAT SHE IS PHYSICALLY, MENTALLY AND OTHERWISE COMPETENT TO SAFELY PRACTICE INCLUDING AT A MINIMUM REPORTS FROM TREATING PHYSICIAN, COMPETENCY EXAMS OR ANY THERAPIST; SHALL COMPLY WITH TERMS OF ARIZONA ORDER; SHALL PROVIDE COPIES OF REPORTS SENT TO OR RECEIVED FROM ARIZONA BOARD UPON REQUEST; SHALL SURRENDER TEXAS CONTROLLED SUBSTANCES

CERTIFICATES AND UNUSED TRIPLICATE PRESCRIPTION FORMS; SHALL NOT SEEK REREGISTRATION WITHOUT PERMISSION.

LAMURE, DAVID S SR MD, LICENSE NUMBER 00D6695, OF DEXTER, NM, WAS DISCIPLINED BY TEXAS ON OCTOBER 9, 1992.
DISCIPLINARY ACTION: LICENSE REVOCATION
OFFENSE: CRIMINAL CONVICTION OR PLEA OF GUILTY, NOLO CONTENDERE, OR NO CONTEST TO A CRIME
NOTES: CONVICTION OF A FELONY.

LANE, RICHARD A DO, LICENSE NUMBER 00D2028, OF DALLAS, TX, WAS DISCIPLINED BY TEXAS ON OCTOBER 1, 1987.
DISCIPLINARY ACTION: RESTRICTION PLACED ON CONTROLLED SUBSTANCE LICENSE
OFFENSE: OVERPRESCRIBING OR MISPRESCRIBING DRUGS
NOTES: EXHIBITED UNPROFESSIONAL OR DISHONORABLE CONDUCT LIKELY TO DECEIVE, DEFRAUD OR INJURE PUBLIC; PRESCRIBED OR ADMINISTERED DRUGS OR TREATMENT NONTHERAPEUTICALLY; PRESCRIBED, ADMINISTERED OR DISPENSED CONTROLLED SUBSTANCES IN MANNER INCONSISTENT WITH PUBLIC HEALTH AND WELFARE; FAILED TO PRACTICE MEDICINE IN ACCEPTABLE MANNER CONSISTENT WITH PUBLIC HEALTH AND WELFARE. LICENSE RESTRICTED UNDER CERTAIN CONDITIONS INCLUDING PROHIBITING HIM FROM TREATING PATIENTS FOR WEIGHT CONTROL WITH SCHEDULE II DRUGS.

LANE, RICHARD A DO OF DALLAS, TX, WAS DISCIPLINED BY MISSOURI ON DECEMBER 21, 1988.
DISCIPLINARY ACTION: 24-MONTH PROBATION
OFFENSE: DISCIPLINARY ACTION BY ANOTHER STATE OR AGENCY
NOTES: MISPRESCRIBING; NEGLIGENCE

LANGE, GERALD T MD, LICENSE NUMBER 00D7139, OF BEAUMONT, TX, WAS DISCIPLINED BY TEXAS ON AUGUST 1, 1988.
DISCIPLINARY ACTION: SURRENDER OF LICENSE

LANGE, GERALD T MD, DATE OF BIRTH MARCH 7, 1944, OF 6810 HIALEAH, BEAUMONT, TX, WAS DISCIPLINED BY MEDICARE ON JANUARY 24, 1989.
DISCIPLINARY ACTION: EXCLUSION FROM THE MEDICARE AND/OR MEDICAID PROGRAMS
OFFENSE: DISCIPLINARY ACTION BY ANOTHER STATE OR AGENCY
NOTES: LICENSE REVOCATION OR SUSPENSION.

LATONN, EDWARD D MD, LICENSE NUMBER 0G15030, OF WILMINGTON, DE, WAS DISCIPLINED BY CALIFORNIA ON JULY 15, 1994.
DISCIPLINARY ACTION: LICENSE REVOCATION
OFFENSE: DISCIPLINARY ACTION BY ANOTHER STATE OR AGENCY
NOTES: DISCIPLINED BY DELAWARE BOARD FOR OVERPRESCRIBING OR INAPPROPRIATE PRESCRIBING TO 24 PATIENTS. DEFAULT DECISION.

LATONN, EDWARD DALE MD WAS DISCIPLINED BY DELAWARE ON JUNE 12, 1991.
DISCIPLINARY ACTION: 1-MONTH LICENSE SUSPENSION; REQUIRED TO TAKE ADDITIONAL MEDICAL EDUCATION
OFFENSE: PROFESSIONAL MISCONDUCT
NOTES: GROSS MISCONDUCT, NEGLIGENCE, OR INCOMPETENCE IN THE PRACTICE OF MEDICINE. REQUIRED TO ATTEND A MINI-RESIDENCY IN PRESCRIBING CONTROLLED DANGEROUS SUBSTANCES; MAY NOT APPLY FOR REINSTATEMENT OF HIS FEDERAL OR STATE CONTROLLED SUBSTANCES REGISTRATIONS FOR ONE YEAR FROM THE DATE OF HIS STIPULATION WITH THE BOARD'S INVESTIGATIVE COMMITTEE; UPON REINSTATEMENT HIS PRACTICE SHALL BE MONITORED BY THE BOARD OR ITS DESIGNEE FOR A PERIOD OF TWO YEARS.

LATONN, EDWARD DALE MD, LICENSE NUMBER 00E1647, OF WILMINGTON, DE, WAS DISCIPLINED BY TEXAS ON DECEMBER 4, 1991.
DISCIPLINARY ACTION: 1-MONTH LICENSE SUSPENSION; 24-MONTH PROBATION
OFFENSE: DISCIPLINARY ACTION BY ANOTHER STATE OR AGENCY
NOTES: DISCIPLINARY ACTION TAKEN BY DELAWARE BOARD ON 1/12/91. TWO YEAR SUSPENSION STAYED, PROBATION INCLUDES FOLLOWING CONDITIONS: MUST SUCCESSFULLY COMPLETE "MINI-RESIDENCY IN PRESCRIBING CONTROLLED DANGEROUS SUBSTANCES"; SHALL NOT APPLY FOR REINSTATEMENT OF FEDERAL CONTROLLED SUBSTANCES REGISTRATION FOR ONE YEAR FROM 4/2/91; MEDICAL PRACTICE SHALL BE MONITORED, INCLUDING BUT NOT LIMITED TO, THE REVIEW OF ANY AND ALL PATIENT RECORDS; SHALL APPEAR BEFORE BOARD ONCE A YEAR; SHALL PROVIDE COPIES OF REPORTS SENT TO DELAWARE TO TEXAS BOARD; SHALL APPEAR BEFORE BOARD PRIOR TO PRACTICING IN TEXAS; TIME SPENT OUT OF TEXAS OR DELAWARE DOES NOT COUNT TOWARD PROBATION; SHALL COOPERATE WITH BOTH BOARDS IN MONITORING COMPLIANCE; SHALL ADVISE BOARD OF ANY CHANGE OF ADDRESS WITHIN 10 DAYS.

LAWRENCE, RICHARD BURNETT III MD, DATE OF BIRTH FEBRUARY 22, 1948, LICENSE NUMBER 00E2671, OF 1925 DARTMOOR COURT, FORT WORTH, TX, WAS DISCIPLINED BY TEXAS ON JUNE 17, 1992.
DISCIPLINARY ACTION: RESTRICTION PLACED ON LICENSE; REPRIMAND
OFFENSE: SUBSTANDARD CARE, INCOMPETENCE, OR NEGLIGENCE
NOTES: FAILING TO SUPERVISE ADEQUATELY THE ACTIVITIES OF THOSE ACTING UNDER THE SUPERVISION OF THE PHYSICIAN, AND PROFESSIONAL FAILURE TO PRACTICE MEDICINE IN AN ACCEPTABLE MANNER CONSISTENT WITH PUBLIC HEALTH AND WELFARE. ON 8/20/93 ORDER TERMINATED AND LICENSE FREE AND CLEAR OF ANY PREVIOUS RESTRICTIONS.

LEAMON, ROY L MD OF 711 WEST 38TH ST SUITE E4, AUSTIN, TX, WAS DISCIPLINED BY DEA ON OCTOBER 9, 1990.
DISCIPLINARY ACTION: RESTRICTION PLACED ON CONTROLLED SUBSTANCE LICENSE
OFFENSE: OVERPRESCRIBING OR MISPRESCRIBING DRUGS
NOTES: OVERPRESCRIBED TO KNOWN ADDICT.

LEAMON, ROY LESLIE MD, LICENSE NUMBER 00C5140, OF AUSTIN, TX, WAS DISCIPLINED BY TEXAS ON SEPTEMBER 28, 1990.
DISCIPLINARY ACTION: 60-MONTH PROBATION; RESTRICTION PLACED ON LICENSE
NOTES: MAY ASSIST BUT MAY NOT PERFORM SURGERY BY HIMSELF OR AS PRIMARY SURGEON; HAVE REGISTRATION CERTIFICATES TO BE AMENDED TO DELETE SCHEDULES II, II-N, III-N AND V AND SHALL NOT REREGISTER WITHOUT PRIOR BOARD AUTHORITY; MAINTAIN FILE COPY OF CERTAIN PRESCRIPTIONS; NOT TELEPHONE ANY CONTROLLED SUBSTANCE OR DANGEROUS DRUG PRESCRIPTION TO PHARMACY; SUBMIT FOR PSYCHIATRIC EVALUATION AND FOLLOW

ANY RECOMMENDATIONS REGARDING CONTINUING CARE AND TREATMENT; IF CHOOSING TO PRACTICE IN FIELD OF MEDICINE OTHER THAN ORTHOPEDICS, SHALL FIRST OBTAIN APPROVAL OF COURSE OR PROGRAM HE PROPOSES TO ATTEND TO DEVELOP PROFICIENCY OR CURRENCY IN PROPOSED NEW SPECIALTY. ON 9/30/94 PROBATION TERMINATED.

LEBLEU, BENNIE MD OF 101 S. FLORENCE, ROTAN, TX, WAS DISCIPLINED BY MEDICARE ON SEPTEMBER 15, 1987.
DISCIPLINARY ACTION: 12-MONTH EXCLUSION FROM THE MEDICARE AND/OR MEDICAID PROGRAMS
OFFENSE: SUBSTANDARD CARE, INCOMPETENCE, OR NEGLIGENCE
NOTES: GROSSLY SUBSTANDARD CARE OF 4 PATIENTS. INCORRECT USE OF AVAILABLE DATA TO DIAGNOSE AND TREAT SEVERELY ILL PATIENTS. TREATING PATIENTS ACCORDING TO SYMPTOMS ONLY, BELIEF THAT LONG-TERM KNOWLEDGE OF PATIENTS IS MORE IMPORTANT IN DIAGNOSIS THAN AVAILABLE LABORATORY STUDIES

LECONEY, THOMAS RATCLIFF MD, LICENSE NUMBER 00H0552, OF FORT WORTH, TX, WAS DISCIPLINED BY TEXAS ON AUGUST 19, 1994.
DISCIPLINARY ACTION: REQUIRED TO TAKE ADDITIONAL MEDICAL EDUCATION; MONITORING OF PHYSICIAN
OFFENSE: DRUG OR ALCOHOL ABUSE
NOTES: HE HAS HAD THREE SINUS SURGERIES TRYING TO CORRECT A MEDICAL CONDITION THAT PRODUCED SEVERE HEADACHES; HIS PHYSICIAN PRESCRIBED CERTAIN DRUGS FOR HIM INCLUDING DALGAN FOR A LEGITIMATE MEDICAL CONDITION; BECAME HABITUATED TO DALGAN; REALIZED THIS AND HAS SOUGHT ASSISTANCE; IS FOLLOWING AN AFTERCARE PROGRAM INCLUDING ATTENDING AA, A WEEKLY CADUCEUS MEETING AND ASSISTANCE FROM AN IMPAIRED PHYSICIANS GROUP AND MEETING WITH PSYCHIATRISTS. CONDITIONS OF FIVE YEAR RESTRICTION: SHALL ABSTAIN FROM THE CONSUMPTION OF ALCOHOL/CHEMICAL SUBSTANCES IN ANY FORM UNLESS PRESCRIBED BY ANOTHER PHYSICIAN FOR LEGITIMATE AND THERAPEUTIC PURPOSES; SHALL NOT TREAT OR OTHERWISE SERVE AS PHYSICIAN, PRESCRIBE, DISPENSE OR ADMINISTER DRUGS THAT MAY BE SUBJECT TO ABUSE TO HIMSELF OR ANY MEMBER OF HIS FAMILY; SHALL SUBMIT HIMSELF FOR APPROPRIATE EXAMS INCLUDING DRUG OR ALCOHOL SCREENS; SHALL CONTINUE TREATMENT WITH PRESENT PSYCHIATRIST WITH QUARTERLY REPORTS; SHALL PARTICIPATE IN AA'S PROGRAM NOT LESS THAN THREE TIMES A WEEK WITH QUARTERLY REPORTS TO THE BOARD; SHALL PARTICIPATE IN ACTIVITIES OF A PHYSICIAN HEALTH AND REHABILITATION COMMITTEE AND ATTEND WEEKLY MEETINGS WITH QUARTERLY REPORTS; SHALL ATTEND AT LEAST 50 HOURS PER YEAR OF CONTINUING MEDICAL EDUCATION; SHALL APPEAR BEFORE THE BOARD TWICE A YEAR; SHALL GIVE A COPY OF THIS ORDER TO ANY HEALTH CARE ENTITY WHERE HE HAS PRIVILEGES; SHALL COOPERATE WITH THE BOARD IN VERIFYING COMPLIANCE; SHALL INFORM BOARD OF CHANGE OF ADDRESS WITHIN 10 DAYS OR IF HE LEAVES THE STATE; TIME SPENT OUT OF TEXAS DOES NOT COUNT TOWARD RESTRICTION. SHALL NOT SEEK MODIFICATION FOR ONE YEAR.

LEDLIE, WILLIAM BOYER MD, DATE OF BIRTH JANUARY 4, 1950, LICENSE NUMBER 00E4475, OF 9218 MONTFORD, HOUSTON, TX, WAS DISCIPLINED BY TEXAS ON AUGUST 24, 1991.
DISCIPLINARY ACTION: SURRENDER OF CONTROLLED SUBSTANCE LICENSE; 36-MONTH PROBATION
OFFENSE: DRUG OR ALCOHOL ABUSE
NOTES: LICENSE SUSPENDED, STAYED; PROBATION TERMS ARE AS FOLLOWS: SHALL APPEAR BEFORE THE BOARD TWICE A YEAR; SHALL SURRENDER DEA AND DPS CONTROLLED SUBSTANCES REGISTRATION CERTIFICATES AND NOT ATTEMPT TO REREGISTER WITHOUT BOARD APPROVAL; SHALL SURRENDER ALL UNUSED TRIPLICATE PRESCRIPTION FORMS AND NOT ATTEMPT TO ORDER MORE WITHOUT BOARD APPROVAL; SHALL SURRENDER ALL CONTROLLED SUBSTANCES, INCLUDING SAMPLES; SHALL NOT TREAT OR OTHERWISE SERVE AS THE PHYSICIAN, PRESCRIBE, DISPENSE, OR ADMINISTER CONTROLLED SUBSTANCES, OR ANY OTHER DRUGS THAT MAY BE SUBJECT TO ABUSE, FOR SELF OR ANY MEMBER OF IMMEDIATE FAMILY; MAY ADMINISTER TO SELF OR IMMEDIATE FAMILY ONLY SUCH DRUGS AS ARE PRESCRIBED BY OTHER PHYSICIANS; SHALL ABSTAIN FROM CONSUMPTION OF ALCOHOL, CONTROLLED SUBSTANCES, DANGEROUS DRUGS, OR PRESCRIPTION DRUGS IN ANY FORM; SHALL PARTICIPATE WITH IMPAIRED PHYSICIANS PROGRAM; SHALL SUBMIT FOR ALCOHOL OR DRUG SCREENING; SHALL CONTINUE TREATMENT FROM TALBOTT-MARSH RECOVERY PROGRAM; SHALL FURNISH WRITTEN REPORTS WHEN REQUESTED; SHALL PARTICIPATE IN AA. ON 1/29/93 MODIFICATION OF ORDER GIVING HIM PERMISSION TO REAPPLY TO THE DRUG ENFORCEMENT ADMINISTRATION AND THE TEXAS DEPARTMENT OF PUBLIC SAFETY FOR SCHEDULES II, IIN, III, IIIN, IV OR V CONTROLLED SUBSTANCE AUTHORITY. ALL OTHER TERMS AND CONDITIONS REMAIN IN EFFECT.

LEDLIE, WILLIAM BOYER MD OF HOUSTON, TX, WAS DISCIPLINED BY UTAH ON MAY 7, 1992.
DISCIPLINARY ACTION: SURRENDER OF LICENSE; SURRENDER OF CONTROLLED SUBSTANCE LICENSE
OFFENSE: DISCIPLINARY ACTION BY ANOTHER STATE OR AGENCY
NOTES: ENGAGING IN THE INTEMPERATE USE OF A CONTROLLED SUBSTANCE RESULTING IN DISCIPLINARY ACTION AGAINST HIS LICENSE IN TEXAS. AGREED NOT TO REAPPLY FOR LICENSURE FOR 2 1/2 YEARS.

LEE, CHUN SHON MD, LICENSE NUMBER 00E3991, OF TAIWAN, REPUBLIC OF CHINA, WAS DISCIPLINED BY TEXAS ON OCTOBER 1, 1987.
DISCIPLINARY ACTION: RESTRICTION PLACED ON LICENSE
OFFENSE: LOSS OR RESTRICTION OF HOSPITAL PRIVILEGES
NOTES: INSTRUCTED TO NOTIFY BOARD IF HE RETURNS TO TEXAS TO PRACTICE MEDICINE AND PROVIDE BOARD WITH NAMES OF APPROPRIATE SUPERVISING PHYSICIANS IN SUCH EVENT.

LEE, CHUN SHON MD WAS DISCIPLINED BY HAWAII ON APRIL 20, 1988.
DISCIPLINARY ACTION: 3-MONTH LICENSE SUSPENSION

LEE, CHUN SHON MD, LICENSE NUMBER 015960E, OF KAOHSIUNG, TAIWAN, WAS DISCIPLINED BY PENNSYLVANIA ON MAY 23, 1989.
OFFENSE: DISCIPLINARY ACTION BY ANOTHER STATE OR AGENCY
NOTES: HAD LICENSE AND HOSPITAL PRIVILEGES SUSPENDED IN TEXAS BASED ON DEFICIENT RECORD KEEPING IN

FOUR INSTANCES AND IMPROPER TREATMENT IN FOUR INSTANCES. IF HE ASSUMES PRACTICE IN PENNSYLVANIA MUST NOTIFY BOARD OF NAMES AND ADDRESSES OF ONE OR MORE PHYSICIANS WILLING TO REVIEW HIS MEDICAL RECORDS EVERY SIX MONTHS FOR TWO YEARS.

LEE, HOWARD MONROE JR MD, LICENSE NUMBER 00F1738, OF EL PASO, TX, WAS DISCIPLINED BY TEXAS ON OCTOBER 5, 1991.
DISCIPLINARY ACTION: 60-MONTH PROBATION; REQUIRED TO TAKE ADDITIONAL MEDICAL EDUCATION
OFFENSE: SUBSTANDARD CARE, INCOMPETENCE, OR NEGLIGENCE
NOTES: ON OR ABOUT 12/20/88 MADE AN ERROR IN PERFORMING LUMBAR SURGERY FOR A HERNIATED DISC, WHICH RESULTED IN A DURAL LEAK AND OTHER COMPLICATIONS, CAUSING THE PATIENT TO HAVE SEVERAL ADDITIONAL OPERATIONS TO CORRECT HIS MISTAKE; DID NOT RELEASE HER MEDICAL RECORDS IN A TIMELY MANNER BECAUSE HE WAS EMBARRASSED ABOUT HIS MISTAKE. CONDITIONS OF PROBATION INCLUDE: COMPLETION OF AT LEAST 50 HOURS PER EACH YEAR OF CONTINUING MEDICAL EDUCATION; MUST APPEAR BEFORE THE BOARD ONCE A YEAR; SHALL COOPERATE WITH BOARD IN VERIFYING COMPLIANCE; SHALL ADVISE BOARD OF ANY ADDRESS CHANGE WITHIN 10 DAYS; TIME SPENT OUT OF TEXAS DOES NOT COUNT TOWARD PROBATION. ON 11/3/94 PROBATION TERMINATED.

LEGGETT, JOSEPH E MD OF COEUR D'ALENE, ID, WAS DISCIPLINED BY IDAHO ON SEPTEMBER 11, 1992.
DISCIPLINARY ACTION: SURRENDER OF LICENSE
OFFENSE: SEXUAL ABUSE OF OR SEXUAL MISCONDUCT WITH A PATIENT
NOTES: CHARGED WITH HAVING SEX WITH PATIENTS. HAS APPEALED AN ORDER OF THE BOARD TO THE IDAHO SUPREME COURT. IN 11/91 DISTRICT COURT REJECTED AN APPEAL TO THE COURT. THE EARLIER APPEAL RESULTED IN A STAY OF THE REVOCATION ORDER OF 9/15/89. JUDGE CALLED FOR ADDITIONAL CONSIDERATION BY BOARD. A SECOND HEARING WAS CONDUCTED MAY 8-9 1990. IN A SETTLEMENT CONFERENCE IT WAS AGREED THE FINDINGS OF THE BOARD WOULD STAND.

LEGGETT, JOSEPH EDWARD MD, LICENSE NUMBER 00E2676, OF HUNTSVILLE, TX, WAS DISCIPLINED BY TEXAS ON JUNE 17, 1992.
DISCIPLINARY ACTION: RESTRICTION PLACED ON LICENSE
NOTES: RESTRICTED TO THE TREATMENT OF MALE PATIENTS WITHIN THE DEPARTMENT OF CORRECTIONS UNTIL SUCH TIME THAT THE IDAHO BOARD'S ACTION IS RESOLVED.

LEGGETT, JOSEPH EDWARD MD, LICENSE NUMBER 00E2676, OF HUNTSVILLE, TX, WAS DISCIPLINED BY TEXAS ON NOVEMBER 19, 1993.
DISCIPLINARY ACTION: 120-MONTH PROBATION; RESTRICTION PLACED ON LICENSE
OFFENSE: DISCIPLINARY ACTION BY ANOTHER STATE OR AGENCY
NOTES: ON 9/29/89 IDAHO BOARD REVOKED HIS MEDICAL LICENSE AFTER FINDING HE HAD ENGAGED IN IMPROPER SEXUAL CONDUCT WITH TWO PATIENTS; HE DENIED THESE CHARGES AND APPEALED THE RULING; THE DISTRICT COURT AFFIRMED THE BOARD'S RULING ON 11/22/91; HE APPEALED TO THE IDAHO SUPREME COURT; PRIOR TO A RULING BY THE COURT HE AND THE IDAHO BOARD ENTERED INTO A STIPULATION FOR DISMISSAL WITH PREJUDICE WHEREBY THE APPEAL WAS DISMISSED AND HE WAS ALLOWED TO SURRENDER HIS LICENSE IN LIEU OF REVOCATION; WAS ALSO INDICTED IN WYOMING FOR ALLEGED SEXUAL MISCONDUCT INVOLVING FEMALE PATIENTS; IS CONTESTING THESE ALLEGATIONS AND A TRIAL WAS PENDING AS OF THE ORDER DATE; HIS EMPLOYER IN TEXAS HAS PLACED HIM IN A PURELY ADMINISTRATIVE ROLE. TEXAS LICENSE SUSPENDED. SUSPENSION STAYED. CONDITIONS OF PROBATION: RESTRICTED FROM THE TREATMENT OF ANY PATIENT PENDING THE OUTCOME OF THE CRIMINAL MATTERS IN WYOMING; IF THIS DOES NOT RESULT IN A FINDING OF GUILT OR A CONVICTION MAY RETURN TO THE PRACTICE OF MEDICINE BUT MAY ONLY TREAT MALE PRISONERS. OTHER CONDITIONS INCLUDE: SHALL APPEAR BEFORE THE BOARD ONCE A YEAR; SHALL ATTEND AT LEAST 50 HOURS OF CONTINUING MEDICAL EDUCATION PER YEAR; SHALL GIVE A COPY OF THIS ORDER TO ANY HEALTH CARE ENTITY WHERE HE HAS PRIVILEGES; SHALL COOPERATE WITH THE BOARD IN VERIFYING COMPLIANCE; SHALL INFORM BOARD OF CHANGE OF ADDRESS WITHIN 10 DAYS OR IF HE LEAVES THE STATE; TIME SPENT OUT OF TEXAS DOES NOT COUNT TOWARD PROBATION. IF HE IS FOUND GUILTY OF THE PENDING CHARGES IN WYOMING, TEXAS LICENSE WILL BE REVOKED. SHALL NOT SEEK MODIFICATION FOR ONE YEAR.

LEGGETT, JOSEPH EDWARD MD, LICENSE NUMBER 00E2676, OF HUNTSVILLE, TX, WAS DISCIPLINED BY TEXAS ON SEPTEMBER 20, 1994.
DISCIPLINARY ACTION: LICENSE REVOCATION
OFFENSE: CRIMINAL CONVICTION OR PLEA OF GUILTY, NOLO CONTENDERE, OR NO CONTEST TO A CRIME
NOTES: ON 9/14/94 IN WYOMING HE ENTERED PLEAS OF NOLO CONTENDERE TO CHARGES OF SECOND DEGREE SEXUAL ASSAULT; THE COURT ORDERED HIM PLACED ON FIVE YEARS OF SUPERVISED PROBATION UNDER CONDITIONS.

LEHMILLER, JOHN ERICH MD, LICENSE NUMBER 00J3340, OF GALVESTON, TX, WAS DISCIPLINED BY TEXAS ON MAY 26, 1994.
DISCIPLINARY ACTION: EMERGENCY SUSPENSION
OFFENSE: DRUG OR ALCOHOL ABUSE
NOTES: AVAILABLE EVIDENCE AND INFORMATION INDICATE THAT BETWEEN 12/3/93 AND 4/18/94 CONSUMED COCAINE THREE TIMES AND ENGAGED IN INTEMPERATE USE OF ALCOHOL.

LEHMILLER, JOHN ERICH MD, LICENSE NUMBER 00J3340, OF GALVESTON, TX, WAS DISCIPLINED BY TEXAS ON AUGUST 19, 1994.
DISCIPLINARY ACTION: LICENSE SUSPENSION
OFFENSE: DRUG OR ALCOHOL ABUSE
NOTES: HE HAS ADMITTED TO A HISTORY OF POLYSUBSTANCE ABUSE AS RECENTLY AS 7/94 AND DATING BACK A NUMBER OF YEARS; HE CLAIMS A SOBRIETY DATE OF 7/10/94. LICENSE SUSPENDED UNTIL HE APPEARS BEFORE THE BOARD AND PROVIDES SUFFICIENT EVIDENCE THAT HE IS PHYSICALLY, MENTALLY AND OTHERWISE COMPETENT TO SAFELY PRACTICE.

LEHRER, LLOYD MICHAEL MD, LICENSE NUMBER 00G4025, OF HOUSTON, TX, WAS DISCIPLINED BY TEXAS ON DECEMBER 3, 1990.

DISCIPLINARY ACTION: 36-MONTH PROBATION; REQUIRED TO TAKE ADDITIONAL MEDICAL EDUCATION
NOTES: MUST MAINTAIN COMPLETE AND ACCURATE RECORDS OF PURCHASES AND DISPOSALS OF CONTROLLED SUBSTANCES.

LEHRER, LLOYD MICHAEL MD, LICENSE NUMBER 00G4025, OF HOUSTON, TX, WAS DISCIPLINED BY TEXAS ON AUGUST 20, 1992.
DISCIPLINARY ACTION: SURRENDER OF LICENSE
OFFENSE: PHYSICAL OR MENTAL ILLNESS INHIBITING THE ABILITY TO PRACTICE WITH SKILL AND SAFETY
NOTES: INABILITY TO PRACTICE MEDICINE WITH REASONABLE SKILL AND SAFETY TO PATIENTS BY REASON OF ILLNESS. RETIREMENT UNDER TERMS AND CONDITIONS.

LENGYEL, MIRCEA IAON MD, LICENSE NUMBER 00D2805, OF HOUSTON, TX, WAS DISCIPLINED BY TEXAS ON JUNE 13, 1989.
DISCIPLINARY ACTION: 36-MONTH PROBATION
NOTES: 3 YEAR SUSPENSION/STAYED. PROBATION TERMS PROHIBIT ASSOCIATION WITH FALSE ADVERTISING.

LENGYEL, MIRCEA IAON MD, LICENSE NUMBER 00D2805, OF HOUSTON, TX, WAS DISCIPLINED BY TEXAS ON JANUARY 12, 1991.
DISCIPLINARY ACTION: 12-MONTH PROBATION
NOTES: SHALL NOT TREAT OR SERVE AS PHYSICIAN, PRESCRIBE, DISPENSE, OR ADMINISTER CONTROLLED SUBSTANCES OR OTHER DRUGS THAT MAY BE SUBJECT TO ABUSE, OR WRITE PRESCRIPTIONS FOR CONTROLLED SUBSTANCES OR OTHER DRUGS THAT MAY BE SUBJECT TO ABUSE, FOR ANY MEMBER OF IMMEDIATE FAMILY OR SELF, AND ADMINISTER TO SELF OR IMMEDIATE FAMILY ONLY SUCH DRUGS AS PRESCRIBED BY OTHER PHYSICIANS.

LENTINO, EDUARDO P MD, LICENSE NUMBER 00E7649, OF HOUSTON, TX, WAS DISCIPLINED BY TEXAS ON DECEMBER 1, 1990.
DISCIPLINARY ACTION: REPRIMAND
NOTES: STIPULATED ORDER.

LENTINO, JORGE A MD, LICENSE NUMBER 00E3994, OF HOUSTON, TX, WAS DISCIPLINED BY TEXAS ON DECEMBER 1, 1990.
DISCIPLINARY ACTION: REPRIMAND
NOTES: STIPULATED ORDER.

LEONG, DANIEL K DO, LICENSE NUMBER 00G1462, OF DALLAS, TX, WAS DISCIPLINED BY TEXAS ON SEPTEMBER 28, 1990.
DISCIPLINARY ACTION: 120-MONTH PROBATION; RESTRICTION PLACED ON CONTROLLED SUBSTANCE LICENSE
NOTES: MUST SUBMIT FOR PSYCHIATRIC EVALUATION AND FOLLOW ANY RECOMMENDATIONS REGARDING CARE; NOT SERVE AS PHYSICIAN, PRESCRIBE, DISPENSE, OR ADMINISTER CONTROLLED SUBSTANCES OR OTHER DRUGS THAT MAY BE SUBJECT TO ABUSE OR WRITE PRESCRIPTIONS FOR CONTROLLED SUBSTANCES OR OTHER DRUGS THAT MAY BE SUBJECT TO ABUSE FOR SELF OR IMMEDIATE FAMILY MEMBERS; ADMINISTER TO SELF OR IMMEDIATE FAMILY ONLY SUCH DRUGS AS PRESCRIBED BY OTHER PHYSICIANS; REFRAIN FROM PRESCRIBING OR UTILIZING HALCION IN HIS MEDICAL PRACTICE FOR SELF, FAMILY, OR PATIENTS; COMPLETE PRECEPTORSHIP ON PREVENTION AND TREATMENT OF DRUG ABUSE; ATTEND CONTINUING MEDICAL EDUCATION; REFRAIN FROM ORDERING MEDICATIONS FROM PHARMACEUTICAL SUPPLIER OR WHOLESALER FOR DISPENSING OR SUPPLYING TO PATIENTS; IF EMPLOYED IN HOSPITAL EMERGENCY ROOMS OR UNDER OTHER CIRCUMSTANCES REQUIRING FREQUENT TRAVEL, SHALL PROVIDE TRAVEL OR WORK SCHEDULE TO THE BOARD; IF ORDERING ADMINISTRATION OF CONTROLLED SUBSTANCES FOR EMERGENCY ROOM OR HOSPITAL IN-PATIENTS OR PRESCRIBING CONTROLLED SUBSTANCES IN WRITING OR BY TELEPHONE FOR SAID PATIENTS, HE SHALL RECORD SAID PRESCRIPTIONS OR MEDICATION ORDERS IN LOG, SPECIFYING CERTAIN DATA, AND HAVE LOG AVAILABLE FOR INSPECTION; IF PRESCRIBING CONTROLLED SUBSTANCES IN OFFICE OR CLINIC SETTING, SHALL OBTAIN AND UTILIZE DUPLICATE, SERIALLY-NUMBERED PRESCRIPTIONS AND RETAIN DUPLICATES OF CONTROLLED SUBSTANCES FOR INSPECTION BY BOARD REPRESENTATIVES; APPEAR BEFORE BOARD OR BOARD COMMITTEE TWICE YEARLY.

LESHNOWER, ALAN C MD, LICENSE NUMBER 00G0756, OF ODESSA, TX, WAS DISCIPLINED BY TEXAS ON NOVEMBER 19, 1993.
DISCIPLINARY ACTION: 36-MONTH PROBATION; RESTRICTION PLACED ON LICENSE
OFFENSE: SUBSTANDARD CARE, INCOMPETENCE, OR NEGLIGENCE
NOTES: DURING 1991 IN THE COURSE OF TREATING THREE PATIENTS HE FAILED TO ADEQUATELY DOCUMENT THEIR RECORDS AND TO ENSURE THAT PROPER FOLLOW-UP CARE WAS PROVIDED FOLLOWING BYPASS SURGERY; TREATMENT WAS SUBSTANDARD AND CONTRIBUTED TO THE COMBINATION OF FACTORS WHICH LED TO THEIR DEATHS; AT THE TIME WAS PRACTICING AT A FACILITY WHICH DID NOT HAVE A CARDIOLOGIST READILY AVAILABLE AND WHICH WAS NOT ADEQUATELY SUITED TO PROVIDE SUFFICIENT SUPPORT FOR HIGH-RISK CARDIAC SURGERIES. SUSPENSION STAYED. CONDITIONS OF PROBATION: SHALL ATTEND AT LEAST 50 HOURS PER YEAR OF CONTINUING MEDICAL EDUCATION TO INCLUDE AT LEAST ONE COURSE IN CARDIOVASCULAR SURGERY AND ONE IN PHARMACOLOGY; SHALL REFER ALL HIGH-RISK CARDIOVASCULAR SURGERY CANDIDATES TO OTHER PHYSICIANS AND FACILITIES WHICH ARE ADEQUATELY SUITED AND EQUIPPED TO PERFORM HIGH-RISK CARDIOVASCULAR SURGERY; SHALL ENSURE AND DOCUMENT THAT EACH OF HIS SURGICAL PATIENTS RECEIVES ADEQUATE HOSPITAL CARE DURING THE 48 HOURS FOLLOWING SURGERY; SHALL MAINTAIN AN UP-TO-DATE LIST OF ALL HIS SURGICAL CASES AVAILABLE FOR REVIEW; SHALL SUBMIT A REPORT THREE TIMES A YEAR REFLECTING THE MORTALITY RATE FOR PATIENTS UNDER HIS CARE; SHALL APPEAR BEFORE THE BOARD TWICE A YEAR; SHALL GIVE A COPY OF THIS ORDER TO ANY HEALTH CARE ENTITY WHERE HE HAS PRIVILEGES; SHALL COOPERATE WITH THE BOARD IN VERIFYING COMPLIANCE; SHALL INFORM BOARD OF CHANGE OF ADDRESS WITHIN 10 DAYS OR IF HE LEAVES THE STATE; TIME SPENT OUT OF TEXAS DOES NOT COUNT TOWARD PROBATION. SHALL NOT SEEK MODIFICATION FOR ONE YEAR. ON 6/28/95 BOARD GRANTED TERMINATION OF THIS ORDER BASED ON HIS HISTORY OF COMPLIANCE, HIS COOPERATION WITH BOARD REPRESENTATIVES, AND BECAUSE THE HOSPITAL FACILITY WHERE HE PRACTICES HAS BEEN UPGRADED

AND NOW PROVIDES SUPPORT FOR HIGH-RISK CARDIAC SURGERIES.

LETT, CHARLES R MD, LICENSE NUMBER 0009543, OF 3938 SOUTH FRANKLIN, DALLAS, TX, WAS DISCIPLINED BY GEORGIA ON JULY 1, 1990.
DISCIPLINARY ACTION: LICENSE REVOCATION
OFFENSE: DISCIPLINARY ACTION BY ANOTHER STATE OR AGENCY
NOTES: FAILURE TO RENEW AND DISCIPLINARY ACTION IN ANOTHER STATE. ADMINISTRATIVE REVOCATION.

LETT, CHARLES REGINALD MD, DATE OF BIRTH MAY 31, 1936, LICENSE NUMBER 00D3635, OF TENNESSEE COLONY, TX, WAS DISCIPLINED BY TEXAS ON MARCH 31, 1990.
DISCIPLINARY ACTION: 60-MONTH RESTRICTION PLACED ON CONTROLLED SUBSTANCE LICENSE; REQUIRED TO TAKE ADDITIONAL MEDICAL EDUCATION
OFFENSE: DRUG OR ALCOHOL ABUSE
NOTES: STIPULATED ORDER. MUST SUBMIT FOR PSYCHIATRIC EVALUATION AND ANY RECOMMENDED TREATMENT, PARTICIPATE IN AA OR NARCOTICS ANONYMOUS, OBTAIN CONTINUING MEDICAL EDUCATION, REQUEST MODIFICATION OF CONTROLLED SUBSTANCES REGISTRATIONS TO ELIMINATE SCHEDULES II, II-N, III AND III-N AND NOT REREGISTER WITHOUT BOARD AUTHORITY, SURRENDER UNUSED TRIPLICATE PRESCRIPTION FORMS AND NOT ORDER MORE UNTIL BOARD WILL PERMIT, NOT TREAT SELF FOR RECURRING MEDICAL CONDITIONS OR ADMINISTER OR PRESCRIBE CONTROLLED SUBSTANCES FOR SELF, PARTICIPATE IN ACTIVITIES OF COUNTY MEDICAL SOCIETY'S COMMITEE ON PHYSICIAN HEALTH AND REHABILITATION, COMPLETE PRECEPTORSHIP ON PREVENTION AND TREATMENT OF DRUG ABUSE, AND SUBMIT FOR APPROPRIATE EXAMINATIONS TO DETERMINE FREEDOM FROM ALCOHOL AND DRUGS EXCEPT THOSE PRESCRIBED BY ANOTHER PHYSICIAN FOR VALID MEDICAL PURPOSE.

LETT, CHARLES REGINALD MD, DATE OF BIRTH MAY 31, 1936, LICENSE NUMBER 00D3635, OF 131 MEMORY LANE #912, PALESTINE, TX, WAS DISCIPLINED BY TEXAS ON OCTOBER 5, 1991.
DISCIPLINARY ACTION: LICENSE SUSPENSION; 60-MONTH PROBATION
OFFENSE: FAILURE TO COMPLY WITH A PREVIOUS BOARD ORDER
NOTES: FAILED TO COMPLY WITH 3/31/90 BOARD ORDER CONCERNING RECOMMENDATIONS OF BOARD-APPROVED PSYCHIATRIST, INCLUDING: ENROLLING AND PARTICIPATING IN AN OUT-OF-STATE DRUG TREATMENT PROGRAM, ATTENDING WEEKLY MEETINGS WITH THE IMPAIRED PHYSICIANS GROUP IN DALLAS UPON COMPLETION OF THE ABOVE PROGRAM, SUBMITTING TO FOUR RANDOM URINE DRUG SCREENS PER YEAR, PARTICIPATING IN WEEKLY OUT-PATIENT PSYCHOTHERAPY FOR TWO YEARS, ATTENDING AA MEETINGS FIVE TIMES A WEEK; ALSO FAILED TO SUBMIT PROOF OF COMPLETION OF 50 HOURS OF CATEGORY I CONTINUING MEDICAL EDUCATION BY 1/31/91, AND FAILED TO ENROLL IN A TWO-WEEK PRECEPTORSHIP ON THE PREVENTION AND TREATMENT OF DRUG ABUSE. REVOCATION STAYED, PROBATION WITH FOLLOWING CONDITIONS: LICENSE SUSPENDED UNTIL HE COMPLETES OUT-OF-STATE DRUG TREATMENT PROGRAM; SHALL COMPLETE A TWO-WEEK PRECEPTORSHIP ON THE PREVENTION AND TREATMENT OF DRUG ABUSE WITHIN 14 MONTHS OF FINISHING THAT PROGRAM; SHALL PARTICIPATE IN THE FOLLOWING ACTIVITIES FOR A COMBINED TOTAL OF FIVE TIMES A WEEK DURING THE FIRST SIX MONTHS FROM THE DATE OF THIS ORDER: AA OR NARCOTICS ANONYMOUS, INCLUDING A 12-STEP PROGRAM; ANY COUNTY MEDICAL SOCIETY'S IMPAIRED PHYSICIAN PROGRAM, INCLUDING PARTICIPATION IN WEEKLY MEETINGS WITH QUARTERLY REPORTS TO THE BOARD; MUST CONTINUE PSYCHIATRIC TREAMENT WITH QUARTERLY REPORTS; SHALL OBTAIN AT LEAST 50 HOURS OF CATEGORY I CONTINUING MEDICAL EDUCATION IN GENERAL MEDICAL COURSES, WHERE AT LEAST TEN HOURS SHALL INCLUDE TOPICS RELATED TO PSYCHOPHARMACOLOGY; SHALL LIMIT HIS CONTROLLED SUBSTANCE SCHEDULES TO IV AND V; SHALL SURRENDER ALL UNUSED TRIPLICATE PRESCRIPTION FORMS; SHALL NOT TREAT HIMSELF FOR ANY RECURRING MEDICAL CONDITION, AND SHALL NOT UNDER ANY CIRCUMSTANCES ADMINISTER OR PRESCRIBE CONTROLLED SUBSTANCES FOR HIMSELF; SHALL SUBMIT HIMSELF FOR EXAMINATIONS, INCLUDING SCREENING FOR ALCOHOL OR DRUGS; SHALL COOPERATE WITH BOARD IN VERIFYING COMPLIANCE; SHALL ADVISE THE BOARD IF HE CHANGES ADDRESS WITHIN 10 DAYS; TIME SPENT OUT OF TEXAS DOES NOT COUNT TOWARDS PROBATION; SHALL NOT PETITION FOR REINSTATEMENT FOR AT LEAST ONE YEAR. ON 1/29/93, THIS ORDER AMENDED SO THAT HE APPEAR BEFORE THE BOARD OR A COMMITTEE OF THE BOARD TWICE A YEAR DURING EACH YEAR OF PROBATION.

LETT, CHARLES REGINALD MD, LICENSE NUMBER 0004069, OF 131 MEMORY LANE #912, PALESTINE, TX, WAS DISCIPLINED BY DEA ON APRIL 27, 1992.
DISCIPLINARY ACTION: RESTRICTION PLACED ON CONTROLLED SUBSTANCE LICENSE
OFFENSE: PROFESSIONAL MISCONDUCT
NOTES: BOARD NUMBER RETIRED 11/01/86 AND 11/01/88 AS DELINQUENT. RESTRICTION PLACED ON REGISTRATION DUE TO HIS PRESCRIBING 7,162 DOSAGE UNITS FIORINAL FOR HIMSELF BETWEEN 10/27/87 AND 04/12/89. VOLUNTARY SURRENDER OF CONTROLLED SUBSTANCES PRIVILEGES.

LEVIN, ALFRED H MD OF DALLAS, TX, WAS DISCIPLINED BY TEXAS ON JULY 1, 1986.
DISCIPLINARY ACTION: SURRENDER OF LICENSE

LEVIN, IRA MARK MD, LICENSE NUMBER 0186535, OF 2 BEEKMAN PLACE, SUITE #5G, NEW YORK, NY, WAS DISCIPLINED BY DEA ON AUGUST 10, 1993.
DISCIPLINARY ACTION: SURRENDER OF CONTROLLED SUBSTANCE LICENSE

LEVIN, IRA MARK MD, LICENSE NUMBER 00J3142, OF AUSTIN, TX, WAS DISCIPLINED BY TEXAS ON MAY 5, 1994.
DISCIPLINARY ACTION: EMERGENCY SUSPENSION
OFFENSE: DRUG OR ALCOHOL ABUSE
NOTES: AVAILABLE EVIDENCE AND INFORMATION INDICATE THE FOLLOWING: ON 3/11/94 AND 4/20/94 HE PURCHASED LARGE QUANTITIES OF SCHEDULE II NARCOTICS; MEDICAL PRACTICE IS LIMITED TO SERVING AS A LOCUM TENEMS PHYSICIAN WITH NO NECESSITY FOR HIM TO POSSESS THE LARGE QUANTITIES OF DRUGS PURCHASED; HAS A HISTORY OF SUBSTANCE ABUSE AND TREATMENT; ACQUIRED THE DRUGS EITHER FOR

SELF-USE OR TO DIVERT FOR USE BY ANOTHER INDIVIDUAL(S) OR FOR BOTH PURPOSES.

LEVIN, IRA MARK MD, LICENSE NUMBER 00J3142, OF AUSTIN, TX, WAS DISCIPLINED BY TEXAS ON SEPTEMBER 30, 1994.
DISCIPLINARY ACTION: LICENSE SUSPENSION
OFFENSE: CRIMINAL CONVICTION OR PLEA OF GUILTY, NOLO CONTENDERE, OR NO CONTEST TO A CRIME
NOTES: WROTE PRESCRIPTIONS FOR CONTROLLED SUBSTANCES FOR HIS OWN USE AND WAS SUBSEQUENTLY ARRESTED BY DEA AGENTS FOR POSSESSION WITH INTENT TO DISTRIBUTE; CHARGE WAS REDUCED TO A MISDEMEANOR TO WHICH HE PLED GUILTY; ATTENDED A 28 DAY INPATIENT TREATMENT PROGRAM AND WAS AT A HALF-WAY HOUSE FOR SUBSTANCE ABUSERS AS OF THE DATE OF THIS ORDER. SUSPENSION UNTIL SUCH TIME AS HE APPEARS BEFORE THE BOARD AND PROVIDES SUFFICIENT EVIDENCE THAT HE IS PHYSICALLY, MENTALLY AND OTHERWISE COMPETENT TO SAFELY PRACTICE INCLUDING BUT NOT LIMITED TO A COMPLETE MEDICAL ASSESSMENT WITH PSYCHOLOGICAL AND NEUROPSYCHIATRIC EVALUATIONS.

LEVIN, MITCHELL L MD, LICENSE NUMBER 0049508, OF KISSIMMEE, FL, WAS DISCIPLINED BY FLORIDA ON APRIL 11, 1990.
DISCIPLINARY ACTION: FINE; REPRIMAND
OFFENSE: PROFESSIONAL MISCONDUCT
NOTES: CHARGED WITH PAYING OR RECEIVING A COMMISSION, BONUS, KICKBACK, OR REBATE, OR ENGAGING IN A SPLIT FEE ARRANGEMENT WITH A PHYSICIAN, ORGANIZATION, AGENCY OR PERSON, EITHER DIRECTLY OR INDIRECTLY FOR PATIENTS REFERRED TO PROVIDERS OF HEALTH CARE GOODS AND SERVICES, INCLUDING BUT NOT LIMITED TO HOSPITALS, NURSING HOMES, CLINICAL LABORATORIES, AMBULATORY SURGICAL CENTERS OR PHARMACIES; SOLICITING PATIENTS, EITHER PERSONALLY OR THROUGH AN AGENT, THROUGH THE USE OF FRAUD, INTIMIDATION, UNDUE INFLUENCE, OR A FORM OF OVERREACHING OR VEXATIOUS CONDUCT. MUST PAY $5000 FINE; REPRIMAND; MUST REVIEW APPLICABLE LAWS AND RULES AND PROVIDE AFFIDAVIT DETAILING SAME IN LIEU OF FURTHER PROSECUTION.

LEVIN, MITCHELL L MD, LICENSE NUMBER 0049508, OF ST CLOUD, FL, WAS DISCIPLINED BY FLORIDA ON APRIL 8, 1992.
DISCIPLINARY ACTION: 24-MONTH PROBATION; FINE
OFFENSE: SUBSTANDARD CARE, INCOMPETENCE, OR NEGLIGENCE
NOTES: FAILING TO PRACTICE MEDICINE WITH AN ACCEPTABLE LEVEL OF CARE AND SKILL. $1,000 FINE.

LEVIN, MITCHELL L MD, LICENSE NUMBER 0049508, OF KISSIMMEE, FL, WAS DISCIPLINED BY FLORIDA ON AUGUST 10, 1993.
DISCIPLINARY ACTION: FINE
OFFENSE: FAILURE TO COMPLY WITH A PREVIOUS BOARD ORDER
NOTES: CHARGED WITH VIOLATING A PREVIOUS BOARD ORDER; FAILING TO INCLUDE IN HIS ADVERTISEMENT LETTER THE DISCLAIMER REQUIRED. IN LIEU OF FURTHER PROSECUTION, CONSENTED TO $1,500 FINE; SHALL APPEAR BEFORE THE BOARD AND EXPLAIN CIRCUMSTANCES OF THIS CASE AND HOW SUBSEQUENT TRAINING AND PRESENT APPROACH HAVE AND WILL PREVENT FUTURE OCCURRENCES.

LEVIN, MITCHELL LEE MD, DATE OF BIRTH JANUARY 16, 1954, LICENSE NUMBER 00G5819, OF 921 N MAIN STREET SUITE 201, KISSIMMEE, FL, WAS DISCIPLINED BY TEXAS ON JUNE 15, 1993.
DISCIPLINARY ACTION: SURRENDER OF LICENSE
NOTES: DOES NOT WISH TO PRACTICE IN TEXAS; SURRENDER IS PERMANENT.

LEVIN, MITCHELL LEE DR OF OTTAWA, IL, WAS DISCIPLINED BY ILLINOIS ON JULY 1, 1994.
DISCIPLINARY ACTION: LICENSE SUSPENSION
OFFENSE: DISCIPLINARY ACTION BY ANOTHER STATE OR AGENCY
NOTES: DISCIPLINED IN FLORIDA. SUSPENSION FOR A MINIMUM OF 5 YEARS.

LEWIS, ALVIN M MD OF RICHMOND, TX, WAS DISCIPLINED BY TEXAS ON SEPTEMBER 1, 1985.
DISCIPLINARY ACTION: 60-MONTH PROBATION
OFFENSE: OVERPRESCRIBING OR MISPRESCRIBING DRUGS
NOTES: PRESCRIBED CONTROLLED SUBSTANCES NONTHERAPEUTICALLY AND FAILED TO PRACTICE MEDICINE IN ACCEPTABLE MANNER CONSISTENT WITH PUBLIC HEALTH AND WELFARE. REVOCATION STAYED

LEWIS, ALVIN M MD OF RICHMOND, TX, WAS DISCIPLINED BY NORTH CAROLINA ON JULY 29, 1986.
DISCIPLINARY ACTION: 60-MONTH PROBATION
OFFENSE: DISCIPLINARY ACTION BY ANOTHER STATE OR AGENCY
NOTES: LICENSE REVOKED IN TEXAS, UNPROFESSIONAL CONDUCT. REVOCATION STAYED, BASED ON COMPLIANCE WITH PROBATIONARY CONDITIONS.

LEWIS, ELBERT HAMPTON MD, DATE OF BIRTH JANUARY 2, 1929, LICENSE NUMBER 00C3124, OF DALLAS, TX, WAS DISCIPLINED BY TEXAS ON DECEMBER 4, 1991.
DISCIPLINARY ACTION: 120-MONTH PROBATION; REQUIRED TO ENTER AN IMPAIRED PHYSICIAN PROGRAM OR DRUG OR ALCOHOL TREATMENT
OFFENSE: DRUG OR ALCOHOL ABUSE
NOTES: USING ALCOHOL, DEMEROL, AND HALCION, PROVIDED DEMEROL TO HIS MOTHER FOR SELF-ADMINISTRATION WHICH WAS PRESCRIBED IN THE NAME OF A PATIENT, FAILED TO KEEP RECORDS OF CONTROLLED SUBSTANCES ON HAND ON THE DATE INVENTORY IS TAKEN, AND FAILED TO KEEP RECORDS FOR RECEIVING AND DISPOSING OF CONTROLLED SUBSTANCES. TEN YEAR SUSPENSION STAYED, PROBATION ISSUED WITH FOLLOWING CONDITIONS: SHALL PARTICIPATE IN DALLAS COUNTY MEDICAL SOCIETY COMMITTEE ON PHYSICIAN HEALTH AND REHABILITATION, INCLUDING PARTICIPATION IN THE WEEKLY MEETINGS; SHALL PARTICIPATE IN THE ACTIVITIES AND PROGRAMS OF ALCOHOLICS ANONYMOUS, INCLUDING A 12-STEP PROGRAM NOT LESS THAN THREE TIMES PER WEEK, WITH QUARTERLY REPORTS TO THE BOARD; SHALL ABSTAIN FROM THE CONSUMPTION OF ALCOHOL/CHEMICAL SUBSTANCES IN ANY FORM; SHALL SUBMIT HIMSELF FOR ALCOHOL AND DRUG SCREENING EXAMINATIONS; DEA AND TEXAS CONTROLLED SUBSTANCES REGISTRATIONS SHALL REMAIN LIMITED TO SCHEDULES III, III-N, IV, AND V; SHALL NOT TREAT OR SERVE AS PHYSICIAN, PRESCRIBE, DISPENSE, OR ADMINISTER CONTROLLED SUBSTANCES OR ANY OTHER DRUGS THAT MAY BE SUBJECT TO ABUSE FOR HIMSELF OR HIS FAMILY; SHALL MAINTAIN A FILE CONSISTING OF A COPY OF EVERY PRESCRIPTION WRITTEN FOR CONTROLLED SUBSTANCES OR DANGEROUS DRUGS BY DATE

ISSUED; SHALL NOT TELEPHONE ANY PRESCRIPTION TO A PHARMACY FOR CONTROLLED SUBSTANCES OR DANGEROUS DRUGS; SHALL COOPERATE WITH BOARD IN VERIFYING COMPLIANCE; SHALL ADVISE THE BOARD IF HE CHANGES ADDRESS WITHIN 10 DAYS; TIME SPENT OUT OF TEXAS DOES NOT COUNT TOWARDS PROBATION; SHALL NOT PETITION FOR MODIFICATION OF ORDER FOR FIVE YEARS; SHALL APPEAR BEFORE BOARD TWO TIMES A YEAR.

LEWIS, ELBERT HAMPTON MD, DATE OF BIRTH JANUARY 2, 1929, LICENSE NUMBER 00C3124, OF DALLAS, TX, WAS DISCIPLINED BY TEXAS ON AUGUST 20, 1992.
DISCIPLINARY ACTION: 120-MONTH PROBATION
OFFENSE: DRUG OR ALCOHOL ABUSE
NOTES: INABILITY TO PRACTICE MEDICINE WITH REASONABLE SKILL AND SAFETY TO PATIENTS BY REASON OF ILLNESS, DRUNKENNESS, EXCESSIVE USE OF DRUGS, NARCOTICS, CHEMICALS, OR ANY OTHER TYPE OF MATERIAL OR AS A RESULT OF ANY MENTAL OR PHYSICAL CONDITION. LICENSE SUSPENDED, SUSPENSION STAYED.

LEWIS, ELBERT HAMPTON MD, DATE OF BIRTH JANUARY 2, 1929, LICENSE NUMBER 00C3124, OF DALLAS, TX, WAS DISCIPLINED BY TEXAS ON NOVEMBER 13, 1992.
DISCIPLINARY ACTION: EMERGENCY SUSPENSION
OFFENSE: FAILURE TO COMPLY WITH A PREVIOUS BOARD ORDER
NOTES: VIOLATION OF 8/20/92 AGREED ORDER.

LEWIS, ELBERT HAMPTON MD, DATE OF BIRTH JANUARY 2, 1929, LICENSE NUMBER 00C3124, OF 7137 LAKEHURST AVENUE, DALLAS, TX, WAS DISCIPLINED BY TEXAS ON JANUARY 29, 1993.
DISCIPLINARY ACTION: SURRENDER OF LICENSE
OFFENSE: PHYSICAL OR MENTAL ILLNESS INHIBITING THE ABILITY TO PRACTICE WITH SKILL AND SAFETY
NOTES: INABILITY TO PRACTICE MEDICINE WITH REASONABLE SKILL AND SAFETY BY REASON OF ILLNESS. HE HAS CHOSEN TO PERMANENTLY RETIRE; SHALL SURRENDER HIS TEXAS AND DEA CONTROLLED SUBSTANCES REGISTRATIONS.

LEWIS, GEORGE E JR MD OF SAN ANTONIO, TX, WAS DISCIPLINED BY TEXAS ON DECEMBER 1, 1986.
DISCIPLINARY ACTION: LICENSE REVOCATION
OFFENSE: CRIMINAL CONVICTION OR PLEA OF GUILTY, NOLO CONTENDERE, OR NO CONTEST TO A CRIME
NOTES: CONVICTION OF FELONY

LEWIS, HAROLD D DO, LICENSE NUMBER 00E6126, OF AUSTIN, TX, WAS DISCIPLINED BY TEXAS ON FEBRUARY 16, 1990.
DISCIPLINARY ACTION: 12-MONTH RESTRICTION PLACED ON LICENSE
NOTES: STIPULATED ORDER. FOR PATIENTS LEWIS TREATS FOR ALLERGY SYMPTOMS BY USE OF MEDICATIONS CONTAINING STERIODS, MUST SEEK CONSULTATION OR REFER PATIENTS IF RELIEF OF SYMPTOMS NOT SHOWN WITHIN THREE MONTHS.

LEWIS, KENNETH D MD, DATE OF BIRTH OCTOBER 24, 1957, OF 7905 BORIXA STREET, HOUSTON, TX, WAS DISCIPLINED BY MEDICARE ON MAY 23, 1993.
DISCIPLINARY ACTION: EXCLUSION FROM THE MEDICARE AND/OR MEDICAID PROGRAMS
OFFENSE: FAILURE TO COMPLY WITH A PROFESSIONAL RULE
NOTES: DEFAULTED ON HEALTH EDUCATION ASSISTANCE LOAN. REINSTATED ON 9/2/93.

LEWIS, MICHAEL L MD, DATE OF BIRTH DECEMBER 1, 1953, OF 3106 SOUTHMORE, HOUSTON, TX, WAS DISCIPLINED BY MEDICARE ON APRIL 16, 1994.
DISCIPLINARY ACTION: EXCLUSION FROM THE MEDICARE AND/OR MEDICAID PROGRAMS
OFFENSE: FAILURE TO COMPLY WITH A PROFESSIONAL RULE
NOTES: DEFAULTED ON PUBLIC HEALTH SERVICE EDUCATION LOAN.

LIDSTONE, JOHN D DR WAS DISCIPLINED BY TENNESSEE ON AUGUST 16, 1988.
DISCIPLINARY ACTION: 12-MONTH RESTRICTION PLACED ON LICENSE; 24-MONTH REQUIRED TO ENTER AN IMPAIRED PHYSICIAN PROGRAM OR DRUG OR ALCOHOL TREATMENT
NOTES: RECIPROCITY REQUEST; RESTRICTIONS INCLUDE: MAINTAIN CONTRACT WITH IMPAIRED PHYSICIANS PROGRAM FOR TWO YEARS AND PRACTICE IN A SUPERVISED METRO AREA FOR ONE YEAR.

LIDSTONE, JOHN DAVID MD, LICENSE NUMBER 00G7411, OF MADISON, TN, WAS DISCIPLINED BY TEXAS ON AUGUST 18, 1990.
OFFENSE: DISCIPLINARY ACTION BY ANOTHER STATE OR AGENCY
NOTES: STIPULATED ORDER. MUST COMPLY WITH TENNESSEE BOARD RESTRICTIONS AND RECEIVE APPROVAL OF TEXAS BOARD PRIOR TO PRACTICING MEDICINE IN TEXAS. HAS FULLY COMPLIED WITH THE CONDITIONS OF TENNESSEE ORDER AND ON 10/20/94 TEXAS ORDER TERMINATED.

LIEBMAN, JACOB MD, LICENSE NUMBER 00F7820, OF ARLINGTON, TX, WAS DISCIPLINED BY TEXAS ON OCTOBER 27, 1989.
DISCIPLINARY ACTION: REPRIMAND
NOTES: STIPULATED ORDER.

LIEGEL, JOYCE M MD, DATE OF BIRTH MARCH 14, 1946, OF 3217 DURHILL STREET, HOUSTON, TX, WAS DISCIPLINED BY MEDICARE ON MAY 23, 1993.
DISCIPLINARY ACTION: EXCLUSION FROM THE MEDICARE AND/OR MEDICAID PROGRAMS
OFFENSE: FAILURE TO COMPLY WITH A PROFESSIONAL RULE
NOTES: DEFAULTED ON HEALTH EDUCATION ASSISTANCE LOAN.

LIGHTFOOT, STANLEY A MD, LICENSE NUMBER 00D0946, OF TYLER, TX, WAS DISCIPLINED BY TEXAS ON DECEMBER 1, 1990.
DISCIPLINARY ACTION: LICENSE SUSPENSION
OFFENSE: CRIMINAL CONVICTION OR PLEA OF GUILTY, NOLO CONTENDERE, OR NO CONTEST TO A CRIME
NOTES: LICENSE SUSPENDED WHILE PHYSICIAN SERVES PRISON TERM IN PENITENTIARY.

LIGHTFOOT, STANLEY A MD, LICENSE NUMBER 00D0946, WAS DISCIPLINED BY TEXAS ON SEPTEMBER 16, 1991.
DISCIPLINARY ACTION: 60-MONTH PROBATION; RESTRICTION PLACED ON LICENSE
NOTES: SUSPENSION OF LICENSE TERMINATED. CONDITIONS OF PROBATION: SHALL APPEAR BEFORE THE BOARD TWICE A YEAR; SHALL NOT PETITION FOR MODIFICATION FOR AT LEAST ONE YEAR; PRACTICE LIMITED TO PATHOLOGY; SHALL COMPLY WITH TERMS OF PROBATION UNDER THE U.S. DISTRICT COURT OR FEDERAL CORRECTIONAL SYSTEM; SHALL GIVE A COPY OF ORDER TO ALL INSTITUTIONS WHERE HE HAS PRIVILEGES; SHALL COOPERATE WITH BOARD IN VERIFYING COMPLIANCE; SHALL ADVISE THE BOARD OF CHANGE OF ADDRESS WITHIN 10 DAYS; TIME SPENT OUT OF TEXAS DOES NOT COUNT TOWARDS

PROBATION.

LIGHTFOOT, STANLEY AUGUSTUS MD OF 119 EAST HOUSTON, TYLER, TX, WAS DISCIPLINED BY OKLAHOMA ON MAY 9, 1992.
DISCIPLINARY ACTION: 60-MONTH PROBATION; RESTRICTION PLACED ON LICENSE
OFFENSE: DISCIPLINARY ACTION BY ANOTHER STATE OR AGENCY
NOTES: ON 2/25/78, LICENSE REVOKED BY TEXAS, REVOCATION STAYED, PLACED ON FIVE YEARS PROBATION; FULLY REINSTATED 3/83. ON 5/15/90, PLED GUILTY TO FOUR COUNTS OF MAKING FALSE STATEMENTS TO BANKS FOR LOANS, SENTENCED TO TWO YEARS IN PRISON AND FIVE YEARS PROBATION; TEXAS LICENSE SUSPENDED 8/18/90. ON 8/23/91, TEXAS LICENSE REINSTATED UNDER FIVE YEARS PROBATION. OKLAHOMA LICENSE GRANTED WITH TEXAS TERMS AND CONDITIONS IMPOSED. SHALL APPEAR BEFORE BOARD TWICE A YEAR; SHALL NOT PETITION FOR MODIFICATION FOR ONE YEAR; PRACTICE LIMITED TO PATHOLOGY; SHALL NOT SUPERVISE A PHYSICIAN ASSISTANT; SHALL FURNISH BOARD WITH ADDRESS AND/OR CHANGE OF ADDRESS; SHALL APPEAR BEFORE BOARD UPON REQUEST; SHALL NOTIFY ANY HOSPITAL WHERE HE HOLDS STAFF PRIVILEGES, OR CLINIC OR GROUP OF THE TERMS AND CONDITIONS.

LINSTRUM, TOM ELTON MD, DATE OF BIRTH MARCH 20, 1925, LICENSE NUMBER 00C4411, OF 310 BROOK LANE, MCKINNEY, TX, WAS DISCIPLINED BY TEXAS ON JUNE 15, 1993.
DISCIPLINARY ACTION: RESTRICTION PLACED ON LICENSE
OFFENSE: PROFESSIONAL MISCONDUCT
NOTES: PENDING INVESTIGATION CHARGING HIM WITH SEXUAL IMPROPRIETIES WITH A CHILD NOT HIS PATIENT AND IMPROPER MEDICAL TREATMENT OF AN ADULT PATIENT; HE HAS REQUESTED THAT THE BOARD'S PROCEEDINGS BE DEFERRED PENDING FINAL RESOLUTION OF FELONY CRIMINAL CHARGES FILED AGAINST HIM IN TEXAS AND COLORADO; HAS AGREED TO REFRAIN FROM PRACTICING IN TEXAS AND ALL OTHER STATES UNTIL THE BOARD'S PENDING PROCEEDINGS HAVE BEEN RESOLVED. SHALL NOTIFY BOARD IN WRITING WITHIN 10 DAYS OF EACH COURT DECISION; SHALL GIVE A COPY OF THIS ORDER TO ANY HEALTH CARE ENTITY WHERE HE HAS PRIVILEGES; SHALL COOPERATE WITH THE BOARD IN VERIFYING COMPLIANCE.

LINSTRUM, TOM ELTON MD, DATE OF BIRTH MARCH 20, 1925, LICENSE NUMBER 00C4411, OF MCKINNEY, TX, WAS DISCIPLINED BY TEXAS ON APRIL 15, 1994.
DISCIPLINARY ACTION: SURRENDER OF LICENSE
OFFENSE: CRIMINAL CONVICTION OR PLEA OF GUILTY, NOLO CONTENDERE, OR NO CONTEST TO A CRIME
NOTES: ON 12/9/93 HE WAS FOUND GUILTY OF THE FELONY OFFENSE OF INDECENCY WITH A CHILD; WHILE NOT ADMITTING HE HAS VIOLATED THE MEDICAL PRACTICE ACT HE SURRENDERED HIS LICENSE IN LIEU OF FURTHER INVESTIGATION. SHALL NOT PETITION FOR REINSTATEMENT OF LICENSE.

LIPSEY, BILLY CLINT MD, LICENSE NUMBER 00C3126, OF VAN HORN, TX, WAS DISCIPLINED BY TEXAS ON AUGUST 1, 1988.
DISCIPLINARY ACTION: REPRIMAND
OFFENSE: OVERPRESCRIBING OR MISPRESCRIBING DRUGS
NOTES: PRESCRIBED CONTROLLED SUBSTANCES IN THAT HE DID NOT PERFORM ADEQUATE PHYSICAL EXAMINATION PRIOR TO PRESCRIPTION OF CONTROLLED SUBSTANCES. OFFICIALLY COMMENDED FOR SERVICE AND CARE TO HIS COMMUNITY.

LIU, KUO TAI MD, LICENSE NUMBER 00E3047, OF MARLIN, TX, WAS DISCIPLINED BY TEXAS ON APRIL 14, 1989.
DISCIPLINARY ACTION: 12-MONTH RESTRICTION PLACED ON LICENSE; REQUIRED TO TAKE ADDITIONAL MEDICAL EDUCATION
NOTES: SHALL COUNSEL WITH SELECTED PHYSICIAN WHO WILL MONITOR PRACTICE, RECORD KEEPING, ETC., AS TO DEFICIENCIES

LIU, KUO TAI MD, LICENSE NUMBER 00E3047, OF MARLIN, TX, WAS DISCIPLINED BY TEXAS ON DECEMBER 4, 1991.
DISCIPLINARY ACTION: 60-MONTH PROBATION; RESTRICTION PLACED ON LICENSE
OFFENSE: SUBSTANDARD CARE, INCOMPETENCE, OR NEGLIGENCE
NOTES: FAILED TO DEMONSTRATE ADEQUATE KNOWLEDGE AND SKILLS IN TREATING FOUR PATIENTS AND PREPARING THEIR MEDICAL RECORDS. SUSPENSION STAYED; CONDITIONS OF PROBATION: SHALL LIMIT PRACTICE TO TREATING PATIENTS AT GOLDEN YEARS AND ELMWOOD NURSING HOMES ONLY; SHALL OBTAIN A BOARD-APPROVED MONITORING PHYSICIAN WHO SHALL REPORT TO THE BOARD EVERY SIX MONTHS; A COPY OF THIS ORDER SHALL BE PROVIDED TO THE MONITOR AND ALL INSTITUTIONS WHERE HE HAS PRIVILEGES; SHALL REFRAIN FROM PRESCRIBING ANY DRUG UNLESS MEDICALLY INDICATED AND IN THERAPEUTIC DOSES, AND WITH AN APPROPRIATE MEDICAL HISTORY AND EXAM; SHALL CONDUCT FOLLOW-UP EXAMS TO DETERMINE IF DRUG REGIMEN IS WORKING AND IF IT SHOULD BE ALTERED; WITHIN THREE MONTHS SHALL COMPLETE A TWO WEEK MINIRESIDENCY COURSE; WITHIN NINE MONTHS MUST PASS THE SPEX EXAM; WITHIN SIX MONTHS SHALL COMPLETE A REMEDIAL PHARMACOLOGY COURSE; SHALL COOPERATE WITH BOARD IN VERIFYING COMPLIANCE; SHALL ADVISE THE BOARD OF A CHANGE OF ADDRESS WITHIN 10 DAYS; TIME SPENT OUT OF TEXAS DOES NOT COUNT TOWARDS PROBATION; SHALL APPEAR BEFORE THE BOARD TWICE A YEAR; SHALL NOT APPLY FOR MODIFICATION OF ORDER FOR ONE YEAR.

LIU, KUO TAI MD, LICENSE NUMBER 0010449, WAS DISCIPLINED BY OKLAHOMA ON JANUARY 15, 1993.
NOTES: IN LIEU OF ANY FURTHER FORMAL PROCEEDINGS BOARD AGREED TO ACCEPT APPLICATION FOR PHYSICIAN EMERITUS STATUS (RETIRED STATUS, NOT ACTIVE TO PRACTICE) WITH THE PROVISION THAT HE FILES WITHIN 10 DAYS.

LOCKHART, ALBERT B MD, LICENSE NUMBER 00F6012, OF RICHARDSON, TX, WAS DISCIPLINED BY TEXAS ON AUGUST 1, 1988.
DISCIPLINARY ACTION: 12-MONTH RESTRICTION PLACED ON LICENSE
OFFENSE: SUBSTANDARD CARE, INCOMPETENCE, OR NEGLIGENCE
NOTES: FAILED TO PRACTICE MEDICINE IN ACCEPTABLE MANNER CONSISTENT WITH PUBLIC HEALTH; WAS REMOVED, SUSPENSION OR HAD DISCIPLINARY ACTION TAKEN BY PEERS IN PROFESSIONAL MEDICAL ASSOCIATION

LOCKHART, ALBERT BELVILLE MD, LICENSE NUMBER 0034111, OF

RICHARDSON, TX, WAS DISCIPLINED BY FLORIDA ON DECEMBER 16, 1988.
DISCIPLINARY ACTION: FINE; REPRIMAND
NOTES: $2500 FINE; SHALL NOT PRACTICE IN FLORIDA UNTIL HE DEOMONSTRATES ABILITY TO PRACTICE WITH SKILL AND SAFETY.

LOCKHART, ALBERT BELVILLE MD, LICENSE NUMBER 0034111, OF RICHARDSON, TX, WAS DISCIPLINED BY FLORIDA ON OCTOBER 29, 1990.
DISCIPLINARY ACTION: LICENSE SUSPENSION
OFFENSE: FAILURE TO COMPLY WITH A PREVIOUS BOARD ORDER
NOTES: FOUND GUILTY OF VIOLATING A LAWFUL ORDER OF THE BOARD PREVIOUSLY ENTERED IN A DISCIPLINARY HEARING BY FAILING TO PAY THE FINE. LICENSE SUSPENDED UNTIL SUCH TIME AS HE COMPLIES WITH THE ORDER OF 12/16/88 BY PAYING THE ADMINISTRATIVE FINE IMPOSED BY THAT ORDER AND UNTIL HE APPEARS BEFORE THE BOARD AND ESTABLISHES HIS ABILITY TO PRACTICE MEDICINE WITH SKILL AND SAFETY.

LOCKHART, ALBERT BELVILLE MD, LICENSE NUMBER 0034111, OF RICHARDSON, TX, WAS DISCIPLINED BY FLORIDA ON SEPTEMBER 23, 1991.
DISCIPLINARY ACTION: LICENSE SUSPENSION; FINE
OFFENSE: FAILURE TO COMPLY WITH A PROFESSIONAL RULE
NOTES: FAILED TO SUBMIT DOCUMENTATION VERIFYING CONTINUING MEDICAL EDUCATION IN RESPONSE TO THE BOARD'S RANDOM AUDIT. $5,000 FINE; LICENSE SUSPENDED UNTIL FINE IS PAID AND HE HAS COMPLETED AN ADDITIONAL 35 HOURS CATEGORY I CONTINUING MEDICAL EDUCATION, AND FIVE HOURS OF RISK MANAGEMENT.

LOCKWOOD, RICHARD L MD, LICENSE NUMBER 00G7083, OF HOUSTON, TX, WAS DISCIPLINED BY TEXAS ON AUGUST 18, 1990.
DISCIPLINARY ACTION: LICENSE SUSPENSION; REQUIRED TO TAKE ADDITIONAL MEDICAL EDUCATION
OFFENSE: DRUG OR ALCOHOL ABUSE
NOTES: STIPULATED ORDER. LICENSE INDEFINITELY SUSPENDED COMMENCING UPON BOARD VERBAL APPROVAL OF ORDER (8/17/90). MUST SUBMIT FOR PSYCHIATRIC EVALUATIONS AND RECOMMENDED TREATMENTS, PARTICIPATE IN HARRIS COUNTY MEDICAL SOCIETY COMMITTEE ON PHYSICAIN HEALTH AND REHABILITATION AND AA, SUBMIT FOR APPROPRIATE EXAMINATIONS TO DETERMINE FREEDOM FROM DRUGS AND ALCOHOL, AND OBTAIN CONTINUING MEDICAL EDUCATION.

LOCKWOOD, RICHARD L MD, LICENSE NUMBER 00G7083, OF 1404 MISSOURI ST, HOUSTON, TX, WAS DISCIPLINED BY DEA ON OCTOBER 2, 1990.
DISCIPLINARY ACTION: SURRENDER OF CONTROLLED SUBSTANCE LICENSE
OFFENSE: DRUG OR ALCOHOL ABUSE
NOTES: OKLAHOMA MEDICAL LICENSE REVOKED 06/08/90; TESTED POSITIVE ON URINE DRUG SCREEN FOR BENZODIAZEPINE METABOLITES 11/10/89 AND 04/04/90; TREATED FOR ABUSE OF FENTANYL AND SODIUM PENTOTHAL 12/87.

LOCKWOOD, RICHARD L MD, LICENSE NUMBER 00G7083, OF IRVING, TX, WAS DISCIPLINED BY TEXAS ON APRIL 29, 1991.
DISCIPLINARY ACTION: PROBATION
NOTES: REINSTATED FROM SUSPENSION; PROBATION CONDITIONS INCLUDE: PARTICIPATION IN IMPAIRED PHYSICIANS PROGRAM; MUST PARTICIPATE IN AA; MUST SUBMIT TO ALCOHOL OR DRUG SCREENS; SHALL ATTEND AT LEAST 50 HOURS OF CATEGORY I CONTINUING MEDICAL EDUCATION IN FAMILY PRACTICE.

LOFTIS, M DEAN MD OF LONGVIEW, TX, WAS DISCIPLINED BY TEXAS ON SEPTEMBER 1, 1985.
DISCIPLINARY ACTION: 60-MONTH PROBATION
OFFENSE: CRIMINAL CONVICTION OR PLEA OF GUILTY, NOLO CONTENDERE, OR NO CONTEST TO A CRIME
NOTES: CONVICTION OF A FELONY; REVOCATION STAYED

LOFTIS, M DEAN MD, LICENSE NUMBER C037364, OF LONGVIEW, TX, WAS DISCIPLINED BY CALIFORNIA ON FEBRUARY 6, 1987.
DISCIPLINARY ACTION: LICENSE REVOCATION
OFFENSE: DISCIPLINARY ACTION BY ANOTHER STATE OR AGENCY
NOTES: DISCIPLINED BY TENNESSEE MEDICAL BOARD. ALSO FEDERAL CONVICTION FOR ATTEMPTED MURDER BY SENDING A BOMB THROUGH THE MAIL

LOFTIS, M DEAN MD, LICENSE NUMBER 00E2274, OF LUBBOCK, TX, WAS DISCIPLINED BY TEXAS ON JANUARY 14, 1994.
DISCIPLINARY ACTION: LICENSE REVOCATION
OFFENSE: CRIMINAL CONVICTION OR PLEA OF GUILTY, NOLO CONTENDERE, OR NO CONTEST TO A CRIME
NOTES: ON 5/28/93 WAS SENTENCED TO 151 MONTHS OF IMPRISONMENT AFTER BEING CONVICTED IN THE U.S. DISTRICT COURT EASTERN DISTRICT OF TEXAS FOR ONE COUNT OF POSSESSION AND RECEIPT OF FIREARMS; TWO COUNTS OF RECEIVING AND CONCEALING STOLEN FIREARMS AND TWO COUNTS OF POSSESSION OF UNREGISTERED FIREARMS; INCARCERATED AS OF THE ORDER DATE. ORDER WILL BECOME FINAL WHEN ALL APPEALS HAVE BEEN EXHAUSTED.

LONG, JOSEPH MERL MD, DATE OF BIRTH JANUARY 31, 1945, LICENSE NUMBER 00E0095, OF 2710 HOSPITAL DRIVE #104, VICTORIA, TX, WAS DISCIPLINED BY TEXAS ON JANUARY 29, 1993.
DISCIPLINARY ACTION: 36-MONTH PROBATION; RESTRICTION PLACED ON CONTROLLED SUBSTANCE LICENSE
OFFENSE: OVERPRESCRIBING OR MISPRESCRIBING DRUGS
NOTES: TREATED A PATIENT FOR A LONG HISTORY OF BACK PAIN, ULCERS, ESOPHAGEAL RUPTURE AND DEPRESSION BEGINNING IN 1982; FAILED TO DOCUMENT REASONS FOR PRESCRIBING CONTROLLED SUBSTANCES; WAS AWARE PATIENT WAS RECEIVING PERCODAN FROM OTHER PHYSICIANS; ATIVAN AND HALCION; DR. LONG WROTE PRESCRIPTIONS FOR DALMANE, VALIUM, FASTIN AND ALUPENT; FROM 1989 THROUGH 3/91 EXCESSIVE AMOUNTS OF DRUGS WERE PRESCRIBED. 3 YEAR SUSPENSION STAYED. CONDITIONS OF PROBATION: SHALL ATTEND AT LEAST 50 HOURS PER YEAR OF CONTINUING MEDICAL EDUCATION APPROVED FOR CATEGORY I CREDITS 25 OF WHICH SHALL BE ASSOCIATED WITH INSTRUCTION IN PAIN MANAGEMENT; SHALL LEARN AND UNDERSTAND THE POTENTIAL FOR ABUSE OF CONTROLLED SUBSTANCES AND OTHER PRESCRIPTION DRUGS; SHALL SURRENDER ALL UNUSED TRIPLICATE PRESCRIPTION FORMS; SHALL NOT POSSESS, ADMINISTER, DISPENSE OR PRESCRIBE ANY CONTROLLED SUBSTANCES, BUT MAY ORDER SUCH TO BE ADMINISTERED TO HOSPITAL PATIENTS; SHALL APPEAR BEFORE THE BOARD ONCE A YEAR; SHALL

GIVE A COPY OF THIS ORDER TO ANY HEALTH CARE ENTITY WHERE HE HAS PRIVILEGES; SHALL COOPERATE WITH THE BOARD IN VERIFYING COMPLIANCE; SHALL INFORM BOARD OF CHANGE OF ADDRESS WITHIN 10 DAYS OR IF HE LEAVES THE STATE; TIME SPENT OUT OF TEXAS DOES NOT COUNT TOWARD PROBATION. SHALL NOT SEEK MODIFICATION FOR 1 YEAR. ON 6/22/94 BASED ON HISTORY OF COMPLIANCE, AND COMPLETION OF CONTINUING MEDICAL EDUCATION THE ORDER WAS TERMINATED.

LONG, WALTER KEIRN JR MD, LICENSE NUMBER 00C4177, OF KINGWOOD, TX, WAS DISCIPLINED BY TEXAS ON APRIL 15, 1994.
DISCIPLINARY ACTION: RESTRICTION PLACED ON LICENSE
OFFENSE: SUBSTANDARD CARE, INCOMPETENCE, OR NEGLIGENCE
NOTES: ADMITTED THAT PATIENTS UNDER HIS TREATMENT HAD DEVELOPED COMPLICATIONS RELATED TO GASTRIC STAPLING PROCEDURES; SUCH COMPLICATIONS ARE COMMON AND ARE NOT INDICATIVE OF NEGLIGENCE PER SE; PROFESSIONAL FAILURE TO PRACTICE MEDICINE IN AN ACCEPTABLE MANNER CONSISTENT WITH PUBLIC HEALTH AND WELFARE. SHALL NOT PERFORM ANY GASTRIC REDUCTION SURGERY FOR OBESITY; SHALL GIVE A COPY OF THIS ORDER TO ANY HEALTH CARE ENTITY WHERE HE HAS PRIVILEGES; SHALL COOPERATE WITH THE BOARD IN VERIFYING COMPLIANCE; SHALL INFORM BOARD OF CHANGE OF ADDRESS WITHIN 10 DAYS. SHALL NOT SEEK MODIFICATION FOR ONE YEAR.

LONGINO, JOSEPH B MD OF 530 N. DAVIS, SULPHUR SPRINGS, TX, WAS DISCIPLINED BY MEDICARE ON DECEMBER 24, 1986.
DISCIPLINARY ACTION: 60-MONTH EXCLUSION FROM THE MEDICARE AND/OR MEDICAID PROGRAMS
OFFENSE: SUBSTANDARD CARE, INCOMPETENCE, OR NEGLIGENCE
NOTES: GROSSLY SUBSTANDARD CARE OF 4 PATIENTS. TREATED PATIENTS WITH UNPROVEN OR ANECDOTAL THERAPIES. RELUCTANCE TO OBTAIN CONSULTATIONS. POOR DIAGNOSES; LENGTH OF EXCLUSION WAS LISTED BY THE DEPARTMENT OF HEALTH AND HUMAN SERVICES AS 36 MONTHS AS OF OCTOBER 31, 1989

LOONEY, GEORGE R MD, LICENSE NUMBER 00G6125, OF DALLAS, TX, WAS DISCIPLINED BY TEXAS ON DECEMBER 4, 1989.
DISCIPLINARY ACTION: REPRIMAND
NOTES: STIPULATED ORDER.

LOVELACE, CHARLES RAY JR DO, DATE OF BIRTH NOVEMBER 1, 1954, LICENSE NUMBER 00G9871, OF 423 RIGGS CIRCLE, MESQUITE, TX, WAS DISCIPLINED BY TEXAS ON APRIL 30, 1993.
DISCIPLINARY ACTION: 120-MONTH PROBATION; MONITORING OF PHYSICIAN
OFFENSE: DRUG OR ALCOHOL ABUSE
NOTES: HAS A 10 YEAR HISTORY OF POLYSUBSTANCE ABUSE INCLUDING ALCOHOL, MARIJUANA, HYDROCODONE, XANAX, DIAZEPAM, ATIVAN AND FIORICET. UNDERWENT EIGHT WEEKS OF INPATIENT ADDICTION TREATMENT IN 1988; AFTER COMPLETING OUTPATIENT MONITORING HE RELAPSED AND IN ORDER TO OBTAIN CONTROLLED SUBSTANCES WROTE PRESCRIPTIONS IN THE NAMES OF OTHER PEOPLE AND HE DIVERTED THESE PRESCRIPTIONS FOR HIS OWN USE; AGREED TO ENTER INTO TREATMENT IN 6/92 AND COMPLETED IT IN 12/92; PRESENTLY UNDER A CONTINUING CARE CONTRACT AND HAS ADHERED TO ITS REQUIREMENTS. SUSPENSION STAYED. CONDITIONS OF PROBATION: SHALL COMPLY WITH THE TERMS OF HIS CONTINUING CARE CONTRACT WITH QUARTERLY REPORTS TO THE BOARD; SHALL ABSTAIN FROM THE CONSUMPTION OF ALCOHOL/DRUGS IN ANY FORM UNLESS PRESCRIBED BY ANOTHER PHYSICIAN FOR A LEGITIMATE AND THERAPEUTIC PURPOSE; SHALL SUBMIT HIMSELF FOR EVALUATION AND TREATMENT TO A BOARD-APPROVED PSYCHIATRIST TO WHOM HE WILL PROVIDE A COPY OF THIS ORDER; SHALL SUBMIT HIMSELF FOR APPROPRIATE EXAMS INCLUDING DRUG OR ALCOHOL SCREENS; SHALL CONTINUE TO PARTICIPATE IN AA NOT LESS THAN 3 TIMES A WEEK WITH QUARTERLY REPORTS TO THE BOARD; SHALL NOT TREAT OR OTHERWISE SERVE AS PHYSICIAN, PRESCRIBE, DISPENSE OR ADMINISTER DRUGS THAT MAY BE SUBJECT TO ABUSE TO HIMSELF OR ANY MEMBER OF HIS FAMILY; SHALL NOT POSSESS, PRESCRIBE, DISPENSE OR ADMINISTER CONTROLLED SUBSTANCES EXCEPT TO HOSPITALIZED PATIENTS AND THEN ONLY WHEN MEDICALLY INDICATED AND IN THERAPEUTIC DOSES; SHALL KEEP A SEPARATE FILE OF SUCH PRESCRIPTIONS SUBJECT TO INSPECTION; SHALL BE MONITORED BY A BOARD-APPROVED PHYSICIAN WITH QUARTERLY REPORTS TO THE BOARD; SHALL ATTEND AT LEAST 50 HOURS PER YEAR OF CONTINUING MEDICAL EDUCATION; SHALL APPEAR BEFORE THE BOARD TWICE A YEAR; SHALL GIVE A COPY OF THIS ORDER TO ANY HEALTH CARE ENTITY WHERE HE HAS PRIVILEGES; SHALL COOPERATE WITH THE BOARD IN VERIFYING COMPLIANCE; SHALL INFORM THE BOARD OF A CHANGE OF ADDRESS WITHIN 10 DAYS OR IF HE LEAVES THE STATE; TIME SPENT OUT OF TEXAS DOES NOT COUNT TOWARD PROBATION. SHALL NOT SEEK MODIFICATION OF THIS ORDER FOR ONE YEAR.

LUHAR, HARASHADA K MD, LICENSE NUMBER 00G9872, OF AUSTIN, TX, WAS DISCIPLINED BY TEXAS ON NOVEMBER 3, 1994.
DISCIPLINARY ACTION: REPRIMAND
OFFENSE: LOSS OR RESTRICTION OF HOSPITAL PRIVILEGES
NOTES: ON 12/28/93 THE QUALITY ASSURANCE COMMITTEE AT ONE HOSPITAL RECOMMENDED THE FOLLOWING IN REGARDS TO ONE CASE; OFFICIAL WARNING OF FAILURE TO MEET STANDARD OF CARE, RECOMMENDATION OF ADDITIONAL CONTINUING MEDICAL EDUCATION IN NEONATAL INTENSIVE CARE, MANDATORY CONSULTATION ON THE NEXT 12 CASES PRESENTING WITH SIGNIFICANT RESPIRATORY IMPAIRMENT; THE BOARD FOUND THAT SHE MISHANDLED THIS PATIENT'S RESPIRATORY ACIDOSIS BY HER FAILURE TO PROMPTLY INTUBATE THE PATIENT AND BY TREATING THE PATIENT WITH BICARBONATE IN LIEU OF INTUBATION AND WITHOUT ADEQUATE INDICATION.

LUKER, JOHN ALONZO MD, LICENSE NUMBER 00E2689, OF DALLAS, TX, WAS DISCIPLINED BY TEXAS ON APRIL 14, 1989.
DISCIPLINARY ACTION: 60-MONTH PROBATION; REQUIRED TO TAKE ADDITIONAL MEDICAL EDUCATION
NOTES: SUSPENSION STAYED; CONDITIONS TO INCLUDE SEMI-ANNUAL BOARD APPEARANCES AND CONTINUING MEDICAL EDUCATION

LUKER, JOHN ALONZO MD, LICENSE NUMBER 00E2689, OF BASTROP, TX, WAS DISCIPLINED BY TEXAS ON JUNE 12, 1990.
DISCIPLINARY ACTION: 120-MONTH PROBATION; RESTRICTION PLACED ON CONTROLLED SUBSTANCE LICENSE

NOTES: STIPULATED ORDER. CONDITIONS OF PROBATION INCLUDE: APPEAR BEFORE BOARD SEMI-ANNUALLY, SUBMIT FOR APPROPRIATE EXAMINATIONS TO DETERMINE FREEDOM FROM DRUGS AND ALCOHOL, NOT TREAT OR OTHERWISE SERVE AS PHYSICIAN, PRESCRIBE, DISPENSE OR ADMINISTER CONTROLLED SUBSTANCES OR OTHER DRUGS SUBJECT TO ABUSE, OR WRITE PRESCRIPTIONS FOR CONTROLLED SUBSTANCES OR DRUGS SUBJECT TO ABUSE, FOR HIMSELF OR ANY MEMBER OF HIS IMMEDIATE FAMILY, AND ADMINISTER TO HIMSELF OR HIS IMMEDIATE FAMILY ONLY SUCH DRUGS AS PRESCRIBED BY OTHER PHYSICIANS; NOT POSSESS, ADMINISTER, DISPENSE OR PRESCRIBE ANY CONTROLLED SUBSTANCE BUT MAY ORDER SUCH CONTROLLED SUBSTANCE TO BE ADMINISTERED TO HOSPITAL OR NURSING HOME PATIENTS FOR MEDICAL NEEDS; SUBMIT FOR PSYCHIATRIC EVALUATION AND FOLLOW RECOMMENDATIONS, IF ANY, REGARDING CONTINUING CARE AND TREATMENT; PARTICIPATE IN AA/NARCOTICS ANONYMOUS; CONTINUE CONTINUING MEDICAL EDUCATION. ON 8/19/94 ORDER MODIFIED AS FOLLOWS: HE IS GRANTED PERMISSION TO REAPPLY TO THE DRUG ENFORCEMENT ADMINISTRATION AND THE TEXAS DEPARTMENT OF PUBLIC SAFETY FOR SCHEDULES III, IV AND V CONTROLLED SUBSTANCES AUTHORITY; SHALL NOT ATTEMPT TO REGISTER FOR SCHEDULES II, IIN OR IIIN WITHOUT FIRST OBTAINING WRITTEN AUTHORITY FROM THE BOARD; SHALL NOT TREAT OR OTHERWISE SERVE AS PHYSICIAN, PRESCRIBE, DISPENSE OR ADMINISTER CONTROLLED SUBSTANCES OR ANY OTHER DRUGS THAT MAY BE SUBJECT TO ABUSE TO HIMSELF OR A MEMBER OF HIS FAMILY; MAY ADMINISTER TO HIS FAMILY ONLY SUCH DRUGS AS PRESCRIBED BY OTHER PHYSICIANS, AND IN COMPLIANCE WITH THEIR ORDERS AND DIRECTIONS; SEPARATE FROM PATIENT RECORDS, HE SHALL MAINTAIN A FILE CONSISTING OF A COPY OF EVERY PRESCRIPTION WRITTEN FOR CONTROLLED SUBSTANCES OR DANGEROUS DRUGS WHICH HAVE A POTENTIAL FOR ABUSE, BY DATE ISSUED WHICH SHALL BE AVAILABLE FOR INSPECTION BY THE BOARD; SHALL NOT TELEPHONE ANY PRESCRIPTION TO A PHARMACY FOR CONTROLLED SUBSTANCES OR DANGEROUS DRUGS; SHALL SURRENDER ALL CONTROLLED SUBSTANCES AND DANGEROUS DRUGS, INCLUDING SAMPLES, TO REPRESENTATIVES OF THE BOARD OR A REPRESENTATIVE OF THE TEXAS DEPARTMENT OF PUBLIC SAFETY NARCOTIC SERVICE. IN THE FUTURE, HE MAY NOT POSSESS ANY CONTROLLED SUBSTANCES OR DANGEROUS DRUGS EXCEPT AS OTHERWISE PROVIDED FOR IN THE BOARD ORDER AS MODIFIED.

LUTHERER, BERTA DEL CARMEN MD, LICENSE NUMBER 00E1030, OF LUBBOCK, TX, WAS DISCIPLINED BY TEXAS ON APRIL 10, 1992.
DISCIPLINARY ACTION: REPRIMAND
OFFENSE: SUBSTANDARD CARE, INCOMPETENCE, OR NEGLIGENCE
NOTES: PROFESSIONAL FAILURE TO PRACTICE MEDICINE IN AN ACCEPTABLE MANNER CONSISTENT WITH PUBLIC HEALTH AND WELFARE.

LYNN, ROBERT J MD WAS DISCIPLINED BY NEBRASKA ON FEBRUARY 22, 1988.
DISCIPLINARY ACTION: PROBATION
OFFENSE: DISCIPLINARY ACTION BY ANOTHER STATE OR AGENCY

LYNN, ROBERT J DR, LICENSE NUMBER 0015188, WAS DISCIPLINED BY MINNESOTA ON NOVEMBER 17, 1990.
DISCIPLINARY ACTION: LICENSE REVOCATION

LYNN, ROBERT J MD, DATE OF BIRTH JUNE 26, 1923, LICENSE NUMBER 0014121, OF 512 E BLUEBRIAR, GRANITE SHOALS, TX, WAS DISCIPLINED BY IOWA ON NOVEMBER 19, 1992.
DISCIPLINARY ACTION: LICENSE REVOCATION
OFFENSE: PROFESSIONAL MISCONDUCT
NOTES: FRAUDULENT APPLICATION.

LYNN, WILLIAM SANFORD JR MD OF UNIV TEXAS MEDICAL BRANCH, GALVESTON, TX, WAS DISCIPLINED BY DEA ON AUGUST 27, 1990.
DISCIPLINARY ACTION: SURRENDER OF CONTROLLED SUBSTANCE LICENSE
OFFENSE: OVERPRESCRIBING OR MISPRESCRIBING DRUGS
NOTES: WROTE EXCESSIVE PRESCRIPTIONS FOR TUSSIONEX SUSPENSION AND PERCODAN FROM 01/31/87 TO 07/13/90.

MABRIE, IMELDA ROSE MD, LICENSE NUMBER 00F6893, OF HOUSTON, TX, WAS DISCIPLINED BY TEXAS ON DECEMBER 4, 1989.
DISCIPLINARY ACTION: 24-MONTH RESTRICTION PLACED ON CONTROLLED SUBSTANCE LICENSE; 24-MONTH MONITORING OF PHYSICIAN
NOTES: STIPULATED ORDER. SHALL SURRENDER UNUSED TRIPLICATE PRESCRIPTION FORMS AND NOT ORDER MORE OR ADMINISTER OR PRESCRIBE PRESCRIPTION DRUG FOR SELF WITHOUT BOARD PERMISSION. SHALL ALSO AUTHORIZE TREATING PHYSICIAN TO PROVIDE BOARD REPORTS CONCERNING MENTAL AND PHYSICAL CONDITION.

MACELUCH, JOHN J DO, LICENSE NUMBER 00E5151, OF PANAMA CITY, FL, WAS DISCIPLINED BY TEXAS ON AUGUST 18, 1990.
NOTES: STIPULATED ORDER. AGREED SETTLEMENT WHEREBY HE MUST OBTAIN APPROVAL OF THE BOARD BEFORE RETURNING TO PRACTICING IN TEXAS.

MACELUCH, JOHN J DO, DATE OF BIRTH AUGUST 26, 1941, LICENSE NUMBER 0001460, OF 600 N COVE BLVD, PANAMA CITY, FL, WAS DISCIPLINED BY IOWA ON JUNE 29, 1992.
NOTES: BEFORE RETURNING TO IOWA TO PRACTICE MEDICINE HE MUST REQUEST A PERSONAL INTERVIEW WITH THE BOARD AND OBTAIN WRITTEN PERMISSION TO PRACTICE IN IOWA.

MACHEN, ROBERT N MD, LICENSE NUMBER 00C5781, OF DALLAS, TX, WAS DISCIPLINED BY TEXAS ON MARCH 31, 1990.
DISCIPLINARY ACTION: RESTRICTION PLACED ON CONTROLLED SUBSTANCE LICENSE
NOTES: STIPULATED ORDER. MUST REFRAIN FROM DISPENSING, PRESCRIBING, OR ADMINISTERING CERTAIN MEDICATIONS TO PATIENTS SEEKING TREATMENT FOR WEIGHT CONTROL.

MADAN, VEENA MD, DATE OF BIRTH NOVEMBER 11, 1944, LICENSE NUMBER 0022595, OF DENVER, CO, WAS DISCIPLINED BY COLORADO ON FEBRUARY 21, 1993.
DISCIPLINARY ACTION: 60-MONTH PROBATION; MONITORING OF PHYSICIAN
OFFENSE: SUBSTANDARD CARE, INCOMPETENCE, OR NEGLIGENCE
NOTES: SUBSTANDARD CARE. PROBATION INCLUDES RESIDENCY TRAINING AND PRACTICE MONITORING.

MADAN, VEENA MD, LICENSE NUMBER 00F1768, OF PLANO, TX, WAS DISCIPLINED BY TEXAS ON AUGUST 19, 1994.
DISCIPLINARY ACTION: RESTRICTION PLACED ON LICENSE; REQUIRED TO TAKE ADDITIONAL MEDICAL EDUCATION
OFFENSE: DISCIPLINARY ACTION BY ANOTHER STATE OR AGENCY
NOTES: ON 2/12/93 ENTERED INTO A STIPULATION AND ORDER WITH THE COLORADO BOARD RESTRICTED COLORADO LICENSE. CONDITIONS ON TEXAS LICENSE: SHALL NOT INDEPENDENTLY TREAT ANY PATIENT UNTIL SHE COMPLETES A BOARD-APPROVED THREE MONTH REFRESHER MINI-RESIDENCY IN ANESTHESIOLOGY AND PERSONALLY APPEARS BEFORE THE BOARD AND PROVIDES SUFFICIENT INFORMATION WHICH SHOWS THAT SHE IS ABLE TO SAFELY PRACTICE. ON 5/13/95 BOARD GRANTED HER PETITION REQUESTING TERMINATION OF ORDER SINCE SHE HAD SATISFIED ALL CONDITIONS.

MAHAFFEY, GENE F DO, LICENSE NUMBER 0012415, OF 2465 S DOWNING #103, DENVER, CO, WAS DISCIPLINED BY DEA ON MARCH 12, 1990.
DISCIPLINARY ACTION: SURRENDER OF CONTROLLED SUBSTANCE LICENSE
OFFENSE: DISCIPLINARY ACTION BY ANOTHER STATE OR AGENCY
NOTES: REVOCATION OF STATE LICENSE DUE TO CONTINUING TO PRESCRIBE AMPHETAMINES AND DIURETICS WITHOUT MEDICAL INDICATION AND PRACTICING MEDICINE WHILE STATE LICENSE SUSPENDED.

MAHAFFEY, GENE F DO, DATE OF BIRTH OCTOBER 13, 1927, OF 3537 SOUTH HILLCREST DR, DENVER, CO, WAS DISCIPLINED BY MEDICARE ON JULY 26, 1990.
DISCIPLINARY ACTION: EXCLUSION FROM THE MEDICARE AND/OR MEDICAID PROGRAMS
OFFENSE: DISCIPLINARY ACTION BY ANOTHER STATE OR AGENCY
NOTES: LICENSE REVOCATION OR SUSPENSION.

MAHAFFEY, GENE F DO OF DENVER, CO, WAS DISCIPLINED BY MISSOURI ON JANUARY 25, 1991.
DISCIPLINARY ACTION: LICENSE REVOCATION
OFFENSE: DISCIPLINARY ACTION BY ANOTHER STATE OR AGENCY
NOTES: REVOCATION OF COLORADO LICENSE BASED ON VIOLATION OF COLORADO BOARD STIPULATION/ORDER BY PRESCRIBING DRUGS RESTRICTED BY THE BOARD'S ORDER AND FAILING TO MEET WITH PATIENTS; FAILING TO KEEP CHARTS AND ADEQUATELY SUPERVISE STAFF IN THE TREATMENT OF ONE PATIENT; PRACTICING MEDICINE WHILE UNDER ORDER OF SUMMARY SUSPENSION.

MAHAFFEY, GENE FRANCIS DO, LICENSE NUMBER 00C3141, OF DENVER, CO, WAS DISCIPLINED BY TEXAS ON AUGUST 25, 1989.
DISCIPLINARY ACTION: 36-MONTH PROBATION; 36-MONTH RESTRICTION PLACED ON CONTROLLED SUBSTANCE LICENSE
OFFENSE: DISCIPLINARY ACTION BY ANOTHER STATE OR AGENCY
NOTES: REVOCATION STAYED. PROBATION CONDITIONS TO COMPLY WITH TERMS OF COLORADO BOARD ORDER AND PROVIDE REPORTS TO EACH BOARD. REFRAIN FROM PRESCRIBING, DISPENSING, ADMINISTERING, POSSESSING AMPHETAMINE-LIKE ACTION DRUGS OR EQUIVALENT.

MAHAFFEY, GENE FRANCIS DO, LICENSE NUMBER 00C3141, OF DENVER, CO, WAS DISCIPLINED BY TEXAS ON JULY 1, 1990.
DISCIPLINARY ACTION: SURRENDER OF LICENSE
NOTES: LICENSE CANCELLED WITH PROVISIONS; EARLIER BOARD ORDER (LICENSE REVOCATION, STAY OF REVOCATION, THREE YEAR PROBATION) TO BE REINSTATED SHOULD PHYSICIAN APPLY FOR LICENSE REINSTATEMENT. IF HE APPLIES FOR REINSTATEMENT FIVE YEARS FROM 1/27/90, HE MUST ALSO PASS A SPECIAL PURPOSE EXAMINATION.

MAJORS, IRVING RICHARD MD OF TROUP, TX, WAS DISCIPLINED BY LOUISIANA ON MARCH 26, 1993.
DISCIPLINARY ACTION: REVOCATION OF CONTROLLED SUBSTANCE LICENSE; 36-MONTH LICENSE SUSPENSION
OFFENSE: SUBSTANDARD CARE, INCOMPETENCE, OR NEGLIGENCE
NOTES: PROFESSIONAL OR MEDICAL INCOMPETENCE; PRESCRIBING, DISPENSING, OR ADMINISTERING CONTROLLED SUBSTANCES IN OTHER THAN A LEGAL OR LEGITIMATE MANNER. MUST PASS SPEX EXAMINATION AND APPEAR BEFORE THE BOARD AS A CONDITION OF REINSTATEMENT. PROHIBITED FOR LIFE FROM PRESCRIBING CONTROLLED SUBSTANCES, AND ORDERED TO PAY FINE OF $5,000 AND COSTS OF ADMINISTRATIVE PROCEEDING.

MAJORS, IRVING RICHARD MD, DATE OF BIRTH SEPTEMBER 8, 1926, LICENSE NUMBER 00C2718, OF P.O. BOX 671, TROUP, TX, WAS DISCIPLINED BY TEXAS ON JULY 9, 1993.
DISCIPLINARY ACTION: EMERGENCY SUSPENSION
OFFENSE: DISCIPLINARY ACTION BY ANOTHER STATE OR AGENCY
NOTES: AVAILABLE EVIDENCE AND INFORMATION INDICATES THAT HE ENGAGED IN ILLEGAL POSSESSION OF A CONTROLLED DANGEROUS DRUG, CONSPIRACY TO ILLEGALLY DISTRIBUTE A CONTROLLED DANGEROUS DRUG AND DISTRIBUTION OF A CONTROLLED DANGEROUS DRUG; ARKANSAS LICENSE WAS SUSPENDED ON 3/26/92 PENDING FINAL DISCIPLINARY ACTION AND LOUISIANA LICENSE WAS SUSPENDED FOR THREE YEARS ON 4/28/93 AS A RESULT OF THESE CHARGES; HOSPITAL PRIVILEGES REVOKED ON 1/6/92 DUE TO OFFENSIVE NATURE WITH STAFF AND PATIENTS; FAILING TO CONDUCT ADEQUATE EXAMS AND TESTS LEADING TO INAPPROPRIATE TREATMENT; LACK OF JUDGEMENT IN PERFORMING CPR; REFUSING TO SEE PATIENTS IN EMERGENCY ROOM; LEAVING EMERGENCY ROOM PRIOR TO THE END OF HIS PERIOD OF COVERAGE.

MAJORS, IRVING RICHARD MD, DATE OF BIRTH SEPTEMBER 8, 1926, LICENSE NUMBER 00C2718, OF TROUP, TX, WAS DISCIPLINED BY TEXAS ON JANUARY 14, 1994.
DISCIPLINARY ACTION: LICENSE REVOCATION
OFFENSE: DISCIPLINARY ACTION BY ANOTHER STATE OR AGENCY
NOTES: ILLEGALLY PRESCRIBED NARCOTICS TO AN UNDERCOVER AGENT IN LOUISIANA; LOUISIANA AND ARKANSAS LICENSES SUSPENDED BASED ON THESE CHARGES AND HOSPITAL PRIVILEGES WERE REVOKED IN TEXAS DUE TO THE DEATH OF A PATIENT UNDER HIS CARE. CONTINUED PRACTICE IS AN IMMINENT PERIL TO THE PUBLIC HEALTH, SAFETY, AND WELFARE REQUIRING IMMEDIATE EFFECT TO AN ORDER REVOKING HIS LICENSE.

MALABANAN, BEN C MD, LICENSE NUMBER 00E0258, OF DALLAS, TX, WAS DISCIPLINED BY TEXAS ON JANUARY 6, 1995.
DISCIPLINARY ACTION: 60-MONTH PROBATION; FINE
OFFENSE: SUBSTANDARD CARE, INCOMPETENCE, OR NEGLIGENCE
NOTES: FROM 1988 TO 1989 WORKED ON A SALARY BASIS FOR A CLINIC OWNED BY A NON-PHYSICIAN AND PROVIDED

MEDICAL CARE TO PATIENTS ESTABLISHED UNDER THEIR GUIDELINES; A REVIEW OF PATIENT RECORDS FOUND INADEQUACIES INCLUDING, LACK OF DOCUMENTATION TO INDICATE A PHYSICAL WAS PERFORMED OR A HISTORY OBTAINED, OBTAINED NUMEROUS LAB STUDIES WITHOUT THE PATIENT BEING FIRST SEEN BY A PHYSICIAN, COMMITTING TO VAGUE, UNSUPPORTED OR BORDERLINE DIAGNOSIS, OMITTING THE DIAGNOSIS OF OBESITY WHEN CLEARLY IT SHOULD HAVE BEEN INCLUDED; PLACED AN INSULIN DEPENDENT DIABETIC ON A STRINGENT WEIGHT LOSS DIET WHILE STOPPING HER INSULIN WITHOUT CLOSE MONITORING, AND ALLOWED OTHERS TO LIST ERRONEOUS DIAGNOSES WITH INTENT TO DEFRAUD INSURANCE CARRIERS; NEITHER ADMITS NOR DENIES ALLEGATIONS. CONDITIONS OF PROBATION: SHALL PASS THE SPEX EXAM WITHIN ONE YEAR AND THE TEXAS MEDICAL JURISPRUDENCE EXAM; PRACTICE SHALL BE MONITORED BY A BOARD-APPROVED PHYSICIAN WITH QUARTERLY REPORTS; SHALL MIANTAIN ADEQUATE MEDICAL RECORDS ON ALL PATIENT OFFICE VISITS WHICH SHALL BE AVAILABLE FOR INSPECTION; SHALL NOT SIGN ANY PATIENT RECORD UNLESS HE HAS PERSONALLY EXAMINED THE PATIENT OR CLEARLY NOTES IN THE RECORD THAT HE DID NOT; SHALL PERSONALLY EXAMINE AND/OR TREAT PATIENTS IN ANY INSTANCE IN WHICH AN INITIAL DIAGNOSIS OR EXAM IS PERFORMED; SHALL OBTAIN AT LEAST 50 HOURS PER YEAR OF CONTINUING MEDICAL EDUCATION AND 10 HOURS PER YEAR OF AN ETHICS COURSE OR PROGRAM; SHALL PERFORM 100 HOURS PER YEAR OF COMMUNITY SERVICE; SHALL PAY A $2,500 ADMINISTRATIVE PENALTY WITHIN FOUR MONTHS; SHALL APPEAR BEFORE THE BOARD ONCE A YEAR OR UPON REQUEST; SHALL COOPERATE WITH THE BOARD IN VERIFYING COMPLIANCE; SHALL ADEQUATELY SUPERVISE THOSE UNDER HIS SUPERVISION; SHALL GIVE A COPY OF THIS ORDER TO ANY HEALTH CARE ENTITY WHERE HE HAS OR APPLIES FOR PRIVILEGES AND ANYONE ELSE WHO ASKS FOR IT; SHALL ENSURE ANY INQUIRIES REGARDING HIS TEXAS LICENSURE STATUS ARE ANSWERED BY REFERENCING THIS ORDER; SHALL INFORM BOARD OF CHANGE OF ADDRESS WITHIN 10 DAYS OR IF HE LEAVES THE STATE; TIME SPENT OUT OF TEXAS DOES NOT COUNT TOWARD PROBATION. SHALL NOT SEEK MODIFICATION FOR ONE YEAR.

MANGOLD, WILLIAM J SR MD OF P.O. BOX 37, LOCKNEY, TX, WAS DISCIPLINED BY MEDICARE ON NOVEMBER 13, 1986.
DISCIPLINARY ACTION: 12-MONTH EXCLUSION FROM THE MEDICARE AND/OR MEDICAID PROGRAMS
OFFENSE: SUBSTANDARD CARE, INCOMPETENCE, OR NEGLIGENCE
NOTES: GROSSLY SUBSTANDARD CARE OF SEVEN PATIENTS. FAILURE TO HAVE TESTS DONE WHICH WERE AVAILABLE AT LOCKNEY GENERAL HOSPITAL

MANION, ROBERT A MD, LICENSE NUMBER 00G6806, OF GRAND PRAIRIE, TX, WAS DISCIPLINED BY TEXAS ON NOVEMBER 19, 1993.
DISCIPLINARY ACTION: 60-MONTH PROBATION; MONITORING OF PHYSICIAN
OFFENSE: DRUG OR ALCOHOL ABUSE
NOTES: SUFFERS FROM ALCOHOLISM AND UNDERWENT INPATIENT TREATMENT IN 7/91 BUT LEFT AGAINST MEDICAL ADVICE; HAS CONSUMED ALCOHOL SINCE THEN ON MORE THAN ONE OCCASION AND AS RECENTLY AS 8/11/93. SUSPENSION STAYED. CONDITIONS OF PROBATION: SHALL ABSTAIN FROM THE CONSUMPTION OF ALCOHOL/CHEMICAL SUBSTANCES IN ANY FORM UNLESS PRESCRIBED BY ANOTHER PHYSICIAN FOR A LEGITIMATE AND THERAPEUTIC PURPOSE; SHALL NOT TREAT OR OTHERWISE SERVE AS PHYSICIAN, PRESCRIBE, DISPENSE OR ADMINISTER DRUGS THAT MAY BE SUBJECT TO ABUSE TO HIMSELF OR ANY MEMBER OF HIS FAMILY; SEPARATE FROM PATIENT RECORDS SHALL MAINTAIN A FILE OF EVERY PRESCRIPTION WRITTEN FOR CONTROLLED SUBSTANCES OR DANGEROUS DRUGS WHICH SHALL BE AVAILABLE FOR INSPECTION; SHALL SUBMIT HIMSELF FOR EVALUATION AND TREATMENT TO A BOARD-APPROVED ADDICTIONOLOGIST WITH QUARTERLY REPORTS; SHALL PARTICIPATE IN ACTIVITIES OF A PHYSICIAN HEALTH AND REHABILITATION COMMITTEE AND ATTEND WEEKLY MEETINGS WITH QUARTERLY REPORTS; SHALL PARTICIPATE IN AA'S PROGRAM NOT LESS THAN THREE TIMES A WEEK WITH QUARTERLY REPORTS; SHALL FURNISH QUARTERLY REPORTS TO THE BOARD REGARDING HIS MEDICAL CONDITION AND COMPLIANCE WITH THIS ORDER; SHALL SUBMIT HIMSELF FOR APPROPRIATE EXAMS INCLUDING DRUG OR ALCOHOL SCREENS; SHALL APPEAR BEFORE THE BOARD ONCE A YEAR; SHALL GIVE A COPY OF THIS ORDER TO ANY HEALTH CARE ENTITY WHERE HE HAS PRIVILEGES; SHALL COOPERATE WITH THE BOARD IN VERIFYING COMPLIANCE; SHALL INFORM BOARD OF CHANGE OF ADDRESS WITHIN 10 DAYS OR IF HE LEAVES THE STATE; TIME SPENT OUT OF TEXAS DOES NOT COUNT TOWARD PROBATION. SHALL NOT SEEK MODIFICATION FOR ONE YEAR.

MANN, PAUL MICHAEL MD, LICENSE NUMBER 00D7443, OF HUMBLE, TX, WAS DISCIPLINED BY TEXAS ON DECEMBER 4, 1991.
NOTES: BOARD ALLEGES THAT THE FOLLOWING DELEGATED OPHTHALMOLOGIC PROCEDURES ARE NOT IN THE BEST INTERESTS OF THE PATIENT: THE PERFORMANCE OF SCLERAL GROOVES; CREATION OF THE SCLERAL BED; CLOSING AND SUTURING OF THE EYE WOUND; AND PARACENTESIS PROCEDURES. NO FORMAL COMPLAINT HAS BEEN BROUGHT. HE NEITHER ADMITS NOR DENIES ALLEGATIONS, AND DENIES ANY VIOLATION OF THE MEDICAL PRACTICE ACT. AGREED THAT HE WILL NOT DELEGATE THESE PROCEDURES TO NONPHYSICIANS. ON 3/5/94 ORDER TERMINATED.

MANTAS, MICHAEL A MD, LICENSE NUMBER 00F4240, OF DALLAS, TX, WAS DISCIPLINED BY TEXAS ON JULY 28, 1989.
DISCIPLINARY ACTION: SURRENDER OF CONTROLLED SUBSTANCE LICENSE; REQUIRED TO TAKE ADDITIONAL MEDICAL EDUCATION
NOTES: SURRENDER CONTROLLED SUBSTANCES CERTIFICATES; SUBMIT TO PSYCHIATRIC EVALUATION AND RECOMMENDATIONS; COMPLETE PRECEPTORSHIP ON PREVENTION AND TREATMENT OF DRUG ABUSE; OBTAIN CONTINUING MEDICAL EDUCATION. ON 4/20/91 PERMISSION GRANTED TO REAPPLY FOR DEA AND DPS SCHEDULE V REGISTRATIONS. RESTRICTIONS TERMINATED EFFECTIVE 6/26/92; LICENSE FREE OF ANY RESTRICTION OR LIMITATION.

MANTAS, MICHAEL A MD, LICENSE NUMBER 0DPSW00, OF 1050 WEST MOCKINGBIRD, DALLAS, TX, WAS DISCIPLINED BY DEA ON AUGUST 10, 1989.

DISCIPLINARY ACTION: SURRENDER OF CONTROLLED SUBSTANCE LICENSE
OFFENSE: OVERPRESCRIBING OR MISPRESCRIBING DRUGS
NOTES: ORDERED OR PRESCRIBED EXCESSIVE QUANTITIES OF MEDICATION FOR PATIENT DURING HOSPITALIZATION. VOLUNTARY SURRENDER OF REGISTRATION 08/08/89.

MARES, ALBERTO MD, LICENSE NUMBER 00F9774, OF SAN ANTONIO, TX, WAS DISCIPLINED BY TEXAS ON AUGUST 1, 1988.
DISCIPLINARY ACTION: 3-MONTH LICENSE SUSPENSION; 33-MONTH PROBATION
OFFENSE: PROFESSIONAL MISCONDUCT
NOTES: THREE-YEAR SUSPENSION STAYED FOR ALL BUT FIRST 90 DAYS AND MARES PLACED ON STIPULATED PROBATION FOR SUSPENSION PERIOD; FAILED TO PRACTICE MEDICINE IN ACCEPTABLE MANNER CONSISTENT WITH PUBLIC HEALTH

MARES, ALBERTO MD, LICENSE NUMBER 00F9774, OF SAN ANTONIO, TX, WAS DISCIPLINED BY TEXAS ON AUGUST 21, 1992.
DISCIPLINARY ACTION: LICENSE REVOCATION
OFFENSE: SUBSTANDARD CARE, INCOMPETENCE, OR NEGLIGENCE
NOTES: NONTHERAPEUTIC PRESCRIBING; FAILURE TO PRACTICE MEDICINE IN AN ACCEPTABLE MANNER CONSISTENT WITH PUBLIC HEALTH AND WELFARE; UNPROFESSIONAL OR DISHONORABLE CONDUCT LIKELY TO DECEIVE, DEFRAUD OR INJURE THE PUBLIC. HE OBTAINED A TEMPORARY RESTRAINING ORDER FROM THE COURTS AND THE REVOCATION OF HIS LICENSE HAS BEEN LIFTED. ON 2/16/95 ORDER VACATED AND REMANDED BACK TO THE BOARD.

MARKEWICH, GARY STEVEN MD OF COLORADO SPRINGS, CO, WAS DISCIPLINED BY TEXAS ON DECEMBER 1, 1986.
DISCIPLINARY ACTION: PROBATION
OFFENSE: DISCIPLINARY ACTION BY ANOTHER STATE OR AGENCY
NOTES: THREE-YEAR SUSPENSION STAYED

MARKSTROM, CARL ERIC MD, DATE OF BIRTH FEBRUARY 13, 1932, LICENSE NUMBER 00D1463, OF SEAGOVILLE, TX, WAS DISCIPLINED BY TEXAS ON AUGUST 18, 1990.
DISCIPLINARY ACTION: REQUIRED TO ENTER AN IMPAIRED PHYSICIAN PROGRAM OR DRUG OR ALCOHOL TREATMENT; MONITORING OF PHYSICIAN
OFFENSE: DRUG OR ALCOHOL ABUSE
NOTES: STIPULATED ORDER. MUST SUBMIT FOR PSYCHIATRIC EVALUATION AND FOLLOW RECOMMENDATIONS, IF ANY, REGARDING TREATMENT, PARTICIPATE IN DALLAS COUNTY MEDICAL SOCIETY'S COMMITTEE ON PHYSICIAN HEALTH AND REHABILITATION, ENTER INTO A DRUG REHABILITATION PROGRAM; SUBMIT FOR APPROPRIATE EXAMINATIONS TO DETERMINE FREEDOM FROM DRUGS AND ALCOHOL, AND REFRAIN FROM USE OF, AND NOT ADMINISTER OR PRESCRIBE TO SELF, DANGEROUS DRUGS OR CONTROLLED SUBSTANCES UNLESS SUCH ARE PRESCRIBED, ADMINISTERED OR DISPENSED BY ANOTHER PHYSICIAN TREATING HIM FOR LEGITIMATE MEDICAL NEED. RESTRICTIONS MODIFIED EFFECTIVE 6/17/92. ORDER TERMINATED ON 6/15/93; LICENSE FREE AND CLEAR OF ANY RESTRICTIONS.

MARON, BARRY P MD, DATE OF BIRTH NOVEMBER 30, 1938, LICENSE NUMBER 0021140, OF BOX 1707, BORGER, TX, WAS DISCIPLINED BY NEW JERSEY ON NOVEMBER 2, 1994.
NOTES: AGREES TO COMPLY WITH ALL REQUIREMENTS OF AN ORDER DATED 06/16/93 ISSUED BY THE BOARD OF MEDICAL EXAMINERS OF ARIZONA. SHALL PROVIDE NOTICE TO NEW JERSEY OF ANY CHANGE IN ANY OF THE TERMS OF THE ARIZONA AGREEMENT OR HIS MEDICAL CONDITION. PRIOR TO ENGAGING IN ACTIVE PRACTICE IN NEW JERSEY, SHALL APPEAR BEFORE THE BOARD OR A COMMITTEE OF THE BOARD TO RESPOND TO QUESTIONS CONCERNING HIS STATUS, HEALTH AND PLANS.

MARRACK, DAVID MD, LICENSE NUMBER 00D1318, OF HOUSTON, TX, WAS DISCIPLINED BY TEXAS ON MARCH 6, 1992.
DISCIPLINARY ACTION: 36-MONTH PROBATION
OFFENSE: PROFESSIONAL MISCONDUCT
NOTES: AIDING OR ABETTING, DIRECTLY OR INDIRECTLY, THE PRACTICE OF MEDICINE BY ANY PERSON, PARTNERSHIP, ASSOCIATION, OR CORPORATION NOT DULY LICENSED TO PRACTICE MEDICINE BY THE BOARD. LICENSE SUSPENDED, SUSPENSION STAYED; PROBATION UNDER TERMS AND CONDITIONS.

MARRACK, DAVID MD, LICENSE NUMBER 00D1318, OF HOUSTON, TX, WAS DISCIPLINED BY TEXAS ON APRIL 15, 1994.
DISCIPLINARY ACTION: RESTRICTION PLACED ON LICENSE
OFFENSE: FAILURE TO COMPLY WITH A PREVIOUS BOARD ORDER
NOTES: VIOLATED TERMS OF 3/6/92 ORDER IN THAT HE FAILED TO PROVIDE IN A TIMELY MANNER, UPON REQUEST, EVIDENCE RELATING TO HIS CURRENT EMPLOYMENT SITUATION WHICH WOULD DEMONSTRATE COMPLIANCE WITH THE PROVISION THAT HE WOULD NOT ACCEPT EMPLOYMENT OR ENTER INTO CONTRACTUAL RELATIONSHIPS WHERE HE WAS PAID TO TREAT PATIENTS BY ANYONE OTHER THAN LICENSED PHYSICIANS. THE FOLLOWING PROVISION WAS ADDED TO THAT ORDER: SHALL PROVIDE TO THE BOARD UPON REQUEST WRITTEN DOCUMENTATION TO ESTABLISH THE TERMS OF ANY EMPLOYMENT AGREEMENT HE ENTERS INTO. IF NO WRITTEN CONTRACT OF EMPLOYMENT EXISTS HE SHALL PROVIDE THE BOARD A WRITTEN NARRATIVE OF THE TERMS OF SUCH AGREEMENT. HE WILL NOTIFY THE BOARD WITHIN 10 DAYS OF ANY MODIFICATION OF THE TERMS OF THE AGREEMENT; ALL OTHER TERMS AND CONDITIONS OF THE 3/92 ORDER ARE IN EFFECT. SHALL NOT SEEK MODIFICATION FOR ONE YEAR.

MARTIN, ALLAN B MD OF INDIANAPOLIS, IN, WAS DISCIPLINED BY OHIO ON NOVEMBER 8, 1989.
DISCIPLINARY ACTION: DENIAL OF LICENSE REINSTATEMENT

MARTIN, ALLAN B MD, LICENSE NUMBER 0128864, OF 2991 EAST CHESTNUT AVE #8A, VINELAND, NJ, WAS DISCIPLINED BY NEW YORK ON JULY 6, 1992.
DISCIPLINARY ACTION: SURRENDER OF LICENSE
OFFENSE: PROVIDING FALSE INFORMATION TO THE BOARD
NOTES: DID NOT CONTEST CHARGES THAT HE PRACTICED THE PROFESSION FRAUDULENTLY BY PROVIDING FALSE INFORMATION TO THE NEW JERSEY BOARD OF MEDICAL EXAMINERS.

MARTIN, ALLAN B MD, DATE OF BIRTH JULY 17, 1947, LICENSE NUMBER 0034654, OF 2991 E CHESTNUT AVE #8A, VINELAND, NJ, WAS DISCIPLINED BY NEW JERSEY ON SEPTEMBER 16, 1992.
DISCIPLINARY ACTION: LICENSE SUSPENSION; REQUIRED TO ENTER AN IMPAIRED PHYSICIAN PROGRAM OR DRUG OR ALCOHOL TREATMENT
NOTES: MAY PETITION FOR PARTIAL OR COMPLETE

REINSTATEMENT OF LICENSE UPON DEMONSTRATION THAT HE HAS SUCCESSFULLY COMPLETED INPATIENT TREATMENT FOR ALCOHOLISM, AND THAT HE HAS FULLY COOPERATED WITH THE PHYSICIANS' HEALTH PROGRAM REGARDING HIS IMPAIRMENT PROBLEM.

MARTIN, ALLAN B MD, DATE OF BIRTH JULY 17, 1947, LICENSE NUMBER 0034654, OF 2991 EAST CHESTNUT AVE, #8A, VINELAND, NJ, WAS DISCIPLINED BY NEW JERSEY ON JULY 14, 1993.
DISCIPLINARY ACTION: RESTRICTION PLACED ON LICENSE; MONITORING OF PHYSICIAN
NOTES: LICENSE RESTORED WITH CONDITIONS: MAY BE EMPLOYED AS A SURGICAL ASSISTANT UNDER THE SPECIFIC CIRCUMSTANCES DESCRIBED IN THE BOARD ORDER AND SHALL UNDERTAKE NO OTHER MEDICAL POSITION OR EMPLOYMENT WITHOUT WRITTEN APPROVAL FROM THE BOARD. SHALL CONTINUE TO COOPERATE WITH THE PHYSICIANS HEALTH PROGRAM AND SHALL AUTHORIZE AND CAUSE QUARTERLY REPORTS FROM THE CHIEF OF SURGERY AND MEDICAL DIRECTOR AT PERTH AMBOY GENERAL HOSPITAL AND OLD BRIDGE HOSPITAL RELATIVE TO EMPLOYMENT.

MARTIN, ALLAN BRADLEY MD, LICENSE NUMBER 00G2769, OF VINELAND, NJ, WAS DISCIPLINED BY TEXAS ON JUNE 22, 1994.
DISCIPLINARY ACTION: SURRENDER OF LICENSE
OFFENSE: DISCIPLINARY ACTION BY ANOTHER STATE OR AGENCY
NOTES: ON 9/16/92 LICENSE WAS SUSPENDED WITH ADDITIONAL CONDITIONS BY THE NEW JERSEY BOARD BASED ON ALLEGATIONS THAT HE DELIBERATELY LIED IN WRITTEN MATERIALS SUBMITTED TO THE BOARD; A NEW JERSEY HOSPITAL SUSPENDED HIS PRIVILEGES BECAUSE OF CONCERN ABOUT ALCOHOL ABUSE. TEXAS LICENSE SURRENDERED IN LIEU OF FURTHER INVESTIGATION; SHALL NOT PETITION FOR REINSTATEMENT OF LICENSE.

MARTIN, MARY ANNE MD, LICENSE NUMBER 00D5094, OF MESQUITE, TX, WAS DISCIPLINED BY TEXAS ON DECEMBER 15, 1988.
DISCIPLINARY ACTION: EMERGENCY SUSPENSION; 60-MONTH PROBATION
NOTES: TEMPORARY LICENSE SUSPENSION TO REMAIN IN FORCE UNTIL BOARD APPROVAL OF PHYSICIAN REPORT STATING RESPONDENT DOES NOT REPRESENT DANGER TO HEALTH OF HER PATIENTS; ON PROBATION FROM 12/6/88; SUSPENSION LIFTED 3/3/89

MARTIN, MARY ANNE MD, LICENSE NUMBER 00D5094, OF MESQUITE, TX, WAS DISCIPLINED BY TEXAS ON DECEMBER 17, 1991.
DISCIPLINARY ACTION: LICENSE REVOCATION
NOTES: VIOLATION OF SEVERAL SECTIONS OF THE MEDICAL PRACTICE ACT, INCLUDING INABILITY TO PRACTICE MEDICINE WITH REASONABLE SKILL AND SAFETY TO PATIENTS.

MARTIN, PATRICK DO OF DALLAS, TX, WAS DISCIPLINED BY TEXAS ON JULY 1, 1986.
DISCIPLINARY ACTION: EMERGENCY SUSPENSION
NOTES: UNABLE TO PRACTICE MEDICINE WITH REASONABLE SKILL AND SAFETY TO PATIENTS BY REASON OF ILLNESS, DRUNKENESS, EXCESSIVE USE OF DRUGS, NARCOTICS, CHEMICALS OR OTHER TYPE MATERIAL OR AS A RESULT OF ANY MENTAL OR PHYSICAL CONDITION. REQUIRED TO UNDERGO PSYCHIATRIC AND PHYSICAL EVALUATION

MARTIN, PATRICK DO, LICENSE NUMBER 00C8820, OF DALLAS, TX, WAS DISCIPLINED BY TEXAS ON DECEMBER 1, 1989.
DISCIPLINARY ACTION: LICENSE REVOCATION
OFFENSE: FAILURE TO COMPLY WITH A PREVIOUS BOARD ORDER
NOTES: PROBATION VIOLATION; UNPROFESSIONAL AND DISHONORABLE CONDUCT LIKELY TO DECEIVE, DEFRAUD AND INJURE PUBLIC; PRESCRIBED OR ADMINISTERED DRUG NONTHERAPEUTICALLY; FAILED TO PRACTICE MEDICINE IN ACCEPTABLE MANNER CONSISTENT WITH PUBLIC HEALTH AND WELFARE.

MARTIN, PATRICK DO, DATE OF BIRTH APRIL 12, 1927, OF 905 N MONTGOMERY, CLARKSVILLE, AR, WAS DISCIPLINED BY MEDICARE ON OCTOBER 21, 1991.
DISCIPLINARY ACTION: EXCLUSION FROM THE MEDICARE AND/OR MEDICAID PROGRAMS
OFFENSE: DISCIPLINARY ACTION BY ANOTHER STATE OR AGENCY
NOTES: LICENSE REVOCATION OR SUSPENSION.

MARTIN, RAYMOND A MD, LICENSE NUMBER 00F4946, OF AMARILLO, TX, WAS DISCIPLINED BY TEXAS ON APRIL 14, 1989.
DISCIPLINARY ACTION: 24-MONTH REQUIRED TO ENTER AN IMPAIRED PHYSICIAN PROGRAM OR DRUG OR ALCOHOL TREATMENT; 24-MONTH MONITORING OF PHYSICIAN
OFFENSE: DRUG OR ALCOHOL ABUSE
NOTES: SHALL ABSTAIN FROM ALCOHOL AND OTHER MOOD-ALTERING SUBSTANCES UNLESS PRESCRIBED BY ANOTHER PHYSICIAN FOR VALID MEDICAL PURPOSE; SHALL NOT PRESCRIBE FOR SELF; SHALL PARTICIPATE IN PROGRAMS OF AA OR NARCOTICS ANONYMOUS; SHALL AUTHORIZE AND REQUEST REPORTING OF ANY ALCOHOL AND DRUG SCREENINGS REVEALING PRESENCE OF ALCOHOL OR OTHER MOOD-ALTERING SUBSTANCES AND COOPERATE WITH REQUESTS FOR LABORATORY ANALYSES; SHALL REPORT QUARTERLY FROM PERSONAL TREATING PHYSICIAN REGARDING REHABILITATION PROGRESS.

MARTIN, THOMAS STERLING MD, LICENSE NUMBER 00C5160, OF EL PASO, TX, WAS DISCIPLINED BY TEXAS ON JUNE 13, 1989.
DISCIPLINARY ACTION: 60-MONTH REQUIRED TO ENTER AN IMPAIRED PHYSICIAN PROGRAM OR DRUG OR ALCOHOL TREATMENT; 60-MONTH MONITORING OF PHYSICIAN
NOTES: PARTICIPATE IN COUNTY MEDICAL SOCIETY ON PHYSICIAN HEALTH AND REHABILITATION; ALCOHOLICS ANONYMOUS; MEET WITH RECOVERING ABUSE SPONSOR; SUBMIT TO ALCOHOL AND DRUG SCREENING.

MARTIN, THOMAS STERLING MD, LICENSE NUMBER 00C5160, OF EL PASO, TX, WAS DISCIPLINED BY TEXAS ON APRIL 15, 1994.
DISCIPLINARY ACTION: 12-MONTH PROBATION
OFFENSE: FAILURE TO COMPLY WITH A PREVIOUS BOARD ORDER
NOTES: VIOLATED ORDER OF 6/13/89 IN THAT HE FAILED TO HAVE QUARTERLY REPORTS SUBMITTED TO THE BOARD FROM THE PHYSICIAN HEALTH AND REHABILITATION COMMITTEE AND HIS RECOVERING ABUSE SPONSOR. THE PROBATION AND OTHER CONDITIONS OF THAT ORDER WILL BE EXTENDED ONE YEAR; ALL OTHER TERMS AND CONDITIONS REMAIN IN EFFECT. SHALL NOT SEEK MODIFICATION FOR ONE YEAR.

MARTIN, WILLIAM C MD, LICENSE NUMBER 00D4213, OF WEATHERFORD, TX, WAS DISCIPLINED BY TEXAS ON MARCH 31, 1990.
DISCIPLINARY ACTION: REPRIMAND; REQUIRED TO TAKE

ADDITIONAL MEDICAL EDUCATION
NOTES: STIPULATED ORDER.

MARTINEZ, DIONISIO F MD OF VERNON, TX, WAS DISCIPLINED BY MISSOURI ON JUNE 25, 1990.
DISCIPLINARY ACTION: 1-MONTH LICENSE SUSPENSION
OFFENSE: SUBSTANDARD CARE, INCOMPETENCE, OR NEGLIGENCE
NOTES: ALSO PRESCRIPTION VIOLATIONS AND NONCOMPLIANCE: FAILURE TO INFORM BOARD OF ADDRESS CHANGE

MARTINEZ, MANUEL A JR MD, LICENSE NUMBER 00D4214, OF DEL RIO, TX, WAS DISCIPLINED BY TEXAS ON MARCH 31, 1990.
DISCIPLINARY ACTION: REQUIRED TO TAKE ADDITIONAL MEDICAL EDUCATION
NOTES: STIPULATED ORDER.

MARTINEZ, MANUEL A JR MD, LICENSE NUMBER 00D4214, OF DEL RIO, TX, WAS DISCIPLINED BY TEXAS ON AUGUST 19, 1994.
DISCIPLINARY ACTION: 60-MONTH PROBATION; RESTRICTION PLACED ON LICENSE
OFFENSE: SUBSTANDARD CARE, INCOMPETENCE, OR NEGLIGENCE
NOTES: SUBSTANDARD TREATMENT IN THE CARE OF SEVERAL PATIENTS BETWEEN 9/87 AND 2/90 INCLUDING: ORDERING GLYCERIN SUPPOSITORIES FOR AN INFANT ALTHOUGH THERE WAS NO INDICATION FOR THEM; DID NOT PLACE A PAP SMEAR IN SOLUTION SOON ENOUGH AFTER IT WAS TAKEN. CYTOLOGY RESULTS WERE NEGATIVE AND THE PAP SMEAR WAS NOT REPEATED, ANOTHER PAP SMEAR WAS DONE BY ANOTHER DOCTOR THREE MONTHS LATER WHICH REVEALED AN ENDOCERVICAL TUMOR MASS WHICH WAS MALIGNANT; THE PATIENT DIED FIVE MONTHS LATER; GIVING A 4 MONTH OLD PATIENT COMPAZINE AND TERRAMYCIN FOR VOMITING AND GASTROENTERITIS THE USE OF WHICH IS CONTRAINDICATED IN PATIENTS OF THIS AGE; GAVE A 2 MONTH OLD INFANT TERRAMYCIN WHICH IS NOT INDICATED FOR A CHILD THIS AGE -- NO DOCUMENTATION THAT AN ABDOMINAL EXAM WAS DONE ALTHOUGH HE SAID THAT ONE WAS PERFORMED; FAILED TO DOCUMENT ANY VITAL SIGNS IN THE COURSE OF TREATING PATIENT FOR HYPERTENSION FOR 12 MONTHS. SUSPENSION STAYED. CONDITIONS OF PROBATION: SHALL APPEAR BEFORE THE BOARD TWICE A YEAR; SHALL CONTINUE TO ATTEND AT LEAST 50 HOURS PER YEAR OF CONTINUING MEDICAL EDUCATION WITH AT LEAST ONE COURSE PER YEAR IN RISK MANAGEMENT AND ONE IN PHARMACOLOGY WITH AN EMPHASIS ON ANTIBIOTICS; SHALL BE SUPERVISED BY A BOARD-APPROVED PHYSICIAN WITH QUARTERLY REPORTS; SHALL MAINTAIN ADEQUATE MEDICAL RECORDS ON ALL PATIENT OFFICE VISITS WHICH SHALL BE AVAILABLE FOR INSPECTION; SHALL NOT SIGN ANY PATIENT RECORD UNLESS HE HAS PERSONALLY EXAMINED THE PATIENT OR CLEARLY NOTES IN THE RECORD THAT HE DID NOT; SHALL TAKE AND PASS THE 9/13/94 SPEX EXAM; SHALL NOT PRACTICE OBSTETRICS OR TREAT PATIENTS UNDER TWO YEARS OF AGE; SHALL GIVE A COPY OF THIS ORDER TO ANY HEALTH CARE ENTITY WHERE HE HAS PRIVILEGES; SHALL COOPERATE WITH THE BOARD IN VERIFYING COMPLIANCE; SHALL INFORM BOARD OF CHANGE OF ADDRESS WITHIN 10 DAYS OR IF HE LEAVES THE STATE; TIME SPENT OUT OF TEXAS DOES NOT COUNT TOWARD PROBATION. SHALL NOT SEEK MODIFICATION FOR ONE YEAR.

MASEIKA, BARTIS T DO, LICENSE NUMBER 00G0474, OF HURST, TX, WAS DISCIPLINED BY TEXAS ON DECEMBER 1, 1988.
DISCIPLINARY ACTION: SURRENDER OF LICENSE

MASON, EDWARD J JR MD, LICENSE NUMBER 00C8755, OF DALLAS, TX, WAS DISCIPLINED BY TEXAS ON APRIL 14, 1989.
DISCIPLINARY ACTION: RESTRICTION PLACED ON LICENSE; REQUIRED TO TAKE ADDITIONAL MEDICAL EDUCATION
NOTES: SHALL OBTAIN CONTINUING MEDICAL EDUCATION OR SPECIFIC EQUIVALENT HOURS; SHALL OBTAIN SECOND OPINION FROM CONSULTING SPECIALIST ON CERTAIN PATIENTS FOR REHOSPITALIZATION

MASON, EDWARD J MD, LICENSE NUMBER 00G6181, OF DALLAS, TX, WAS DISCIPLINED BY CALIFORNIA ON JUNE 10, 1992.
DISCIPLINARY ACTION: LICENSE REVOCATION
OFFENSE: DISCIPLINARY ACTION BY ANOTHER STATE OR AGENCY
NOTES: DISCIPLINE BY TEXAS BOARD. DEFAULT DECISION.

MASON, WALTER LEE MD, LICENSE NUMBER 00F1139, OF ALLEN, TX, WAS DISCIPLINED BY TEXAS ON AUGUST 20, 1992.
DISCIPLINARY ACTION: 36-MONTH RESTRICTION PLACED ON LICENSE
OFFENSE: PROFESSIONAL MISCONDUCT
NOTES: OVERTREATING. ON 9/30/94 ORDER TERMINATED.

MASSEY, CHARLES R JR MD, LICENSE NUMBER 00G5341, OF FREDERICKSBURG, TX, WAS DISCIPLINED BY TEXAS ON AUGUST 24, 1991.
DISCIPLINARY ACTION: 60-MONTH PROBATION; MONITORING OF PHYSICIAN
OFFENSE: DRUG OR ALCOHOL ABUSE
NOTES: SUSPENSION STAYED; CONDITIONS OF PROBATION INCLUDE: SHALL CONTINUE TO PARTICIPATE IN AA AND CO-DEPENDENCY GROUP; SHALL SUBMIT FOR ALCOHOL OR DRUG SCREENS; SHALL CONTINUE TREATMENT FROM BOARD-DESIGNATED PHYSICIAN; SHALL APPEAR BEFORE THE BOARD ONE TIME A YEAR.

MATHIS, JAMES EDWARD MD, DATE OF BIRTH MARCH 10, 1930, LICENSE NUMBER 00C5162, OF 11300 HARWIN, HOUSTON, TX, WAS DISCIPLINED BY TEXAS ON APRIL 30, 1993.
DISCIPLINARY ACTION: REPRIMAND
OFFENSE: FAILURE TO COMPLY WITH A PROFESSIONAL RULE
NOTES: FAILED TO SUBMIT A COMPLETED MEDICAL PRACTICE ACT QUESTIONNAIRE AND LIABILITY CLAIM INFORMATION ON FOUR PATIENTS AFTER SEVERAL REQUESTS BY A BOARD INVESTIGATOR. SHALL GIVE A COPY OF THIS ORDER TO ANY HEALTH CARE ENTITY WHERE HE HAS PRIVILEGES.

MAURER, ANNE R MD, LICENSE NUMBER 00H3493, OF LEXINGTON, KY, WAS DISCIPLINED BY TEXAS ON APRIL 20, 1991.
DISCIPLINARY ACTION: 60-MONTH PROBATION; MONITORING OF PHYSICIAN
NOTES: UPON RETURN TO PRACTICE IN TEXAS, SHALL UNDERGO COMPLETE PSYCHIATRIC EXAM AND FOLLOW RECOMMENDATIONS; SUBMIT TO ALCOHOL OR DRUG SCREENS.

MAUSKAR, ANANT NILKANTH MD, LICENSE NUMBER 00E9300, OF 8300 HOMESTEAD ROAD #5, HOUSTON, TX, WAS DISCIPLINED BY DEA ON NOVEMBER 16, 1993.
DISCIPLINARY ACTION: REVOCATION OF CONTROLLED SUBSTANCE LICENSE

OFFENSE: OVERPRESCRIBING OR MISPRESCRIBING DRUGS
NOTES: ARRESTED 01/23/92 IN HOUSTON, TEXAS FOR ILLEGALLY PRESCRIBING CODEINE. ALIAS ANANT MAUSKER, ANAN MAUSKAUR.

MAZEIKA, BARTIS T DO OF FORT WORTH, TX, WAS DISCIPLINED BY TEXAS ON JULY 1, 1986.
DISCIPLINARY ACTION: LICENSE SUSPENSION
NOTES: INDEFINITE SUSPENSION

MAZEIKA, BARTIS T DO, DATE OF BIRTH OCTOBER 18, 1950, OF 1717 PRECINCT ROAD, #202, HURST, TX, WAS DISCIPLINED BY MEDICARE ON DECEMBER 23, 1988.
DISCIPLINARY ACTION: EXCLUSION FROM THE MEDICARE AND/OR MEDICAID PROGRAMS
OFFENSE: DISCIPLINARY ACTION BY ANOTHER STATE OR AGENCY
NOTES: LICENSE REVOCATION OR SUSPENSION.

MAZEIKA, BARTIS T DO, LICENSE NUMBER 0004979, OF KETTERING, OH, WAS DISCIPLINED BY OHIO ON MARCH 20, 1990.
DISCIPLINARY ACTION: 60-MONTH PROBATION; REPRIMAND
OFFENSE: DISCIPLINARY ACTION BY ANOTHER STATE OR AGENCY
NOTES: DISCIPLINARY ACTIONS BY THE TEXAS AND ILLINOIS MEDICAL BOARDS, COMMISSION OF FRAUD, MISREPRESENTATION OR DECEPTION IN APPLYING FOR OHIO LICENSE; LICENSE GRANTED SUBJECT TO FIVE YEAR PROBATION, INELIGIBLE TO HOLD DEA CERTIFICATE WITHOUT PRIOR BOARD APPROVAL.

MAZEIKA, BARTIS T DO, LICENSE NUMBER 0004979, OF KETTERING, OH, WAS DISCIPLINED BY OHIO ON JANUARY 16, 1991.
DISCIPLINARY ACTION: 1-MONTH LICENSE SUSPENSION; 60-MONTH PROBATION
OFFENSE: FAILURE TO COMPLY WITH A PREVIOUS BOARD ORDER
NOTES: VIOLATION OF CONDITIONS OF LIMITATION PREVIOUSLY IMPOSED BY BOARD. REVOCATION STAYED; INDEFINITE SUSPENSION, MINIMUM 30 DAYS; PROBATION FOR MINIMUM OF FIVE YEARS; CONDITIONS FOR REINSTATEMENT; INELIGIBLE TO HOLD DEA CERTIFICATE WITHOUT PRIOR BOARD APPROVAL. PROBATION AFFIRMED BY COMMON PLEAS COURT ON 10/8/91.

MAZEIKA, BARTIS T DO, LICENSE NUMBER 0004979, OF KETTERING, OH, WAS DISCIPLINED BY OHIO ON JUNE 1, 1991.
NOTES: TEMPORARY TRAINING CERTIFICATE ISSUED AUTHORIZING ENTRY INTO RESIDENCY TRAINING PROGRAM CONTINGENT ON CONTINUING COMPLIANCE WITH MONITORING CONDITIONS; LICENSE REMAINS SUSPENDED BY PREVIOUS BOARD ORDER.

MAZEIKA, BARTIS T DO, LICENSE NUMBER 0004979, OF KETTERING, OH, WAS DISCIPLINED BY OHIO ON JULY 8, 1992.
DISCIPLINARY ACTION: REPRIMAND
OFFENSE: PROFESSIONAL MISCONDUCT
NOTES: SIGNED A SWORN STATEMENT ATTESTING THAT HE WAS DULY LICENSED IN OHIO WHEN, IN FACT, LICENSE HAD BEEN SUSPENDED EFFECTIVE 1/16/91 BY BOARD ORDER OF 1/9/91.

MAZEIKA, BARTIS T DO, LICENSE NUMBER 0004979, OF KETTERING, OH, WAS DISCIPLINED BY OHIO ON SEPTEMBER 9, 1992.
OFFENSE: FAILURE TO COMPLY WITH A PREVIOUS BOARD ORDER
NOTES: VIOLATED LIMITATIONS IMPOSED ON TEMPORARY TRAINING CERTIFICATE BY INGESTING ALCOHOL. BOARD ORDERED THAT TEMPORARY TRAINING CERTIFICATE ISSUED 6/13/91 BE RECOGNIZED AS EXPIRED, AND THAT DOCTOR MAZEIKA NOT BE ELIGIBLE TO APPLY FOR REINSTATEMENT OR ANY FUTURE TEMPORARY TRAINING CERTIFICATE.

MAZIQUE, EMORY E MD, LICENSE NUMBER 00D3647, OF HOUSTON, TX, WAS DISCIPLINED BY TEXAS ON AUGUST 24, 1991.
DISCIPLINARY ACTION: SURRENDER OF CONTROLLED SUBSTANCE LICENSE; 36-MONTH PROBATION
OFFENSE: OVERPRESCRIBING OR MISPRESCRIBING DRUGS
NOTES: NONTHERAPEUTIC PRESCRIBING. SUSPENSION STAYED; CONDITIONS OF PROBATION: SHALL COMPLETE A TWO WEEK PRECEPTORSHIP ON THE PREVENTION AND TREATMENT OF DRUG ABUSE; SHALL ISSUE NO PRESCRIPTIONS FOR, NOR DISTRIBUTE OR DISPENSE, SCHEDULE II THROUGH V CONTROLLED SUBSTANCES WITHOUT ANOTHER PRACTIONER'S APPROVAL; SHALL NOT POSSESS ANY SUCH SUBSTANCES; SHALL MAINTAIN COPIES OF ALL PRESCRIPTIONS ISSUED BY THE CONCURRING MEDICAL PRACTITIONER ON HIS BEHALF FOR PATIENTS FOR ALL DRUGS; SHALL SURRENDER DEA AND DPS CONTROLLED SUBSTANCES CERTIFICATES AND SHALL NOT ATTEMPT TO REREGISTER WITHOUT PRIOR BOARD APPROVAL; SHALL APPEAR BEFORE THE BOARD TWICE A YEAR.

MCAFEE, ALPHONSO C III MD, LICENSE NUMBER 00G5963, OF SPRING, TX, WAS DISCIPLINED BY TEXAS ON AUGUST 20, 1992.
DISCIPLINARY ACTION: REPRIMAND
OFFENSE: PROFESSIONAL MISCONDUCT
NOTES: OVERTREATING OF PATIENTS.

MCCALL, VICTOR E MD, LICENSE NUMBER 00D3509, OF DUNCANVILLE, TX, WAS DISCIPLINED BY TEXAS ON FEBRUARY 22, 1991.
DISCIPLINARY ACTION: 120-MONTH PROBATION; REQUIRED TO TAKE ADDITIONAL MEDICAL EDUCATION
NOTES: MUST COMPLETE COURSE IN GENERAL PHARMACOLOGY; COMPLETE COURSE IN ADVANCED CARDIAC LIFE SUPPORT; RESEARCH AND WRITE A PAPER SUITABLE FOR PUBLICATION REGARDING RADIOLOGICAL TECHNICIANS AND THE PROCEDURES OR TREATMENTS THAT CAN BE DELEGATED FROM A PHYSICIAN TO A TECHNICIAN; MAINTAIN ADEQUATE MEDICAL RECORDS FOR A RADIOLOGIST ON ALL PATIENT OFFICE VISITS; ADEQUATELY SUPERVISE ALL "EMPLOYEES OR DELEGATES"; APPEAR FOR SEMIANNUAL REPORTS TO BOARD. ON 11/3/94 PROBATION TERMINATED.

MCCALL, VICTOR EUGENE MD, LICENSE NUMBER 0015667, OF 6236 INDIAN CREEK DRIVE, FORT WORTH, TX, WAS DISCIPLINED BY OKLAHOMA ON SEPTEMBER 9, 1994.
DISCIPLINARY ACTION: 60-MONTH PROBATION
OFFENSE: DISCIPLINARY ACTION BY ANOTHER STATE OR AGENCY
NOTES: ON 2/22/91 THE TEXAS BOARD ISSUED AN ORDER PLACING LICENSE ON PROBATION FOR 10 YEARS WITH CONDITIONS FOR DELEGATING TO A RADIOLOGIC TECHNICIAN THE RESPONSIBILITY FOR CALCULATING A DOSAGE FOR CHLORAL HYDRATE WHICH WAS INCORRECTLY CALCULATED AND LED TO THE DEATH OF THE PATIENT. EXPECTS TEXAS TO VACATE ITS ORDER; AGREES TO SUBMIT TO PROBATION IN OKLAHOMA. CONDITIONS OF PROBATION: SHALL PROVIDE THE BOARD WITH ANY DOCUMENTATION

REQUESTED RELATED TO HIS PRACTICE AND SHALL PAY COSTS.

MCCALLUM, MICHAEL H MD, LICENSE NUMBER 00G6128, OF AUSTIN, TX, WAS DISCIPLINED BY TEXAS ON AUGUST 18, 1990.
DISCIPLINARY ACTION: 60-MONTH PROBATION; MONITORING OF PHYSICIAN
OFFENSE: DRUG OR ALCOHOL ABUSE
NOTES: STIPULATED ORDER. MUST APPEAR BEFORE BOARD OR BOARD COMMITTEE ANNUALLY, PARTICIPATE IN AA, SUBMIT FOR APPROPRIATE EXAMINATIONS TO DETERMINE FREEDOM FROM DRUGS AND ALCOHOL, AND COMPLY WITH TERMS OF AFTER-CARE AGREEMENT WITH SUBSTANCE ABUSE CENTER.

MCCALLUM, MICHAEL H MD, LICENSE NUMBER 00G6128, OF NEW BRAUNFELS, TX, WAS DISCIPLINED BY TEXAS ON DECEMBER 4, 1991.
DISCIPLINARY ACTION: 120-MONTH PROBATION; RESTRICTION PLACED ON LICENSE
OFFENSE: FAILURE TO COMPLY WITH A PREVIOUS BOARD ORDER
NOTES: ON 3/23/91 HE WAS RELIEVED FROM DUTY FOR THE DAY AT BRACKENRIDGE HOSPITAL FOR BEING ON DUTY WHILE UNDER THE INFLUENCE OF ALCOHOL, AND HIS CONTRACT WITH EMCARE WAS TERMINATED IN MARCH OR EARLY APRIL, 1991; THE HOSPITAL SUSPENDED HIS PRIVILEGES; ALCOHOL USE VIOLATED TERMS OF 8/17/90 BOARD ORDER; RELAPSE WAS IN 1/91; ENTERED TREATMENT ON 3/26/91, WAS TRANSFERRED TO A DIFFERENT PROGRAM ON 4/15/91, AND WAS DISCHARGED ON 8/3/91; ALSO EXECUTED A TWO YEAR CONTINUING CARE CONTRACT WITH TALBOTT/MARSH RECOVERY CENTER AND ANOTHER WITH THE TRAVIS COUNTY MEDICAL SOCIETY. SUSPENSION STAYED; CONDITIONS OF PROBATION: SHALL CONTINUE TO PARTICIPATE IN IMPAIRED PHYSICIANS PROGRAM, WITH WRITTEN QUARTERLY REPORTS TO BOARD; SHALL CONTINUE WITH AA OR OTHER BOARD-APPROVED PROGRAM, AND ATTEND AT LEAST FIVE TIMES A WEEK, WITH QUARTERLY REPORTS TO BOARD; TREATING PHYSICIAN SHALL SUBMIT QUARTERLY REPORTS TO THE BOARD; SHALL PARTICIPATE IN BIOLOGICAL ALCOHOL/DRUG SCREENS AS DIRECTED BY TREATING PHYSICIAN; FOR FIRST SIX MONTHS SHALL SUBMIT TO BODILY FLUID SCREENS AT LEAST ONCE WEEKLY, THEREAFTER SCREENS SHALL BE RANDOM; PRACTICE LIMITED TO MCKENNA HOSPITAL, WITH A SUPERVISING PHYSICIAN AND QUARTERLY REPORTS TO THE BOARD; SHALL COMPLY WITH TERMS OF CONTINUING AND AFTERCARE CONTRACTS; SHALL APPEAR BEFORE THE BOARD TWICE A YEAR; SHALL GIVE A COPY OF THIS ORDER TO ANY INSTITUTION WHERE HE HAS PRIVILEGES; SHALL COOPERATE WITH BOARD IN VERIFYING COMPLIANCE; SHALL ADVISE THE BOARD OF ANY CHANGE OF ADDRESS WITHIN 10 DAYS; TIME SPENT OUT OF TEXAS DOES NOT COUNT TOWARDS PROBATION; SHALL NOT SEEK MODIFICATION OF THE ORDER FOR ONE YEAR. ON 1/14/94 ORDER MODIFIED AS FOLLOWS: HE SHALL REQUEST A MEETING, MEET PERIODICALLY AND PARTICIPATE IN ACTIVITIES RECOMMENDED BY A SPECIFIED MEDICAL SOCIETY COMMITTEE AND HAVE QUARTERLY WRITTEN REPORTS SUBMITTED TO THE BOARD; SHALL PARTICIPATE IN BIOLOGICAL ALCOHOL/DRUG SCREENS WHICH SHALL BE MADE AVAILABLE TO THE BOARD UPON REQUEST; HIS MEDICAL PRACTICE SHALL BE LIMITED TO TEACHING EMERGENCY MEDICINE AT LBJ AND HERMAN HOSPITALS IN HOUSTON, TEXAS; HE SHALL NOT MAINTAIN AN OFFICE PRACTICE; IF HE DOES RECEIVE APPROVAL TO PRACTICE AT ANOTHER HOSPITAL, HIS MEDICAL PRACTICE, RECORD KEEPING AND PATIENT CHARTS SHALL BE MONITORED BY A PHYSICIAN ACCEPTABLE TO THE BOARD.

MCCASKILL, BERNIE L MD, LICENSE NUMBER 00E9799, OF DALLAS, TX, WAS DISCIPLINED BY TEXAS ON AUGUST 20, 1992.
DISCIPLINARY ACTION: REPRIMAND
OFFENSE: SUBSTANDARD CARE, INCOMPETENCE, OR NEGLIGENCE
NOTES: PROFESSIONAL FAILURE TO PRACTICE MEDICINE IN AN ACCEPTABLE MANNER CONSISTENT WITH PUBLIC HEALTH AND WELFARE.

MCCLELLAN, DAVID MARK MD, DATE OF BIRTH OCTOBER 30, 1953, LICENSE NUMBER 00G0476, OF 5911 FM 2100, CROSBY, TX, WAS DISCIPLINED BY TEXAS ON JANUARY 29, 1993.
DISCIPLINARY ACTION: 120-MONTH PROBATION; RESTRICTION PLACED ON LICENSE
OFFENSE: SEXUAL ABUSE OF OR SEXUAL MISCONDUCT WITH A PATIENT
NOTES: FROM 9/4/91 THROUGH 9/9/91 HE BEHAVED INAPPROPRIATELY TOWARDS ONE PATIENT IN THAT HE MADE SEXUAL ADVANCES BY CALLING HER HOME ON TWO OCCASIONS. SUSPENSION STAYED. CONDITIONS OF PROBATION: SHALL SUBMIT HIMSELF FOR EVALUATION AND TREATMENT TO A BOARD-APPROVED PSYCHIATRIST WITHIN 30 DAYS WITH MONTHLY REPORTS TO THE BOARD; WILL FURNISH A COPY OF THIS ORDER TO THE PSYCHIATRIST; SHALL ATTEND AT LEAST 50 HOURS PER YEAR OF CONTINUING MEDICAL EDUCATION, 10 OF WHICH SHALL BE IN RISK MANAGEMENT AND ETHICS COMBINED; SHALL APPEAR BEFORE THE BOARD TWICE A YEAR; SHALL HAVE A CHAPERONEE IN ATTENDANCE AT ALL TIMES THAT HE EXAMINES FEMALE PATIENTS; SHALL GIVE A COPY OF THIS ORDER TO ANY HEALTH CARE ENTITY WHERE HE HAS PRIVILEGES; SHALL COOPERATE WITH THE BOARD IN VERIFYING COMPLIANCE; SHALL INFORM BOARD OF ADDRESS CHANGE WITHIN 10 DAYS OR IF HE LEAVES THE STATE; TIME SPENT OUT OF TEXAS DOES NOT COUNT TOWARD PROBATION. SHALL NOT SEEK MODIFICATION FOR FIVE YEARS. ON 3/5/94 ORDER MODIFIED SUCH THAT HE SUBMITS TO FOLLOW-UP TREATMENT AND EVALUATION ONCE A YEAR AND SHALL FOLLOW PSYCHIATRIST'S RECOMMENDATIONS REGARDING FURTHER CARE AND TREAMENT.

MCCLURE, ROBERT A MD, LICENSE NUMBER 00C3133, OF HOUSTON, TX, WAS DISCIPLINED BY TEXAS ON OCTOBER 27, 1989.
DISCIPLINARY ACTION: REPRIMAND
NOTES: STIPULATED ORDER. SHALL NOT ADMINISTER OR SUPERVISE ADMINISTRATION OF GENERAL ANESTHESIA FOR PATIENTS UNLESS APPROPRIATE DIAGNOSTIC STUDIES AND LAB TESTS HAVE BEEN PERFORMED TO ALLOW LICENSEE TO PROPERLY ASSESS PATIENTS' FITNESS FOR SURGERY.

MCCORKLE, BRANDT DO OF 715 MIMOSA DRIVE, MINEOLA, TX, WAS DISCIPLINED BY MEDICARE ON JANUARY 6, 1987.
DISCIPLINARY ACTION: 12-MONTH EXCLUSION FROM THE MEDICARE AND/OR MEDICAID PROGRAMS
OFFENSE: SUBSTANDARD CARE, INCOMPETENCE, OR NEGLIGENCE

NOTES: GROSSLY SUBSTANDARD CARE OF FIVE PATIENTS. LACK OF KNOWLEDGE OF CARDIOLOGY, PULMONARY MEDICINE, INFECTIOUS DISEASES, GENERAL MEDICINE AND PHARMACOLOGY

MCCORKLE, BRANDT HALBERT DO, DATE OF BIRTH NOVEMBER 14, 1953, LICENSE NUMBER 00F4260, OF 104 DOGWOOD LOOP, MINEOLA, TX, WAS DISCIPLINED BY TEXAS ON AUGUST 6, 1993.
DISCIPLINARY ACTION: EMERGENCY SUSPENSION
OFFENSE: DRUG OR ALCOHOL ABUSE
NOTES: ON 2/15/93 HE ATTEMPTED SUICIDE; DURING SUBSEQUENT HOSPITAL STAY HE UNDERWENT A PSYCHIATRIC EVALUATION IN WHICH HE ADMITTED THAT HE WAS EXPERIENCING SEVERE MOOD SWINGS FOR SEVERAL YEARS; PRIOR MEDICAL HISTORY DENOTES HISTORY OF TOURETTE'S SYNDROME FOR WHICH HE WAS TREATED WITH HALDOL; WAS HOSPITALIZED BY HIS NEUROLOGIST AND TREATED WITH TALWIN FOR ANALGESIA; BECAME HABITUATED TO THIS DRUG AND CONTINUED TO ABUSE IT; SELF MEDICATED HIMSELF WITH TENORMIN AND DYNACIRC FOR HYPERTENSION AND PROSOM FOR INSOMNIA; ON 4/29/93 HIS DOCTOR'S IMPRESSION WAS RELAPSE IN MAJOR DRUG ABUSE AND REFERRED HIM FOR INPATIENT DETOXIFICATION; ALSO PRESCRIBED MEDICATIONS TO PATIENTS HE KNEW WERE ADDICTED; THEIR RECORDS WERE VERY POOR AND DID NOT DENOTE A HISTORY AND PHYSICAL OR OTHER WORKUP.

MCCORKLE, BRANDT HALBERT DO, DATE OF BIRTH NOVEMBER 14, 1953, LICENSE NUMBER 00F4260, OF 104 DOGWOOD LOOP, MINEOLA, TX, WAS DISCIPLINED BY TEXAS ON AUGUST 20, 1993.
DISCIPLINARY ACTION: LICENSE SUSPENSION
OFFENSE: DRUG OR ALCOHOL ABUSE
NOTES: INDEFINITE SUSPENSION. PRIOR TO PRACTICING SHALL OBTAIN APPROVAL OF THE BOARD; SHALL SUBMIT TO A FULL PSYCHIATRIC, PSYCHOLOGICAL AND NEUROLOGICAL EXAM PRIOR TO SEEKING APPROVAL.

MCCORKLE, BRANDT HALBERT DO, LICENSE NUMBER 0004260, OF 1060 N PACIFIC, MINEOLA, TX, WAS DISCIPLINED BY DEA ON SEPTEMBER 27, 1993.
DISCIPLINARY ACTION: SURRENDER OF CONTROLLED SUBSTANCE LICENSE
OFFENSE: DISCIPLINARY ACTION BY ANOTHER STATE OR AGENCY
NOTES: MEDICAL LICENSE SUSPENDED ON 08/06/93 IN TEXAS AND SUSPENDED INDEFINITELY ON 08/20/93. VOLUNTARY SURRENDER OF REGISTRATION ON 09/09/93.

MCCORKLE, CARTER W DO OF P.O. BOX 627, MINEOLA, TX, WAS DISCIPLINED BY MEDICARE ON MARCH 2, 1987.
DISCIPLINARY ACTION: 48-MONTH EXCLUSION FROM THE MEDICARE AND/OR MEDICAID PROGRAMS
OFFENSE: SUBSTANDARD CARE, INCOMPETENCE, OR NEGLIGENCE
NOTES: GROSSLY SUBSTANDARD CARE IN 11 CASES; LACK OF KNOWLEDGE IN BASIC SKILLS IN THE EVALUATION OF CARDIOLOGY AND PULMONARY PROBLEMS, INFECTIOUS DISEASES, GENERAL MEDICINE AND PHARMACOLOGY. DISCHARGING PATIENTS BEFORE THEY ACHIEVE MEDICAL STABILITY

MCCORKLE, CARTER W DO, LICENSE NUMBER 00C8662, OF MINEOLA, TX, WAS DISCIPLINED BY TEXAS ON AUGUST 25, 1989.
DISCIPLINARY ACTION: 60-MONTH REQUIRED TO TAKE ADDITIONAL MEDICAL EDUCATION

MCCORKLE, CARTER W DO OF MINEOLA, TX, WAS DISCIPLINED BY MISSOURI ON AUGUST 2, 1990.
OFFENSE: DISCIPLINARY ACTION BY ANOTHER STATE OR AGENCY
NOTES: MUST APPEAR BEFORE BOARD BEFORE RETURNING TO PRACTICE IN MISSOURI

MCCOY, MARTIN LEMUEL MD OF DALLAS, TX, WAS DISCIPLINED BY NORTH CAROLINA ON FEBRUARY 3, 1988.
NOTES: CONSENT ORDER, UNSPECIFIED.

MCDONALD, DEWARD D MD, LICENSE NUMBER 00C5174, OF LONGVIEW, TX, WAS DISCIPLINED BY TEXAS ON AUGUST 25, 1989.
DISCIPLINARY ACTION: 60-MONTH PROBATION; REQUIRED TO TAKE ADDITIONAL MEDICAL EDUCATION
OFFENSE: LOSS OR RESTRICTION OF HOSPITAL PRIVILEGES
NOTES: CONTINUE PSYCHIATRIC CARE, OBTAIN CONTINUING MEDICAL EDUCATION; COMPLY WITH RESTRICTIONS PREVIOUSLY PLACED ON HOSPITAL PRIVILEGES.

MCGREGORY, SCOTT DUNCAN DO, DATE OF BIRTH SEPTEMBER 5, 1953, OF 2211 DANIEL WAY, CARROLLTON, TX, WAS DISCIPLINED BY MEDICARE ON SEPTEMBER 5, 1993.
DISCIPLINARY ACTION: EXCLUSION FROM THE MEDICARE AND/OR MEDICAID PROGRAMS
OFFENSE: FAILURE TO COMPLY WITH A PROFESSIONAL RULE
NOTES: DEFAULTED ON HEALTH EDUCATION ASSISTANCE LOAN.

MCKELLAR, DUNCAN L MD, LICENSE NUMBER 00E8267, OF PLANO, TX, WAS DISCIPLINED BY TEXAS ON AUGUST 1, 1988.
DISCIPLINARY ACTION: LICENSE SUSPENSION
OFFENSE: CRIMINAL CONVICTION OR PLEA OF GUILTY, NOLO CONTENDERE, OR NO CONTEST TO A CRIME
NOTES: REVOCATION STAYED, PLACED ON STIPULATED SUSPENSION FOR PERIOD OF INCARCERATION; FOLLOWING RELEASE, LICENSE RESTORED WITH STIPULATIONS; CONVICTED OF FELONY

MCLAUGHLIN, BLAINE EDMUND MD, DATE OF BIRTH NOVEMBER 15, 1914, LICENSE NUMBER 00D7856, OF 6201 GREENWAY, FORT WORTH, TX, WAS DISCIPLINED BY TEXAS ON MARCH 26, 1993.
DISCIPLINARY ACTION: SURRENDER OF LICENSE
OFFENSE: PHYSICAL OR MENTAL ILLNESS INHIBITING THE ABILITY TO PRACTICE WITH SKILL AND SAFETY
NOTES: RETIREMENT IS PERMANENT; SHALL NOT SEEK TO REACTIVATE LICENSE.

MCLAUGHLIN, BLAINE EDMUND MD, DATE OF BIRTH NOVEMBER 15, 1914, LICENSE NUMBER 00D7856, OF 800 8TH AVENUE SUITE 316, FORT WORTH, TX, WAS DISCIPLINED BY DEA ON JULY 19, 1993.
DISCIPLINARY ACTION: SURRENDER OF CONTROLLED SUBSTANCE LICENSE
OFFENSE: DISCIPLINARY ACTION BY ANOTHER STATE OR AGENCY
NOTES: VOLUNTARY SURRENDER RESULTING FROM BOARD ACTION. ILL HEALTH OF PRACTITIONER.

MCLAUGHLIN, RICHARD A MD, LICENSE NUMBER 00E3063, OF HOUSTON, TX, WAS DISCIPLINED BY TEXAS ON OCTOBER 27, 1989.
DISCIPLINARY ACTION: 60-MONTH RESTRICTION PLACED ON LICENSE; REQUIRED TO TAKE ADDITIONAL MEDICAL EDUCATION
NOTES: STIPULATED ORDER. SHALL NOT CONDUCT CERTAIN EXAMINATIONS WITHOUT CHAPERONEE, MUST INSTITUTE CHARTING METHOD.

MCLAUGHLIN, RICHARD A DR OF HOUSTON, TX, WAS DISCIPLINED BY ILLINOIS ON OCTOBER 1, 1991.
DISCIPLINARY ACTION: LICENSE SUSPENSION
OFFENSE: DISCIPLINARY ACTION BY ANOTHER STATE OR AGENCY
NOTES: TEXAS LICENSE WAS DISCIPLINED FOR INADEQUATE CHARTING. INDEFINITE SUSPENSION.

MCLAUGHLIN, RICHARD A MD, LICENSE NUMBER 00E3063, OF MARLOW HEIGHTS, MD, WAS DISCIPLINED BY TEXAS ON NOVEMBER 9, 1991.
DISCIPLINARY ACTION: EMERGENCY SUSPENSION
OFFENSE: CRIMINAL CONVICTION OR PLEA OF GUILTY, NOLO CONTENDERE, OR NO CONTEST TO A CRIME
NOTES: CONVICTED IN A DISTRICT COURT OF HARRIS COUNTY, TEXAS, ON 9/10/91 OF RAPE OF A 34 YEAR OLD FEMALE PATIENT DURING A GYNECOLOGICAL EXAM IN HIS OFFICE; WAS SENTENCED TO FOUR YEARS IN THE TEXAS DEPARTMENT OF CORRECTIONS BEGINNING 9/20/91; AT THE TRIAL ANOTHER PATIENT ALSO TESTIFIED SHE HAD BEEN SEXUALLY ASSAULTED DURING A GYNECOLOGICAL EXAM. HE GAVE NOTICE OF APPEAL ON 9/20/91.

MCLAUGHLIN, RICHARD A MD, LICENSE NUMBER 00E3063, OF MARLOW HEIGHTS, MD, WAS DISCIPLINED BY TEXAS ON AUGUST 21, 1992.
DISCIPLINARY ACTION: LICENSE REVOCATION
OFFENSE: CRIMINAL CONVICTION OR PLEA OF GUILTY, NOLO CONTENDERE, OR NO CONTEST TO A CRIME
NOTES: CONVICTION OF FELONY INVOLVING MORAL TURPITUDE.

MCLAUGHLIN, RICHARD A JR MD, LICENSE NUMBER 0107914, OF 1301 FRANKLIN, HOUSTON, TX, WAS DISCIPLINED BY NEW YORK ON DECEMBER 17, 1993.
DISCIPLINARY ACTION: LICENSE REVOCATION
OFFENSE: DISCIPLINARY ACTION BY ANOTHER STATE OR AGENCY
NOTES: CONVICTED OF SEXUALLY ASSAULTING A PATIENT; FOUND GUILTY OF MISCONDUCT BY THE TEXAS BOARD.

MCLEAN, PAUL EUGENE II MD, LICENSE NUMBER 00E2719, OF CORPUS CHRISTI, TX, WAS DISCIPLINED BY TEXAS ON AUGUST 19, 1994.
DISCIPLINARY ACTION: SURRENDER OF CONTROLLED SUBSTANCE LICENSE; PROBATION
OFFENSE: DRUG OR ALCOHOL ABUSE
NOTES: HE HAS SUFFERED FROM A LONG HISTORY OF CHEMICAL DEPENDENCY AND HAS SOUGHT TREATMENT SINCE 1980; LICENSE WAS SUSPENDED ON 6/11/86 AND HE SURRENDERED CONTROLLED SUBSTANCES CERTIFICATES; REQUESTED TERMINATION OF THE SUSPENSION ON 2/26/88 AND WAS DENIED; CONTINUED TO SUFFER RELAPSES FROM 1988 TO 1994; COMPLETED TREATMENT ON 2/5/93 AND HAS SINCE RETURNED FOR CONTINUING CARE VISTS, REGULARLY ATTENDS AA MEETINGS, AND FOLLOWS TWO AFTERCARE CONTRACTS; AS REQUIRED BY THE 6/11/86 ORDER HE HAS PROVIDED SUFFICIENT EVIDENCE THAT HE IS ABLE TO PRACTICE IN A MANNER CONSISTENT WITH PUBLIC WELFARE. SUSPENSION IMPOSED BY THE 1986 ORDER STAYED. CONDITIONS OF INDEFINITE PROBATION: PRACTICE RESTRICTED TO A SIX-MONTH MINI-FELLOWSHIP OR MINI-RESIDENCY WITH A BOARD-APPROVED SUPERVISOR WITH BIMONTHLY REPORTS TO THE BOARD; WITHIN ONE YEAR SHALL PASS THE SPEX EXAM; SHALL ABSTAIN FROM THE CONSUMPTION OF ALCOHOL/CHEMICAL SUBSTANCES IN ANY FORM UNLESS PRESCRIBED BY ANOTHER PHYSICIAN FOR A LEGITIMATE AND THERAPEUTIC PURPOSE; SHALL SURRENDER DEA AND TEXAS CONTROLLED SUBSTANCES CERTIFICATES AND ALL UNUSED TRIPLICATE PRESCRIPTION FORMS; SHALL NOT ATTEMPT TO REREGISTER WITHOUT PERMISSION; SEPARATE FROM PATIENT RECORDS SHALL MAINTAIN A FILE OF EVERY PRESCRIPTION WRITTEN FOR DANGEROUS DRUGS WHICH SHALL BE AVAILABLE FOR INSPECTION; SHALL NOT TREAT OR OTHERWISE SERVE AS PHYSICIAN, PRESCRIBE, DISPENSE OR ADMINISTER ANY DRUGS THAT MAY BE SUBJECT TO ABUSE TO HIMSELF OR ANY MEMBER OF HIS FAMILY; SHALL PARTICIPATE IN THE ACTIVITIES OF A PHYSICIAN HEALTH AND REHABILITATION COMMITTEE AND ATTEND WEEKLY MEETINGS WITH QUARTERLY REPORTS; SHALL FOLLOW ANY AFTERCARE CONTRACT HE HAS ENTERED INTO; SHALL CONTINUE TO PARTICIPATE IN AA'S PROGRAM NOT LESS THAN THREE TIMES A WEEK WITH QUARTERLY REPORTS TO THE BOARD; SHALL SUBMIT HIMSELF FOR APPROPRIATE EXAMS INCLUDING DRUG OR ALCOHOL SCREENS; WITHIN 30 DAYS SHALL UNDERGO A COMPLETE PHYSICAL EXAM FROM A BOARD-APPROVED PHYSICIAN AND SHALL PLACE HIMSELF UNDER THE CARE OF THIS PHYSICIAN FOR TREATMENT OF ANY CONDITION; SHALL SUBMIT HIMSELF FOR EVALUATION AND TREATMENT TO A BOARD-APPROVED PSYCHIATRIST WITH REPORTS TO THE BOARD; SHALL APPEAR BEFORE THE BOARD TWICE A YEAR; SHALL ATTEND AT LEAST 50 HOURS PER YEAR OF CONTINUING MEDICAL EDUCATION; SHALL GIVE A COPY OF THIS ORDER TO ANY HEALTH CARE ENTITY WHERE HE HAS PRIVILEGES; SHALL COOPERATE WITH THE BOARD IN VERIFYING COMPLIANCE; SHALL INFORM BOARD OF CHANGE OF ADDRESS WITHIN 10 DAYS OR IF HE LEAVES THE STATE; TIME SPENT OUT OF TEXAS SHALL NOT COUNT TOWARD PROBATION. SHALL NOT SEEK MODIFICATION FOR ONE YEAR.

MCLEROY, ROBERT LEE MD, LICENSE NUMBER 00C4428, OF GAINESVILLE, TX, WAS DISCIPLINED BY TEXAS ON AUGUST 25, 1989.
DISCIPLINARY ACTION: 120-MONTH RESTRICTION PLACED ON CONTROLLED SUBSTANCE LICENSE
NOTES: CANNOT TREAT PATIENTS FOR OBESITY OR WEIGHT LOSS BY PRESCRIBING DRUGS OR DISPENSING NONPRESCRIPTION DRUGS.

MCNARY, ROBERT E MD OF LETCHER, SD, WAS DISCIPLINED BY TEXAS ON DECEMBER 1, 1986.
DISCIPLINARY ACTION: SURRENDER OF LICENSE

MCNEILL, ARCHIBALD J MD, LICENSE NUMBER 00B4282, OF DALLAS, TX, WAS DISCIPLINED BY TEXAS ON JUNE 17, 1992.
DISCIPLINARY ACTION: SURRENDER OF LICENSE
OFFENSE: PHYSICAL OR MENTAL ILLNESS INHIBITING THE ABILITY TO PRACTICE WITH SKILL AND SAFETY
NOTES: INABILITY TO PRACTICE MEDICINE WITH REASONABLE SKILL AND SAFETY TO PATIENTS BY REASON OF ILLNESS. LICENSE PERMANENTLY AND VOLUNTARILY RETIRED.

MEALY, KATHERINE E MD, LICENSE NUMBER C041436, OF SAN JOSE, CA, WAS DISCIPLINED BY CALIFORNIA ON AUGUST 15, 1991.

DISCIPLINARY ACTION: 2-MONTH LICENSE SUSPENSION; 58-MONTH PROBATION
OFFENSE: SUBSTANDARD CARE, INCOMPETENCE, OR NEGLIGENCE
NOTES: GROSS NEGLIGENCE, INCOMPETENCE, REPEATED NEGLIGENT ACTS, EXCESSIVE USE OF DIAGNOSTIC SERVICES AT CENTER FOR WOMEN'S DISORDERS AND WEIGHT CONTROL. REVOCATION STAYED.

MEALY, KATHERINE E MD, LICENSE NUMBER 00G7688, OF SAN JOSE, CA, WAS DISCIPLINED BY TEXAS ON APRIL 10, 1992.
DISCIPLINARY ACTION: SURRENDER OF LICENSE
NOTES: LICENSE VOLUNTARILY SURRENDERED IN LIEU OF FURTHER DISCIPLINARY ACTION.

MEDINA, AMANTE D MD OF ODESSA, TX, WAS DISCIPLINED BY TEXAS ON DECEMBER 1, 1986.
DISCIPLINARY ACTION: LICENSE REVOCATION
OFFENSE: CRIMINAL CONVICTION OR PLEA OF GUILTY, NOLO CONTENDERE, OR NO CONTEST TO A CRIME
NOTES: CONVICTED OF FELONY INVOLVING CONTROLLED SUBSTANCES

MEDINA, AMANTE DE LEON MD, LICENSE NUMBER 00E4521, OF KEENE, TX, WAS DISCIPLINED BY TEXAS ON AUGUST 24, 1991.
DISCIPLINARY ACTION: RESTRICTION PLACED ON CONTROLLED SUBSTANCE LICENSE
NOTES: PROBATION MODIFIED TO ALLOW DR. MEDINA TO POSSESS, ADMINISTER, PRESCRIBE, AND DISPENSE SCHEDULE II AND IIN CONTROLLED SUBSTANCES WHILE PERFORMING DUTIES AS AN EMERGENCY ROOM PHYSICIAN IN A HOSPITAL EMERGENCY ROOM SETTING.

MEDINA, MATIAS R MD, LICENSE NUMBER 00E9803, OF HOUSTON, TX, WAS DISCIPLINED BY TEXAS ON JANUARY 14, 1994.
DISCIPLINARY ACTION: REPRIMAND; REQUIRED TO TAKE ADDITIONAL MEDICAL EDUCATION
OFFENSE: PROFESSIONAL MISCONDUCT
NOTES: FAILED TO ADEQUATELY SUPERVISE AN ACUPUNCTURIST UNDER HIS SUPERVISION; SEVERED THE RELATIONSHIP WHEN HE WAS INFORMED THERE WAS A PROBLEM. SHALL GIVE A COPY OF THIS ORDER TO ANY HEALTH CARE ENTITY WHERE HE HAS PRIVILEGES; SHALL TERMINATE ANY CURRENT SUPERVISION OF ACUPUNCTURISTS AND MUST PETITION FOR PERMISSION TO SUPERVISE ACUPUNCTURISTS IN THE FUTURE; SHALL TAKE AN ETHICS COURSE WITHIN THE NEXT YEAR; SHALL PASS THE TEXAS MEDICAL JURISPRUDENCE EXAM.

MEHARRY, ROGER ALVIN MD, LICENSE NUMBER 00E5172, OF RUSK, TX, WAS DISCIPLINED BY TEXAS ON FEBRUARY 22, 1991.
DISCIPLINARY ACTION: 60-MONTH PROBATION; REQUIRED TO TAKE ADDITIONAL MEDICAL EDUCATION
NOTES: MUST NOT PRESCRIBE OR ADMINISTER ANY DRUG FOR ANY PATIENT UNLESS SUCH DRUG IS THERAPEUTIC IN THE MANNER SUCH DRUG IS PRESCRIBED; LEARN AND UNDERSTAND THE POTENTIAL FOR ABUSE OF CONTROLLED SUBSTANCES AND OTHER PRESCRIPTION DRUGS; CONDUCT ADEQUATE FOLLOW-UP EXAMINATION ON ALL PATIENTS; NOT PERMIT ANY PERSON NOT LICENSED BY THIS BOARD TO TELEPHONE A PRESCRIPTION TO ANY PHARMACY ON HIS BEHALF WITHOUT FIRST PERFORMING A MEDICALLY APPROPRIATE EXAMINATION AND ARRIVING AT A DIAGNOSIS; MAINTAIN SEPARATE FILE OF EVERY PRESCRIPTION FOR CONTROLLED SUBSTANCES OR DANGEROUS DRUGS BY DATE ISSUED; COMPLETE PRECEPTORSHIP ON PREVENTION AND TREATMENT OF DRUG ABUSE; MAINTAIN ADEQUATE MEDICAL RECORDS ON ALL PATIENT OFFICE VISITS; ATTEND CONTINUING MEDICAL EDUCATION COURSES; NOT ATTEMPT TO REREGISTER FOR CONTROLLED SUBSTANCE REGISTRATION CERTIFICATES FROM DEA AND TDPS WITHOUT WRITTEN AUTHORITY FROM THE BOARD.

MEHARRY, ROGER ALVIN MD, LICENSE NUMBER 00E5172, OF RUSK, TX, WAS DISCIPLINED BY TEXAS ON JUNE 17, 1992.
DISCIPLINARY ACTION: REPRIMAND
OFFENSE: FAILURE TO COMPLY WITH A PROFESSIONAL RULE
NOTES: SEVERAL VIOLATIONS OF THE MEDICAL PRACTICE ACT.

MEHARRY, ROGER ALVIN MD, DATE OF BIRTH APRIL 8, 1936, LICENSE NUMBER 0031117, OF POST OFFICE BOX 516, RUSK, TX, WAS DISCIPLINED BY MICHIGAN ON JUNE 16, 1993.
DISCIPLINARY ACTION: 32-MONTH PROBATION
OFFENSE: SUBSTANDARD CARE, INCOMPETENCE, OR NEGLIGENCE
NOTES: NEGLIGENCE/INCOMPETENCE.

MEHARRY, ROGER ALVIN MD, LICENSE NUMBER 00E5172, OF RUSK, TX, WAS DISCIPLINED BY TEXAS ON AUGUST 19, 1994.
DISCIPLINARY ACTION: 24-MONTH PROBATION; FINE
OFFENSE: SUBSTANDARD CARE, INCOMPETENCE, OR NEGLIGENCE
NOTES: FAILED TO KEEP ADEQUATE RECORDS REFLECTIVE OF HIS CARE AND TREATMENT, REFERRAL AND FOLLOW-UP OF TWO PATIENTS; CONDITIONS OF THE 2/22/91 ORDER ARE EXTENDED AN ADDITIONAL TWO YEARS WITH THESE ADDITIONS: SHALL MAINTAIN ADEQUATE MEDICAL RECORDS ON ALL PATIENT OFFICE VISITS WHICH SHALL BE AVAILABLE FOR INSPECTION; SHALL PERSONALLY EXAMINE PATIENTS WHENEVER A FORM CERTIFIES A PERSONAL EXAM HAS BEEN PERFORMED, WHERE STATE LAW REQUIRES THIS OR WHERE AN INITIAL DIAGNOSIS OF PROBABLE DISEASE OR INJURY HAS BEEN MADE; SHALL PESONALLY EXAMINE THE PATIENT DURING THE FIRST VISIT; SHALL NOT SIGN ANY PATIENT RECORD UNLESS HE HAS PERSONALLY EXAMINED THE PATIENT OR CLEARLY NOTES IN THE RECORD THAT HE HAS NOT; SHALL ATTEND AT LEAST 50 HOURS PER YEAR OF CONTINUING MEDICAL EDUCATION INCLUDING AN ADDITIONAL 10 HOURS IN RISK MANAGEMENT AND 25 HOURS IN PHARMACOLOGY/ADDICTIONOLOGY DURING THE FIRST YEAR; SHALL APPEAR BEFORE THE BOARD ONCE A YEAR; SHALL PAY A $500 ADMINISTRATIVE PENALTY; SHALL GIVE A COPY OF THIS ORDER TO ANY HEALTH CARE ENTITY WHERE HE HAS PRIVILEGES; SHALL COOPERATE WITH THE BOARD IN VERIFYING COMPLIANCE; SHALL INFORM BOARD OF ADDRESS CHANGE WITHIN 10 DAYS OR IF HE LEAVES THE STATE; TIME SPENT OUT OF TEXAS DOES NOT COUNT TOWARD PROBATION. SHALL NOT SEEK MODIFICATION FOR ONE YEAR.

MELENYZER, CHARLES L MD OF SAN ANTONIO, TX, WAS DISCIPLINED BY TEXAS ON JULY 1, 1986.
DISCIPLINARY ACTION: LICENSE REVOCATION
OFFENSE: OVERPRESCRIBING OR MISPRESCRIBING DRUGS
NOTES: EXHIBITED UNPROFESSIONAL OR DISHONORABLE CONDUCT LIKELY TO INJURE, DECEIVE OR DEFRAUD PUBLIC AND WROTE FALSE OR FICTITIOUS

PRESCRIPTIONS.

MERLICH, EARLE D MD OF EL PASO, TX, WAS DISCIPLINED BY TEXAS ON DECEMBER 1, 1986.
DISCIPLINARY ACTION: SURRENDER OF LICENSE

MERWORTH, ROY W MD OF EL PASO, TX, WAS DISCIPLINED BY TEXAS ON SEPTEMBER 1, 1985.
DISCIPLINARY ACTION: 4-MONTH LICENSE SUSPENSION; 120-MONTH PROBATION
OFFENSE: OVERPRESCRIBING OR MISPRESCRIBING DRUGS
NOTES: PRESCRIBED CONTROLLED SUBSTANCES NONTHERAPEUTICALLY AND FAILED TO PRACTICE MEDICINE IN ACCEPTABLE MANNER; REVOCATION STAYED;

MERWORTH, ROY W MD OF NORTH HOLLYWOOD, CA, WAS DISCIPLINED BY TEXAS ON DECEMBER 1, 1986.
DISCIPLINARY ACTION: SURRENDER OF LICENSE

MESERVE, FRANCIS BRUCE MD, LICENSE NUMBER 0005909, OF 121 N DAVIS DR, WARNER ROBINS, GA, WAS DISCIPLINED BY GEORGIA ON MAY 12, 1988.
DISCIPLINARY ACTION: LICENSE REVOCATION
OFFENSE: DRUG OR ALCOHOL ABUSE
NOTES: PERSONAL ADDICTION.

MESERVE, FRANCIS BRUCE MD, DATE OF BIRTH DECEMBER 23, 1920, OF 14674C PERTHSHIRE, HOUSTON, TX, WAS DISCIPLINED BY MEDICARE ON JANUARY 24, 1989.
DISCIPLINARY ACTION: EXCLUSION FROM THE MEDICARE AND/OR MEDICAID PROGRAMS
OFFENSE: DISCIPLINARY ACTION BY ANOTHER STATE OR AGENCY
NOTES: LICENSE REVOCATION OR SUSPENSION.

MESHEL, WILLIAM N MD OF GALVESTON, TX, WAS DISCIPLINED BY TEXAS ON DECEMBER 1, 1986.
DISCIPLINARY ACTION: 60-MONTH PROBATION; RESTRICTION PLACED ON LICENSE
OFFENSE: DISCIPLINARY ACTION BY ANOTHER STATE OR AGENCY

MESSINA, JOEL MICHAEL DO, DATE OF BIRTH SEPTEMBER 5, 1929, LICENSE NUMBER 00C5180, OF 500 VONDERBURG, BOX 1329, BRANDON, FL, WAS DISCIPLINED BY TEXAS ON JANUARY 29, 1993.
DISCIPLINARY ACTION: RESTRICTION PLACED ON LICENSE
OFFENSE: DISCIPLINARY ACTION BY ANOTHER STATE OR AGENCY
NOTES: ON 7/27/90 FLORIDA BOARD RESTRICTED HIS LICENSE SUCH THAT HE COULD NOT PRACTICE OBSTETRICS OR TERMINATE PREGNANCIES FOR TWO YEARS, REPRIMANDED HIM AND FINED HIM $2,000; HE WAS ALSO PLACED UNDER SUPERVISION OF A MONITORING PHYSICIAN FOR TWO YEARS. TEXAS RESTRICTED HIS LICENSE INDEFINITELY SUCH THAT HE SHALL NOT TREAT ANY PATIENTS FOR OBSTETRICAL MATTERS OR TERMINATE PREGNANCIES; PRIOR TO PRACTICING IN TEXAS HE SHALL APPEAR BEFORE THE BOARD; SHALL GIVE A COPY OF THIS ORDER TO ANY HEALTH CARE ENTITY WHERE HE HAS PRIVILEGES; SHALL COOPERATE WITH THE BOARD IN VERIFYING COMPLIANCE; SHALL INFORM BOARD OF CHANGE OF ADDRESS WITHIN 10 DAYS OR IF HE LEAVES THE STATE; TIME SPENT OUT OF TEXAS DOES NOT COUNT TOWARD RESTRICTION.

METZNER, WESLEY R T MD, LICENSE NUMBER 00C1662, OF SAN ANTONIO, TX, WAS DISCIPLINED BY TEXAS ON MAY 1, 1985.
DISCIPLINARY ACTION: 120-MONTH PROBATION
NOTES: SUSPENSION STAYED

METZNER, WESLEY R T MD, LICENSE NUMBER 00C1662, OF SAN ANTONIO, TX, WAS DISCIPLINED BY TEXAS ON AUGUST 23, 1986.
DISCIPLINARY ACTION: LICENSE REVOCATION
OFFENSE: FAILURE TO COMPLY WITH A PREVIOUS BOARD ORDER
NOTES: VIOLATED PROBATIONARY TERMS

MEZA, ALFONSO MD, LICENSE NUMBER 00E9308, OF PORT ARTHUR, TX, WAS DISCIPLINED BY TEXAS ON FEBRUARY 16, 1990.
DISCIPLINARY ACTION: REQUIRED TO TAKE ADDITIONAL MEDICAL EDUCATION
NOTES: STIPULATED ORDER. SHALL PERFORM PATIENT EVALUATIONS THAT ARE CLINICALLY ADEQUATE TO SUPPORT DIAGNOSES AND MAKE TREATMENT DECISIONS AFTER DIAGNOSTIC INFORMATION OBTAINED. ORDER EFFECTIVE FOR ONE YEAR.

MICKISH, ALAN B MD, LICENSE NUMBER 00E1059, OF FORT WORTH, TX, WAS DISCIPLINED BY TEXAS ON OCTOBER 9, 1992.
DISCIPLINARY ACTION: 36-MONTH PROBATION
OFFENSE: PROFESSIONAL MISCONDUCT
NOTES: COMMITTED SEVERAL VIOLATIONS OF THE MEDICAL PRACTICE ACT, INCLUDING AIDING AND ABETTING, DIRECTLY OR INDIRECTLY, THE PRACTICE OF MEDICINE BY ANY PERSON, PARTNERSHIP, ASSOCIATION, OR CORPORATION NOT DULY LICENSED TO PRACTICE MEDICINE BY THE BOARD. SUSPENSION STAYED. PROBATION ON TERMS AND CONDITIONS.

MICKISH, ALAN B MD, DATE OF BIRTH JANUARY 2, 1947, LICENSE NUMBER 0021568, OF IRVING, TX, WAS DISCIPLINED BY COLORADO ON AUGUST 20, 1993.
DISCIPLINARY ACTION: REPRIMAND

MIKESKY, GREGORY R MD, DATE OF BIRTH MARCH 21, 1959, OF 511 SUMMIT STREET, SCHULENBURG, TX, WAS DISCIPLINED BY MEDICARE ON JUNE 12, 1993.
DISCIPLINARY ACTION: EXCLUSION FROM THE MEDICARE AND/OR MEDICAID PROGRAMS
OFFENSE: FAILURE TO COMPLY WITH A PROFESSIONAL RULE
NOTES: DEFAULTED ON HEALTH EDUCATION ASSISTANCE LOAN.

MILES, PATRICK KELLY DO, LICENSE NUMBER 00D8037, OF ABELINE, TX, WAS DISCIPLINED BY TEXAS ON OCTOBER 27, 1993.
DISCIPLINARY ACTION: EMERGENCY SUSPENSION
OFFENSE: PHYSICAL OR MENTAL ILLNESS INHIBITING THE ABILITY TO PRACTICE WITH SKILL AND SAFETY
NOTES: HISTORICALLY SUFFERS FROM CONFIRMED BIPOLAR DISORDER AND PROBABLE CYCLOTHYMIC DISORDER WHICH IS NOT ADEQUATELY CONTROLLED AS REPRESENTED BY BEHAVIORS AND ACTIVITIES INCLUDING THE FOLLOWING: ON 9/16/93 ATTEMPTED TO HAVE A PATIENT RELEASED WHO HAD BEEN INVOLUNTARILY COMMITTED TO A STATE HOSPITAL BECAUSE OF A CASE INVOLVING THE CHARGE OF MURDER AGAINST THE PATIENT; FROM INVOLUNTARY COMMITMENT BECAUSE OF A CASE INVOLVING MURDER; FALSE REPRESENTATIONS TO MEMBERS OF THE MEDICAL COMMUNITY AND OTHER REGARDING HIS PROFESSIONAL EXPERIENCE AND ASSOCIATIONS; REPRESENTATIONS TO MEMBERS OF THE MEDICAL COMMUNITY WHICH DEMONSTRATE FAILURE TO MAINTAIN ADEQUATE BOUNDARIES IN PHYSICIAN-PATIENT RELATIONSHIPS; EXTREME AND

INAPPROPRIATE REACTION TO NORMAL EVENTS AND CIRCUMSTANCES.

MILES, PATRICK KELLY DO, LICENSE NUMBER 00D8037, OF ABILENE, TX, WAS DISCIPLINED BY TEXAS ON MARCH 5, 1994.
DISCIPLINARY ACTION: 60-MONTH PROBATION; RESTRICTION PLACED ON LICENSE
NOTES: AFTER 10/27/93 EMERGENCY SUSPENSION, HE WAS EVALUATED BY A BOARD-APPROVED PSYCHIATRIST ON 1/26/94 WHO MADE A DIAGNOSIS OF AN ATYPICAL CYCLOTHYMIA AND SIGNIFICANT ANXIETY BUT FELT THAT DR. MILES CONDITION DID NOT PREVENT HIM FROM PRACTICING ALTHOUGH WITH RESTRICTIONS. FIVE YEAR SUSPENSION STAYED. CONDITIONS OF PROBATION: PRACTICE RESTRICTED TO THAT ASSOCIATED WITH A BOARD-APPROVED INSTITUTIONAL OR RESEARCH SETTING; SUPERVISOR WILL MAKE QUARTERLY REPORTS TO THE BOARD; SHALL CONTINUE TO RECEIVE TREATMENT FROM A PSYCHIATRIST WITH QUARTERLY REPORTS; SHALL APPEAR BEFORE THE BOARD ONCE A YEAR; SHALL GIVE A COPY OF THIS ORDER TO ANY HEALTH CARE ENTITY WHERE HE HAS PRIVILEGES; SHALL COOPERATE WITH THE BOARD IN VERIFYING COMPLIANCE; SHALL INFORM BOARD OF CHANGE OF ADDRESS WITHIN 10 DAYS OR IF HE LEAVES THE STATE; TIME SPENT OUT OF TEXAS DOES NOT COUNT TOWARD PROBATION. SHALL NOT SEEK MODIFICATION FOR ONE YEAR.

MILLER, MILTON M DO, LICENSE NUMBER 0003318, WAS DISCIPLINED BY MICHIGAN ON JULY 20, 1987.
DISCIPLINARY ACTION: LICENSE REVOCATION

MILLER, MILTON M DO WAS DISCIPLINED BY IOWA ON FEBRUARY 12, 1988.
DISCIPLINARY ACTION: LICENSE REVOCATION
OFFENSE: DISCIPLINARY ACTION BY ANOTHER STATE OR AGENCY

MILLER, MILTON M DO, LICENSE NUMBER 00DO494, OF DETROIT, MI, WAS DISCIPLINED BY TEXAS ON AUGUST 1, 1988.
DISCIPLINARY ACTION: LICENSE REVOCATION
OFFENSE: CRIMINAL CONVICTION OR PLEA OF GUILTY, NOLO CONTENDERE, OR NO CONTEST TO A CRIME
NOTES: CONVICTED OF FELONY INVOLVING CONTROLLED SUBSTANCES.

MILLER, VERLYN MICHAEL MD OF DES MOINES, IA, WAS DISCIPLINED BY NORTH DAKOTA ON NOVEMBER 17, 1989.
DISCIPLINARY ACTION: DENIAL OF NEW LICENSE
OFFENSE: PROVIDING FALSE INFORMATION TO THE BOARD
NOTES: FALSIFIED APPLICATION FOR LICENSE.

MILLER, VERLYN MICHAEL MD, DATE OF BIRTH APRIL 19, 1927, LICENSE NUMBER 0019579, OF P.O. BOX 381668, DUNCANVILLE, TX, WAS DISCIPLINED BY IOWA ON OCTOBER 7, 1993.
DISCIPLINARY ACTION: LICENSE SUSPENSION
OFFENSE: PROFESSIONAL MISCONDUCT
NOTES: MAKING MISLEADING, DECEPTIVE, AND UNTRUE REPRESENTATION IN HIS PRACTICE OF MEDICINE. INDEFINITE SUSPENSION.

MILLWEE, ROBERT H MD, LICENSE NUMBER 00B5977, OF DALLAS, TX, WAS DISCIPLINED BY TEXAS ON OCTOBER 1, 1987.
DISCIPLINARY ACTION: SURRENDER OF LICENSE

MIMS, ROBERT LEWIS MD, DATE OF BIRTH JUNE 11, 1955, LICENSE NUMBER 00F9827, OF 3221 OMEGA DRIVE, ARLINGTON, TX, WAS DISCIPLINED BY TEXAS ON MARCH 26, 1993.
DISCIPLINARY ACTION: 60-MONTH PROBATION; REQUIRED TO TAKE ADDITIONAL MEDICAL EDUCATION
OFFENSE: SUBSTANDARD CARE, INCOMPETENCE, OR NEGLIGENCE
NOTES: FROM 4/87 TO 10/90 EXCESSIVELY PRESCRIBED LOMOTIL (AVERAGE OF 200 DOSAGE UNITS PER DAY) TO A PATIENT WITHOUT ADEQUATE CONSULTATION WITH A GASTROENTEROLOGIST; ALSO FAILED TO HOSPITALIZE THE PATIENT. 5 YEAR SUSPENSION STAYED. CONDITIONS OF PROBATION: SHALL APPEAR BEFORE THE BOARD ONCE A YEAR; SHALL ATTEND AT LEAST 50 HOURS PER YEAR OF CONTINUING MEDICAL EDUCATION AND SHALL LEARN AND UNDERSTAND THE POTENTIAL FOR ABUSE OF CERTAIN PRESCRIPTION DRUGS; SHALL GIVE A COPY OF THIS ORDER TO ANY HEALTH CARE ENTITY WHERE HE HAS PRIVILEGES; SHALL COOPERATE WITH THE BOARD IN VERIFYING COMPLIANCE; SHALL INFORM BOARD OF CHANGE OF ADDRESS WITHIN 10 DAYS OR IF HE LEAVES THE STATE; TIME SPENT OUT OF TEXAS DOES NOT COUNT TOWARD PROBATION. SHALL NOT SEEK MODIFICATION FOR ONE YEAR. ON 5/11/95 BOARD GRANTED HIS PETITION FOR TERMINATION OF THIS ORDER BASED ON COMPLIANCE WITH THE TERMS OF THE ORDER.

MINOR, OFELIA M MD, LICENSE NUMBER 00D1738, OF HOUSTON, TX, WAS DISCIPLINED BY TEXAS ON MAY 17, 1994.
DISCIPLINARY ACTION: SURRENDER OF LICENSE
NOTES: RETIREMENT IS PERMANENT AND SHE WILL NOT PETITION FOR REINSTATEMENT OF HER LICENSE.

MIRON, MORTON A MD, DATE OF BIRTH APRIL 30, 1938, OF 404 WEST BERLIN, TERRELL, TX, WAS DISCIPLINED BY MEDICARE ON AUGUST 17, 1994.
DISCIPLINARY ACTION: EXCLUSION FROM THE MEDICARE AND/OR MEDICAID PROGRAMS
OFFENSE: DISCIPLINARY ACTION BY ANOTHER STATE OR AGENCY
NOTES: LICENSE REVOKED FOR REASONS BEARING ON PROFESSIONAL PERFORMANCE.

MIRON, MORTON ARTHUR MD, LICENSE NUMBER 00D2534, OF TERRELL, TX, WAS DISCIPLINED BY TEXAS ON AUGUST 28, 1992.
DISCIPLINARY ACTION: EMERGENCY SUSPENSION
OFFENSE: PROFESSIONAL MISCONDUCT
NOTES: ALLEGATIONS OF UNPROFESSIONAL OR DISHONORABLE CONDUCT LIKELY TO DECEIVE, DEFRAUD, OR INJURE THE PUBLIC.

MIRON, MORTON ARTHUR MD, LICENSE NUMBER 00D2534, OF TERRELL, TX, WAS DISCIPLINED BY TEXAS ON OCTOBER 27, 1993.
DISCIPLINARY ACTION: LICENSE REVOCATION
OFFENSE: SEXUAL ABUSE OF OR SEXUAL MISCONDUCT WITH A PATIENT
NOTES: BETWEEN 1984 AND 1992 REPEATEDLY ENGAGED IN INAPPROPRIATE TOUCHING OF 8 PATIENTS MANY OF WHOM WORKED AT A COMPANY FOR WHICH HE WAS THE ONLY DOCTOR THEY COULD SEE FOR COMPANY PHYSICALS WITHOUT PAYING. HAS 20 DAYS TO FILE A MOTION FOR REHEARING. ORDER WILL BECOME FINAL WHEN ALL APPEALS HAVE BEEN EXHAUSTED.

MIRON, MORTON ARTHUR MD, LICENSE NUMBER 00D2534, OF TERRELL, TX, WAS DISCIPLINED BY TEXAS ON JANUARY 14, 1994.
DISCIPLINARY ACTION: LICENSE REVOCATION
OFFENSE: SEXUAL ABUSE OF OR SEXUAL MISCONDUCT WITH A

PATIENT
NOTES: IN THE CASE OF TWO PATIENTS HE ENGAGED IN INAPPROPRIATE TOUCHING OF A SEXUAL NATURE; ACTIONS WERE INDIVIDUALLY AND COLLECTIVELY INAPPROPRIATE AND WITHOUT SUFFICIENT MEDICAL JUSTIFICATION; ONE PATIENT ARRANGED WITH TV CAMERAS TO VIDEOTAPE A 6/3/92 VISIT. ORDER WILL BECOME FINAL WHEN ALL APPEALS HAVE BEEN EXHAUSTED. HE HAS 20 DAYS TO FILE A MOTION FOR REHEARING.

MIRZATUNY, ARDASHES MD, LICENSE NUMBER 00F9830, OF TERRELL, TX, WAS DISCIPLINED BY TEXAS ON AUGUST 18, 1990.
DISCIPLINARY ACTION: 72-MONTH PROBATION; RESTRICTION PLACED ON LICENSE
NOTES: STIPULATED ORDER. MUST APPEAR BEFORE BOARD TWICE ANNUALLY, CONTINUE PSYCHIATRIC TREATMENT UNTIL RELEASED BY PSYCHIATRIST, AND LIMIT HIS PRACTICE TO ADULTS.

MITCHELL, RODERICK LEE MD, LICENSE NUMBER 00F9834, OF MARSHALL, TX, WAS DISCIPLINED BY TEXAS ON JUNE 10, 1991.
DISCIPLINARY ACTION: RESTRICTION PLACED ON LICENSE
NOTES: SHALL REFRAIN FROM ACCEPTING EMPLOYMENT OR ENTERING INTO CONTRACTUAL RELATIONSHIPS WHEREIN HE WOULD BE COMPENSATED TO DIAGNOSE AND/OR TREAT PATIENTS BY A LAYPERSON, CORPORATION, OR OTHER ENTITY NOT COMPRISED EXCLUSIVELY OF LICENSED PHYSICIANS, AND WHEREIN SAID PERSON OR ENTITY THEN WOULD RECEIVE AND RETAIN THE FEES PAID BY OR ON BEHALF OF PATIENTS FOR THE PHYSICIAN'S PROFESSIONAL SERVICES. ON 11/3/94 ORDER TERMINATED.

MODDERS, ROBERT E DO, LICENSE NUMBER 00C8053, OF GRAND PRAIRIE, TX, WAS DISCIPLINED BY TEXAS ON FEBRUARY 24, 1989.
DISCIPLINARY ACTION: SURRENDER OF LICENSE
NOTES: PLACED ON RETIREMENT STATUS TO RECEIVE WRITTEN BOARD AUTHORITY PRIOR TO ANY RETURN TO PRACTICE

MOLNAR, EUGENE M MD, LICENSE NUMBER A024674, OF LOS ANGELES, CA, WAS DISCIPLINED BY CALIFORNIA ON DECEMBER 29, 1989.
DISCIPLINARY ACTION: 3-MONTH LICENSE SUSPENSION; 57-MONTH PROBATION
OFFENSE: SUBSTANDARD CARE, INCOMPETENCE, OR NEGLIGENCE
NOTES: GROSS NEGLIGENCE IN COSMETIC SURGERY AND FALSE INSURANCE BILLING. ALSO DISCIPLINED BY NEVADA FOR FALSE STATEMENT IN RENEWAL APPLICATION.

MOLNAR, EUGENE M MD, LICENSE NUMBER 00D7193, OF NEWPORT BEACH, CA, WAS DISCIPLINED BY TEXAS ON AUGUST 24, 1991.
DISCIPLINARY ACTION: 60-MONTH PROBATION
OFFENSE: DISCIPLINARY ACTION BY ANOTHER STATE OR AGENCY
NOTES: REVOCATION STAYED. BEFORE PRACTICING IN TEXAS SHALL APPEAR BEFORE AND RECEIVE APPROVAL FROM THE TEXAS BOARD.

MOLNAR, EUGENE MICHAEL MD, LICENSE NUMBER 0015405, WAS DISCIPLINED BY ARIZONA ON APRIL 12, 1991.
DISCIPLINARY ACTION: LICENSE REVOCATION
OFFENSE: DISCIPLINARY ACTION BY ANOTHER STATE OR AGENCY
NOTES: CALIFORNIA LICENSE WAS REVOKED ON 7/28/89 WITH REVOCATION STAYED TO 5 YEARS PROBATION, ALLEGING IMPROPER SURGICAL PROCEDURES AND INSURANCE FRAUD, AIDING THREE PERSONS IN THE UNAUTHORIZED PRACTICE OF NURSING, AND LYING ON A NEVADA REGISTRATION APPLICATION.

MOLNAR, EUGENE MICHAEL DR OF NEWPORT BEACH, CA, WAS DISCIPLINED BY ILLINOIS ON SEPTEMBER 1, 1991.
DISCIPLINARY ACTION: LICENSE SUSPENSION
OFFENSE: DISCIPLINARY ACTION BY ANOTHER STATE OR AGENCY
NOTES: DISCIPLINED BY CALIFORNIA. INDEFINITE SUSPENSION.

MONROE, ELLIOT F MD, LICENSE NUMBER 0019670, OF PANAMA CITY, FL, WAS DISCIPLINED BY FLORIDA ON DECEMBER 30, 1991.
DISCIPLINARY ACTION: LICENSE REVOCATION
OFFENSE: SUBSTANDARD CARE, INCOMPETENCE, OR NEGLIGENCE
NOTES: PRESCRIBING, DISPENSING, ADMINISTERING, MIXING, OR OTHERWISE PREPARING A LEGEND DRUG OTHER THAN IN THE COURSE OF PROFESSIONAL PRACTICE; FAILING TO PRACTICE MEDICINE WITH AN ACCEPTABLE LEVEL OF CARE AND SKILL; FAILING TO KEEP MEDICAL RECORDS JUSTIFYING THE COURSE OF TREATMENT OF A PATIENT; IMMORAL OR UNPROFESSIONAL CONDUCT, INCOMPETENCE, NEGLIGENCE, OR WILLFUL MISCONDUCT.

MONROE, ELLIOT F MD OF 4000 THIRD ST, PANAMA CITY, FL, WAS DISCIPLINED BY DEA ON JULY 2, 1992.
DISCIPLINARY ACTION: REVOCATION OF CONTROLLED SUBSTANCE LICENSE
OFFENSE: DISCIPLINARY ACTION BY ANOTHER STATE OR AGENCY
NOTES: ON 06/13/89 FLORIDA SUSPENDED HIS MEDICAL LICENSE AND ON 12/30/91 REVOKED IT, THEREBY TERMINATING HIS AUTHORITY TO PRESCRIBE, DISPENSE, ADMINISTER OR OTHERWISE HANDLE CONTROLLED SUBSTANCES. CURRENTLY LICENSED TO PRACTICE MEDICINE IN TEXAS.

MONROE, ELLIOT F MD OF 2236 DOGWOOD, PAMPA, TX, WAS DISCIPLINED BY DEA ON MARCH 30, 1993.
DISCIPLINARY ACTION: DENIAL OF NEW LICENSE
OFFENSE: DISCIPLINARY ACTION BY ANOTHER STATE OR AGENCY
NOTES: ON 12/30/91 FLORIDA BOARD REVOKED HIS MEDICAL LICENSE DUE TO FINDINGS OF UNPROFESSIONAL CONDUCT, INCOMPETENCE AND NEGLIGENCE. ON 12/2/92 FOUND GUILTY OF KNOWINGLY AND INTENTIONALLY FURNISHING FALSE AND FRAUDULENT INFORMATION ON HIS DEA APPLICATIONS AND WAS SENTENCED TO A TERM OF THREE MONTHS INCARCERATION TO BE FOLLOWED BY A TERM OF SUPERVISED RELEASE FOR A PERIOD OF ONE YEAR.

MONROE, ELLIOTT F MD, LICENSE NUMBER 0019670, OF PANAMA CITY, FL, WAS DISCIPLINED BY FLORIDA ON JUNE 15, 1989.
DISCIPLINARY ACTION: LICENSE SUSPENSION

MONROE, ELLIOTT F MD WAS DISCIPLINED BY LOUISIANA ON AUGUST 28, 1989.
DISCIPLINARY ACTION: LICENSE REVOCATION
OFFENSE: DISCIPLINARY ACTION BY ANOTHER STATE OR AGENCY
NOTES: REVOCATION OF TEXAS AND ALABAMA LICENSES

MONROE, ELLIOTT F MD, LICENSE NUMBER 0019670, OF PANAMA CITY, FL, WAS DISCIPLINED BY FLORIDA ON SEPTEMBER 23, 1991.
DISCIPLINARY ACTION: LICENSE REVOCATION
OFFENSE: SUBSTANDARD CARE, INCOMPETENCE, OR

NEGLIGENCE
NOTES: FAILURE TO PRACTICE WITH AN ACCEPTABLE LEVEL OF CARE AND SKILL; FAILING TO KEEP MEDICAL RECORDS JUSTIFYING THE COURSE OF TREATMENT OF A PATIENT.

MONROE, ELLIOTT FAIL MD, DATE OF BIRTH JUNE 26, 1943, LICENSE NUMBER 00G2436, OF SAN DIEGO, TX, WAS DISCIPLINED BY TEXAS ON AUGUST 1, 1988.
DISCIPLINARY ACTION: 60-MONTH PROBATION
OFFENSE: LOSS OR RESTRICTION OF HOSPITAL PRIVILEGES
NOTES: FIVE-YEAR SUSPENSION STAYED. ENGAGED IN INTEMPERATE USE OF ALCOHOL THAT COULD ENDANGER PATENTS' LIVES; ENGAGED IN UNPROFESSIONAL OR DISHONORABLE CONDUCT; DISCIPLINED BY HOSPITAL

MONROE, ELLIOTT FAIL MD, DATE OF BIRTH JUNE 26, 1943, WAS DISCIPLINED BY MISSISSIPPI ON JULY 19, 1990.
DISCIPLINARY ACTION: DENIAL OF NEW LICENSE
NOTES: LICENSE BY RECIPROCITY DENIED.

MONROE, ELLIOTT FAIL MD, DATE OF BIRTH JUNE 26, 1943, OF 2709 ARDEN AVENUE, PANAMA CITY, FL, WAS DISCIPLINED BY MEDICARE ON FEBRUARY 10, 1992.
DISCIPLINARY ACTION: EXCLUSION FROM THE MEDICARE AND/OR MEDICAID PROGRAMS
OFFENSE: DISCIPLINARY ACTION BY ANOTHER STATE OR AGENCY
NOTES: LICENSE REVOCATION OR SUSPENSION.

MONROE, ELLIOTT FAIL MD, DATE OF BIRTH JUNE 26, 1943, LICENSE NUMBER 00G2436, OF P.O. BOX 108, CLINTON, AL, WAS DISCIPLINED BY TEXAS ON MARCH 27, 1993.
DISCIPLINARY ACTION: LICENSE REVOCATION
OFFENSE: DISCIPLINARY ACTION BY ANOTHER STATE OR AGENCY
NOTES: DISCIPLINARY ACTION BY ANOTHER STATE; UNPROFESSIONAL CONDUCT. APPLICATION FOR REINSTATEMENT MAY NOT BE MADE FOR ONE YEAR FROM THE DATE THIS ORDER BECOMES FINAL. ORDER WILL BECOME FINAL WHEN ALL APPEALS HAVE BEEN EXHAUSTED.

MONTE, MELVILLE R MD, LICENSE NUMBER 00C3528, OF LUBBOCK, TX, WAS DISCIPLINED BY TEXAS ON AUGUST 25, 1989.
DISCIPLINARY ACTION: RESTRICTION PLACED ON LICENSE
NOTES: RESTRICTED TO TAKING HISTORIES AND/OR PERFORMING PHYSICALS.

MOORE, ANTHONY J MD OF DURHAM, NC, WAS DISCIPLINED BY NORTH CAROLINA ON JUNE 1, 1992.
DISCIPLINARY ACTION: SURRENDER OF LICENSE

MOORE, ANTHONY JOSEPH MD OF DURHAM, NC, WAS DISCIPLINED BY NORTH CAROLINA ON JANUARY 25, 1990.
DISCIPLINARY ACTION: SURRENDER OF LICENSE

MOORE, ANTHONY JOSEPH MD OF DURHAM, NC, WAS DISCIPLINED BY NORTH CAROLINA ON OCTOBER 16, 1990.
DISCIPLINARY ACTION: LICENSE REINSTATEMENT
NOTES: TEMPORARY LICENSE ISSUED WITH CONDITIONS.

MOORE, ANTHONY JOSEPH MD, LICENSE NUMBER 00C9232, OF BUTNER, NC, WAS DISCIPLINED BY TEXAS ON OCTOBER 5, 1991.
DISCIPLINARY ACTION: 60-MONTH PROBATION
OFFENSE: DISCIPLINARY ACTION BY ANOTHER STATE OR AGENCY
NOTES: ON 1/25/90 HE VOLUNTARILY SURRENDERED HIS NORTH CAROLINA LICENSE; THAT BOARD FOUND HE WAS A RECOVERING ALCOHOLIC; HIS NORTH CAROLINA LICENSE WAS REINSTATED ON 10/16/90 FOR FOUR MONTHS, AND WAS LATER EXTENDED UNTIL 7/31/91. SUSPENSION STAYED; CONDITIONS OF PROBATION: SHALL NOT PETITION FOR MODIFICATION FOR AT LEAST ONE YEAR; SHALL PROVIDE TEXAS ANY REPORTS HE SUBMITS TO NORTH CAROLINA, AND SHALL COMPLY WITH TERMS OF NORTH CAROLINA ORDERS; SHALL APPEAR BEFORE BOARD BEFORE PRACTICING IN TEXAS; SHALL COOPERATE WITH BOARD IN VERIFYING COMPLIANCE; SHALL ADVISE THE BOARD OF ANY CHANGE OF ADDRESS WITHIN 10 DAYS.

MOORE, ANTHONY JOSEPH MD, LICENSE NUMBER 00C9232, OF BUTNER, NC, WAS DISCIPLINED BY TEXAS ON OCTOBER 5, 1991.
DISCIPLINARY ACTION: 60-MONTH PROBATION
OFFENSE: DISCIPLINARY ACTION BY ANOTHER STATE OR AGENCY
NOTES: INTEMPERATE USE OF ALCOHOL OR DRUGS. LICENSE SUSPENDED, SUSPENSION STAYED; PROBATION UNDER TERMS AND CONDITIONS.

MOORE, BEN HAROLD JR MD, DATE OF BIRTH FEBRUARY 4, 1937, LICENSE NUMBER 00D1743, OF MISSOURI CITY, TX, WAS DISCIPLINED BY TEXAS ON AUGUST 25, 1989.
DISCIPLINARY ACTION: 60-MONTH PROBATION; 60-MONTH REQUIRED TO TAKE ADDITIONAL MEDICAL EDUCATION
NOTES: OBTAIN REVIEW OF PATIENT RECORDS; MAINTAIN ADEQUATE MEDICAL RECORDS ON PATIENT OFFICE VISITS. ORDER VACATED ON 6/15/93; LICENSE FREE AND CLEAR OF ANY RESTRICTIONS OR LIMITATION.

MOORE, M J MD, LICENSE NUMBER 00D4531, OF ORANGE, TX, WAS DISCIPLINED BY TEXAS ON JANUARY 28, 1989.
DISCIPLINARY ACTION: RESTRICTION PLACED ON LICENSE; RESTRICTION PLACED ON CONTROLLED SUBSTANCE LICENSE
NOTES: PROHIBITED FROM PRESCRIBING, DISPENSING, ADMINISTERING OR POSSESSING CERTAIN DRUGS AND MEDICATIONS; MUST PROPERLY REFER PATIENTS; SHALL NOT TREAT PATIENTS OUTSIDE ORTHOPEDIC SURGERY; SHALL COMPLETE A PRECEPTORSHIP ON PREVENTION AND TREATMENT OF DRUG ABUSE; SHALL MAINTAIN PRESCRIPTION FILE FOR CONTROLLED SUBSTANCES FOR THREE YEARS AND SHALL NOT TELEPHONE DANGEROUS DRUG PRESCRIPTION TO PHARMACY;

MOORE, M J MD, LICENSE NUMBER 00D4531, OF ORANGE, TX, WAS DISCIPLINED BY TEXAS ON NOVEMBER 3, 1994.
DISCIPLINARY ACTION: SURRENDER OF CONTROLLED SUBSTANCE LICENSE; 120-MONTH PROBATION
OFFENSE: DRUG OR ALCOHOL ABUSE
NOTES: HAS PRESCRIBED TO HIS RELATIVES, PEOPLE HE LIVES WITH AND HIMSELF; STATED TO AN INVESTIGATOR ON 6/16/93 THAT HE DID NOT DRINK AND THAT HE HAD TAKEN PAIN MEDICATIONS OCCASIONALLY AFTER OPEN HEART SURGERY; DID NOT HAVE MEDICAL RECORDS FOR THE PEOPLE HE PRESCRIBED FOR REFERENCED ABOVE AND SAID HE MAY HAVE DESTROYED THEM; AGREED TO SURRENDER HIS CONTROLLED SUBSTANCES REGISTRATION SCHEDULES II THROUGH V BY 9/3/93 BASED UPON ALLEGATIONS OF NON-THERAPEUTIC PRESCRIBING OF DARVOCET N-1OO TO AN UNDERCOVER AGENT; DR. MOORE HAS RECEIVED TREATMENT RELATED TO HIS ABUSE OF MEDICATIONS; SOBRIETY DATE IS 9/10/93; IS CURRENTLY UNDER THE CARE OF A PSYCHIATRIST AND ATTENDS AA. SUSPENSION STAYED. CONDITIONS

OF PROBATION: SHALL SURRENDER HIS DEA AND TEXAS CONTROLLED SUBSTANCES CERTIFICATES, ALL UNUSED TRIPLICATE PRESCRIPTION FORMS AND ALL CONTROLLED SUBSTANCES IN HIS POSSESSION INCLUDING SAMPLES; SHALL NOT ATTEMPT TO REREGISTER WITHOUT PERMISSION; SHALL ABSTAIN FROM THE CONSUMPTION OF ALCOHOL/CHEMICAL SUBSTANCES IN ANY FORM UNLESS PRESCRIBED BY ANOTHER PHYSICIAN FOR A LEGITIMATE AND THERAPEUTIC PURPOSE; SHALL SUBMIT HIMSELF FOR APPROPRIATE EXAMS INCLUDING DRUG OR ALCOHOL SCREENS; SHALL SUBMIT HIMSELF FOR EVALUATION AND TREATMENT TO A BOARD-APPROVED PSYCHIATRIST WITH REPORTS TO THE BOARD; SHALL CONTINUE TO PARTICIPATE IN AA'S PROGRAM NOT LESS THAN THREE TIMES A WEEK WITH QUARTERLY REPORTS TO THE BOARD; SEPARATE FROM PATIENT RECORDS SHALL MAINTAIN A LOG OF EVERY PRESCRIPTION WRITTEN FOR DANGEROUS DRUGS WHICH SHALL BE AVAILABLE FOR INSPECTION; SHALL NOT TELEPHONE TO A PHARMACY ANY PRESCRIPTION FOR DANGEROUS DRUGS WITH A POTENTIAL FOR ABUSE; SHALL NOT TREAT OR OTHERWISE SERVE AS PHYSICIAN, PRESCRIBE, DISPENSE OR ADMINISTER DRUGS THAT MAY BE SUBJECT TO ABUSE TO HIMSELF OR ANY MEMBER OF HIS FAMILY; SHALL BE SUPERVISED BY A BOARD-APPROVED PHYSICIAN WITH QUARTERLY REPORTS; SHALL MAINTAIN A LIST OF ALL PRESCRIPTIONS FOR CONTROLLED SUBSTANCES OR DANGEROUS DRUGS PRESCRIBED BY HIS PHYSICIAN WHICH HE SHALL PROVIDE TO EACH PRESCRIBING PHYSICIAN AT EACH VISIT FOR THEM TO INITIAL; SHALL GIVE A COPY OF THIS ORDER TO ANY HEALTH CARE ENTITY WHERE HE HAS PRIVILEGES; SHALL COOPERATE WITH THE BOARD IN VERIFYING COMPLIANCE; SHALL INFORM BOARD OF CHANGE OF ADDRESS WITHIN 10 DAYS OR IF HE LEAVES THE STATE; TIME SPENT OUT OF TEXAS DOES NOT COUNT TOWARD PROBATION. SHALL NOT SEEK MODIFICATION FOR ONE YEAR.

MOORE, MILTON JOE MD OF ORANGE, TX, WAS DISCIPLINED BY LOUISIANA ON FEBRUARY 15, 1990.
OFFENSE: DISCIPLINARY ACTION BY ANOTHER STATE OR AGENCY
NOTES: DISCIPLINED BY TEXAS, ALSO INVESTIGATION OF SUSPECTED DISPENSING OF CONTROLLED SUBSTANCES IN OTHER THAN A LEGITIMATE MANNER; MUST COMPLY WITH TERMS AND CONDITIONS MANDATED BY TEXAS, MUST INFORM BOARD OF INTENT TO RELOCATE TO LOUISIANA.

MOORE, MILTON JOE MD OF 1309 WEST PARK, ORANGE, TX, WAS DISCIPLINED BY DEA ON SEPTEMBER 7, 1993.
DISCIPLINARY ACTION: SURRENDER OF CONTROLLED SUBSTANCE LICENSE
OFFENSE: CRIMINAL CONVICTION OR PLEA OF GUILTY, NOLO CONTENDERE, OR NO CONTEST TO A CRIME
NOTES: SURRENDERED DEA REGISTRATION IN PLEA BARGAIN. SEARCH WARRANT EXECUTED ON 08/19/93 IN ORANGE, TX TO OBTAIN MEDICAL RECORDS. JUDGEMENT FILED AGAINST HIM FOR UNLAWFUL DISPENSING OF CONTROLLED SUBSTANCE. ORDERED TO PAY FINE.

MOORE, SHIRLEY ANN MD OF ORLANDO, FL, WAS DISCIPLINED BY TEXAS ON DECEMBER 1, 1986.
DISCIPLINARY ACTION: LICENSE REVOCATION
OFFENSE: DISCIPLINARY ACTION BY ANOTHER STATE OR AGENCY

MOOREHEAD, WILL EARL MD, LICENSE NUMBER C033088, OF SAN FRANCISCO, CA, WAS DISCIPLINED BY CALIFORNIA ON AUGUST 18, 1986.
DISCIPLINARY ACTION: 60-MONTH PROBATION
OFFENSE: CRIMINAL CONVICTION OR PLEA OF GUILTY, NOLO CONTENDERE, OR NO CONTEST TO A CRIME
NOTES: CONVICTION FOR FILING FALSE MEDI-CAL CLAIMS. REVOCATION STAYED.

MOOREHEAD, WILL EARL MD, LICENSE NUMBER C033088, OF HOUSTON, TX, WAS DISCIPLINED BY CALIFORNIA ON MARCH 17, 1989.
DISCIPLINARY ACTION: LICENSE REVOCATION
OFFENSE: FAILURE TO COMPLY WITH A PREVIOUS BOARD ORDER
NOTES: LACK OF COOPERATION AND FAILURE TO COMPLY WITH PROBATION OF PRIOR DISCIPLINE . DEFAULT DECISION.

MOOREHEAD, WILL EARL MD, LICENSE NUMBER C033088, OF 1801 BUSH STREET, STE 106, SAN FRANCISCO, CA, WAS DISCIPLINED BY DEA ON APRIL 19, 1989.
DISCIPLINARY ACTION: SURRENDER OF CONTROLLED SUBSTANCE LICENSE
OFFENSE: INSURANCE, MEDICARE, OR MEDICAID FRAUD
NOTES: FOUND GUILTY OF SUBMITTING FALSE MEDI-CAL CLAIMS AND ACCEPTING PAYMENT FOR SAME; PLACED ON 5 YEARS PROBATION. CALIFORNIA MEDICAL LICENSE REVOKED.

MOOREHEAD, WILL EARL MD, DATE OF BIRTH OCTOBER 26, 1943, LICENSE NUMBER 0013230, OF 5600 S WILLOW SUITE 206, HOUSTON, TX, WAS DISCIPLINED BY GEORGIA ON JULY 17, 1991.
DISCIPLINARY ACTION: LICENSE SUSPENSION; FINE
OFFENSE: DISCIPLINARY ACTION BY ANOTHER STATE OR AGENCY
NOTES: DUE TO REVOCATION OF LICENSE IN CALIFORNIA. $1500 FINE MUST BE PAID WITHIN 60 DAYS.

MORALES, MAX JR MD, LICENSE NUMBER 00C9083, OF PLANO, TX, WAS DISCIPLINED BY TEXAS ON JANUARY 28, 1989.
DISCIPLINARY ACTION: 24-MONTH RESTRICTION PLACED ON LICENSE
NOTES: MUST OBTAIN SPECIFIC INFORMATION FROM PATIENTS SEEKING TREATMENT BY WEIGHT REDUCTION PROGRAM AND TREAT SUCH PATIENTS IN SPECIFIC MANNER; SHALL PROPERLY DELEGATE TO APPROPRIATELY TRAINED AND EXPERIENCED PERSONNEL;

MORAN, WILMER JR MD, LICENSE NUMBER 00E1684, OF HOUSTON, TX, WAS DISCIPLINED BY TEXAS ON AUGUST 19, 1994.
DISCIPLINARY ACTION: FINE; REPRIMAND
OFFENSE: PROFESSIONAL MISCONDUCT
NOTES: AIDED AND ABETTED THE UNLICENSED PRACTICE OF MEDICINE IN THAT HE ENGAGED IN THE CORPORATE PRACTICE OF MEDICINE BY VIRTUE OF HIS EMPLOYMENT BY GALLERIA DIAGNOSTIC SERVICE ON A SALARY BASIS IN THE FALL OF 1991; CEASED PRACTICE AS SOON AS HE LEARNED IT WAS ILLEGAL. SHALL NOT ACCEPT EMPLOYMENT OR ENTER INTO CONTRACTUAL RELATIONSHIPS WHERE HE WOULD BE COMPENSATED BY ANY ENTITY NOT COMPRISED EXCLUSIVELY OF TEXAS LICENSED PHYSICIANS WHERE THEY WOULD RECEIVE AND RETAIN THE FEES; SHALL PAY A $1,000 ADMINISTRATIVE PENALTY; SHALL GIVE A COPY OF THIS ORDER TO ANY HEALTH CARE ENTITY WHERE HE HAS PRIVILEGES; SHALL COOPERATE WITH THE BOARD IN VERIFYING COMPLIANCE; SHALL INFORM BOARD OF

CHANGE OF ADDRESS WITHIN 10 DAYS.

MORGAN, CHARLES III MD, LICENSE NUMBER MD14095, OF CLACKAMAS, OR, WAS DISCIPLINED BY OREGON ON OCTOBER 11, 1984.
DISCIPLINARY ACTION: 120-MONTH PROBATION
NOTES: NO LONGER ON PROBATION AS OF 8/10/90.

MORGAN, CHARLES III MD OF LAKE OSWEGO, OR, WAS DISCIPLINED BY TEXAS ON DECEMBER 1, 1986.
DISCIPLINARY ACTION: 120-MONTH PROBATION
OFFENSE: DISCIPLINARY ACTION BY ANOTHER STATE OR AGENCY
NOTES: REVOCATION STAYED

MORGAN, JERRY MELDON MD, LICENSE NUMBER 00E5863, OF DESOTO, TX, WAS DISCIPLINED BY TEXAS ON APRIL 14, 1989.
NOTES: SHALL NOT DELEGATE TASK OF TELEPHONING CONTROLLED SUBSTANCE PRESCRIPTIONS TO PHARMACIST; SHALL MAINTAIN ADEQUATE MEDICAL RECORDS ON PATIENT OFFICE VISITS TO INCLUDE CERTAIN INFORMATION; SHALL ADEQUATELY SUPERVISE EMPLOYEE TO DETERMINE THERE ARE NO VIOLATIONS OF LAWS TO PRACTICE MEDICINE; SHALL MAINTAIN FILE OF EVERY PRESCRIPTION WRITTEN BY HIM FOR CONTROLLED SUBSTANCES. ORDER TERMINATED ON 11/19/93.

MORGAN, RICHARD DOUGLAS DO, LICENSE NUMBER 00H4565, OF BRADY, TX, WAS DISCIPLINED BY TEXAS ON APRIL 15, 1994.
DISCIPLINARY ACTION: 60-MONTH PROBATION; REQUIRED TO TAKE ADDITIONAL MEDICAL EDUCATION
OFFENSE: DISCIPLINARY ACTION BY ANOTHER STATE OR AGENCY
NOTES: IN 8/93 DISCIPLINED BY THE U.S. AIR FORCE FOR THEFT OF STADOL, FALSE OFFICIAL STATEMENTS AND DERELICTION OF DUTIES FOR SELF-PRESCRIBING OF STADOL; SELF-ADMINISTERED STADOL BEFORE (FOR HEADACHES) AND AFTER HIS CAR ACCIDENT IN 6/92; USED STADOL FOR LOCAL ANESTHETIC PURPOSES WHICH WAS FOUND TO BE INAPPROPRIATE; PATIENT NAMES WERE USED TO DOCUMENT THAT STADOL WAS RECEIVED WHEN IN FACT THE PATIENTS DID NOT RECEIVE THE DRUGS; FALSIFIED MEDICAL RECORDS AND PHARMACY ACCOUNTING FORMS; PRESCRIBED STADOL TO HIS FATHER; HOSPITAL PRIVILEGES WERE SUSPENDED BASED ON THESE FINDINGS; AFTER SEPARATION FROM AIR FORCE HAS SUBMITTED TO THE CARE OF A FAMILY PHYSICIAN. SUSPENSION STAYED. CONDITIONS OF PROBATION: SHALL APPEAR BEFORE THE BOARD TWICE A YEAR; SHALL ATTEND AT LEAST 50 HOURS PER YEAR OF CONTINUING MEDICAL EDUCATION INCLUDING 20 HOURS IN PHARMACOLOGY/ADDICTIONOLOGY DURING THE FIRST YEAR; SHALL BE SUPERVISED BY A BOARD-APPROVED PHYSICIAN WITH QUARTERLY REPORTS; SHALL MAINTAIN ADEQUATE MEDICAL RECORDS ON ALL PATIENT OFFICE VISITS WHICH SHALL BE AVAILABLE FOR REVIEW; SHALL NOT PERSONALLY USE, POSSESS, ADMINISTER OR PRESCRIBE ANY PRESCRIPTION DRUG UNLESS PRESCRIBED, ADMINISTERED OR DISPENSED BY ANOTHER PHYSICIAN FOR A LEGITIMATE MEDICAL NEED; SHALL NOT TREAT OR OTHERWISE SERVE AS PHYSICIAN, PRESCRIBE, DISPENSE OR ADMINISTER DRUGS THAT MAY BE SUBJECT TO ABUSE TO HIMSELF OR ANY MEMBER OF HIS FAMILY; SEPARATE FROM PATIENT RECORDS, SHALL MAINTAIN A FILE OF EVERY PRESCRIPTION WRITTEN FOR CONTROLLED SUBSTANCES OR DANGEROUS DRUGS WHICH SHALL BE AVAILABLE FOR INSPECTION; SHALL ABSTAIN FROM THE CONSUMPTION OF ALCOHOL/CHEMICAL SUBSTANCES IN ANY FORM UNLESS PRESCRIBED BY ANOTHER PHYSICIAN FOR A LEGITIMATE MEDICAL PURPOSE; SHALL SUBMIT HIMSELF FOR APPROPRIATE EXAMS INCLUDING DRUG AND ALCOHOL SCREENS; WITHIN 60 DAYS SHALL ENTER AN IN-PATIENT BOARD-APPROVED PAIN MANAGEMENT PROGRAM WITH REPORTS TO THE BOARD; SHALL UNDERGO A COMPLETE EXAMINATION BY A BOARD-APPROVED PHYSICIAN UPON REQUEST; IN COMPLIANCE WITH CONDITIONS SET OUT BY SHANNON MEDICAL CENTER SHALL NOT POSSESS A KEY OR HAVE ACCESS TO ANY MEDICINE CABINET CONTAINING CONTROLLED SUBSTANCES OR DANGEROUS DRUGS AND SHALL SUBMIT TO ANY DRUG SCREENS ORDERED; SHALL GIVE A COPY OF THIS ORDER TO ANY HEALTH CARE ENTITY WHERE HE HAS PRIVILEGES; SHALL COOPERATE WITH THE BOARD IN VERIFYING COMPLIANCE; SHALL INFORM BOARD OF CHANGE OF ADDRESS WITHIN 10 DAYS OR IF HE LEAVES THE STATE; TIME SPENT OUT OF TEXAS DOES NOT COUNT TOWARD PROBATION. SHALL NOT SEEK MODIFICATION FOR ONE YEAR.

MORRIS, WILFORD JR DO OF SEALY, TX, WAS DISCIPLINED BY KANSAS ON JUNE 22, 1990.
NOTES: STIPULATION AND ENFORCEMENT ORDER.

MORRIS, WILFORD V JR DO, LICENSE NUMBER 00E3382, OF SEALY, TX, WAS DISCIPLINED BY TEXAS ON JULY 28, 1989.
DISCIPLINARY ACTION: 29-MONTH RESTRICTION PLACED ON CONTROLLED SUBSTANCE LICENSE; 29-MONTH REQUIRED TO TAKE ADDITIONAL MEDICAL EDUCATION
NOTES: PRESCRIBE NO SEDATIVES OR STIMULANTS FOR OVER 3 WEEKS; PRESCRIBE NO NARCOTIC DRUG OR MEDICATION FOR OVER 6 WEEKS; MAINTAIN COPIES OF CONTROLLED SUBSTANCE PRESCRIPTIONS; COMPLETE PRECEPTORSHIP ON PREVENTION AND TREATMENT OF DRUG ABUSE.

MORRISON, RICHARD FRANK MD, LICENSE NUMBER 00F4308, OF DALLAS, TX, WAS DISCIPLINED BY TEXAS ON MARCH 5, 1994.
DISCIPLINARY ACTION: 60-MONTH PROBATION; MONITORING OF PHYSICIAN
OFFENSE: DRUG OR ALCOHOL ABUSE
NOTES: IN 1983 AND 1991 WAS CONVICTED OF DRIVING WHILE INTOXICATED; IS CURRENTLY UNDER TREATMENT FOR DEPRESSION. FIVE YEAR SUSPENSION STAYED. CONDITIONS OF PROBATION: SHALL APPEAR BEFORE THE BOARD TWICE A YEAR; SHALL CONTINUE TO RECEIVE TREATMENT FOR DEPRESSION WITH QUARTERLY REPORTS TO THE BOARD; SHALL ABSTAIN FROM THE CONSUMPTION OF ALCOHOL OR OTHER DRUGS IN ANY FORM UNLESS PRESCRIBED BY ANOTHER PHYSICIAN FOR A LEGITIMATE MEDICAL PURPOSE; SHALL SUBMIT HIMSELF FOR APPROPRIATE EXAMS INCLUDING DRUG OR ALCOHOL SCREENS; SHALL NOT TREAT OR OTHERWISE SERVE AS PHYSICIAN, PRESCRIBE, DISPENSE OR ADMINISTER DRUGS THAT MAY BE SUBJECT TO ABUSE TO HIMSELF OR FOR ANY MEMBER OF HIS FAMILY; SHALL FURNISH WRITTEN REPORTS TO THE BOARD VERIFYING COMPLIANCE; SHALL GIVE A COPY OF THIS ORDER TO ANY HEALTH CARE ENTITY WHERE HE HAS PRIVILEGES; SHALL COOPERATE WITH THE BOARD IN VERIFYING COMPLIANCE; SHALL INFORM BOARD OF CHANGE OF ADDRESS WITHIN 10 DAYS OR IF THE LEAVES THE

STATE; TIME SPENT OUT OF TEXAS DOES NOT COUNT TOWARD PROBATION. SHALL NOT SEEK MODIFICATION FOR ONE YEAR.

MUIJSSONARNOLD, INGRID DO, DATE OF BIRTH JULY 5, 1953, OF 4725 GUS THOMASSON, MESQUITE, TX, WAS DISCIPLINED BY MEDICARE ON APRIL 1, 1988.
DISCIPLINARY ACTION: 36-MONTH EXCLUSION FROM THE MEDICARE AND/OR MEDICAID PROGRAMS
OFFENSE: CRIMINAL CONVICTION OR PLEA OF GUILTY, NOLO CONTENDERE, OR NO CONTEST TO A CRIME
NOTES: PROGRAM-RELATED CONVICTION.

MUIJSSONARNOLD, INGRID DO, LICENSE NUMBER 00F6978, OF MESQUITE, TX, WAS DISCIPLINED BY TEXAS ON APRIL 14, 1989.
DISCIPLINARY ACTION: 120-MONTH RESTRICTION PLACED ON LICENSE; REQUIRED TO TAKE ADDITIONAL MEDICAL EDUCATION
NOTES: SHALL UTILIZE SYSTEM OF PATIENT RECORD-KEEPING TO INCLUDE CERTAIN INFORMATION; SHALL REFRAIN FROM ACCEPTING TOO LARGE A PATIENT LOAD; SHALL OBTAIN CONTINUING MEDICAL EDUCATION; SHALL APPEAR ANNUALLY BEFORE BOARD; SHALL NOT FILE INSURANCE CLAIMS FOR SERVICES RENDERED AFTER 3/1/89 TO PATIENTS BUT MAY FILE HOSPITALIZATION CHARGES

MULDOON, THOMAS N MD, LICENSE NUMBER 0093458, OF ANTHONY, TX, WAS DISCIPLINED BY NEW YORK ON JUNE 14, 1989.
DISCIPLINARY ACTION: LICENSE REVOCATION

MULDOON, THOMAS N MD, DATE OF BIRTH JUNE 3, 1936, OF FED CORR INST - PO BOX 1000, ANTHONY, NM, WAS DISCIPLINED BY MEDICARE ON FEBRUARY 10, 1992.
DISCIPLINARY ACTION: EXCLUSION FROM THE MEDICARE AND/OR MEDICAID PROGRAMS
OFFENSE: DISCIPLINARY ACTION BY ANOTHER STATE OR AGENCY
NOTES: LICENSE REVOCATION OR SUSPENSION.

MULLEN, JOHN P MD, DATE OF BIRTH OCTOBER 11, 1940, LICENSE NUMBER 0027156, OF 1614 COLQUITT, SAN ANTONIO, TX, WAS DISCIPLINED BY NEW JERSEY ON APRIL 15, 1992.
NOTES: SHALL APPEAR BEFORE A PRELIMINARY EVALUATION COMMITTEE OF THE BOARD OF MEDICAL EXAMINERS PRIOR TO COMMENCING THE PRACTICE OF MEDICINE IN NEW JERSEY. BOARD RESERVES THE RIGHT TO IMPOSE A REASSESSMENT OF HIS SKILLS AND REEDUCATION AT THAT TIME.

MUNCRIEF, KIM IVAN DO, LICENSE NUMBER 00G7284, OF COLBERT, OK, WAS DISCIPLINED BY TEXAS ON JANUARY 27, 1990.
DISCIPLINARY ACTION: PROBATION
OFFENSE: DISCIPLINARY ACTION BY ANOTHER STATE OR AGENCY
NOTES: STIPULATED ORDER. REVOCATION STAYED, INDEFINITE PROBATION. SHALL COMPLY WITH CONDITIONS OF OKLAHOMA BOARD ORDER, SUBMIT REPORTS TO TEXAS BOARD AS SUBMITTED TO OKLAHOMA BOARD, AND MUST SECURE BOARD APPROVAL BEFORE PRACTICING. PROBATION TERMINATED EFFECTIVE 1/9/92; LICENSE FREE OF ANY RESTRICTION OR LIMITATION.

MURPHY, FRANK STUART DO, LICENSE NUMBER 00J3167, OF THE COLONY, TX, WAS DISCIPLINED BY TEXAS ON APRIL 15, 1994.
DISCIPLINARY ACTION: LICENSE SUSPENSION
OFFENSE: LOSS OR RESTRICTION OF HOSPITAL PRIVILEGES
NOTES: IN 3/93 BEGAN TO CONDUCT PSYCHOTHERAPY WITH A FEMALE PATIENT SUFFERING FROM BIPOLAR DISORDER WHICH LASTED FOR SIX THERAPY SESSIONS OVER TWO WEEKS; REPORTED TO HIS SUPERVISOR THAT HE EXPERIENCED STRONG FEELINGS OF COUNTERTRANSFERENCE AND THERAPY WAS TERMINATED; HE THEN INITIATED A SEXUAL RELATIONSHIP WITH HIS FORMER PATIENT; HAD ADMITTED TO A HISTORY OF POLYSUBSTANCE ABUSE AS RECENTLY AS 6/93; ENGAGED IN THE ABUSE OF STREET DRUGS WITH HIS FORMER PATIENT; HOSPITAL PRIVILEGES WERE SUSPENDED ON 6/17/93; WAS DISCHARGED FROM TREATMENT ON 12/15/93; CLAIMS A SOBRIETY DATE OF 6/13/93. SUSPENSION UNTIL SUCH TIME AS HE APPEARS BEFORE THE BOARD AND PROVIDES SUFFICIENT EVIDENCE THAT HE IS PHYSICALLY, MENTALLY OR OTHERWISE COMPETENT TO SAFELY PRACTICE MEDICINE INCLUDING AT A MINIMUM, BUT SHALL NOT BE LIMITED TO, COMPLETE MEDICAL RECORDS AND REPORTS OF PSYCHOLOGICAL AND NEUROPSYCHIATRIC EVALUATIONS.

MURPHY, FRANK STUART DO, LICENSE NUMBER 00J3167, OF DALLAS, TX, WAS DISCIPLINED BY TEXAS ON AUGUST 19, 1994.
DISCIPLINARY ACTION: SURRENDER OF CONTROLLED SUBSTANCE LICENSE; 120-MONTH PROBATION
OFFENSE: DRUG OR ALCOHOL ABUSE
NOTES: LICENSE SUSPENDED 4/15/94 DUE TO INTEMPERATE USE OF DRUGS OR ALCOHOL AND UNPROFESSIONAL OR DISHONORABLE CONDUCT. HAS SATISFIED THE MINIMUM REQUIREMENTS AS SET OUT IN THE 4/15/94 ORDER AND SUSPENSION IS NOW STAYED. CONDITIONS OF PROBATION: SHALL ABSTAIN FROM THE CONSUMPTION OF ALCOHOL/CHEMICAL SUBSTANCES IN ANY FORM UNLESS PRESCRIBED BY ANOTHER PHYSICIAN FOR A LEGITIMATE AND THERAPEUTIC PURPOSE; SHALL SUBMIT HIMSELF FOR APPROPRIATE EXAMS INCLUDING DRUG OR ALCOHOL SCREENS; SHALL NOT TREAT OR OTHERWISE SERVE AS PHYSICIAN, PRESCRIBE, DISPENSE OR ADMINISTER DRUGS THAT MAY BE SUBJECT TO ABUSE FOR HIMSELF OR ANY MEMBER OF HIS FAMILY; SHALL SURRENDER DEA AND TEXAS CONTROLLED SUBSTANCES CERTIFICATES, ALL UNUSED TRIPLICATE PRESCRIPTION FORMS AND ALL CONTROLLED SUBSTANCES IN HIS POSSESSION INCLUDING SAMPLES; SHALL NOT SEEK TO REREGISTER WITHOUT APPROVAL; SEPARATE FROM PATIENT RECORDS, SHALL MAINTAIN A FILE OF EVERY PRESCRIPTION WRITTEN FOR DANGEROUS DRUGS WHICH SHALL BE AVAILABLE FOR INSPECTION; SHALL PARTICIPATE IN THE ACTIVITIES OF A PHYSICIAN ASSISTANCE PROGRAM AND ABIDE BY THEIR AFTERCARE PROGRAM CONTRACT WITH QUARTERLY REPORTS TO THE BOARD; SHALL PARTICIPATE IN AA'S PROGRAMS NOT LESS THAN THREE TIMES A WEEK WITH QUARTERLY REPORTS TO THE BOARD; SHALL SUBMIT HIMSELF TO EVALUATION AND TREATMENT BY A BOARD-APPROVED PSYCHIATRIST WITH QUARTERLY REPORTS; SHALL ATTEND AT LEAST 50 HOURS PER YEAR OF CONTINUING MEDICAL EDUCATION; SHALL APPEAR BEFORE THE BOARD TWICE A YEAR; SHALL GIVE A COPY OF THIS ORDER TO ANY HEALTH CARE ENTITY WHERE HE HAS PRIVILEGES; SHALL COOPERATE WITH THE BOARD IN VERIFYING COMPLIANCE; SHALL INFORM BOARD OF CHANGE OF ADDRESS WITHIN 10 DAYS OR IF HE LEAVES THE STATE; TIME SPENT OUT OF TEXAS DOES NOT COUNT TOWARD PROBATION. SHALL NOT

SEEK MODIFICATION FOR ONE YEAR.

MURPHY, JACK P JR MD OF KENNER, LA, WAS DISCIPLINED BY TEXAS ON DECEMBER 1, 1986.
DISCIPLINARY ACTION: LICENSE REVOCATION
OFFENSE: CRIMINAL CONVICTION OR PLEA OF GUILTY, NOLO CONTENDERE, OR NO CONTEST TO A CRIME
NOTES: CONVICTED OF FELONY.

MURRAY, ROBERT VINCENT JR MD, LICENSE NUMBER 00B8502, OF AUSTIN, TX, WAS DISCIPLINED BY TEXAS ON APRIL 15, 1994.
DISCIPLINARY ACTION: 60-MONTH PROBATION; REQUIRED TO TAKE ADDITIONAL MEDICAL EDUCATION
OFFENSE: SUBSTANDARD CARE, INCOMPETENCE, OR NEGLIGENCE
NOTES: FAILED TO FOLLOW UP ON LAB VALUES INDICATING A PATIENT WAS ANEMIC; ALTHOUGH HE STATES HE DOES MAKE HOME VISITS, HE FAILED TO VISIT OR INSIST AN 86 YEAR OLD PATIENT COME INTO THE OFFICE TO BE EVALUATED FOR ONSET SEIZURES, INSTEAD PRESCRIBING DILANTIN OVER THE PHONE; FAILED TO ADDRESS EXCEPT IN A PALLIATIVE MANNER A PATIENT'S COMPLAINT OF EXTREME SHORTNESS OF BREATH AND CHEST X-RAY SHOWING LUNG INFILTRATE EVEN THOUGH PATIENT HAD A HISTORY OF BREAST CANCER; FAILED TO RECOGNIZE SIGNS AND SYMPTOMS OF POSSIBLE PULMONARY EMBOLUS IN ANOTHER PATIENT; AFTER THIS PATIENT DIED HOSPITAL COMMITTEE SUGGESTED SEVERAL PROCEDURES SHOULD HAVE BEEN DONE. SUSPENSION STAYED. CONDITIONS OF PROBATION: SHALL WITHIN ONE YEAR COMPLETE A BOARD-APPROVED INTERNAL MEDICINE COURSE; SHALL ATTEND AT LEAST 50 HOURS PER YEAR OF CONTINUING MEDICAL EDUCATION; SHALL APPLY FOR BOARD APPROVAL TO TAKE 6/94 SPEX EXAM; IF HE FAILS LICENSE WILL IMMEDIATELY BE SUSPENDED; IF HE PASSES MAY PETITION BOARD FOR EARLY TERMINATION OR MODIFICATION OF THIS ORDER; SHALL APPEAR BEFORE THE BOARD ONCE A YEAR; SHALL GIVE A COPY OF THIS ORDER TO ANY HEALTH CARE ENTITY WHERE HE HAS PRIVILEGES; SHALL COOPERATE WITH THE BOARD IN VERIFYING COMPLIANCE; SHALL INFORM BOARD OF CHANGE OF ADDRESS WITHIN 10 DAYS OR IF HE LEAVES THE STATE; TIME SPENT OUT OF TEXAS DOES NOT COUNT TOWARD PROBATION. SHALL NOT SEEK MODIFICATION FOR ONE YEAR. ON 11/03/94 ORDER WAS TERMINATED.

MURTHA, CARROLL E MD, LICENSE NUMBER 00C0429, OF ABILENE, TX, WAS DISCIPLINED BY TEXAS ON MARCH 31, 1990.
DISCIPLINARY ACTION: 36-MONTH RESTRICTION PLACED ON CONTROLLED SUBSTANCE LICENSE; REQUIRED TO TAKE ADDITIONAL MEDICAL EDUCATION
NOTES: STIPULATED ORDER. MUST COMPLETE PRECEPTORSHIP ON PREVENTION AND TREATMENT OF DRUG ABUSE, PASS SPECIAL PURPOSE EXAMINATION, MUST NOT PRESCRIBE, DISPENSE, ADMINISTER OR POSSESS CERTAIN AMPHETAMINE-LIKE ACTION DRUGS OR ANORECTIC AGENTS.

MYRICK, ANDREW J II MD, LICENSE NUMBER 00G6354, OF FLORENCE, AL, WAS DISCIPLINED BY TEXAS ON DECEMBER 1, 1988.
NOTES: SETTLEMENT AGREEMENT AND UNSPECIFIED DISCIPLINARY ACTION

NACOL, WILLIAM S JR MD, LICENSE NUMBER 00C5814, OF BATON ROUGE, LA, WAS DISCIPLINED BY TEXAS ON MAY 24, 1990.
DISCIPLINARY ACTION: SURRENDER OF LICENSE
NOTES: STIPULATED ORDER.

NACOL, WILLIAM S JR MD OF BATON ROUGE, LA, WAS DISCIPLINED BY LOUISIANA ON NOVEMBER 15, 1990.
DISCIPLINARY ACTION: LICENSE REVOCATION
OFFENSE: DISCIPLINARY ACTION BY ANOTHER STATE OR AGENCY
NOTES: CHARGED WITH CONVICTION OF A FELONY; PRESCRIBING, DISPENSING, OR ADMINISTERING CONTROLLED SUBSTANCES IN OTHER THAN A LEGAL OR LEGITIMATE MANNER; DISPENSATION OF MEDICATIONS WITHOUT CURRENT REGISTRATION; PROFESSIONAL AND MEDICAL INCOMPETENCY; DISCIPLINED BY ANOTHER STATE.

NACOL, WILLIAM S JR MD, DATE OF BIRTH DECEMBER 2, 1925, OF 12509 COURSEY BLVD, BATON ROUGE, LA, WAS DISCIPLINED BY MEDICARE ON MARCH 16, 1992.
DISCIPLINARY ACTION: 120-MONTH EXCLUSION FROM THE MEDICARE AND/OR MEDICAID PROGRAMS
OFFENSE: CRIMINAL CONVICTION OR PLEA OF GUILTY, NOLO CONTENDERE, OR NO CONTEST TO A CRIME
NOTES: CONVICTION RELATING TO CONTROLLED SUBSTANCES.

NACOL, WILLIAM SAMUEL JR MD OF 3703 TWIN CITY HIGHWAY, PORT ARTHUR, TX, WAS DISCIPLINED BY DEA ON APRIL 30, 1990.
DISCIPLINARY ACTION: SURRENDER OF CONTROLLED SUBSTANCE LICENSE
OFFENSE: CRIMINAL CONVICTION OR PLEA OF GUILTY, NOLO CONTENDERE, OR NO CONTEST TO A CRIME
NOTES: MEDICAL LICENSE REVOKED BY TEXAS BOARD OF MEDICAL EXAMINERS FOR INDISCRIMINATE PRESCRIBING OF HORMONES. CONSPIRED TO OBTAIN 100,000 DOSAGE UNITS PYRIBENZAMINE 10/82 TO 11/82 FOR DISTRIBUTING IN BEAUMONT AND HOUSTON TEXAS. INDICTED 04/03/87 FOR DISTRIBUTION, CONSPIRACY, UNLAWFUL USES OF COMMUNICATION AND UNLAWFUL REMOVAL OF A SYMBOL OF CONTROLLED SUBSTANCES. INVOLVED IN ILLEGAL DISTRIBUTION OF PYRIBENZAMINE AND TALWIN IN PORT ARTHUR AND BRIDGE CITY TEXAS AREAS. PLED GUILTY 03/90 IN JEFFERSON COUNTY TEXAS AND AGREED TO SURRENDER OF MEDICAL LICENSE AND REGISTRATION FOR TALWIN DISTRIBUTION. PLED GUILTY 03/08/90 IN TEXAS TO CONSPIRACY TO DISTRIBUTE AND POSSESSION WITH INTENT TO DISTRIBUTE TALWIN. SENTENCED 04/27/90 TO 1000 HOURS COMMUNITY SERVICE, FIVE YEARS PROBATION, $5000 FINE AND SURRENDERED CONTROLLED SUBSTANCE REGISTRATION VOLUNTARILY. INVOLVED IN DISPENSING ANORECTICS WITHOUT MEDICAL JUSTIFICATION. MEDICAL LICENSE REVOKED. VOLUNTARY SURRENDER OF REGISTRATION 02/05/91; CHARGES DISMISSED 08/22/91 IN TEXAS.

NAIFEH, JEROME G MD, LICENSE NUMBER 0C37560, OF IRVING, TX, WAS DISCIPLINED BY CALIFORNIA ON MAY 24, 1984.
DISCIPLINARY ACTION: 9-MONTH LICENSE SUSPENSION; 51-MONTH PROBATION
OFFENSE: CRIMINAL CONVICTION OR PLEA OF GUILTY, NOLO CONTENDERE, OR NO CONTEST TO A CRIME
NOTES: REVOCATION STAYED; CONVICTION FOR GRAND THEFT INVOLVING BILLINGS TO MEDI-CAL AND INSURANCE COMPANY.

NAIFEH, JEROME G MD WAS DISCIPLINED BY PENNSYLVANIA ON AUGUST 13, 1986.
DISCIPLINARY ACTION: LICENSE REVOCATION

NAIFEH, JEROME G MD, LICENSE NUMBER 015075E, OF PITTSBURGH, PA, WAS DISCIPLINED BY PENNSYLVANIA ON MARCH 25, 1987.
DISCIPLINARY ACTION: PREVIOUS BOARD ACTION OVERRULED; PROBATION
NOTES: 1986 REVOCATION REVERSED; LICENSE PLACED ON PROBATION WITH TERMS AND CONDITIONS. MUST PROVIDE THE BOARD WITH CERTAIN DOCUMENTATION AND INFORMATION.

NEESE, WILLIAM DEAN DO, LICENSE NUMBER 00E5869, OF ATLANTIC BEACH, FL, WAS DISCIPLINED BY TEXAS ON JANUARY 24, 1992.
DISCIPLINARY ACTION: SURRENDER OF LICENSE
NOTES: LICENSE VOLUNTARILY SURRENDERED IN LIEU OF FURTHER DISCIPLINARY ACTION.

NELSON, STUART L MD, LICENSE NUMBER 00E7688, OF ALVARADO, TX, WAS DISCIPLINED BY TEXAS ON AUGUST 18, 1990.
DISCIPLINARY ACTION: REPRIMAND; REQUIRED TO TAKE ADDITIONAL MEDICAL EDUCATION
NOTES: STIPULATED ORDER. MUST OBTAIN CONTINUING MEDICAL EDUCATION, PREPARE LIST OF PATIENTS BEING REIMBURSED UNDER WORKERS' COMPENSATION INSURANCE AND ALLOW INSPECTION BY BOARD REPRESENTATIVES OF SUCH PATIENTS' MEDICAL RECORDS. ORDER EFFECTIVE FOR THREE YEARS.

NELSON, STUART L MD, LICENSE NUMBER 00E7688, OF ALVARADO, TX, WAS DISCIPLINED BY TEXAS ON JULY 1, 1995.
DISCIPLINARY ACTION: SURRENDER OF LICENSE
NOTES: IN LIEU OF FURTHER INVESTIGATION INTO ALLEGATIONS THAT HE MAY HAVE VIOLATED THE MEDICAL PRACTICE ACT. SHALL NOT PETITION FOR REINSTATEMENT.

NEUFELD, NEWTON D DO OF SPRINGFIELD, MO, WAS DISCIPLINED BY MISSOURI ON MARCH 11, 1991.
DISCIPLINARY ACTION: 12-MONTH SURRENDER OF CONTROLLED SUBSTANCE LICENSE; 36-MONTH PROBATION
OFFENSE: OVERPRESCRIBING OR MISPRESCRIBING DRUGS
NOTES: WHILE LICENSED IN TEXAS, HE WROTE CONTROLLED DRUG PRESCRIPTIONS FOR A MISSOURI PATIENT; THE PRESCRIPTION DID NOT MEET ALL OF THE TECHNICAL REQUIREMENTS OF TEXAS LAW; HE DID NOT HAVE THE AUTHORITY TO PRESCRIBE CONTROLLED DRUGS IN MISSOURI; TEXAS ISSUED AN ORAL REPRIMAND.

NEUFELD, NEWTON D DO, LICENSE NUMBER 00C2895, OF SPRINGFIELD, MO, WAS DISCIPLINED BY TEXAS ON AUGUST 24, 1991.
DISCIPLINARY ACTION: SURRENDER OF LICENSE
NOTES: SURRENDER IN LIEU OF FURTHER DISCIPLINARY ACTION.

NEUFELD, NEWTON D DO OF MOUNT VERNON, MO, WAS DISCIPLINED BY MISSOURI ON APRIL 28, 1993.
DISCIPLINARY ACTION: 24-MONTH PROBATION
OFFENSE: DISCIPLINARY ACTION BY ANOTHER STATE OR AGENCY
NOTES: DISCIPLINE TAKEN BY TEXAS WHERE HE SURRENDERED HIS TEXAS MEDICAL LICENSE WITHOUT ADMITTING ANY VIOLATION OF TEXAS ADMINISTRATIVE PROCEDURES. PROBATION TIME ADDED TO PREVIOUS PROBATION.

NEWMAN, NICK J MD, LICENSE NUMBER 0076783, OF 1900 S COULTER, SUITE H, AMARILLO, TX, WAS DISCIPLINED BY DEA ON JANUARY 25, 1994.
DISCIPLINARY ACTION: RESTRICTION PLACED ON CONTROLLED SUBSTANCE LICENSE
OFFENSE: DRUG OR ALCOHOL ABUSE
NOTES: MEDICAL LICENSE SUSPENDED AROUND 7/89 FOR CHEMICAL DEPENDENCY IMPAIRMENT. USED XANAX SAMPLES TAKEN FROM PLACE OF EMPLOYMENT AROUND 6/93. REQUEST FOR SURRENDER OF REGISTRATION 10/20/93. REGISTRATION EXPIRED 10/31/93.

NEWMAN, NICK JAY MD, LICENSE NUMBER 00H8284, WAS DISCIPLINED BY TEXAS ON DECEMBER 4, 1991.
DISCIPLINARY ACTION: MONITORING OF PHYSICIAN
OFFENSE: DRUG OR ALCOHOL ABUSE
NOTES: ON 8/18/90 THE BOARD TERMINATED INDEFINITE SUSPENSION AND PLACED HIM ON PROBATION FOR THREE YEARS PROVIDING IN PART: SHALL SUBMIT FOR SCREENS OF BODILY FLUIDS; SHALL BE MONITORED BY BOARD-APPROVED PHYSICIAN WITH QUARTERLY REPORTS TO THE BOARD. HE NOW DESIRES TO RELOCATE AND FINDS THE MONITORING REQUIREMENTS BURDENSOME, AS WELL AS A BARRIER TO ADMISSION TO A RESIDENCY PROGRAM; THERE IS NO EVIDENCE THAT PRIOR INTEMPERATE USE CAUSED ANY PROBLEMS WITH PATIENT CARE; HE IS IN COMPLIANCE WITH EARLIER BOARD ORDER AND MONITORING PHYSICIAN FINDS HE CONTINUES TO FUNCTION WITHOUT DIFFICULTY. PREVIOUS ORDER MODIFIED SUCH THAT HE IS PLACED ON PROBATION FOR REMAINDER OF THREE YEAR PERIOD; MUST REFRAIN FROM USE OF CONTROLLED SUBSTANCES AND GIVE HIS TREATING PHYSICIAN A COPY OF THE ORDER; SHALL SUBMIT TO RANDOM BODILY FLUID SCREENS; SHALL PARTICIPATE IN AA OR OTHER BOARD-APPROVED PROGRAM, FREQUENCY DEPENDING ON AVAILABILITY OF PROGRAM WHERE HE RESIDES, WITH QUARTERLY REPORTS TO THE BOARD; SHALL GIVE A COPY OF THIS ORDER TO ALL INSTITUTIONS WHERE HE HAS PRIVILEGES; SHALL COOPERATE WITH THE BOARD IN VERIFYING COMPLIANCE; SHALL ADVISE THE BOARD OF ANY ADDRESS CHANGE WITHIN 10 DAYS; TIME SPENT OUT OF TEXAS DOES NOT COUNT TOWARDS PROBATION; SHALL NOT SEEK MODIFICATION OF THE ORDER FOR ONE YEAR.

NEWMAN, NICK JAY MD, LICENSE NUMBER 00H8284, OF TEMPLE, TX, WAS DISCIPLINED BY TEXAS ON OCTOBER 1, 1993.
DISCIPLINARY ACTION: LICENSE SUSPENSION
OFFENSE: FAILURE TO COMPLY WITH A PREVIOUS BOARD ORDER
NOTES: VIOLATED 8/18/90 AND 12/4/91 BOARD ORDERS IN THAT HE CONSUMED TWO SAMPLES OF XANAX THAT HE TOOK FROM THE MEDICINE CABINET OF THE FACILITY WHERE HE WAS EMPLOYED IN 6/93; APPEARED TO BE IMPAIRED WHILE PERFORMING MEDICAL DUTIES; ENTERED A CHEMICAL ABUSE PROGRAM AND WAS DISCHARGED 7/26/93. IN LIEU OF AN EMERGENCY SUSPENSION HEARING HE AGREED TO THE VOLUNTARY SUSPENSION OF HIS LICENSE PENDING COMPLETION OF SATISFACTORY INPATIENT TREATMENT AND SUBSEQUENT PROOF THAT HE IS COMPETENT TO PRACTICE; SHALL GIVE A COPY OF

THIS ORDER TO ANY HEALTH CARE ENTITY WHERE HE HAS PRIVILEGES; SHALL COOPERATE WITH THE BOARD IN VERIFYING COMPLIANCE; SHALL INFORM THE BOARD OF CHANGE OF ADDRESS WITHIN 10 DAYS.

NEWMAN, NICK JAY MD, LICENSE NUMBER 00H8284, OF TEMPLE, TX, WAS DISCIPLINED BY TEXAS ON JANUARY 5, 1995.
OFFENSE: DRUG OR ALCOHOL ABUSE
NOTES: SUSPENSION STAYED. LICENSE REINSTATED UNDER TERMS AND CONDITIONS FOR 10 YEARS.

NGUYEN, DUC TUE MD OF 1701 B WEBSTER, HOUSTON, TX, WAS DISCIPLINED BY DEA ON DECEMBER 14, 1993.
DISCIPLINARY ACTION: SURRENDER OF CONTROLLED SUBSTANCE LICENSE

NIX, DARRYL D DO, LICENSE NUMBER 00F9883, OF ARLINGTON, TX, WAS DISCIPLINED BY TEXAS ON JANUARY 6, 1995.
DISCIPLINARY ACTION: REPRIMAND; 36-MONTH REQUIRED TO TAKE ADDITIONAL MEDICAL EDUCATION
OFFENSE: FAILURE TO COMPLY WITH A PROFESSIONAL RULE
NOTES: FAILED TO KEEP ADEQUATE RECORDS OF HIS CARE AND TREATMENT OF ONE PATIENT; AGREED TO THIS ORDER IN LIEU OF FURTHER INVESTIGATION. CONDITIONS ON LICENSE FOR THREE YEARS: SHALL MAINTAIN ADEQUATE MEDICAL RECORDS ON ALL PATIENT OFFICE VISITS WHICH SHALL BE AVAILABLE FOR INSPECTION; SHALL OBTAIN AT LEAST 50 HOURS PER YEAR OF CONTINUING MEDICAL EDUCATION INCLUDING AT LEAST 25 HOURS IN RISK MANAGEMENT AND GENERAL OR ADDICTIVE PHARMACOLOGY; SHALL APPEAR BEFORE THE BOARD ONCE A YEAR; SHALL COOPERATE WITH THE BOARD IN VERIFYING COMPLIANCE; SHALL GIVE A COPY OF THIS ORDER TO ANY HEALTH CARE ENTITY WHERE HE HAS OR APPLIES FOR PRIVILEGES OR ANY ONE ELSE WHO REQUESTS IT; SHALL ENSURE ANY INQUIRIES REGARDING HIS TEXAS LICENSURE STATUS ARE ANSWERED BY REFERENCING THIS ORDER; SHALL INFORM BOARD OF CHANGE OF ADDRESS WITHIN 10 DAYS OR IF HE LEAVES THE STATE; TIME SPENT OUT OF TEXAS DOES NOT COUNT TOWARD RESTRICTION. SHALL NOT SEEK MODIFICATION FOR ONE YEAR.

NKONGHO, ANDREW L LACHE II MD, LICENSE NUMBER 00G4365, OF TEANECK, NJ, WAS DISCIPLINED BY TEXAS ON OCTOBER 1, 1993.
DISCIPLINARY ACTION: 24-MONTH PROBATION; MONITORING OF PHYSICIAN
OFFENSE: DISCIPLINARY ACTION BY ANOTHER STATE OR AGENCY
NOTES: ON 11/9/92 NEW YORK PLACED LICENSE ON PROBATION BASED ON 4 CASES OF INAPPROPRIATE OR INCORRECT SURGERY IN 1984 AND 1985 DURING OR AFTER WHICH THE PATIENTS DIED; ALSO IN 1986 PRACTICED WHILE IMPAIRED BY ALCOHOL; TEXAS LICENSE SUSPENSION STAYED. PLACED ON PROBATION UNDER THE TERMS AND CONDITIONS OF NEW YORK ORDER; ADDITIONAL PROBATIONARY CONDITIONS; PRIOR TO PRACTICING IN TEXAS SHALL OBTAIN PERMISSION FROM THE BOARD; ANYTIME SPENT OUTSIDE NEW YORK OR TEXAS DOES NOT COUNT TOWARD PROBATION; WHEN NEW YORK REMOVES RESTRICTIONS HE MAY APPLY TO HAVE TEXAS RESTRICTIONS REMOVED. SHALL NOT SEEK MODIFICATION FOR ONE YEAR.

NORDLUND, PAUL CLEMENS MD, LICENSE NUMBER 00D4247, OF UPLAND, CA, WAS DISCIPLINED BY TEXAS ON JUNE 17, 1992.
DISCIPLINARY ACTION: PROBATION
OFFENSE: DISCIPLINARY ACTION BY ANOTHER STATE OR AGENCY
NOTES: REVOCATION STAYED, PLACED ON PROBATION UNDER TERMS AND CONDITIONS FOR THE REST OF HIS LIFE.

NOVOSAD, CHARLES L JR MD OF 210 NORTH HIGHWAY 285, POJOAQUE, NM, WAS DISCIPLINED BY NEW MEXICO ON MAY 20, 1994.
DISCIPLINARY ACTION: LICENSE REVOCATION
OFFENSE: OVERPRESCRIBING OR MISPRESCRIBING DRUGS
NOTES: UNPROFESSIONAL CONDUCT; INJUDICIOUS PRESCRIBING.

NOVOSAD, CHARLES LOUIS JR MD, LICENSE NUMBER 00C4483, OF POJOAQUE, NM, WAS DISCIPLINED BY TEXAS ON JANUARY 6, 1995.
OFFENSE: DISCIPLINARY ACTION BY ANOTHER STATE OR AGENCY
NOTES: ON 5/20/94 NEW MEXICO BOARD REVOKED HIS LICENSE ON THE GROUNDS OF INJUDICIOUS PRESCRIBING TO SEVERAL PATIENTS; PRESENTLY SEEKING JUDICIAL REVIEW OF THIS ORDER. SHALL NOT PRACTICE IN TEXAS UNTIL HE REQUESTS PERMISSION IN WRITING FROM THE TEXAS BOARD TO RESUME PRACTICE, PERSONALLY APPEARS BEFORE THE BOARD AND PROVIDES SUFFICIENT EVIDENCE THAT HE IS PHYSICALLY, MENTALLY AND OTHERWISE COMPETENT TO PRACTICE INCLUDING AT A MINIMUM CERTIFICATION OF REVERSAL OF THE NEW MEXICO REVOCATION; SHALL COOPERATE WITH THE BOARD IN VERIFYING COMPLIANCE; SHALL INFORM BOARD OF CHANGE OF ADDRESS WITHIN 10 DAYS.

NUNNALLY, CLEON S MD, LICENSE NUMBER 00C6458, WAS DISCIPLINED BY TEXAS ON OCTOBER 5, 1991.
DISCIPLINARY ACTION: REPRIMAND
OFFENSE: FAILURE TO COMPLY WITH A PROFESSIONAL RULE
NOTES: PRESCRIBED DEMEROL TO HIS WIFE OUT OF OFFICE ACCOUNT, AND FAILED TO KEEP COMPLETE AND ACCURATE RECORDS TO SUPPORT THE USE OF DEMEROL IN HIS WIFE'S TREATMENT.

NUTT, CLINTON DEWITT DO, LICENSE NUMBER 00C3337, OF HOUSTON, TX, WAS DISCIPLINED BY TEXAS ON DECEMBER 1, 1988.
NOTES: SETTLEMENT AGREEMENT AND UNSPECIFIED DISCIPLINARY ACTION. ON 04/20/91, PROBATION TERMINATED; LICENSE FREE OF ANY RESTRICTION OR LIMITATION.

O'BRIEN, ROBERT BURNS MD, DATE OF BIRTH OCTOBER 2, 1927, LICENSE NUMBER 00C5818, OF 2600 N GESSNER SUITE 168, HOUSTON, TX, WAS DISCIPLINED BY TEXAS ON MARCH 26, 1993.
DISCIPLINARY ACTION: LICENSE REVOCATION
OFFENSE: LOSS OR RESTRICTION OF HOSPITAL PRIVILEGES
NOTES: ALLOWED HIS BROTHER TO PRACTICE IN HIS PLACE AND AS A PHYSICIAN'S ASSISTANT AFTER THE BROTHER'S MEDICAL LICENSE HAD BEEN REVOKED. IN 1/91 MEMORIAL MEDICAL CENTER RESTRICTED HIS HOSPITAL PRIVILEGES IN THAT HE WAS REQUIRED TO INITIATE APPROPRIATE CONSULTATIONS WITHIN 24 HOURS OF ADMITTING PATIENTS; VOLUNTARILY PLACED HIS PRIVILEGES ON 90 DAY SUSPENSION AFTER HE FAILED TO OBTAIN THESE CONSULTATIONS; ALSO WITH RESPECT TO 1 PATIENT HE WAS GUILTY OF MISDIAGNOSIS, GROSS MISMANAGEMENT AND A DELAY IN TREATMENT; HE REFUSED TO COOPERATE WITH THE BOARD'S INVESTIGATION. ORDER WILL BECOME FINAL

WHEN ALL APPEALS HAVE BEEN EXHAUSTED.

O'BRIEN, ROBERT BURNS MD, DATE OF BIRTH OCTOBER 2, 1927, OF 2600 N GESSNER SUITE 168, HOUSTON, TX, WAS DISCIPLINED BY MEDICARE ON AUGUST 30, 1994.
DISCIPLINARY ACTION: EXCLUSION FROM THE MEDICARE AND/OR MEDICAID PROGRAMS
OFFENSE: DISCIPLINARY ACTION BY ANOTHER STATE OR AGENCY
NOTES: LICENSE REVOKED FOR REASONS BEARING ON PROFESSIONAL COMPETENCE.

O'NEILL, PHILIP MD, LICENSE NUMBER 00D0586, OF ODESSA, TX, WAS DISCIPLINED BY TEXAS ON DECEMBER 5, 1988.
DISCIPLINARY ACTION: 60-MONTH REQUIRED TO ENTER AN IMPAIRED PHYSICIAN PROGRAM OR DRUG OR ALCOHOL TREATMENT; 60-MONTH MONITORING OF PHYSICIAN
OFFENSE: DRUG OR ALCOHOL ABUSE
NOTES: TO PARTICIPATE IN AA AND IMPAIRED PHYSICIAN GROUP PROGRAMS; SHALL SUBMIT HIMSELF FOR APPROPRIATE EXAMS TO DETERMINE FREEDOM FROM DRUGS AND ALCOHOL; SHALL OBTAIN RECOVERY ABUSE SPONSOR; SHALL ABSTAIN FROM ALCOHOL AND OTHER MOOD-ALTERING SUBSTANCES; SHALL APPEAR BEFORE THE BOARD UPON WRITTEN REQUEST. ON 12/04/91, RESTRICTIONS ON LICENSE REMOVED.

OBRIEN, RICHARD F MD, LICENSE NUMBER 00C5193, OF HOUSTON, TX, WAS DISCIPLINED BY TEXAS ON AUGUST 1, 1988.
DISCIPLINARY ACTION: LICENSE REVOCATION
OFFENSE: CRIMINAL CONVICTION OR PLEA OF GUILTY, NOLO CONTENDERE, OR NO CONTEST TO A CRIME
NOTES: CONVICTION OF FELONY

OCAMPO, JOSE MD OF TUCSON, AZ, WAS DISCIPLINED BY TEXAS ON DECEMBER 1, 1986.
DISCIPLINARY ACTION: LICENSE REVOCATION
OFFENSE: DISCIPLINARY ACTION BY ANOTHER STATE OR AGENCY

OFFUTT, DONALD NIXON MD, LICENSE NUMBER 00D5805, OF DALLAS, TX, WAS DISCIPLINED BY TEXAS ON APRIL 15, 1994.
DISCIPLINARY ACTION: 60-MONTH PROBATION; REQUIRED TO TAKE ADDITIONAL MEDICAL EDUCATION
OFFENSE: DRUG OR ALCOHOL ABUSE
NOTES: ADMITS HE IS AN ALCOHOLIC; VOLUNTARILY ADMITTED HIMSELF FOR INPATIENT TREATMENT ON 8/27/93; CURRENTLY MAINTAINING A HALF-TIME OUTPATIENT PSYCHIATRIC PRACTICE. SUSPENSION STAYED. CONDITIONS OF PROBATION: SHALL ABSTAIN FROM THE CONSUMPTION OF ALCOHOL/CHEMICAL SUBSTANCES IN ANY FORM UNLESS PRESCRIBED BY ANOTHER PHYSICIAN FOR A LEGITIMATE AND THERAPEUTIC PURPOSE; SHALL NOT TREAT OR OTHERWISE SERVE AS PHYSICIAN, PRESCRIBE, DISPENSE, OR ADMINISTER DRUGS THAT MAY BE SUBJECT TO ABUSE TO HIMSELF OR ANY MEMBER OF HIS FAMILY; SHALL PARTICIPATE IN AA'S PROGRAM NOT LESS THAN THREE TIMES A WEEK WITH QUARTERLY REPORTS TO THE BOARD AND SHALL INFORM THE BOARD OF HIS AA SPONSOR WITHIN 30 DAYS; SHALL SUBMIT HIMSELF FOR APPROPRIATE EXAMS INCLUDING DRUG OR ALCOHOL SCREENS; SHALL CONTINUE TO RECEIVE PSYCHIATRIC TREATMENT WITH QUARTERLY REPORTS; SHALL CONTINUE TO PARTICIPATE IN ACTIVITIES OF A PHYSICIAN HEALTH AND REHABILITATION COMMITTEE AND ATTEND WEEKLY MEETINGS WITH QUARTERLY REPORTS; SHALL ATTEND AT LEAST 50 HOURS PER YEAR OF CONTINUING MEDICAL EDUCATION INCLUDING COURSES IN ADDICTIONOLOGY AND SUBSTANCE ABUSE; SHALL PERFORM TWO HOURS PER MONTH OF COMMUNITY SERVICE FOR FIVE YEARS; PRIOR TO INCREASING HIS HOURS ABOVE HALFTIME OR ANY OTHER CHANGE IN THE NATURE OF HIS PRACTICE SHALL APPEAR BEFORE AND RECEIVE BOARD APPROVAL; SHALL APPEAR BEFORE THE BOARD FOUR TIMES A YEAR; SHALL GIVE A COPY OF THIS ORDER TO ANY HEALTH CARE ENTITY WHERE HE HAS PRIVILEGES; SHALL COOPERATE WITH THE BOARD IN VERIFYING COMPLIANCE; SHALL INFORM BOARD OF CHANGE OF ADDRESS WITHIN 10 DAYS OR IF HE LEAVES THE STATE; TIME SPENT OUT OF TEXAS DOES NOT COUNT TOWARD PROBATION. SHALL NOT SEEK MODIFICATION FOR ONE YEAR.

OGLE, ROBERT CURTIS DO, DATE OF BIRTH FEBRUARY 3, 1947, OF ROUTE 2 BOX 150, TENNESSEE COLONY, TX, WAS DISCIPLINED BY MEDICARE ON JULY 23, 1991.
DISCIPLINARY ACTION: 240-MONTH EXCLUSION FROM THE MEDICARE AND/OR MEDICAID PROGRAMS
OFFENSE: CRIMINAL CONVICTION OR PLEA OF GUILTY, NOLO CONTENDERE, OR NO CONTEST TO A CRIME
NOTES: CONVICTION RELATING TO FRAUD.

OGLE, ROBERT CURTIS DO OF 406 HERITAGE, ROCKWALL, TX, WAS DISCIPLINED BY DEA ON NOVEMBER 16, 1993.
DISCIPLINARY ACTION: RESTRICTION PLACED ON CONTROLLED SUBSTANCE LICENSE
OFFENSE: CRIMINAL CONVICTION OR PLEA OF GUILTY, NOLO CONTENDERE, OR NO CONTEST TO A CRIME
NOTES: DIVERTING 10,000+ DOSAGE UNTIS OF CONTROLLED SUBSTANCES MONTHLY THROUGH PRESCRIPTIONS FOR NONMEDICAL PURPOSES. PLED GUILTY 08/17/83 TO DISPENSING QUAALUDE NOT FOR MEDICAL PURPOSE AND SURRENDERED BD. SENTENCED 09/28/83 TO PRISON, SPECIAL PAROLE AND FINE. PREVIOUS REGISTRATION VOLUNTARILY SURRENDERED AND RETIRED 07/31/84. WITHDRAWAL OF APPLICATION 02/24/89. APPROVAL OF APPLICATION; RESTRICTED TO SCHEDULES III, IIIN, IV AND V.

OLSON, ROBERT J MD OF SPRINGFIELD, MO, WAS DISCIPLINED BY TEXAS ON JULY 1, 1986.
DISCIPLINARY ACTION: SURRENDER OF LICENSE

ORLOWSKI, FRANCIS JOHN DO, LICENSE NUMBER 00C2088, OF BEDFORD, TX, WAS DISCIPLINED BY TEXAS ON JUNE 12, 1990.
DISCIPLINARY ACTION: SURRENDER OF LICENSE
NOTES: STIPULATED ORDER. LICENSE IMMEDIATELY AND PERMANENTLY RETIRED IN LIEU OF INVESTIGATION AND SUBSEQUENT HEARING. MUST ALSO IMMEDIATELY SURRENDER CONTROLLED SUBSTANCE REGISTRATIONS AND TRIPLICATE PRESCRIPTION PADS.

ORLOWSKI, FRANK J DO OF 813 BROWN TRAIL STE 4, BEDFORD, TX, WAS DISCIPLINED BY DEA ON JUNE 26, 1990.
DISCIPLINARY ACTION: SURRENDER OF CONTROLLED SUBSTANCE LICENSE
NOTES: ALIASES FRANK A. ORLOWSKI, FRANK P. ORLOWSKI.

ORTEGA-MORA, JUAN ANTONIO MD, DATE OF BIRTH MARCH 6, 1943, LICENSE NUMBER 00E3593, OF PO BOX 111428, HOUSTON, TX, WAS DISCIPLINED BY TEXAS ON AUGUST 20, 1993.
DISCIPLINARY ACTION: 36-MONTH PROBATION; REPRIMAND
OFFENSE: LOSS OR RESTRICTION OF HOSPITAL PRIVILEGES

NOTES: ON 5/29/92 HOSPITAL PRIVILEGES WERE RESTRICTED BASED UPON PEER REVIEW OF 18 MEDICAL CHARTS WHICH FOCUSED ON ON-CALL EMERGENCY ROOM PEDIATRIC PATIENTS. RECORD KEEPING FOR THESE PATIENTS REFLECTED INADEQUATE DOCUMENTATION OF DAILY EVALUATION, MEDICAL CARE OR TREATMENT PLANS; HE WAS ALSO SEVERAL MONTHS LATE IN COMPLETING DISCHARGE SUMMARIES; AS A RESULT OF THIS REVIEW HE AGREED TO TERMINATE FUTURE ON-CALL DUTIES FOR THE EMERGENCY ROOM AND TO A SIX MONTH PROCTORSHIP WHEREBY HIS ADMITTANCE OF PATIENTS WERE REVIEWED BY A PROCTOR; NO INJURY OR ILLNESSES RESULTED FROM LAPSES OF DOCUMENTATION. THREE YEAR SUSPENSION STAYED. CONDITIONS OF PROBATION: SHALL APPEAR BEFORE THE BOARD ONCE A YEAR; SHALL ATTEND AT LEAST 50 HOURS PER YEAR OF CONTINUING MEDICAL EDUCATION INCLUDING AT LEAST ONE COURSE IN RISK MANAGEMENT DURING THE FIRST YEAR; HOSPITAL PRACTICE SHALL BE MONITORED BY A BOARD-APPROVED SUPERVISOR WITH REPORTS TO THE BOARD EVERY FOUR MONTHS; SHALL ATTEND FIVE HOURS OF AN ETHICS COURSE FOR ONE YEAR; SHALL NOT SIGN ANY PATIENT RECORD UNLESS HE HAS PERSONALLY EXAMINED THE PATIENT OR CLEARLY NOTES IN THE RECORD THAT HE DID NOT. SHALL GIVE A COPY OF THIS ORDER TO ANY HEALTH CARE ENTITY WHERE HE HAS PRIVILEGES; SHALL COOPERATE WITH THE BOARD IN VERIFYING COMPLIANCE; SHALL INFORM BOARD OF CHANGE OF ADDRESS WITHIN 10 DAYS OR IF HE LEAVES THE STATE; TIME SPENT OUT OF TEXAS DOES NOT COUNT TOWARD PROBATION. SHALL NOT SEEK MODIFICATION FOR ONE YEAR.

ORZECK, ERIC A MD, LICENSE NUMBER 00D6513, OF HOUSTON, TX, WAS DISCIPLINED BY TEXAS ON JULY 28, 1989.
DISCIPLINARY ACTION: 6-MONTH REQUIRED TO TAKE ADDITIONAL MEDICAL EDUCATION
NOTES: COMPLETE PRECEPTORSHIP ON PREVENTION AND TREATMENT OF DRUG ABUSE; TRAINING PROGRAM TO IMPROVE SKILLS IN PATIENT CHRONIC PAIN MANAGEMENT.

OTERO, HUMBERTO MD OF KENNER, LA, WAS DISCIPLINED BY LOUISIANA ON JANUARY 24, 1987.
DISCIPLINARY ACTION: EMERGENCY SUSPENSION
OFFENSE: SUBSTANDARD CARE, INCOMPETENCE, OR NEGLIGENCE

OTERO, HUMBERTO MD OF KENNER, LA, WAS DISCIPLINED BY LOUISIANA ON JUNE 1, 1987.
DISCIPLINARY ACTION: PROBATION; REQUIRED TO TAKE ADDITIONAL MEDICAL EDUCATION
OFFENSE: SUBSTANDARD CARE, INCOMPETENCE, OR NEGLIGENCE
NOTES: INABILITY TO PRACTICE MEDICINE WITH REASONABLE SKILL AND SAFETY OF PATIENTS. PROBATION TERMS: COMPLIANCE WITH TERMS OF AFTERCARE TREATMENT CONTRACT; PROFESSIONAL WORK HOURS RESTRICTED TO SPECIFIC SCHEDULE; 50 HOURS OF COMMUNITY MEDICAL EDUCATION ANNUALLY.

OTERO, HUMBERTO MD OF 5620 N UTICA STREET, METAIRIE, LA, WAS DISCIPLINED BY ILLINOIS ON AUGUST 1, 1988.
DISCIPLINARY ACTION: LICENSE SUSPENSION
OFFENSE: DISCIPLINARY ACTION BY ANOTHER STATE OR AGENCY
NOTES: INDEFINITE SUSPENSION; LICENSE ON PROBATION IN LOUISIANA FOR ALCOHOLISM.

OTERO, HUMBERTO MD OF KENNER, LA, WAS DISCIPLINED BY LOUISIANA ON OCTOBER 20, 1989.
DISCIPLINARY ACTION: LICENSE REVOCATION
OFFENSE: FAILURE TO COMPLY WITH A PREVIOUS BOARD ORDER
NOTES: ALCOHOL ABUSE, VIOLATION OF PREVIOUS CONSENT ORDER

OTERO, HUMBERTO MD, DATE OF BIRTH AUGUST 6, 1940, OF 3645 WILLIAMS BLVD #103, KENNER, LA, WAS DISCIPLINED BY MEDICARE ON APRIL 24, 1990.
DISCIPLINARY ACTION: EXCLUSION FROM THE MEDICARE AND/OR MEDICAID PROGRAMS
OFFENSE: DISCIPLINARY ACTION BY ANOTHER STATE OR AGENCY
NOTES: LICENSE REVOCATION OR SUSPENSION.

OTERO, HUMBERTO MD, DATE OF BIRTH AUGUST 6, 1940, LICENSE NUMBER 0006949, OF 76 GRANATA DRIVE, KENNER, LA, WAS DISCIPLINED BY MISSISSIPPI ON MAY 17, 1990.
DISCIPLINARY ACTION: LICENSE REVOCATION
OFFENSE: DISCIPLINARY ACTION BY ANOTHER STATE OR AGENCY

OTERO, HUMBERTO MD, LICENSE NUMBER 00E3079, OF KENNER, LA, WAS DISCIPLINED BY TEXAS ON JULY 1, 1990.
DISCIPLINARY ACTION: LICENSE REVOCATION
OFFENSE: DISCIPLINARY ACTION BY ANOTHER STATE OR AGENCY
NOTES: LOUISIANA LICENSE REVOKED.

OWENS, GUY MD, DATE OF BIRTH JANUARY 25, 1926, LICENSE NUMBER 0013413, OF 40 HART STREET, NEW BRITAIN, CT, WAS DISCIPLINED BY CONNECTICUT ON SEPTEMBER 18, 1990.
DISCIPLINARY ACTION: REPRIMAND; MONITORING OF PHYSICIAN
OFFENSE: SUBSTANDARD CARE, INCOMPETENCE, OR NEGLIGENCE
NOTES: INCOMPETENCE/NEGLIGENCE. WILL NEED WRITTEN CONSULTING OPINION FOR SURGICAL AND OTHER PROCEDURES; MUST KEEP DEPARTMENT NOTIFIED OF HIS PRIVILEGE STATUS.

OWENS, GUY MD, LICENSE NUMBER 00C4913, OF NEW BRITAIN, CT, WAS DISCIPLINED BY TEXAS ON JUNE 17, 1992.
DISCIPLINARY ACTION: RESTRICTION PLACED ON LICENSE
OFFENSE: DISCIPLINARY ACTION BY ANOTHER STATE OR AGENCY

OWENS, RONALD HUBERT DO, LICENSE NUMBER 00C9475, OF DALLAS, TX, WAS DISCIPLINED BY TEXAS ON JANUARY 12, 1991.
DISCIPLINARY ACTION: LICENSE SUSPENSION
OFFENSE: PHYSICAL OR MENTAL ILLNESS INHIBITING THE ABILITY TO PRACTICE WITH SKILL AND SAFETY
NOTES: MUST BEGIN AND CONTINUE PSYCHIATRIC EVALUATION AND TREATMENT; SUSPENSION TO CONTINUE UNTIL SUCH TIME AS HE CAN SHOW BOARD HE IS NO LONGER IMPAIRED BY MENTAL CONDITION AND CAN PRACTICE MEDICINE WITH REASONABLE SKILL AND SAFETY TO PATIENTS.

PARET, ROBERT W MD, LICENSE NUMBER 00D6915, OF OAK RIDGE, TN, WAS DISCIPLINED BY TEXAS ON MARCH 6, 1992.
DISCIPLINARY ACTION: 48-MONTH PROBATION
OFFENSE: PROFESSIONAL MISCONDUCT
NOTES: UNPROFESSIONAL OR DISHONORABLE CONDUCT LIKELY TO DECEIVE, DEFRAUD OR INJURE THE PUBLIC. LICENSE SUSPENDED, SUSPENSION STAYED. ON 04/08/93, TERMINATION OF PROBATION GRANTED. LICENSE FREE AND CLEAR OF ANY RESTRICTIONS AND

LIMITATIONS.

PARIKH, KIRAN RAJEN MD, LICENSE NUMBER 00G5825, OF RICHMOND, TX, WAS DISCIPLINED BY TEXAS ON OCTOBER 5, 1991.
DISCIPLINARY ACTION: 60-MONTH PROBATION; REQUIRED TO TAKE ADDITIONAL MEDICAL EDUCATION
OFFENSE: SUBSTANDARD CARE, INCOMPETENCE, OR NEGLIGENCE
NOTES: FAILED TO REFER PATIENT TO AN OPHTHALMOLOGIST IN A TIMELY FASHION AND DEMONSTRATED EXTREMELY POOR DOCUMENTATION IN PATIENT'S CHART. FIVE YEAR SUSPENSION STAYED; CONDITIONS OF PROBATION: SHALL ATTEND AT LEAST HOURS PER YEAR OF CATEGORY I CONTINUING MEDICAL EDUCATION WITH VERIFICATION TO BOARD; SHALL CONSULT WITH AN OPHTHALMOLOGIST WITHIN 7 DAYS OF ANY NONRESPONSIVE EYE PROBLEM; SHALL MAINTAIN ADEQUATE MEDICAL RECORDS ON ALL OFFICE VISITS AND MAKE THESE AVAILABLE TO BOARD; SHALL NOT MAKE ANY NOTES ON PATIENT RECORD UNLESS HAS PERSONALLY SEEN AND EXAMINED THE PATIENT UNLESS EXCEPTIONS ARE NOTED IN THE RECORD; SHALL PERSONALLY EXAMINE PATIENT DURING FIRST VISIT AND WHEN A DIAGNOSIS OF A NEW OR DIFFERENT DISEASE OR INJURY OCCURS; SHALL COOPERATE WITH BOARD IN VERIFYING COMPLIANCE; SHALL ADVISE BOARD OF ADDRESS CHANGE WITHIN 10 DAYS; TIME SPENT OUT OF TEXAS DOES NOT COUNT TOWARD PROBATION; SHALL APPEAR BEFORE THE BOARD TWICE A YEAR; SHALL NOT SEEK MODIFICATION OF THE ORDER FOR ONE YEAR. PROBATION TERMINATED ON 11/19/93.

PARKER, WAYLON M MD, LICENSE NUMBER 00G7301, OF GULFPORT, MS, WAS DISCIPLINED BY TEXAS ON AUGUST 19, 1994.
DISCIPLINARY ACTION: SURRENDER OF LICENSE
OFFENSE: OVERPRESCRIBING OR MISPRESCRIBING DRUGS
NOTES: ALLEGATIONS OF NON-THERAPEUTIC PRESCRIBING; HE DOES NOT ADMIT THIS BUT WISHES TO AVOID EXPENSE OF LITIGATION; SURRENDER IN LIEU OF FURTHER INVESTIGATION. SHALL NOT PETITION FOR REINSTATEMENT OF LICENSE.

PARSONS, JAMES T MD, LICENSE NUMBER 00C6816, OF HOUSTON, TX, WAS DISCIPLINED BY TEXAS ON JANUARY 26, 1990.
DISCIPLINARY ACTION: RESTRICTION PLACED ON LICENSE
NOTES: STIPULATED ORDER. MUST LIMIT PRACTICE OF MEDICINE TO OFFICE PRACTICE AND PERFORM NO ENDOSCOPIC PROCEDURES.

PARSONS, JAMES T MD, LICENSE NUMBER 0C24969, OF HOUSTON, TX, WAS DISCIPLINED BY CALIFORNIA ON APRIL 12, 1992.
DISCIPLINARY ACTION: SURRENDER OF LICENSE
NOTES: VOLUNTARY SURRENDER WHILE CHARGES PENDING.

PARSONS, JAMES T MD, LICENSE NUMBER 00C6816, OF HOUSTON, TX, WAS DISCIPLINED BY TEXAS ON JUNE 22, 1994.
DISCIPLINARY ACTION: 120-MONTH PROBATION; REQUIRED TO TAKE ADDITIONAL MEDICAL EDUCATION
OFFENSE: PROFESSIONAL MISCONDUCT
NOTES: ON 10/20/92 PERFORMED AN UNNECESSARY TENDON REPAIR ON ONE PATIENT; HIS OFFICE STAFF ERRONEOUSLY BILLED THE PATIENT FOR A SECOND PROCEDURE AS WELL; HE ALSO HAD NO MEDICAL RECORDS FOR TWO PATIENTS WHO PHARMACY RECORDS SHOW HAD PRESCRIPTIONS FROM HIM; HE HAD FAILED TO ADEQUATELY SUPERVISE ACTIVITIES OF HIS OFFICE NURSE, THEREBY ALLOWING HER TO CALL IN THE PRESCRIPTIONS USING HIS DEA NUMBER; FIRED THE NURSE UPON LEARNING OF THIS; 1/26/90 ORDER IS INDEPENDENT OF THIS ORDER; TEN YEAR SUSPENSION STAYED. CONDITIONS OF PROBATION: SHALL APPEAR BEFORE THE BOARD TWICE A YEAR; SHALL ATTEND AT LEAST 50 HOURS PER YEAR OF CONTINUING MEDICAL EDUCATION FOR EACH YEAR OF PROBATION AND SIX HOURS PER YEAR OF AN ETHICS COURSE FOR TWO YEARS; SHALL ADEQUATELY SUPERVISE ALL OF HIS EMPLOYEES; SHALL PERFORM EIGHT HOURS PER MONTH OF COMMUNITY SERVICE FOR FOUR YEARS; WITHIN ONE YEAR SHALL PASS THE JURISPRUDENCE EXAM; SHALL GIVE A COPY OF THIS ORDER TO ANY HEALTH CARE ENTITY WHERE HE HAS PRIVILEGES; SHALL COOPERATE WITH THE BOARD IN VERIFYING COMPLIANCE; SHALL INFORM BOARD OF CHANGE OF ADDRESS WITHIN 10 DAYS OR IF HE LEAVES THE STATE; TIME SPENT OUT OF TEXAS DOES NOT COUNT TOWARD PROBATION. SHALL NOT SEEK MODIFICATION FOR ONE YEAR.

PASKOW, JAMES ANDREW MD, DATE OF BIRTH JANUARY 19, 1960, LICENSE NUMBER 00H8790, OF 38 DEERFERN PLACE, THE WOODLANDS, TX, WAS DISCIPLINED BY TEXAS ON APRIL 30, 1993.
DISCIPLINARY ACTION: REPRIMAND
OFFENSE: PROFESSIONAL MISCONDUCT
NOTES: DURING THE SECOND YEAR IN A FAMILY PRACTICE PROGRAM ON 4/7/91 PERFORMED A C-SECTION ON A PATIENT DURING WHICH HORSEPLAY ENSUED; HE DISCHARGED A STAPLING GUN INTO HIS SUPERVISING PHYSICIAN'S ARM; CLAIMED THIS WAS AN ACCIDENT; AS A RESULT WAS NOT ALLOWED TO PERFORM C-SECTIONS FOR 3 MONTHS. HE UNDERSTANDS THE SERIOUSNESS OF THE INCIDENT AND ADMITS THAT THE INCIDENT DEMONSTRATED A LACK OF GOOD JUDGEMENT. SHALL GIVE A COPY OF THIS ORDER TO ANY HEALTH CARE ENTITY WHERE HE HAS PRIVILEGES; SHALL COOPERATE WITH THE BOARD IN VERIFYING COMPLIANCE; SHALL INFORM BOARD OF CHANGE OF ADDRESS WITHIN 10 DAYS.

PASSIAS, JAMES N DO OF NEWARK, OH, WAS DISCIPLINED BY OHIO ON MARCH 10, 1989.
NOTES: CONSENT AGREEMENT, UNSPECIFIED

PASSIAS, JAMES N DO, LICENSE NUMBER 00H2078, OF NEWARK, OH, WAS DISCIPLINED BY TEXAS ON JULY 28, 1989.
DISCIPLINARY ACTION: 36-MONTH REQUIRED TO ENTER AN IMPAIRED PHYSICIAN PROGRAM OR DRUG OR ALCOHOL TREATMENT; 36-MONTH MONITORING OF PHYSICIAN
NOTES: SUBMIT TO PSYCHIATRIC EVALUATION; MEDICAL PRACTICE MONITORED BY PHYSICIAN; ALCOHOL/DRUG SCREENING; PARTICIPATE IN ALCOHOLICS OR NARCOTICS ANONYMOUS.

PASSIAS, JAMES N DO, LICENSE NUMBER A006534, OF 2709 MARY LANE, PORT NECHES, TX, WAS DISCIPLINED BY DEA ON DECEMBER 5, 1989.
DISCIPLINARY ACTION: SURRENDER OF CONTROLLED SUBSTANCE LICENSE
OFFENSE: DRUG OR ALCOHOL ABUSE
NOTES: ON PROBATION WITH STATE MEDICAL BOARD DUE TO CONTROLLED SUBSTANCE ABUSE. REGISTRATION RESTRICTED 11/21/89; VOLUNTARY SURRENDER OF

REGISTRATION 12/05/89.

PASSIAS, JAMES N DO OF NEWARK, OH, WAS DISCIPLINED BY MISSOURI ON DECEMBER 20, 1989.
DISCIPLINARY ACTION: 60-MONTH PROBATION
OFFENSE: LOSS OR RESTRICTION OF HOSPITAL PRIVILEGES

PASSIAS, JAMES N DO, LICENSE NUMBER 0004232, OF DUBLIN, OH, WAS DISCIPLINED BY OHIO ON DECEMBER 22, 1989.
DISCIPLINARY ACTION: RESTRICTION PLACED ON LICENSE; RESTRICTION PLACED ON CONTROLLED SUBSTANCE LICENSE
OFFENSE: DRUG OR ALCOHOL ABUSE
NOTES: REVISED CONSENT AGREEMENT IMPOSING CONDITIONS ON PRACTICE DUE TO HISTORY OF CHEMICAL DEPENDENCY, DEA LIMITATIONS. ON 6/13/91 PROBATION TERMINATED; LICENSE TO PRACTICE UNRESTRICTED.

PATEL, RAMESHBHAI F MD, LICENSE NUMBER 0036995, WAS DISCIPLINED BY MICHIGAN ON AUGUST 10, 1989.
DISCIPLINARY ACTION: LICENSE REVOCATION

PATEL, RAMESHBHAI F MD, DATE OF BIRTH DECEMBER 9, 1943, OF REG 10479039 FED CORR INST, FT WORTH, TX, WAS DISCIPLINED BY MEDICARE ON DECEMBER 3, 1991.
DISCIPLINARY ACTION: 120-MONTH EXCLUSION FROM THE MEDICARE AND/OR MEDICAID PROGRAMS
OFFENSE: CRIMINAL CONVICTION OR PLEA OF GUILTY, NOLO CONTENDERE, OR NO CONTEST TO A CRIME
NOTES: PROGRAM-RELATED CONVICTION.

PATRICK, JOSEPH J MD OF HOUSTON, TX, WAS DISCIPLINED BY OHIO ON FEBRUARY 8, 1989.
DISCIPLINARY ACTION: LICENSE SUSPENSION
NOTES: INDEFINITE SUSPENSION

PATRICK, JOSEPH J MD, LICENSE NUMBER 0G41400, OF HOUSTON, TX, WAS DISCIPLINED BY CALIFORNIA ON SEPTEMBER 26, 1992.
DISCIPLINARY ACTION: SURRENDER OF LICENSE
NOTES: VOLUNTARY SURRENDER WHILE CHARGES PENDING.

PATTEN, EDWARD L MD, DATE OF BIRTH JANUARY 16, 1949, OF 3332 SOUTHMORE BLVD & CIR, HOUSTON, TX, WAS DISCIPLINED BY MEDICARE ON MAY 24, 1991.
DISCIPLINARY ACTION: 240-MONTH EXCLUSION FROM THE MEDICARE AND/OR MEDICAID PROGRAMS
OFFENSE: CRIMINAL CONVICTION OR PLEA OF GUILTY, NOLO CONTENDERE, OR NO CONTEST TO A CRIME
NOTES: PROGRAM-RELATED CONVICTION.

PATTEN, EDWARD LEE MD, LICENSE NUMBER 00F0282, OF HOUSTON, TX, WAS DISCIPLINED BY TEXAS ON JANUARY 12, 1991.
DISCIPLINARY ACTION: SURRENDER OF CONTROLLED SUBSTANCE LICENSE; PROBATION
OFFENSE: CRIMINAL CONVICTION OR PLEA OF GUILTY, NOLO CONTENDERE, OR NO CONTEST TO A CRIME
NOTES: PLACED ON PROBATION FOR THE PENDENCY OF HIS APPEAL FROM HIS U.S. DISTRICT COURT CONVICTION UNDER CONDITIONS INCLUDING: RESTRICTION OF MEDICAL LICENSE TO PRACTICE OF MEDICINE AT RIVERSIDE HOSPITAL, HOUSTON, TEXAS, BUT NOT TO PRACTICE SURGERY; SURRENDER CONTROLLED SUBSTANCES REGISTRATION CERTIFICATES AND NOT ATTEMPT TO REREGISTER OR OBTAIN REGISTRATIONS WITHOUT PRIOR WRITTEN AUTHORITY FROM BOARD; SUBMIT TO APPROPRIATE EXAMINATIONS TO DETERMINE FREEDOM FROM DRUGS AND ALCOHOL.

PATTEN, EDWARD LEE MD, LICENSE NUMBER 00F0282, OF HOUSTON, TX, WAS DISCIPLINED BY TEXAS ON OCTOBER 5, 1991.
DISCIPLINARY ACTION: LICENSE SUSPENSION
OFFENSE: CRIMINAL CONVICTION OR PLEA OF GUILTY, NOLO CONTENDERE, OR NO CONTEST TO A CRIME
NOTES: ORDER OF PROBATION OF 1/12/91 EXPIRED WHEN HE WAS INCARCERATED ON ABOUT 3/11/91; IS SERVING A PRISON TERM OF 84 MONTHS. LICENSE SUSPENDED WHILE HE IS IN PRISON.

PEAKE, REGINALD T MD, LICENSE NUMBER 00E2780, OF MIDLAND, TX, WAS DISCIPLINED BY TEXAS ON OCTOBER 1, 1987.
DISCIPLINARY ACTION: 60-MONTH PROBATION; COMMUNITY SERVICE
OFFENSE: PROFESSIONAL MISCONDUCT
NOTES: EXHIBITED UNPROFESSIONAL OR DISHONORABLE CONDUCT LIKELY TO DECEIVE, DEFRAUD OR INJURE PUBLIC; AIDED OR ABETTED PRACTICE OF MEDICINE BY PERSON, PARTNERSHIP, ASSOCIATION OR CORPORATION NOT DULY LICENSED BY BOARD TO PRACTICE MEDICINE. MUST PROVIDE 30 DAYS FREE PUBLIC SERVICE TO COMMUNITY.

PEARL, CONRAD R DO, DATE OF BIRTH DECEMBER 19, 1931, LICENSE NUMBER 0004524, OF 27676 CHERRY HILL ROAD, GARDEN CITY, MI, WAS DISCIPLINED BY MICHIGAN ON NOVEMBER 17, 1993.
DISCIPLINARY ACTION: 6-MONTH SUSPENSION OF CONTROLLED SUBSTANCE LICENSE; FINE
OFFENSE: PROFESSIONAL MISCONDUCT
NOTES: DRUG RELATED. DRUG CONTROL LICENSE REVOKED; $2,500 FINE.

PEARL, CONRAD R DO, DATE OF BIRTH DECEMBER 19, 1931, LICENSE NUMBER 0004524, OF 27676 CHERRY HILL ROAD, GARDEN CITY, MI, WAS DISCIPLINED BY MICHIGAN ON DECEMBER 2, 1993.
DISCIPLINARY ACTION: 12-MONTH PROBATION; FINE
OFFENSE: SUBSTANDARD CARE, INCOMPETENCE, OR NEGLIGENCE
NOTES: NEGLIGENCE/INCOMPETENCE. $2,500 FINE; LICENSE LIMITED.

PEARL, CONRAD ROBERT DO, LICENSE NUMBER 00D6842, OF GARDEN CITY, MI, WAS DISCIPLINED BY TEXAS ON JANUARY 6, 1995.
DISCIPLINARY ACTION: SURRENDER OF LICENSE
NOTES: IN LIEU OF FURTHER INVESTIGATION OR A HEARING ON ALLEGATIONS THAT HE VIOLATED THE MEDICAL PRACTICE ACT. SHALL NOT PETITION FOR REINSTATEMENT.

PEARSON, LYNN L MD OF JASPER, TX, WAS DISCIPLINED BY DEA ON JULY 1, 1994.
DISCIPLINARY ACTION: DENIAL OF NEW LICENSE
OFFENSE: CRIMINAL CONVICTION OR PLEA OF GUILTY, NOLO CONTENDERE, OR NO CONTEST TO A CRIME
NOTES: IN 5/86 CONVICTED OF TWO FELONY COUNTS OF THE UNLAWFUL DISPENSING OF PERCODAN, DILAUDID AND DOLOPHINE, ALL SCHEDULE II CONTROLLED SUBSTANCES. DEA REGISTRATION REVOKED 7/31/87; ON 2/8/88 TEXAS BOARD ORDERED THAT HIS MEDICAL LICENSE BE REVOKED, STAYED THAT REVOCATION, AND PLACED HIS LICENSE TO PRACTICE MEDICINE ON PROBATION FOR TWO YEARS. LIMITED HIM TO

PRACTICE MEDICINE WITHOUT PAY AT A LOCAL COMMUNITY HEALTH CENTER AND PROHIBITED HIM FOR POSSESSING, DISPENSING OR PRESCRIBING ANY CONTROLLED SUBSTANCE; REISSUED CONTROLLED SUBSTANCE REGISTRATION 2/92 AND ABLE TO APPLY FOR SCHEDULE II THROUGH V.

PEARSON, LYNN LANIER MD, LICENSE NUMBER 00D4441, OF WEBSTER, TX, WAS DISCIPLINED BY TEXAS ON OCTOBER 1, 1987.
DISCIPLINARY ACTION: LICENSE REVOCATION
OFFENSE: CRIMINAL CONVICTION OR PLEA OF GUILTY, NOLO CONTENDERE, OR NO CONTEST TO A CRIME
NOTES: CONVICTED OF FELONY INVOLVING CONTROLLED SUBSTANCES.

PEARSON, LYNN LANIER MD, LICENSE NUMBER 00D4441, OF SEABROOK, TX, WAS DISCIPLINED BY TEXAS ON AUGUST 1, 1988.
DISCIPLINARY ACTION: 120-MONTH PROBATION
OFFENSE: CRIMINAL CONVICTION OR PLEA OF GUILTY, NOLO CONTENDERE, OR NO CONTEST TO A CRIME
NOTES: CONVICTED OF FELONY INVOLVING CONTROLLED SUBSTANCES. REVOCATION STAYED. STAY OF REVOCATION CONTINGENT UPON US DISTRICT COURT DECISION AS TO WHETHER OR NOT TO INCARCERATE RESPONDENT. IF INCARCERATION OCCURS, STAY OF REVOCATION BECOMES NULL AND VOID SIMULTANEOUS TO COURT ORDER OF INCARCERATION, AND REVOCATION OF LICENSE IN EFFECT FROM DATE OF BOARD ORDER. NOT YET SENTENCED AS OF APRIL 1990.

PENNINGTON, KAREN MD, LICENSE NUMBER 00E4592, OF KNOX CITY, TX, WAS DISCIPLINED BY TEXAS ON NOVEMBER 3, 1994.
DISCIPLINARY ACTION: LICENSE SUSPENSION
OFFENSE: DRUG OR ALCOHOL ABUSE
NOTES: ALLEGATIONS INVOLVING INTEMPERATE USE OF ALCOHOL OR DRUGS THAT COULD ENDANGER THE LIVES OF PATIENTS AND INABILITY TO PRACTICE WITH REASONABLE SKILL AND SAFETY; ON 9/21/94 AT HER REQUEST WAS TAKEN TO HOSPITAL WITH AN INITIAL DIAGNOSIS OF GASTROINTESTINAL BLEEDING, WEIGHT LOSS AND PNEUMONIA AND WAS CONSIDERED CRITICALLY ILL: ILLNESS IS A RESULT OF HER SELF-PRESCRIBING OF TYLENOL #4, DARVOCET AND PERCODAN WITHOUT A LEGITIMATE MEDICAL PURPOSE; STATES SHE BEGAN SELF-PRESCRIBING FOUR OR FIVE MONTHS AGO FOR ABDOMINAL PAIN; PREVIOUS SANCTIONS WERE 12/11/78 SUSPENSION FOR SELF-PRESCRIBING, 12/9/79 PROBATION, 8/28/82 REVOCATION DUE TO VIOLATION OF THE PROBATION; 5/24/90 LICENSE REINSTATED WITHOUT RESTRICTION. SUSPENSION UNTIL SHE PERSONALLY APPEARS BEFORE THE BOARD AND PROVIDES SUFFICIENT EVIDENCE THAT SHE IS PHYSICALLY, MENTALLY AND OTHERWISE COMPETENT TO SAFELY PRACTICE INCLUDING BUT NOT LIMITED TO MEDICAL RECORDS AND REPORTS OF PSYCHOLOGICAL AND NEUROPSYCHIATRIC EVALUATIONS.

PEREZ, DONALD H MD, LICENSE NUMBER 00E2316, OF SAN ANTONIO, TX, WAS DISCIPLINED BY TEXAS ON DECEMBER 1, 1989.
DISCIPLINARY ACTION: LICENSE SUSPENSION
OFFENSE: PHYSICAL OR MENTAL ILLNESS INHIBITING THE ABILITY TO PRACTICE WITH SKILL AND SAFETY
NOTES: MENTAL CONDITION; LICENSE SUSPENDED UNTIL BOARD CAN BE SHOWN HE IS NO LONGER IMPAIRED.

PETRUS, EDWARD J JR MD, LICENSE NUMBER 00D6520, OF AUSTIN, TX, WAS DISCIPLINED BY TEXAS ON DECEMBER 1, 1988.
DISCIPLINARY ACTION: 24-MONTH PROBATION; COMMUNITY SERVICE
OFFENSE: CRIMINAL CONVICTION OR PLEA OF GUILTY, NOLO CONTENDERE, OR NO CONTEST TO A CRIME
NOTES: REVOCATION STAYED. PROBATION CONDITIONS INCLUDE COMMUNITY SERVICE CONTRIBUTION. CONVICTED OF FELONY INVOLVING MEDICARE AND MEDICAID VIOLATIONS AND OBSTRUCTION OF JUSTICE.

PETTEY, THOMAS D MD, LICENSE NUMBER 00G9187, OF FORT WORTH, TX, WAS DISCIPLINED BY TEXAS ON AUGUST 18, 1990.
DISCIPLINARY ACTION: 60-MONTH PROBATION; RESTRICTION PLACED ON LICENSE
NOTES: STIPULATED ORDER. MUST OBTAIN CONTINUING MEDICAL EDUCATION, ALLOW RANDOM REVIEW BY BOARD STAFF OF OFFICE PATIENT RECORDS TO ENSURE COMPLIANCE WITH ORDER AND TO ASCERTAIN THAT DOCUMENTATION HAS IMPROVED, AND REFRAIN FROM OBSTETRICS PRACTICE UNTIL PERMITTED TO DO SO BY BOARD (SUCH RESTRICTION INDEPENDENT OF AND SHALL SURVIVE PROBATIONARY PERIOD).

PETTEY, THOMAS DAVID MD, LICENSE NUMBER 0008789, OF FORT WORTH, TX, WAS DISCIPLINED BY MISSISSIPPI ON JANUARY 16, 1992.
DISCIPLINARY ACTION: PROBATION
OFFENSE: DISCIPLINARY ACTION BY ANOTHER STATE OR AGENCY
NOTES: ACTION TAKEN IN TEXAS. FIVE-YEAR SUSPENSION, EFFECTIVE AUGUST 7, 1991, STAYED.

PETTY, PRESTON D MD, LICENSE NUMBER C034876, OF BIG SPRING, TX, WAS DISCIPLINED BY CALIFORNIA ON MAY 8, 1989.
DISCIPLINARY ACTION: REPRIMAND
OFFENSE: DISCIPLINARY ACTION BY ANOTHER STATE OR AGENCY
NOTES: DISCIPLINE BY TEXAS MEDICAL BOARD

PETTY, PRESTON D MD, LICENSE NUMBER 0028630, OF ODESSA, TX, WAS DISCIPLINED BY FLORIDA ON OCTOBER 22, 1991.
DISCIPLINARY ACTION: REQUIRED TO TAKE ADDITIONAL MEDICAL EDUCATION
OFFENSE: DISCIPLINARY ACTION BY ANOTHER STATE OR AGENCY
NOTES: IF EVER RETURNS TO PRACTICE MEDICINE IN FLORIDA, HIS LICENSE SHALL BE RESTRICTED IN THAT HE SHALL NOT PRESCRIBE, ADMINISTER, DISPENSE, MIX, OR ORDER SCHEDULED DRUGS UNTIL HE COMPLETES THE COURSE: "PROTECTING YOUR MEDICAL PRACTICE, CLINICAL, LEGAL, AND ETHICAL ISSUES IN PRESCRIBING ABUSABLE DRUGS", OR A BOARD-APPROVED EQUIVALENT.

PHUOC, HO TAN MD, LICENSE NUMBER 00F7052, OF HOUSTON, TX, WAS DISCIPLINED BY TEXAS ON AUGUST 24, 1991.
DISCIPLINARY ACTION: RESTRICTION PLACED ON LICENSE
NOTES: MAY PERFORM CERTAIN PROCEDURES ON PATIENTS UNDER 12 ONLY IN HOSPITALS OR LICENSED SURGICAL CENTERS.

PIAZZA, KENNETH M MD, LICENSE NUMBER 00E8112, OF JASPER, TX, WAS DISCIPLINED BY TEXAS ON OCTOBER 29, 1988.
DISCIPLINARY ACTION: 120-MONTH PROBATION; 120-MONTH RESTRICTION PLACED ON CONTROLLED SUBSTANCE LICENSE
NOTES: SUSPENSION STAYED; SHALL NOT REREGISTER FOR CONTROLLED SUBSTANCES WITHOUT PRIOR BOARD APPROVAL; SHALL NOT TREAT PATIENTS FOR WEIGHT CONTROL WITH CONTROLLED SUBSTANCES OR OVER

THE COUNTER DRUGS, SHALL APPEAR FOR SEMI-ANNUAL REPORTS; SHALL OBTAIN 50 HOURS CONTINUING MEDICAL EDUCATION PER YEAR. ON 4/15/94 ORDER MODIFIED AS FOLLOWS: APPEARANCES BEFORE BOARD REDUCED TO ONCE A YEAR; HE IS GRANTED PERMISSION TO REAPPLY TO THE DRUG ENFORCEMENT ADMINISTRATION AND THE TEXAS DEPARTMENT OF PUBLIC SAFETY FOR SCHEDULES IV AND V CONTROLLED SUBSTANCES AUTHORITY; SEPARATE FROM PATIENT RECORDS, HE SHALL MAINTAIN A FILE CONSISTING OF A COPY OF EVERY PRESCRIPTION WRITTEN BY HIM FOR CONTROLLED SUBSTANCES AND FOR ANY DANGEROUS DRUGS WHICH HAVE ADDICTIVE QUALITIES WHICH SHALL BE AVAILABLE TO THE BOARD; SHALL NOT TELEPHONE ANY PRESCRIPTION TO A PHARMACY FOR ANY DANGEROUS DRUGS WHICH MAY BE HABIT-FORMING; SHALL NOT TREAT OR OTHERWISE SERVE AS PHYSICIAN, PRESCRIBE, DISPENSE OR ADMINISTER CONTROLLED SUBSTANCES OR ANY OTHER DRUGS THAT MAY BE SUBJECT TO ABUSE FOR HIMSELF OR ANY MBMER OF HIS FAMILY; MAY ADMINISTER SUCH DRUGS AS PRESCRIBED BY OTHER PHYSICIANS TO HIMSELF OR HIS FAMILY IN COMPLIANCE WITH THE ORDERS AND DIRECTIONS OF SUCH OTHER PHYSICIANS; SHALL NOT TREAT ANY PATIENT FOR WEIGHT CONTROL OR OBESITY WITH ANY CONTROLLED SUBSTANCES, DANGEROUS DRUGS OR OVER-THE-COUNTER DRUGS; MAY ONLY TREAT WEIGHT CONTROL PATIENTS WITH COUNSELING, DIET AND EXERCISE.

PIERSON, ROBERT L MD WAS DISCIPLINED BY NEBRASKA ON MARCH 13, 1986.
DISCIPLINARY ACTION: LICENSE REVOCATION

PIERSON, ROBERT L MD WAS DISCIPLINED BY IOWA ON AUGUST 15, 1986.
DISCIPLINARY ACTION: SURRENDER OF LICENSE
OFFENSE: CRIMINAL CONVICTION OR PLEA OF GUILTY, NOLO CONTENDERE, OR NO CONTEST TO A CRIME
NOTES: CONVICTION RELATED TO DRUG PRESCRIBING AND SEXUAL IMPROPRIETIES WITH PATIENT.

PIERSON, ROBERT L MD WAS DISCIPLINED BY NEBRASKA ON FEBRUARY 16, 1990.
DISCIPLINARY ACTION: RESTRICTION PLACED ON LICENSE

PIERSON, ROBERT L MD OF 7709 CAMBRIDGE, HOUSTON, TX, WAS DISCIPLINED BY VERMONT ON JULY 20, 1991.
DISCIPLINARY ACTION: DENIAL OF NEW LICENSE
OFFENSE: DISCIPLINARY ACTION BY ANOTHER STATE OR AGENCY
NOTES: HAD CRIMINAL CONVICTIONS FOR FAILING TO KEEP DRUG RECORDS REQUIRED BY LAW AND FOR SHOPLIFTING; VOLUNTARILY SURRENDERED IOWA LICENSE AFTER INVESTIGATION REVEALED EVIDENCE OF SEXUAL INVOLVEMENT WITH PATIENTS AND PRESCRIBING DEPO-PROVERA, WHICH WAS NOT FDA APPROVED FOR PURPOSES OF BIRTH CONTROL; NEBRASKA LICENSE REVOKED IN 1986 AND REINSTATED IN 1990 WITH MULTIPLE CONDITIONS; NORTH DAKOTA THEN DENIED HIS LICENSE APPLICATION.

PIERSON, ROBERT L MD, LICENSE NUMBER 0016506, OF GREENSBORO, AL, WAS DISCIPLINED BY ALABAMA ON JUNE 3, 1992.
DISCIPLINARY ACTION: RESTRICTION PLACED ON LICENSE
NOTES: IN CONNECTION WITH LICENSURE APPLICATION. MUST ABIDE BY REQUIREMENTS OF PHYSICIANS RECOVERY NETWORK.

PILLSBURY, CURTIS BRYANT MD, DATE OF BIRTH JANUARY 11, 1921, LICENSE NUMBER 00C2954, OF RICHARDSON, TX, WAS DISCIPLINED BY TEXAS ON MAY 20, 1989.
DISCIPLINARY ACTION: RESTRICTION PLACED ON LICENSE; REQUIRED TO TAKE ADDITIONAL MEDICAL EDUCATION
NOTES: SHALL NOT PRACTICE ANESTHESIA OR WEIGHT CONTROL MEDICINE OR HAVE DIRECT PATIENT CONTACT; SHALL BE LIMITED TO GIVING PHYSICALS, TAKING HISTORIES AND MAY WRITE PRESCRIPTIONS; SHALL SUBMIT TO PSYCHIATRIC EVALUATION AND FOLLOW RECOMMENDATIONS; SHALL APPLY TO TAKE SPECIAL PURPOSE EXAM. AND PASS; IF UNSUCCESSFUL, SHALL WITHDRAW FROM PRACTICE UNTIL PASSAGE

PILLSBURY, CURTIS BRYANT MD, DATE OF BIRTH JANUARY 11, 1921, LICENSE NUMBER 00C2954, OF 2803 TAM OSHANTER, RICHARDSON, TX, WAS DISCIPLINED BY TEXAS ON APRIL 30, 1993.
DISCIPLINARY ACTION: SURRENDER OF LICENSE
OFFENSE: FAILURE TO COMPLY WITH A PREVIOUS BOARD ORDER
NOTES: HAS HAD PRACTICAL DIFFICULTIES IN FULLY COMPLYING WITH TERMS OF 5/89 ORDER. SURRENDER IS PERMANENT.

PINO, WILBERT B MD, DATE OF BIRTH OCTOBER 11, 1961, OF 3817 QUILL COURT, EL PASO, TX, WAS DISCIPLINED BY MEDICARE ON APRIL 16, 1994.
DISCIPLINARY ACTION: EXCLUSION FROM THE MEDICARE AND/OR MEDICAID PROGRAMS
OFFENSE: FAILURE TO COMPLY WITH A PROFESSIONAL RULE
NOTES: DEFAULTED ON PUBLIC HEALTH SERVICE EDUCATION LOAN. REINSTATED ON 4/22/94.

PITTARD, CARLTON DUWAIN MD, DATE OF BIRTH DECEMBER 3, 1931, LICENSE NUMBER 00C6476, OF 1600 WEST COLLEGE SUITE 110, GRAPEVINE, TX, WAS DISCIPLINED BY TEXAS ON JUNE 15, 1993.
DISCIPLINARY ACTION: 60-MONTH PROBATION
OFFENSE: FAILURE TO COMPLY WITH A PROFESSIONAL RULE
NOTES: FAILED TO KEEP COMPLETE AND ACCURATE RECORDS OF THE PURCHASES AND DISPOSALS OF CONTROLLED SUBSTANCES, MAINTAIN AN INITIAL OR BIENNIAL INVENTORIES, MAINTAIN DISPENSATION CHARTS OF CONTROLLED SUBSTANCES, AND STORE SUCH DRUGS IN ACCORDANCE WITH FEDERAL AND STATE REQUIREMENTS; A 5/5/92 AUDIT NOTED MANY DEFICIENCIES IN THESE AREAS; IN 3/91 HE ORDERED SAMPLES OF TALWIN AND DISPENSED ENTIRE SUPPLY TO A PATIENT WHOSE SON USED THE DRUGS TO COMMIT SUICIDE; HAS SECURED THE ASSISTANCE OF A LAW FIRM IN BRINGING OFFICE INTO COMPLIANCE WITH STATE AND FEDERAL REGULATIONS. FIVE YEAR SUSPENSION STAYED. CONDITIONS OF PROBATION: SHALL MAINTAIN ADEQUATE MEDICAL RECORDS ON ALL PATIENT OFFICE VISITS AND MAKE THEM AVAILABLE FOR INSPECTION; SHALL COMPLY WITH ALL STATUES, RULES AND REGULATIONS PERTAINING TO THE PRESCRIBING, ADMINISTERING, DISPENSING OR SUPPLYING OF DANGEROUS DRUGS OR CONTROLLED SUBSTANCES; SHALL ADEQUATELY SUPERVISE THE ACTIVITIES OF ALL EMPLOYEES; SHALL APPEAR

BEFORE THE BOARD ONCE A YEAR; SHALL GIVE A COPY OF THIS ORDER TO ANY HEALTH CARE ENTITY WHERE HE HAS PRIVILEGES; SHALL COOPERATE WITH THE BOARD IN VERIFYING COMPLIANCE; SHALL INFORM BOARD OF CHANGE OF ADDRESS WITHIN 10 DAYS OR IF HE LEAVES THE STATE; TIME SPENT OUT OF TEXAS DOES NOT COUNT TOWARD PROBATION. SHALL NOT SEEK MODIFICATION FOR ONE YEAR. ON 8/19/94 REQUEST FOR TERMINATION WAS DENIED. ON 10/13/95 ORDER TERMINATED BASED ON COMPLIANCE WITH TERMS.

POEHLMANN, KURT S MD, LICENSE NUMBER 00D1771, OF COMANCHE, TX, WAS DISCIPLINED BY TEXAS ON JUNE 22, 1994.
DISCIPLINARY ACTION: RESTRICTION PLACED ON LICENSE; REQUIRED TO TAKE ADDITIONAL MEDICAL EDUCATION
OFFENSE: SUBSTANDARD CARE, INCOMPETENCE, OR NEGLIGENCE
NOTES: RESIGNED FROM A HOSPITAL WHILE PRIVILEGE STATUS WAS UNDER INVESTIGATION; FAILED TO PRACTICE IN AN ACCEPTABLE MANNER ON EIGHT PATIENTS INVOLVING OBSTETRICS AND MYOCARDIAL INFARCTIONS; EXERCISED POOR JUDGEMENT IN ALLOWING PATIENTS TO MAKE THE DECISION FOR SURGERY. LICENSE IS RESTRICTED IN THAT HE SHALL NOT PRACTICE OBSTETRICS AND GYNECOLOGY EXCEPT THAT WHICH MAY ARISE IN EITHER AN EMERGENCY ROOM OR GENERAL FAMILY PRACTICE SETTING NOR SHALL HE PRACTICE INPATIENT SURGERY EXCEPT WHEN ASSISTING; SHALL ATTEND AT LEAST 50 HOURS PER YEAR OF CONTINUING MEDICAL EDUCATION INCLUDING AT LEAST 20 HOURS PER YEAR IN CARDIOLOGY COURSES; SHALL APPEAR BEFORE THE BOARD ONCE A YEAR; SHALL WITHIN THREE MONTHS UNDERGO A COMPLETE PHYSICAL EXAM INCLUDING BUT NOT LIMITED TO AN OPHTHALMOLOGICAL AND NEUROPSYCHOLOGICAL EVALUATION BY BOARD-APPROVED PHYSICIANS; SHALL GIVE A COPY OF THIS ORDER TO ANY HEALTH CARE ENTITY WHERE HE HAS PRIVILEGES; SHALL COOPERATE WITH THE BOARD IN VERIFYING COMPLIANCE; SHALL INFORM BOARD OF CHANGE OF ADDRESS WITHIN 10 DAYS. SHALL NOT SEEK MODIFICATION FOR ONE YEAR.

POLINGER, IRIS SANDRA MD, LICENSE NUMBER 00E8117, OF STAFFORD, TX, WAS DISCIPLINED BY TEXAS ON JANUARY 24, 1992.
DISCIPLINARY ACTION: PROBATION
OFFENSE: PROFESSIONAL MISCONDUCT
NOTES: SEVERAL VIOLATIONS OF THE MEDICAL PRACTICE ACT, INCLUDING PERSISTENTLY AND FLAGRANTLY OVERCHARGING OR OVERTREATING PATIENTS. THREE-YEAR SUSPENSION, STAYED; PROBATION UNDER TERMS AND CONDITIONS. ON 3/5/94 PROBATION TERMINATED.

POLLNOW, ROBERT E MD, DATE OF BIRTH JANUARY 30, 1946, LICENSE NUMBER 0027751, OF 4205 SQUIRE DRIVE, BETTENDORF, IA, WAS DISCIPLINED BY IOWA ON FEBRUARY 4, 1992.
DISCIPLINARY ACTION: 60-MONTH PROBATION
OFFENSE: DRUG OR ALCOHOL ABUSE
NOTES: ALLEGATIONS OF EXCESSIVE USE OF ALCOHOL.

POLLNOW, ROBERT EDWARD MD, LICENSE NUMBER 0018141, WAS DISCIPLINED BY OKLAHOMA ON JUNE 26, 1992.
DISCIPLINARY ACTION: 60-MONTH PROBATION; RESTRICTION PLACED ON LICENSE
OFFENSE: DRUG OR ALCOHOL ABUSE
NOTES: EVIDENCE INDICATED THAT HE PREVIOUSLY MISUSED ALCOHOL; HAS COMPLETED APPROPRIATE SUBSTANCE ABUSE TREATMENT; PRESENTLY IN RECOVERY. LICENSE GRANTED UNDER PROBATIONARY TERMS AND CONDITIONS: SHALL NOT PRESCRIBE, ADMINISTER OR DISPENSE ANY MEDICATIONS FOR HIS PERSONAL USE; SHALL TAKE NO MEDICATION UNLESS PRESCRIBED BY TREATING PHYSICIAN; SHALL ABSTAIN FROM ALCOHOL OR ANY SUBSTANCE WHICH WOULD ADVERSELY AFFECT HIS ABILITY TO PRACTICE; SHALL SUBMIT BIOLOGICAL FLUID SPECIMENS FOR ANALYSIS; SHALL MAINTAIN FORMAL RELATIONSHIP WITH PHYSICIAN RECOVERY COMMITTEE AND PARTICIPATE IN THEIR MEETINGS AND ACTIVITIES; SHALL NOT SUPERVISE A PHYSICIAN ASSISTANT; SHALL FURNISH BOARD WITH ADDRESS AND/OR CHANGE OF ADDRESS; SHALL APPEAR BEFORE BOARD UPON REQUEST; SHALL NOTIFY ANY HOSPITAL WHERE HE HOLDS STAFF PRIVILEGES OR CLINIC OR GROUP OF THE TERMS AND CONDITIONS.

POLLNOW, ROBERT EDWARD MD, DATE OF BIRTH JANUARY 30, 1946, LICENSE NUMBER 00E2321, OF 4205 SQUIRE DRIVE, BETTENDORF, IA, WAS DISCIPLINED BY TEXAS ON APRIL 30, 1993.
DISCIPLINARY ACTION: 60-MONTH PROBATION; MONITORING OF PHYSICIAN
OFFENSE: DISCIPLINARY ACTION BY ANOTHER STATE OR AGENCY
NOTES: ON 1/23/92 PLACED ON PROBATION WITH CONDITIONS BY IOWA BOARD DUE TO ALCOHOL ABUSE; ON 7/2/92 HE WAS GRANTED LICENSURE BY OKLAHOMA ON PROBATION WITH CONDITIONS. FIVE YEAR SUSPENSION STAYED. CONDITIONS OF PROBATION: PRIOR TO PRACTICING IN TEXAS SHALL APPEAR BEFORE THE BOARD; SHALL PROVIDE THE TEXAS BOARD COPIES OF REPORTS SUBMITTED TO IOWA AND OKLAHOMA UPON REQUEST; SHALL PARTICIPATE IN ACTIVITIES OF A PHYSICIAN HEALTH AND REHABILITATION COMMITTEE AND ATTEND WEEKLY MEETINGS WITH QUARTERLY REPORTS; SHALL PARTICIPATE IN AA OR ANY SUBSTANTIALLY SIMILAR PROGRAM NOT LESS THAN TWICE A WEEK WITH QUARTERLY REPORTS TO THE BOARD; SHALL SUBMIT HIMSELF FOR APPROPRIATE EXAMS INCLUDING DRUG OR ALCOHOL SCREENS; SHALL SUBMIT HIMSELF FOR EVALUATION AND TREATMENT TO A BOARD-APPROVED PSYCHIATRIST; SHALL ABSTAIN FROM THE CONSUMPTION OF ALCOHOL/CHEMICAL SUBSTANCES IN ANY FORM; SHALL NOT TREAT OR OTHERWISE SERVE AS THE PHYSICIAN, PRESCRIBE, DISPENSE OR ADMINISTER DRUGS THAT MAY BE SUBJECT TO ABUSE FOR HIMSELF OR ANY MEMBER OF HIS FAMILY; SHALL FURNISH WRITTEN REPORTS TO THE BOARD REGARDING HIS MEDICAL CONDITION UPON REQUEST; SHALL GIVE A COPY OF THIS ORDER TO ANY HEALTH CARE ENTITY WHERE HE HAS PRIVILEGES; SHALL COOPERATE WITH THE BOARD IN VERIFYING COMPLIANCE; SHALL INFORM BOARD OF CHANGE OF ADDRESS WITHIN 10 DAYS OR IF HE LEAVES THE STATE; TIME SPENT OUT OF TEXAS DOES NOT COUNT TOWARD PROBATION. SHALL NOT SEEK MODIFICATION FOR ONE YEAR.

POLLNOW, ROBERT EDWARD MD, LICENSE NUMBER 0018141, WAS DISCIPLINED BY OKLAHOMA ON NOVEMBER 19, 1994.
OFFENSE: FAILURE TO COMPLY WITH A PREVIOUS BOARD ORDER
NOTES: CURRENTLY ON LEVEL II PROBATION WHICH REQUIRES

HIM TO SUBMIT MONTHLY COMPLIANCE REPORTS ON A TIMELY BASIS; HAS FAILED TO SUBMIT REPORTS ON A TIMELY BASIS. LICENSE PLACED ON LEVEL I PROBATION AND SHALL BE REVIEWED IN SIX MONTHS.

POPE, DONALD D MD, LICENSE NUMBER 00F4386, OF COLEMAN, TX, WAS DISCIPLINED BY TEXAS ON DECEMBER 1, 1988.
NOTES: SETTLEMENT AGREEMENT AND UNSPECIFIED DISCIPLINARY ACTION

PRANGLE, ROBERT E DO, DATE OF BIRTH JANUARY 30, 1944, LICENSE NUMBER 00D9870, OF 13310 BEAMER #G, HOUSTON, TX, WAS DISCIPLINED BY TEXAS ON JANUARY 29, 1993.
DISCIPLINARY ACTION: REPRIMAND
OFFENSE: OVERPRESCRIBING OR MISPRESCRIBING DRUGS
NOTES: NONTHERAPEUTICALLY PRESCRIBED EXCESSIVE AMOUNTS OF VICODIN AND FIORINAL TO A PATIENT WHEN HE KNEW SHE WAS HABITUATED TO THE MEDICATIONS AND FAILED TO KEEP ADEQUATE MEDICAL RECORDS FOR THIS PATIENT. SHALL GIVE A COPY OF THIS ORDER TO ANY HEALTH CARE ENTITY WHERE HE HAS PRIVILEGES; SHALL INFORM BOARD OF CHANGE OF ADDRESS WITHIN 10 DAYS.

PRATER, WILLIAM WARREN MD, LICENSE NUMBER 00F4390, OF PLANO, TX, WAS DISCIPLINED BY TEXAS ON AUGUST 19, 1994.
DISCIPLINARY ACTION: EMERGENCY SUSPENSION
OFFENSE: DRUG OR ALCOHOL ABUSE
NOTES: AVAILABLE EVIDENCE AND INFORMATION INDICATES: THAT HE IS CHEMICALLY DEPENDENT AND EXHIBITING BEHAVIOR WHICH CAUSES HIS CONTINUED PRACTICE TO CONSTITUTE A THREAT TO THE PUBLIC WELFARE; HAS ENGAGED IN THE USE OF VARIOUS MEDICATIONS INCLUDING NARCOTIC ANALGESICS, A STIMULANT, AN ANTIDEPRESSANT AND A BENZODIAZEPINE WITHOUT ANY LEGITIMATE MEDICAL OR THERAPEUTIC PURPOSE; HAS ENGAGED IN THE ILLEGAL USE OF VARIOUS STREET DRUGS INCLUDING COCAINE, MARIJUANA AND LSD; HAS ABANDONED HIS CARE OF ALL PATIENTS WITHOUT ADEQUATE NOTICE AND IN DOING SO MAY HAVE PUT THEM AT RISK; HAS WRITTEN FALSE OR FICTITIOUS PRESCRIPTIONS FOR DANGEROUS DRUGS IN THE NAMES OF OFFICE STAFF, PATIENTS, FRIENDS AND FAMILY WHICH HE DIVERTED FOR HIS OWN USE; FAILED TO KEEP ACCURATE RECORDS OF PURCHASES AND DISPOSALS OF LARGE QUANTITIES OF MEDICATIONS.

PUCEK, MARK DOUGLASS MD, DATE OF BIRTH JANUARY 5, 1956, LICENSE NUMBER 00G3707, OF 1414 S LOOP WEST #200, HOUSTON, TX, WAS DISCIPLINED BY TEXAS ON AUGUST 20, 1993.
DISCIPLINARY ACTION: 60-MONTH PROBATION; RESTRICTION PLACED ON LICENSE
OFFENSE: PROFESSIONAL MISCONDUCT
NOTES: IN 1990 ENTERED INTO A VERBAL CONTRACT WITH GALLERIA DIAGNOSTIC SERVICES TO EVALUATE PERSONAL INJURY PATIENTS; HE BILLED THEM FOR SERVICES RENDERED; THEY THEN BILLED INSURANCE COMPANIES FOR PATIENT TREATMENT FOR SOME SERVICES USING HIS NAME; HE SAID HE DID NOT KNOW THEY HAD DONE THIS; TWO PATIENTS WERE GIVEN EXCESSIVE TREATMENT WITHOUT PHYSICIANS ORDERS AND BILLING WAS ALSO EXCESSIVE. FIVE YEAR SUSPENSION STAYED. CONDITIONS OF PROBATION: SHALL APPEAR BEFORE THE BOARD TWICE A YEAR; SHALL ATTEND SIX HOURS OF AN ETHICS COURSE PER YEAR FOR TWO YEARS; SHALL UTILIZE AN ACCURATE SYSTEM OF PATIENT RECORD KEEPING; SHALL NOT ACCEPT EMPLOYMENT OR ENTER INTO CONTRACTUAL RELATIONSHIPS WHEREIN HE WOULD BE COMPENSATED TO DIAGNOSE AND/OR TREAT PATIENTS BY A LAYPERSON, CORPORATION, OR OTHER ENTITY NOT COMPRISED EXCLUSIVELY OF TEXAS LICENSED PHYSICIANS AND WHEREIN THE PERSON OR ENTITY WOULD RECEIVE AND RETAIN THE FEES PAID BY OR ON BEHALF OF PATIENTS FOR THE PHYSICIAN'S PROFESSIONAL SERVICES; SHALL GIVE A COPY OF THIS ORDER TO ALL HEALTH CARE ENTITIES WHERE HE HAS PRIVILEGES; SHALL COOPERATE WITH THE BOARD IN VERIFYING COMPLIANCE; SHALL INFORM BOARD OF CHANGE OF ADDRESS WITHIN 10 DAYS OR IF HE LEAVES THE STATE; TIME SPENT OUT OF TEXAS DOES NOT COUNT TOWARD PROBATION. SHALL NOT SEEK MODIFICATION FOR ONE YEAR.

PUGH, MARION JR MD, LICENSE NUMBER 0C13537, OF DALLAS, TX, WAS DISCIPLINED BY CALIFORNIA ON DECEMBER 2, 1987.
DISCIPLINARY ACTION: LICENSE REVOCATION
OFFENSE: DISCIPLINARY ACTION BY ANOTHER STATE OR AGENCY
NOTES: DISCIPLINE BY FLORIDA MEDICAL BOARD; DEFAULT

PUGH, MARION MD, LICENSE NUMBER 0021586, OF DALLAS, TX, WAS DISCIPLINED BY COLORADO ON OCTOBER 10, 1990.
DISCIPLINARY ACTION: SURRENDER OF LICENSE
OFFENSE: DRUG OR ALCOHOL ABUSE
NOTES: HABITUAL INTEMPERANCE AND EXCESSIVE USE OF ALCOHOLIC BEVERAGES.

PUGH, MARION C JR MD, LICENSE NUMBER 00D5159, OF AUSTIN, TX, WAS DISCIPLINED BY TEXAS ON JANUARY 24, 1992.
DISCIPLINARY ACTION: 60-MONTH PROBATION
OFFENSE: DRUG OR ALCOHOL ABUSE
NOTES: INABILITY TO PRACTICE MEDICINE WITH REASONABLE SKILL AND SAFETY TO PATIENTS. LICENSE SUSPENDED, SUSPENSION STAYED; PROBATION UNDER TERMS AND CONDITIONS.

PULLIAM, ALBERT LEON MD OF 6711 BELLFORT BLVD, #400, HOUSTON, TX, WAS DISCIPLINED BY DEA ON NOVEMBER 7, 1989.
DISCIPLINARY ACTION: SURRENDER OF CONTROLLED SUBSTANCE LICENSE
OFFENSE: CRIMINAL CONVICTION OR PLEA OF GUILTY, NOLO CONTENDERE, OR NO CONTEST TO A CRIME
NOTES: INVOLVED IN DIVERSION OF CONTROLLED SUBSTANCES AND PRESCRIBED VALIUM 60 UNITS 10 MG, 40 UNITS TYLENOL 4, AND 8 OZS OF TUSSIONEX SUSPENSION 09/15/88 AND 11/02/88 HOUSTON, TEXAS; ARRESTED 12/07/88 IN TX; CHARGED WITH DISPENSING TYLENOL WITH CODEINE, TUSSIONEX AND VALIUM FOR NON-LEGITIMATE MEDICAL PURPOSES. ALSO PRESCRIBING DIAZEPAM AND HYDROCODONE; PLED GUILTY 05/23/89 TO UNLAWFUL DISPENSING OF CONTROLLED SUBSTANCE AND 09/18/89 TO POSSESSION WITH INTENT TO DISTRIBUTE CONTROLLED SUBSTANCE; SENTENCED TO 30 DAYS JAIL, 5 YEARS PROBATION, 100 HOURS COMMUNITY SERVICE YEARLY FOR 3 YEARS, AND $10,000 FINE; DEA REGISTRATION REVOKED 10/18/89 IN HOUSTON, TX ; VOLUNTARY SURRENDER OF REGISTRATION 11/06/89.

PULLIAM, ALBERT LEON MD, DATE OF BIRTH DECEMBER 29, 1939, LICENSE NUMBER 00E9340, OF HOUSTON, TX, WAS DISCIPLINED BY TEXAS ON MARCH 31, 1990.
DISCIPLINARY ACTION: SURRENDER OF CONTROLLED SUBSTANCE

LICENSE; 60-MONTH PROBATION
NOTES: STIPULATED ORDER. REVOCATION STAYED. MUST COMPLETE PRECEPTORSHIP ON PREVENTION AND TREATMENT OF DRUG ABUSE, APPEAR BEFORE BOARD SEMI-ANNUALLY, SURRENDER CONTROLLED SUBSTANCES REGISTRATIONS AND NOT REREGISTER WITHOUT BOARD AUTHORITY, AND COMPLY WITH TERMS OF CRIMINAL PROBATION. ON 4/30/93, MODIFICATION OF ORDER SO THAT HE MAY REAPPLY TO TEXAS DEPARTMENT OF PUBLIC SAFETY AND THE DRUG ENFORCEMENT ADMINISTRATION FOR REINSTATEMENT OF HIS CONTROLLED SUBSTANCE REGISTRATION IN ALL SCHEDULES AND FOR ISSUANCE OF TRIPLICATE PRESCRIPTION FORMS.

PULLIAM, ALBERT LEON MD, DATE OF BIRTH DECEMBER 29, 1939, LICENSE NUMBER 0036501, OF 6711 BELLFORT BOULEVARD #400, HOUSTON, TX, WAS DISCIPLINED BY MICHIGAN ON AUGUST 30, 1993.
DISCIPLINARY ACTION: 6-MONTH LICENSE SUSPENSION
NOTES: DRUG RELATED.

PULLIAM, KATHY A MD, DATE OF BIRTH FEBRUARY 10, 1955, LICENSE NUMBER 0012699, OF 48 MEADOWOODS TERRACE, JACKSON, MS, WAS DISCIPLINED BY MISSISSIPPI ON SEPTEMBER 26, 1991.
DISCIPLINARY ACTION: RESTRICTION PLACED ON LICENSE
OFFENSE: DRUG OR ALCOHOL ABUSE
NOTES: RECENTLY SUFFERED A RELAPSE OF HER CHEMICAL DEPENDENCY. CONSENT AGREEMENT PROHIBITS THE PRACTICE OF MEDICINE IN MISSISSIPPI UNTIL SUCH TIME AS CERTAIN REQUIREMENTS ARE MET.

PULLIAM, KATHY A MD, DATE OF BIRTH FEBRUARY 10, 1955, LICENSE NUMBER 0012699, OF 48 MEADOWOODS TERRACE, JACKSON, MS, WAS DISCIPLINED BY MISSISSIPPI ON MARCH 19, 1992.
DISCIPLINARY ACTION: RESTRICTION PLACED ON LICENSE; RESTRICTION PLACED ON CONTROLLED SUBSTANCE LICENSE
NOTES: PERMISSION TO RE-ENTER THE PRACTICE OF MEDICINE IN MISSISSIPPI SUBJECT TO TERMS AND CONDITIONS: PRACTICE LIMITED TO MISSISSIPPI STATE DEPARTMENT OF HEALTH; NO DRUG ENFORCEMENT ADMINISTRATION CERTIFICATE; PROHIBITED FROM ORDERING, MANUFACTURING, DISTRIBUTING, POSSESSING, DISPENSING, ADMINISTERING OR PRESCRIBING STADOL AND NUBAIN, OR THEIR GENERICS.

PULLIAM, KATHY A MD, LICENSE NUMBER 00F9982, OF JACKSON, MS, WAS DISCIPLINED BY TEXAS ON JUNE 17, 1992.
DISCIPLINARY ACTION: 120-MONTH PROBATION
OFFENSE: DRUG OR ALCOHOL ABUSE
NOTES: INABILITY TO PRACTICE MEDICINE WITH REASONABLE SKILL AND SAFETY TO PATIENTS BY REASON OF USE OF DRUGS. SUSPENSION STAYED.

PULLIAM, KATHY A MD, DATE OF BIRTH FEBRUARY 10, 1955, LICENSE NUMBER 0012699, OF 5613 BOGGS DRIVE, STONE MOUNTAIN, GA, WAS DISCIPLINED BY MISSISSIPPI ON JULY 16, 1992.
DISCIPLINARY ACTION: LICENSE SUSPENSION
OFFENSE: FAILURE TO COMPLY WITH A PREVIOUS BOARD ORDER
NOTES: SUFFERED RELAPSE OF HER CHEMICAL DEPENDENCY IN VIOLATION OF THE MARCH 19, 1992 BOARD ORDER. BOARD RATIFIED THE ORDER OF IMMEDIATE SUSPENSION OF HER MEDICAL LICENSE DATED JUNE 2, 1992, THE EFFECTIVE DATE OF THIS ORDER. ON 1/20/94 HER REQUEST FOR REINSTATEMENT WAS DENIED. AFTER ONE YEAR SHE MAY PETITION THE BOARD FOR RECONSIDERATION.

PULLIAM, KATHY A MD, LICENSE NUMBER 00F9982, OF JACKSON, MS, WAS DISCIPLINED BY TEXAS ON OCTOBER 9, 1992.
DISCIPLINARY ACTION: 24-MONTH LICENSE SUSPENSION
OFFENSE: FAILURE TO COMPLY WITH A PREVIOUS BOARD ORDER
NOTES: VIOLATED PREVIOUS ORDER OF 06/17/92.

PULLIAM, KATHY ANN MD, LICENSE NUMBER 0010342, OF GA, WAS DISCIPLINED BY ALABAMA ON MARCH 2, 1993.
DISCIPLINARY ACTION: LICENSE REVOCATION
OFFENSE: DISCIPLINARY ACTION BY ANOTHER STATE OR AGENCY
NOTES: UNABLE TO PRACTICE MEDICINE WITH REASONABLE SKILL AND SAFETY DUE TO EXCESSIVE USE OF DRUGS; MISSISSIPPI LICENSE HAD BEEN SUSPENDED DUE TO A VIOLATION OF A PREVIOUS CONSENT AGREEMENT.

PULLIAM, KATHY ANN MD OF STONE MOUNTAIN, GA, WAS DISCIPLINED BY LOUISIANA ON MARCH 22, 1993.
DISCIPLINARY ACTION: LICENSE SUSPENSION
OFFENSE: DISCIPLINARY ACTION BY ANOTHER STATE OR AGENCY
NOTES: ACTION TAKEN BY BOTH MISSISSIPPI AND TEXAS; HABITUAL AND RECURRING ABUSE OF DRUGS, INCLUDING ALCOHOL; PROVIDING FALSE SWORN INFORMATION TO THE BOARD.

PULSE, TERRY L MD, LICENSE NUMBER 00F3295, OF GRAND PRAIRIE, TX, WAS DISCIPLINED BY TEXAS ON OCTOBER 27, 1989.
DISCIPLINARY ACTION: 36-MONTH RESTRICTION PLACED ON CONTROLLED SUBSTANCE LICENSE
NOTES: STIPULATED ORDER. PROHIBITED FROM CALLING PRESCRIPTIONS IN AND FROM WRITING PRESCRIPTIONS WHICH ALLOW REFILLS, MUST MAINTAIN SEPARATE FILE FOR PRESCRIPTIONS OF CONTROLLED SUBSTANCES, SUBMIT TO PSYCHIATRIC EVALUATION AND FOLLOW ANY RECOMMENDATIONS REGARDING CARE, MAINTAIN COMPLETE AND ACCURATE RECORDS OF PURCHASES AND DISPOSALS OF CONTROLLED SUBSTANCES, AND ADEQUATELY SUPERVISE EMPLOYEE ACTIVITIES TO DETERMINE THEY ARE NOT VIOLATING LAWS INVOLVING PRACTICE OF MEDICINE NOR CAUSING LICENSEE TO VIOLATE SUCH LAWS.

QUENNEVILLE, KENNETH B MD, LICENSE NUMBER 0065096, OF 2300 WEST MICHIGAN AVENUE, MIDLAND, TX, WAS DISCIPLINED BY DEA ON SEPTEMBER 24, 1990.
DISCIPLINARY ACTION: SURRENDER OF CONTROLLED SUBSTANCE LICENSE
OFFENSE: PRACTICING WITHOUT A VALID LICENSE OR PRESCRIBING WITHOUT A VALID CONTROLLED SUBSTANCE LICENSE
NOTES: DISPENSING CONTROLLED DRUGS WITHOUT DEA REGISTRATION; SURRENDERED DEA REGISTRATION UPON ORDER FROM STATE OF TX; MEDICAL LICENSE SUSPENDED 02/16/90 FOR INTEMPERATE USE OF ALCOHOL AND DANGEROUS DRUGS. LICENSE REINSTATED 06/11/90 AND PLACED ON FIVE YEARS PROBATION.

QUENNEVILLE, KENNETH BRUCE MD, DATE OF BIRTH JANUARY 26, 1954, LICENSE NUMBER 00H1404, OF MIDLAND, TX, WAS DISCIPLINED BY TEXAS ON FEBRUARY 16, 1990.
DISCIPLINARY ACTION: SURRENDER OF CONTROLLED SUBSTANCE

LICENSE; EMERGENCY SUSPENSION
OFFENSE: DRUG OR ALCOHOL ABUSE
NOTES: STIPULATED ORDER. LICENSE SUSPENDED UNTIL PSYCHIATRIST FINDS PHYSICIAN CAPABLE OF PRACTICING MEDICINE WITH REASONABLE SAFETY TO SELF AND PATIENTS. MUST PASS SPECIAL PURPOSE EXAMINATION. WHEN CONDITIONS SATISFIED, SUSPENSION TERMINATED AND LICENSE PROBATED WITH FOLLOWING TERMS: MUST SURRENDER CONTROLLED SUBSTANCES REGISTRATIONS AND NOT REREGISTER WITHOUT BOARD AUTHORITY, SURRENDER TRIPLICATE PRESCRIPTION FORMS AND NOT ORDER MORE UNTIL BOARD AUTHORIZES, PARTICIPATE IN AA OR NARCOTICS ANONYMOUS, REPORT ANY INCIDENT IN WHICH HE PARTAKES OF ALCOHOL OR USES CONTROLLED SUBSTANCES NOT PRESCRIBED BY ANOTHER PHYSICIAN FOR LEGITIMATE, THERAPEUTIC CONDITION, AND SUBMIT FOR EXAMINATIONS TO DETERMINE FREEDOM FROM DRUGS AND ALCOHOL.

QUENNEVILLE, KENNETH BRUCE MD, DATE OF BIRTH JANUARY 26, 1954, LICENSE NUMBER 00H1404, OF 411 S ORIENT STREET, STAMFORD, TX, WAS DISCIPLINED BY TEXAS ON JUNE 28, 1991.
DISCIPLINARY ACTION: 60-MONTH PROBATION
NOTES: TERMS OF PROBATION: SHALL CONTINUE TREATMENT FROM PHYSICIAN APPROVED BY BOARD; SHALL ATTEND AT LEAST 50 HOURS PER YEAR OF CATEGORY I CONTINUING MEDICAL EDUCATION; SHALL APPEAR BEFORE THE BOARD ONCE A YEAR; SHALL PARTICIPATE FOUR TIMES A WEEK IN A 12-STEP PROGRAM OF AA OR NARCOTICS ANONYMOUS; SHALL IMMEDIATELY REPORT TO THE BOARD ANY USE OF ALCOHOL OR CONTROLLED SUBSTANCE NOT PRESCRIBED BY ANOTHER PHYSICIAN FOR A LEGITIMATE AND THERAPEUTIC CONDITION; SHALL SUBMIT TO DRUG OR ALCOHOL SCREENS. PROBATION MODIFIED EFFECTIVE 4/11/92. PROBATION MODIFIED EFFECTIVE 8/20/92. ON 8/20/93 ORDER TERMINATED AND LICENSE FREE AND CLEAR OF ANY PREVIOUS RESTRICTIONS.

RAINE, DAVID BURTON MD OF DAYTON, TX, WAS DISCIPLINED BY TEXAS ON JULY 1, 1986.
DISCIPLINARY ACTION: SURRENDER OF LICENSE

RAMAKRISHNAN, VASUKI MD, LICENSE NUMBER 00F5712, OF STAFFORD, TX, WAS DISCIPLINED BY TEXAS ON APRIL 15, 1994.
DISCIPLINARY ACTION: 120-MONTH MONITORING OF PHYSICIAN
OFFENSE: PROFESSIONAL MISCONDUCT
NOTES: ON 10/5/93 PLACED ON PROBATION FOR ONE YEAR WITH DEFERRED ADJUDICATION FOR ENDANGERMENT OF HER SON IN DISTRICT COURT OF HARRIS COUNTY; REQUIRED TO CONTINUE COUNSELING AND PERFORM 100 HOURS OF COMMUNITY SERVICE; PREVIOUSLY HAD A HISTORY OF PSYCHOLOGICAL DIFFICULTIES COUPLED WITH INTERVENTION BY LAW ENFORCEMENT AND SOCIAL SERVICE AGENCIES; STRESS ARISES FROM SETTINGS OUTSIDE OF HER MEDICAL PRACTICE AND, AT THIS TIME, THE BOARD DOES NOT HAVE EVIDENCE THAT THERE HAS BEEN AN ADVERSE IMPACT ON HER PRACTICE; CURRENTLY RECEIVING CARE AND COUNSELING BY A PSYCHIATRIST. CONDITIONS OF MONITORING: SHALL CONTINUE TO RECEIVE CARE FROM HER CURRENT PSYCHIATRIST WITH QUARTERLY REPORTS; SHALL APPEAR BEFORE THE BOARD TWICE A YEAR; SHALL GIVE A COPY OF THIS ORDER TO ANY HEALTH CARE ENTITY WHERE SHE HAS PRIVILEGES; SHALL COOPERATE WITH THE BOARD IN VERIFYING COMPLIANCE; SHALL INFORM BOARD OF CHANGE OF ADDRESS WITHIN 10 DAYS OR IF SHE LEAVES THE STATE; TIME SPENT OUT OF TEXAS DOES NOT COUNT TOWARD MONITORING. SHALL NOT SEEK MODIFICATION FOR ONE YEAR.

RAMESHWAR, ANTHONY B MD, LICENSE NUMBER 00G3059, OF THE WOODLANDS, TX, WAS DISCIPLINED BY TEXAS ON OCTOBER 5, 1991.
DISCIPLINARY ACTION: 36-MONTH PROBATION; REQUIRED TO TAKE ADDITIONAL MEDICAL EDUCATION
OFFENSE: PROFESSIONAL MISCONDUCT
NOTES: IMPROPERLY BILLED FOR HOSPITAL VISITS AND PSYCHIATRIC SERVICES RENDERED TO ONE PATIENT. SUSPENSION STAYED; CONDITIONS OF PROBATION: SHALL ATTEND AT LEAST 10 HOURS CONTINUING MEDICAL EDUCATION PER YEAR IN RISK MANAGEMENT OR BILLING PROCEDURES AND SUBMIT PROOF TO THE BOARD; SHALL NOT SIGN OR INDICATE ANYTHING IN A PATIENT RECORD WITHOUT PERSONALLY SEEING AND EXAMINING THE PATIENT, UNLESS THE CHART CLEARLY REFLECTS THIS; SHALL NOT BACK DATE ANY ENTRY; SHALL UTILIZE A SYSTEM OF RECORD KEEPING THAT WILL INSURE ACCURACY; SHALL COOPERATE WITH THE BOARD IN VERIFYING COMPLIANCE; SHALL ADVISE THE BOARD OF ANY CHANGE OF ADDRESS WITHIN 10 DAYS; MAY NOT APPLY FOR REINSTATEMENT FOR AT LEAST A YEAR; TIME SPENT OUT OF TEXAS WILL NOT COUNT TOWARDS PROBATION. ON 1/14/94 PROBATION TERMINATED.

RAMIREZ, HUGO A MD, LICENSE NUMBER 00D9872, OF PASADENA, TX, WAS DISCIPLINED BY TEXAS ON OCTOBER 1, 1987.
DISCIPLINARY ACTION: LICENSE REVOCATION
OFFENSE: SUBSTANDARD CARE, INCOMPETENCE, OR NEGLIGENCE
NOTES: PRESCRIBED OR ADMINISTERED DRUGS OR TREATMENT NONTHERAPEUTICALLY; FAILED TO ADEQUATELY SUPERVISE ACTIVITIES OF THOSE ACTING UNDER HIS SUPERVISION; USED FALSE, MISLEADING OR DECEPTIVE ADVERTISING; FAILED TO PRACTICE MEDICINE IN ACCEPTABLE MANNER CONSISTENT WITH PUBLIC HEALTH AND WELFARE; LIPOSUCTION PRACTICES CAUSED TWO DEATHS. ON 12/03/87 REVOCATION OVERTURNED IN U.S. DISTRICT COURT IN HOUSTON. ON 5/3/88 THE U.S. FIFTH CIRCUIT COURT OF APPEALS OVERRULED THE U.S. DISTRICT COURT'S EARLIER ACTION AND REIMPOSED THE MEDICAL BOARD'S ORDER OF REVOCATION.

RAMIREZ, HUGO A MD, DATE OF BIRTH FEBRUARY 19, 1939, OF PO BOX 7304, PASADENA, TX, WAS DISCIPLINED BY MEDICARE ON JULY 24, 1989.
DISCIPLINARY ACTION: EXCLUSION FROM THE MEDICARE AND/OR MEDICAID PROGRAMS
OFFENSE: DISCIPLINARY ACTION BY ANOTHER STATE OR AGENCY
NOTES: LICENSE REVOCATION OR SUSPENSION.

RAMIREZ, HUGO A MD OF PASADENA, TX, WAS DISCIPLINED BY OHIO ON SEPTEMBER 13, 1989.
DISCIPLINARY ACTION: DENIAL OF LICENSE REINSTATEMENT

RAMIREZ, HUGO A MD, LICENSE NUMBER 031320L, OF PASADENA, TX, WAS DISCIPLINED BY PENNSYLVANIA ON OCTOBER 11, 1990.
DISCIPLINARY ACTION: LICENSE REVOCATION

OFFENSE: DISCIPLINARY ACTION BY ANOTHER STATE OR AGENCY
NOTES: LICENSE WAS REVOKED ON 7/24/87 BY THE TEXAS STATE BOARD OF MEDICAL EXAMINERS FOR UNPROFESSIONAL OR DISHONORABLE CONDUCT AND FOR NEGLIGENTLY FAILING TO PRACTICE MEDICINE IN AN ACCEPTABLE MANNER CONSISTENT WITH THE PUBLIC HEALTH AND WELFARE, WHICH RESULTED IN THE DEATH OF TWO PATIENTS. 10/31/90 ORDER GRANTED STAY OF HEARING EXAMINER'S ORDER OF REVOCATION PENDING REVIEW BY THE BOARD.

RAMIREZ, HUGO A MD WAS DISCIPLINED BY TEXAS ON OCTOBER 5, 1991.
DISCIPLINARY ACTION: DENIAL OF LICENSE REINSTATEMENT
NOTES: LICENSE REVOKED 8/21/87.

RAMIREZ, HUGO A MD OF ROLLING HILLS HOSP 60 E TOWNSHIP, ELKINS PARK, PA, WAS DISCIPLINED BY DEA ON MAY 11, 1992.
DISCIPLINARY ACTION: DENIAL OF NEW LICENSE
OFFENSE: DISCIPLINARY ACTION BY ANOTHER STATE OR AGENCY
NOTES: MEDICAL LICENSE REVOKED BY PENNSYLVANIA EFFECTIVE 10/30/90 BASED ON PRIOR REVOCATION BY TEXAS ON 08/21/87. TEXAS ACTION DUE TO FINDING THAT HE FAILED TO INSURE A STERILE ENVIRONMENT DURING LIPOSUCTION PROCEDURES AND FAILED TO ORDER PROPER TESTS AND TO PROPERLY MONITOR PATIENTS AFTER THE PROCEDURES WERE COMPLETED. THEREFORE HE IS NOT AUTHORIZED TO PRESCRIBE, DISPENSE, ADMINISTER OR OTHERWISE HANDLE CONTROLLED SUBSTANCES.

RAMIREZ, JAIME MD, LICENSE NUMBER 00G7422, OF PLANO, TX, WAS DISCIPLINED BY TEXAS ON JUNE 10, 1991.
DISCIPLINARY ACTION: 60-MONTH PROBATION; RESTRICTION PLACED ON LICENSE
OFFENSE: LOSS OR RESTRICTION OF HOSPITAL PRIVILEGES
NOTES: SUBMITTED FALSE OR MISLEADING STATEMENT, DOCUMENT, OR CERTIFICATE TO BOARD IN AN APPLICATION FOR EXAMINATION OR LICENSURE; UNPROFESSIONAL OR DISHONORABLE CONDUCT LIKELY TO DECEIVE, DEFRAUD, OR INJURE THE PUBLIC; PROFESSIONAL FAILURE TO PRACTICE MEDICINE IN AN ACCEPTABLE MANNER CONSISTENT WITH PUBLIC HEALTH AND WELFARE; NONTHERAPEUTIC PRESCRIBING; LOSS OF HOSPITAL PRIVILEGES. SIX MONTH SUSPENSION STAYED; TERMS OF PROBATION: SHALL APPEAR BEFORE THE BOARD ONCE A YEAR; SHALL ATTEND AT LEAST 50 HOURS OF CATEGORY I CONTINUING MEDICAL EDUCATION, AN ADVANCED TRAUMA LIFE SUPPORT COURSE, AND AN ADVANCED CARDIAC LIFE SUPPORT COURSE TO OBTAIN RECERTIFICATION IN THESE COURSES; SHALL NOT ACCEPT EMPLOYMENT OR ENTER INTO CONTRACTUAL RELATIONSHIPS WHEREIN HE WOULD BE COMPENSATED TO DIAGNOSE AND/OR TREAT PATIENTS BY A LAYPERSON, CORPORATION, OR OTHER ENTITY NOT COMPRISED EXCLUSIVELY OF LICENSED PHYSICIANS, AND WHEREIN SAID PERSON OR ENTITY THEN WOULD RECEIVE AND RETAIN THE FEES PAID BY OR ON BEHALF OF PATIETNS FOR THE PHYSICIAN'S PROFESSNAL SERVICES.

RAMIREZ, JAIME MD, LICENSE NUMBER 00G7422, OF PLANO, TX, WAS DISCIPLINED BY TEXAS ON JUNE 22, 1994.
DISCIPLINARY ACTION: FINE; REPRIMAND
OFFENSE: FAILURE TO COMPLY WITH A PREVIOUS BOARD ORDER
NOTES: HAS ENGAGED IN THE CORPORATE PRACTICE OF MEDICINE IN VIOLATION OF A CONDITION OF 6/10/91 ORDER IN THAT HE ENTERED INTO AN AGREEMENT WITH THE OAK LAWN MEDICAL CENTER AGREEING TO PROVIDE PROFESSIONAL SERVICES FOR A SET RATE OF COMPENSATION; THIS WAS DONE FOR TAX PURPOSES. SHALL PAY A $5,000 ADMINISTRATIVE PENALTY WITHIN 90 DAYS; SHALL NOT ACCEPT EMPLOYMENT OR ENTER INTO CONTRACTUAL RELATIONSHIPS WHERE HE WOULD BE COMPENSATED TO DIAGNOSE AND/OR TREAT PATIENTS BY ANY ENTITY NOT COMPRISED EXCLUSIVELY OF TEXAS LICENSED PHYSICIANS; SHALL GIVE A COPY OF THIS ORDER TO ANY HEALTH CARE ENTITY WHERE HE HAS PRIVILEGES; SHALL COOPERATE WITH BOARD IN VERIFYING COMPLIANCE; SHALL INFORM BOARD OF CHANGE OF ADDRESS OR IF HE LEAVES THE STATE; TIME SPENT OUT OF TEXAS DOES NOT COUNT TOWARD RESTRICTION. SHALL NOT SEEK MODIFICATION FOR ONE YEAR.

RAMOS, BALTAZAR JR MD, LICENSE NUMBER 00D8391, OF BEAUMONT, TX, WAS DISCIPLINED BY TEXAS ON DECEMBER 1, 1988.
DISCIPLINARY ACTION: LICENSE REVOCATION
OFFENSE: CRIMINAL CONVICTION OR PLEA OF GUILTY, NOLO CONTENDERE, OR NO CONTEST TO A CRIME
NOTES: EXHIBITED UNPROFESSIONAL OR DISHONORABLE CONDUCT LIKELY TO DECEIVE, DEFRAUD OR INJURE PUBLIC. CONVICTED OF FELONY

RAMPOLDI, JAMES MOSES MD, LICENSE NUMBER 00E3829, OF DENTON, TX, WAS DISCIPLINED BY TEXAS ON MARCH 5, 1994.
DISCIPLINARY ACTION: 60-MONTH PROBATION; RESTRICTION PLACED ON LICENSE
OFFENSE: SUBSTANDARD CARE, INCOMPETENCE, OR NEGLIGENCE
NOTES: FROM 1/90 THROUGH 8/91 HE FAILED TO ADEQUATELY DOCUMENT EVALUATIONS AND TREATMENT RENDERED TO A NURSING HOME PATIENT AND FAILED TO PERSONALLY EVALUATE HER ON A SUFFICIENTLY REGULAR BASIS TO ENABLE HIM TO RENDER ADEQUATE CARE TO HER. FIVE YEAR SUSPENSION STAYED. CONDITIONS OF PROBATION: SHALL MAINTAIN ADEQUATE MEDICAL RECORDS AND UTILIZE A SYSTEM TO INSURE THIS; SHALL NOT SIGN ANY PATIENT RECORD UNLESS HE HAS PERSONALLY EXAMINED THE PATIENT OR CLEARLY NOTES IN THE RECORD THAT HE DID NOT; SHALL PERSONALLY EXAMINE A PATIENT WHEN STATE LAW REQUIRES THAT A PHYSICIAN PERFORM THE EXAMINATION; SHALL ATTEND AT LEAST 50 HOURS PER YEAR OF CONTINUING MEDICAL EDUCATION IN FAMILY PRACTICE MEDICINE; SHALL RESPOND IN A TIMELY MANNER TO ALL BOARD REQUESTS FOR MEDICAL RECORDS OR OTHER INFORMATION; SHALL NOT SEE, TREAT OR SERVE AS A PHYSICIAN FOR NURSING HOME PATIENTS; SHALL APPEAR BEFORE THE BOARD ONCE A YEAR; SHALL GIVE A COPY OF THIS ORDER TO ANY HEALTH CARE ENTITY WHERE HE HAS PRIVILEGES; SHALL COOPERATE WITH THE BOARD IN VERIFYING COMPLIANCE; SHALL INFORM THE BOARD OF CHANGE OF ADDRESS WITHIN 10 DAYS OR IF HE LEAVES THE STATE; TIME SPENT OUT OF TEXAS DOES NOT COUNT TOWARD PROBATION. SHALL NOT SEEK MODIFICATION FOR ONE YEAR.

RANELLE, JOHN DO OF WOLFE CITY, TX, WAS DISCIPLINED BY

MISSOURI ON AUGUST 22, 1990.
OFFENSE: DISCIPLINARY ACTION BY ANOTHER STATE OR AGENCY
NOTES: ACTION TAKEN IN TEXAS BASED ON EXCESSIVE PRESCRIBING AND INADEQUATE PATIENT RECORDS. MUST APPEAR BEFORE BOARD BEFORE RETURNING TO PRACTICE IN MISSOURI. NO DATE LISTED BY DEA.

RANELLE, JOHN B DO, LICENSE NUMBER 00E9349, OF WOLFE CITY, TX, WAS DISCIPLINED BY TEXAS ON FEBRUARY 16, 1990.
DISCIPLINARY ACTION: 36-MONTH RESTRICTION PLACED ON CONTROLLED SUBSTANCE LICENSE; 36-MONTH MONITORING OF PHYSICIAN
NOTES: STIPULATED ORDER. SHALL APPEAR BEFORE BOARD EVERY SIX MONTHS, AUTHORIZE BOARD TO OBTAIN URINE OR BLOOD SAMPLES FOR DRUG AND ALCOHOL SCREENS, SURRENDER TRIPLICATE PRESCRIPTION FORMS AND NOT ORDER MORE UNTIL BOARD PERMITS, REQUEST MODIFICATION OF CONTROLLED SUBSTANCES REGISTRATIONS TO ELIMINATE SCHEDULES II AND II-N AND NOT REREGISTER FOR SAME UNTIL BOARD APPROVAL, NOT PRESCRIBE, DISPENSE, ADMINISTER OR POSSESS SPECIFIC AMPHETAMINE-LIKE ACTION DRUGS OR ANORECTIC AGENTS, REFRAIN FROM CONSUMING PRESCRIPTION DRUGS UNLESS PRESCRIBED BY ANOTHER PHYSICIAN FOR VALID MEDICAL PURPOSES, MAINTAIN ADEQUATE MEDICAL RECORDS ON ALL PATIENT OFFICE VISITS TO INCLUDE CERTAIN INFORMATION, AND MAINTAIN SEPARATE FILE OF PRESCRIPTIONS FOR CONTROLLED SUBSTANCES.

RANELLE, JOHN BARRY DO OF 1805 N GARRETT, DALLAS, TX, WAS DISCIPLINED BY DEA ON JANUARY 1, 1986.
DISCIPLINARY ACTION: RESTRICTION PLACED ON CONTROLLED SUBSTANCE LICENSE
OFFENSE: OVERPRESCRIBING OR MISPRESCRIBING DRUGS
NOTES: EXCESSIVE PURCHASING OF PRELUDIN. NO DATE LISTED BY DEA.

RANELLE, JOHN BARRY DO, LICENSE NUMBER 00E9349, OF DALLAS, TX, WAS DISCIPLINED BY TEXAS ON MARCH 6, 1992.
DISCIPLINARY ACTION: LICENSE SUSPENSION
OFFENSE: DRUG OR ALCOHOL ABUSE
NOTES: UNPROFESSIONAL OR DISHONORABLE CONDUCT LIKELY TO DECEIVE, DEFRAUD OR INJURE THE PUBLIC, AND INTEMPERATE USE OF ALCOHOL OR DRUGS. LIFTING OF THE SUSPENSION WILL NOT BE CONSIDERED UNTIL CERTAIN MINIMUM REQUIREMENTS ARE MET. SUSPENSION TERMINATED ON 9/28/92.

RANELLE, JOHN BARRY DO, LICENSE NUMBER 00E9349, OF EULESS, TX, WAS DISCIPLINED BY TEXAS ON SEPTEMBER 28, 1992.
DISCIPLINARY ACTION: 60-MONTH PROBATION
NOTES: SUSPENSION TERMINATED.

RANELLE, JOHN BARRY DO, LICENSE NUMBER 00E9349, OF EULESS, TX, WAS DISCIPLINED BY TEXAS ON JUNE 22, 1994.
DISCIPLINARY ACTION: 60-MONTH PROBATION; RESTRICTION PLACED ON LICENSE
OFFENSE: FAILURE TO COMPLY WITH A PREVIOUS BOARD ORDER
NOTES: ON 3/3/93 AND 7/30/93 PRESCRIBED DEMEROL A SCHEDULE II CONTROLLED SUBSTANCE AND FAILED TO ADEQUATELY DOCUMENT PRESCRIPTIONS IN PATIENT CHARTS IN VIOLATION OF 9/28/92 BOARD ORDER. SUSPENSION STAYED. CONDITIONS OF PROBATION; SHALL APPEAR BEFORE THE BOARD TWICE A YEAR; SHALL ABSTAIN FROM THE CONSUMPTION OF ALCHOL/CHEMICAL SUBSTANCES IN ANY FORM UNLESS PRESCRIBED BY ANOTHER PHYSICIAN FOR A LEGITIMATE AND THERAPEUTIC PURPOSE; SHALL SUBMIT HIMSELF FOR APPROPRIATE EXAMS INCLUDING DRUG OR ALCOHOL SCREENS; SHALL SURRENDER DEA AND TEXAS CONTROLLED SUBSTANCES REGISTRATION CERTIFICATES, ALL UNUSED TRIPLICATE PRESCRIPTION FORMS AND ALL CONTROLLED SUBSTANCES IN HIS POSSESSION INCLUDING SAMPLES; SHALL NOT ATTEMPT TO REREGISTER WITHOUT PERMISSION; SHALL NOT PRESCRIBE, DISPENSE, ADMINISTER OR POSSESS ANY OF A LIST OF AMPHETAMINE-LIKE ACTION DRUGS UNDER ANY CIRCUMSTANCES; SHALL NOT TREAT OR OTHERWISE SERVE AS PHYSICIAN, PRESCRIBE, DISPENSE OR ADMINISTER DRUGS THAT MAY BE SUBJECT TO ABUSE FOR HIMSELF OR ANY MEMBER OF HIS FAMILY; SHALL MAINTAIN ADEQUATE MEDICAL RECORDS ON ALL PATIENT OFFICE VISITS WHICH SHALL BE AVAILABLE FOR INSPECTION; SEPARATE FROM PATIENT RECORDS SHALL MAINTAIN A FILE OF EVERY PRESCRIPTION WRITTEN FOR DANGEROUS DRUGS WHICH HAVE POTENTIAL FOR ABUSE WHICH SHALL BE AVAILABLE FOR INSPECTION; SHALL NOT TELEPHONE IN ANY PRESCRIPTIONS FOR DANGEROUS DRUGS; SHALL BE SUPERVISED BY A SPECIFIED PHYSICIAN WITH BIMONTHLY REPORTS; SHALL CONTINUE TO RECEIVE PSYCHIATRIC TREATMENT WITH QUARTERLY REPORTS; SHALL GIVE A COPY OF THIS ORDER TO ANY HEALTH CARE ENTITY WHERE HE HAS PRIVILEGES; SHALL COOPERATE WITH THE BOARD IN VERIFYING COMPLIANCE; SHALL INFORM BOARD OF CHANGE OF ADDRESS WITHIN 10 DAYS OR IF HE LEAVES THE STATE; TIME SPENT OUT OF TEXAS DOES NOT COUNT TOWARD PROBATION. THIS ORDER SUPERCEDES THAT OF 9/28/92. SHALL NOT SEEK MODIFICATION FOR ONE YEAR.

RANHEIM, RICHARD O MD OF MANSURA, LA, WAS DISCIPLINED BY TEXAS ON DECEMBER 1, 1986.
DISCIPLINARY ACTION: LICENSE REVOCATION
OFFENSE: DISCIPLINARY ACTION BY ANOTHER STATE OR AGENCY

RANKIN, DOUG HALL MD, LICENSE NUMBER 00F2867, OF 515 CAPITOL OF TEXAS HGWY 101, AUSTIN, TX, WAS DISCIPLINED BY DEA ON MARCH 15, 1994.
DISCIPLINARY ACTION: RESTRICTION PLACED ON CONTROLLED SUBSTANCE LICENSE
NOTES: VOLUNTARY SURRENDER OF REGISTRATION.

RANKIN, DOUGLAS HALL MD, LICENSE NUMBER 00F2867, OF AUSTIN, TX, WAS DISCIPLINED BY TEXAS ON DECEMBER 4, 1991.
DISCIPLINARY ACTION: SURRENDER OF CONTROLLED SUBSTANCE LICENSE; 120-MONTH PROBATION
OFFENSE: DRUG OR ALCOHOL ABUSE
NOTES: IS ADDICTED TO NUBAIN AND STADOL; HAS COMPLETED THE SOLUTIONS OUTPATIENT REHABILITATION AND IS CONTINUING IN WEEKLY AFTERCARE. SUSPENSION STAYED; CONDITIONS OF PROBATION: SHALL APPEAR BEFORE THE BOARD TWICE A YEAR TO VERIFY COMPLIANCE; SHALL NOT PETITION FOR MODIFICATION FOR AT LEAST ONE YEAR; SHALL SURRENDER HIS DEA AND TEXAS CONTROLLED SUBSTANCES REGISTRATIONS; SHALL SURRENDER ALL UNUSED TRIPLICATE PRESCRIPTION FORMS AND SHALL NOT ORDER MORE WITHOUT BOARD PERMISSION; SHALL SURRENDER ALL CONTROLLED SUBSTANCES,

INCLUDING SAMPLES; SHALL REPORT TO THE BOARD WITHIN 24 HOURS IF HE PARTAKES OF ALCOHOL OR ANY OTHER CHEMICAL SUBSTANCES; SHALL ABSTAIN FROM CONSUMPTION OF ALCOHOL/CHEMICAL SUBSTANCES IN ANY FORM; SHALL PARTICIPATE IN THE IMPAIRED PHYSICIANS GROUP WEEKLY; SHALL PARTICIPATE IN AA, INCLUDING A 12-STEP PROGRAM, NOT LESS THAN 3 TIMES PER WEEK, WITH WRITTEN REPORTS TO THE BOARD EVERY 3 MONTHS; SHALL SUBMIT TO RANDOM SCREENS OF BODILY FLUIDS; SHALL CONTINUE TREATMENT WITH REPORTS TO THE BOARD FROM TREATING PHYSICIAN; SHALL COMPLY WITH RECOMMENDATIONS OF AFTERCARE PROGRAM; SHALL NOTIFY THE BOARD IMMEDIATELY IF HE DISCONTINUES MEDICAL CARE; SHALL SUPPLY WRITTEN REPORTS TO BOARD WHEN REQUESTED, AND COOPERATE WITH BOARD IN MONITORING COMPLIANCE; SHALL ADVISE THE BOARD OF ANY CHANGE OF ADDRESS WITHIN 10 DAYS; DURATION OF PROBATION NOT SERVED BY TIME SPENT OUT OF STATE; SHALL APPEAR BEFORE THE BOARD TWICE A YEAR. ON 1/14/94 ORDER MODIFIED AS FOLLOWS: HE IS GRANTED PERMISSION TO REAPPLY TO THE DRUG ENFORCEMENT ADMINISTRATION AND THE TEXAS DEPARTMENT OF PUBLIC SAFETY FOR SCHEDULES III, IV AND V ONLY; SEPARATE FROM PATIENT RECORDS, HE SHALL MAINTAIN A FILE CONSISTING OF A COPY OF EVERY PRESCRIPTION WRITTEN BY HIM FOR CONTROLLED SUBSTANCES OR DANGEROUS DRUGS BY DATE ISSUED WHICH SHALL BE AVAILABLE TO THE BOARD FOR INSPECTION; HE AND HIS STAFF SHALL NOT TELEPHONE ANY PRESCRIPTION TO A PHARMACY FOR CONTROLLED SUBSTANCES OR DANGEROUS DRUGS; SHALL NOT PRESCRIBE, DISPENSE, ADMINISTER, OR POSSESS STADOL, NUBAIN, SOMA OR THEIR GENERIC OR CHEMICAL EQUIVALENTS. ALL OTHER PROVISIONS OF THIS ORDER REMAIN IN EFFECT.

RANKIN, MANLY W JR MD, LICENSE NUMBER 00C0107, OF LAKE DALLAS, TX, WAS DISCIPLINED BY TEXAS ON DECEMBER 1, 1988.
DISCIPLINARY ACTION: SURRENDER OF LICENSE

RANKIN, MANLY W JR MD, DATE OF BIRTH OCTOBER 3, 1925, OF POST OFFICE BOX 788, LAKE DALLAS, TX, WAS DISCIPLINED BY MEDICARE ON APRIL 13, 1989.
DISCIPLINARY ACTION: EXCLUSION FROM THE MEDICARE AND/OR MEDICAID PROGRAMS
OFFENSE: DISCIPLINARY ACTION BY ANOTHER STATE OR AGENCY
NOTES: LICENSE REVOCATION OR SUSPENSION.

RANKIN, MANLY W JR MD, LICENSE NUMBER 0005811, OF HUNTSVILLE, TX, WAS DISCIPLINED BY SOUTH CAROLINA ON OCTOBER 24, 1989.
DISCIPLINARY ACTION: SURRENDER OF LICENSE
NOTES: NOT ELIGIBLE FOR REINSTATEMENT

RASKIN, MILTON MD, LICENSE NUMBER 0026124, WAS DISCIPLINED BY MASSACHUSETTS ON OCTOBER 19, 1988.
DISCIPLINARY ACTION: LICENSE SUSPENSION
OFFENSE: DISCIPLINARY ACTION BY ANOTHER STATE OR AGENCY
NOTES: DISCIPLINED IN TEXAS; CONTROLLED SUBSTANCE PROBLEMS; SUSPENSION OF THE RIGHT TO RENEW HIS LICENSE.

RASKIN, MILTON MD, LICENSE NUMBER 0008865, OF 7908 PARKLAND STREET, EL PASO, TX, WAS DISCIPLINED BY GEORGIA ON FEBRUARY 8, 1990.
DISCIPLINARY ACTION: NONRENEWAL OF LICENSE
OFFENSE: DISCIPLINARY ACTION BY ANOTHER STATE OR AGENCY
NOTES: DISCIPLINARY ACTION TAKEN BY MASSACHUSETTS.

RASKIN, MILTON MD, LICENSE NUMBER 00D4840, OF EL PASO, TX, WAS DISCIPLINED BY TEXAS ON JANUARY 6, 1995.
DISCIPLINARY ACTION: SURRENDER OF LICENSE
OFFENSE: FAILURE TO COMPLY WITH A PROFESSIONAL RULE
NOTES: ALLEGATIONS INCLUDE BILLING FOR SERVICES WITHOUT A DOCUMENTED INDICATION, BILLING FOR SERVICES WHICH THE RECORDS DO NOT INDICATE WERE PERFORMED, AND HAVING ENTERED INTO A CONTRACTUAL RELATIONSHIP WHICH WOULD CONSTITUTE A VIOLATION OF STATE STATUTES REGARDING ILLEGAL REMUNERATION AND/OR A VIOLATION OF THE CORPORATE PRACTICE OF MEDICINE PROHIBITION; SURRENDER IN LIEU OF FURTHER INVESTIGATION OR HEARING ON THE ALLEGATIONS. SHALL NOT PETITION FOR REINSTATEMENT.

READING, WILLIAM H MD, LICENSE NUMBER 00G8363, OF VICTORIA, TX, WAS DISCIPLINED BY TEXAS ON AUGUST 20, 1992.
DISCIPLINARY ACTION: 60-MONTH PROBATION
OFFENSE: SUBSTANDARD CARE, INCOMPETENCE, OR NEGLIGENCE
NOTES: UNPROFESSIONAL OR DISHONORABLE CONDUCT THAT IS LIKELY TO DECEIVE, DEFRAUD OR INJURE THE PUBLIC; NONTHERAPEUTIC PRESCRIBING; OVERCHARGING OR OVERTREATING PATIENTS; FAILURE TO SUPERVISE ADEQUATELY THE ACTIVITIES OF THOSE ACTING UNDER THE SUPERVISION OF THE PHYSICIAN; PROFESSIONAL FAILURE TO PRACTICE MEDICINE IN AN ACCEPTABLE MANNER CONSISTENT WITH PUBLIC HEALTH AND WELFARE. LICENSE SUSPENDED, SUSPENSION STAYED. PROBATION UNDER TERMS AND CONDITIONS.

RECKENTHALER, KARL J MD, DATE OF BIRTH JANUARY 29, 1931, LICENSE NUMBER 0010766, OF GRANT MEMORIAL HOSPITAL, PETERSBURG, WV, WAS DISCIPLINED BY WEST VIRGINIA ON JANUARY 24, 1994.
DISCIPLINARY ACTION: FINE; REPRIMAND
OFFENSE: PROFESSIONAL MISCONDUCT
NOTES: PERMITTED FABRICATION OF THE MINUTES OF THE MEETINGS OF THE RADIATION SAFETY COMMITTEE AT GRANT MEMORIAL HOSPITAL AND FAILED TO EXERCISE HIS RESPONSIBILITY AS RADIATION SAFETY OFFICER AND HOLD MEETINGS; ASSESSED A FINE OF $1,000 AND WITHIN FIVE DAYS MUST PROVIDE A COPY OF THIS ORDER TO ANY HEALTH CARE FACILITY WHERE HE HAS PRIVILEGES.

RECKENTHALER, KARL J MD, LICENSE NUMBER 00C7103, OF PETERSBURG, WV, WAS DISCIPLINED BY TEXAS ON JANUARY 6, 1995.
DISCIPLINARY ACTION: SURRENDER OF LICENSE
NOTES: IN LIEU OF FURTHER INVESTIGATION OR A HEARING. SHALL NOT PETITION FOR REINSTATEMENT.

REDDIX-NORMAN, IRANCE E MD, DATE OF BIRTH OCTOBER 4, 1960, OF 1246 KINGS CREEK TRAIL, MISSOURI CITY, TX, WAS DISCIPLINED BY MEDICARE ON AUGUST 13, 1993.
DISCIPLINARY ACTION: EXCLUSION FROM THE MEDICARE AND/OR MEDICAID PROGRAMS
OFFENSE: FAILURE TO COMPLY WITH A PROFESSIONAL RULE

NOTES: DEFAULTED ON HEALTH EDUCATION ASSISTANCE LOAN.

REDDY, GADDUM J M MD OF ALEXANDRIA, LA, WAS DISCIPLINED BY LOUISIANA ON AUGUST 23, 1990.
DISCIPLINARY ACTION: REQUIRED TO TAKE ADDITIONAL MEDICAL EDUCATION; 12-MONTH MONITORING OF PHYSICIAN
OFFENSE: SUBSTANDARD CARE, INCOMPETENCE, OR NEGLIGENCE
NOTES: SUSPECTED CONTINUING OR RECURRING MEDICAL PRACTICE FAILING TO SATISFY PREVAILING AND USUALLY ACCEPTED STANDARDS OF PRACTICE. MUST PAY $1500 COSTS, COMPLETE CONTINUING MEDICAL EDUCATION, AND HAVE PRACTICE SUPERVISED FOR 12 MONTHS BY BOARD-APPROVED PHYSICIAN.

REDDY, GADDUM J M MD, LICENSE NUMBER 0008168, OF TX, WAS DISCIPLINED BY ALABAMA ON JANUARY 23, 1991.
DISCIPLINARY ACTION: PROBATION
OFFENSE: DISCIPLINARY ACTION BY ANOTHER STATE OR AGENCY
NOTES: LOUISIANA BOARD DISCIPLINED LICENSE BASED ON QUALITY OF CARE ISSUES. ON 10/12/92 PROBATION TERMINATED AFTER FINDING THAT LOUISIANA LICENSE HAD BEEN REINSTATED TO FULL, UNRESTRICTED STATUS AND ALL TERMS AND CONDITIONS HAD BEEN COMPLIED WITH.

REDDY, KALPANA Y MD, LICENSE NUMBER 00H3149, OF SHOREVIEW, MN, WAS DISCIPLINED BY TEXAS ON MARCH 7, 1992.
DISCIPLINARY ACTION: LICENSE REVOCATION
OFFENSE: DISCIPLINARY ACTION BY ANOTHER STATE OR AGENCY
NOTES: SEVERAL VIOLATIONS OF THE MEDICAL PRACTICE ACT, INCLUDING DISCIPLINARY ACTION TAKEN BY A PEER REVIEW ENTITY.

REDELFS, JOHN W MD, LICENSE NUMBER C016552, OF SAN JOSE, CA, WAS DISCIPLINED BY CALIFORNIA ON JUNE 25, 1991.
DISCIPLINARY ACTION: SURRENDER OF LICENSE
NOTES: VOLUNTARY SURRENDER WHILE CHARGES PENDING.

REDELFS, JOHN WRIGHT MD, LICENSE NUMBER 00C4867, OF SAN JOSE, CA, WAS DISCIPLINED BY TEXAS ON JANUARY 24, 1992.
DISCIPLINARY ACTION: SURRENDER OF LICENSE
NOTES: LICENSE VOLUNTARILY SURRENDERED IN LIEU OF FURTHER DISCIPLINARY ACTION.

REECE, DOUGLAS L DO, LICENSE NUMBER 0006242, WAS DISCIPLINED BY MICHIGAN ON MAY 11, 1977.
DISCIPLINARY ACTION: LICENSE REVOCATION

REECE, DOUGLAS L DO, LICENSE NUMBER 0006242, WAS DISCIPLINED BY MICHIGAN ON JULY 3, 1980.
DISCIPLINARY ACTION: PROBATION

REECE, DOUGLAS L DO, LICENSE NUMBER 0006242, WAS DISCIPLINED BY MICHIGAN ON JUNE 27, 1984.
DISCIPLINARY ACTION: LICENSE REVOCATION

REECE, DOUGLAS L DO, LICENSE NUMBER 00E1398, OF LUBBOCK, TX, WAS DISCIPLINED BY TEXAS ON OCTOBER 26, 1990.
DISCIPLINARY ACTION: 84-MONTH PROBATION; RESTRICTION PLACED ON LICENSE
NOTES: SUSPENSION STAYED; MUST LIVE AND PRACTICE IN LUBBOCK COUNTY UNLESS PRACTICE RELOCATION APPROVED BY BOARD; COMPLETE PRECEPTORSHIP RELATED TO DIAGNOSIS AND TREATMENT OF PATIENTS IN FAMILY PRACTICE, SPECIFICALLY INCLUDING PEDIATRICS; OBTAIN CONTINUING MEDICAL EDUCATION; SUBJECT TO MONITORING BY MEANS OF RETROSPECTIVE CHART REVIEW AND PERSONAL OBSERVATION; MUST NOT PRESCRIBE, ADMINISTER, OR DISPENSE DRUG WITH POTENTIAL OF ABUSE TO PERSON UNTIL SATISFIED OF LEGITIMATE MEDICAL AND THERAPEUTIC NEED, AFTER MEDICAL HISTORY AND EXAMINATION; CONDUCT ADEQUATE FOLLOW-UP EXAMINATION; MAINTAIN COPY OF PRESCRIPTIONS SEPARATE FROM PATIENTS' MEDICAL CHARTS AND MAKE COPIES AVAILABLE FOR INSPECTION BY PHYSICIANS MONITORING PRACTICE OR BY BOARD REPRESENTATIVES; NOT TREAT PATIENTS FOR WEIGHT CONTROL OR OBESITY WITH CONTROLLED SUBSTANCES OR OVER-THE-COUNTER DRUGS; NOT TREAT OBSTETRICAL PATIENTS; CONTINUE TO SEEK CARE FROM PSYCHOLOGIST OR PSYCHIATRIST AND FOLLOW ANY RECOMMENDATIONS; APPEAR BEFORE BOARD TWICE YEARLY.

REECE, DOUGLAS L DO, DATE OF BIRTH JANUARY 26, 1942, OF 2901 AVENUE Q, LUBBOCK, TX, WAS DISCIPLINED BY MEDICARE ON FEBRUARY 1, 1993.
DISCIPLINARY ACTION: 60-MONTH EXCLUSION FROM THE MEDICARE AND/OR MEDICAID PROGRAMS
OFFENSE: CRIMINAL CONVICTION OR PLEA OF GUILTY, NOLO CONTENDERE, OR NO CONTEST TO A CRIME
NOTES: CONVICTED AND SENTENCED TO 10 YEARS PROBATION FOR MAKING A FALSE STATEMENT TO MEDICAID.

REECE, DOUGLAS L DO, LICENSE NUMBER 00E1398, OF LUBBOCK, TX, WAS DISCIPLINED BY TEXAS ON OCTOBER 1, 1993.
DISCIPLINARY ACTION: EMERGENCY SUSPENSION
OFFENSE: PHYSICAL OR MENTAL ILLNESS INHIBITING THE ABILITY TO PRACTICE WITH SKILL AND SAFETY
NOTES: AT A 9/17/93 MEETING BEFORE BOARD, PRESENTATION AND RESPONSE DEMONSTRATED A MARKED LACK OF CLARITY IN HIS MENTAL PROCESS; UNDERWENT A PSYCHIATRIC EVALUATION ON 9/23/93 WHICH REPORTED THAT HE DEMONSTRATED "COGNITIVE SLIPPAGE" AND THAT "JUDGMENT ABILITY AND INSIGHT SEEMED QUESTIONABLE."

REECE, DOUGLAS L DO, LICENSE NUMBER 0050096, OF 2901 AVENUE Q, LUBBOCK, TX, WAS DISCIPLINED BY DEA ON NOVEMBER 29, 1993.
DISCIPLINARY ACTION: SURRENDER OF CONTROLLED SUBSTANCE LICENSE
OFFENSE: DISCIPLINARY ACTION BY ANOTHER STATE OR AGENCY

REECE, DOUGLAS L DO, LICENSE NUMBER 00E1398, OF LUBBOCK, TX, WAS DISCIPLINED BY TEXAS ON MARCH 5, 1994.
DISCIPLINARY ACTION: 60-MONTH PROBATION; RESTRICTION PLACED ON LICENSE
OFFENSE: CRIMINAL CONVICTION OR PLEA OF GUILTY, NOLO CONTENDERE, OR NO CONTEST TO A CRIME
NOTES: ON 5/5/92 PLED GUILTY TO TAMPERING WITH GOVERNMENT RECORDS AND WAS SENTENCED TO 10 YEARS PROBATION UNDER AN ORDER FOR DEFERRED ADJUDICATION; ON 1/12/93 WAS EXCLUDED FROM MEDICARE PROGRAM FOR FIVE YEARS; APPEARED BEFORE BOARD IN SEPTEMBER AND EXHIBITED BEHAVIORS WHICH CAUSED CONCERN REGARDING HIS MENTAL CONDITION; ON 10/15/93 HE WAS EVALUATED BY A BOARD-APPROVED PSYCHIATRIST WHO FELT HE COULD PRACTICE IN A STRUCTURED SUPERVISED SETTING. SUSPENSION STAYED. CONDITIONS OF

PROBATION: PRACTICE RESTRICTED TO A BOARD-APPROVED INSTITUTIONAL OR CLINICAL SETTING WITH SUPERVISOR MAKING QUARTERLY REPORTS; SHALL SUBMIT HIMSELF FOR EVALUATION AND TREATMENT TO A BOARD-APPROVED PSYCHIATRIST WITH REPORTS; SHALL APPEAR BEFORE THE BOARD ONCE A YEAR; SHALL GIVE A COPY OF THIS ORDER TO ANY HEALTH CARE ENTITY WHERE HE HAS PRIVILEGES; SHALL COOPERATE WITH THE BOARD IN VERIFYING COMPLIANCE; SHALL INFORM BOARD OF CHANGE OF ADDRESS WITHIN 10 DAYS OR IF LEAVING THE STATE; TIME SPENT OUT OF TEXAS DOES NOT COUNT TOWARD PROBATION. SHALL NOT SEEK MODIFICATION FOR ONE YEAR.

REES, SEARLE B MD, LICENSE NUMBER 0026772, OF ROUTE 7, BOX 160, GILMER, TX, WAS DISCIPLINED BY MASSACHUSETTS ON NOVEMBER 9, 1994.
OFFENSE: DISCIPLINARY ACTION BY ANOTHER STATE OR AGENCY
NOTES: DISCIPLINE BY TEXAS; CONTROLLED SUBSTANCE VIOLATION; FAILURE TO RESPOND TO BOARD. REVOCATION OF INCHOATE RIGHT TO RENEW LICENSE.

REES, SEARLE BEAUFORT MD, DATE OF BIRTH OCTOBER 7, 1927, LICENSE NUMBER 00G4434, OF 300 WEST UPSHUR STREET, GLADEWATER, TX, WAS DISCIPLINED BY TEXAS ON JANUARY 29, 1993.
DISCIPLINARY ACTION: 60-MONTH PROBATION; RESTRICTION PLACED ON LICENSE
OFFENSE: OVERPRESCRIBING OR MISPRESCRIBING DRUGS
NOTES: PRESCRIBED FASTIN FOR SIX MONTHS AS THE SOLE WEIGHT CONTROL MEASURE FOR TWO PATIENTS; SUCH PRESCRIBING IS NONTHERAPEUTIC IN NATURE OR THE MANNER PRESCRIBED. 5 YEAR SUSPENSION STAYED. CONDITIONS OF PROBATION: SHALL APPEAR BEFORE THE BOARD TWICE A YEAR; SHALL ATTEND AT LEAST 50 HOURS PER YEAR OF CONTINUING MEDICAL EDUCATION INCLUDING AT LEAST 10 HOURS IN WEIGHT LOSS MANAGEMENT THE FIRST YEAR; SHALL NOT TREAT ANY PATIENT FOR WEIGHT CONTROL WITH ANY DRUGS; SHALL CONTINUE TO RECEIVE TREATMENT FROM HIS PRESENT DOCTOR; SHALL NOT TREAT OR OTHERWISE SERVE AS PHYSICIAN, PRESCRIBE, DISPENSE OR ADMINISTER DRUGS THAT MAY BE SUBJECT TO ABUSE TO HIMSELF OR ANY MEMBER OF HIS FAMILY; SHALL GIVE A COPY OF THIS ORDER TO ANY HEALTH CARE ENTITY WHERE HE HAS PRIVILEGES; SHALL COOPERATE WITH THE BOARD IN VERIFYING COMPLIANCE; SHALL NOTIFY BOARD OF CHANGE OF ADDRESS WITHIN 10 DAYS OR IF HE LEAVES THE STATE; TIME SPENT OUT OF TEXAS DOES NOT COUNT TOWARD PROBATION. SHALL NOT SEEK MODIFICATION FOR 1 YEAR.

REES, SEARLE BEAUFORT MD, DATE OF BIRTH OCTOBER 7, 1927, LICENSE NUMBER 00G4434, OF ROUTE 7 BOX 160, GILMER, TX, WAS DISCIPLINED BY TEXAS ON AUGUST 6, 1993.
DISCIPLINARY ACTION: EMERGENCY SUSPENSION
OFFENSE: OVERPRESCRIBING OR MISPRESCRIBING DRUGS
NOTES: ON 1/29/93 ENTERED INTO AGREEMENT WITH BOARD RESULTING IN A STAYED SUSPENSION WITH FIVE YEAR PROBATION BASED ON NON-THERAPEUTIC PRESCRIBING OF FASTIN AS THE SOLE WEIGHT CONTROL MEASURE FOR TWO PATIENTS; BETWEEN 11/92 AND 3/93 AN UNDERCOVER NARCOTICS AGENT MADE SEVEN BUYS FROM HIM USING A FICTITIOUS PATIENT NAME; ON 2/26/93 DEA AGENTS RECEIVED PRESCRIPTIONS FOR TALWIN, VALIUM AND AXOTAL WITH NO PHYSICAL EXAMS AND NO MEDICAL NEED OR JUSTIFICATION; HE AND HIS WIFE WERE ARRESTED ON 3/16/93 FOR POSSESSION WITH INTENT TO DISTRIBUTE AND DISTRIBUTION OF SCHEDULE II, III AND IV CONTROLLED SUBSTANCES; SURRENDERED DEA AND TEXAS CONTROLLED SUBSTANCES REGISTRATIONS ON 3/29/93; HAS CONTINUED TO PRESCRIBE (OVER 80 PRESCRIPTIONS) SINCE THIS SURRENDER; ONE OF HIS PATIENTS OVERDOSED ON VALIUM AND ALCOHOL 5 DAYS AFTER HE PRESCRIBED/DISPENSED 100 TABLETS OF DEMEROL. HE SUFFERS FROM DEPRESSION, IS TAKING LITHIUM AND IS UNDER MEDICAL CARE.

REES, SEARLE BEAUFORT MD, DATE OF BIRTH OCTOBER 7, 1927, LICENSE NUMBER 00G4434, OF ROUTE 7 BOX 160, GILMER, TX, WAS DISCIPLINED BY TEXAS ON AUGUST 20, 1993.
DISCIPLINARY ACTION: SURRENDER OF LICENSE
OFFENSE: FAILURE TO COMPLY WITH A PREVIOUS BOARD ORDER
NOTES: CONTINUED TO PRESCRIBE CONTROLLED SUBSTANCES TO NUMEROUS PATIENTS AFTER HE HAD SURRENDERED CONTROLLED SUBSTANCES REGISTRATION ON 3/29/93. SURRENDER IN LIEU OF FURTHER PROCEEDINGS.

REINER, MICHAEL D MD, DATE OF BIRTH MARCH 31, 1957, OF 15031 YORKTOWN COLONY DR, HOUSTON, TX, WAS DISCIPLINED BY MEDICARE ON NOVEMBER 9, 1989.
DISCIPLINARY ACTION: 48-MONTH EXCLUSION FROM THE MEDICARE AND/OR MEDICAID PROGRAMS
OFFENSE: CRIMINAL CONVICTION OR PLEA OF GUILTY, NOLO CONTENDERE, OR NO CONTEST TO A CRIME
NOTES: PROGRAM-RELATED CONVICTION.

REINER, MICHAEL DAVID MD, LICENSE NUMBER 0026184, OF 8200 E BELVIEW, STE 100, ENGLEWOOD, CO, WAS DISCIPLINED BY DEA ON MAY 15, 1989.
DISCIPLINARY ACTION: SURRENDER OF CONTROLLED SUBSTANCE LICENSE
OFFENSE: CRIMINAL CONVICTION OR PLEA OF GUILTY, NOLO CONTENDERE, OR NO CONTEST TO A CRIME
NOTES: AUDIT OF CONTROLLED SUBSTANCE USAGE 02/12/87. SEARCH WARRANT EXECUTED AT BUSINESS 01/23/87 IN OAK CREEK, COLORADO AND RESULTED IN SEIZURE OF SAMPLE CONTAINING LESS THAN ONE PERCENT COCAINE AND DEMEROL SAMPLE CONTAINING LESS THAN ONE PERCENT MEPERIDINE. ARRESTED 06/30/87 IN GRAND COUNTY, CO FOR VIOLATION OF CONTROLLED SUBSTANCE ACT. CONVICTED 09/11/87 FOR THEFT IN EXCESS OF $11,000, OBTAINING CONTROLLED SUBSTANCES BY FRAUD AND DECEIT, AND FAILING TO MAINTAIN RECORDS OF CONTROLLED SUBSTANCES; SENTENCED TO 1 YEAR SUSPENSION AND $1,500 FINE. COLORADO MEDICAL LICENSE SUSPENDED FOR 1.5 YEARS AND LIFETIME PROBATION WITH RESTRICTIONS. PLACED UNDER 5 YEAR SUSPENSION. WITHDRAWAL OF APPLICATION FOR RENEWAL 03/06/89 AND SURRENDER OF REGISTRATION 04/17/89.

REINER, MICHAEL DAVID MD, LICENSE NUMBER 0026184, OF HOUSTON, TX, WAS DISCIPLINED BY COLORADO ON OCTOBER 10, 1990.
DISCIPLINARY ACTION: PROBATION
NOTES: REINSTATEMENT SOUGHT FROM SUSPENSION ORDER ENTERED ON 12/5/88. REINSTATEMENT SUBJECT TO

PROBATIONARY TERMS AND CONDITIONS.

REISCHMANN, EDDY DO, LICENSE NUMBER 00D8603, OF PORTER, TX, WAS DISCIPLINED BY TEXAS ON MARCH 6, 1992.
DISCIPLINARY ACTION: 60-MONTH PROBATION
OFFENSE: OVERPRESCRIBING OR MISPRESCRIBING DRUGS
NOTES: SEVERAL VIOLATIONS OF THE MEDICAL PRACTICE ACT, INCLUDING NONTHERAPEUTIC PRESCRIBING. LICENSE SUSPENDED, SUSPENSION STAYED; PROBATION UNDER TERMS AND CONDITIONS.

REISCHMANN, EDDY DO, LICENSE NUMBER 00D8603, OF PORTER, TX, WAS DISCIPLINED BY TEXAS ON NOVEMBER 14, 1992.
DISCIPLINARY ACTION: LICENSE SUSPENSION
OFFENSE: FAILURE TO COMPLY WITH A PREVIOUS BOARD ORDER
NOTES: FAILED TO PASS THE SPEX EXAMINATION AS REQUIRED BY THE PREVIOUS BOARD ORDER.

REYES, LUCIO ARTURO MD, LICENSE NUMBER 00J0787, OF CONROE, TX, WAS DISCIPLINED BY TEXAS ON OCTOBER 9, 1992.
DISCIPLINARY ACTION: EMERGENCY SUSPENSION
OFFENSE: SUBSTANDARD CARE, INCOMPETENCE, OR NEGLIGENCE
NOTES: UNPROFESSIONAL OR DISHONORABLE CONDUCT THAT IS LIKELY TO DECEIVE, DEFRAUD OR INJURE THE PUBLIC; AND PROFESSIONAL FAILURE TO PRACTICE MEDICINE IN AN ACCEPTABLE MANNER CONSISTENT WITH PUBLIC HEALTH AND WELFARE. LICENSE TEMPORARILY SUSPENDED PENDING A HEARING.

REYES, LUCIO ARTURO MD, LICENSE NUMBER 00J0787, OF CONROE, TX, WAS DISCIPLINED BY TEXAS ON SEPTEMBER 30, 1994.
DISCIPLINARY ACTION: LICENSE REVOCATION
OFFENSE: CRIMINAL CONVICTION OR PLEA OF GUILTY, NOLO CONTENDERE, OR NO CONTEST TO A CRIME
NOTES: ON 6/14/94 WAS CONVICTED IN THE DISTRICT COURT OF WALKER COUNTY, TEXAS OF SEXUAL ASSAULT COMMITTED ON 8/17/92 A SECOND DEGREE FELONY AND ATTEMPTED SEXUAL ASSAULT COMMITTED ON 9/19/92 A THIRD DEGREE FELONY; HE ENTERED GUILTY PLEAS TO BOTH OFFENSES.

RHEA, IRA E MD, LICENSE NUMBER 00E5606, OF EAGLEVILLE, TN, WAS DISCIPLINED BY TEXAS ON JULY 1, 1989.
NOTES: MUST RECEIVE APPROVAL FROM BOARD BEFORE PRACTICING IN TEXAS

RHOADES, JOE WALKER DO, LICENSE NUMBER 00C3186, OF FORT WORTH, TX, WAS DISCIPLINED BY TEXAS ON JANUARY 6, 1995.
DISCIPLINARY ACTION: REQUIRED TO TAKE ADDITIONAL MEDICAL EDUCATION; MONITORING OF PHYSICIAN
OFFENSE: OVERPRESCRIBING OR MISPRESCRIBING DRUGS
NOTES: OVER THE COURSE OF SEVERAL YEARS, HAS PRESCRIBED CONTROLLED SUBSTANCES TO TWO PATIENTS WITHOUT ADEQUATE DOCUMENTATION AND WITHOUT ADEQUATE FOLLOW-UP EVALUATIONS, REFERRAL OR DRUG COUNSELING; ACTION IN LIEU OF FURTHER INVESTIGATION. CONDITIONS OF THREE YEAR RESTRICTION: SEPARATE FROM PATIENT RECORDS SHALL MAINTAIN A FILE OF EVERY PRESCRIPTION WRITTEN FOR CONTROLLED SUBSTANCES OR DANGEROUS DRUGS WITH ADDICTIVE POTENTIAL WHICH SHALL BE AVAILABLE FOR INSPECTION; SHALL NOT TELEPHONE TO A PHARMACY ANY PRESCRIPTION OR REFILL FOR SUCH DRUGS; SHALL MAINTAIN ADEQUATE MEDICAL RECORDS ON ALL OFFICE VISITS WHICH SHALL BE AVAILABLE FOR INSPECTION; SHALL OBTAIN AT LEAST 50 HOURS PER YEAR OF CONTINUING MEDICAL EDUCATION; SHALL APPEAR BEFORE THE BOARD ONCE A YEAR OR UPON REQUEST; SHALL COOPERATE WITH THE BOARD IN VERIFYING COMPLIANCE; SHALL GIVE A COPY OF THIS ORDER TO ANY HEALTH CARE ENTITY WHERE HE HAS OR APPLIES FOR PRIVILEGES OR ANYONE ELSE WHO ASKS FOR IT; SHALL ENSURE INQUIRIES REGARDING HIS TEXAS LICENSURE STATUS ARE ANSWERED BY REFERENCING THIS ORDER; SHALL INFORM BOARD OF CHANGE OF ADDRESS WITHIN 10 DAYS OR IF HE LEAVES THE STATE; TIME SPENT OUT OF TEXAS DOES NOT COUNT TOWARD RESTRICTION. SHALL NOT SEEK MODIFICATION FOR ONE YEAR.

RICE, KARL WOODS MD, LICENSE NUMBER 00D9626, OF LONGVIEW, TX, WAS DISCIPLINED BY TEXAS ON AUGUST 20, 1992.
DISCIPLINARY ACTION: 60-MONTH PROBATION
OFFENSE: DRUG OR ALCOHOL ABUSE
NOTES: INTEMPERATE USE OF ALCOHOL. LICENSE SUSPENDED, SUSPENSION STAYED. PROBATION UNDER TERMS AND CONDITIONS. ON 9/30/94 PETITION FOR TERMINATION OF ORDER DENIED.

RICH, DOMINIC RICHARD DO, LICENSE NUMBER 00C4188, OF CORPUS CHRISTI, TX, WAS DISCIPLINED BY TEXAS ON OCTOBER 1, 1993.
DISCIPLINARY ACTION: SURRENDER OF LICENSE
NOTES: IN LIEU OF FURTHER INVESTIGATION INTO ALLEGATIONS. SHALL NOT PETITION FOR REINSTATEMENT OF LICENSE.

RICHTER, JAMES K MD, LICENSE NUMBER 00C4518, OF SAN ANTONIO, TX, WAS DISCIPLINED BY TEXAS ON AUGUST 19, 1994.
DISCIPLINARY ACTION: REQUIRED TO TAKE ADDITIONAL MEDICAL EDUCATION; MONITORING OF PHYSICIAN
OFFENSE: OVERPRESCRIBING OR MISPRESCRIBING DRUGS
NOTES: FROM 1989 THROUGH 1993 HE PRESCRIBED CONTROLLED STIMULANT MEDICATIONS FOR THE TREATMENT OF OBESITY TO MULTIPLE PATIENTS WITHOUT SUFFICIENTLY ESTABLISHING AND DOCUMENTING AN APPROPRIATE DIAGNOSIS AND BASIS FOR SUCH A DIAGNOSIS; ALSO FAILED TO ADEQUATELY DOCUMENT THE PRESCRIBING AND DISPENSING OF MEDICATIONS. CONDITIONS OF FIVE YEAR RESTRICTION: SHALL APPEAR BEFORE THE BOARD ONCE A YEAR; SHALL MAINTAIN ADEQUATE MEDICAL RECORDS ON ALL PATIENT OFFICE VISITS WHICH SHALL BE AVAILABLE FOR INSPECTION; SEPARATE FROM PATIENT RECORDS, SHALL MAINTAIN A FILE OF EVERY PRESCRIPTION WRITTEN FOR CONTROLLED SUBSTANCES OR DANGEROUS DRUGS WHICH SHALL BE AVAILABLE FOR INSPECTION; SHALL ATTEND AT LEAST 50 HOURS PER YEAR OF CONTINUING MEDICAL EDUCATION; PRIOR TO PRACTICING IN THE SPECIALTY OF FAMILY PRACTICE SHALL COMPLETE A BOARD-APPROVED MINI-RESIDENCY; WITHIN ONE YEAR SHALL PASS THE MEDICAL JURISPRUDENCE EXAM; SHALL GIVE A COPY OF THIS ORDER TO ANY HEALTH CARE ENTITY WHERE HE HAS PRIVILEGES; SHALL COOPERATE WITH THE BOARD IN VERIFYING COMPLIANCE; SHALL INFORM BOARD OF CHANGE OF ADDRESS WITHIN 10 DAYS OR IF HE LEAVES THE STATE; TIME SPENT OUT OF TEXAS DOES NOT COUNT TOWARD RESTRICTION. SHALL NOT SEEK MODIFICATION FOR ONE YEAR.

RIEDWEG, EDWARD A MD, LICENSE NUMBER 0022008, OF 301 EAST DIVISION, GREENVILLE, TX, WAS DISCIPLINED BY DEA ON JULY 30, 1993.
DISCIPLINARY ACTION: SURRENDER OF CONTROLLED SUBSTANCE LICENSE
OFFENSE: DISCIPLINARY ACTION BY ANOTHER STATE OR AGENCY

RIEDWEG, EDWARD ALBERT MD, DATE OF BIRTH NOVEMBER 26, 1941, LICENSE NUMBER 00E3757, OF DALLAS, TX, WAS DISCIPLINED BY TEXAS ON JUNE 17, 1992.
DISCIPLINARY ACTION: 60-MONTH PROBATION
OFFENSE: DRUG OR ALCOHOL ABUSE
NOTES: SEVERAL VIOLATIONS OF THE MEDICAL PRACTICE ACT, INCLUDING INTEMPERATE USE OF ALCOHOL OR DRUGS. LICENSE SUSPENDED, SUSPENSION STAYED. PROBATION UNDER TERMS AND CONDITIONS.

RIEDWEG, EDWARD ALBERT MD, DATE OF BIRTH NOVEMBER 26, 1941, LICENSE NUMBER 00E3757, OF 4401 A I-35 NORTH SUITE 210, DENTON, TX, WAS DISCIPLINED BY TEXAS ON APRIL 30, 1993.
DISCIPLINARY ACTION: EMERGENCY SUSPENSION
OFFENSE: FAILURE TO COMPLY WITH A PREVIOUS BOARD ORDER
NOTES: IN A 6/17/92 ORDER CONDITIONS OF PROBATION INCLUDED THAT HE ABSTAIN FROM CONSUMING ANY ALCOHOL OR OTHER DRUGS AND IF HE DID USE THEM WOULD REPORT THIS TO THE BOARD WITHIN 24 HOURS; ON 2/20/93 HE ADMITTED HE WAS DRINKING AND WAS RELIEVED OF HIS DUTIES IN THE EMERGENCY ROOM; WAS ADMITTED TO INPATIENT HOSPITALIZATION ON 3/22/93.

RIEDWEG, EDWARD ALBERT MD, DATE OF BIRTH NOVEMBER 26, 1941, LICENSE NUMBER 00E3757, OF 4401 AI35 NORTH SUITE 210, DENTON, TX, WAS DISCIPLINED BY TEXAS ON JUNE 15, 1993.
DISCIPLINARY ACTION: LICENSE SUSPENSION
OFFENSE: FAILURE TO COMPLY WITH A PREVIOUS BOARD ORDER
NOTES: BY USING ALCOHOL WAS NOT COMPLYING WITH 6/17/92 ORDER. SUSPENSION FOR A MINIMUM OF ONE YEAR; SHALL THEN MAKE APPLICATION FOR REINSTATEMENT; BOARD SHALL REQUIRE AN INDEPENDENT MENTAL AND PHYSICAL EXAM; SHALL PROVIDE PROOF OF A DOCUMENTED AFTERCARE PROGRAM SATISFACTORY TO THE BOARD; SHALL INFORM BOARD OF CHANGE OF ADDRESS WITHIN 10 DAYS OR IF HE LEAVES THE STATE; TIME SPENT OUT OF TEXAS DOES NOT COUNT TOWARD SUSPENSION.

RIEDWEG, EDWARD ALBERT MD, DATE OF BIRTH NOVEMBER 26, 1941, LICENSE NUMBER 00E3757, OF KERRVILLE, TX, WAS DISCIPLINED BY TEXAS ON JULY 14, 1994.
OFFENSE: DRUG OR ALCOHOL ABUSE
NOTES: SINCE LICENSE SUSPENSION, HAS WORKED ON A VOLUNTEER BASIS ASSISTING IN UTILIZATION REVIEW; SIGNED A CONTINUING CARE CONTRACT WITH PHYSICIANS HEALTH AND REHABILITATION COMMITTEE; A PHYSICIAN HAS AGREED TO SUPERVISE HIS MEDICAL PRACTICE AND HE WAS EVALUATED BY A PSYCHIATRIST AND AN INTERNAL MEDICINE PHYSICIAN, NEITHER OF WHOM FOUND ANY PROBLEM THAT WOULD PREVENT HIM FOR PRACTICING MEDICINE. LICENSE REINSTATED FROM 6/3/93 SUSPENSION. HOWEVER, HE SHALL NOT PRACTICE MEDICINE UNTIL SUCH TIME AS HE UNDERGOES A 96 HOUR EVALUATION FOR CHEMICAL DEPENDENCY WHICH INDICATES HE IS ABLE TO SAFELY PRACTICE AND HE APPEARS BEFORE THE BOARD. UPON RETURN TO PRACTICE HE SHALL BE SUBJECT TO PROBATIONARY TERMS AND CONDITIONS.

RIEDWEG, EDWARD ALBERT MD, DATE OF BIRTH NOVEMBER 26, 1941, LICENSE NUMBER 00E3757, OF KERRVILLE, TX, WAS DISCIPLINED BY TEXAS ON AUGUST 20, 1994.
DISCIPLINARY ACTION: SURRENDER OF CONTROLLED SUBSTANCE LICENSE; 120-MONTH PROBATION
OFFENSE: DRUG OR ALCOHOL ABUSE
NOTES: LICENSE REINSTATED FROM SUSPENSION OF 6/3/93; ON 7/26/94 HE SUBMITTED TO A 96 HOUR MULTIDISCIPLINARY EVALUATION. THE EVALUATION INDICATED THAT HE IS ABLE TO SAFELY RETURN TO THE PRACTICE OF MEDICINE UNDER CERTAIN TERMS AND CONDITIONS. SUSPENSION STAYED. CONDITIONS OF PROBATION: SHALL APPEAR BEFORE THE BOARD TWICE A YEAR; PRACTICE SHALL BE SUPERVISED BY PRESENT SUPERVISOR WITH QUARTERLY REPORTS; SHALL ABSTAIN FROM THE CONSUMPTION OF ALCOHOL/CHEMICAL SUBSTANCES IN ANY FORM UNLESS PRESCRIBED BY ANOTHER PHYSICIAN FOR A LEGITIMATE AND THERAPEUTIC PURPOSE; SHALL CONTINUE TO PARTICIPATE WITH A PHYSICIANS HEALTH AND REHABILITATION COMMITTEE AND ATTEND WEEKLY MEETINGS WITH QUARTERLY REPORTS; SHALL CONTINUE TO PARTICIPATE IN AA'S PROGRAM NOT LESS THAN THREE TIMES A WEEK WITH QUARTERLY REPORTS TO THE BOARD; SHALL CONTINUE TO RECEIVE TREATMENT FROM CURRENT PSYCHIATRIST WITH QUARTERLY REPORTS; SHALL SUBMIT TO WEEKLY PSYCHOTHERAPY WITH A BOARD-APPROVED PSYCHOTHERAPIST WITH AT LEAST QUARTERLY REPORTS; SHALL SUBMIT HIMSELF FOR APPROPRIATE DRUG OR ALCOHOL SCREENS; SHALL NOT TREAT OR OTHERWISE SERVE AS PHYSICIAN, PRESCRIBE, DISPENSE OR ADMINISTER DRUGS THAT MAY BE SUBJECT TO ABUSE TO HIMSELF OR ANY MEMBER OF HIS FAMILY; SHALL ATTEND AT LEAST 50 HOURS PER YEAR OF CONTINUING MEDICAL EDUCATION INCLUDING AT LEAST 20 HOURS PER YEAR OF ADDICTIONOLOGY/PHARMACOLOGY; SHALL SURRENDER HIS DEA AND TEXAS CONTROLLED SUBSTANCES CERTIFICATE AND SHALL NOT ATTEMPT TO REREGISTER WITHOUT PERMISSION; SHALL GIVE A COPY OF THIS ORDER TO ANY HEALTH CARE ENTITY WHERE HE HAS PRIVILEGES; SHALL COOPERATE WITH THE BOARD IN VERIFYING COMPLIANCE; SHALL INFORM BOARD OF CHANGE OF ADDRESS WITHIN 10 DAYS OR IF HE LEAVES THE STATE; TIME SPENT OUT OF TEXAS DOES NOT COUNT TOWARD PROBATION. SHALL NOT SEEK MODIFICATION FOR ONE YEAR.

RIGGLE, KENNETH BURTON DO, LICENSE NUMBER 00C2963, OF PASADENA, TX, WAS DISCIPLINED BY TEXAS ON MARCH 6, 1992.
DISCIPLINARY ACTION: SURRENDER OF LICENSE
NOTES: LICENSE RETIRED IN LIEU OF FURTHER DISCIPLINARY ACTION.

RIVERA, RAUL MD, LICENSE NUMBER 00C8420, OF EL PASO, TX, WAS DISCIPLINED BY TEXAS ON OCTOBER 27, 1989.
DISCIPLINARY ACTION: 60-MONTH PROBATION; REQUIRED TO ENTER AN IMPAIRED PHYSICIAN PROGRAM OR DRUG OR ALCOHOL TREATMENT
OFFENSE: DRUG OR ALCOHOL ABUSE
NOTES: STIPULATED ORDER. REVOCATION STAYED. MUST PARTICIPATE IN CHEMICAL ABUSE PROGRAM AND IMPAIRED PHYSICIANS PROGRAM, SUBMIT FOR EVALUATION TO PSYCHIATRIST OR SUBSTANCE ABUSE PHYSICIAN AND FOLLOW ANY RECOMMENDED CARE, SUBMIT FOR EXAMINATIONS TO DETERMINE FREEDOM

FROM DRUGS AND ALCOHOL, ABSTAIN FROM ALCOHOL AND CONTROLLED SUBSTANCES NOT PRESCRIBED BY ANOTHER PHYSICIAN, AND APPEAR ANNUALLY BEFORE BOARD.

RIVERA, RAUL MD, LICENSE NUMBER 0C27288, OF EL PASO, TX, WAS DISCIPLINED BY CALIFORNIA ON APRIL 8, 1992.
DISCIPLINARY ACTION: 60-MONTH PROBATION
OFFENSE: DISCIPLINARY ACTION BY ANOTHER STATE OR AGENCY
NOTES: DISCIPLINE BY TEXAS BOARD FOR EXCESSIVE USE OF ALCOHOL. REVOCATION, STAYED. PROBATION WITH TERMS AND CONDITIONS.

RIVERIA, JAIME H MD, LICENSE NUMBER 0131829, OF HOUSTON, TX, WAS DISCIPLINED BY NEW YORK ON AUGUST 26, 1986.
DISCIPLINARY ACTION: 12-MONTH PROBATION
NOTES: 1 YEAR SUSPENSION, STAYED

RIVERO, MANUEL S MD OF PRESB. HOSP. PROFL. BLDG, KAUFMAN, TX, WAS DISCIPLINED BY MEDICARE ON DECEMBER 9, 1986.
DISCIPLINARY ACTION: 60-MONTH EXCLUSION FROM THE MEDICARE AND/OR MEDICAID PROGRAMS
OFFENSE: SUBSTANDARD CARE, INCOMPETENCE, OR NEGLIGENCE
NOTES: OVERTURNED BY APPEALS COUNCIL FEBRUARY 6, 1989. ORIGINALLY FOUND TO HAVE PROVIDED GROSSLY SUBSTANDARD CARE IN SIX CASES. CITED FOR FAILURE TO ACT PROMPTLY AND AGGRESSIVELY IN THE THERAPEUTIC MANAGEMENT OF LIFE-THREATENING ILLNESSES AND FOR POOR UNDERSTANDING OF CARDIAC PATHOPHYSIOLOGY AND PHARMACOLOGIC INTERVENTION. APPEALS COUNCIL DECISION SAID CARE WAS NOT SUBSTANDARD

RIZOV, VLADIMIR Z MD, LICENSE NUMBER 00G4694, OF AUSTIN, TX, WAS DISCIPLINED BY TEXAS ON AUGUST 18, 1990.
DISCIPLINARY ACTION: 60-MONTH PROBATION; REPRIMAND
NOTES: STIPULATED ORDER. MUST OBTAIN CONTINUING MEDICAL EDUCATION.

ROBERSON, FRED MD, LICENSE NUMBER 0033929, WAS DISCIPLINED BY MINNESOTA ON SEPTEMBER 12, 1992.
DISCIPLINARY ACTION: RESTRICTION PLACED ON LICENSE
NOTES: AMENDED ORDER ON 7/16/94.

ROBERSON, FRED M MD OF ZUMBROTA, MN, WAS DISCIPLINED BY LOUISIANA ON DECEMBER 2, 1993.
DISCIPLINARY ACTION: 36-MONTH PROBATION
OFFENSE: DISCIPLINARY ACTION BY ANOTHER STATE OR AGENCY
NOTES: ACTION TAKEN BY MINNESOTA; PRESCRIBING CONTROLLED SUBSTANCES IN OTHER THAN A LEGAL OR LEGITIMATE MANNER. LICENSE PLACED ON PROBATION FOR TERM CONCURRENT WITH ORDER PREVIOUSLY ENTERED BY MINNESOTA BOARD, SUBJECT TO COMPLIANCE WITH MINNESOTA ORDER, PROHIBITION ON MEDICAL PRACTICE IN LOUISIANA FOR THREE YEARS, PRIOR NOTICE TO BOARD OF INTENT TO RELOCATE TO LOUISIANA AFTER EXPIRATION OF THREE YEARS AND PROVISION OF QUARTERLY MEDICAL REPORTS TO THE BOARD.

ROBERSON, FRED MCRAE MD, LICENSE NUMBER 00D4552, OF ZUMBROTA, MN, WAS DISCIPLINED BY TEXAS ON NOVEMBER 19, 1993.
DISCIPLINARY ACTION: 60-MONTH PROBATION; MONITORING OF PHYSICIAN
OFFENSE: DISCIPLINARY ACTION BY ANOTHER STATE OR AGENCY
NOTES: ON 9/12/92 MINNESOTA BOARD RESTRICTED HIS LICENSE BASED ON THE FACT THAT HE SELF-PRESCRIBED NUMEROUS MEDICATIONS TO HIMSELF FROM 11/1/90 THROUGH 11/12/91 AVERAGING 3.7 TABLETS PER DAY OF PRIMARILY PAIN MEDICATION FOR TREATMENT RELATING TO AN ANKLE AND BACK INJURY; HE KEPT NO RECORD OF THE AMOUNT PRESCRIBED AND HAS BEEN SELF-PRESCRIBING INTERMITTENTLY SINCE 1979 OR 1980; BETWEEN 10/22/90 AND 7/5/91 PRESCRIBED NUMEROUS MEDICATIONS TO HIS WIFE FOLLOWING SURGERY FOR BREAST CANCER; HE KEPT NO RECORD OF THE AMOUNT PRESCRIBED; ADMITTED THAT ONE OF THESE PRESCRIPTIONS WAS FOR HIMSELF; MINNESOTA RESTRICTED HIS LICENSE SUCH THAT HE SHALL NOT PRESCRIBE OR SELF-ADMINISTER CONTROLLED SUBSTANCES FOR HIS OWN USE OR FOR THE USE OF HIS FAMILY; SHALL MAKE ARRANGEMENTS WITH A MONITORING/TREATING PHYSICIAN TO PROVIDE THE BOARD WITH QUARTERLY REPORTS REGARDING HIS PAIN MANAGEMENT. IN TEXAS FIVE YEAR SUSPENSION STAYED. CONDITIONS OF PROBATION: SAME TERMS AS MINNESOTA ORDER; PRIOR TO PRACTICING IN TEXAS SHALL APPEAR BEFORE THE BOARD; SHALL INFORM THE BOARD IF HE LEAVES TEXAS OR MINNESOTA; TIME SPENT OUT OF TEXAS OR MINNESOTA SHALL NOT COUNT TOWARD PROBATION. SHALL NOT SEEK MODIFICATION FOR ONE YEAR.

ROBERTSON, GERALD MELVIN MD, LICENSE NUMBER 0005670, OF CALHOUN, LA, WAS DISCIPLINED BY MISSISSIPPI ON NOVEMBER 21, 1991.
NOTES: IN VIEW OF THE LAPSED STATUS OF LICENSE, PENDING DISCIPLINARY ACTION WAS PLACED IN ABEYANCE WITH THE BOARD HAVING THE RIGHT TO ACTIVATE THE DISCIPLINARY ACTION IN THE EVENT HE ELECTS TO RENEW.

ROBERTSON, GERALD MELVIN MD, LICENSE NUMBER 00D9875, OF WEST MONROE, LA, WAS DISCIPLINED BY TEXAS ON AUGUST 20, 1992.
DISCIPLINARY ACTION: RESTRICTION PLACED ON LICENSE
OFFENSE: DISCIPLINARY ACTION BY ANOTHER STATE OR AGENCY

ROBERTSON, LESTER E MD, LICENSE NUMBER 00C5854, OF MCGREGOR, TX, WAS DISCIPLINED BY TEXAS ON OCTOBER 29, 1988.
NOTES: MUST PROMPTLY DOCUMENT ADMINISTRATION OR ORDER OF CONTROLLED SUBSTANCES OR DANGEROUS DRUGS FOR PATIENTS, THE MEDICAL REASON AND PHYSICAL EXAM RESULTS; SHALL CONDUCT FOLLOW-UP EXAMS TO DETERMINE TREATMENT; SHALL ASSURE PATIENTS ON MOOD ALTERING DRUGS RECEIVE APPROPRIATE WARNINGS; ORDER IN EFFECT FOR TWO YEARS

ROBERTSON, WILLIAM C MD, LICENSE NUMBER 00C8423, OF MCGREGOR, TX, WAS DISCIPLINED BY TEXAS ON OCTOBER 29, 1988.
NOTES: MUST PROMPTLY DOCUMENT ADMIN. OR ORDER OF CONTROLLED SUBSTANCES OR DANGEROUS DRUGS FOR PATIENTS, THE MEDICAL REASON AND PHYSICAL EXAM RESULTS; SHALL CONDUCT FOLLOW-UP EXAMS TO DETERMINE TREATMENT; SHALL ASSURE THAT PATIENTS ON MOOD-ALTERING DRUGS RECEIVE WARNING ABOUT SIDE EFFECTS; ORDER IN EFFECT

FOR TWO YEARS

ROBINETT, KELLY E DO, LICENSE NUMBER 00G7576, OF BURLESON, TX, WAS DISCIPLINED BY TEXAS ON NOVEMBER 13, 1992.
DISCIPLINARY ACTION: 60-MONTH PROBATION
OFFENSE: DRUG OR ALCOHOL ABUSE
NOTES: UNPROFESSIONAL OR DISHONORABLE CONDUCT THAT IS LIKELY TO DECEIVE, DEFRAUD OR INJURE THE PUBLIC. LICENSE SUSPENDED, SUSPENSION STAYED. ON 11/3/94 ORDER MODIFIED AS FOLLOWS: SHALL ABSTAIN FROM THE CONSUMPTION OF ALCOHOL, DANGEROUS DRUGS, OR CONTROLLED SUBSTANCES IN ANY FORM UNLESS PRESCRIBED BY ANOTHER PHYSICIAN FOR A LEGITIMATE AND THERAPEUTIC PURPOSE; DANGEROUS DRUGS OR CONTROLLED SUBSTANCES FROM ANOTHER PHYSICIAN MUST BE REPORTED IMMEDIATELY TO THE BOARD CONCERNING THE MEDICAL CONDITION BEING TREATED AND THE SUBSTANCE PRESCRIBED, DISPENSED OR ADMINISTERED; SHALL SUBMIT HIMSELF FOR APPROPRIATE EXAMINATIONS, INCLUDING SCREENING FOR ALCOHOL OR DRUGS; SHALL CONTINUE TO PARTICIPATE IN THE ACTIVITIES OF COMMITTEE ON PHYSICIAN HEALTH AND REHABILITATION INCLUDING WEEKLY MEETINGS WITH QUARTERLY REPORTS; SHALL CONTINUE TO PARTICIPATE IN THE ACTIVITIES AND PROGRAMS OF ALCOHOLICS ANONYMOUS OR ANOTHER BOARD-APPROVED PROGRAM ON A REGULAR BASIS OF NOT LESS THAN TWICE A WEEK WITH QUARTERLY REPORTS TO THE BOARD; HE IS GRANTED PERMISSION TO REAPPLY TO THE DRUG ENFORCEMENT ADMINISTRATION AND THE TEXAS DEPARTMENT OF PUBLIC SAFETY FOR SCHEDULES II, IIN, III, IIIN IV OR V; SEPARATE FROM PATIENT RECORDS SHALL MAINTAIN A COPY OF EVERY PRESCRIPTION WRITTEN FOR DANGEROUS DRUGS WHICH HAVE POTENTIAL FOR ABUSE BY DATE ISSUED WHICH SHALL BE AVAILABLE TO THE BOARD FOR INSPECTION; SHALL NOT TELEPHONE ANY PRESCRIPTION TO A PHARMACY FOR CONTROLLED SUBSTANCES OR DANGEROUS DRUGS; MAY ORDER CONTROLLED SUBSTANCES TO BE ADMINISTERED TO HOSPITAL OR NURSING HOME PATIENTS FOR THEIR MEDICAL NEEDS; SHALL NOT TREAT OR OTHERWISE SERVE AS PHYSICIAN, PRESCRIBE, DISPENSE OR ADMINISTER CONTROLLED SUBSTANCES OR ANY OTHER DRUGS THAT MAY BE SUBJECT TO ABUSE FOR HIMSELF OR ANY MEMBER OF HIS FAMILY; MAY ADMINISTER TO HIS IMMEDIATE FAMILY ONLY SUCH DRUGS AS ARE PRESCRIBED BY OTHER PHYSICIANS IN COMPLIANCE WITH THEIR ORDERS; SHALL SURRENDER ALL UNUSED TRIPLICATE PRESCRIPTION FORMS IN HIS POSSESSION; SHALL NOT ATTEMPT TO ORDER ANY MORE TRIPLICATE PRESCRIPTION FORMS UNTIL HE HAS BOARD AUTHORITY; SHALL APPEAR BEFORE THE BOARD ONCE A YEAR DURING EACH YEAR OF PROBATION TO REPORT ON HIS COMPLIANCE; SHALL GIVE A COPY OF THIS ORDER TO HEALTH CARE ENTITIES WHERE HE HAS PRIVILEGES; SHALL INFORM BOARD OF CHANGE OF ADDRESS WITHIN 10 DAYS OR IF HE LEAVES THE STATE; SHALL COOPERATE WITH BOARD IN VERIFYING COMPLIANCE; TIME SPENT OUT OF TEXAS DOES NOT COUNT TOWARD PROBATION; SHALL NOT SEEK MODIFICATION FOR ONE YEAR.

ROBINSON, HERBERT J MD, LICENSE NUMBER 00D5568, OF SAN ANTONIO, TX, WAS DISCIPLINED BY TEXAS ON DECEMBER 5, 1988.
DISCIPLINARY ACTION: LICENSE SUSPENSION
OFFENSE: FAILURE TO COMPLY WITH A PROFESSIONAL RULE
NOTES: FAILED TO COMPLY WITH BOARD SUBPOENAS. SUSPENSION UNTIL HE COMPLIES WITH SUBPOENAS AND APPEARS AS SCHEDULED

ROBINSON, HERBERT J MD OF SAN ANTONIO, TX, WAS DISCIPLINED BY DEA ON MARCH 14, 1994.
DISCIPLINARY ACTION: REVOCATION OF CONTROLLED SUBSTANCE LICENSE
OFFENSE: PROVIDING FALSE INFORMATION TO THE BOARD
NOTES: IN 1987, THE TEXAS BOARD SUBPOENAED PATIENT RECORDS FROM HIM WHICH HE REFUSED TO PROVIDE. ON 09/24/88 THE BOARD SUSPENDED HIS MEDICAL LICENSE INDEFINITELY UNTIL HE PROVIDED THE RECORDS IN QUESTION. SUSPENSION TERMINATED ON 1/12/91 AFTER HE PROVIDED THE RECORDS. IN A 1991 DEA APPLICATION HE LIED ABOUT THIS STATE LICENSE SUSPENSION.

ROBINSON, LUKE E MD, LICENSE NUMBER 00E4642, OF VICTORIA, TX, WAS DISCIPLINED BY TEXAS ON OCTOBER 5, 1991.
DISCIPLINARY ACTION: 60-MONTH PROBATION; REQUIRED TO ENTER AN IMPAIRED PHYSICIAN PROGRAM OR DRUG OR ALCOHOL TREATMENT
OFFENSE: DRUG OR ALCOHOL ABUSE
NOTES: FROM 1/90 THROUGH 12/12/90 HE ABUSED BENZODIAZEPAM AND ALCOHOL FOR NON-MEDICAL PURPOSES; PARTICIPATED IN A TREATMENT PROGRAM FOR TREATMENT OF CHEMICAL DEPENDENCY FROM 12/13/90 TO 1/25/91; EXECUTED A TWO YEAR CONTINUING CARE CONTRACT ON 1/25/91; IMPAIRMENT CAUSED HIM TO EXPERIENCE MEMORY BLACKOUTS AND CANCEL SCHEDULED SURGERIES AND APPOINTMENTS. SUSPENSION STAYED; CONDITIONS OF PROBATION: SHALL REFRAIN FROM CONSUMING ANY MOOD-ALTERING DRUGS, INCLUDING ALCOHOL; SHALL SUBMIT HIMSELF FOR RANDOM SCREENING OF BODILY FLUIDS; SHALL PARTICIPATE IN IMPAIRED PHYSICIANS PROGRAM WITH WEEKLY MEETINGS AND QUARTERLY REPORTS TO THE BOARD; SHALL PARTICIPATE IN AA, INCLUDING A 12-STEP PROGRAM, NOT LESS THAN TWICE A WEEK, WITH QUARTERLY REPORTS TO THE BOARD; SHALL COMPLY WITH CONDITIONS OF CONTINUING CARE CONTRACT; SHALL CONTINUE TO RECEIVE TREATMENT, WITH QUARTERLY REPORTS TO THE BOARD; SHALL APPEAR BEFORE THE BOARD TWICE A YEAR; SHALL COOPERATE WITH THE BOARD IN VERIFYING COMPLIANCE; SHALL ADVISE BOARD OF ANY CHANGE OF ADDRESS WITHIN 10 DAYS; TIME SPENT OUT OF TEXAS DOES NOT COUNT TOWARDS PROBATION; SHALL NOT PETITION FOR MODIFICATION FOR ONE YEAR. ON 4/15/94 REQUEST FOR TERMINATION OF THIS ORDER DENIED. ORDER MODIFIED AS FOLLOWS: APPEARANCES BEFORE BOARD REDUCED TO ONCE A YEAR DURING EACH YEAR OF PROBATION TO REPORT ON HIS COMPLIANCE; HE MAY REQUEST MODIFICATION OR TERMINATION OF THIS ORDER ONCE EVERY SIX MONTHS. ALL OTHER CONDITIONS OF THIS ORDER REMAIN IN EFFECT. ON 11/3/94 PROBATION TERMINATED.

ROBINSON, RALPH R MD, DATE OF BIRTH JULY 7, 1913, LICENSE NUMBER 0011914, WAS DISCIPLINED BY KENTUCKY ON MARCH 24, 1988.

DISCIPLINARY ACTION: 60-MONTH PROBATION; FINE
NOTES: NO SCHEDULE II, IIN, III OR IIIN CONTROLLED SUBSTANCE PRIVILEGES DURING PROBATION; 15 HOURS OF CONTINUING MEDICAL EDUCATION IN AREA OF PHARMACOLOGY PER YEAR FOR 2 YEARS; FINED $1,000

ROBINSON, RALPH R MD OF MIDDLESBORO, KY, WAS DISCIPLINED BY OHIO ON JANUARY 11, 1989.
DISCIPLINARY ACTION: LICENSE SUSPENSION
NOTES: INDEFINITE SUSPENSION

ROBINSON, RALPH R MD OF MIDDLESBORO, KY, WAS DISCIPLINED BY OHIO ON MAY 13, 1989.
DISCIPLINARY ACTION: SURRENDER OF LICENSE

ROBINSON, RALPH R MD, LICENSE NUMBER 0008135, OF MIDDLESBORO, KY, WAS DISCIPLINED BY SOUTH CAROLINA ON JULY 14, 1989.
DISCIPLINARY ACTION: SURRENDER OF LICENSE
NOTES: NOT ELIGIBLE FOR REINSTATEMENT

ROBINSON, RALPH R MD OF MIDDLESBORO, KY, WAS DISCIPLINED BY MISSOURI ON SEPTEMBER 15, 1989.
DISCIPLINARY ACTION: 120-MONTH PROBATION
OFFENSE: DISCIPLINARY ACTION BY ANOTHER STATE OR AGENCY
NOTES: LIMITATION OF CONTROLLED SUBSTANCE PRESCRIBING AUTHORITY BY ANOTHER STATE OR AGENCY.

ROBINSON, RALPH R MD WAS DISCIPLINED BY WASHINGTON ON FEBRUARY 16, 1990.
DISCIPLINARY ACTION: PROBATION; RESTRICTION PLACED ON CONTROLLED SUBSTANCE LICENSE
OFFENSE: DISCIPLINARY ACTION BY ANOTHER STATE OR AGENCY
NOTES: ON 12/6/89 BOARD ISSUED A STATEMENT OF CHARGES REGARDING FREQUENTLY PRESCRIBING, DISPENSING OR ADMINISTERING CONTROLLED SUBSTANCES FOR UNDIAGNOSED PAIN, FOR PROLONGED PERIODS OF TIME AND IN INAPPROPRIATE COMBINATIONS; HIS LICENSE HAS BEEN RESTRICTED IN KENTUCKY, ALABAMA, OKLAHOMA AND NORTH CAROLINA. THE FOLLOWING PROVISIONS OF THE KENTUCKY ORDER ARE ADOPTED BY WASHINGTON: UNABLE TO PRESCRIBE, ADMINISTER, OR DISPENSE SCHEDULE II, IIN, III, OR IIIN CONTROLLED DANGEROUS SUBSTANCES DURING PROBATION; MUST OBTAIN 15 HOURS PER YEAR OF CONTINUING MEDICAL EDUCATION IN PHARMACOLOGY FOR THE FIRST 2 YEARS OF PROBATION. WHEN HIS PRESCRIBING PRIVILEGES ARE REINSTATED IN COMMONWEALTH OF KENTUCKY, MAY APPLY FOR REINSTATEMENT IN WASHINGTON.

ROBINSON, RALPH R MD OF MIDDLESBORO, KY, WAS DISCIPLINED BY TENNESSEE ON MAY 14, 1990.
DISCIPLINARY ACTION: 60-MONTH PROBATION; RESTRICTION PLACED ON CONTROLLED SUBSTANCE LICENSE
OFFENSE: DISCIPLINARY ACTION BY ANOTHER STATE OR AGENCY
NOTES: MAY NOT PRESCRIBE SCHEDULE II OR III DRUGS DURING PROBATION, HOWEVER, PHYSICIAN MAY REAPPLY FOR FULL DEA PRIVILEGES AFTER TWO YEARS. MUST COMPLETE CONTINUING MEDICAL EDUCATION COURSE IN PHARMACOLOGY

ROBINSON, RALPH R MD WAS DISCIPLINED BY WASHINGTON, D.C. ON SEPTEMBER 5, 1990.
DISCIPLINARY ACTION: PROBATION
OFFENSE: DISCIPLINARY ACTION BY ANOTHER STATE OR AGENCY
NOTES: DISCIPLINED BY KENTUCKY FOR CONDUCT THAT WOULD BE GROUNDS FOR DISCIPLINARY ACTION IN THE DISTRICT OF COLUMBIA; FILED WITH THE BOARD A DOCUMENT HE KNEW OR SHOULD HAVE KNOWN WAS FALSE OR MISLEADING.

ROBINSON, RALPH R MD, LICENSE NUMBER C019518, OF MIDDLESBORO, KY, WAS DISCIPLINED BY CALIFORNIA ON JANUARY 10, 1991.
DISCIPLINARY ACTION: SURRENDER OF LICENSE
NOTES: VOLUNTARY SURRENDER WHILE CHARGES PENDING.

ROBINSON, RALPH R MD OF MIDDLESBORO, KY, WAS DISCIPLINED BY VIRGINIA ON APRIL 9, 1991.
DISCIPLINARY ACTION: PROBATION
OFFENSE: DISCIPLINARY ACTION BY ANOTHER STATE OR AGENCY
NOTES: DISCIPLINARY ACTION IN OTHER STATES.

ROBINSON, RALPH R MD, DATE OF BIRTH JULY 7, 1913, LICENSE NUMBER 0011914, OF BELL COUNTY, KY, WAS DISCIPLINED BY KENTUCKY ON MARCH 4, 1993.
DISCIPLINARY ACTION: SURRENDER OF LICENSE
NOTES: IN LIEU OF INQUIRY CONCERNING MEDICAL PRACTICE.

ROBINSON, RALPH R MD, LICENSE NUMBER 0016797, OF MIDDLESBORO, KY, WAS DISCIPLINED BY VIRGINIA ON FEBRUARY 17, 1994.
OFFENSE: DISCIPLINARY ACTION BY ANOTHER STATE OR AGENCY
NOTES: ON 2/18/93 KENTUCKY BOARD ACCEPTED HIS RETIREMENT FROM THE ACTIVE PRACTICE OF MEDICINE IN THAT JURISDICTION AND AGREED TO TERMINATE INQUIRY INTO HIS PRESCRIBING OF CONTROLLED SUBSTANCES UNTIL HE REACTIVATES HIS KENTUCKY LICENSE. SURRENDER OF PRIVILEGE TO RENEW VIRGINIA LICENSE IN LIEU OF FURTHER ADMINISTRATIVE PROCEEDINGS.

ROBINSON, RALPH ROLLIN MD OF KY, WAS DISCIPLINED BY NORTH CAROLINA ON JANUARY 31, 1989.
DISCIPLINARY ACTION: 60-MONTH PROBATION

ROBINSON, RALPH ROLLIN MD, LICENSE NUMBER 00E7253, OF MIDDLESBORO, KY, WAS DISCIPLINED BY TEXAS ON DECEMBER 1, 1990.
DISCIPLINARY ACTION: LICENSE REVOCATION
NOTES: PHYSICIAN, UNDER BOARD DISCIPLINARY ORDER, REQUESTED CANCELLATION OF LICENSE. IF HE REAPPLIES, BOARD DISCIPLINARY ORDER WILL BE REACTIVATED.

ROBY, RUSSELL R MD, LICENSE NUMBER 00E1255, OF AUSTIN, TX, WAS DISCIPLINED BY TEXAS ON DECEMBER 1, 1989.
DISCIPLINARY ACTION: REQUIRED TO TAKE ADDITIONAL MEDICAL EDUCATION
OFFENSE: SUBSTANDARD CARE, INCOMPETENCE, OR NEGLIGENCE
NOTES: CONTINUE PREVIOUS PROBATIONARY TERMS AND IMPOSE NEW TERMS REGARDING PATIENT CHARTS AND CONTINUING MEDICAL EDUCATION

RODRIGUEZ, MARIO A MD, LICENSE NUMBER 00G9302, OF ARLINGTON, TX, WAS DISCIPLINED BY TEXAS ON APRIL 26, 1991.
DISCIPLINARY ACTION: LICENSE REVOCATION
OFFENSE: PHYSICAL OR MENTAL ILLNESS INHIBITING THE ABILITY TO PRACTICE WITH SKILL AND SAFETY
NOTES: FAILURE TO PRACTICE MEDICINE WITH REASONABLE SAFETY AND SKILL NECESSARY BY REASON OF A

MENTAL CONDITION.

RODRIGUEZ, SERGIO LUIS MD, LICENSE NUMBER 00D9276, OF LIBERTY, TX, WAS DISCIPLINED BY TEXAS ON APRIL 20, 1991.
DISCIPLINARY ACTION: SURRENDER OF LICENSE
NOTES: LICENSE VOLUNTARILY SURRENDERED IN LIEU OF FURTHER DISCIPLINARY PROCEEDINGS.

RODRIGUEZ, SERGIO LUIS MD, LICENSE NUMBER 0C38767, OF LIBERTY, TX, WAS DISCIPLINED BY CALIFORNIA ON NOVEMBER 28, 1994.
DISCIPLINARY ACTION: LICENSE REVOCATION
OFFENSE: DISCIPLINARY ACTION BY ANOTHER STATE OR AGENCY
NOTES: DISCIPLINED BY TEXAS BOARD FOR MENTAL IMPAIRMENT AFFECTING SAFE PRACTICES. DEFAULT DECISION.

RODRIGUEZ, VINCENT MD, LICENSE NUMBER 0028371, OF HUNT, TX, WAS DISCIPLINED BY COLORADO ON APRIL 10, 1991.
DISCIPLINARY ACTION: LICENSE REVOCATION
OFFENSE: CRIMINAL CONVICTION OR PLEA OF GUILTY, NOLO CONTENDERE, OR NO CONTEST TO A CRIME
NOTES: ACTION BASED ON HABITUAL OR EXCESSIVE USE OF CONTROLLED SUBSTANCES AND FELONY CONVICTION FOR CARRYING A CONCEALED WEAPON.

RODRIGUEZ, VINCENT MD OF 9950 W 80TH AVENUE #16, ARVADA, CO, WAS DISCIPLINED BY DEA ON AUGUST 1, 1991.
DISCIPLINARY ACTION: REVOCATION OF CONTROLLED SUBSTANCE LICENSE
OFFENSE: DISCIPLINARY ACTION BY ANOTHER STATE OR AGENCY
NOTES: ON 4/10/91 COLORADO REVOKED HIS LICENSE. IN HIS STATEMENT HE CONTENDS COLORADO ACTION WAS BASED ON FLORIDA'S EMERGENCY SUSPENSION OF HIS LICENSE ON 2/6/90 AND THAT HE HAD ENTERED INTO AN AGREEMENT WITH FLORIDA PERMITTING HIM TO SEEK REINSTATEMENT ON 5/6/91. DEA FOUND THESE FACTS IRRELEVANT TO THE FACT THAT HE DID NOT HAVE PRESCRIBING AUTHORITY IN COLORADO.

RODRIGUEZ, VINCENT MD WAS DISCIPLINED BY NEBRASKA ON DECEMBER 7, 1994.
DISCIPLINARY ACTION: SURRENDER OF LICENSE
OFFENSE: FAILURE TO COMPLY WITH A PREVIOUS BOARD ORDER
NOTES: CHARGES OF MISREPRESENTATION OF FACTS; PROBATION VIOLATION. CHARGES DISMISSED IN LIEU OF SURRENDER OF LICENSE.

RODRIGUEZ, VINCENT J MD, DATE OF BIRTH AUGUST 23, 1959, OF PO BOX 1, HUNT, TX, WAS DISCIPLINED BY MEDICARE ON DECEMBER 20, 1991.
DISCIPLINARY ACTION: EXCLUSION FROM THE MEDICARE AND/OR MEDICAID PROGRAMS
OFFENSE: DISCIPLINARY ACTION BY ANOTHER STATE OR AGENCY
NOTES: LICENSE REVOCATION OR SUSPENSION.

RODRIGUEZ, VINCENT JOHN MD, LICENSE NUMBER 0053547, OF TALLAHASSEE, FL, WAS DISCIPLINED BY FLORIDA ON FEBRUARY 6, 1990.
DISCIPLINARY ACTION: EMERGENCY SUSPENSION
NOTES: INABILITY TO PRACTICE WITH REASONABLE SKILL BY REASON OF THE USE OF DRUGS OR AS A RESULT OF A MENTAL OR PHYSICAL CONDITION; PRESCRIBING TO HIMSELF.

RODRIGUEZ, VINCENT JOHN MD, LICENSE NUMBER 0053547, OF HUNT, TX, WAS DISCIPLINED BY FLORIDA ON MAY 6, 1991.
DISCIPLINARY ACTION: LICENSE SUSPENSION; 60-MONTH PROBATION
NOTES: CHARGED WITH BEING UNABLE TO PRACTICE BY REASON OF THE USE OF DRUGS OR AS A RESULT OF ANY MENTAL OR PHYSICAL CONDITION. IN LIEU OF FURTHER PROSECUTION, STIPULATED TO SUSPENSION UNTIL HE CAN PROVE HE IS ABLE TO PRACTICE WITH REASONABLE SKILL AND SAFETY, WHICH SHALL INCLUDE SATISFACTORY PSYCHIATRIC AND PHYSICAL EVALUATIONS; ACTIVE PHYSICIANS RECOVERY NETWORK CONTRACT; BOARD-APPROVED PLAN FOR RENTRY TO PRACTICE. UPON REINSTATEMENT, PROBATION WITH TERMS AND CONDITIONS TO BE SET, WHICH SHALL INCLUDE CONTINUATION OF ACTIVE PHYSICIAN'S RECOVERY NETWORK CONTRACT.

RODRIGUEZSILVA, MARIO A MD, LICENSE NUMBER 0049850, OF ARLINGTON, TX, WAS DISCIPLINED BY FLORIDA ON MAY 6, 1991.
DISCIPLINARY ACTION: 24-MONTH LICENSE SUSPENSION; REQUIRED TO TAKE ADDITIONAL MEDICAL EDUCATION
OFFENSE: SUBSTANDARD CARE, INCOMPETENCE, OR NEGLIGENCE
NOTES: CHARGED WITH FAILING TO PRACTICE MEDICINE WITH AN ACCEPTABLE LEVEL OF CARE AND SKILL; FAILING TO KEEP WRITTEN MEDICAL RECORDS JUSTIFYING THE COURSE OF TREATMENT OF A PATIENT; PRESCRIBING, DISPENSING, ADMINISTERING, MIXING, OR OTHERWISE PREPARING LEGEND DRUGS NOT IN THE BEST INTEREST OF THE PATIENT. IN LIEU OF FURTHER PROSECUTION, STIPULATED TO ESTABLISH SATISFACTORY COMPLETION OF AN ACGME ACCREDITED RESIDENCY PROGRAM OF AT LEAST ONE YEAR. UPON REINSTATEMENT, BOARD MAY PLACE LICENSE ON PROBATION FOR A PERIOD NOT TO EXCEED 18 MONTHS WITH TERMS AND CONDITIONS.

ROGERS, CHERYL J MD, LICENSE NUMBER 1032007, OF 5211 W 9TH AVENUE #202, AMARILLO, TX, WAS DISCIPLINED BY INDIANA ON OCTOBER 6, 1989.
DISCIPLINARY ACTION: 3-MONTH EMERGENCY SUSPENSION

ROGERS, CHERYL J MD, LICENSE NUMBER 1032007, OF PO BOX 292265, LOUISVILLE, TX, WAS DISCIPLINED BY INDIANA ON APRIL 17, 1990.
DISCIPLINARY ACTION: 26-MONTH PROBATION; MONITORING OF PHYSICIAN
OFFENSE: DRUG OR ALCOHOL ABUSE
NOTES: ABUSED DEMEROL WHICH SHE SELF-PRESCRIBED. EMERGENCY SUSPENSION LIFTED. THE FOLLOWING TERMS AND CONDITIONS WERE ATTACHED TO PROBATION WHICH FOLLOWED SUSPENSION: MUST SUBMIT COPIES OF RESULTS OF ANY AND ALL BLOOD AND/OR URINE SCREENS, MUST SUBMIT REPORTS CONCERNING ATTENDANCE AT AA, NARCOTICS ANONYMOUS AND CADUCEUS MEETINGS AND QUARTERLY REPORTS ON AFTERCARE PROGRAM. INDEFINITE PROBATION ISSUED AND STAYED, TO BEGIN 07/01/92, WHICH INCLUDES THE FOLLOWING TERMS AND CONDITIONS: POSSESSION OF AN UNLIMITED LICENSE TO PRACTICE MEDICINE DURING PROBATIONARY PERIOD, PROHIBITED FROM POSSESSING AN INDIANA CONTROLLED SUBSTANCE REGISTRATION PERMIT, PARTICIPATION IN AA OR NARCOTICS ANONYMOUS MEETINGS A MINIMUM OF THREE TIMES A WEEK, COMPLETION OF FOUR HOURS OF COMMUNITY SERVICE A WEEK FOR 46 WEEKS A YEAR, SUBMISSION TO RANDOM BLOOD AND URINE

SCREENS. ASSESSED COSTS OF $150.

ROMAN, ERNEST T MD, LICENSE NUMBER 00H6938, OF MCALLEN, TX, WAS DISCIPLINED BY TEXAS ON JANUARY 6, 1995.
DISCIPLINARY ACTION: 36-MONTH PROBATION; MONITORING OF PHYSICIAN
OFFENSE: PROFESSIONAL MISCONDUCT
NOTES: DURING 10/93 FAILED TO EXAMINE AND EVALUATE A PATIENT DURING THE PATIENT'S CARE AND TREATMENT INSTEAD DELEGATING AND RELYING ENTIRELY ON THE EVALUATION OF A MEDICAL ASSISTANT WHICH RESULTED IN A MISDIAGNOSIS; IN LIEU OF FURTHER INVESTIGATION. SUSPENSION STAYED. CONDITIONS OF PROBATION: SHALL ADEQUATELY SUPERVISE ALL INDIVIDUALS UNDER HIS CONTROL OR SUPERVISION OR IN WHICH HE HAS AN OWNERSHIP INTEREST; SHALL PERSONALLY EXAMINE AND OR TREAT PATIENTS WHEN A FORM REPRESENTS THIS OR ANY TIME AN INITIAL DIAGNOSIS OR EXAM IS PERFORMED; WITHIN SIX MONTHS SHALL PROVIDE A NOTARIZED REPORT DETAILING THE BILLING PRACTICES OF CLINICS UNDER HIS CONTROL OR SUPERVISION OR IN WHICH HE HAS AN OWNERSHIP INTEREST; SHALL APPEAR BEFORE THE BOARD ONCE A YEAR OR UPON REQUEST; SHALL COOPERATE WITH BOARD IN VERIFYING COMPLIANCE; SHALL GIVE A COPY OF THIS ORDER TO ANY HEALTH CARE ENTITY WHERE HE HAS OR APPLIES FOR PRIVILEGES OR ANYONE ELSE WHO ASKS; SHALL ENSURE ANY INQUIRIES REGARDING HIS TEXAS LICENSURE STATUS ARE ANSWERED BY REFERENCING THIS ORDER; SHALL INFORM BOARD OF CHANGE OF ADDRESS WITHIN 10 DAYS OR IF HE LEAVES THE STATE; TIME SPENT OUT OF TEXAS DOES NOT COUNT TOWARD PROBATION. SHALL NOT SEEK MODIFICATION FOR ONE YEAR.

ROOT, LAWRENCE GORDON MD, LICENSE NUMBER 00E4644, OF HOUSTON, TX, WAS DISCIPLINED BY TEXAS ON OCTOBER 29, 1988.
DISCIPLINARY ACTION: 58-MONTH RESTRICTION PLACED ON LICENSE
NOTES: MUST REFRAIN FROM PRESCRIBING TO KNOWN ADDICT AND PRESCRIBING, ADMINISTERING OR DISPENSING TO PATIENTS UNLESS SUCH IS THERAPEUTIC; SHALL MAINTAIN ADEQUATE MEDICAL RECORDS ON PATIENTS; SHALL REFER TO PROPER PHYSICIAN THOSE PATIENTS HAVING NEED OF MEDICAL SERVICES OTHER THAN FOR PSYCHIATRIST. PROBATION TERMINATED EFFECTIVE 8/20/92; LICENSE FREE OF ANY RESTRICTION OR LIMITATION.

ROSA, SAMUEL MD WAS DISCIPLINED BY IOWA ON AUGUST 24, 1987.
DISCIPLINARY ACTION: SURRENDER OF LICENSE
OFFENSE: PHYSICAL OR MENTAL ILLNESS INHIBITING THE ABILITY TO PRACTICE WITH SKILL AND SAFETY

ROSA, SAMUEL MD WAS DISCIPLINED BY IOWA ON JANUARY 26, 1989.
DISCIPLINARY ACTION: 24-MONTH PROBATION; RESTRICTION PLACED ON LICENSE
NOTES: LICENSE REISSUED; CANNOT PRACTICE OB-GYN; MUST MAINTAIN RECORD OF ALL CONTROLLED DRUGS PRESCRIBED

ROSA, SAMUEL MD, LICENSE NUMBER 00D3970, OF COUNCIL BLUFFS, IA, WAS DISCIPLINED BY TEXAS ON APRIL 14, 1989.
DISCIPLINARY ACTION: RESTRICTION PLACED ON LICENSE
OFFENSE: DISCIPLINARY ACTION BY ANOTHER STATE OR AGENCY
NOTES: SHALL AGREE TO BE BOUND BY CONSENT AGREEMENT WITH IOWA BOARD INCLUDING SAME RESTRICTIONS ON TEXAS LICENSE AND ANY VIOLATION OF IOWA AGREEMENT TO BE DEEMED VIOLATION OF TEXAS ORDER; SHALL NOTIFY TEXAS BOARD IF EVER RESUMING PRACTICE OF OBSTETRICS. ON 06/10/91 PROBATION TERMINATED; LICENSE FREE OF ANY RESTRICTION OR LIMITATION.

ROSE, TERRANCE L MD, LICENSE NUMBER 00G0028, OF RED OAK, TX, WAS DISCIPLINED BY TEXAS ON JANUARY 26, 1990.
DISCIPLINARY ACTION: SURRENDER OF CONTROLLED SUBSTANCE LICENSE; 3-MONTH LICENSE SUSPENSION
NOTES: STIPULATED ORDER. REVOCATION STAYED. FOLLOWING LICENSE SUSPENSION, LICENSE REINSTATED UPON 10-YEAR PROBATION. MUST SUBMIT TO PSYCHIATRIC EVALUATION AND TREATMENT, SURRENDER CONTROLLED SUBSTANCES REGISTRATION CERTIFICATES AND UNUSED TRIPLICATE PRESCRIPTION FORMS AND NOT OBTAIN REGISTRATIONS WITHOUT BOARD PERMISSION, COMPLETE PRECEPTORSHIP ON PREVENTION AND TREATMENT OF DRUG ABUSE, APPEAR BEFORE BOARD ANNUALLY, OBTAIN CONTINUING MEDICAL EDUCATION, MAINTAIN ADEQUATE MEDICAL RECORDS ON PATIENT OFFICE VISITS, REFRAIN FROM ISSUING PRESCRIPTIONS AND FROM ADMINISTERING OR DISPENSING DANGEROUS DRUGS TO PATIENTS UNLESS PHYSICIAN CONCLUDED SUCH DRUG THERAPEUTIC FOR MEDICAL CONDITION, SHALL NOT PRESCRIBE, ADMINISTER, OR DISPENSE DRUGS WITH ABUSE POTENTIAL UNTIL SATISFIED OF LEGITIMATE MEDICAL AND THERAPEUTIC NEED AND AFTER EXAMINATION, AND MAINTAIN SEPARATE FILE OF PRESCRIPTIONS FOR DANGEROUS DRUGS.

ROSE, TERRANCE LYNN MD OF 140 A OVILLA ROAD, RED OAK, TX, WAS DISCIPLINED BY DEA ON MARCH 23, 1990.
DISCIPLINARY ACTION: SURRENDER OF CONTROLLED SUBSTANCE LICENSE

ROSENKRANTZ, MILTON P MD OF CHALMETTE, LA, WAS DISCIPLINED BY LOUISIANA ON JULY 19, 1990.
DISCIPLINARY ACTION: 6-MONTH LICENSE SUSPENSION; 2-MONTH RESTRICTION PLACED ON CONTROLLED SUBSTANCE LICENSE
OFFENSE: SUBSTANDARD CARE, INCOMPETENCE, OR NEGLIGENCE
NOTES: PRESCRIBING, DISPENSING, OR ADMINISTERING CONTROLLED SUBSTANCES WITHOUT LEGITIMATE MEDICAL JUSTIFICATION, PROFESSIONAL INCOMPETENCY, CONTINUING OR RECURRING MEDICAL PRACTICE FAILING TO SATISFY PREVAILING STANDARDS OF PRACTICE. PROBATION OF 4 1/2 YEARS AFTER MEDICAL LICENSE SUSPENSION TO INCLUDE THE FOLLOWING CONDITIONS: PROHIBITION ON PRESCRIPTION OF CONTROLLED SUBSTANCES FOR ONE YEAR; LIFETIME PROHIBITION ON PRESCRIPTION OF SCHEDULE II CONTROLLED SUBSTANCES; MAINTENANCE OF PRESCRIPTION LOG FOR DURATION OF PROBATION; COMPLETION OF SPECIFIED CONTINUING MEDICAL EDUCATION; 100 HOURS COMMUNITY SERVICE PER YEAR FOR FIVE YEARS; $5000 FINE.

ROSENKRANTZ, MILTON PAUL MD, LICENSE NUMBER 005140B, OF

401 W GENIE STREET, CHALMETTE, LA, WAS DISCIPLINED BY DEA ON SEPTEMBER 14, 1990.
DISCIPLINARY ACTION: SURRENDER OF CONTROLLED SUBSTANCE LICENSE; FINE
NOTES: PAID $5,000 FINE; WITHDRAWAL OF APPLICATION.

ROSENKRANTZ, MILTON PAUL MD, LICENSE NUMBER 00E4646, OF NEW ORLEANS, LA, WAS DISCIPLINED BY TEXAS ON DECEMBER 3, 1990.
DISCIPLINARY ACTION: 14-MONTH LICENSE SUSPENSION; PROBATION
OFFENSE: DISCIPLINARY ACTION BY ANOTHER STATE OR AGENCY
NOTES: ON 7/19/90 LOUISIANA BOARD SUSPENDED HIS LICENSE AND IMPOSED TERMS OF PROBATION AND FINE FOR PRESCRIBING CONTROLLED SUBSTANCES, PRIMARILY NARCOTIC ANALGESICS IN ALLEGEDLY EXCESSIVE QUANTITIES TO 19 PATIENTS. SUSPENSION UNTIL 2/15/91; MUST COMPLY WITH TERMS OF LOUISIANA ORDER; MUST RECEIVE PERMISSION FROM TEXAS BOARD BEFORE RETURNING TO PRACTICE IN TEXAS AND BE SUBJECT TO ANY TERMS IMPOSED. REQUEST TO PRACTICE IN TEXAS GRANTED 3/23/92; SHALL COMPLY WITH TERMS OF THIS ORDER, APPEAR ANNUALLY BEFORE THE BOARD AND PERFORM 100 HOURS PER YEAR OF COMMUNITY SERVICE.

ROTTNER, MARK H MD OF 4105 HUBBY AVENUE, WACO, TX, WAS DISCIPLINED BY MEDICARE ON MAY 23, 1984.
DISCIPLINARY ACTION: 36-MONTH EXCLUSION FROM THE MEDICARE AND/OR MEDICAID PROGRAMS
OFFENSE: CRIMINAL CONVICTION OR PLEA OF GUILTY, NOLO CONTENDERE, OR NO CONTEST TO A CRIME
NOTES: PROGRAM-RELATED CONVICTION.

ROTTNER, MARK H MD, LICENSE NUMBER 0040926, OF BRONX, NY, WAS DISCIPLINED BY NEW YORK ON AUGUST 17, 1987.
DISCIPLINARY ACTION: SURRENDER OF LICENSE

RUBINSTEIN, BARNEY MD, LICENSE NUMBER 00C7116, OF SAN ANTONIO, TX, WAS DISCIPLINED BY TEXAS ON OCTOBER 1, 1993.
DISCIPLINARY ACTION: 84-MONTH PROBATION; RESTRICTION PLACED ON CONTROLLED SUBSTANCE LICENSE
OFFENSE: OVERPRESCRIBING OR MISPRESCRIBING DRUGS
NOTES: ENGAGED IN EXCESSIVE PRESCRIBING OF VICODIN TO A MEMBER OF HIS FAMILY OVER TWO YEARS BEGINNING IN 1991 WITHOUT SUFFICIENT CLINICAL INDICATIONS TO JUSTIFY THE AMOUNT AND DURATION. SUSPENSION STAYED. CONDITIONS OF PROBATION: SHALL NOT POSSESS, ADMINISTER, DISPENSE OR PRESCRIBE ANY CONTROLLED SUBSTANCES UNLESS PRESCRIBED TO HIM BY ANOTHER PHYSICIAN; SHALL NOT TREAT OR OTHERWISE SERVE AS PHYSICIAN, PRESCRIBE, DISPENSE OR ADMINISTER DRUGS THAT MAY BE SUBJECT TO ABUSE TO HIMSELF OR HIS IMMEDIATE FAMILY; SHALL SURRENDER ALL UNUSED TRIPLICATE PRESCRIPTION FORMS; DURING FIRST YEAR OF PROBATION SHALL COMPLETE A BOARD-APPROVED COURSE IN CHRONIC PAIN MANAGEMENT AND 50 HOURS PER YEAR OF CONTINUING MEDICAL EDUCATION; SHALL APPEAR BEFORE THE BOARD ONCE A YEAR; SHALL GIVE A COPY OF THIS ORDER TO ANY HEALTH CARE ENTITY WHERE HE HAS PRIVILEGES; SHALL COOPERATE WITH THE BOARD IN VERIFYING COMPLIANCE; SHALL INFORM BOARD OF CHANGE OF ADDRESS WITHIN 10 DAYS OR IF HE LEAVES THE STATE; TIME SPENT OUT OF TEXAS DOES NOT COUNT TOWARD PROBATION. SHALL NOT SEEK MODIFICATION FOR ONE YEAR.

RUSSOL, FREDERICK JOSEPH MD, LICENSE NUMBER 00E8876, OF ODESSA, TX, WAS DISCIPLINED BY TEXAS ON JANUARY 14, 1994.
DISCIPLINARY ACTION: REPRIMAND
OFFENSE: PROFESSIONAL MISCONDUCT
NOTES: AIDING AND ABETTING THE UNLICENSED PRACTICE OF MEDICINE IN THAT IN 1991 HE SERVED AS AN UNPAID MEDICAL DIRECTOR FOR A LAB OWNED AND OPERATED BY A NON-PHYSICIAN WHO PERFORMED ALLERGY TESTING AND TREATMENT OF ALLERGY WHICH INVOLVED INJECTIONS PURSUANT TO A PROTOCOL APPROVED BY DR. RUSSOL; PATIENTS WERE NOT REFERRALS FROM DR. RUSSOL AND SOME WERE NEVER EXAMINED BY HIM; LAB WAS NOT ASSOCIATED WITH HIS PRACTICE; DR. RUSSOL IS NO LONGER ASSOCIATED WITH THE LAB.

SABATES, FELIX NABOR JR MD, LICENSE NUMBER 00J2773, OF HOUSTON, TX, WAS DISCIPLINED BY TEXAS ON JUNE 22, 1994.
DISCIPLINARY ACTION: 60-MONTH PROBATION; REQUIRED TO TAKE ADDITIONAL MEDICAL EDUCATION
OFFENSE: DRUG OR ALCOHOL ABUSE
NOTES: ON 10/15/93 VOLUNTARILY ADMITTED HIMSELF FOR EVALUATION DUE TO ALCOHOL AND COCAINE ABUSE AND A HISTORY OF A SUICIDE ATTEMPT IN 1992; HE WAS DISCHARGED FROM INPATIENT TREATMENT ON 12/93; IS UNDER PSYCHIATRIC TREATMENT AND HIS PSYCHIATRIST BELIEVES THAT HIS INVOLVEMENT WITH DRUGS WAS RELATED TO HIS PREVIOUSLY UNDIAGNOSED BIPOLAR DISORDER. SUSPENSION STAYED. CONDITIONS OF PROBATION: SHALL CONTINUE TREATMENT WITH HIS CURRENT PSYCHIATRIST WITH QUARTERLY REPORTS; SHALL ABSTAIN FROM THE CONSUMPTION OF ALCOHOL/CHEMICAL SUBSTANCES IN ANY FORM UNLESS PRESCRIBED BY A PHYSICIAN FOR A LEGITIMATE AND THERAPEUTIC PURPOSE; SHALL SUBMIT HIMSELF FOR APPROPRIATE EXAMS INCLUDING DRUG OR ALCOHOL SCREENS; SHALL PARTICIPATE IN AA'S PROGRAM NOT LESS THAN TWO TIMES A WEEK WITH QUARTERLY REPORTS; SHALL NOT TREAT OR OTHERWISE SERVE AS PHYSICIAN, PRESCRIBE, DISPENSE OR ADMINISTER DRUGS THAT MAY BE SUBJECT TO ABUSE TO HIMSELF OR ANY MEMBER OF HIS FAMILY; SHALL ATTEND AT LEAST 50 HOURS PER YEAR OF CONTINUING MEDICAL EDUCATION; SEPARATE FROM PATIENT RECORDS, SHALL MAINTAIN A FILE OF EVERY PRESCRIPTION WRITTEN FOR CONTROLLED SUBSTANCES AND DANGEROUS DRUGS WHICH SHALL BE AVAILABLE FOR INSPECTION; SHALL PARTICIPATE IN CADUCEUS MEETINGS WEEKLY WITH QUARTERLY REPORTS; SHALL APPEAR BEFORE THE BOARD ONCE A YEAR; SHALL GIVE A COPY OF THIS ORDER TO ANY HEALTH CARE ENTITY WHERE HE HAS PRIVILEGES; SHALL COOPERATE WITH THE BOARD IN VERIFYING COMPLIANCE; SHALL INFORM BOARD OF CHANGE OF ADDRESS WITHIN 10 DAYS OR IF HE LEAVES THE STATE; TIME SPENT OUT OF TEXAS DOES NOT COUNT TOWARD PROBATION. SHALL NOT SEEK MODIFICATION FOR ONE YEAR.

SAMBERSON, RANDALL RAY MD, DATE OF BIRTH MAY 22, 1951, LICENSE NUMBER 00E6598, OF AMARILLO, TX, WAS DISCIPLINED BY TEXAS ON SEPTEMBER 28, 1990.
DISCIPLINARY ACTION: 36-MONTH RESTRICTION PLACED ON LICENSE; REQUIRED TO TAKE ADDITIONAL MEDICAL EDUCATION

NOTES: MAY PERFORM NO GYNECOLOGICAL SURGERY WITHOUT BOARD CERTIFIED OR BOARD ELIGIBLE OBSTETRICIAN-GYNECOLOGIST AS SURGICAL ASSISTANT. EFFECTIVE 4/30/93 LICENSE FREE OF ANY RESTRICTION OR LIMITATION.

SANCHEZ, DANILO ABUD MD, DATE OF BIRTH JANUARY 18, 1952, OF 1891 NORTH LEE TREVINO, EL PASO, TX, WAS DISCIPLINED BY MEDICARE ON JULY 20, 1992.
DISCIPLINARY ACTION: 48-MONTH EXCLUSION FROM THE MEDICARE AND/OR MEDICAID PROGRAMS
OFFENSE: CRIMINAL CONVICTION OR PLEA OF GUILTY, NOLO CONTENDERE, OR NO CONTEST TO A CRIME
NOTES: CONVICTION RELATING TO FRAUD.

SANCHEZLEAL, HENRY R MD, LICENSE NUMBER 000T503, OF COLUMBIA, SC, WAS DISCIPLINED BY SOUTH CAROLINA ON NOVEMBER 6, 1989.
NOTES: TEMPORARY LICENSE ISSUED WITH CONDITIONS

SANCHEZLEAL, HENRY R MD, LICENSE NUMBER 000T503, OF COLUMBIA, SC, WAS DISCIPLINED BY SOUTH CAROLINA ON MARCH 6, 1990.
DISCIPLINARY ACTION: SURRENDER OF LICENSE
NOTES: NOT ELIGIBLE FOR REINSTATEMENT

SANCHEZLEAL, HENRY R MD, LICENSE NUMBER 00G0052, OF KERRVILLE, TX, WAS DISCIPLINED BY TEXAS ON SEPTEMBER 28, 1990.
DISCIPLINARY ACTION: MONITORING OF PHYSICIAN
NOTES: MUST SUBMIT FOR APPROPRIATE EXAMINATIONS TO DETERMINE FREEDOM FROM DRUGS AND ALCOHOL; PARTICIPATE IN ALCOHOLICS/NARCOTICS ANONYMOUS; SUBMIT FOR PSYCHIATRIC EVALUATION AND FOLLOW ANY RECOMMENDATIONS REGARDING CARE.

SANDERS, MARK S MD, LICENSE NUMBER 00H0002, OF TEXAS CITY, TX, WAS DISCIPLINED BY TEXAS ON JANUARY 6, 1995.
DISCIPLINARY ACTION: REPRIMAND
OFFENSE: SUBSTANDARD CARE, INCOMPETENCE, OR NEGLIGENCE
NOTES: ON 2/11/93 HE PERFORMED A CARPAL TUNNEL RELEASE ON A PATIENT WHERE HE DEVIATED FROM THE STANDARD OF CARE BY PERFORMING THIS SURGERY WITHOUT ADEQUATE INTRAVENOUS ACCESS IN CASE ANY COMPLICATIONS AROSE; FAILED TO ADEQUATELY INFORM PATIENT AS TO THE NATURE OF THE PROCEDURE AND THEREFORE FAILED TO TRUELY OBTAIN INFORMED CONSENT; NEITHER ADMITS NOR DENIES THE ALLEGATIONS. SHALL GIVE A COPY OF THIS ORDER TO ANY HEALTH CARE ENTITY WHERE HE HAS OR APPLIES FOR PRIVILEGES OR ANYONE ELSE WHO ASKS FOR IT. SHALL ENSURE ANY INQUIRIES REGARDING HIS TEXAS LICENSURE STATUS ARE ANSWERED BY REFERENCING THIS ORDER.

SANDS, LARRY REX MD, LICENSE NUMBER 00G0884, OF BROWNWOOD, TX, WAS DISCIPLINED BY TEXAS ON APRIL 21, 1990.
DISCIPLINARY ACTION: 24-MONTH RESTRICTION PLACED ON LICENSE
NOTES: STIPULATED ORDER. WILL OBTAIN SPECIFIC INFORMATION FROM PATIENTS SEEKING WEIGHT LOSS TREATMENT, FOR THOSE WITH NO CONTRAINDICATION FOR SUCH TREATMENT, HE SHALL FOLLOW SPECIFICATIONS INCLUDING: PATIENTS RECEIVING CONTROLLED SUBSTANCE PRESCRIPTIONS SHALL RECEIVE WRITTEN INFORMATION DETAILING RISK OF HABITUATION; CONDUCT FOLLOW-UP EXAMINATIONS. MAY USE TRAINED PERSONNEL FOR THIS PROVIDED HE DOES NOT DELEGATE DIAGNOSIS AND TREATMENT RESPONSIBILITIES TO UNLICENSED ASSISTANTS.

SANDS, LARRY REX MD, LICENSE NUMBER 00G0884, OF BROWNWOOD, TX, WAS DISCIPLINED BY TEXAS ON OCTOBER 1, 1993.
DISCIPLINARY ACTION: 120-MONTH PROBATION; RESTRICTION PLACED ON LICENSE
OFFENSE: CRIMINAL CONVICTION OR PLEA OF GUILTY, NOLO CONTENDERE, OR NO CONTEST TO A CRIME
NOTES: ON 7/2/92 HE PLED GUILTY TO ONE COUNT OF MAIL FRAUD AND WAS PLACED ON PROBATION FOR FIVE YEARS, FINED AND ORDERED TO SUBMIT TO A HOME CONFINEMENT PROGRAM FOR NOT LONGER THAN 120 DAYS. TEN YEAR SUSPENSION STAYED. CONDITIONS OF PROBATION: SHALL APPEAR BEFORE THE BOARD TWICE A YEAR; SHALL ATTEND AT LEAST 50 HOURS PER YEAR OF CONTINUING MEDICAL EDUCATION AND SIX HOURS OF AN ETHICS COURSE OR PROGRAM PER YEAR FOR 10 YEARS; SHALL BE SUPERVISED BY A BOARD-APPROVED PHYSICIAN WITH THREE-TIMES-A-YEAR REPORTS TO THE BOARD; SHALL NOT PARTICIPATE IN THE BILLING PROCEDURE FOR ANY INDIVIDUAL OR THIRD-PARTY PAYER; SHALL SUBMIT HIMSELF FOR EVALUATION TO A BOARD-APPROVED PSYCHIATRIST WITH REPORTS TO THE BOARD; SHALL PRACTICE ONLY IN A GROUP PRACTICE IN A MEDICALLY UNDER-SERVED AREA; SHALL NOT CHANGE THIS WITHOUT WRITTEN APPROVAL; SHALL INFORM THE BOARD IF HE LEAVES THE STATE; TIME SPENT OUT OF TEXAS DOES NOT COUNT TOWARD PROBATION; SHALL PERFORM 100 HOURS PER YEAR OF COMMUNITY SERVICE.

SARIOL, OSCAR MD, LICENSE NUMBER 0017404, OF FT LAUDERDALE, FL, WAS DISCIPLINED BY FLORIDA ON JUNE 8, 1993.
DISCIPLINARY ACTION: FINE; REQUIRED TO TAKE ADDITIONAL MEDICAL EDUCATION
OFFENSE: SUBSTANDARD CARE, INCOMPETENCE, OR NEGLIGENCE
NOTES: CHARGED WITH GROSS OR REPEATED MALPRACTICE OR FAILING TO PRACTICE MEDICINE WITH AN ACCEPTABLE LEVEL OF CARE AND SKILL. IN LIEU OF FURTHER PROSECUTION, CONSENTED TO $1,000 FINE; MUST COMPLETE 20 HOURS OF CONTINUING MEDICAL EDUCATION IN THE AREAS OF CYTOLOGY, PATHOLOGY, AND/OR OBSTETRICS/GYNECOLOGY WITHIN ONE YEAR.

SARIOL, OSCAR MD, LICENSE NUMBER 00E3765, OF FORT LAUDERDALE, FL, WAS DISCIPLINED BY TEXAS ON JANUARY 14, 1994.
DISCIPLINARY ACTION: SURRENDER OF LICENSE
NOTES: WAIVES THE RIGHT TO A SHOW COMPLIANCE PROCEEDING. LICENSE IS PERMANENTLY CANCELLED.

SARTORI, HELLFRIED E MD, LICENSE NUMBER 0D24475, WAS DISCIPLINED BY MARYLAND ON SEPTEMBER 20, 1984.
DISCIPLINARY ACTION: LICENSE REVOCATION

SARTORI, HELLFRIED E MD OF WASHINGTON, DC, WAS DISCIPLINED BY VIRGINIA ON JUNE 5, 1985.
DISCIPLINARY ACTION: LICENSE REVOCATION

SARTORI, HELLFRIED E MD WAS DISCIPLINED BY PENNSYLVANIA ON JULY 12, 1985.
DISCIPLINARY ACTION: LICENSE REVOCATION

SARTORI, HELLFRIED E MD OF 1350 BEVERLY ROAD, MCLEAN, VA, WAS DISCIPLINED BY MEDICARE ON AUGUST 27, 1986.
DISCIPLINARY ACTION: 120-MONTH EXCLUSION FROM THE MEDICARE AND/OR MEDICAID PROGRAMS
OFFENSE: PROFESSIONAL MISCONDUCT
NOTES: HE BILLED MEDICARE FOR CHELATION THERAPY FOR THE TREATMENT OF ARTERIOSCLEROSIS OR ORGANIC LEAD INTOXICATION WHICH IS NOT A PROFESSIONALLY RECOGNIZED TREATMENT FOR THIS DIAGNOSIS. HE ALSO BILLED MEDICARE FOR THE FOLLOWING DIAGNOSTIC TECHNIQUES NOT ACCEPTED BY THE MEDICAL PROFESSION FOR THE PURPOSES FOR WHICH HE USED THEM: CYTOTOXIC TESTING FOR FOOD ALLERGIES; THERMOGRAPHY TO DIAGNOSE VASCULAR INSUFFICIENCY; HAIR ANALYSIS TO DIAGNOSE SYSTEMIC HEAVY METAL OR LEAD INTOXICATION; AND HEIDELBERG PH CAPSULE AND TRANSMITTER TO DIAGNOSE HYPER OR HYPOACIDITY IN THE GASTROINTESTINAL TRACT. MARYLAND LICENSE WAS REVOKED. LICENSES IN NORTH CAROLINA, VIRGINIA, WASHINGTON, THE DISTRICT OF COLUMBIA AND PENNSYLVANIA HAVE ALSO BEEN REVOKED OR SUSPENDED.

SARTORI, HELLFRIED E MD, LICENSE NUMBER 00E9973, OF WASHINGTON, DC, WAS DISCIPLINED BY TEXAS ON OCTOBER 1, 1987.
DISCIPLINARY ACTION: LICENSE REVOCATION
OFFENSE: DISCIPLINARY ACTION BY ANOTHER STATE OR AGENCY
NOTES: DISCIPLINARY ACTION BY MARYLAND, PENNSYLVANIA, VIRGINIA AND WASHINGTON.

SAUCEDA, FRANCISCO BASIL MD, LICENSE NUMBER 00H8375, OF HOUSTON, TX, WAS DISCIPLINED BY TEXAS ON APRIL 10, 1992.
DISCIPLINARY ACTION: 6-MONTH LICENSE SUSPENSION; 60-MONTH PROBATION
OFFENSE: DRUG OR ALCOHOL ABUSE
NOTES: SUSPENSION SHALL REMAIN IN EFFECT UNTIL SUCH TIME AS HE IS EVALUATED BY AN APPROVED PSYCHIATRIST SPECIALIZING IN ADDICTIONOLOGY AND REPORTS ARE FURNISHED INDICATING THAT HE IS BOTH MENTALLY AND PHYSICALLY ABLE TO SAFELY PRACTICE MEDICINE. AFTER SUCH TIME, LICENSE IS SUSPENDED, SUSPENSION STAYED, AND PLACED ON PROBATION UNDER TERMS AND CONDITIONS. ON 10/14/93 ORDER MODIFIED AS FOLLOWS: HE MAY APPLY FOR DRUG ENFORCEMENT ADMINISTRATION AND TEXAS DEPARTMENT OF PUBLIC SAFETY CONTROLLED SUBSTANCES REGISTRATION CERTIFICATES; SEPARATE FROM PATIENT RECORDS, HE SHALL MAINTAIN A FILE CONSISTING OF A COPY OF EVERY PRESCRIPTION WRITTEN BY HIM FOR CONTROLLED SUBSTANCES AND DANGEROUS DRUGS BY DATE ISSUED WHICH SHALL BE AVAILABLE TO BOARD FOR INSPECTION; HE SHALL NOT TELEPHONE ANY PRESCRIPTION TO A PHARMACY FOR CONTROLLED SUBSTANCES OR DANGEROUS DRUGS. ALL OTHER PROVISIONS OF THIS ORDER REMAIN IN EFFECT.

SAVAGE, PATRICK JOSEPH MD, LICENSE NUMBER 00F7600, OF 311 EAST MATTHEWS, JONESBORO, AR, WAS DISCIPLINED BY DEA ON JANUARY 29, 1990.
DISCIPLINARY ACTION: SURRENDER OF CONTROLLED SUBSTANCE LICENSE

SAVAGE, PATRICK JOSEPH MD, LICENSE NUMBER 00F7600, OF JONESBORO, AR, WAS DISCIPLINED BY TEXAS ON OCTOBER 26, 1990.
DISCIPLINARY ACTION: REQUIRED TO ENTER AN IMPAIRED PHYSICIAN PROGRAM OR DRUG OR ALCOHOL TREATMENT
NOTES: COMPLY WITH PROVISIONS OF AFTERCARE CONTRACT EXECUTED WITH PHYSICIANS' HEALTH COMMITTEE OF ARKANSAS MEDICAL SOCIETY; IF WISHING TO PRACTICE IN TEXAS, MUST DEMONSTRATE CAPACITY TO PRACTICE WITH REASONABLE SKILL AND SAFETY AND PROVIDE REPORT ON STATUS OF ARKANSAS LICENSE AND COMPLIANCE WITH AFTERCARE CONTRACT; IF GRANTED PERMISSION TO PRACTICE IN TEXAS, BOARD MAY IMPOSE CONDITIONAL TERMS AS DEEMED APPROPRIATE.

SAVAGE, PATRICK JOSEPH MD, DATE OF BIRTH JANUARY 21, 1949, LICENSE NUMBER 0008541, OF 1812 MACARTHUR PARK, JONESBORO, AR, WAS DISCIPLINED BY MISSISSIPPI ON NOVEMBER 15, 1990.
DISCIPLINARY ACTION: PROBATION
NOTES: REVOCATION STAYED; CONSENT AGREEMENT.

SCARLETT, MAXWELL CURTIS MD, LICENSE NUMBER 00E6910, OF FORT WORTH, TX, WAS DISCIPLINED BY TEXAS ON FEBRUARY 1, 1991.
DISCIPLINARY ACTION: RESTRICTION PLACED ON LICENSE; REQUIRED TO TAKE ADDITIONAL MEDICAL EDUCATION
OFFENSE: LOSS OR RESTRICTION OF HOSPITAL PRIVILEGES
NOTES: DISCIPLINED BY HOSPITAL OR HOSPITAL MEDICAL STAFF INCLUDING REMOVAL, SUSPENSION, OR LIMITATION OF HOSPITAL PRIVILEGES OR OTHER DISCIPLINARY ACTIONS; FAILURE TO PRACTICE MEDICINE IN ACCEPTABLE MANNER CONSISTENT WITH PUBLIC HEALTH AND WELFARE. MUST PERFORM NO MAJOR SURGERY UNTIL AFTER COMPLETION OF APPROVED GENERAL SURGICAL RESIDENCY AND BOARD CERTIFICATION; COMPLETION OF 50 HOURS CONTINUING MEDICAL EDUCATION EACH YEAR WITH PROOF OF COMPLETION.

SCHAFFNER, LEROY MD OF 303 S. ARCHER, HENRIETTA, TX, WAS DISCIPLINED BY MEDICARE ON NOVEMBER 14, 1986.
DISCIPLINARY ACTION: 24-MONTH EXCLUSION FROM THE MEDICARE AND/OR MEDICAID PROGRAMS
OFFENSE: SUBSTANDARD CARE, INCOMPETENCE, OR NEGLIGENCE
NOTES: GROSSLY SUBSTANDARD CARE OF 5 PATIENTS

SCHEFFEY, ERIC H MD OF BAYTOWN, TX, WAS DISCIPLINED BY TEXAS ON JULY 1, 1986.
DISCIPLINARY ACTION: LICENSE SUSPENSION; 120-MONTH PROBATION
OFFENSE: DRUG OR ALCOHOL ABUSE
NOTES: REVOCATION STAYED; SUSPENSION UNTIL SATISFACTION OF TERMS; ON APPEAL AS OF APRIL 1990

SCHEFFEY, ERIC H MD, LICENSE NUMBER 0008573, OF BAYTOWN, TX, WAS DISCIPLINED BY SOUTH CAROLINA ON AUGUST 31, 1987.
DISCIPLINARY ACTION: PROBATION
OFFENSE: DISCIPLINARY ACTION BY ANOTHER STATE OR AGENCY
NOTES: SANCTIONED IN TEXAS FOR SUBSTANCE ABUSE

SCHOETTLE, ROY W DO OF 13630 NIGHTINGALE DRIVE, HOUSTON,

TX, WAS DISCIPLINED BY MEDICARE ON JUNE 17, 1986.
DISCIPLINARY ACTION: 84-MONTH EXCLUSION FROM THE MEDICARE AND/OR MEDICAID PROGRAMS; FINE

SCHOOLER, JOE F MD OF 4833B BRENTWOOD STAIR RD., FORT WORTH, TX, WAS DISCIPLINED BY DEA ON APRIL 28, 1988.
DISCIPLINARY ACTION: DENIAL OF NEW LICENSE
OFFENSE: DISCIPLINARY ACTION BY ANOTHER STATE OR AGENCY
NOTES: ALLEGEDLY DISPENSED STIMULANT CONTROLLED SUBSTANCES FROM THE TRUNK OF HIS CAR OR FROM VACANT BUILDINGS; BY 1982, HE WAS DENIED PRIVILEGES IN ALL FORT WORTH AREA HOSPITALS AND HAD BEEN DENIED MEMBERSHIP IN THE TARRANT COUNTY MEDICAL SOCIETY. INDICTED ON MAY 12, 1983 IN US DISTRICT COURT FOR THE NORTHERN DISTRICT OF TEXAS, FORT WORTH DIVISION, OF 12 FELONY COUNTS RELATED TO CONTROLLED SUBSTANCES. EXECUTED A PRETRIAL DIVERSION AGREEMENT THAT HE SURRENDER HIS CONTROLLED SUBSTANCES REGISTRATION AND NEVER AGAIN APPLY FOR REGISTRATION. TEXAS MEDICAL BOARD SUSPENDED HIS LICENSE FOR 6 MONTHS ON JUNE 27, 1983 AND PLACED HIM ON PROBATION FOR 10 YEARS. HE WAS ORDERED TO SURRENDER HIS DEA AND TEXAS CONTROLLED SUBSTANCE REGISTRATIONS AND NOT TO REAPPLY. ON DEC 23, 1986, THE BOARD PERMITTED HIM TO REAPPLY FOR SCHEDULE III, IV AND V CONTROLLED SUBSTANCE REGISTRATIONS; ON JANUARY 26, 1987 HE LIED ON DEA APPLICATION, STATING HE WAS AUTHORIZED TO HANDLE CONTROLLED SUBSTANCES IN TEXAS.

SCHULTZ, FRED MICHAEL MD, LICENSE NUMBER 00TXDPS, OF 2410 CROCKETT DRIVE, BROWNWOOD, TX, WAS DISCIPLINED BY DEA ON APRIL 19, 1989.
DISCIPLINARY ACTION: RESTRICTION PLACED ON CONTROLLED SUBSTANCE LICENSE
OFFENSE: OVERPRESCRIBING OR MISPRESCRIBING DRUGS
NOTES: FEDERAL CRIMINAL ACTION REGARDING PRESCRIBING PRELUDIN FOR NON-MEDICAL PURPOSES.

SCHULTZE, JORGE MD, LICENSE NUMBER 00D6164, OF SANTA CRUZ, BOLIVIA, WAS DISCIPLINED BY TEXAS ON DECEMBER 1, 1990.
DISCIPLINARY ACTION: LICENSE REVOCATION
OFFENSE: CRIMINAL CONVICTION OR PLEA OF GUILTY, NOLO CONTENDERE, OR NO CONTEST TO A CRIME
NOTES: CONVICTION OF MISDEMEANOR INVOLVING MORAL TURPITUDE, USE OF ADVERTISING STATEMENT THAT WAS FALSE.

SCHULZE, JOHN P MD, LICENSE NUMBER 00C5311, OF CORPUS CHRISTI, TX, WAS DISCIPLINED BY TEXAS ON JANUARY 6, 1995.
DISCIPLINARY ACTION: 60-MONTH RESTRICTION PLACED ON LICENSE; REQUIRED TO TAKE ADDITIONAL MEDICAL EDUCATION
OFFENSE: OVERPRESCRIBING OR MISPRESCRIBING DRUGS
NOTES: FROM 1987 THROUGH 7/1/92 PRESCRIBED DANGEROUS DRUGS AND CONTROLLED SUBSTANCES TO ONE PATIENT WITHOUT PERFORMING OR ADEQUATELY DOCUMENTING APPROPRIATE PHYSICAL EXAMS AND LAB STUDIES; FAILED TO APPROPRIATELY MONITOR THE PATIENT FOR HYPERTENSION AND WEIGHT LOSS AND CONDUCT APPROPRIATE FOLLOW-UP EXAMS; REPORTS HIS OFFICE STAFF IMPROPERLY ALLOWED THE PATIENT TO OBTAIN REFILLS OF MEDICATIONS WITHOUT REQUIRING HIM TO EXAMINE THE PATIENT; AGREED ORDER IN LIEU OF FURTHER INVESTIGATION OR A HEARING ON THE ALLEGATIONS. CONDITIONS OF FIVE YEAR RESTRICTION: SEPARATE FROM PATIENT RECORDS SHALL MAINTAIN A FILE OF EVERY PRESCRIPTION WRITTEN FOR CONTROLLED SUBSTANCES OR DANGEROUS DRUGS WHICH SHALL BE AVAILABLE FOR INSPECTION; SHALL NOT TELEPHONE A PRESCRIPTION TO A PHARMACY FOR SUCH DRUGS OR PERMIT ANY INDIVIDUAL TO DO SO ON HIS BEHALF; WITHIN 30 DAYS SHALL DEVELOP AND ENSURE COMPLIANCE WITH A WRITTEN OFFICE POLICY FOR PATIENT MONITORING AND FOLLOW-UP EXAMS WHICH SHALL BE DISTRIBUTED TO ALL OF HIS EMPLOYEES AND MADE AVAILABLE FOR REVIEW; SHALL MAINTAIN ADEQUATE MEDICAL RECORDS OF ALL OFFICE VISITS WHICH SHALL BE AVAILABLE FOR INSPECTION; SHALL NOT SIGN ANY PATIENT RECORD UNLESS HE HAS PERSONALLY EXAMINED THE PATIENT OR CLEARLY NOTES IN THE RECORD THAT HE DID NOT; SHALL PERSONALLY EXAMINE AND TREAT A PATIENT ANY TIME AN INITIAL DIAGNOSIS OR EXAM IS DONE; SHALL ADEQUATELY SUPERVISE THE ACTIVITIES OF ALL INDIVIDUALS UNDER HIS SUPERVISION; SHALL ATTEND AT LEAST 50 HOURS PER YEAR OF CONTINUING MEDICAL EDUCATION INCLUDING AT LEAST 15 HOURS IN RISK MANAGEMENT, MEDICAL RECORD KEEPING AND PHARMACOLOGY; SHALL APPEAR BEFORE THE BOARD ONCE A YEAR OR UPON REQUEST; SHALL COOPERATE WITH THE BOARD IN VERIFYING COMPLIANCE; SHALL EXECUTE ANY RELEASES NEEDED TO OBTAIN EMPLOYMENT RECORDS; SHALL GIVE A COPY OF THIS ORDER TO ANY HEALTH CARE ENTITY WHERE HE HAS OR HAS APPLIED FOR PRIVILEGES OR ANYONE ELSE WHO ASKS FOR IT; SHALL ENSURE INQUIRIES REGARDING HIS TEXAS LICENSURE STATUS ARE ANSWERED BY REFERENCING THIS ORDER; SHALL INFORM BOARD OF CHANGE OF ADDRESS WITHIN 10 DAYS OR IF HE LEAVES THE STATE; TIME SPENT OUT OF TEXAS DOES NOT COUNT TOWARD RESTRICTION. SHALL NOT SEEK MODIFICATION FOR ONE YEAR.

SCHWARTZ, HAROLD ROBERT MD, LICENSE NUMBER 00B8522, OF HOUSTON, TX, WAS DISCIPLINED BY TEXAS ON JUNE 22, 1994.
DISCIPLINARY ACTION: REQUIRED TO TAKE ADDITIONAL MEDICAL EDUCATION; MONITORING OF PHYSICIAN
OFFENSE: OVERPRESCRIBING OR MISPRESCRIBING DRUGS
NOTES: BETWEEN 3/24 AND 4/21/92 HE PRESCRIBED TO AN UNDERCOVER SHERIFF'S DEPARTMENT OFFICER TYLENOL #4 WITH CODEINE AND VALIUM ON THREE SEPARATE OCCASIONS WITHOUT ANY VALID MEDICAL JUSTIFICATION; MAINTAINED THAT HE PRESCRIBED THIS AS TREATMENT FOR DOCUMENTED HYPERTENSION ALTHOUGH ADMITS IT WAS POOR JUDGMENT PRESCRIBING IT WITH OTHER MEDICATIONS; VOLUNTARILY SURRENDERED DEA AND TEXAS CONTROLLED SUBSTANCES REGISTRATIONS; GRAND JURY CHOSE NOT TO PROCEED WITH CRIMINAL ACTION; TEXAS CONTROLLED SUBSTANCE REGISTRATION REINSTATED PRIOR TO THE DATE OF THIS ORDER. HIS DEA REGISTRATION HAS NOT BEEN REISSUED AS OF ORDER DATE. CONDITIONS OF THREE YEAR RESTRICTION ON LICENSE: SHALL ATTEND AT LEAST 50 HOURS PER YEAR OF CONTINUING MEDICAL EDUCATION SIX HOURS OF WHICH SHALL BE IN THE AREA OF RECORD KEEPING OR RISK MANAGEMENT; SHALL BE SUPERVISED BY A BOARD-APPROVED PHYSICIAN WITH QUARTERLY REPORTS; WITHIN ONE YEAR SHALL PASS THE SPEX EXAM; IN THE EVENT HE

DOES NOT PASS THE SPEX EXAM WITHIN ONE YEAR HIS LICENSE SHALL BE IMMEDIATELY SUSPENDED; SHALL GIVE A COPY OF THIS ORDER TO ANY HEALTH CARE ENTITY WHERE HE HAS PRIVILEGES; SHALL COOPERATE WITH THE BOARD IN VERIFYING COMPLIANCE; SHALL INFORM BOARD OF CHANGE OF ADDRESS WITHIN 10 DAYS OR IF HE LEAVES THE STATE; TIME SPENT OUT OF TEXAS DOES NOT COUNT TOWARD RESTRICTION. SHALL NOT SEEK MODIFICATION FOR ONE YEAR.

SCOTT, HILLARD L MD OF NORMANDY, MO, WAS DISCIPLINED BY MISSOURI ON JULY 27, 1990.
DISCIPLINARY ACTION: 1-MONTH LICENSE SUSPENSION; 36-MONTH PROBATION
OFFENSE: OVERPRESCRIBING OR MISPRESCRIBING DRUGS
NOTES: PROBATION RETROACTIVE TO 7/1/90

SCOTT, HILLARD L MD, LICENSE NUMBER 00F7605, OF NORMANDY, MO, WAS DISCIPLINED BY TEXAS ON APRIL 20, 1991.
DISCIPLINARY ACTION: 36-MONTH PROBATION
OFFENSE: DISCIPLINARY ACTION BY ANOTHER STATE OR AGENCY
NOTES: DISCIPLINED BY ANOTHER STATE FOR SIGNING BLANK PRESCRIPTION FORMS. PRIOR TO PRACTICING IN TEXAS SHALL APPEAR BEFORE AND RECEIVE APPROVAL OF BOARD.

SEGGER, FRANZJOSEF MD, LICENSE NUMBER 00D7789, OF HOUSTON, TX, WAS DISCIPLINED BY TEXAS ON AUGUST 18, 1990.
DISCIPLINARY ACTION: 60-MONTH REQUIRED TO ENTER AN IMPAIRED PHYSICIAN PROGRAM OR DRUG OR ALCOHOL TREATMENT; 60-MONTH MONITORING OF PHYSICIAN
OFFENSE: DRUG OR ALCOHOL ABUSE
NOTES: STIPULATED ORDER. MUST SUBMIT HIMSELF TO PSYCHIATRIST FOR EVALUATION AND TREATMENT AND FOLLOW RECOMMENDATIONS, IF ANY, SUBMIT FOR APPROPRIATE EXAMINATIONS TO DETERMINE FREEDOM FROM DRUGS AND ALCOHOL, AND PARTICIPATE IN HOUSTON DOCTOR'S GROUP, AN IMPAIRED PHYSICIANS PROGRAM. ON 1/6/95 ORDER TERMINATED.

SEXTON, ROBERT L MD, LICENSE NUMBER 00E5933, OF WEST MONROE, LA, WAS DISCIPLINED BY TEXAS ON OCTOBER 29, 1988.
OFFENSE: DISCIPLINARY ACTION BY ANOTHER STATE OR AGENCY
NOTES: MODIFY PRESCRIBING AND ADMINISTRATION PRACTICES AS DIRECTED; SHALL COMPLY WITH LOUISIANA BOARD ORDER REGARDING PERSONAL HEALTH AND PROFESSIONAL CONDUCT; SHALL RECEIVE BOARD APPROVAL BEFORE PRACTICING IN TEXAS

SEYLER, LOUIS WALTER MD OF COMMERCE, TX, WAS DISCIPLINED BY TEXAS ON JULY 1, 1986.
DISCIPLINARY ACTION: SURRENDER OF LICENSE

SHAH, ARUNKUMAR J MD, LICENSE NUMBER 00F6323, OF HOUSTON, TX, WAS DISCIPLINED BY TEXAS ON FEBRUARY 22, 1991.
DISCIPLINARY ACTION: 24-MONTH PROBATION; RESTRICTION PLACED ON CONTROLLED SUBSTANCE LICENSE
NOTES: MUST APPEAR BEFORE BOARD ANNUALLY; ATTEND CONTINUING MEDICAL EDUCATION COURSES; MAINTAIN ADEQUATE MEDICAL RECORDS ON ALL PATIENT OFFICE VISITS; NOT SIGN OR INDICATE IN ANY MANNER ON ANY PATIENT RECORD, ANY VISIT, EVALUATION, MEDICAL TREATMENT, MEDICAL OPINION, OR MEDICATION ORDER WITHOUT HAVING SEEN AND EXAMINED THE PATIENT, NOR MAKE ANY LATER ENTRY WITHOUT SO NOTING; REFRAIN FROM PRESCRIBING OR ADMINISTERING ANY DRUG FOR ANY PATIENT UNLESS IN HIS MEDICAL JUDGMENT SUCH DRUG IS THERAPEUTIC IN THE MANNER SUCH DRUG IS PRESCRIBED, NOR PRESCRIBE, ADMINISTER, OR DISPENSE ANY DRUG WITH A POTENTIAL FOR ABUSE TO ANY PERSON UNLESS SATISFIED THAT THERE IS A LEGITIMATE MEDICAL AND THERAPEUTIC NEED; MAINTAIN A FILE OF EVERY PRESCRIPTION WRITTEN FOR CONTROLLED SUBSTANCES OR DANGEROUS DRUGS BY DATE ISSUED; NOT ATTEMPT TO REREGISTER OR OTHERWISE OBTAIN CONTROLLED SUBSTANCE REGISTRATIONS WITHOUT PRIOR WRITTEN AUTHORITY FROM THE BOARD AFTER PERSONAL APPEARANCE BEFORE THE BOARD.

SHAH, ARUNKUMAR J MD OF HOUSTON, TX, WAS DISCIPLINED BY DEA ON FEBRUARY 5, 1993.
DISCIPLINARY ACTION: DENIAL OF NEW LICENSE
OFFENSE: DISCIPLINARY ACTION BY ANOTHER STATE OR AGENCY
NOTES: ALLEGEDLY WROTE PRESCRIPTIONS TO UNDERCOVER OFFICERS WITHOUT A VALID MEDICAL INDICATION ON THREE OCCASIONS, SURRENDERED HIS TEXAS MEDICAL LICENSE AND CONTROLLED SUBSTANCE REGISTRATION AND HIS DEA CERTIFICATE OF REGISTRATION HAD BEEN PREVIOUSLY REVOKED.

SHAH, ARUNKUMAR JAYANTLAL MD OF 150 WEST PARKER ROAD SUITE 605, HOUSTON, TX, WAS DISCIPLINED BY DEA ON MAY 21, 1990.
DISCIPLINARY ACTION: SURRENDER OF CONTROLLED SUBSTANCE LICENSE
NOTES: SURRENDERED MEDICAL LICENSE AND CEASED MEDICAL PRACTICE FOR ONE YEAR BEGINNING 07/31/89 AND PLACED IN PRE-TRIAL DIVERSION PROGRAM FOR ONE YEAR.

SHAH, DAULAT MD, LICENSE NUMBER 00G4399, OF HOUSTON, TX, WAS DISCIPLINED BY TEXAS ON AUGUST 19, 1994.
DISCIPLINARY ACTION: LICENSE SUSPENSION; 60-MONTH PROBATION
OFFENSE: LOSS OR RESTRICTION OF HOSPITAL PRIVILEGES
NOTES: IN 2/94 HE ANSWERED NO TO A MEDICAL PRACTICE ACT QUESTIONNAIRE QUERY ASKING WHETHER HIS MEDICAL PRIVILEGES HAD EVER BEEN DISCIPLINED BY ANY HEALTH CARE FACILITY; IN 1985 HE WAS PLACED ON COURTESY PROBATION FOR ONE YEAR AT ONE HOSPITAL FOR FAILURE TO ATTEND MEETINGS AND FOR LACK OF ADMISSIONS; IN 6/88 HE WAS DENIED PRIVILEGES AT ONE HOSPITAL FOR FAILURE TO REVEAL THAT PRIVILEGES AT ANOTHER HOSPITAL HAD BEEN DENIED DUE TO FAILURE TO ATTEND SURGERY COMMITTEE MEETINGS; SUSPENDED FROM EMERGENCY ROOM CALL IN GENERAL SURGERY ON 5/19/93 AT ANOTHER HOSPITAL WHICH CONCLUDED THAT HE "SHOWED POOR JUDGMENT WITH REGARD TO TREATMENT" IN THE CASE OF ONE PATIENT AND AN INDEPENDENT REVIEW OF RECORDS INDICATED THAT HE DEVIATED FROM ACCEPTED STANDARDS OF CARE; HOSPITAL SUSPENSION WAS TO LAST UNTIL HE COMPLETED SPECIFIED CONTINUING MEDICAL EDUCATION WHICH HE HAS. SUSPENSION STAYED AFTER 14 DAYS. CONDITIONS OF PROBATION: SHALL ATTEND AT LEAST 50 HOURS PER YEAR OF CONTINUING MEDICAL EDUCATION AND DURING THE

FIRST YEAR OF PROBATION SHALL SUCCESSFULLY COMPLETE ADVANCED CARDIAC LIFE SUPPORT AND ADVANCED TRAUMA LIFE SUPPORT TRAINING; WITHIN ONE YEAR SHALL PASS THE SPEX EXAM; SHALL APPEAR BEFORE THE BOARD ONCE A YEAR; SHALL GIVE A COPY OF THIS ORDER TO ANY HEALTH CARE ENTITY WHERE HE HAS PRIVILEGES; SHALL COOPERATE WITH THE BOARD IN VERIFYING COMPLIANCE; SHALL INFORM BOARD OF CHANGE OF ADDRESS WITHIN 10 DAYS OR IF HE LEAVES THE STATE; TIME SPENT OUT OF TEXAS DOES NOT COUNT TOWARD PROBATION. SHALL NOT SEEK MODIFICATION FOR ONE YEAR.

SHARP, DOUGLAS ROBERT DO, DATE OF BIRTH MARCH 22, 1950, LICENSE NUMBER 00F1242, OF 6206 HWY 6 SOUTH, HOUSTON, TX, WAS DISCIPLINED BY TEXAS ON APRIL 30, 1993.
DISCIPLINARY ACTION: SURRENDER OF CONTROLLED SUBSTANCE LICENSE; 120-MONTH PROBATION
OFFENSE: DRUG OR ALCOHOL ABUSE
NOTES: ON 1/22/92 HE CONTACTED PHYSICIAN'S ASSISTANCE PROGRAM INFORMING THEM OF HIS SELF-MEDICATING FOR UPPER BACK AND NECK PAIN; MEDICATION ABUSE INCLUDED UP TO 40-50 LORTABS PER DAY AND DEMEROL INJECTIONS; WAS PLACED ON PROBATION FOR TWO YEARS FOR DRIVING WHILE INTOXICATED IN 1990; IN 9/92 RELAPSED AND ENTERED ANOTHER INPATIENT PROGRAM WHICH HE SUCCESSFULLY COMPLETED; IN 2/93 ENTERED A CONTINUING CARE CONTRACT WITH THE PHYSICIANS ASSISTANCE PROGRAM. REVOCATION STAYED. CONDITIONS OF PROBATION: SHALL APPEAR BEFORE THE BOARD TWICE A YEAR; SHALL SURRENDER DEA AND TEXAS CONTROLLED SUBSTANCES REGISTRATION CERTIFICATES AND SHALL NOT ATTEMPT TO REREGISTER WITHOUT BOARD PERMISSION; SHALL SURRENDER ALL CONTROLLED SUBSTANCES INCLUDING SAMPLES IN HIS POSSESSION; SHALL REFRAIN FROM THE PERSONAL USE OF AND NOT PERSONALLY POSSESS, ADMINISTER OR PRESCRIBE ANY CONTROLLED SUBSTANCE OR PRESCRIPTION DRUG UNLESS GIVEN BY ANOTHER PHYSICIAN FOR A LEGITIMATE AND THERAPEUTIC PURPOSE; SHALL NOT TREAT OR OTHERWISE SERVE AS PHYSICIAN, PRESCRIBE, DISPENSE OR ADMINISTER DRUGS THAT MAY BE SUBJECT TO ABUSE TO HIMSELF OR ANY MEMBER OF HIS FAMILY; SHALL ABSTAIN FROM THE CONSUMPTION OF ALCOHOL AND CHEMICAL SUBSTANCES IN ANY FORM; SHALL PARTICIPATE IN ACTIVITIES OF AN IMPAIRED PHYSICIAN COMMITTEE AND ATTEND WEEKLY MEETINGS WITH QUARTERLY REPORTS; SHALL PARTICIPATE IN AA MEETINGS NOT LESS THAN THREE TIMES A WEEK; SHALL SUBMIT HIMSELF FOR APPROPRIATE EXAMS INCLUDING DRUG OR ALCOHOL SCREENS; SHALL SUBMIT HIMSELF TO A BOARD-APPROVED PSYCHIATRIST FOR EVALUATION AND TREATMENT TO WHOM HE WILL PROVIDE COPIES OF THIS ORDER; THIS PSYCHIATRIST WILL SUBMIT REPORTS TO THE BOARD UPON REQUEST; SHALL FURNISH WRITTEN REPORTS TO THE BOARD REGARDING HIS MEDICAL CONDITION AND COMPLIANCE UPON REQUEST; SHALL COMPLY WITH THE TERMS OF HIS CONTRACT WITH THE TEXAS OSTEOPATHIC MEDICAL ASSOCIATION; SHALL LIMIT HIS PRACTICE TO THAT OF A BOARD-APPROVED GROUP SETTING; SHALL BE MONITORED OR SUPERVISED BY A BOARD-APPROVED SUPERVISOR WITH REPORTS TO THE BOARD EVERY FOUR MONTHS; SHALL GIVE A COPY OF THIS ORDER TO ANY HEALTH CARE ENTITY WHERE HE HAS PRIVILEGES; SHALL COOPERATE WITH THE BOARD IN VERIFYING COMPLIANCE; SHALL INFORM THE BOARD OF CHANGE OF ADDRESS WITHIN 10 DAYS OR IF HE LEAVES THE STATE; TIME SPENT OUT OF TEXAS DOES NOT COUNT TOWARD PROBATION. SHALL NOT SEEK MODIFICATION FOR ONE YEAR.

SHAUGHNESSY, DENNIS M MD, DATE OF BIRTH SEPTEMBER 9, 1941, LICENSE NUMBER 00F7913, OF 105 MANOR ROAD, SAN MARCOS, TX, WAS DISCIPLINED BY TEXAS ON APRIL 21, 1990.
DISCIPLINARY ACTION: 120-MONTH RESTRICTION PLACED ON LICENSE; 120-MONTH MONITORING OF PHYSICIAN
OFFENSE: DRUG OR ALCOHOL ABUSE
NOTES: STIPULATED ORDER. MUST IMMEDIATELY REPORT ANY INCIDENT IN WHICH HE CONSUMES ALCOHOL OR USES CONTROLLED SUBSTANCE NOT PRESCRIBED BY ANOTHER PHYSICIAN FOR VALID MEDICAL PURPOSE, CONTINUE TO PARTICIPATE IN AA, SUBMIT FOR APPROPRIATE EXAMINATIONS TO DETERMINE FREEDOM FROM DRUGS AND ALCOHOL, NOT RESUME PRACTICE OF GENERAL OR FAMILY MEDICINE, GENERAL SURGERY, OR WORK IN HOSPITAL EMERGENCY ROOMS UNLESS HE HAS PASSED SPECIAL PURPOSE EXAMINATION AND OBTAINED APPROVAL OF BOARD (BUT MAY PROVIDE SUBSTANCE ABUSE CARE AND TREATMENT AND/OR ADDICTIONOLOGY SERVICES FOR PATIENTS) AND APPEAR SEMI-ANNUALLY BEFORE BOARD. ON 3/26/93 MODIFICATION OF HIS ORDER REDUCING REQUIRED ATTENDANCE OF ALCOHOLICS ANONYMOUS MEETINGS FROM FOUR TO TWO WEEKLY. ALL OTHER TERMS OF THIS ORDER REMAIN IN EFFECT.

SHAUGHNESSY, DENNIS M MD, DATE OF BIRTH SEPTEMBER 9, 1941, LICENSE NUMBER 00F7913, OF 105 MANOR ROAD, SAN MARCOS, TX, WAS DISCIPLINED BY TEXAS ON AUGUST 20, 1993.
OFFENSE: FAILURE TO COMPLY WITH A PREVIOUS BOARD ORDER
NOTES: BY BOARD ORDER OF 4/21/90 HE IS RESTRICTED FROM CONSUMING ANY ALCOHOL AND THAT HE REPORT ANY USE IMMEDIATELY; ONCE IN 3/93 AND ONCE IN 6/93 CONSUMED ALCOHOL ON AN AIRPLANE ENROUTE TO A BUSINESS MEETING; DID NOT REPORT THESE INCIDENTS TO THE BOARD UNTIL SEVERAL DAYS AFTER THE SECOND INCIDENT. PREVIOUS ORDER MODIFIED SUCH THAT HE SHALL APPEAR BEFORE THE BOARD EVERY THREE MONTHS DURING EACH YEAR OF HIS REMAINING PROBATION.

SHAUGHNESSY, DENNIS M MD, DATE OF BIRTH SEPTEMBER 9, 1941, LICENSE NUMBER 00F7913, OF MIDLAND, TX, WAS DISCIPLINED BY TEXAS ON JUNE 22, 1994.
DISCIPLINARY ACTION: LICENSE SUSPENSION
OFFENSE: CRIMINAL CONVICTION OR PLEA OF GUILTY, NOLO CONTENDERE, OR NO CONTEST TO A CRIME
NOTES: IN 4/21/90 ORDER WAS RESTRICTED FROM CONSUMING ALCOHOL; CONSUMED ALCOHOL ON 2/15/94 AND SUBSEQUENTLY PLEADED NOLO CONTENDERE TO DRIVING WHILE INTOXICATED; FINED AND PLACED ON PROBATION FOR ONE YEAR; HAD DISCONTINUED USE OF ANTABUSE PRIOR TO THIS INCIDENT; HAS RESUMED USE SINCE THEN. SUSPENSION UNTIL HE PERSONALLY APPEARS BEFORE BOARD AND PROVIDES SUFFICIENT EVIDENCE THAT HE IS PHYSICALLY, MENTALLY AND OTHERWISE COMPETENT TO SAFELY PRACTICE MEDICINE.

SHAUGHNESSY, DENNIS M MD, DATE OF BIRTH SEPTEMBER 9, 1941, LICENSE NUMBER 00F7913, OF MIDLAND, TX, WAS DISCIPLINED BY TEXAS ON OCTOBER 10, 1994.
DISCIPLINARY ACTION: SURRENDER OF CONTROLLED SUBSTANCE LICENSE; 120-MONTH PROBATION
OFFENSE: DRUG OR ALCOHOL ABUSE
NOTES: SUSPENSION OF 6/22/94 STAYED. CONDITIONS OF PROBATION: SHALL ABSTAIN FROM THE CONSUMPTION OF ALCOHOL/CHEMICAL SUBSTANCES IN ANY FORM UNLESS PRESCRIBED BY ANOTHER PHYSICIAN FOR A LEGITIMATE AND THERAPEUTIC PURPOSE; SHALL SUBMIT HIMSELF FOR APPROPRIATE EXAMS INCLUDING DRUG OR ALCOHOL SCREENS; SHALL NOT TREAT OR OTHERWISE SERVE AS PHYSICIAN, PRESCRIBE, DISPENSE OR ADMINISTER DRUGS THAT MAY BE SUBJECT TO ABUSE TO HIMSELF OR ANY MEMBER OF HIS FAMILY; SHALL NOT USE, POSSESS, ADMINISTER OR PRESCRIBE ANY CONTROLLED SUBSTANCE OR DANGEROUS DRUGS UNLESS PRESCRIBED, ADMINISTERED OR DISPENSED BY ANOTHER PHYSICIAN WHO IS TREATING HIM FOR A LEGITIMATE MEDICAL NEED; SHALL SURRENDER DEA AND TEXAS CONTROLLED SUBSTANCES CERTIFICATES, ALL UNUSED TRIPLICATE PRESCRIPTION FORMS AND ALL CONTROLLED SUBSTANCES IN HIS POSSESSION INCLUDING SAMPLES; SHALL NOT REREGISTER WITHOUT PERMISSION; SEPARATE FROM PATIENT RECORDS SHALL MAINTAIN A FILE OF EVERY PRESCRIPTION WRITTEN FOR DANGEROUS DRUGS WHICH SHALL BE AVAILABLE FOR INSPECTION; SHALL NOT TELEPHONE ANY PRESCRIPTIONS TO A PHARMACY FOR DANGEROUS DRUGS THAT MAY BE HABIT-FORMING; SHALL BE SUPERVISED BY A BOARD-APPROVED PHYSICIAN WITH QUARTERLY REPORTS; SHALL CONTINUE TO PARTICIPATE IN AA'S PROGRAM NOT LESS THAN FOUR TIMES A WEEK WITH QUARTERLY REPORTS TO THE BOARD; SHALL SUBMIT HIMSELF FOR EVALUATION AND TREATMENT TO A BOARD-APPROVED PSYCHIATRIST WITH REPORTS TO THE BOARD; SHALL CONTINUE ANTABUSE TREATMENT UNTIL TREATMENT IS TERMINATED BY MONITORING PHYSICIAN OR TREATING PSYCHIATRIST; SHALL ATTEND AT LEAST 50 HOURS PER YEAR OF CONTINUING MEDICAL EDUCATION; SHALL ATTEND AT LEAST SIX HOURS OF CONTINUING EDUCATION ON THE SUBJECT OF ETHICS WITHIN 12 MONTHS; SHALL APPEAR BEFORE THE BOARD FOUR TIMES A YEAR; SHALL GIVE A COPY OF THIS ORDER TO ANY HEALTH CARE ENTITY WHERE HE HAS PRIVILEGES; SHALL COOPERATE WITH BOARD IN VERIFYING COMPLIANCE; SHALL INFORM BOARD OF CHANGE OF ADDRESS WITHIN 10 DAYS OR IF HE LEAVES THE STATE; TIME SPENT OUT OF TEXAS DOES NOT COUNT TOWARD PROBATION. SHALL NOT SEEK MODIFICATION FOR ONE YEAR. THIS ORDER TAKES THE PLACE OF THE 4/21/90 ORDER AS MODIFIED.

SHERP, GARY ALLAN MD, LICENSE NUMBER 00F3335, OF DALLAS, TX, WAS DISCIPLINED BY TEXAS ON AUGUST 24, 1991.
DISCIPLINARY ACTION: 60-MONTH PROBATION; REQUIRED TO ENTER AN IMPAIRED PHYSICIAN PROGRAM OR DRUG OR ALCOHOL TREATMENT
OFFENSE: LOSS OR RESTRICTION OF HOSPITAL PRIVILEGES
NOTES: SUBSTANCE ABUSE AND LOSS OF HOSPITAL PRIVILEGES. SUSPENSION STAYED; TERMS OF PROBATION: SHALL PARTICIPATE IN AN IMPAIRED PHYSICIANS PROGRAM WITH WRITTEN REPORTS TO BOARD; SHALL PARTICIPATE IN AA; SHALL SUBMIT TO DRUG OR ALCOHOL SCREENS; SHALL APPEAR BEFORE THE BOARD TWICE A YEAR.

SHERP, GARY ALLAN MD, LICENSE NUMBER 00F3335, WAS DISCIPLINED BY TEXAS ON NOVEMBER 9, 1991.
DISCIPLINARY ACTION: EMERGENCY SUSPENSION
OFFENSE: DRUG OR ALCOHOL ABUSE
NOTES: PERFORMED ANESTHESIOLOGY WHILE UNDER THE INFLUENCE OF SUFENTA IV FOR NON-MEDICAL PURPOSES, AND WAS SEEN DOZING DURING SURGERY ON ONE OR MORE OCCASIONS; ON AT LEAST ONE OCCASION, HE FAILED TO PROVIDE ADEQUATE ANESTHESIA TO A PATIENT, WHICH RESULTED IN THE PATIENT BEING AROUSABLE DURING SURGERY; ON ONE OR MORE OCCASIONS HE USED SUFENTA IV IMMEDIATELY BEFORE AND OR DURING SURGERY; THESE ACTS COULD HAVE ENDANGERED PATIENTS LIVES; DRUGS WERE OBTAINED THORUGH DIVERTING DRUGS INTENDED FOR HIS PATIENTS AND RECORDS SUBSEQUENTLY FALSIFIED BY HIM.

SHERP, GARY ALLAN MD, LICENSE NUMBER 00F3335, OF DALLAS, TX, WAS DISCIPLINED BY TEXAS ON JANUARY 24, 1992.
DISCIPLINARY ACTION: LICENSE REVOCATION
OFFENSE: FAILURE TO COMPLY WITH A PROFESSIONAL RULE
NOTES: VIOLATION OF PREVIOUS BOARD ORDER FOR FAILURE TO PRACTICE MEDICINE IN AN ACCEPTABLE MANNER CONSISTENT WITH PUBLIC HEALTH AND WELFARE.

SHICKMAN, BARRY L MD, LICENSE NUMBER 0G15109, OF HOUSTON, TX, WAS DISCIPLINED BY CALIFORNIA ON JUNE 6, 1985.
DISCIPLINARY ACTION: SURRENDER OF LICENSE

SHICKMAN, BARRY L MD WAS DISCIPLINED BY PENNSYLVANIA ON DECEMBER 14, 1986.
DISCIPLINARY ACTION: LICENSE REVOCATION

SHIELDS, FREDERICK S MD, LICENSE NUMBER 00C7772, OF VICTORIA, TX, WAS DISCIPLINED BY TEXAS ON OCTOBER 5, 1991.
DISCIPLINARY ACTION: SURRENDER OF LICENSE
OFFENSE: DRUG OR ALCOHOL ABUSE
NOTES: HE PERFORMED A DILATION AND CURETAGE ON 7/8/88, DURING WHICH THE PATIENT STARTED HEMORRHAGING; SHE WAS TRANSFERRED TO A HOSPITAL FOR EMERGENCY CARE, WHERE SHE DIED. ALLEGED TO HAVE FAILED TO STOP DRINKING ALCOHOL, AS AGREED WITH THE EXECUTIVE COMMITTEE OF CITIZENS MEDICAL CENTER IN 3/90. EXECUTIVE COMMITTEE OF CITIZENS MEDICAL CENTER ACCEPTED HIS SURRENDER OF ADMITTING PRIVILEGES IN RESOLUTION OF A PEER REVIEW COMPLAINT ON 4/10/90.

SHIPKEY, FREDERICK H JR MD, LICENSE NUMBER 00D5474, OF JACKSON, MS, WAS DISCIPLINED BY TEXAS ON JANUARY 12, 1991.
OFFENSE: DISCIPLINARY ACTION BY ANOTHER STATE OR AGENCY
NOTES: AGREED ORDER AS A RESULT OF HAVING BEEN DISCIPLINED BY MISSISSIPPI BOARD. MUST RECIEVE PERMISSION OF TEXAS BOARD BEFORE RETURNING TO PRACTICE MEDICINE IN TEXAS AND BE SUBJECT TO TERMS IMPOSED, IF ANY, INCLUDING A COMPLETE REPORT ON THE STATUS OF HIS MISSISSIPPI LICENSE.

SHORT, LUKE HENRY MD, LICENSE NUMBER 00C7145, OF 449 W

NORTH STREET, MOUNTAIN HOME, AR, WAS DISCIPLINED BY ARKANSAS ON APRIL 8, 1994.
DISCIPLINARY ACTION: EMERGENCY SUSPENSION

SHORT, LUKE HENRY MD, LICENSE NUMBER 00C7145, OF 449 W NORTH STREET, MOUNTAIN HOME, AR, WAS DISCIPLINED BY ARKANSAS ON JUNE 21, 1994.
DISCIPLINARY ACTION: 24-MONTH PROBATION
OFFENSE: DRUG OR ALCOHOL ABUSE
NOTES: EXCESSIVE USE OF NARCOTICS IN A HABITUAL, INTEMPERATE AND EXCESSIVE MANNER FOR NONMEDICAL REASONS; VIOLATION OF LAW REGULATING THE POSSESSION, DISTRIBUTION AND USE OF NARCOTICS AND CONTROLLED DRUGS. GRANTED TEMPORARY PERMIT TO PRACTICE 9/94.

SHORT, LUKE HENRY MD, LICENSE NUMBER 00J3222, OF MOUNTAIN HOME, AR, WAS DISCIPLINED BY TEXAS ON JANUARY 6, 1995.
DISCIPLINARY ACTION: SURRENDER OF LICENSE
OFFENSE: FAILURE TO COMPLY WITH A PREVIOUS BOARD ORDER
NOTES: IN VIOLATION OF A 12/7/92 BOARD ORDER HE SUFFERED A RELAPSE THROUGH THE INGESTION OF FENTANYL IN 2/94; WAS ADMITTED FOR TREATMENT OF CHEMICAL DEPENDENCY; SELF-REPORTED THE RELAPSE TO THE BOARD; DISCHARGED FROM INPATIENT TREATMENT ON 6/25/94 AND ENTERED AFTERCARE. SHALL NOT PETITION FOR REINSTATEMENT.

SHORT, MARVIN JOHN II MD, DATE OF BIRTH JULY 28, 1932, LICENSE NUMBER 00D1124, OF 604 GROVE ROAD, GREENVILLE, SC, WAS DISCIPLINED BY TEXAS ON JUNE 15, 1993.
OFFENSE: DISCIPLINARY ACTION BY ANOTHER STATE OR AGENCY
NOTES: ON 8/11/92 SOUTH CAROLINA LICENSE PLACED ON INDEFINITE PROBATION AFTER A $10,000 FINE AND SURRENDER OF CONTROLLED SUBSTANCES REGISTRATIONS. PRIOR TO PRACTICING IN TEXAS SHALL APPEAR BEFORE THE BOARD TO OBTAIN APPROVAL; SHALL PROVIDE TEXAS WITH ANY REPORTS SUBMITTED TO SOUTH CAROLINA; SHALL GIVE A COPY OF THIS ORDER TO ANY HEALTH CARE ENTITY WHERE HE HAS PRIVILEGES; SHALL COOPERATE WITH THE BOARD IN VERIFYING COMPLIANCE; SHALL INFORM BOARD OF CHANGE OF ADDRESS WITHIN 10 DAYS. SHALL NOT SEEK MODIFICATION FOR ONE YEAR.

SIEBENLIST, BUD ROGER MD OF JONESVILLE, TX, WAS DISCIPLINED BY LOUISIANA ON APRIL 4, 1989.
DISCIPLINARY ACTION: PROBATION; REQUIRED TO TAKE ADDITIONAL MEDICAL EDUCATION
OFFENSE: DISCIPLINARY ACTION BY ANOTHER STATE OR AGENCY
NOTES: TEXAS RESTRICTED LICENSE; HABITUAL OR RECURRING ABUSE OF ALCOHOL; INDEFINITE PROBATION CONDITIONED ON STRICT COMPLIANCE WITH TERMS OF TEXAS ORDER INCLUDING PASSAGE OF SPEX EXAM, PARTICIPATION IN AA, SUBMISSION TO SPONTANEOUS DRUG SCREENS, AND PRIOR NOTICE TO BOARD BEFORE RELOCATION OF PRACTICE TO LOUISIANA

SIMMS, JOHN H II MD, LICENSE NUMBER 00C8439, OF BEAUMONT, TX, WAS DISCIPLINED BY TEXAS ON OCTOBER 27, 1989.
DISCIPLINARY ACTION: REPRIMAND
NOTES: STIPULATED ORDER.

SIMON, JEAN-CHARLES MD, LICENSE NUMBER 00G1776, OF SPRING, TX, WAS DISCIPLINED BY TEXAS ON NOVEMBER 3, 1994.
DISCIPLINARY ACTION: 120-MONTH PROBATION; RESTRICTION PLACED ON LICENSE
OFFENSE: OVERPRESCRIBING OR MISPRESCRIBING DRUGS
NOTES: IN SIX CASES IN 1987 AND 1988 TESTS PERFORMED WITHOUT ADEQUATE INDICATION OR PRIOR TO ANY PHYSICAL EXAMINATION; IN FIVE CASES IN 1991 AND 1992 TREATMENTS AND CHARGES WERE EXCESSIVE IN RELATION TO THE INJURY AND THEIR MEDICAL RECORDS FAILED TO SUPPORT THE TREATMENT METHODS AND CHARGES OR TO DEMONSTRATE THAT ANY HOME SELF-CARE INSTRUCTION WAS GIVEN; IN SEVERAL CASES BETWEEN 1987 AND 1990 PATIENTS WERE PRESCRIBED MEDICATIONS WITHOUT EITHER ADEQUATE ASSESSMENT, FOLLOW-UP, OR DOCUMENTATION; SOME OF THESE PRESCRIPTIONS WERE REFILLED OR PRESCRIBED FOR LONG PERIODS OF TIME WITHOUT PROPER INDICATION; IN SOME CASES NO PROPER HISTORY OR PHYSICAL EXAM WAS PERFORMED AND IN ONE CASE THERE WAS INDICATION OF DRUG ABUSE; ENGAGED IN THE CORPORATE PRACTICE OF MEDICINE BY HIS SALARIED EMPLOYMENT AT A CLINIC OWNED AND OPERATED BY A NON-PHYSICIAN; SIGNED A MEMORANDUM OF AGREEMENT WITH THE DEA ON 3/21/94 REGARDING PREVIOUS SURRENDER OF CONTROLLED SUBSTANCES REGISTRATIONS. HE NEITHER ADMITS NOR DENIES THESE CHARGES. REVOCATION STAYED. CONDITIONS OF PROBATION: SHALL APPEAR BEFORE THE BOARD TWICE A YEAR; WITHIN ONE YEAR SHALL TAKE THE TEXAS MEDICAL JURISPRUDENCE EXAM; SHALL NOT ACCEPT EMPLOYMENT OR ENTER INTO CONTRACTUAL RELATIONSHIPS WHERE HE WOULD BE COMPENSATED TO DIAGNOSE OR TREAT PATIENTS BY ANY ENTITY NOT COMPOSED OF TEXAS LICENSED PHYSICIANS AND WHERE THE ENTITY WOULD RECEIVE AND RETAIN FEES PAID FOR THE PHYSICIAN'S PROFESSIONAL SERVICES; ORDER CONSTITUTES A PUBLIC REPRIMAND; SHALL PERSONALLY EXAMINE PATIENTS WHEN A FORM CERTIFIES THIS OR WHERE AN INITIAL DIAGNOSIS OF PROBABLE DISEASE OR INJURY HAS BEEN MADE; SHALL PERFORM 10 HOURS PER MONTH OF COMMUNITY SERVICE FOR TWO YEARS; SHALL FOLLOW TERMS OF AGREEMENT WITH DEA; SHALL NOT ADMINISTER, DISPENSE, OR PRESCRIBE ANY SCHEDULE II OR IIN CONTROLLED SUBSTANCES ALTHOUGH MAY ORDER THESE CONTROLLED SUBSTANCES FOR HOSPITAL OR NURSING HOME PATIENTS; SHALL BE SUPERVISED BY A BOARD-APPROVED PHYSICIAN WITH QUARTERLY REPORTS; SHALL NOT TREAT ANY PATIENT FOR WEIGHT CONTROL OR OBESITY WITH ANY DRUGS; SEPARATE FROM PATIENT RECORDS, SHALL MAINTAIN A FILE OF EVERY PRESCRIPTION WRITTEN FOR CONTROLLED SUBSTANCES OR DANGEROUS DRUGS WHICH SHALL BE AVAILABLE FOR INSPECTION; SHALL NOT TELEPHONE ANY PRESCRIPTION FOR THESE DRUGS TO A PHARMACY; SHALL NOT PRESCRIBE, DISPENSE, ADMINISTER OR POSSESS ANY OF A SPECIFIED LIST OF AMPHETAMINE-LIKE DRUGS; SHALL NOT TREAT OR OTHERWISE SERVE AS PHYSICIAN, PRESCRIBE, DISPENSE OR ADMINISTER DRUGS THAT MAY BE SUBJECT TO ABUSE TO HIMSELF OR ANY MEMBER OF HIS FAMILY; SHALL NOT SIGN ANY PATIENT RECORD UNLESS HE HAS PERSONALLY EXAMINED THE PATIENT OR CLEARLY NOTES IN THE RECORD THAT HE DID NOT; SHALL MAINTAIN ADEQUATE MEDICAL RECORDS ON ALL PATIENT OFFICE VISITS WHICH

SHALL BE AVAILABLE FOR INSPECTION; SHALL ATTEND SIX HOURS OF AN ETHICS COURSE OR PROGRAM PER YEAR FOR TWO YEARS AND SHALL ATTEND AT LEAST 75 HOURS OF CONTINUING MEDICAL EDUCATION INCLUDING 25 IN PHARMACOLOGY/ADDICTIONOLOGY; SHALL GIVE A COPY OF THIS ORDER TO ANY HEALTH CARE ENTITY WHERE HE HAS PRIVILEGES; SHALL COOPERATE WITH THE BOARD IN VERIFYING COMPLIANCE; SHALL INFORM BOARD OF CHANGE OF ADDRESS WITHIN 10 DAYS OR IF HE LEAVES THE STATE; TIME SPENT OUT OF TEXAS DOES NOT COUNT TOWARD PROBATION. SHALL NOT SEEK MODIFICATION FOR TWO YEARS.

SINCLARE, ROSS MD, LICENSE NUMBER 00F2928, OF HOUSTON, TX, WAS DISCIPLINED BY TEXAS ON JANUARY 28, 1989.
DISCIPLINARY ACTION: SURRENDER OF LICENSE
OFFENSE: CRIMINAL CONVICTION OR PLEA OF GUILTY, NOLO CONTENDERE, OR NO CONTEST TO A CRIME
NOTES: REQUESTED BOARD ACCEPT VOLUNTARY SURRENDER IN LIEU OF FURTHER PROCEEDINGS AS CONDITION OF PLEA BARGAIN AGREEMENT WITH U.S. DISTRICT COURT

SINCLARE, ROSS G MD, DATE OF BIRTH DECEMBER 31, 1930, OF 1703 MISSION SPRINGS, KATY, TX, WAS DISCIPLINED BY MEDICARE ON JULY 10, 1990.
DISCIPLINARY ACTION: 60-MONTH EXCLUSION FROM THE MEDICARE AND/OR MEDICAID PROGRAMS
OFFENSE: CRIMINAL CONVICTION OR PLEA OF GUILTY, NOLO CONTENDERE, OR NO CONTEST TO A CRIME
NOTES: PROGRAM-RELATED CONVICTION.

SJOBERG, WALTER EUGENE JR MD, LICENSE NUMBER 00C5884, OF AUSTIN, TX, WAS DISCIPLINED BY TEXAS ON APRIL 15, 1994.
DISCIPLINARY ACTION: 60-MONTH RESTRICTION PLACED ON LICENSE; MONITORING OF PHYSICIAN
OFFENSE: LOSS OR RESTRICTION OF HOSPITAL PRIVILEGES
NOTES: HOSPITAL PRIVILEGES WERE RESTRICTED AS FOLLOWS IN 1993 FOR 12 MONTHS DUE TO USE OF ANTICOAGULANTS WITH A PATIENT WHO EXPIRED DUE TO AN INTRACRANIAL HEMORRHAGE: MANDATORY CONSULTATIONS ARE REQUIRED FOR ONE YEAR ON ALL ADMISSIONS INVOLVING ANTICOAGULANTS AND THE NEXT 20 CASES FOR ALL OTHER ADMISSIONS; THE CARE PROVIDED WAS DETERMINED BY THE HOSPITAL TO BE A SIGNIFICANT DEVIATION FROM THE STANDARD OF CARE. CONDITIONS OF RESTRICTIONS: OBTAIN MANDATORY CONSULTATION ON ALL HOSPITAL ADMISSIONS INVOLVING ANTICOAGULANTS AND ON THE NEXT 20 CASES FOR ALL HOSPITAL ADMISSIONS; SHALL COOPERATE WITH THE BOARD IN VERIFYING COMPLIANCE; SHALL INFORM BOARD OF CHANGE OF ADDRESS WITHIN 10 DAYS OR IF HE LEAVES THE STATE; TIME SPENT OUT OF TEXAS DOES NOT COUNT TOWARD RESTRICTION; SHALL APPEAR BEFORE THE BOARD ONCE A YEAR; SHALL GIVE A COPY OF THIS ORDER TO ANY HEALTH CARE ENTITY WHERE HE HAS PRIVILEGES; SHALL NOT SEEK MODIFICATION FOR ONE YEAR. ON 5/11/95 BOARD GRANTED HIS PETITION FOR TERMINATION OF THIS ORDER; RESTRICTIONS PLACED ON HOSPITAL PRIVILEGES HAVE BEEN TERMINATED.

SKARBOVIG, PETER JENS JR DO, LICENSE NUMBER 00F7174, OF KINGWOOD, TX, WAS DISCIPLINED BY TEXAS ON SEPTEMBER 28, 1990.
DISCIPLINARY ACTION: SURRENDER OF LICENSE
OFFENSE: PHYSICAL OR MENTAL ILLNESS INHIBITING THE ABILITY TO PRACTICE WITH SKILL AND SAFETY
NOTES: INABILITY TO PRACTICE MEDICINE WITH REASONABLE SKILL AND SAFETY TO PATIENTS BY REASON OF ILLNESS, DRUNKENESS, EXCESSIVE USE OF DRUGS, NARCOTICS, CHEMICALS, OR ANY OTHER TYPE OF MATERIAL, OR AS RESULT OF ANY MENTAL OR PHYSICAL CONDITION. SURRENDER IN LIEU OF FUTURE DISCIPLINARY HEARING.

SLEVIN, DANIEL DO, LICENSE NUMBER 00D1169, WAS DISCIPLINED BY TEXAS ON DECEMBER 4, 1991.
NOTES: AGREEMENT DATED 11/19/86, WHERE LICENSE WAS RESTRICTED, IS TERMINATED; LICENSE IS FREE OF ANY AND ALL RESTRICTIONS.

SMILEY, EVELYN J K MD, LICENSE NUMBER 00C6518, OF LAMESA, TX, WAS DISCIPLINED BY TEXAS ON AUGUST 20, 1992.
DISCIPLINARY ACTION: 60-MONTH PROBATION
OFFENSE: SUBSTANDARD CARE, INCOMPETENCE, OR NEGLIGENCE
NOTES: FAILURE TO PRACTICE MEDICINE IN AN ACCEPTABLE MANNER CONSISTENT WITH PUBLIC HEALTH AND WELFARE. LICENSE SUSPENDED, SUSPENSION STAYED. PROBATION UNDER TERMS AND CONDITIONS.

SMILEY, EVELYN J MD, LICENSE NUMBER 0C20354, OF LAMESA, TX, WAS DISCIPLINED BY CALIFORNIA ON JUNE 30, 1994.
DISCIPLINARY ACTION: 60-MONTH PROBATION
OFFENSE: DISCIPLINARY ACTION BY ANOTHER STATE OR AGENCY
NOTES: DISCIPLINED BY THE TEXAS BOARD FOR FAILING TO PRACTICE MEDICINE IN AN ACCEPTABLE MANNER CONSISTENT WITH PUBLIC HEALTH AND WELFARE IN THE CARE AND TREATMENT OF THREE PATIENTS. ONE YEAR SUSPENSION STAYED.

SMITH, ART GLENN MD, LICENSE NUMBER 00H3344, OF SAN ANTONIO, TX, WAS DISCIPLINED BY TEXAS ON NOVEMBER 9, 1993.
DISCIPLINARY ACTION: EMERGENCY SUSPENSION
OFFENSE: SEXUAL ABUSE OF OR SEXUAL MISCONDUCT WITH A PATIENT
NOTES: IN 8/93 ENGAGED IN ALLEGED INAPPROPRIATE AND UNPROFESSIONAL CONTACT WITH ONE PATIENT WHICH LED HER TO BELIEVE HE WAS ATTEMPTING TO INITIATE A SEXUAL RELATIONSHIP WITH HER; FROM 4/93 AND CONTINUING TO DATE OF ORDER HE HAS ENGAGED IN BEHAVIORS WHICH MAY BE INDICATIVE OF PSYCHIATRIC IMPAIRMENT SUCH AS STATEMENTS INDICATING PARANOID IDEATION, INAPPROPRIATE BEHAVIORS INCLUDING YELLING AND BEING ABUSIVE WITH STAFF AND PATIENTS OVER MINOR INCIDENTS AND CARRYING ON A CONVERSATION WITH A TELEPHONE WHICH WAS NOT CONNECTED TO ANY OTHER PARTY.

SMITH, CHARLES D MD, LICENSE NUMBER 00C7906, OF CRYSTAL CITY, TX, WAS DISCIPLINED BY TEXAS ON MAY 20, 1989.
DISCIPLINARY ACTION: SURRENDER OF CONTROLLED SUBSTANCE LICENSE
NOTES: SHALL APPLY TO TAKE SPECIAL PURPOSE EXAMINATION (SPEX) AND PASS; IF UNSUCCESSFUL AT PASSAGE OF SPEX SHALL WITHDRAW FROM PRACTICE OF MEDICINE UNTIL SUCH PASSAGE; SHALL SUBMIT TO PSYCHIATRIC AND PHYSICAL EVALUATIONS AND FOLLOW RECOMMENDATIONS

SMITH, SALLY TOW MD, LICENSE NUMBER 00C8477, OF SAN ANTONIO, TX, WAS DISCIPLINED BY TEXAS ON DECEMBER 1, 1988.
NOTES: SETTLEMENT AGREEMENT AND UNSPECIFIED DISCIPLINARY ACTION

SMITH, THOMAS E MD, LICENSE NUMBER 00C7497, OF BAYTOWN, TX, WAS DISCIPLINED BY TEXAS ON OCTOBER 29, 1988.
DISCIPLINARY ACTION: 23-MONTH RESTRICTION PLACED ON CONTROLLED SUBSTANCE LICENSE; 24-MONTH REQUIRED TO TAKE ADDITIONAL MEDICAL EDUCATION
NOTES: MUST SUBMIT TO NEUROPSYCHIATRIC EVALUATION AND FOLLOW TREATMENT RECOMMENDATIONS; TO OBTAIN 50 HOURS CONTINUING MEDICAL EDUCATION PER YEAR FOR TWO YEARS; SURRENDER ALL CONTROLLED SUBSTANCE REGISTRATIONS FOR SCHEDULES II THROUGH IV AND NOT REREGISTER FOR SAME WITHOUT PRIOR BOARD APPROVAL; ATTEND APPROPRIATE PROGRAM REGARDING RISK MANAGEMENT FOR DRUGS

SMITH, THOMAS E MD, LICENSE NUMBER 0TXC749, OF 6019 EAST THOMPSON ROAD, BAYTOWN, TX, WAS DISCIPLINED BY DEA ON MARCH 16, 1989.
DISCIPLINARY ACTION: RESTRICTION PLACED ON CONTROLLED SUBSTANCE LICENSE
OFFENSE: OVERPRESCRIBING OR MISPRESCRIBING DRUGS
NOTES: OVERPRESCRIBED CONTROLLED SUBSTANCES TO PATIENTS THAT WERE KNOWN HABITUAL USERS; PROFESSIONAL FAILURE TO PRACTICE MEDICINE.

SNEAD, EVA LEE MD OF SAN ANTONIO, TX, WAS DISCIPLINED BY TEXAS ON JULY 1, 1986.
DISCIPLINARY ACTION: LICENSE REVOCATION
OFFENSE: PROFESSIONAL MISCONDUCT
NOTES: MOTION FOR REHEARING DENIED. APPEAL DISMISSED

SNYDER, JOHN T MD OF 1113 REDBUD, CHANNELVIEW, TX, WAS DISCIPLINED BY DEA ON JANUARY 29, 1990.
DISCIPLINARY ACTION: SURRENDER OF CONTROLLED SUBSTANCE LICENSE
OFFENSE: PROFESSIONAL MISCONDUCT
NOTES: DISPENSED PHENTERMINE FOR ILLEGITIMATE MEDICAL PURPOSE.

SOLANKI, KIRIT MD OF 5451 INDEPENDENCE, PLANO, TX, WAS DISCIPLINED BY MEDICARE ON JULY 10, 1986.
DISCIPLINARY ACTION: 24-MONTH EXCLUSION FROM THE MEDICARE AND/OR MEDICAID PROGRAMS
OFFENSE: CRIMINAL CONVICTION OR PLEA OF GUILTY, NOLO CONTENDERE, OR NO CONTEST TO A CRIME
NOTES: PROGRAM-RELATED CONVICTION.

SOLANKI, KIRIT V MD WAS DISCIPLINED BY WISCONSIN ON DECEMBER 5, 1985.
DISCIPLINARY ACTION: SURRENDER OF LICENSE

SOLANKI, KIRIT V MD OF PLANO, TX, WAS DISCIPLINED BY TEXAS ON DECEMBER 1, 1986.
DISCIPLINARY ACTION: 6-MONTH LICENSE SUSPENSION; 24-MONTH PROBATION
OFFENSE: CRIMINAL CONVICTION OR PLEA OF GUILTY, NOLO CONTENDERE, OR NO CONTEST TO A CRIME
NOTES: CONVICTED OF FELONY

SOMMERS, GUY H JR MD OF ATLANTA, GA, WAS DISCIPLINED BY TEXAS ON DECEMBER 1, 1986.
DISCIPLINARY ACTION: PROBATION
OFFENSE: DISCIPLINARY ACTION BY ANOTHER STATE OR AGENCY
NOTES: THREE-YEAR SUSPENSION STAYED

SONIK, SIMON MD, DATE OF BIRTH JANUARY 22, 1931, LICENSE NUMBER 00F0318, OF 9660 HILLCROFT SUITE 550, HOUSTON, TX, WAS DISCIPLINED BY TEXAS ON JANUARY 29, 1993.
DISCIPLINARY ACTION: REPRIMAND
OFFENSE: FAILURE TO COMPLY WITH A PROFESSIONAL RULE
NOTES: FAILED TO KEEP ADEQUATE RECORDS OF THE MEDICAL CARE GIVEN TO A PATIENT. SHALL GIVE A COPY OF ORDER TO ANY HEALTH CARE ENTITY WHERE HE HAS PRIVILEGES; SHALL INFORM THE BOARD OF CHANGE OF ADDRESS WITHIN 10 DAYS.

SORIANO, SALVADOR L MD, LICENSE NUMBER 00D3405, OF DUNCANVILLE, TX, WAS DISCIPLINED BY TEXAS ON OCTOBER 5, 1991.
DISCIPLINARY ACTION: 60-MONTH PROBATION; MONITORING OF PHYSICIAN
OFFENSE: DRUG OR ALCOHOL ABUSE
NOTES: MADE HOSPITAL ROUNDS ON OR ABOUT 10/21/90 WHILE UNDER THE INFLUENCE OF A COMBINATION OF ALCOHOL AND AN ANTIDEPRESSANT, WHICH CAUSED HIS SPEECH TO BE SLURRED, EYES RED, AND UNABLE TO ACCURATELY COMMUNICATE INFORMATION ABOUT HIS PATIENT; HAD BEEN DEPRESSED SINCE 9/90; FAILED TO COMPLETE ADMISSION NOTES ON A PATIENT WITHIN 24 HOURS OF ADMISSION, LATER FALSIFIED RECORDS. DENIES THESE ALLEGATIONS BUT AGREED TO DISPOSE OF MATTER BY AGREED SETTLEMENT. SUSPENSION STAYED, PROBATION INCLUDES FOLLOWING CONDITIONS: SHALL SUBMIT HIMSELF FOR APPROPRIATE EXAMINATIONS, INCLUDING SCREENING FOR ALCOHOL OR DRUGS, THROUGH TESTS OF BODILY FLUIDS; SHALL SUBMIT IN WRITING TO BOARD THE NAMES OF THREE PSYCHIATRISTS FOR BOARD APPROVAL, AND SHALL EXPEDITIOUSLY SUBMIT HIMSELF FOR EVALUATION AND TREATMENT, FOLLOWING THE PSYCHIATRIST'S RECOMMENDATIONS, IF ANY, REGARDING CONTINUING CARE AND TREATMENT; SHALL APPEAR BEFORE THE BOARD TWICE A YEAR; MUST COOPERATE WITH THE BOARD IN VERIFYING COMPLIANCE; MUST ADVISE THE BOARD OF ANY CHANGE OF ADDRESS WITHIN 10 DAYS; TIME SPENT OUT OF TEXAS DOES NOT COUNT TOWARDS PROBATION.

SOROOSH, FARHANG MD OF 1401 E LAKE MEAD BLVD, N LAS VEGAS, NV, WAS DISCIPLINED BY MEDICARE ON NOVEMBER 5, 1984.
DISCIPLINARY ACTION: 108-MONTH EXCLUSION FROM THE MEDICARE AND/OR MEDICAID PROGRAMS
OFFENSE: DISCIPLINARY ACTION BY ANOTHER STATE OR AGENCY
NOTES: PEER REVIEW ORGANIZATION RECOMMENDATION. NO LONGER LISTED AS EXCLUDED AS OF 9/30/92.

SOROOSH, FARHANG MD OF LAS VEGAS, NV, WAS DISCIPLINED BY TEXAS ON SEPTEMBER 1, 1985.
DISCIPLINARY ACTION: SURRENDER OF LICENSE

SOROOSH, FARHANG MD, LICENSE NUMBER 0100411, OF NORTH LAS VEGAS, NV, WAS DISCIPLINED BY NEW YORK ON AUGUST 26, 1986.
DISCIPLINARY ACTION: 36-MONTH PROBATION
NOTES: REVOCATION STAYED

SOROOSH, FARHANG MD, LICENSE NUMBER C039705, OF NORTH LAS VEGAS, NV, WAS DISCIPLINED BY CALIFORNIA ON OCTOBER 26, 1987.
DISCIPLINARY ACTION: SURRENDER OF LICENSE

SORRELS, WILLIAM F DO, LICENSE NUMBER 00F7187, OF SD, WAS DISCIPLINED BY TEXAS ON SEPTEMBER 30, 1994.
DISCIPLINARY ACTION: LICENSE SUSPENSION
OFFENSE: DISCIPLINARY ACTION BY ANOTHER STATE OR AGENCY
NOTES: ON 3/2/94 SIGNED AN AGREED DISPOSITION WITH THE SOUTH DAKOTA BOARD AGREEING TO A TWO YEAR STAYED SUSPENSION TO PROBATION; THERE HAD BEEN ALLEGATIONS OF UNLAWFUL USE OF COCAINE. SUSPENSION UNTIL HE PERSONALLY APPEARS BEFORE THE BOARD TO REQUEST PERMISSION TO PRACTICE AND PROVIDES SUFFICIENT EVIDENCE THAT HE IS PHYSICALLY, MENTALLY AND OTHERWISE COMPETENT TO SAFELY PRACTICE; SHALL GIVE A COPY OF THIS ORDER TO ANY HEALTH CARE ENTITY WHERE HE HAS PRIVILEGES; SHALL COOPERATE WITH THE BOARD IN VERIFYING COMPLIANCE; SHALL INFORM BOARD OF CHANGE OF ADDRESS WITHIN 10 DAYS; SHALL SURRENDER TEXAS CONTROLLED SUBSTANCES CERTIFICATE AND ALL UNUSED TRIPLICATE PRESCRIPTION FORMS; SHALL NOT ATTEMPT TO REREGISTER WITHOUT PERMISSION; SHALL COMPLY WITH ALL TERMS OF THE SOUTH DAKOTA BOARD ORDER.

SOSA, ROBERT MD, LICENSE NUMBER 0022595, WAS DISCIPLINED BY MICHIGAN ON JUNE 11, 1979.
DISCIPLINARY ACTION: PROBATION; REPRIMAND

SOSA, ROBERT MD, LICENSE NUMBER 0022595, WAS DISCIPLINED BY MICHIGAN ON AUGUST 28, 1983.
DISCIPLINARY ACTION: RESTRICTION PLACED ON LICENSE

SOSA, ROBERT MD OF GRAND RAPIDS, MI, WAS DISCIPLINED BY TEXAS ON SEPTEMBER 1, 1985.
DISCIPLINARY ACTION: SURRENDER OF LICENSE

SOSA, ROBERT MD, LICENSE NUMBER 0022595, WAS DISCIPLINED BY MICHIGAN ON MARCH 13, 1986.
DISCIPLINARY ACTION: LICENSE REVOCATION

SOTOODEH, BAGHER MD, DATE OF BIRTH JULY 3, 1915, LICENSE NUMBER 00C5976, OF 105 E LAUREL STREET, SAN ANTONIO, TX, WAS DISCIPLINED BY TEXAS ON JANUARY 29, 1993.
DISCIPLINARY ACTION: RESTRICTION PLACED ON LICENSE
OFFENSE: SUBSTANDARD CARE, INCOMPETENCE, OR NEGLIGENCE
NOTES: HAD A HIGHER THAN AVERAGE COMPLICATION RATE AS WELL AS PROBLEMS IN SURGICAL TECHNIQUE IN PERFORMANCE OF CATARACT INTRAOCULAR LENS SURGERIES. SHALL NOT PERFORM ANY OF THE FOLLOWING MAJOR INVASIVE PROCEDURES OR ANY OTHER PROCEDURES NOT SPECIFIED IN THE ORDER AS MINOR PROCEDURES: CATARACT INTRAOCULAR LENS APPLICATION; GLAUCOMA FILTERING; LACERATION OF THE EYE; INTRAOCULAR FOREIGN BODY REMOVAL; MASTOIDECTOMY; STAPEDECTOMY; TYMPANOPLASTY; TONSILLECTOMY; LARYNGOSCOPY; RADIAL KERATOTOMY; ARGON PHOTO COAGULATION; AND YAG LASER IRIDOTOMY AND CAPSILOTOMY. SHALL GIVE A COPY OF THIS ORDER TO ANY HEALTH CARE ENTITY WHERE HE HAS PRIVILEGES; SHALL COOPERATE WITH THE BOARD TO VERIFY COMPLIANCE; SHALL INFORM BOARD OF CHANGE OF ADDRESS WITHIN 10 DAYS; TIME SPENT OUT OF TEXAS DOES NOT COUNT TOWARD RESTRICTION; SHALL NOT SEEK MODIFICATION TO THIS ORDER FOR 12 MONTHS.

SOUDA, ROBERT M MD, LICENSE NUMBER 00D1497, OF DALLAS, TX, WAS DISCIPLINED BY TEXAS ON NOVEMBER 30, 1994.
DISCIPLINARY ACTION: SURRENDER OF LICENSE
NOTES: DENIES ALLEGATIONS CONCERNING POSSIBLE VIOLATIONS OF THE MEDICAL PRACTICE ACT BUT SURRENDERS LICENSE IN LIEU OF FURTHER INVESTIGATION. SHALL NOT PETITION FOR REINSTATEMENT OF LICENSE.

SPEAK, KENNETH EDWIN DO, LICENSE NUMBER 00C4555, OF KERENS, TX, WAS DISCIPLINED BY TEXAS ON JANUARY 11, 1991.
DISCIPLINARY ACTION: 6-MONTH LICENSE SUSPENSION; REQUIRED TO TAKE ADDITIONAL MEDICAL EDUCATION
OFFENSE: SUBSTANDARD CARE, INCOMPETENCE, OR NEGLIGENCE
NOTES: ADMINISTERED DRUG OR TREATMENT THAT WAS NONTHERAPEUTIC IN NATURE; FAILED PROFESSIONALLY TO PRACTICE MEDICINE IN ACCEPTABLE MANNER CONSISTENT WITH PUBLIC HEALTH AND WELFARE. SUSPENSION FOR AT LEAST SIX MONTHS AND THEREAFTER UNTIL SUCCESSFUL COMPLETION OF MINI-RESIDENCY IN FAMILY PRACTICE AND SUCCESSFUL COMPLETION OF SPECIAL PURPOSE EXAMINATION. MOTION FOR REHEARING FILED.

SPRINGER, GEORGE O MD, DATE OF BIRTH JULY 9, 1957, OF 3001 TYLER STREET, EL PASO, TX, WAS DISCIPLINED BY MEDICARE ON JANUARY 3, 1995.
DISCIPLINARY ACTION: EXCLUSION FROM THE MEDICARE AND/OR MEDICAID PROGRAMS
OFFENSE: FAILURE TO COMPLY WITH A PROFESSIONAL RULE
NOTES: DEFAULTED ON PUBLIC HEALTH SERVICE EDUCATION LOAN.

SPURLOCK, CHARLES E MD OF BATON ROUGE, LA, WAS DISCIPLINED BY TEXAS ON DECEMBER 1, 1986.
DISCIPLINARY ACTION: LICENSE REVOCATION
OFFENSE: DISCIPLINARY ACTION BY ANOTHER STATE OR AGENCY
NOTES: PROBATIONARY PROVISIONS ISSUED BY LOUISIANA BOARD ADOPTED AND INCORPORATED.

STAFFORD, JOHN S MD, LICENSE NUMBER 00G5640, OF SANTA FE, TX, WAS DISCIPLINED BY TEXAS ON OCTOBER 27, 1989.
DISCIPLINARY ACTION: 24-MONTH RESTRICTION PLACED ON LICENSE
NOTES: STIPULATED ORDER. SHALL NOT SUPERVISE OR EMPLOY PHYSICIAN ASSISTANT WITHOUT BOARD APPROVAL. IF APPROVAL OBTAINED, SHALL NOT AUTHORIZE PHYSICIAN ASSISTANT TO EXAMINE AND/OR TREAT PATIENTS UNLESS PHYSICALLY PRESENT IN OFFICE OR READILY AVAILABLE, SHALL COMPLY WITH RULES ON SUPERVISION OF PHYSICIAN ASSISTANTS.

STANTON, ELBERT MD, LICENSE NUMBER 00C5894, OF HUNTSVILLE, TX, WAS DISCIPLINED BY TEXAS ON OCTOBER 1, 1987.
DISCIPLINARY ACTION: LICENSE SUSPENSION
OFFENSE: CRIMINAL CONVICTION OR PLEA OF GUILTY, NOLO CONTENDERE, OR NO CONTEST TO A CRIME
NOTES: CONVICTION OF FELONY; PRESCRIBED DRUGS NON-THERAPEUTICALLY. LICENSE SUSPENDED

PENDING APPEAL OF CONVICTION AS OF AUTUMN 1987; LICENSE TO BE REVOKED IF APPEAL FAILS. REMAINED SUSPENDED AS OF MAY 1990

STANTON, JAMES M MD OF 1201 BERING DRIVE, HOUSTON, TX, WAS DISCIPLINED BY DEA ON DECEMBER 23, 1992.
DISCIPLINARY ACTION: REVOCATION OF CONTROLLED SUBSTANCE LICENSE
OFFENSE: DISCIPLINARY ACTION BY ANOTHER STATE OR AGENCY
NOTES: THE TEXAS BOARD OF MEDICAL EXAMINERS FOUND THAT CONTROLLED SUBSTANCES PRESCRIBED AND ADMINISTERED BY HIM WERE NOT PRESCRIBED OR ADMINISTERED FOR A VALID MEDICAL REASON. FROM 01/04/89 TO 11/29/90 HE ISSUED 201 PRESCRIPTIONS OF CODEINE PRODUCTS IN HIS MOTHER'S NAME, WHICH WERE ACTUALLY FOR HIS PERSONAL USE. THE BOARD CONCLUDED THAT THE PUBLIC WAS PUT IN DANGER BY HIS SELF-ADMINISTRATION OF CONTROLLED SUBSTANCES AND THAT HE ENGAGED IN UNPROFESSIONAL OR DISHONORABLE CONDUCT THAT WAS LIKELY TO DECEIVE OR DEFRAUD OR INJURE THE PUBLIC. MEDICAL LICENSE REVOKED IN TEXAS ON 10/10/91. THEREFORE, HE IS NOT AUTHORIZED TO HANDLE CONTROLLED SUBSTANCES.

STANTON, JAMES MICHAEL MD, DATE OF BIRTH NOVEMBER 14, 1946, LICENSE NUMBER 00E3779, OF MISSOURI CITY, TX, WAS DISCIPLINED BY TEXAS ON OCTOBER 10, 1991.
DISCIPLINARY ACTION: LICENSE REVOCATION
OFFENSE: FAILURE TO COMPLY WITH A PREVIOUS BOARD ORDER
NOTES: ON 9/3/87 HE ENTERED INTO AN AGREEMENT WITH THE BOARD IN WHICH HE AGREED NOT TO PRESCRIBE, ADMINISTER, OR DISPENSE ANY CONTROLLED SUBSTANCES FOR HIMSELF OR HIS IMMEDIATE FAMILY EXCEPT IN EMERGENCIES; AGREEMENT WAS IN EFFECT UNTIL 9/30/90. HE ISSUED APPROXIMATELY 169 PRESCRIPTIONS OF CONTROLLED SUBSTANCES DURING THE PERIOD 1/4/89 THROUGH 9/2/90 IN THE NAME OF HIS MOTHER; HE SELF-ADMINISTERED THESE CONTROLLED SUBSTANCES. HE ISSUED APPROXIMATELY 201 PRESCRIPTIONS OF CONTROLLED SUBSTANCES IN THE NAME OF HIS MOTHER AND SELF-ADMINISTERED THEM DURING THE PERIOD 1/4/89 TO 11/29/90. PRESCRIPTIONS WRITTEN WERE FALSE AND FICTITIOUS.

STANTON, JAMES MICHAEL MD, DATE OF BIRTH NOVEMBER 14, 1946, LICENSE NUMBER 00E3779, OF 1201 BERING #99, HOUSTON, TX, WAS DISCIPLINED BY TEXAS ON NOVEMBER 30, 1992.
DISCIPLINARY ACTION: SURRENDER OF CONTROLLED SUBSTANCE LICENSE; LICENSE REINSTATEMENT
OFFENSE: DRUG OR ALCOHOL ABUSE
NOTES: SINCE 10/10/91 REVOCATION, HAS UNDERGONE OVER FIVE MONTHS OF IN-PATIENT TREATMENT FOR IMPAIRED PHYSICIANS; PROVIDED RESULTS OF URINE SCREENS CONDUCTED IN 1992 WHICH INDICATE THAT DRUGS OR THEIR METABOLITES WERE NOT DETECTED IN HIS URINE; PROVIDED FAVORABLE LETTERS REGARDING HIS PROFESSIONAL CHARACTER, ABILITIES AND REHABILITATION EFFORTS. PLACED ON TEN-YEAR PROBATION UNDER TERMS AND CONDITIONS: SHALL ATTEND AT LEAST 50 HOURS PER YEAR OF CONTINUING MEDICAL EDUCATION APPROVED FOR CATEGORY I CREDITS; SHALL BE MONITORED OR SUPERVISED BY A BOARD-APPROVED PHYSICIAN WHO WILL MONITOR HIS MEDICAL PRACTICE, RECORD KEEPING AND PATIENT CHARTS AND WILL REPORT TO BOARD QUARTERLY; SHALL MAKE PATIENT MEDICAL RECORDS AVAILABLE FOR EVALUATION BY BOARD; SHALL ABSTAIN FROM CONSUMPTION OF ALCOHOL AND CHEMICAL SUBSTANCES IN ANY FORM, AND SHALL IMMEDIATELY REPORT TO BOARD ANY LAPSE; SHALL SURRENDER ALL CONTROLLED SUBSTANCES PRESENTLY IN HIS OFFICE OR POSSESSION AND MAY NOT POSSESS ANY IN THE FUTURE; SHALL NOT ATTEMPT TO REREGISTER FOR DEA CONTROLLED SUBSTANCES REGISTRATION CERTIFICATE WITHOUT PRIOR APPROVAL; SHALL CONTINUE TO PARTICIPATE IN ALCOHOLICS ANONYMOUS OR SIMILAR PROGRAM, AND IN A COUNTY IMPAIRED PHYSICIANS GROUP WITH QUARTERLY REPORTS; SHALL SUBMIT HIMSELF FOR APPROPRIATE EXAMINATIONS, INCLUDING URINE OR BLOOD SCREENINGS FOR ALCOHOL OR DRUGS; SHALL APPEAR BEFORE THE BOARD TWICE A YEAR; SHALL GIVE A COPY OF THE ORDER TO HOSPITALS WHERE HE HAS PRIVILEGES; SHALL COOPERATE WITH THE BOARD IN VERIFYING COMPLIANCE; SHALL ADVISE THE BOARD OF ANY ADDRESS CHANGE; TIME SPENT OUT OF THE STATE DOES NOT COUNT TOWARDS PROBATION; AFTER ONE YEAR MAY SEEK TERMINATION OR MODIFICATION OF THIS ORDER. BOARD DENIED HIS REQUEST FOR MODIFICATION OF THIS ORDER ON 6/22/94.

STARLING, KENNETH A MD, LICENSE NUMBER 00D3093, OF CHARLESTON, WV, WAS DISCIPLINED BY TEXAS ON DECEMBER 1, 1988.
NOTES: SETTLEMENT AGREEMENT AND UNSPECIFIED DISCIPLINARY ACTION

STARLING, KENNETH ALLEN MD, LICENSE NUMBER 0014214, OF CHARLESTON, WV, WAS DISCIPLINED BY WEST VIRGINIA ON MAY 28, 1987.
DISCIPLINARY ACTION: 36-MONTH PROBATION; MONITORING OF PHYSICIAN
OFFENSE: DRUG OR ALCOHOL ABUSE
NOTES: IN 5/86 BOARD REMOVED PROBATIONARY STATUS AND CONDITIONS IMPOSED IN 5/86. IN 3/87 THE BOARD RECEIVED NOTICE HE HAD TAKEN A LEAVE OF ABSENCE FOR PARTICIPATION IN A 4 MONTH TREATMENT PROGRAM FOR ALCOHOLISM; UPON COMPLETION OF TREATMENT HE PRESENTED TO THE BOARD A COPY OF HIS AFTERCARE CONTRACT WITH THE IMPAIRED HEALTH PROFESSIONALS PROGRAM IN ORDER TO RETURN TO WORK. CONDITIONS OF PROBATION: MUST PRACTICE ONLY WITH BOARD-APPROVED SUPERVISOR WHO SHALL SUBMIT BIMONTHLY REPORTS TO THE BOARD; MUST SUBMIT TO RANDOM BODILY FLUID TESTING BIWEEKLY FOR THE FIRST YEAR, AND 4 TIMES ANNUALLY FOR THE NEXT TWO YEARS; MUST REFRAIN FROM THE USE OF CONTROLLED SUBSTANCES; MUST ATTEND AT LEAST 300 AA MEETINGS ANNUALLY, WITH A LOG REVIEWED BY SUPERVISING PHYSICIAN; MUST PROVIDE A COPY OF ORDER TO HIS SUPERVISING PHYSICIAN AND AA SPONSOR; MUST PROVIDE COPIES OF ANY AGREEMENT WITH CAMC WITH IMPAIRED HEALTH PROFESSIONALS PROGRAM IN GEORGIA TO THE BOARD.

STARR, THOMAS PIERCE SR MD, LICENSE NUMBER 00G6877, OF SAN ANTONIO, TX, WAS DISCIPLINED BY TEXAS ON AUGUST 25, 1989.
DISCIPLINARY ACTION: SURRENDER OF CONTROLLED SUBSTANCE LICENSE; MONITORING OF PHYSICIAN

OFFENSE: OVERPRESCRIBING OR MISPRESCRIBING DRUGS
NOTES: AIDING AND ABETTING PATIENTS IN THEIR CHRONIC ALCOHOLIC STATE BY PRESCRIBING CONTROLLED SUBSTANCES FOR THEM; PRESENTS AS A VICTIM OF HIS PATIENTS RATHER THAN A PERPETRATOR OF HIS PROBLEMS WITH THE BOARD. SUBMIT TO PSYCHIATRIC EVALUATION TO INCLUDE DRUG ANALYSIS OF URINE OR BLOOD; SHALL COOPERATE WITH THE BOARD; SHALL PROVIDE BOARD WITH ADDRESS CHANGE; ON 11/14/92, THIS ORDER MODIFIED SUCH THAT HE MAY APPLY FOR ISSUANCE OF DEA CERTIFICATE; SHALL KEEP SUCH PRESCRIPTIONS SEPARATE FROM OTHER PATIENT RECORDS.

STARR, THOMAS PIERCE SR MD OF 3203 NACOGDOCHES RD, SAN ANTONIO, TX, WAS DISCIPLINED BY DEA ON SEPTEMBER 19, 1989.
DISCIPLINARY ACTION: SURRENDER OF CONTROLLED SUBSTANCE LICENSE
OFFENSE: OVERPRESCRIBING OR MISPRESCRIBING DRUGS
NOTES: FOUND GUILTY OF NONTHERAPEUTIC PRESCRIBING; SURRENDERED REGISTRATION 07/27/89.

STARR, THOMAS PIERCE MD OF SAN ANTONIO, TX, WAS DISCIPLINED BY NORTH CAROLINA ON JULY 8, 1991.
DISCIPLINARY ACTION: LICENSE REVOCATION

STAYER, DAVID SHELLENBERGER MD, LICENSE NUMBER 00D4900, OF IRVING, TX, WAS DISCIPLINED BY TEXAS ON DECEMBER 4, 1991.
DISCIPLINARY ACTION: REPRIMAND
OFFENSE: OVERPRESCRIBING OR MISPRESCRIBING DRUGS
NOTES: REFILLED PRESCRIPTION FOR WEIGHT CONTROL WITHOUT GIVING PATIENT A PHYSICAL EXAMINATION.

STEELE, JOHN GILBERT MD, LICENSE NUMBER 00C9149, OF IRVING, TX, WAS DISCIPLINED BY TEXAS ON JUNE 22, 1994.
DISCIPLINARY ACTION: 60-MONTH PROBATION; MONITORING OF PHYSICIAN
OFFENSE: DRUG OR ALCOHOL ABUSE
NOTES: HE ADMITS HE IS AN ALCOHOLIC; LAST SOBRIETY DATE STATED TO BE 1/3/92; HAS HAD NO DRUG/ALCOHOL SCREENS PERFORMED SINCE THEN; IS UNDER PSYCHIATRIC CARE AND ACTIVE IN AA; MAINTAINS AN OFFICE PRACTICE IN ORTHOPEDICS AND HAS NOT PERFORMED SURGERY FOR TWO YEARS. FIVE YEAR SUSPENSION STAYED. CONDITIONS OF PROBATION: SHALL CONTINUE PSYCHIATRIC TREATMENT WITH QUARTERLY REPORTS; SHALL PARTICIPATE IN AA'S PROGRAM NOT LESS THAN THREE TIMES A WEEK WITH QUARTERLY REPORTS TO THE BOARD; SHALL PARTICIPATE IN THE ACTIVITIES OF A PHYSICIAN HEALTH AND REHABILITATION COMMITTEE AND ATTEND WEEKLY MEETINGS WITH QUARTERLY REPORTS; SHALL SUBMIT HIMSELF FOR APPROPRIATE EXAMS INCLUDING DRUG OR ALCOHOL SCREENS; SHALL ABSTAIN FROM THE CONSUMPTION OF ALCOHOL/CHEMICAL SUBSTANCES IN ANY FORM UNLESS PRESCRIBED BY ANOTHER PHYSICIAN FOR A LEGITIMATE AND THERAPEUTIC PURPOSE; SHALL REFRAIN FROM THE PERSONAL USE OF AND SHALL NOT POSSESS OR ADMINISTER TO HIMSELF ANY PRESCRIPTION DRUG UNLESS PRESCRIBED, ADMINISTERED OR DISPENSED BY ANOTHER PHYSICIAN FOR A LEGITIMATE MEDICAL NEED; SHALL NOT TREAT OR OTHERWISE SERVE AS PHYSICIAN, PRESCRIBE, DISPENSE, OR ADMINISTER DRUGS THAT MAY BE SUBJECT TO ABUSE TO HIMSELF OR ANY MEMBER OF HIS FAMILY; SHALL SUBMIT HIMSELF FOR EVALUATION TO A BOARD-APPROVED NEUROPSYCHIATRIST; PRIOR TO PERFORMING SURGERY SHALL RECEIVE APPROVAL FROM BOARD AFTER SUBMITTING A PROPOSAL FOR A PERIOD OF ONLY ASSISTING AT SURGERY WITH BOARD-APPROVED SURGEON; SHALL APPEAR BEFORE THE BOARD TWICE A YEAR; SHALL GIVE A COPY OF THIS ORDER TO ALL HEALTH CARE ENTITIES WHERE HE HAS PRIVILEGES; SHALL COOPERATE WITH BOARD IN VERIFYING COMPLIANCE; SHALL INFORM BOARD OF CHANGE OF ADDRESS WITHIN 10 DAYS OR IF HE LEAVES THE STATE; TIME SPENT OUT OF TEXAS DOES NOT COUNT TOWARD PROBATION. SHALL NOT SEEK MODIFICATION FOR SIX MONTHS.

STEGMAN, RONALD R DO, DATE OF BIRTH OCTOBER 13, 1937, OF 12222 C IT ROAD, DALLAS, TX, WAS DISCIPLINED BY MEDICARE ON FEBRUARY 28, 1994.
DISCIPLINARY ACTION: EXCLUSION FROM THE MEDICARE AND/OR MEDICAID PROGRAMS
OFFENSE: DISCIPLINARY ACTION BY ANOTHER STATE OR AGENCY
NOTES: LICENSE REVOKED FOR REASONS BEARING ON UNPROFESSIONAL AND DISHONORABLE CONDUCT AS A PHARMACIST PRACTICING WITHOUT A LICENSE.

STEGMAN, RONALD REGIS DO, DATE OF BIRTH OCTOBER 13, 1937, LICENSE NUMBER 00D2303, OF 12222 COIT ROAD, DALLAS, TX, WAS DISCIPLINED BY TEXAS ON JANUARY 29, 1993.
DISCIPLINARY ACTION: LICENSE REVOCATION
OFFENSE: OVERPRESCRIBING OR MISPRESCRIBING DRUGS
NOTES: ON OR ABOUT 11/14/90 A BOARD INVESTIGATOR CONDUCTED A COMPLIANCE INSPECTION WITH DRUG RECORD AND INVENTORY LAWS OF DR. STEGMAN'S OFFICE; LARGE QUANTITIES OF CONTROLLED SUBSTANCES PREPACKAGED FOR DISPENSING WERE FOUND; HE DISPENSED PRESCRIPTION DRUGS/CONTROLLED SUBSTANCES FOR A SEPARATE FEE WITHOUT HAVING A PHARMACIST'S LICENSE; FAILED TO KEEP COMPLETE AND ACCURATE RECORDS OF ALL PURCHASES AND DISPOSALS OF CONTROLLED SUBSTANCES AS REQUIRED BY DEPARTMENT OF PUBLIC SAFETY DRUG RULES; PRESCRIBED 110 SHOTS OF DEMEROL TO A PATIENT WHICH WAS NONTHERAPEUTIC IN NATURE OR THE MANNER IN WHICH IT WAS ADMINISTERED; FAILED TO SUBMIT REQUIRED TRIPLICATE PRESCRIPTION FORMS FOR DEMEROL. SHALL SURRENDER TO THE BOARD HIS DEA AND TEXAS CONTROLLED SUBSTANCES CERTIFICATES. SHALL NOT SEEK REINSTATEMENT FOR ONE YEAR. ORDER APPEALED TO THE COURTS; WILL BECOME FINAL WHEN ALL APPEALS HAVE BEEN EXHAUSTED.

STEGMAN, RONALD REGIS DO OF 12222 COIT ROAD, DALLAS, TX, WAS DISCIPLINED BY DEA ON AUGUST 27, 1993.
DISCIPLINARY ACTION: SURRENDER OF CONTROLLED SUBSTANCE LICENSE

STENGER, EARL M MD, LICENSE NUMBER 00D7315, OF SAN ANTONIO, TX, WAS DISCIPLINED BY TEXAS ON APRIL 14, 1989.
DISCIPLINARY ACTION: RESTRICTION PLACED ON LICENSE
NOTES: SHALL TREAT NON-EMERGENCY PATIENTS ONLY UPON ADEQUATE MEDICAL EVALUATION, SHALL MAINTAIN PRESCRIPTION AND MEDICAL RECORDS AS DIRECTED;SHALL MODIFY CRITERIA FOR PRESCRIBING AND ADMINISTERING CERTAIN MEDICATIONS; SHALL NOT TREAT OR SERVE AS PHYSICIAN FOR SELF OR FAMILY; SHALL REEVALUATE FEE STRUCTURE

STERN, STEVEN EMERY MD, LICENSE NUMBER 00E4701, OF HOUSTON, TX, WAS DISCIPLINED BY TEXAS ON NOVEMBER 19, 1993.
DISCIPLINARY ACTION: REPRIMAND
OFFENSE: OVERPRESCRIBING OR MISPRESCRIBING DRUGS
NOTES: FROM 1/1/90 THROUGH 12/29/92 EXCESSIVELY PRESCRIBED FIORINAL WITH CODEINE #3 TO A FAMILY MEMBER IN AN EFFORT TO TREAT CHRONIC TENSION HEADACHES; WHEN HE BECAME AWARE THAT THIS PERSON HAD DEVELOPED A DEPENDENCE ON THE MEDICATION HE TERMINATED THE MEDICATION AND MADE ARRANGEMENTS FOR CARE BY ANOTHER PHYSICIAN; HAS HAD NO OTHER COMPLAINTS AGAINST HIM FILED WITH BOARD.

STILL, ROBERT L JR MD, LICENSE NUMBER 00F7201, OF SAN ANTONIO, TX, WAS DISCIPLINED BY TEXAS ON JUNE 22, 1994.
DISCIPLINARY ACTION: 60-MONTH PROBATION; REPRIMAND
OFFENSE: DRUG OR ALCOHOL ABUSE
NOTES: ENTERED INPATIENT TREATMENT FOR ALCOHOLISM IN 9/90; CONTINUES TO ATTEND AA AND STATES A SOBRIETY DATE OF 9/27/90; VOLUNTARILY DISCLOSED THIS TO THE BOARD. SUSPENSION STAYED. CONDITIONS OF PROBATION: SHALL APPEAR BEFORE THE BOARD ONCE A YEAR; SHALL NOT TREAT OR OTHERWISE SERVE AS PHYSICIAN, PRESCRIBE, DISPENSE OR ADMINISTER DRUGS THAT MAY BE SUBJECT TO ABUSE TO HIMSELF OR ANY MEMBER OF HIS IMMEDIATE FAMILY; SHALL ABSTAIN FROM THE CONSUMPTION OF ALCOHOL/CHEMICAL SUBSTANCES IN ANY FORM UNLESS PRESCRIBED BY ANOTHER PHYSICIAN FOR A LEGITIMATE AND THERAPEUTIC PURPOSE; SHALL SUBMIT HIMSELF FOR APPROPRIATE EXAMS INCLUDING DRUG OR ALCOHOL SCREENS; SHALL CONTINUE TO PARTICIPATE IN AA'S PROGRAM NOT LESS THAN THREE TIMES A WEEK WITH QUARTERLY REPORTS TO THE BOARD; SHALL CONTINUE TO PARTICIPATE IN ACTIVITIES OF A PHYSICIAN HEALTH AND REHABILITATION COMMITTEE AND PARTICIPATE IN WEEKLY MEETINGS WITH QUARTERLY REPORTS; SHALL ATTEND AT LEAST 50 HOURS PER YEAR OF CONTINUING MEDICAL EDUCATION; SHALL MAINTAIN ADEQUATE MEDICAL RECORDS ON ALL PATIENT OFFICE VISITS WHICH SHALL BE AVAILABLE FOR INSPECTION; SHALL NOT SIGN ANY PATIENT RECORD UNLESS HE HAS PERSONALLY EXAMINED THE PATIENT OR CLEARLY NOTES IN THE RECORD THAT HE DID NOT; SHALL GIVE A COPY OF THIS ORDER TO ANY HEALTH CARE ENTITY WHERE HE HAS PRIVILEGES; SHALL COOPERATE WITH THE BOARD IN VERIFYING COMPLIANCE; SHALL INFORM BOARD OF CHANGE OF ADDRESS WITHIN 10 DAYS OR IF HE LEAVES THE STATE; TIME SPENT OUT OF TEXAS DOES NOT COUNT TOWARD PROBATION. SHALL NOT SEEK MODIFICATION FOR ONE YEAR.

STIVERS, ROBERT R MD, DATE OF BIRTH AUGUST 31, 1934, LICENSE NUMBER 0012202, OF 2182 SPRING CREEK RD, ATLANTA, GA, WAS DISCIPLINED BY GEORGIA ON APRIL 5, 1991.
DISCIPLINARY ACTION: EMERGENCY SUSPENSION
OFFENSE: DRUG OR ALCOHOL ABUSE
NOTES: CHEMICAL DEPENDENCY (ALCOHOLISM) RELAPSE.

STIVERS, ROBERT R MD, DATE OF BIRTH AUGUST 31, 1934, LICENSE NUMBER 0012202, OF 2182 SPRING CREEK RD, DECATUR, GA, WAS DISCIPLINED BY GEORGIA ON JUNE 1, 1992.
DISCIPLINARY ACTION: 60-MONTH LICENSE SUSPENSION
OFFENSE: DRUG OR ALCOHOL ABUSE
NOTES: PERSONAL USE OR ADDICTION (NARCOTIC VIOLATION), UNABLE TO PRACTICE MEDICINE WITH REASONABLE SKILL AND SAFETY TO THE PUBLIC BY REASON OF IMPAIRMENT. MAY PETITION FOR REINSTATEMENT AFTER TWO YEARS.

STIVERS, ROBERT RUTHERFORD MD, LICENSE NUMBER 00D4319, OF DECATUR, GA, WAS DISCIPLINED BY TEXAS ON APRIL 16, 1994.
DISCIPLINARY ACTION: LICENSE REVOCATION
OFFENSE: DISCIPLINARY ACTION BY ANOTHER STATE OR AGENCY
NOTES: ON 4/5/91 GEORGIA BOARD ENTERED AN ORDER OF EMERGENCY SUSPENSION BECAUSE OF HIS RELAPSE INTO ALCOHOL DEPENDENCY; ON 6/1/92 GEORGIA SUSPENDED HIS LICENSE DUE TO HIS INABILITY TO PRACTICE MEDICINE WITH REASONABLE SKILL AND SAFETY BY REASON OF USE OF ALCOHOL; HE HAS NOT COMMUNICATED WITH TEXAS BOARD ABOUT THIS ACTION AND DID NOT APPEAR AT DISCIPLINARY HEARING CONCERNING THIS MATTER.

STOCKTON, ROBERT LOUIS MD, LICENSE NUMBER 00C8855, OF WACO, TX, WAS DISCIPLINED BY TEXAS ON JANUARY 26, 1990.
DISCIPLINARY ACTION: 60-MONTH PROBATION; RESTRICTION PLACED ON LICENSE
NOTES: STIPULATED ORDER. MUST OBTAIN CONCURRING NEUROLOGICAL CONSULTAION PRIOR TO SURGERY ON ANY CASE WHICH HAS OR MAY HAVE NEUROSURGICAL IMPLICATIONS.

STOCKTON, ROBERT LOUIS MD, LICENSE NUMBER 0007457, WAS DISCIPLINED BY OKLAHOMA ON NOVEMBER 8, 1991.
DISCIPLINARY ACTION: 60-MONTH PROBATION; MONITORING OF PHYSICIAN
NOTES: PROBATION RETROACTIVE TO 1/26/90 WITH FOLLOWING TERMS AND CONDITIONS: PRIOR TO PERFORMING SURGERY ON ANY CASE WHICH HAS OR MAY HAVE NEUROSURGICAL IMPLICATIONS, SHALL FIRST OBTAIN A WRITTEN CONCURRING NEUROLOGICAL CONSULTATION FROM AN ABMS BOARD-CERTIFIED NEUROSURGEON OR NEUROLOGIST; SHALL NOTIFY ANY HOSPITAL WHERE HE HOLDS STAFF PRIVILEGES OR CLINIC OR GROUP WHERE HE PRACTICES OF TERMS AND CONDITIONS; SHALL FURNISH BOARD WITH ADDRESS AND/OR CHANGE OF ADDRESS; SHALL APPEAR BEFORE BOARD UPON REQUEST. THIS PROBATION SHALL RUN CONCURRENTLY WITH THE EXISTING PROBATION TO THE TEXAS STATE BOARD OF MEDICAL EXAMINERS WITH REPORTS TO OKLAHOMA BOARD; SHALL APPEAR BEFORE OKLAHOMA BOARD BEFORE RESUMING PRACTICE IN THE STATE.

STOCKTON, ROBERT LOUIS MD, LICENSE NUMBER 00C8855, OF WACO, TX, WAS DISCIPLINED BY TEXAS ON JANUARY 14, 1994.
DISCIPLINARY ACTION: SURRENDER OF LICENSE
NOTES: DOES NOT ADMIT ALLEGATIONS BUT SURRENDERS LICENSE IN LIEU OF FURTHER INVESTIGATION. SHALL NOT PETITION THE BOARD FOR REINSTATEMENT.

STOCKTON, ROBERT LOUIS MD OF 824 N 18TH STREET, WACO, TX, WAS DISCIPLINED BY DEA ON FEBRUARY 14, 1994.
DISCIPLINARY ACTION: SURRENDER OF CONTROLLED SUBSTANCE LICENSE
OFFENSE: DISCIPLINARY ACTION BY ANOTHER STATE OR AGENCY

STOERMER, DIETRICH A MD WAS DISCIPLINED BY NEVADA ON

MARCH 5, 1993.
DISCIPLINARY ACTION: RESTRICTION PLACED ON CONTROLLED SUBSTANCE LICENSE; REPRIMAND
OFFENSE: OVERPRESCRIBING OR MISPRESCRIBING DRUGS
NOTES: FAILED TO MAKE MEDICAL RECORDS AVAILABLE TO PATIENTS AND EXCESSIVE PRESCRIBING OF CONTROLLED SUBSTANCES. CONDITIONS: SUSPENDED FROM PRESCRIBING SCHEDULE II DRUGS UNTIL FURTHER ORDER OF THE BOARD; MUST COMPLETE CONTINUING MEDICAL EDUCATION ON CHRONIC PAIN MANAGEMENT INCLUDING INAPPROPRIATE WRITING OF PRESCRIPTIONS FOR CONTROLLED SUBSTANCES AND A COURSE ON APPROPRIATE MEDICAL RECORD KEEPING/DOCUMENTATION.

STOERMER, DIETRICH ALBERT MD, LICENSE NUMBER 00E5952, OF LAS VEGAS, NV, WAS DISCIPLINED BY TEXAS ON AUGUST 19, 1994.
DISCIPLINARY ACTION: RESTRICTION PLACED ON CONTROLLED SUBSTANCE LICENSE; REQUIRED TO TAKE ADDITIONAL MEDICAL EDUCATION
OFFENSE: DISCIPLINARY ACTION BY ANOTHER STATE OR AGENCY
NOTES: LICENSE WAS DISCIPLINED BY ARIZONA BOARD ON 3/18/93. PRIOR TO PRACTICING IN TEXAS SHALL APPEAR BEFORE THE BOARD AND BE SUBJECT TO THE FOLLOWING RESTRICTIONS; SHALL NOT PRESCRIBE OR ADMINISTER SCHEDULE II CONTROLLED SUBSTANCES; SHALL ATTEND AT LEAST 50 HOURS PER YEAR OF CONTINUING MEDICAL EDUCATION INCLUDING AT LEAST 15 HOURS IN PAIN MANAGEMENT AND 6 HOURS IN RISK MANAGEMENT PER YEAR; SHALL GIVE A COPY OF THIS ORDER TO ANY HEALTH CARE ENTITY WHERE HE HAS PRIVILEGES; SHALL COOPERATE WITH THE BOARD IN VERIFYING COMPLIANCE; SHALL INFORM BOARD OF CHANGE OF ADDRESS WITHIN 10 DAYS. SHALL NOT SEEK MODIFICATION FOR ONE YEAR.

STOWE, ROBERT HOMAN MD, LICENSE NUMBER 00H2814, OF EL PASO, TX, WAS DISCIPLINED BY TEXAS ON APRIL 15, 1994.
DISCIPLINARY ACTION: 120-MONTH PROBATION; RESTRICTION PLACED ON LICENSE
OFFENSE: LOSS OR RESTRICTION OF HOSPITAL PRIVILEGES
NOTES: HAD A HISTORY OF ALCOHOL USE STARTING BACK IN HIGH SCHOOL; PERIODICALLY ABUSED ALCOHOL SINCE RESIDENCY; ADMITS THAT ON OCCASIONS HE PRACTICED MEDICINE WHEN HE WAS USING DRUGS OR UNDER THE INFLUENCE OF DRUGS; HOSPITAL PRIVILEGES WERE SUMMARILY SUSPENDED ON 3/3/93 PENDING THE OUTCOME OF DRUG TREATMENT AND REHABILITATION BASED ON A POSITIVE DRUG SCREEN; DISCHARGED FROM INPATIENT TREATMENT ON 7/13/93; IS CURRENTLY UNDER TREATMENT ON AN OUTPATIENT BASIS; SOBRIETY DATE 4/22/93; SINCE COMPLETION OF TREATMENT PROGRAM HAS BEEN ATTENDING AA ON A DAILY BASIS. TEN YEAR SUSPENSION STAYED. CONDITIONS OF PROBATION: SHALL ABSTAIN FROM THE CONSUMPTION OF ALCOHOL/CHEMICAL SUBSTANCES IN ANY FORM UNLESS PRESCRIBED BY ANOTHER PHYSICIAN FOR A LEGITIMATE AND THERAPEUTIC PURPOSE; SHALL NOT TREAT OR OTHERWISE SERVE AS PHYSICIAN, PRESCRIBE, DISPENSE OR ADMINISTER DRUGS THAT MAY BE SUBJECT TO ABUSE TO HIMSELF OR ANY MEMBER OF HIS FAMILY; SHALL PARTICIPATE IN ACTIVITIES OF A PHYSICIAN HEALTH AND REHABILITATION COMMITTEE AND ATTEND MEETINGS WITH QUARTERLY REPORTS; SHALL LIMIT HIS MEDICAL PRACTICE SOLELY TO THE PRACTICE OF ANESTHESIOLOGY IN HOSPITAL AND LICENSED AMBULATORY SURGERY SETTINGS; SHALL NOT POSSESS, ADMINISTER, DISPENSE OR PRESCRIBE ANY CONTROLLED SUBSTANCES EXCEPT TO ORDER THEM FOR HOSPITAL AND SURGICAL CENTER PATIENTS AND WHILE UNDER THE OBSERVATION OF A LICENSED PHYSICIAN OR REGISTERED NURSE; SHALL MAINTAIN A NOTEBOOK CONTAINING COPIES OF ALL PATIENT ANESTHESIA RECORDS AVAILABLE FOR INSPECTION; SHALL CONTINUE TO PARTICIPATE IN AA'S PROGRAM NOT LESS THAN THREE TIMES A WEEK WITH QUARTERLY REPORTS TO THE BOARD; SHALL SUBMIT HIMSELF FOR APPROPRIATE EXAMS INCLUDING DRUG OR ALCOHOL SCREENS; SHALL CONTINUE TO RECEIVE TREATMENT FROM A SPECIFIED PHYSICIAN WITH QUARTERLY REPORTS; SHALL HAVE RANDOM DRUG SCREENS BY HAIR ANALYSIS AT LEAST FOUR TIMES PER YEAR; SHALL APPEAR BEFORE THE BOARD TWICE A YEAR.

STRICKLAND, ALAN D MD, LICENSE NUMBER 00E2885, OF RICHARDSON, TX, WAS DISCIPLINED BY TEXAS ON DECEMBER 1, 1990.
DISCIPLINARY ACTION: 24-MONTH PROBATION
OFFENSE: SUBSTANDARD CARE, INCOMPETENCE, OR NEGLIGENCE
NOTES: ADMINISTERED DRUG OR TREATMENT THAT WAS NONTHERAPEUTIC IN NATURE. FAILED PROFESSIONALLY TO PRACTICE MEDICINE IN ACCEPTABLE MANNER CONSISTENT WITH PUBLIC HEALTH AND WELFARE. RESTRICTIONS INCLUDE REFRAINING FROM RESEARCHING OR ADMINISTERING NONAPPROVED DRUGS WITHOUT INFORMED WRITTEN CONSENT AND REFRAINING FROM CONDUCTING EXPERIMENTS OR RESEARCH WITHOUT EXPRESS APPROVAL OF PROPER HOSPITAL AUTHORITY OR REVIEW COMMITTEE. MOTION FILED FOR REHEARING.

STRICKLAND, ANN ROBERTSHAW MD, DATE OF BIRTH JULY 29, 1951, LICENSE NUMBER 00F8330, OF 2476 BOLSOVER BOX 471, HOUSTON, TX, WAS DISCIPLINED BY TEXAS ON JUNE 15, 1993.
DISCIPLINARY ACTION: LICENSE SUSPENSION
OFFENSE: PHYSICAL OR MENTAL ILLNESS INHIBITING THE ABILITY TO PRACTICE WITH SKILL AND SAFETY
NOTES: SUFFERS FROM A COMPLEX PARTIAL SEIZURE DISORDER, FIBROMYALGIA, AND OSTEOPOROSIS WITH ASSOCIATED FATIGUE AND PHYSICAL DIFFICULTIES AS WELL AS DEPRESSION AND CHRONIC POST TRAUMATIC STRESS DISORDER; AILMENTS ARE SO SEVERE SHE IS PRESENTLY UNABLE TO PRACTICE. LICENSE SUSPENDED UNTIL SHE PERSONALLY APPEARS BEFORE THE BOARD AND PROVIDES SUFFICIENT EVIDENCE TO SHOW THAT SHE IS PHYSICALLY, MENTALLY AND OTHERWISE COMPETENT TO PRACTICE INCLUDING PSYCHIATRIC REPORTS AND CURRENT PHYSICAL EXAMS; SHALL GIVE A COPY OF THIS ORDER TO ANY HEALTH CARE ENTITY WHERE SHE HAS PRIVILEGES; SHALL COOPERATE WITH THE BOARD IN VERIFYING COMPLIANCE; SHALL INFORM BOARD OF CHANGE OF ADDRESS.

STRINGER, DRENNON DURWOOD MD, LICENSE NUMBER 00F2953, OF DALLAS, TX, WAS DISCIPLINED BY TEXAS ON MARCH 5, 1994.
DISCIPLINARY ACTION: REPRIMAND
OFFENSE: OVERPRESCRIBING OR MISPRESCRIBING DRUGS
NOTES: DISPENSED MEDICATIONS TO A PATIENT WHEN ACCESS TO A PHARMACY WAS POSSIBLE. SHALL GIVE A COPY

OF THIS ORDER TO ANY HEALTH CARE ENTITY WHERE HE HAS PRIVILEGES.

STUBBLEFIELD, WAYNE MD, LICENSE NUMBER 0005893, WAS DISCIPLINED BY TENNESSEE ON OCTOBER 17, 1988.
DISCIPLINARY ACTION: SURRENDER OF CONTROLLED SUBSTANCE LICENSE
OFFENSE: DRUG OR ALCOHOL ABUSE
NOTES: HEARING CONTINUED, STUBBLEFIELD IS IN TREATMENT

STUBBLEFIELD, WAYNE MD, LICENSE NUMBER 0005893, WAS DISCIPLINED BY TENNESSEE ON JANUARY 25, 1989.
DISCIPLINARY ACTION: 12-MONTH SUSPENSION OF CONTROLLED SUBSTANCE LICENSE; 60-MONTH PROBATION
OFFENSE: DISCIPLINARY ACTION BY ANOTHER STATE OR AGENCY
NOTES: MUST MAINTAIN CONTINUED CONTACT WITH IMPAIRED PHYSICIAN PROGRAM; SUBMIT TO MONTHLY RANDOM URINE SCREENS TO BE REPORTED TO IMPAIRED PHYSICIANS WITH ANNUAL REPORTS TO THE BOARD; MUST APPEAR BEFORE BOARD TO REQUEST LIFTING OF RESTRICTIONS; SUSPENDED IN ARKANSAS FOR FAILING TO APPEAR TO ANSWER CHARGES OF WRITING FICTITIOUS CONTROLLED SUBSTANCE PRESCRIPTIONS. HAS ENGAGED IN DRUG-SEEKING BEHAVIOR CHARACTERISTIC OF CHEMICAL DEPENDENCY, HAS ORDERED COCAINE WHEN HIS PRACTICE DID NOT JUSTIFY IT AND HAS PRESCRIBED CONTROLLED SUBSTANCES TO FAMILY MEMBERS FOR EXTENDED PERIODS

STUBBLEFIELD, WAYNE MD, LICENSE NUMBER 0016809, OF 1001 SW 44, OKLAHOMA CITY, OK, WAS DISCIPLINED BY OKLAHOMA ON FEBRUARY 23, 1989.
DISCIPLINARY ACTION: 60-MONTH PROBATION; RESTRICTION PLACED ON CONTROLLED SUBSTANCE LICENSE
OFFENSE: DRUG OR ALCOHOL ABUSE
NOTES: RECOVERING FROM SUBSTANCE ABUSE; HAS SUCCESSFULLY COMPLETED IN-PATIENT HOSPITALIZATION. PROBATION UNDER TERMS AND CONDITIONS: SHALL NOT PRESCRIBE, ADMINISTER OR DISPENSE ANY MEDICATIONS FOR HIS PERSONAL USE; SHALL TAKE NO MEDICATION UNLESS PRESCRIBED BY TREATING PHYSICIAN; SHALL ABSTAIN FROM ALCOHOL OR ANY SUBSTANCE WHICH WOULD ADVERSELY AFFECT HIS ABILITY TO PRACTICE; SHALL SUBMIT BIOLOGICAL FLUID SPECIMENS FOR ANALYSIS; MAY PRESCRIBE, ADMINISTER OR DISPENSE CONTROLLED DANGEROUS SUBSTANCES ONLY TO HOSPITAL ROOM INPATIENTS AND EMERGENCY ROOM OUTPATIENTS; SHALL CONTINUE ALL SUPPORTIVE PROGRAMS, INCLUDING PHYSICIAN RECOVERY COMMITTEE AND PSYCHIATRIC CARE IF SO DIRECTED; SHALL FURNISH BOARD WITH ADDRESS AND/OR CHANGE OF ADDRESS; SHALL APPEAR BEFORE BOARD UPON REQUEST. ON 11/8/91 SUPERVISION REDUCED FROM LEVEL I TO LEVEL II.

STUBBLEFIELD, WAYNE MD, LICENSE NUMBER 0005893, WAS DISCIPLINED BY TENNESSEE ON MARCH 3, 1989.
DISCIPLINARY ACTION: 24-MONTH SURRENDER OF CONTROLLED SUBSTANCE LICENSE; MONITORING OF PHYSICIAN
NOTES: SHALL PARTICIPATE WITH IMPAIRED PHYSICIAN PROGRAM; RANDOM DRUG SCREENS; MUST APPEAR BEFORE BOARD BEFORE RESTRICTIONS CAN BE LIFTED.

STUBBLEFIELD, WAYNE MD OF 11317 S. WESTERN, OKLAHOMA CITY, OK, WAS DISCIPLINED BY DEA ON SEPTEMBER 19, 1989.
DISCIPLINARY ACTION: SURRENDER OF CONTROLLED SUBSTANCE LICENSE
OFFENSE: OVERPRESCRIBING OR MISPRESCRIBING DRUGS
NOTES: MEDICAL LICENSE REVOKED FOR WRITING PRESCRIPTIONS FOR CONTROLLED SUBSTANCES TO FICTITIOUS PERSONS 07/13/89; INVOLVED IN COCAINE; TENNESSEE MEDICAL LICENSE ON 5 YEAR PROBATION FOR WRITING FICTITIOUS DRUG PRESCRIPTIONS; STATE REGISTRATION DENIED UNTIL 12/03/90; WITHDRAWAL OF APPLICATION 05/15/90.

STUBBLEFIELD, WAYNE MD, LICENSE NUMBER 00F2955, OF OKLAHOMA CITY, OK, WAS DISCIPLINED BY TEXAS ON AUGUST 18, 1990.
OFFENSE: DISCIPLINARY ACTION BY ANOTHER STATE OR AGENCY
NOTES: STIPULATED ORDER. MUST COMPLY WITH TENNESSEE BOARD AGREED ORDER AND OKLAHOMA BOARD FINAL ORDER. IF DESIRING TO PRACTICE MEDICINE IN TEXAS, MUST DEMONSTRATE TO BOARD CAPACITY TO PRACTICE MEDICINE WITH REASONABLE SKILL AND SAFETY. IF AUTHORIZED TO PRACTICE IN TEXAS, MUST FOLLOW ANY ADDITIONAL TERMS OF PROBATION AS MAY BE IMPOSED.

STUBBLEFIELD, WAYNE MD, LICENSE NUMBER 0005893, OF OKLAHOMA CITY, OK, WAS DISCIPLINED BY TENNESSEE ON FEBRUARY 8, 1994.
DISCIPLINARY ACTION: LICENSE REVOCATION; FINE
OFFENSE: FAILURE TO COMPLY WITH A PREVIOUS BOARD ORDER
NOTES: VIOLATION OF TERMS OF PROBATION; MAKING FALSE STATEMENTS IN OBTAINING ADMISSION TO PRACTICE IN ANOTHER STATE; FAILURE TO RENEW TENNESSEE LICENSE. ASSESSED $1400 IN CIVIL PENALTIES.

STUBBLEFIELD, WAYNE MD, LICENSE NUMBER 0016809, OF 1001 SW 44, OKLAHOMA CITY, OK, WAS DISCIPLINED BY OKLAHOMA ON FEBRUARY 17, 1994.
DISCIPLINARY ACTION: 24-MONTH PROBATION; MONITORING OF PHYSICIAN
OFFENSE: FAILURE TO COMPLY WITH A PREVIOUS BOARD ORDER
NOTES: IN VIOLATION OF 1/12/89 PROBATION ORDER HE FAILED TO PRODUCE DUPLICATE PRESCRIPTIONS TO THE BOARD AND ON ONE OCCASION RECEIVED NECESSARY SCHEDULED DRUGS FROM A DENTIST BUT DID NOT INFORM THE DENTIST OF HIS HISTORY OF ADDICTION. PROBATION EXTENDED FOR TWO YEARS. CONDITIONS OF EXTENDED PROBATION: SHALL NOT PRESCRIBE, ADMINISTER OR DISPENSE ANY MEDICATIONS FOR HIS PERSONAL USE; SHALL NOT TAKE ANY MEDICATION UNLESS AUTHORIZED BY ANOTHER PHYSICIAN FOR A LEGITIMATE MEDICAL NEED; SHALL ABSTAIN FROM THE CONSUMPTION OF ALCOHOL OR ANY SUBSTANCE WHICH WOULD ADVERSELY AFFECT HIS ABILITY TO PRACTICE; SHALL SUBMIT BIOLOGICAL FLUID SPECIMENS; SHALL ONLY PRESCRIBE, ADMINISTER OR DISPENSE CONTROLLED SUBSTANCES ON DUPLICATE, SERIALLY-NUMBERED PRESCRIPTION PADS WITH COPIES AVAILABLE FOR INSPECTION; SHALL CONTINUE SUPPORTIVE PROGRAMS INCLUDING PHYSICIANS RECOVERY COMMITTEE AND PSYCHIATRIC CARE IF ORDERED; SHALL FURNISH BOARD WITH ADDRESS AND/OR CHANGE OF ADDRESS; SHALL APPEAR BEFORE THE BOARD UPON REQUEST AND PROVIDE REQUIRED REPORTS; SHALL PAY COSTS. LEVEL OF SUPERVISION REDUCED FROM LEVEL I TO LEVEL II.

SULLIVAN, BRIAN LOREN MD, LICENSE NUMBER 00E1946, OF AUSTIN, TX, WAS DISCIPLINED BY TEXAS ON APRIL 20, 1991.
DISCIPLINARY ACTION: 24-MONTH PROBATION
NOTES: SHALL NOT TREAT OR OTHERWISE SERVE AS THE PHYSICIAN, PRESCRIBE, DISPENSE, OR ADMINISTER CONTROLLED SUBSTANCES OR ANY OTHER DRUGS THAT MAY BE SUBJECT TO ABUSE, OR WRITE PRESCRIPTIONS FOR CONTROLLED SUBSTANCES, FOR ANY MEMBER OF IMMEDIATE FAMILY; SHALL ADMINISTER TO IMMEDIATE FAMILY ONLY DRUGS THAT ARE PRESCRIBED BY OTHER PHYSICIANS; SHALL HAVE NO CONTROLLED SUBSTANCES, INCLUDING SAMPLES, IN HIS RESIDENCE UNLESS PRESCRIBED BY A PHYSICIAN OTHER THAN SELF AND ARE IN ORIGINAL CONTAINER AS DISPENSED; SHALL APPEAR BEFORE THE BOARD ANNUALLY.

SUMMERS, LARRY B MD, LICENSE NUMBER 00C7797, OF ABILENE, TX, WAS DISCIPLINED BY TEXAS ON DECEMBER 1, 1988.
NOTES: SETTLEMENT AGREEMENT AND UNSPECIFIED DISCIPLINARY ACTION

SWATE, TOMMY ERNEST MD, LICENSE NUMBER 00E3781, OF HOUSTON, TX, WAS DISCIPLINED BY TEXAS ON JANUARY 24, 1992.
DISCIPLINARY ACTION: 60-MONTH PROBATION
OFFENSE: SUBSTANDARD CARE, INCOMPETENCE, OR NEGLIGENCE
NOTES: PROFESSIONAL FAILURE TO PRACTICE MEDICINE IN AN ACCEPTABLE MANNER CONSISTENT WITH PUBLIC HEALTH AND WELFARE, AND REPEATED OR RECURRING MERITORIOUS HEALTH-CARE LIABILITY CLAIMS. LICENSE SUSPENDED, SUSPENSION STAYED; PROBATION UNDER TERMS AND CONDITIONS.

SWATE, TOMMY ERNEST MD OF HOUSTON, TX, WAS DISCIPLINED BY LOUISIANA ON JANUARY 28, 1993.
DISCIPLINARY ACTION: 48-MONTH PROBATION
OFFENSE: DISCIPLINARY ACTION BY ANOTHER STATE OR AGENCY
NOTES: ACTION TAKEN BY TEXAS. TERMS AND CONDITIONS OF PROBATION AS FOLLOWS: SUBJECT TO COMPLIANCE WITH TERMS AND CONDITIONS OF DISCIPLINARY ORDER OF TEXAS BOARD; PRIOR NOTIFICATION TO BOARD OF INTENT TO RELOCATE TO LOUISIANA.

SWERSKY, ERNEST DOUGLAS MD, LICENSE NUMBER 00F1263, OF DALLAS, TX, WAS DISCIPLINED BY TEXAS ON NOVEMBER 3, 1994.
DISCIPLINARY ACTION: 60-MONTH PROBATION; RESTRICTION PLACED ON LICENSE
OFFENSE: PROFESSIONAL MISCONDUCT
NOTES: IN THE CASE OF FOUR PATIENTS FAILED TO DOCUMENT CARE AND TREATMENT IN THAT HE PROVIDED PSYCHOTHERAPY SESSIONS IN THE EVENING AFTER REGULAR OFFICE HOURS; DID NOT DOCUMENT IN THEIR RECORDS ANY INDICATIONS OF EMOTIONAL OR PSYCHOLOGICAL DIFFICULTIES OR ANY COUNSELING SESSIONS; DID NOT CHARGE THEM FOR THESE SESSIONS; FAILED TO MAINTAIN APPROPRIATE BOUNDARIES WITH ONE PATIENT BY DEVELOPING A PERSONAL AND SOCIAL RELATIONSHIP; ENGAGED IN PSYCHIATRIC COUNSELING OF PATIENTS WITHOUT APPROPRIATE TESTING, EVALUATION AND REFERRAL. SUSPENSION STAYED. CONDITIONS OF PROBATION: SHALL SUBMIT HIMSELF FOR EVALUATION AND TREATMENT BY A BOARD-APPROVED PSYCHIATRIST WITHIN 30 DAYS; SHALL REFRAIN FROM PERFORMING ANY PSYCHIATRIC COUNSELING; SHALL BE MONITORED BY A PHYSICIAN ACCEPTABLE TO THE BOARD; SHALL NOT PRESCRIBE ANY PSYCHOTROPIC DRUGS WITHOUT CONSULTATION WITH A BOARD-APPROVED PHYSICIAN; MONITORING PHYSICIAN SHALL SUBMIT REPORTS EVERY FOUR MONTHS; SHALL MAINTAIN ADEQUATE MEDICAL RECORDS ON ALL PATIENT OFFICE VISITS WHICH SHALL BE AVAILABLE FOR INSPECTION; SHALL NOT SIGN ANY PATIENT RECORD UNLESS HE HAS PERSONALLY EXAMINED THE PATIENT OR CLEARLY NOTES IN THE RECORD THAT HE DID NOT; SHALL ATTEND AT LEAST 50 HOURS PER YEAR OF CONTINUING MEDICAL EDUCATION; SHALL HAVE A CHAPERONEE PRESENT ANY TIME HE PERFORMS A PHYSICAL EXAM ON A FEMALE PATIENT WITH THIS DOCUMENTED IN THE CHART; SHALL PERFORM 10 HOURS PER MONTH OF COMMUNITY SERVICE FOR A HOMELESS SHELTER OR OTHER SIMILAR PROGRAM; SHALL APPEAR BEFORE THE BOARD ONCE A YEAR; SHALL GIVE A COPY OF THIS ORDER TO ANY HEALTH CARE ENTITY WHERE HE HAS PRIVILEGES; SHALL COOPERATE WITH THE BOARD IN VERIFYING COMPLIANCE; SHALL INFORM BOARD OF CHANGE OF ADDRESS WITHIN 10 DAYS OR IF HE LEAVES THE STATE; TIME SPENT OUT OF TEXAS DOES NOT COUNT TOWARD PROBATION. SHALL NOT SEEK MODIFICATION FOR ONE YEAR.

SYRQUIN, ABRAHAM FINKELBERG MD, LICENSE NUMBER 00D4325, OF GRAND PRAIRIE, TX, WAS DISCIPLINED BY TEXAS ON JUNE 26, 1992.
DISCIPLINARY ACTION: REPRIMAND
OFFENSE: PROFESSIONAL MISCONDUCT
NOTES: UNPROFESSIONAL OR DISHONORABLE CONDUCT THAT IS LIKELY TO DECEIVE, DEFRAUD OR INJURE THE PUBLIC.

TABATABAI, JAFAR MD, DATE OF BIRTH DECEMBER 23, 1925, LICENSE NUMBER 0014868, OF 1039 3RD STREET, STONE MOUNTAIN, GA, WAS DISCIPLINED BY GEORGIA ON DECEMBER 6, 1990.
DISCIPLINARY ACTION: 6-MONTH LICENSE SUSPENSION; 60-MONTH PROBATION
OFFENSE: OVERPRESCRIBING OR MISPRESCRIBING DRUGS
NOTES: NARCOTIC VIOLATION. CANNOT PRESCRIBE SCHEDULE II, IIN, III, IIIN IN OFFICE PRACTICE. EFFECTIVE 10/7/93 HE IS ALLOWED TO USE DEA REGISTRATION FOR SCHEDULES II, IIN, III, AND IIIN IN HIS OFFICE PRACTICE. MUST MAINTAIN LOG OF THESE SCHEDULES.

TABATABAI, JAFAR MD, LICENSE NUMBER 00D3792, OF STONE MOUNTAIN, GA, WAS DISCIPLINED BY TEXAS ON AUGUST 24, 1991.
DISCIPLINARY ACTION: 60-MONTH PROBATION
OFFENSE: DISCIPLINARY ACTION BY ANOTHER STATE OR AGENCY
NOTES: SUSPENSION STAYED. SHALL COMPLY WITH TERMS OF GEORGIA BOARD ORDER; PRIOR TO PRACTICING IN TEXAS, SHALL APPEAR BEFORE AND RECEIVE APPROVAL OF TEXAS BOARD.

TABATABAI, JAFAR MD, LICENSE NUMBER 0104547, OF 1039 3 STREET, STONE MOUNTAIN, GA, WAS DISCIPLINED BY NEW YORK ON JULY 2, 1992.
DISCIPLINARY ACTION: SURRENDER OF LICENSE
OFFENSE: DISCIPLINARY ACTION BY ANOTHER STATE OR AGENCY
NOTES: DID NOT CONTEST THE CHARGE OF BEING FOUND GUILTY OF IMPROPER PROFESSIONAL PRACTICE BY THE GEORGIA BOARD.

TABOADA, LUIS ENRIQUE MD, LICENSE NUMBER 00F2961, OF SAN ANTONIO, TX, WAS DISCIPLINED BY TEXAS ON NOVEMBER 3, 1994.
DISCIPLINARY ACTION: FINE; REPRIMAND
OFFENSE: PROFESSIONAL MISCONDUCT
NOTES: FAILED TO MAINTAIN PROPER BOUNDARIES IN AN INTERPERSONAL RELATIONSHIP WITH AN ADULT FEMALE PATIENT WHOM HE INITIALLY MET IN A SOCIAL SETTING. $1,000 ADMINISTRATIVE PENALTY; SHALL WITHIN SIX MONTHS RESEARCH AND WRITE A PAPER ON APPROPRIATE AND INAPPROPRIATE INTERPERSONAL RELATIONSHIPS BETWEEN PHYSICIANS AND PATIENTS; SHALL GIVE A COPY OF THIS ORDER TO ANY HEALTH CARE ENTITY WERE HE HAS PRIVILEGES; SHALL COOPERATE WITH THE BOARD IN VERIFYING COMPLIANCE; SHALL INFORM BOARD OF CHANGE OF ADDRESS WITHIN 10 DAYS. SHALL NOT SEEK MODIFICATION FOR SIX MONTHS.

TALMAGE, EDWARD ARTHUR MD, LICENSE NUMBER 00D2722, OF HOUSTON, TX, WAS DISCIPLINED BY TEXAS ON NOVEMBER 12, 1990.
DISCIPLINARY ACTION: REPRIMAND
OFFENSE: LOSS OR RESTRICTION OF HOSPITAL PRIVILEGES
NOTES: DISCIPLINED BY HOSPITAL OR HOSPITAL MEDICAL STAFF INCLUDING REMOVAL, SUSPENSION, OR LIMITATION OF HOSPITAL PRIVILEGES OR OTHER DISCIPLINARY ACTIONS; PROFESSIONAL FAILURE TO PRACTICE MEDICINE IN ACCEPTABLE MANNER CONSISTENT WITH PUBLIC HEALTH AND WELFARE.

TAMEZ, RICHARD JOSEPH DO, DATE OF BIRTH DECEMBER 12, 1928, LICENSE NUMBER 00C4571, OF 323 NW 24TH STREET, SAN ANTONIO, TX, WAS DISCIPLINED BY TEXAS ON AUGUST 20, 1993.
DISCIPLINARY ACTION: 30-MONTH PROBATION; MONITORING OF PHYSICIAN
OFFENSE: DRUG OR ALCOHOL ABUSE
NOTES: HAS SUFFERED FROM THE DISEASE OF ALCOHOLISM FOR APPROXIMATELY 10 YEARS AND HAS HAD SEVERAL RELAPSES THE LAST ONE TERMINATING IN 2/92 WHEN HE ENTERED INTO A TWO YEAR CONTRACT WITH THE PHYSICIAN HEALTH AND REHABILITATION COMMITTEE; RECEIVED INPATIENT TREATMENT IN 1987; CURRENTLY RECEIVING PSYCHIATRIC COUNSELING. SUSPENSION STAYED. CONDITIONS OF PROBATION: SHALL ABSTAIN FROM THE CONSUMPTION OF ALCOHOL/DRUGS IN ANY FORM UNLESS PRESCRIBED BY ANOTHER PHYSICIAN FOR A LEGITIMATE MEDICAL PURPOSE; SHALL SUBMIT HIMSELF FOR APPROPRIATE EXAMS INCLUDING DRUG OR ALCOHOL SCREENS; SHALL PARTICIPATE IN ACTIVITIES OF A PHYSICIAN HEALTH AND REHABILITATION COMMITTEE AND ATTEND WEEKLY MEETINGS WITH QUARTERLY REPORTS; SHALL PARTICIPATE IN AA'S 12 STEP PROGRAM NOT LESS THAN TWICE A WEEK WITH QUARTERLY REPORTS TO THE BOARD; SHALL COMPLY WITH TERMS OF 2/92 CONTRACT; SHALL CONTINUE TO RECEIVE PSYCHIATRIC COUNSELING WITH QUARTERLY REPORTS TO THE BOARD; SHALL APPEAR BEFORE THE BOARD TWICE A YEAR; SHALL COOPERATE WITH THE BOARD IN VERIFYING COMPLIANCE; SHALL INFORM BOARD OF CHANGE OF ADDRESS WITHIN 10 DAYS OR IF HE LEAVES THE STATE; TIME SPENT OUT OF TEXAS DOES NOT COUNT TOWARD PROBATION. SHALL NOT SEEK MODIFICATION FOR ONE YEAR.

TAN, EARL ENG-CHOW MD, DATE OF BIRTH APRIL 1, 1932, OF 6909 LYONS AVENUE, HOUSTON, TX, WAS DISCIPLINED BY MEDICARE ON JANUARY 2, 1994.
DISCIPLINARY ACTION: 36-MONTH EXCLUSION FROM THE MEDICARE AND/OR MEDICAID PROGRAMS
OFFENSE: OVERPRESCRIBING OR MISPRESCRIBING DRUGS
NOTES: PLED GUILTY TO DELIVERY OF A PRESCRIPTION WITHOUT A VALID PURPOSE.

TAN, EARL ENG-CHOW MD, LICENSE NUMBER 00F6196, OF HOUSTON, TX, WAS DISCIPLINED BY TEXAS ON MARCH 5, 1994.
DISCIPLINARY ACTION: SURRENDER OF LICENSE
NOTES: HE ADMITS HE VIOLATED THE MEDICAL PRACTICE ACT. VOLUNTARY SURRENDERS HIS LICENSE IN LIEU OF FURTHER INVESTIGATION OR A HEARING ON THE ALLEGATIONS. SHALL NOT PETITION FOR REINSTATEMENT.

TANO, LEONEL MD, LICENSE NUMBER 00E7516, OF SAN ANTONIO, TX, WAS DISCIPLINED BY TEXAS ON AUGUST 18, 1990.
DISCIPLINARY ACTION: RESTRICTION PLACED ON CONTROLLED SUBSTANCE LICENSE; REQUIRED TO TAKE ADDITIONAL MEDICAL EDUCATION
NOTES: STIPULATED ORDER. MUST REFRAIN FROM PRESCRIBING OR DISPENSING CONTROLLED SUBSTANCES TO KNOWN DRUG ABUSERS, INCLUDING METHADONE PATIENTS, AND COMPLETE RISK MANAGEMENT COURSE.

TAYLOR, PAT GEORGE EDWARD MD, LICENSE NUMBER 00F7222, OF 1315 DOCTORS DRIVE, TYLER, TX, WAS DISCIPLINED BY DEA.
NOTES: SURRENDER OF REGISTRATION, APPROVAL OF APPLICATION, MODIFICATION OF REGISTRATION. ALIAS TAYLOR P.G. EDWARDS.

TAYLOR, ROOSEVELT JR MD, LICENSE NUMBER 00D9896, OF AUSTIN, TX, WAS DISCIPLINED BY TEXAS ON JUNE 10, 1991.
DISCIPLINARY ACTION: REPRIMAND; REQUIRED TO TAKE ADDITIONAL MEDICAL EDUCATION
OFFENSE: SUBSTANDARD CARE, INCOMPETENCE, OR NEGLIGENCE
NOTES: ACTS WHICH CONSTITUTED UNPROFESSIONAL AND/OR DISHONORABLE CONDUCT LIKELY TO DECEIVE OR DEFRAUD THE PUBLIC, AND PROFESSIONAL FAILURE TO PRACTICE MEDICINE IN AN ACCEPTABLE MANNER CONSISTENT WITH PUBLIC HEALTH AND WELFARE. SHALL ATTEND FIVE HOURS OF AN ETHICS COURSE PER YEAR FOR FIVE YEARS.

TAYLOR, ROOSEVELT JR MD, DATE OF BIRTH OCTOBER 11, 1938, LICENSE NUMBER 0D11816, WAS DISCIPLINED BY MARYLAND ON JULY 22, 1992.
DISCIPLINARY ACTION: REPRIMAND
OFFENSE: DISCIPLINARY ACTION BY ANOTHER STATE OR AGENCY
NOTES: ON JUNE 10, 1991, THE TEXAS STATE BOARD OF MEDICAL EXAMINERS REPRIMANDED HIM AND ORDERED HIM TO ATTEND 5 HOURS OF ETHICS COURSES EACH YEAR FOR FIVE YEARS AFTER FINDING HE HAD EXHIBITED "UNPROFESSIONAL OR DISHONORABLE CONDUCT." ON HIS MARYLAND RENEWAL APPLICATION IN 1991 HE STATED THAT HE HAD NOT BEEN DISCIPLINED BY ANY OTHER BODY.

TAYLOR, ROOSEVELT JR MD, DATE OF BIRTH OCTOBER 11, 1938, LICENSE NUMBER 0023506, OF 1910 E MARTIN LUTHER KING JR BLV, AUSTIN, TX, WAS DISCIPLINED BY NEW JERSEY ON NOVEMBER 23, 1992.
DISCIPLINARY ACTION: REPRIMAND

OFFENSE: PROFESSIONAL MISCONDUCT
NOTES: ENGAGED IN CONDUCT CONSTITUTING UNPROFESSIONAL OR DISHONORABLE CONDUCT IN TEXAS. PRIOR TO RESUMING PRACTICE IN NEW JERSEY, SHALL APPEAR BEFORE A COMMITTEE OF THE BOARD FOR A STATUS CONFERENCE.

TAYLOR, STANLEY KAY MD, LICENSE NUMBER 00D1079, OF ASPERMONT, TX, WAS DISCIPLINED BY TEXAS ON AUGUST 19, 1994.
DISCIPLINARY ACTION: REPRIMAND; REQUIRED TO TAKE ADDITIONAL MEDICAL EDUCATION
OFFENSE: FAILURE TO COMPLY WITH A PROFESSIONAL RULE
NOTES: FAILED TO ADEQUATELY DOCUMENT HIS CARE AND TREATMENT OF ONE PATIENT INCLUDING ADEQUATE DOCUMENTATION THAT THIS INITIAL DIAGNOSIS OF HEPATITIS A WAS A TENTATIVE WORKING DIAGNOSIS, THAT THE PATIENT PRESENTED MANAGEMENT DIFFICULTIES, THAT THE PATIENT WAS THOROUGHLY ADVISED OF HER CONDITION AND POSSIBLE COURSES OF ACTION AND THAT APPROPRIATE REFERRALS HAD BEEN MADE. SHALL MAINTAIN ADEQUATE MEDICAL RECORDS ON ALL PATIENT OFFICE VISITS WHICH SHALL BE AVAILABLE FOR INSPECTION; SHALL NOT "BACK DATE" ANY ENTRY OR RECORD OF PATIENT CARE; FOR FIVE YEARS SHALL ATTEND AT LEAST 50 HOURS PER YEAR OF CONTINUING MEDICAL EDUCATION; DURING THE FIRST YEAR 25 HOURS SHALL BE IN INTERNAL MEDICINE OR GASTROENTEROLOGY; SHALL GIVE A COPY OF THIS ORDER TO ANY HEALTH CARE ENTITY WHERE HE HAS PRIVILEGES; SHALL COOPERATE WITH THE BOARD IN VERIFYING COMPLIANCE; SHALL INFORM BOARD OF CHANGE OF ADDRESS WITHIN 10 DAYS OR IF HE LEAVES THE STATE; TIME SPENT OUT OF TEXAS DOES NOT COUNT TOWARDS RESTRICTION. SHALL NOT SEEK MODIFICATION FOR ONE YEAR. ON 10/13/95 ORDER TERMINATED BASED ON COMPLIANCE WITH CONDITIONS.

TAYLOR, TIM C MD, LICENSE NUMBER 00F4590, OF HOUSTON, TX, WAS DISCIPLINED BY TEXAS ON AUGUST 26, 1988.
DISCIPLINARY ACTION: REQUIRED TO TAKE ADDITIONAL MEDICAL EDUCATION; MONITORING OF PHYSICIAN
OFFENSE: PROFESSIONAL MISCONDUCT
NOTES: ALLEGED THAT HE DISPENSED TO WEIGHT CONTROL PATIENTS CONTROLLED SUBSTANCES IN EXCESS OF THEIR IMMEDIATE NEEDS; FAILED TO KEEP COMPLETE AND ACCURATE RECORDS OF PURCHASES AND DISPOSALS OF PHENTERMINE AND PHENDIMETRAZINE. CONDITIONS OF ORDER: SHALL ATTEND AT LEAST 50 HOURS PER YEAR OF CONTINUING MEDICAL EDUCATION IN GENERAL MEDICAL COURSES; SHALL HAVE A BOARD-APPROVED PRACTICE MONITOR WITH QUARTERLY REPORTS; ADVISE THE BOARD OF ADDRESS CHANGE. ON 4/22/91, REQUEST TO TERMINATE PROBATION WAS DENIED. PROBATION TERMINATED EFFECTIVE 6/17/92; LICENSE FREE OF ANY RESTRICTION OR LIMITATION.

TEKELL, GORDON S MD, LICENSE NUMBER 0007235, OF YUMA, AZ, WAS DISCIPLINED BY ARIZONA ON JANUARY 21, 1993.
DISCIPLINARY ACTION: RESTRICTION PLACED ON CONTROLLED SUBSTANCE LICENSE; REQUIRED TO TAKE ADDITIONAL MEDICAL EDUCATION
OFFENSE: OVERPRESCRIBING OR MISPRESCRIBING DRUGS
NOTES: ALLEGATIONS THAT HE HAD BEEN PRESCRIBING LARGE AMOUNTS OF SCHEDULED DRUGS. SHALL SUCCESSFULLY COMPLETE 40 HOURS OF CONTINUING MEDICAL EDUCATION ACCEPTABLE TO THE BOARD WITHIN SIX MONTHS OF THE EFFECTIVE DATE OF THIS ORDER IN THE SUBJECT OF THE USE OF NARCOTICS FOR PAIN CONTROL AND CHRONIC PAIN MANAGEMENT; CONSULT WITH AN INDEPENDENT ORGANIZATION ACCEPTABLE TO THE BOARD REGARDING THE PROPER CREATION, MANAGEMENT AND MAINTENANCE OF MEDICAL RECORDS; EFFECTIVE TWO WEEKS FROM 01/21/93, CEASE ANY AND ALL PRESCRIBING, DISPENSING, OR ADMINISTRATION OF ALL SCHEDULE II AND III CONTROLLED SUBSTANCES, EXCEPT FOR THOSE PATIENTS IN A RECOGNIZED HOSPICE PROGRAM. SUCCESSFULLY FULFILLED THE TERMS OF THIS STIPULATION AND ORDER, SO AS OF 07/15/93 THIS STIPULATION AND ORDER IS TERMINATED.

TEKELL, GORDON SILAS MD, LICENSE NUMBER 00C9159, OF YUMA, AZ, WAS DISCIPLINED BY TEXAS ON NOVEMBER 3, 1994.
DISCIPLINARY ACTION: SURRENDER OF CONTROLLED SUBSTANCE LICENSE; LICENSE SUSPENSION
OFFENSE: DISCIPLINARY ACTION BY ANOTHER STATE OR AGENCY
NOTES: ARIZONA BOARD INITIATED DISCIPLINARY ACTION BASED ON ALLEGATIONS THAT HE HAD OVERPRESCRIBED VARIOUS PRESCRIPTION MEDICATIONS INCLUDING CONTROLLED SUBSTANCES; ENTERED INTO A WRITTEN STIPULATION WITH ARIZONA ON 3/18/93 WHICH REQUIRED HIM TO CEASE ANY PRESCRIBING OF SCHEDULE II AND III CONTROLLED SUBSTANCES EXCEPT IN A RECOGNIZED HOSPICE PROGRAM; THIS ORDER WAS TERMINATED ON 7/15/93. SUSPENSION UNTIL HE APPEARS BEFORE THE BOARD AND PROVIDES SUFFICIENT EVIDENCE THAT HE IS PHYSICALLY, MENTALLY AND OTHERWISE COMPETENT TO SAFELY PRACTICE; SHALL GIVE A COPY OF THIS ORDER TO ANY HEALTH CARE ENTITY WHERE HE HAS PRIVILEGES; SHALL COOPERATE WITH THE BOARD IN VERIFYING COMPLIANCE; SHALL INFORM BOARD OF CHANGE OF ADDRESS WITHIN 10 DAYS; SHALL SURRENDER TEXAS CONTROLLED SUBSTANCES CERTIFICATE AND ALL UNUSED TRIPLICATE PRESCRIPTION FORMS; SHALL NOT ATTEMPT TO REREGISTER WITHOUT PERMISSION.

TESTER, LEWIS KLEIN MD, LICENSE NUMBER 00B4470, OF SAN ANTONIO, TX, WAS DISCIPLINED BY TEXAS ON OCTOBER 1, 1987.
DISCIPLINARY ACTION: SURRENDER OF LICENSE

THOMAS, CLYDE E JR MD OF 411 E. 9TH STREET, BIG SPRING, TX, WAS DISCIPLINED BY MEDICARE ON MARCH 16, 1989.
DISCIPLINARY ACTION: EXCLUSION FROM THE MEDICARE AND/OR MEDICAID PROGRAMS
OFFENSE: SUBSTANDARD CARE, INCOMPETENCE, OR NEGLIGENCE
NOTES: PERMANENT EXCLUSION; GROSSLY SUBSTANDARD CARE OF 9 PATIENTS. SUBSTANDARD CARE OF 8 OTHERS. LACK OF BASIC MEDICAL KNOWLEDGE; POOR UNDERSTANDING OF PHARMACOLOGY. NO LONGER LISTED AS EXCLUDED AS OF 9/30/92.

THOMAS, CLYDE E MD, DATE OF BIRTH NOVEMBER 1, 1913, OF 411 E 9TH ST PO BOX 2071, BIG SPRING, TX, WAS DISCIPLINED BY MEDICARE ON NOVEMBER 13, 1991.
DISCIPLINARY ACTION: 120-MONTH EXCLUSION FROM THE MEDICARE AND/OR MEDICAID PROGRAMS
OFFENSE: DISCIPLINARY ACTION BY ANOTHER STATE OR AGENCY

NOTES: PEER REVIEW ORGANIZATION RECOMMENDATION.

THOMAS, FRED BEHMAN DO, LICENSE NUMBER 00C7319, OF DALLAS, TX, WAS DISCIPLINED BY TEXAS ON JUNE 12, 1990.
DISCIPLINARY ACTION: 36-MONTH RESTRICTION PLACED ON CONTROLLED SUBSTANCE LICENSE; REQUIRED TO TAKE ADDITIONAL MEDICAL EDUCATION
OFFENSE: PROFESSIONAL MISCONDUCT
NOTES: HAD FAILED TO KEEP RECORDS AND MAINTAIN INVENTORIES OF CONTROLLED SUBSTANCES DISPENSED AND DISPENSED AN ANORECTIC DRUG TO PATIENTS SEEKING TREATMENT FOR OBESITY IN QUANTITIES THAT EXCEEDED THOSE NECESSARY. HE HAS NEITHER DENIED OR ADMITTED THE CHARGES. STIPULATED ORDER. MUST COMPLETE PRECEPTORSHIP ON PREVENTION AND TREATMENT OF DRUG ABUSE, MAINTAIN ADEQUATE MEDICAL RECORDS ON PATIENT OFFICE VISITS. OTHER THAN SAMPLES, NOT DISPENSE MEDICATIONS TO PATIENTS IN QUANTITIES GREATER THAN NECESSARY FOR TREATMENT UNTIL ACCESS TO PHARMACY POSSIBLE. EXCEPT IN EMERGENCIES, MAY NOT ADMINISTER, PRESCRIBE, OR DISPENSE CONTROLLED SUBSTANCES TO SELF, MAINTAIN IN SEPARATE FILE COPY OF PRESCRIPTIONS WRITTEN FOR CONTROLLED SUBSTANCES, SUBMIT FOR PSYCHIATRIC EVALUATION AND FOLLOW RECOMMENDATIONS, IF ANY, REGARDING CONTINUING CARE AND TREATMENT AND APPEAR BEFORE BOARD SEMI-ANNUALLY. SHALL INFORM THE BOARD OF ADDRESS CHANGE. PROBATION MODIFIED, EFFECTIVE 3/6/92 REDUCING APPEARANCES BEFORE BOARD TO ANNUALLY.

THOMAS, JACK M MD, LICENSE NUMBER 00E4718, OF DENISON, TX, WAS DISCIPLINED BY TEXAS ON DECEMBER 4, 1991.
DISCIPLINARY ACTION: LICENSE REVOCATION
OFFENSE: FAILURE TO COMPLY WITH A PROFESSIONAL RULE
NOTES: ALLEGATIONS OF ILLEGAL DIVERSION TO UNKNOWN SOURCES OF QUANTITIES OF DILAUDID PRESCRIBED FOR PATIENTS; FAILURE TO KEEP COMPLETE AND ACCURATE RECORDS OF PURCHASES AND DISPOSALS OF CONTROLLED SUBSTANCES INCLUDING, BUT NOT LIMITED TO, DILAUDID; FAILURE TO COMPLY WITH A SUBPOENA RECEIVED IN HIS OFFICE ON 3/19/91; WRITING OF PRESCRIPTIONS DURING THE PERIOD OF 6/11/90 FOR PERCOCET, DEMEROL, AND DILAUDID TO A PERSON WHEN IN FACT SUCH PERSON WAS NOT A PATIENT DURING THE ABOVE PERIOD; CONTINUING MEDICAL DISABILITY AS REFLECTED BY HIS LAWYER'S ADMISSION DATED 9/12/91 COUPLED WITH HIS HOSPITALIZATION IN 3/91 FOR SEVERE DEPRESSION AND EPISODES REGARDING SUICIDAL THOUGHTS. HE WAS UNWILLING TO RESPOND TO ALLEGATIONS DUE TO HIS MENTAL IMPAIRMENT AND PENDING THE OUTCOME OF CRIMINAL CHARGES.

THOMAS, JAMES H JR MD, LICENSE NUMBER 00G0199, OF HOUSTON, TX, WAS DISCIPLINED BY TEXAS ON MARCH 31, 1990.
DISCIPLINARY ACTION: REPRIMAND
NOTES: STIPULATED ORDER.

THOMAS, STEPHEN C MD, LICENSE NUMBER 0176191, OF 22 WILLOWBREEZE, BUFFALO, NY, WAS DISCIPLINED BY DEA ON JANUARY 5, 1990.
DISCIPLINARY ACTION: SURRENDER OF CONTROLLED SUBSTANCE LICENSE
NOTES: SURRENDERED STATE MEDICAL LICENSE.

THOMAS, STEPHEN CROCKETT MD, LICENSE NUMBER 00J5036, OF LUBBOCK, TX, WAS DISCIPLINED BY TEXAS ON JUNE 22, 1994.
DISCIPLINARY ACTION: 120-MONTH PROBATION; RESTRICTION PLACED ON CONTROLLED SUBSTANCE LICENSE
OFFENSE: DISCIPLINARY ACTION BY ANOTHER STATE OR AGENCY
NOTES: DURING HIS RESIDENCY IN NEW YORK STARTING IN 1987 HE ABUSED PRESCRIPTION MEDICATION WITH CODEINE, PERCOCET, PERCODAN AS WELL AS BENZODIAZEPINES; ON 12/19/89 AFTER BEING APPROACHED ABOUT THIS HE SURRENDERED HIS NEW YORK LICENSE; ENTERED INPATIENT AND OUTPATIENT TREATMENT PROGRAMS AT THIS TIME; WAS SUSPENDED FROM HIS RESIDENCY PROGRAM DURING TREATMENT AND IN 5/90 WAS REINSTATED ON PROBATION; NEW YORK LICENSE RESTORED ON 11/19/90 SUBJECT TO CONDITIONS; ON 6/2/92 DEA ISSUED HIM A CERTIFICATE WITH RESTRICTIONS; REMAINS IN PHYSICIANS HEALTH PROGRAM; GAVE INACCURATE ANSWERS ON APPLICATION FORMS REGARDING THESE ACTIONS BUT APPEARS TO HAVE CORRECTED THESE. CONDITIONS OF PROBATION: SHALL APPEAR BEFORE THE BOARD TWICE A YEAR; SHALL BE SUPERVISED BY A BOARD-APPROVED PHYSICIAN WITH REPORTS THREE TIMES A YEAR; SHALL COMPLETE A TWO WEEK PRECEPTORSHIP ON PREVENTION AND TREATMENT OF DRUG ABUSE; SHALL NOT APPLY FOR OR MAINTAIN DEA OR TEXAS CONTROLLED SUBSTANCES CERTIFICATES; SHALL NOT TREAT OR OTHERWISE SERVE AS PHYSICIAN, PRESCRIBE, DISPENSE OR ADMINISTER DRUGS THAT MAY BE SUBJECT TO ABUSE FOR HIMSELF OR ANY MEMBER OF HIS FAMILY; SHALL ABSTAIN FROM THE CONSUMPTION OF ALCOHOL/CHEMICAL SUBSTANCES IN ANY FORM UNLESS PRESCRIBED BY ANOTHER PHYSICIAN FOR A LEGITIMATE AND THERAPEUTIC PURPOSE; SHALL CONTINUE TO PARTICIPATE IN A PHYSICIAN HEALTH AND REHABILITATION GROUP AND ATTEND WEEKLY MEETING WITH QUARTERLY REPORTS; SHALL CONTINUE TO PARTICIPATE IN AA'S PROGRAM NOT LESS THAN THREE TIMES A WEEK WITH QUARTERLY REPORTS TO THE BOARD; SHALL SUBMIT HIMSELF FOR APPROPRIATE EXAMS INCLUDING DRUG OR ALCOHOL SCREENS; SHALL FURNISH WRITTEN REPORTS TO THE BOARD UPON REQUEST VERIFYING COMPLIANCE; SHALL INFORM BOARD OF CHANGE OF ADDRESS WITHIN 10 DAYS OR IF HE LEAVES THE STATE; TIME SPENT OUT OF TEXAS DOES NOT COUNT TOWARD PROBATION. SHALL NOT SEEK MODIFICATION FOR ONE YEAR. THIS ORDER TAKES THE PLACE OF 8/28/93 ORDER.

THOMPSON, FRANK WILLIAM DO, LICENSE NUMBER 00D3694, OF DALLAS, TX, WAS DISCIPLINED BY TEXAS ON APRIL 15, 1994.
DISCIPLINARY ACTION: REPRIMAND
OFFENSE: OVERPRESCRIBING OR MISPRESCRIBING DRUGS
NOTES: NONTHERAPEUTIC PRESCRIBING IN THE MANNER IN WHICH A DRUG WAS USED IN THAT ON 2/14/89 HE FAILED TO OBTAIN RECORDS OF BASELINE STUDIES FOR ONE PATIENT PRIOR TO INITIATING TREATMENT OF HER PSORIASIS WITH METHOTREXATE, WHICH IS KNOWN TO HAVE SIDE EFFECTS AND COMPLICATIONS.

THOMPSON, LLOYD G MD, LICENSE NUMBER 00C9161, OF DALLAS, TX, WAS DISCIPLINED BY TEXAS ON JUNE 17, 1992.
DISCIPLINARY ACTION: REPRIMAND
OFFENSE: FAILURE TO COMPLY WITH A PROFESSIONAL RULE
NOTES: SEVERAL VIOLATIONS OF THE MEDICAL PRACTICE ACT,

INCLUDING MISLEADING ADVERTISEMENT.

THOMPSON, PEYTON L MD, LICENSE NUMBER 00D9687, OF HOUSTON, TX, WAS DISCIPLINED BY TEXAS ON JUNE 10, 1991.
DISCIPLINARY ACTION: REPRIMAND
OFFENSE: PROFESSIONAL MISCONDUCT
NOTES: UNPROFESSIONAL OR DISHONORABLE CONDUCT LIKELY TO DECEIVE, DEFRAUD, OR INJURE THE PUBLIC.

THOMPSON, STEPHEN KELLY MD, DATE OF BIRTH JUNE 6, 1953, LICENSE NUMBER 00G2582, OF 1714 N HENDERSON, DALLAS, TX, WAS DISCIPLINED BY TEXAS ON MARCH 31, 1990.
OFFENSE: DISCIPLINARY ACTION BY ANOTHER STATE OR AGENCY
NOTES: STIPULATED ORDER. MUST COMPLY WITH GEORGIA ORDER AND MUST DEMONSTRATE CAPACITY TO PRACTICE MEDICINE WITH REASONABLE SKILL AND SAFETY IF HE DESIRES TO PRACTICE IN TEXAS. IF GRANTED PERMISSION TO PRACTICE IN TEXAS WHILE GEORGIA ORDER EFFECTIVE, TEXAS BOARD MAY IMPOSE PROBATIONARY TERMS AS IT DEEMS APPROPRIATE. ON 8/20/93 ORDER TERMINATED AND LICENSE FREE AND CLEAR OF ANY RESTRICTIONS.

THOMPSON, WALTER F DO OF 712 S. FIFTH STREET, KNOX CITY, TX, WAS DISCIPLINED BY MEDICARE ON MAY 1, 1986.
DISCIPLINARY ACTION: 12-MONTH EXCLUSION FROM THE MEDICARE AND/OR MEDICAID PROGRAMS
OFFENSE: SUBSTANDARD CARE, INCOMPETENCE, OR NEGLIGENCE
NOTES: SUBSTANDARD TREATMENT OF ONE PATIENT, RESULTING IN THE PATIENT'S DEATH; FAILED TO PROVIDE CARDIAC MONITORING, OBTAIN SERIAL EKG'S OBTAIN SERUM ELECTROLYTES, OR OBTAIN SERIAL MONITORING OF BLOOD GLUCOSE

THOMPSON, WALTER FRED DO, LICENSE NUMBER 00E7301, OF KNOX CITY, TX, WAS DISCIPLINED BY TEXAS ON NOVEMBER 19, 1993.
DISCIPLINARY ACTION: REPRIMAND
OFFENSE: SUBSTANDARD CARE, INCOMPETENCE, OR NEGLIGENCE
NOTES: ON 9/24/91 HIS SON WAS INVOLVED IN AN AUTO ACCIDENT AT WHICH TIME DR. THOMPSON TRANSPORTED HIM TO THE FAMILY PHYSICIAN RATHER THAN TO A CLOSER HOSPITAL; DEMONSTRATES AN ERROR IN JUDGEMENT; HE CONTENDS HE WAS EMOTIONALLY AFFECTED AT THE TIME. SHALL GIVE A COPY OF THIS ORDER TO ANY HEALTH CARE ENTITY WHERE HE HAS PRIVILEGES; SHALL COOPERATE WITH THE BOARD IN VERIFYING COMPLIANCE; SHALL INFORM BOARD OF CHANGE OF ADDRESS WITHIN 10 DAYS.

THOMSON, ALTON L JR MD, LICENSE NUMBER 00D8461, OF STUART, FL, WAS DISCIPLINED BY TEXAS ON SEPTEMBER 30, 1994.
DISCIPLINARY ACTION: SURRENDER OF LICENSE
NOTES: ALLEGATIONS THAT HE VIOLATED THE MEDICAL PRACTICE ACT; HE DID NOT ADMIT ALLEGATIONS. SURRENDER IN LIEU OF FURTHER INVESTIGATION. PERMANENT CANCELLATION.

THORNTON, THOMAS L MD, LICENSE NUMBER 00D4335, OF ALLEN, TX, WAS DISCIPLINED BY TEXAS ON APRIL 20, 1991.
NOTES: LICENSE PLACED ON RETIRED STATUS IN LIEU OF DISCIPLINARY ACTION; IF DESIRES TO PRACTICE IN TEXAS, SHALL OBTAIN PRIOR APPRVAL FROM THE BOARD.

TICAS, ROBERTO MD, LICENSE NUMBER 00H8865, OF LAKE JACKSON, TX, WAS DISCIPLINED BY TEXAS ON JANUARY 6, 1995.
DISCIPLINARY ACTION: 60-MONTH PROBATION; RESTRICTION PLACED ON CONTROLLED SUBSTANCE LICENSE
OFFENSE: DRUG OR ALCOHOL ABUSE
NOTES: ON JULY 30 AND AUGUST 6 1994 EXHIBITED BEHAVIORAL CHANGES AND CONCERNS WERE RAISED THAT HIS CAPACITY TO FUNCTION AS A PHYSICIAN HAD BEEN REDUCED; REPORTED THAT HE SELF-MEDICATED FOR DEPRESSION AND ASTHMA AND CONSUMED BEER WHILE ON MEDICATIONS HE SELF-PRESCRIBED; AGREED TO A PHYSICAL AND MENTAL EXAM WHICH INDICATED HIS ABILITY WAS IMPAIRED BY ALCOHOL USE. SUSPENSION STAYED. CONDITIONS OF PROBATION: SHALL ABSTAIN FROM THE CONSUMPTION OF ALCOHOL/CHEMICAL SUBSTANCES IN ANY FORM UNLESS PRESCRIBED BY ANOTHER PHYSICIAN FOR A LEGITIMATE AND THERAPEUTIC PURPOSE; SHALL SUBMIT HIMSELF FOR APPROPRIATE EXAMS INCLUDING DRUG OR ALCOHOL SCREENS; SHALL SUBMIT HIMSELF TO A BOARD-APPROVED PSYCHIATRIST FOR EVALUATION AND TREATMENT WITH REPORTS TO THE BOARD; SHALL PARTICIPATE IN AA'S PROGRAM NOT LESS THAN THREE TIMES A WEEK WITH QUARTERLY REPORTS TO THE BOARD; SHALL PARTICIPATE IN ACTIVITIES OF A PHYSICIANS HEALTH AND REHABILITATION COMMITTEE INCLUDING WEEKLY MEETINGS WITH QUARTERLY REPORTS; SHALL COMPLY WITH CONDITIONS OF ANY AGREEMENT ENTERED INTO FOR HOSPITAL PRIVILEGES AND SHALL REPORT THESE TO THE BOARD; SHALL NOT POSSESS ALCOHOL OR DRUGS WITH POTENTIAL FOR ABUSE EXCEPT AS OTHERWISE PROVIDED IN THIS ORDER; SHALL SURRENDER ALL SUCH SUBSTANCES IN HIS POSSESSION INCLUDING SAMPLES; SHALL NOT TELEPHONE A PRESCRIPTION FOR CONTROLLED SUBSTANCES OR DANGEROUS DRUGS TO A PHARMACY; SEPARATE FROM PATIENT RECORDS SHALL MAINTAIN A FILE OF EVERY PRESCRIPTION WRITTEN FOR CONTROLLED SUBSTANCES OR DANGEROUS DRUGS WHICH SHALL BE AVAILABLE FOR INSPECTION; SHALL NOT POSSESS, ADMINISTER OR DISPENSE ANY DANGEROUS DRUGS OR CONTROLLED SUBSTANCES BUT MAY PRESCRIBE SUCH DRUGS FOR OUTPATIENTS AND MAY ORDER SUCH DRUGS FOR HOSPITAL INPATIENTS; MEDICAL PRACTICE SHALL BE MONITORED BY A BOARD-APPROVED PHYSICIAN WITH QUARTERLY REPORTS; SHALL MAINTAIN ADEQUATE MEDICAL RECORDS ON ALL OFFICE VISITS WHICH SHALL BE AVAILABLE FOR INSPECTION; SHALL OBTAIN AT LEAST 50 HOURS PER YEAR OF CONTINUING MEDICAL EDUCATION; SHALL PASS THE SPEX EXAM WITHIN ONE YEAR; SHALL APPEAR BEFORE THE BOARD TWICE A YEAR AND WHEN REQUESTED; SHALL COOPERATE WITH THE BOARD IN VERIFYING COMPLIANCE; SHALL EXECUTE RELEASES NECESSARY TO OBTAIN MEDICAL TREATMENT RECORDS AND PEER REVIEW RECORDS; SHALL GIVE A COPY OF THIS ORDER TO ANY HEALTH CARE ENTITY WHERE HE HAS OR APPLIES FOR PRIVILEGES OR ANYONE ELSE WHO REQUESTS IT; SHALL ENSURE INQUIRIES REGARDING HIS TEXAS LICENSURE STATUS ARE ANSWERED BY REFERENCING THIS ORDER; SHALL INFORM BOARD OF CHANGE OF ADDRESS WITHIN 10 DAYS OR IF HE LEAVES THE STATE; TIME SPENT OUT OF TEXAS DOES

NOT COUNT TOWARD PROBATION. SHALL NOT SEEK MODIFICATION FOR ONE YEAR.

TINSLEY, MARK S MD, LICENSE NUMBER 0014907, WAS DISCIPLINED BY ARIZONA ON JUNE 8, 1990.
OFFENSE: FAILURE TO COMPLY WITH A PREVIOUS BOARD ORDER
NOTES: VIOLATED BOARD ORDER OF 10/7/88 BY USING ILLICIT DRUGS AND FAILING TO RESPOND TO A REQUEST FOR A URINE SPECIMEN. LICENSE PLACED ON INACTIVE STATUS IN ORDER FOR HIM TO ENTER A LONG-TERM DRUG DEPENDENCY PROGRAM.

TINSLEY, MARK S MD, LICENSE NUMBER 0014907, WAS DISCIPLINED BY ARIZONA ON JUNE 19, 1991.
DISCIPLINARY ACTION: 60-MONTH PROBATION; RESTRICTION PLACED ON CONTROLLED SUBSTANCE LICENSE
OFFENSE: DRUG OR ALCOHOL ABUSE
NOTES: ON 1/15/88 BOARD RECEIVED INFORMATION HE HAD BEEN TERMINATED FROM HIS SURGICAL RESIDENCY FOR FAILURE TO PERFORM IN ACCORDANCE WITH HIS CONTRACT AND FOR CONCERNS REGARDING HIS CLINICAL ABILITIES. ON 6/9/88 HE ENTERED AN INPATIENT CHEMICAL DEPENDENCY TREATMENT PROGRAM WHICH HE SUCCESSFULLY COMPLETED ON 09/29/88. ON 4/13/89 THE BOARD ISSUED A LETTER OF CONCERN REGARDING A MALPRACTICE COMPLAINT FOR FAILURE TO CORRECTLY DIAGNOSE TORSION OF THE PATIENT'S TESTICLE. IN EARLY 1990 HE WAS FIRED FROM HIS POSITION AS AN EMERGENCY ROOM PHYSICIAN. IN MAY 1990 HE ACKNOWLEDGED MISUSING DRUGS BETWEEN 4/7/90 AND 5/17/90. IN JUNE 1990 HE REQUESTED THE BOARD PLACE HIS LICENSE ON INACTIVE STATUS. ENTERED INPATIENT CHEMICAL DEPENDENCY TREATMENT ON 7/15/90 AND COMPLETED THE PROGRAM ON 8/17/90. ENTERED A SECOND INPATIENT CHEMICAL DEPENDENCY TREATMENT PROGRAM ON 8/29/90 AND WAS DISCHARGED ON 3/30/91. ON 6/19/91 HE ASKED THE BOARD TO RETURN HIS LICENSE TO ACTIVE STATUS. CONDITIONS OF PROBATION: SHALL SURRENDER HIS DEA REGISTRATION FOR SCHEDULE II SUBSTANCES AND SHALL NOT APPLY FOR REINSTATEMENT WITHOUT BOARD APPROVAL; SHALL PARTICIPATE IN THE ARIZONA MEDICAL ASSOCIATION'S MONITORED AFTERCARE TREATMENT PROGRAM; MUST HAVE THERAPIST SUBMIT QUARTERLY REPORTS TO THE BOARD AND OPEN HIS RECORDS TO THE BOARD; MUST ATTEND A MINIMUM OF 90 MEETINGS OF A 12 STEP RECOVERY PROGRAM WITHIN 90 DAYS AND THREE MEETINGS PER WEEK AFTER THAT; MUST OBTAIN ONE BOARD-APPROVED TREATING PHYSICIAN; MUST ABSTAIN FROM ALCOHOL AND OTHER DRUGS; MUST COMPLY WITH REQUESTS FOR RANDOM SCREENING OF BODILY FLUIDS; MUST MAINTAIN A LOG OF ALL MEDICATION; MUST SUBMIT TO MENTAL, PHYSICAL OR MEDICAL COMPETENCY EXAMS AS REQUESTED BY BOARD; MUST SUBMIT TO ANY THERAPY ORDERED BY BOARD; MUST APPEAR BEFORE BOARD FOR INTERVIEWS UPON REQUEST AND INFORM THE BOARD IF HE CHANGES ADDRESS OR WILL BE AWAY FOR MORE THAN FIVE DAYS. ON 1/25/92 BOARD GAVE WRITTEN PERMISSION FOR HIM TO REAPPLY FOR DEA CONTROLLED SUBSTANCES REGISTRATION FOR SCHEDULE II NARCOTICS DUE TO HIS ONGOING REHABILITATION EFFORTS. EFFECTIVE 10/16/93 HIS REQUEST TO CHANGE SUPPORT GROUPS WAS APPROVED. EFFECTIVE 4/16/94 PROBATION TERMINATED AND HE MUST ENTER INTO A STIPULATION WITH THE SAME TERMS AS HIS PROBATIONARY ORDER. ON 4/8/95 ORDER TERMINATED.

TINSLEY, MARK STANLY MD, LICENSE NUMBER 00G5693, OF PHOENIX, AZ, WAS DISCIPLINED BY TEXAS ON JULY 28, 1989.
OFFENSE: DISCIPLINARY ACTION BY ANOTHER STATE OR AGENCY
NOTES: FOLLOW TERMS OF ARIZONA ORDER THROUGH DURATION OF ARIZONA ORDER.

TINSLEY, MARK STANLY MD, LICENSE NUMBER 00G5693, OF PHOENIX, AZ, WAS DISCIPLINED BY TEXAS ON MARCH 6, 1992.
DISCIPLINARY ACTION: 60-MONTH PROBATION
OFFENSE: DISCIPLINARY ACTION BY ANOTHER STATE OR AGENCY
NOTES: DISCIPLINARY ACTION TAKEN BY ANOTHER STATE BOARD FOR INTEMPERATE USE OF ALCOHOL OR DRUGS. LICENSE SUSPENDED, SUSPENSION STAYED; PROBATION UNDER TERMS AND CONDITIONS.

TIPPIT, NATHANIEL G MD, LICENSE NUMBER 00C2104, OF SAN ANTONIO, TX, WAS DISCIPLINED BY TEXAS ON DECEMBER 1, 1988.
NOTES: SETTLEMENT AGREEMENT AND UNSPECIFIED DISCIPLINARY ACTION

TITUS, PATRICK A MD, LICENSE NUMBER 00C8730, OF HOUSTON, TX, WAS DISCIPLINED BY TEXAS ON DECEMBER 1, 1988.
NOTES: SETTLEMENT AGREEMENT AND UNSPECIFIED DISCIPLINARY ACTION

TIZARD, GARY T MD, LICENSE NUMBER 0012551, OF HENDERSONVILLE, TN, WAS DISCIPLINED BY TENNESSEE ON JULY 17, 1990.
DISCIPLINARY ACTION: EMERGENCY SUSPENSION; RESTRICTION PLACED ON LICENSE
OFFENSE: PROFESSIONAL MISCONDUCT
NOTES: ALLEGED SEXUAL MISCONDUCT, PERSON UNSPECIFIED

TIZARD, GARY T MD, LICENSE NUMBER 00D7334, OF HENDERSONVILLE, TN, WAS DISCIPLINED BY TEXAS ON OCTOBER 26, 1990.
DISCIPLINARY ACTION: LICENSE SUSPENSION
OFFENSE: DISCIPLINARY ACTION BY ANOTHER STATE OR AGENCY
NOTES: SUSPENDED PENDING OUTCOME OF FINAL HEARING BEFORE TENNESSEE BOARD; MUST AUTHORIZE TENNESSEE BOARD TO RELEASE INFORMATION TO TEXAS AS TO STATUS AND COMPLIANCE WITH PROBATION; RECEIVE APPROVAL OF TEXAS BOARD PRIOR TO PRACTICING MEDICINE IN TEXAS.

TIZARD, GARY T MD WAS DISCIPLINED BY ARIZONA ON JANUARY 23, 1992.
DISCIPLINARY ACTION: LICENSE REVOCATION
OFFENSE: DISCIPLINARY ACTION BY ANOTHER STATE OR AGENCY
NOTES: LICENSE WAS SUSPENDED IN TENNESSEE FOR UNPROFESSIONAL CONDUCT. TEXAS ENTERED INTO AN AGREED ORDER WITH DOCTOR TIZARD'S SURRENDERING HIS TEXAS LICENSE AS A RESULT OF ACTIONS TAKEN IN TENNESSEE. DR. TIZARD SIGNED A CANCELLATION OF HIS ARIZONA LICENSE WITH CAUSE WHICH REQUIRES BOARD ACTION.

TIZARD, GARY TIFFANY MD, DATE OF BIRTH JUNE 17, 1944, OF 111 WILLIAM SHY DR, HENDERSONVILLE, TN, WAS DISCIPLINED BY MEDICARE ON AUGUST 18, 1991.

DISCIPLINARY ACTION: EXCLUSION FROM THE MEDICARE AND/OR MEDICAID PROGRAMS
OFFENSE: DISCIPLINARY ACTION BY ANOTHER STATE OR AGENCY
NOTES: LICENSE REVOCATION OR SUSPENSION.

TODD, EUGENE RAY MD, LICENSE NUMBER 00C7144, OF DALLAS, TX, WAS DISCIPLINED BY TEXAS ON JUNE 22, 1994.
DISCIPLINARY ACTION: REQUIRED TO TAKE ADDITIONAL MEDICAL EDUCATION; MONITORING OF PHYSICIAN
OFFENSE: FAILURE TO COMPLY WITH A PROFESSIONAL RULE
NOTES: TREATED A FAMILY MEMBER WITH PAIN MEDICATIONS; FAILED TO KEEP ANY MEDICAL RECORDS REGARDING THIS; AUDITED BY DEA WHICH FOUND THAT HIS RECORD KEEPING FOR STEROIDS WAS INADEQUATE. LICENSE RESTRICTED FOR THREE YEARS WITH THE FOLLOWING CONDITIONS: SHALL ATTEND AT LEAST 50 HOURS PER YEAR OF CONTINUING MEDICAL EDUCATION WITH AT LEAST 10 OF THESE IN RISK MANAGEMENT OR RECORD KEEPING COURSES; SHALL MAINTAIN ADEQUATE MEDICAL RECORDS ON ALL PATIENT OFFICE VISITS WHICH SHALL BE AVAILABLE FOR INSPECTION; SHALL NOT SIGN ANY PATIENT RECORD UNLESS HE HAS PERSONALLY EXAMINED THE PATIENT OR CLEARLY NOTES IN THE RECORD THAT HE DID NOT; SHALL NOT TREAT OR OTHERWISE SERVE AS PHYSICIAN, PRESCRIBE, DISPENSE OR ADMINISTER DRUGS THAT MAY BE SUBJECT TO ABUSE TO HIMSELF OR ANY MEMBER OF HIS FAMILY; SHALL APPEAR BEFORE THE BOARD ONCE A YEAR; SHALL GIVE A COPY OF THIS ORDER TO ANY HEALTH CARE ENTITY WHERE HE HAS PRIVILEGES; SHALL COOPERATE WITH THE BOARD IN VERIFYING COMPLIANCE; SHALL INFORM BOARD OF CHANGE OF ADDRESS WITHIN 10 DAYS OR IF HE LEAVES THE STATE; TIME SPENT OUT OF TEXAS DOES NOT COUNT TOWARD RESTRICTION. SHALL NOT SEEK MODIFICATION FOR ONE YEAR.

TODD, WILLIAM D MD, DATE OF BIRTH JANUARY 23, 1946, LICENSE NUMBER 0017077, OF KERRVILLE, TX, WAS DISCIPLINED BY KENTUCKY ON OCTOBER 20, 1994.
DISCIPLINARY ACTION: SURRENDER OF LICENSE

TODD, WILLIAM DAVID MD, LICENSE NUMBER 00E2093, OF BIG SPRING, TX, WAS DISCIPLINED BY TEXAS ON MARCH 5, 1994.
DISCIPLINARY ACTION: 60-MONTH PROBATION; REQUIRED TO TAKE ADDITIONAL MEDICAL EDUCATION
OFFENSE: DISCIPLINARY ACTION BY ANOTHER STATE OR AGENCY
NOTES: ON 9/1/93 KENTUCKY BOARD PLACED LICENSE ON A FIVE YEAR PROBATION WHICH REQUIRES PARTICIPATION WITH KENTUCKY IMPAIRED PHYSICIANS COMMITTEE AND AA, AND SHALL SUBMIT TO RANDOM BIOLOGICAL FLUID TESTING; HE IS AN ALCOHOLIC; CURRENTLY WORKING IN A HOSPITAL AS A PSYCHIATRIST AND IS SUPERVISED. FIVE YEAR SUSPENSION STAYED. CONDITIONS OF PROBATION: SHALL ABSTAIN FROM THE CONSUMPTION OF DRUGS/CHEMICAL SUBSTANCES IN ANY FORM UNLESS PRESCRIBED BY ANOTHER PHYSICIAN FOR A LEGITIMATE AND THERAPEUTIC PURPOSE; SHALL NOT TREAT OR OTHERWISE SERVE AS PHYSICIAN, PRESCRIBE, DISPENSE, OR ADMINISTER DRUGS SUBJECT TO ABUSE TO HIMSELF OR ANY MEMBER OF HIS FAMILY; SHALL PARTICIPATE IN AA'S PROGRAMS NOT LESS THAN THREE TIMES A WEEK WITH QUARTERLY REPORTS TO THE BOARD; SHALL SUBMIT HIMSELF FOR APPROPRIATE EXAMS INCLUDING BLOOD OR ALCOHOL SCREENS; SHALL SUBMIT HIMSELF FOR EVALUATION AND TREATMENT BY A BOARD-APPROVED PSYCHIATRIST WITH QUARTERLY REPORTS; SHALL CONTINUE TO BE MONITORED BY HIS SUPERVISOR WITH QUARTERLY REPORTS; SHALL ATTEND AT LEAST 50 HOURS PER YEAR OF CONTINUING MEDICAL EDUCATION AT LEAST FIVE HOURS PER YEAR SHALL BE IN THE AREA OF SUBSTANCE ABUSE; SHALL PERFORM EIGHT HOURS PER MONTH OF COMMUNITY SERVICE FOR FIVE YEARS; SHALL APPEAR BEFORE THE BOARD FOUR TIMES A YEAR FOR THE FIRST YEAR AND TWICE A YEAR AFTER THAT; SHALL GIVE A COPY OF THIS ORDER TO ANY HEALTH CARE ENTITY WHERE HE HAS PRIVILEGES; SHALL COOPERATE WITH THE BOARD IN VERIFYING COMPLIANCE; SHALL INFORM BOARD OF CHANGE OF ADDRESS WITHIN 10 DAYS OR IF HE LEAVES THE STATE; TIME SPENT OUT OF TEXAS DOES NOT COUNT TOWARD PROBATION. SHALL NOT SEEK MODIFICATION FOR ONE YEAR.

TOMASEVIC, MIRA MD, DATE OF BIRTH APRIL 7, 1937, OF FISHER COUNTY HOSPITAL, ROTAN, TX, WAS DISCIPLINED BY IOWA ON JULY 21, 1986.
DISCIPLINARY ACTION: SURRENDER OF LICENSE
OFFENSE: DISCIPLINARY ACTION BY ANOTHER STATE OR AGENCY
NOTES: EFFECTIVE 11/12/92 UPON PROOF OF SUCCESSFUL COMPLETION AND PASSING SCORE OF SPEX, MEDICAL LICENSE WILL BE REINSTATED.

TOMASEVIC, MIRA MD OF 426 WEST BARRY, CHICAGO, IL, WAS DISCIPLINED BY MEDICARE ON AUGUST 12, 1986.
DISCIPLINARY ACTION: 36-MONTH EXCLUSION FROM THE MEDICARE AND/OR MEDICAID PROGRAMS
OFFENSE: CRIMINAL CONVICTION OR PLEA OF GUILTY, NOLO CONTENDERE, OR NO CONTEST TO A CRIME
NOTES: PROGRAM-RELATED CONVICTION.

TOMASEVIC, MIRA MD OF CHICAGO, IL, WAS DISCIPLINED BY TEXAS ON DECEMBER 1, 1986.
DISCIPLINARY ACTION: 6-MONTH LICENSE SUSPENSION; 24-MONTH PROBATION
OFFENSE: CRIMINAL CONVICTION OR PLEA OF GUILTY, NOLO CONTENDERE, OR NO CONTEST TO A CRIME
NOTES: CONVICTED OF FELONY.

TOMASEVIC, MIRA MD, LICENSE NUMBER 00G8764, OF ASPERMONT, TX, WAS DISCIPLINED BY TEXAS ON APRIL 10, 1992.
DISCIPLINARY ACTION: 60-MONTH PROBATION
OFFENSE: DISCIPLINARY ACTION BY ANOTHER STATE OR AGENCY
NOTES: UNPROFESSIONAL OR DISHONORABLE CONDUCT LIKELY TO DECEIVE, DEFRAUD OR INJURE THE PUBLIC, AND DISCIPLINARY ACTION BY A PEER REVIEW ENTITY. LICENSE REVOKED, REVOCATION STAYED; PROBATION UNDER TERMS AND CONDITIONS. ON 10/1/93 ORDER MODIFIED SO THAT WITHIN SIX MONTHS SHE SHALL ENROLL IN, BEGIN PARTICIPATION IN, AND SUBSEQUENTLY COMPLETE A PHARMACOLOGY RETRAINING COURSE ACCEPTABLE TO THE BOARD.

TRAN, VAN THI MD, LICENSE NUMBER 00F3644, OF N. TEXAS MED CENTER, MCKINNEY, TX, WAS DISCIPLINED BY TEXAS ON AUGUST 1, 1988.
DISCIPLINARY ACTION: RESTRICTION PLACED ON LICENSE; REQUIRED TO TAKE ADDITIONAL MEDICAL EDUCATION
NOTES: SHALL OBTAIN 50 CONTINUING MEDICAL EDUCATION HOURS PER YEAR; PRACTICE THE SAME AS SCOPE OF PRIVILEGES AT NORTH TEXAS MEDICAL CENTER IN MCKINNEY; OBTAIN SEMI-ANNUAL PROGRESS REPORT

BY HOSPITAL CHIEFS OF OB/GYN; APPEAR ANNUALLY BEFORE THE BOARD; AND OBTAIN CURRENCY IN ADVANCED CARDIAC LIFE SUPPORT.

TRIMBLE, ROBERT H MD, LICENSE NUMBER 00D1087, OF HOUSTON, TX, WAS DISCIPLINED BY TEXAS ON JUNE 17, 1992.
DISCIPLINARY ACTION: REPRIMAND
NOTES: ADVISED NOT TO ENGAGE IN THE CORPORATE PRACTICE OF MEDICINE.

ULDRICH, DENNIS ALAN MD, DATE OF BIRTH JULY 27, 1955, LICENSE NUMBER 00H7841, OF 647 CYPRESS GREEN, SAN ANTONIO, TX, WAS DISCIPLINED BY TEXAS ON JANUARY 29, 1993.
DISCIPLINARY ACTION: SURRENDER OF CONTROLLED SUBSTANCE LICENSE; 60-MONTH PROBATION
OFFENSE: DRUG OR ALCOHOL ABUSE
NOTES: DURING 1/92 AND PRECEDING MONTHS, HE HAD INGESTED THE DRUGS PHENERGAN, ATIVAN, BENADRYL AND FENTANYL ON MULTIPLE OCCASIONS WITHOUT A VALID MEDICAL REASON; ON 1/20/92 WAS FOUND UNCONSCIOUS AND CYANOTIC DUE TO DRUG ABUSE; RECEIVED INPATIENT TREATMENT FOR DRUG DEPENDENCE IN 1/92 AND 3/92 AT AN AIR FORCE HOSPITAL AND FROM 3/92 THROUGH 6/92 AT AN ARMY HOSPITAL; HE FULLY COOPERATED WITH BOARD IN ITS INVESTIGATION; ON 7/14/92 ENTERED A MONITORED TREATMENT PROGRAM CONTRACT IN WHICH HE ACKNOWLEDGED HIS CHEMICAL DEPENDENCE. SUSPENSION STAYED. CONDITIONS OF PROBATION: SHALL ATTEND 50 HOURS PER YEAR OF CONTINUING MEDICAL EDUCATION APPROVED FOR CATEGORY I CREDITS; SHALL BE EVALUATED AND TREATED BY A BOARD-APPROVED PSYCHIATRIST TO WHOM HE WILL PROVIDE A COPY OF THIS ORDER WITH REPORTS TO THE BOARD; SHALL ABSTAIN FROM THE CONSUMPTION OF ALCOHOL OR OTHER DRUGS IN ANY FORM; SHALL SURRENDER ALL CONTROLLED SUBSTANCES INCLUDING SAMPLES; SHALL SURRENDER DEA AND TEXAS CONTROLLED SUBSTANCES REGISTRATION; SHALL NOT ATTEMPT TO REREGISTER FOR THESE WITHOUT BOARD AUTHORIZATION; SHALL PARTICIPATE IN ACTIVITIES OF A COUNTY IMPAIRED PHYSICIANS GROUP AND ATTEND WEEKLY MEETINGS WITH QUARTERLY REPORTS; SHALL SUBMIT HIMSELF FOR APPROPRIATE EXAMS INCLUDING DRUG OR ALCOHOL SCREENS; SHALL APPEAR BEFORE THE BOARD AT LEAST ONCE A YEAR; SHALL GIVE A COPY OF THIS ORDER TO ANY HEALTH CARE ENTITY WHERE HE HAS PRIVILEGES; SHALL COOPERATE WITH THE BOARD IN VERIFYING COMPLIANCE; SHALL INFORM BOARD OF CHANGE OF ADDRESS WITHIN 10 DAYS OR IF HE LEAVES THE STATE; TIME SPENT OUT OF TEXAS DOES NOT COUNT TOWARD PROBATION; SHALL COMPLY WITH ALL PROVISIONS OF TREATMENT CONTRACT ENTERED 7/14/92. SHALL NOT SEEK MODIFICATION FOR 1 YEAR OR UNTIL HE IS DISCHARGED FROM THE AIR FORCE WHICHEVER IS EARLIER. ON 1/14/94 THIS ORDER MODIFIED AS FOLLOWS: CONTINUING MEDICAL EDUCATION REQUIREMENT DROPPED FOR THE TIME HE IS IN A RESIDENCY TRAINING PROGRAM; HE MAY REAPPLY FOR CONTROLLED SUBSTANCES AUTHORITY IN SCHEDULES II THROUGH V BUT SHALL POSSESS, PRESCRIBE OR ADMINISTER THEM ONLY FOR PURPOSES OF RESIDENCY TRAINING; SEPARATE FROM OTHER RECORDS SHALL KEEP A LOG OF ALL CONTROLLED SUBSTANCES ADMINISTERED, DISPENSED OR PRESCRIBED; SHALL GIVE A COPY OF THE ORIGINAL ORDER AND THIS MODIFICATION TO THE HEAD OF HIS RESIDENCY PROGRAM.

ULDRICH, DENNIS ALAN MD, LICENSE NUMBER 0051767, OF EL PASO, TX, WAS DISCIPLINED BY OHIO ON AUGUST 19, 1993.
DISCIPLINARY ACTION: PROBATION; RESTRICTION PLACED ON LICENSE
OFFENSE: DISCIPLINARY ACTION BY ANOTHER STATE OR AGENCY
NOTES: PRIOR ACTION BY TEXAS BOARD WHICH WAS BASED ON HIS HISTORY OF SUBSTANCE ABUSE. AGREEMENT TO REMAIN IN EFFECT FOR A MINIMUM OF TWO YEARS PRIOR TO ANY REQUEST FOR TERMINATION.

ULDRICH, DENNIS ALAN MD, DATE OF BIRTH JULY 27, 1955, LICENSE NUMBER 00H7841, OF EL PASO, TX, WAS DISCIPLINED BY TEXAS ON AUGUST 19, 1994.
DISCIPLINARY ACTION: EMERGENCY SUSPENSION
OFFENSE: FAILURE TO COMPLY WITH A PREVIOUS BOARD ORDER
NOTES: AVAILABLE EVIDENCE AND INFORMATION INDICATE THAT: IN VIOLATION OF 1/29/93 ORDER HE INGESTED PROPOFOL ON 2/14/94 WHICH HE REPORTED TO THE BOARD; THE INGESTION WAS NOT PURSUANT TO A PRESCRIPTION FROM HIS PRIMARY CARE PHYSICIAN; ENTERED A RECOVERY PROGRAM AND WAS DISCHARGED ON 7/9/94 AND TRANSFERRED TO A TRANSITIONAL LIVING FACILITY; LEFT THE FACILITY ON 8/5/94 WITHOUT THE CONSENT OF THE STAFF.

VALVERDE, WILLIAM MARK MD, LICENSE NUMBER 00E1957, OF HOUSTON, TX, WAS DISCIPLINED BY TEXAS ON AUGUST 19, 1994.
DISCIPLINARY ACTION: LICENSE SUSPENSION
OFFENSE: PHYSICAL OR MENTAL ILLNESS INHIBITING THE ABILITY TO PRACTICE WITH SKILL AND SAFETY
NOTES: ALLEGATIONS WHICH IF TRUE COULD INDICATE HE SUFFERS FROM AN INABILITY TO PRACTICE WITH REASONABLE SKILL AND SAFETY BECAUSE OF A MENTAL OR EMOTIONAL CONDITION; WHILE NOT ADMITTING THE ALLEGATIONS HE WISHES TO AVOID THE EXPENSE OF LITIGATION AND INSTEAD VOLUNTARILY UNDERGO A PSYCHIATRIC EVALUATION. SUSPENSION UNTIL SUCH TIME AS HE APPEARS BEFORE THE BOARD AND PROVIDES SUFFICIENT EVIDENCE THAT HE IS PHYSICALLY, MENTALLY AND OTHERWISE COMPETENT TO SAFELY PRACTICE; SHALL COOPERATE WITH THE BOARD IN VERIFYING COMPLIANCE; SHALL INFORM BOARD OF CHANGE OF ADDRESS WITHIN 10 DAYS.

VAN BOLDEN, VERNON II MD, LICENSE NUMBER 00G0854, OF NEW ORLEANS, LA, WAS DISCIPLINED BY TEXAS ON OCTOBER 9, 1992.
DISCIPLINARY ACTION: LICENSE REVOCATION
OFFENSE: SUBSTANDARD CARE, INCOMPETENCE, OR NEGLIGENCE
NOTES: PROFESSIONAL FAILURE TO PRACTICE MEDICINE IN AN ACCEPTABLE MANNER CONSISTENT WITH PUBLIC HEALTH AND WELFARE.

VAN BOLDEN, VERNON II MD OF LUBBOCK, TX, WAS DISCIPLINED BY LOUISIANA ON JUNE 21, 1993.
DISCIPLINARY ACTION: LICENSE REVOCATION
OFFENSE: DISCIPLINARY ACTION BY ANOTHER STATE OR AGENCY
NOTES: FRAUD, DECEIT OR PERJURY IN OBTAINING A LICENSE.

VANBUSKIRK, RONALD MD, LICENSE NUMBER 00F6338, OF MOUNT PLEASANT, TX, WAS DISCIPLINED BY TEXAS ON JUNE 17, 1992.
DISCIPLINARY ACTION: 60-MONTH RESTRICTION PLACED ON

LICENSE; REPRIMAND
OFFENSE: OVERPRESCRIBING OR MISPRESCRIBING DRUGS
NOTES: NONTHERAPEUTIC PRESCRIBING. LICENSE RESTRICTED UNDER TERMS AND CONDITIONS. ON 8/19/94 REQUEST FOR TERMINATION OF THIS ORDER WAS DENIED.

VANCE, ROBERT BLISS DO, LICENSE NUMBER 00C7973, OF LAS VEGAS, NV, WAS DISCIPLINED BY TEXAS ON OCTOBER 1, 1987.
DISCIPLINARY ACTION: SURRENDER OF LICENSE

VANGORDER, PAUL N MD, LICENSE NUMBER 00F4628, OF NASHVILLE, TN, WAS DISCIPLINED BY TEXAS ON DECEMBER 1, 1988.
NOTES: SETTLEMENT AGREEMENT AND UNSPECIFIED DISCIPLINARY ACTION

VAUSE, DAVID DWIGHT MD, DATE OF BIRTH JANUARY 5, 1934, LICENSE NUMBER 00E3490, OF PO BOX 189, BLANCO, TX, WAS DISCIPLINED BY TEXAS ON APRIL 30, 1993.
DISCIPLINARY ACTION: 60-MONTH PROBATION; REQUIRED TO TAKE ADDITIONAL MEDICAL EDUCATION
OFFENSE: SUBSTANDARD CARE, INCOMPETENCE, OR NEGLIGENCE
NOTES: FAILED TO RELEASE MEDICAL RECORDS OF TWO PATIENTS OR TO RESPOND TO THE BOARD ABOUT SAME; FAILED TO ESTABLISH A PROTOCOL FOR TIMES WHEN HE IS ON CALL AS HE HAS NO ANSWERING SERVICE TO TAKE EMERGENCY CALLS; FAILED TO ADDRESS THE HIGH RISK PREGNANCY OF A 39 YEAR OLD PATIENT AND FAILED TO PROVIDE PROPER PRENATAL CARE WHICH COULD HAVE PREVENTED THE BIRTH OF HER STILLBORN CHILD; FAILED TO DIAGNOSE DIABETES IN TWO PATIENTS AND LEUKEMIA IN ONE; PRESCRIBED FASTIN FOR WEIGHT LOSS TO 3 PATIENTS WITHOUT TAKING A HISTORY AND PHYSICAL; KEPT AND USED DANGEROUS DRUGS AT HIS OFFICE WHICH WERE OUTDATED AND SHOULD HAVE BEEN DESTROYED; DISPENSED DRUGS OUT OF HIS OFFICE AFTER HE SUBSTITUTED AND RELABELED BOTTLES; HE NEITHER ADMITS NOR DENIES THE CHARGES. FIVE YEAR SUSPENSION STAYED. CONDITIONS OF PROBATION: SHALL TAKE THE SPEX EXAM ON 6/16/93; IF HE FAILS, HIS LICENSE WILL BE SUSPENDED UNTIL EXAM IS PASSED; SHALL WITHIN SIX MONTHS ENROLL IN AND SUBSEQUENTLY COMPLETE A PHARMACOLOGY RETRAINING COURSE; SHALL TAKE A BOARD-APPROVED PERSONALIZED CONTINUING MEDICAL EDUCATION ACUTE MINI-RESIDENCY AND COMPLETE WITHIN SIX MONTHS; SHALL ATTEND AT LEAST 75 HOURS PER YEAR OF CONTINUING MEDICAL EDUCATION; SHALL BE MONITORED OR SUPERVISED BY A BOARD-APPROVED PHYSICIAN WHO WILL MAKE BIMONTHLY REPORTS TO THE BOARD; SHALL MAINTAIN ADEQUATE MEDICAL RECORDS ON ALL PATIENT OFFICE VISITS; SHALL NOT SIGN ANY PATIENT RECORD UNLESS HE PERSONALLY SAW AND EXAMINED THE PATIENT AND THIS IS SO INDICATED IN THE RECORD; SHALL PERSONALLY EXAMINE PATIENTS DURING THEIR FIRST VISIT; SHALL PERFORM EIGHT HOURS PER MONTH OF COMMUNITY SERVICE; SHALL APPEAR BEFORE THE BOARD ONCE A YEAR; SHALL GIVE A COPY OF THIS ORDER TO ANY HEALTH CARE ENTITY WHERE HE HAS PRIVILEGES; SHALL COOPERATE WITH THE BOARD IN VERIFYING COMPLIANCE; SHALL INFORM BOARD OF CHANGE OF ADDRESS WITHIN 10 DAYS OR IF HE LEAVES THE STATE; TIME SPENT OUT OF TEXAS DOES NOT COUNT TOWARD PROBATION. SHALL NOT SEEK MODIFICATION FOR FIVE YEARS UNLESS FURTHER APPLICATION IS MADE TO THE BOARD.

VEGA, JULIO MD, LICENSE NUMBER 00F5082, OF BUENA PARK, CA, WAS DISCIPLINED BY TEXAS ON MARCH 31, 1990.
DISCIPLINARY ACTION: 120-MONTH PROBATION
OFFENSE: DISCIPLINARY ACTION BY ANOTHER STATE OR AGENCY
NOTES: STIPULATED ORDER. REVOCATION STAYED. BOUND BY CERTAIN CONDITIONS OF CALIFORNIA BOARD. MUST OBTAIN APPROVAL BEFORE PRACTICING MEDICINE IN TEXAS.

VEGGEBERG, KERMIT ROGER MD, LICENSE NUMBER 00D1172, OF HOUSTON, TX, WAS DISCIPLINED BY TEXAS ON AUGUST 19, 1994.
DISCIPLINARY ACTION: 36-MONTH PROBATION; REQUIRED TO TAKE ADDITIONAL MEDICAL EDUCATION
OFFENSE: SUBSTANDARD CARE, INCOMPETENCE, OR NEGLIGENCE
NOTES: HAD TREATED ONE PATIENT FOR A TOTAL HIP REPLACEMENT IN 1977 AND SUBSEQUENTLY PERFORMED SEVERAL REVISIONS; MADE ASSUMPTIONS ABOUT THE SIZES OF THE PROSTHETIC BALL AND CUP WHICH LED TO A MISMATCH WHICH RESULTED IN THE PATIENT EXPERIENCING MANY HIP DISLOCATIONS, EVENTUALLY NECESSITATING FURTHER SURGERIES WITH THE ATTENDANT PAIN AND RECOVERY PERIODS; HE WAS NOT IN THE HABIT OF DOCUMENTING PATIENTS' LEVELS OF PAIN. SUSPENSION STAYED. CONDITIONS OF PROBATION: SHALL ATTEND AT LEAST 100 HOURS OF CONTINUING MEDICAL EDUCATION DURING THE FIRST YEAR OF PROBATION AND 50 HOURS PER YEAR AFTER THAT; 75 HOURS OF THE FIRST YEAR SHALL BE IN THE AREA OF ORTHOPEDICS AND 25 SHALL BE IN THE AREA OF RADIOLOGY; SHALL BE MONITORED BY A BOARD-APPROVED PHYSICIAN WITH REPORTS THREE TIMES A YEAR; SHALL APPEAR BEFORE THE BOARD TWICE A YEAR; SHALL GIVE A COPY OF THIS ORDER TO ANY HEALTH CARE ENTITY WHERE HE HAS PRIVILEGES; SHALL COOPERATE WITH THE BOARD IN VERIFYING COMPLIANCE; SHALL INFORM BOARD OF CHANGE OF ADDRESS WITHIN 10 DAYS OR IF HE LEAVES THE STATE; TIME SPENT OUT OF TEXAS DOES NOT COUNT TOWARD PROBATION. SHALL NOT SEEK MODIFICATION FOR ONE YEAR.

VICKERS, FRANK ALLEN MD, LICENSE NUMBER 00C9172, OF HUNTSVILLE, TX, WAS DISCIPLINED BY TEXAS ON NOVEMBER 9, 1993.
DISCIPLINARY ACTION: EMERGENCY SUSPENSION
OFFENSE: DRUG OR ALCOHOL ABUSE
NOTES: IN 6/93 AND AS RECENTLY AS 11/5/93 ENGAGED IN THE INTEMPERATE USE OF DRUGS BY CONSUMING VARIOUS CONTROLLED SUBSTANCES INCLUDING STADOL, NUBAIN, DARVON, ATIVAN AND XANAX WITHOUT A LEGITIMATE MEDICAL REASON; DURING 10/93 HIS PHYSICAL AND MENTAL CONDITION HAS UNDERGONE A RAPID DETERIORATION CREATING AN INCREASE IN THE POTENTIAL FOR DANGER TO PATIENTS.

VICKERS, FRANK ALLEN MD OF 1528 AVE O, HUNTSVILLE, TX, WAS DISCIPLINED BY DEA ON JANUARY 13, 1994.
DISCIPLINARY ACTION: SURRENDER OF CONTROLLED SUBSTANCE LICENSE

VICKERS, FRANK ALLEN MD, LICENSE NUMBER 00C9172, OF HOUSTON, TX, WAS DISCIPLINED BY TEXAS ON JUNE 22, 1994.
DISCIPLINARY ACTION: LICENSE SUSPENSION
OFFENSE: DRUG OR ALCOHOL ABUSE
NOTES: HE WAS TREATED FOR SUBSTANCE ABUSE AS AN INPATIENT FROM 8/83 THROUGH 12/83; REGULARLY ATTENDED MEETINGS OF AA AND A PHYSICIANS HEALTH AND REHABILITATION COMMITTEE UNTIL 1989; SUBSEQUENTLY RELAPSED AND RECEIVED INPATIENT TREATMENT IN 6/93; ON 11/5/93 WAS ARRESTED AND CHARGED WITH PUBLIC INTOXICATION THROUGH BEING UNDER THE INFLUENCE OF DRUGS; HAD IN HIS POSSESSION XANAX, ATIVAN, NUBAIN INJECTABLE, DARVON, AND PLACIDYL SUPPOSITORIES; WAS ADMITTED FOR INPATIENT TREATMENT ON 11/6/93 AND SINCE 2/4/94 HAS BEEN IN AN AFTERCARE RECOVERY AND SUPERVISION PROGRAM; HAS ADMITTED TO TAKING CONTROLLED SUBSTANCES AND DANGEROUS DRUGS WHICH HAVE POTENTIAL FOR ABUSE FROM SAMPLES LEFT IN HIS OFFICE, FROM SUPPLIES PURCHASED FOR OFFICE USE AND FROM UNUSED PORTIONS OF PRESCRIPTIONS LEFT IN HIS OFFICE BY PATIENTS; CLAIMS 11/5/93 AS A SOBRIETY DATE. SUSPENSION UNTIL SUCH TIME AS HE APPEARS BEFORE THE BOARD AND PROVIDES SUFFICIENT EVIDENCE THAT HE IS PHYSICALLY, MENTALLY AND OTHERWISE COMPETENT TO SAFELY PRACTICE.

VICKERS, FRANK ALLEN MD, LICENSE NUMBER 00C9172, OF HOUSTON, TX, WAS DISCIPLINED BY TEXAS ON NOVEMBER 23, 1994.
DISCIPLINARY ACTION: SURRENDER OF CONTROLLED SUBSTANCE LICENSE; 120-MONTH PROBATION
OFFENSE: DRUG OR ALCOHOL ABUSE
NOTES: HAS SATISFIED THE MINIMUM REQUIREMENTS OF 6/22/94 SUSPENSION AND SUSPENSION IS NOW STAYED. CONDITIONS OF PROBATION: PRACTICE RESTRICTED TO AN INSTITUTIONAL OR SUPERVISED SETTING WITH A BOARD-APPROVED SUPERVISOR WITH QUARTERLY REPORTS; SHALL ABSTAIN FROM THE CONSUMPTION OF ALCOHOL/CHEMICAL SUBSTANCES IN ANY FORM UNLESS PRESCRIBED BY ANOTHER PHYSICIAN FOR A LEGITIMATE AND THERAPEUTIC PURPOSE; SHALL SUBMIT HIMSELF FOR APPROPRIATE EXAMS INCLUDING DRUG OR ALCOHOL SCREENS; SHALL NOT TREAT OR OTHERWISE SERVE AS PHYSICIAN, PRESCRIBE DISPENSE OR ADMINISTER DRUGS THAT MAY BE SUBJECT TO ABUSE TO HIMSELF OR ANY MEMBER OF HIS FAMILY; SHALL SURRENDER DEA AND TEXAS CONTROLLED SUBSTANCES CERTIFICATES, ALL UNUSED TRIPLICATE PRESCRIPTION FORMS AND ALL CONTROLLED SUBSTANCES IN HIS POSSESSION INCLUDING SAMPLES; SHALL NOT SEEK TO REREGISTER WITHOUT PERMISSION; SEPARATE FROM PATIENT RECORDS, SHALL MAINTAIN A FILE OF EVERY PRESCRIPTION WRITTEN FOR DANGEROUS DRUGS WHICH SHALL BE AVAILABLE FOR INSPECTION; SHALL PARTICIPATE IN ACTIVITIES OF A PHYSICIANS COUNSELING COMMITTEE WITH QUARTERLY REPORTS; SHALL PARTICIPATE IN AA'S PROGRAM NOT LESS THAN THREE TIMES A WEEK WITH QUARTERLY REPORTS TO THE BOARD; SHALL ABIDE BY ALL TERMS OF 2/4/94 CONTRACT WITH HOSPITAL; SHALL SUBMIT HIMSELF FOR EVALUATION AND TREATMENT TO A BOARD-APPROVED PSYCHIATRIST; SHALL ATTEND AT LEAST 50 HOURS PER YEAR OF CONTINUING MEDICAL EDUCATION; SHALL APPEAR BEFORE THE BOARD TWICE A YEAR; SHALL GIVE A COPY OF THIS ORDER TO ANY HEALTH CARE ENTITY WHERE HE HAS PRIVILEGES; SHALL COOPERATE WITH THE BOARD IN VERIFYING COMPLIANCE; SHALL INFORM BOARD OF CHANGE OF ADDRESS WITHIN 10 DAYS OR IF HE LEAVES THE STATE; TIME SPENT OUT OF TEXAS DOES NOT COUNT TOWARD PROBATION. SHALL NOT SEEK MODIFICATION FOR ONE YEAR.

VIGDERMAN, DAVID L DO, LICENSE NUMBER 00F7654, OF BIG SPRING, TX, WAS DISCIPLINED BY TEXAS ON JANUARY 25, 1992.
DISCIPLINARY ACTION: 3-MONTH EMERGENCY SUSPENSION
OFFENSE: DISCIPLINARY ACTION BY ANOTHER STATE OR AGENCY
NOTES: LICENSE TEMPORARILY SUSPENDED. A FORMAL HEARING IS PENDING.

VIGDERMAN, DAVID L DO, LICENSE NUMBER 00F7654, OF BIG SPRING, TX, WAS DISCIPLINED BY TEXAS ON NOVEMBER 30, 1992.
DISCIPLINARY ACTION: LICENSE REVOCATION
OFFENSE: DISCIPLINARY ACTION BY ANOTHER STATE OR AGENCY
NOTES: DISCIPLINARY ACTION TAKEN BY ANOTHER STATE BOARD FOR UNPROFESSIONAL OR DISHONORABLE CONDUCT LIKELY TO DECEIVE, DEFRAUD OR INJURE THE PUBLIC.

VILLEGAS, LEO III DO, LICENSE NUMBER 0058965, OF 2162 TEXAS AVENUE, BRIDGE CITY, TX, WAS DISCIPLINED BY DEA ON SEPTEMBER 30, 1993.
DISCIPLINARY ACTION: RESTRICTION PLACED ON CONTROLLED SUBSTANCE LICENSE
OFFENSE: OVERPRESCRIBING OR MISPRESCRIBING DRUGS
NOTES: PRESCRIBING LARGE QUANTITIES OF CONTROLLED SUBSTANCES WITHOUT LEGITIMATE MEDICAL REASONS. RESTRICTED 08/20/93 ORDER FROM SCHEDULES II AND III CONTROLLED SUBSTANCES. REGISTRATION MODIFIED 09/30/93.

VILLEGAS, LEOPOLD III DO, LICENSE NUMBER 00G7763, WAS DISCIPLINED BY TEXAS ON AUGUST 20, 1993.
DISCIPLINARY ACTION: 60-MONTH PROBATION; RESTRICTION PLACED ON CONTROLLED SUBSTANCE LICENSE
OFFENSE: DRUG OR ALCOHOL ABUSE
NOTES: DIVERTED TYLOX PRESCRIPTIONS FOR HIS OWN USE; SUFFERS FROM POLIOMYELITIS RESIDUAL EFFECTS. FIVE YEAR SUSPENSION STAYED. CONDITIONS OF PROBATION: SHALL APPEAR BEFORE A COMMITTEE OF THE BOARD TWICE A YEAR; SHALL BE MONITORED BY A BOARD-APPROVED PHYSICIAN WHO SHALL REPORT TO THE BOARD THREE TIMES A YEAR; SHALL WITHIN 6 MONTHS ENROLL IN A TWO WEEK PRECEPTORSHIP ON THE PREVENTION AND TREATMENT OF DRUG ABUSE; ON 4/11/94, SINCE THE SPECIFIED COURSE WAS NOT OFFERED AT THIS TIME THIS PROVISION WAS DROPPED; SHALL NOT TREAT OR OTHERWISE SERVE AS PHYSICIAN, PRESCRIBE, DISPENSE OR ADMINISTER DRUGS THAT MAY BE SUBJECT TO ABUSE FOR HIMSELF OR ANY MEMBER OF HIS FAMILY; DEA AND CONTROLLED SUBSTANCES REGISTRATION LIMITED TO SCHEDULES IV AND V; SHALL ABSTAIN FROM THE CONSUMPTION OF ALCOHOL/CHEMICAL SUBSTANCES IN ANY FORM UNLESS PRESCRIBED BY ANOTHER PHYSICIAN FOR A LEGITIMATE AND THERAPEUTIC PURPOSE; SHALL ENTER A DRUG REHABILITATION PROGRAM WITHIN 20 DAYS WITH REPORTS TO THE BOARD; SHALL UNDERGO EXAMS AND ANY NECESSARY TREATMENT BY A BOARD-APPROVED NEUROLOGIST AND PSYCHIATRIST; SHALL FOLLOW THIS

NEUROLOGIST'S RECOMMENDATIONS CONCERNING RESTRICTIONS ON HIS MEDICAL PRACTICE; SHALL PARTICIPATE IN THE ACTIVITIES OF AA NOT LESS THAN THREE TIMES A WEEK; SHALL PARTICIPATE IN ACTIVITIES OF A PHYSICIAN HEALTH AND REHABILITATION COMMITTEE AND ATTEND WEEKLY MEETINGS WITH QUARTERLY REPORTS; SHALL SUBMIT HIMSELF FOR APPROPRIATE EXAMS INCLUDING DRUG OR ALCOHOL SCREENS; SHALL GIVE A COPY OF THIS ORDER TO ANY HEALTH CARE ENTITY WHERE HE HAS PRIVILEGES; SHALL COOPERATE WITH THE BOARD IN VERIFYING COMPLIANCE; SHALL INFORM BOARD OF CHANGE OF ADDRESS WITHIN 10 DAYS OR IF HE LEAVES THE STATE; TIME SPENT OUT OF TEXAS DOES NOT COUNT TOWARD PROBATION. SHALL NOT SEEK MODIFICATION FOR ONE YEAR.

VINSON, JACK R DO, LICENSE NUMBER 00C6109, OF DALLAS, TX, WAS DISCIPLINED BY TEXAS ON MAY 24, 1990.
DISCIPLINARY ACTION: MONITORING OF PHYSICIAN
NOTES: STIPULATED ORDER. MUST MAINTAIN ADEQUATE MEDICAL RECORDS OF PATIENT OFFICE VISITS TO INCLUDE CERTAIN INFORMATION, ADEQUATELY ASCERTAIN LEGAL-MEDICAL STATUS OF PATIENTS, I.E. WHETHER OR NOT PATIENT HAS GUARDIAN OR SIGNED POWER OF ATTORNEY PRIOR TO INITIATING CERTAIN THERAPY, ASCERTAIN LEGAL CAPACITY AND AUTHORITY OF THOSE PERSONS WHO SIGN INFORMED CONSENT ON BEHALF OF PATIENT, AND OBTAIN CONSULTATION FORM BOARD-APPROVED INTERNIST FOR CERTAIN PATIENTS.

VINSON, RUSSELL L II DO, LICENSE NUMBER 00F4637, OF FORT WORTH, TX, WAS DISCIPLINED BY TEXAS ON FEBRUARY 24, 1989.
DISCIPLINARY ACTION: RESTRICTION PLACED ON CONTROLLED SUBSTANCE LICENSE
NOTES: SHALL NOT PRESCRIBE CERTAIN AMPHETAMINE-LIKE DRUGS, ANORECTIC AGENTS OR GENERIC EQUIVALENTS; SHALL NOT TREAT PATIENTS FOR WEIGHT CONTROL OR OBESITY WITH CONTROLLED SUBSTANCES OR OVER THE COUNTER DRUGS; SHALL MAINTAIN PROPER RECORDS OF CONTROLLED SUBSTANCES

VINSON, RUSSELL L DO, LICENSE NUMBER 00C4586, OF FORT WORTH, TX, WAS DISCIPLINED BY TEXAS ON APRIL 14, 1989.
DISCIPLINARY ACTION: RESTRICTION PLACED ON CONTROLLED SUBSTANCE LICENSE
NOTES: SHALL NOT PRESCRIBE, DISPENSE, ADMINISTER OR POSSESS CERTAIN AMPHETAMINE-LIKE DRUGS, ANORECTIC AGENTS OR GENERIC EQUIVALENTS; SHALL NOT TREAT PATIENTS FOR WEIGHT CONTROL OR OBESITY WITH CONTROLLED SUBSTANCES OR OVER THE COUNTER DRUGS; SHALL MAINTAIN PROPER RECORDS OF CONTROLLED SUBSTANCES

VIOLA, CARLOS A MD, LICENSE NUMBER 00E5273, OF SAN JUAN, ARGENTINA, WAS DISCIPLINED BY TEXAS ON OCTOBER 1, 1987.
DISCIPLINARY ACTION: LICENSE REVOCATION
OFFENSE: SUBSTANDARD CARE, INCOMPETENCE, OR NEGLIGENCE
NOTES: FAILED TO PRACTICE MEDICINE IN ACCEPTABLE MANNER CONSISTENT WITH PUBLIC HEALTH AND WELFARE.

VU, THONG T MD OF MCKINNEY, TX, WAS DISCIPLINED BY MISSOURI ON AUGUST 25, 1989.
DISCIPLINARY ACTION: 24-MONTH PROBATION
OFFENSE: DISCIPLINARY ACTION BY ANOTHER STATE OR AGENCY
NOTES: PROBATION TO BEGIN UPON RETURN TO MISSOURI.

VU, THONG TIEN MD, LICENSE NUMBER 00F3654, OF N. TEXAS MED CENTER, MCKINNEY, TX, WAS DISCIPLINED BY TEXAS ON AUGUST 1, 1988.
DISCIPLINARY ACTION: RESTRICTION PLACED ON LICENSE; REQUIRED TO TAKE ADDITIONAL MEDICAL EDUCATION
NOTES: SHALL OBTAIN 50 CONTINUING MEDICAL EDUCATION HOURS PER YEAR; PRACTICE THE SAME AS SCOPE OF PRIVILEGES AT NORTH TEXAS MEDICAL CENTER IN MCKINNEY; OBTAIN SEMI-ANNUAL PROGRESS REPORT BY HOSPITAL CHIEFS OF OB/GYN; APPEAR ANNUALLY BEFORE THE BOARD; AND OBTAIN CURRENCY IN ADVANCED CARDIAC LIFE SUPPORT

VU, THONG TIEN MD WAS DISCIPLINED BY NEBRASKA ON AUGUST 25, 1989.
DISCIPLINARY ACTION: PROBATION
OFFENSE: DISCIPLINARY ACTION BY ANOTHER STATE OR AGENCY
NOTES: DISHONORABLE CONDUCT (UNFITNESS); UNPROFESSIONAL CONDUCT

WAKEFIELD, CORNELIUS III MD, LICENSE NUMBER 00G1799, OF EL PASO, TX, WAS DISCIPLINED BY TEXAS ON JANUARY 28, 1989.
DISCIPLINARY ACTION: 24-MONTH REQUIRED TO ENTER AN IMPAIRED PHYSICIAN PROGRAM OR DRUG OR ALCOHOL TREATMENT; 24-MONTH MONITORING OF PHYSICIAN
OFFENSE: DRUG OR ALCOHOL ABUSE
NOTES: SHALL ABSTAIN FROM ALCOHOL AND OTHER MOOD-ALTERING DRUGS UNLESS PRESCRIBED FOR VALID MEDICAL PURPOSE BY ANOTHER PHYSICIAN; SHALL NOT PRESCRIBE FOR HIMSELF; SHALL PARTICIPATE IN AA PROGRAMS; SHALL AUTHORIZE REPORTING TO BOARD OF RESULTS OF ANALYSES WHICH REVEAL PRESENCE OF ALCOHOL OR MOOD ALTERING DRUGS; SHALL AUTHORIZE DESIGNATED PHYSICIAN TO REPORT PROGRESS;

WALDEN, ARCHIE DON MD, DATE OF BIRTH NOVEMBER 23, 1933, LICENSE NUMBER 0016414, OF 546 GENERAL DISPENSARY, UNIT 29920 BOX 17 APO AE, WAS DISCIPLINED BY MINNESOTA ON NOVEMBER 14, 1992.
DISCIPLINARY ACTION: FINE; REPRIMAND
OFFENSE: SEXUAL ABUSE OF OR SEXUAL MISCONDUCT WITH A PATIENT
NOTES: IMPROPER MANAGEMENT OF MEDICAL RECORDS; PRESCRIBING A DRUG OR DEVICE FOR OTHER THAN MEDICALLY ACCEPTED THERAPEUTIC PURPOSES; ENGAGING IN CONDUCT WITH A PATIENT WHICH IS SEXUAL OR MAY REASONABLY BE INTERPRETED BY THE PATIENT AS SEXUAL. SHALL PAY A CIVIL PENALTY OF $5,000.

WALDEN, ARCHIE DON MD, LICENSE NUMBER 00C7814, OF PEACHTREE CITY, GA, WAS DISCIPLINED BY TEXAS ON MARCH 5, 1994.
DISCIPLINARY ACTION: REPRIMAND
OFFENSE: DISCIPLINARY ACTION BY ANOTHER STATE OR AGENCY
NOTES: ON 10/21/92 THE MINNESOTA BOARD SANCTIONED HIM FOR NUMEROUS CASES OF PATIENT TREATMENT IN WHICH LACK OF DOCUMENTATION OF MEDICATIONS, VITAL SIGNS, WEIGHTS, AND LABORATORY VALUES PROVIDED INADEQUATE INFORMATION FOR FOLLOW-UP CARE AND MEDICAL MANAGEMENT OF PATIENTS WHICH RESULTED IN FRAGMENTED MEDICAL CARE. SHALL NOT

PRACTICE MEDICINE IN TEXAS BEFORE APPEARING BEFORE BOARD AND PROVIDING INFORMATION THAT SHOWS HE IS ABLE TO SAFELY PRACTICE MEDICINE; BOARD MAY IMPOSE ADDITIONAL RESTRICTIONS AT THAT TIME.

WALL, HAROLD JAMES MD, LICENSE NUMBER 0013803, OF PO BOX 189, BERTRAM, TX, WAS DISCIPLINED BY GEORGIA ON FEBRUARY 5, 1986.
DISCIPLINARY ACTION: SURRENDER OF LICENSE
OFFENSE: DISCIPLINARY ACTION BY ANOTHER STATE OR AGENCY
NOTES: ACTION IN FLORIDA. LICENSE PLACED ON INACTIVE STATUS. MAY NOT APPLY TO REACTIVATE WITHOUT BOARD APPROVAL.

WALLACE, C B MD, LICENSE NUMBER 00F3656, WAS DISCIPLINED BY TEXAS ON OCTOBER 5, 1991.
NOTES: ALL RESTRICTIONS PLACED ON LICENSE 6/8/85 ARE TERMINATED.

WALLACE, ROBERT D MD WAS DISCIPLINED BY UTAH ON FEBRUARY 21, 1984.
DISCIPLINARY ACTION: 12-MONTH PROBATION
NOTES: DRUG RELATED; UNPROFESSIONAL CONDUCT; ALSO KNOWN AS R. DUNCAN WALLACE

WALLACE, ROBERT D MD HAD AN ACTION TAKEN BY UTAH ON FEBRUARY 20, 1985.
NOTES: PROBATION COMPLETED. ALSO KNOWN AS R. DUNCAN WALLACE

WALLACE, ROBERT D MD OF SALT LAKE CITY, UT, WAS DISCIPLINED BY TEXAS ON SEPTEMBER 1, 1985.
OFFENSE: DISCIPLINARY ACTION BY ANOTHER STATE OR AGENCY
NOTES: MUST OBTAIN PRIOR BOARD APPROVAL IF HE WISHES TO RETURN TO TEXAS TO PRACTICE

WALLACE, ROBERT D MD, LICENSE NUMBER 0C29427, OF SALT LAKE CITY, UT, WAS DISCIPLINED BY CALIFORNIA ON JANUARY 8, 1988.
DISCIPLINARY ACTION: 60-MONTH PROBATION
OFFENSE: DISCIPLINARY ACTION BY ANOTHER STATE OR AGENCY
NOTES: REVOCATION STAYED; DISCIPLINED BY UTAH AND TEXAS

WALTERS, RONALD S DR OF 1411 NEW TREE LANE, MISSOURI CITY, TX, WAS DISCIPLINED BY ILLINOIS ON FEBRUARY 1, 1989.
DISCIPLINARY ACTION: LICENSE SUSPENSION
OFFENSE: DISCIPLINARY ACTION BY ANOTHER STATE OR AGENCY
NOTES: ENTERED INTO AGREEMENT WITH TEXAS BOARD FOR PRESCRIBING NONTHERAPUTIC DRUG

WARREN, BRUCE HUNTINGTON MD, LICENSE NUMBER 00D9316, OF SAN ANTONIO, TX, WAS DISCIPLINED BY TEXAS ON OCTOBER 1, 1993.
DISCIPLINARY ACTION: 60-MONTH PROBATION; REQUIRED TO TAKE ADDITIONAL MEDICAL EDUCATION
OFFENSE: SEXUAL ABUSE OF OR SEXUAL MISCONDUCT WITH A PATIENT
NOTES: VIOLATED THE BOUNDARIES OF THE DOCTOR-PATIENT RELATIONSHIP WITH ONE PATIENT WITH WHOM HE ENGAGED IN A PERSONAL RELATIONSHIP FROM 3/85 THROUGH 10/86 WHILE HE PROVIDED PSYCHIATRIC TREATMENT TO HER; GAVE HER MONEY ON SEVERAL OCCASIONS AND A GIFT ON AT LEAST ONE OCCASION; TOOK HER OUT TO LUNCH AND DINNER; THE PATIENT ALLEGES THEY HAD SEX ON AT LEAST TWO OCCASIONS WHICH HE DENIES. SUSPENSION STAYED. CONDITIONS OF PROBATION: SHALL ENROLL IN AND COMPLETE ONE BOARD-APPROVED ETHICS COURSE REGARDING SEXUAL ABUSE; SHALL SUBMIT HIMSELF FOR EVALUATION TO A BOARD-APPROVED PSYCHIATRIST AND WILL FOLLOW TREATMENT RECOMMENDATIONS WITH REPORTS TO THE BOARD; SHALL APPEAR BEFORE THE BOARD ONCE A YEAR; SHALL COOPERATE WITH THE BOARD IN VERIFYING COMPLIANCE; SHALL INFORM BOARD OF CHANGE OF ADDRESS WITHIN 10 DAYS OR IF HE LEAVES THE STATE; TIME SPENT OUT OF TEXAS DOES NOT COUNT TOWARD PROBATION. SHALL NOT SEEK MODIFICATION FOR ONE YEAR.

WARREN, BRUCE HUNTINGTON MD OF 2914 WAR FEATHER DRIVE, SAN ANTONIO, TX, WAS DISCIPLINED BY DEA ON MARCH 1, 1994.
DISCIPLINARY ACTION: SURRENDER OF CONTROLLED SUBSTANCE LICENSE

WATSON, JAMES R DO, DATE OF BIRTH JULY 6, 1944, LICENSE NUMBER 0001405, OF 1032 SOUTH W W WHITE, SAN ANTONIO, TX, WAS DISCIPLINED BY IOWA ON DECEMBER 23, 1991.
DISCIPLINARY ACTION: PROBATION; FINE
OFFENSE: SEXUAL ABUSE OF OR SEXUAL MISCONDUCT WITH A PATIENT
NOTES: ACTION BASED ON ALLEGATIONS OF IMPROPER SEXUAL CONTACT WITH PATIENTS. $5,000 CIVIL PENALTY ASSESSED; INDEFINITE PROBATION.

WAYNE, BRYAN MATTHEW MD, LICENSE NUMBER 00G8492, OF HOUSTON, TX, WAS DISCIPLINED BY TEXAS ON MAY 26, 1994.
DISCIPLINARY ACTION: EMERGENCY SUSPENSION
OFFENSE: PROFESSIONAL MISCONDUCT
NOTES: AVAILABLE EVIDENCE AND INFORMATION INDICATE THE FOLLOWING: ON 3/11/94 DISCHARGED A WEAPON INTO HIS NEIGHBOR'S RESIDENCE AND DISCHARGED A SHOTGUN SEVERAL TIMES INTO THE AIR; THEN BARRICADED HIMSELF IN HIS RESIDENCE WHERE HE GAVE HIMSELF UP TO A SWAT TEAM THREE HOURS LATER; CHARGED WITH AGGRAVATED ASSAULT WITH A DEADLY WEAPON; HAS NOT PRACTICED MEDICINE SINCE 3/93 WHEN HE WAS DISCHARGED FROM HIS JOB; BOARD STAFF REQUESTED HIM TO SUBMIT TO A COMPLETE PSYCHIATRIC EXAM BY MAIL; HAS NOT RECEIVED A REPLY AND LETTER RETURNED TO BOARD MARKED UNCLAIMED.

WAYNE, BRYAN MATTHEW MD, LICENSE NUMBER 00G8492, OF HOUSTON, TX, WAS DISCIPLINED BY TEXAS ON AUGUST 19, 1994.
DISCIPLINARY ACTION: LICENSE SUSPENSION
OFFENSE: PROFESSIONAL MISCONDUCT
NOTES: ON 3/11/94 HE WAS INVOLVED IN A DISTURBANCE WHICH RESULTED IN POLICE INTERVENTION; POLICE REPORT HE DISCHARGED A HAND HELD WEAPON INTO A NEIGHBORING BUSINESS AND DISCHARGED A SHOTGUN INTO THE AIR FOR UNKNOWN REASONS; THEY ALSO REPORT HE BARRICADED HIMSELF INSIDE HIS RESIDENCE FOR THREE HOURS UNTIL HE GAVE HIMSELF UP; WAS CHARGED WITH AGGRAVATED ASSAULT WITH A DEADLY WEAPON; HE STATES HE HAD PREVIOUS PROBLEMS WITH THE NEIGHBORING BUSINESS REGARDING DISRUPTIVE BEHAVIOR AND THAT HE TOLD THEM TWICE TO BE QUIET; THEN HE FIRED A BB PELLET GUN IN THEIR DIRECTION, WENT TO SLEEP AND AWOKE TO FIND A MESSAGE FROM THE POLICE ON HIS ANSWERING MACHINE; HE THEN

TALKED TO THE POLICE AND AT THEIR REQUEST WENT OUTSIDE HIS RESIDENCE WHERE HE WAS ARRESTED; DENIES HE USED THE SHOTGUN OR THAT HE WAS BARRICADED; TRIAL DATE HAS BEEN POSTPONED. SUSPENSION UNTIL SUCH TIME AS HE PERSONALLY APPEARS BEFORE THE BOARD AND PROVIDES SUFFICIENT EVIDENCE THAT HE IS PHYSICALLY, MENTALLY AND OTHERWISE COMPETENT TO SAFELY PRACTICE MEDICINE.

WAYNE, BRYAN MATTHEW MD, LICENSE NUMBER 00G8492, OF HOUSTON, TX, WAS DISCIPLINED BY TEXAS ON OCTOBER 10, 1994.
DISCIPLINARY ACTION: 60-MONTH PROBATION; MONITORING OF PHYSICIAN
NOTES: HE HAS SATISFIED THE MINIMUM REQUIREMENTS OF 8/19/94 ORDER SUSPENDING HIS LICENSE. THAT SUSPENSION NOW STAYED. CONDITIONS OF PROBATION: SHALL CONTINUE PSYCHIATRIC TREATMENT WITH QUARTERLY REPORTS; SHALL ABSTAIN FROM THE CONSUMPTION OF ALCOHOL/CHEMICAL SUBSTANCES IN ANY FORM UNLESS PRESCRIBED BY ANOTHER PHYSICIAN FOR A LEGITIMATE AND THERAPEUTIC PURPOSE; SHALL SUBMIT HIMSELF FOR APPROPRIATE EXAMS INCLUDING DRUG OR ALCOHOL SCREENS; SHALL APPEAR BEFORE THE BOARD ONCE A YEAR; SHALL GIVE A COPY OF THIS ORDER TO ANY HEALTH CARE ENTITY WHERE HE HAS PRIVILEGES; SHALL COOPERATE WITH THE BOARD IN VERIFYING COMPLIANCE; SHALL INFORM BOARD OF CHANGE OF ADDRESS WITHIN 10 DAYS OR IF HE LEAVES THE STATE; TIME SPENT OUT OF TEXAS DOES NOT COUNT TOWARD PROBATION. SHALL NOT SEEK MODIFICATION FOR ONE YEAR.

WAYNE, BRYAN MATTHEW MD, LICENSE NUMBER 00G8492, OF HOUSTON, TX, WAS DISCIPLINED BY TEXAS ON DECEMBER 20, 1994.
DISCIPLINARY ACTION: EMERGENCY SUSPENSION
NOTES: EVIDENCE AND INFORMATION INDICATING THAT HE POSES A CONTINUING THREAT TO THE HEALTH AND WELFARE OF PATIENTS.

WEEKS, BOB LEE DO OF OKLAHOMA CITY, OK, WAS DISCIPLINED BY TEXAS ON DECEMBER 1, 1986.
DISCIPLINARY ACTION: PROBATION
OFFENSE: DISCIPLINARY ACTION BY ANOTHER STATE OR AGENCY
NOTES: FIVE-YEAR SUSPENSION STAYED

WEEKS, BOB LEE DO, LICENSE NUMBER 00F7290, OF QUINTON, OK, WAS DISCIPLINED BY TEXAS ON DECEMBER 1, 1988.
OFFENSE: DISCIPLINARY ACTION BY ANOTHER STATE OR AGENCY
NOTES: DISCIPLINARY ACTION TAKEN AGAINST HIM BY OKLAHOMA BOARD. TEXAS ORDER MODIFIED TO REFLECT STIPULATIONS ATTACHED TO PROBATION TERMINATION ORDER BY OKLAHOMA BOARD.

WEHMER, RALPH E JR MD, DATE OF BIRTH JULY 29, 1948, OF 1007 WATER ST APT 102, BASTROP, TX, WAS DISCIPLINED BY MEDICARE ON AUGUST 10, 1990.
DISCIPLINARY ACTION: 60-MONTH EXCLUSION FROM THE MEDICARE AND/OR MEDICAID PROGRAMS
OFFENSE: CRIMINAL CONVICTION OR PLEA OF GUILTY, NOLO CONTENDERE, OR NO CONTEST TO A CRIME
NOTES: PROGRAM-RELATED CONVICTION.

WEHMER, RALPH EDWARD JR MD, LICENSE NUMBER 00G3899, OF BASTROP, TX, WAS DISCIPLINED BY TEXAS ON JUNE 10, 1991.
DISCIPLINARY ACTION: 36-MONTH PROBATION
OFFENSE: PROFESSIONAL MISCONDUCT
NOTES: UNPROFESSIONAL OR DISHONORABLE CONDUCT LIKELY TO DECEIVE, DEFRAUD, OR INJURE THE PUBLIC. TERMS OF PROBATION: MUST APPEAR ONCE A YEAR BEFORE THE BOARD; MUST MAINTAIN ADEQUATE RECORDS ON ALL PATIENT OFFICE VISITS; MUST REFRAIN FROM NONTHERAPEUTIC PRESCRIBING; MUST CONDUCT ADEQUATE FOLLOW-UP EXAMS ON ALL PATIENTS TO DETERMINE WHETHER THE COURSE OF TREATMENT IS APPROPRIATE. ON 1/14/94 ORDER AMENDED TO INCLUDE ADDITION OF THE FOLLOWING: BEFORE THE DATE OF EXPIRATION OF THIS ORDER, HE MUST OBTAIN AT LEAST 50 HOURS OF CONTINUING MEDICAL EDUCATION IN THE AREAS OF EMERGENCY ROOM MEDICINE, DOCUMENTATION, CENTRAL INTRAVENOUS ACCESS, ADVANCED CARDIAC LIFE SUPPORT, AND ADVANCED TRAUMA LIFE SUPPORT AND SHALL SUBMIT PROOF OF SUCCESSFUL COMPLETION OF EACH COURSE.

WEISS, STEPHEN JOEL MD, LICENSE NUMBER 00E5985, OF HOUSTON, TX, WAS DISCIPLINED BY TEXAS ON JUNE 22, 1994.
DISCIPLINARY ACTION: 60-MONTH PROBATION; REQUIRED TO TAKE ADDITIONAL MEDICAL EDUCATION
OFFENSE: PROFESSIONAL MISCONDUCT
NOTES: ON NUMEROUS PATIENTS BETWEEN 11/88 AND 9/92 HE: FAILED TO ACCURATELY INTERPRET AND RECORD DIAGNOSTIC FINDINGS; FAILED TO FORMULATE OR DOCUMENT APPROPRIATE TREATMENT PLANS OR CLINICAL RATIONALE FOR SUBSEQUENT TESTING; RECOMMENDED SURGICAL INTERVENTION EVEN THOUGH PATIENTS WERE POOR CANDIDATES; ORDERED UNNECESSARY REFERRALS; ORDERED PHYSICAL THERAPY FOR PERIODS OF MORE THAN A YEAR; CONSIDERED CHEMONUCLEOLYSIS AND PERFORMED MULTIPLE IMAGING STUDIES IN SPITE OF THE ABSENCE OF SUFFICIENT OBJECTIVE PHYSICAL FINDINGS, REPRODUCIBLE RADICULOPATHY AND PREVIOUS NEGATIVE TEST RESULTS; ASSESSED CONFLICTING IMPAIRMENT RATINGS; THESE ACTIONS CONSTITUTED FLAGRANT OVERCHARGING AND OVERTREATING PATIENTS. SUSPENSION STAYED. CONDITIONS OF PROBATION: SHALL OBTAIN A WRITTEN SECOND OPINION ON EACH PATIENT FOR WHOM HE PRESCRIBES PHYSICAL THERAPY BEYOND SIX WEEKS FOR A 12-MONTH PERIOD; ALL DISCOGRAMS HE ORDERS SHALL BE PERFORMED AND READ BY A RADIOLOGIST; SHALL ATTEND AT LEAST 50 HOURS PER YEAR OF CONTINUING MEDICAL EDUCATION ONE-HALF OF WHICH SHALL BE IN THE AREA OF PAIN MANAGEMENT; SHALL MAINTAIN ADEQUATE MEDICAL RECORDS ON ALL PATIENT OFFICE VISITS WHICH SHALL BE AVAILABLE FOR INSPECTION; SHALL NOT SIGN ANY PATIENT RECORD UNLESS HE HAS PERSONALLY EXAMINED THE PATIENT OR CLEARLY NOTES IN THE RECORD THAT HE DID NOT; SHALL GIVE A COPY OF THIS ORDER TO ANY HEALTH CARE ENTITY WHERE HE HAS PRIVILEGES; SHALL COOPERATE WITH THE BOARD IN VERIFYING COMPLIANCE; SHALL INFORM BOARD OF CHANGE OF ADDRESS WITHIN 10 DAYS OR IF HE LEAVES THE STATE; TIME SPENT OUT OF TEXAS DOES NOT COUNT TOWARD PROBTION. SHALL NOT SEEK MODIFICATION FOR ONE YEAR.

WERNER, MARK ALLEN MD, LICENSE NUMBER 00E6682, OF

WEBSTER, TX, WAS DISCIPLINED BY TEXAS ON JUNE 10, 1991.
DISCIPLINARY ACTION: SURRENDER OF CONTROLLED SUBSTANCE LICENSE
OFFENSE: DISCIPLINARY ACTION BY ANOTHER STATE OR AGENCY
NOTES: DISCIPLINARY ACTION TAKEN BY ANOTHER STATE DUE TO INTEMPERATE USE OF ALCOHOL OR DRUGS, AND UNPROFESSIONAL OR DISHONORABLE CONDUCT LIKELY TO DECEIVE, DEFRAUD, OR INJURE THE PUBLIC. MUST COMPLY WITH TERMS OF NEW MEXICO'S BOARD ORDER. ADDITIONAL TERMS AND CONDITIONS AS FOLLOWS: MUST REFRAIN FROM THE USE OF AND SHALL NOT POSSESS, ADMINISTER, OR PRESCRIBE ANY CONTROLLED SUBSTANCES OR ANY OTHER PRESCRIPTION MEDICATION UNLESS PRESCRIBED BY ANOTHER PHYSICIAN FOR A LEGITIMATE MEDICAL NEED; PRIOR TO PRACTICING IN TEXAS, SHALL RECEIVE BOARD APPROVAL; MUST SURRENDER ALL UNUSED TRIPLICATE PRESCRIPTION FORMS; SHALL NOT ATTEMPT TO RDER MORE TRIPLICATE PRESCRIPTION FORMS UNTIL WRITTEN PERMISSION IS GRANTED; MUST SURRENDER DPS CONTROLLED SUBSTANCE REGISTRATION CERTIFICATE AND CANCEL DPS REGISTRATION; MUST NOT ATTEMPT TO REREGISTER CONTROLLED SUBSTANCES LICENSES WITHOUT PRIOR WRITTEN AUTHORITY FROM THE BOARD.

WESELY, OREST MD, LICENSE NUMBER 0110186, OF STOCKTON, CA, WAS DISCIPLINED BY NEW YORK ON MARCH 19, 1985.
DISCIPLINARY ACTION: 24-MONTH PROBATION
NOTES: 1 YEAR SUSPENSION, STAYED

WESELY, OREST MD OF STOCKTON, CA, WAS DISCIPLINED BY TEXAS ON DECEMBER 1, 1986.
DISCIPLINARY ACTION: SURRENDER OF LICENSE

WESELY, OREST MD OF 2740 RANIER AVENUE, STOCKTON, CA, WAS DISCIPLINED BY VIRGINIA ON AUGUST 19, 1988.
DISCIPLINARY ACTION: LICENSE REVOCATION
OFFENSE: DISCIPLINARY ACTION BY ANOTHER STATE OR AGENCY

WEST, PATRICIA BEATY MD, LICENSE NUMBER 00C8019, OF VERNON, TX, WAS DISCIPLINED BY TEXAS ON AUGUST 24, 1991.
DISCIPLINARY ACTION: 6-MONTH LICENSE SUSPENSION
OFFENSE: DRUG OR ALCOHOL ABUSE
NOTES: INTEMPERATE USE OF ALCOHOL OR DRUGS AND INABILITY TO PRACTICE MEDICINE WITH REASONABLE SKILL AND SAFETY TO PATIENTS BY REASON OF ILLNESS AND DRUNKENNESS.

WESTBROOK, MARK DENTON MD, LICENSE NUMBER 00G3902, OF HOUSTON, TX, WAS DISCIPLINED BY TEXAS ON NOVEMBER 19, 1993.
DISCIPLINARY ACTION: 60-MONTH MONITORING OF PHYSICIAN
OFFENSE: DRUG OR ALCOHOL ABUSE
NOTES: HAS SUFFERED FROM ALCOHOLISM AND ABUSE OF HISTUSSIN IN RESPONSE TO HIS WIFE'S DIVING ACCIDENT FOLLOWED SHORTLY BY HIS MOTHER'S DEATH; HAS BEGUN ATTENDANCE AT AA AND HAS SOUGHT INDIVIDUAL AND GROUP PSYCHIATRIC TREATMENT ON HIS OWN INITIATIVE. LICENSE RESTRICTED UNDER THE FOLLOWING CONDITIONS: SHALL ABSTAIN FROM THE CONSUMPTION OF ALCOHOL/CHEMICAL SUBSTANCES IN ANY FORM UNLESS PRESCRIBED BY ANOTHER PHYSICIAN FOR A LEGITIMATE AND THERAPEUTIC PURPOSE; SHALL NOT TREAT OR OTHERWISE SERVE AS PHYSICIAN, PRESCRIBE, DISPENSE OR ADMINSTER DRUGS THAT MAY BE SUBJECT TO ABUSE TO HIMSELF OR ANY MEMBER OF HIS FAMILY; SHALL CONTINUE TO PARTICIPATE IN AA'S PROGRAM NOT LESS THAN THREE TIMES A WEEK WITH QUARTERLY REPORTS TO THE BOARD; SHALL CONTINUE TO PARTICIPATE IN INDIVIDUAL THERAPY AND THE SUNRISE PROGRAM WITH REPORTS TO THE BOARD; SHALL SUBMIT HIMSELF FOR APPROPRIATE EXAMS INCLUDING DRUG OR ALCOHOL SCREENS; SHALL COOPERATE WITH THE BOARD IN VERIFYING COMPLIANCE; SEPARATE FROM PATIENT RECORDS HE SHALL MAINTAIN A FILE OF EVERY PRESCRIPTION WRITTEN FOR DANGEROUS DRUGS WHICH SHALL BE AVAILABLE FOR INSPECTION; SHALL APPEAR BEFORE THE BOARD TWICE A YEAR; SHALL GIVE A COPY OF THIS ORDER TO ANY HEALTH CARE ENTITY WHERE HE HAS PRIVILEGES; SHALL INFORM BOARD OF CHANGE OF ADDRESS WITHIN 10 DAYS OR IF HE LEAVES THE STATE; TIME SPENT OUT OF TEXAS DOES NOT COUNT TOWARD RESTRICTION. SHALL NOT SEEK MODIFICATION FOR ONE YEAR.

WESTBROOK, MARK DENTON MD, LICENSE NUMBER 00G3902, OF HOUSTON, TX, WAS DISCIPLINED BY TEXAS ON AUGUST 19, 1994.
DISCIPLINARY ACTION: 120-MONTH PROBATION; RESTRICTION PLACED ON CONTROLLED SUBSTANCE LICENSE
OFFENSE: FAILURE TO COMPLY WITH A PREVIOUS BOARD ORDER
NOTES: ENTERED AN AGREED ORDER ON 11/19/93; BETWEEN 12/14/93 AND 1/19/94 HE SUFFERED A RELAPSE AND INGESTED ALCOHOL; SELF-REPORTED HIS RELAPSE ON 1/20/94; SINCE THEN HAS RECEIVED TREATMENT, IS IN INDIVIDUAL AND GROUP THERAPY AND IS UNDER THE CARE OF A PSYCHIATRIST. SUSPENSION STAYED. CONDITIONS OF PROBATION: SHALL ABSTAIN FROM THE CONSUMPTION OF ALCOHOL/CHEMICAL SUBSTANCES IN ANY FORM UNLESS PRESCRIBED BY ANOTHER PHYSICIAN FOR A LEGITIMATE AND THERAPEUTIC PURPOSE; SHALL NOT POSSESS SAMPLES OF DANGEROUS DRUGS WHICH HAVE POTENTIAL FOR ABUSE; SHALL SURRENDER ALL UNUSED TRIPLICATE PRESCRIPTION FORMS; SHALL NOT POSSESS, ADMINISTER DISPENSE OR PRESCRIBE ANY CONTROLLED SUBSTANCES BUT MAY ORDER THEM TO BE ADMINISTERED TO HOSPITAL OR NURSING HOME PATIENTS; SHALL NOT TREAT OR OTHERWISE SERVE AS PHYSICIAN, PRESCRIBE, DISPENSE OR ADMINISTER DRUGS THAT MAY BE SUBJECT TO ABUSE TO HIMSELF OR ANY MEMBER OF HIS FAMILY; SHALL CONTINUE TO PARTICIPATE IN AA'S PROGRAM NOT LESS THAN THREE TIMES A WEEK WITH QUARTERLY REPORTS TO THE BOARD; SHALL SUBMIT HIMSELF FOR APPROPRIATE EXAMS INCLUDING DRUG OR ALCOHOL SCREENS; SEPARATE FROM PATIENT RECORDS SHALL MAINTAIN A FILE CONSISTING OF EVERY PRESCRIPTION WRITTEN FOR DANGEROUS DRUGS WITH A POTENTIAL FOR ABUSE WHICH SHALL BE AVAILABLE FOR INSPECTION; SHALL NOT TELEPHONE ANY PRESCRIPTION TO A PHARMACY FOR DANGEROUS DRUGS; SHALL APPEAR BEFORE THE BOARD TWICE A YEAR; SHALL CONTINUE TO RECEIVE PSYCHIATRIC TREATMENT WITH QUARTERLY REPORTS; SHALL GIVE A COPY OF THIS ORDER TO ANY HEALTH CARE ENTITY WHERE HE HAS PRIVILEGES; SHALL COOPERATE WITH THE BOARD IN VERIFYING COMPLIANCE; SHALL INFORM BOARD OF CHANGE OF ADDRESS WITHIN 10 DAYS OR IF HE LEAVES THE STATE; TIME SPENT OUT OF TEXAS DOES NOT COUNT TOWARD PROBATION. SHALL NOT

SEEK MODIFICATION FOR ONE YEAR. ORDER TAKES THE PLACE OF THE ORDER OF 11/19/93.

WHITCOMB, DONALD D MD, LICENSE NUMBER 00C7510, OF GRAND PRAIRIE, TX, WAS DISCIPLINED BY TEXAS ON JULY 28, 1989.
DISCIPLINARY ACTION: 36-MONTH RESTRICTION PLACED ON LICENSE; 36-MONTH REQUIRED TO TAKE ADDITIONAL MEDICAL EDUCATION
NOTES: CEASE TREATING CERTAIN PATIENTS EXCEPT IN LIFE-THREATENING EMERGENCIES.

WHITCOMB, DONALD DALE MD OF 1005 S W THIRD PO BOX 451, GRAND PRAIRIE, TX, WAS DISCIPLINED BY DEA ON MAY 31, 1990.
DISCIPLINARY ACTION: SURRENDER OF CONTROLLED SUBSTANCE LICENSE

WHITE, JAMES HARRISON \ MD, LICENSE NUMBER 00D4357, OF CORONA DEL MAR, CA, WAS DISCIPLINED BY TEXAS ON NOVEMBER 13, 1992.
DISCIPLINARY ACTION: LICENSE REVOCATION
OFFENSE: CRIMINAL CONVICTION OR PLEA OF GUILTY, NOLO CONTENDERE, OR NO CONTEST TO A CRIME
NOTES: CONVICTION OF FELONY INVOLVING MORAL TURPITUDE.

WHITE, ROLAND L MD, LICENSE NUMBER 00B8191, OF 8535 FERNDALE #7, DALLAS, TX, WAS DISCIPLINED BY DEA ON FEBRUARY 2, 1990.
DISCIPLINARY ACTION: SURRENDER OF CONTROLLED SUBSTANCE LICENSE

WHITMAN, PAUL F MD, LICENSE NUMBER 0059522, OF 1000 N COCKRELL HILL ROAD, DESOTO, TX, WAS DISCIPLINED BY DEA ON AUGUST 10, 1993.
DISCIPLINARY ACTION: SURRENDER OF CONTROLLED SUBSTANCE LICENSE
OFFENSE: DRUG OR ALCOHOL ABUSE
NOTES: ADMITTED SELF ABUSE OF FENTANYL FROM HOSPITAL PHARMACY STOCKS.

WHITMAN, PAUL F JR MD, LICENSE NUMBER 00G8506, OF DESOTO, TX, WAS DISCIPLINED BY TEXAS ON JANUARY 14, 1994.
DISCIPLINARY ACTION: 60-MONTH PROBATION; RESTRICTION PLACED ON LICENSE
OFFENSE: DRUG OR ALCOHOL ABUSE
NOTES: PRIOR TO 7/7/93 ON NUMEROUS OCCASIONS DIVERTED FENTANYL FROM THE OPERATING ROOM WHERE HE SERVED AS AN ANESTHESIOLOGIST WHICH HE ADMINISTERED TO HIMSELF; AFTER INTERVENTION BY A HOSPITAL PHARMACIST HE VOLUNTARILY SURRENDERED HIS CONTROLLED SUBSTANCES CERTIFICATES; COMPLETED TREATMENT ON 11/6/93. SUSPENSION STAYED. CONDITIONS OF PROBATION: SHALL ABSTAIN FROM THE CONSUMPTION OF ALCOHOL/CHEMICAL SUBSTANCES IN ANY FORM UNLESS PRESCRIBED BY ANOTHER PHYSICIAN FOR A LEGITIMATE AND THERAPEUTIC PURPOSE; SHALL SUBMIT HIMSELF FOR APPROPRIATE EXAMS INCLUDING DRUG OR ALCOHOL SCREENS; SHALL LIMIT PRACTICE SOLELY TO THE PRACTICE OF ANESTHESIOLOGY IN A HOSPITAL SETTING; SHALL NOT POSSESS, ADMINISTER, DISPENSE OR PRESCRIBE ANY DANGEROUS DRUGS EXCEPT AS MEDICALLY NECESSARY FOR TREATMENT OF INPATIENTS; SHALL BE UNDER THE OBSERVATION OF A PHYSICIAN OR NURSE WHILE ADMINISTERING OR SUPERVISING THE ADMINISTRATION OF ANESTHESIA; SHALL CONTINUE TO RECEIVE TREATMENT FROM PSYCHIATRIST WITH QUARTERLY REPORTS; SHALL PARTICIPATE IN ACTIVITIES OF A PHYSICIAN HEALTH AND REHABILITATION COMMITTEE AND ATTEND WEEKLY MEETINGS WITH QUARTERLY REPORTS; SHALL ATTEND AT LEAST 50 HOURS PER YEAR OF CONTINUING MEDICAL EDUCATION; SHALL GIVE A COPY OF THIS ORDER TO ANY HEALTH CARE ENTITY WHERE HE HAS PRIVILEGES; SHALL COOPERATE WITH THE BOARD IN VERIFYING COMPLIANCE; SHALL INFORM BOARD OF CHANGE OF ADDRESS WITHIN 10 DAYS OR IF HE LEAVES THE STATE; TIME SPENT OUT OF TEXAS DOES NOT COUNT TOWARD PROBATION; SHALL APPEAR BEFORE THE BOARD ONCE A YEAR. SHALL NOT SEEK MODIFICATION FOR ONE YEAR. ON 11/3/94 ORDER MODIFIED AS FOLLOWS; LIMITATION OF PRACTICE OF ANESTHESIOLOGY TO A HOSPITAL SETTING AND TO PRESCRIBING CONTROLLED SUBSTANCES ONLY IN THAT SETTING MODIFIED TO ALLOW HIM TO PRACTICE PAIN MANAGEMENT IN A GROUP SETTING AND TO PRESCRIBE IN THIS SETTING; REQUIREMENT THAT HE BE OBSERVED WHILE ADMINISTERING OR SUPERVISING THE ADMINISTRATION OF ANESTHESIA IS DROPPED; CONDITION ADDED THAT HE MAINTAIN A FILE OF PRESCRIPTIONS WRITTEN FOR CONTROLLED SUBSTANCES OR DANGEROUS DRUGS WHICH SHALL BE AVAILABLE FOR INSPECTION.

WHITNEY, RICHARD N MD, LICENSE NUMBER 00G1802, OF PLANO, TX, WAS DISCIPLINED BY TEXAS ON DECEMBER 3, 1990.
DISCIPLINARY ACTION: 60-MONTH PROBATION; REQUIRED TO ENTER AN IMPAIRED PHYSICIAN PROGRAM OR DRUG OR ALCOHOL TREATMENT
NOTES: MUST ATTEND AA MEETINGS ON A REGULAR BASIS; SUBMIT FOR APPROPRIATE EXAMINATIONS TO DETERMINE FREEDOM FROM DRUGS AND ALCOHOL; CONTINUE MONITORING BY SMITH COUNTY COMMITTEE FOR IMPAIRED PHYSICIANS; ABIDE BY CONTRACT WITH TALBOT RECOVERY SYSTEM; APPEAR BEFORE BOARD ONCE A YEAR.

WHITTAKER, JOHN NORMAN MD, LICENSE NUMBER 00F1305, OF DE SOTO, TX, WAS DISCIPLINED BY TEXAS ON JANUARY 24, 1992.
DISCIPLINARY ACTION: 24-MONTH RESTRICTION PLACED ON LICENSE; REPRIMAND
OFFENSE: PROFESSIONAL MISCONDUCT
NOTES: OVERTREATING OF PATIENTS.

WILCOX, LOUISE NELLIE MD, LICENSE NUMBER 00G1252, OF HOUSTON, TX, WAS DISCIPLINED BY TEXAS ON JUNE 17, 1992.
DISCIPLINARY ACTION: REPRIMAND
NOTES: INVOLVED IN THE CORPORATE PRACTICE OF MEDICINE.

WILKERSON, WILLIAM GEORGE MD, DATE OF BIRTH JANUARY 26, 1932, LICENSE NUMBER 00E0215, OF 1121 ELLIS AVENUE, LUFKIN, TX, WAS DISCIPLINED BY TEXAS ON MARCH 26, 1993.
DISCIPLINARY ACTION: SURRENDER OF LICENSE
NOTES: LICENSE PERMANENTLY SURRENDERED IN LIEU OF FURTHER DISCIPLINARY ACTION; DOCTOR RETIRED FROM PRACTICE.

WILLIAMS, ALFRED VAUGHN MD, DATE OF BIRTH NOVEMBER 14, 1940, LICENSE NUMBER 00D4361, OF 4402 VANCE JACKSON, SUITE 100, SAN ANTONIO, TX, WAS DISCIPLINED BY TEXAS ON MAY 24, 1990.
DISCIPLINARY ACTION: PROBATION; 60-MONTH MONITORING OF PHYSICIAN

NOTES: STIPULATED ORDER. MUST SUBMIT HIMSELF FOR PSYCHIATRIC EVALUATION AND FOLLOW ANY RECOMMENDATIONS REGARDING CARE, SUBMIT HIMSELF FOR APPROPRIATE EXAMINATIONS TO DETERMINE FREEDOM FROM DRUGS AND ALCOHOL, AND MAINTAIN SEPARATE FILE OF PRESCRIPTIONS WRITTEN FOR CONTROLLED SUBSTANCES. ON 8/20/93 BOARD MODIFIED ORDER GRANTING HIM PERMISSION TO REAPPLY TO THE DRUG ENFORCEMENT ADMINISTRATION AND TEXAS DEPARTMENT OF PUBLIC SAFETY FOR SCHEDULES II AND IIN CONTROLLED SUBSTANCES. SHOULD HE BE GRANTED THESE APPLICATIONS SCHEDULE II AND IIN ARE LIMITED TO HOSPITAL PATIENTS ONLY. ALL OTHER TERMS OF THIS ORDER REMAIN IN EFFECT.

WILLIAMS, ALFRED VAUGHN MD, LICENSE NUMBER 00D4365, OF 4402 VANCE JACKSON, SAN ANTONIO, TX, WAS DISCIPLINED BY DEA ON AUGUST 24, 1990.
DISCIPLINARY ACTION: RESTRICTION PLACED ON CONTROLLED SUBSTANCE LICENSE
OFFENSE: DRUG OR ALCOHOL ABUSE
NOTES: PERSONAL USE OF DILAUDID.

WILLIAMS, AUBREY DUDLEY DO, LICENSE NUMBER 00D0756, OF PARKVILLE, MO, WAS DISCIPLINED BY TEXAS ON JUNE 10, 1991.
DISCIPLINARY ACTION: SURRENDER OF LICENSE
OFFENSE: DISCIPLINARY ACTION BY ANOTHER STATE OR AGENCY
NOTES: DISCIPLINARY ACTION TAKEN BY ANOTHER STATE DUE TO UNPROFESSIONAL CONDUCT.

WILLIAMS, BARNEY KENNETH JR MD, LICENSE NUMBER 00C3911, WAS DISCIPLINED BY TEXAS ON AUGUST 20, 1993.
DISCIPLINARY ACTION: 60-MONTH PROBATION; REQUIRED TO TAKE ADDITIONAL MEDICAL EDUCATION
OFFENSE: LOSS OR RESTRICTION OF HOSPITAL PRIVILEGES
NOTES: IN 1991 ENTERED INTO AN AGREEMENT WITH SID PETERSON MEMORIAL HOSPITAL FOR MEDICAL STAFF PRIVILEGES WHICH REQUIRED HIM TO BE MONITORED AND SCREENED FOR ALCOHOL CONSUMPTION; IN 11/92 RELAPSED WHILE ALONE ON A FISHING TRIP; HOSPITAL SUSPENDED PRIVILEGES ON 11/25/92 AND HE WAS REINSTATED ON 12/30/92 WITH A TWO YEAR SCREENING AND MONITORING CONTRACT. FIVE YEAR SUSPENSION STAYED. CONDITIONS OF PROBATION: SHALL ATTEND AT LEAST 50 HOURS PER YEAR OF CONTINUING MEDICAL EDUCATION; SHALL ABSTAIN FROM THE CONSUMPTION OF ALCOHOL/CHEMICAL SUBSTANCES IN ANY FORM; SHALL PARTICIPATE IN ACTIVITIES OF A PHYSICIAN HEALTH AND REHABILITATION COMMITTEE AND ATTEND WEEKLY MEETINGS WITH QUARTERLY REPORTS; SHALL PARTICIPATE IN AA NOT LESS THAN THREE TIMES A WEEK WITH QUARTERLY REPORTS; SHALL SUBMIT HIMSELF FOR APPROPRIATE EXAMS INCLUDING DRUG OR ALCOHOL SCREENS; SHALL APPEAR BEFORE THE BOARD ONCE A YEAR; SHALL NOT TREAT OR OTHERWISE SERVE AS PHYSICIAN, PRESCRIBE, DISPENSE OR ADMINISTER DRUGS THAT MAY BE SUBJECT TO ABUSE FOR HIMSELF OR ANY MEMBER OF HIS FAMILY; SHALL ABIDE BY THE TERMS OF HIS TWO YEAR CONTRACT WITH SID PETERSON MEMORIAL HOSPITAL; SHALL COOPERATE WITH THE BOARD IN VERIFYING COMPLIANCE; SHALL INFORM BOARD OF CHANGE OF ADDRESS WITHIN 1O DAYS OR IF HE LEAVES THE STATE; TIME SPENT OUT OF TEXAS DOES NOT COUNT TOWARD PROBATION. MAY NOT SEEK MODIFICATION FOR ONE YEAR. ON 9/30/94 BOARD DENIED A REQUEST TO TERMINATE PROBATION.

WILLIAMS, CONRAD REX MD, DATE OF BIRTH SEPTEMBER 13, 1932, LICENSE NUMBER 0012492, WAS DISCIPLINED BY KENTUCKY ON AUGUST 31, 1989.
DISCIPLINARY ACTION: 36-MONTH PROBATION; 36-MONTH RESTRICTION PLACED ON CONTROLLED SUBSTANCE LICENSE
NOTES: RESTRICTIONS ON PRESCRIBING PRIVILEGES; NO SCHEDULE II OR IIN FOR 2 YEARS, NO SCHEDULE III, IIIN IV OR V AMPHETAMINES WITHOUT CONSULTATION FROM PSYCHIATRIST. ORDER OF DISCHARGE FROM PROBATION EFFECTIVE 8/31/92.

WILLIAMS, CONRAD REX MD, LICENSE NUMBER 00C7512, OF COLORADO SPRINGS, CO, WAS DISCIPLINED BY TEXAS ON MARCH 31, 1990.
DISCIPLINARY ACTION: SURRENDER OF LICENSE
NOTES: STIPULATED ORDER.

WILLIAMS, DEBRA N MD, LICENSE NUMBER 00F2116, OF BEAUMONT, TX, WAS DISCIPLINED BY TEXAS ON JANUARY 26, 1990.
DISCIPLINARY ACTION: 60-MONTH PROBATION; RESTRICTION PLACED ON CONTROLLED SUBSTANCE LICENSE
NOTES: STIPULATED ORDER. REVOCATION STAYED. MUST REFRAIN FROM ACCEPTING CERTAIN EMPLOYMENT OR ENTERING INTO CONTRACTUAL RELATIONSHIPS, REFRAIN FROM ISSUING PRESCRIPTIONS, ADMINISTERING OR DISPENSING DRUGS TO PATIENTS UNLESS THERAPEUTIC, MUST NOT PRESCRIBE, ADMINISTER, OR DISPENSE DRUGS WITH ABUSE POTENTIAL UNTIL SATISFIED OF LEGITIMATE MEDICAL AND THERAPEUTIC NEED AND AFTER EXAMINATION, MUST MAINTAIN COMPLETE AND ACCURATE RECORDS OF PURCHASES AND DISPOSALS OF CONTROLLED SUBSTANCES AND MAINTAIN SEPARATE FILE OF COPIES OF PRESCRIPTIONS FOR CONTROLLED SUBSTANCES OR DANGEROUS DRUGS, MUST NOT CALL IN CONTROLLED SUBSTANCES OR DANGEROUS DRUG PRESCRIPTIONS TO PHARMACIES AND MUST COMPLETE PRECEPTORSHIP ON PREVENTION AND TREATMENT OF DRUG ABUSE.

WILLIAMS, HARVEY E DO, DATE OF BIRTH APRIL 5, 1945, LICENSE NUMBER 00E5643, OF PO BOX 5673, SCOTTSDALE, AZ, WAS DISCIPLINED BY TEXAS ON JANUARY 29, 1993.
DISCIPLINARY ACTION: RESTRICTION PLACED ON LICENSE
OFFENSE: DISCIPLINARY ACTION BY ANOTHER STATE OR AGENCY
NOTES: ON 7/25/92 ARIZONA BOARD RESTRICTED HIM FROM PERFORMING ANY BREAST SURGERY DEFINED AS ALL BREAST IMPLANTS, LIFTS, RECONSTRUCTION, OR OTHER SURGERIES RELATED TO THE BREAST AND PERFORMED EITHER ENTIRELY OR PARTIALLY FOR COSMETIC PURPOSES BASED ON HIS INABILITY TO APPROPRIATELY PERFORM SUCH SURGERY BASED ON SIX COMPLAINTS. HE IS PERMANENTLY RESTRICTED FROM PERFORMING SUCH SURGERY IN TEXAS; PRIOR TO PRACTICING IN TEXAS SHALL APPEAR BEFORE THE BOARD. SHALL NOT SEEK MODIFICATION FOR ONE YEAR.

WILLIAMS, HARVEY E DO, DATE OF BIRTH APRIL 5, 1945, LICENSE NUMBER 00E5643, OF SCOTTSDALE, AZ, WAS DISCIPLINED BY TEXAS ON SEPTEMBER 30, 1994.
DISCIPLINARY ACTION: SURRENDER OF LICENSE
NOTES: ALLEGATIONS CONCERNING POSSIBLE VIOLATIONS OF

THE MEDICAL PRACTICE ACT; DID NOT ADMIT ALLEGATIONS; SURRENDER IN LIEU OF FURTHER INVESTIGATION. SHALL NOT PETION FOR REINSTATEMENT OF LICENSE.

WILLIAMS, PHILLIP EARLE JR MD, LICENSE NUMBER 00D2172, OF DALLAS, TX, WAS DISCIPLINED BY TEXAS ON APRIL 26, 1994.
DISCIPLINARY ACTION: RESTRICTION PLACED ON LICENSE; REPRIMAND
OFFENSE: LOSS OR RESTRICTION OF HOSPITAL PRIVILEGES
NOTES: WAS THE SUBJECT OF DISCIPLINARY PROCEEDINGS AT A HOSPITAL WHICH RESULTED IN AN AGREEMENT THAT HIS PRACTICE BE RESTRICTED TO CERTAIN PROCEDURES THAT HE HAD ALREADY VOLUNTARILY RESTRICTED HIMSELF TO; WAS PLACED ON PROBATION BY THE HOSPITAL FOR ONE YEAR; HE HAS FULLY COMPLIED WITH THESE RESTRICTIONS; VEHEMENTLY DISAGREES THAT THE ACTION OF THE HOSPITAL WAS CORRECT BUT VOLUNTARILY ENTERS INTO THIS AGREEMENT. SURGICAL PRACTICE LIMITED TO THOSE PROCEDURES HE WAS CREDENTIALED FOR BY THE HOSPITAL AS OF 3/1/94; SHALL BE SUPERVISED BY CHIEF OF NEUROSURGERY AT HIS HOSPITAL WITH QUARTERLY REPORTS; SHALL ATTEND AT LEAST 50 HOURS PER YEAR OF CONTINUING MEDICAL EDUCATION; SHALL GIVE A COPY OF THIS ORDER TO ANY HEALTH CARE ENTITY WHERE HE HAS PRIVILEGES; SHALL COOPERATE WITH THE BOARD IN VERIFYING COMPLIANCE; SHALL INFORM BOARD OF CHANGE OF ADDRESS WITHIN 10 DAYS OR IF HE LEAVES THE STATE; TIME SPENT OUT OF TEXAS DOES NOT COUNT TOWARD RESTRICTION. SHALL NOT SEEK MODIFICATION FOR ONE YEAR.

WILLIAMSON, MARK A MD, LICENSE NUMBER 00H4855, OF WEBSTER, TX, WAS DISCIPLINED BY TEXAS ON JANUARY 6, 1995.
DISCIPLINARY ACTION: 60-MONTH PROBATION; REQUIRED TO TAKE ADDITIONAL MEDICAL EDUCATION
OFFENSE: DRUG OR ALCOHOL ABUSE
NOTES: ADMITS TO POLYSUBSTANCE ABUSE FOR MANY YEARS INCLUDING BUT NOT LIMITED TO COCAINE AND ALCOHOL; REPORTS A SOBRIETY DATE OF 10/23/93; HAS BEEN ATTENDING AA AND ENTERED INTO AN AFTERCARE RECOVERY CONTRACT; RECEIVES OUTPATIENT AND PSYCHIATRIC TREATMENT. SUSPENSION STAYED. CONDITIONS OF PROBATION: SHALL ABSTAIN FROM THE CONSUMPTION OF ALCOHOL/CHEMICAL SUBSTANCES IN ANY FORM UNLESS PRESCRIBED BY ANOTHER PHYSICIAN FOR A LEGITIMATE AND THERAPEUTIC PURPOSE; SHALL SUBMIT HIMSELF FOR APPROPRIATE EXAMS INCLUDING DRUG OR ALCOHOL SCREENS; SHALL CONTINUE SUBSTANCE ABUSE TREATMENT WITH QUARTERLY REPORTS; SHALL PARTICIPATE IN AA'S PROGRAM NOT LESS THAN FIVE TIMES A WEEK WITH QUARTERLY REPORTS TO THE BOARD; SHALL PARTICIPATE WITH PHYSICIAN'S COUNSELING COMMITTEE AND ATTEND WEEKLY MEETINGS WITH QUARTERLY REPORTS; SHALL COMPLY WITH CONDITIONS OF CONTINUING CARE CONTRACT WITH THE HARRIS COUNTY MEDICAL SOCIETY WITH QUARTERLY REPORTS; SHALL COMPLY WITH CONDITIONS OF ANY AGREEMENT ENTERED INTO FOR HOSPITAL PRIVILEGES; SHALL NOT TREAT OR OTHERWISE SERVE AS PHYSICIAN, PRESCRIBE, DISPENSE OR ADMINISTER DRUGS THAT MAY BE SUBJECT TO ABUSE TO HIMSELF OR ANY MEMBER OF HIS FAMILY; SEPARATE FROM PATIENT RECORDS SHALL MAINTAIN A COPY OF EVERY PRESCRIPTION WRITTEN FOR CONTROLLED SUBSTANCES OR DANGEROUS DRUGS WHICH SHALL BE AVAILABLE FOR INSPECTION; SHALL MAINTAIN A LOGBOOK FOR ALL PRESCRIPTIONS OR REFILLS OF SUCH DRUGS TELEPHONED IN; SHALL OBTAIN AT LEAST 50 HOURS PER YEAR OF CONTINUING MEDICAL EDUCATION; SHALL APPEAR BEFORE THE BOARD ONCE A YEAR OR UPON REQUEST; SHALL COOPERATE WITH THE BOARD IN VERIFYING COMPLIANCE; SHALL EXECUTE RELEASES FOR RECORDS OF TREATMENT OR OF HIS PARTICIPATION WITH THE MEDICAL SOCIETY; SHALL GIVE A COPY OF THIS ORDER TO ANY HEALTH CARE ENTITY WHERE HE HAS OR HAS APPLIED FOR PRIVILEGES; SHALL ENSURE INQUIRIES REGARDING HIS TEXAS LICENSURE STATUS ARE ANSWERED BY REFERENCING THIS ORDER; SHALL INFORM BOARD OF CHANGE OF ADDRESS WITHIN 10 DAYS OR IF HE LEAVES THE STATE; TIME SPENT OUT OF TEXAS DOES NOT COUNT TOWARD PROBATION. SHALL NOT SEEK MODIFICATION FOR ONE YEAR.

WILSON, LARRY D MD, DATE OF BIRTH JANUARY 26, 1953, LICENSE NUMBER 00H1333, OF 6633 HWY 290E, SUITE 302, AUSTIN, TX, WAS DISCIPLINED BY TEXAS ON JANUARY 29, 1993.
DISCIPLINARY ACTION: 36-MONTH PROBATION; RESTRICTION PLACED ON LICENSE
OFFENSE: PROFESSIONAL MISCONDUCT
NOTES: BETWEEN 3/89 AND 8/90 HE WAS THE MEDICAL DIRECTOR AT AN OUTPATIENT METHADONE THERAPY CLINIC FOR NARCOTIC DEPENDENT PERSONS; RECEIVED NO COMPENSATION FOR THESE SERVICES; FAILED TO MEET PROGRAM REQUIREMENTS RELATING TO REPORTING OF ADVERSE REACTIONS, WRITTEN JUSTIFICATION OF INCREASED DOSES OF MEDICATION, DOCUMENTATION OF PHYSICAL EXAMS, OBTAINING PROPER DOCUMENTATION FOR TRANSFER PATIENTS, DOCUMENTATION OF ADDICTION, AND REGULAR ATTENDANCE ON THE PREMISES OF THE PROGRAM; THESE FAILURES PERMITTED NON-QUALIFIED EMPLOYEES TO EXERCISE INDEPENDENT MEDICAL JUDGEMENT WHICH CONSTITUTED IMPROPER DELEGATION OF RESPONSIBILITY AND PERMITTED THE PRACTICE OF MEDICINE BY A BUSINESS ENTITY NOT LICENSED TO DO SO; THIS MAY HAVE CONTRIBUTED TO ONE PATIENT'S DEATH. 3 YEAR SUSPENSION STAYED. CONDITIONS OF PROBATION: SHALL ATTEND AT LEAST 50 HOURS PER YEAR OF CONTINUING MEDICAL EDUCATION; SHALL NOT ACCEPT EMPLOYMENT OR ENTER INTO CONTRACTUAL RELATIONSHIPS WHERE HE WOULD BE COMPENSATED TO DIAGNOSE AND/OR TREAT PATIENTS BY A LAYPERSON, CORPORATION OR OTHER ENTITY NOT COMPRISED EXCLUSIVELY OF TEXAS LICENSED PHYSICIANS AND WHEREIN THE PERSON OR ENTITY WOULD RECEIVE AND RETAIN THE FEES PAID BY OR ON BEHALF OF PATIENTS FOR THE PHYSICIAN'S PROFESSIONAL SERVICES; SHALL PERFORM 12 HOURS PER MONTH OF COMMUNITY SERVICE FOR A NONPROFIT CHARITABLE ORGANIZATION FOR THE FIRST YEAR OF PROBATION; SHALL APPEAR BEFORE THE BOARD TWICE A YEAR; SHALL GIVE A COPY OF THIS ORDER TO ANY HEALTH CARE ENTITY WHERE HE HAS PRIVILEGES; SHALL COOPERATE WITH THE BOARD IN VERIFYING COMPLIANCE; SHALL INFORM BOARD OF CHANGE OF ADDRESS WITHIN 10 DAYS OR IF HE LEAVES THE STATE; TIME SPENT OUT OF TEXAS DOES NOT COUNT

TOWARD PROBATION; SHALL NOT SEEK MODIFICATION FOR ONE YEAR. ON 6/22/94, BASED ON HISTORY OF COMPLIANCE AND EXEMPLARY COMMUNITY SERVICE THE ORDER WAS TERMINATED.

WILSON, MARK DANIEL MD, LICENSE NUMBER 00F4697, OF DENTON, TX, WAS DISCIPLINED BY TEXAS ON MARCH 31, 1990.
DISCIPLINARY ACTION: RESTRICTION PLACED ON CONTROLLED SUBSTANCE LICENSE
NOTES: STIPULATED ORDER. MUST REFRAIN FROM PRESCRIPTION OR ADMINISTRATION OF ANY DRUG UNLESS IT IS THERAPEUTIC, MUST NOT PRESCRIBE, ADMINISTER OR DISPENSE DRUG WITH POTENTIAL OF ABUSE WITHOUT APPROPRIATE MEDICAL HISTORY AND CLINICALLY ADEQUATE EXAMINATION, MUST UNDERSTAND POTENTIAL FOR ABUSE OF CONTROLLED SUBSTANCES OR DANGEROUS DRUGS, SHALL NOT PRESCRIBE, DISPENSE, OR ADMINISTER DRUG OR MEDICATION HAVING ANORECTIC EFFECT WITHOUT PERMISSION FROM BOARD, MUST CONDUCT ADEQUATE FOLLOW-UP EXAMINATIONS ON PATIENTS TO DETERMINE WHETHER TREATMENT COURSE APPROPRIATE AND MUST MAINTAIN COPIES OF ANORECTIC AGENT PRESCRIPTIONS. RESTRICTIONS TERMINATED EFFECTIVE 6/16/92; LICENSE FREE OF ANY RESTRICTION OR LIMITATION.

WINSLOW, DAVID EVERETT DO, DATE OF BIRTH APRIL 10, 1959, LICENSE NUMBER 00H4804, OF 2745 VALWOOD PARKWAY, DALLAS, TX, WAS DISCIPLINED BY TEXAS ON JANUARY 29, 1993.
DISCIPLINARY ACTION: 120-MONTH PROBATION; RESTRICTION PLACED ON LICENSE
OFFENSE: SUBSTANDARD CARE, INCOMPETENCE, OR NEGLIGENCE
NOTES: FAILED TO KEEP ADEQUATE RECORDS OF WEIGHT CONTROL PATIENTS; FAILED TO DOCUMENT PHYSICAL EXAMS; FAILED TO ADEQUATELY ADDRESS PATIENT SYMPTOMS/COMPLAINTS. 10 YEAR SUSPENSION STAYED. SHALL APPEAR BEFORE THE BOARD ONCE A YEAR; SHALL ATTEND AT LEAST 50 HOURS PER YEAR OF CONTINUING MEDICAL EDUCATION; SHALL MAINTAIN ADEQUATE MEDICAL RECORDS ON ALL PATIENT OFFICE VISITS; SHALL NOT SIGN ANY PATIENT RECORD UNLESS HE HAS PERSONALLY SEEN AND EXAMINED THE PATIENT UNLESS THIS IS SO NOTED IN THE RECORD; SHALL TAKE THE SPEX EXAM WITHIN 1 YEAR; SHALL NOT TREAT ANY PATIENT FOR WEIGHT CONTROL WITH DRUGS; SHALL GIVE A COPY OF THIS ORDER TO ANY HEALTH CARE ENTITY WHERE HE HAS PRIVILEGES; SHALL COOPERATE WITH THE BOARD IN VERIFYING COMPLIANCE; SHALL INFORM BOARD OF ADDRESS CHANGE WITHIN 10 DAYS OR IF HE LEAVES THE STATE; TIME SPENT OUT OF TEXAS DOES NOT COUNT TOWARD PROBATION.

WINSTEAD, GLENN C MD, DATE OF BIRTH DECEMBER 17, 1944, LICENSE NUMBER 0006542, OF 2200 BOX ELDER, MILES CITY, MT, WAS DISCIPLINED BY MONTANA ON AUGUST 24, 1990.
DISCIPLINARY ACTION: PROBATION
OFFENSE: CRIMINAL CONVICTION OR PLEA OF GUILTY, NOLO CONTENDERE, OR NO CONTEST TO A CRIME
NOTES: FEDERAL FELONY CONVICTION INVOLVING MORAL TURPITUDE - COUNTERFEITING. PROBATION UNTIL FURTHER ORDER OF THE BOARD.

WINSTEAD, GLENN C MD, LICENSE NUMBER 00D9324, OF STEVENSVILLE, MT, WAS DISCIPLINED BY TEXAS ON FEBRUARY 22, 1991.
NOTES: MUST APPEAR BEFORE TEXAS BOARD AND RECEIVE APPROVAL BEFORE PRACTICING IN TEXAS.

WINSTEAD, GLENN C MD, LICENSE NUMBER 0021097, OF GREAT FALLS, MT, WAS DISCIPLINED BY VIRGINIA ON APRIL 19, 1993.
DISCIPLINARY ACTION: LICENSE REVOCATION
OFFENSE: CRIMINAL CONVICTION OR PLEA OF GUILTY, NOLO CONTENDERE, OR NO CONTEST TO A CRIME
NOTES: BASED ON FELONY CONVICTION.

WITHERSPOON, ROBERT GLYNN JR MD, LICENSE NUMBER 00E4772, OF MOUNT PLEASANT, TX, WAS DISCIPLINED BY TEXAS ON JUNE 17, 1992.
DISCIPLINARY ACTION: 60-MONTH PROBATION
OFFENSE: SUBSTANDARD CARE, INCOMPETENCE, OR NEGLIGENCE
NOTES: NONTHERAPEUTIC PRESCRIBING AND PROFESSIONAL FAILURE TO PRACTICE MEDICINE IN AN ACCEPTABLE MANNER CONSISTENT WITH PUBLIC HEALTH AND WELFARE. SUSPENSION STAYED.

WOLF, GARY DUKE DO, LICENSE NUMBER 00E9029, OF MANSFIELD, TX, WAS DISCIPLINED BY TEXAS ON JANUARY 6, 1995.
DISCIPLINARY ACTION: REQUIRED TO TAKE ADDITIONAL MEDICAL EDUCATION; MONITORING OF PHYSICIAN
OFFENSE: OVERPRESCRIBING OR MISPRESCRIBING DRUGS
NOTES: FROM 1985 TO 1993 PRESCRIBED CONTROLLED SUBSTANCES TO VARIOUS PATIENTS WITHOUT ADEQUATE INDICATIONS AND SUFFICIENT MONITORING OR FOLLOW-UP; CARE AND TREATMENT APPEARS TO BE WELL DOCUMENTED AND HE REPORTS THAT PATIENTS HAVE BEEN WEANED OFF THE DRUGS PRESCRIBED; AGREEMENT IN LIEU OF FURTHER INVESTIGATION OR A HEARING. CONDITIONS OF THREE YEAR RESTRICTION: SHALL OBTAIN AT LEAST 50 HOURS PER YEAR OF CONTINUING MEDICAL EDUCATION INCLUDING 25 HOURS IN PHARMACOLOGY, SUBSTANCE ABUSE OR PAIN MANAGEMENT IN THE FIRST YEAR; SEPARATE FROM PATIENT RECORDS, SHALL MAINTAIN A FILE OF EVERY PRESCRIPTION WRITTEN FOR CONTROLLED SUBSTANCES OR DANGEROUS DRUGS WHICH SHALL BE AVAILABLE FOR INSPECTION; SHALL MAINTAIN A LOGBOOK FOR ALL PRESCRIPTIONS OR REFILLS OF SUCH DRUGS TELEPHONED IN, WHICH SHALL BE AVAILABLE FOR INSPECTION; SHALL APPEAR BEFORE THE BOARD ONCE A YEAR OR UPON REQUEST; SHALL COOPERATE WITH THE BOARD IN VERIFYING COMPLIANCE; SHALL EXECUTE RELEASES NECESSARY TO OBTAIN PEER REVIEW RECORDS; SHALL GIVE A COPY OF THIS ORDER TO ANY HEALTH CARE ENTITY WHERE HE HAS OR HAS APPLIED FOR PRIVILEGES OR ANYONE ELSE WHO REQUESTS IT; SHALL ENSURE INQUIRIES REGARDING HIS TEXAS LICENSURE STATUS ARE ANSWERED BY REFERENCING THIS ORDER; SHALL INFORM BOARD OF CHANGE OF ADDRESS WITHIN 10 DAYS OR IF HE LEAVES THE STATE; TIME SPENT OUT OF TEXAS DOES NOT COUNT TOWARD RESTRICTION. SHALL NOT SEEK MODIFICATION FOR ONE YEAR.

WOLF, RENE JR MD, DATE OF BIRTH MARCH 8, 1949, LICENSE NUMBER 00F3672, OF DALLAS, TX, WAS DISCIPLINED BY TEXAS ON FEBRUARY 22, 1991.
NOTES: MUST COMPLY WITH HAWAII BOARD ORDER; OBTAIN PERMISSION FROM TEXAS BOARD BEFORE PRACTICING MEDICINE IN TEXAS, AND FOLLOW SUCH TERMS AS

MAY BE IMPOSED. ORDER TERMINATED ON 6/15/93; LICENSE FREE AND CLEAR OF RESTRICTIONS.

WOLF, RENE JR MD, DATE OF BIRTH MARCH 8, 1949, LICENSE NUMBER 00F3672, OF 4500 PEAR RIDGE #738, DALLAS, TX, WAS DISCIPLINED BY TEXAS ON DECEMBER 16, 1991.
DISCIPLINARY ACTION: 24-MONTH PROBATION
NOTES: GRANTED PERMISSION TO PRACTICE IN TEXAS. PROBATION UNDER TERMS AND CONDITIONS. ON 1/29/93 MODIFICATION GRANTED SO THAT HE MAY REAPPLY FOR LIFTING OF PROBATIONARY CONDITIONS NO SOONER THAN 6/1/93 AND ALL OTHER TERMS IMPOSED BY THIS ORDER REMAIN IN EFFECT.

WOLFE, ALVIN E DO OF WICHITA, KS, WAS DISCIPLINED BY KANSAS ON APRIL 27, 1989.
DISCIPLINARY ACTION: RESTRICTION PLACED ON LICENSE

WOLFE, ALVIN E DO, LICENSE NUMBER 00D7715, OF WICHITA, KS, WAS DISCIPLINED BY TEXAS ON APRIL 21, 1990.
NOTES: STIPULATED ORDER. MUST REQUEST PERSONAL INTERVIEW BEFORE BOARD TO DISCUSS PRESENT STATUS, LOCATION AND TYPE OF PRACTICE DESIRED TO ENTER INTO, AND RECEIVE APPROVAL PRIOR TO PRACTICING IN TEXAS.

WOLFE, ALVIN E DO, DATE OF BIRTH AUGUST 15, 1932, LICENSE NUMBER 0015428, OF WICHITA, KS, WAS DISCIPLINED BY COLORADO ON OCTOBER 18, 1991.
DISCIPLINARY ACTION: SURRENDER OF LICENSE
OFFENSE: DISCIPLINARY ACTION BY ANOTHER STATE OR AGENCY
NOTES: ADMINISTERING, DISPENSING OR PRESCRIBING A HABIT FORMING DRUG NOT IN THE COURSE OF LEGITIMATE MEDICAL PRACTICE. PERMANENT SURRENDER OF COLORADO MEDICAL LICENSE. ACTION TAKEN BY KANSAS BOARD.

WOMACK, GROVER KENNETH MD, DATE OF BIRTH JULY 6, 1925, LICENSE NUMBER 00C5304, OF HOUSTON, TX, WAS DISCIPLINED BY TEXAS ON DECEMBER 1, 1988.
NOTES: SETTLEMENT AGREEMENT AND UNSPECIFIED DISCIPLINARY ACTION

WOMACK, GROVER KENNETH MD, DATE OF BIRTH JULY 6, 1925, LICENSE NUMBER 00C5304, OF FORT WORTH, TX, WAS DISCIPLINED BY TEXAS ON JUNE 10, 1991.
DISCIPLINARY ACTION: 60-MONTH PROBATION; MONITORING OF PHYSICIAN
OFFENSE: FAILURE TO COMPLY WITH A PREVIOUS BOARD ORDER
NOTES: VIOLATED TERMS OF PREVIOUS BOARD ORDER; UNPROFESSIONAL OR DISHONORABLE CONDUCT LIKELY TO DECEIVE, DEFRAUD, OR INJURE THE PUBLIC. TERMS OF PROBATION: SHALL APPEAR ONCE A YEAR BEFORE THE BOARD; SHALL BE MONITORED BY BOARD-APPROVED PHYSICIAN; SHALL ABSTAIN FROM CONSUMPTION OF ALCOHOL/CHEMICAL SUBSTANCES; SHALL IMMEDIATELY REPORT ANY USAGE OF ALCOHOL OR CHEMICAL SUBSTANCES NOT PRESCRIBED BY ANOTHER PHYSICIAN FOR A LEGITIMATE AND THERAPEUTIC CONDITION TO THE BOARD; SHALL PARTICIPATE IN AA; SHALL SUBMIT TO ALCOHOL OR DRUG SCREENS; SHALL CONTINUE TREATMENT WITH BOARD-APPROVED PHYSICIAN; SHALL FURNISH WRITTEN REPORTS TO THE BOARD. ORDER TERMINATED ON 6/15/93; LICENSE FREE AND CLEAR OF ANY RESTRICTIONS.

WOMACK, JAMES C MD OF 1300 CEDAR, BANDERA, TX, WAS DISCIPLINED BY DEA ON FEBRUARY 5, 1993.
DISCIPLINARY ACTION: DENIAL OF LICENSE REINSTATEMENT
OFFENSE: PRACTICING WITHOUT A VALID LICENSE OR PRESCRIBING WITHOUT A VALID CONTROLLED SUBSTANCE LICENSE
NOTES: ON 12/16/91 HAD SURRENDERED DEA CERTIFICATE OF REGISTRATION BASED UPON PERSONAL ABUSE OF CONTROLLED SUBSTANCES; THEREFORE HE HAD NO AUTHORITY TO PRESCRIBE OR OTHERWISE HANDLE CONTROLLED SUBSTANCES, YET CONTINUED TO PRESCRIBE SUCH SUBSTANCES USING HIS FATHER'S DEA NUMBER. WHILE HE DID DEMONSTRATE REHABILITATION FROM SUBSTANCE ABUSE, HE FAILED TO DEMONSTRATE THAT HIS BEHAVIOR WAS IN ANY WAY JUSTIFIED OR THAT SUCH BEHAVIOR WAS NOT LIKELY TO RECUR. HOWEVER, GIVEN HIS REHABILITATION FROM SUBSTANCE ABUSE AND CONTRIBUTION IN MEDICALLY UNDERSERVED AREA, AN APPLICATION FOR DEA REGISTRATION MADE AFTER ONE YEAR WILL BE FAVORABLY CONSIDERED, PROVIDED NO ADDITIONAL EVIDENCE OF WRONGDOING.

WOMACK, JAMES CHANSLOR MD, LICENSE NUMBER 00G8516, OF SAN ANTONIO, TX, WAS DISCIPLINED BY TEXAS ON JULY 28, 1989.
DISCIPLINARY ACTION: SURRENDER OF CONTROLLED SUBSTANCE LICENSE; 120-MONTH PROBATION
OFFENSE: DRUG OR ALCOHOL ABUSE
NOTES: SUSPENSION STAYED; CANNOT PRESCRIBE, DISPENSE, ADMINISTER CONTROLLED SUBSTANCES OR DRUGS FOR SELF OR FAMILY; SUBMIT TO ALCOHOL/DRUG SCREENING; PARTICIPATE IN ACTIVITIES OF COMMITTEE ON PHYSICIAN HEALTH AND REHABILITATION; SUBMIT TO PSYCHIATRIC EVALUATION AND FOLLOW RECOMMENDATIONS; PARTICIPATE IN ALCOHOLICS OR NARCOTICS ANONYMOUS. ON 3/5/94 ORDER TERMINATED.

WOMACK, JAMES CHANSLOR MD, LICENSE NUMBER 00G8516, OF 1300 CEDAR 1, POB 1120, BANDERA, TX, WAS DISCIPLINED BY DEA ON AUGUST 31, 1989.
DISCIPLINARY ACTION: SURRENDER OF CONTROLLED SUBSTANCE LICENSE
OFFENSE: OVERPRESCRIBING OR MISPRESCRIBING DRUGS
NOTES: ADMITTED 08/31/90 IN SAN ANTONIO, TEXAS TO PHONING IN PRESCRIPTIONS AND USING FATHER'S BOARD REGISTRATION; PRESCRIBING PRIVILEGES REVOKED 07/28/89 AND SURRENDERED REGISTRATION 08/30/89.

WONNACOTT, JAMES B MD OF 3515 OAK FOREST DRIVE, HOUSTON, TX, WAS DISCIPLINED BY DEA ON AUGUST 27, 1993.
DISCIPLINARY ACTION: SURRENDER OF CONTROLLED SUBSTANCE LICENSE

WONNACOTT, JAMES BRIAN MD, LICENSE NUMBER 00F1313, OF PORTLAND, TX, WAS DISCIPLINED BY TEXAS ON JANUARY 6, 1995.
DISCIPLINARY ACTION: REPRIMAND; REQUIRED TO TAKE ADDITIONAL MEDICAL EDUCATION
OFFENSE: PROFESSIONAL MISCONDUCT
NOTES: DESPITE RECEIVING WRITTEN REQUESTS, HE FAILED TO TIMELY PROVIDE MEDICAL RECORDS OF VARIOUS PATIENTS DURING OCTOBER THROUGH DECEMBER 1993 AND IN VARIOUS MONTHS IN 1994; DID NOT PROVIDE A WRITTEN EXPLANATION TO PATIENTS OR INCLUDE THIS IN THE WRITTEN RECORDS; MAINTAINS

HE WAS UNABLE TO PROVIDE RECORDS DUE TO CHANGING OFFICE LOCATION AND IMPOUNDMENT OF RECORDS BY THE IRS IN 2/94; ALSO DURING THIS TIME PRESCRIBED VARIOUS MEDICATIONS OVER THE PHONE WITHOUT A PHYSICAL EXAM OR ACCESS TO THE MEDICAL RECORDS OF THE PATIENTS. CONDITIONS OF FIVE YEAR RESTRICTION: SHALL MAINTAIN ADEQUATE MEDICAL RECORDS ON ALL PATIENT OFFICE VISITS WHICH SHALL BE AVAILABLE FOR INSPECTION; SHALL BECOME FAMILIAR WITH AND COMPLY WITH PROVISIONS OF THE MEDICAL PRACTICE ACT REGARDING TIMELY RELEASE OF MEDICAL RECORDS; SHALL ATTEND AT LEAST 50 HOURS PER YEAR OF CONTINUING MEDICAL EDUCATION INCLUDING AT LEAST 10 HOURS IN THE AREA OF RISK MANAGEMENT; WITHIN ONE YEAR SHALL TAKE AND PASS THE TEXAS MEDICAL JURISPRUDENCE EXAM; SHALL APPEAR BEFORE THE BOARD ONCE A YEAR OR UPON REQUEST; SHALL COOPERATE WITH THE BOARD IN VERIFYING COMPLIANCE; SHALL GIVE A COPY OF THIS ORDER TO ANY HEALTH CARE ENTITY WHERE HE HAS OR HAS APPLIED FOR PRIVILEGES OR ANYONE ELSE WHO REQUESTS IT; SHALL ENSURE INQUIRIES REGARDING HIS TEXAS LICENSURE STATUS ARE ANSWERED BY REFERENCING THIS ORDER; SHALL INFORM BOARD OF CHANGE OF ADDRESS WITHIN 10 DAYS OR IF HE LEAVES THE STATE; TIME SPENT OUT OF TEXAS DOES NOT COUNT TOWARD RESTRICTION. SHALL NOT SEEK MODIFICATION FOR ONE YEAR.

WOOD, HAROLD LEE MD, LICENSE NUMBER 00C7978, OF KILLEEN, TX, WAS DISCIPLINED BY TEXAS ON OCTOBER 1, 1987.
DISCIPLINARY ACTION: SURRENDER OF LICENSE

WOODS, THOMAS ALAN MD, LICENSE NUMBER 00D0354, OF DALLAS, TX, WAS DISCIPLINED BY TEXAS ON NOVEMBER 13, 1992.
DISCIPLINARY ACTION: REPRIMAND
OFFENSE: PROFESSIONAL MISCONDUCT
NOTES: UNPROFESSIONAL OR DISHONORABLE CONDUCT THAT IS LIKELY TO DECEIVE, DEFRAUD OR INJURE THE PUBLIC.

WOODWARD, ROBERT A MD OF MINDEN, LA, WAS DISCIPLINED BY LOUISIANA ON OCTOBER 22, 1992.
DISCIPLINARY ACTION: LICENSE SUSPENSION; REQUIRED TO ENTER AN IMPAIRED PHYSICIAN PROGRAM OR DRUG OR ALCOHOL TREATMENT
OFFENSE: DRUG OR ALCOHOL ABUSE
NOTES: HABITUAL OR RECURRING ABUSE OF DRUGS; PRESCRIBING, DISPENSING OR ADMINISTERING CONTROLLED SUBSTANCES WITHOUT LEGITIMATE MEDICAL JUSTIFICATION OR IN OTHER THAN A LEGAL OR LEGITIMATE MANNER. SUSPENDED PENDING SPECIFIED INPATIENT SUBSTANCE ABUSE TREATMENT. SUPERSEDING ORDER ENTERED 12/3/92 REINSTATING LICENSE ON PROBATION FOR FIVE YEARS SUBJECT TO CONTINUING AFTERCARE; PARTICIPATION IN IMPAIRED PHYSICIANS PROGRAM; ABSTINENCE FROM THE USE OF MOOD-ALTERING SUBSTANCES; LIFETIME PROHIBITION ON PRESCRIPTION, DISPENSATION OR ADMINISTRATION OF CONTROLLED SUBSTANCES; AND OBTAINING SPECIFIED CONTINUING MEDICAL EDUCATION.

WOODWARD, ROBERT ALAN MD, DATE OF BIRTH FEBRUARY 28, 1957, LICENSE NUMBER 00G8518, OF 211 CARROLLTON, SHREVEPORT, LA, WAS DISCIPLINED BY TEXAS ON JANUARY 29, 1993.
DISCIPLINARY ACTION: 60-MONTH PROBATION; RESTRICTION PLACED ON CONTROLLED SUBSTANCE LICENSE
OFFENSE: DISCIPLINARY ACTION BY ANOTHER STATE OR AGENCY
NOTES: ACTION BASED ON THE 10/22/92 LOUISIANA ACTION FOR INTEMPERATE USE OF ALCOHOL OR DRUGS; UNPROFESSIONAL OR DISHONORABLE CONDUCT LIKELY TO DEFRAUD OR INJURE THE PUBLIC AND WRITING FALSE OR FICTITIOUS PRESCRIPTIONS FOR DANGEROUS DRUGS. 5 YEAR SUSPENSION STAYED. CONDITIONS OF PROBATION: WILL ABIDE BY THE CONDITIONS OF THE LOUISIANA PROBATION INCLUDING SHALL CONTINUE UNDER TREATMENT WITH QUARTERLY REPORTS; SHALL APPEAR BEFORE THE BOARD UPON REQUEST; LIFETIME PROHIBITION ON PRESCRIBING, DISPENSING OR ADMINISTERING ANY CONTROLLED SUBSTANCE EXCEPT FOR IN A HOSPITAL TO PROVIDE EMERGENCY SERVICES; LIFETIME ABSTINENCE FROM THE USE OF ANY MOOD-ALTERING SUBSTANCE EXCEPT AS PROVIDED BY ANOTHER PHYSICIAN FOR A LEGITIMATE MEDICAL PURPOSE; SHALL OBTAIN AT LEAST 50 HOURS WORTH OF CONTINUING MEDICAL EDUCATION PER YEAR. PRIOR TO PRACTICING IN TEXAS SHALL APPEAR BEFORE THE BOARD; SHALL INFORM THE BOARD IF HE LEAVES EITHER TEXAS OR LOUISIANA; TIME SPENT OUTSIDE THESE TWO STATES DOES NOT COUNT TOWARD PROBATION. SHALL NOT SEEK MODIFICATION FOR 1 YEAR.

WRAY, ROBERT E DO, LICENSE NUMBER 00G1314, OF TYLER, TX, WAS DISCIPLINED BY TEXAS ON APRIL 14, 1989.
DISCIPLINARY ACTION: REPRIMAND

WRIGHT, ARTHUR GLENN JR MD, DATE OF BIRTH JANUARY 16, 1929, LICENSE NUMBER 00C3922, OF 4225 DRIFTWOOD, CORPUS CHRISTI, TX, WAS DISCIPLINED BY TEXAS ON JANUARY 29, 1993.
DISCIPLINARY ACTION: REPRIMAND
OFFENSE: FAILURE TO COMPLY WITH A PROFESSIONAL RULE
NOTES: FROM 4/86 TO 4/92 FOR ONE PATIENT HE FAILED TO KEEP ADEQUATE RECORDS CONCERNING MEDICAL CONDITION OR PRESCRIBED MEDICATIONS; ALSO FAILED TO DOCUMENT WHETHER EFFORTS WERE MADE TO CONSULT OTHER PHYSICIANS CONCERNING THIS PATIENT'S INCONTINENCE, GASTRIC ULCERS, DUMPING SYNDROME OR SEVERE ARTHRITIS. SHALL GIVE A COPY OF THIS ORDER TO ANY HEALTH CARE ENTITY WHERE HE HAS PRIVILEGES; SHALL COOPERATE WITH THE BOARD IN VERIFYING COMPLIANCE; SHALL INFORM BOARD OF CHANGE OF ADDRESS WITHIN 10 DAYS.

WRIGHT, JOHN L JR MD, LICENSE NUMBER 00B8970, OF BIG LAKE, TX, WAS DISCIPLINED BY TEXAS ON JANUARY 24, 1992.
DISCIPLINARY ACTION: SURRENDER OF LICENSE
NOTES: INABILITY TO PRACTICE MEDICINE WITH REASONABLE SKILL AND SAFETY TO PATIENTS. LICENSE PERMANENTLY RETIRED IN LIEU OF FURTHER DISCIPLINARY ACTION.

WYCKOFF, STUART M MD WAS DISCIPLINED BY NEVADA ON JANUARY 19, 1991.
DISCIPLINARY ACTION: RESTRICTION PLACED ON LICENSE; REPRIMAND
OFFENSE: SUBSTANDARD CARE, INCOMPETENCE, OR NEGLIGENCE
NOTES: TREATED PATIENTS IN A MATTER NOT RECOGNIZED

SCIENTIFICALLY AS BEING BENEFICIAL, FAILED TO EXERCISE SKILL OR DILIGENCE, SPECIFICALLY IN THE AREA OF ADOLESCENT PSYCHIATRY, REPEATED MALPRACTICE. CANNOT PROVIDE PSYCHIATRIC TREATMENT TO ANY PERSON UNDER 18; LICENSE STATUS INACTIVE FOR 3 YEARS SUBJECT TO CONDITIONS FOR REINSTATEMENT TO ACTIVE STATUS.

WYCKOFF, STUART M MD, LICENSE NUMBER 00E2955, OF FORT FAIRFIELD, ME, WAS DISCIPLINED BY TEXAS ON OCTOBER 5, 1991.
DISCIPLINARY ACTION: 60-MONTH PROBATION; RESTRICTION PLACED ON LICENSE
OFFENSE: DISCIPLINARY ACTION BY ANOTHER STATE OR AGENCY
NOTES: MAINE BOARD FOUND THAT DURING HIS TREATMENT OF ADOLESCENT PATIENTS WHILE PRACTICING AS A PSYCHIATRIST IN NEVADA, HE VIOLATED STANDARDS OF PROFESSIONAL BEHAVIOR IN THE PRACTICE OF PSYCHIATRY, INCLUDING THE INAPPROPRIATE USE OF PROFANITY, CONFRONTATIONAL STYLE, AND EXTREME AND INAPPROPRIATE DISCIPLINARY MEASURES; LICENSE RESTRICTED IN BOTH MAINE AND NEVADA. FIVE YEAR SUSPENSION STAYED, PROBATION ISSUED UNDER FOLLOWING CONDITIONS: SHALL TREAT NO INVOLUNTARY PATIENTS IN ANY PRACTICE SETTING; SHALL TREAT ONLY THOSE PATIENTS WHO SEEK HIS SERVICES INTENTIONALLY WITHOUT COERCION OF ANY KIND; SHALL NOT PROVIDE PROFESSIONAL TREATMENT TO ANY PERSON UNDER THE AGE OF 18 IN ANY PRACTICE SETTING EXCEPT UNDER CERTAIN CONDITIONS, INCLUDING GROUP OR FAMILY THERAPY; SUPERVISORY ROLE LIMITED TO ADMINISTRATIVE PERSONNEL; SHALL PROVIDE TEXAS WITH COPIES OF REPORTS SENT TO MAINE; MUST APPEAR BEFORE BOARD BEFORE PRACTICING; TIME SPENT OUTSIDE OF TEXAS OR MAINE DOES NOT COUNT TOWARD PROBATION; SHALL COOPERATE WITH BOARD IN VERIFYING COMPLIANCE; SHALL APPEAR BEFORE BOARD ONCE A YEAR; MAY FILE FOR TERMINATION OF ORDER AFTER 8/1/92.

WYCKOFF, STUART MORELY MD, DATE OF BIRTH OCTOBER 13, 1949, LICENSE NUMBER 0013113, OF PO BOX 612, FORT FAIRFIELD, ME, WAS DISCIPLINED BY MAINE ON MAY 31, 1991.
DISCIPLINARY ACTION: RESTRICTION PLACED ON LICENSE
OFFENSE: PROFESSIONAL MISCONDUCT
NOTES: ISSUED MODIFIED, CONDITIONAL LICENSE BASED ON UNPROFESSIONAL CONDUCT ALLEGED TO HAVE OCCURRED IN NEVADA.

YASHAR, JAMES J MD, LICENSE NUMBER 0003910, OF ONE RANDALL SQUARE, PROVIDENCE, RI, WAS DISCIPLINED BY RHODE ISLAND ON AUGUST 11, 1993.
DISCIPLINARY ACTION: REPRIMAND; MONITORING OF PHYSICIAN
OFFENSE: LOSS OR RESTRICTION OF HOSPITAL PRIVILEGES
NOTES: VIOLATED A HOSPITAL OPEN HEART SURGERY GUIDELINE WHICH STATES THAT "ONE OF THE DESIGNATED CARDIAC SURGEONS WILL BE PHYSICALLY PRESENT IN THE HOSPITAL AFTER AN OPEN HEART SURGICAL CASE UNTIL THE PATIENT IS STABLE AND WILL REMAIN AVAILABLE FOR ANY EMERGENCY. THIS IN-HOUSE COVERAGE WILL BE CONTINUED WHEN THE PATIENT IS UNSTABLE, OR IF THE CARDIAC PHYSICIAN ASSISTANT IS UNAVAILABLE OR NEEDS ASSISTANCE IN CARING FOR A HEART PATIENT;" HOSPITAL SUSPENDED HIS PRIVILEGES FOR 20 DAYS AND SUBSEQUENTLY REACHED AN AGREEMENT WITH HIM TO REDEFINE HIS WORKLOAD. BOARD SHALL MONITOR COMPLIANCE WITH HOSPITAL AGREEMENT THROUGH QUARTERLY REPORTS WHICH MUST BE SENT TO THE BOARD BY THE HOSPITAL AND THE PHYSICIAN'S HEALTH COMMITTEE. MAY PETITION BOARD FOR RELIEF FROM RESTRICTIONS UPON SHOWING THAT AN ACCEPTABLE SURGICAL ASSISTANT HAS BEEN RECRUITED. ADMINISTRATIVE FEE OF $1,500 SHALL BE PAYABLE WITHIN 60 DAYS. ON 8/10/94 HE WAS GRANTED RELIEF FROM RESTRICTIONS.

YASHAR, JAMES J MD, LICENSE NUMBER 0035150, OF 1 RANDALL SQUARE, PROVIDENCE, RI, WAS DISCIPLINED BY MASSACHUSETTS ON NOVEMBER 30, 1994.
DISCIPLINARY ACTION: REPRIMAND
OFFENSE: DISCIPLINARY ACTION BY ANOTHER STATE OR AGENCY
NOTES: DISCIPLINE BY RHODE ISLAND; MISCONDUCT, GENERAL.

YASHAR, JAMES JAMSHID MD, LICENSE NUMBER 00D4367, OF PROVIDENCE, RI, WAS DISCIPLINED BY TEXAS ON JANUARY 6, 1995.
DISCIPLINARY ACTION: SURRENDER OF LICENSE
OFFENSE: DISCIPLINARY ACTION BY ANOTHER STATE OR AGENCY
NOTES: ON 4/30/93 ENTERED A CONSENT ORDER WITH RHODE ISLAND CONSTITUTING A PUBLIC REPRIMAND FOR FAILING TO MAINTAIN STANDARDS ESTABLISHED BY PEER REVIEW REQUIRING THAT AFTER AN OPEN HEART SURGICAL CASE, THE SURGEON WILL BE PHYSICALLY PRESENT IN THE HOSPITAL UNTIL THE PATIENT IS STABLE; HAS NO INTENTION OF PRACTICING IN TEXAS IN THE IMMEDIATE FUTURE; IN LIEU OF FURTHER INVESTIGATION OR HEARING. MAY PETITION FOR REINSTATEMENT.

YERGER, DAVID H MD, LICENSE NUMBER 0014447, OF PO BOX 5249, BILOXI, MS, WAS DISCIPLINED BY GEORGIA ON JULY 1, 1992.
DISCIPLINARY ACTION: NONRENEWAL OF LICENSE
OFFENSE: DISCIPLINARY ACTION BY ANOTHER STATE OR AGENCY
NOTES: DISCIPLINARY ACTION IN AIR FORCE. ADMINISTRATIVE REVOCATION FOR FAILURE TO RENEW.

YERGER, DAVID H MD, DATE OF BIRTH DECEMBER 12, 1939, LICENSE NUMBER 0011884, OF HCR3, BOX 22 QUAIL RUN I, DEL RIO, TX, WAS DISCIPLINED BY MISSISSIPPI ON JANUARY 21, 1993.
OFFENSE: LOSS OR RESTRICTION OF HOSPITAL PRIVILEGES
NOTES: DISCIPLINARY ACTION TAKEN AGAINST STAFF PRIVILEGES AT KEESLER MEDICAL CENTER IN BILOXI, MS; ACTION IN CALIFORNIA. PROVISIONS INCLUDE: IF HE CHOOSES TO RETURN TO MISSISSIPPI TO PRACTICE MEDICINE, SHALL NOTIFY THE BOARD IN WRITING PRIOR TO DOING SO; SHALL APPEAR BEFORE THE BOARD. BOARD MAY PLACE ANY AND ALL RESTRICTIONS WHICH IT DEEMS NECESSARY TO DETERMINE HIS COMPETENCY TO PRACTICE MEDICINE AND TO PROTECT THE PUBLIC, INCLUDING BUT NOT LIMITED TO, LIMITATIONS ON LICENSEE'S SURGICAL PRACTICE/PRIVILEGES AND/OR RESTRICTIONS TO PRACTICE PRIMARY CARE.

YILMAZ, SALIH M MD OF 500 E. WASHINGTON AVE, NAVASOTA, TX, WAS DISCIPLINED BY MEDICARE ON APRIL 13, 1987.
DISCIPLINARY ACTION: 12-MONTH EXCLUSION FROM THE MEDICARE AND/OR MEDICAID PROGRAMS
OFFENSE: SUBSTANDARD CARE, INCOMPETENCE, OR NEGLIGENCE
NOTES: GROSSLY SUBSTANDARD CARE IN FIVE CASES,

INCLUDING TWO FOR WHICH HOSPITAL ADMISSIONS WERE UNNECESSARY. FAILURE TO ASSESS PATIENTS AND TO FORMULATE A DIAGNOSTIC AND THERAPEUTIC PROGRAM RELATING TO CARDIAC PATIENTS, CRITICAL CARE, ANTIBIOTIC SELECTION AND DIABETIC MANAGEMENT

YONG, GABRIEL Y MD, LICENSE NUMBER 00F3006, OF HOUSTON, TX, WAS DISCIPLINED BY TEXAS ON SEPTEMBER 24, 1988.
OFFENSE: DISCIPLINARY ACTION BY ANOTHER STATE OR AGENCY
NOTES: SHALL INFORM BOARD CONCERNING DISCIPLINARY ACTION AGAINST HIM IN BRITISH COLUMBIA; SHALL RECEIVE BOARD APPROVAL BEFORE RETURNING TO TEXAS

YOUNG, ALAN W DO, DATE OF BIRTH AUGUST 8, 1954, OF SAN ANTONIO, TX, WAS DISCIPLINED BY IOWA ON AUGUST 1, 1990.
DISCIPLINARY ACTION: DENIAL OF NEW LICENSE
NOTES: APPLICATION FOR LICENSURE DENIED DUE TO INELIGIBILITY.

ZALUD, MIROSLAV DR OF HOUSTON, TX, WAS DISCIPLINED BY VERMONT ON AUGUST 31, 1988.
NOTES: MUST MEET WITH BOARD BEFORE BEGINNING ANY PRACTICE IN VERMONT.

ZAMORA, CARLOS E MD, DATE OF BIRTH JULY 7, 1944, OF 2002 C MEDICAL PLAZA, SAN MARCOS, TX, WAS DISCIPLINED BY MEDICARE ON OCTOBER 28, 1988.
DISCIPLINARY ACTION: 60-MONTH EXCLUSION FROM THE MEDICARE AND/OR MEDICAID PROGRAMS
OFFENSE: CRIMINAL CONVICTION OR PLEA OF GUILTY, NOLO CONTENDERE, OR NO CONTEST TO A CRIME
NOTES: PROGRAM-RELATED CONVICTION.

ZAVALA, ALFONSO G MD, DATE OF BIRTH SEPTEMBER 8, 1952, OF 7665 PHOENIX #1127, HOUSTON, TX, WAS DISCIPLINED BY MEDICARE ON MAY 12, 1992.
DISCIPLINARY ACTION: EXCLUSION FROM THE MEDICARE AND/OR MEDICAID PROGRAMS
OFFENSE: FAILURE TO COMPLY WITH A PROFESSIONAL RULE
NOTES: DEFAULT ON HEALTH EDUCATION LOAN OR SCHOLARSHIP OBLIGATIONS.

ZUAZU, GREGORIO B MD, LICENSE NUMBER 0039137, OF KINGWOOD, TX, WAS DISCIPLINED BY FLORIDA ON MAY 7, 1991.
DISCIPLINARY ACTION: FINE; REPRIMAND
OFFENSE: PROVIDING FALSE INFORMATION TO THE BOARD
NOTES: FOUND GUILTY OF RENEWAL OF LICENSE BY FRAUDULENT MISREPRESENTATION IN THAT HE FALSELY CERTIFIED THAT HE COMPLETED THE CONTINUING MEDICAL EDUCATION REQUIREMENTS FOR LICENSE RENEWAL; VIOLATING A BOARD RULE IN THAT HE FAILED TO COMPLETE CONTINUING MEDICAL EDUCATION COURSES IN RESPONSE TO BOARD'S RANDOM AUDIT. MUST PAY $100O FINE AND SUBMIT DOCUMENTATION TO DEMONSTRATE COMPLETION OF ALL CONTINUING MEDICAL EDUCATION REQUIREMENTS FOR 1988-89 BIENNIUM WITHIN 6 MONTHS; DOCUMENT COMPLETION OF CONTINUING MEDICAL EDUCATION REQUIREMENTS WITH CERTIFICATES FOR 1990-91 BIENNIUM.

Public Citizen is a nonprofit membership organization in Washington, D.C., dedicated to advancing consumer rights through lobbying, litigation, research, publications, and information services.

Since its founding by Ralph Nader in 1971, Public Citizen has fought for consumer rights in the marketplace, for safe and secure health care, for fair trade, for clean and safe energy sources, and for corporate and government accountability.

Public Citizen accepts no corporate or government funds.

If you would like to join Public Citizen or purchase a publication, please complete the form at right and mail it with your check or money order made out to Public Citizen to:

Public Citizen
1600 20th Street, N.W.
Washington, D.C. 20009

Combination Membership ($35) includes the bimonthly *Public Citizen* magazine and the monthly *Health Letter.*

Basic Membership includes *Public Citizen* magazine.

Public Citizen Membership

Qty	Item	Price	Total
	Combination Membership	$35.00	
	Basic Membership	$25.00	
		Membership Subtotal	

Publications Orders

Qty	Item	Price	Total
	Delivering a Better Childbirth Experience	$15.00	
	Encouraging the Use of Nurse-Midwives	$15.00	
	Worst Pills Best Pills II	$15.00	
	Worst Pills Best Pills News (one year)	$10.00	
	13,012 Questionable Doctors (3 vol. set)	$250.00	
	Questionable Doctors (please specify state)	$15.00	
	Continental U.S. Postage and Handling $ 4.00 for First Item		
	Postage and Handling $ 1.00 for Each Additional Item		
		Publications Subtotal	

PUBLICATIONS/MEMBERSHIP TOTAL	

QD3396

☐ Charge to credit card

☐ VISA ☐ MasterCard ☐ American Express

☐ Payment enclosed (check or money order payable to "Public Citizen")

☐ From time to time, Public Citizen makes members' names available to other groups seeking public support. Please check this box if you would prefer we not make your name available in this way.

Credit Card # ____________________ Exp Date ________

Signature ____________________

Ordered By/Gift From:

Name (Please Print) ____________________

Address ____________________
(must be street address for publication orders shipped via UPS)

City ____________ State ______ Zip ______

Phone number: (____) ____________________

Send/Gift To:

Name (Please Print) ____________________

Address ____________________
(must be street address for publication orders shipped via UPS)

City ____________ State ______ Zip ______

Phone number: (____) ____________________

Please allow 4 to 6 weeks for delivery of publications; 6 to 8 weeks for your first issue of magazine/newsletters.

To order publications by phone, get information on overnight delivery, or orders outside the continental U.S., or for information on membership call 202/588-1000, Mon.–Fri., 9 a.m.–5 p.m. EST.

Public Citizen membership/subscriptions and publications make wonderful gifts. To send a gift, simply choose a category from above and fill out the recipient's name and address in the "Gift to:" section of this form, then print your name and address in the "Gift From:" section.

Delivering a Better Childbirth Experience

A Consumer's Guide to Nurse-Midwifery

Public Citizen

Public Citizen's Health Research Group
November 1995

Encouraging the Use of Nurse-Midwives

A Report for Policymakers

Public Citizen

Public Citizen's Health Research Group
November 1995

Delivering a Better Childbirth Experience

$15

Encouraging the Use of Nurse-Midwives

$15

Now Available from Public Citizen

Two new reports look at the increasingly important role certified nurse-midwives are playing in the future of obstetric care.

Delivering a Better Childbirth Experience
A Consumers' Guide

This new consumer guide answers common questions about nurse-midwives and includes descriptions for 414 nurse-midwifery practices in 47 states across the country that attend in-hospital births as well as 41 freestanding birth center practices.

Health Research Group

Encouraging the Use of Nurse-Midwives
A Policymakers' Guide

This new policy report explores certified nurse-midwives' role in improving the health status of newborns and curbing the excessive use of costly, and sometimes dangerous, medical interventions during births. The report also outlines a set of recommendations for state and federal policymakers and administrators, promoting nurse-midwifery as the standard of care for low-risk pregnant women.

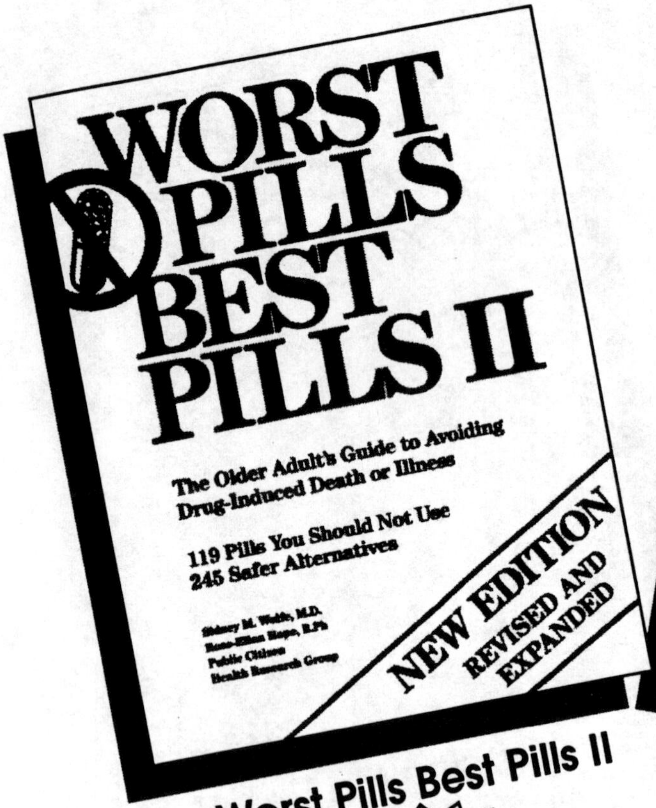

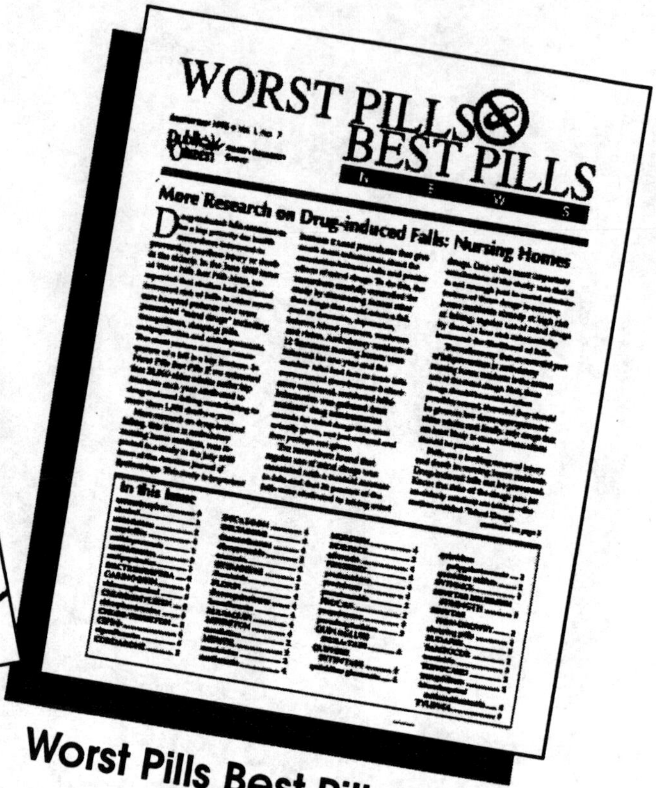